ENCYCLOPEDIA
of the
UNITED STATES

3

NORTH DAKOTA
WYOMING

SOMERSET PUBLISHERS, INC.
1532 State Street
Santa Barbara, California 93101

Editor and Publisher
FRANK H. GILLE

Managing Editor
KARIN RICKERT

Art and Production
KEVIN HEDENSTAD

Assistant Editor
COURTNEY E. KING

Associate Editor
GAIL HAMLIN-WILSON

CONTRIBUTORS
Jan Onofrio-Grimm
Mary Anne Kenealy
Margarite Mercado

NORTH DAKOTA
The Peace Garden State

Knife River Indian Villages - Stanton

Frontier Army Days - Fort Abraham Lincoln State Park

GOVERNOR
Edward T. Schafer

Petrified Forest
Badlands

Buffalo in the Badlands

Lewis and Clark Interpretive Center
Washburn

Elk in the Badlands

INTRODUCTION

North Dakota is bounded on the north by Canada, on the south by South Dakota, on the east by Minnesota, and on the west by Montana. Identified as one of seven north-central states, its terrain spreads through three regions from east to west, and incorporates parts of two major physiographic provinces that separate the Rocky Mountain and Appalachian Mountain systems.

Early in its history, North Dakota was the home of hunting and agricultural Indians. It later became a trading area for white fur traders. Still later, its rich farming soil provided crops for the new settlers who sought to establish themselves here. Today, the State remains primarily rural, agricultural, and sparsely populated, with vast cattle ranches and grain farms spread out across much of its total land area.

STATE NAME

Dakota Territory was created in 1861, and was named for the Native Americans who inhabited the region. When the territory was divided into North and South Dakota by an omnibus bill passed in 1889, the name was retained for both divisions. Dakota is a Sioux word meaning "friends" or "allies."

STATE NICKNAME

Three nicknames are given for North Dakota. They include the Sioux State, Land of the Dakotas, and the Flickertail State. The nicknames of Sioux State and Land of the Dakotas are given out of recognition for the Dakota tribe, also called the Sioux. The Flickertail State refers to the flickertail squirrel, which inhabits the State.

STATE SEAL

A territorial seal was approved for Dakota in 1863. When North Dakota became a state in 1889, the new legislature retained the seal of the territory as the State seal. It is described as follows: "The seal is hereby declared to be and hereby constituted the great seal of the state of North Dakota, to wit: a tree in the open field, the trunk of which is surrounded by three bundles of wheat; on the right a plow, anvil, and sledge; on the left, a bow crossed with three arrows, and an Indian on horseback pursuing a buffalo toward the setting sun; the foliage of the tree arched by a half circle of forty-two stars, surrounded by the motto 'Liberty and Union Now and Forever, One and Inseparable'; the words 'Great Seal' at the top; the words 'State of North Dakota' at the bottom; 'October 1st' on the left and '1889' on the right. The seal to be two and one-half inches in diameter."

STATE FLAG

The official State flag for North Dakota was adopted in 1911. In 1959, an amendment was made to the original act. The current law reads as follows: "The flag of North Dakota shall consist of a field of blue silk or material which will withstand the elements four feet four inches (132.08 centimeters) on the pike and five feet six inches (167.64 centimeters) on the fly, with a border of knotted yellow fringe two and one-half inches (6.35 centimeters) wide. On each side of said flag in the center thereof, shall be embroidered or stamped an eagle with outspread wings and with opened beak. The eagle shall be three feet four inches (101.6 centimeters) from tip to tip of wing, and one foot ten inches (55.88 centimeters) from top of head to bottom of olive branch hereinafter described. The left foot of the eagle shall grasp a sheaf of arrows, the right foot shall grasp an olive branch showing three red berries. On the breast of the eagle shall be displayed a shield, the lower part showing seven red and six white stripes placed alternately. Through the open beak of the eagle shall pass a scroll bearing the words 'E Pluribus Unum.' Beneath the eagle there shall be a scroll on which shall be borne the words 'North Dakota.' Over the scroll carried through the eagle's beak shall be shown thirteen five-pointed stars, the whole device being surmounted by a sunburst. The flag shall conform in all respects as to color, form, size, and device with the regimental flag carried by the First North Dakota Infantry in the Spanish American War and Philippine Insurrection, except in the words shown on the scroll below the eagle."

STATE MOTTO

North Dakota adopted its State motto in 1889, at the same time the State seal was designated. It is "Liberty and Union Now and Forever, One and Inseparable." The motto is a quotation from Daniel Webster's "Reply to Hayne."

STATE BIRD

In 1947, the legislature of North Dakota adopted the meadowlark, *Sturnella neglecta*, as the official State bird. It ranges in the western United States, southwestern Canada, and northwestern Mexico; and east to the prairie areas of the Mississippi Valley in Iowa, Minnesota, Missouri, and Texas.

The head and back of the meadowlark's neck are a pale, dull buffy or white with broad lateral crown stripes of pale grayish brown. Lower sides of the head are mostly yellow, topped by a dull grayish white area streaked with gray. Outermost tail feathers are mostly white, and the throat, breast, and abdomen are deep yellow, sometimes with an orange hue. The yellow area is relieved by a black horseshoe-shaped patch on the chest.

The western meadowlark is an oriole. Its diet consists mostly of insects, with about one-third consisting of grains. It has a loud, distinctive song, and may hammer out as many as 200 notes per minute. Fledglings leave the nest early, while they are still unable to fly. However, they remain under the protection of their parents until they can care for themselves, because they can become easy prey for skunks, snakes, weasels, owls, and hawks.

STATE FLOWER

The North Dakota legislature designated the wild prairie rose, *Rosa blanda* or *R. arkansana* as the official floral emblem of the State in 1907. The rose is an erect shrub, with stems that are usually free of prickles. Occasionally the stems have a few slender thorns. The pink flowers bloom in June or July.

STATE TREE

The American elm, *Ulmus americana* was named the State tree of North Dakota in 1947. It is also called the white elm, soft elm, water elm, gray elm, swamp elm, and rock elm. It is native to the eastern half of the United States and Canada.

The American elm is a large, spreading tree with gray bark, deeply furrowed with broad, forking, scaly ridges. Twigs are soft and hairy, becoming smooth. Fruits are elliptical and flat, from three eighths to one half inch long. Leaves are in two rows, elliptical, from three to six inches long, and coarsely and doubly toothed with unequal teeth. Leaves are dark green and smooth or slightly rough above, and pale and usually soft and hairy underneath. The two sides of the leaf are unequal.

STATE SONG

In 1947, North Dakota's legislature adopted "North Dakota Hymn" as the official State song. It was composed by Dr. C.S. Putnam with lyrics by James W. Foley. In 1989, a State march was also designated by the legislature. "Flickertail March" was written by James D. Ployhar; it is to be played at appropriate state functions.

STATE LICENSE PLATE

The State first required North Dakota vehicle owners to register their vehicles and display front and back plates in 1911. The first plate had a black background and gold letters. Annual plates in a variety of colors were issued (excepting 1949) until 1958, when a four-year plate program was undertaken. In 1974, a multiyear plate program was begun.

The current plate for North Dakota features a blue sky over a yellow prairie with bronze mountains in the background. Above the numbers and centered across the top is lettered "Discover the Spirit.' 'North Dakota' is centered across the bottom in a black band with white letters. Beneath the state name lettered in brown is the slogan "The Peace Garden State." At the bottom right is a depiction of wheat, and at the bottom left is a buffalo.

STATE POSTAGE STAMP

In 1939, North Dakota was one of four states, including Washington, South Dakota, and Montana, to commemorate its fifty-year anniversary of statehood. A purple three-cent stamp was issued with all four states depicted; issue dates in each State capital corresponded to the anniversary date of entrance into the Union. For North Dakota, the stamp was issued on November 2, 1939 in Bismarck. The stamp features each of the four states highlighted on a map of the northwestern United States, and the name of each state's capital. A.R. Meissner designed the stamp, and M.D. Fenton and W.B. Wells were the engravers. A total of 66,835,000 of the stamp were printed.

OTHER STATE DESIGNATIONS

Over the years, the North Dakota legislature has adopted a number of additional symbols to represent officially the State. Included are the State beverage as milk (1983); the State fossil as Teredo petrified wood (1967); the State grass as western wheat grass (1977); and the State railroad museum as Mandan Railroad Museum (1989).

STATE CAPITOL

In 1930, fire destroyed the original capitol located in the city of Bismarck, which is sometimes called the "Skyscraper Capital of the Plains." A new capitol building was constructed and completed in 1934.

The Indiana-limestone building has nineteen stories and was designed in modern American style by Holabrid and Root of Chicago; Joseph Bell De Remer of Grand Forks; and William F. Kurke of Fargo. In the 1970s, a four-story judicial wing and State office building were added to the original structure. The annex was finished in limestone to match the capital, and it added another 100,000 square feet of space. Between 1971 and 1981, more than ten million dollars were spent on a variety of renovation projects.

OTHER FACTS ABOUT NORTH DAKOTA

Total area: 70,702 square miles
Land area: 69,300 square miles
Water area: 1,403 square miles
Average elevation: 1,900 feet
Highest point: White Butte, Slope County, 3,506 feet
Lowest point: Red River, 750 feet
Highest temperature: 121 degrees Fahrenheit
Lowest temperature: -60 degrees Fahrenheit
Population in 1990: 638,800
Population density in 1990: 9.26 persons per square mile
Population 1980-1990: -2.1 percent change
Population projected for year 2000: 629,000
Asian/Pacific Islander population in 1990: 3,462
Black population in 1990: 3,524
Hispanic population in 1990: 4,665
Native American population in 1990: 25,917
White population in 1990: 604,142
Capital: Bismarck
Admitted to Union: November 2, 1889
Order of Statehood: 39
Electoral votes: 3

CHRONOLOGY

1738 December. French explorer Pierre Gaultier de Varennes, Sieur de La Verendrye, visits Mandan Indians at what is now Menoken; he is first white in North Dakota.

1775 American Revolution begins; fighting starts in Concord, Massachusetts, with George Washington commanding Continental Army.

1781 October 19. British forces surrender.

1783 Treaty of Paris is signed.

1797-98 English explorer David Thompson visits Mandan and Hidatsa Indians in central region of North Dakota.

1801 Alexander Henry of North West Company establishes fur-trading post at Pembina.
– X, Y, and Hudson's Bay Company establish trading posts at Pembina.

1803 December. U.S. receives most of North Dakota in Louisiana Purchase.

1804 October. Meriwether Lewis and William Clark, en route to Pacific Northwest, arrive in North Dakota; they create winter quarters on Missouri River near present-day Washburn, engage in services of Toussaint Charbonneau and Sacajawea, his Shoshone wife, for trip west.

1806 Lewis and Clark party returns from exploration of Pacific Northwest.

1812 Group of dispossessed Scottish and Irish peasants sponsored by Thomas Douglas, Earl of Selkirk, establish farming settlement at Pembina.
– War of 1812 begins after conflict between U.S. and Great Britain over trade with France and continuing role of British in Indian hostilities
– North Dakota becomes part of Missouri Territory.

1814 British burn U.S. Capitol and White House.
– Francis Scott Key writes Star Spangled Banner.
December. Treaty of Ghent is signed.

1818 Anglo-American treaty establishes northern border of what is now North Dakota, and most of Pembina colonists return north into Canada.

1823 December. President James Monroe delivers *Monroe Doctrine* speech, declares that U.S. and rest of Americas are not open to future colonization or interference by European powers.

1832 Steamboat *Yellowstone* ascends Missouri from St. Louis to Fort Union, just beyond present North Dakota-Montana border.

1846 Mexican War begins; General Zachary Taylor seizes disputed Texas territory claimed by Mexico; U.S. declares war after border clashes.

1847 September. U.S. troops capture Mexico City.

1848 February. Treaty cedes territory to U.S.

1851 Settlers arrive at Pembina from Minnesota to form first permanent white agricultural community in North Dakota.

1857 Fort Abercrombie, first military post in North Dakota, is established on Red River of the North near Wahpeton.
– In *Dred Scott* Decision, Supreme Court rules 6-3 that slaves are not free when brought into free state, that Congress cannot restrict slavery from a territory, and that blacks cannot be citizens; ruling leads to Civil War.

1859 First steamboat on Red River arrives at Fort Garry.

1861 Dakota Territory is organized, including what are now North and South Dakota.
April 12. Civil War begins.

1863 January. Free land becomes available under Homestead Act, which provides 160 acres to settlers cultivating portion of it for five years.
– Chippewa Indians sell ten million acres in northwestern Minnesota and northeastern North Dakota for $500,000.
– Emancipation Proclamation decree issued by President Abraham Lincoln abolishes slavery in rebel states.

1863-64 In retaliation for uprising of Santee Sioux (Dakota) in Minnesota in 1862, federal troops conduct punitive expeditions on upper Missouri against Sioux tribes, most of which had taken no part in fighting.

1865 Civil War ends.

1867 Fort Totten Indian Reservation, south of Devils Lake, is created for Sisseton, Wahpeton, and Cut-Head Sioux.

1868 Treaty defines reservation boundaries for other Sioux tribes, including part of Standing Rock Reservation in what is now North Dakota.

1870 Fort Berthold Reservation in northwest North Dakota is set aside for Mandan, Arikara, and Hidatsa Indians.

1871 Northern Pacific Railroad seeks European immigration to settle on land grants, comprising almost one quarter of what later becomes North Dakota.

1873 Northern Pacific Railroad reaches Bismarck.
July. First issue of Bismarck *Tribune* appears; it is State's oldest newspaper.

1876 First of bonanza farms (giant wheat farms) is established near Casselton; total of 91 farms of more than 3,000 acres are established by around 1885, after which they are broken up.
May. Federal troops under George A. Custer leave Fort Abraham Lincoln near Mandan to fight in campaign against Sioux that results in major defeat at Little Big Horn.

1881 Sitting Bull's forces, who fled to Canada after defeating Custer, surrender and return to reservations.
– Northern Pacific reaches Montana border.

1882 Nine million acres of north central North Dakota are opened to public despite protests from Turtle Mountain Chippewa, who do not cede the land until 1892.

1883 Bismarck becomes capital of Dakota Territory by offering best bid – $100,000 and 160 acres of land.
– University of North Dakota opens at Grand Forks.
– Theodore Roosevelt comes to North Dakota for health reasons and begins ranching near Medora.

1884 First commercial mining of North Dakota's abundant lignite is undertaken.

1885 First land boom peaks; population has grown from 37,000 in 1880 to 152,000.

1886 Thirteenth Amendment to Constitution abolishes all slavery in U.S.

1889 November. North and South Dakota are admitted simultaneously as 39th and 40th states of Union.

1890 North Dakota ranks second to Minnesota in production of wheat.
– Population is 190,183; forty-three percent are foreign born, including 25,773 from Norway and 23,045 from Canada.

1898 April-December. Spanish American War is fought between U.S. and Spain over treatment of American interests in Cuba; Battleship *Maine* is blown up in Havana on February 15; Treaty of Paris cedes Guam, Philippines, and Puerto Rico to U.S.

1906 Second wave of land fever reaches peak with homestead filing of 2.7 million acres, mostly in arid western region of North Dakota.

1914 June 28. World War I begins; U.S. is neutral.

1915 Nonpartisan League is formed to further farmers' interests, and fight out-of-state grain milling and elevator companies; league enters candidates in Republican Party primaries.

1916 Lynn J. Frazier, Nonpartisan League's candidate, is elected governor.

1917 April 6. U.S. declares war on Germany, after attacks on U.S. shipping.

1918 July. One million troops are in Europe.
November 11. World War I ends.

1919 Bank of North Dakota is created; it is only state-owned bank in United States.
– Graduated income tax, inheritance tax are adopted.
June 28. Treaty of Versailles is signed.

1920 Women's Suffrage Movement leads to ratification of 19th Amendment, giving women right to vote in all elections.

1922 State-owned grain mill and elevator are opened in Grand Forks.

1929 Drought conditions in Great Plains begin to affect farm production.

1930 Dry weather continues; vast amounts of topsoil are blown away by high winds; dry conditions will prevail until 1936.

1932 Nineteen-story State capital is built; it is tallest building in North Dakota.
– Voters repeal State constitution's prohibition clause.

1933 State's per capita income is $145, far lower than U.S. average of $375.
– Moratorium on foreclosure of farm mortgages continues.

1935 State adopts retail sales tax.

1936 Wheat crop drops to 19 tons due to prevailing severe drought conditions.
– Sale of liquor is legalized.

1939 World War II begins.

1941 International Peace Garden is established on border with Canada.
– U.S. enters World War II.
– Blizzard hits North Dakota, three other midwestern states; sixty-two die in storm.
– Senator Gerald Nye urges defeat of Lend-Lease bill, attacking Great Britain as greatest aggressor in all modern history.

1947 Almost one decade of farm prosperity raises per capita income to $1,446, exceeding national average of $1,316.
– Construction of Garrison Dam begins on Missouri River.
– Tornado hits U.S.-Canadian border near Grand Forks; eleven are dead.

1949 Theodore Roosevelt National Memorial Park is dedicated at Medora; park honors Roosevelt's concern for conservation of natural resources and wildlife.

1951 Oil is struck in Williston Basin near Tioga.

1954 Standard Oil of Indiana opens 30,000 barrel per day refinery at Mandan.

1956 Nonpartisan League joins Democratic Party.

1958 State's GOP convention in Bismarck rejects Senator William Langer's bid for renomination; legislators vote to endorse Lieutenant Governor Clyde Duffy for seat.

1959 Governor John Davis (R), appoints former governor Norman Brunsdale to Senate seat vacated by death of William Langer.

1960 Garrison Dam is completed, creating 200-mile-long Lake Sakakawea, which inundates 550,000 acres.

1961 State ranks 10th in nation in oil production.

1963 State's first modern lignite-burning electrical generating station is put into operation.

1966 Democrat William A. Guy wins record fourth term as governor.

1969 At Grand Fork, construction begins on $5.7 billion antiballistic missile complex for defense of Minuteman II missiles.

1971 State ranks first in nation in barley production, second in wheat, third in hay and oats.

1973 Canada requests one-year moratorium on $500 million Garrison diversion project until determination can be made that irrigation runoff will not pollute Red and Souris rivers, which flow into Manitoba.
– In effort to save fuel, President Nixon signs bill to put most of U.S. on year-round daylight savings time for two years; only Alaska and Hawaii are exempted.

1974 Gasoline shortage situation worsens; federal allocations are reduced in North Dakota, nine other states.
– U.S. government informs Canadian embassy that it will continue preliminary work on Garrison irrigation project in State, but pledges to abide by treaty obligations to Canada.
– Former Governor William L. Guy (D) wins senatorial nomination.

1975 Antiballistic missile complex is decommissioned after agreement with Soviet Union.

1976 Supreme Court approves coal strip mining in North Dakota, three other states; approval rejects Sierra Club request for delay until regional environmental impact study is completed.

1977 FEA orders refineries in North Dakota, three other north-central states to produce more heating oil for customers.

1979 North Dakota is one of thirteen states to pass law authorizing arbitration of medical malpractice claims.

1980 Construction begins on nation's first commercial-scale synthetic fuels plant at Beulah.
– U.S. Census Bureau reports population total of 652,695 in 1980; State will have one representative in 98th Congress in 1982.

1981 State outranks Kansas in wheat production, with record of 328 million bushels.

1982 Democrats take control of State house.

1983 North Dakota resident, Gordon Kahl, who called federal income tax "work of Satan" is indicted by federal grand jury for murder after killing two U.S. marshals.
– Tax protester Gordon Kahl is shot and killed in northeastern Arkansas; Kahl became fugitive after gunning down two U.S. marshals while they attempted to stop him for parole violations.

1984 After November election, Republicans gain control of both houses.

1985 Default of $1.5 billion in federally-guaranteed loans causes synthetic fuels plant at Beulah to pass into hands of U.S. Department of Energy, which is unable to find buyer.
– Makeshift State Supreme Court rules that Democrat George Sinner has been legal governor since start of year; ruling is made after Republican outgoing Governor Allen I. Olson, refuses to vacate office until Jan. 6, exactly four years after he took office; at issue are two vacancies on Supreme Court and Sinner's plan to impose hiring freeze, challenge year-end bonuses for 100 State employees.

1986 Garrison water project is approved by House.

1987 North Dakota wins finals of National Collegiate Athletic Association hockey tournament against Michigan State.

1988 Study at North Dakota State University reports that spring drought has wiped out about forty percent of wheat crop.

1989 Congress names Des Lacs as one of many national wildlife refuges being despoiled by human activities; power boating, water-skiing have disturbed migratory bird nesting and nurturing of broods, according to General Accounting Office (GAO) report.

1990 State residents reject proposed temporary hike in sales tax; one percent increase, slated to last one year, would have raised $42 million for public education.

1991 North Dakota is one of three states, including Montana and California, with highest tax hikes in nation.

1992 Republican Edward Schafer is governor.

1993 North Dakota is one of fourteen states in U.S. without capital punishment.

1994 Democrats lose control of State Senate.

1995 Thomas Keith Glennan, born in North Dakota in 1905, dies after suffering stroke; Glennan was first administrator of NASA, represented U.S. at International Atomic Energy Agency.

1996 Governor Schafer wins reelection.

1997 Supreme Court declares unconstitutional 1984 law barring American Indians from passing small parcels of land to heirs; justices hold that takings clause of Fifth Amendment bars government from taking private property from individuals without just compensation.

1998 Protest arises after agricultural trade pact is reached between U.S. and Canada; North Dakota, two other states block entry points for Canadian trucks hauling farm products for several hours.

1999 In trial of President Bill Clinton, both United States senators from North Dakota, Kent Conrad and Byron Dorgan, vote not guilty on two impeachment articles.

DIRECTORY OF STATE SERVICES

OFFICE OF THE GOVERNOR
600 E Boulevard
Bismarck, ND 58505-0001
Governor: 701-328-2200
Fax: 701-328-2205

LIEUTENANT GOVERNOR
600 E Boulevard
Bismarck, ND 58505-0001
Lieutenant Governor: 701-328-2200
Fax: 701-328-2205

ATTORNEY GENERAL
600 E Boulevard Ave.
Bismarck, ND 58505-0040
Attorney General: 701-328-2210
Fax: 701-328-2226

SECRETARY OF STATE
600 E Boulevard
Bismarck, ND 58505-0500
Secretary of State: 701-328-2900
Fax: 701-328-2992

Athletic Commission
600 E Boulevard
Bismarck, ND 58505
Athletic Commissioner: 701-328-3665
Fax: 701-328-2992

TREASURER
600 E Boulevard
Bismarck, ND 58505
State Treasurer: 701-328-2643
Fax: 701-328-3002

ADJUTANT GENERAL
Box 5511
Bismarck, ND 58506-5511
Adjutant General: 701-224-5102
Fax: 701-224-5180

AGRICULTURAL DEPARTMENT
600 E Boulevard
Bismarck, ND 58505
Commissioner: 701-328-2231
Fax: 701-328-4567

AUDITOR
600 E Boulevard
Bismarck, ND 58505
State Auditor: 701-328-2241
Fax: 701-328-3000

BANKING ANDFINANCIAL INSTITUTIONS DEPARTMENT
600 E Boulevard
Bismarck, ND 58505-0080
Commissioner: 701-328-2253
Fax: 701-328-3000

CORRECTIONS ANDREHABILITATION DEPARTMENT
P.O. Box 1898
Bismarck, ND 58502-1898
Director: 701-328-6390
Fax: 701-328-6651

ECONOMIC DEVELOPMENT AND FINANCE DEPARTMENT
1833 E Bismarck Expressway
Bismarck, ND 58504
Director: 701-328-5300
Fax: 701-328-5320

GAME AND FISH DEPARTMENT
100 N Bismarck Expressway
Bismarck, ND 58501-5095
Director: 701-328-6300
Fax: 701-328-6352

HEALTH AND CONSOLIDATED LABORATORIES DEPARTMENT
600 E Boulevard
Bismarck, ND 58505
State Health Officer: 701-328-2372
Fax: 701-328-4727

Administrative Services Section
600 E Boulevard
Bismarck, ND 58505-0200
Chief: 701-328-2392
Fax: 701-328-4727

Toxicology Laboratory
P.O. Box 937
Bismarck, ND 58502-5520
Director: 701-328-6141
Fax: 701-328-4727

Environmental Health Section
P.O. Box 5520
Bismarck, ND 58502-5520
Chief: 701-328-5150
Fax: 701-328-5200

Health Resources Section
600 E Boulevard
Bismarck, ND 58505
Chief: 701-328-2352
Fax: 701-328-4727

Preventative Health Section
600 E Boulevard
Bismarck, ND 58505
Chief: 701-328-2493
Fax: 701-328-4727

HUMAN SERVICES DEPARTMENT
600 E Boulevard
Bismarck, ND 58505
Executive Director: 701-328-2310
Fax: 701-328-2359

INSURANCE DEPARTMENT
600 E Boulevard
Bismarck, ND 58505
Commissioner: 701-328-2440
Fax: 701-328-4880

LABOR DEPARTMENT
600 E Boulevard
Bismarck, ND 58505
Commissioner: 701-328-2660
Fax: 701-328-2031

LAND DEPARTMENT
P.O. Box 5523
Bismarck, ND 58506-5523
Commissioner: 701-328-2800
Fax: 701-328-3650

PARKS AND TOURISM DEPARTMENT
1835 E Bismarck Expressway
Bismarck, ND 58504
Director: 701-328-5357
Fax: 701-328-5363

PUBLIC INSTRUCTION DEPARTMENT
600 E Boulevard
Bismarck, ND 58505-0440
State Superintendent: 701-328-4572
Fax: 701-328-2461

State Library
604 E Boulevard Ave.
Bismarck, ND 58505-0800
State Librarian: 701-328-2492
Fax: 701-328-2040

SECURITIES DEPARTMENT
600 E Boulevard
Bismarck, ND 58505
Commissioner: 701-328-2910
Fax: 701-255-3113

TAX DEPARTMENT
600 E Boulevard
Bismarck, ND 58505
Commissioner: 701-328-2770
Fax: 701-328-3700

TRANSPORTATION DEPARTMENT
608 E Boulevard Ave.
Bismarck, ND 58505-0700
Commissioner & Director: 701-328-2581
Fax: 701-328-4545

VETERANS AFFAIRS DEPARTMENT
P.O. Box 9003
Fargo, ND 58106-9003
Commissioner: 701-239-7165
Fax: 701-239-7166

AERONAUTICS COMMISSION
Box 5020
Bismarck, ND 58502
Chairman: 701-328-2748
Fax: 701-328-2780

AGRICULTURAL PRODUCTS UTILIZATION COMMISSION
600 E Boulevard
Bismarck, ND 58505
Chairman: 701-328-4760
Fax: 701-328-4567

ANIMAL HEALTH BOARD
600 E Boulevard
Bismarck, ND 58505-0390
Exec Officer & State Veterinarian: 701-328-2654
Fax: 701-328-3000

ARTS COUNCIL
Black Bldg, 114 Broadway, Rm. 606
Fargo, ND 58102
Executive Director: 701-231-8962

ATMOSPHERIC RESOURCE BOARD
900 E Boulevard
Bismarck, ND 58505
Director: 701-328-2788
Fax: 701-328-4749

BEEF COMMISSION
4023 N State St.
Bismarck, ND 58501
Executive Director: 701-328-5120
Fax: 701-328-5119

FOREST SERVICE AND STATE FORESTER
1st & Brander St.
Bottineau, ND 58318
State Forester / Director: 701-228-5422
Fax: 701-228-5448

HERITAGE FOUNDATION
P.O. Box 1976
Bismarck, ND 58502-0200
Executive Director: 701-222-1966

HIGHER EDUCATION BOARD
600 E Boulevard
Bismarck, ND 58505
Chancellor: 701-328-2960
Fax: 701-328-2961

HIGHWAY PATROL
600 E Boulevard
Bismarck, ND 58505
Superintendent: 701-328-2459
Fax: 701-328-3000

HISTORICAL SOCIETY
612 E Boulevard
Bismarck, ND 58505
Superintendent: 701-328-2667
Fax: 701-328-3710

HOUSING FINANCE AGENCY
P.O. Box 1535
Bismarck, ND 58502-1535
Executive Director: 701-328-3434
Fax: 701-328-3420

INDIAN AFFAIRS COMMISSION
600 E Boulevard
Bismarck, ND 58505
Chairman: 701-328-3722

INDUSTRIAL COMMISSION
600 E Boulevard
Bismarck, ND 58505
Chairman: 701-328-3722

JOB SERVICE
P.O. Box 5507
Bismarck, ND 58506-5507
Executive Director: 701-328-2836
Fax: 701-328-4000

LEGISLATIVE COUNCIL
600 E Boulevard
Bismarck, ND 58505
Director: 701-328-2916

MANAGEMENT AND BUDGET OFFICE
600 E Boulevard
Bismarck, ND 58505
Director: 701-328-2680
Fax: 701-328-3230

MILK STABILIZATION BOARD
206 N 6th Street
Bismarck, ND 58501
Executive Secretary: 701-328-2988

MUNICIPAL BOND BANK
418 E Broadway, Ste 246
Bismarck, ND 58501-3980
Executive Director: 701-328-3980

NURSING BOARD
919 S 7th St., Ste 504
Bismarck, ND 58504
Executive Director: 701-328-2974
Fax: 701-328-4614

PROTECTION ADVOCACY PROJECT
400 E Broadway, Ste 515
Bismarck, ND 58501
Director: 701-328-2972
Fax: 701-328-3934

PUBLIC EMPLOYEES RETIREMENT SYSTEM
P.O. Box 1214
Bismarck, ND 58502
Executive Director: 701-328-3900
Fax: 701-328-3820

PUBLIC SERVICE COMMISSION
State Capitol, 12th Fl.
Bismarck, ND 58505-0480

Executive Secretary: 701-328-2400
Fax: 701-328-2410

RADIO COMMUNICATIONS
P.O. Box 5511
Bismarck, ND 58502-5511
Director: 701-328-2127
Fax: 701-328-2126

REAL ESTATE COMMISSION
P.O. Box 727
Bismarck, ND 58502-0727
Secretary-Treasurer: 701-328-2749
Fax: 701-328-4150

SOIL CONSERVATION COMMITTEE
600 E Boulevard Ave., 18th Fl.
Bismarck, ND 58505-0790
Executive Director: 701-328-2651
Fax: 701-328-4143

TEACHERS RETIREMENT ANDINVESTMENT FUND
P.O. Box 7100
Bismarck, ND 58507-7100
Executive Director: 701-328-4885
Fax: 701-328-4897

TECHNICAL ANDVOCATIONAL EDUCATION BOARD
600 E Boulevard
Bismarck, ND 58505-0610
Director / Executive Officer: 701-328-3180
Fax: 701-328-1255

WATER COMMISSION
900 East Boulevard
Bismarck, ND 58505
State Engineer / Secretary: 701-328-4940
Fax: 701-328-3696

WHEAT COMMISSION
4023 State St.
Bismarck, ND 58501
Administrator: 701-328-5111
Fax: 701-328-5115

WORKERS COMPENSATION BUREAU
500 E Front Ave.
Bismarck, ND 58504-5685
Executive Director: 701-328-3800
Fax: 701-328-3820

MEMBERS OF CONGRESS

SENATE

SEN. KENT CONRAD (D) (b. 1948), 3rd Term;
Phone: 202-224-2043; Fax: 202-224-7776;
E-mail: senator@conrad.senate.gov

www.senate.gov/~conrad/

SEN. BYRON L. DORGAN (D) (b. 1942), 2nd Term;
Phone: 202-224-2551; Fax: 202-224-1193;
E-mail: senator@dorgan.senate.gov

www.senate.gov/~dorgan/

HOUSE

EARL POMEROY (D-At Large) (b. 1952), 4th Term;
Phone: 202-225-2611; Fax: 202-226-0893;
E-mail: rep.earl.pomeroy@mail.house.gov

www.house.gov/pomeroy

TWENTIETH CENTURY GOVERNORS

FANCHER, FREDERICK BARTLETT (1852-1944), sixth governor of North Dakota (1899-1901), was born in Kenyonville, New York on April 2, 1852. Fancher attended the State Normal School in Ypsilanti, Michigan. He subsequently moved to Chicago, Illinois, where he found employment at the Continental Insurance Company, as an insurance underwriter. In 1881 he migrated to Jamestown, North Dakota, where he was involved in farming and real estate ventures. Fancher also worked as an agent for eastern firms where he was overseer of thousands of acres of land. Eventually, he founded his own insurance firm, the Alliance Insurance Company, which spanned five states. In 1894 he was elected State Insurance Commissioner, a post he held until 1898.

A member of the Republican Party, Fancher secured the North Dakota governorship in 1898, taking office on January 2, 1899. During his tenure, several new railroad lines were established throughout the State, the Board of Pardons was organized, and a twine and cordage plant was constructed within the State Penitentiary. Fancher was going to run for a second term, but frail health prevented him from doing so, and he stepped down from office on January 7, 1901. He subsequently relocated to Sacramento, California, where he owned and operated a grocery business until 1925, when he retired in Los Angeles.

Fancher was married to Florence S. Van Voorhies. He died on January 10, 1944.

WHITE, FRANK (1856-1940), seventh governor of North Dakota (1901-1905), was born in Stillman Valley, Illinois on December 12, 1856. He attended the University of Illinois, graduating in 1880, then subsequently found work with the Chicago, Milwaukee and St. Paul Railroad. In 1882 he relocated to Valley City, North Dakota, where he owned and operated a farm.

Entering politics, White was elected to the North Dakota House of Representatives in 1891, where he served until 1893. In that year, he secured a seat in the State Senate, resigning from that post in 1898. In 1900 White ran for and won the North Dakota governorship on the Republican ticket, taking office on January 7, 1901. He also won a second term the following year. During his tenure, a wing of the State Capitol Building was completed, plus a facility for the mentally retarded was constructed. Also, the Eighth Judicial District was established.

White stepped down from office on January 2, 1905, and returned to his business interests. In 1915 he was named to the State Board of Regents, and between 1917 and 1919, during World War I, White served in the United States Army. In 1921 White was appointed Treasurer of the United States, a post he held until 1928, after which he became president of the Middlewest Trust Company.

White was married to Elsie Hadley, the couple had one child. White died on March 23, 1940.

SARLES, ELMORE YOCUM (1859-1929), eighth governor of North Dakota (1905-1907), was born in Wonewoc, Wisconsin on January 15, 1859. He studied for one year at Wisconsin's Galesville University. Sarles was employed in banking for a time, then served as secretary-treasurer of the Wonewoc Manufacturing Company during 1878-79. In 1880 he worked at a lumber enterprise, then the following year, partnered with his brother to establish a bank in Hillsboro, North Dakota. In 1882 he managed O.C. Sarles and Co. Lumber, which later became Valley Lumber Company. In 1885 Sarles founded the First National Bank of Hillsboro, eventually serving as its president.

Entering politics, Sarles served as Mayor of Hillsboro for two years. In 1904 he ran for and won the North Dakota governorship on the Republican ticket, taking office on January 2, 1905. During his tenure, the State Banking Board was organized to oversee all State banks. In addition, the Pure Food and Drug Act was adopted, as was an irrigation code. In addition, regulations were implemented on the sale of dairy products, and the office of Inspector of Weights and Measures was created.

Sarles lost his reelection bid in 1906, and stepped down from office on January 9, 1907, returning to his numerous business interests. He was married to Anna York, and the couple had four children. Sarles died on February 14, 1929.

BURKE, JOHN (1859-1937), ninth governor of North Dakota (1907-1913), was born in Sigourney, Iowa on February 25, 1859. He attended the University of Iowa between 1882 and 1886. From the latter year until 1888, he was in the law partnership of Burke and Burke.

In 1891 Burke entered politics with a seat in the North Dakota House of Representatives, then in 1893, became a member of the State Senate, where he served until 1895. In 1896 he was named Judge of the Rolette County Court, a post he held until 1906. In that year Burke secured the North Dakota governorship, the first Democrat in the history of the State to win that office and was inaugurated on January 9, 1907. He went on to win two more terms, in 1908 and 1910.

During Burke's tenure, one of the first laws to be passed was legislation authorizing a plan to provide seed grain for struggling farmers. In addition, approval was given by the State Legislature for the State Capitol to be established in Bismarck, and for the construction of a State Tuberculosis Sanitarium. In addition, funding was put aside for the building of a library for the Legislature.

Burke stepped down from the governorship on January 8, 1913. Burke was married Mary E. Kane, and the couple had three children. Burke died on May 14, 1937.

HANNA, LOUIS BENJAMIN (1861-1948), tenth governor of North Dakota (1913-1917), was born in New Brighton, Pennsylvania on August 9, 1861. He received a public school education in both Cleveland, Ohio and New York City. He subsequently worked at a number of different jobs, including banking, farming, and mercantile. In 1900 he founded the First National Bank of Page, and served as its president until 1926. Between 1900 and 1912, he was president of the Fargo Street Railway Company and also owned the Carrington and Casey farm.

Hanna entered politics in 1895 when he won a seat in the North Dakota House of Representatives, serving until 1901, then from 1905 to 1909, he was a member of the State Senate. In 1909 he won a term in the United States House of Representatives. In 1912 he successfully sought the North Dakota governorship on the Republican ticket, taking office on January 8, 1913, and went on to win a second term the following year. During his tenure, regulations were implemented, both on the district courts and on the State Supreme Court. Also, inheritance taxes were established, and funding was provided to teachers for their retirements. In addition, a law was adopted that disallowed established criminals and insane persons from having children.

Hanna stepped down from the governorship on January 3, 1917. He was married to Lottie L. Thatcher, with whom he had three children. Hanna died on April 23, 1948.

FRAZIER, LYNN JOSEPH (1874-1947), eleventh governor of North Dakota (1917-1921), was born on December 21, 1874 in Steele County, Minnesota. After a public school education, Frazier attended the University of North Dakota from 1898 to 1901. He subsequently made his living as a farmer.

Frazier was politically active as a member of the Nonpartisan League, which successfully nominated him for the North Dakota governorship in 1916. In the primary race, Frazier ran on the Republican ticket, and won the election, taking office on January 3, 1917. He went on to win another term in 1918.

During Frazier's administration, several laws were adopted that included: provisions for the initiative and referendum, revision of the State's land registration code, and a guarantee on bank deposits, and women were given the right to vote. Frazier, known as a progressive administrator, persuaded the State Legislature to organize the State Industrial Commission, with the purpose of regulating corporations. In addition, he established a State Bank, which was the repository for all funds regarding State business, such as schools, counties, townships, etc. Also, during that time, the North Dakota Mill and Elevator Association was organized.

In 1920 Frazier was elected to a third term; however, the new State Bank was a big issue of contention at that time, along with his other progressive programs, all of which led to a recall election in October of 1921. Frazier lost the race to Ragnvald Nestos, of the Independent Republican Party. Frazier stepped down from office on November 23, 1921, and went on to win three terms to the United States Senate, in 1922, 1928 and 1934. After his last term, he retired from politics and returned to his farming interests.

Frazier was married twice: to Lottie J. Stafford, and after her death, to Cathrine Behrens Paulson. He had five children from his first union. Frazier died on January 11, 1947.

NESTOS, RAGNVALD ANDERSON (1877-1942), twelfth governor of North Dakota (1921-1925), was born in Voss, Norway, on April 12, 1877. At the age of sixteen he immigrated to the United States, and lived with relatives in Buxton, North Dakota. Nestos attended the University of Wisconsin, earning a Ph.D. in 1902, then continued his studies at the University of North Dakota, where he took his LL.B. degree in 1904. That same year he began his law work with the firm of Johnson and Nestos in Monit, North Dakota, subsequently going into the law partnership of Nestos and Herigstad.

Nestos entered the political arena with his election to the North Dakota House of Representatives in 1911. He served until the following year, then in 1913, was named State's Attorney for Ward County, a post he held until 1916, when he made an unsuccessful bid for the United States Senate. A member of the Independent Republican Party, Nestos was elected to the North Dakota governorship in a special recall election held on October 28, 1921, defeating the two-term incumbent, Lynn J. Frazier, and taking office on November 23, 1921. In November of the following year, Nestos was reelected to a second term.

During Nestos's tenure, the State Banking Administration operations were revamped, a State Health Officer was appointed,

and the State of North Dakota was added to the national registration rolls for the listing of births and deaths.

Nestos lost his reelection bid in 1924, and stepped down from office on January 5, 1925, returning to his law work. Never married, he died on July 15, 1942.

SORLIE, ARTHUR GUSTAV (1874-1928), thirteenth governor of North Dakota (1925-1928), was born on April 26, 1874 in Albert Lea, Minnesota. He studied for three years at the Albert Lea Lutheran Academy, and relocated to Buxton, North Dakota, in 1894. He found work in various occupations, including as a bank clerk, manager of a general store, and a traveling shoe salesman. Between 1903 and 1907 Sorlie was a cracker factory manager, and went on to start up a number of businesses that included gas stations, car dealerships and feed stores. In addition, he was named vice-president of the Douglas State Bank.

Sorlie entered politics with a two-term stint on the Grand Forks City Council. A member of the Nonpartisan League, in 1924 he ran for and won the North Dakota governorship, taking office on January 5, 1925, and won a second term in 1926. During his tenure, Sorlie was able to bring his business expertise to the running of the State government. Things got tenuous when the State Legislature asked for an investigation concerning his handling of the operations of the State-owned grain mill and elevator, but Sorlie made the plight of the farmers his first priority, supporting them in their fight for fair prices for their product.

Sorlie decided not to seek reelection, but became ill before the expiration of his term, and died on August 28, 1928. He was married twice: to Jennie Odegard, and after her death, to Grace Hilleboe. He had three children from each marriage.

MADDOCK, WALTER JEREMIAH (1880-1951), acting governor of North Dakota (1928-1929), was born on September 13, 1880, in Grand Forks, North Dakota. He studied at Northwestern Business College, and subsequently engaged in farming.

Politically active early on, Maddock was one of the organizers of the North Dakota branch of the Non-Partisan League. Beginning in 1914, he served several terms in the North Dakota House of Representatives, then became the State's Lieutenant Governor. As such, when incumbent Governor Arthur Sorlie died while in office, Maddock assumed the governorship. After finishing the unexpired term, he made a reelection bid on the Democratic ticket, but lost the race. Stepping down from office, he returned to his farming ventures, which included his organizing a number of farmers' cooperatives. Due to his expertise, Maddock was named senior administrative officer of the regional branch of the Agricultural Adjustment Administration in 1933. In 1937, he was appointed to oversee the North Dakota branch of the Farm Security Administration, a post he held until 1950.

Maddock was married to Marguerite Tierney, and the couple had six children. He died on January 25, 1951.

SHAFER, GEORGE F. (1888-1948), fourteenth governor of North Dakota (1929-1933), was born on November 23, 1888 in Mandan, North Dakota. He studied at the University of North Dakota between 1908 and 1912, passed the bar that same year, then went into private law practice. Between 1915 and 1919, Shafer served as State's Attorney for McKenzie County. During 1921-22, he was Assistant Attorney General of North Dakota, then in the latter year, became Attorney General, leaving that post in 1929. In 1928 Shafer successfully ran for the North Dakota governorship on the Independent Republican ticket, and won a second term in 1930.

Shafer's biggest priorities during his tenure included dealing with the effect that the severe droughts were having on the State at that time, plus the plight of the State's farmers, who were not able to get a fair price for their products. Shafer attempted to solve these situations, and by the end of his term, the profit margin for the State-owned grain mill and elevator showed a substantial increase due to his expertise.

With his second term coming to an end, Shafer decided to run for the United States Senate in 1932, but lost his bid. He was married to Frances Kellogg, and the couple had four children. Shafer died on August 13, 1948.

LANGER, WILLIAM (1886-1959), fifteenth and seventeenth governor of North Dakota (1933-1934, 1937-1939), was born on September 30, 1886 in Everest, Dakota Territory. He attended the University of North Dakota, earning an LL.B. degree in 1906, then continued his schooling at Columbia University, where he received an A.B. degree in 1910. The following year he started his law practice in Mandan, North Dakota, and between 1914 and 1916, was State's Attorney for Morton County. In the latter year, with help from the Non-Partisan League, Langer secured the post of Attorney General, serving for two terms.

In 1920, Langer ran unsuccessfully for the North Dakota governorship, then left politics until 1932, when he sought that office again. Running on the Republican ticket, with some help from the Nonpartisan League, he won the election. Like his predecessor, Langer sought to help North Dakota farmers during the time of economic depression by such methods as wheat embargoes, and moratoriums on farm foreclosures. In 1934 he found himself in the midst of a scandal, being accused of soliciting money from federal and State workers, and was removed from the governorship. Eventually he was able to disprove all of the charges, and in 1936, successfully ran for his former office once again, on the Independent ticket. During his second term, he continued his efforts to help the State's farmers. In 1938 he ran unsuccessfully for the United States Senate on the Independent ticket, but in 1940, secured that post as a Republican and went on to win three more terms, in 1946, 1952, and 1958.

Langer was married to Lydia Cady, and the couple had four children. He died on November 8, 1959.

OLSON, OLE H. (1872-1954), acting governor of North Dakota (1934-1935), was born in Mondoir, Wisconsin on September 19, 1872. He moved to Moorhead, Minnesota to attend Concordia College, from which he graduated. He then migrated to North Dakota in 1892, eventually running a homestead in Eddy County.

Several years after moving to North Dakota, Olson entered politics when he was elected to the North Dakota House of Representatives, serving from 1916 to 1918. In the latter year he secured a seat in the State Senate, where he served until 1930. Between 1932 and 1934, he was North Dakota's Lieutenant Governor. As such, when the incumbent Governor, William Langer, was removed from office in July of 1934, Olson assumed the governorship for a short time. During that period, North Dakota's political climate was in upheaval, and the State Capitol was filled with demonstrators, forcing Olson to call out the National Guard.

Olson stepped down from office on January 7, 1935 and returned his farming interests, as well as other various business ventures. He was married to Julia Ramberget, and the couple had ten children. Olson died on January 29, 1954.

MOODIE, THOMAS HENRY (1878-1948), sixteenth governor of North Dakota (1935), was born in Winona, Minnesota on May 26, 1878. When he was ten, he and his mother relocated to Wadena, Minnesota. As a young man, he found employment in the printing department of the Wadena *Pioneer*, where he subsequently worked as a reporter. For a short period, Moodie also worked for the Northern Pacific Railroad as a brakeman. Eventually, he resumed his association with the newspaper business as a printer, and later got a position as cub reporter with the Bismarck *Tribune*. For a number of years after that, he continued either working as a printer, a reporter or an editor for a number of North Dakota newspapers and also wrote editorials for the Minneapolis *Tribune* from 1930 to 1932. In addition, Moodie also owned and operated several weekly newspapers.

In 1933, President Franklin D. Roosevelt appointed Moodie to a committee organized to oversee the issuance of federal grants for public buildings. In November of 1934, Moodie ran for the North Dakota governorship on the Democratic ticket, taking office on January 7, 1935. Moodie would serve a little over a year before being removed from the governor's post, due to an eligibility problem. All candidates for the governorship were required to reside in North Dakota for five consecutive years, and when it was discovered that Moodie had not done so, the State Supreme Court ruled that he was ineligible to serve, and he was forced to leave office on February 16, 1936.

After stepping down, Moodie continued to be involved in public service, first as head of the North Dakota Federal Housing Administration, and then as deputy administrator of the State War Finance Committee, in Montana. In later years, he was associated with the Spokane *Chronicle* as their financial editor, and as confidential agent for the paper's publisher.

Moodie was married to Julia Edith McMurray. He died on March 3, 1948.

WELFORD, WALTER (1869-1952), acting governor of North Dakota (1935-1937), was born on May 21, 1869 in England. When he was ten years old, he came to the United States, and during his younger years, grew up in North Dakota.

For twenty years, beginning in 1900, Welford served as township clerk of Pembina, North Dakota. In 1906 he entered politics with a seat in the North Dakota House of Representatives, serving for two terms, then in 1916, began a two-term stint in the State Senate. In 1934 Welford became North Dakota's Lieutenant Governor. As such, when incumbent Governor Thomas Moodie was forced to relinquish the office on February 2, 1936, Welford assumed the governorship. During his administration, North Dakota, like the rest of the country, was still suffering the effects of the Great Depression. In order to help provide unemployment payments to needy citizens, as well as support the State's public school system, Welford helped push through a sales tax. In addition, a drought had caused a severe drop in agricultural production, and Welford managed to persuade President Roosevelt to provide assistance to the farmers that had been debilitated by the situation.

Welford lost his 1936 campaign for reelection and stepped down from office. Married to Edith Bachmann, he died on June 2, 1952.

MOSES, JOHN (1885-1945), eighteenth governor of North Dakota (1939-1945), was born on June 12, 1885 in Strand, Norway. In 1905 he migrated to the United States, and the following year he found employment with the Great Northern Railway, where he worked until 1911. In 1912 he began attending the University of North Dakota, where he earned an A.B. degree in 1914 and a J.D. degree in 1915, passing the bar in the latter year.

Moses practiced law for a time, then got involved in Democratic Party politics, serving as Mercer County State's Attorney from 1919 to 1923, and again later, between 1927 and 1933. In 1934 he made an unsuccessful bid for the post of Attorney General of North Dakota, and also lost a bid for the governor's chair in 1936. In 1938 he tried again and won the governorship, securing two additional terms in 1940 and 1942.

During his tenure, Moses sought to streamline every aspect of the State government and also run it on a balanced budget. In addition, he tried to lure wartime industries to North Dakota in order to help boost the State's economy. In 1944 Moses won a seat in the United States Senate, but became ill soon after his term began, and died on March 3, 1945. Moses was married to Ethel Joslyn, and the couple had four children.

AANDAHL, FRED GEORGE (1897-1966), nineteenth governor of North Dakota (1945-1951), was born on April 9, 1897 in Litchville, North Dakota. He studied at the University of North Dakota, from where he graduated in 1921. He subsequently engaged in farming and in 1922, was named Superintendent of Litchville High School, serving in that post until 1927. In 1931 he was elected to the North Dakota State Senate, also serving in 1939 and 1941.

In 1944 Aandahl successfully ran for the North Dakota governorship on the Republican ticket, and went on to secure two more terms, in 1946 and 1948. A dedicated conservationist, one of Aandahl's priorities concerned North Dakota's natural resources. He chaired the North Dakota Water Conservation Commission, and battled for the State's right to manage its own conservation issues.

Aandahl successfully sought a seat in the United States House of Representatives in 1950, and stepped down from the governorship. In 1952 he lost a bid for a seat in the United States Senate. However, due to his interest and expertise regarding natural resources, he was appointed by President Dwight D. Eisenhower to serve as Assistant Secretary of the Interior for Water and Power Development, a post he held from 1953 to 1960.

Aandahl was married to Luella Brekke, and the couple had three children. He died on April 7, 1966.

BRUNSDALE, CLARENCE NORMAN (1891-1978), twentieth governor of North Dakota (1951-1957), was born on July 9, 1891 in Sherbrooke, North Dakota. He attended Luther College, earning a B.A. degree in 1913. Brunsdale was the overseer of his family's farming enterprises for a number of years, and during 1913-14, was a business instructor. Between 1918 and 1950, he was director, then vice president of the Goose River Bank in Mayville. In addition, he served as director of the First and Farmers' Bank in Portland, North Dakota.

Politically active, Brunsdale was elected to the State Senate in 1927, and served again later, between 1940 and 1951. In 1950 he successfully sought the North Dakota governorship on the Republican ticket, and won an additional two terms, in 1952 and 1954. During his tenure, his first priority was to make sure that all State-run ventures got his full attention so that they ran smoothly. Also, the oil industry boomed in North Dakota during that time, and Brunsdale sought to solve the problems that came with that situation. Water development within North Dakota was another pressing issue during his administration, and he worked in tandem with other governors, as well as with the federal government, in order to reach an equitable solution. In addition, he sought to lure new industry to North Dakota.

Brunsdale stepped down from office in 1957. In November of 1959, he was asked to serve out an unexpired term in the United States Senate, left vacant by the death of William Langer. Brunsdale held that post until August of 1960.

Brunsdale was married to Carrie Lajord, and the couple had two children. He died on January 27, 1978.

DAVIS, JOHN EDWARD (1913-), twenty-first governor of North Dakota (1957-1961), was born in Minneapolis, Minnesota on April 18, 1913. He studied at the University of North Dakota, graduating in 1935. That same year, while overseeing his family's ranching interests, he was also named vice-president of the First National Bank of McClusky, North Dakota. In 1941, during World War II, he was stationed in Europe while serving in the United States Army and in 1945, was discharged at the rank of lieutenant colonel.

Upon returning home to North Dakota, Davis resumed his banking ventures, and soon after, decided to pursue a political career. Between 1946 and 1952, Davis, a Republican, served as Mayor of McClusky. In the latter year, he secured a seat in the North Dakota State Senate for two terms. In 1956 Davis successfully sought the governorship on the Republican ticket, and won an additional term in 1958. During his tenure, he backed the North Dakota Economic Development Corporation in an effort to bring about more industry to the State. Davis supported the addition of new highways and the upgrading of those in existence, and also sought to strengthen health and welfare statutes. Toward the end of his administration he made an unsuccessful run for a vacant United States Senate seat, but nevertheless remained active in Republican Party politics. In 1969 he was named Director of Civil Defense in the Office of the Secretary of the Army, and in 1972, was appointed Director of the Defense Civil Preparedness Agency of the Department of Defense.

Davis is married to Pauline Huntley, and the couple has three children.

GUY, WILLIAM LEWIS (1919-), twenty-second governor of North Dakota (1961-1973), was born on September 30, 1919 in Devil's Lake, North Dakota. He studied at North Dakota State University, earning a B.S. degree in 1941. Beginning 1942, during World War II, he served in the United States Navy, and was discharged in 1945.

After returning to the U.S., Guy continued his education at the University of Minnesota, taking his M.A. degree in 1946. The following year he returned home to North Dakota, where he was named Assistant County Agent for Cass County. Also, from 1947 to 1950, he owned and operated the Guy-Bean Farm Store in West Fargo. Between 1952 and 1958, Guy was an instructor at North Dakota State University, where he taught agricultural economics.

Deciding to pursue politics, Guy won a seat in the North Dakota House of Representatives in 1959, serving until 1961. Successfully running for the North Dakota governorship on the Democratic ticket in 1960, he was the first Democrat to secure that office in sixteen years, and went on to win three more terms. In the 1964 race, the terms stretched from two to four years.

During his administration, taxes were often an issue of contention between Guy and the State Legislature, and at one point, he requested a special session in order to revamp the sales tax statute. In addition, he successfully sought to tighten the State's authority over the State-owned grain mill and elevator. In 1967, President Lyndon Johnson requested that Guy make a trip to South Vietnam in order to observe their elections. Also, in 1967 and 1968, he chaired the National Governors Conference, and in the former year, headed the Council of State Governments.

Eschewing a fourth term, Guy stepped down from office in 1973, and subsequently served as a political science instructor at Concordia College. In 1975 he was named Staff Director of the Western Governors' Regional Energy Policy Office, located in Denver.

Guy is married to Jean Mason, and the couple has five children.

LINK, ARTHUR A. (1914-), twenty-third governor of North Dakota (1973-1981), was born in Alexander, North Dakota on May 24, 1914. He studied at North Dakota Agricultural College (later, North Dakota State University). Politically active early on, Link, a Democrat, held a seat in the North Dakota House of Representatives between 1947 and 1971. During that time, from 1969 to 1971, he chaired the State Advisory Council for Vocational Education. In 1970 he ran for and won a seat in the United States House of Representatives.

In 1972 Link successfully sought the North Dakota governorship on the Democratic ticket. During his tenure, North Dakota's agricultural climate was prosperous, with farmers able to make a profit on their crops. Also, income and property tax laws were revised. However, the biggest issue during that time was probably the energy crisis, as it was throughout the rest of the country. North Dakota's mineral wealth attracted those who sought to exploit it, a point of view that didn't sit well with citizens who were worried about the environment, especially concerning the issue of strip mining. Link, keeping in mind that much of the wealth of minerals often sat directly beneath the State's most prolific agricultural areas, wanted tighter controls on the strip mining industry. He also fought for more water rights for North Dakota. During his time in office, he served as Chairman of the Resolutions Committee of the Farmers Union Grain Terminal Association for three years and in 1979, was Chairman of the National Governors' Association Committee on Agriculture.

Link's decisions concerning North Dakota's energy and conservation issues were not always popular, especially his support of a substantial severance tax on the mining of the State's mineral supplies, and it was surmised that this was the reason for the loss of his third gubernatorial bid in 1980.

After stepping down from office, Link served on a number of boards for such organizations as the Lewis and Clark Trail Museum and the Williston University Center Foundation. Link is married to Grace Johnson, and the couple has six children.

OLSON, ALLEN INGVAR (1938-), twenty-fourth governor of North Dakota (1981-1985), was born in Rolla, North Dakota on November 5, 1938. He attended the University of North Dakota, where he received a B.A. degree in 1960 and an LL.B. degree in 1963. In the latter year he enlisted in the United States Army, where he was an attorney in the Judge Advocate General Corps, serving at the Pentagon in Washington, D.C., and also in Germany.

After his discharge in 1967, Olson returned to North Dakota where he was named Assistant Director of the Legislative Council. In that post, working from the State Capitol in Bismarck, Olson oversaw extensive research concerning the long-term effects of strip mining and land reclamation. Olson subsequently entered into private law practice as a member of the firm of Conmy, Rosenberg, Lucas and Olson, between 1969 to 1972.

In the latter year, Olson, a Republican, successfully ran for North Dakota Attorney General, and was reelected to that post in 1976. In the 1980 gubernatorial election, Olson won the race on the Republican ticket, taking office on January 6, 1981. During his tenure, he was outspoken in his belief that the State of North Dakota should have more autonomy concerning the issue of coal development, which he felt should be increased. Also, since State revenues were dwindling, he was forced to make several budget cuts, which included State raises and funding earmarked for construction of State buildings. While in office, Olson served on a number of boards and commissions, including the Board of Pardons, the Board of University and School Lands, the Indian Affairs Commission, and North Dakota's Emergency Commission.

It was assumed that Olson would join the Republican sweep during Ronald Reagan's landslide victory for the presidency in 1984, but in a surprise upset, Olson lost his bid for reelection, and stepped down from office the following year. He continued to be involved in public service after his governorship, serving as chairman of such organizations as the National Governors' Association Soil Conservation Task Force, and the Legal Committee of the Interstate Oil Compact Commission, plus he was also a member of the Executive Committee of the National Governors' Association.

Olson is married to Barbara Benner, and the couple has three children.

SINNER, GEORGE A. (1928-), twenty-fifth governor of North Dakota (1985-1993), was born in Fargo, North Dakota, but spent his youth in Casselton, a town that produced a number of other North Dakota governors. Sinner attended St. John's University, earning a philosophy degree in 1950. During 1950-51 he was a member of the United States Air Force, and in 1952, went into partnership with his brothers in a diversified farming venture called Sinner Brothers and Bresnahan.

Sinner served in the North Dakota State Senate from 1962 to 1966. Several years later, in 1982, he ran for and won a seat in the North Dakota State House of Representatives. During his political years Sinner served with a number of professional and educational organizations, including the North Dakota Wheat Growers Association Board, the North Dakota Board of Higher Education, the American Soybean Association, the North Dakota Stockmen's Association, and the North Dakota Farm Bureau, plus he served as president of the Red River Valley Sugarbeet Growers Association from 1975 to 1979.

In 1985 Sinner successfully secured the North Dakota governorship on the Democratic ticket. During his tenure, a reorganization of the State government took place, most notably within the Economic Development Commission. In addition, the governor had to deal with the farm crisis brought on by a debilitating drought throughout the State. Also during his time in office, Sinner was co-chairman of the United States-Canada Task Force of the National Governor's Association, as well as chairman of the NGA's Committee on Agriculture and Rural Development.

Sinner stepped down from the governor's chair in 1993.

SCHAFER, EDWARD T. (1946-), twenty-sixth governor of North Dakota (1993-current), was born in Bismarck, North Dakota, on August 8, 1946. He attended the University of North Dakota, from which he graduated with a business administration degree in 1969, then studied at Denver University, receiving his Master's Degree. Schafer served in several executive posts at Gold Seal Company, and was named president of the firm in 1976.

In 1992 Schafer successfully ran for the North Dakota governorship on the Republican ticket, and secured a second term in 1996. During his tenure, Schafer has been able to create a solid economic base from which to generate funding for such State needs as health, education, and safety programs, all without raising taxes. In addition, the job rate has increased and unemployment has dropped significantly. Education has been a priority as well, with educational programs receiving more funding, and over seventy million dollars has been earmarked for North Dakota's senior citizens. He has also pushed for water development in the State, especially water service for those living in rural areas. In addition, a progressive welfare reform program has been implemented during his administration.

Also while in office, Schafer has served as Chairman of such organizations as the Western Governors' Association, the Midwestern Governors' Association, and the Interstate Oil and Gas Compact, and is currently the lead governor for the TRUST Coalition (Transportation Revenues Used Solely for Transportation) and vice-chair of the National Governors' Association Natural Resources Committee.

Schafer is married to Nancy Jones, and the couple has four children. His current term is set to expire in 2001.

DICTIONARY OF PLACES

Population figures and demographic information are official U.S. Census Bureau finals for 1990. When two figures are shown, separated by a slash, the first figure is the 1990 and the second is the Census Bureau 1999 estimate – the most recent available. Year 2000 census supplements will be available in the fall of 2001.

ABERCROMBIE, City; Richland County; Pop. 260 / 232; Zip Code 58001; Elev. 936; Lat. 46-26-33 N, Long. 096-43-30 W; The town is named after Fort Abercrombie, a military post in intermittent use in the 1660s.

ADAMS, City; Walsh County; Pop. 303 / 228; Zip Code 58210; Lat. 48-25-41 N, Long. 098-04-32 W; Named by early settlers for Adams County, Wisconsin.

ALAMO, City; Williams County; Pop. 122 / 63; Zip Code 58830; Elev. 2115; Lat. 48-34-44 N, Long. 103-27-46 W; Alamo is Spanish for cottonwood. The town is named for both the nearby cottonwood stands and the famous mission in Texas.

ALEXANDER, City; McKenzie County; Pop. 358 / 174; Zip Code 58831; Lat. 47-50-22 N, Long. 103-38-36 W; Founded in 1905 and named for prominent political leader, Alexander McKenzie.

ALMONT, City; Morton County; Pop. 146 / 125; Zip Code 58520; Lat. 46-43-18 N, Long. 101-30-32 W; Founded in 1906 and named for nearby Altamount Buttes, a glacial moraine.

ANAMOOSE, City; McHenry County; Pop. 355 / 264; Zip Code 58710; Lat. 47-52-58 N, Long. 100-14-17 W; The town's name honors U.S. District Court Judge Chales Anamoose.

ANETA, City; Nelson County; Pop. 341 / 269; Zip Code 58212; Elev. 1503; Lat. 47-40-46 N, Long. 097-59-32 W; Aneta is named for Mrs. Annetta Mitchell who was the first woman resident of the townsite.

ANTLER, City; Bottineau County; Pop. 101 / 65; Zip Code 58711; Elev. 2430; Lat. 48-58-17 N, Long. 101-17-02 W; Descriptively named for a set of streams flowing through the area that resembles a deer's horns.

ARGUSVILLE, City; Cass County; Pop. 147 / 157; Zip Code 58005; Lat. 47-03-21 N, Long. 096-56-05 W; The town is named after the *Forge Argus* newspaper, which was the first daily newspaper in North Dakota.

ARTHUR, City; Cass County; Pop. 445 / 426; Zip Code 58006; Lat. 47-06-18 N, Long. 097-13-03 W; The town's name honors U.S. President Chester A. Arthur.

ASHLEY, City; McIntosh County Seat; Pop. 1,192 / 863; Zip Code 58413; Lat. 46-02-08 N, Long. 099-22-17 W; The railroad came through in 1887. Railroad officials named it for Ashley Morrow, who was part of the construction company.

BALTA, City; Pierce County; Pop. 139 / 67; Zip Code 58313; Elev. 1542; Lat. 48-10-03 N, Long. 100-02-11 W; Early Russian immigrants named the town for Balta in the Russian Ukraine.

BEACH, City; Stark County; Pop. 1,274 / 1,040; Zip Code 58621; Lat. 46-54-54 N, Long. 104-00-14 W; Named for a local settler.

BELFIELD, City; Stark County; Pop. 1,274 / 864; Zip Code 58622; Elev. 2592; Lat. 46-53-05 N, Long. 103-11-53 W; The town is named for the beautiful prairie bluebell flowers on the nearby hills.

BERTHOLD, City; Ward County; Pop. 485 / 409; Zip Code 58710; Lat. 48-19-49 N, Long. 101-49-45 W; Bartholomew Berthold established a trading post at the townsite in 1845. Later a fort, the town was named in his honor.

BEULAH, City; Mercer County; Pop. 2,878 / 3,162; Zip Code 58523; Elev. 1750; Lat. 47-15-53 N, Long. 101-46-46 W; Originally called Tray, New York, the name was later changed to Beulah after a niece of the land company agent.

BINFORD, City; Griggs County; Pop. 293 / 195; Zip Code 58416; Lat. 47-33-38 N, Long. 098-20-40 W; Originally called Blooming Prairie, the town was renamed Binford for the attorney representing the original landowners.

BISBEE, City; Towner County; Pop. 257 / 193; Zip Code 583+; Lat. 48-37-25 N, Long. 099-30-03 W; The town's name remembers Civil War veteran Colonel Bisbee who lived nearby.

BISMARCK, City; Burleigh County Seat and Capital of North Dakota; Pop. 44,485 / 55,109; Zip Code 585+; Lat. 46-48-51 N, Long. 100-47-06 W; Northern Pacific Railroad officials named the town for Germany's famous Chancellor, Otto Von Bismarck.

BOTTINEAU, City; Bottineau County Seat; Pop. 2,829 / 2,434; Zip Code 58318; Elev. 1635; Lat. 48-49-38 N, Long. 100-26-30 W; The city's name honors early explorer Pierre Bottineau.

BOWBELLS, City; Burke County Seat; Pop. 587 / 370; Zip Code 58721; Lat. 48-48-14 N, Long. 102-14-51 W; Named by English stockholders of the Soo railroad for the famous Bow Bells in London, England.

BOWMAN, City; Bowman County Seat; Pop. 2,071 / 1,595; Zip Code 58623; Elev. 2960; Lat. 46-10-52 N, Long. 103-23-53 W; Originally called Lowden, the name was changed to honor William Bowman, a well-known territorial legislator.

BUFFALO, City; Cass County; Pop. 226 / 197; Zip Code 58011; Elev. 1197; Lat. 46-55-16 N, Long. 097-32-58 W; The town is named for Buffalo, New York.

BURLINGTON, City; Ward County; Pop. 762 / 993; Zip Code 587+; Lat. 48-16-44 N, Long. 101-25-36 W; Originally called Colton, the name was changed in 1884 to Burlington, for Burlington, Iowa.

CANDO, City; Towner County Seat; Pop. 1,496 / 1,251; Zip Code 58324; Elev. 1486; Lat. 48-26-25 N, Long. 099-11-52 W; Established in 1884 and given the name "can do" by county commissioners overruling a challenge to their authority.

CARRINGTON, City; Foster County Seat; Pop. 2,641 / 2,187; Zip Code 58421; Elev. 1587; Lat. 47-26-59 N, Long. 099-07-11 W; The town was named in honor of M.D. Carrington, general manager of a land company with large holdings in the area.

CARSON, City; Grant County Seat; Pop. 469 / 274; Zip Code 58529; Lat. 46-25-12 N, Long. 101-34-00 W; Early settlers coined the name to honor pioneer businessmen Frank Carter and the Pederson brothers.

CASSELTON, City; Cass County; Pop. 1,661 / 1,630; Zip Code 58012; Elev. 936; Lat. 46-54-07 N, Long. 097-12-43 W; Named in honor of Northern Pacific Railway president George Cass.

CAVALIER, City; Pembina County Seat; Pop. 1,505 / 1,414; Zip Code 58220; Lat. 48-47-33 N, Long. 097-37-22 W; The town is named in honor of Charles Cavalier, the earliest settler.

CENTER, City; Oliver County Seat; Pop. 900 / 274; Zip Code 58530; Lat. 47-07-03 N, Long. 101-17-56 W; The town's early residents named it for its central location in the county.

COGSWELL, City; Sargent County; Pop. 227 / 167; Zip Code 58017; Lat. 46-06-22 N, Long. 097-46-59 W; Founded in 1889 and named after a Soo Railroad official.

COLEHARBOR, City; Mclean County; Pop. 150 / 77; Zip Code 58531; Lat. 47-32-37 N, Long. 101-13-06 W; Named by Soo Railroad officials for one of their employees, W.A. Cole.

COLUMBUS, City; Burke County; Pop. 325 / 146; Zip Code 58727; Lat. 48-54-19 N, Long. 102-46-48 W; The town takes its name from the second postmaster, Columbus Larson.

COOPERSTOWN, City; Griggs County Seat; Pop. 1,308 / 1,090; Zip Code 58425; Elev. 1437; Lat. 47-26-38 N, Long. 098-07-12 W; The town is named in honor of Rollin C. Cooper a well-to-do farmer who settled the area in 1880.

CROSBY, City; Divide County Seat; Pop. 1,469 / 968; Zip Code 58730; Elev. 1964; Lat. 48-54-47 N, Long. 103-17-29 W; In 1903 local lawyer, S.A. Crosby platted the area and founded the town. It is named in his honor.

DAVENPORT, City; Cass County; Pop. 195 / 213; Zip Code 58021; Lat. 46-42-50 N, Long. 097-04-01 W; Founded in 1872 and named by one of the town's founders for Alice Davenport, wife of the Governor of Massachusetts.

DAWSON, City; Kidder County; Pop. 144 / 68; Zip Code 58428; Lat. 46-52-04 N, Long. 099-45-06 W; Founded in 1873 and named in honor of former and banker J. Dawson Thompson.

DES LACS, City; Ward County; Pop. 212 / 215; Zip Code 58733; Elev. 1931; Lat. 46-15-22 N, Long. 101-33-32 W; The town is named after the river and lakes of the same name.

DEVILS LAKE, City; Ramsey County Seat; Pop. 7,442 / 7,480; Zip Code 58301; Elev. 1475; Lat. 48-06-46 N, Long. 098-51-44 W; Originally called Creelsburg, the town's name was later changed to Devil's Lake after the nearby lake.

DICKINSON, City; Stark County Seat; Pop. 15,924 / 16,301 Zip Code 586+; Elev. 2417; Lat. 46-52-57 N, Long. 102-47-24 W; The town is named after the original landowner Wells S. Dickinson.

DRAKE, City; McHenry County; Pop. 479 / 291; Zip Code 58736; Elev. 1682; Lat. 47-55-17 N, Long. 100-22-21 W; Herman Drake homesteaded the town in 1899. Soo Railroad Company officials named it in his honor.

DRAYTON, City; Pembina County; Pop. 1,082 / 845; Zip Code 58225; Elev. 801; Lat. 48-33-45 N, Long. 097-10-29 W; Canadian settlers named the town after their former home in Drayton, Ontario.

DUNN CENTER, City; Rolette County; Pop. 625 / 118; Zip Code 58626; Elev. 2182; Lat. 47-21-13 N, Long. 102-37-21 W; Named for an early settler.

ELGIN, City; Grant County; Pop. 930 / 597; Zip Code 58533; Elev. 1545; Lat. 46-23-53 N, Long. 101-50-48 W; Originally called Staley, the name was changed to Elgin when a local citizen suggested the name after his Elgin watch.

ELLENDALE, City; Dickey County Seat; Pop. 1,967 / 1,701; Zip Code 58436; Elev. 1456; Lat. 46-00-06 N, Long. 098-31-27 W; A railroad townsite, it is named in honor of Mary Ellen Dole Merrill, the wife of the local railroad superintendent.

EMERADO, City; Grand Forks County; Pop. 596 / 449; Zip Code 58228; Lat. 47-55-00 N, Long. 097-21-59 W; The town's name derives from Emery Farm, part of the original townsite.

ENDERLIN, City; Cass & Ransom Counties; Pop. 1,151 / 935; Zip Code 58027; Lat. 46-37-09 N, Long. 097-36-02 W; A humorous corruption of "end of the line," and referring to a temporary terminus of the railroad.

ESMOND, City; Benson County; Pop. 337 / 181; Zip Code 58332; Elev. 1623; Lat. 48-02-01 N, Long. 099-45-59 W; Founded in 1901 and named by railroad construction engineer E. Smith after Thockeray's novel, *Henry Esmond*.

FAIRMOUNT, City; Richland County; Pop. 480 / 400; Zip Code 58030; Elev. 984; Lat. 46-03-22 N, Long. 096-35-57 W; Founded in 1881 and named by original settlers after Fairmount Park in Philadelphia, Pa.

FARGO, City; Cass County Seat; Pop. — / 88,128; Zip Code 58102; Lat. 46-52-45 N long. 096-47-44 W; Founded in 1871 and named by Northern Pacific Railroad officials in honor of William Fargo, the founder of Wells-Fargo.

FESSENDEN, City; Wells County Seat; Pop. 761 / 571; Zip Code 58438; Elev. 1608; Lat. 47-39-01 N, Long. 099-37-26 W; Named in honor of surveyor, General Cortez Fessenden who surveyed the area in the early 1880s.

FINLEY, City; Steele County Seat; Pop. 718 / 495; Zip Code 58230; Elev. 1457; Lat. 47-30-54 N, Long. 097-50-06 W; Originally called Gilbert, it was renamed in 1896 to honor Great Northern Railway Vice-President, W.W. Finley.

FLASHER, City; Morton County; Pop. 410 / 296; Zip Code 585+; Lat. 46-27-14 N, Long. 101-13-42 W; The town was founded in 1902 and named in honor of homesteader Mabel Flasher.

FORDVILLE, City; Walsh County; Pop. 326 / 267; Zip Code 58231; Elev. 1144; Lat. 48-15-08 N, Long. 097-47-53 W; Originally called Medford, the name was combined with Belleville to give Fordville.

FORMAN, City; Sargent County Seat; Pop. 629 / 538; Zip Code 58032; Lat. 46-06-26 N, Long. 097-38-06 W; Founded in 1883 and named after Colonel Colnglius Forman who settled in the area.

FORT YATES, City; Sioux County Seat; Pop. 771 / 203; Zip Code 58528; Lat. 46-24-46 N, Long. 100-38-13 W; The town is named in honor of Captain George Yates, who was killed at Custer's last stand in 1876.

FULLERTON, City; Dickey County; Pop. 107 / 80; Zip Code 58441; Elev. 1455; Lat. 46-09-47 N, Long. 098-25-39 W; Original landowner E.F. Sweet settled in the area in 1882. He named the town for his father-in-law, P.C. Fuller.

GACKLE, City; Logan County; Pop. 456 / 403; Zip Code 58442; Lat. 46-37-35 N, Long. 099-08-21 W; Founded in 1903 and named for merchant George Gackle.

GALESBURG, City; Traill County; Pop. 165 / 153; Zip Code 58035; Lat. 47-16-11 N, Long. 097-24-35 W; Named after the original landowner, J.H. Gale, who settled in the area in 1883.

GARRISON, City; McLean County; Pop. 1,830 / 1,463, Zip Code 58540; Elev. 1920; Lat. 47-39-18 N, Long. 101-24-45 W; The town is named from Garrison Stream. The stream was named in 1864 by troops garrisoned at nearby Fort Stevenson.

GILBY, City; Grand Forks County; Pop. 283 / 229; Zip Code 58235; Lat. 48-05-09 N, Long. 097-28-12 W; The town is named for the Gibley brothers who were early settlers.

GLADSTONE, City; Stark County; Pop. 317 / 224; Zip Code 58630; Elev. 2354; Lat. 46-51-35 N, Long. 102-34-09 W; Early settlers named the town for English statesman William Gladstone.

GLEN ULLIN, City; Morton County; Pop. 1,125 / 869; Zip Code 58631; Elev. 2072; Lat. 46-48-48 N, Long. 101-49-51 W; Founded in 1883 and given a Gaelic name, *Glen* means "volley" and *ullin* is from an English ballad, *Lord's Ullin Daughter*.

GRAFTON, City; Walsh County Seat; Pop. 5,293 / 5,123; Zip Code 58237; Elev. 826; Lat. 48-25-04 N, Long. 097-24-37 W; The first settler, Thomas Cooper, named the town for his wife's former home in Grafton County, New Hampshire.

GRAND FORKS, City; Grand Forks County Seat; Pop. 43,765 / 45,967; Zip Code 58201; Elev. 834; Lat. 47-56-12 N, Long. 097-12-00 W; French for traders named the Site Grand Forks for the union of the Red River and Red Lake River.

GWINNER, City; Sargent County; Pop. 725 / 692; Zip Code 58020; Elev. 1263; Lat. 46-11-58 N, Long. 097-57-38 W; Northern Pacific Railway officials named the town in honor of Major Stockholder and European banker Arthur Gwinner.

HALLIDAY, City; Dunn County; Pop. 355 / 243; Zip Code 58636; Elev. 2044; Lat. 47-21-05 N, Long. 102-20-15 W; The town's name honors Nathan Holiday, the first postmaster.

HANKINSON, City; Richland County; Pop. 1,158 / 978; Zip Code 58041; Elev. 1067; Lat. 46-04-26 N, Long. 096-53-37 W; Civil War soldier Richard Hankinson homesteaded the site. The town is named in his honor.

HARVEY, City; Wells County; Pop. 2,527 / 2,044; Zip Code 58341; Elev. 1600; Lat. 47-46-10 N, Long. 099-55-49 W; The town's name honors Colonel James Harvey, a director and stockholder of the Soo Railroad.

HARWOOD, City; Cass County; Pop. 326 / 615; Zip Code 58042; Elev. 889; Lat. 46-58-41 N, Long. 096-52-41 W; The town is named after Fargo real-estate agent A.J. Harwood, who invested heavily in the region.

HATTON, City; Traill County; Pop. 787 / 778; Zip Code 58240; Elev. 1081; Lat. 47-38-16 N, Long. 097-27-33 W; The town's name honors assistant U.S. Postmaster Frank Hatton.

HAZEN, City; Mercer County; Pop. 2,365 / 2,545; Zip Code 58545; Elev. 1743; Lat. 47-24-09 N, Long. 101-32-27 W; The city was founded in 1885 and named for assistant U.S. Postmaster, A.D. Hazen.

HEBRON, City; Morton County; Pop, 1,078 / 797; Zip Code 58638; Elev. 2167; Lat. 46-54-23 N, Long. 102-02-39 W; Originally called Knife River, the name was changed to Hebron, a biblical valley in 1904.

HETTINGER, City; Adams County Seat; Pop. 1,739 / 1,334; Zip Code 58639; Lat. 46-00-00 N, Long. 102-37-57 W; U.S. surveyor E.A. Williams named the town after his father-in-law, Mathias Hettinger.

HILLSBORO, City; Trail County Seat; Pop. 1,600 / 1,493; Zip Code 580+; Elev. 908; Lat. 47-20-45 N, Long. 097-13-10 W; Founded in 1880 as Comstock, but later renamed Hillsboro to honor railroad magnate James J. Hill.

HOPE, City; Steele County; Pop. 406 / 253; Zip Code 58046; Elev. 1240; Lat. 47-19-31 N, Long. 097-43-01 W; Founded in 1882 and named for Hope Steele, wife of the land company treasurer who bought 50,000 acres of wheat land from the railroad for one dollar per acre.

HUNTER, City; Cass County; Pop. 369 / 307; Zip Code 58048; Elev. 978; Lat. 47-11-36 N, Long. 097-13-22 W; The town's name remembers John C. Hunter who owned extensive landholdings in the area.

INKSTER, City; Grand Forks County; Pop. 135 / 78; Zip Code 58244; Elev. 1029; Lat. 48-09-14 N, Long. 097-38-44 W; The town is named for the first settler George Inkster.

JAMESTOWN, City; Stutsman County Seat; Pop. 16,280 / 15,100; Zip Code 584+; Elev. 1413; Lat. 46-54-12 N, long, 098-42-30 W; The town is located on the James River. Construction Engineer T.L. Rosser, a Virginian, named it after Jamestown, Virginia.

KENMARE, City; Ward County; Pop. 1,456 / 1,315; Zip Code 58746; Lat. 48-40-36 N, Long. 102-04-40 W; Settled in the 1890s and named for a community in Ireland.

KILLDEER, City; Dunn County; Pop. 790 / 623; Zip Code 58640; Elev. 1433; Lat. 47-22-11 N, Long. 102-45-10 W; The town is named for the nearby ten-mile long Killdeer hills.

KULM, City; La Moure County; Pop. 570 / 395; Zip Code 58456; Lat. 46-18-09 N, Long. 098-56-56 W; The city's name honors settlers from Kulm, Russia and Kulm, Germany.

LA MOURE, City; La Moure County Seat; Pop. 1,077 / 865; Zip Code 58458; Lat. 46-21-25 N, Long. 098-17-34 W; Founded in 1882 and named in honor of pioneer and territorial politician Judson La Moure.

LARIMORE, City; Grand Forks County; Pop. 1,524 / 1,281 Zip Code 58251; Elev. 1136; Lat. 47-54-21 N, Long. 097-37-42 W; The town is named in honor of Bonanza farmer N.G. Larimore, who held 15,000 acres in the area.

LEEDS, City; Benson County; Pop. 678 / 515; Zip Code 583+; Elev. 1514; Lat. 48-11-14 N, Long. 099-19-13 W; Officials of the Great Northern and Northern Pacific Railroads named the town after Leeds, England.

LEONARD, City; Cass County; Pop. 289 / 289; Zip Code 58052; Lat. 46-39-00 N, Long. 097-14-46 W; The town is named in honor of pioneer settler Leonard Stroble.

LINTON, City; Emmons County Seat; Pop. 1,561 / 1,266; Zip Code 58552; Elev. 1708; Lat. 46-16-01 N, Long. 100-14-01 W; Established in 1899 and named in honor of George Lynn, a prominent pioneer attorney.

LISBON, City; Ransom County Seat; Pop. 2,283 / 2,213; Zip Code 58054; Elev. 1091; Lat. 46-26-17 N, Long. 097-41-15 W; Early settlers named the new town for their former homes in Illinois and New York.

MADDOCK, City; Benson County; Pop. 677 / 526; Zip Code 58348; Elev. 588; Lat. 47-57-41 N, Long. 099-31-41 W; Originally called Ellwood, but later renamed Maddock to honor early settlers.

MANDAN, City; Morton County Seat; Pop. 15,513 / 15,970; Zip Code 58554; Elev. 1657; The town is named in honor of the Mandan Indians.

MAPLETON, City; Cass County; Pop. 306 / 638; Zip Code 58059; Elev. 808; Lat. 46-53-27 N, Long. 097-02-23 W; Founded in 1876 and named for its location on the Maple River.

MAYVILLE, City; Trail County; Pop. 2,255 / 2,109; Zip Code 58219; Elev. 976; Lat. 47-27-28 N, Long. 096-53-02 W; An early settler, Alvin Arnold, named the town for his second daughter, May.

MCCLUSKY, City; Sheridan County Seat; Pop. 658 / 306; Zip Code 58463; Elev. 1925; Lat. 47-28-58 N, Long. 100-26-32 W; The city is named for William McClusky, who settled in the area in 1902.

MEDINA, City; Stutsman County; Pop. 521 / 352; Zip Code 58467; Lat. 46-53-29 N, Long. 099-14-15 W; Founded in 1873 and originally called Midway. The name was later changed to Medina.

MICHIGAN CITY, City; Nelson County; Pop. 502 / 346; Zip Code 58224; Elev. 1516; Lat. 48-09-26 N, Long. 097-55-47 W; In the 1880s settlers from Michigan named the town after their former home.

MILNOR, City; Sargent County; Pop. 716 / 644; Zip Code 58060; Lat. 46-15-36 N, Long. 097-27-19 W; Northern Pacific Railroad officials named the town for two of their employees.

MINOT, City; Ward County Seat; Pop. 32,843 / 35,673; Zip Code 58701; Lat. 48-19-38 N, Long. 101-18-54 W; Founded in 1886 and named for Eastern Railroad investor Henry Davis Minot.

MINTO, City; Walsh County; Pop. 592 / 537; Zip Code 58261; Elev. 820; Lat. 48-17-35 N, Long. 097-22-30 W; Settled by Canadians, who named it for their former home in Canada.

MOHALL, City; Renville County Seat; Pop. 1,049 / 865; Zip Code 58761; Elev. 1639; Lat. 48-45-58 N, Long. 101-30-28 W; The town is named for Martin O. Hall, who settled in the area in 1901.

MOTT, City; Hettinger County Seat; Pop. 1,315 / 867; Zip Code 58646; Elev. 2377; Lat. 46-22-24 N, Long. 102-19-24 W; The town's name honors C.W. Mott, a general agent for the Northern Pacific Railroad.

MUNICH, City; Cavalier County; Pop. 300 / 251; Zip Code 58352; Lat. 48-40-09 N, Long. 098-49-49 W; Town founder, William Budge named the city for the famous town in Germany.

NAPOLEON, City; Logan County Seat; Pop. 1,103 / 791; Zip Code 58561; Lat. 46-30-22 N, Long. 099-46-16 W; Founded in 1886 and named for Napoleon Goodsill, the president of the local land company.

NEW ENGLAND, City; Hettinger County; Pop. 825 / 536; Zip Code 58647; Elev. 2592; Lat. 46-32-25 N, Long. 102-52-00 W; Founded in 1887 by New Englanders and named for their former regional home.

NEW ROCKFORD, City; Eddy County Seat; Pop. 1,791 / 1,445; Zip Code 58356; Lat. 47-40-47 N, Long. 099-08-10 W; Pioneer Charles Gregory named the town for his former home in Rockford, Illinois.

NEW TOWN, City; Mountrail County; Pop. 1,335 / 1,308; Zip Code 58763; Lat. 47-58-52 N, Long. 102-28-44 W; Founded in 1950 to replace several towns flooded by the Garrison Dam Reservoir.

NORTHWOOD, City; Grand Forks County; Pop. 1,240 / 1,042; Zip Code 58267; Elev. 1113; Lat. 47-44-04 N, Long. 097-34-25 W; Early settlers from Northwood, Iowa gave the town its name.

OAKES, City; Dickey County; Pop. 2,112 / 1,760; Zip Code 58474; Elev. 1313; Lat. 46-08-19 N, Long. 098-05-12 W; The town is named in honor of Northern Pacific Railway manager Thomas Oakes.

PAGE, City; Cass County; Pop. 329 / 246; Zip Code 58064; Lat. 47-09-46 N, Long. 097-34-24 W; A large landowner named Colonel Morton named the town in honor of his brother-in-law, E.E. Page.

PARK RIVER, City; Walsh County; Pop. 1,844 / 1,619; Zip Code 58270; Elev. 1006; Lat. 48-23-44 N, Long. 097-44-36 W; Named for the Park River, which flows through the town.

PARSHALL, City; Mountrail County; Pop. 1,059 / 949; Zip Code 58770; Lat. 47-57-11 N, Long. 102-07-58 W; Founded in 1913 and named in honor of George Parshall, a pioneer stagecoach driver.

PEMBINA, City; Pembina County; Pop. 673 / 618; Zip Code 58271; Lat. 48-58-02 N, Long. 097-14-41 W; Derived from the Chippewa Indian word for "summer berry."

PLAZA, City; Mountrail County; Pop. 222 / 170; Zip Code 58771; Lat. 48-01-30 N, Long. 101-57-32 W; Founded in 1906 and descriptively named for a plaza in the town's business district.

PORTAL, City; Burke County; Pop. 238 / 138; Zip Code 58772; Lat. 48-59-42 N, Long. 102-32-38 W; Founded in the 1890s as a railroad division point and named for its closeness to the international border.

RAY, City; Williams County; Pop. 766 / 598; Zip Code 58849; Lat. 48-18-15 N, Long. 103-10-00 W; Founded in 1901 and named in honor of early pioneer Ray Payton.

REEDER, City; Adams County; Pop. 355 / 206; Zip Code 58649; Lat. 46-06-19 N, Long. 102-56-30 W; The town is named in honor of Milwaukee Railroad Engineer, E.A. Reeder.

RHAME, City; Bowman County; Pop. 222 / 168; Zip Code 58651; Lat. 46-13-57 N, Long. 103-39-21 W; Settled in 1907 and named for railroad district engineer, Mitchell Rhame.

ROLETTE, City; Rolette County; Pop. 667 / 727; Zip Code 58366; Elev. 1623; Lat. 48-39-46 N, Long. 099-50-11 W; The town's name honors pioneer fur trader and legislator Joseph Rolette.

ROLLA, City; Rolette County Seat; Pop. 1,538 / 1,536; Zip Code 8367; Lat. 48-51-40 N, Long. 099-36-51 W; The city's name is either a contraction of the county name or is named after Rolla, Missouri.

RUGBY, City; Pierce County Seat; Pop. 3,335 / 2,774; Zip Code 58315; Elev. 1550; Lat. 48-30-21 N, Long. 100-10-29 W; Founded in 1885 and named by English railroad stockholders for Rugby, England.

ST. JOHN, City; Rolette County; Pop. 401 / 419; Zip Code 58369; Lat. 48-56-43 N, Long. 099-42-31 W; An old trading center, St. John was named by an early settler for his former home of St. John, Canada.

SAWYER, City; Ward County; Pop. 417 / 315; Zip Code 58781; Elev. 1542; Lat. 48-05-21 N, Long. 101-03-03 W; Founded in 1882 and named by Soo railroad officials for a company employee named Sawyer.

SCRANTON, City; Bowman County; Pop. 415 / 265; Zip Code 58653; Lat. 46-08-55 N, Long. 103-08-16 W; Established in 1907 and named for another coal mining town, Scranton, Pa.

SELFRIDGE, City; Sioux County; Pop. 273 / 253; Zip Code 58568; Elev. 2184; Lat. 46-02-29 N, Long. 100-55-26 W; Named either for a Soo railroad official or an early army aviator hero.

SHERWOOD, City; Renville County; Pop. 294 / 251; Zip Code 58782; Lat. 48-57-41 N, Long. 101-37-49 W; The town is named for original landowner Sherwood Sleeper.

SHEYENNE, City; Eddy County; Pop. 307 / 282; Zip Code 58374; Lat. 47-49-37 N, Long. 099-06-57 W; The town is named after the river, and the river, in turn, is named for the Chetening Indians.

STANLEY, City; Mountrail County Seat; Pop. 1,631 / 1,243; Zip Code 58784; Lat. 48-18-45 N, Long. 102-23-01 W; Settled in 1895 and named for an early homesteader, King Stanley.

STANTON, City; Mercer County Seat; Pop. 623 / 462; Zip Code 58571; Elev. 1701; Lat. 47-19-14 N, Long. 101-22-57 W; The McGrath brothers settled here in 1882 and gave it their mother's maiden name.

STEELE, City; Kidder County Seat; Pop. 796 / 603; Zip Code 58482; Elev. 1865; Lat. 46-51-11 N, Long. 099-55-05 W; In 1881 Colonel Wilbur Steele platted a townsite on his homestead. The town is named in his honor.

STRASBURG, City; Emmons County; Pop. 623 / 504; Zip Code 5573; Elev. 1804; Lat. 46-08-04 N, Long. 100-09-50 W; Founded in 1902 and named for the city in Europe's Rhineland.

SURREY, City; Ward County; Pop. 999 / 848; Zip Code 58785; Elev. 1625; Lat. 48-14-03 N, Long. 101-07-54 W; Founded in 1900 and named by railroad officials for Surrey, England.

TAPPEN, City; Kidder County; Pop. 271 / 209; Zip Code 58487; Lat. 46-52-15 N, Long. 099-37-47 W; Tappen is named after Bonanza former S. Toppen, who ran a 10,000 acre farm there in the 1880s.

THOMPSON, City; Grand Forks County; Pop. 785 / 886; Zip Code 58278; Lat. 47-46-36 N, Long. 097-06-20 W; Originally called Norton, but renamed for the first postmaster, Albert Thompson.

TIOGA, City; Williams County; Pop. 1,597 / 1,236; Zip Code 58852; Elev. 2238; Lat. 48-23-56 N, Long. 102-56-15 W; Settlers from Tioga, New York settled here in 1902. The name is an Iroquois Indian word meaning "peaceful valley."

TOWNER, City; McHenry County Seat; Pop. 867 / 554; Zip Code 58788; Elev. 1186; Lat. 48-20-53 N, Long. 100-24-18 W; Settled in 1886 and named for Colonel O.M. Towner, a Civil War veteran, and an early rancher.

TURTLE LAKE, City; McLean County; Pop. 707 / 611; Zip Code 58575; Elev. 1875; Lat. 47-31-19 N, Long. 100-53-12 W; The town is named for the nearby turtle-shaped lake.

UNDERWOOD, City; McLean County; Pop. 1,329 / 912; Zip Code 58576; Elev. 2026; Lat. 47-27-14 N, Long. 101-08-13 W; Founded in 1903 and named in honor of local railroad vice-president Fred Underwood.

UPHAM, City; McHenry County; Pop. 227 / 194; Zip Code 58789; Elev. 1445; Lat. 48-34-53 N, Long. 100-43-48 W; Founded in 1905 and named in honor of explorer and geologist Dr. Warren Upham.

VALLEY CITY, City; Barnes County Seat; Pop. 7,774 / 6,966; Zip Code 58072; Elev. 1222; Lat. 46-55-34 N, Long. 097-59-55 W; Founded in 1881 and given a descriptive name.

VELVA, City; McHenry County; Pop, 1,101 / 820; Zip Code 58790; Lat. 48-03-34 N, Long. 100-55-53 W; Soo railroad officials descriptively named the town for the velvet-like appearance of the Mouse River Valley.

WAHPETON, City; Richland County Seat; Pop. 9,064 / 9,213; Zip Code 58024; Elev. 963; Lat. 46-18-06 N, Long. 096-44-19 W; The town is named after the local Indian tribe, the Wahpetons.

WALHALLA, City; Pembina County; Pop. 1,429 / 1,111; Zip Code 58282; Lat. 48-55-13 N, Long. 097-55-11 W; An English translation of a German word meaning "home of the gods."

WASHBURN, City; McLean County Seat; Pop. 1,767 / 1,400; Zip Code 58577; Elev. 7731; Lat. 47-17-16 N, Long. 101-01-31 W; The town was founded in 1882 and named by its founders for C.C. Washburn, the Governor of Wisconsin in 1872.

WATFORD CITY, City; McKenzie County Seat; Pop. 2,119 / 1,494; Zip Code 58854; Lat. 47-48-07 N, Long. 103-16-56 W; Originally named Banks, the local physician, V.G. Morris, renamed it for his former home in Ontario, Canada.

WEST FARGO, City; Cass County; Pop. 10,099 / 14,477; Zip Code 58078; Lat. 46-54-48 N, Long. 096-49-23 W; Originally called Haggart, the town's name was changed to West Fargo to reflect its proximity to Fargo, N.D.

WILLISTON, City; Williams County Seat; Pop. 13,336 / 12,463; Zip Code 58801; Elev. 1882; Lat. 48-09-17 N, Long. 103-37-28 W; Great Northern Railroad Director James Hill named the town after hit friend D. Willis James of New York.

WILTON, City; McLean County; Pop. 688 / 660; Zip Code 58579; Elev. 2183; Lat. 47-09-36 N, Long. 100-47-06 W; Minneapolis flour magnate W.D. Washburn founded the town in 1898 and named it for his former home in Maine.

WISHEK, City; McIntosh County; Pop. 1,345 /972; Zip Code 58495; Lat. 46-15-36 N, Long. 099-33-44 W; Surveyed in 1898 and named in honor of original landowner John Wishek.

WYNDMERE, City; Richland County; Pop. 550 / 545; Zip Code 58008; Elev. 1059; Lat. 46-15-58 N, Long. 096-59-51 W; Settled in the 1880s and given an English peace name meaning "narrow marshy lone."

OHIO
The Buckeye State

Scioto Downs - Columbus

The Yacht Club Basin on Lake Erie, Rocky River

GOVERNOR
Bob Taft

Columbus celebrates

Horse and Buggie auction in Amish Country near Farmerstown

The "Valley Gem" takes a tour
through the Ohio River Valley

Cleveland's skyline

INTRODUCTION

THE BUCKEYE STATE

Ohio is truly a land of variety, a microcosm of the rest of America's landscape, culture, and economy. About 2,500 lakes dot this small (thirty-fourth in size) State, including Lake Erie, which forms its northern border. In fact, the towns along Erie can be considered ocean ports because of their access to the Atlantic Ocean via the St. Lawrence. Ohio is also a land of rivers, namely the Muskingum, Scioto, Maumee, and Miami, as well as the great Ohio and its many tributaries.

A variety of geographical features make for cultural differences. In Ohio, there are three distinct ways of life determined by the natural surroundings. In cities such as Toledo and Cleveland along the banks of ocean-going Lake Erie, life is cosmopolitan and carries much of New England's heritage. The southern part of the State is centered on Cincinnati and the great Ohio River upon which it was built; here, trade with western and southern states is important. The heartland area of rivers, valleys, and hills is taken up mainly by farmlands that spread outward from the capital.

Even before it was named the seventeenth state in the Union on March 1, 1803, Ohio experienced growth due to its service as a passageway to the Northwest Territory. Small settlements of New Englanders developed the area into several major cities. Canals, railroads, and highways traveling in and out of the State were built to provide transportation.

The later need for steel was accompanied by Ohio's importance as the holder of fine lake and river transportation between the iron ore deposits of Minnesota and Michigan, and the coal mines of the east. In 1870, about 2,600,000 persons lived in Ohio. By the time of the 1970 census, 10,657,423 persons were residing here, with two-thirds of the population in nine urban areas; the State had become the sixth largest in population, with a reputation as a nationwide provider of manufactured items such as steel and rubber products as well as farm goods. By 1980, the State's population was 10,772,342, an increase of 1.1 percent from 1970 Census. In 1990, population had grown to 10,847,115, a 0.5 percent increase over 1980 figures. And the U.S. Census for 2000 listed Ohio's population at 11,353,140, with 506,140 new residents, an increase of 4.7 percent over 1990 figures.

THE STATE NAME

Ohio was named after the river that flows along its southern border. The French took the name from a Wyandot Indian word, O-*he-zuh*, meaning "great, grand, fair to look upon," and pronounced it Ohio. The Iroquois also had a word, *Oheo*, which meant "beautiful;" some historians suggest that the Wyandots may have used this word in naming the river. Other Iroquoian words, such as *O-y-o*, meaning "a stream very white with froth," and *Ohion-hiio*, or "beautiful river," are also possible roots for the State's name.

One historian suggests that there may be a connection between the Delaware Indian name Kittanning, or "at the Great River," and an Iroquoian word, *Ohio*, meaning the same thing. The secondary meaning of *io*, he says, was "grand" and "beautiful," and was applied to the Ohio River only after the French arrived.

In any case, the French first brought the word into common usage to describe the section of the country now known as Ohio.

STATE NICKNAMES

Ohio's nicknames are as follows: the Buckeye State, the Mother of Modern Presidents, and the Yankee State.

The nickname of "Buckeye" is derived from a legendary incident before Ohio became a State. The first court conducted by the settlers in Ohio was located at Marietta, in a large wooden fortress known as the Campus Martius. On September 2, 1788, while the judges marched in a body to the fort, a large, robust man named Colonel Sproat so impressed a group of onlooking Iroquois Indians that they excitedly shouted, "Hetuck! Hetuck!" which meant *Big Buckeye*. From that incident, in addition to the fact that there were many buckeye trees (*Aesculus glabra*) in the area, Ohio became known as the Buckeye State. However, the nickname was not made official until 1840, when it was approved by the Legislature after a bitter fight.

Ohio's reputation as the "Mother of Modern Presidents" stems from the fact that eight presidents hail from the State: James A. Garfield, Ulysses S. Grant, Warren G. Harding, Benjamin Harrison, William H. Harrison, Rutherford B. Hayes, William McKinley, and William H. Taft.

Before 1820, the more staid settlers in Virginia and Kentucky called Ohio the "Yankee State" because of its more freewheeling institutions.

THE STATE SEAL

In 1803, the Legislature of the new State of Ohio approved a State seal designed by Secretary of State, William Creighton. The seal was inspired by a view of the rising sun between the hills of Mount Logan, as seen from the home of U.S. Senator Thomas Worthington. In the foreground of the seal were a sheaf of wheat and a bundle of seventeen arrows, and in the background was the sun spreading its rays over a mountain, signifying that Ohio was both the seventeenth State and the first State west of the Alleghenies.

The first law authorizing this seal was repealed in 1805, and various other seals were introduced until 1868, when an act reinstated the original seal with a minor change: the single mountain was replaced with a range of hills. Surrounding the circular sign were the words, "The Great Seal of the State of Ohio." The current seal of Ohio was revised in 1967, with the revision based on the original seal of 1803, as follows:

"The great seal of the state shall be two and one-half inches in diameter and shall consist of the coat of arms of the state within a circle, having a diameter of one and three-fourths inches, surrounded by the words 'THE GREAT SEAL OF THE STATE OF OHIO' in news gothic capitals."

The coat of arms used in the seal was also revised in 1967:

"The coat of arms of the state shall consist of the following device: a circular shield; in the right foreground of the shield a full sheaf of wheat bound and standing erect; in the left foreground, a cluster of seventeen arrows bound in the center and resembling in form the sheaf of wheat; in the background, a representation of Mount Logan, Ross County, as viewed from Adena state memorial; over the mount, a rising sun three-quarters exposed and radiating seventeen rays, the exterior extremities of which form a semicircle; and uniting the background and foreground, a representation of the Scioto River and cultivated fields; when the coat of arms of the state is reproduced in color, the colors used shall be substantially the same as the natural color of the terrain and objects shown."

THE STATE FLAG

Ohio was already nearly a century old when the first State flag was designed in 1901, to be shown at the Pan-American Exposition in Buffalo, New York. The State Legislature approved the flag on May 9, 1902. Designed by John Eisenmann, the official flag has three red and two white horizontal stripes (symbolizing the roads and waterways), a blue triangular field in which there are seventeen white, five-pointed stars, (symbolizing Ohio as the seventeenth State), all grouped around a red disc, superimposed over a white "O" for Ohio.

In 1953, an amendment was made to change the flag as follows:

"The flag of the state shall be pennant shaped. It shall have three red and two white horizontal stripes. The union of the flag shall be seventeen five-pointed stars, white in a blue triangular field, the base of which shall be the staff end, or vertical edge of the flag, and the apex of which shall be the center of the middle red stripe. The stars shall be grouped around a red disc, superimposed upon a white circular 'O.' The proportional dimensions of the flag and of its various parts shall be according to the official design on file in the office of the Secretary of State. One State flag of uniform dimensions shall be furnished to each company of the organized militia."

In 1963, descriptions of other official flags were passed by the Legislature:

"The flag of the Governor of this State will be of scarlet wool bunting, six feet eight inches hoist, by ten feet six inches fly. In each of the four corners will be a white five-pointed star with one point upward. The centers of these stars will be twelve inches from the long edges and seventeen inches from the short edges of the flag. In the center of the flag will be a reproduction of the great seal of Ohio in proper colors, three feet in diameter, surrounded by thirteen white stars equally spaced with their centers on an imaginary circle four feet three inches in diameter. All stars shall be of such size that their points would lie on the circumference of an imaginary circle ten inches in diameter.

"The official colors of the Governor of Ohio will be of scarlet silk, four feet four inches on the pike by five feet six inches fly, of the same design as the flag of the Governor of Ohio, with the seal and stars proportionately reduced in size and embroidered. The colors will be trimmed on three edges with a knotted fringe of yellow silk two and one half inches wide. Attached below the head of the pike will be a silk cord of scarlet and white eight feet six inches in length with a tassel at each end.

"The naval flag of the Governor of Ohio will be of scarlet wool bunting, three feet hoist by four feet fly. The design will be the same as the flag of the Governor of Ohio with the seal and the stars proportionately reduced in size.

"The automobile flag of the Governor of Ohio will be of scarlet silk, or wool bunting, one foot, six inches on the staff by two feet, six inches on the fly. The design will be the same as the flag of the Governor of Ohio with the seal and stars proportionately reduced in size. The flag will be trimmed on three edges with a knotted fringe of silk or wool one and one half inches wide."

THE STATE MOTTO

Between the years 1865 and 1868, the State had as its motto, *Imperium In Impeno*, Latin for "An empire within an empire." However, this motto offended many settlers in the State because it sounded too much like a passage from *The Life and Times of Thomas Becket* that read: "The Church, an imperium in impeno, however corrupt in practise, was encroaching on the state with organized system..." (Froude, Sir James Anthony, New York 1878).

Between 1868 and 1959, the State was without a motto. On October 1, 1959, a new State motto was enacted: "With God, All Things are Possible." This saying was taken from Matthew 19:26 in the Bible, and was suggested by James Mastronardo, a twelve-year old boy from Cincinnati.

THE STATE BIRD

The songbird *cardinalis cardinalis*, or red cardinal, was adopted as Ohio's favorite bird in 1933 by an act of the Legislature. The cardinal ranges in the eastern United States, west to the Great Plains, southern Arizona to northwestern Mexico, and south through Georgia to the Gulf States. Total length of the cardinal is seven to eight inches; its tail length is four inches. A member of the finch species, it is crested and thick-billed. Its tail is longer than its short and rounded wings. Adult males are bright red, except for a black patchy band from the eye to the throat on both sides of the bill. The female is brownish above and dull tawny or pale buff below, with a dull grayish patch on the face and throat. The crest, wings, and tail are dull reddish in color, and the under wing feathers are pinkish red.

Cardinals build their nests in shrubs and bushes, sometimes in areas of close proximity to humans. Eggs are whitish with brown spots; the incubation period lasts between twelve to thirteen days. Both parents attend to the young with frequent feedings of insects. As the young birds mature, they become primarily fruit and grain eaters, although insects still make up a third of their diet. The cardinal is a colorful bird, whose songs are loud, flutelike whistles, the trills lasting about three seconds.

THE STATE FLOWER

The State Legislature in 1904 adopted the scarlet carnation (*Dianthus*) as the State flower, in memory of Ohio-born President William McKinley. McKinley wore the bloom in his buttonhole as a good luck piece. He began this tradition during an early campaign for a seat in the U.S. House of Representatives, when his opponent gave him a red carnation for his buttonhole. After he won the election, he decided to wear the carnation during later campaigns.

McKinley was assassinated three years before adoption of the State flower, but the State legislators had not forgotten the president's use of the carnation. "It is fitting and proper that a state should honor and perpetuate the memory of its illustrious sons," the 1904 law read. Ohio also adopted an official State wildflower, the white trillium (*Trillium grandiflorum*), in 1987.

THE STATE TREE

In 1953, the buckeye tree (*Aesculus glabra*) was designated the official tree of Ohio. Also called the Ohio buckeye, fetid buckeye, stinking buckeye, and American horse chestnut, the tree is native to the Midwestern United States, primarily the Ohio and Mississippi Valley regions.

The buckeye is a small to medium-sized tree with gray bark, much furrowed, and broken into scaly plates. Leaves are paired together with leafstalks from four to six inches long. Leaflets are five per leafstalk, from three to five inches in length, long, pointed, narrow at the base, and finely toothed. Flowers are pale greenish yellow, with petals almost as long as the flower; they grow in branched clusters from four to six inches long. Seeds are poisonous and are from one to one and one half inches wide, encased in a prickly fruiting capsule from one and one quarter to two inches in diameter.

The buckeye tree received its name from the Indians; it was thought that the seed looked like the "eye of the buck," in the Native American language, the *hetuck*.

THE STATE SONG

In 1969, "Beautiful Ohio" was designated the official song of Ohio. Written by Ballard McDonald and composed by Mary Earl, special lyrics were written by Wilbert B. White to the 1918 waltz. The song does not refer specifically to the State of Ohio, but to the river.

Beautiful Ohio
Long, long ago,
Someone I know
Had a little red canoe
In it room for only two
Love found its start,
Then in my heart
And like a flower it grew.
Chorus:
Drifting with the current
down a moonlit stream
While above the Heavens
in their glory gleam
And the stars on high—
Twinkle in the sky—
Seeming in a Paradise
of love divine
Dreaming of a pair of eyes
that looked in mine
Beautiful Ohio,
in dreams again I see
Visions of what used to be.
(Copyright 1911 by Shapiro, Bernstein and Co., New York, N.Y.)

THE STATE LICENSE PLATE

The first year the State of Ohio issued plates was 1908; a total of 10,649 plates were issued for the year. By 1909, the number of registered vehicles in the State had more than doubled, for a total of 23,003. An undated porcelain plate was used for the first two years. From 1910 to 1974, except for the years 1943 and 1952, annually issued plates had a variety of color combinations with no particular pattern. In 1910, 1914, 1930, 1934,1946, 1959, 1965, 1968, and 1976, red and white combinations were used. In 1908, 1909, 1920, 1922, 1924, 1932,1936, 1939, 1940, 1944, 1945, 1951, 1955, 1958, 1963,1967, 1969, blue and white combinations were used.

Multiyear plates came into use in 1974. The most current Ohio license plate, issued in 1996, is a combination of red, white, gold, and blue. The background of the plate is white and gold; "Ohio" appears in blue lettering in the top center; the slogan "The Heart of It All" is below the State name in red script. Numbers and letters in the center of the plate are blue.

THE STATE POSTAGE STAMP

The State of Ohio issued a three-cent sesquicentennial stamp on March 2, 1953 in Chillicothe, the first capital city. Engraved by M.D. Fenton and G.A. Payne, the stamp is brown and tan in color. At the top of the stamp are the words "Ohio Sesquicentennial." On both the right and left sides is a border of eight stars; the sixteen stars represent the states that preceded Ohio into the Union. The dates 1803 and 1953 are printed just inside the star borders on the right and left. A lone star representing Ohio is located at top center, just above a map of Ohio on which is printed the State seal. To the bottom left is a leaf from the Ohio State tree, the buckeye. A total of 118,706,000 stamps were issued.

OTHER STATE DESIGNATIONS

Ohio has several other official State-designated symbols. The white-tailed deer is the State animal (1988); the State gem (1965) is Ohio flint; the invertebrate fossil of the State is Isotelus (1985).

THE CAPITOL BUILDING

Ohio's capital was first located in Chillicothe. It was moved to Zanesville in 1809 and moved back to Chillicothe in 1812. In 1817, the Legislature sought to build a capital city in the center of the State and voted to locate the capital in Columbus, which at the time possessed no name.

Ground was broken for the Ohio capitol building at Columbus in 1838. It was designed by Henry Walter of Cincinnati, Martin E. Thompson of New York City, and Thomas Cole of Catskill, New York. In 1840, construction was stopped when the Legislature repealed the authorization; work was not resumed until 1846. In 1848, supervising architects were William Russell West and J.O. Sawyer. When William West resigned in 1854, and N.B. Kelly was appointed to take his place, all the stonework but the cupola had already been finished. By 1856, Thomas U. Walter and Richard Upjohn were consulting architects, and the legislative chambers had been completed. In 1858, Isaiah Rogers was appointed the architect to complete the interior designs.

The Ohio statehouse is "built of limestone taken from the State-owned quarry, five miles northwest of the city. The labor was done by convicts from the state penitentiary." The architecture is Doric Greek. At 304 feet long, 184 feet wide, and 158 feet high, the capitol building was completed in 1861 at a cost of 1,359,121 dollars.

An annex, or judicial building, constructed on the east front of the structure, was begun in 1898 and dedicated in 1901. This addition, 220 feet long and ninety-nine feet wide, and constructed of the same material as the building proper, cost 450,000 dollars.

OTHER FACTS ABOUT OHIO

Total area: 44,827 square miles
Land area: 40,953 square miles
Water area: 3,875 square miles
Rank in total area: 34
Average elevation: 850 feet
Highest point: Campbell Hill, 1,549 feet
Lowest point: Ohio River, 455 feet
Highest temperature: 113 degrees Fahrenheit, July 21, 1934, Gallipolis
Lowest temperature: -39 degrees Fahrenheit, February 10, 1899, Milligan
Population in 1990: 10,847,115
Population density in 1990: 264.87 persons per square mile
Population 1980-1990: + 0.5 percent change
Population in 2000: 11,353,140
Population 1990-2000: +4.7 percent change
Population difference 1990 – 2000: 506,025 persons
Black population in 1990: 1,154,826
Hispanic population in 1990:139,696
Native American population in 1990: 20,358
Per capita income 1998: $26,073
Per capita income est. 1999: $27,081
Resident: Ohioan
Capital: Columbus
Admitted to Union: March 1, 1803
Order of Statehood: 17
Electoral votes: 21

CHRONOLOGY

20,000 B.C. Primitive man from Asia arrives in the North American continent; these early hunters scatter out over the entire continent.

5,000 B.C. Glacial Age ends.
– Traveling south from Canada, the first primitive man enters the Ohio Valley; these early settlers, known as the Archaic Indians, lead a sedentary life, but leave little trace of their existence.

800 B.C. Indians, known commonly as Mound Builders, begin settling in Ohio; Adena Indians, the first of five successive mound-building cultures in the region, live in circular dwellings, grow vegetables, make pottery and elaborate ornaments of mica and copper, and build mounds for burying their great men.

600 B.C. Indians of the Hopewell Culture begin settling in the State; more artistic and skillful than Adena Indians, they build mounds in geometric patterns and live in highly organized communities.
– A distinct culture during the same period, the "Cole Complex," is considered to be a degenerate form of the Hopewell Culture.

200 A.D. Beginning of the Fort Ancient culture; these farmers, hunters, and fishermen survive until shortly before Columbus comes to America; living in rectangular houses, they make baskets and weave clothing.

1000 - 1655 The last mound building culture, the Erie or Cat Nation, flourishes in Ohio; artistic and highly skillful as their predecessors, these prehistoric Indians are destroyed by their warlike enemies from the North, the Iroquois; after their destruction until the American Revolutionary War, there are few Indian settlements in the State.

1669 - 1670 Sieur de la Salle, a young French nobleman, enters the Ohio Valley, giving France the first non-Indian claim to the land.

1689 - 1697 Onset of King William War, between France and England, over colonial possessions.
– Treaty of Ryswick gives France official possession of western wilderness; to secure its new possession, the French government in Quebec builds chain of forts from the Great Lakes to the Gulf, including the Ohio Valley.

1745 Fort Sandoski is built on Sandusky Bay by the British.

1747 Ohio Indians travel to Philadelphia to make alliance with fur trader, George Croghan.

1748 Ohio Land Company is organized.

1749 Hoping to further legitimize its claim to the west, provincial French government of Quebec sends expedition to the Ohio River area, led by Celeron de Bienville; burying lead markers, the group proclaims the region a possession of King Louis XV of France.

1750 After receiving half million acre grant in the Ohio Valley, Ohio Land Company sends Christopher Gist to explore the region.

1752 Ottawa Indians help in French capture of Pickawillany.

1753 George Washington, 19 years old, is sent to the Forks of the Ohio to warn French to stop their encroachment into British land.

1756 French-Indian War begins.

1758 Western lands come under English rule when Fort Duquesne at the Forks of the Ohio is captured by Gen. John Forbes.

1761 First permanent dwelling in Ohio, a log cabin, is constructed by Christian F. Post near Bolivar.

1763 Ottawa Chief, Pontiac, leads unsuccessful conspiracy against the white intruders.
– French-Indian War ends with signing of Treaty of Versailles; France officially loses all possessions in America.

1764 Colonel Henry Bouquet leads 1500 men into region, rescuing white prisoners from Indians and bringing peace to the region for 10 years to come.

1772 David Zeisberger and John Heckewelder establish Moravian community of Schoenbrunn, with help of Indians converted to Christianity.

1773 Missionaries at Schoenbrunn open first school west of the Allegheny Mountains.
– Christian Indian children are taught to read and write.

1774 Governor Dunmore of Virginia launches personal war against Indians.
– At Point Pleasant, Shawnee leader, Cornstalk, and 1000 braves attack part of Dunmore's contingent, inflicting heavy losses to the troops.
– Cornstalk is forced to cede land south of the Ohio River to Dunmore and the Western movement.

1775 American Revolution begins.

1777 Chief Cornstalk and his son are vengefully murdered when they try to warn garrison at Pt. Pleasant of impending Indian attacks.
– Schoenbrunn is abandoned; Moravian mission is established near Coshocton.

1778 Fort Laurens is built in present day Tuscarawas County; it is the first American post in Ohio.
– Kentucky volunteers attempt to destroy Shawnee headquarters in Ohio.

1780 George Rogers Clark and 1000 backwoodsmen destroy Shawnee Indian village on Mad River.

1782 Ninety-six Christian Indians, including 34 children, are massacred at Gnadenhutten, a Moravian mission in Tuscarawas Valley, by Colonel Williamson and militiamen.
– Indians burn Col. William Crawford at stake near upper Sandusky.
– Garrison at Fort Henry is saved by Betty Zane.

1783 United States receives Ohio Valley as part of Treaty of Paris.

1784 Ordinance of 1784, written by Thomas Jefferson, creates first form of government for the region, but it is never put into use.

1785 Land Ordinance of 1785 is passed, allowing distribution of land in the Ohio Area.
– Fort Harmar is established at mouth of Muskingum River.

1787 Ordinance of 1787 is passed, creating first actual instrument of government in Northwest Territory; it also provides for free speech, press, and assembly, while prohibiting slavery.
– General Arthur St. Clair is appointed first governor of territory.
– Zeisberger establishes settlement at Milan, with converted Indians' help.
– U.S. geographer, Thomas Hutchins, assisted by Rufus Putnam and others, completes first four surveys of Northwest Territory in southeastern Ohio, thus allowing first congressional auction of land.

1788 Marietta, first permanent white settlement in Ohio, is established at mouth of Muskingum River by Rufus Putnam and 48 pioneers.

1789 Fort Washington construction begins at new settlement of Losantiville.

1790 Losantiville is renamed Cincinnati by St. Clair; it becomes capital of territory.

– Indians defeat Josiah Harmar's army at present-day city of Fort Wayne.
– Five hundred French artisans and craftsmen found city of Gallipolis.

1791 Gen. St. Clair's army is defeated by Indians while attempting to eliminate the confederacy of Indian tribes in the Northwest Territory near present-day Recovery.
– Fort Hamilton and Fort Jefferson are built.

1793 *The Sentinel of the North-Western Territory* begins publishing in Cincinnati; it is the first newspaper north and west of Ohio River; William Maxwell is its publisher.

1794 Fort Defiance is built.
– Maj. Gen. "Mad Anthony" Wayne defeats Chief Blue Jacket and 2000 braves at Battle of Fallen Timber, bringing end to Indian wars in Ohio.

1795 Treaty of Greenville is signed, officially ending hostilities with Indians; all remaining Indian lands in southern Ohio are ceded to government.

1796 General Moses Cleveland establishes town site at mouth of Cuyahoga River.
– William Maxwell publishes the first book in Ohio, *Maxwell's Code*, a collection of the laws in the Northwest Territory.
– Ebenezer Zane is authorized by Congress to survey Zane's Trace.

1799 First legislature of Northwest Territory, a 22-man House of Representatives, meets in Cincinnati.
– William H. Harrison is appointed the first territory representative to Washington.

1800 The *Scioto Gazette* begins publishing in Chillicothe.
– Chillicothe is named the capital of Northwest Territory.
– Harrison Land Act is passed by Congress, lowering the amount of land settlers must purchase.
– Muskingum Academy is founded; Marietta College is later derived from this institution.
– Population is 43,365.

1801 John Chapman, later known as Johnny Appleseed, plants orchards along the banks of Licking Creek near Etna.

1802 Enabling Act is passed by Congress, establishing boundaries for the future State and calling for a constitutional convention.
– Dr. Edward Tiffin chairs constitutional convention in Chillicothe; document is submitted to Congress, requesting admission into the Union.

1803 Ohio becomes the 17th state in the Union.
– Edward Tiffin is elected Ohio's first governor.
– Coonskin Library opens at Amesville in Athens County.

1804 Ohio University is founded in Athens; it is the first institution of higher learning north and west of Ohio River.

1806 Aaron Burr leads conspiracy for establishment of new nation in southwest; Burr and fellow conspirator, Harman Blennerhasset, are captured, ending the revolt.

1809 Ohio legislature establishes Miami University.

1810 Zanesville is made State capital.
– Population is 230,760.

1811 Gen. William H. Harrison attacks Indian settlement in Tippecanoe Creek in northern Indiana, ending Tecumseh Indian confederacy in Northwest.
– The *Orleans* becomes the first steamboat to travel the Ohio River.

1812 War of 1812 begins; 26,000 Ohio residents volunteer for U.S. army duty.
– Chillicothe is named State capital.
– The first permanent seat of government is established.

1813 Oliver Hazard Perry defeats superior British Navy in Put-in-Bay, ending war in Northwest area.

1814 War of 1812 ends.

1815 Ohio's first abolition society, the Union Humane Society, is established in St. Clairsville by Benjamin Lundy.

1816 Ohio Legislature holds its first meeting in Columbus.

1817 Charles Osborn publishes *The Philanthropist* in Mount Pleasant; it is the first abolitionist paper in the United States.
– Cutler Hall is constructed at Ohio University (Athens).
– United States Bank establishes branch in Cincinnati.

1818 United States Bank establishes branch in Chillicothe.
– First steamboat on Lake Erie, *Walk-in-Water*, arrives in Cleveland.

1819 An experiment in communal living, which will last for 79 years, begins at Zoar by the Society of Separatists.

1820 Martin Baum House is completed in Cincinnati; it is later known as the Taft House.
– Population is 501,434.

1823 The last Moravian mission in Ohio is closed when Christian Indians in Goshen cede their land to State.
– John Stewart establishes the first Methodist mission in the State at Upper Sandusky.

1824 Theological Seminary of the Protestant Episcopal Church is founded at Gambier; it is now known as Kenyon College.

1825 Miami and Erie Canal construction begins.

1826 First labor union in Ohio, the Franklin Typographical Society, is organized at Cincinnati.
– Western Reserve Academy opens at Hudson.

1827 First stretch of Ohio and Erie Canal opens between Cleveland and Massillon.
– First daily newspaper west of Philadelphia, Cincinnati's *Daily Gazette*, begins publishing.

1829 Boat service begins on Miami and Erie Canal.

1830 First Charter granted to medical school in Ohio is used to start college.
– Worthington Medical College is opened.
– Capital University is founded at Canton.
– Population is 937,903.

1831 Capital University moves to Columbus.
– Granville Literary and Theological Institution is founded in Granville; today it is known as Denison University.
– Jesuits establish Xavier University in Cincinnati.
– Joseph Smith, leader of the Mormons, comes to Kirkland seeking converts.
– First labor paper in the United States, *Working Man's Shield*, is published in Cincinnati.

1832 Robert Lucas is elected governor; he is the first Jacksonian governor in the State.
– Ohio State School for the Deaf is opened.
– Ohio legislature charters Mad River Railroad to run from Dayton to Sandusky.
– Construction of Ohio and Erie Canal is completed.

1833 First institution in America to admit blacks and whites on an equal basis, Oberlin College, is founded.
– National Road stretches to Columbus.

1834 Prisoners begin being housed in buildings at present day Ohio Penitentiary in Columbus.
– Construction of first Mormon temple in the United States begins in Kirkland.

1835 Five-year-old "Toledo War" ends, establishing firmly the border between Ohio and Michigan.
– The first strike in Ohio occurs when Cincinnati's Harnessmakers' Union demands higher wages and a 10-hour day.
– Marietta College is chartered.

1836 Pro-slavery sympathizers destroy James Birney's abolitionist press in Cincinnati.
– First railroad from Toledo to Adrian, Michigan, is completed. Mormons complete Kirkland Temple.

1837 The first school for the blind in the United States, the Ohio State School for the Blind, opens in Columbus.
– The first hot-blast furnace in the United States, the Vesuvius Furnace, begins operating in Ohio.
– Abolitionists hold first convention in nation's history in Mount Pleasant.
– Oberlin College becomes first coeducational college in the world.
– United Presbyterian Church is founded Muskingum College at New Concord.
– Ohio receives $2.6 million from federal government; using the money as loans to counties, the State hopes to raise income from the loans' interest to establish common schools.

1838 First kindergarten in America is established in Columbus by German immigrants.

1839 Cornerstone of the Ohio capitol is laid at Columbus.
– Milan is linked to Lake Erie by canal.
– Milan marks beginning as a wheat shipping center.
– Strict fugitive slave law is enacted.

1840 William H. Harrison becomes the first of eight Ohio residents elected president; he is elected the ninth president of the United States.
– Population is 1,519,467.

1842 Ohio Wesleyan University is chartered at Delaware.

1845 "State Bank of Ohio" opens, following passage of Kelley Bank Act.
– Lutheran Church founds Wittenburg College in Springfield.
– State Board of Agriculture is established.
– Miami and Erie Canal is completed.

1846 United States war with Mexico begins; 7000 Ohio residents serve in country's armed forces over the next two years.
– Squire and Davis lead archaeological dig at Hopewell Mound Group.
– Methodist Episcopal Church is founded Mount Union College at Alliance.

1847 System of graded schools is established by Akron legislature.
– Thomas A. Edison, electrical wizard and one of America's foremost inventors, is born in Milan.
– United Brethren Church is founded Otterbein University at Westerville; today it is known as Otterbein College.

1848 Oxford College for Women is founded at Oxford.

1849 Law is enacted creating separate schools for blacks.
– Cincinnati's German populace inaugurates first annual Saengerfest; Norwegian violinist, Ole Bull, helps establish this predecessor to Cincinnati's biennial May festival.
– Cholera epidemic ravages Cincinnati; 7,500 residents are killed. At Sandusky, another 400 are killed by the disease.

1850 Second Constitutional Convention is held in Columbus.
– Western Reserve Eclectic Institute is founded in Niles; later it will become Hiram College.
– Defiance Female Seminary is founded by Disciples of Christ.
– Heidelberg College is founded in Tiffin.
– Swedenborgian Church founds Urbana University, today known as Urbana Junior College.
– Roman Catholics found St. Marys Institute in Dayton; today it is known as Dayton University.
– Cincinnati is site of first State fair.
– Ohio women hold women's rights convention in Salem.
– Population is 1,980,329.

1851 Electorate approves new State constitution in special election; district courts are created, and several State offices become elected positions.

1852 Harriet Beecher Stowe publishes anti-slavery novel, *Uncle Tom's Cabin*.
– Women hold second rights convention in Massillon, and form permanent association.
– Ohio becomes first State in nation to enact 10-hour work day for women and children; also enacted is legislation forbidding children under age of 12 to be hired for work in mines.

1853 Antioch College is founded in Yellow Springs.

1855 Anti-Slavery leader, Salmon P. Chase, is elected governor.

1856 Wilberforce College is established; both whites and blacks are allowed to enroll; later the institution will become Wilberforce University.

1857 Willoughby Female Seminary helped charter Lake Erie College at Painesville.
– Great Panic of 1857; Ohio Life Insurance and Trust Company is one of several companies to fold, while unemployment rises rapidly.

1858 University of Cincinnati is founded.
– Runaway slave, John Price, is captured by United States deputy Marshall in Oberlin; irate mob frees Price and helps him escape to Canada.

1859 Religious, anti-slavery zealot, John Brown, captures Harper's Ferry with help of five sons and others; two days later, Robert E. Lee recaptures the small town in West Virginia, killing 10 of Brown's men and capturing the others; Brown is convicted of treason and hung, becoming a martyr to Ohio's abolitionists. Pike's Opera House opens in Cincinnati.

1860 Maria Longworth Storer establishes Rockwood Potteries in Cincinnati.
– Population is 2,339,511.

1861 Civil War begins.
– Union party candidate, David Tod, is elected governor.
– First society in the United States to offer aid to soldiers is established by Cleveland women.

1862 James J. Andrew leads 24 men in an unsuccessful raid on Western and Atlantic Railroad.
– Johnson Isle is used as prison camp for Confederate soldiers.
– Dayton *Empire* editor, J.F. Bollmeyer, is murdered as political tension from war mounts.

1863 Gen. John Hunt Morgan leads an unsuccessful raid to free Confederate soldiers imprisoned in Ohio.
– Franklin College opens at Topper's Plain.
– Wilberforce College becomes the first solely black owned and operated college in the nation.

1864 Captains Charles H. Cole and John Y. Beall lead unsuccessful attempt to free Confederate soldiers held at Johnson Isle Prison.

1865 Civil War ends; Ohio has supplied 319,189 men to fight with the Union army; some 35,000 Ohio residents have been killed in the war.

– First college music department in the United States is established at Oberlin College (the Oberlin Conservatory of Music).

1866 Presbyterians found College of Wooster.

1867 Clara Baur founds Cincinnati Conservatory of Music.
– State Commission of Railroads is established.

1868 Ohio native, Ulysses S. Grant, is elected 18th U.S. President.

1869 Country's first professional baseball team, the Red Stockings, is established in Cincinnati.

1870 Ohio allows first black delegate to attend Republican State Convention.
– Standard Oil Company is established in Cleveland by John D. Rockefeller.
– Dr. Benjamin F. Goodrich begins manufacturing fire hoses and other rubber goods at his Akron home.
– Diamond Match Company is founded by Ohio Columbus Barber.
– Buchte College is established in Akron by members of the Universalist Church.
– Ohio Agricultural and Mechanical College is established in Columbus; today it is known as Ohio State University.
– Franklin College moves to Wilmington; it is renamed Wilmington College.
– Population is 2,665,260.

1871 Toledo University of Arts and Trades is established; later it will become University of Toledo.
– Methodists establish Northwestern Ohio Normal School in Ada, known today as Ohio Northern University.

1873 Third Constitutional convention is held.
– Eliza Jane Trimble Thompson helps launch Women's Temperance Crusade in Hillsboro.
– First Cincinnati Music Festival is held.

1874 Voters reject changes in State constitution.

1876 Native Ohio resident, Rutherford B. Hayes, is elected 19th President.
– Baptists found Rio Grande College.

1877 Railroad workers hold strike in Newark; Governor declares state of Martial Law to end strike.

1878 First link in Scripps-Howard newspaper chain is established when Edward W. Scripp purchases Cleveland's *Penny Press*.
– German Baptists' found Ashlen College.

1880 Native Ohio resident, James A. Garfield, is elected 20th President.
– Case School of Applied Science opens in Cleveland.
– Population is 3,198,062.

1881 President Garfield is assassinated.

1882 Western Reserve College moves to Cleveland.

1883 Prohibition bill is defeated by voters.

1884 Western Reserve College is chartered as Western Reserve University.
– Miners striking in New Straitsville start fire in coal mines that is smoldering to this day.
– Rioting erupts in Cincinnati; courthouse is destroyed; 300 persons are killed or injured.
– Findlay College is founded.

1885 Ohio State Reformatory opens in Mansfield.

1886 American Federation of Labor is established at labor convention in Columbus.
– Charles Martin Hall, Thompson native and Oberlin College graduate, discovers an electrolytic process for making aluminum; later, his discovery helps form the Aluminum Company of America.
– Catholics found St. Ignatius College in Cleveland.

1887 Reformed Presbyterian Church is founded: Cedarville College.
– Law passes allowing women to control their own property.

1888 Native Ohio resident, Benjamin Harris, is elected 23rd President of the United States.
– Youngstown College is founded.

1890 Population is 3,672,329.

1893 Howard Russell founds Ohio Anti-Saloon League in Oberlin.
– Financial crisis, "Panic of 1893," erupts; strikes, unemployment are rampant throughout State.
– Women gain rights to vote in school board elections, act as legal guardians, execute bills, and sue and be sued.

1894 Jacob S. Coxey leads an army of unemployed workers ("Coxey's Army") to Washington to demand government approval of a $500 million government works program to help ease the 1893 crisis.

1896 Native Ohio resident, William McKinley, is elected 27th President.
– Anti-lynching law is passed.

1897 Social reformer, Samuel M. Jones, is elected Toledo Mayor.

1898 Spanish-American war begins; 15,345 Ohio residents will join the United States Army to fight in the war.
– Society of Separatists at Zoar is dissolved; the property of the experiment in communal living is divided among the members.

1899 J. Ward Packard produces the first Packard automobile in Warren.

1900 Mennonite Church founds Bluffton College.
– Population is 4,157,545.

1901 Tom L. Johnson, champion of social and political reform, is elected Cleveland mayor.

1902 Defiance College is founded as offshoot of Defiance Female Seminary.

1903 Dayton natives, Orville and Wilbur Wright, make their historic aircraft flight at Kittyhawk, North Carolina.
– Big Brothers of America is founded in Cincinnati by Irvin Westheimer.

1905 Social reformer, Brand Whitlock, is elected Toledo mayor.

1906 University of Ohio is established as a cooperative system of education.

1908 Cincinnati native, William Howard Taft, is elected 27th President.

1909 Anti-Saloon League's headquarters is established in Westerville.

1910 Kent State University is founded.
– Population is 4,767,121.

1911 Social and political reformist, Henry Hunt, is elected Cincinnati mayor; election ends Boss Cox's corrupt leadership of the city.
– Ohio legislature approves Workman's Compensation law.
– A Cincinnati resident becomes the first U.S. citizen to be issued a radio license.

1912 Fourth constitutional convention is held; voters approve major constitutional changes, but deny women suffrage.

1913 Ohio River floods, killing 430 and causing an estimated $250 million in damages.
– Buchtel College becomes University of Akron.
– Baldwin Institute and German-Wallace College merge, becoming Baldwin-Wallace, a Methodist school in Beren.

1914 After the Great Ohio Flood of 1913, legislature adopts Conservatory Law to produce funds for building dams and locks so catastrophe won't be repeated; law also creates Miami Conservatory District.
– Last passenger pigeon in world dies in Cincinnati's Zoological Gardens.
– Bowling Green State Normal School opens.

1916 WWI begins; Ohio contributes 250,000 soldiers until war's end; over 7,000 Ohio residents will die in war.
– Cleveland Museum of Art opens.
– Rioting erupts in Youngstown following steel-workers strike.

1917 Camp Sherman (near Chillicothe) opens as Army training center; Selective Service Act is approved.
– Presidential suffrage approved.

1918 Influenza kills 1,100 Ohio residents stationed at Camp Sherman.

– Ohio citizens approve statewide prohibition against alcoholic beverages.
– WWI ends.

1919 Ohio becomes fifth state to ratify 19th amendment, allowing women's suffrage.
– Jack Dempsey defeats Jess Willard in world championship heavy weight fight in Toledo.
– Chicago White Sox's acceptance of bribes taints World Series victory for Cincinnati Reds.

1920 Ohio resident, Warren G. Harding, defeats James M. Cox, another Ohio resident, and becomes 27th President of the U.S.
– National Football League is organized in Canton.
– Population is 5,759,394.

1921 Bing Act is adopted; mandatory school age is raised to 18 years.

1922 Ohio resident, Florence E. Allen, becomes first woman in United States to serve as a State Supreme Court judge.

1923 President Harding dies in office.
– Restoration of Moravian village of Schoenbrunn begins.
– St. Ignatius College becomes John Carroll University.

1924 Tornado ravages Lorain; seventy-five are killed and an estimated $25 million in damages is caused.

1925 Fourteen people are killed when the dirigible *Shenandoah* crashes near Ava.

1929 Port Columbus is completed, becoming first air-rail service in the world.
– Stock Market crash marks beginning of the Great Depression.
– Massive unemployment and poverty spread throughout State.

1930 Eighty-two workers are killed in Millfield mine disaster in Athens County.
– 318 persons are killed in fire at Ohio Penitentiary.
– Population is 6,646,697.

1931 Cleveland stadium opens.
– Depression causes 125 Ohio banks to close.

1932 Ohio residents help elect Franklin D. Roosevelt over Herbert Hoover for President by 75,000 votes.
– George White is elected first Democratic governor in sixteen years.

1933 Unemployment continues to rise; Ohio wage-earners have fallen from 1929 high of 740,000 to low of 472,000; production during the same period falls from $5 billion to $3.3 billion.
– Franklin D. Roosevelt begins social reform programs to give jobs to the unemployed.
– Cincinnati's Union Terminal is completed.

1934 Labor strikes in Toledo create turmoil; federal troops are ordered in to quell disorder.
– Federally-subsidized Muskingum Watershed Project begins providing jobs for the needy.
– Farm production falls as drought stretches throughout the summer.

– Wayne National Forest is created.

1935 Legislature enacts a three-cent sales tax to help fight State's economic woes.
– Taft-Hartley Labor-Management Act is introduced in Congress by Ohio Senator, Robert A. Taft.
– Labor-management dispute in Toledo brings rise to Toledo Industrial Peace Plan.

1936 Cleveland hosts Great Lakes Exposition.

1937 Ohio River floods, causing immense damage throughout Ohio Valley.
– Congress of Industrial Organizations (CIO) leads major strike against steel companies throughout State.

1938 Muskingum Watershed is completed.

1939 Major fire destroys eight stores in downtown Sandusky, causing $1 million in damages.

1940 Democrats choose Martin L. Davey as gubernatorial candidate, despite accusations of his excessive expenditures in State Supreme Court suit; State Senate investigates other complaints of excessive expenditures by several candidates.
– Republican candidate, John W. Bricker, is elected governor.
– National Guard Armory is robbed in Cincinnati.
– Communists, Socialists, and Social-Labor party fail to qualify for ballot.
– Cleveland holds International Exposition.

1941 The Marietta opens; it is the first river museum shop on the Ohio River.
– Cleveland holds International Exposition.
– *Cincinnati Enquirer* marks 100th anniversary with special centennial edition.
– WW II begins; Ohio sends 839,000 men and women to fight in the United States armed forces; by war's end, some 23,000 Ohio residents will be killed.

1942 Communist and Social-Labor parties are barred from election ballots.
– Cleveland *Plain Dealer* newspaper celebrates its 100th anniversary.

1943 U.S. Civil Service commission refuses payment to Unemployment Compensation Bureau, after Bureau is cited for Hatch Act violation.
– Ohio State Penitentiary in Columbus receives WPB National Service Award.

1944 Franklin County Election board is ordered by court not to drop service personnel from ballot rolls.
– University of Cincinnati celebrates 125th anniversary.
– Governor Bricker calls special legislative session to create supplementary ballot for federal soldiers.
– State adopts armed forces absentee ballot law to solve war-time voting problem.
– Cleveland Mayor, Frank Lausche, is elected governor.
– Scarlet Fever outbreak causes suspension of classes at University of Cincinnati.

1945 Sen. Harold H. Burton is appointed to the United States Supreme Court.
– Cleveland Electric Illuminating Company cuts electrical output following coal miners strike; U.S. Army is called in to end the strike.

1946 Thomas J. Herbert defeats Lausche in his reelection bid for governor.
– President Harry S. Truman helps Cleveland celebrate its 150th anniversary.
– Coal miners strike forces voluntary brown-outs in some cities.
– Cleveland Electric Utility Company begins shift away from coal use to oil.

1947 U.S. Constitutional amendment limiting presidential tenure is ratified.
– Leading Ohio Democrats assail State Republican Party for using Communist "bugaboo" as campaign issue in previous year's election.
– Taft-Hartley law goes into effect, despite heavy opposition from labor groups.
– Justice Department questions the loyalty of the Ohio School of Social Sciences to the United States.
– Mill Creek Dam is completed on the Ohio River.

1948 Governor Thomas Hubert is defeated by Frank J. Lausche in reelection attempt.

1949 Bill requiring loyalty oaths of all public employees is approved by House.
– Farm and labor groups, upset over passage of Taft-Hartley Act, join forces in attempt to oust Sen. Taft in next election.

1950 Despite massive campaigning by farm and labor groups, Taft is reelected by record vote.
– Lausche is reelected governor.
– Representative Brehm is cited in charges of accepting campaign contributions from two employees.
– Ohio River channel is deepened by three feet.

1951 Brehm is convicted of five counts of violating Federal Corrupt Practices Act; conviction stems from political contributions Brehm received from one of two employees; he is fined, but is allowed to retain his seat.
– University of Ohio institutes rule requiring advanced screening of campus speakers; faculty, church, and community groups protest curb on "disloyal" speakers; several conventions and speaking appearances are cancelled.

1952 Lausche is reelected governor.
– 1,600 inmates riot at Columbus penitentiary over food; riot ends after inmates confer with warden; one inmate is killed, three wounded, and $1 million in damages caused.
– Taft family attempts to purchase *Cincinnati Enquirer*, but are outbid by a coalition of employees.

1953 State's Sesquicentennial is celebrated.
– Congress approves resolution officially recognizing Ohio's entry into the state on March 1, 1803.
– Communist scare continues; Ohio State University professor is suspended, then dismissed for refusing to answer House Un-American Activities Commission queries on alleged Communist ties.

– Cincinnati Ohio Planning Commission director is forced to resign for attending Marxist study in 1946.

1954 State legislature enacts loyalty test for State employees.
– Colonial Dames of America donate 166-year-old land office at Marietta to State.
– Constitutional amendment is adopted, lengthening governor's term to four years.
– Lausche is reelected governor for fifth and last term.
– Modernization of Ohio River begins.

1955 Open Meeting Law is enacted, requiring all meetings of local governing boards, committees, and agencies to be public.
– Ohio turnpike is opened.

1957 After being elected senator, Lausche resigns governorship; Lt. Gov. John W. Brown become Ohio's governor.

1958 Michael V. DiSalle is elected governor.
– Ohio State University dedicates E. Pyle Memorial Library.
– Wesleyan University president is named House, Education and Welfare Department Secretary.
– Cleveland is named "typical American city" by U.S. Junior Chamber of Commerce.
– Cincinnati *Times-Star* merges with the *Post* after being purchased by E.W. Scripps Company.

1959 Voting age is lowered from 21 to 18 years.
– Official State motto is adopted: "With God all Things Are Possible."
– Ohio adopts nation's first Truth-In-Advertising Law.

1960 L.C. Hanna Jr. bequests $33,455,298 to Cleveland Museum of Art.
– *Cleveland News* is sold to Scripps-Howard; publication is suspended.
– *Cleveland Press* becomes *Cleveland Press* and *Cleveland News*.

1961 State Treasury begins year with no funds and a $66 million deficit because of legislative battle.
– First link in billion dollar chain of 19 new locks and dams is completed along the Ohio River in New Cumberland, costing $40 million; project is scheduled to take 20 years to complete.
– Urban Renewal Administration gives Cincinnati $9 million to aid slum cleanup program.
– Cincinnati College Conservatory of Music merges with University of Cincinnati.

1962 Rhodes defeats DiSalle for governor in campaign tainted with personal attacks.
– $54 million Greenup Lock and Dam Project, along Ohio River, is dedicated.
– Cleveland downtown renewal project begins.
– Cincinnati approves downtown renewal project.
– Ohio native, John Glenn, is first American to orbit Earth.
– Racial restriction of homeownership is removed by legislature.

1963 $250 million bond is approved by voters for capital improvements.
– William Walker becomes first black Ohio cabinet member.

1964 Use of municipal halls by singing groups, such as the Beatles, is banned in Cleveland.
– Voters approve $500 million bond issue for State highway construction.

1965 Tomato juice is approved by Senate as official State drink.
– State law is enacted, giving State employees time off for all legal holidays.
– Voters approve $290 million capital improvements bond issue.
– Two hundred and fifty students sit-in outside administration office at Ohio State University to protest university control over speakers lecturing to student groups; despite protest and recommendation by faculty, Trustees vote to continue practice.
– Ohio native, Jerrie Mock, is the first woman to fly solo around globe.

1966 Robert E. Henry is appointed Springfield mayor, becoming the first black mayor in an important city in the U.S.

1967 Black candidate, Carl Stokes, defeats white candidate, Locker, in race-oriented contest for mayor of Cleveland; Stokes becomes the first popularly elected black mayor in a major American city.

1968 U.S. Supreme Court rules that State's election laws violate 14th amendment equal protection clause.
– George Wallace and the American Independent Party order is placed on ballot.
– Violence on university campuses flare; at the University of Ohio, 110 blacks take over administration building in a protest over discrimination; at Ohio University (Athens), 650 National Guardsmen are called out to end student rioting; blacks riot at Kent State.

1969 Thirty-four black students are indicted for 1968 takeover of Ohio State University administration building; rioting continues at several universities.
– Stokes is reelected Cleveland mayor.
– "Beautiful Ohio" is adopted as State song.
– Native Ohio resident, Neil Armstrong, becomes first man to walk on the moon.

1970 Rioting continues on university campuses; Governor Rhodes calls out National Guardsmen to quell disorder at Ohio State; guardsmen, firing hundreds of rounds of tear gas and shot gun charges, injure over 100 students in chaotic spring quarter.
– Campus violence climaxes when National Guardsmen fatally shoot four students, wound another eight after breaking up rally of 1,000 in Kent State's commons; protests at Ohio University (Athens) denouncing Kent State shootings force closure of university.
– Over 1,200 municipal workers strike in Cincinnati over wages; labor council holds one-day sympathy strike by 100,000 workers.
– State loan scandal begins; Republican outcome in State elections affected.
– Population is 10,652,017.
– Ohio loses one congressional seat following 1970 census.
– Construction boom begins in downtown Cleveland.

1971 E.W. Scripp sells *Cincinnati Enquirer* to American Financial Corporation.
– Ohio legislature battles nine months over budget, decides to initiate income tax.

1972 Last two inmates on death row at Ohio Penitentiary transferred to prison reception center, following U.S. Supreme Court ruling of death penalty as unconstitutional.

1973 U.S. District Court rules that members of National Socialists White Peoples Party be allowed to wear swastika armbands at Cleveland City Council meetings.

1974 2,000 prison guards, mental health workers, and other State employees strike for higher pay.
– Watergate deeply hurts Republican candidates in State elections; among surprise winners, former astronaut, John Glenn, overwhelms Republican opponent, Ralph Perks, in Senate race.
– State lottery inaugurated.
– Ohio's first national park created in Cuyahoga Valley.
– Xenia rampaged by tornado.

1975 Ohio is first of 31 states to restore death penalty since 1972 Supreme Court decision ruling as unconstitutional.
– Fifth generation of Taft family of Ohio enters politics after 33-year-old Robert Taft II appointed to legislature as Cincinnati Representative.
– State officials, National Guard troops found innocent by Grand Jury of negligence in 1970 shooting at Kent State.

1976 U.S. Representative Wayne Hays exposed in sex scandal with Elizabeth Ray; congressional powers shattered, Hays withdraws as candidate for seat he held for 28 years.
– University of Cincinnati becomes part of Ohio State University system.
– Ohio's last commuter train, running from Cleveland to Youngstown, discontinued.

1977 Census Bureau estimates that Ohio has second largest outward population migration from state in nation.
– Natural gas shortage forces Gov. James A. Rhodes to declare "energy crisis."
– Cold weather leaves 75,000 people jobless in one of Ohio's worst recorded winters.
– 31-year-old political maverick, Dennis J. Kucinich, elected youngest mayor of a major American city by Cleveland voters.

1978 State has second devastating winter in a row.
– Fierce blizzard paralyzes Ohio, causing $100 million loss in State's economy.
– Trustees of Ohio State University vote to eliminate university holdings in South Africa, becoming first State institution to do so.
– Cleveland Mayor, Dennis Kucinich, survives first political test in defeating recall forces in special election; Cleveland defaults when it fails to repay $15.5 million in loans; City Council approves Kucinich's proposal to raise city income taxes to get out of debt.
– Ohio's death penalty declared unconstitutional by U.S. Supreme Court.
– Wayne Hays elected State Representative.

1979 Cleveland defaults on $5 million employee pension fund payment; voters approve 50 percent increase in city income tax to bail city out of crisis.
– Kucinich defeated by George Voinovich in mayoral election.
– Eleven concertgoers trampled to death in Cincinnati waiting in line to see rock group "The Who."

– Cleveland begins massive busing of students to achieve racial balance in schools; U.S. Supreme Court rules Dayton and Columbus must also bus.
– State financing of schools through property taxes ruled unconstitutional.

1980 U.S. Supreme Court declares victory for Ohio in 14-year-long dispute with Kentucky over Ohio River border between states.
– Ohio auditor declares Cleveland in state of financial emergency.
– Population is 10,797,419 (only 1.3 increase over 1970).
– State Auditor, Thomas Ferguson, declares Cleveland to be in state of fiscal emergency; action allows creation of special commission to supervise city's financial planning.
– Cleveland teachers approve new contract to end 11-week strike; cost of new contract estimated at $32 million to $33.5 million.
– In Cincinnati, U.S. Sixth District Court of Appeals upholds federal ruling that U.S. Steel Corp. can close Youngstown, Ohio area plants, but orders trial on question of whether company's refusal to sell plants to workers is antitrust violation.

1981 Ohio River boundary dispute settled; Kentucky gives up claim to sole taxing authority on river activities where river touches Ohio and Indiana.
– Tornadoes hit Midwest; Cardington, Ohio reports four deaths, damage to 200 homes and 45 businesses from storm.

1982 Coldest temperatures of century recorded throughout State.
– Recession affects State's traditional steel and automotive industries adversely; many businesses shut down or cut down employees drastically.
– Unemployment reaches highest levels since Great Depression.
– United Rubber Workers Union resolve bargaining on 3-year contracts; Akron's Goodrich Co. plant approves separate contract, special concessions to keep plant from closing.
– U.S. Justice Dept. suit in Cincinnati forces 23 companies and two individuals to share cost of cleaning 10-acre hazardous-waste dump in Hamilton; site considered among largest hazardous-waste dumps in country.
– Four FBI agents and two others killed when Cessna 411 plane crashes into bookstore in Montgomery; store completely destroyed, at least four persons in store injured.
June 17. Afternoon daily newspaper, *Cleveland Press*, publishes last edition, leaving Ohio's largest city with only one newspaper, morning *Plain Dealer*.

1983 U.S. Steel Corp. announces plant closings to reduce annual steel producing by about 20 percent; steel finishing plant in Cleveland is among those cited to be closed.

1986 Earthquake with epicenter 30 miles northeast of Cleveland briefly shakes nine states and Ontario; magnitude 5.5 on Richter scale, minor by world standards but strong for region; no damages or injuries reported.

1988 Ashland Oil Co. storage tank spills nearly one million gallons of diesel fuel into Monongahela River; listed among largest inland fuel spills in U.S. history, oil slick moves downriver into Steubenville, where officials close down intake system after oil smell and taste detected.

– Energy Department undersecretary, Joseph Salgado, says costs will total one billion dollars to begin cleaning radioactive uranium dust and leaks from storage silos at aging foundry in Fernald along Great Miami River, 18 miles NW of Cincinnati.

1989 Harold Friedman, Ohio Teamsters official, fined $35,000 and sentenced to four years probation; Friedman convicted of embezzlement, racketeering, and filing false reports with government.
– Senate Ethics Committee votes unanimously to hire special counsel investigating allegations of improprieties against six senators, among them John Glenn (D), from Ohio; probe results from implications in Lincoln savings and loan collapse.
– Cincinnati Archbishop Daniel E. Pilarczyk named president of conference for Roman Catholic Bishops.

1992 Tornadoes rip through 11 states in South and Midwest, from Texas to Ohio.
– December 21. Using religious freedom argument, Ku Klux Klan receives city permit to erect eight-foot high wooden cross in downtown square in Cincinnati until December 31; cross attacked and toppled several times by protesters.

1993 Five Amish children killed, three others seriously injured after being struck by out-of-control automobile about three miles from Fredericksburg; driver Eric Bache arraigned on five felony counts of vehicular homicide.
– Eleven-day siege of Southern Ohio Correctional Facility near Lucasville ends after inmates reach agreement with prison officials calling for improvements in conditions; five remaining hostages released; at least nine inmates and one guard reported killed in rioting, begun April 11 in recreational yard of cellblock.
– General Electric Co. cuts 4,000 jobs from GE Aircraft Engines subsidiary; most cuts scheduled to take place at unit's headquarters in Cincinnati.
– Cincinnati-based Procter & Gamble Co., among largest consumer-products companies in nation, announces plans to close 30 factories and eliminate 13,000 jobs.
– Ohio Senator, Howard Metzenbaum, after three terms, announces he will not seek reelection in 1994.

1994 Cleveland designated "supplemental" empowerment area by Clinton administration; city will receive one-time grant of $90 million from fund of Department of Housing and Urban Development.
– New Lexington judge rules that State school funding system is unconstitutional because it prevents students in poorer districts from receiving same quality of education offered in wealthier districts; Judge Linton Lewis rules that Ohio's financing system, which relied largely on local property taxes, violates equal education guarantees; State officials ordered to draw up new funding plan to submit to Legislature.
– Michael Mower shoots and wounds two deputies, then shoots mother and self, after police surround hotel where he resides near Dayton; Secret Service officials say Mower reportedly had history of mental illness, wrote threatening letter to President Bill Clinton in March; stand-off ensues after two Montgomery County sheriff's deputies visit hotel to question Mower about letter.

1995 High court agrees to decide on case of *Capitol Square Review and Advisory Board v. Pinette*, after Ku Klux Klan successfully sues agency that runs public park in Columbus because of ban to erect 10-foot cross on premises; Klan suit alleges that group was denied free-speech rights, noting permission of other groups to place Christmas tree and menorah in park; State agency asserts it was justified because cross display is exclusively religious symbol.
– Lancaster white supremist pleads guilty to one count of wire fraud; Larry Wayne Harris accused of improperly buying bubonic plague cultures through mail, after ordering freeze-dried bacterium from Maryland medical supply company; three counts of wire fraud and one count of mail fraud charged for ordering bacterium; guilt in wire fraud is part of plea bargaining agreement.
– Supreme Court strikes down statute banning distribution of anonymous political literature; justices rule 7-2 that law requiring political literature to include name and address of person responsible violates individuals' free-speech rights.
– U.S. 6th Circuit Court of Appeals in Cincinnati upholds amendment to city charter that voided 1993 law protecting homosexuals from discrimination and barring any such future laws; ruling reverses 1994 federal judge's decision to strike down amendment; decision makes void existing protections for gays in employment and housing.

1996 National Football League approves Cleveland Brown's proposed move to Baltimore, Maryland; compromise reached between team owner, Art Modell, and city after agreement that Modell's team will receive new name, the Ravens.
– Supreme Court agrees to consider conditions under which State police may conduct extended interrogations of drivers they stop for routine traffic violations; court rules that police conducted unreasonable search of motorist's car in case of *Ohio v. Robinette*.
– Federal judge lifts desegregation order compelling Cleveland school district to integrate public schools; ruling ends 17 years of enforced busing in Cleveland school system.
– Nine die after fire sweeps through fireworks store in Scottown; Todd Martin arrested, charged with eight counts of involuntary manslaughter after lighting box of firecrackers that sets off chain reaction.
– Carl Burton Stokes, first black American to become mayor of a major city, dies at age 68; Stokes was mayor of Cleveland from 1967 to 1971, and municipal judge of Cleveland from 1983 to 1994.

1997 Supreme Court rejects petition brought by General Motors to strike down tax imposed by State on natural gas purchased from out-of-state companies; justices rule that Ohio can impose tax even though State did not impose similar tax on natural gas purchased from Ohio-based utilities.
– Ohio River flooding results in at least 30 deaths, and major property damage to residents of Ohio, Kentucky, Indiana, Tennessee, and West Virginia.

1998 Forty-four police and corrections officers are arrested for selling protection to suspected cocaine traffickers in and around Cleveland; officers are accused of taking money to provide security to drug dealers and those smuggling illegal gambling machines into region; some are also accused of selling illegal drugs.
– Ohio Environmental Protection Agency awards $90,00 in grants to aid 10 groups in building coalitions and developing action plans to protect local water resources; State Department of Natural Resources contributes additional $45,000 to effort.

1999 Governor's Community Council executive director Kitty Burcsu announces that thousands of Ohioans will participate in service activities for communities and neighbors on King Holiday honoring Martin Luther King, Jr.

– Cleveland Municipal Schools are released from fiscal emergency status; schools have been in state of fiscal emergency since November 1996, when district was placed under control of financial planning and supervision commission.

2000 With 65,000 trees planted and more than 60,000 volunteer hours for urban forestry efforts, State remains national leader in number of Tree City USA communities; Ohio celebrates 18th consecutive year as top participant in nation's most prestigious urban forestry program.
– Department of Education announces that fourth, sixth, ninth, and twelfth-grade proficiency tests given to students in school year 1999-2000 can be downloaded from department's web site.
– Criminal Justice Information System Initiative's Office of Criminal Justice Services awards Columbus $231,000 for Columbus Police Division grant that will provide easy, unified, and secure access to inter-agency information for law enforcement agencies in central Ohio.

DIRECTORY OF STATE SERVICES

OFFICE OF THE GOVERNOR
77 High St., 30th Fl.
Columbus, OH 43266-0601
Fax: 614-466-9354
Governor: 614-644-0813
Internet (URL) address: http://www.ohio.gov/gov/

Washington, DC Office
444 N. Capitol St. NW, Suite 546
Washington, DC 20001
Fax: 202-624-5847
Director: 202-624-5844

OFFICE OF THE LIEUTENANT GOVERNOR
77 S. High St. 30th Fl.
Columbus, OH 43215
Fax: 614-644-0575
Lieutenant Governor: 614-466-3396
Internet (URL) address: http://www.ohio.gov/sos

OFFICE OF THE ATTORNEY GENERAL
30 E Broad St.
Columbus, OH 43215-3428
Fax: 614-466-5087
Attorney General: 614-466-3376
Internet (URL) address: http://www.ag.ohio.gov/

Criminal Identification and Investigation Bureau
P.O. Box 365
London, OH 43140
Fax: 614-852-1603
Superintendent: 614-466-8204

Peace Officers Training Camp
P.O. Box 309
1650 SR 56
London, OH 43140
Superintendent: 614-466-7771

OFFICE OF THE SECRETARY OF STATE
30 E Broad St., 14th Fl.
Columbus, OH 43266-0418
Fax: 614-466-2892
Secretary of State: 614-466-4980
Internet (URL) address: http://www.ohio.gov/sos/

DEPARTMENT OF TREASURY
30 E Broad St. 9th Fl.
Columbus, OH 43266-0421
Fax: 614-644-7313
Treasurer: 614-466-2160
Internet (URL) address: http://www.ohio.gov/treasurer/

ADJUTANT GENERAL
2825 W Dublin Granville Rd.
Columbus, OH 43235-2789
Fax: 614-336-7074
Adjutant General: 614-336-7070
Internet (URL) address: http://www.state.oh.us/adj/

AUDITOR OF STATE
88 E Broad St., 5th Fl.
Columbus, OH 43216-1140
Fax: 614-466-4490
Auditor of State: 614-466-4490
Internet (URL) address: http://www.auditor.ohio.gov/auditor

DEPARTMENTS

ADMINISTRATIVE SERVICES DEPARTMENT
30 E Broad St., Room 4040
Columbus, OH 43266-0401
Fax: 614-644-8151
Director: 614-466-6511
Internet (URL) address: http://www.state.oh.us/das/

Computer and Information System Services Division
30 E Broad St., 39th Fl.
Columbus, OH 43215
Fax: 614-644-9152
Deputy Director: 614-466-5860

Equal Opportunity Center
30 E Broad St., 39th Fl.
Columbus, OH 43215
Fax: 614-728-5628
Deputy Director: 614-466-8380

General Services Division
4200 Surface Rd.
Columbus, OH 43328-1395
Fax: 614-466-1040
Deputy Director: 614-466-4277

Human Resources Division
30 E Broad St., 28th Fl.
Columbus, OH 43215
Fax: 614-728-2785
Deputy Director: 614-466-3485

AGING DEPARTMENT
50 W. Broad St., 9th Fl.
Columbus, OH 43215-5928
Fax: 614-466-5741
Director: 614-466-5500

AGRICULTURE DEPARTMENT
8995 E. Main St.
Reynoldsburg, OH 43068-3399
Fax: 614-466-6124
Director: 614-466-2732
Internet (URL) address: http://www.ohio.gov/agr/

Administration Division
8995 E Main St.
Reynoldsburg, OH 43068
Fax: 614-466-6124
Deputy Director: 614-466-2732

Regulation Division
8995 E. Main St.
Reynoldsburg, OH 43068
Fax: 614-466-6124
Deputy Director: 614-466-2732

ALCOHOL AND DRUG ADDICTION SERVICES DEPARTMENT
280 N. High St., 12th Fl.
Columbus, OH 43215-2537
Fax: 614-752-8645
Director: 614-466-3445
Internet (URL) address: http://www.ohio.gov/ada/odada/htm

BUDGET AND MANAGEMENT DEPARTMENT
30 E Broad St., 34th Fl.
Columbus, OH 43266-0411
Fax: 614-466-3813
Director: 614-466-4034
Internet (URL) address: http://www.ohio.gov/obm/

COMMERCE DEPARTMENT
77 High St., 23rd Fl.
Columbus, OH 43266-0544
Fax: 614-644-8292
Director: 614-466-3636
Internet (URL) address: http://www.ohio.gov/commerce/

Fire Marshal Division
8895 E Main St.
Reynoldsburg, OH 43068
Fax: 614-752-7213
Fire Marshal: 614-752-8200

Industrial Compliance Division
6606 Tussing Rd.
Box 4009
Reynoldsburg, OH 43068-9009
Fax: 614-644-2618
Superintendent: 614-644-2223

Liquor Control Division
P.O. Box 4005
Reynoldsburg, OH 43068-9005
Fax: 614-644-2480
Superintendent: 614-644-2472

DEVELOPMENT DEPARTMENT
P.O. Box 1001
Columbus, OH 43216-1001
Fax: 614-644-0745

Director: 614-466-3379
Internet (URL) address: http://www.odod.ohio.gov/

Community Development Division
P.O. Box 1001
Columbus, OH 43226-1001
Fax: 614-466-4708
Director: 614-466-5863

Housing Finance Agency
77 S High St., 26th Fl.
Columbus, OH 43215
Fax: 614-644-5393
Director: 614-466-7970

Operations Division
77 High St., 29th Fl.
P.O. Box 1001
Columbus, OH 43215
Fax: 614-628-4920
Director: 614-466-7611

EDUCATION DEPARTMENT
65 S Front St., Room 810
Columbus, OH 43215-4183
Fax: 614-644-5960
Superintendent: 614-466-7578
Internet (URL) address: http://www.ode.ohio.gov/

Assessment and Evaluation Division
65 S. Front St., Room 202
Columbus, OH 43215-4183
Fax: 614-728-7434
Director: 614-466-3224

Child Nutrition Division
65 S. Front St., Room 709
Columbus, OH 43215-48183
Fax: 614-752-7613
Director: 614-466-2945

Early Childhood Education Division
65 S. Front St., Room 309
Columbus, OH 43215-4183
Director: 614-466-0224

Federal Assistance Bureau
933 High St.
Worthington, OH 43085-4087
Fax: 614-728-1622
Director: 614-466-4161

Information Management Services Division
1320 Arthur E Adams Dr.
Columbus, OH 43221-3595
Fax: 614-466-0022
Director: 614-466-7000

Professional Development, Licensing Division
65 S. Front St., Room 1009
Columbus, OH 43215-4183
Fax: 614-728-3058
Director: 614-466-2761

School Finance Division
65 S. Front St., Room 815
Columbus, OH 43215-4183
Fax: 614-728-3058
Director: 614-466-6266

School for the Blind
5220 N. High St.
Columbus, OH 43214
Fax: 614-752-1713
Superintendent: 614-752-1152

School for the Deaf
500 Morse Rd.
Columbus, OH 43214-1833
Fax: 614-728-4060
Superintendent: 614-728-4030

Special Education Division
933 High St.
Worthington, OH 43085
Fax: 614-728-1097
Director: 614-466-2650

Vocational and Adult Education Division
65 S. Front St., Room 907
Columbus, OH 43215-4183
Fax: 614-644-5702
Director: 614-466-3430

HEALTH DEPARTMENT
P.O. Box 118
Columbus, OH 43266-0588
Fax: 614-644-0085
Director: 614-466-2253
Internet (URL) address: http://www.odh.state.oh.us/

Chief Operations Officer
246 N. High St.
Columbus, OH 43266-0588
Fax: 614-644-0085
Chief Operations Officer: 614-466-1101

Health Programs Assistant Director
246 N. High St.
Columbus, OH 43266-0588
Fax: 614-644-0085
Director: 614-466-4237

Family and Community Health Services Division
246 N. High St.
Columbus, OH 43216-1603
Fax: 614-728-3616
Chief: 614-466-3263

Prevention Division
245 N. High St.
Columbus, OH 43215
Fax: 614-644-7740
Chief: 614-466-0302

Quality Assurance Division
246 N High St.
Columbus, OH 43266-0588

Fax: 614-644-0208
Chief: 614-466-7857

HUMAN SERVICES DEPARTMENT
30 E Broad St., 32nd Fl.
Columbus, OH 43266-0423
Fax: 614-466-2815
Director: 614-466-6282
Internet (URL) address: http://www.ohio.gov/odhs/

INSURANCE DEPARTMENT
2100 Stella Ct.
Columbus, OH 43215-0167
Fax: 614-644-3743
Director: 614-644-2658
Internet (URL) address: http://www.ohio.gov/ins/

MENTAL HEALTH DEPARTMENT
30 E Broad St., 8th Fl.
Columbus, OH 43215
Fax: 614-752-9453
Director: 614-466-2337
Internet (URL) address: http://www.mh.state.oh.us/

MENTAL RETARDATION AND DEVELOPMENTAL DISABILITIES DEPARTMENT
30 Broad St., Room 1280
Columbus, OH 43266-0415
Fax: 614-644-5013
Director: 614-466-5214
Internet (URL) address: http://www.ohio.gov/dmr/

NATURAL RESOURCES DEPARTMENT
1930 Belcher Drive, Building D-3
Columbus, OH 43224
Fax: 614-261-9601
Director: 614-265-6875
Internet (URL) address: http://www.dnr.ohio.gov/

PUBLIC SAFETY DEPARTMENT
1970 W Broad St.
P.O. Box 182081
Columbus, OH 43218-2081
Fax: 614-466-0433
Director: 614-466-3383
Internet (URL) address: http://www.ohio.gov/odps/

Motor Vehicles Bureau
1970 W Broad St.
Columbus, OH 43266-0020
Fax: 614-752-7973
Registrar: 614-752-7500

Ohio State Highway Patrol
1970 W Broad St.
Columbus, OH 43218-2074
Fax: 614-752-6409
Superintendent: 614-466-2990

Emergency Management Agency
2855 Dublin Granville Rd.
Columbus, OH 43235
Fax: 614-889-7183
Executive Director: 614-889-7150

Emergency Medical Services
1970 W. Broad St.
Columbus, OH 43218-2073
Fax: 614-466-9461
Executive Administrator: 614-466-9447

REHABILITATION AND CORRECTION DEPARTMENT
1050 Freeway Dr. N
Columbus, OH 43229
Main Fax: 614-752-1086
Director Fax: 614-752-1171
Director: 614-752-1162
Internet (URL) address: http://www.drc.ohio.gov/

TAXATION DEPARTMENT
P.O. Box 530
Columbus, OH 43266-0030
Fax: 614-466-6401
Tax Commissioner: 614-466-2166
Internet (URL) address: http://www.state.oh.us/tax/

Taxpayer Service and Compliance Division
1030 Freeway Dr. N
Columbus, OH 43229
Fax: 614-433-7834
Executive Administrator: 614-433-7654

Estate Tax Division
1880 E Dublin Granville Rd.
Columbus, OH 43229
Fax: 614-895-5727
Director: 614-895-5710

Income Tax Operations
1030 Freeway Dr. North
Columbus, OH 43229
Fax: 614-846-9504
Executive Administrator: 614-433-7602

Income Tax Service Center Department
1030 Freeway Dr. N
Columbus, OH 43229
Fax: 614-433-7884
Administrator: 614-438-5302

Public Utility Tax
P.O. Box 530
Columbus, OH 43226-0030
Fax: 614-752-2496
Administrator: 614-466-7371

Motor Fuel, Excise and Tax Division
P.O. Box 530
Columbus, OH 43266-0030
Fax: 614-752-8644
Administrator: 614-466-3053

Personal Property Tax Division
P.O. Box 530
Columbus, OH 43266-0030
Fax: 614-466-8654
Administrator: 614-466-3280

Sales and Use Tax Division
P.O. Box 530
Columbus, OH 43266
Fax: 614-466-4977
Administrator: 614-466-7350

Tax Equalization Division
P.O. Box 530
Columbus, OH 43266
Fax: 614-466-8654
Administrator: 614-466-5744

TRANSPORTATION DEPARTMENT
1980 W Broad St.
Columbus, OH 43223
Fax: 614-644-0587
Director: 614-466-2335
Internet (URL) address: http://www.dot.state.oh.us/

Business Management
1980 W Broad St.
Columbus, OH 43223
Fax: 614-644-2587
Assistant Director: 614-466-3599

Field Operations
1980 W Broad St., 2nd Fl.
Columbus, OH 43223
Fax: 614-644-0587
Assistant Director: 614-446-2448

Transportation Policy
1980 W Broad
Columbus, OH 43223
Fax: 614-644-0587
Assistant Director: 614-466-8990

YOUTH SERVICES DEPARTMENT
51 N High St.
Columbus, OH 43215
Fax: 614-752-9078
Director: 614-466-8783

BOARDS AND COMMISSIONS

ACCOUNTANCY BOARD
77 S. High St., 18th Fl.
Columbus, OH 43266-0301
Fax: 614-466-2628
Director: 614-466-4135
Internet (URL) address: http://www.ohio.gov/acc/

AIR QUALITY DEVELOPMENT AUTHORITY
50 W. Broad St., Suite 1901
Columbus, OH 43215
Fax: 614-752-9188
Executive Director: 614-466-6825

ARCHITECTS AND LANDSCAPE EXAMINERS BOARD
77 S. High St., 16th Fl.
Columbus, OH 43266-0303
Fax: 614-644-9048
Executive Director: 614-466-2316

ARTS COUNCIL
727 E Main St.
Columbus, OH 43205-1796
Fax: 614-466-4494
Executive Director: 614-466-2613
Internet (URL) address: http://www.oac.ohio.gov/

BUILDING AUTHORITY
30 E Broad St., Suite 4020
Columbus, OH 43215
Fax: 614-644-6478
Executive Director: 614-466-5959

CIVIL RIGHTS COMMISSION
1111 E Broad St., Suite 4020
Columbus, OH 43215
Fax: 614-644-6478
Executive Director: 614-466-5959

CRIMINAL JUSTICE SERVICES OFFICE
400 E Town St., Suite 300
Columbus, OH 43215
Fax: 614-466-5025
Director: 614-466-0280

EMPLOYMENT SERVICES BUREAU
145 S Front St.
Columbus, OH 43215
Fax: 614-466-5025
Administrator: 614-466-2100
Internet (URL) address: http://www.state.oh.us/obes/

ENVIRONMENTAL PROTECTION AGENCY
P.O. Box 1049
Columbus, OH 43266-1049
Fax: 614-644-3184
Director: 614-644-2782
Internet (URL) address: http://www.epa.ohio.gov/

Hazardous Waste Facility Board
P.O. Box 1049
Columbus, OH 43216-1049
Fax: 614-644-3439
Executive Director: 614-644-2742

ETHICS COMMISSION
8 E. Long St., 10th Fl.
Columbus, OH 43215-2940
Fax: 614-466-8368
Executive Director: 614-466-7090

HIGHER EDUCATION FACILITIES COMMISSION
30 E Broad St., 36th Fl.
Columbus, OH 43266-0417
Fax: 614-466-5866
Chairman: 614-466-6000

HISTORICAL SOCIETY
17th & Interstate 71
Columbus, OH 43211-2497
Fax: 614-297-2411
Director: 614-297-2392
Internet (URL) address:
  http://winslo.ohio.gov/ohswww/ohshome.html

INDUSTRIAL COMMISSION
30 W Spring St.
Columbus, OH 43215-2233
Fax: 614-752-6610
Chairman: 614-466-3711

LIBRARY
65 S Front St.
Columbus, OH 43215
Fax: 614-466-3584
State Librarian: 614-644-7061
Internet (URL) address: http://winnslo.ohio.gov/

LIQUOR CONTROL COMMISSION
77 S High St., 18th Fl.
Columbus, OH 43266-0565
Fax: 614-466-4564
Chairman: 614-466-3132

LOTTERY COMMISSION
615 Superior Ave. W
Cleveland, OH 44113
Fax: 216-787-3313
Executive Director: 216-787-3344

PUBLIC DEFENDER
8 E Long St., 11th Fl.
Columbus, OH 43215
Fax: 614-644-9972
Public Defender: 614-466-5393

PUBLIC EMPLOYEES RETIREMENT SYSTEM
277 E Town St.
Columbus, OH 43215
Fax: 614-466-5837
Executive Director: 614-466-2822

PUBLIC FACILITIES COMMISSION
30 E Broad St., 34th Fl.
Columbus, OH 43215
Fax: 614-466-3813
Chairman: 614-466-0691

PUBLIC UTILITIES COMMISSION
180 E Broad St.
Columbus, OH 43215-3793
Fax: 614-466-7954
Chairman: 614-466-3204
Internet (URL) address: http://mabel.puc.ohio.gov/

RACING COMMISSION
77 S. High St., 18th Fl.
Columbus, OH 43266
Fax: 614-466-3813
Executive Director: 614-466-0691

REGENTS BOARD
30 E Broad St., 36th Fl.
Columbus, OH 43266-0417
Fax: 614-466-5866
Chancellor: 614-466-6000
Internet (URL) address: http://www.bor.ohio.gov/

REHABILITATION SERVICES COMMISSION
400 Campus View Blvd.
Columbus, OH 43235-4604
Fax: 614-438-1257
Administrator: 614-438-1210

Disability Determination Bureau
P.O. Box 359001
Columbus, OH 43235-9001
Director: 614-438-1500

SCHOOL FACILITIES COMMISSION
88 E Broad St., Suite 1400
Columbus, OH 43215
Fax: 614-466-7749
Chairman: 614-466-6290
Internet (URL) address: http://www.osfc.state.oh.us/

TAX APPEALS BOARD
30 E Broad St., 24th Fl.
Columbus, OH 43215
Fax: 614-644-5196
Chairman: 614-466-6700
Internet (URL) address: http://www.ohio.gov/bta

TURNPIKE COMMISSION
682 Prospect St.
Berea, OH 44017
Fax: 614-234-4618
Executive Director: 614-234-2081

WATER DEVELOPMENT AUTHORITY
88 E Broad St., Suite 1300
Columbus, OH 43215
Fax: 614-644-9964
Executive Director: 614-466-5822

WORKERS COMPENSATION BUREAU
30 W Spring St., 29th Fl.
Columbus, OH 43265-2256
Fax: 614-752-8428
Chairman: 614-466-8751

MEMBERS OF CONGRESS

SENATE

SEN. MIKE DeWINE (R) (b. 1947); 1st Term;
Phone: 202-224-2315; Fax: 202-224-6519;
E-mail: senatordewine@dewine.senate.gov.

www.senate.gov/~dewine/

SEN. GEORGE V. VOINOVICH (R) (b. 1936); 1st Term;
Phone: 202-224-3353; Fax: 202-228-1382;
E-mail: senator_voinovich@voinovich.senate.gov.

www.senate.gov/~voinovich

HOUSE

STEVE CHABOT (R-1st) (b. 1953); 3rd Term;
Phone: 202-225-2216; Fax: 202-225-3012;
E-mail: oh01@legislators.com.

www.house.gov/chabot

ROB J. PORTMAN (R-2nd) (b. 1955); 4th Term;
Phone: 202-225-3164; Fax: 202-225-1992;
E-mail: portmail@mail.house.gov.

www.house.gov/portman/

TONY P. HALL (D-3rd) (b. 1942); 11th Term;
Phone: 202-225-6465; Fax: (None);
E-mail: oh03@legislators.com.

www.house.gov/tonyhall

MICHAEL G. OXLEY (R-4th) (b. 1944); 9th Term;
Phone: 202-225-2676; Fax: 202-226-0577;
E-mail: mike.oxley@mail.house.gov.

www.house.gov/oxley

PAUL E. GILLMOR (R-5th) (b. 1939); 6th Term;
Phone: 202-225-6405; Fax: 202-225-1985;
E-mail: oh05@legislators.com.

www.house.gov/gillmor/

TED STRICKLAND (D-6th) (b. 1941); 3rd Term;
Phone: 202-225-5705; Fax: 202-225-5907;
E-mail: oh06@legislators.com.

www.house.gov/strickland/

DAVID HOBSON (R-7th) (b. 1936); 5th Term;
Phone: 202-225-4324; Fax: (None); E-mail: (None).

www.house.gov/hobson/

JOHN A. BOEHNER (R-8th) (b. 1949); 5th Term;
Phone: 202-225-6205; Fax: 202-225-0704;
E-mail: john.boehner@mail.house.gov.

www.house.gov/boehner

MARCY KAPTUR (D-9th) (b. 1946); 9th Term;
Phone: 202-225-4146; Fax: 202-225-7711;
E-mail: rep.kaptur@mail.house.gov.

www.gov/kaptur/

DENNIS J. KUCINICH (D-10th) (b. 1946); 2nd Term;
Phone: 202-225-5871; Fax: 202-225-5745; E-mail: (None).

www.house.gov/kucinich

STEPHANIE TUBBS JONES (D-11th) (b. 1949); 1st Term;
Phone: 202-225-7032; Fax: 202-225-1339;
E-mail: Stephanie.Tubbs.Jones@mail.house.gov.

www.house.gov/tubbsjones

JOHN R. KASICH (R-12th) (b. 1952); 9th Term;
Phone: 202-225-5355; Fax: (None);
E-mail: oh12@legislators.com.

www.house.gov/kasich/

SHERROD BROWN (D-13th) (b. 1952); 4th Term;
Phone: 202-225-3401; Fax: 202-225-2266;
E-mail: oh13@legislators.com.

www.house.gov/sherrodbrown/

THOMAS C. SAWYER (D-14th) (b. 1945); 7th Term;
Phone: 202-225-5231; Fax: 202-225-5278;
E-mail: oh14@legislators.com.

www.house.gov/sawyer/

DEBORAH PRYCE (R-15th) (b. 1951); 4th Term;
Phone: 202-225-2015; Fax: (None);
E-mail: pryce.oh15@mail.house.gov.

www.house.gov/pryce/

RALPH REGULA (R-16th) (b. 1924); 14th Term;
Phone: 202-225-3876; Fax: 202-225-3059;
E-mail: oh16@legislators.com.

www.house.gov/regula/

JAMES A. TRAFICANT, Jr. (D-17th) (b. 1941); 8th Term;
Phone: 202-225-5261; Fax: 202-225-3719;
E-mail: telljim@mail.house.gov.

www.house.gov/traficant/

BOB NEY (R-18th) (b. 1954); 3rd Term;
Phone: 202-225-6265; Fax: 202-225-3394;
E-mail: bobney@mail.house.gov.

www.house.gov/ney/

STEVEN C. LaTOURETTE (R-19th) (b. 1954); 3rd Term;
Phone: 202-225-5731; Fax: 202-225-3307;
E-mail: oh19@legislators.com.

www.house.gov/latourette

TWENTIETH CENTURY GOVERNORS

NASH, GEORGE KILBON (1842-1904), was the forty-first Governor of Ohio (1900-04). Born in York, Ohio, to Electra Branch and Asa Nash, he received his early education in the nearby public schools then studied at Western Reserve Academy before entering Oberlin College when he was twenty.

After two years at Oberlin, Nash dropped out to serve in the Union Army during the Civil War. Remaining in the army for only a short period of time, he began studying law in 1865 and was admitted to the State bar two years later. He then opened a law practice in Columbus. For a few months in 1869, he served as chief clerk to Ohio's Secretary of State.

In 1870, Nash was elected to his first of two consecutive terms as Franklin County Prosecuting Attorney. After an unsuccessful bid for Congress in 1876 and for State Attorney General in 1877, he was elected State Attorney General in 1879 for a three-year term. In 1883, he was appointed to a State Supreme Court Commission to help the court finish hearing all its cases.

Active in the State's Republican Party, Nash was elected to his first term as Governor in 1899. During his tenure, he was considered an able and forceful leader. He successfully pushed through the legislature laws giving the Governor more control in local management of the State. Besides raising corporate taxes and decreasing property taxes, Nash instituted regular audits of all State-run institutions.

Deciding against seeking reelection at the end of his term, Nash retired from public life. He was married to Ada Deshler. He died in Columbus in 1904.

HERRICK, MYRON (1854-1929), forty-second Governor of Ohio (1904-06), was born in Huntington, Ohio, to Mary Hulbert and Timothy Herrick. After receiving an early education in Huntington and Wellington public schools, he worked as a newspaper reporter and a schoolteacher. A few years later, after saving enough money, he was educated at Oberlin and Ohio Wesleyan University.

Herrick was admitted to the State bar in 1878, and shortly afterwards opened a law office in Cleveland. Over the next two decades, he was involved in several profitable businesses, white also making close ties with the leaders of the State's Republican Party. He was elected to the Cleveland City Council in 1885, retaining that position for six years. In 1901, he was elected President of the American Bankers Association. Two years later, he was elected to his only term as Governor.

During his tenure, Herrick was saddled in his decision-making ability by a major rift, which had been growing in his Party over the past several years. Although Herrick paid close attention to the State finances, his vetoes of several major bills caused his defeat in a reelection bid in 1905.

After returning to his business interests for a few years, Herrick was appointed by President William H. Taft in 1912 as Ambassador to France. Herrick received national recognition for his important contributions to the two countries. During World War I, the French government honored him with the Legion of Honor cross. Herrick returned home for a short time after the war, and ran unsuccessfully for the U.S. Senate.

Herrick was reappointed to his ambassadorial position in 1921, and retained that post until his death in 1929. He was married to Carolyn M. Parmely in 1880.

PATTISON, JOHN M. (1854-1929), forty-third governor of Ohio (1906), was born in Owensville, Ohio, the son of Mary Duckwall and William Pattison. After receiving an early education in Clermont County public schools, he began clerking in his father's store. When the Civil War broke out, he enlisted in the Ohio Voluntary Infantry, serving as a drummer. At the war's end, Pattison enrolled at Ohio Wesleyan University and began teaching in nearby public schools.

After graduating in 1869, Pattison worked as an agent for the Union Central Life Insurance Company in Illinois. Simultaneously, he attended Cincinnati Law School and read law in the office of Alfred Yaple. He was admitted to the bar in 1871.

For a few months in 1873, Pattison served as assistant attorney for the Cincinnati and Marietta Railroad. Later that year, he was elected to the State Legislature and was forced to resign his former job. After his two-year term expired, he became a partner in Yaple's law firm and a member of an anti-corruption organization in Cincinnati. He also edited the *Ohio Law Review*. In 1881, he was elected Vice President of the Union Central Life Insurance Company. After ten years as Vice President, he became president of the company.

In addition to retaining his presidency of the Union Central for most of the remainder of his life, Pattison was also active in many other business ventures. In 1890, he was elected to the State Senate, and in 1891, to the U.S. House of Representatives.

After deciding against reelection, Pattison returned to his numerous business interests. In 1905, with the support of the State's temperance groups, he was elected to his only term as Governor. However, before he could be inaugurated, he became extremely ill. Although he survived his first legislative session, ill health forced him to return to his Milford home in April.

Pattison died in 1929, before his term expired. He was married to Alethia Williams in 1879. After her death in 1891, he married her younger sister, Anna Margaret Williams.

HARRIS, ANDREW LINTNER (1835-1915), forty-fourth governor of Ohio (1906-1909), was born in Butler County, Ohio, the son of Nancy Lintner and Benjamin Harris. After receiving an early education in local public schools, he attended Miami University. He graduated in 1860 and began studying law at the firm of Thompson and Eaton. During the Civil War, Harris enlisted in the Ohio Volunteer Infantry and served in eighteen battles, including Gettysburg; and was wounded. He was discharged as a brigadier general in 1865. Later that year, he was admitted to the Ohio Bar. He was elected to the State Senate for a two-year term in 1866, and then opened a law office in Easton, with Robert Miller as his partner.

From 1875 to 1882, Harris served as Probate Judge of Preble County. In 1885, he was elected to the State General Assembly, retaining the position until 1891, when he was elected Lieutenant Governor of Ohio. In 1893, he was reelected to that position, serving both terms under Governor William McKinley. When McKinley became president, he appointed Harris to the United States Industrial Commission on Trusts and Industrial Combinations. He served in that post until 1902. Again elected Lieutenant Governor in 1905, Harris became Governor in 1906, when John Pattison died in office. He remained in the office for three years because of a constitutional change adopted in 1905, which moved State elections to every even-numbered year.

During his term, Harris was instrumental in the passage of numerous temperance laws, including the Rose Law, which allowed major portions of the State to prohibit alcohol. He also helped establish a Bureau of Vital Statistics, a reorganized Bureau of Forestry, and a Pure Food and Drug law.

Although his administration did much to help the State, Harris's support of the temperance laws ultimately caused his defeat in a bid for reelection in 1908. When his term ended, he returned to his Easton farm and retired from public life. Harris was married to Caroline Conger in 1865. He died in Easton in 1915.

HARMON, JUDSON (1846-1927), forty-fifth Governor of Ohio (1909-1913), was born in Newton, Ohio, the son of Julia Bronson and Franklin Harmon. After receiving his early education in local public schools and from his father, he graduated from Denison University at age twenty.

Joining the home guard near the end of the Civil War, Harmon fought against Morgan's Raiders. After teaching school for a year in Columbia, he began studying law in the office of George Hoadly, shortly before Hoadly was elected governor. He received his law degree from the Cincinnati School of Law in 1869, and was then admitted to the State Bar.

Harmon was elected to the Court of Common Pleas in Cincinnati in 1876, but was subsequently ousted by the State Senate. Two years later, he was elected to a Superior Court seat. He resigned from the Superior Court in 1887, and became a partner in the prominent Cincinnati law firm of Hoadly, Johnson and Colston. Appointed Attorney General in 1895 by President Grover Cleveland, he returned to his law practice two years later.

After a short stint as a United States Special Investigator assigned to investigate kickbacks by the Atchison, Topeka & Santa Fe Railroad, Harmon announced his candidacy for governor. He was elected to the first of two consecutive terms by over 17,000 votes. A Republican prior to the Civil War, and a Democrat afterwards, he quickly rose in popularity. Two years later, he was reelected by over 100,000 votes.

During his administration, Harmon fought triumphantly against corruption and for numerous reform legislations. By 1912, his reputation had made him a popular-son candidate for the Presidency. But his lack of support of the statewide initiative and referendum process caused his defeat. In 1913, he resumed his successful practice as a corporation lawyer, and as a professor at Cincinnati Law School. He died in Cincinnati in 1927.

COX, JAMES MIDDLETON (1870-1957), forty-sixth and forty eighth governor of Ohio (1913-1915 and 1917-1921), was born near Jacksonburg in Butler County, Ohio, the son of Eliza Andrew and Gilbert Cox. He received his early education in the local county schools, and attended high school in Amanda for two years before becoming a reporter for the Middletown *News Signal*. Earning a reputation as a competent reporter and political writer, he was hired by the Cincinnati *Enquirer* where he served as a railroad editor. He left the *Enquirer* in 1894 to work as Congressman Paul Sorg's private secretary. Cox purchased the Dayton *Daily News* in 1898. Over the next few years, he brought prosperity to the financially floundering newspaper, while making it one of the State's most influential voices.

In 1903, Cox purchased the Springfield *Daily News*. In 1908, he was elected to the United States House of Representatives. He remained in Congress until 1913, when he was elected to the first of three terms as Governor of Ohio. During his administration, he became one of the Ohio Progressive Movement's most outspoken leaders. Among numerous programs he was instrumental in instituting in the State were the first workmen's compensation law, a system for administering pensions for mothers, a child labor code, a reorganization of the public school system, Ohio's first public utilities commission, the introduction of direct primaries in State elections, a massive reform in State courts and prisons, and passage of a State banking code.

Although Cox was defeated in his reelection bid two years later, he was elected to the governorship again in 1915 and 1917. In 1920, he ran unsuccessfully for President of the United States. After his defeat, which many considered a result of his support of the unpopular League of Nations, Cox returned to his numerous publishing interests. Before his death, he owned over one half-dozen newspapers throughout the State, three radio stations, and a television broadcasting station.

In 1925, Cox co-founded the University of Miami. In 1933, he was named Vice President of the United States Delegation to the World Economic Conference in London. He refused an appointment to the United States Senate in 1946. Considered one of the State's most humanitarian and progressive governors, he was honored by the city of Dayton in 1952, when it renamed its municipal airport the James M. Cox Dayton Municipal Airport, in tribute of his many years of service to the people of the State. Cox was married twice. He died in 1957.

WILLIS, FRANK BARTLETT (1871-1928), forty-seventh Governor of Ohio (1915-1917), was born at Lewis Center in Delaware County, Ohio, the son of Jay B. Willis. After receiving his early education in local public schools, he spent much of his youth working on his father's farm. He taught high school for a short time before graduating from Ohio Northern University in 1894.

Willis became a professor of History and Economics at the university while studying law. From 1900 to 1904, he served in the State House of Representatives. He was admitted to the State bar in 1901. In 1902, he received a Masters degree, and in 1906, earned a law degree from Ohio Northern University. He left his chairmanship of the History and Economics Department and began teaching law.

Willis was elected to his first of two consecutive terms to the United States Congress in 1910. When he defeated incumbent Governor James M. Cox for the governorship in 1914, he resigned from Congress. During his administration, the progressive movement was at its height in Ohio, and he pushed for economic and legislative restraint. He was instrumental in the codification of highway laws, the construction of better highways throughout the State, and the institution of public health laws. Defeated in a re-election bid in 1917, he ran in the next election under the first political platform in the State calling for women's suffrage and alcohol prohibition, but was again defeated. From 1921 to 1927, Willis served in the United States Senate. He was nominated as a Presidential candidate in 1928, but died in Delaware, Ohio, at a political rally, before the election took place. He was married to Allie Dustin in 1894. He died in 1928.

DAVIS, HARRY LYMAN (1878-1950), forty-ninth governor of Ohio (1921-1923), was born in Cleveland, Ohio, the son of Barbara James and Evan Hicks Davis; his father was a Welsh immigrant. After receiving his early education in the Cleveland public schools, he began working in the city's steel mills when he was thirteen years old.

Davis enrolled in the Euclid Avenue Business College while still in his teens and was appointed a page in the State House of Representatives after his father was elected to the legislature. Simultaneously with his work as a page, he worked in the Metropolitan Parks System of Cleveland.

Over the next several years, Davis held a series of jobs in the Cleveland area. In 1909, he was elected Treasurer of the city. After being defeated in a mayoral bid in 1913, he was elected to the first of three consecutive terms to that post in 1915. Achieving widespread popularity as a mayor, he was overwhelmingly elected to his only term as Governor in 1920, defeating Warren G. Harding.

During his administration, Davis spent much of his time trying to solve the legislative battle, which was brewing over State taxes. Near the end of his first term, when Senate and House leaders could not agree on pending tax legislation, he exercised a seldom used amendment to the State Constitution which allowed him to adjourn the legislative session for the year.

A few months later, when the nationwide coal miners' strike threatened the State's economy, Davis called a special legislative session to solve the crisis. He also pushed through the divided legislature an emergency measure reorganizing the State government into departments similar to those on the Federal level. Passage of the legislation as an emergency measure was criticized because it avoided a referendum vote. An ensuing legal battle ended with the State Supreme Court ruling the legislature had the right to determine what constitutes an emergency.

Deciding against seeking reelection in 1922, Davis lost a gubernatorial election bid again in 1924. He formed the Harry L.

Davis Insurance Company after leaving office, and presided over the company until his death. He also served as Cleveland's Mayor in 1934-1935, after leading a successful campaign to end Cleveland's city manager system. Davis was married to Lucy V. Forgan in 1902. He died in Cleveland in 1950.

DONAHEY, ALVIN VICTOR (1873-1946), fiftieth governor of Ohio (1923-1929), was born near Cadwallader in Tuscarawas County, Ohio, to Catherine Chaney and John C. Donahey. After receiving his early education in West Chester and New Philadelphia, he dropped out of high school to become a printer in Masillon.

At age twenty, Donahey borrowed money and bought a printing shop in New Philadelphia. He began a successful political career in 1898 when he was elected clerk of the Goshen Township Board of Trustees. He served as Auditor of Tuscarawas County in 1904, retaining the position for two years. From 1902 to 1911, he served on the New Philadelphia Board of Education.

Donahey was State Auditor from 1912 to 1921. In the latter year, he ran unsuccessfully for Governor of Ohio, but in 1923, he was elected to his first of three consecutive terms as Chief of State. During his administration, he spent much of his time contending with a staunchly Republican legislature. As a Democrat, in his first term alone, he vetoed seventy-four bills and eleven acts sent to him by the legislature.

Donahey had several major accomplishments, however, especially in highway construction and prison reform. Opposed to prohibition enforcement, which he felt was unfairly directed against the poor, he pardoned 256 prisoners during his first term alone, and over 2,000 prisoners in all during his three terms of gubernatorial office. At the end of his last term, Donahey returned to his Indian Lake home and established the Motorists' Mutual Insurance Company of Columbus. Elected to the United States Senate in 1934, he served one term before retiring from public life. Donahey was married to Mary Edith Harvey in 1897. He died in 1946.

COOPER, MYERS YOUNG (1873-1958), fifty-first governor of Ohio (1929-1931), was born near Saint Louisville in Licking County, Ohio, the son of Lemuel Cooper and Anne Greenlee Cooper.

After receiving his early education in the public schools of Licking County, Cooper enrolled in the Lebanon National Normal University for two years. In the early 1890s, Cooper opened a real estate business in Cincinnati with his brothers. In about a decade, his business interests mushroomed when he opened the Hyde Park Lumber Company, the Hyde Park Savings Bank, and Norward National Bank. He remained in control of the three Norward companies throughout his life. A Taft supporter in 1908, Cooper was affiliated with the Bull Moose Party for a short time before becoming actively involved in the State Republican Party in 1915. After serving in a variety of Republican Party posts, he ran unsuccessfully for the governorship in 1926. Two years later, he was elected to gubernatorial office, defeating Ohio's future governor, Martin Luther Davey.

During his administration, Cooper saw the legislature pass most of the bills he recommended with little conflict. Among the laws he implemented were the Blue Sky Law to safeguard investors, new regulations controlling the State's Public Utilities Commission, a tighter conservation law, revised banking and election laws, and the establishment of a social welfare program in the State.

After losing a reelection bid to George White in 1930, Cooper left office at the end of his term and returned to his business interests. He was active in numerous educational and civic functions. Cooper was marred to Martha Kinney in 1897. He died in Cincinnati in 1958.

WHITE, GEORGE (1872-1953), fifty-second governor of Ohio (1931-1935), was born in Elmira, New York, to Mary Black and Charles White. After receiving his early education in the local public schools of Titusville, Pennsylvania, he graduated from Princeton University in 1895.

White taught school in Titusville for a time after earning his degree. He then worked as a laborer for a Pittsburgh oil company. In 1898, later departing for Alaska to mine gold. Upon his return to Ohio in 1902, he began working for several oil companies in Ohio and neighboring states. He later became an independent oil producer. White's political career began with an election to the State House of Representatives. In 1910, he was elected to his first of two consecutive terms in the United States House. After a defeat for reelection in 1914, he was again reelected in 1916.

In 1930, White was elected to his first of two consecutive terms as Ohio's Governor. During his administration, he spent most of his time trying to deal with the national and State economic woes resulting from the Great Depression. Almost immediately after his inauguration, he cut the State budget by twenty million dollars, a reduction of fifteen percent. Besides instituting a relief system for the State's unemployed, he pushed through the legislature a revised tax system which reduced property taxes and introduced sales taxes on such items as cigarettes, cosmetics, and other non-essential items. He was also responsible for the creation of the State Highway Patrol.

At the end of his second term, White ran unsuccessfully for the U.S. Senate. After two further unsuccessful bids for the position, he retired from public life and devoted himself to his many business and civic interests. White was married twice. He died in West Palm Beach, Florida in 1953.

DAVEY, MARTIN LUTHER (1884-1946), fifty-third governor of Ohio (1935-1939), was born at Kent in Portage County, Ohio, to Bertha Reeves and John Davey. After receiving his early education in the State public school system and Oberlin Academy, he attended Oberlin College for three years. He dropped out of school in 1907 to assist in his father's tree surgery business. The senior Davey was later known as the "father of tree surgery." In 1909, Davey and his father organized the Davey Tree Expert Company, of which Davey was the general manager. When his father died in 1923, Davey became the company's president. Later he also expanded the business nationwide and into Canada, carrying what he had learned from his father's expertise in tree care and cultivation to all corners of the country.

Davey served as Kent's mayor from 1914 to 1918. He was appointed to the United States House of Representatives, and reelected three more times before becoming a United States Senator in 1923. When his Senate term expired in 1929, he ran unsuccessfully for governor.

Davey was elected Ohio's Governor in 1935. During his administration, he spent much of his time trying to solve the economic problems from the Great Depression. After the State legislature refused to drop the newly created sales tax on food during his first term, he succeeded in getting the law repealed by incorporating it as a legislative amendment, where it was overwhelmingly opposed by the State voters. In other conflicts with the legislature, he was able to get several laws passed to guarantee State funds for local school and old age pensioners. He was also instrumental in Ohio becoming the first state to pay unemployment insurance benefits. Defeated in his reelection bid in

1938 and 1940, Davey retired from public office and returned to his tree business. He was married to Berenice Chrisman in 1907. He died in Kent in 1946.

BRICKER, JOHN WILLIAM (1893-1986), fifty-fourth governor of Ohio (1939-1945), was born in Madison County, Ohio, the son of Laura King and Lemuel Spencer Bricker. After receiving an early education in the local schools, he taught school for a time before graduating from Ohio State University in 1916. In 1917, he was admitted to the State bar.

Bricker was denied entry into the military during World War I because of a low pulse rate; after gaining support from his church, however, he was able to enter into the Army Chaplain Corps as a first lieutenant. At the end of the war, he established a law practice in Columbus.

From 1920 to 1928, Bricker served as Solicitor of Grand View Heights. He was Assistant Attorney General of the State from 1923 to 1927. After running unsuccessfully for Attorney General in 1928, he served on the Public Utilities Commission. In 1932, he left the commission when he was elected to his first of two consecutive terms as Attorney General.

After his defeat in a gubernatorial bid in 1936, Bricker was elected Ohio's governor in 1938. During his three terms of office, he managed to turn the State's massive deficit into a surplus. He also oversaw increases in the old-age pension allowable in the State, and in the level of subsidies given to the schools by the State.

Defeated in a presidential bid in 1944, Bricker was elected to the United States Senate in 1946. As a senator, Bricker introduced the controversial Bricker Amendment to the Constitution, which would have limited the President's treaty-making powers. After a defeat in his reelection bid for a third term, he left public office and returned to his law practice. Bricker was married to Harriet Day in 1920. He died on March 22, 1986.

LAUSCHE, FRANK JOHN (1895-1990), fifty-fifth and fifty-seventh Governor of Ohio (1945-47, 1949-57), was born in Cleveland, Ohio, the son of Frances Milavec and Louis Lausche. At age twelve, after his father's death, he began working odd jobs to earn money. He also attended Central Institute Preparatory School before entering the United States Army in 1918.

At the end of the war, Lausche was discharged a second Lieutenant, and entered the John Marshall School of Law. He graduated from the institute in 1920. Later that year, he was admitted to the Cleveland bar. After an unsuccessful bid for the State House in 1922 and the State Senate in 1924, he served on the Cleveland Municipal Court from 1932 to 1937. In 1937, Lausche was elected to the Cuyahoga County Court of Common Pleas. He remained a judge in the Pleas Court until his election to Cleveland Mayor in 1941. Reelected to the mayoral position two years later, he resigned in 1944 after winning his first gubernatorial race in the State.

After a defeat by Thomas Herbert in 1946, Lausche was elected again two years later. In all, he was Ohio's Governor for five terms. During his tenure, he was fiscally conservative, denying salary increases to himself and his underlings. Despite his frugal policies, he pushed for the construction of a 336 million dollars turnpike across the State, and an expansion of the State's welfare system.

An avid conservationist, Lausche also created a Department of Natural Resources, introduced legislation to control strip-mining, and called for a statewide campaign to plant more trees. He also oversaw the creation of the State Board of Education. In 1957, Lausche resigned his gubernatorial position to become a

United States Senator. He retired from politics in 1968, after losing a reelection bid. He was married to Jane Sheal in 1928. He died on April 21, 1990.

HERBERT, THOMAS J. (1894-1974), fifty-sixth Governor of Ohio (1947-49), was born in Cleveland, Ohio, the son of Jane Jones and John Herbert. After receiving an early education in the public schools of Cleveland, he attended Adelbert College for a short time before graduating from Western Reserve University in 1915.

Herbert attended Western Reserve University Law School, graduated in 1920, and was admitted to the State bar shortly afterwards. His studies were interrupted by World War I, when he enlisted in the United States Air Force. After being seriously injured in combat, he was discharged from the service.

For a short time after the war, Herbert served as Cleveland's Assistant Director of Law. Later, he was named Cuyahoga County Assistant Prosecuting Attorney. In 1929, he began a four-year stint as Assistant Attorney General of Ohio. After an unsuccessful bid as State Attorney General in 1936, he was elected to that post in 1938. He lost a bid for the governorship in 1944, but two years later was elected to his only term in that position.

A conservative Republican, Herbert pushed hard to eliminate State taxes during his tenure. Although he did much to support the war veterans and improve State services, he was defeated in his reelection bid two years later. He returned to his law practice following the defeat. In the early 1950s, Herbert was named to the United States Subversive Control Board. In 1951, he was elected to the State Supreme Court. Resigning from his court seat eleven years later, he left public office for good. He died in Grove City, Ohio in 1974.

BROWN, JOHN WILLIAM (1913-1993), fifty-eighth Governor of Ohio (1957), was born in Athens, Ohio, the son of Daisy Foster and James Brown. After receiving an early education in the public schools of Athens and Fairfield County, where his father worked as a coal miner, Brown embarked in a series of business ventures around the Medina area—from insurance to real estate.

For a time, Brown served in the Ohio Highway Patrol. After the outbreak of World War II, he enlisted in the United States Coast Guard, and attained the rank of Commander. As his business interests grew, Brown became interested in politics.

In 1950, Brown entered the political arena when he was elected Mayor of Medina. Two years later, he was elected Lieutenant Governor of Ohio. Brown became Ohio's Governor in 1957, when Governor Frank J. Lausche resigned. He held his gubernatorial position for only eleven days.

The most notable contribution of Brown's tenure was his success in ending a vicious strike against the Ohio Consolidated Telephone Company. Defeated in a bid for Governor in 1956, he ran successfully for the State House of Representatives in 1959. In 1960, he was elected to the State Senate, and two years later, he was again elected Lieutenant Governor of the State. He retained the position until 1975. He was married to Violet Helman in 1943. He died in 1993.

O'NEILL, CRANE WILLIAM, (1916-1978), fifty-ninth Governor of Ohio (1957-59), was born in Marietta, Ohio, to Jesse Arnold and Charles O'Neill; his father was an attorney. After receiving an early education in Marietta's public schools, he graduated from Marietta High School in 1934.

O'Neill attended Marietta College, graduating in 1938, and Ohio State University College of Law, from which he graduated in 1942. At twenty-two, he was elected to his first of six consecutive terms to the State House of Representatives. Shortly after receiving his law degree, he joined his father's law firm. During World War II, he served four years in the U.S. Army under General George Patton, and was discharged as a Sergeant in 1946. O'Neill was a leading Republican spokesmen by the end of his six terms in the State legislature, and was elected State Attorney General for the first of three consecutive terms in 1950. In 1956, he made one of his most controversial rulings as Attorney General when he announced that the State Board of Education could withhold funds to school districts allowing segregation. Later that year, O'Neill was elected to his only term as Governor.

During his administration, O'Neill did much to increase the pay of lower level State employees. He also pushed through the legislature an emergency measure, which called for the construction of major highways throughout the State. Although most of the legislation he introduced in the State House met with success, he was defeated in a reelection bid in 1958.

After leaving office, O'Neill returned to his law practice and a Professorship at Bethany College. He was named to the State Supreme Court in 1960, and from 1970 until his death, he served as Chief Justice of the Court. Honored by many civic and educational groups for his activities in the State, O'Neill died in Columbus. O'Neill was married to Betty Hewson in 1945. He died in 1978.

DISALLE, MICHAEL VINCENT (1908-1981), sixtieth Governor of Ohio (1959-63), was born in New York City, the son of Assunta Arcangelo and Anthony DiSalle. After receiving an early education in Toledo's public schools and at Central Catholic High School in Toledo, he graduated from Georgetown University in 1931.

Passing the Ohio bar examination in 1932, DiSalle began practicing law in Toledo. In 1933 and 1934, he worked for the Home Owner's Loan Corporation, serving as an Assistant District Counsel. In 1936, he was elected to the State House of Representatives for a two-year term. Although named one of the five most outstanding House members shortly after taking office, he lost a bid for the State Senate two years later. During World War II he served in the National Guard.

In 1939, DiSalle became Assistant City Law Director of Toledo. In 1941, he was elected to his first of five consecutive terms as a Toledo City Councilman. For the last two terms, he served as Vice-Mayor. He entered national prominence in 1945 when he originated and began chairing the Toledo Labor-Management Citizens Committee. In 1947, he was elected Mayor of Toledo. DiSalle resigned from his second term as Mayor in 1950 to become President Harry Truman's Director of Price Stabilization. Defeated in a senatorial bid in 1952 and a gubernatorial bid in 1956, he was elected in 1958 to his only term as Governor.

DiSalle was the first Governor to serve a single four-year term. During his tenure, he increased State taxes to give additional money to numerous State programs. Although he did much to improve services in Ohio, he defeated in a reelection bid in 1962. After his defeat, DiSalle continued to practice law. He was married to Myrtle Eugene England in 1929. He died on September 14, 1981.

RHODES, JAMES ALLEN (1909-), sixty-first and sixty-third Governor of Ohio (1963-71, 1975-83), was born at Coalton in Jackson County, Ohio, the son of Susan Howe and Jesse Allen Rhodes. After his father died in a coal mining accident when James was seven years old, the family moved to Springfield.

Rhodes received his early education in the public schools of Springfield. Throughout his early life, he also took on a number of odd jobs to help his family financially. After graduating from high school, he attended Ohio State University before he was forced to drop out because of financial difficulties.

Becoming active in the State's Republican Party while still in college, Rhodes was elected to the Columbus Board of Education in 1937. Near the end of his term, he was appointed City Auditor. Two years later, he was elected to a full four-year term to that post. In 1944, he resigned his post as City Auditor to become Mayor of Columbus. Reelected twice as Mayor, he served as the United States representative to the London Olympic Games during that period. The publicity from the Olympic post brought him statewide recognition, but he still failed in the gubernatorial bid in 1952.

In 1953, Rhodes began a ten-year stint as State Auditor. As Auditor, Rhodes established himself as an able director of State monies. He also co-wrote three historical novels. In 1962, he was elected to his first of four terms as Ohio's Governor. During the first eight years of his administration, Rhodes cut back the extensive State programs instituted by his predecessor, Michael DiSalle. By tightening controls on financial aid to the needy, decreasing taxes of small businesses, and cutting hundreds of State employees from Ohio's payroll, he tried to improve the faltering economic climate in the State. His austerity in State spending overturned the State deficit. Rhodes retired from gubernatorial office at the end of his second term, but was again reelected in 1974 and 1978. His fourth term ended in 1982. He married Helen Rawlins in 1941.

GILLIGAN, JOHN JOYCE (1921-), sixty-second Governor of Ohio (1971-75), was born in Cincinnati, Ohio, to Blanche Joyce and Harry Joseph Gilligan. After receiving an early education in Cincinnati schools, he graduated from Notre Dame University in 1943.

During World War II, Gilligan served as a destroyer gunnery officer in the United States Navy. Attaining the rank of Lieutenant before his 1945 discharge, he was decorated for his gallantry. In 1947, he graduated from University of Cincinnati with an M.A. in literature. During the next six years, he taught literature at Xavier University.

Gilligan began his political career in 1953 with an election to the Cincinnati City Council. He served in that post until 1967. After an unsuccessful bid for a United States Congress seat in 1962, he was elected to the United States House of Representatives in 1964. He was defeated in a reelection bid in 1966 by Robert Taft Jr. He became a partner in the Sauter, Gilligan and Associated Insurance Company in 1968, and also made an unsuccessful bid for the U.S. Senate.

In 1970, Gilligan was elected to his only term as Ohio's Governor. During his tenure, he attempted to overturn the austerity in State services created by his Republican predecessor. His proposals met with opposition from traditional liberal laborists and conservatives who dominated the two State Houses, but eventually he signed into law a new two-year budget, increasing State spending by 47 percent by raising personal and corporate income taxes.

Gilligan was defeated by Rhodes in his reelection bid in 1974. At the end of his term, he returned to his numerous business and educational interests. He was appointed by President Jimmy Carter to head the Agency for International Development shortly after leaving office, but resigned the post in 1979. He began teaching at Notre Dame University in South Bend, Indiana. He was married to Mary Kathryn Dixon in 1945.

CELESTE, RICHARD F. (1937-), sixty-fourth governor of Ohio (1983-1991), was born in Cleveland, Ohio, the son of Frank Celeste. He received a B.A. in history and graduated summa cum laude from Yale University in 1959. He taught at Yale for one year as a Carnegie Teaching Fellow, and attended Oxford University from 1960 to 1962 as a Rhodes scholar.

In 1963, Celeste began a career with the Peace Corps, first as a regular staff member in Washington, D.C., and then as an assistant to the ambassador to India from 1963 to 1967. He returned to Ohio and served as a member of the State Legislature from 1970 to 1974, and was elected majority whip in the latter two years.

Celeste was elected Lieutenant Governor of the State in 1974. At the end of his term, President Jimmy Carter named him Director of the Peace Corps, a post in which he served until Carter left office in 1981.

Celeste became Governor of Ohio in 1983. During his administration, he sought to help Ohio businesses compete in the global marketplace; his efforts resulted in new global links for over seventy-five Ohio firms. His aggressive program to promote international trade and investment moved the State from last place nationally in job creation to one of the top five generators of new jobs.

During his tenure, Celeste ambitiously fostered science and technology as a key to economic development. Ohio's Thomas Edison Centers, where government, universities, and industry have cooperated to develop new applications of technology, have earned the State national recognition from the National Academy of Sciences and the National Science Foundation.

While he was Chief of State, Celeste also chaired the National Governors' Association Committee on Science and Technology, and was the first elected official to be invited to sit on the National Academy of Sciences prestigious Government-University-Industry Research Roundtable.

At the end of his term, Celeste began a partnership with Celeste & Sabety Ltd., a small consulting firm specializing in public policy strategy regarding international trade, health care, and science and technology issues. In 1993, President Bill Clinton appointed him to chair the National Health Care Campaign. Celeste was married to Dagmar Braun in 1962. The couple has six children and seven grandchildren.

VOINOVICH, GEORGE V. (1936-), sixty-fifth governor of Ohio (1991-2000), was born July 15, 1936. He received his education at Ohio University, graduating with a B.A. in government in 1958. He then attended Ohio State University College of Law, and graduated in 1961 with a law degree.

Voinovich was elected Ohio's Assistant Attorney General in 1963; he worked in the Trial Section of the Workmen's Compensation Division located in Cleveland. In 1967, he was elected to the State House of Representatives and served on several committees during his three terms, including a vice-chairmanship on the Environmental and Natural Resources Committee. He successfully stopped oil drilling in Lake Erie, and was instrumental in creating the Ohio Environmental Agency.

In 1971, Voinovich was elected Cuyahoga County Auditor. He was nationally recognized in 1976 as a recipient of the "Outstanding Public Service Award," from the National Association of County Officials for his pioneering efforts in computer-assisted mass appraisal of residential and small commercial properties. He was also a leader in overhauling the State real estate appraisal laws and eliminating unvoted, non-charter real estate taxes.

In 1977-1978, Voinovich became Cuyahoga County Commissioner. Seeking to promote more efficient management of county business, he established three new offices: Budget and Management, Personnel, and Economic Development.

Voinovich became Cleveland's mayor in 1979, and held the office for a decade. He earned national recognition for his outstanding management of the city and his commitment to public service. The June 1986 issue of *National Journal* named him one of five local and state officials to make a difference in Washington. And in 1987, *City and State* magazine recognized him as one of three top mayors in the nation.

Voinovich was elected Governor of Ohio in November 1990. During his administration, he worked aggressively to create jobs in the State; his efforts resulted in the passing of key legislation to establish new jobs in Ohio. His efforts to reform the education system focused on improving student performance in the "basics," stricter accountability for teachers and schools, and funding equity for school systems. State support dramatically increased for programs to help children and families, while also cutting government costs and holding the budget to its lowest growth in twenty-five years.

Voinovich was reelected in 1994. He has been chairman of the Council of Great Lakes Governors, and has chaired, co-chaired and been a member of many committees of the National Governors Association, including the N.G.A. Education Action Team on School Readiness and the N.G.A. Child Support Enforcement Work Group. He and his wife, Janet, have three surviving children; their youngest daughter died in a fatal traffic accident when she was nine years old.

TAFT, BOB (1942-) was sworn in as Ohio's sixty seventh governor on January 11, 1999 at noon in the Ohio Theater in Columbus, Ohio.

Born in Boston, Taft earned his Juris Doctorate from the University of Cincinnati in 1976, his Master of Arts in Government from Princeton University in 1967, and his B.A. from Yale University in 1963.

Taft served as Secretary of State for Ohio from 1991-99. His political background also includes: Hamilton County Commissioner (1981-1990), and member of the Ohio House of Representatives (1976-1980).

Governor Taft's father and grandfather were United States Senators. His great-grandfather was William Howard Taft, the twenty seventh president of the United States and Chief Justice of the United States from 1921-30.

Taft and his wife, Hope, have one daugher.

DICTIONARY OF PLACES

Population figures and demographic information are official U.S. Census Bureau finals for 1990. When two figures are shown, separated by a slash, the first figure is the 1990 and the second is the U.S. Census Bureau 1999 estimate—the most recent available. Year 2000 census supplements will be available in the Fall of 2001.

ABERDEEN, Village; Brown County; Pop. 1,532 / 1,875; Zip Code 45101; Elev. 500; Lat. 38-39-20 N, Long. 083-45-40 W; SW Ohio; Named for the Scottish city.

ADA, Village; Hardin County; Pop. 5,646 / 5,505; Zip Code 45810; Lat. 40-46-10 N, Long. 083-49-22 W; 6 mi. E of Lirna in NW Ohio; Established in 1853 as Johnstown.

ADDYSTON, Village; Hamilton County; Pop. 1,200 / 436; Zip Code 45001; Elev. 510; Lat. 39-08-12 N, Long. 084-42-33 W; SW Ohio; Had a few settlers as early as 1789, but did not become a town until 1871, when Matthew Addy of Cincinnati established a large pipe foundry here.

AKRON, City; Seat of Summit County; Pop. 237,005 / 211,822; Zip Code 443+; Elev. 950; Lat. 41-04-53 N, Long. 081-31-09 W; on the little Cuyahoga River. Akron is derived from the Greek *akros*, meaning "high".

ALLIANCE, City; Mahoning and Stark Counties; Pop. 24,322 / 22,474; Zip Code 44601; Elev. 1174; Lat. 40-54-55 N, Long. 081-06-22 W; 14 mi. NE of Canton in NE central Ohio; In 1805, three rival towns sprang up near by and prospered—Greendom, Williamsport, and Mount Union. In 1854 the four communities were united under the name Alliance, and the town was incorporated in 1889.

AMBERLEY, Village; Hamilton County; Pop. 3,428 / 3,140; Elev. 803; Lat. 39-12-17 N, Long. 084-25-41 W; NE of Cincinnati in SW Ohio; is mainly a suburban community.

AMELIA, Village, Clermont County; Pop. 1,104 / 937; Zip Code 45102; Lat. 39-01-42 N, Long. 084-13-04 W; SW Ohio; 21 mi. SE of Cincinnati.

AMHERST, City; Lorain County; Pop. 10,620 / 11,470; Zip Code 44001; Lat. 41-23-52 N, Long. 082-13-21 W; 25 mi. SW of Cleveland in N Ohio. Named after the city in New Jersey.

ANDOVER, Village; Ashtabula County; Pop. 1,205 / 1,246; Zip Code 44004; Elev. 1,095; Lat. 41-36-24 N, Long. 080-34-21 W; NE Ohio. Named after the city in Maine.

ANSONIA, Village, Darke County; Pop. 1,271 / 1,207; Zip Code 45303; Elev. 1009; Lat. 40-12-52 N, Long. 084-38-13 W; W Ohio.

ANTWERP, Village; Paulding County; Pop. 1,768 / 1,760; Zip Code 45813; Elev. 732; Lat. 41-10-53 N, Long. 084-44-26 W; NW Ohio; Named by Dutch and Germans who settled here.

APPLE CREEK, Village; Wayne County; Pop. 742 / 1,094; Zip Code 44606; Lat. 40-45-06 N, Long. 081-50-22 W; SE of Wooster in NE Ohio. Descriptively named.

ARCANUM, Village; Darke County; Pop. 2,017 / 1,949; Zip Code 45304; Lat. 39-59-28 N, Long. 084-33-08 W; W Ohio; 14 mi. SE of Greenville along Twin Creek.

ARCHBOLD, Village; Fulton County; Pop. 3,322 / 4,256; Zip Code 43502; Elev. 734; Lat. 41-31-17 N, Long. 084-18-26 W; NW Ohio.

ARLINGTON, Village; Fulton County; Pop. 3,322 / 1,367; Zip Code 45814; Elev. 869; Lat. 40-53-47 N, Long. 083-39-01 W; Ohio. The village was named after the district in Virginia.

ASHLAND, City; Seat of Ashland County; Pop. 20,252 / 21,193; Zip Code 44805; Elev. 1,077; Lat. 40-52-07 N, Long. 082-19-06 W; N central Ohio, NE of Mansfield. In 1822 the growing town was renamed Ashland, after Henry Clay's estate at Lexington, Kentucky.

ASHLEY, Village; Delaware County; Pop. 1,056 / 1,109; Zip Code 43003; Elev. 989; Lat. 40-24-32 N, Long. 082-57-20 W; 40 mi. N of Columbus on the E shore of the Delaware Reservoir in central Ohio.

ASHTABULA, City; Ashtabula County; Pop. 23,354 / 21,130; Zip Code 44004; Elev. 688; Lat. 41-51-54 N, Long. 080-47-24 W; 50 mi. NE of Cleveland in NE Ohio; Lies on the shore of Lake Erie. The name is an Indian word thought to mean "River of Many Fish."

ASHVILLE, Village; Pickaway County; Pop. 2,046 / 2,747; Zip Code 43103; Elev. 709; Lat. 39-42-56 N, Long. 082-57-11 W; S central Ohio; 30 mi. S of Columbus.

ATHENS, City; Seat of Athens County; Pop. 19,801 / 21,967; Zip Code 45701; Elev. 723; Lat. 39-19-45 N, Long. 082-06-05 W; 30 mi. W of Marietta; named after the famous Greek city.

AURORA, City; Portage County; Pop. 8,174 / 12,440; Zip Code 44202; Elev. 1130; Lat. 41-19-03 N, Long. 081-20-44 W; 21 mi. SE of Cleveland and 21 mi. NE of Akron in NE Ohio. Given the Roman name for the Goddess of Dawn.

AVON, City; Lorain County; Pop. 7,265 / 11,701; Zip Code 44011; Elev. 670; Lat. 41-27-06 N, Long. 082-02-08 W; S of Lake Erie shoreline in N Ohio. Named for the English river.

AVON LAKE, City; Lorain County; Pop. 13,184 / 16,947; Zip Code 44012; Elev. 628; Lat. 41-30-19 N, Long. 082-01-42 W; 19 mi. W of Cleveland in NE Ohio.

BAINBRIDGE, Village; Ross County; Pop. 1,030 / 1,065; Zip Code 45612; Elev. 716; Lat. 39-13-39 N, Long. 083-16-14 W; S central Ohio. The village was named for Commander William Bainbridge of War of 1812 fame.

BALTIMORE, Village; Fairfield County; Pop. 2,694 / 3,242; Zip Code 43105; Lat. 39-50-43 N, Long. 082-36-03 W; S central Ohio; 30 mi. SE of Columbus.

BARBERTON, City; Summit County; Pop. 29,732 / 27,360; Zip Code 44203; Elev. 969; Lat. 41-00-46 N, Long. 081-36-19 W; 7 mi. SW of Akron in NE Ohio; Barberton was laid out in 1891 by Ohio Columbus Barber.

BARNESVILLE, Village; Belmont County; Pop. 4,640 / 4,500; Zip Code 43713; Lat. 39-59-17 N, Long. 081-10-36 W; 40 mi. SW of Steubenville in SE Ohio; in a hilly region. The town was named after James Barnes who was the founder in 1808.

BATAVIA, Village; Seat of Clermont County; Pop. 1,890 / 2,361; Zip Code 45103; Elev. 594; Lat. 39-04-37 N, Long. 084-10-37 W; on the E fork of the Miami River, 20 mi. E of Cincinnati in SW Ohio.

BAY VILLAGE, City; Cuyahoga County; Pop. 17,239 / 15,459; Zip Code 44140; Elev. 630; Lat. 41-29-05 N, Long. 081-55-20 W; NE Ohio; is a suburb of Cleveland overlooking Lake Erie.

BEACHWOOD, City; Cuyahoga County; Pop. 9,618 / 10,754; Zip Code 44122; Lat. 41-27-52 N, Long. 081-30-32 W; NE Ohio; Near Cleveland on Lake Erie; Suburban.

BEDFORD, City; Cuyahoga County; Pop. 15,003 / 13,478; Zip Code 44146; Elev. 946; Lat. 41-23-35 N, Long. 081-32-12 W; 10 mi. SE of Cleveland in NE Ohio; was the site of a temporary settlement by Moravian missionaries in 1786; The name was chosen after the same town in Connecticut.

BEDFORD HEIGHTS, City; Cuyahoga County; Pop. 13,187 / 11,203; Lat. 41-25-01 N, Long. 081-31-39 W.

BELLAIRE, City; Belmont County; Pop. 8,231 / 4,893; Zip Code 43906; Elev. 653; Lat. 40-00-45 N, Long. 080-45-39 W; 35 mi. S of Steubenville on the Ohio River in E Ohio.

BELLBROOK, City; Greene County; Pop. 5,182 / 6,150; Zip Code 45305; Elev. 796; Lat. 39-38-08 N, Long. 084-04-15 W; 14 mi. SE of Dayton in SW Ohio; suburban; is named after Stephen Bell in 1816.

BELLEFONTAINE, City; Seat of Logan County; Pop. 11,798 / 13,380; Zip Code 43311; Elev. 1,251; Lat. 40-21-40 N, Long. 083-45-35 W; is 30 mi. N of Springfield in W Ohio; was named for the springs of limestone according to an early writer.

BELLEVUE, City; Huron and Sandusky Counties; Pop. 8,193 / 8,119; Zip Code 44811; Elev. 753; Lat. 41-16-25 N, Long. 082-50-30 W; 15 mi. SW of Sandusky in N Ohio; first settled in 1815; Named in 1839 by James Bell, who was then building the Mad River and Lake Erie Railroad from Sandusky.

BELOIT, Village; Mahoning County; Pop. 1,100 / 1,089; Zip Code 44609; Elev. 1132; Lat. 40-55-23 N, Long. 080-59-38 W; E Ohio; 30 mi. SW of Youngstown. Named for the French explorer.

BELPRE, City; Washington County; Pop. 7,155 / 6,960; Zip Code 45714; Elev. 622; Lat. 39-16-26 N, Long. 081-34-23 W; S Ohio; The name means beautiful meadows in French.

BEREA, City; Cuyahoga County; Pop. 19,636 / 18,210; Zip Code 44017; Elev. 788; Lat. 41-21-58 N, Long. 081-51-16 W; 10 mi. SW of Cleveland in N Ohio.

BETHEL, Village; Clermont County; Pop. 2,230 / 2,945; Zip Code 45106; Elev. 892; Lat. 38-57-49 N, Long. 084-04-51 W; SW Ohio; 30 mi. SE of Cincinnati. A Biblical name meaning hope.

BETHESDA, Village; Belmont County; Pop. 1,453 / 1,067; Zip Code 43719; Lat. 40-00-58 N, Long. 081-04-22 W; E Ohio; Hilly region.

BEVERLY, Village; Washington County; Pop. 1,468 / 1,475; Zip Code 45715; Elev. 631; Lat. 39-32-52 N, Long. 081-38-23 W; SE Ohio; was settled in 1789.

BEXLEY, City; Franklin County; Pop. 13,396 / 12,519; Zip Code 43209; Elev. 775; Lat. 39-58-08 N, Long. 082-56-16 W; E side of Columbus in central Ohio.

BLANCHESTER, Village; Clinton County; Pop. 3,302 / 4,249; Zip Code 45107; Elev. 953; Lat. 40-43-55 N, Long. 083-38-37 W; approx. 30 mi. NE of Cincinnati in SW Ohio; The town was first settled in 1832.

BLOOMVILLE, Village, Seneca County; Pop. 1,020 / 640; Zip Code 44818; Lat. 41-03-07 N, Long. 083-00-54 W; N Central Ohio.

BLUE ASH, City; Hamilton County; Pop. 9,482 / 12,093; Lat. 39-13-55 N, Long. 084-22-42 W; NE of Cincinnati; Residential.

BLUFFTON, Village; Allen County; Pop. 3,308 / 3,845; Zip Code 45817; Elev. 824; Lat. 40-53-43 N, Long. 083-53-20 W; 14 mi. NE of Lima in NW Ohio; Founded in 1833, Bluffton took its present name from a Mennonite community in Indiana.

BOTKINS, Village; Shelby County; Pop. 1,376 / 1,252; Zip Code 45306; Elev. 1011; Lat. 40-28-04 N, Long. 084-10-50 W; W Ohio; Rural.

BOWLING GREEN, City; Seat of Wood County; Pop. 25,745 / 29,168; Zip Code 43402; Elev. 700; Lat. 41-22-29 N, Long. 083-39-05 W; 20 mi. SW of Toledo in NW central Ohio; Laid out in 1835 and named by Joseph Gordon for his home town in Kentucky.

BRADFORD, Village; Miami County; Pop. 2,171 / 2,039; Zip Code 45308; Elev. 989; Lat. 40-07-56 N, Long. 084-25-51 W; 15 mi. W of Greenville.

BRADNER, Village; Wood County; Pop. 1,172 / 1,098; Zip Code 43406; Lat. 41-19-27 N, Long. 083-26-19 W; NW Ohio.

BRATENAHL, Village; Cuyahoga County; Pop. 1,483 / 1,373; Zip Code (with Cleveland); Lat. 41-32-33 N, Long. 081-37-35 W; NE Ohio; On Lake Erie.

BRECKSVILLE, City; Cuyahoga County; Pop. 10,133 / 12,260; Zip Code 44141; Elev. 955; Lat. 41-19-11 N, Long. 081-37-37 W; was settled about 1811 and named for John and Robert Broth, early landowners in the region.

BREMEN, Village; Fairfield County; Pop. 1,435 / 1,447; Zip Code 43107; Lat. 39-42-06 N, Long. 082-25-37 W; 10 mi. E of Lancaster in N central Ohio; is named for the German City.

BREWSTER, Village; Stark County; Pop. 2,312 / 2,234; Zip Code 44613; Lat. 40-42-25 N, Long. 081-35-54 W; NE Ohio; 18 mi. SW of Canton; Along the Sugar Creek.

BRIDGEPORT, Village; Belmont County; Pop. 2,642 / 1,995; Zip Code 43912; Elev. 660; Lat. 40-04-11 N, Long. 080-44-25 W; On the Ohio River in E Ohio; Across the river is Wheeling, West Virginia.

BRILLIANT, Village; Jefferson County; Pop. 1,756; Zip Code 43913; Lat. 40-15-53 N, Long. 080-37-35 W; E Ohio; On the Ohio River, 7 mi. S of Steubenville.

BROADVIEW HEIGHTS, City; Cuyahoga County; Pop. 10,909 / 14,211; Zip Code (with Cleveland); Lat. 41-18-50 N, Long. 081-41-07 W; NE Ohio; Suburban development, 20 mi. S of Cleveland.

BROOKLYN, City; Cuyahoga County; Pop. 12,324 / 11,090; Zip Code 44144; Elev. 765; Lat. 41-26-23 N, Long. 081-44-08 W; NE Ohio; S suburb of Cleveland; Named after the city in New York.

BROOK PARK, City; Cuyahoga County; Pop. 26,195 / 21,600; Zip Code 44142; Lat. 41-23-54 N, Long. 081-48-17 W; NE Ohio; SW suburb of Cleveland.

BROOKVILLE, Village; Montgomery County; Pop. 4,317 / 5,120; Zip Code 45309; Elev. 1033; Lat. 39-50-12 N, Long. 084-24-41 W; SW central Ohio; 20 mi. NW of Dayton.

BRUNSWICK, City; Medina County; Pop. 27,645 / 32,849; Zip Code 44212; Lat. 41-14-17 N, Long. 081-50-31 W; 25 mi. SW of Cleveland in N Ohio; is named for Brunswick township.

BRYAN, City; Seat of Williams County; Pop. 7,880 / 8,357; Zip Code 43506; Elev. 764; Lat. 41-28-29 N, Long. 084-33-09 W; 50 mi. W of Toledo in NW Ohio; is named for Hon. John A. Bryon who held offices in the state and also developed this part of the state.

BUCYRUS, City; Seat of Crawford County; Pop. 13,413 / 13,452; Zip Code 44820; Elev. 1,006; Lat. 40-48-30 N, Long. 082-58-32 W; 20 mi. NE of Marion in N central Ohio, along the Sandusky River; Because Cyrus, a leader of the ancient Persians, was one of the founder's favorite heroes, and because the country was attractive, he is said to have named the community by prefixing Cyrus with "bu," signifying "beautiful."

BURTON, Village; Geauga County; Pop. 1,401 / 1,366; Zip Code 44021; Elev. 1,310; Lat. 41-28-14 N, Long. 081-08-43 W; NE Ohio; near the Cuyahoga River; is named for the son of the founder.

BYESVILLE, Village; Guernsey County; Pop. 4,050 / 2,539; Zip Code 45820; Elev. 804; Lat. 39-58-11 N, Long. 081-32-12 W; E Ohio; Named for Jonathan Bye, who built the first flour mill in the vicinity early in the nineteenth century.

CADIZ, Village; Seat of Harrison County; Pop. 4,050 / 3,407; Zip Code 43907; Elev. 1,280; Lat. 40-16-22 N, Long. 080-59-49 W; 20 mi. SW of Steubenville in E Ohio. Named after the Spanish city.

CALDWELL, Village; Seat of Noble County; Pop. 1,942 / 4,306; Zip Code 43724; Elev. 744; Lat. 39-44-52 N, Long. 081-31-00 W; 27 mi. N of Marietta in a rich coal mining region in SE Ohio. Founded in 1857. It is named for the owners of the town site.

CAMBRIDGE, City; Seat of Guernsey County; Pop. 13,450 / 11,887; Zip Code 43725; Elev. 799; 20 mi. NE of Zanesville in E Ohio. In 1806 Jacob Gomber and Zacheus Beatty laid out the town and named it for Cambridge, Maryland, from which came many of the first settlers.

CAMDEN, Village; Preble County; Pop. 1,965 / 2,562; Zip Code 45311; Lat. 39-46-01 N, Long. 080-56-42 W; SW Ohio; On Seven-mile Creek, 19 mi. N of Hamilton. Named for the city in New Jersey.

CAMPBELL, City; Mahoning County; Pop. 11,591 / 9,180; Zip Code 44405; Lat. 41-04-42 N, Long. 080-35-58 W; on the Mahoning River, 5 mi. SE of Youngstown in NE Ohio; Suburb.

CANAL FULTON, Village; Stark County; Pop. 3,481 / 4,939; Zip Code 44614; Elev. 947; Lat. 40-53-23 N, Long. 081-35-52 W; NE Ohio; Formerly Milan, it changed its name to Canal Fulton in honor of Robert Fulton, inventor of the steamboat.

CANFIELD, City; Mahoning County; Pop. 5,530 / 6,266; Zip Code 44406; Elev. 1161; Lat. 41-01-30 N, Long. 080-45-40 W; 10

mi. SW of Youngstown in NE Ohio; Named for Johnathan Canfield, an early landowner.

CANTON, City; Seat of Stark County; Pop. 94,635 / 78,582; Zip Code 444+; Elev. 1,050; Lat. 40-47-56 N, Long. 081-22-43 W; 20 mi. SE of Akron in NE Ohio. The city takes its name from the famous Chinese port.

CARDINGTON, Village; Morrow County; Pop. 1,665 / 2,130; Zip Code 43315; Elev. 1014; Lat. 40-30-02 N, Long. 082-53-37 W; N central Ohio; 14 mi. SE of Marion.

CAREY, Village; Wyandot County; Pop. 3,681 / 3,559; Zip Code 43316; Elev. 823; Lat. 40-57-09 N, Long. 083-22-57 W; 15 mi. SE of Findlay NW central Ohio; the place was named for Judge John Carey.

CARLISLE, Village; Warren and Montgomery Counties; Pop. 4,271 / 5,140; Zip Code 45005; Lat. 39-44-44 N, Long. 081-21-50 W; 15 mi. SW of Dayton in SW Ohio; Between the Twin and Miami Rivers; Near Middletown.

CARROLLTON, Village; Seat of Carroll County; Pop. 3,054 / 3,620; Zip Code 44615; Elev. 1130; Lat. 40-34-22 N, Long. 081-05-09 W; 20 mi. SE of Canton in E Ohio; was named for Charles Carroll, who signed the Declaration of Independence.

CEDARVILLE, Village; Greene County; Pop. 2,804 / 3,662; Zip Code 45314; Elev. 1,055; Lat. 39-44-39 N, Long. 083-48-31 W; NE of Xenia in SW central Ohio; Was named for cedar trees in the area. The place was formerly known as Milford but was changed for postal reasons.

CELINA, City; Seat of Mercer County; Pop. 9,127 / 11,042; Zip Code 45822; Elev. 768; Lat. 40-32-56 N, Long. 084-34-13 W; on the W end of Lake St. Marys in W Ohio; was named for a New York town, Salina. Settled in 1834.

CENTERVILLE, City; Montgomery County; Pop. 18,953 / 23,285; Zip Code 454+; Lat. 39-58-33 N, Long. 080-57-56 W; 10 mi. S of Dayton in SW central Ohio. Named for its geographical position.

CHAGRIN FALLS, City; Cuyahoga County; Pop. 4,306 / 3,837; Zip Code 44022; Elev. 985; Lat. 41-25-47 N, Long. 081-23-27 W; NE Ohio; Lies in a wide loop of the Chagrin River, which is said to have been named by Moses Cleaveland and his party of surveyors. The Indian word meaning clear water sounds like *Shagreen*.

CHARDON, Village; Seat of Geauga County; Pop. 4,417 / 5,117; Zip Code 44024; Elev. 1,230; Lat. 41-36-51 N, Long. 081-08-57 W; 25 mi. NE of Cleveland in NE Ohio; The town is named for Peter Chardon Brooks, first owner of the site.

CHAUNCEY, Village; Athens County; Pop. 1,048 / 1,339; Zip Code 45719; Elev. 659; Lat. 39-23-52 N, Long. 082-07-46 W; SE Ohio.

CHESAPEAKE, Village; Lawrence County; Pop. 1,382 / 1,314; Zip Code 45619; Lat. 38-25-40 N, Long. 082-27-26 W; S Ohio; On the Ohio River across from Huntington, West Virginia. Named after the Chesapeake Bay.

CHEVIOT, City; Hamilton County; Pop. 9,842 / 8,887; Lat. 39-09-25 N, Long. 084-36-48 W; 10 mi. NW of Cincinnati in SW Ohio.

CHILLICOTHE, City; Seat of Ross County; Pop. 23,384 / 22,550; Zip Code 45601; Elev. 643; Lat. 39-19-59 N, Long. 082-58-57 W; A Shawnee Indian word meaning "a place where people dwell."

CINCINNATI, City; Pop. 383,114 / 330,914; Elev. 683; Lat. 39-09-43 N, Long. 084-27-25 W; Cincinnati was named by Gen. Arthur St. Clair in 1709 in honor of the "Order of Cincinnati," an association of American Revolution Veterans.

CIRCLEVILLE, City; Seat of Pickaway County; Pop. 11,682 / 13,054; Zip Code 43114; Elev. 702; Lat. 39-36-02 N, Long. 082-56-46 W; on Scioto River 25 mi. S of Columbus in S central Ohio. Circleville was laid out inside the round enclosure from which it took its name.

CLEVELAND, City; Cuyahoga County Seat; Pop. 572,657 / 501,662; Zip Code 441+; Elev. 665. The city was named for General Moses Cleaveland who platted a town site here for the Connecticut Land Company in 1796. Legend has it that the simplified spelling resulted when a newly launched newspaper called itself the Cleveland Gazette and Commercial Register, dropping the first "A" so that the name would more neatly fit its masthead.

CLEVELAND HEIGHTS, City; Cuyahoga County; Pop. 56,308 / 53,277; Zip Code 44118; Elev. 915; Lat. 41-31-12 N, Long. 081-33-23 W; 10 mi. E of Cleveland on an Appalachian Plateau above Lake Erie in NE Ohio.

CLEVES, Village; Hamilton County; Pop. 2,109 / 2,396; Zip Code 45002; Elev. 496; Lat. 39-09-42 N, Long. 084-44-57 W; SW Ohio; the village was named for early proprietor John Cleves Symmes.

COLUMBUS, City; Franklin County Seat; Pop. 562,462 / 671,247; Zip Code 430+, 432+; Elev. 760. This city. the state capital, was named in honor of Christopher Columbus by the Honorable Joseph Foos, a senator from Franklin County, in 1816.

CORTLAND, City; Trumbull County; Pop. 5,001 / 6,702; Zip Code 44410; Lat. 41-19-49 N, Long. 080-43-32 W; Named by the Company Railroad that came through here in the 1800s. The place was originally known as Baconsburgh for Enos Bacon who owned a store here in 1829.

COSHOCTON, City; Seat of Coshocton County; Pop. 13,418 / 12,282; Zip Code 43812; Elev. 770; Lat. 40-16-19 N, Long. 081-51-35 W; SE central Ohio; The town's name was probably taken from one of two Delaware Indian names; Cush-og-wenk, meaning "black bear town," or Coshac-gung, meaning "union of waters."

COVINGTON, Village; Miami County; Pop. 2,614 / 2,655; Zip Code 45318; Elev. 930; Lat. 40-07-02 N, Long. 084-21-14 W; 5 mi. W of Piqua in SW Ohio; on Stillwater Creek.

CRAIG BEACH, Village; Mahoning County; Pop. 1,666 / 1,762; Lat. 41-07-01 N, Long. 080-59-01 W; On a widened area of the Mohoning River. W of Youngstown.

CRESTLINE, City; Crawford County; Pop. 5,404 / 4,924; Zip Code 44827; Lat. 40-47-15 N, Long. 082-44-12 W; 10 mi. W of Mansfield on the Sandusky River in N central Ohio; The name comes from the watershed located here.

CRESTON, Village; Wayne County; Pop. 1,821 / 2,197; Zip Code 44217; Elev. 985; Lat. 40-59-13 N, Long. 081-53-38 W; NE Central Ohio.

CRIDERSVILLE, Village; Auglaize County; Pop. 1,841 / 1,942; Zip Code 45806; Elev. 890; Lat. 40-39-15 N, Long. 084-09-03 W; 10 mi. S of Lima in W central Ohio.

CROOKSVILLE, Village; Perry County; Pop. 2,773 / 3,270; Zip Code 43731; Lat. 39-46-08 N, Long. 082-05-32 W; 10 mi. S of Zanesville in SE central Ohio.

CUYAHOGA FALLS, City; Summit County; Pop. 43,708 / 49,193; Zip Code 442+; Lat. 41-08-02 N, Long. 081-29-05 W; 5 mi. N of Akron in NE Ohio; Named because it lies along a rapids area of the Cuyahoga River.

DALTON, Village; Wayne County; Pop. 1,351 / 1,574; Zip Code 44618; Lat. 40-47-56 N, Long. 081-41-44 W; 7 mi. W of Massillon in NE central Ohio.

DANVILLE, Village; Knox County; Pop. 1,123 / 987; Zip Code 43014; Lat. 39-08-41 N, Long. 083-44-17 W; N central Ohio.

DAYTON, City; Seat of Montgomery County; Pop. 190,323 / 169,338; Zip Code 454+; Lat. 39-45-32 N, Long. 084-11-30 W; in SW Ohio. Named for the early landowner Johnathan Dayton, who platted the town in 1795.

DEER PARK, City; Hamilton County; Pop. 6,501 / 5,820; Zip Code 45236; Lat. 39-12-19 N, Long. 084-23-41 W; 10 mi. NE of Cincinnati in SW corner of Ohio.

DEFIANCE, City; Seat of Defiance County; Pop. 16,783 / 16,185; Zip Code 43512; Elev. 712; Lat. 41-17-04 N, Long. 084-21-21 W; 40 mi. NW of Lima in NW Ohio; Named for Fort Defiance.

DE GRAFF, Village; Logan County; Pop. 1,361 / 1,326; Zip Code 43318; Elev. 1007; Lat. 40-18-43 N, Long. 083-54-57 W; 12 mi. SW of Bellefontaine in W central Ohio.

DELAWARE, City; Seat of Delaware County; Pop. 17,629 / 24,931; Zip Code 43015; Elev. 900; Lat. 40-17-55 N, Long. 083-04-05 W; central Ohio. The Delaware Indians, for whom the city and the county are named, had a village here.

DELPHOS, City; Allen and Van Wert Counties; Pop. 7,317 / 6,965; Zip Code 45833; Elev. 750; 10 mi. NW of Lima in NW Ohio.

DELTA, Village; Fulton County; Pop. 2,750 / 3,163; Zip Code 43515; Lat. 41-34-25 N, Long. 084-00-19 W; Approx. 25 mi. W of Toledo.

DENNISON, Village; Tuscarawas County; Pop. 3,391 / 3,267; Zip Code 44621; Elev. 862; Lat. 40-23-36 N, Long. 081-20-02 W; 30 mi. S of Canton in E Ohio; Named for William Dennison, a Civil War governor of Ohio.

DOVER, City; Tuscarawas County; Pop. 11,500 / 12,214; Zip Code 44622; Elev. 900; Lat. 40-31-14 N, Long. 081-28-27 W; E Ohio. Named after the English city.

DOYLESTOWN, Village; Wayne County; Pop. 2,487 / 2,972; Zip Code 44230; Lat. 40-58-12 N, Long. 081-41-48 W; NE central Ohio.

DUBLIN, City; Delaware and Franklin Counties; Pop. 16,366 / 27,360; Zip Code 43017; Elev. 805; Lat. 41-00-11 N, Long. 080-47-09 W; Central Ohio; on the W bank of the Scioto River; named after the city of the same name in Ireland.

EAST CANTON, Village; Stark County; Pop. 1,719 / 1,694; Zip Code 44730; Elev. 1,050; Lat. 40-47-14 N, Long. 081-16-58 W; 5 mi. E of Canton in NE Ohio; originally named as Osnaburg, the name was changed to East Canton in 1918.

EAST CLEVELAND, City; Cuyahoga County; Pop. 36,694 / 29,077; Zip Code 44112; Elev. 730; Lat. 41-31-59 N, Long. 081-34-45 W; NE Ohio; Suburb of Cleveland.

EASTLAKE, City; Lake County; Pop. 21,954 / 21,618; Zip Code 44094; NE Ohio; 20 mi. NE of Cleveland on Lake Erie shoreline.

EAST LIVERPOOL, City; Columbiana County; Pop. 16,517 / 12,848; Zip Code 43920; Elev. 686; Lat. 40-37-07 N, N of Steubenville in E Ohio; Named because many of the inhabitants had come from the English city of Liverpool. Later the name was changed to East Liverpool.

EAST PALESTINE, City; Columbiana County; Pop. 5,303 / 8,408; Zip Code 44413; Elev. 1,015; Lat. 40-50-02 N, Long. 080-32-26 W; 20 mi. S of Youngstown in E Ohio; Established in 1828 by Thomas McCalla and William Grate.

EATON, City; Seat of Preble County; Pop. 6,830 / 8,000; Zip Code 45320; Elev. 1,040; Lat. 39-44-38 N, Long. 084-38-12 W; 20 mi. W of Dayton in SW Ohio; was founded in 1806 and named after General William Eaton, hero of the Tripolitan War of 1805.

EDGERTON, Village; Williams County; Pop. 1,815 / 2,105; Zip Code 43517; Lat. 41-26-55 N, Long. 084-44-53 W; 40 mi. NE of Fort Wayne, Indiana in NW Ohio; It is named for Alfred P. Edgerton, a land developer of this area of the state.

ELIDA, Village; Allen County; Pop. 1,335 / 1,862; Zip Code 45807; Lat. 40-47-19 N, Long. 084-12-14 W; NW Ohio; 7 mi. NW of Lima.

ELMORE, Village; Ottawa County; Pop. 1,270 / 1,310; Zip Code 43416; Lat. 41-28-34 N, Long. 083-17-45 W; N Ohio; On the Portage River, just off the Ohio Turnpike (U.S. 80).

ELMWOOD PLACE, Village; Hamilton County; Pop. 2,822 / 2,580; Zip Code 45216; Lat. 39-11-14 N, Long. 084-29-17 W; SW Ohio; On Mill Creek just N of Cincinnati city center.

ELYRIA, City; Seat of Lorain County; Pop. 57,039 / 55,826; Zip Code 440+; Elev. 730; Lat. 41-22-06 N, Long. 082-06-28 W; N Ohio; Settlement began in 1817 when Herman Ely, a New Englander, acquired 12,500 acres around the falls of the Black River. The name was derived by combining Ely with ria because his wife's name was Maria.

ENGLEWOOD, City; Montgomery County; Pop. 11,320 / 12,296; Zip Code 45322; Elev. 922; Lat. 39-52-39 N, Long. 084-18-08 W; 10 mi. NW of Dayton in SW Ohio.

ENON, Village; Clark County; Pop. 2,595 / 2,747; Zip Code 45323; Lat. 39-52-41 N, Long. 083-56-13 W; W Ohio; 10 mi. SW of Springfield.

EUCLID, City; Cuyahoga County; Pop. 59,951; Zip Code 44117; Elev. 648; Lat. 41-35-35 N, Long. 081-31-37 W; on Lake Erie in N Ohio; This suburb of Cleveland, first settled in 1798, was named for the Greek mathematician by surveyors in the party of Moses Cleaveland.

FAIRBORN, City; Greene County; Pop. 29,747 / 33,775; Zip Code 45324; Lat. 39-49-15 N, Long. 084-01-10 W; 10 mi. NE of Dayton in SW Ohio; The name came from combining the names of two towns in 1950.

FAIRFAX, Village; Hamilton County; Pop. 2,233 / 1,838; Lat. 39-08-43 N, Long. 084-23-36 W; SW Ohio; N of Cincinnati; a residential area.

FAIRFIELD, City; Butler County; Pop. 30,816 / 42,242; Zip Code 45014; Lat. 39-20-45 N, Long. 084-33-38 W; 20 mi. N of Cincinnati in SW Ohio.

FAIRLAWN, City; Summit County; Pop. 6,105 / 6,500; Zip Code 44313; Elev. 1005; Lat. 41-07-40 N, Long. 081-36-36 W; NE central Ohio; Residential area on the Cuyahoga River, just N of Akron.

FAIRVIEW PARK, City; Cuyahoga County; Pop. 19,283 / 16,519; Zip Code 44126; Lat. 41-26-29 N, 081-51-52 W; NE Ohio; 10 mi. SW of Cleveland city center.

FINDLAY, City; Seat of Hancock County; Pop. 35,533 / 38,509; Zip Code 45840; Elev. 777; Lat. 41-02-39 N, Long. 083-39-00 W; 41 mi. S of Toledo in NW Ohio; Named for Fort Findlay, one of the outposts built here under the direction of General Hull during his march to Detroit in the War of 1812.

FLUSHING, Village; Belmont County; Pop. 1,272 / 904; Zip Code 43977; Elev. 1132; Lat. 40-08-58 N, Long. 081-03-59 W; Approx. 40 mi. SW of Steubenville in E Ohio in a former coal mining area. The village was named for a place in Holland.

FOREST PARK, City; Hamilton County; Pop. 18,770 / 19,240; Elev. 836; Lat. 39-17-25 N, Long. 084-30-15 W; Zip Code 454+; Approx. 20 mi. N of downtown Cincinnati.

FORT RECOVERY, Village; Mercer County; Pop. 1,366 / 1,374; Zip Code 45846; Elev. 948; Lat. 40-24-46 N, Long. 084-46-35 W; W Ohio; Fort Recovery is the site of Gen. Arthur St. Clair's defeat in 1791, and of General Anthony Wayne's "recovery" of the area in 1793, after the erection of a fort here.

FORT SHAWNEE, Village; Allen County; Pop. 4,533 / 3,892; Elev. 866; Lat. 40-41-12 N, Long. 084-08-16 W; NW Ohio; nearby is the Shawnee State Forest, the largest forested area in Ohio, covering 33,410 acres.

FOSTORIA, City; Seneca County; Pop. 15,717 / 13,834; Zip Code 44830; Elev. 780; Lat. 41-09-25 N, Long. 083-25-01 W; N Ohio. Because C.W. Foster had much to do with local development in the real estate, merchandising, and banking fields, the community was named for him.

FRANKFORT, Village; Ross County; Pop. 1,016 / 1,109; Zip Code 45628; Elev. 740; Lat. 41-38-38 N, Long. 083-51-23 W; S Ohio.

FRAZEYBURG, Village; Muskingum County; Pop. 1,022 / 540; Zip Code 43822; Lat. 40-07-02 N, Long. 082-07-10 W; 15 mi. N of Zanesville in a hilly region in SE central Ohio; Was named for Samuel Frazey.

FREMONT, City; Seat of Sandusky County; Pop. 17,887 / 17,065; Zip Code 43420; Elev. 636; Lat. 41-21-01 N, Long. 083-07-19 W; 45 mi. W of Cleveland on the Sandusky River in N Ohio; named for the explorer John C. Fremont,

GALION, City; Crawford County; Pop. 12,391 / 11,510; Zip Code 44833; Elev. 1,169; Lat. 40-44-01 N, Long. 082-47-24 W; 15 mi. W of Mansfield in N central Ohio; Settled by German Lutherans from Pennsylvania in 1831.

GALLIPOLIS, City; Seat of Gallia County; Pop. 5,576 / 5,412; Zip Code 45631; Elev. 576; Lat. 38-48-35 N, Long. 082-12-09 W; on the Ohio River, 30 mi. NE of Ironton in S Ohio near the West Virginia border. Gallipolis was established in 1790. It was the third settlement in Ohio.

GAMBIER, Village; Knox County; Pop. 2,056 / 2,098; Zip Code 43022; Lat. 40-22-32 N, Long. 082-23-50 W; 5 mi. E of Mount Vernon on the Walhonding River in N central Ohio; named for Lord James Gambier, an English Admiral.

GARFIELD HEIGHTS, City; Cuyahoga County; Pop. 33,380 / 28,390; Zip Code 441+; Lat. 41-25-01 N, Long. 081-36-22 W; NE Ohio, S suburb of Cleveland bordered to the W by the Cuyahoga River-Ohio Canal; Residential, with some industry.

GARRETTSVILLE, Village; Portage County; Pop. 1,769 / 2,205; Zip Code 44231; Lat. 41-17-03 N, Long. 081-05-48 W; 20 mi. W of Warren in NE Ohio; named for Col. John Garrett, who was the first settler here.

GATES MILLS, Village; Cuyahoga County; Pop. 2,236 / 2,454; Zip Code 44040; Lat. 41-31-03 N, Long. 081-24-13 W; 15 mi. E of Cleveland, outside of the busy metropolitan area in NE Ohio; Named for Halsey Gates, who settled here in 1812.

GENEVA, City; Ashtabula County; Pop. 6,655 / 6,952; Zip Code 44041; Elev. 685; Lat. 39-39-43 N, Long. 082-26-01 W; 10 mi. SW of Ashtabula in NE Ohio; Named for Switzerland town.

GENEVA-ON-THE-LAKE, Village; Ashtabula County; Pop. 1,634 / 1,721; Zip Code 44043; Elev. 605; Lat. 41-51-34 N, Long. 080-57-15 W; N of the city of Geneva in NE Ohio, on Lake Erie shoreline.

GENOA, Village; Ottawa County; Pop. 2,213 / 2,258; Zip Code 43430; Lat. 41-31-05 N, Long. 083-21-33 W; N Ohio; 15 mi. S of Lake Erie shoreline and 20 mi. SE of Toledo.

GEORGETOWN, Village; Seat of Brown County; Pop. 3,467 / 4,113; Zip Code 45121; Elev. 930; Lat. 38-51-52 N, Long.

083-54-15 W; SW Ohio near the Ohio River. It was surveyed in 1819 and named for Georgetown, Kentucky.

GERMANTOWN, Village; Montgomery County; Pop. 5,015 / 5,309; Zip Code 45327; Elev. 756; Lat. 39-35-02 N, Long. 081-19-04 W; 15 mi. SW of Dayton in SW central Ohio; Early settlers of German descent gave this town its name after the same town name in Pennsylvania.

GIBSONBURG, Village; Sandusky County; Pop. 2,479 / 2,467; Zip Code 43431; Lat. 41-23-04 N, Long. 083-19-14 W; N Ohio; 24 mi. SE of Toledo.

GIRARD, City; Trumbull County; Pop. 12,517 / 10,798; Zip Code 44420; Elev. 866; Lat. 41-09-14 N, Long. 080-42-06 W; NE Ohio; named for Stephen Girard, philanthropist and founder of Girard College at Philadelphia, Pennsylvania.

GLENDALE, Village; Hamilton County; Pop. 2,368 / 2,500; Zip Code 45246; Elev. 630; Lat. 39-16-14 N, Long. 084-27-34 W; 15 mi. N of Cincinnati in SW Ohio.

GNADENHUTTEN, Village; Tuscarawas County; Pop. 1,320 / 1,258; Zip Code 44629; Elev. 835; Lat. 40-21-30 N, Long. 081-26-04 W; 10 mi. S of New Philadelphia on the Tuscarawas River in E central Ohio. A group of Christian Indians led by Joshua, a Mohican elder, came here in 1772 and founded this town, calling it after the German word for "tents of grace," which they had learned from Moravian missionaries.

GOLF MANOR, City; Hamilton County; Pop. 4,317 / 3,831; Lat. 39-11-14 N, Long. 084-26-47 W; SW Ohio; Residential development just N of downtown Cincinnati; In a hilly area; named for the golf facilities in the city.

GRAFTON, Village; Lorain County; Pop. 2,231 / 4,602; Zip Code 44044; Lat. 41-16-21 N, Long. 082-03-17 W; N Ohio, along the Black River just S of Elyria.

GRAND RAPIDS, Village; Wood County; Pop. 962 / 1,004; Zip Code 43522; Elev. 654; Lat. 41-24-43 N, Long. 083-51-52 W; NW Ohio; Along the Maumee River, 7 mi. W of Bowling Green; Residential area, with a large state park nearby.

GRANDVIEW HEIGHTS, City; Franklin County; Pop. 7,420 / 6,329; Zip Code (with Columbus); Lat. 40-11-08 N, Long. 083-58-13 W; Central Ohio; On the Olentangy River, just W of downtown Columbus.

GRANVILLE, Village; Licking County; Pop. 3,851 / 4,518; Zip Code 43023; Elev. 960; Lat. 40-04-05 N, Long. 082-31-11 W; 10 mi. W of Newark in a rich farming area in central Ohio; Named for the town in Massachusetts.

GREENFIELD, City; Seat of Highland County; Pop. 5,034 / 5,639; Zip Code 45123; Lat. 39-21-07 N, Long. 083-22-58 W; 20 mi. W of Chillicothe along Paint Creek in S Ohio. The name describes the locality.

GREENHILLS, City; Hamilton County; Pop. 4,927 / 4,056; Zip Code 45218; Elev. 968; Lat. 39-16-05 N, Long. 084-31-23 W; SW Ohio, N suburb of Cincinnati, first developed in 1937 by the Federal Works Project Administration.

GREEN SPRINGS, Village; Sandusky and Seneca Counties; Pop. 1,568 / 1,521; Zip Code 44836; N Ohio; 10 mi. SE of Fremont.

GREENVILLE, City; Darke County; Pop. 13,002 / 12,886; Zip Code 45331; Elev. 1,020; Lat. 40-06-10 N, Long. 084-37-59 W; 30 mi. NW of Dayton in W Ohio. Site of Fort Greenville, built in 1793. Once the home of Tecumseh, Shawnee Indian chief. The place is named for General Nathaniel Greene.

GREENWICH, Village; Huron County; Pop. 1,458 / 1,588; Zip Code 44837; Elev. 1,031; Lat. 41-01-48 N, Long. 082-30-57 W; N Ohio; in a large farming area. Named for Greenwich, CT.

GROVE CITY, City; Franklin County; Pop. 16,793 / 27,856; Zip Code 43123; Elev. 835; Lat. 39-52-53 N, Long. 083-05-35 W; Central Ohio; Just S of Columbus; Named by William F. Bruck for the description of the area.

GROVEPORT, Village; Franklin County; Pop. 3,286 / 3,311; Zip Code 43125; Lat. 39-52-42 N, Long. 082-53-02 W; Central Ohio; Between the Hocking River and Big Walnut Creek, SE of Columbus city center; First named Wert's Grove by Jacob Wert in 1843 for the walnut groves here. A year later, nearby, John Rareysport, a great horse trainer, started a settlement. In 1846 the names were combined.

HAMILTON, City; Seat of Butler County; Pop. 63,169 / 60,901; Zip Code 450 +; Lat. 39-23-58 N, Long. 084-33-41 W; 20 mi. N of Cincinnati in SW Ohio. It lies on the Great Miami River; named after Alexander Hamilton.

HARRISON, City; Hamilton County; Pop. 5,855 / 7,680; Zip Code 45030; Elev. 820; Lat. 39-15-43 N, Long. 084-49-12 W; SW Ohio; Named for General William Henry Harrison.

HEATH, City; Licking County; Pop. 6,961 / 7,828; Zip Code 43055; Lat. 40-01-22 N, Long. 082-26-41 W; S central Ohio; Just W of Newark.

HEBRON, Village; Licking County; Pop. 2,036 / 2,154; Zip Code 43025; Elev. 889; Lat. 39-57-42 N, Long. 082-29-29 W; S central Ohio; 9 mi. SW of Newark on a branch of the Licking river. Named after the Biblical region.

HICKSVILLE, Village; Defiance County; Pop. 3,743 / 3,706; Zip Code 43526; Elev. 766; Lat. 41-17-35 N, Long. 084-45-43 W; 20 mi. W of Defiance, just W of the Indiana state line in NW Ohio. Named for Henry W. Wicks who laid out this town in 1836 with a New York state group named "American Land Co."

HILLIARD, City; Franklin County; Pop. 7,996 / 20,529; Zip Code 43026; Lat. 40-02-00 N, Long. 083-09-30 W; S central Ohio; W of Columbus; Named for the man who laid out this place in 1853.

HILLSBORO, City; Seat of Highland County; Pop. 6,344 / 7,520; Zip Code 45133; Elev. 1,129; Lat. 39-12-08 N, Long. 083-36-42 W; S Ohio. Descriptively named.

HOLGATE, Village; Henry County; Pop. 1,320 / 1,250; Zip Code 43527; Elev. 714; Lat. 41-14-56 N, Long. 084-07-59 W; NW Ohio; 11 mi. S of Napoleon.

HUBRARD, City; Trumbull County; Pop. 9,262 / 7,793; Zip Code 44425; Elev. 935; Lat. 41-09-23 N, Long. 080-34-10 W; NE Ohio; 10 mi. N of Youngstown, just W of the Pennsylvania state line; This town was named for Nehemiah Hubbard, who purchased the surrounding township in 1801.

HUDSON, Village; Summit County; Pop. 4,612; Zip Code 44236; Elev. 1,409; Lat. 41-14-24 N, Long. 081-26-27 W; 10 mi. NE of Akron in NE Ohio. In 1799, David Hudson and a group from Connecticut settled this site.

HURON, City; Erie County; Pop. 7,075 / 7,249; Zip Code 44839; Elev. 599; Lat. 41-22-25 N, Long. 082-33-17 W; 10 mi. ESE of Sandusky in N Ohio; at the mouth of the Huron River. Named for the Indian tribe.

INDEPENDENCE, City; Cuyahoga County; Pop. 6,612 / 6,406; Zip Code 44131; Elev. 728; Lat. 41-23-40 N, Long. 081-38-27 W; NE Ohio; Just S of Cleveland along the old Ohio Canal; Industrial suburb.

IRONTON, City; Seat of Lawrence County; Pop. 14,178 / 12,930; Zip Code 45638; Elev. 547; Lat. 38-32-12 N, Long. 082-40-59 W; S Ohio; On the Ohio River across from the Kentucky state line; Named after iron ore was discovered here in 1826.

JACKSON, City; Seat of Jackson County; Pop. 6,670 / 5,719; Zip Code 45640; Elev. 670; Lat. 39-03-07 N, Long. 082-38-12 W; S Ohio; Plotted in 1817. Named after Gen. Andrew Jackson.

JAMESTOWN, Village; Greene County; Pop. 1,703 / 1,962; Zip Code 45335; Elev. 1,053; Lat. 39-39-29 N, Long. 083-44-06 W; SW Ohio; Named for Jamestown, VA.

JEFFERSON, Village; Seat of Ashtabula County; Pop. 2,964 / 3,438; Zip Code 44047; Elev. 700; Lat. 41-44-19 N, Long. 080-46-12 W; NE corner of Ohio; 10 mi. S of Ashtabula. Named for Thomas Jefferson.

JEFFERSON, Village; Madison County; Pop. 4,433 / 3,438; Zip Code 43162; Lat. 39-48-50 N, Long. 082-45-39 W; SW central Ohio; 15 mi. W of Columbus. Named for Thomas Jefferson.

JEFFERSONVILLE, Village; Fayette County; Pop. 1,247 / 1,276; Zip Code 43128; Elev. 1049; Lat. 39-39-13 N, Long. 023-33-50 W; SW central Ohio near Paint Creek; Named for Thomas Jefferson.

JOHNSTOWN, Village; Licking County; Pop. 3,158 / 3,383; Zip Code 43031; Elev. 1,166; Lat. 40-09-13 N, Long. 082-41-07 W; 20 mi. NE of Columbus in N central Ohio. Named for Capt. James Johnston who was an early landowner.

KALIDA, Village; Putnam County; Pop. 1,019 / 1,132; Zip Code 45853; Elev. 727; Lat. 40-58-58 N, Long. 084-11-58 W; 20 mi. N of Lima in NW Ohio along the Ottawa River. Named for the Greek word meaning beautiful.

KENT, City; Portage County; Pop. 26,142 / 25,780; Zip Code 44240; Elev. 1097; Lat. 41-09-13 N, Long. 081-21-29 W; 10 mi. E of Akron on the Cuyahoga River in NE central Ohio.

KETTERING, City; Montgomery County; Pop. 61,223 / 57,156; Zip Code 454+; Lat. 39-41-22 N, Long. 084-10-08 W; SW Ohio; On the southern outskirts of Dayton; Named after Charles F. Kettering.

KINGSTON, Village; Ross County; Pop. 1,299 / 1,285; Zip Code 45644; Elev. 797; Lat. 39-28-26 N, Long. 082-54-39 W; S central Ohio; 11 mi. NE of Chillicothe in a rolling farmlands region.

KIRTLAND, City; Lake County; Pop. 5,915 / 6,619; Zip Code (with Euclid); Elev. 660; Lat. 41-37-44 N, Long. 081-21-42 W; a suburban village on the brow of a hill overlooking the Chargrin River.

LAGRANGE, Village; Lorain County; Pop. 1,253 / 1,630; Zip Code 44050; N Ohio; Elev. 825; Lat. 41-14-14 N, Long. 082-07-12 W; 10 mi. S of Elyria near the Black River.

LAKEMORE, Village; Summit County; Pop. 2,746 / 2,568; Zip Code 44250; Lat. 41-01-15 N, Long. 081-26-10 W; NE Ohio; Just SE of Akron on the N tip at Springfield Lake.

LAKEVIEW, Village; Logan County; Pop. 1,089 / 997; Zip Code 43331; Lat. 39-55-19 N, Long. 081-26-00 W; W Ohio on Indian Lake, 15 mi. NW of Bellefontaine; Descriptively named for its lakeside location.

LAKEWOOD, City; Cuyahoga County; Pop. 61,921 / 54,222; Zip Code 44107; Elev. 685; Lat. 41-28-55 N, Long. 081-47-54 W; NE Ohio; On Lake Erie; Named for its setting along the wooded shore of Lake Erie.

LANCASTER, City; Seat of Fairfield County; Pop. 34,925 / 36,714; Zip Code 43130; Elev. 898; Lat. 39-42-49 N, Long. 082-35-58 W; S central Ohio; Named for Lancaster, PA.

LEBANON, City; Seat of Warren County; Pop. 9,602 / 14,966; Zip Code 45036; Elev. 969; Lat. 39-36-28 N, Long. 081-16-24 W; 20 mi. E of Hamilton in SW Ohio; was founded in 1803 and named after the Biblical country.

LEESBURG, Village; Highland County; Pop. 1,021 / 1,201; Zip Code 45135; Elev. 1,025; Lat. 39-20-42 N, Long. 083-33-11 W; SW central Ohio; 10 mi. N of Hillsboro.

LEIPSIC, Village; Putnam County; Pop. 2,170 / 2,231; Zip Code 45856; Elev. 766; Lat. 41-05-54 N, Long. 083-59-05 W; 30 mi. N of Lima in NW Ohio. Named by the settlers for their hometown in Germany.

LEWISBURG, Village; Preble County; Pop. 1,452 / 1,701; Zip Code 45338; Elev. 1,019; Lat. 39-50-46 N, Long. 084-32-23 W; 22 mi. NW of Dayton in SW Ohio; Industrial center of a large agricultural region.

LEXINGTON, Village; Richland County; Pop. 3,826 / 4,493; Zip Code 44904; Elev. 1,180; Lat. 40-40-43 N, Long. 082-34-57 W; 10 mi. SW of Mansfield in N central Ohio; Laid out in 1812, and named in honor of Lexington. Massachusetts.

LIMA, City; Seat of Allen County; Pop. 47,354 / 42,635; Zip Code 458+; Elev. 878; Lat. 40-44-33 N, Long. 084-06-19 W; NW Ohio, Named after the city in South America.

LINCOLN HEIGHTS, City; Hamilton County; Pop. 5,214 / 4,397; Zip Code (with Cincinnati); Lat. 39-14-20 N, Long. 084-27-20 W; SW Ohio; N suburb of Cincinnati, set amidst the hills encircling the city.

LISBON, Seat of Columbia County; Pop. 3,157 / 2,899; Zip Code 44432; Elev. 955; Lat. 39-51-39 N, Long. 083-38-07 W; 15 mi. NW of East Liverpool in E Ohio; Founded in 1802 and named for the great city in Portugal.

LOCKLAND, Village; Hamilton County; Pop. 4,256 / 4,343; Zip Code 45215; SW Ohio; Just N of Cincinnati an Mill Creek.

LODI, Village; Median County; Pop. 2,924 / 3,094; Zip Code 44254; Elev. 927; Lat. 41-02-00 N, Long. 082-00-44 W; N Ohio. Named after Bonaparte's Italian Campaign victory, the Battle of Lodi.

LOGAN, City; Seat of Hocking County; Pop. 6,557 / 7,576; Zip Code 48138; Elev. 728; Lat. 39-32-24 N, Long. 082-24-26 W; S Ohio; Named for the Mingo Chief.

LONDON, City; Seat of Madison County; Pop. 6,916 / 8,529; Zip Code 43140; Elev. 1,046; Lat. 39-53-11 N, Long. 083-26-54 W; SW central Ohio. Named after the English city.

LORAIN, City; Lorain County; Pop. 74,580 / 67,377; Zip Code 440+; Elev. 610; Lat. 41-27-10 N, Long. 082-10-57 W; 25 mi. W of Cleveland in N Ohio where Black River flows into Lake Erie; Named for the French, Lorraine by Judge Herman Ely from his European travels.

LOUDONVILLE, Village; Ashland County; Pop. 2,933 / 2,933; Zip Code 44842; Elev. 974; Lat. 40-38-07 N, Long. 062-14-00 W; N central Ohio; Named after James Loudon, a priest who laid out the town with Stephen Butler in 1814.

LOUISVILLE, City; Stark County; Pop. 7,839 / 8,373; Zip Code 44641; Elev. 900; Lat. 38-59-34 N, Long. 083-27-52 W; 5 mi. NE of Canton in NE central Ohio; A land owner named Henry Loutzenheiser named the place after his son Lewis Heald.

LOVELAND, City; Hamilton and Clermont Counties; Pop. 9,096 / 12,472; Zip Code 45140; Elev. 728; Lat. 39-17-59 N, Long. 084-15-48 W; SW Ohio; 16 mi. NE of Cincinnati on the Little Miami River; Named for Colonel Loveland.

LOWELLVILLE, Village; Mahoning County; Pop. 1,559 / 1,478; Zip Code 44436; Lat. 41-02-07 N, Long. 080-32-12 W; 5 mi. SE of Youngstown in NE Ohio.

LYNCHBURG, Village; Highland County; Pop. 1,207 / 1,365; Zip Code 45142; Lat. 40-44-28 N, Long. 080-59-58 W; 15 mi. NW of Hillsboro in S Ohio. Named by early settlers from Virginia for their original hometown.

LYNDHURST, City; Cuyahoga County; Pop. 18,093 / 14,748; Zip Code 44124; Lat. 41-31-12 N, Long. 081-29-20 W; NE Ohio; Approx. 10 mi. E of downtown Cleveland in a residential area.

MACEDONIA, City; Summit County; Pop. 6,562 / 9,302; Zip Code 44056; Elev. 989; Lat. 41-18-49 N, Long. 081-30-31 W; NE Ohio; At a midpoint between Cleveland and Akron; Named for the ancient kingdom in Europe.

MADEIRA, City; Hamilton County; Pop. 9,342 / 8,643; Zip Code 45243; Elev. 772; Lat. 39-11-27 N, Long. 084-21-49 W; SW Ohio; Approx. 15 mi. NE of Cincinnati in a residential area.

MADISON, Village; Lake County; Pop. 2,278 / 3,168; Zip Code 44057; Elev. 744; Lat. 41-46-16 N, Long. 081-03-00 W; 15 mi. SW of Ashtabula in NE Ohio; Named for President James Madison.

MALVERN, Village; Carroll County; Pop. 1,023 / 1,221; Zip Code 44644; Elev. 997; Lat. 40-41-30 N, Long. 081-10-53 W; 16 mi. SE of Canton on Sandy Creek in E Ohio; Named after the town in Pennsylvania by the two landowners, Joseph Tidbald and Lewis Vail.

MANCHESTER, Village; Adams County; Pop. 2,333 / 2,649; Zip Code 45144; Elev. 511; Lat. 38-41-17 N, Long. 023-36-34 W; S Ohio; Named after Manchester, England.

MANSFIELD, City; Seat of Richland County; Pop. 53,907 / 51,326; Zip Code 449+; Elev. 1,240; Lat. 40-45-30 N, Long. 082-30-56 W; N central Ohio; Named in 1808 under the direction of Jared Mansfield, Surveyor General of the United States.

MANTUA, Village; Portage County; Pop. 1,041 / 1,052; Zip Code 44255; Lat. 41-17-02 N, Long. 081-13-27 W; 30 mi. SE of Cleveland in NE Ohio on the Cuyahoga River. Named by John Leavitt for a town in Italy.

MAPLE HEIGHTS, City; Cuyahoga County; Pop. 29,465 / 24,636; Zip Code 44137; Lat. 41-24-55 N, Long. 081-33-58 W; NE Ohio; SE suburb of Cleveland; Residential area named for the trees that line many of the streets.

MARIEMONT, Village; Hamilton County; Pop. 3,274 / 2,814; Zip Code 45227; Elev. 650; Lat. 39-08-42 N, Long. 084-22-28 W; SW Ohio; Overlooking the Little Miami River; Laid out in 1922 on land owned by Marie Emery of Cincinnati.

MARIETTA, City; Seat of Washington County; Pop. 16,462 / 15,489; Zip Code 45750; Elev. 620; Lat. 39-24-55 N, Long. 081-27-18 W; SE Ohio; 45 mi. SE of Zanesville where the Ohio and Muskingum Rivers merge; Named after Queen Marie Antoinette of France for her assistance in the American Revolution.

MARION, City; Seat of Marion County; Pop. 37,071 / 36,362; Zip Code 43302; Elev. 986; Lat. 40-35-19 N, Long. 083-07-43 W; Central Ohio; Named for General Francis Marion, a Revolutionary War hero.

MARTINS FERRY, City; Belmont County; Pop. 9,304 / 12,522; Zip Code 43935; Elev. 660; Lat. 40-05-45 N, Long. 080-43-29 W; E Ohio; In 1835 the place was known as Martinsville after Ebenezer Martin. The name was later changed by the post office to Martins Ferry.

MARYSVILLE, City; Seat of Union County; Pop. 7,403 / 14,183; Zip Code 43040; Elev. 999; Lat. 39-56-50 N, Long. 081-36-13 W; W central Ohio; Settled in 1816 by Jonathan Summers, and platted in 1820 by Samuel Culbertson, who named the village for his daughter Mary.

MASON, City; Warren County; Pop. 8,696 / 21,097; Zip Code 45040; Lat. 39-21-36 N, Long. 084-18-36 W; SW Ohio; 20 mi. E of Cincinnati in a hilly residential area.

MASSILLON, City; Stark County; Pop. 30,422 / 30,634; Zip Code 44646; Elev. 1,030; Lat. 40-47-48 N, Long. 081-31-18 W; 10 mi. W of Canton in NE central Ohio. Named after the famous French divine Jean Batiste Massillon.

MAUMEE, City; Lucas County; Pop. 15,752 / 15,303; Zip Code 43537; Lat. 41-33-46 N, Long. 083-39-14 W; NW Ohio; adjacent to and S of Toledo on the Maumee River; Early a trading post and fort (1680) later the British Ft. Miami (1764). The present name is a variation of Miami.

MAYFIELD, Village; Cuyahoga County; Pop. 3,552 / 3,270; Lat. 39-29-41 N, Long. 084-22-22 W; 15 mi. E of Cleveland in NE Ohio; Residential.

MAYFIELD HEIGHTS, City; Cuyahoga County; Pop. 21,383 / 18,313; Lat. 41-31-09 N, Long. 081-27-29 W; 15 mi. E of Cleveland, just S of Village of Mayfield; Residential development.

MCARTHUR, Village; Seat of Vinton County; Pop. 1,919 / 1,979; Zip Code 45651; Elev. 767; Lat. 39-14-47 N, Long. 082-28-43 W; S Ohio; Named McArthurstown for General Duncan McArthur, later governor of Ohio.

MCCOMB, Village; Hancock County; Pop. 1,606 / 1,610; Zip Code 45858; Elev. 778; Lat. 41-06-27 N, Long. 083-47-34 W; NW Ohio; 10 mi. NW of Findlay.

MCDONALD, Village; Trumbull County; Pop. 3,738 / 3,500; Zip Code 44437; Lat. 39-51-45 N, Long. 081-50-50 W; NE Ohio, just S of Niles and Warren.

MECHANICSBURG, Village; Champaign County; Pop. 1,782 / 1,689; Zip Code 43044; Lat. 40-04-19 N, Long. 083-33-23 W; W Ohio; 30 mi. W of Columbus in a farming region.

MEDINA, City; Seat of Medina County; Pop. 15,307 / 23,012; Zip Code 44256; Elev. 1,086; Lat. 41-08-18 N, Long. 081-51-50 W; 20 mi. NW of Akron in N Ohio. The name was changed to Medina in 1825 for the ancient capital of Arabia.

MENTOR, City; Lake County; Pop. 41,903 / 51,686; Zip Code 44060; Elev. 65; Lat. 41-39-58 N, Long. 081-20-23 W; NE Ohio, just S of the Lake Erie shoreline; Named for the great teacher from Greek history.

MENTOR-ON-THE-LAKE, City; Lake County; Pop. 7,894 / 8,962; Zip Code 44060; Lat. 41-42-18 N, Long. 081-21-38 W; Just S of Lake Erie shoreline.

MIAMISBURG, City; Montgomery County; Pop. 15,327 / 18,766; Zip Code 45342; Elev. 711; Lat. 39-38-34 N, Long. 084-17-12 W; SW Ohio; Named for its location on the Great Miami River, S of Dayton.

MIDDLEBURG HEIGHTS, City; Cuyahoga County; Pop. 16,228 / 14,744; Zip Code (With Parma); Lat. 41-21-41, Long. 081-48-47 W; 15 mi. SW of Cleveland in a suburban-residential area.

MIDDLEFIELD, Village; Geauga County; Pop. 2,001 / 2,194; Zip Code 44062; Elev. 1126; Lat. 41-27-43 N, Long. 081-04-26 W; NE Ohio; Named for its geographic location between Warren and Painesville.

MIDDLEPORT, Village; Meigs County; Pop. 2,967 / 2,840; Zip Code 45760; Elev. 564; Lat. 39-00-06 N, Long. 082-02-56; SE Ohio; 40 mi. SW of Marietta.

MIDDLETOWN, City; Butler County; Pop. 43,693 / 52,922; Zip Code 45042; Lat. 39-30-54 N, Long. 084-23-54; SW Ohio; On the Miami River, 35 mi. N of Cincinnati; Named for its location between Dayton and Cincinnati.

MILAN, Village; Erie and Huron Counties; Pop. 1,564 / 1,398; Zip Code 44846; Elev. 602; Lat. 41-17-51 N, Long. 032-36-20 W; N Ohio; Named after the famous Italian city.

MILFORD, Village; Clermont County; Pop. 5,227 / 7,007; Zip Code 45150; Lat. 39-10-31 N, Long. 084-17-40 W; SW Ohio; 12 mi. NE of Cincinnati in an industrial area.

MILLERSBURG, Village; Seat of Holmes County; Pop. 3,225 / 3,921; Zip Code 44654; Elev. 818; Lat. 40-33-16 N, Long. 081-55-05 W; NE central Ohio; Named after Charles Miller who settled here in 1824 along with Adam Johnson.

MINERVA, Village; Stark & Carroll Counties; Pop. 4,547 / 4,409; Zip Code 44657; Elev. 1,050; Lat. 40-43-47 N, Long. 081-06-20 W; NE central Ohio on the Sandy River. It was named for the niece of John Whitacre, the founder.

MINERVA PARK, Village; Franklin County; Pop. 1,617 / 1,463; Lat. 40-04-35 N, Long. 082-56-38 W; central Ohio.

MINGO JUNCTION, City, Jefferson County; Pop. 4,844 / 3,628; Zip Code 43938; Elev. 675; Lat. 40-19-18 N, Long. 080-36-36 W; E Ohio; On the Ohio River.

MINSTER, Village; Auglaize County; Pop. 2,556 / 2,896; Zip Code 45864; Elev. 967; Lat. 40-23-35 N, Long. 084-22-34 W; W Ohio; On E shore of Loramie Lake.

MOGADORE, Village; Portage & Summit Counties; Pop. 4,192 / 3,849; Zip Code 44260; Lat. 41-02-47 N, Long. 081-23-53 W; NE Ohio; Named after the city of the same name in Morocco, North Africa.

MONROE, City; Warren County; Pop. 4,259 / 7,300; Zip Code 45050; Elev. 823; Lat. 39-26-25 N, Long. 084-21-44 W; SW Ohio; Approx. 30 mi. N of Cincinnati. Named after President James Monroe.

MONTGOMERY, City; Hamilton County; Pop. 15,090 / 10,005; Zip Code 45242; Lat. 39-13-41 N, Long. 084-21-15 W; SW Ohio; 15 mi. NE of Cincinnati in a residential area.

MONTPELIER, Village; Williams County; Pop. 4,426 / 4,243; Zip Code 43543; Elev. 860; 50 mi. W of Toledo in NW Ohio on the St. Joseph River; Named after the French city.

MORAINE, City; Montgomery County; Pop. 5,250 / 7,825; Lat. 39-42-22 N, Long. 084-13-10 W; 5 mi. S of Dayton in SW Ohio. Named after the local geological feature.

MORROW, Village; Warren County; Pop. 1,247 / 1,487; Zip Code 45152; Elev. 640; Lat. 39-21-16 N, Long. 084-07-38 W; SW Ohio; Settled in 1844 and named for Jeremiah Morrow, Governor of Ohio from 1822 to 1826.

MOUNT GILEAD, Village; Seat of Morrow County; Pop. 2,894 / 3,305; Zip Code 43338; Elev. 1,083; Lat. 40-32-57 N, Long. 082-49-39 W; Named to honor Mount Gilead, Virginia.

MOUNT HEALTHY, City; Hamilton County; Pop. 7,553 / 7,119; Zip Code 45231; Elev. 855; Lat. 39-14-01 N, Long. 084-32-45 W; SW Ohio; 14 mi. N of Cincinnati surrounding a large hill by the same name.

MOUNT ORAB, Village; Brown County; Pop. 1,869 / 2,536; Zip Code 45154; Elev. 922; Lat. 39-01-39 N, Long. 083-55-11 W; SW Ohio; In a hilly region near Lake Grant.

MOUNT STERLING, Village; Madison County; Pop. 1,616 / 1,761; Zip Code 43149; Elev. 906; Lat. 39-43-10 N, Long. 083-15-55 W; SW central Ohio; On Deer Creek; 23 mi. SW of Columbus.

MOUNT VERNON, City; Seat of Knox County; Pop. 14,362 / 16,040; Zip Code 43050; Lat. 40-23-36 N, Long. 082-29-09 W; 35 mi. NE of Columbus in central Ohio on the Kokosing River. Named after George Washington's estate.

MUNROE FALLS, City; Summit County; Pop. 4,729 / 5,368; Zip Code 44262; Lat. 41-08-40 N, Long. 081-26-24 W; NE central Ohio; Named for founder Edmund Munroe.

NAPOLEON, City; Seat of Henry County; Pop. 8,615 / 9,175; Zip Code 43545; Elev. 689; Lat. 41-23-32 N, Long. 084-07-31 W; NW Ohio. Named in honor of the great French soldier.

NAVARRE, Village; Stark County; Pop. 1,344 / 1,689; Zip Code 44662; Elev. 940; Lat. 40-43-28 N, Long. 081-31-20 W; NE Ohio; Named in honor of King Henry IV of France and Navarre by the French speaking wife of James Duncan.

NELSONVILLE, City; Athens County; Pop. 4,571 / 5,001; Zip Code 45764; Elev. 1,044; Lat. 39-27-31 N, Long. 082-13-55 W; S Ohio; Originally known as Englishtown, the town changed its name in 1824 to honor Daniel Nelson, the settlement's most enterprising citizen.

NEW ALBANY, Village; Franklin County; Pop. 398 / 3,105; Zip Code 43054; Lat. 40-56-32 N, Long. 080-50-10 W; Central Ohio; 13 mi. NE of Columbus. Named for Albany, New York.

NEWARK, City; Seat of Licking County; Pop. 41,162 / 47,612; Zip Code 43055; Elev. 836; Lat. 40-03-29 N, Long. 082-24-05 W; 35 mi. E of Columbus. Founded in 1802 by General William Schenck, the settlement was named after a New Jersey community.

NEW BOSTON, Village; Scioto County; Pop. 3,177 / 2,725; Zip Code 45662; Lat. 38-45-08 N, Long. 082-56-13 W; S Ohio; On the Ohio River, 5 mi. E of Portsmouth. Named after Boston, Massachusetts.

NEW BREMEN, Village; Auglaize County; Pop. 2,401 / 3,137; Zip Code 45869; Elev. 941; Lat. 40-26-13 N, Long. 084-22-47 W; W central Ohio; On the St. Marys River. Named for the city in Germany.

NEWBURGH HEIGHTS, Village; Cuyahoga County; Pop. 2,671 / 2,035; Zip Code 441+; Lat. 41-27-00 N, Long. 081-39-49 W; NE Ohio; Just S of downtown Cleveland off the Willow Freeway (U.S. 77).

NEW CARLISLE, City; Clark County; Pop. 6,435 / 6,168; Zip Code 45344; Elev. 906; Lat. 39-56-10 N, Long. 084-01-32 W; W central Ohio; 12 mi. W of Springfield. Named after Carlisle, New Jersey.

NEWCOMERSTOWN, Village; Tuscarawas County; Pop. 3,955 / 4,091; Zip Code 43832; Elev. 849; Lat. 40-16-20 N, Long. 081-36-22 W; E Ohio; Located on the site of the old Delaware capital of Gekelemukpechunk , the area is near the Tuscarawas River.

It was to this place that Chief Eagle Feather's second wife, called "the newcomer" by his first wife, Mary Harris, fled after circumstantial evidence pointed to her guilt in his murder. It is said to have taken its final name from "the newcomer.

NEW CONCORD, Village; Muskingum County; Pop. 1,858 / 2,389; Zip Code 43762; Lat. 39-59-37 N, Long. 081-44-03 W; 8 mi. W of Cambridge in SE central Ohio. Named after Concord, Massachusetts.

NEW LEBANON, Village; Montgomery County; Pop. 4,498 / 4,169; Zip Code 45345; Elev. 913; Lat. 39-44-43 N, Long. 084-23-06 W; 10 mi. W of Dayton in SW Ohio. Named after the biblical country.

NEW LEXINGTON, Village; Perry County Seat; Pop. 5,174 / 5,326; Zip Code 43764; Elev. 958; Lat. 39-42-50 N, Long. 082-12-31 W; SE central Ohio; 19 mi. SW of Zanesville. Named for the famous town in Massachusetts.

NEW LONDON, Village; Huron County; Pop. 2,439 / 2,877; Zip Code 44851; 45 mi. SW of Cleveland near the Vermillion River in N central Ohio. The village is named for the city in Connecticut.

NEW MADISON, Village; Darke County; Pop. 1,016 / 928; Zip Code 45346; Lat. 39-58-04 N, Long. 084-42-33 W; W Ohio; 11 mi. S of Greenville.

NEW MIAMI, Village; Butler County; Pop. 2,991 / 3,374; Lat. 39-26-05 N, Long. 084-32-13 W; E Ohio. Named after the local Miami Indians.

NEW MIDDLETOWN, Village; Mahoning County; Pop. 2,189 / 2,154; Lat. 40-51-52 N, Long. 080-54-55 W; 12 mi. SE of Youngstown.

NEW PHILADELPHIA, City; Seat of Tuscarawas County; Pop. 16,921 / 17,616; Zip Code 44663; Elev. 901; Lat. 40-29-23 N, Long. 081-26-45 W; E Ohio; Founded by John Kinisely in 1804.

NEW RICHMOND, Village; Clermont County; Pop. 2,773 / 2,833; Zip Code 45157; Elev. 510; Lat. 38-56-55 N, Long. 084-16-48 W; SW Ohio; is a union of two villages.

NEWTON FALLS, City; Trumbull County; Pop. 4,954 / 4,927; Zip Code 44444; Elev. 924; Lat. 41-11-18 N, Long. 080-58-42 W; NE Ohio; On the Mahoning River, 10 mi. W of Warren.

NEWTOWN, Village; Hamilton County; Pop. 1,816 / 2,399; Zip Code 45244; Lat. 39-07-26 N, Long. 084-21-42 W; SW Ohio; Just E of Cincinnati. Descriptively named upon its founding.

NEW VIENNA, Village; Clinton County; Pop. 1,133 / 1,010; Zip Code 45159; Lat. 39-19-25 N, Long. 083-41-28 W; SW central Ohio; 13 mi. SE of Wilmington. Named for the Austrian capital.

NEW WASHINGTON, Village; Crawford County; Pop. 1,211 / 953; Zip Code 44854; Lat. 40-57-44 N, Long. 082-51-16 W; N central Ohio; 20 mi. NW of Mansfield. The village is named after George Washington.

NILES, City; Trumball County; Pop. 23,072 / 20,251; Zip Code 44446; Elev. 912; Lat. 41-10-58 N, Long. 080-45-56 W; Just S of Warren in NE central Ohio. Named after a Baltimore newspaper editor.

NORTH BALTIMORE, Village; Wood County; Pop. 3,124 / 3,210; Zip Code 45872; Lat. 41-10-58 N, Long. 083-40-42 W; NW Ohio; 20 mi. S of Bowling Green.

NORTH CANTON, City; Stark County; Pop. 14,189 / 16,011; Zip Code 447+; Elev. 1160; Lat. 40-52-33 N, Long. 081-24-09 W; NE central Ohio; Just N of city of Canton; Site of Walsh College.

NORTH COLLEGE HILL, City; Hamilton County; Pop. 11,066 / 10,085; Zip Code 45239; Elev. 712; Lat. 39-13-06 N, Long. 084-33-03 W; 10 mi. N of Cincinnati in SW Ohio; Suburban.

NORTHFIELD, Village; Summit County; Pop. 2,918 / 642; Zip Code 44067; Elev. 1044; Lat. 41-20-42 N, Long. 081-31-43 W; 20 mi. S of Cleveland in NE Ohio; The first earlier settlers were from Massachusetts and named it after their hometown.

NORTH KINGSVILLE, Village; Ashtabula County; Pop. 2,922 / 2,998; Zip Code 44068; Elev. 715; Lat. 41-54-21 N, Long. 080-41-26 W; NE Ohio; Just S of the Lake Erie shoreline; Suburban.

NORTH OLMSTED, City; Cuyahoga County; Pop. 36,480 / 32,978; Zip Code 44070; Lat. 41-24-56 N, Long. 081-55-25 W; NE Ohio; 15 mi. W of Cleveland, just S of the Lake Erie shoreline; Suburban.

NORTH RIDGEVILLE, City; Lorain County; Pop. 21,237 / 23,939; Zip Code 44039; Lat. 41-22-13 N, Long. 082-02-43 W; N Ohio; N suburb of Elyria; Residential.

NORTH ROYALTON, City; Cuyahoga County; Pop. 17,705 / 25,394; Zip Code 44133; Elev. 1197; Lat. 41-18-49 N, Long. 081-43-29 W; NE Ohio; 20 mi. S of Cleveland in a residential area.

NORTHWOOD, Village; Wood County; Pop. 5,482 / 5,913; Zip Code (with Toledo); Lat. 40-28-22 N, Long. 083-43-57 W; NW Ohio; Across the Maumee River from Toledo in a residential area.

NORTON, City; Summit County; Pop. 12,241; Zip Code 44203; Elev. 946; Lat. 40-26-02 N, Long. 083-04-26 W; NE central Ohio; Residential suburb, just S of Akron and Barberton.

NORWALK, City; Seat of Huron County; Pop. 14,348 / 15,896; Zip Code 44857; Elev. 719; Lat. 41-14-33 N, Long. 082-36-57 W; N central Ohio; It was named for the Connecticut town because many of its settlers left that State to make homes here on their "Firelands" grants.

NORWOOD, City; Hamilton County; Pop. 26,126 / 21,651; Zip Code 452+; Lat. 39-09-20 N, Long. 084-27-35 W; SW Ohio; surrounded by the city of Cincinnati.

OAK HARBOR, Village; Ottawa County; Pop. 2,683 / 2,637; Zip Code 43449; N Ohio; On the Portage River, 11 mi. W of Port Clinton. Named for the many oaks once in the area.

OAK HILL, Village; Jackson County; Pop. 1,715 / 1,830; Zip Code 45656; Elev. 967; Lat. 40-24-51 N, Long. 082-14-28 W; 12 mi. S of the city of Jackson.

OAKWOOD, City; Montgomery County; Pop. 9,404 / 8,352; Zip Code (with Dayton); Elev. 64; Lat. 41-23-09 N, Long. 081-29-20 W; SW central Ohio; A suburb of Dayton.

OAKWOOD, Village; Cuyahoga County; Pop. 3,783 / 643; Zip Code (with Cleveland); Lat. 39-43-31 N, Long. 084-10-27 W; 15 mi. SE of Cleveland in NE Ohio. Residential suburb.

OBERLIN, City; Lorain County; Pop. 8,600 / 7,900; Zip Code 44074; Lat. 41-17-38 N, Long. 082-13-03 W; N Ohio; 20 mi. SW of Cleveland. Named after Rev. Johann Friedrich Oberlin, it was one of the first colleges to admit African American students.

OBETZ, Village; Franklin County; Pop. 3,098 / 3,903; Lat. 39-52-44 N, Long. 082-57-03 W; central Ohio.

OLMSTED FALLS, City; Cuyahoga County; Pop. 5,868 / 8,209; Zip Code 44138; Elev. 774; Lat. 41-22-30 N, Long. 081-54-30 W; NE Ohio; 15 mi. SW of Cleveland along Rocky Creek.

ONTARIO, Village; Richland County; Pop. 4,122 / 4,909; Zip Code 44862; Lat. 40-45-34 N, Long. 082-35-25 W; N central Ohio; Just W of Mansfield. Named after the Canadian province.

ORANGE, Village; Cuyahoga County; Pop. 2,368 / 3,024; Zip Code (with Cleveland); Lat. 40-17-17 N, Long. 081-40-59 W; Suburban-residential.

OREGON, City; Lucas County; Pop. 18,682 / 19,102; Zip Code 436+; Lat. 41-38-37 N, Long. 083-29-13 W; 10 mi. E of Toledo in NW Ohio, just S of Maumee Bay. Named after the state.

ORRVILLE, City; Wayne County; Pop. 7,507 / 8,449; Zip Code 44667; Elev. 1064; Lat. 40-50-37 N, Long. 081-45-51 W; 44 mi. S of Cleveland in NE central Ohio.

OTTAWA, Village; Seat of Putnam County; Pop. 3,870 / 4,449; Zip Code 45875; Elev. 729; Lat. 41-01-09 N, Long. 084-02-50 W; NW Ohio; 20 mi. N of Lime. The village was established in 1833, shortly after the last of the Ottawa Indians had been removed to their western reservations.

OTTAWA HILLS, Village; Lucas County; Pop. 4,053 / 4,161; Lat. 41-39-51 N, Long. 083-38-36 W; NW Ohio.

OXFORD, City; Butler County; Pop. 17,669 / 21,198; Zip Code 45056; Elev. 972; Lat. 39-30-25 N, Long. 084-44-43 W; SW Ohio; 25 mi. SW of Dayton, named for the great English university town.

PAINESVILLE, City; Seat of Lake County; Pop. 16,351 / 15,700; Zip Code 44077; Elev. 702; Lat. 41-43-28 N, Long. 081-14-45 W; 30 mi. NE of Cleveland in NE Ohio; It was named for General Edward Paine, an officer in the Revolutionary War, who arrived here in the early 1800s.

PANDORA, Village; Putnam County; Pop. 977 / 1,036; Zip Code 45877; Elev. 773; Lat. 40-56-53 N, Long. 083-57-40 W; NW Ohio; 18 mi. NE of Lima. Named for the Greek mythological character.

PARMA, City; Cuyahoga County; Pop. 92,578 / 81,207; Zip Code 441+; Lat. 41-24-17 N, Long. 081-43-23 W; 10 mi. S of Cleveland in N Ohio; named after the Italian city.

PATASKALA, Village; Licking County; Pop. 2,285 / 9,539; Zip Code 43062; Lat. 39-59-44 N, Long. 082-40-28 W; 20 mi. E of Columbus in central Ohio; farming area. Named for the Indian word meaning "Salt Lick."

PAULDING, Village; Seat of Paulding County; Pop. 2,760 / 3,088; Zip Code 45879; Elev. 723; Lat. 41-08-17 N, Long. 084-34-50 W; 40 mi. NW of Lima in NW Ohio; Named for John Paulding of Peekskill, NY, one of the three men who captured Major Andre during the Revolution,

PAYNE, Village; Paulding County; Pop. 1,397 / 1,242; Zip Code 45880; Elev. 753; Lat. 41-04-39 N, Long. 084-43-38 W; NW Ohio; 35 mi. E of Fort Wayne, Indiana.

PEEBLES, Village; Adams County; Pop. 1,791 / 1,979; Zip Code 45660; Elev. 813; Lat. 38-56-56 N, Long. 083-24-21 W; Approx. 30 mi. NW of Portsmouth in S Ohio.

PEPPER PIKE, City; Cuyahoga County; Pop. 6,175 / 5,997; Elev. 1050; Lat. 41-28-42 N, Long. 081-27-50 W; 10 mi. E of Cleveland in N Ohio.

PERRYSBURG, City; Wood County; Pop. 10,196 / 15,807; Zip Code 43551; Elev. 628; Lat. 41-33-25 N, Long. 083-37-38 W; NW Ohio; Overlooks the Maumee River and the city of Maumee; Named for the War of 1812 hero Commander Oliver Hazard Perry.

PICKERINGTON, Village; Fairfield & Franklin Counties; Pop. 3,887 / 9,521; Zip Code 43147; Elev. 842; Lat. 39-53-03 N, Long. 082-45-13 W; 10 mi. NW of Lancaster; Named for Abraham Pickerington, who bought land here in 1811.

PIKETON, Village; Pike County; Pop. 1,726 / 1,875; Zip Code 45661; Elev. 578; Lat. 39-04-05 N, Long. 083-00-52 W; S Ohio; 10 mi. S of Waverley; Named for General Zebulon Montgomery Pike.

PIONEER, Village; Williams County; Pop. 1,127 / 1,302; Zip Code 43554; Elev. 874; Lat. 41-40-48 N, Long. 084-33-11 W; NW corner, Ohio; Just S of Michigan state line.

PIQUA, City; Miami County; Pop. 20,466 / 20,694; Zip Code 45358; Elev. 899; Lat. 40-08-41 N, Long. 084-14-33 W; W Ohio; Situated on the Great Miami River. Named for a tribe of the Shawnee who established themselves in this region after 1763. The name *Piqua* means "a man risen out of the ashes."

PLAIN CITY, Village; Madison and Union Counties; Pop. 2,114 / 2,601; Zip Code 43064; Elev. 935; Lat. 40-06-27 N, Long. 083-16-03 W; SW central Ohio. Laid out in 1818 by Issac Bigelow, named Plain City in 1851 because it is situated on Big Darby Plain.

PLEASANT HILL, Village; Miami County; Pop. 1,056 / 1,101; Zip Code 45359; Lat. 39-40-17 N, Long. 082-30-29 W; W central Ohio.

PLYMOUTH, Village; Huron and Richland Counties; Pop. 1,941 / 2,000; Zip Code 44865; Lat. 41-49-33 N, Long. 080-44-46 W; N central Ohio; On the W branch of the Huron River, named after the city in Massachusetts.

POMEROY, Village; Seat of Meigs County; Pop. 2,781 / 2,401; Zip Code 45769; Elev. 590; Elev. 39-01-39 N, Long. 082-02-02 W; SE Ohio, 40 mi. SE of Marietta; Named for Samuel Pomeroy, a Boston merchant who in 1804 purchased 262 acres of land on the site of the city.

PORT CLINTON, City; Seat of Ottawa County; Pop. 7,229 / 7,058; Elev. 580; Lat. 41-30-43 N, Long. 082-56-16 W; N Ohio; 30 mi. SE of Toledo. The town was named in honor of Dewitt Clinton, New York governor.

PORTSMOUTH, City; Seat of Scioto County; Pop. 25,993 / 22,996; Zip Code 45662; Elev. 527; Lat. 38-43-54 N, Long. 082-59-52 W; S Ohio; Was founded in 1803 by a Virginia land speculator, Major Henry Massie.

POWHATAN POINT, Village; Belmont County; Pop. 2,183 / 1,649; Zip Code 43942; Elev. 638; Lat. 39-51-36 N, Long. 080-48-56 W; E Ohio.

PROSPECT, Village; Marion County; Pop. 1,164 / 1,688; Zip Code 43342; Lat. 40-27-01 N, Long. 083-11-19 W; Central Ohio; Along the Scioto River, 12 mi. S of Marion.

RAVENNA, City; Seat of Portage County; Pop. 11,956 / 11,532; Zip Code 44266; Elev. 1,138; Lat. 41-09-27 N, Long. 081-14-32 W; NE Ohio; It was named for the Italian city after its settlement in 1799.

READING, City; Hamilton County; Pop. 12,819 / 11,218; Elev. 660; Lat. 40-50-06 N, Long. 081-01-53 W; SW Ohio; 10 mi. NE of the city in a residential area. Reading was given its present name in honor of Redingbo, William Penn's son-in-law.

REYNOLDSBURG, City; Franklin County; Pop. 20,513 / 30,282; Zip Code 43068; Lat. 39-57-17 N, Long. 082-48-44 W; Central Ohio; 10 mi. E of Columbus. The current name is in honor of John C. Reynolds.

RICHFIELD, Village; Summit County; Pop. 3,424 / 3,680; Zip Code 44286; Elev. 1,148; Lat. 41-44-23 N, Long. 081-38-18 W; NE Ohio.

RICHMOND HEIGHTS, City; Cuyahoga County; Pop. 10,090 / 9,461; Zip Code 44143; Lat. 41-33-10 N, Long. 081-30-37 W; NE Ohio; 15 mi. NE of Cleveland in a residential area just S of Lake Erie.

RICHWOOD, Village; Union County; Pop. 2,176 / 2,289; Zip Code 43344; Lat. 40-25-35 N, Long. 083-17-49 W; 15 mi. S of Marion in W central Ohio.

RIPLEY, Village; Brown County; Pop. 2,193 / 2,222; Zip Code 45167; Elev. 447; Lat. 38-44-44 N, Long. 083-50-42 W; SW Ohio. The current name is in honor of General Eleazer Wheelock Ripley.

RITTMAN, City; Wayne & Medina Counties; Pop. 6,066 / 6,617; Zip Code 44270; Elev. 979; Lat. 40-58-41 N, Long. 081-46-56 W; 40 mi. S of Cleveland.

ROCKY RIVER, City; Cuyahoga County; Pop. 21,070 / 24,165; Zip Code 44116; Lat. 41-28-32 N, Long. 081-50-22 W; NE Ohio; At the mouth of the Rocky River on Lake Erie, 10 mi. W of Cleveland city center.

ROSSFORD, City; Wood County; Pop. 5,983 / 5,861; Zip Code 43460; Elev. 630; Lat. 41-36-35 N, Long. 083-33-52 W; NW Ohio.

RUSSELLS POINT, Village; Logan County; Pop. 1,158 / 1,593; Zip Code 43348; Lat. 40-28-16 N, Long. 083-53-34 W; W Ohio; On S Indian Lake, 13 mi. NW of Bellefontaine.

SABINA, Village; Clinton County; Pop. 2,807 / 2,852; Zip Code 45169; Elev. 1,051; Lat. 39-29-19 N, Long. 083-38-13 W; SW Ohio; 11 mi. NE of Wilmington.

ST. CLAIRSVILLE, City; Seat of Belmont County; Pop. 5,425 / 4,736; Zip Code 43950; Elev. 1,260; Lat. 40-04-50 N, Long. 080-54-01 W; E Ohio; Named for Arthur St. Clair, first governor of the Northwest Territory.

ST. MARYS, City; Auglaize County; Pop. 8,368 / 8,572; Zip Code 45885; Elev. 926; Lat. 40-32-32 N, Long. 084-23-22 W; 80 mi. NW of Columbus in W Ohio; Named for an early church.

SALEM, City, Columbia County; Pop. 12,865 / 11,850; Zip code 44460; Elev. 1,230; Lat. 40-54-03 N, Long. 080-51-25 W; SW of Youngstown in E. Ohio; named after Salem, Massachusetts.

SALINEVILLE, Village; Columbia County; Pop. 1,637 / 1,358; Zip Code 43945; Elev. 950; Lat. 40-37-21 N, Long. 080-50-17 W; 18 mi. W of East Liverpool in E Ohio; Named for the salt springs in the area.

SPRINGFIELD, City; Clark County Seat; Pop. 72,263 / 65,154; Zip Code 455+; Elev. 980; Incorporated a town in 1801; city in 1850, Christened Springfield because of the spring water flowing down the hills that bordered the valley of Buck Creek.

STEUBENVILLE, City; Jefferson County Seat; Pop. 26,287 / 21,970; Zip Code 43952; Elev. 830. This town became a city in

1851 and was named after Fort Steuben, which was named after Baron von Steuben, a Prussian drill master and Revolutionary War supporter.

SUGARCREEK, Village; Tuscarawas County; Pop. 1,969 / 2,417; Zip Code 44681; Lat. 39-22-56 N, Long. 082-04-45 W; 8 mi. W of Dover in E Ohio; Along a branch of the Sugar Creek; Named in 1818 after the township.

SUNBURY, Village; Delaware County; Pop. 1,895 / 2,558; Zip Code 43074; Elev. 965; Lat. 40-14-33 N, Long. 082-51-33 W; Central Ohio; 12 mi. SE of Delaware city.

SWANTON, Village; Fulton County; Pop. 3,423 / 4,103; Zip Code 43558; Lat. 41-35-19 N, Long. 083-53-28 W; NW Ohio.

SYCAMORE, Village; Wyandot County; Pop. 1,057 / 897; Zip Code 44882; Elev. 826; Lat. 39-17-00 N, Long. 084-19-01 W; 14 mi. S of Tiffin in NW central Ohio. Named for the creek that runs through the place.

SYLVANIA, City; Lucas County; Pop. 15,556 / 19,274; Zip Code 43560; Lat. 41-43-08 N, Long. 083-42-47 W; W Ohio; 11 mi. NW of Toledo, just S of the Michigan state line.

TALLMADGE, City; Summit County; Pop. 15,238 / 15,962; Zip Code 44278; Elev. 1114; Lat. 41-06-05 N, Long. 081-26-31 W; NE central Ohio; Just E of Akron; Named in honor of founder Colonel Benjamin Tallmadge.

TIFFIN, City; Seat of Seneca County; Pop. 19,567 / 17,991; Zip Code 44883; Elev. 761; Lat. 41-06-52 N, Long. 083-10-41 W; N Ohio; On the Sandusky River. Named after Edward Tiffin, first governor of Ohio.

TILTONSVILLE, Village; Jefferson County; Pop. 1,755 / 1,293; Zip Code 43963; Lat. 40-10-00 N, Long. 080-42-00 W; E Ohio; On the Ohio River, about 20 mi. S of Steubenville. Named after John Tilton, who plotted out the town in 1806.

TIPP CITY, City; Miami County; Pop. 5,601 / 8,709; Zip Code 45371; Lat. 39-57-30 N, Long. 084-10-20 W; W central Ohio; Along the Miami River about 7 mi. S of Troy.

TOLEDO, City; Lucas County Seat; Pop. 354,558 / 307,946; Zip Code 436+; Elev. 587. The first permanent settlement here was named Port Lawrence, which, a year later, merged with Vistula, a river settlement to the north. The residents chose the name Toledo. Legend has it that it was suggested by Willard J. Daniels, a merchant, because it "is easy to pronounce, pleasant in sound, and there is no other city by that name on the American Continent."

TORONTO, City; Jefferson County; Pop. 6,869 / 5,455; Zip Code 43964; Elev. 695; Lat. 40-27-51 N, Long. 080-36-04 W; E Ohio; Toronto was named after the Canadian city.

TRENTON, City; Butler County; Pop. 6,375 / 8,988; Zip Code 45067; Elev. 653; Lat. 39-28-51 N, Long. 084-27-28 W; 35 mi. N of Cincinnati in SW Ohio; named after Trenton, New Jersey.

TROY, City; Seat of Miami County; Pop. 19,008 / 20,639; Zip Code 45373; Elev. 840; Lat. 40-02-22 N, Long. 084-12-12 W; W central Ohio. The city is named after Troy, New York.

TWINSBURG, City, Summit County; Pop. 7,627 / 15,516; Zip Code 44087; Elev. 985; Lat. 41-18-45 N, Long. 081-26-25 W; NE Ohio; Clusters about its six-acre village square, a gift of the Wilcox twins, Moses and Aaron, for whom the town was named.

UHRICHSVILLE, City; Tuscarawas County; Pop. 6,139 / 5,917; Zip Code 44683; Elev. 856; Lat. 40-23-35 N, Long. 081-20-48 W; E Ohio; Settled in 1804 by Michael Uhrich of Pennsylvania.

UNION, Village; Montgomery County; Pop. 5,109 / 6,221; Zip Code 45322; Lat. 39-53-52 N, Long. 084-18-23 W; SW central Ohio.

UNIVERSITY HEIGHTS, City; Cuyahoga County; Pop. 15,380 / 13,162; Zip Code 44118; Elev. 600; Lat. 41-29-52 N, Long. 081-32-15 W; 10 mi. W of Cleveland in NE Ohio.

UPPER ARLINGTON, City; Franklin County; Pop. 35,624 / 31,553; Zip Code 43221; Lat. 39-30-58 N, Long. 084-22-35 W; Central Ohio; Just NW of Columbus.

URBANA, City; Seat of Champaign County; Pop. 10,774 / 11,138; Zip Code 43078; Elev. 1,031; Lat. 40-06-30 N, Long. 083-45-09 W; W central Ohio.

UTICA, Village; Knox and Licking Counties; Pop. 2,235 / 2,223; Zip Code 43080; Elev. 961; Lat. 40-14-03 N, Long. 082-27-05 W; Central Ohio; On the Licking River, 14 mi. N of Newark. In 1815 first known as Wilmington. The name was changed to Utica for the city in New York.

VANDALIA, City; Montgomery County; Pop. 13,164 / 14,411; Zip Code 45377; Elev. 994; Lat. 39-53-26 N, Long. 084-11-56 W; SW Ohio; Settled in 1838, and when it appeared that the National Road would end here instead of at Vandalia, Illinois, the community took the name of the Illinois town.

VAN WERT, City; Seat of Van Wert County; Pop. 11,022 / 10,628; Zip Code 45891; Elev. 788; Lat. 40-52-10 N, Long. 084-35-03 W; NW Ohio; 70 mi. SW of Toledo. Named for Issac Van Wert, Revolutionary war hero. Spelling of name was modified later.

VERMILION, City; Erie and Lorain Counties; Pop. 11,011 / 11,190; Zip Code 44099; Elev. 664; Lat. 41-25-19 N, Long. 082-21-53 W; on Lake Erie in N Ohio just E of Sandusky; settled in 1808, lies along the winding Vermilion River.

VERSAILLES, Village; Darke County; Pop. 2,300 / 2,428; Zip Code 45380; Elev. 978; Lat. 40-13-21 N, Long. 084-29-04 W; W Ohio; 40 mi. NW of Dayton. Named after the French estate.

WADSWORTH, City; Medina County; Pop. 15,187 / 21,395; Zip Code 44281; Elev. 1,173; Lat. 41-01-32 N, Long. 081-43-48 W; NE central Ohio; 35 mi. S of Cleveland. Named after the township, which was named for Gen. Elijah Wadsworth, who was the largest landowner in the Western Reserve.

WAPAKONETA, City; Seat of Auglaize County; Pop. 8,379 / 9,709; Zip Code 45895; Elev. 898; Lat. 40-34-04 N, Long. 084-11-37 W; According to local history, Wapaghkonetta (the town's original name) was derived from the names of an Indian chief and his squaw, Wapaugh and Konetta.

WARREN, City; Trumbull County; Pop. 55,471 / 47,845; Zip Code 444+; Elev. 904; Lat. 41-14-15 N, Long. 080-49-07 W; 15 mi. NW of Youngstown in NE Ohio; Named for Moses Warren, a county surveyor, in 1798.

WASHINGTON COURT HOUSE, City; Seat of Fayette County; Pop. 12,648; Zip Code 43160; Elev. 973; Lat. 39-32-11 N, Long. 083-26-21 W; 30 mi. NW of Chillicothe in SW Ohio; Originally named Washington, the city adopted the larger name in 1810 after the first court of common pleas was held in the cabin of one of the town's resident's, John Devault.

WATERVILLE, Village; Lucas County; Pop. 3,885 / 4,954; Zip Code 43567; Elev. 654; Lat. 41-30-03 N, Long. 083-43-06 W; NW Ohio; Plotted in 1818 by John Pray.

WAUSEON, Village; Seat of Fulton County; Pop. 6,170 / 6,847; Zip Code 4356; Elev. 757; Lat. 41-32-57 N, Long. 084-08-30 W; W of Toledo in NW Ohio.

WAVERLY CITY, City; Seat of Pike County; Pop. 4,573 / 4,248; Zip Code 45690; Elev. 604; 15 mi. S of Chillicothe in S Ohio; founded in 1829 and named after the sir Walter Scott's novel, *Waverly*.

WESTON, Village; Wood County; Pop. 1,700 / 1,887; Zip Code 43569; Lat. 41-20-41 N, Long. 083-47-50 W; NW Ohio; 8 mi. W of Bowling Green; Residential area.

WEST SALEM, Village; Wayne County; Pop. 1,356 / 1,823; Zip Code 44287; Elev. 1,092; Lat. 40-58-17 N, Long. 082-06-36 W; NE central Ohio; Laid out in 1834 by the Rickel brothers.

WEST UNION, Village; Seat of Adams County; Pop. 2,790 / 3,610; Zip Code 45693; Elev. 967; Lat. 38-47-40 N, Long. 083-32-43 W; 55 mi. SE of Cincinnati; 10 mi. N of Kentucky state line in S Ohio.

WHITEHALL, City; Franklin County; Pop. 21,295 / 19,240; Zip Code 43213; Central Ohio; 6 mi. E of Columbus, over-looking the city on Big Walnut Creek; Named after the famous English estate.

WHITEHOUSE, Village; Lucas County; Pop. 2,132 / 2,811; Zip Code 43571; NW Ohio; 20 mi. SW of Toledo in a section outside of the city area.

WICKLIFFE, City; Lake County; Pop. 16,800 / 13,742; Zip Code 44092; 15 NE of Cleveland, just S of the Lake Erie shoreline.

WILLARD, City; Huron County; Pop. 5,666 / 6,641; Zip Code 44890; N central Ohio; 20 mi. N of Mansfield.

WILLIAMSBURG, Village; Clermont County; Pop. 1,948 / 3,162; Zip Code 45176; SW Ohio; On the E Fork of the Miami River, 25 mi. E of Cincinnati. Named for the town in Virginia.

WILLOUGHBY, City; Lake County; Pop. 19,290 / 21,312; Zip Code 44094; Elev. 649; 20 mi. NE of Cleveland in NE Ohio. Originally called Chagrin, this city was named for an instructor in the Willoughby Medical College.

WILLOWICK, City; Lake County; Pop. 17,758 / 14,233; Zip Code 44094; 10 mi. NE of Cleveland, in a suburban area near Willoughby on Lake Erie in NE Ohio; Residential.

WILMINGTON, City; Seat of Clinton County; Pop. 10,442 / 11,961; Zip Code 45177; Elev. 1,033; Lat. 39-26-43 N, Long. 083-49-43 W; 30 mi. SE of Dayton; Founded in 1810. Named after Wilmington, N.C. and originally known as Clinton.

WINCHESTER, Village; Adams County; Pop. 1,086 / 997; Zip Code 45697; Lat. 38-56-30 N, Long. 083-39-03 W; S Ohio; 45 mi. E of Cincinnati.

WOODSFIELD, Village; Seat of Monroe County; Pop. 3,127 / 2,912; Zip Code 43793; Elev. 1213; Lat. 39-45-45 N, Long. 081-06-56 W; 30 mi. NE of Marietta in SE Ohio; Archibald Woods founded the town in 1815.

WOODVILLE, Village; Sandusky County; Pop. 2,053 / 2,096; Zip Code 43469; Lat. 39-15-18 N, Long. 084-00-40 W; N Ohio; 25 mi. SE of Toledo. Named for the man who laid the town out in 1838, Amos Wood.

WOOSTER, City; Seat of Wayne County; Pop. 19,273 / 24,308; Zip Code 44691; Elev. 910; Lat. 40-48-18 N, Long. 081-56-07 W; NE central Ohio. Named for the Revolutionary War general, David Wooster.

WORTHINGTON, City; Franklin County; Pop. 14,956 / 14,080; Zip Code 43085; Elev. 908; Lat. 40-05-35 N, Long. 083-01-05 W; Central Ohio; 10 mi. N of Columbus; Named Worthington in 1803 after a parish in Connecticut.

WYOMING, City; Hamilton County; Pop. 8,247 / 8,161; Zip Code (with Cincinnati); Lat. 39-13-52 N, Long. 084-27-57 W; SW Ohio; 10 mi. N of Cincinnati in a residential area; Named for the county in Pennsylvania.

XENIA, Seat of Greene County; Pop. 24,712 / 25,598; Zip Code 45385; Elev. 925; Lat. 39-41-05 N, Long. 083-55-47 W; 15 mi. SE of Dayton and 3 mi. E of the Little Miami River in SW Ohio.

YELLOW SPRINGS, Village; Greene County; Pop. 4,074 / 4,192; Zip Code 45387; Elev. 974; Lat. 39-48-23 N, Long. 083-53-13 W; SW Ohio; 9 mi. S of Springfield; It was founded in 1804 and took its name from the yellow discharges of the neighboring iron springs whose health-giving waters attracted visitors here for several decades.

YORKVILLE, Village; Belmont and Jefferson Counties; Pop. 1,443 / 1,063; Zip Code 43971; Elev. 669; Lat. 40-09-16 N, Long. 080-42-38 W; E Ohio; Named for its early settlers who came from York, Pennsylvania.

YOUNGSTOWN, City; Seat of Mahoning County; Pop. 115,429 / 82,757; Zip Code 445+; Elev. 861; Lat. 41-05-59 N, Long. 080-38-59 W; On Mahoning river 45 mi. E of Akron in NE Ohio. Named after pioneer John Young of Whitestown, New York and his party of settlers, who arrived in 1797.

ZANESVILLE, City; Seat of Muskingum County; Pop. 28,600 / 26,989; Zip Code 43701; Lat. 39-56-25 N, Long. 082-00-48 W; On Muskingum river 50 mi. E of Columbus in SE central Ohio; The land once belonged to Issac Zane, about whom center many of the events in early Ohio history.

OKLAHOMA
The Sooner State

End of the Trail Statue-National Cowboy Hall of Fame

Oklahoma City skyline

GOVERNOR
Frank Keating

Blue Bell Saloon
Guthrie

Downtown Tulsa skyline

Will Rogers Museum
Clare more

Route 66 Museum
Clinton

INTRODUCTION

Oklahoma is a southern state in the western south central region of the United States. It is bordered on the north by Colorado and Kansas; on the south by the Red River and Texas; on the east by Mississippi and Arkansas; and on the west by Texas and New Mexico.

The State ranks twentieth in area among the fifty states. Its total area is 69,903 square miles, with a land area of 68,679 square miles and inland water area of 1,224 square miles.

Oklahoma is a transitional state, and occupies an area where the Coastal Plain, Interior Highlands, and Central Lowland come together. Cotton and corn grow in the more moist and warm region of the southeast; in the drier, cooler northwest, wheat is the primary crop. Along the Oklahoma Panhandle is a dry, elevated strip extending west along the top of Texas; this High Plains terrain is best for grazing. Coal, gas, and oil deposits are plentiful all over the State.

In the great Oklahoma Land Rush of April 22, 1889, some 10,000 settlers raced to stake their claims; however, they were beaten to the punch by the "Sooners" (defined as a person who settled on land in the early West before its official opening to settlement in order to gain prior claim allowed by law to the first settler after official opening) who sneaked ahead and took the best land.

Oklahoma was admitted into the Union on November 16, 1907; it was the 46th state to become part of the United States.

STATE NAME

The bill creating the Territory of Oklahoma was signed on May 2, 1890. President Theodore Roosevelt issued a proclamation on November 16, 1907 that admitted Oklahoma as a State in the Union. Most historians agree that the name Oklahoma is derived from the two Choctaw words, *ukla*, signifying "person," and *huma* meaning "red;" consequently the name signifies "red people."

The word Oklahoma first appeared in the 1866 Choctaw-Chickasaw Treaty. The land that later became the State of Oklahoma was first designated as the "Indian Territory," and this name was used as the name of the division admitted as a territory; the name of Oklahoma was afterwards employed for the Territory; finally the name was used for the State of Oklahoma.

Joseph B. Thoburn, former Curator of the Oklahoma Historical Society, explained that he obtained the facts about the naming of the territory from a friend and neighbor of the Reverend Allen Wright. According to the story, Wright represented the Choctaws in the proceedings before Congress, which officially created the Indian Territory. During the proceedings "the Commissioner of Indian Affairs rather abruptly asked: 'What would you call your territory?' To this inquiry, Wright impulsively replied 'Oklahoma!' Whereas, several of the Cherokee delegates were said to have shown signs of displeasure" because they considered themselves elder brothers and should have been entitled to be heard first. The matter was then dropped, but "Wright wrote the name 'Territory of Oklahoma' into the Choctaw-Chickasaw treaty with the United States Government as that of the 'proposed new territory.'"

When the bill for organization of the Indian Territory came up before the Forty-first Congress, "the name 'Oklahoma' is said to have been suggested to the House Committee on Indian Affairs by Col. Elias C. Boudinot, of the Cherokee Nation, out of deference to the clause in the Choctaw-Chickasaw Treaty of 1866 which specified that the proposed intertribal commonwealth should be called 'The Territory of Oklahoma.'"

STATE NICKNAMES

Sobriquets applied to Oklahoma include the Boomer's Paradise and the Sooner State. Both of these nicknames derive from the opening of the Oklahoma Territory to settlement in 1889.

Oklahoma has been nicknamed the Boomer's Paradise because when President Harrison opened up the territory to settlement on April 22, 1889, great processions of "boomers" poured into the new territory.

The sobriquet the Sooner State was given to Oklahoma from the fact that "when the lands of Oklahoma were opened to settlement at a given hour, those who did not await the appointed time, but who slipped in clandestinely ahead of time, were dubbed 'sooners' because they did not wait as required by law, but tried to gain an unfair advantage by entering the forbidden precincts too soon.

THE GREAT SEAL

Oklahoma's Constitution of 1906 specifies that the State seal shall be designed as follows:

"In the center shall be a five pointed star, with one ray directed upward. The center of the star shall contain the central device of the seal of the Territory of Oklahoma, including the words, 'Labor Omnia Vincit.' The upper left hand ray shall contain the symbol of the ancient seal of the Cherokee Nation, namely: A seven pointed star partially surrounded by a wreath of oak leaves. The ray directed upward shall contain the symbol of the ancient seal of the Chickasaw Nation, namely: An Indian warrior standing upright with a bow and shield. The lower left hand ray shall contain the symbol of the ancient seal of the Creek Nation, namely: A sheaf of wheat and a plow. The upper right hand ray shall contain the symbol of the ancient seal of the Choctaw Nation, namely: A tomahawk, bow, and three crossed arrows. The lower right hand ray shall contain the symbol of the ancient seal of the Seminole Nation, namely: A village with houses and a factory beside a lake upon which an Indian is paddling a canoe. Surrounding the central star and grouped between its rays shall be forty-five small stars, divided into five clusters of nine stars each, representing the forty-five states of the Union, to which the forty-sixth is now added. In a circular band surrounding the whole device shall be inscribed, 'GREAT SEAL OF THE STATE OF OKLAHOMA 1907.' The impression of the seal shows no insignia on the lower right band ray."

STATE FLAG

The Oklahoma State flag was adopted on April 2, 1925. In 1941, the law was amended to add the name of the State to the flag. The law reads as follows:

"The banner, or flag, of the design prescribed by Senate Concurrent Resolution No. 25, Third Legislature of the State of Oklahoma shall be, and it hereby is superseded and replaced by one of the following design, to-wit:

"A sky blue field with a circular rawhide shield of an American Indian Warrior, decorated with six painted crosses on the face thereof; the lower half of the shield to be fringed with seven pendant eagle feathers and superimposed upon the face of the shield a calumet or peace pipe, crossed at right angles by an olive branch, as illustrated by the design accompanying this resolution, and underneath said shield or design in white letters shall be placed the word 'Oklahoma,' and the same is hereby adopted as the official flag and banner of the State of Oklahoma."

The same section describing the flag also set out the official salute to the flag as follows:

"I salute the flag of the state of Oklahoma: Its symbols of peace unite all people." This salute was adopted in 1982.

In 1957, the State Legislature also approved a governor's flag as follows:

"The flag of the Governor of the State of Oklahoma shall be forest green, bearing on each side the following: the Great Seal of the State of Oklahoma, centered, surrounded by five equidistant white stars with one of the stars placed directly above the Great Seal; and the flag to be edged with golden fringe."

STATE MOTTO

The State motto of Oklahoma is *Labor Omnia Vincit*, meaning "Labor conquers all things." The motto was adopted in 1906 as part of the State seal.

The motto is a classical quotation from Virgil; it speaks to the virtue of hard work in the settlement and growth of the State.

STATE BIRD

The scissor-tailed flycatcher, *Muscivora forticata*, was designated as the State bird of Oklahoma by joint resolution of the Legislature in 1951. The adoption of this bird was endorsed by numerous ornithologists, biologists, and wildlife societies in the State.

In the joint resolution, it was noted that the flycatcher's nesting range is centered in Oklahoma, and because its diet consists of harmful and useless insects, the flycatcher was believed to be of great economic value.

The range of the scissor-tailed flycatcher is Texas to Kansas, and less commonly in Missouri, Arkansas, and Louisiana; it migrates to Central America and Mexico. The total length of the bird is eleven to thirteen inches, with a tail length of six to nine inches. The head of the male is clear pale gray with a small, concealed, orange-red patch on the center of the crown. The back is light gray, strongly suffused with a pink wine color. Upper tail feathers are black or dusky, margined with gray. The six middle tail feathers are black. The three outermost tail feathers on each side are white, strongly tinged with salmon pink, terminally black. The tail is deeply forked, especially the male lateral tail feathers, which are more than twice as tong as the middle pair and longer than the wing. The cheek, chin, and throat are white, shading into gray on the breast. The sides and flanks are salmon to red in color. A concealed patch of bright orange-red is on either side of the breast.

The female is similar to the male, but duller in color, with breast patches more restricted and orange; the concealed crown spot is often missing.

The flycatcher likes open terrain; it perches on telephone poles and wires. Its diet consists primarily of noxious insects such as beetles, wasps, and bees, although it also favors crickets and grasshoppers. Ironically, the flycatcher is not fond of flies. The bird is extremely energetic when provoked or frightened. When it builds its nest, it often leaves strings and twine hanging from it in a sloppy manner. Eggs are creamy white in color, spotted with brown and gray.

STATE FLOWER

The State floral emblem of Oklahoma is the mistletoe, (*Phoradendron serotinum*). It was adopted by the Territorial Legislature on February 11, 1893. There are more than 100 American species in the mistletoe family. A shrub, the mistletoe has the dubious distinction of being a tree parasite.

STATE TREE

The Oklahoma Legislature, on March 30, 1937, adopted the redbud tree (*Cercis canadensis*) as the official State tree. The resolution is as follows:

"Be it Resolved by the Senate and the House of Representatives of the Sixteenth Legislature of the State of Oklahoma:

"Whereas, In the beginning of this great commonwealth, when the sturdy and hardy pioneers thereof trekked across its rolling hills and plains, one of the first sights to greet them, spread out in a glorious panorama, was the redbud tree—a tree, that as it arose in the Spring from the verdant fields, was emblematic of the eternal renewal of all life; a tree that in its beauty renewed the worn spirit and gave hope to the tired heart of a people seeking homes in a new land, and,

"Whereas, It is the will of this Legislature that the adoption of the redbud tree as the official State tree of the State of Oklahoma would be small, but fitting tribute, to the part it has played in, and the beauty it has lent to, the lives of the people of this State.

"Now, Therefore, be it Resolved by the Senate of the State of Oklahoma and the House of Representatives of the State of Oklahoma.

"That the redbud tree be adopted and the same be made the official tree of this State."

The redbud tree is also known as the Judas tree, red Judas tree, Canadian Judas tree, and salad-tree. It is native to the north central and eastern part of the United States.

The redbud is a small tree with branches of ten to fifteen feet from the ground. It forms a narrow and erect or a spreading, flattened, or rounded head. The ornamental tree flowers in late February to April with a profusion of small, light pink to purple blossoms.

THE STATE SONG

In 1953, the Oklahoma Legislature declared the song "Oklahoma," composed and written by Richard Rogers and Oscar Hammerstein, as the official State song. The 1953 act repealed a 1935 act that had designated "Oklahoma (A Toast)" by Harriet Parker Camden as the official song of the State.

STATE LICENSE PLATE

The State of Oklahoma began to issue license plates in 1915. Until 1943, annual plates were issued. Because of the metal shortage during the World War II effort, the 1943 plate was actually a window sticker plate. In 1947, a metal validation tab replaced a new plate. However, annual plates were still being issued until 1980, when the State began to issue multi year plates. The slogan "Oklahoma is OK" appeared on all plates until the 1989 issue, which changed the slogan slightly to read "OK!" in buckskin color beneath the word "Oklahoma" in black across the top.

License plates in Oklahoma have experienced some controversy. An attempt at using school colors—in 1968, the orange black of Oklahoma State, and in 1969, the red and white of the University of Oklahoma—resulted in a 1970 law that prohibited school colors from being used on State plates. The official colors of the State of green and white then became the standard.

Oklahoma's 1989 issue did not invalidate the two previous issues. The plate has green lettering on a white background. Centered between the numerals is the emblem that appears on the State flag.

Oklahoma's current license plate was first issued in 1995. The plate has dark lettering over a green background. Centered between the numerals remains the emblem that appears on the State flag. Across the top, the plate spells out "OKLAHOMA" in all capital letters; across the bottom the plate displays "NATIVE AMERICA" in all capital letters.

STATE POSTAGE STAMP

On June 14, 1957, a three-cent stamp was issued in Oklahoma City to commemorate the State's fiftieth anniversary of statehood. The stamp was designed by William K. Schrage and engraved by M.D. Fenton and G.L. Huber.

The stamp carries the theme of "Arrows to Atoms," progressively depicted in symbols by the arrow that pierces the orbital emblem above the deep blue outline of a map of Oklahoma. A total of 102,219,500 of the stamp were printed.

OTHER STATE DESIGNATIONS

Across the years, the Legislature of Oklahoma has designated a number of additional symbols to recognize the State. Included are the State colors (1915) as green and white; the State animal (1972) as the American buffalo; the State fish (1974) as the white bass; the State reptile (1969) as the collared lizard; and the State rock (1968) as the barite rose.

THE CAPITOL BUILDING

The capitol of the State is located in Oklahoma City. The structure was designed by the firm of Layton-Smith. It is modern classic in style, based on Greek and Roman architecture. Construction of the capitol began in 1914 and was completed in 1917.

The outside walls are built of Indiana limestone with a base of pink and black granite. Built in the form of a huge cross, the statehouse is 480 feet east to west, and 380 feet north to south. There are five main floors, excluding the basement, and the dome and legislative chambers are two stories in height. The facade of the exterior is ornamented with smooth columns and Corinthian capitals. The total cost for building the capitol was thirty-five million dollars. A seal was inlaid in the rotunda in 1966 at a cost of 4,000 dollars.

OTHER FACTS ABOUT OKLAHOMA

Total area: 69,956 square miles
Land area: 68,655 square miles
Water area: 1,301 square miles
Average elevation: 1,300 feet
Highest point: Black Mesa, 4,973 feet
Lowest point: Little River, 289 feet
Highest temperature: 120 degrees Fahrenheit
Lowest temperature: -27 degrees Fahrenheit
Population in 1990: 3,145,585
Population density in 1990: 45.80 persons per square mile
Population 1980-1990: +4.0 percent change
Population projected for year 2000: 3,376,000
African American population in 1990: 233,801
Hispanic American population in 1990: 86,160
Native American population in 1990: 252,420
European American population in 1990: 2,583,512
Capital: Oklahoma City
Admitted to Union: November 16, 1907
Order of Statehood: 46
Electoral votes: 8

CHRONOLOGY

1541 Francisco Vasquez de Coronado crosses western Oklahoma in search of golden city of Quivira, claims land for Spain but makes no permanent settlement.
– Hernando de Soto explores along present eastern border of Oklahoma.

1650 Don Diego de Castillo spends six months in Wichita Mountains prospecting for gold and silver.

1682 Rene Robert Cavelier, Sieur de la Salle, claims for King of France all lands drained by Mississippi River (including Oklahoma) under name of Louisiana.

1719 Bernard de la Harpe crosses southeastern Oklahoma from Red River to vicinity of present Muskogee.
– Charles Claude du Tisne visits Pawnee villages near present site of Chelsea.

1762 Louisiana (including Oklahoma) is ceded to Spain by France.

1800 Louisiana is retro-ceded to France by Spain.

1802 United States makes compact with Georgia to remove Creeks and Cherokees as soon as it can be done peaceably and on favorable terms.

– Pierre Chouteau induces some of Osages to remove from Missouri to northeastern Oklahoma and opens up a profitable trade with them.

1803 United States purchases Louisiana from France. President Thomas Jefferson draws up a proposal for exchanging land occupied by Indians in eastern states for "equivalent portions" in Louisiana.

1804 All of Louisiana north of thirty-third parallel is designated as District of Louisiana and placed under the administration of Indiana Territory; William Henry Harrison thus becomes first American governor of Oklahoma.

1805 District of Louisiana is organized as Territory of Louisiana with seat of government at St. Louis.

1806 Lieutenant James B. Wilkinson descends Arkansas River, crossing northeastern Oklahoma.

1808 Several Cherokee chiefs and headmen inform President Jefferson that a portion of tribe wishes to emigrate to West.

1812 Territory of Louisiana is organized as Territory of Missouri.
– George C. Sibley, United States Indian agent, explores Great Salt Plains near present Cherokee.

1817 Cherokees sign first removal treaty, obtaining land in the present stale of Arkansas; movement of one-third of tribe to new location begins.
– Fort Smith is established on present border of Oklahoma to protect immigrant Indians.

1819 That portion of the Territory of Missouri south of 36 degrees 30' is organized as Territory of Arkansas, including all of Oklahoma except a strip along the present northern boundary.
– Thomas Nuttall, English naturalist, visits Oklahoma, studies flora and fauna.
– Boundary between United States and Spanish possessions is fixed at Red River and one-hundredth meridian, thus establishing southern and western limits of Oklahoma.

1820 Choctaws purchase area south of Canadian and Arkansas rivers; they are first eastern Indian tribe to acquire land in Oklahoma, but few remove to new location.
– Arkansas legislature passes act creating Miller County in southeastern Oklahoma and establishing the Miller Courthouse, first court within present State.

1821 Rev. Epaphras Chapman founds Union Mission on Grand River among Osages; it is first Protestant mission in Oklahoma.
– Sequoyah completes Cherokee alphabet.

1824 First post office in Oklahoma opens at Miller Courthouse.
– Fort Gibson—first fort in Oklahoma—is established on Grand River.
– Fort Towson is established on Red River near mouth of Kiamichi.

1825 Treaty with Choctaws fixes present eastern boundary of Oklahoma from Fort Smith to Red River.

1826 Creeks purchase tract of land in Oklahoma, and a portion of tribe prepares to emigrate.
– Military road is constructed from Fort Gibson to Fort Smith; it is first road established in Oklahoma.

1828 First immigrant Creeks arrive in Oklahoma and begin to lay out farms in Arkansas valley.
– Cherokees in Arkansas exchange their land for tract in Oklahoma; boundary established by this treaty fixes remainder of present eastern boundary of State.

1829 Arkansas Cherokees begin removal to Oklahoma; Sequoyah settles in present Sequoyah County.
– Dwight Mission, established by Presbyterians for Arkansas Cherokees, is removed to Oklahoma.
– Sam Houston, after resigning as governor of Tennessee, settles near Fort Gibson and is granted full citizenship rights by the Cherokee Council.
– President Andrew Jackson, in his message to Congress, advises removal of all Indians remaining in the East.

1830 Indian Removal Act is passed by Congress.
– Choctaws cede remainder of their land in Mississippi and prepare to remove to Oklahoma; main removals take place during succeeding three years.
– Presbyterian church is organized among Creeks in Arkansas Valley.

1832 Cherokee Council provides for opening of five schools; it is first school law enacted in the present state of Oklahoma.
– Washington Irving accompanies United States rangers on expedition from Fort Gibson to present site of Norman, recording his experiences in *A Tour on the Prairies*.
– Creeks cede remainder of their land in the East, thus paving the way for removal of succeeding four years.
– Presbyterian church is organized among immigrant Choctaws at Wheelock, and a Baptist church among the Creeks.

1833 Seminoles are tricked into signing removal treaty, which is followed by long and exhausting Seminole War and final colonization of the tribe in Oklahoma.

1834 United States Commissioners draw up territorial form of government for immigrant Indians, first of many futile attempts to create Indian state of Oklahoma.
– Leavenworth-Dodge Expedition from Fort Gibson visits southwestern Oklahoma, establishes friendly relations with tribes.

1835 Comanche and Wichita Indians enter into treaty relations with United States at council near present site of Lexington.
– Criminal jurisdiction of federal courts of Arkansas is extended over Oklahoma.
– Cherokees remaining in East cede their land to United States, thus paving way for removals of succeeding three years.
– Samuel A. Worcester installs printing press at Union Mission and publishes first book printed in Oklahoma.

1837 Chickasaws surrender their lands in East and begin their removal to Oklahoma.

1838 Choctaws complete a council house of hewn logs near present site of Tuskahoma, the first capitol built in Oklahoma.

1839 Newly arrived Cherokees and "Old Settler Cherokees" adopt new constitution and establish council grounds at Tahlequah.

1842 Fort Washita is established to protect Chickasaw settlements from wild tribes of Southwest.
– Choctaw congregation at Wheelock builds stone church, which still stands as oldest church building in Oklahoma.

1843 Great council of eighteen Indian tribes is held at Tahlequah, and a code of intertribal law drawn up and adopted by Cherokees, Creeks, and Osages.

1844 *Cherokee Messenge*, first newspaper published in Oklahoma, is issued at Baptist missionary station north of present Westville; it is followed a month later by *The Cherokee Advocate*, published at Tahlequah.
– First cotton gin in Cherokee Nation (probably first in Oklahoma) is constructed on Arkansas, fifteen miles above Fort Smith.

1849 First Masonic Lodge established by Indian tribe is organized at Tahlequah.
– Hordes of California gold-seekers follow well-defined trail across Oklahoma.

1850 Texas relinquishes land north of 36 degrees 30', thus forming southern boundary of Oklahoma Panhandle.

1851 Fort Arbuckle is established.

1852 Tahlequah is incorporated under Cherokee law; it is the first incorporated town in Oklahoma.

1854 Kansas-Nebraska Act defines southern boundary of Kansas at 37 degrees, thus fixing northern boundary of Oklahoma.

1856 Seminoles separate from Creeks and form their own government.
– Chickasaws set up tribal government, adopt constitution, and establish Tishomingo as their capital.

1858 Butterfield stage and mail route is laid out, crossing Oklahoma from Fort Smith west and south to Red River.

1859 Intertribal law code is drawn up by the Five Civilized Tribes (Cherokees, Choctaws, Chickasaws, Creeks, and Seminoles) at North Fork Town.
– Fort Cobb is established on western frontier of civilized Indian settlement.

1860 Choctaws adopt constitution under which their government functions until end of tribal period.

1861 Civil War begins.
– United States abandons forts in Oklahoma; most of Indian tribes align with Confederates; thousands of Union Indians flee to Kansas.

1862 Union military expedition from Kansas penetrates to Fort Gibson.

1863 Union forces defeat Confederates at Honey Springs; it is most important battle fought in Oklahoma during Civil War.

1865 Confederate Indians surrender to Union forces more than two months after Appomattox; United States officials hold council with Indians, lay down terms for resumption of treaty relations.

1866 Five Civilized Tribes sign treaties with United States freeing their slaves, ceding western half of Oklahoma for settlement of other Indians, and agreeing to tentative intertribal organization.
– The name Oklahoma is first suggested by Allen Wright, member of Choctaw treaty delegation.
– Congress grants franchises for construction of first two railroads across Oklahoma.

1867 United States makes first of a series of treaties, assigning reservations to Indian tribes in ceded territory.
– Creeks adopt their final constitution.

1869 Fort Sill is established as base of operations against Plains Indians.

1870 Construction is started on Missouri-Kansas-Texas Railroad, first to enter the Oklahoma area.
– Federal government begins survey of Chickasaw district, establishing initial point from which all of Oklahoma except Panhandle is eventually surveyed.
– First meeting of intertribal council is convened at Okmulgee.

1872 First coal mining on commercial scale begins at McAlester in Choctaw Nation.

1874 Fort Reno is established.

1875 Resistance of Plains Indians to European encroachment is finally crushed.
– Intertribal council at Okmulgee holds last session.

1876 Last buffalo herd is reported in Oklahoma.

1879 First telephone in Oklahoma is set up, connecting Fort Sill and Fort Reno.
– "Boomers" begin their attempts to settle on "Oklahoma Lands."
– Will Rogers is born in the Cherokee Nation near Oologah.
– Population of Indian Territory is estimated at 81,381; this includes Indians, a few white residents, and former slaves of Indians.

1882 Isparhecher begins rebellion against the Creek government known as Green Peach War.
– Atlantic and Pacific Railroad establishes station in Creek Nation at place called "Tulsey Town" by Indians.

1883 Isparhecher faction makes peace with constitutional Creek government.
– Cherokee Strip Live Stock Association leases "Outlet" from Cherokee Nation.

1884 Company of Choctaw citizens drills for oil near Atoka.

1887 Congress passes Dawes Act, providing for breaking up Indian reservations into individual allotments and opening surplus land to white settlement.

1889 First federal court in Oklahoma is established in Muskogee.
– Oklahoma's first producing oil well is drilled near Chelsea.
– First Run opens area in Oklahoma to European settlement; Oklahoma City, Guthrie, Norman, and other cities and towns are established.

1890 Congress creates Territorial government for settlers in "Oklahoma Lands."
– Guthrie becomes capital.
– George W. Steele is appointed governor.
– First Territorial Legislature adopts code of laws, establishes school system.
– Panhandle is joined to Territory of Oklahoma.
– First federal census shows population of 78,475 in Oklahoma Territory and 180,182 in area of Five Civilized Tribes.

1891 First statehood convention is held in Oklahoma City.
– First Territorial college (later Central State College) opens at Edmond.
– Oklahoma Agricultural and Mechanical College opens at Stillwater.
– Sac and Fox, Iowa, Shawnee, and Potawatomi reservations are opened for settlement, adding two new counties.

1892 University of Oklahoma opens at Norman.
– Cheyenne and Arapaho country is opened for settlement, adding six new counties.

1893 Dawes Commission is created for purpose of liquidating affairs of Five Civilized Tribes.
– Oklahoma Historical Society is founded at Kingfisher.
– Cherokee Outlet is opened to white settlement by greatest of all the settlement runs in Oklahoma.

1896 Greer County is awarded to United States by Supreme Court decision and joined to Territory of Oklahoma.

1897 Choctaws, Chickasaws, and Seminoles make agreements with Dawes Commission.

1898 Congress passes Curtis Act, providing for compulsory liquidation of Five Civilized Tribes.
– Many Oklahoma and Indian Territory frontiersmen serve with Roosevelt's Rough Riders in Spanish-American War.

1899 United States takes over schools, Dawes Commission starts allotting the lands, and first town sites are platted for Five Civilized Tribes.

1900 Federal census shows population of 398,331 in Territory of Oklahoma, and 392,060 in Five Civilized Tribes area.
– First course in geology is taught at University of Oklahoma.

1901 Kiowa-Comanche and Wichita reservations are opened to settlement, the last opening in Oklahoma.
– Tulsa becomes oil center.
– Red Fork-Tulsa Oilfield opens.

– Republican William M. Jenkins becomes Governor.
– William Grimes (R) serves as acting Governor.

1905 Inhabitants of Five Tribes area hold Convention, draw up constitution for a state to be named Sequoyah.
– Glenn Oil Pool is discovered.
– Republican Thomas B. Ferguson is elected as Governor.

1906 Congress passes Enabling Act, providing statehood for Oklahoma; constitutional convention meets at Guthrie.
– Republican Frank Frantz is Governor.

1907 November 16. Oklahoma is admitted to Union as forty-sixth state.
– Special federal census enumerates population of 1,414,177 for new State.
– First election reveals overwhelming Democratic majority.
– Democrat Charles N. Haskell, first governor, is inaugurated at Guthrie.

1910 Population is 1,657,155.
– State capital is moved from Guthrie to Oklahoma City.

1911 State legislature provides for placing statue of Sequoyah in Statuary Hall in national Capitol.
– Democrat Lee Cruce is inaugurated governor.

1912 Cushing Oil Pool is discovered.

1913 Healdton Oil Field is discovered.

1915 Robert L. Williams is inaugurated as governor.

1916 Oklahoma National Guard sees service on Mexican Border.

1917 World War I; United States declares war on Germany.
In first draft, Oklahoma registers 173,744.
– Green Corn Rebellion breaks out when farmers and Indians protest draft.

1918 End of World War I, for which Oklahoma has furnished 88,496 men in uniform and purchased $116,368,045 worth of Liberty Bonds.

1919 J.B.A. Robertson is inaugurated governor of Oklahoma.

1920 For the first time in its history, Oklahoma votes Republican.
– Oil fields in Osage County begin spectacular production. Population is 2,028,283.

1923 Democrat John C. Walton begins serving as Governor; after impeachment charges are brought against him, he is suspended and Lieutenant Governor Martin E. Trapp becomes acting Governor.

1926 Greater Seminole Oil Field is developed, bringing serious over-production in oil industry.

1927 Democrat Henry S. Johnston becomes Governor.

1928 Oklahoma City Oil Field is opened.

1929 Governor Johnston is impeached and removed from office; William J. Holloway becomes governor.

1930 Population is 2,396,040.

1931 William H. ("Alfalfa Bill") Murray is inaugurated as governor.
– Governor Murray closes Oklahoma oil wells in effort to stabilize prices.
– Wiley Post, noted Oklahoma air pilot, completes round-the-world flight of 16,474 miles in 8 days, 15 hours, 51 minutes.

1934-35 Wheat and cotton crops ruined by severe drought.
– Farmers abandon farms and begin migration to California.
– Democrat Earnest W. Marland is Governor.

1935 E.W. Marland is inaugurated as governor.
– Will Rogers and Wiley Post die in airplane crash in Alaska.

1937 Construction begins on $22,750,000 Grand River Dam in eastern Oklahoma.

1939 Leon C. ("Red") Phillips becomes governor.

1940 Population is 2,336,434, loss of 59,606 since census of 1930.

1941-1945 Thousands enter armed forces for World War II effort.
– Large amounts of State's petroleum and agricultural products benefit Allied forces.

1943 Robert S. Kerr becomes governor, the first born in Oklahoma.

1944 Oklahoma votes for Franklin D. Roosevelt for fourth term as President.

1945 More than two hundred thousand Oklahomans are in armed services of United States.

1947 Roy J. Turner begins term as governor.
– Legislature authorizes turnpike connecting Oklahoma City with Tulsa.
– Reforms are initiated by Governor Roy Turner that will remove institutions from politics.

1948 Oklahoma votes for Harry S. Truman for President over Thomas F. Dewey.
– United States Supreme Court rules that legal education opportunities for African Americans in State must be equal to those for European Americans.

1949 Oklahoma City and Tulsa become first two cities in State to begin television broadcasting: WKY-TV in former, and KOTV in latter.

1950 Population is 2,233,351.

1951 Johnston Murray, son of "Alfalfa Bill," is inaugurated as governor.

1952 Oklahoma casts vote for Dwight D. Eisenhower over Adlai E. Stevenson, a total vote of 948,984, largest in State's history.
– Oklahoma is declared disaster area by President Harry S. Truman due to prolonged severe drought.

1953 Turner Turnpike from Oklahoma City to Tulsa is completed.

1955 Raymond Gary becomes governor.
– Racial segregation in Oklahoma schools to be abandoned.
– Oklahoma City selected as site of National Cowboy Hall of Fame.
– Severe tornadoes cause damage.

1956 Oklahoma again votes for Eisenhower over Stevenson.

1959 For first time in 51 years, Oklahoma voters legalize beer sales; local option and mixed drinks are rejected.
– J. Howard Edmondson (D) is Governor.

1962 A 7 million-dollar bond issue for University of Oklahoma Medical Center to build 600-bed hospital is approved by voters.

1963 Edmondson resigns to take seat in U.S. Senate; Democrat George Nigh becomes acting Governor.
– Republican Henry Bellmon is elected as Governor.

1964 National Cowboy Hall of Fame dedicated as memorial to men and women who developed the West.
– Wildcat oil well blows out near Canton; gas from well ignites, and fire cannot be brought under control until June 11, 1965.

1967 Will Rogers World Airport Terminal is opened in Oklahoma City.
– Republican Dewey Barlett is Governor.

1970 American Civil Liberties Union sues State on grounds that files of some 6,000 "potential troublemakers" are being used to prevent persons from entering college or getting jobs.

1971 Democrat David Hall becomes Governor.

1973 Riot erupts in State prison, resulting in death for seven prisoners, injuries to guards, officials, and other prisoners, and over 20 million dollars in property damage.

1975 Democrat David L. Boren is Governor.

1976 Prison construction bill is passed after long delays.

1978 Fifty-seven of State's 77 counties declared federal disaster area after prolonged summer drought.

1979 Democrat George Nigh is Governor.

1981 Oklahoma raises teachers' salaries by average of $1,600 per year in midst of oil boom.

1986 Heavy floods cause severe property damage.

1987 Twenty-nine banks fail.
– Republican Henry Bellmon becomes Governor.

1991 Tornadoes hit Oklahoma and Kansas; thirty are killed, 300 are injured.
– University of Oklahoma law professor Anita F. Hill accuses U.S. Supreme Court nominee Clarence Thomas of sexual harassment before Senate Judiciary Committee.
– Per capita income is 15,827 dollars, a 2.4 percent increase over 1990.
– David Walters (D) is Governor.

1992 Republican Don Nickles wins election for U.S. Senator.
– Ernest Jim elected to U.S. Congress; U.S. House now has four Democrats, two Republicans.

1993 Governor David Walters announces he will not seek a second term in 1994; announcement comes after Walters pleads guilty to misdemeanor charge of accepting illegal contribution during 1990 campaign.

1995 Car bomb explodes at Alfred P. Murrah building in Oklahoma City; total of 168 people killed, including 19 children; more than 500 injured; Attorney General Janet Reno seeks death penalty against bombers.
– State Representative Frank D. Lucas defeats former congressional aide Dan Webber Jr. in special election to replace Rep. Glenn English, who rehired in January.
– Miss Oklahoma, Shawntel Smith, is crowned Miss America.
– Supreme Court rules that sales made on Indian tribal territories cannot be subjected to State excise taxes.
– Frank Keating (R) serves as Governor.

1996 Republican Senator James M. Inhofe is elected for full six-year term (Inhofe won special election in 1994 to fill David L. Boren's seat after he retired).

1997 Republican Senator Don Nickles, along with Sam Brownback of Kansas, is target of Senate committee investigating campaign-finance abuses in 1996 election; committee releases documents identifying conservative donors who contributed to consulting firm that helped them get around federal campaign finance restrictions.
– After six-week trial, Timothy McVeigh is convicted on 11 counts in Oklahoma City bombing; jury later sentences him to death for crimes.
– Couple agrees to plead guilty to charges that they participated in scheme to funnel some 50,000 dollars to Democratic candidates in 1994 and 1995; Eugene and Nora Lum sign plea agreements regarding illegal donations to Senator Edward Kennedy (D. Massachusetts), and W. Stuart Price (D. Oklahoma), who had an unsuccessful bid for seat in U.S. House in 1994.
– Supreme Court rules unanimously that State is required to grant hearing to inmate discharged from State penitentiary under early release program and then ordered back to prison; under ruling, Ernest E. Harper is released from prison, and State is told it may order re-imprisonment only if early release program terms are violated.

1998 Don Carroll defeats Jacquelyn Ledgerwood, a dead woman, in runoff election to select Democratic nominee for U.S. Senate seat held by Republican Don Nickles; Ledgerwood receives 25 percent of vote, despite her death in July, since State law requires that her name remain on ballot for runoff election after coming in second in four-way primary in August.
– Republican Representative Wes Watkins (who changed party affiliation from Democrat to Republican) reverses April decision to retire from public office for health reasons; Watkins, who served in House from 1977 to 1990 as Democrat, says his health is improved enough to run in November election.
– Four State Democrats run in primary to determine opponent for Representative Wes Watkins; two top contenders, Walt Roberts and Daryll Roberts, who are unrelated, will face off in September runoff election.
– Oklahoma is one of three states to ban controversial late-term abortions since April; at least 28 states now have passed laws banning the procedure.

1999 May 3. Tornadoes hit Oklahoma and Kansas killing at least forty people. Damages are estimated at over 225 million dollars.

DIRECTORY OF STATE SERVICES

OFFICE OF THE GOVERNOR
State Capitol, Rm. 212
Oklahoma City, OK 73105
Fax: 405-521-3353
Governor: 405-521-2342

Women's Commission
State Capitol, Rm. 212
Oklahoma City, OK 73105
Fax: 405-524-6942
Chairperson: 405-521-2342

OFFICE OF LIEUTENANT GOVERNOR
211 State Capitol
Oklahoma City, OK 73105
Fax: 405-525-2702
Lieutenant Governor: 405-521-2161

OFFICE OF ATTORNEY GENERAL
112 State Capitol Bldg.
Oklahoma City, OK 73105
Fax: 405-521-6246
Attorney General: 405-521-3921

OFFICE OF SECRETARY OF STATE
101 State Capitol Bldg.
Oklahoma City, OK 73105
Fax: 405-521-3771
Secretary of State: 405-521-3911

DEPARTMENT OF TREASURY
217 State Capitol Bldg.
Oklahoma City, OK 73105
Fax: 405-521-4994
Treasurer: 405-521-3191

AGRICULTURE DEPARTMENT
2800 N. Lincoln Blvd.
Oklahoma City, OK 73105
Fax: 405-521-4912
Commissioner: 405-521-3864

AUDITOR AND INSPECTOR
100 State Capitol Bldg.
Oklahoma City, OK 73105
Fax: 405-521-3426
State Auditor & Inspector: 405-521-3495

BANKING DEPARTMENT
4545 N. Lincoln Blvd., Ste. 164
Oklahoma City, OK 73105
Fax: 405-525-9701
Commissioner: 405-521-2782

CENTRAL SERVICES DEPARTMENT
104 State Capitol Bldg.
Oklahoma City, OK 73105
Fax: 405-521-6403
Director: 405-521-2121

CIVIL EMERGENCY MANAGEMENT DEPARTMENT
P.O. Box 53365
Oklahoma City, OK 73152
Fax: 405-521-4053
Director: 405-521-2481

COMMERCE DEPARTMENT
P.O. Box 26980
Oklahoma City, OK 73126-0980
Fax: 405-841-5199
Executive Director: 405-843-9770

CONSUMER CREDIT DEPARTMENT
4545 N. Lincoln Blvd., Ste. 104
Oklahoma City, OK 73105
Fax: 405-521-6740
Administrator: 405-521-3653

Examinations Services
440 S. Houston, Ste. 581
Tulsa, OK 74127
Fax: 405-521-2599
Senior Examiner: 405-581-2771

CORRECTIONS DEPARTMENT
P.O. Box 11400
Oklahoma City, OK 73136
Fax: 405-425-2064
Director: 405-425-2505

EDUCATION DEPARTMENT
2500 N. Lincoln Blvd.
Oklahoma City, OK 73105
Fax: 405-521-6205
Superintendent: 405-521-3301

Federal Fiscal Services
2500 N. Lincoln Blvd.
Oklahoma City, OK 73105
Fax: 405-521-6205

Assistant Superintendent: 405-521-2578

Financial Services
2500 N. Lincoln Blvd.
Oklahoma City, OK 73105
Fax: 405-521-6205
Assistant Superintendent: 405-521-3371

Professional Services
2500 N. Lincoln Blvd.
Oklahoma City, OK 73105
Fax: 405-521-6205
Assistant Superintendent: 405-521-4311

School Improvement and Standards
2500 N. Lincoln Blvd.
Oklahoma City, OK 73105
Fax: 405-521-6205
Deputy Superintendent: 405-521-4891

Special Education Services
2500 N. Lincoln Blvd.
Oklahoma City, OK 73105
Fax: 405-521-6205
Assistant Superintendent: 405-521-3351

ENVIRONMENTAL QUALITY DEPARTMENT
1000 NE 10th Street
Oklahoma City, OK 73117-1212
Fax: 405-271-8425
Executive Director: 405-271-8056

HEALTH DEPARTMENT
1000 NE 10th St., P.O. Box 53551
Oklahoma City, OK 73152
Fax: 405-271-7339
Commissioner: 405-271-4200

Administrative Services and State Registrar
1000 NE 10th St., P.O. Box 53551
Oklahoma City, OK 73152
Fax: 405-271-3431
Deputy Commissioner/State Registrar: 405-271-5615

Health Promotion and Policy Analysis
1000 NE 10th St., P.O. Box 53551
Oklahoma City, OK 73152
Fax: 405-271-3431
Deputy Commissioner: 405-271-4200

Personal Health Services
1000 NE 10th St., P.O. Box 53551
Oklahoma City, OK 73152
Fax: 405-271-3431
Deputy Commissioner: 405-271-4200

Special Health Services
1000 NE 10th St., P.O. Box 53551
Oklahoma City, OK 73152
Fax: 405-271-3431
Deputy Commissioner: 405-271-6868

HUMAN SERVICES DEPARTMENT
P.O. Box 25352
Oklahoma City, OK 73152
Fax: 405-521-6458
Director: 405-521-3646

INSURANCE DEPARTMENT
P.O. Box 53408
Oklahoma City, OK 73152-3408
Fax: 405-521-6652
Commissioner: 405-521-2828

LABOR DEPARTMENT
4001 Lincoln Blvd.
Oklahoma City, OK 73105
Fax: 405-528-5751
Commissioner: 405-528-1500

LIBRARIES DEPARTMENT
200 NE 18th
Oklahoma City, OK 73105
Fax: 405-525-7804
Director: 405-521-2502

MENTAL HEALTH DEPARTMENT
P.O. Box 53277
Oklahoma City, OK 73152-3277
Fax: 405-522-3650
Commissioner: 405-522-3908

MILITARY DEPARTMENT
3501 Military Circle
Oklahoma City, OK 73111-4398
Fax: 405-425-8524
Adjutant General: 405-425-8000

MINES DEPARTMENT
4040 N. Lincoln Blvd., Ste. 107
Oklahoma City, OK 73105
Fax: 405-424-4932
Director: 405-521-3859

PUBLIC SAFETY DEPARTMENT
P.O. Box 11415
Oklahoma City, OK 73136-1415
Fax: 405-425-2324
Commissioner: 405-425-2001

REHABILITATIVE SERVICES DEPARTMENT
P.O. Box 36659
Oklahoma City, OK 73136
Fax: 405-427-3027
Director: 405-522-6377

School for the Blind
3300 Gibson St.
Muskogee, OK 74401
Fax: 918-682-1651
Director: 918-682-6641

School for the Deaf
E 10th & Tahlequh
Sulfur, OK 73086
Fax: 405-622-2104

Director: 405-622-3186

SECURITIES DEPARTMENT
621 N. Robinson, Ste. 400
Oklahoma City, OK 73102
Chairperson: 405-235-0230

TOURISM AND RECREATION DEPARTMENT
2401 N. Lincoln Blvd., Ste. 500
Oklahoma City, OK 73105
Fax: 405-521-4883
Executive Director: 405-521-2413

TRANSPORTATION DEPARTMENT
200 NE 21st St.
Oklahoma City, OK 73105
Fax: 405-521-6528
Director: 405-521-2631

Aeronautics Commission
200 NE 21st St.
Oklahoma City, OK 73105
Fax: 405-521-6528
Chairperson: 405-521-2377

Operations
200 NE 21st St.
Oklahoma City, OK 73105
Fax: 405-521-6528
Assistant Director: 405-521-4675

Preconstruction
200 NE 21st St.
Oklahoma City, OK 73105
Fax: 405-521-2524
Assistant Director: 405-521-2688

VETERANS AFFAIRS DEPARTMENT
P.O. Box 53067
Oklahoma City, OK 73152
Fax: 405-521-6533
Director: 405-521-3684

VOCATIONAL AND TECHNICAL EDUCATION DEPARTMENT
1500 W. 7th Ave.
Stillwater, OK 74074-4364
Fax: 405-743-5541
Director: 405-377-2000

WILDLIFE CONSERVATION DEPARTMENT
P.O. Box 53465
Oklahoma City, OK 73152
Fax: 405-521-6535
Director: 405-521-3851

ACCOUNTANCY BOARD
4545 N. Lincoln Blvd., Ste. 165
Oklahoma City, OK 73105-3413
Fax: 405-521-3118
Chairperson: 405-521-2397

ALCOHOLIC BEVERAGE LAWS ENFORCEMENT COMMISSION
4545 N. Lincoln Blvd., Ste. 270
Oklahoma City, OK 73105
Fax: 405-521-6578
Chairperson: 405-521-3484

ARCHITECTS BOARD
6801 N. Broadway, Ste. 201
Oklahoma City, OK 73116-9037
Fax: 405-843-6278
Chairperson: 405-848-6596

ARTS COUNCIL
P.O. Box 52001-2001
Oklahoma City, OK 73152-2001
Fax: 405-521-6418
Chairperson: 405-521-2931

CONSERVATION COMMISSION
2800 N. Lincoln Blvd., Ste. 160
Oklahoma City, OK 73105
Fax: 405-521-6686
Chairperson: 405-521-2384

CORPORATION COMMISSION
2101 N. Lincoln Blvd.
Oklahoma City, OK 73105
Fax: 405-521-6045
Chairperson: 405-521-2211

DEVELOPMENT FINANCE AUTHORITY
301 NW 63rd St., Ste. 225
Oklahoma City, OK 73116
Fax: 405-848-3314
President: 405-848-9761

EDUCATIONAL TELEVISION AUTHORITY
P.O. Box 14190
Oklahoma City, OK 73113
Fax: 405-841-9216
Chairperson: 405-848-8501

ELECTION BOARD
P.O. Box 53156
Oklahoma City, OK 73152
Fax: 405-521-6457
Chairperson: 405-521-2391

EMPLOYMENT SECURITY COMMISSION
2401 N. Lincoln Blvd.
Oklahoma City, OK 73152-2003
Fax: 405-557-7256
Executive Director: 405-557-0200

FIRE MARSHAL
4545 N. Lincoln Blvd., Ste. 280
Oklahoma City, OK 73105
Fax: 405-524-9810
State Fire Marshal: 405-524-9610

HANDICAPPED CONCERNS OFFICE
4300 N. Lincoln Blvd., Ste. 200
Oklahoma City, OK 73105

Fax: 405-424-1782
Director: 405-521-3756

HEALTH CARE AUTHORITY
4545 N. Lincoln Blvd., Ste. 124
Oklahoma City, OK 73105
Fax: 405-521-0455
Director: 405-530-3439

HISTORICAL SOCIETY
2100 N. Lincoln Blvd.
Oklahoma City, OK 73105-4997
Fax: 405-525-3272
Executive Director: 405-521-2491

HOUSING FINANCE AUTHORITY
1140 NW 63rd St., Ste. 200
Oklahoma City, OK 73116
Fax: 405-842-2537
Executive Director: 405-848-1144

HUMAN RIGHTS COMMISSION
2101 N. Lincoln Blvd., Rm. 480
Oklahoma City, OK 73105
Fax: 405-522-3635
Director: 405-521-3441

HUMAN SERVICES COMMISSION
P.O. Box 25352
Oklahoma City, OK 73125
Fax: 405-524-6458
Secretary: 405-521-3646

INDIAN AFFAIRS COMMISSION
4545 N. Lincoln Blvd., Ste. 282
Oklahoma City, OK 73105
Fax: 405-521-0902
Chairperson: 405-521-3828
Executive Director: 405-521-3828

INVESTIGATION BUREAU
P.O. Box 11497
Oklahoma City, OK 73136
Fax: 405-843-3804
Director: 405-848-6724

LIQUIFIED PETROLEUM GAS ADMINISTRATION
2101 N. Lincoln Blvd., Ste. B45
Oklahoma City, OK 73105
Fax: 405-521-6037
Chairperson: 405-521-2458

MERIT PROTECTION COMMISSION
310 NE 28th St., Ste. 201
Oklahoma City, OK 73105
Fax: 405-528-6245
Director: 405-525-9144

MOTOR VEHICLE COMMISSION
4400 Will Rogers Pkwy., Ste. 205
Oklahoma City, OK 73108
Fax: 405-521-6096
Executive Director: 405-521-2375

NARCOTICS AND DANGEROUS DRUGS CONTROL
BUREAU
4545 N. Lincoln Blvd., Ste. 11
Oklahoma City, OK 73105
Fax: 405-530-3189
Director: 405-521-2885

PERSONNEL MANAGEMENT OFFICE
2101 N. Lincoln Blvd., Rm. G80
Oklahoma City, OK 73105
Fax: 405-524-6942
Administrator: 405-521-2177

PUBLIC EMPLOYEES RETIREMENT SYSTEM
P.O. Box 53007
Oklahoma City, OK 73152
Fax: 405-521-3569
Executive Director: 405-521-2381

STATE FAIR
P.O. Box 74943
Oklahoma City, OK 73147
Fax: 405-948-6828
President & General Mgr.: 405-948-6700

STATE FINANCE OFFICE
122 State Capitol Bldg.
Oklahoma City, OK 73105
Fax: 405-521-3902
Director: 405-521-2141

STUDENT LOAN AUTHORITY
P.O. Box 54530
Oklahoma City, OK 73154
Fax: 405-556-9255
Chairperson: 405-556-9210

TAX COMMISSION
2501 Lincoln Blvd.
Oklahoma City, OK 73194
Fax: 405-521-2035
Chairperson: 405-521-3115
Administrator: 405-521-3214

TEACHERS RETIREMENT SYSTEM
P.O. Box 53524
Oklahoma City, OK 73152
Fax: 405-521-3810
Executive Secretary: 405-521-2387

WATER RESOURCES BOARD
P.O. Box 150
Oklahoma City, OK 73101-0150
Fax: 405-231-2600
Chairperson: 405-231-2500

WHEAT COMMISSION
800 NE 63rd St.
Oklahoma City, OK 73105
Fax: 405-848-0372
Executive Director: 405-521-2796

TWENTIETH CENTURY GOVERNORS

HASKELL, CHARLES NATHANIEL (1860-1933), first governor of Oklahoma (1907-1911), was born in Leipsic, Ohio on March 13, 1860.

After working as a schoolteacher for a time, Haskell began to study law, and in 1880 was admitted to the Ohio Bar, going into private law practice the following year. Later on, he switched careers and became employed as a construction worker, which included railroad work. In April of 1901, Haskell settled in Muskogee, Oklahoma, where he founded the Territorial Trust and Banking Company, and also purchased the *New State Tribune*.

Haskell's first foray into politics was when he served as a member of the Sequoyah Constitutional Convention in 1905. In 1907 Haskell ran for the Oklahoma governorship on the Democratic ticket, and by defeating his Republican opponent, Frank Frantz, became the State's first governor, taking office on November 16, 1907. During his tenure, Haskell guided the establishment of several of the State's institutions, and helped pass a number of legislative bills that were intended to bring Oklahoma into a new era. They included a bank guaranty law and a comprehensive labor code. In addition, after it was decided by election that the State capital was to be moved from Guthrie to Oklahoma City, Haskell instigated the move on June 11, 1910, by moving the State Seal to a hotel in the new city. Although this was in violation of the Oklahoma Enabling Act, Haskell's action was upheld by both the Oklahoma Supreme Court and the United States Supreme Court. Also, it was during his administration that the "Grandfather Clause" and the "Jim Crow Code" were implemented.

The original Oklahoma Constitution prohibited governors from serving more than one consecutive term, and as such, Haskell stepped down from office on January 9, 1911. The following year he made an unsuccessful bid for the United States Senate, and subsequently engaged in the oil business.

Haskell was married twice: to Lucy Pomeroy, who died in 1888, and to Lillian Elizabeth Gallup. He had three children by each marriage. Haskell died on July 5, 1933.

CRUCE, LEE (1863-1933), second governor of Oklahoma (1911-1915), was born near Marion, Kentucky on July 8, 1863.

Cruce attended Vanderbilt University for a time, but was unable to finish because of failing health. Instead, he studied law privately, and in 1888, was admitted to the Kentucky Bar. However, it wasn't until 1891, when he moved to Ardmore, Oklahoma, that he actually began to practice law, which he did until 1901. Then from 1901 to 1903, Cruce served as a cashier at the Ardmore National Bank. In the latter year he was named president of that institution, a post he served in until 1910.

Cruce's first foray into politics was in 1899, with his election as alderman of Ardmore. In 1910 he ran for the Oklahoma governorship on the Democratic ticket, defeating his Republican opponent, J.W. McNeal, and taking office on January 9, 1911. During his tenure, Cruce was often at odds with the State Legislature over such issues as higher education and congressional reapportionment. Also during his administration, two new counties, Harmon and Cotton, were organized, and the State Highway Department was created. Due to his opposition to capital punishment, no criminal was executed during Cruce's time in office. Supporting a number of "Blue Laws," he declared martial law in order to curb horse racing, gambling, prize fighting and bootlegging. His periodic stubbornness with the Legislature instigated an investigation of his office, followed by a resolution for impeachment, which failed by only one vote.

Unable by law to succeed himself as governor, Cruce stepped down from office on January 11, 1915. He made an unsuccessful bid for the United States Senate in 1930 and subsequently engaged in such business ventures as real estate and oil.

He was married to Chickie LaFlore, and the couple had one child. Cruce died on January 16, 1933.

WILLIAMS, ROBERT LEE (1868-1948), third governor of Oklahoma (1915-1919), was born in Brundidge, Alabama on December 20, 1868.

Williams attended Southern University, graduating in 1894. He taught school for a year, then began to study law privately, passing the Alabama Bar in 1891. After practicing law in Troy, Alabama, Williams moved to Guthrie, Oklahoma in 1893. He studied Methodist ministry in Alabama, then returned to Oklahoma, settling first in Atoka in 1896, then in Durant.

Between 1907 and 1914, Williams served as Chief Justice of the Oklahoma Supreme Court. In the latter year he left that post to run for the Oklahoma governorship on the Democratic ticket, defeating Republican candidate, John Fields and Socialist nominee Fred W. Holt, taking office on January 11, 1915.

Fiscally prudent, during Williams's tenure several State agencies and State institutions were eliminated, appropriations were reduced, and taxes were raised. Also, the State Board of Affairs was established and the new Capitol Building was ready for use. Although the United States Supreme Court declared Oklahoma's "Grandfather Clause" unconstitutional in 1915, Williams called a special session of the State Legislature to pass a registration law that would hinder African-American voters. In addition, with the start of World War I came the "Green Corn Rebellion," a passionate protest by some Oklahoma citizens against the U.S. draft, which was quickly extinguished by Williams.

Unable by law to succeed himself as governor, Williams stepped down from office on January 13, 1919. From that year until 1937, he served as United States Judge for the Eastern District of Oklahoma, then from 1937 to 1939, he was United States Circuit Judge of the Tenth Circuit Court. Between 1938 and 1948, he was president of the Oklahoma Historical Society.

Williams never married. He died on April 10, 1948.

ROBERTSON, JAMES BROOKS (1871-1938), fourth governor of Oklahoma (1919-1923), was born in Keokuk County, Iowa on March 15, 1871.

Between 1887 and 1897, Robertson worked as a schoolteacher, and during those years he settled in Chandler, Oklahoma. Having studied law privately, he passed the Oklahoma Bar in 1898. From 1900 to 1902 he served as County Attorney of Lincoln County. During 1909-10 he was Judge of the Tenth District of Oklahoma. In 1911, he was a member of the Capitol Commission, and from 1911 to 1914, he was a member of the Oklahoma Supreme Court Commission. In the latter year he made an unsuccessful bid for the governorship. However, in 1918 he ran for that office on the Democratic ticket, and defeated Republican candidate Horace G. McKeever, taking office on January 13, 1919.

During Robertson's tenure, over 1,000 miles of new highway were completed, and the State Legislature ratified the eighteenth and nineteenth amendments to the United States Constitution. The United States Supreme Court, in a series of several verdicts handed down, settled a long dispute over the Red River boundary by bequeathing the river rights to the State of Oklahoma. In addition, during his time in office, Oklahoma suffered a severe economic depression, the National Guard was used to eradicate a coal miners' strike, and the Ku Klux Klan increased their visibility. In 1922, Robertson was also involved in a scandal with bribery

charges leveled against him, but avoided being impeached by one vote in the State Legislature. Although he was indicted, he was not convicted.

Unable by law to succeed himself, Robertson stepped down on January 8, 1923. He made another attempt at the governorship in 1930, but did not receive the nomination. After leaving office, Robertson continued practicing law, and from 1935 to 1938, served as Chief Council for the Oklahoma Corporation Commission.

Robertson was married to Olive Stubblefield, and the couple had two children. He died on March 7, 1933.

WALTON, JOHN C. (1881-1949), fifth governor of Oklahoma (1923), was born near Indianapolis, Indiana on March 6, 1881.

As a young boy Walton moved with his family to Nebraska, then later to Arkansas. In 1898 he graduated from Fort Smith, Arkansas Commercial College. Walton served in the Spanish-American War, then studied engineering. In 1903 he settled in Oklahoma City. During World War I, Walton served in the Engineering Corps. From 1917 to 1919, he served as the Oklahoma City Commissioner of Public Works, and between 1919 and 1923, was Mayor of Oklahoma City.

In 1922, Walton ran for the Oklahoma governorship on the Democratic ticket, defeating his Republican opponent, John Fields, and taking office on January 8, 1923. During his tenure, he was often at odds with several members of the State Legislature, a situation instigated by the Ku Klux Klan who were making themselves more visible. In order to curb the group's violence, Walton caused himself a lot of trouble by pronouncing Tulsa County to be under martial law, then putting himself in violation of the Oklahoma Constitution by suspending habeas corpus. When a grand jury tried to investigate his decision, Walton then declared the entire state to be under martial law, and went as far as using the National Guard to prevent the Legislature from convening. However, an initiative petition was passed that allowed a special legislative session to be held. Walton was brought up on impeachment charges on October 23, 1923 and was suspended from the governor's office, with Lieutenant Governor Martin E. Trapp stepping in as acting governor. Walton was then convicted and forced to step down on November 19, 1923.

Walton made a bid for the United States Senate in 1924, and although he won the nomination, he was defeated in the general election. In 1931, he also lost the race for Mayor of Oklahoma City. However, he was elected to the Oklahoma Corporation Commission, serving from 1932 to 1939. He tried running for governor twice more, in 1934 and 1938, but was defeated both times.

Walton was married to Madeliene Cecile, and the couple had two children. He died on November 24, 1949.

TRAPP, MARTIN EDWIN (1877-1970), sixth governor of Oklahoma (1923-1927), was born in Robinson, Kansas on April 18, 1877.

As a young boy, Trapp moved with his family to Oklahoma Territory in 1889. He later attended Capitol City College in Guthrie, Oklahoma, graduating in 1898. He later attended Capitol City College in Guthrie, Oklahoma, graduating in 1898. After privately studying law, Trapp passed the Oklahoma Bar in 1912. Between 1904 and 1907, he served as County Clerk of Logan County, in Oklahoma Territory. In the latter year he was elected State Auditor of Oklahoma, serving until 1911. From 1914 to 1923 Trapp was Lieutenant Governor of Oklahoma.

On October 23, 1923, when incumbent Governor John C. Walton was brought up on impeachment charges, Trapp became acting governor, then stepped in as Governor of Oklahoma on November 19, 1923, when Walton was removed from office after being convicted. During his tenure, the Fish and Game Commission and the Forestry Commission were created, as was the Conservation Commission. Also, funds from a State gasoline tax were used to construct a number of State highways. In addition, to minimize the influence of the Ku Klux Klan, an "antimask law" was adopted during Trapp's time in office.

Trapp was well liked by the citizens of his state, and held on to the title of "acting governor," hoping to bypass the constitutional rule about governors not being allowed to succeed themselves in office. However, after a ruling by the Oklahoma Supreme Court was handed down, stating that Trapp was indeed "governor" and was not allowed to run for a successive second term, he stepped down on January 10, 1927. In 1930 he made a bid for the governorship, but did not make it past the Democratic primary. Afterward he became an investment securities dealer.

Trapp was married to Lou Strang, and the couple had one child. Trapp died on July 26, 1951.

JOHNSTON, HENRY SIMPSON (1867-1970), seventh governor of Oklahoma (1927-1929), was born near Evansville, Indiana on December 30, 1867.

As a young boy, Johnston moved with his family to Kansas, and there he attended both Baker University and Methodist College. After later settling in Colorado and privately studying law, he passed the Colorado Bar in 1891. In 1893 he migrated to Perry, Oklahoma Territory. From 1897 to 1904, Johnston served as a member of the Oklahoma Territorial Council, and from 1901 to 1904, was County Attorney for Noble County, Oklahoma Territory. During 1907-08, Johnston served in the Oklahoma State Senate, and was also President Pro Tempore of that body.

In 1926 Johnston ran for the governorship on the Democratic ticket and defeated his Republican opponent, Omar K. Benedict, taking office on January 10, 1927. Johnston's tenure was tumultuous, ranging from his bitter dissension with the State Legislature over how many people were to be chosen to the State Highway Commission, to his declaring martial law in order to prevent the Legislature from investigating his office. Part of their anger was reportedly caused by Johnston's private secretary, Mrs. O.O. Howard, who was said to have been the cause of his inaccessibility to them, coupled with their blaming him for the 1928 Republican sweep in State government. Impeachment charges were ultimately brought against him by the Legislature, with Lieutenant Governor William J. Holloway stepping in as acting governor. Johnston was forced to leave office on March 20, 1929.

Between 1932 and 1936, Johnston served in the Oklahoma Senate, then returned to private law practice. He was married to Ethel L. Littleton, and adopted her four children. He died on January 28, 1970.

HOLLOWAY, WILLIAM JUDSON (1888-1970), eighth governor of Oklahoma (1929-1931), was born in Arkadelphia, Arkansas on December 15, 1888.

Holloway attended Ouachita College, earning a B.A. degree in 1910, then studied for a short time at the University of Chicago. Holloway subsequently moved to Hugo, Oklahoma, where he secured the position of principal of Hugo High School, serving from 1911 to 1914. He next attended Cumberland University where he received a LL.B. degree in 1915, and later that year, he passed the Oklahoma Bar.

Between 1916 and 1918 Holloway served as County Attorney of Choctaw County, in Oklahoma. After a short stint in the United States Army Officers Training School, he began practicing law, then in 1920 he was elected to the Oklahoma Senate, serving until

1926. During his last year, he was President Pro Tempore of that body, then during 1925-26, served as acting Lieutenant Governor. In 1927 he was elected Lieutenant Governor of Oklahoma on the Democratic ticket, serving until 1929, when he succeeded to the governorship after incumbent Governor Henry S. Johnston was impeached and removed from office on March 20 of that year.

During Holloway's tenure the State Legislature, with his support, passed a bill implementing a runoff primary election system within Oklahoma. In addition a new mining code was created, several child labor laws were expanded, and the State Highway Commission was revamped. While Holloway was serving as governor, the United States was hit with the Great Depression, with Oklahoma suffering especially hard, causing many of its citizens to migrate west, hoping to improve their lot. It was also the catalyst for a huge jump in the number of people seeking political jobs, with 103 candidates filing for several elective posts in 1930.

Unable by law to succeed himself in office, Holloway stepped down on January 12, 1931, and returned to his private law practice. When the Interstate Oil Compact Commission was formed, Holloway attended as Oklahoma's representative.

Holloway was married to Amy Arnold, and the couple had one child. Holloway died on January 28, 1970.

MURRAY, WILLIAM HENRY (1869-1956), ninth governor of Oklahoma (1931-1935), was born in Spring Creek, Texas on November 21, 1869.

Murray attended College Hill Institute in Springtown, Texas, graduating in 1889. He subsequently became a schoolteacher, and also published a newspaper. After privately studying law, he passed the Texas Bar in 1895. In 1898 he migrated to Tishomingo, Chickasaw Nation. After marrying a Chickasaw woman, Mary Alice Hearrell, he was made a citizen of the Nation. Eventually, Murray served as the personal attorney of Chickasaw Governor Douglas Johnston. In 1905 he served as a delegate to the Sequoyah Convention, and the following year, was a delegate to the Oklahoma Constitutional Convention. A Democrat, during 1907-08, Murray served in the Oklahoma House of Representatives, and was also Speaker of that body. Between 1914 and 1918 he was a member of the United States House of Representatives.

Murray made two unsuccessful bids for the Oklahoma governorship—in 1910 and in 1918. He then moved to the country of Bolivia in 1924, hoping to organize a colony, but five years later, returned home to Oklahoma. In 1930 Murray made his third try for the governorship on the Democratic ticket, this time winning over Republican Ira Hill, and taking office on January 12, 1931.

Oklahoma, as well as the rest of the country, was still deep in the midst of the Great Depression, and Murray was part of the problem where the State of Oklahoma was concerned, due to his rejection of many of President Franklin D. Roosevelt's New Deal programs. This ultimately caused a huge amount of financial chaos that included an extensive amount of foreclosures and bank failures, as well as a 5,000,000 dollars deficit. He requested funds from the State Legislature to help the desperately poor, and then requested that a National Council on Relief be organized to help solve the situation. Also during his tenure, Murray called out the National Guard for such duties as maintaining segregation and enforcing a limit on the production of oil, as well as a moratorium on banks.

In 1932, Murray made an unsuccessful attempt at the presidency on the Democratic ticket. Unable by law to succeed himself as governor, Murray stepped down from office on January 14, 1935 and returned to his farming interests. In 1942 he made one last attempt at public office, unsuccessfully running for the United States Senate.

Murray and his wife Mary Alice had five children. He died on October 15, 1956.

MARLAND, EARNEST WHITWORTH (1874-1935), tenth governor of Oklahoma (1935-1939), was born in Pittsburgh, Pennsylvania on May 8, 1874.

Marland attended the University of Michigan, earning a LL.B. degree in 1893. After practicing law for a short time, Marland decided instead to enter into the oil business, and in 1908, moved to Ponca City, Oklahoma, where he learned every end of the oil industry, including refining, production, and marketing. Eventually he started his own firm, the Marland Oil Company, which had a number of subsidiaries throughout the United States and Mexico.

Marland entered the political arena in 1933 when he secured a seat in the United States House of Representatives, serving until 1935. In 1934 he ran for the Oklahoma governorship on the Democratic ticket, and defeated his Republican opponent, William B. Pine, taking office on January 15, 1935.

Marland saw great potential for the citizens of Oklahoma, and came up with what he called the "Little New Deal," in which he proposed over 100,000 working homesteads, pushed for better education within the State's school system, supported out-of-state industry within Oklahoma, and asked for an increase of hydroelectric power. Since the country was in the midst of the Great Depression, some of his ideas were vetoed by the State Legislature. However, he was able to get the State sales tax increased to two percent, which provided funds used for relief programs, with schools also receiving extra money. In addition, the State Planning and Resources Board was created in order to attract new industry to Oklahoma. Marland was also responsible for having several oil-producing states take part in the Interstate Oil Compact, which was initiated to stabilize oil prices and support oil conservation.

Unable by law to succeed himself as governor, Marland stepped down on January 9, 1939, and returned to his business ventures. He was married twice: to Mary Virginia Collins, who died in 1926; and to Lydie Miller Roberts, who brought two children to the marriage. Marland died on October 3, 1941.

PHILLIPS, LEON CHASE (1890-1958), eleventh governor of Oklahoma (1939-1943), was born in Worth County, Missouri on December 9, 1890.

While Phillips was still a baby, his family moved to Oklahoma Territory. During 1908-09, Phillips was a schoolteacher. He later studied at Epworth University, then attended the University of Oklahoma, earning a LL.B. degree in 1916. Later that year he went into private law practice in Okemah, Oklahoma.

Phillips first foray into politics was in 1933 when he became a member of the Oklahoma House of Representatives, where he served until 1938. During 1935 he was Speaker of the House, and in 1937 he was Democratic Minority Leader.

In 1938 Phillips ran for the Oklahoma governorship on the Democratic ticket, defeating Republican Ross Rizley, and taking office on January 9, 1939. During his tenure, Phillips made the balancing of the State budget a top priority. When the Grand River Dam Project was in its beginning stages, Phillips, who was strongly against the proposed building, went as far as to ask the National Guard to impede its construction; however a federal court overruled his opposition. With World War II looming, Oklahoma, like many states at that time, became involved in the war effort, a cause that helped revive the State's economy.

Unable by law to succeed himself in office, Phillips stepped down on January 11, 1943 and returned to practicing law. He was married to Myrtle Ellenberger, who brought two children to the marriage. He died on March 27, 1958.

KERR, ROBERT SAMUEL (1896-1963), twelfth governor of Oklahoma (1943-1947), was born near Ada, Chickasaw Nation, on September 11, 1896.

During 1911-12 Kerr attended Oklahoma Baptist University, then studied at the University of Oklahoma during 1915-16. In the latter year he began teaching school. After taking private law study, Kerr passed the Oklahoma Bar in 1922. In 1926 he founded and operated an oil well drilling company, which twenty years later became Kerr-McGee Oil Industries, Inc.

In 1931 Kerr was named Special Justice of the Oklahoma Supreme Court. A Democrat, he ran for the Oklahoma governorship in 1942, defeating Republican William J. Otjen, and taking office on January 11, 1943.

During Kerr's tenure, in anticipation of a major Republican upset in the 1944 elections, a Ballot Separation Law was passed. Also, the State Pardon and Parole Board was organized, the primary election runoff system was reinstated, and the public school system was provided with free textbooks. During World War II Oklahoma became deeply involved in the war effort, with forty-one military installations and several P.O.W. camps being constructed throughout the State.

Although Kerr and many other Democrats were against a fourth term for President Franklin D. Roosevelt, Kerr did not desert his party, and gave the keynote speech at the 1944 Democratic National Convention. Unable by law to succeed himself as governor, Kerr stepped down on January 13, 1947. The following year he was elected to the United States Senate, serving until 1963.

Kerr was married twice: to Reba Shelton, who died in 1924 and to Grace Breene. He had four children. Kerr died on January 1, 1963.

TURNER, ROY JOSEPH (1894-1951), thirteenth governor of Oklahoma (1947-1951), was born in Lincoln County, Oklahoma Territory on November 6, 1894.

Turner attended Hill's Business College, and subsequently began working as a bookkeeper from 1911 to 1915. During 1916 he was employed as a salesman, and between 1920 and 1928 he was a real estate agent. In the latter year he co-founded the Harper-Turner Oil Company. In 1933, he became owner of the 10,000 acre Turner Ranch, and within two years, had his own purebred Hereford cattle.

Turner delved into politics in 1946 when he ran for the Oklahoma governorship on the Democratic ticket, defeating Republican Olney F. Flynn and taking office on January 13, 1947. During his tenure, the Board of Regents for State Colleges was organized, as was the Oklahoma Turnpike Authority, and both the State Planning and Resources Board and the State Highway Department were revamped. In addition, segregation in the State's colleges and universities was abolished. The State Legislature failed to pass his public education financing reform bill, and Oklahoma voters rejected his proposed revision of the State Constitution.

Unable by law to succeed himself as governor, Turner stepped down on January 8, 1951, returning to his oil and cattle ventures. His last public post was between 1959 and 1963, when he served on the State Highway Commission.

Turner was married to Jessica B. Grimm, who brought two children to the marriage. He died on June 11, 1973.

MURRAY, JOHNSON (1902-1974), fourteenth governor of Oklahoma (1951-1955), was born in Emet, Chickasaw Nation on July 21, 1902.

Murray attended the Murray State School of Agriculture, graduating in 1924. Several years later he continued his studies at Oklahoma City University, earning an LL.B. degree in 1946. Murray worked as a newspaperman for a time, then moved to Bolivia for a few years (1924-1930) with his father. Upon his return he went to work in the Oklahoma oil fields, until 1942, when he became employed at Douglas Aircraft Company until 1944. From 1944 to 1946 he worked in various jobs including law clerk, and investigator. After receiving his law degree he opened his own law office in Oklahoma City, Oklahoma.

In 1950 Murray ran for the Oklahoma governorship on the Democratic ticket, defeating his Republican opponent, Jo O. Ferguson, and taking office on January 8, 1951. During his tenure, Murray's main focus was to slash all forms of waste in State government, along with eliminating the need for new taxes. As such, his first order of business was to establish the Governor's Joint Committee on Reorganization of State Government in an effort to streamline all levels of Oklahoma's governmental structure. Murray became known for his liberal use of the veto, invoking it forty times during his four-year term. In addition, during his time in office, the Oklahoma Constitution was amended to allow women to serve jury duty.

Unable by law to succeed himself in office, Murray stepped down on January 10, 1955, and along with returning to his private law practice, he acted as consulting attorney for the Oklahoma Department of Welfare.

Murray was married to Willie Roberta Emerson, and the couple had one child. He died on April 16, 1974.

GARY, RAYMOND D. (1908-1993), fifteenth governor of Oklahoma (1955-1959), was born in Marshall County, Oklahoma on January 21, 1908.

Gary attended Southeastern State College between 1928 and 1932, and also taught school during those years. In 1932 he was elected Marshall County Superintendent of Schools, serving in that post until 1936. From 1936 to 1941 he owned and operated the Gary Furniture Manufacturing Company. Beginning in 1946 he was named president of the Sooner Oil Company.

From 1940 to 1954 Gary served in the Oklahoma Senate. In the latter year he ran for the Oklahoma governorship on the Democratic ticket, winning over his Republican opponent Reuben K. Sparks, taking office on January 10, 1955. During his tenure, school integration was firmly established, especially after the State Constitution was amended to withhold State funds from segregated schools, and racial barriers were brought down in almost all facets throughout the State, due to Gary's influence. In addition, the State of Oklahoma turned fifty years old, with a celebration being planned by the Oklahoma Semi-Centennial Commission. Other issues Gary involved himself in included the vast improvement of the State highways, with over 3,500 built between 1955 and 1959, along with the establishment of both the Water Study Commission, and the Department of Commerce and Industry.

Unable by law to succeed himself as governor, Gary stepped down on January 8, 1959, and returned to his various business ventures. He was married to Emma Mae Purser, and the couple had two children. Gary died Dec. 11, 1993.

EDMONDSON, JAMES HOWARD (1925-1971), sixteenth governor of Oklahoma (1959-1963), was born in Muskogee, Oklahoma on September 27, 1925.

After serving a stint in the United States Army Air Corps between 1942 and 1945, Edmondson attended the University of Oklahoma, where he earned an LL.B. degree in 1948. Between

the latter year and 1953, Edmondson had his own private law practice. During 1953 he served as Chief Prosecutor in the Tulsa County Attorney's Office, then from 1954 to 1958, he held the post of Tulsa County Attorney.

Edmondson ran for the Oklahoma governorship on the Democratic ticket in 1958, defeating his Republican opponent Phil Ferguson, and taking office on January 12, 1959. During his tenure he was continually at odds with the State Legislature, with a big point of contention being the issue of prohibition; Edmondson had promised his constituency that Oklahoma's Legislature would take an early vote regarding the repeal of the standing law. After much maneuvering, the law was repealed and the Alcoholic Beverage Control Board was created to help keep the new situation in check. In addition, during his administration a State merit system was organized, as was the State Industrial Finance Authority. Even more friction between Edmondson and other Democratic leaders was created when he became almost the lone voice in his support of John F. Kennedy for the Democratic presidential nomination in 1960.

After Oklahoma's U.S. Senator Robert S. Kerr died on January 1, 1963, Edmondson resigned from the governorship a few days later, with Lieutenant Governor George P. Nigh succeeding to office. The State Constitution dictated that the governor was to choose Kerr's successor until the next election, and Nigh appointed Edmondson to fill Kerr's unexpired term. Edmondson's attempt at the Senate seat by general election in 1964 was unsuccessful, and he returned to private law practice in Oklahoma City, Oklahoma.

Edmondson was married to Jeannette Bartleston and the couple had three children. He died on November 17, 1971.

NIGH, GEORGE PATTERSON (1927-), acting governor, and twenty-first governor of Oklahoma (1963, 1979-1987), was born in McAlester, Oklahoma on June 9, 1927. He attended Eastern Oklahoma Agricultural and Mechanical College during 1946-47. Continuing his studies at East Central State College, he earned a B.A. degree in 1950. Between 1952 and 1958 Nigh was a schoolteacher, and from 1956 until 1960, he was a partner in Nigh Grocery.

Nigh's first foray into politics was his 1950 run for the Oklahoma House of Representatives, where he served until 1958. In the latter year he became Lieutenant Governor of Oklahoma under Governor James Edmondson. When the governor resigned on January 6, 1963, Nigh succeeded to that office.

Although only governor for nine days, one of Nigh's first decisions was to appoint Edmondson to the unexpired U.S. senatorial term of Robert S. Kerr, who had died on January 1, 1963.

Even with his short time in office, he was not allowed by law to succeed himself, and Nigh stepped down on January 14, 1963. He successfully ran for Lieutenant Governor in 1966, and won three more terms in that office. In 1978 he ran for the governorship on the Democratic ticket, and was elected, defeating his Republican opponent, Ron Shotts, and taking office on January 3, 1979. By this time, Oklahoma's Constitution had been amended, and he was able to serve several more terms, finally stepping down in 1987.

Beginning in 1992, Nigh became president of the University of Central Oklahoma, in Edmond. He is married to Donna Mashburn, and the couple has two children.

BELLMON, HENRY LOUIS (1921-), seventeenth and twenty-second governor of Oklahoma (1963-1967, 1987-1991), was born in Tonkawa, Oklahoma on September 3, 1921.

Bellmon attended Oklahoma State University, earning a B.S. degree in Agriculture in 1942, then did his graduate work at Colorado State University. Between 1942 and 1946 he served in the United States Marine Corps, and was awarded the Silver Star. After his discharge he returned to his farming interests. Bellmon served in the Oklahoma House of Representatives from 1946 to 1948. Much later, in 1962, he ran for the Oklahoma governorship on the Republican ticket, defeating his Democratic opponent, W.P. "Bill" Atkinson, and taking office on January 14, 1963, a victory that made him the first Republican governor in the State's history.

During Bellmon's tenure, the United States Supreme Court ruled that urban areas needed a more equitable share of representation, forcing a reapportionment of the State Legislature. Bellmon, intent on improving the public school system throughout the State, proposed his "Giant Stride" program, which he was ultimately unable to implement due to a lack of funds, a situation that caused sanctions to be imposed on Oklahoma by the National Education Association. In addition, during his term, two judges on the Oklahoma Supreme Court were involved in a bribery scandal, forcing one to resign and the other to be impeached. Also, the Industrial Development and Park Commission was established, a code for higher education was implemented, and a district attorney's office was created.

Another big change during Bellmon's administration was the amendment of the Oklahoma Constitution allowing governors to serve more than one consecutive term. Unfortunately, Bellmon could not take advantage of the new law and stepped down on January 9, 1967. Roughly a year and a half later, he ran for and won a seat in the United States Senate.

Bellmon is married to Shirley Osborn, and the couple has three children.

BARTLETT, DEWEY FOLLETT (1919-1979), eighteenth governor of Oklahoma (1967-1971), was born in Marietta, Ohio on March 28, 1919.

Bartlett attended Princeton University, earning a B.S. degree in Geological Engineering in 1942 and supported himself during his college years by working in the oil fields of Oklahoma. After a stint in the United States Marine Corps Aviation, he settled in Tulsa, Oklahoma in 1945 and became a partner in the Keener Oil Company. Between 1953 and 1956 he was president of the Dewey Supply Company, and in 1958, went into the ranching business.

Bartlett served in the Oklahoma Senate from 1963 to 1965. In 1966 he ran for the Oklahoma governorship on the Republican ticket, defeating his Democratic opponent, Preston J. Moore, and taking office on January 9, 1967.

During Bartlett's tenure, the State's judicial system was revamped so that State judges were no longer appointed, instead they had to be elected by the voters. In addition, a State Constitutional amendment was adopted, allowing money earmarked for education to be deposited in public banks. Also a Board of Legislative Compensation was created, and the Legislative Conflict of Interest Law was adopted. Bartlett was also instrumental in getting taxes removed on certain types of personal property, and in implementing reforms of Oklahoma tax laws.

Allowed by a new State Constitutional amendment to succeed himself in office, Bartlett ran for a second term, but was defeated by Democrat David Hall. After stepping down on January 11, 1971, Bartlett returned to his business ventures. However, the following year he ran for the United States Senate, and was elected.

Bartlett married Ann Chilton Smith, and the couple had three children. He died on March 1, 1979.

HALL, DAVID (1930-), nineteenth governor of Oklahoma (1971-1975), was born in Oklahoma City, Oklahoma on October 20, 1930.

Hall attended the University of Oklahoma, earning a B.A. degree in Government and History in 1952. He continued his studies at Harvard University during 1955-56, and at the University of Tulsa, receiving an LL.B. degree from the latter school in 1959.

From 1959 to 1962 Hall served as Assistant County Attorney in Tulsa County, then became County Attorney in the latter year, serving in that post until 1966, when he went into private law practice. Later that year he made an unsuccessful run for the governorship on the Democratic ticket. Two years later he became Professor of Law at the University of Tulsa.

In 1970 Hall made a second try for the governorship, defeating the Republican candidate, incumbent Governor Dewey F. Bartlett, and taking office on January 11, 1971. During his tenure, the voting age was dropped to eighteen, the "silent vote" was abolished, and the Oklahoma Grand Jury system was revamped, as was the State's tax system. Being allowed by a recent constitutional amendment to run for a succeeding term, he did so, but was defeated in the Democratic primary contest, and stepped down on January 13, 1975.

After leaving office, Hall received a three-year sentence in federal prison after being convicted of bribery and extortion while governor of Oklahoma.

Hall is married to Jo Evans Hall, and the couple has three children.

BOREN, DAVID LYLE (1941-), twentieth governor of Oklahoma (1975-1979), was born in Washington, D.C. on April 21, 1941.

Boren attended Yale University where he received a B.A. degree, summa cum laude, in 1963. Boren continued his schooling at Oxford University in England, earning an M.A. degree in 1965. Three years later he received a J.D. degree from the University of Oklahoma.

Between 1960 and 1962 Boren was Assistant to the Director of Liaison for the Office of Civil and Defense Mobilization. During 1962-63 he served with the United States Information Agency in London, England, as a Propaganda Analyst in Soviet Affairs. During 1965-66 he served on the Resident Counseling Staff at the University of Oklahoma. From 1969 to 1974, Boren served as both Professor of Political Science, and as Chairman of the Social Studies Division at Oklahoma Baptist University.

Between 1967 and 1974, Boren was a member of the Oklahoma House of Representatives. In the latter year, he ran for the Oklahoma governorship on the Democratic ticket, defeating the Republican candidate, Jim Inhofe, and taking office on January 13, 1975.

Boren's intent for his administration was to eliminate waste in spending, and revamp the State government. One of his bigger decisions was the consolidation of several departments, including the Highway Safety Office, the Railroad Maintenance Authority, the Aeronautics Commission, and the Highway Department, to fall under the heading of the Department of Transportation.

Although allowed to run for a second term in 1978, Boren decided instead to run for the United States Senate seat vacated by the ailing Dewey F. Bartlett. Serving for several years, Boren stepped down from his Senate post in 1994 in order to take the position of president of the University of Oklahoma, in Norman.

Boren was married to Janna Lou Little, with whom he had two children. After their divorce, he married Molly W. Shi.

WALTERS, DAVID (1951-), twenty-third governor of Oklahoma (1991-1995), was born on November 20, 1951.

Walters attended the University of Oklahoma, earning a B.A. degree in 1973, and continued his education at Harvard University, receiving an M.B.A in 1977. During 1975 he served as management systems and project administrator at the University of Oklahoma. With an interest in Democratic politics, Walters served as project manager during the administration of Governor David Boren in 1976. Between 1977 and 1980 Walters was assistant provost at the Health Science Center, and associate provost from 1980 to 1982. Between 1982 and 1985 he was president of the Burks Group, and during 1985-86, was president of American Fidelity Property Company. From 1986 to 1990, Walters was owner and president of The Walters Company, and beginning in 1992, served chairman of the Interstate Oil & Gas Compact Commission. During that year he also served as national chairman for the Clinton/Gore Campaign.

Walters ran for and won the governorship of Oklahoma in 1990, serving between 1991 and 1995. Declining to run for a second term, he pled guilty to misdemeanor charges for accepting illegal contributions during his 1990 campaign. He is married to Rhonda Smith, and the couple has three children.

KEATING, FRANK (1944-), twenty-fourth governor of Oklahoma (1995-), was born in St. Louis, Missouri, on February 10, 1944, but grew up from the age of six months in Tulsa, Oklahoma.

Keating first studied at Georgetown University where he received a B.A. degree in 1966, then earned a law degree at the University of Oklahoma College of Law in 1969. Keating subsequently went into law enforcement, becoming a special agent with the Federal Bureau of Investigation, then later became an assistant district attorney in his hometown of Tulsa.

Deciding to enter politics, Keating, a Republican, ran for and won a seat in the Oklahoma House of Representatives in 1972, then two years later, was elected to the Oklahoma State Senate. In 1981, President Ronald Reagan chose Keating to serve as U.S. Attorney for the Northern District of Oklahoma. Five years later he was appointed Assistant Secretary of the U.S. Treasury (1986-88), and was subsequently named Associate Attorney General (1988-89). While serving in the latter posts, he was overseer of some of the federal government's most important agencies, including the Federal Bureau of Prisons, the U.S. Customs Service, the Bureau of Alcohol, Tobacco and Firearms, and the Secret Service.

In November of 1994, Keating won the governorship of Oklahoma, and within the first three months of his tenure in 1995, he was faced with a major crisis when the Alfred P. Murrah Federal Office Building in Oklahoma City was bombed, causing 168 deaths. Both the Governor and the First Lady immediately mobilized rescue crews and relief organizations, and due to their efforts, in 1996 the Salvation Army bestowed upon them the William Booth Award.

Other achievements by Keating during his time in office included his proposal of a State income tax cut across the board, including sales, unemployment and state taxes, which became a reality due to his perseverance. Several reforms were initiated by Keating as well, such as worker's compensation, substantial investments in higher education, and several million dollars earmarked for the State's roads and highways. He was also the architect of the Animal Waste and Water Quality Protection Task Force, organized in an effort to address environmental concerns.

Frank Keating was reelected to the Oklahoma governorship in 1998. He and his wife Cathy have three children.

DICTIONARY OF PLACES

Population figures and demographic information are official U.S. Census Bureau finals for 1990. When two figures are shown, separated by a slash, the first figure is the 1990 and the second is the Census Bureau 1999 estimate – the most recent available. Year 2000 census supplements will be available in the fall of 2001.

ACHILLE, Town; Bryan County; Pop. 480 / 551; Zip Code 74720; Elev. 685; Lat. 33-50-08 N, Long. 096-23-11 W; The town's name is loosely based on the Cherokee word *astila*, which means "fire."

ADA, City; Pontotoc County Seat; Pop. 15,902 / 15,268; Zip Code 74820; Elev. 1010; Lat. 34-46-32 N, Long. 096-4005 W; The town is named for the daughter of the first postmaster, William Reed.

ADAIR, Town; Mayes County; Pop. 508 / 702; Zip Code 74330; Elev. 680; Lat. 36-26-18 N, Long. 095-16-11 W; Adair is named after William Penn Adair, a well-known Cherokee leader.

AFTON, Town; Ottawa County; Pop. 1,174 / 874; Zip Code 74331; Elev. 792; Lat. 36-39-29 N, Long. 094-56-20 W; Railroad surveyor, Anton Aires, named his daughter for the Afton River in Scotland. The town was named in her honor.

ALEX, Town; Grady County; Pop. 769 / 670; Zip Code 73002; Elev. 1048; Lat. 34-54-41 N, Long. 097-46-59 W; The town's name honors the first postmaster, William Alexander.

ALLEN, Town; Hughes & Pontotoc Counties; Pop. 998 / 1,047; Zip Code 74825; Lat. 34-52-45 N, Long. 096-24-18 W; The town is named for the son of a deputy U.S. Marshall, Allen McCall.

ALTUS, City; Jackson County Seat; Pop. 23,101 / 20,981; Zip Code 73521; Elev. 1395; Lat. 34-39-39 N, Long. 099-19-13 W; After the original townsite was destroyed in a flood, the settlers moved to higher ground and named the new town "altus" - Latin for "high."

ALVA, City; Woods County Seat; Pop. 6,416 / 4,966; Zip Code 73717; Lat. 36-48-00 N, Long. 098-39-59 W; Alva was named for Alva Adams, one time governor of the state of Colorado.

AMETT, Town; Ellis County Seat; Pop. 714; The town is named after an early settler.

ANODARKO, City; Caddo County Seat; Pop. 6,378 / 6,761; Zip Code 73005; Lat. 35-04-21 N, Long. 098-14-30 W; A Caddo Indian name for one of the Caddo tribes.

ANTLERS, Town; Pushmataha County Seat; Pop. 2,989 / 2,591; Zip Code 74523; Elev. 508; Lat. 34-14-06 N, Long. 095-36-57 W; An early camping place was marked by a pair of antlers. The town took its name from this trail mark.

APACHE, Town; Codda County; Pop. 1,560 / 1,461; Zip Code 73006; Elev. 1300; Lat. 34-53-36 N, Long. 098-21-42 W; A Zuni Indian word meaning "enemy."

ARAPAHO, Town; Custer County Seat; Pop. 851 / 745; Zip Code 73620; Elev. 1669; Lat. 35-34-32 N, Long. 098-57-32 W; An Indian word meaning "cloud men."

ARDMORE, City; Carter County Seat; Pop. 23,689 / 24,095; Zip Code 73401; Lat. 34-11-02 N, Long. 097-03-14 W; Named by early settlers for Ardmore, Pennsylvania.

ARKOMA, Town; Le Flore County; Pop. 2,175 / 2,302; Zip Code 74901; Lat. 35-20-58 N, Long. 094-26-28 W; Near the state line the word is a joining of Arkansas and Oklahoma.

ASHER, Town; Pottawatomie County; Pop. 659 / 468; Zip Code 74826; Lat. 34-59-27 N, Long. 096-55-39 W; The town is named in honor of its founder, G.M. Asher.

ATOKA, City; Atoka County Seat; Pop. 3,409 / 3,343; Zip Code 74525; Elev. 583; Lat. 34-23-02 N, Long. 096-07-46 W; The town is named for Captain Atoka, a Choctaw ball-player.

BARNSDALL, City; Osage County; Pop. 1,501 / 1,192; Zip Code 74002; Elev. 773; Lat. 36-33-39 N, Long. 096-09-32 W; The town is named after the Barnsdall Oil Company.

BARTLESVILLE, City; Osage and Washington Counties; Washington County Seat; Pop. 34,568 / 33,693; Zip Code 74003; Lat. 36-44-58 N, Long. 095-58-34 W; Jacob Bartles established a trading post here in 1879. The town is named in his honor.

BEAVER, City; Beaver County Seat; Pop. 1,939 / 1,427; Zip Code 73932; Elev. 2393; Lat. 36-48-49 N, Long. 100-31-28 W; The town is named after the adjacent Beaver River.

BEGGS, City; Okmulgee County; Pop. 1,428 / 1,246; Zip Code 74421; Elev. 732; Lat. 35-44-27 N, Long. 096-04-20 W; Begg's name honors C.H. Beggs, Vice-President of a local railroad.

BETHANY, City; Oklahoma County; Pop. 22,130 / 20,092; Zip Code 73008; Lat. 35-30-47 N, Long. 097-35-04 W; Named after the Biblical community near Jerusalem.

BEHEL ACRES, Town; Pottawatomie County; Pop. 2,314 / 2,137; Zip Code 74724; Elev. 874; Lat. 34-21-29 N, Long. 094-50-51 W; Bethel is a Hebrew word meaning "house of god."

BILLINGS, Town; Noble County; Pop. 632 / 542; Zip Code 74630; Elev. 1020; Lat. 36-32-02 N, Long. 097-26-28 W; A Rock Island Railroad agent named the town after his wife's maiden surname.

BINGER, Town; Caddo County; Pop. 791 / 640; Zip Code 73009; Lat. 35-18-31 N, Long. 098-20-31 W; The town's name honors Binger Hermann, commissioner of the General Land Office from 1897 to 1903.

BIXBY, City; Tulsa & Wagoner Counties; Pop. 6,969 / 13,278; Zip Code 74008; Lat. 35-57-29 N, Long. 095-52-54 W; The town's name honors Tam Bixby, chairman of the Dawes Commission.

BLACKWELL, City; Kay County; Pop. 8,400 / 7,145; Zip Code 74631; Elev. 1014; Lat. 36-47-51 N, Long. 097-17-21 W; Named for its founder Andrew Blackwell.

BLAIR, Town; Jackson County; Pop. 1,092 / 846; Zip Code 73526; Lat. 34-46-42 N, Long. 099-20-03 W; The name honors John Blair, a local railroad official.

BLANCHARD, Town; Grady and McClain Counties; Pop. 1,616 / 2,864; Zip Code 73010; Elev. 1276; Lat. 35-08-21 N, Long. 097-39-25 W; Founded in 1906 and named after town founder, W.G. Blanchard.

BOISE CITY, City; Cimarron County Seat; Pop. 1,761 / 1,345; Zip Code 73933; Elev. 4165; Lat. 36-43-47 N, Long. 102-30-21 W; Named in 1908 for Boise, Idaho.

BOKCHITO, Town; Bryan County; Pop. 628 / 564; Zip Code 74726; Elev. 637; Lat. 34-01-14 N, Long. 096-08-20 W; A Choctaw Indian word meaning "big creek."

BOKOSHE, Town; Le Flore County; Pop. 556 / 448; Zip Code 74930; Lat. 35-11-23 N, Long. 094-47-20 W; A Choctaw Indian word meaning "little creek."

BOLEY, Town; Okfuskee County; Pop. 423 / 872; Zip Code 74829; Lat. 35-29-38 N, Long. 096-28-56 W; Founded in 1903 and named for the local railroad roadmaster, W.H. Boley.

BOSWELL, Town; Choctaw County; Pop. 702 / 638; Zip Code 74727; Elev. 597; Lat. 34-01-39 N, Long. 095-52-00 W; Formerly called Mayhew, Boswell honors civic leader and engineer, A.V. Boswell.

BOWLEGS, Town; Seminole County; Pop. 522 / 385; Zip Code 74830; Lat. 35-08-35 N, Long. 096-40-15 W; In Seminole County; the town as named for Billy Bowlegs, a Seminole chief.

BOYNTON, Town; Muskogee County; Pop. 518 / 405; Zip Code 74422; Lat. 35-38-54 N, Long. 095-39-17 W; The town is named for E.W. Boynton, a chief engineer for a local railway company.

BRAY, Town; Stephens County; Pop. 591 / 1,000; Zip Code 73012; Lat. 34-38-28 N, Long. 097-48-31 W; Bray takes its name from the first postmaster, Thomas Bray.

BRISTOW, City; Creek County; Pop. 4,702 / 4,395; Zip Code 74010; Lat. 35-49-45 N, Long. 096-23-10 W; Founded in 1898 and named for Kansas Senator Joseph Bristow.

BROKEN ARROW, City; Tulsa & Wagoner Counties; Pop. 35,761 / 75,336; Zip Code 740+; Elev. 753; Lat. 36-02-00 N, Long. 095-48-20 W; Near Tulsa, the name comes from a Creek Indian ceremony after the Civil War to symbolize the war's end.

BROKEN BOW, City; McCurtain County; Pop. 3,965 / 4,725; Zip Code 74728; Lat. 34-01-28 N, Long. 094-44-00 W; Founded in 1911 and named by pioneer Dirks family for their former home in Nebraska.

BUFFALO, Town; Harper County Seat; Pop. 1,381 / 1,161; Zip Code 73834; Lat. 36-50-02 N, Long. 099-37-19 W; The town is named for nearby Buffalo Creek.

BURNS FLAT, Town; Washita County; Pop. 2,431 / 941; Zip Code 73624; Lat. 35-21-24 N, Long. 099-10-53 W; Named for the town of Burns immediately to the south.

BYNG, Town; Pontotoc County; Pop. 833 / 1,141; Byng's name honors British Army officer Sir Julian Byng.

CANTON, Town; Blaine County; Pop. 854 / 520; Zip Code 73724; Elev. 1591; Lat. 36-03-21 N, Long. 098-35-22 W; Established in 1905 and named for nearby Cantonment, a one-time military reservation.

CANUTE, Town; Washita County; Pop. 676 / 595; Zip Code 73626; Lat. 35-25-13 N, Long. 099-16-45 W; Originally called Oak, the town was renamed for the famous King Canute of Denmark.

CARMEN, Town; Alfalfa County; Pop. 516 / 359; Zip Code 73726; Elev. 1354; Lat. 36-34-46 N, Long. 098-27-23 W; Founded in 1901 and named for Carmen Diaz, the wife of the president of Mexico.

CARNEGIE, Town; Caddo County; Pop. 2,016 / 1,739; Zip Code 73015; Elev. 1309; Lat. 35-06-21 N, Long. 098-35-58 W; The town is named for industrialist Andrew Carnegie.

CARNEY, Town; Lincoln County; Pop. 622 / 553; Zip Code 74832; Lat. 35-48-15 N, Long. 097-00-44 W; Called Cold Springs originally, the town's name was changed to Carney in honor of its founder.

CASHION, Town; Kingfisher and Logan Counties; Pop. 547 / 550; Zip Code 73016; Lat. 35-47-47 N, Long. 097-41-00 W; The town's name honors Spanish-American War hero Roy Cashion.

CATOOSA, City; Rogers County; Pop. 1,772 / 5,570; Zip Code 74015; Lat. 36-11-19 N, Long. 095-44-48 W; A Cherokee Indian word meaning "new settlement place."

CEMENT, Town; Caddo County; Pop. 884 / 608; Zip Code 73017; Lat. 34-55-55 N, Long. 098-08-20 W; Founded in 1902 and named after nearby cement operations.

CHANDLER, City; Lincoln County Seat; Pop. 2,926 / 2,755; Zip Code 74834; Lat. 35-42-23 N, Long. 096-52-44 W; The name honors George Chandler, assistant secretary of the interior under President Harrison.

CHECOTAH, City; McIntosh County; Pop. 3,454 / 3,650; Zip Code 74426; Elev. 652; Lat. 35-28-12 N, Long. 095-31-16 W; Founded in 1886 and named for a Creek Chief, Samuel Checote.

CHELSEA, City; Rogers County; Pop. 1,754 / 1,954; Zip Code 74016; Lat. 36-32-06 N, Long. 095-25-44 W; Charles Peach, a local railroad official, named the town for his former home in England in 1882.

CHEROKEE, City; Alfalfa County Seat; Pop. 2,105 / 1,485; Zip Code 73728; Elev. 1181; Lat. 36-46-14 N, Long. 098-22-38 W; Established in 1894 and named after the Cherokee Indian nation.

CHEYENNE, Town; Roger Mills County Seat; Pop. 1,207 / 700; Zip Code 73628; Lat. 35-36-46 N, Long. 099-40-18 W; Named after the Cheyenne Indian tribe.

CHICKASHA, City; Grady County Seat; Pop. 15,828 / 16,578; Zip Code 73018; Elev. 1096; Lat. 35-02-04 N, Long. 097-56-56 W. The site of the town was included in the "Swinging Ring" cat-

tle ranch owned by an intermarried citizen of the Chickasaw Indian Nation, the western border of which was nearby.

CHOCTAW, City; Oklahoma County; Pop. 7,520 / 9,988; Zip Code 73020; Lat. 35-28-48 N, Long. 097-16-10 W; The city derives its name from the Choctaw Coal and Railway Company.

CHOUTEAU, Town; Mayes County; Pop. 1,559 / 2,026; Zip Code 74337; Lat. 36-11-15 N, Long. 095-20-30 W; Founded in 1871 and named in honor of the Chouteau family.

CLAREMORE, City; Rogers County Seat; Pop. 12,085 / 21,781; Zip Code 74017; Lat. 36-18-46 N, Long. 095-36-30 W; Established in 1874 and named for an Osage Indian chief, Clermont.

CLAYTON, Town; Pushmataha County; Pop. 833 / 686; Zip Code 74536; Lat. 34-35-13 N, Long. 095-21-19 W; The town is named for Clayton, Missouri.

CLEO SPRINGS, Town; Major County; Pop. 514 / 403; Zip Code 73729; Elev. 283; Lat. 36-24-31 N, Long. 098-26-08 W; Named for nearby Cleo Springs.

CLEVELAND, City; Pawnee County; Pop. 2,972 / 3,009; Zip Code 74020; Elev. 777; Lat. 36-18-23 N, Long. 096-27-54 W; The town is named in honor of Grover Cleveland.

CLINTON, City; Custer County; Pop. 8,796 / 8,649; Zip Code 73601; Elev. 1592; Lat. 35-30-36 N, Long. 098-52-29 W; Founded in 1903 and named for a territorial jurist, Clinton F. Irwin.

COALGATE, City; Coal County Seat; Pop. 2,001 / 1,902; Zip Code 74538; Elev. 623; Lat. 34-31-17 N, Long. 096-13-18 W; The town got its name from nearby coal mines.

COLBERT, Town; Bryan County; Pop. 1,122 / 1,227; Zip Code 74733; Lat. 33-51-22 N, Long. 096-29-59 W; Colbert's name honors early settler, Benjamin Colbert.

COLCORD, Town; Delaware County; Pop. 530 / 797; Zip Code 74338; Lat. 36-15-35 N, Long. 094-41-14 W; The town's name remembers Charles Colcord, an early resident of Oklahoma City.

COLLINSVILLE, City; Rogers & Tulsa Counties; Pop. 3,556 / 4,138; Zip Code 74021; Lat. 36-21-57 N, Long. 095-50-06 W; Founded in 1897 and named for Dr. H.H. Collins, an early settler.

COMANCHE, City; Stephens County; Pop. 1,937 / 1,703; Zip Code 73529; Elev. 984; Lat. 34-21-59 N, Long. 097-58-15 W; Named after the famous Indian tribe.

COMMERCE, City; Ottawa County; Pop. 2,556 / 2,586; Zip Code 74339; Lat. 36-56-28 N, Long. 094-52-33 W; Named by local settlers after their ambitions.

COPAN, Town; Washington County; Pop. 960 / 782; Zip Code 74022; Lat. 36-54-01 N, Long. 095-55-20 W; The city takes its name from the Honduran city.

CORN, Town; Washita County; Pop. 542 / 502; Zip Code 73024; Lat. 35-22-38 N, Long. 098-46-56 W; The original post office was in a cornfield, hence the name.

COVINGTON, Town; Garfield County; Pop. 715 / 608; Zip Code 73730; Lat. 36-18-28 N, Long. 097-35-20 W; John Covington, a well-known pioneer, left his name on the town.

COWETA, City; Wagoner County; Pop. 4,554 / 7,380; Zip Code 74429; Elev. 654; Lat. 36-03-06 N, Long. 095-41-51 W; Presbyterian missionaries named the town after a Creek Indian town in Alabama.

COWLINGTON, Town; Le Flore County; Pop. 546 / 166; Founded in the 1880s and named for early pioneer, A.F. Cowling.

CRESCENT, City; Logan County; Pop. 1,651 / 1,202; Zip Code 73028; Lat. 36-00-15 N, Long. 097-36-40 W; Settled in the 1890s and descriptively named for a nearby crescent-shaped oak grove.

CUSHING, City; Payne County; Pop. 7,720 / 7,933; Zip Code 74023; Marshall Cushing, assistant to the Postmaster General, had the town named in his honor.

CUSTER CITY, Town; Custer County; Pop. 530 / 417; Zip Code 73639; Elev. 1769; Lat. 35-39-43 N, Long. 098-53-06 W; Named in honor of General George Custer, who was killed in 1876 while fighting the Sioux Indians.

CYRIL, Town; Caddo County; Pop. 1,220 / 1,123; Zip Code 73029; Lat. 34-53-02 N, Long. 098-12-06 W; The original landowner, Cyril Lookingglass, had the town named in his honor.

DAVENPORT, Town; Lincoln County; Pop. 974 / 1,002; Zip Code 74026; Lat. 35-42-15 N, Long. 096-45-44 W; The first postmaster, Nettie Davenport, gave the town her family name.

DAVIDSON, Town; Tillman County; Pop. 501 / 457; Zip Code 73530; Lat. 34-14-37 N, Long. 099-04-53 W; Davidson is named in honor of A.J. Davidson, a Director of a local railroad.

DAVIS, City; Murray County; Pop. 2,782 / 2,769; Zip Code 73030; Elev. 846; Lat. 34-30-07 N, Long. 097-06-58 W; Merchant Samuel Davis left his name on the town.

DEL CITY, City; Oklahoma County; Pop. 28,424; A part of the Oklahoma City area, the town is named for Delaphens Campbell, the daughter of the original landowner.

DELAWARE, Town; Nowata County; Pop. 544 / 456; Zip Code 74027; Lat. 36-46-45 N, Long. 095-38-21 W; The town's name remembers the Delaware Indians.

DEPEW, Town; Creek County; Pop. 682 / 563; Zip Code 74028; Lat. 35-47-57 N, Long. 096-30-13 W; Founded in 1901 and named for Chauncey Depew, U.S. Senator from New York.

DEWAR, City; Okmulgee County; Pop. 1,048 / 838; Zip Code 74431; Lat. 35-27-21 N, Long. 095-56-21 W; Established in 1909 and named for a local railroad official, William Dewar.

DEWEY, City; Washington County; Pop. 3,545 / 3,291; Zip Code 74029; Lat. 36-47-48 N, Long. 095-56-05 W; Founded in 1899 and named for Spanish-American War hero, Admiral George Dewey.

DICKSON, Town; Carter County; Pop. 996 / 980; Named for an early pioneer.

DILL CITY, Town; Washita County; Pop. 649 / 685; Zip Code 73641; Lat. 35-16-57 N, Long. 099-07-49 W; Named for prominent Washita County resident D.S. Dill.

DOVER, Town; Kingfisher County; Pop. 570 / 388; Zip Code 73734; Lat. 35-58-58 N, Long. 097-54-39 W; The town is named after Dover, England.

DRUMRIGHT, City; Creek County; Pop. 3,162 / 2,875; Zip Code 74030; Lat. 35-59-11 N, Long. 096-36-55 W; The original landowner, Aaron Drumright, had the town named in his honor.

DUNCAN, City; Stephens County Seat; Pop. 22,517 / 21,795; Zip Code 73533; Elev. 1126; Lat. 34-28-09 N, Long. 097-59-42 W.

DURANT, City; Bryan County Seat; Pop. 11,972 / 12,992; Zip Code 74701; Lat. 33-59-51 N, Long. 096-23-08 W; Established in the 1870s and named in honor of the well-known Durant family.

EAST NINNEKAH, Town; Grady County; Pop. 1,085; The city takes its name from the Choctaw Indian word Ninek, meaning "night" or "darkness."

EDMOND, City; Oklahoma County; Pop. 34,637 / 66,757; Zip Code 730+; Elev. 1,200; Lat. 35-32-46 N, Long. 098-22-50 W. Named for a railroad official.

ELGIN, Town; Comanche County; Pop. 1,003 / 1,000; Zip Code 73538; Lat. 34-46-27 N, Long. 098-17-28 W. The town is named after Elgin, Illinois.

ELK CITY, City; Beckham County; Pop. 9,579 / 11,122; Zip Code 73644; Elev. 1,928; Lat. 35-24-51 N, Long. 099-24-44 W. Named for Elk Creek, which skirts the town's limits.

EL RENO, City; Canadian County Seat; Pop. 15,486 / 15,985; Zip Code 73036; Lat. 35-31-56 N, Long. 097-57-14 W; Founded in 1889 and named for nearby Fort Reno.

ELMORE CITY, Town; Garvin County; Pop. 582 / 521; Zip Code 73035; Lat. 34-37-23 N, Long. 097-23-44 W; The town is named for pioneer J.O. Elmore.

ENID, City; Garfield County Seat; Pop. 50,363 / 45,196; Zip Code 73701; Elev. 1246; Lat. 36-25-08 N, Long. 097-51-55 W; Established in 1893 and taken from the Idylls of the King by Tennyson.

ERICK, City; Beckham County; Pop. 1,375 / 1,126; Zip Code 73645; Lat. 35-12-47 N, Long. 099-52-12 W; The town's developer, Beeks Erick, had the town named in his honor.

EUFAULA, City; McIntosh County Seat; Pop. 3,092 / 3,490; Zip Code 74432; Elev. 617; Lat. 35-17-09 N, Long. 095-34-57 W; Eutoula was the name of a Creek Indian village in Alabama. It means "they left here and went to other places."

FAIRFAX, Town; Osage County; Pop. 1,073 / 1,611; Zip Code 74637; Elev. 342; Lat. 36-34-26 N, Long. 096-42-15 W; The town is named in honor of Fairfax County in Virginia.

FAIRLAND, Town; Ottawa County; Pop. 1,073 / 971; Zip Code 74343; Elev. 838; Lat. 36-45-21 N, Long. 094-50-37 W; A descriptive name for the many prairie flowers in the area.

FAIRVIEW, City; Major County Seat; Pop. 3,370 / 2,660; Zip Code 73737; Lat. 36-16-40 N, Long. 098-28-38 W; The town has a scenic location in a wooded valley east of the Glass Mountains.

FLETCHER, Town; Comanche County; Pop. 1,074 / 998; Zip Code 73541; Lat. 34-48-59 N, Long. 098-14-25 W; In Comanche County; the town was named for pioneer, Fletcher Dodge.

FOREST PARK, Town; Oklahoma County; Pop. 1,148 / 1,250; A part of Oklahoma City, descriptively named for the oak groves in the town.

FORGAN, Town; Beaver County; Pop. 611 / 507; Zip Code 73938; Lat. 36-54-25 N, Long. 100-32-17 W; The town is named for Chicago banker, James B. Forgan.

FORT COBB, Town; Caddo County; Pop. 760 / 636; Zip Code 73038; Elev. 1255; Lat. 35-06-00 N, Long. 098-26-14 W; Established in 1859 and named for Howell Cobb, Secretary of the Treasury under President Buchanan.

FORT GIBSON, Town; Muskagee County; Pop. 2,483 / 3,785; Zip Code 74434; Lat. 35-48-18 N, Long. 095-15-04 W; Founded in 1824, the fort was named for Colonel George Gibson, U.S. Army Commissary Dept.

FORT SUPPLY, Town; Woodward County; Pop. 559 / 357; Zip Code 73841; Elev. 1994; Lat. 36-30-23 N, Long. 099-23-10 W; Established in 1868 as a supply base for General Custer's Indian campaigns.

FORT TOWSON, Town; Choctaw County; Pop. 789 / 528; Zip Code 74735; Lat. 34-01-06 N, Long. 095-15-56 W; Set up as an army base in 1824 and named for Nathan Towson, U.S. Army paymaster general.

FREDERICK, City; Tillman County Seat; Pop. 6,153 / 4,662; Zip Code 73542; Lat. 34-23-31 N, Long. 099-00-50 W; Formerly Gosnell, the town's name was changed to honor Frederick Van Blarcom, the son of a prominent railroad developer.

GAGE, Town; Ellis County; Pop. 667 / 405; Zip Code 73843; Elev. 2136; Lat. 36-19-03 N, Long. 099-45-31 W; In Ellis County; Gage is named in honor of Lyman Gage, William McKinley's Secretary of the Treasury.

GARBER, City; Garfield County; Pop. 1,215 / 909; Zip Code 73738; Elev. 1177; Lat. 36-26-16 N, Long. 097-34-50 W; Once called McCardie, the name was changed in 1894 to honor early resident Martin Garber.

GEARY, City; Blame and Canadian Counties; Pop. 1,700 / 1,155; Zip Code 73040; Elev. 1541; Lat. 35-37-38 N, Long. 098-18-50 W; Established in 1892 and named for Indian scout Ed Geary.

GERONIMO, Town; Comanche County; Pop. 726 / 1,026; Zip Code 73543; Lat. 34-29-10 N, Long. 098-22-49 W; The town is named for the famous Apache Indian chief.

GLENCOE, Town; Payne County; Pop. 490 / 509; Zip Code 74032; Elev. 1046; Lat. 36-13-29 N, Long. 096-55-40 W; Named after Glencoe, Scotland.

GLENPOOL, City; Tulsa County; Pop. 2,706 / 8,265; Zip Code 74033; Lat. 35-57-23 N, Long. 096-00-34 W; The town is named after Ida Glenn, the original landowner of the townsite.

GOLDSBY, Town; McCloin County; Pop. 603 / 1,111; In McCloin County; the town is named for early resident Frank Goldsby.

GOODWELL, Town; Texas County; Pop. 1,166 / 989; Zip Code 73939; Elev. 3293; Lat. 36-35-38 N, Long. 101-37-40 W; The Rock Island Railroad drilled a water well on the site, which proved to be good water; hence the name.

GORE, Town; Sequoyah County; Pop. 445 / 895; Zip Code 74435; Lat. 35-31-49 N, Long. 095-07-04 W; The town's name honors U.S. Senator Thomas P. Gore.

GRACEMONT, Town; Caddo County; Pop. 503 / 334; Zip Code 73042; Lat. 35-11-14 N, Long. 098-15-14 W; The first postmaster Alice Bailey coined the name after two of her friends, Grace and Montgomery.

GRANDFIELD, City; Tulman County; Pop. 1,445 / 1,088; Zip Code 73546; Elev. 1456; Lat. 34-13-46 N, Long. 098-41-20 W; The town's name honors U.S. Postmaster General Charles Grandfield.

GRANITE, Town; Greer County; Pop. 1,617 / 1,943; Zip Code 73547; Lat. 34-57-42 N, Long. 099-23-01 W; Founded in 1889 and named for the large granite formations in the nearby Wichita Mountains.

GROVE, Town; Delaware County; Pop. 3,378 / 5,536; Zip Code 74344; Lat. 36-35-27 N, Long. 094-47-31 W; The nearby Round Grove Civil War landmark gave the town its name.

GUTHRIE, City; Logan County Seat; Pop. 10,312 / 10,169; Zip Code 73044; Lat. 35-52-43 N, Long. 097-25-31 W; Capital of the Oklahoma Territory, the city was named for Kansas jurist John Guthrie.

GUYMON, City; Texas County Seat; Pop. 8,492 / 8,921; Zip Code 73942; Elev. 3121; Lat. 36-41-10 N, Long. 101-28-56 W; The town's name honors E.T. Guyman, the original developer.

HALLETT, Town; Pawnee County; Pop. 196 / 180; Zip Code 74034; Lat. 36-13-45 N, Long. 096-34-06 W; The town's name remembers Lieutenant Charles Hallett of the nineteenth Kansas Cavalry.

HALL PARK, Town; Cleveland County; Pop. 577 / 1,224; Near the city of Norman, Hall is named after original developer Ike Hall.

HAMMON, Town; Custer and Roger Mills Counties; Pop. 866 / 554; Zip Code 73650; Elev. 1736; Lat. 35-37-30 N, Long. 099-22-40 W; Founded in 1894 and named for Indian agent J.H. Hammon.

HARRAH, Town; Oklahoma County; Pop. 2,897 / 5,007; Zip Code 73045; Lat. 35-29-10 N, Long. 097-09-56 W; Businessman and civic leader Frank Harrah had the town take his name.

HARTSHORNE, City; Pittsburg County; Pop. 2,380 / 2,169; Zip Code 74547; Elev. 705; Lat. 34-50-36 N, Long. 095-33-33 W; Founded in 1890 and named for railroad official Dr. Charles Hartshorne.

HASKELL, Town; Muskogee County; Pop. 1,953 / 2,056; Zip Code 74436; Lat. 35-49-12 N, Long. 095-40-33 W; Formerly Sanokla, the town is named after Charles Haskell, longtime resident.

HEALDTON, City; Carter County; Pop. 3,769 / 2,950; Zip Code 73438; Lat. 34-13-58 N, Long. 097-29-12 W; Founded in the 1880s and named after prominent resident Charles Heald.

HEAVENER, City; Le Flore County; Pop. 2,776 / 2,444; Zip Code 74937; Elev. 562; Lat. 34-53-16 N, Long. 094-36-14 W; Established in the 1890s and named for Joseph Heavener, a well-known merchant.

HELENA, Town; Alfalfa County; Pop. 710 / 1,055; Zip Code 73741; Elev. 1397; Lat. 36-32-50 N, Long. 098-16-08 W; The town is named after its first postmaster, Helen S. Monroe.

HENNESSEY, Town; Kingfisher County; Pop. 2,287 / 1,874; Zip Code 73742; Lat. 36-06-27 N, Long. 097-53-55 W; The town's name commemorates freight hauler Pat Hennessey, who was killed in an Indian massacre in 1874.

HENRYETTA, City; Okmulgee County; Pop. 6,432 / 6,057; Zip Code 74437; Lat. 35-28-23 N, Long. 095-55-47 W; In Okmulgee County; The town is named after Henry and Etta Ray Beard.

HOBART, City; Kiowa County Seat; Pop. 4,735 / 3,734; Zip Code 73651; Elev. 1,550; Lat. 35-01-41 N, Long. 099-05-39 W. Named for Garrett A. Hobart, vice president 1897-1899.

HOLDENVILLE, City; Hughes County Seat; Pop. 5,469 / 5,867; Zip Code 74848; Elev. 866; Lat. 35-05-02 N, Long. 096-23-41 W, Named for nearby Lake Holdenville.

HOLLIS, City; Harmon County Seat; Pop. 2,958 / 2,314; Zip Code 73550; Elev. 1,615; Lat. 34-41-08 N, Long. 099-55-02 W. Part of the Red River Territory, which Texas claimed prior to a Supreme Court decision in 1896.

HOMINY, City; Osage County; Pop. 3,130 / 3,122; Zip Code 74035; Elev. 792; Lat. 36-24-49 N, Long. 096-23-32 W; A corruption of the word harmony, possibly referring to a religious mission in Kansas.

HOOKER, City; Texas County; Pop. 1,788 / 1,594; Zip Code 73945; Lat. 36-51-39 N, Long. 101-12-43 W; The town is named for local rancher Joseph Hooker.

HOWE, Town; Le Flore County; Pop. 562 / 516; Zip Code 74940; Lat. 34-56-59 N, Long. 094-38-09 W; The town is named for Kansas Railroad Director, Dr. Herbert Howe.

HUGO, City; Choctaw County Seat; Pop. 7,172 / 5,896; Zip Code 74743; Lat. 34-00-32 N, Long. 095-30-41 W; Hugo is named in honor of the great French novelist, Victor Hugo.

HULBERT, Town; Cherokee County; Pop. 633 / 716; Zip Code 74441; Lat. 34-56-04 N, Long. 095-53-30 W; Hulbert is in Cherokee County, and is named for Ben Hulbert, a well-known Cherokee.

HYDRO, Town; Blaine and Caddo Counties; Pop. 938 / 890; Zip Code 73048; Elev. 1557; Lat. 35-32-53 N, Long. 098-34-42 W; The town is named for the good well water locally available.

IDABEL, City; McCurtain County Seat; Pop. 7,622 / 7,369; Zip Code 74745; Elev. 489; Lat. 33-53-30 N, Long. 094-48-56 W; Founded around 1904 and named for Ida and Belle Purnell, the daughters of a local railroad official.

INOLA, Town; Rogers County; Pop. 1,550 / 1,686; Zip Code 74036; Elev. 600; Lat. 36-09-06 N, Long. 095-35-19 W; A Cherokee word meaning "black fox."

JAY, Town; Delaware County Seat; Pop. 2,100 / 2,464; Zip Code 74346; Elev. 1035; Lat. 36-25-11 N, Long. 094-47-50 W; Jay is named for Jay Washbourne, the grandson of a Cherokee missionary.

JENKS, City; Tulsa County; Pop. 5,876 / 9,703; Zip Code 74037; Lat. 36-01-22 N, Long. 095-58-04 W; In Tulsa County; the town is named after early resident Elmer Jenks.

JONES, Town; Oklahoma County; Pop. 2,270 / 2,470; Zip Code 73049; Lat. 35-33-50 N, Long. 097-17-25 W; The town is named in honor of C.G. Jones, an Oklahoma City industrialist and railroad promoter.

KANSAS, Town; Delaware County; Pop. 491 / 689; Zip Code 74347; Lat. 36-12-15 N, Long. 094-47-49 W; Early settlers named the town after the state of Kansas.

KELLYVILLE, Town; Creek County; Pop. 960 / 1,107; Zip Code 74039; Lat. 35-56-25 N, Long. 096-12-45 W; Merchant James Kelly gave his name to the town.

KEOTA, Town; Haskell County; Pop. 661 / 658; Zip Code 74941; Elev. 4353; Lat. 35-15-34 N, Long. 094-55-10 W; A Choctaw Indian word meaning "the fire gone out," referring to an entire tribe destroyed by disease.

KEYES, Town; Cimarron County; Pop. 557 / 404; Zip Code 73947; Elev. 954; Lat. 36-48-31 N, Long. 102-15-03 W; The town's name honors Santa Fe Railway President, Henry Keyes.

KIEFER, Town; Creek County; Pop. 912 / 1,075; Zip Code 74041; Lat. 35-56-39 N, Long. 096-03-41 W; Formerly called Proper, the town is named for Smith Kiefer, an early resident.

KINGFISHER, City; Kingfisher County Seat; Pop. 4,245 / 4,280; Zip Code 73750; Lat. 35-51-15 N, Long. 097-55-55 W; The town gets is name from Kingfisher Creek.

KINGSTON, Town; Marshall County; Pop. 1,171 / 1,535; Zip Code 73439; Lat. 33-59-430 N, Long. 096-43-17 W; Kingston gets its name from early resident Jeb King.

KIOWA, Town; Pittsburg County; Pop. 866 / 772; Zip Code 74553; Elev. 744; Lat. 34-43-22 N, Long. 095-54-04 W; Named for the Kiowa Indian tribe.

KONAWA, City; Seminole County; Pop. 1,711 / 1,421; Zip Code 74849; Elev. 967; Lat. 34-57-34 N, Long. 096-45-44 W; A Seminole Indian word meaning "a string of beads."

KREBS, City; Pittsburg County; Pop. 1,754 / 1,971; Zip Code 74554; Lat. 34-55-39 N, Long. 095-43-07 W; The town is named for Judge Edmund Krebs, a Choctaw jurist.

LAHOMA, Town; Garfield County; Pop. 537 / 641; Zip Code 73754; Elev. 1236; Lat. 36-23-11 N, Long. 098-05-07 W; A diminutive name for Oklahoma.

LAMONT, Town; Grant County; Pop. 571 / 449; Zip Code 74643; Elev. 1011; Lat. 36-41-27 N, Long. 097-33-33 W; The town is named in honor of Daniel Lamont, President Cleveland's Secretary of War.

LANGLEY, Town; Mayes County; Pop. 582 / 613; Zip Code 74350; Lat. 36-27-51 N, Long. 095-03-04 W; Langley's name honors J. Howard Langley, who was chairman of the Grand River Dam Authority.

LANGSTON, Town; Logan County; Pop. 443 / 1,292; Zip Code 73050; Lat. 35-56-28 N, Long. 097-15-10 W; Black educator and U.S. Congressman, John M. Langston had the town named in his honor.

LAVERNE, Town; Harper County; Pop. 1,563 / 1,126; Zip Code 73848; Lat. 26-42-25 N, Long. 099-53-44 W; Founded in the 1890s and named for early settler Laverne Smith.

LAWTON, City; Comanche County Seat; Pop. 80,054 / 79,927; Zip Code 73501; Lat. 34-36-47 N, Long. 098-24-57 W; The town's name honors General Henry Lawton, who was killed during the Philippine insurrection.

LEXINGTON, Town; Cleveland County; Pop, 1,731 / 1,923; Zip Code 73051; Elev. 1034; Lat. 35-00-57 N, Long. 097-19-53 W; The town is named after Lexington, Kentucky.

LINDSAY, City; Garvin County; Pop. 3,454 / 2,777; Zip Code 73052; Lat. 34-50-20 N, Long. 097-36-39 W; Named for the town's original landowner, Lewis Lindsay.

LOCUST GROVE, Town; Mayes County; Pop. 1,179 / 1,479; Zip Code 74352; Lat. 36-12-04 N, Long. 095-09-59 W; Site of a Civil War battle, the town is named after a prominent grove of locust trees.

LONE GROVE, Town; Carter County; Pop. 3,369 / 4,435; Zip Code 73443; Lat. 34-10-31 N, Long. 097-15-59 W; Descriptively named for a single grove of trees.

LONE WOLF, Town; Kiowa County; Pop. 613 / 499; Zip Code 73655; Elev. 1577; Lat. 34-59-20 N, Long. 099-14-39 W; The town's name honors Kiowa Indian Chief, Lone Wolf.

LUTHER, Town; Oklahoma County; Pop. 1,159 / 1,663; Zip Code 73054; Lat. 35-38-14 N, Long. 097-13-06 W; Founded in the 1890s and named in honor of Oklahoma City businessman Luther Jones.

MADILL, City; Marshall County Seat; Pop. 3,173 / 3,139; Zip Code 73446; Elev. 789; Lat. 34-05-17 N, Long. 096-46-17 W; Railroad attorney George Madill had the town named in his honor.

MANGUM, City; Greer County Seat; Pop. 3,833 / 2,887; Zip Code 73554; Elev. 1606; Lat. 34-52-38 N, Long. 099-30-14 W; Named after the town's original landowner, A.S. Magnum.

MANNFORD, Town; Tulsa County; Pop. 1,786 / 2,035; Zip Code 74044; Lat. 36-07-08 N, Long. 096-20-44 W; Named for an early settler.

MANNSVILLE, Town; Johnston County; Pop. 568 / 375; Zip Code 73447; Lat. 34-11-15 N, Long. 096-51-29 W; The town is named after its first postmaster, Wallace Mann.

MARIETTA, City; Love County Seat; Pop. 2,494 / 2,546; Zip Code 73448; Lat. 33-56-09 N, Long. 097-07-08 W; The city is named after Marietta, Pennsylvania.

MARLOW, City; Stephens County; Pop. 5,017 / 4,545; Zip Code 73055; Elev. 1312; Lat. 34-39-01 N, Long. 097-57-05 W; The city was named after the nearby Marlow Ranch.

MAUD, City; Pottawatomie and Seminole Counties; Pop. 1,444 / 1,267; Zip Code 74854; Elev. 966; Lat. 35-07-54 N, Long. 096-46-46 W; Established in 1896 and named for local resident Maud Tinkle.

MAYSVILLE, Town; Garvin County; Pop. 1,396 / 1,114; Zip Code 73057; Elev. 943; Lat. 34-49-07 N, Long. 097-24-35 W; Founded in 1878 and named for the Mayes brothers, ranchers.

MCALESTER, City; Pittsburg County Seat; Pop. 17,255 / 17,416; Zip Code 74501; Lat. 34-56-03 N, Long. 095-46-08 W; Founded in 1873 and named in honor of businessman and second Lieutenant Governor of Oklahoma, John McAlester.

MCCURTAIN, Town; Kaskell County; Pop. 549 / 476; Zip Code 14944; Lat. 35-09-12 N, Long. 094-57-46 W; The town's name honors Choctaw Chief, Green McCurtain.

MCLOUD, Town; Pottawatomie County; Pop. 4,061 / 2,900; Zip Code 74851; Lat. 35-25-46 N, Long. 097-05-12 W; Railroad attorney John McCloud had the town named in his honor.

MEDFORD, City; Grant County Seat; Pop. 1,419 / 956; Zip Code 73759; Lat. 36-48-25 N, Long. 097-44-09 W; The town is named for Medford, Massachusetts.

MEEKER, Town; Lincoln County; Pop. 1,032 / 1,013; Zip Code 74855; Lat. 35-30-06 N, Long. 096-54-06 W; The town's name remembers Julian Meeker, the original landowner.

MIAMI, City; Ottawa County Seat; Pop. 14,237 / 13,360; Zip Code 743+; Elev. 798; Lat. 36-53-12 N, Long. 094-52-47 W; The town's name honors the nearby Miami Indians.

MIDWEST CITY, City; Oklahoma County; Pop. 49,559 / 54,172; Near Oklahoma City; The town was named after the adjoining Midwest air base.

MINCO, City; Grady County; Pop. 1,489 / 1,552; Zip Code 73059; Lat. 35-19-12 N, Long. 097-55-48 W; The town's name is an Indian word meaning "chief."

MOORE, City; Cleveland County; Pop. 35,063 / 45,431; Santa Fe Railroad conductor Al Moore had the town named in his honor.

MOORELAND, Town; Woodward County; Pop. 1,383 / 1,126; Zip Code 73852; Lat. 36-26-45 N, Long. 099-07-21 W; A descriptive name for the "moor" like landscape near the town.

MORRIS, City; Okmulgee County; Pop. 1,288 / 1,454; Zip Code 74455; Elev. 710; Lat. 35-36-21 N, Long. 095-51-24 W; Railroad official H.E. Morris had the town named in his honor.

MORRISON, Town; Noble County; Pop. 671 / 648; Zip Code 73061; Lat. 36-17-43 N, Long. 097-00-35 W; Original landowner, James Morrison, gave his name to the town.

MOUNDS, Town; Creek County; Pop. 1,086 / 1,029; Zip Code 74047; Elev. 722; Lat. 35-52-30 N, Long. 096-03-31 W; A descriptive name for the large twin mounds near the townsite.

MOUNTAIN PARK, Town; Kiowa County; Pop. 557 / 473; Zip Code 73559; Elev. 1365; Lat. 34-41-52 N, Long. 098-57-06 W; Formerly called Bujord the town took its name from the nearby Wichita Mountains.

MOUNTAIN VIEW, Town; Kiowa County; Pop. 1,189 / 953; Zip Code 73062; Elev. 1336; Lat. 35-06-06 N, Long. 098-44-36 W; Descriptively named for the view of the adjacent Wichita Mountains.

MULDROW, Town; Sequoyah County; Pop. 2,538 / 3,303; Zip Code 74948; Lat. 35-24-25 N, Long. 094-35-52 W; Founded in 1887 and named for Henry Muldrow, Congressman and Assistant Secretary of State.

MUSKOGEE, City; Muskogee County Seat; Pop. 40,011 / 38,432; Zip Code 74401; Lat. 35-45-01 N, Long. 095-21-52 W; Established in 1872 and given the alternate name for the Creek Indians.

MUSTANG, City; Canadian County; Pop. 7,496 / 12,886; Zip Code 73064; Lat. 35-23-14 N, Long. 097-43-16 W; Named for adjacent Mustang Creek.

MUTUAL, Town; Woodward County; Pop. 135 / 65; Zip Code 73853; Elev. 1873; Lat. 36-13-49 N, Long. 099-10-00 W; The post office assigned the name to the town.

NARDIN, Town; Kay County; Pop. 98; Zip Code 74646; Lat. 36-48-22 N, Long. 097-26-36 W; The name honors George Nardin, an early settler.

NEWCASTLE, Town; McClain County; Pop. 3,076 / 5,521; Zip Code 73065; Named after Newcastle, Texas.

NEWKIRK, City; Kay County Seat; Pop. 2,413 / 2,094; Zip Code 74647; Elev. 1154; Lat. 36-52-53 N, Long. 097-03-25 W; A descriptive name applied when the site was chosen two miles from a Santa Fe railway stop known as Kirk.

NICHOLS HILLS, City; Oklahoma County; Pop. 4,171 / 4,022; The city's name honors Oklahoma civic leader G.A. Nichols.

NICOMA PARK, City; Oklahoma County; Pop. 2,588 / 2,313; Zip Code 73066; Lat. 35-29-36 N, Long. 097-19-43 W; A coined word combining the original landowner's name, G.A. Nichols, and Oklahoma.

NOBLE, Town; Cleveland County; Pop. 3,497 / 5,345; Zip Code 73068; Lat. 35-08-34 N, Long. 097-22-58 W; The town's name recalls John Noble, President Benjamin Harrison's Secretary of the Interior.

NORMAN, City; Cleveland County Seat; Pop. 68,020 / 94,193; Zip Code 730+; Lat. 35-13-37 N, Long. 097-25-08 W; Named for Sante Fe Railroad surveyor Aubrey Norman.

NORTH MIAMI, Town; Ottawa County; Pop. 544 / 437; Zip Code 74358; Lat. 36-55-24 N, Long. 094-53-05 W; Miami was the name of a nearby Indian tribe.

NOWATA, City; Nowata County Seat; Pop. 4,270 / 3,705; Zip Code 74048; Lat. 36-41-53 N, Long. 095-38-03 W; A Delaware Indian word meaning "welcome."

OAKLAND, Town; Marshall County; Pop. 485 / 611; Zip Code 73452; Lat. 34-05-58 N, Long. 096-47-33 W; The town is named for the oak groves in the vicinity.

OAKS, Town; Delaware County; Pop. 591 / 524; Zip Code 74359; Lat. 36-10-52 N, Long. 094-50-53 W; Founded in 1842 as a mission and descriptively named for the oak trees nearby.

OILTON, City; Creek County; Pop. 1,244 / 1,166; Zip Code 74052; Lat. 36-04-59 N, Long. 096-35-06 W; Descriptively named during the great oil boom of 1915.

OKARCHE, Town; Canadian & Kingfisher Counties; Pop. 1,064 / 1,198; Zip Code 73762; Lat. 35-43-31 N, Long. 097-58-37 W; Early settler Charles Hunter coined the name from Oklahoma, Arapaho, and Cheyenne.

OKAY, Town; Wagoner County; Pop. 554 / 666; Zip Code 74446; Lat. 35-50-46 N, Long. 095-18-41 W; The town got its name from the local OK Truck Manufacturing Company.

OKEENE, Town; Blaine County; Pop. 1,601 / 1,165; Zip Code 73763; Elev. 1218; Lat. 36-07-00 N, Long. 098-19-03 W; Settler Elmer Brodrick combined the words Oklahoma, Cherokee, and Cheyenne.

OKEMAH, City; Okfuskee County Seat; Pop. 3,381 / 2,855; Zip Code 74859; Lat. 35-25-51 N, Long. 096-18-22 W; Town developer H.B. Dexter gave the town a Creek Indian name meaning "big chief."

OKLAHOMA CITY, City; Oklahoma County Seat; Capital of Oklahoma; Pop. 403,213 / 475,322; Zip Code 731+; Lat. 35-29-21 N, Long. 097-31-02 W; In Choctaw Indian language the name means "red people."

OKMULGEE, City; Okmulgee County Seat; Pop. 16,263 / 13,719; Zip Code 74447; Lat. 35-37-20 N, Long. 095-57-45 W; The name of a Creek town in Alabama.

OOLOGAH, Town; Rogers County; Pop. 798 / 1,014; Zip Code 74053; Elev. 657; Lat. 36-26-50 N, Long. 095-42-24 W; A Cherokee Indian chief, the name means "dark cloud."

OWASSO, City; Tulsa County; Pop. 6,149 / 16,285; Zip Code 74055; Lat. 36-16-12 N, Long. 095,50,59 W; An Osage word meaning "end" and descriptively applied to a branch of the Santa Fe Railroad.

PANAMA, Town; Le Flore County; Pop. 1,164 / 1,722; Zip Code 74951; Lat. 35-10-17 N, Long. 094-40-10 W; Named after the country in Central America.

PAOLI, Town; Garvin County; Pop. 573 / 611; Zip Code 73074; Elev. 962; Lat. 34-49-37 N, Long. 097-15-37 W; The town is named after Paoli, Pennsylvania.

PAULS VALLEY, City; Garvin County Seat; Pop. 5,664 / 5,657; Zip Code 73075; Elev. 876; Lat. 34-44-14 N, Long. 097-13-09 W; The city is named in honor of early settler Smith Paul.

PAWHUSKA, City; Osage County Seat; Pop. 4,771 / 3,607; Zip Code 74009; Elev. 818; Lat. 35-57-29 N, Long. 095-52-54 W; The name of an Osage Indian chief, it means "white hair."

PAWNEE, City; Pawnee County Seat; Pop. 1,688 / 2,106; Zip Code 74058; Elev. 866; Lat. 36-21-09 N, Long. 096-41-46 W; Named after the Pawnee Indians.

PERKINS, Town; Payne County; Pop. 1,762 / 2,090; Zip Code 74059; Lat. 35-58-29 N, Long. 097-02-00 W; Founded in 1890 and named for U.S. Senator from Kansas, B.W. Perkins.

PERRY, City; Noble County Seat; Pop. 5,796 / 5,357; Zip Code 73077; Lat. 36-17-31 N, Long. 097-17-25 W; The Perrys were a prominent Choctaw Indian family. The town is named after them.

PICHER, City; Ottawa County; Pop. 2,180 / 1,743; Zip Code 74360; Lat. 36-59-28 N, Long. 094-49-58 W; The town is named after W.S. Picher of the Eagle-Picher Lead Company.

PIEDMONT, Town; Canadian and Kingfisher Counties; Pop. 2,016 / 3,535; Zip Code 73078; Lat. 35-38-27 N, Long. 097-44-36 W; Named for the Piedmont region of the eastern United States.

POCOLA, Town; Le Flare County; Pop. 3,268 / 3,791; A Choctaw Indian word meaning "ten" and referring to the distance to nearby Fort Smith.

PONCA CITY, City; Kay County; Pop. 26,238 / 26,052; Zip Code 74601; Elev. 1022; Lat. 36-44-59 N, Long. 097-00-24 W; An Indian word meaning "sacred leader."

POND CREEK, City; Grant County; Pop. 949 / 784; Zip Code 73766; Elev. 1048; Lat. 36-40-13 N, Long. 097-47-57 W; Descriptively named for an embedded pond in a local creek.

PORTER, Town; Wagoner County; Pop. 642 / 661; Zip Code 74454; Lat. 35-52-03 N, Long. 095-31-07 W; The town is named for Pleasant Porter, a Creek Indian Chief.

POTEAU, City; Le Flore County Seat; Pop. 7,089 / 7,792; Zip Code 74953; Lat. 35-03-05 N, Long. 094-37-06 W; The name is derived from the adjacent Porteau, or "post," River.

PRAGUE, City; Lincoln County; Pop. 2,208 / 2,332; Zip Code 74864; Lat. 35-29-02 N, Long. 096-41-11 W; The town is named after the famous city in Europe.

PRUE, Town; Osage County; Pop. 554 / 373; Zip Code 74060; Lat. 36-15-22 N, Long. 096-16-06 W; Henry Prue, the original landowner, gave his name to the town.

PRYOR CREEK, City; Mayes County Seat; Pop. 8,483 / 8,986; Pryor Creek is located a few miles from the city. The town is named for this stream.

PURCELL, City; McClain County Seat; Pop. 4,638 / 5,270; Zip Code 73080; Elev. 1106; Lat. 35-00-37 N, Long. 097-21-46 W; Santa Fe Railway Director E.B. Purcell had the town named in his honor.

QUAPAW, Town; Ottawa County; Pop. 1,097 / 911; Zip Code 74363; Lat. 36-56-32 N, Long. 094-43-52 W; The town is named for the Quapaw Indians. The name means "downstream people."

QUINTON, Town; Pittsburg County; Pop. 1,228 / 1,222; Zip Code 74561; Elev. 619; Lat. 35-07-15 N, Long. 095-21-59 W; The town is named after Martha Quinton, a prominent Choctaw Indian.

RAMONA, Town; Washington County; Pop. 567 / 521; Zip Code 74061; Lat. 36-31-49 N, Long. 095-55-14 W; Formerly Banton, the name was changed in 1899 for the novel Ramona by Helen Hunt Jackson.

RANDLETT, Town; Cotton County; Pop. 461 / 511; Zip Code 73562; Lat. 34-10-36 N, Long. 098-27-41 W; Randlett is named in honor of Kiowa-Comanche Indian agent, James Randlett.

RED OAK, Town; Latimer County; Pop. 676 / 556; Zip Code 74563; Lat. 34-56-54 N, Long. 095-04-45 W; Descriptively named for a well-known red oak tree in the town's center.

RINGLING, Town; Jefferson County; Pop. 1,561 / 1,245; Zip Code 73456; Lat. 34-10-09 N, Long. 097-35-45 W; The town's name honors famous circus owner John Ringling.

ROFF, Town; Pontotoc County; Pop. 729 / 682; Zip Code 74865; Elev. 1254; Lat. 34-37-31 N, Long. 096-50-21 W; Rancher J.T. Roff gave his name to the town.

ROLAND, Town; Sequoyah County; Pop. 1,472 / 2,706; Zip Code 74954; Lat. 35-25-07 N, Long. 094-30-19 W; Formerly called Garrison, the town's name was changed to Roland in 1904.

RUSH SPRINGS, Town; Grady County; Pop. 1,451 / 1,293; Zip Code 73082; Lat. 34-46-42 N, Long. 097-57-37 W; Named for the well-known Chisholm Trail watering site, Rush Springs.

RYAN, Town; Jefferson County; Pop. 1,083 / 915; Zip Code 73565; Lat. 34-03-02 N, Long. 097-57-59 W; The town is named for early pioneer Stephen Ryan.

SALINA, Town; Mayes County; Pop. 1,115 / 1,375; Zip Code 74365; Lat. 36-17-48 N, Long. 095-09-12 W; The name is a variant of Saline, so called because of a nearby salt works.

SALLISAW, City; Sequoyah County Seat; Pop. 6,403 / 7,869; Zip Code 74955; Lat. 35-27-47 N, Long. 094-47-10 W; The town is named after Sallisaw Creek. Sallisaw means "salt provisions."

SAND SPRINGS, City; Osage and Tulsa Counties; Pop. 13,246 / 18,434; Zip Code 74063; Lat. 36-07-41 N, Long. 096-02-46 W. Named for the adjacent springs on the north bank of the Arkansas River.

SAPULPA, City; Creek County Seat; Pop. 15,853 / 20,114; Zip Code 74066; Lat. 35-59-41 N, Long. 096-06-20 W; The town's name is derived from a Creek Indian leader who lived nearby, Sus-pul-ber.

SAVANNA, Town; Pittsburg County; Pop. 828 / 976; Zip Code 74565; Elev. 729; Lat. 34-49-43 N, Long. 095-50-23 W; A railroad manager, Robert Stevens, had a private railroad car called Savanna. The town takes its name from that car.

SAYRE, City; Beckham County Seat; Pop. 3,177 / 3,062; Zip Code 73662; Lat. 35-18-07 N, Long. 099-38-16 W; The town's name honors railroad developer Robert Sayre.

SEILING, City; Dewey County; Pop. 1,103 / 711; Zip Code 73663; Elev. 1744; Lat. 36-08-52 N, Long. 098-55-28 W; Seiling is named for its original landowner, Louis Seiling.

SEMINOLE, City; Seminole County; Pop. 8,590 / 6,799; Zip Code 748+; Lat. 35-14-08 N, Long. 096-40-46 W; The city is named after the Seminole Indians.

SENTINEL, City; Washita County; Pop. 1,016 / 1,058; Zip Code 73664; Lat. 35-09-37 N, Long. 099-09-58 W; Established in 1899, the town is named after a local newspaper, the Herald Sentinel.

SHADY POINT, Town; Le Flore County; Pop. 235 / 712; Zip Code 74956; Elev. 447; Lat. 35-07-50 N, Long. 094-39-30 W; Formerly called Harrison, the name was changed to Shady Point in 1894.

SHATTUCK, Town; Ellis County; Pop. 1,759 / 1,369; Zip Code 73858; Elev. 2268; Lat. 36-16-12 N, Long. 099-52-30 W; The town's name honors George Shattuck, a one-time director of the Santa Fe Railway Company.

SHAWNEE, City; Pottawatomie County Seat; Pop. 26,506 / 27,979; Zip Code 74801; Lat. 35-19-54 N, Long. 096-58-33 W. The city takes its name from the Shawnee Indians. Shawnee is an Algonquin Indian word meaning "southerner."

SHIDLER, Town; Osage County; Pop. 708 / 487; Zip Code 74652; Elev. 1167; Lat. 36-46-52 N, Long. 096-39-24 W; E.S. Shidler, the original landowner, had the town named in his honor.

SKIATOOK, Town; Osage and Tulsa Counties; Pop. 3,596 / 5,672; Zip Code 74070; Elev. 834; Lat. 36-21-57 N, Long. 096-W; Founded in 1880 and named for a prominent Osage Indian, Skiatooka.

SNYDER, City; Kiowa County; Pop. 1,848 / 1,408; Zip Code 73566; Elev. 1364; Lat. 34-39-43 N, Long. 098-56-55 W; First postmaster Margaret Snyder had the town named in her honor.

SOUTH COFFEYVILLE, Town; Nowata County; Pop. 873 / 762; Zip Code 74072; Lat. 36-59-38 N, Long. 095-37-04 W; The town is just across the state line south of Coffeyville, Kansas, hence the name.

SPARKS, Town; Lincoln County; Pop. 772 / 220; Zip Code 74869; Elev. 846; Lat. 35-36-40 N, Long. 096-49-09 W; Sparks is named for George Sparks who was a director of the Fort Smith and Western Railway.

SPAVINAW, Town; Mayes County; Pop. 623 / 499; Zip Code 74366; Lat. 36-23-34 N, Long. 095-03-06 W; Founded in 1892 and given phonetic equivalent to two French words *cepee* and *vineux* meaning "young growths" of trees.

SPENCER, City; Oklahoma County; Pop. 4,064 / 3,986; Zip Code 73084; Lat. 35-29-09 N, Long. 097-22-08 W; Spencer is named after railroad developer A.M. Spencer.

SPERRY, Town; Tulsa County; Pop. 1,276 / 979; Zip Code 74073; Lat. 36-17-45 N, Long. 095-59-33 W; The town is named for an English adaptation, Sperry, of settler Henry Spybuck's last name.

SPIRO, Town; Le Flore County; Pop. 2,221 / 2,445; Zip Code 74959; Lat. 35-14-32 N, Long. 094-37-27 W; Named for Abram Spiro of Ft. Smith, Arkansas.

SPRINGER, Town; Carter County; Pop. 679 / 483; Zip Code 73458; Elev. 917; Lat. 34-18-48 N, Long. 097-07-54 W; The town is named in honor of pioneer cattleman, W.A. Springer.

STERLING, Town; Comanche County; Pop. 702 / 626; Zip Code 73567; Lat. 34-44-47 N, Long. 098-10-00 W; Texas ranger Captain Charles Sterling had the town named in his honor.

STIGLER, City; Haskell County Seat; Pop. 2,630 / 2,465; Zip Code 74462; Elev. 583; Lat. 35-19-43 N, Long. 095-03-14 W; Town developer Joseph Stigler had the town named in his honor.

STILLWATER, City; Payne County Seat; Pop. 38,268 / 38,444; Zip Code 740+; Lat. 36-07-22 N, Long. 097-04-07 W; The city takes its name from the nearby tributary of the Cimarron, Stillwater Creek.

STILWELL, City; Adair County; Pop. 2,369 / 3,377; Zip Code 74960; Elev. 1112; Lat. 35-48-52 N, Long. 094-37-24 W; Arthur Stilwell, developer of the Kansas City Southern Railway, had the town named in his honor.

STONEWALL, Town; Pontotoc County; Pop. 672 / 517; Zip Code 74871; Lat. 34-39-06 N, Long. 096-31-24 W; The town's name commemorates General "Stonewall" Jackson, military hero of the confederacy.

STRATFORD, Town; Garvin County; Pop. 1,459 / 1,515; Zip Code 74872; Elev. 1110; Lat. 34-47-42 N, Long. 096-57-32 W; Named for the town of Stratford-on-Avon in England.

STRINGTOWN, Town; Atoka County; Pop. 1,047 / 379; Zip Code 74569; Lat. 34-28-06 N, Long. 096-03-13 W; Originally called Springtown, the name was changed in the 1870s to Stringtown.

STROUD, City; Lincoln County; Pop. 3,139 / 2,917; Zip Code 74079; Lat. 35-44-46 N, Long. 096-39-08 W; Established in 1892 and named for early day merchant James Stroud.

SULPHUR, City; Murray County Seat; Pop. 5,516 / 5,054; Zip Code 73086; Lat. 34-31-54 N, Long. 096-54-54 W; Descriptively named for the nearby sulfur springs.

TAHLEQUAH, City; Cherokee County Seat; Pop. 9,708 / 13,012; Zip Code 74464; Lat. 35-54-25 N, Long. 094-58-31 W; The word is an old Cherokee place name, which the settlers borrowed for their use.

TALIHINA, Town; Le Flore County; Pop. 1,387 / 1,416; Zip Code 74571; Lat. 34-45-14 N, Long. 095-03-28 W; Talihina is the Choctaw Indian word for "railroad."

TECUMSEH, City; Pottawotomie County; Pop. 5,123 / 5,869; Zip Code 74873; Lat. 35-15-31 N, Long. 096-55-55 W; The town is named for the famous Shawnee Indian chief.

TEMPLE, Town; Cotton County; Pop. 1,339 / 1,401; Zip Code 73568; Elev. 1007; Lat. 34-16-11 N, Long. 098-14-04 W; The town's name honors Temple Houston, the son of Sam Houston.

TERRAL, Town; Jefferson County; Pop. 604 / 384; Zip Code 73561; Lat. 33-59-06 N, Long. 097-45-14 W; The first postmaster, John Terral, had the town named in his honor.

TEXHOMA, Town; Texas County; Pop. 785 / 850; Zip Code 73949; Elev. 3487; Lat. 36-29-57 N, Long. 101-47-00 W; A coined name combining Texas and Oklahoma.

THOMAS, Town; Custer County; Pop. 1,515 / 1,146; Zip Code 73669; Lat. 35-44-56 N, Long. 098-45-00 W; Pioneer attorney William Thomas left his name on the city.

TIPTON, Town; Tillman County; Pop. 1,475 / 901; Zip Code 73570; Elev. 1303; Lat. 34-30-06 N, Long. 099-08-12 W; Conductor John Tipton, who worked for a local railroad, had the town named in his honor.

TISHOMINGO, City; Johnston County Seat; Pop. 3,212 / 2,984; Zip Code 73460; Elev. 693; Lat. 34-14-19 N, Long. 096-40-56 W; The town's name remembers the great Chickasaw Indian chief.

TONKOWA, City; Kay County; Pop. 3,524 / 2,983; Zip Code 74653; Lat. 36-40-43 N, Long. 097-18-22 W; Named for the Tonkowa Indian tribe.

TRYON, Town; Lincoln County; Pop. 435 / 555; Zip Code 74875; Lat. 35-52-04 N, Long. 096-57-40 W; Tryon is named in honor of original landowner Fred Tryon.

TULSA, City; Osage and Tulsa Counties; Tulsa County Seat; Pop. 360,919 / 381,579; Zip Code 741+; Lat. 36-09-21 N, Long. 095-58-31 W; A borrowed Creek Indian place name for an Indian town in Alabama.

TUPELO, City; Coal County; Pop. 542 / 374; Zip Code 74572; Elev. 689; Lat. 34-36-05 N, Long. 096-25-10 W; Named for Tupelo, Mississippi.

TUTTLE, Town; Grady County; Pop. 3,051 / 4,222; Zip Code 73089; Lat. 35-18-18 N, Long. 097-46-48 W; Named in honor of local rancher James Tuttle.

TYRONE, Town; Texas County; Pop. 928 / 955; Zip Code 73951; Elev. 2921; Lat. 36-57-18 N, Long. 101-03-57 W; Tyrone is named after County Tyrone in Ireland.

UNION CITY, Town; Canadian County; Pop. 558 / 1,124; Zip Code 73090; Lat. 35-23-25 N, Long. 097-56-13 W; Founded in 1889 and named for the American "union."

VALLEY BROOK, Town; Oklahoma County; Pop. 921 / 725; Part of Oklahoma City's area - given a euphonious name by its incorporators.

VALLIANT, Town; McCurtain County; Pop. 927 / 922; Zip Code 74764; Elev. 512; Lat. 34-00-00 N, Long. 095-05-37 W; The town is named after F.W. Valliant, who was chief engineer on the Arkansas and Choctaw Railroad.

VELMA, City; Stephens County; Pop. 831 / 722; Zip Code 73091; Elev. 1044; Lat. 34-27-23 N, Long. 097-40-18 W; The town is named after the daughter of a local merchant, Velma Dobbins.

VERDEN, Town; Grady County; Pop. 625 / 581; Zip Code 73092; Lat. 35-05-01 N, Long. 098-05-14 W; Named for original landowner, A.N. Verden.

VIAN, Town; Sequoyah County; Pop. 1,521 / 1,404; Zip Code 74962; Lat. 35-29-58 N, Long. 094-58-13 W; Derived from the French word *viande*, or "meat."

VICI, Town; Dewey County; Pop. 845 / 697; Zip Code 73859; Elev. 2265; Lat. 36-08-55 N, Long. 099-17-55 W; Founded in 1900 and named for the last word in the Julius Caesar quote, *veni, vidi, vici* – "I came, I saw, I conquered."

VINITA, City; Craig County Seat; Pop. 6,740 / 5,735; Zip Code 74301; Lat. 36-31-18 N, Long. 095-08-31 W; The town is named in honor of Vinnie Ream, a well-known sculptress.

WAGONER, City; Wagoner County Seat; Pop. 6,191 / 7,392; Zip Code 74467; Lat. 35-57-29 N, Long. 095-22-12 W; Train dispatcher "Big Foot" Wagoner of Parsons, Kansas had the town named after him.

WAKITA, Town; Grant County; Pop. 526 / 473; Zip Code 73771; Elev. 1175; Lat. 36-52-56 N, Long. 097-54-50 W; A Cherokee word meaning "water collected in a depression."

WALTERS, City; Cotton County Seat; Pop. 2,778 / 2,216; Zip Code 73572; Lat. 34-21-15 N, Long. 098-17-58 W; The town's name honors a prominent citizen, William R. Walter.

WARNER, Town; Muskogee County; Pop. 1,310 / 1,612; Zip Code 74469; Lat. 35-29-42 N, Long. 095-18-18 W; The town is named for William Warner, U.S. Senator from Missouri.

WARR ACRES, City; Oklahoma County; Pop. 9,940 / 9,378; Founded in 1948 and named in honor of Oklahoma City civic leader C.B. Warr.

WATONGA, City; Blaine County Seat; Pop. 4,139 / 3,009; Zip Code 73772; Lat. 35-50-52 N, Long. 098-24-51 W; Established in 1892 and named for an Arapaho chief. Translated his name means "black coyote."

WAUKOMIS, Town; Garfield County; Pop. 1,551 / 1,303; Zip Code 73773; Elev. 1238; Lat. 36-16-48 N, Long. 097-54-05 W; According to legend certain railroad officials were stranded and had to "walk home." The name is a phonetic variation of this phrase.

WAURIKA, City; Jefferson County Seat; Pop. 2,258 / 1,740; Zip Code 73573; Elev. 881; Lat. 34-10-08 N, Long. 098-00-02 W; An Indian word meaning "pure water."

WAYNE, Town; McClain County; Pop. 621 / 696; Zip Code 73095; Lat. 34-55-07 N, Long. 097-18-47 W; The town is named after Wayne, Pennsylvania.

WAYNOKA, City; Woods County; Pop. 1,377 / 809; Zip Code 73860; Elev. 1476; Lat. 36-35-10 N, Long. 098-52-31 W; A Cheyenne Indian word meaning "sweet water."

WEATHERFORD, City; Custer County; Pop. 9,640 / 9,761; Zip Code 73096; Elev. 1647; Lat. 35-31-50 N, Long. 098-42-12 W; Deputy Marshal William Weatherford gave his name to the town.

WEBBERS FALLS, Town; Muskogee County; Pop. 461 / 765; Zip Code 74470; Lat. 35-30-54 N, Long. 095-07-40 W; The town's name remembers local Cherokee Chief Walter Webber.

WELCH, Town; Craig County; Pop. 697 / 588; Zip Code 74369; Lat. 36-56-28 N, Long. 095-05-36 W; The town is named after railroad official A.L. Welch.

WELEETKA, Town; Okfuskee County; Pop. 1,195 / 1,010; Zip Code 74880; Lat. 35-21-42 N, Long. 096-05-51 W; A Creek Indian word meaning "running water."

WELLSTON, Town; Lincoln County; Pop. 802 / 1,000; Zip Code 74881; Lat. 35-41-31 N, Long. 097-04-04 W; Indian trader Christian Wells left his name on the town.

WESTVILLE, Town; Adair County; Pop. 1,049 / 1,558; Zip Code 74965; Elev. 1139; Lat. 35-59-28 N, Long. 094-33-51 W; Local resident Samuel West had the town named in his honor.

WETUMKA, City; Hughes County; Pop. 1,725 / 1,470; Zip Code 74883; Lat. 35-14-07 N, Long. 096-14-12 W; A Creek Indian word meaning "tumbling water."

WEWOKA, City; Seminole County Seat; Pop. 5,480 / 3,855; Zip Code 74884; Lat. 35-09-03 N, Long. 096-29-51 W; A Creek Indian word meaning "roaring water."

WILBURTON, City; Latimer County Seat; Pop. 2,996 / 3,162; Zip Code 74578; Lat. 34-55-01 N, Long. 095-18-37 W; The city's name honors Elisha Wilbur, president of the Lehigh Valley Railroad.

WILSON, City; Carter County; Pop. 1,585 / 1,654; Zip Code 73463; Elev. 699; Lat. 34-09-46 N, Long. 097-25-22 W; The town is named in honor of local merchant J.H. Wilson.

WOODWARD, City; Woodward County Seat; Pop. 13,610 / 12,185; Zip Code 738+; Lat. 36-25-59 N, Long. 099-24-11 W; The town's name honors Brinton Woodward, a Santa Fe Railroad Company Director.

WRIGHT CITY, Town; McCurtain County; Pop. 1,168 / 796; Zip Code 74766; Elev. 399; Lat. 34-03-31 N, Long. 095-00-01 W; The town's name honors World War I soldier William Wright, the first local boy killed in action.

WYNNEWOOD, City; Garvin County; Pop. 2,615 / 2,294; Zip Code 73098; Elev. 896; Lat. 34-38-39 N, Long. 097-09-48 W. The center of a farming region, especially noted for its production of pecans.

YUKON, City; Canadian County; Pop. 17,112 / 22,756; Zip Code 73099; Elev. 1,298; Lat. 35-30-03 N, Long. 097-44-50 W. Laid out in 1891 by the Spencer Brothers, who owned the site.

OREGON
The Beaver State

Punch Bowl Falls in the gorge

Mack Arch near Seal Beach

GOVERNOR
John A. Kitzhaber

Timberline Lodge
Mount Hood

Portland Skyline

Downtown Salem

The North Coast near Cannon Beach

INTRODUCTION

The western state of Oregon is one of the Pacific States. It is bordered on the north by the Columbia River and Washington; on the south by Nevada and California; on the east by Idaho and the Snake River; and on the west by the Pacific Ocean.

In area, Oregon ranks ninth among all the states. Its total area comprises 98,386 square miles, with 96,003 square miles of land area, and 2,383 square miles of inland water area.

Oregon has a widely varied terrain. Major forested mountain ranges include the Coast Range along the Pacific Coast, the Klamath Range in the southwestern part of the State, the Cascade Range in the west-central area, and the Blue-Wallowa Mountains in the northeast. Climatic conditions in Oregon are also varied; the Coast Range has about 120 inches of precipitation and the climate of a temperate rain forest, while the central, southeastern, and eastern sections are mainly lava plains, lunar in appearance. Rangeland and revering lowlands cover the remainder of the State.

Economically, the most important agricultural products in Oregon are beef and dairy cattle, wheat, and hay. The timber industry also brings large profits, mainly from softwood-based trees such as Douglas fir, ponderosa pine, and hemlock. Oregon is the nation's top supplier of Christmas trees.

The State abounds in the romance of our country's westward expansion. It is the end of the famous Oregon Trail, which so many pioneers passed in their covered wagons. Meriwether Lewis and William Clark, sent by President Thomas Jefferson to explore the vast area acquired in the Louisiana Purchase, ended their explorations here. Year after year, Americans spend a vast amount of money to enjoy Oregon's magnificent coastline, blue lakes, mountains and forests, the Pendleton Round-up, the Portland Rose Festival, and countless other attractions offered by the State. Visitors to Oregon's national and state parks bring in more than one billion dollars of revenue annually.

STATE NAME

There is much speculation concerning the origin of the name Oregon; however, none has led to a definitive answer. The name Oregon was first applied to the Columbia River, next to a vast undefined territory known as "the countries of the Columbia," later to the Territory of Oregon, and last to the State.

Jonathan Carver first used the name Oregon in a document entitled *Travels through the Interior Parts of North America*, published in London in 1778. Some authorities think Carver's use of the word Oregon was a corruption of the name *Ouragon* or *Ourigan*, "which was communicated to him by Major Robert Rogers, the English commandant of the frontier military and trading post at Mackinac, Michigan, during the years (1766-1767) of Captain Carver's journey to the Upper Valley of the Mississippi river and to lake Superior." It is speculated that Rogers obtained the word *Ouragon* or *Ouragan* from French Canadian voyageurs and traders. However, others suggest that Carver heard the word spoken by the Sioux Indians. The French word *Ouragan* is supposed to be the source of the present English word of "Hurricane." Canadian fur traders probably at one time called the Columbia River "the river of storms."

Another theory supposes that the word Oregon is derived from the Shoshone Indian expression, meaning "The River of the West," originating from the two Shoshone words *ogwa*, meaning "river," and *pe-on* meaning "west," the complete Shoshone word being *ogwa pe-on*.

William O. Steel, first President of the Oregon Geographic Board, said that the word Oregon was derived from the Shoshone word *oyer-un-gon*, denoting "a place of plenty."

Another theory is that the name Oregon came from the term *orejon*, the Spanish word for "big ears." It is speculated that the term was applied by the Spaniards to the tribes of Indians whose warriors had elongated their ears by wearing many heavy ornaments.

Still another possibility is that the name of Oregon came from the Spanish word *oregano*, or wild sage, which was then corrupted to Oregon. Sage grows in abundance in the eastern part of the State.

In his poem *Thanatopsis*, published in 1812, William Cullen Bryant used the word Oregon as the name of the Oregon River, and did much to popularize the name.

STATE NICKNAME

The following sobriquets are attributed to Oregon: the Beaver State, the Hard-case State, the Sunset State, and the Web-foot State.

Oregon is sometimes called the Beaver State, on account of the association of the little fur-bearing animal with the early history of the Oregon country, as well as because of its intelligence, industry, ingenuity, and other admirable qualities. The beaver has been declared the State animal and is depicted on the State flag.

The sobriquet, the Hard-case State, attributed to Oregon, is reference to the rough and hardy life led by the early settlers of the State and the difficulties they encountered.

Oregon is known as the Sunset State, because it reaches a more westerly point than any other American commonwealth, except Washington.

Oregon has been called the Web-foot State, because of the excessive rainfall during the winter months, and because the climate at that season is best appreciated by web-footed animals.

STATE SEAL

The Legislative committee designed the great seal of the State of Oregon in 1857. It was officially adopted on February 24, 1903. It is described as follows:

"The description of the seal of the State of Oregon shall be an escutcheon, supported by thirty-three stars, and divided by an ordinary, with the inscription, 'The Union.' In chief—mountains, an elk with branching antlers, a wagon, the Pacific Ocean, on which there are a British man-of-war departing and an American steamer arriving. The second—quartering with a sheaf, a plow, and a pickax. Crest—the American eagle. Legend—State of Oregon, 1859."

STATE FLAG

The Oregon Legislature adopted a State flag on February 26, 1925. It is described as follows:

"A state flag is adopted to be used on all occasions when the State is officially and publicly represented, with the privilege of use by all citizens upon such occasions as may be fitting and appropriate. It shall bear on one side on a navy blue field the state escutcheon in gold, supported by thirty-three gold stars and bearing above the escutcheon the words 'State of Oregon' in gold and below the escutcheon the figures '1859' in gold, and on the other side on a navy blue field a representation of the beaver in gold."

The official colors of the State of Oregon are navy blue and gold.

STATE MOTTO

The State motto of Oregon is *Alis Volat Propiis*, which is translated as "She Flies with Her Own Wings." The motto was first used on the 1849 seal of the Oregon Territory.

In 1857, a legislative committee recommended the motto of "The Union," and the State Legislature adopted it in 1859. It remained Oregon's motto until 1987, when the Legislature voted to change it back to the motto on the seal.

STATE BIRD

In 1927, by gubernatorial proclamation, the western meadowlark, (*Sturnella neglecta*) was chosen as the official State bird of Oregon. This bird was chosen following a vote by the State's school children sponsored by the Oregon Audubon Society.

The western meadowlark ranges in the western United States, southwestern Canada, northwestern Mexico, east to the prairie areas of the Mississippi Valley, and in Minnesota, Iowa, Missouri, and Texas.

The total length of the western meadowlark is eight to nine inches, with a tail length of 2 ½ to three inches. The head and back of the neck are pale dull buffy or white in color, with broad lateral crown stripes of pale grayish brown. The lower sides of the head are mostly yellow, topped by a dull grayish white area streaked with gray, and mostly buffy or grayish brown above streaked with black. Outermost tail feathers are mostly white; the throat, breast, and abdomen are a deep yellow, sometimes with an orange hue. The yellow area is relieved by a black horseshoe-shaped patch on the chest.

The western meadowlark is an oriole. It has a loud, distinctive song that is considered one of its most appealing qualities; it sometimes sings as many as 200 notes per minute. Fledglings leave the nest early, while they are still unable to fly, but they are protected by the parents until they can fend for themselves; the young birds are easy prey for weasels, skunks, owls, snakes, and hawks. The diet of the western meadowlark consists primarily of insects, although about one-third of its food is grain.

STATE FLOWER

The Oregon grape, *Berberts aquifolium*, was designated the official flower of the State by the Legislature in January 1899.

Also known as the Rocky Mountain grape and the holly-leaf barberry, the Oregon grape is a low trailing shrub. Berries are round, about three inches in diameter, and blue or purple in color. Flowers are small, yellow, and blossom in a cluster.

STATE TREE

In 1939, the Douglas fir, (*Pseudorsuga menziessii*), was declared the official State tree of Oregon. The tree was chosen by the Legislature because Oregon is the major supplier of Douglas fir lumber. Its wood is relatively lightweight when compared with its strength, and it is considered one of the foremost trees in the world for its lumber.

Also known as the Douglas spruce, red fir, yellow fir, Oregon pine, Puget Sound pine, spruce, fir, Douglas tree, and corn-barked Douglas spruce, the tree is native to the Pacific coast and Rocky Mountain region, including Mexico and Canada.

The Douglas fir is a very large tree, next in size to the giant sequoia and the redwood. Bark is reddish brown, thick, and deeply furrowed into broad ridges.

The dark yellow-green or blue-green needles are short stalked, flat, and from three-quarters to one and one-quarter inches long. Cones are from two to four inches long and light brown, with thin, rounded scales and long, three-toothed bracts.

STATE SONG

The Oregon Legislature adopted the song *Oregon, My Oregon* as the State song in 1927. The resolution reads as follows:

"Whereas the State of Oregon has never adopted a state song; and

"Whereas many civic and patriotic bodies have recommended that the song entitled 'Oregon, My Oregon, words by J. A. Buchanon [Buchanan] and music by Henry B. Murtagh, be adopted as the State song of Oregon; and

"Whereas it is eminently proper that a State song should be adopted; therefore,

"Be It Resolved by the Senate of the State of Oregon, the House of Representatives jointly concurring: That the song entitled 'Oregon, My Oregon,' words by J.A. Buchanon [Buchanan] and music by Henry B. Murtagh, be the same hereby is accepted and adopted as the State song of the State of Oregon."

This production was published in 1920 for the Society of Oregon Composers by the Oregon Eilers Music House, Portland, Oregon.

STATE LICENSE PLATE

The State of Oregon began issuing license plates in 1911. The first plate was black numerals on a yellow background. The same color combination was used again in 1915, 1922, 1925, and 1939; the latter plate was of a lighter yellow. Plates in a variety of color combinations were issued annually except for 1930, 1943, 1944, and 1945. In 1950, five-year permanent plates began being issued. Permanent plates validated with tabs or stickers were issued in 1956, 1964, and 1974. After the 1974 blue-on-gold issue, the State changed to graphic plates. The first had a light green fir tree at the center with small gray fir trees below on a tan background.

Oregon's current issue plate is a graphic plate with a dark green fir tree centered between blue numerals in the middle. The word "Oregon," also in dark green, is centered at the top. A white outline silhouettes the mountains beneath a light blue sky, and small, forested peaks across the bottom of the plate are colored the same dark blue as the numerals.

STATE POSTAGE STAMP

On February 14, 1959, a green four-cent Oregon Statehood Commemorative stamp was issued in Astoria, Oregon. It was designed by Robert Hallock and engraved by C.A. Brooks and J.S. Edmondson. Astoria claims to be the oldest settlement west of the Rocky Mountains.

In the center of the stamp is a covered wagon that represents the type used by many early settlers as they headed over the Oregon Trail. In the right background is depicted Mt. Hood, with terrain that slopes gently to the ocean. A total of 120,740,200 of the stamp were printed.

OTHER STATE DESIGNATIONS

Throughout the years, the Legislature of Oregon has adopted several additional symbols to represent the State. Included are the State animal (1969) as the beaver; the State fish (1961) as the Chinook salmon; the State insect (1979) as the swallowtail butterfly; and the State rock (1965) as the thunder egg.

STATE CAPITOL

The Oregon statehouse is located in Salem; it is the third capitol building to be constructed in the city. Like many of the early capitols in other states, the previous two buildings were destroyed by fire. The first capitol was erected in 1854 at a cost of 40,000 dollars. In 1872, another capitol was begun, modeled somewhat after the U.S. Capitol, at a cost of about 325,000 dollars; it was destroyed in 1935. Construction on the present capitol began in 1935 and was completed in 1938.

The four-story Modern Greek capitol was designed by Francis Keally of New York. Constructed of white Vermont marble and bronze, its tower is topped by an 8 ½-ton bronze statue enameled with gold leaf; called the "Golden Pioneer," the statue is turned to the west in tribute to Oregon's early settlers.

The capitol building cost approximately 2 ½ million dollars to construct. In 1977, wings were added to the capitol, which yielded 144,000 more square feet of usable space to the 131,750 feet in the original building, at a cost of 12,025,303 dollars.

CHRONOLOGY

1543 Juan Cabrillo's pilot, Bartolome Ferello, sails along coast of Oregon, to 42 or 44 degrees N.

1579 Francis Drake passes Oregon coast, names region of southwest Oregon and northern California "New Albion."

1592 Apostolus Valerianos (alias Juan de Fuca), Greek pilot, claims discovery of Strait of Anian, long-sought "Northwest Passage."

1602 Sebastian Vizcaino sights Cape Blanco; his lieutenant, Aguila, sailing further along coast, finds and names Cape Blanco and discovers mouth of river near 43 degrees N, possibly Umpqua.

1728 Vitus Bering, Danish navigator sent by Peter the Great of Russia, discovers Bering Sea.

1741 Bering's second expedition reaches Alaskan coast.
– Russian fur-trading post is established in Alaska; Russians eventually extend activities as far south as California.

1765 Major Robert Rogers, in petition asking permission of King George III to explore territory in search of Northwest Passage, is first to call the territory "Oregon"; however, the word is spelled "Guragon."

1774 Juan Perez sails to 54 N lat.; he discovers Nootka Sound.

1775 Bruno Heceta and Bodega y Quadra, Spanish navigators, sight, but do not enter, mouth of Columbia River.

1778 Name of "Oregon" appears for first time in published print in Carver's *Travels*, which mentions "the River Oregon, or the River of the West."
– Gore and Ledyard, with Captain James Cook's expedition, sail along Oregon coast; they are first Americans to visit Pacific Northwest.

1787 Captain Barkley reaches Strait of Anian and names it Juan de Fuca, after its supposed discoverer in 1592.

1788 Captain Meares reaches Strait of Anian and also names it Juan de Fuca.

1789 Spanish Naval force, under Estevan Jose Martinez, builds fort on Vancouver Island, expels English predecessors, and takes possession for Spain.

1792 American Captain Robert Gray discovers and names Columbia River.
– Lieutenant William Broughton of British Navy reaches Cascades after traveling up Columbia River about one hundred miles; he names Mount Hood.
– Captain George Vancouver (British commissioner) maps northwestern coast.

1793 Sir Alexander Mackenzie completes first overland trip across Canada to Pacific coast, at 52 degrees 30 minutes Latitude, opening Pacific Northwest to fur trappers.

1795 First British map bearing name "Columbia River" is published.

1803 United States purchases Louisiana Territory—the land west of Mississippi River and drained by it and its tributaries.

1804 Lewis and Clark, under orders from President Jefferson, lead expedition from St. Louis to mouth of Columbia River.

1810 Winship brothers attempt settlement at Oak Point in lower Columbia; it is a failure.

1811 Astoria, first permanent American foothold La Pacific Northwest, founded as trading post by John Jacob Astor's Pacific Fur Company.

1812 Donald McKenzie explores Willamette River.

1813 Astoria, renamed Fort George, comes under British rule during War of 1812.

1817 William Cullen Bryant's *Thanatopsis*, containing lines "where rolls the Oregon and hears no sound save its own dashings," is published.

1818 Fort Walla Walla is built by North West Company.
– Astoria is returned to United States.
– First Oregon joint occupancy treaty is made with Great Britain, permitting both nations to occupy for ten years disputed region between Columbia River and present north boundary of United States.

1819 Treaty with Great Britain is ratified.
– California-Oregon boundary is fixed at 42 degrees by treaty with Spain.

1824 Southern boundary of Russian possessions is fixed at 54 degrees 40' N.
– Dr. John McLoughlin, chief factor of Hudson's Bay Company, arrives in Oregon, removes headquarters from Fort George to Fort Vancouver on north bank of Columbia.

1827 Second treaty with Great Britain extends provision for joint occupancy of Oregon Territory.

1828 Jedediah S. Smith and party of American trappers (first Americans to enter Oregon from California) ambushed by Indians on Umpqua River; Smith and two or three others survive.

1829 Hudson's Bay Company occupies location at Willamette Falls (Oregon City).

1832 McLeod and La Framboise build Fort Umpqua for Hudson's Bay Company.
– Nathaniel J. Wyeth reaches Vancouver overland and establishes fishery on Sauvie Island at mouth of Willamette River.

1834 Reverend Jason Lee founds Methodist mission on French Prairie in Willamette Valley.

1836 Dr. Marcus Whitman and H.H. Spaulding establish missions in Walla Walla and Clearwater valleys.

1839 First American settlers, "Peoria Party," come to Oregon from Illinois.

1841 Settlers meet to make code of laws for settlements south of Columbia River.
– Lieutenant Charles Wilkes of United States Navy makes survey of Columbia River.
– American timbered *Star of Oregon*, launched from Swan Island, sails for San Francisco.

1842 Oregon Institute (Willamette University) is established at Salem.
– Marcus Whitman goes east, arouses interest in Oregon country.

1843 Influx of immigrants begins with first considerable wagon train west from Fort Hall.
– Provisional government sets up at meeting in Champoeg; it is first American government on Pacific coast.
– Oregon City becomes seat of government; code of laws adopted, executive governing committee constituted; first districts established: Champoeg (Marion), Clackamas, Tualaty (Washington), and Yamhill.

1844 Indian Mission School on Chemeketa Plain is sold to trustees of Oregon Institute.
– Salem is laid out.

1845 George Abernathy installed as first provisional governor on June 3.
– Amended organic law approved by voters July 25.

1846 United States title to Oregon is established; northern boundary line is fixed at 49 degrees N by treaty with Great Britain.
– Publication of Oregon *Spectator* begins at Oregon City.
– First mail contract in Oregon is let to Hugh Burns.

1847 First regular mail service is established.
– Cayuse Indians kill Dr. Whitman, his wife, and twelve others at Waiilatpu.
– First school (private) opens in Portland.

1848 Oregon Territory is established by Congress on August 14.
– Pacific University and Tualatin Academy open at Forest Grove.

1849 General Joseph Latie installed as first Territorial Governor on March 3.
– Oregon Exchange Company coins and circulates five-and ten-dollar gold pieces, known as beaver money.
– Oregon's first school law is adopted.
– First Territorial legislature meets at Oregon City on July 16.

1850 U.S. Census population is 13,294.
– Legislature locates seat of government at Salem, penitentiary at Portland, and university at Corvallis.

– Oregon Donation Act grants each missionary station 640 acres of land; each settler is to be apportioned quantity according to length of residence and marital status.

1851 Major Philip Kearny fights Indians at Rogue River.
– Territorial legislature incorporates Portland.
– First mayor, H.D. O'Bryant, is elected.
– First public school under Oregon school law organized September 21 at West Union as District No. 1, Washington County.
– District No. 2 organized at Cornelius.
– District No. 3 established at Portland.
– Gold discovered on Jackson Creek by James Cluggage and John R. Pool.

1852 Jacksonville founded, following gold discovery.
– Congress decides state capital dispute; seat of government moves from Oregon City to Salem.
– Great immigration takes place across plains into Oregon and northwest country.

1853 Outbreak of Indian Wars; Rogue River tribes involved in southern Oregon.
– Willamette University chartered at Salem.
– Steamer *Gazelle* explodes while docked at Canemah; 24 lives are lost.
– Treaty is made September 8, by which Indians sell Rogue Valley for $60,000.
– Washington Territory is organized, including all Oregon domains north of Columbia River.

1854 Charters granted to Pacific University and Tualatin Academy.
– Salem becomes city; statehouse is built.

1855 Astoria is chartered.
– Legislature votes to locate State capital at Corvallis.
– Legislature begins session in December at Corvallis.
– Fire destroys statehouse at Salem on December 30.

1856 Legislature meeting at Corvallis votes to relocate seat of government at Salem.

1857 Constitutional convention is held at Salem in August and September.
– State constitution is ratified by popular vote.
– Oregonians vote heavily against slavery.
– Freed blacks denied admission to State.

1858 Oregon State Educational Association organized.

1859 Oregon is admitted to Union on February 14 as 33rd State.
– John Whiteaker takes office as State governor on March 3.
– Steamer *Brother Jonathan* reaches Oregon, bringing news of statehood.
– Organization of state government is completed.

1860 Population is 52,465.

1861 Civil War begins; First Oregon Cavalry enlists for three years' service against Oregon Indians.

1862 Grande Ronde Valley settled by immigrants.

– La Grande is founded.
– Oregon receives government grant of 90,000 acres for support of State college.

1863 Idaho Territory set off from Oregon.

1864 Fort Stevens completed at mouth of Columbia River.
– Telegraph line extends from Portland to California points.

1865 First National Bank of Portland, first bank west of Rocky Mountains, is organized.
– Earthquake follows Mount Hood eruption.

1867 Oregon sends cargo of wheat directly to Australia in barge *Whistler*.

1868 Grading begins for two rival railroads.
– First full cargo of wheat is shipped direct to Europe (Liverpool) in *Sally Brown*.
– State agricultural college opens at Corvallis.

1869 Union Pacific and Central Pacific transcontinental railroads connected at Promontory, Utah.

1870 Population is 90,923.

1872 Legislature authorizes erection of permanent capitol.
– Modoc War begins with night attack on November 29 at Captain Jack's camp.

1873 Modoc War ends with capture of Captain Jack's band.
– Oregon State Woman's Suffrage Association meets for first time.
– Public land grant for military road across Oregon is authorized.
– Ground broken for new capitol building at Salem.

1875 Oregon and Washington Fish Propagating Company constructs hatching station near Oregon City.

1876 University of Oregon (chartered in 1872) opens at Eugene City. (First class is graduated June 2, 1878.)
– Legislature meets for first time in new capitol at Salem.

1877 Chief Joseph's War; Nez Perce Indians are involved.

1880 Population is 174,768.

1884 Legislative act creates Drain Normal School.

1885 Legislature passes "local option" bill.
– State Board of Agriculture is created.
– State takes over Corvallis College and establishes Oregon Agriculture College.

1888 Thomas Nast, famous cartoonist, lectures in Portland.

1890 Population is 317,704.

1891 Legislature passes Australian Ballot law, creates state board of charities and corrections.

1893 State capitol is completed.

1894 Forty lose lives in fire at Silver Lake.

1898 Second Volunteers depart for Philippines.

1899 Resolution of legislature designates Oregon grape as State flower.
– Second Volunteers return.

1900 Population is 413,536.
– Next to San Francisco, Portland has largest Chinese community on West Coast.

1902 Constitutional amendment to establish initiative and referendum adopted by voters.
– Crater Lake National Park is created.

1903 Democrat George E. Chamberlain is Governor.

1904 Direct primary law is passed.

1905 Centennial celebration of Lewis and Clark expedition is held in Portland; nearly two million people attend.

1906 City home rule law is passed.

1908 Recall is adopted as constitutional amendment.

1909 Oregon is fourth in nation in lumber output; production has increased from 444 million board feet in 1889 to 1.9 million board feet.
– Governor Chamberlain resigns gubernatorial office to take U.S. Senate seat; Republican Frank W. Benson becomes acting Governor.

1910 Population is 672,765.
– Baldwin Sheep and Land Company has control of 281 square miles of range land in central Oregon.
– Republican Jay Bowerman becomes acting Governor after Benson becomes ill.

1911 Reform movement calls for election of United States senators by popular vote; it is endorsed by Oregon Senate, and calls upon Congress to submit to states a constitutional amendment to carry out reform.
– Democrat Oswald West is Governor.

1912 State legislature enacts women's suffrage law.

1913 Sarah Bernhardt, great French actress, makes first visit to Portland for three performances.
– Workmen's Compensation Act, Widow's Pension Act passed.

1914 Weyerhaeuser Company holds 400,000 acres of ponderosa pine and Douglas fir lands in State for future use.

1915 Republican James Withycombe is Governor.

1916 Oregon troops mobilize for Mexican border service.

1917 Oregon adopts modern highway program, imposes one cent per gallon tax on gasoline.
– Oregon contributes 44,166 to armed forces of United States for World War I; more than 1,000 die in service; 350 Oregonians are cited for distinguished service.

1919 Governor Withycombe dies during second term; Republican Ben W. Olcott becomes acting Governor.

1920 Population is 783,369.
– Special legislative session passes safety law and rehabilitation act, provides increased benefits under compensation law.
– Permanent state tax of two mills for elementary school purposes approved by popular vote.

1921 Compulsory education law passed.

1922 Indian chiefs from Umpqua, Clackamas, and Rogue River tribes arrive in Portland to sue federal government for $12,500,000 for lands bought but not paid for.
– KGW, first commercial broadcasting station in State, opens.
– Astoria is almost wiped out by $15,000,000 fire.

1923 Shrine Hospital for Crippled Children is completed.
– Law forbids aliens from owning land in Oregon; measure is aimed at Japanese and Chinese.
– Democrat Walter M. Pierce is Governor.

1925 Game preserve on ten million acres is created in Harney and Lake counties for antelope refuge.

1926 Queen Marie of Romania visits Oregon.
– 27,000 people attend dedication of Multnomah Civic Stadium.

1927 Western meadowlark is chosen State bird by popular vote of school children.
– Legislature adopts "Oregon, My Oregon" as State song.
– Republican Isaac Lee Patterson is Governor.

1929 State Parks Commission organized.
– Upon death of Governor Patterson, Republican Albin W. Norblad steps up to become acting Governor.

1930 Population is 953,786.
– New $1,300,000 U.S. Veterans Hospital is dedicated at Portland.
– People's utility district law is passed.
– Sheep population peaks in State at 3,319,000.

1931 Department of State Police begins operations.
– Independent candidate Julius L. Meier becomes Governor.

1933 Construction of Bonneville Dam begins on Columbia River.
– Near Tillamook along northern coast, forest fire burns 311,000 acres.

1935 Capitol building destroyed by fire.
– Democrat Charles II Martin is Governor.

1936 *SS Iowa* wrecked at mouth of Columbia; 34 lives are lost.
– Bandon fire wipes out town; 11 die in blaze.
– Sunset Highway appropriations granted by Federal WPA.

1937 Andre Gagnon, "Father of Modern Sawmills" and inventor of Gagnon bandsaw, dies in Portland at age 93.
– President Roosevelt visits Portland, dedicates Timberline Lodge.

1938 Bonneville Dam is completed; first ocean-going vessel, 55 *Charles L. Wheeler* passes through Bonneville Locks.
– First Bonneville Power lines established.
– Voters approve law banning picketing by strikers where less than half of employees are involved.
– Oregon leads nation in lumbering.

1939 Republican Charles A. Sprague becomes Governor.

1940 Population is 1,089,684.

1941 Shipbuilding boom begins at Portland.
– United States declares war on Germany and Japan, following Pearl Harbor attack.

1942-1945 Total of 1,174 ocean vessels are built in Portland area for World War II effort.
– Portland is top shipping port for lend-lease goods to Soviet Union.

1942 Japanese submarine shells Fort Stevens at mouth of Columbia River.
– Vanport, Oregon's second largest city, constructed as temporary war-housing project.
– Wartime construction and employment boom begins.

1943 Republican Earl Snell is Governor.

1945 May 7. Germany surrenders.
August 14. Japan capitulates.

1947 State executives killed in plane crash.
– John H. Hall (R) becomes acting Governor.

1948 Vanport flood occurs, destroying entire city.

1949 Earthquake rocks northern Oregon.
– State adopts fair-employment practices law.
– Law passed in 1923, which forbids aliens from owning land, is ruled unconstitutional.
– Republican Douglas McKay becomes Governor.

1950 Population is 1,510,148.

1952 Oregon has peak lumber production of 9 billion board feet.
– Governor McKay resigns office to become Secretary of Interior in President Eisenhower's cabinet; Paul M. Patterson (R) steps up as acting Governor.

1953 Civil rights law forbids discrimination in public accommodations.

1954 McNary Dam on Columbia River is dedicated.

1955 Government guarantees equal pay for equal work for women.

1956 Republican Elmo E. Smith becomes acting Governor after death of Patterson.

1957 Democrat Robert D. Holmes is Governor.

1959 Fair-housing law is adopted.
– Dalles Dam on Columbia River is dedicated.
– Republican Mark Hatfield is Governor.

1965 State produces record 8,037 million square feet of softwood plywood; it is 65 percent of national total.

1966 Astoria Bridge, which spans Columbia River, is opened.

1967 Republican Thomas L. McCall is Governor.

1968 John Day Dam is dedicated; it includes country's second largest hydroelectric plant.

1971 Oregon becomes first state to pass law-prohibiting use of non-refundable beverage cans and bottles.

1973 Oregon adopts statewide land-use planning.

1975 Unemployment is 11.2 percent in July, highest since Great Depression, caused primarily from high interest rates, and reduced demand for housing and wood products for building.
– Democrat Robert W. Straub is Governor.

1977 Law bans use of fluorocarbon aerosol cans.

1979 Republican Victor Atiyeh is Governor.

1981 A 64,000-acre ranch near Antelope in Wasco County is purchased by followers of Indian guru Bhagwan Shree Rajneesh; it is incorporated as Rajneeshpuram, with population of 1,200.

1987 Democrat Neil Goldschmidt is Governor.

1990 Population is 2,842,321.
– Scientists discover ten new active volcanoes on seabed of Oregon coast.
– Supreme Court rules that government may prohibit use of drugs as part of religious rituals, says ban against peyote by Native Americans does not violate constitutional right to free exercise of religion; peyote has been used for centuries in Indian religious ceremonies.

1991 Seattle district court blocks sale of logging rights on national forest land in Pacific Northwest; ruling is intended to protect habitat of endangered northern spotted owl.
– Per capita income is $17,592, a 2.4 percent increase over 1990.
– Democrat Barbara Roberts is Governor.

1992 Republican Robert W. Packwood wins election as U.S. Senator.
– Elizabeth Furse elected to U.S. Congress; U.S. House now has four Democrats, one Republican.
– State Court of Appeals rules that ballot measure opposing homosexual rights is unconstitutional; measure was passed in 1988.

1993 Wildfires burn parts of State.

1995 Supreme Court rules to uphold random drug-testing program for school athletes in State school Supreme Court rules to uphold random drug testing program for school athletes in State school district; decision marks first ruling on school-sponsored programs and first in which court upholds program to test individuals at random.
– Democrat John A. Kitzhaber is Governor.

1996 Republican Gordon Smith wins close Senate contest against Democrat Tom Bruggere.
– State voters reject referendum requiring voter approval for new taxes.

1997 Don Wolf, U.S. scientist at Oregon Regional Primate Research Center in Beaverton, announces that he and team of researchers have created two monkey clones from embryo cells.
– State residents vote 60 percent in favor of keeping nation's only law that allows physician-assisted suicide; vote reaffirms State's commitment to assisted suicide statute, approved three years earlier, and opens way for its enactment.
– Former Representative Wes S. Cooley is convicted of lying about military service in 1994 voters' pamphlet.

1998 Attorney General Janet Reno announces that Justice Department will not prosecute doctors for prescribing drugs for purpose of suicide under State law permitting physician-assisted suicide; announcement overrules statement in November by Thomas Constantine, administrator of Drug Enforcement Administration, who warned that doctors who wrote such prescriptions could have licenses revoked under Federal Controlled Substances Act.
– Oregon Health Division releases first official tally of terminally ill people who died from lethal medications prescribed under State law that permits physician-assisted suicide; eight people have died under law since it took effect in November 1997; two others were authorized to take lethal drugs but died from illnesses before doing so; nine patients suffered from cancer, one from heart disease; average age was 71.
– Springfield student, Kipland Kinkel, is formally charged with numerous counts of murder and assault after alleged shooting spree in his high school cafeteria; Kinkel is accused of killing parents and two classmates, wounding 22 others.

1999 May 16. In Oregon ballots are counted in the nation's first regular primary election conducted by mail, the estimated response is 47 percent.

DIRECTORY OF STATE SERVICES

OFFICE OF THE GOVERNOR
State Capitol Bldg., Rm. 254
Salem, OR 97310
Fax: 503-378-4863
Governor: 503-378-3111

OFFICE OF ATTORNEY GENERAL
100 Justice Bldg.
Salem, OR 97310
Fax: 503-378-4017
Attorney General: 503-378-6002

OFFICE OF SECRETARY OF STATE
State Capitol, Rm. 136
Salem, OR 97310
Fax: 503-373-7414
Secretary of State: 503-986-1500

Accountancy Board
158 12th St. NE
Salem, OR 97310
Administrator: 503-378-4181

Corporation Division
255 Capitol St. NE
Salem, OR 97310
Fax: 503-373-1166
Director: 503-986-2205

Tax Service Examiners Board
158 12th St. NE, Commerce Bldg.
Salem, OR 97310
Administrator: 503-378-4034

DEPARTMENT OF TREASURY
159 State Capitol
Salem, OR 97310-0840
Fax: 503-373-7051
Treasurer: 503-378-4329

ADMINISTRATIVE SERVICES DEPARTMENT
155 Cottage St. NE
Salem, OR 97310
Fax: 503-378-7643
Director: 503-378-3104

Facilities Division
1225 Ferry St. SE
Salem, OR 97310-1561
Fax: 503-373-7210
Administrator: 503-378-2865

Fiscal Policy Analysis Division
155 Cottage St. NE
Salem, OR 97310
Fax: 503-373-7643
Administrator: 503-378-3103

Information Resources Management Division
155 Cottage St. NE
Salem, OR 97310
Fax: 503-986-3242
Administrator: 503-378-3160

Internal Support Division
1225 Ferry St. SE
Salem, OR 97310
Fax: 503-378-6879
Administrator: 503-373-7245

Human Resource Management Division
155 Cottage St. NE
Salem, OR 97310
Fax: 503-373-7684
Administrator: 503-378-3020

Labor Relations Division
155 Cottage St. NE
Salem, OR 97310
Fax: 503-373-7684
Administrator: 503-378-6061

Risk Management Division
155 Cottage St. NE
Salem, OR 97310
Fax: 503-373-7338
Administrator: 503-373-7475

Telecommunications
1225 Ferry St. SE
Salem, OR 97310
Fax: 503-373-7338
Administrator: 503-373-1549

Transportation, Purchasing and Printing Division
1225 Ferry St. SE
Salem, OR 97310
Fax: 503-373-1626
Director: 503-378-4643

AGRICULTURE DEPARTMENT
635 Capitol St. NE
Salem, OR 97310-0110
Fax: 503-986-4747
Director: 503-986-4551

Agricultural Development and Marketing Division
121 SW Salmon, Ste. 240
Portland, OR 97204-2987
Fax: 503-229-6113
Administrator: 503-229-6734

Commodity Inspection Division
635 Capitol St. NE
Salem, OR 97310-0110
Fax: 503-986-4737
Administrator: 503-986-4620

Livestock Health and Identification Division
635 Capitol St. NE
Salem, OR 97310-0110
Fax: 503-986-4734
Administrator: 503-986-4680

Measurement Standards Division
635 Capitol St. NE
Salem, OR 97310-0110
Fax: 503-986-4734
Administrator: 503-986-4670

Plant Division
635 Capitol St. NE
Salem, OR 97310-0110
Fax: 503-986-4735
Administrator: 503-986-4635

CONSUMER AND BUSINESS SERVICES DEPARTMENT
21 Labor & Industries Bldg.
Salem, OR 97310
Fax: 503-378-6444

Director: 503-378-4100

Insurance Pool Governing Board
796 Winter St. NE
Salem, OR 97310
Fax: 503-378-8365
Administrator: 503-373-1692

Minority, Women and Emerging Small Business Office
11 Labor & Industries Bldg.
Salem, OR 97310
Advocate: 503-378-5651

Worker's Compensation Division
21 Labor & Industries Bldg.
Salem, OR 97310
Fax: 503-945-7581
Administrator: 503-945-7881

Worker's Compensation Board
250 McGilchrist St. NE
Salem, OR 97310
Fax: 503-945-7581
Administrator: 503-378-3308

CORRECTIONS DEPARTMENT
2575 Center St. NE
Salem, OR 97310
Fax: 503-373-1173
Director: 503-945-0920

ECONOMIC DEVELOPMENT DEPARTMENT
775 Summer St. NE
Salem, OR 97310
Fax: 503-581-5115
Director: 503-986-0110

Film and Video
121 SW Salmon, Ste. 3000
Portland, OR 97204
Manager: 503-373-1232

Industry Development
775 Summer St. NE
Salem, OR 97310
Fax: 503-581-5115
Manager: 503-986-0200

Tourism
775 Summer St. NE
Salem, OR 97310
Fax: 503-581-5115
Manager: 503-373-1270

EDUCATION DEPARTMENT
255 Capitol St. NE
Salem, OR 97310-0203
Fax: 503-373-7968
Superintendent of Public Instruction: 503-378-3573

Educational Support Services
255 Capitol St. NE
Salem, OR 97310-0203
Director: 503-378-3573

Management Services Office
255 Capitol St. NE
Salem, OR 97310-0203
Director: 503-378-2997

School for the Blind
700 Church St. SE
Salem, OR 97310
Director: 503-378-3826

School for the Deaf
999 Locust St. NE
Salem, OR 97310
Director: 503-378-3826

EMPLOYMENT DEPARTMENT
875 Union St. NE
Salem, OR 97311
Fax: 503-373-7515
Director: 503-378-8420

ENERGY DEPARTMENT
625 Marion St. NE
Salem, OR 97310
Fax: 503-373-7806
Director: 503-378-4040

ENVIRONMENTAL QUALITY DEPARTMENT
811 SW 6th Ave.
Portland, OR 97204
Fax: 503-229-6124
Director: 503-229-5395

Air Quality Division
811 SW 6th Ave.
Portland, OR 97204
Fax: 503-229-6124
Administrator: 503-229-5397

Laboratory Division
1712 SW 11th Ave.
Portland, OR 97201
Fax: 503-229-6924
Administrator: 503-229-5983

Management Services Division
811 SW 6th Ave.
Portland, OR 97204
Fax: 503-229-5850
Administrator: 503-229-6484

Waste Management and Cleanup Division
811 SW 6th Ave.
Portland, OR 97204
Fax: 503-229-5072
Administrator: 503-229-6853

Water Quality Control Division
811 SW 6th Ave.
Portland, OR 97204
Fax: 503-229-6124
Administrator: 503-229-5279

FISH AND WILDLIFE DEPARTMENT
P.O. Box 59
Portland, OR 97207
Fax: 503-229-6134
Director: 503-229-5406

FORESTRY DEPARTMENT
2600 State St.
Salem, OR 97310
Fax: 503-945-7212
State Forester: 503-945-7211

Administrative Services Division
2600 State St.
Salem, OR 97310
Fax: 503-945-7212
Assistant State Forester: 503-945-7203

Forest Management Division
2600 State St.
Salem, OR 97310
Fax: 503-945-7376
Assistant State Forester: 503-945-7204

Protection Division
2600 State St.
Salem, OR 97310
Fax: 503-945-7454
Assistant State Forester: 503-945-7205

GEOLOGY AND MINERAL INDUSTRIES DEPARTMENT
800 NE Oregon St., #28
Portland, OR 97232
Fax: 503-731-4066
State Geologist: 503-731-4100

HOUSING & COMMUNITY SERVICES DEPARTMENT
1600 State St.
Salem, OR 97310-0302
Fax: 503-986-2020
Director: 503-986-2000

Administrative Operations Division
1600 State St.
Salem, OR 97310-0302
Fax: 503-986-2020
Administrator & CFO: 503-986-2056

Community Development and Finance Division
1600 State St.
Salem, OR 97310-0302
Fax: 503-986-2020
Administrator: 503-986-2103

HUMAN RESOURCES DEPARTMENT
500 Summer St. NE
Salem, OR 97310-1012
Fax: 503-378-2897
Director: 503-945-5944

Adult and Family Services Division
500 Summer St. NE
Salem, OR 97310-1013
Fax: 503-373-7492

Administrator: 503-945-5600

Alcohol and Drug Abuse Program Office
500 Summer St. NE, 3rd Fl.
Salem, OR 97310-1016
Fax: 503-378-8467
Assistant Director: 503-945-5763

Children's Services Division
500 Summer St. NE, 2nd Fl.
Salem, OR 97310-1017
Fax: 503-581-6198
Administrator: 503-945-5909

Health Division
P.O. Box 14450
Portland, OR 97214-0450
Fax: 503-731-4078
Administrator: 503-731-4000

Health Policy Office
800 NE Oregon St., #23, Ste. 640
Portland, OR 97232-2162
Fax: 503-731-4056
Director: 503-731-4091

Medical Assistance Program Office
500 Summer St. NE
Salem, OR 97310-1014
Fax: 503-373-7689
Director: 503-945-5772

Mental Health and Developmental Disabilities Services Division
2575 Bittern St. NE
Salem, OR 97310
Fax: 503-378-3796
Administrator: 503-945-9499

Senior and Disabled Services Division
500 Summer St. NE
Salem, OR 97310-1015
Fax: 503-373-7823
Administrator: 503-945-5811

Vocational Rehabilitation Division
500 Summer St. NE
Salem, OR 97310-1018
Fax: 503-378-3318
Administrator: 503-945-5880

LAND CONSERVATION AND DEVELOPMENT DEPARTMENT
1175 Court St. NE
Salem, OR 97310
Fax: 503-362-6705
Director: 503-373-0050

MILITARY DEPARTMENT
P.O. Box 14350
Salem, OR 97309-5047
Fax: 503-945-3962
Adjutant General: 503-945-3981

PARKS AND RECREATION DEPARTMENT
1115 Commercial St. NE
Salem, OR 97310-1001
Fax: 503-378-6447
Director: 503-378-5019

REVENUE DEPARTMENT
955 Center St. NE
Salem, OR 97310
Fax: 503-945-8738
Director: 503-945-8214

Administrative Services Division
955 Center St. NE
Salem, OR 97310
Fax: 503-945-8738
Administrator: 503-945-8001

Audit Division
955 Center St. NE
Salem, OR 97310
Fax: 503-945-8738
Administrator: 503-945-8460

Collection Division
955 Center St. NE
Salem, OR 97310
Fax: 503-945-8735
Administrator: 503-945-8608

Information Processing Division
955 Center St. NE
Salem, OR 97310
Fax: 503-945-8738
Administrator: 503-945-8211

Property Tax Division
256 Revenue, 955 Center St.
Salem, OR 97310
Fax: 503-945-8738
Administrator: 503-945-8290

STATE POLICE DEPARTMENT
400 Public Service Bldg.
Salem, OR 97310
Fax: 503-378-8282
Superintendent: 503-378-3720

Intergovernmental Services Bureau
400 Public Service Bldg.
Salem, OR 97310
Fax: 503-378-8282
Director: 503-378-3720

Emergency Management
595 Cottage St. NE
Salem, OR 97310
Fax: 503-588-1378
Director: 503-378-4124

Fire Marshal Division
4760 Portland Rd. NE
Salem, OR 97305-1760
Fax: 503-373-1825

Fire Marshal: 503-378-3473

Law Enforcement Data Systems
400 Public Service Bldg.
Salem, OR 97310
Fax: 503-363-8249
Director: 503-378-3054

TRANSPORTATION DEPARTMENT
135 Transportation Bldg.
Salem, OR 97310
Fax: 503-986-3446
Transportation Commission Chairman: 503-986-3200

Driver and Motor Vehicles Services Branch
1905 Lana Ave. NE
Salem, OR 97314
Fax: 503-945-5259
Manager: 503-945-5100

Financial Services Branch
Rm. 434, Transportation Bldg.
Salem, OR 97310
Fax: 503-986-3446
Chief Financial Officer: 503-986-3000

Human Resources and Organization Development Branch
Rm. 102, Transportation Bldg.
Salem, OR 97310
Fax: 503-986-3446
Manager: 503-986-3838

Information Systems Branch
471 Revenue Bldg.
Salem, OR 97310
Fax: 503-986-3446
Manager: 503-986-3500

Maritime Pilots Board
800 NE Oregon St.
Portland, OR 97232
Administrator: 503-731-4044

Support Services Branch
2800 State St.
Portland, OR 97310
Fax: 503-986-2717
Manager: 503-986-2726

Technical Services Branch
Rm. 204, Transportation Bldg.
Salem, OR 97310
Fax: 503-986-3446
Managing Engineer: 503-986-3302

Transportation Development Branch
Rm. 132, Transportation Bldg.
Salem, OR 97310
Fax: 503-986-3446
Manager: 503-986-3420

VETERANS AFFAIRS DEPARTMENT
700 Summer St. NE
Salem, OR 97310-1201

Fax: 503-373-2362
Director: 503-373-2388

WATER RESOURCES DEPARTMENT
158 12th St. NE
Salem, OR 97310-0210
Fax: 503-378-8130
Director: 503-378-3739

ARCHITECT EXAMINERS BOARD
750 Front St. NE, Ste. 260
Salem, OR 97310
Fax: 503-364-6891
Administrator: 503-378-4270

ARTS COMMISSION
775 Summer St. NE
Salem, OR 97301
Fax: 503-581-5115
Executive Director: 503-986-0088

COMMISSION FOR THE BLIND
535 SE 12th St.
Portland, OR 97214
Fax: 503-731-3230
Administrator: 503-731-3223

CONSTRUCTION AND LANDSCAPE CONTRACTORS BOARD
P.O. Box 14140
Salem, OR 97309-5052
Fax: 503-373-2213
Administrator: 503-378-4621

EDUCATIONAL POLICY AND PLANNING OFFICE
255 Capitol St. NE, Ste. 126
Salem, OR 97310-1338
Fax: 503-378-4789
Director: 503-378-3921

EMPLOYMENT APPEALS BOARD
875 Union St. NE
Salem, OR 97303
Fax: 503-378-5023
Chairperson: 503-378-4462

EMPLOYMENT RELATIONS BOARD
528 Cottage St. NE, Ste. 400
Salem, OR 97310
Fax: 503-373-0021
Chairperson: 503-378-3807

ENGINEERING AND GEOLOGISTS EXAMINERS BOARD
750 Front St. NE, Ste. 240
Salem, OR 97310
Fax: 503-364-6891
Administrator: 503-378-4180

GOVERNMENT STANDARDS AND PRACTICES COMMISSION
100 High St. SE, Ste. 220
Salem, OR 97310-1360
Fax: 503-373-1456
Executive Director: 503-378-5105

HIGHER EDUCATION BOARD
P.O. Box 3175
Eugene, OR 97403
Fax: 503-346-5764
Chancellor: 503-346-5794

Public Affairs Office
528 SW Mill St.
Portland, OR 97207
Fax: 503-725-5709
Vice Chancellor: 503-725-5700

LABOR AND INDUSTRIES BUREAU
800 NE Oregon St. #32
Portland, OR 97232
Fax: 503-731-4103
Commissioner: 503-731-4070

LIQUOR CONTROL COMMISSION
P.O. Box 22297
Portland, OR 97269-2297
Fax: 503-652-1380
Administrator: 503-653-3018

LONG TERM CARE OMBUDSMAN PROGRAM
2475 Lancaster Dr. NE, B-9
Salem, OR 97310
Fax: 503-373-0852
Director: 503-378-6533

MARINE BOARD
435 Commercial St. NE
Salem, OR 97310
Fax: 503-378-4597
Director: 503-378-8587

PAROLE AND POST PRISON SUPERVISION BOARD
2575 Center St. NE
Salem, OR 97310
Fax: 503-373-7558
Chairperson: 503-945-0900

PHARMACY BOARD
800 NE Oregon St., Ste. 425
Portland, OR 97232
Fax: 503-731-4067
Administrator: 503-731-4032

PUBLIC BROADCASTING SERVICE
7140 SW Macadam Ave.
Portland, OR 97219-3013
Fax: 503-293-4152
Executive Director: 503-244-9900

PUBLIC DEFENDER
603 Chemeketa St. NE
Salem, OR 97310
Fax: 503-375-9701
Public Defender: 503-378-3349

PUBLIC EMPLOYEES RETIREMENT SYSTEM
P.O. Box 73
Portland, OR 97207-0073
Fax: 503-223-2869

Director: 503-229-5824

PUBLIC UTILITY COMMISSION
550 Capitol St. NE
Salem, OR 97310-1380
Fax: 503-378-5505
Chairperson: 503-378-6611

REAL ESTATE AGENCY
1177 Center St. NE
Salem, OR 97310
Fax: 503-373-7153
Commissioner: 503-378-4170

STATE ACCIDENT INSURANCE FUND CORPORATION
400 High St. SE
Salem, OR 97312
Fax: 503-373-8271
President: 503-373-8001

STATE FAIR AND EXPOSITION CENTER
2330 17th St. NE
Salem, OR 97310
Fax: 503-373-1788
Director: 503-378-3247

STATE LANDS DIVISION
775 Summer St. NE
Salem, OR 97310
Fax: 503-378-4844
Director: 503-378-3805

STATE LIBRARY
State Library Bldg.
Salem, OR 97310-0640
Fax: 503-588-7119
State Librarian: 503-378-4243

STATE LOTTERY
P.O. Box 12649
Salem, OR 97309
Fax: 503-373-0248
Director: 503-373-0202

STATE SCHOLARSHIP COMMISSION
1500 Valley River Dr., Ste. 100
Eugene, OR 97401
Fax: 503-687-7419
Executive Director: 503-687-7400

TEACHERS STANDARDS AND PRACTICES COMMISSION
255 Capitol St. NE, Ste. 105
Salem, OR 97310-1332
Fax: 503-378-4448
Executive Secretary: 503-373-6813

TRAVEL INFORMATION COUNCIL
229 Mardona Ave. SE
Salem, OR 97302
Fax: 503-378-6282
Director: 503-378-4508

MEMBERS OF CONGRESS

SENATE

SEN. RON WYDEN (D) (b. 1949); 2nd Term;
Phone: 202-224-5244; Fax: 202-228-2717;
E-mail: senator@wyden.senate.gov.

www.senate.gov/~wyden/

SEN. GORDON SMITH (R) (b. 1952); 1st Term;
Phone: 202-224-3753; Fax: 202-228-3997;
E-mail: oregon@gsmith.senate.gov.

www.senate.gov/~gsmith

HOUSE

DAVID WU (D-1st) (b. 1955); 1st Term;
Phone: 202-225-0855; Fax: 202-225-9497;
E-mail: david.wu@mail.house.gov.

www.house.gov/wu/

GREG WALDEN (R-2nd) (b. 1957); 1st Term;
Phone: 202-225-6730; Fax: 202-225-5774;
E-mail: greg.walden@mail.house.gov.

www.house.gov/walden

EARL BLUMENAUER (D-3rd) (b. 1948); 3rd Term;
Phone: 202-225-4811; Fax: 202-225-8941;
E-mail: write.earl@mail.house.gov.

www.house.gov/blumenauer/

PETER A. DeFAZIO (D-4th) (b. 1947); 7th Term;
Phone: 202-225-6416; Fax: 202-225-0032;
E-mail: peter.defazio@mail.house.gov.

www.house.gov/defazio/index.htm

DARLENE HOOLEY (D-5th) (b. 1939); 2nd Term;
Phone: 202-225-5711; Fax: 202-225-5699;
E-mail: or05@legislators.com.

www.house.gov/hooley/

TWENTIETH CENTURY GOVERNORS

GEER, THEODORE T. (1851-1924), ninth governor of Oregon (1899-1903), was born near Salem, Oregon on March 12, 1851.

Between 1863 and 1865 Geer attended Oregon Institute, a branch of Willamette University, and for a short time during 1864 he was a member of the "Marion Rifles," a local militia troop. After college, Geer moved to his father's farm in the Grand Rhonde Valley in 1866. By the age of seventeen he was passionately interested in politics, and had his first political article published in the *Blue Mountain Times*. In 1877 he had his own farm near Salem, and for the next twenty years, while maintaining his farmland, he continued to write numerous political essays. With so many of his opinions being printed in newspapers, his name became so well known that in 1880 he was elected to the State Legislature, subsequently winning three more terms.

In the 1896 election, Geer traveled across Oregon stumping for presidential candidate William McKinley, hoping that his efforts might garner him a federal appointment. When that did not happen, he still had enough support from political insiders to run for the Oregon governorship in 1898 on the Republican ticket, during which he defeated his Democrat-Populist challenger, W.R. King, and took office on January 9, 1899. During his tenure, an important constitutional amendment was adopted in 1902, which implemented the initiative and referendum, making Oregon one of only a few states at that time to have such a reform.

Losing in his bid for a second term, Geer stepped down from office on January 14, 1903, and subsequently secured the post of editor for the Salem *Daily Statesman*, and in 1905, became owner of the *Pendleton Tribune*, which he published until 1908. Geer spent his remaining years engaged in his real estate ventures, and in 1911, wrote his memoirs, *Fifty Years in Oregon*. He was married twice: to Nancy Duncan Batte, who died in 1898, and with whom he had three children; and to Isabelle Trullinger. Geer died on February 21, 1924.

CHAMBERLAIN, GEORGE EARLE (1854-1928), tenth governor of Oregon (1903-1909), lawyer, senator, was born near Natchez, Mississippi on January 1, 1854. His father was Charles Thomson Chamberlain, a leading physician of Natchez, whose father had been one of the foremost physicians of Newark, Delaware. Chamberlain's mother was Pamelia H. Archer, whose father was in turn a congressman from Maryland, judge of Mississippi Territory with gubernatorial powers, and at the time of his death, one of the justices of the Court of Appeals of Maryland. Chamberlain's early education was received from private tutors and in the schools of Natchez. From sixteen to eighteen he clerked in a store, but with consciousness of his abilities and his family traditions, he naturally struck out for a professional career, and, attending Washington and Lee University, he received the degrees of Bachelor of Arts and bachelor of law in the same year, June 1876.

Upon arriving in Oregon late in 1876 Chamberlain first taught school in Linn County. From 1877 to 1879 he served as deputy county clerk in the same county, then returned to Natchez. In 1880 Chamberlain was elected to the House of Representatives of the Oregon Legislature, and, having entered upon the active practice of law, he was, in 1884, elected district attorney of the third Judicial District. In 1891 the Office of Attorney General of Oregon was created and Chamberlain was appointed by the governor to that position. At the succeeding general election he was chosen as the Democratic candidate, running some 10,000 votes ahead of his party's ticket. In 1900, having taken up his residence in Portland, he was chosen as district attorney of Multnomah County, his vote leading that of the party ticket by about the ratio with which he had won his previous victories.

Chamberlain was twice elected governor, first in 1902, taking office on January 15, 1903, and again in 1906, finally stepping down on February 28, 1909. As governor he moved quickly to rescue for the people valuable timbered school lands that were being rapidly filched away from them through dummy entrymen. He also used his veto freely to prevent frustration of the people's aims. The federal amendment providing for popular election of United States senators was anticipated in Oregon through the so-called "Statement No. 1," submitted to candidates for election to the Legislature in 1908, through which each could be pledged to vote for the man receiving the highest popular vote. This brought about the unique spectacle of a Legislature strongly Republican, casting its vote in 1909 for Chamberlain, a Democrat, as United States Senator.

In 1915, with direct election of United States senators provided by federal amendment, Chamberlain was again elected. As senator, his attitude and ability had secured immediate recognition and in 1913 he had become Chairman of the Committee on Military Affairs. This position during the years immediately preceding and during American participation in the World War placed weighty responsibilities on Chamberlain's shoulders. He is credited with a large part in the formulation and the handling of the measures providing for the selective draft, food control, and the financing of the war. Dilatoriness of movement in the War Department in the early months of the war aroused him to pronounce a sharp judgment upon it in a New York City speech and to ask for an emergency organization to take over some of that department's duties. Those nearest Chamberlain were inclined to believe that "he considered his efforts in behalf of the boys in service during the late war to have been the finest thing, the thing most fruitful of benefit to humanity that he ever did." His action, however, was bitterly resented by President Wilson and from that time on he was out of favor with the administration. In 1920, defeated for reelection, he stepped down from office, thus ending his political career.

He was large and impressive in appearance and an excellent speaker, whose manner inspired confidence. After his defeat his friends, both Republican and Democrat, secured his appointment as a member of the United States Shipping Board. Chamberlain was married to Sallie M. Welch, of New England ancestry. He died on July 9, 1928.

BENSON, FRANK W. (1858-1911), acting governor of Oregon (1909-1910), was born in San Jose, California on March 20, 1858.

While still a boy Benson moved with his family to Portland, Oregon, then later returned to California to attend the College of the Pacific, where he earned both an A.B. and A.M. degree. In 1880 he was made overseer of the Umpqua Academy in Wilbur. Two years later he was elected County Superintendent of Schools, serving in that post until 1886, when he was named president of a normal school in Drain, Oregon. Benson was elected to two terms as Douglas County Clerk, in 1892, and 1896, while passing the Oregon Bar in the latter year. Beginning in 1898 he had his own law practice in Roseburg, then in 1906, won the office of Secretary of State on the Republican ticket.

When incumbent Governor George Chamberlain resigned to serve in the United States Senate, Benson succeeded to the governorship on March 1, 1909, while still remaining Secretary of State. During his tenure as governor, he called a special two-day session of the Oregon Legislature, during which State funds were earmarked for the upgrade of such State institutions as the reform school, insane asylum, penitentiary, and retired soldiers' home. In addition, working in tandem with the governor of the State of Washington, he made the effort to end a long-time boundary dispute between the two states; however, due to an extended illness, he was forced to step down before it could be resolved.

In order to get well Benson traveled to California, and soon after, asked his private assistant, C.N. McArthur, to contact the President of the State Senate, Jay Bowerman, asking that he "assume the duties of the governorship," which he did on June 17, 1910. Benson intended to return to office, but never did. Instead, later that year, he was elected to another term as Secretary of State. However, still in fragile health, he died on April 14, 1911. Benson was married to Harriet Ruth Benjamin, and the couple had two children.

BOWERMAN, JAY (1876-1957), acting governor of Oregon (1910-1911), was born in Hesper, Iowa on August 15, 1876.

Moving to Salem, Oregon in 1893, Bowerman studied at Willamette University, earning a law degree in 1896, and passing the Oregon Bar the next year. From that time until 1899, he had his own law practice in Salem; then moved to Condon, Oregon, where he went into a law partnership with H.H. Henricks. A Republican, his entry into politics was his 1904 election to the State Senate, where he went on to serve a second term, some of it as president of that body. In June of 1910, when Governor Frank W. Benson needed to leave office due to his ailing health, he requested that Bowerman, in his capacity as President of the Senate, succeed to the governorship, which he did, on June 17, 1910. During his tenure he supported the creation of a Board of Control that would oversee the purchasing for State institutions, a department that would not be organized until the term of his successor.

In 1910 Bowerman ran for the next term of the governorship, but was sabotaged by his own party. In 1904 Oregon voters had passed a direct primary law, which turned the nomination process over to them, rather than the nominating conventions. However, the Republicans chafed at the new system and in 1910 convened at an "assembly," where they nominated Bowerman for the Oregon governorship. Bowerman's opponent, Democrat Oswald West, used it against him during the campaign, convincing Oregon's citizens that Bowerman felt he was above the primary law. Although Bowerman's campaign platform was solid in its support of Oregon's modernization, he lost to West, and stepped down from office on January 8, 1911.

Bowerman settled in Portland and returned to his private law practice, but continued to be politically active as a lobbyist at the State Legislature. He was married to Elizabeth Hoover, and the couple had three children. Bowerman died on October 25, 1957.

WEST, OSWALD (1873-1960), eleventh governor of Oregon (1911-1915), was born on May 20, 1873 in Guelph, Ontario, Canada.

After attending public schools, West quit at the age of sixteen and worked in a bank until 1899, when he left to search for gold in Alaska. In 1903 he received the appointment of State Land Agent from Governor George Chamberlain, during which time he attempted to recover nearly 900,000 acres of school land that had been illegally stolen by land speculators. In 1907 he was asked to serve a four-year term with the Oregon Railroad Commission.

West ran for the Oregon governorship in 1910 on the Democratic ticket, defeating his challenger, Republican incumbent Acting Governor Jay Bowerman, and taking office on January 11, 1911. Almost immediately, West had to contend with the Republican-dominated State Legislature, but managed to get their attention by vetoing more than sixty-three bills they were attempting to pass. He made good use of the initiative and referendum, especially in his efforts to pass such issues as prohibition and women's suffrage. Also during his tenure, the workmen's compensation act was passed by referendum, which was then administered by the newly-created Industrial Accident Commission. In addition, prison reform was made a priority, and a unified purchasing system, originally proposed by West's predecessor, Acting Governor Jay Bowerman, was created in order to oversee the purchasing for State institutions.

An environmentalist, Governor West was intent on preserving the State's natural resources. As such, both the Bureau of Forestry and the Office of State Forester were established, as was the Fish and Game Commission, and the State's beaches were preserved for use by Oregon's citizens.

Although he accomplished a great deal while in office, West decided to serve only the one term and stepped down on January 12, 1915. Settling in Portland, where he went into law practice, he continued to involve himself heavily in political issues, writing numerous articles and essays for newspapers and magazines. In recalling his administration years later, he mused that he had "banished dullness from the Oregon Governorship, and brought worthwhile laws to benefit the commonwealth.'

West was married to Mabel Hutton, and the couple had three children. He died on August 22, 1960.

WITHYCOMBE, JAMES (1843-1919), twelfth governor of Oregon (1915-1919), was born on March 21, 1843 in Devonshire, England.

Withycombe attended school in his native country, then as an adult, moved with his family to America in 1871, settling near Hillsboro, Oregon, and becoming a United States citizen in April of 1900. The family chose to live on a farm, and Withycombe became prolific enough at it to teach farming, eventually buying his own acreage, which he expanded into an even larger property. His extensive knowledge of farming led to a teaching position at Oregon Agricultural College (which would later become Oregon State University) in 1898, in which he offered farmers the latest scientific agricultural methods. Not long after, he was named Director of that school's College Experiment Station.

Withycombe's entry into politics was in 1906, when he ran unsuccessfully for the Oregon governorship on the Republican ticket. In a second attempt in 1914, he defeated the Democratic challenger, Charles Smith, taking office on January 12, 1915. During his tenure, Withycombe urged that the building of new roads be a top priority, noting that the money used would be "the best investment" Oregon could make. He was also instrumental in developing the flax industry within the State by convincing the State Legislature to back the growing and processing of the plant, in order to provide work for penitentiary inmates. After the start of World War I, Withycombe enthusiastically supported the war effort, and encouraged Oregon's citizens to do the same.

Withycombe ran for a second term, defeating the Democratic candidate, Walter M. Pierce. However, two months into his second term, on March 3, 1919, he died. He was married to Isabel Carpenter and the couple had five children.

OLCOTT, BEN (1872-1952), acting governor of Oregon (1919-1923), was born in Keithsburg, Illinois on October 15, 1872.

After attending business college in Dixon, Illinois, Olcott moved to Chicago to work as a clerk. In 1891, he migrated to Salem, Oregon where he became friends with another future governor of Oregon, Oswald West. For the following ten years, Olcott worked at a number of jobs, including shoe salesman, bookkeeper, clerk, bricklayer, and farmhand, and when so inclined, mined for gold in Oregon and Alaska. For a time he worked for his friend, Oswald West, in the State Land Office. Later, although Olcott was Republican and West was a Democrat, the former was overseer of West's campaign for the governorship in 1910. After West was elected, he appointed Olcott to serve as Secretary of State, and he was reelected to the office two more times. In that capacity, he succeeded to the Oregon governorship upon the death of James Withycombe on March 3, 1919.

During Olcott's tenure, he traveled for miles by army planes across Oregon, California and Washington and asked U.S. Army personnel if they would patrol Oregon forests to watch for fires. In that same vein, he requested that the State Legislature pass a bill that would protect the forests that lined State highways. Also while in office, he asked the legislature to forbid the sale of State land to people of Japanese ethnicity.

In May of 1922, only a few days before the primary election for governor, Olcott spoke out about his disdain for the burgeoning power of the Ku Klux Klan, and although he won the primary, he lost the general election to his Democratic opponent, Walter Pierce. The latter had a number of Klan supporters, many of whom disliked Olcott because it was assumed he was a Catholic, and was against the anti-Catholic Compulsory School Bill.

After stepping down on January 8, 1923, Olcott moved to Long Beach, California where he was employed as the manager of a branch of the Bank of Italy. He returned to Oregon in 1924. Olcott was married to Lena Hutton, and the couple had three children. He died on July 21, 1952.

PIERCE, WALTER MARCUS (1861-1954), thirteenth governor of Oregon (1923-1927), was born in Morris, Illinois on May 30, 1861.

In 1883 Pierce migrated to Oregon, settling near Milton. Making his living as a schoolteacher, he served as Superintendent of Schools for Umatilla County between 1886 and 1890. In the latter year, he was named County Clerk, serving until 1894. During this time he successfully sold land, making enough money to return to Illinois and study for a law degree. Attending Northwestern University, he earned a Bachelor of Laws degree in 1896, and made his way back to Oregon, settling in Pendleton, where he practiced law and continued his involvement in real estate. Other successful business pursuits included his breeding of Hereford cattle, and his owning and operating the Grande Ronde Electric Company.

Pierce's entry into politics was his election to the Oregon State Senate in 1902. Although he wasn't reelected for a second term, Pierce continued his involvement in civic matters, such as helping establish both the Oregon Farmers' Union and the Public Power League. A Democrat, in 1912 he unsuccessfully ran for a seat in the United States Senate, but in 1916, returned to the State Senate. In 1918 he made his first bid for the Oregon governorship, but was defeated by the Republican incumbent, James Withycombe, and in 1920, lost his third bid for the State Senate by only a few votes.

In 1922, with backing from the Ku Klux Klan, who supported the Compulsory School Bill, and with the added factor of the anti-Catholic sentiments against his challenger, incumbent governor Ben Olcott, Pierce secured the governorship in 1922, taking office on January 8, 1923. During his tenure he urged the implementation of the State's first income tax, and strongly supported prohibition, as well as a law that denied land ownership to foreigners. Pierce also backed prison reform, pushed for State-owned hydroelectric plants, and supported other progressive legislation, much of which was not passed by the mostly Republican Legislature. Although admired for being a strong governor, ultimately Oregon's mostly Republican voters elected his gubernatorial opponent, I.L. Patterson, in the 1926 election. After stepping down from office on January 10, 1927, Pierce made an unsuccessful try for the United States Congress in 1928, but in 1932, won that seat, and was reelected for an additional five terms, losing in his last attempt in 1942.

Pierce was married three times: to Clara R. Rudio, who died in 1890; to Laura Rudio, who died in 1925, and with whom he had five children; and to Cornelia Marvin. Pierce died on March 27, 1954.

PATTERSON, ISAAC LEE (1859-1929), fourteenth governor of Oregon (1927-1929), was born in Benton County, Oregon on September 17, 1859.

After holding such jobs as grocery clerk and farm laborer, Patterson studied at the Christian College at Monmouth for a year; then became co-owner of a grocery store. Beginning around 1905 he owned and operated his own wool and hide company in Portland. Patterson subsequently organized a brokerage firm, and owned a farm near Salem, where he raised livestock and fruit.

Patterson's entry into politics was in 1895 when he began serving in the Oregon State Senate, leaving in 1899 when he was named by President McKinley to the post of Collector of Customs for the Portland District. In 1902, President Theodore Roosevelt reappointed him to the same position, where he served until 1906. A long-time Republican, Patterson continued his involvement in politics behind the scenes for a while, then in 1918, ran for, and won a seat in the Oregon State Senate. He made an unsuccessful attempt for the Oregon governorship in 1922, but a few years later, was named chairman of the presidential campaign for Calvin Coolidge.

Due to the recognition Patterson gained while in that post, Patterson was successful in his second attempt for the governorship in 1926, defeating his democratic opponent, Walter Pierce, and taking office on January 10, 1927. During his tenure he made somewhat of an effort to revive the State income tax in order to lessen property taxes, but according to the Salem *Capital Journal*, he "championed no special program to the legislature and contented himself with letting it drift without executive guidance." However, Patterson supported a more efficient State government by urging the State Legislature to create one board to oversee all colleges and universities, and also switching the autonomy of the State Penitentiary from the governor's office to the State Board of Control. In addition, Patterson supported the continued expansion of the State's highways.

Patterson died while in office on December 21, 1929. He was married to Mary E. Woodworth, and the couple had two children.

NORBLAD, ALBIN WALTER, (1881-1960), acting governor of Oregon (1929-1931), was born in Malmo, Sweden on March 19, 1881, his original family name being Youngberg, which was later changed by the Swedish government.

While a young boy he moved with his family to Grand Rapids, Michigan, and by the age of twelve, Norblad had left home, supporting himself with several jobs. He later studied at the Grand Rapids Business College for a time, then deciding on a law career, attended the Chicago Law School, graduating in 1902, and passing the bar soon after. He returned to Michigan and went into law practice, then won the post of District Attorney of Delta County. After visiting a friend in Oregon in 1908, Norblad decided to move west, settling in Astoria. From 1910 to 1915, he was the City Attorney for Astoria, and in 1918, was elected to the Oregon State Senate on the Republican ticket, winning a second term in 1926. In between, in 1922, he made an unsuccessful bid for the United States Congress.

Due to Norblad's position as President of the State Senate during 1929, he succeeded to the Oregon governorship on December 22 of that year, with the death of the incumbent, Isaac Patterson. He made his presence known within the first half-hour of his taking office when he immediately declared himself a candidate in the gubernatorial election the following year. However, he was a progressive leader who wanted to see some improvements within the State that included finding a way to stem the escalating unemployment and the State's continuing economic downturn. As such, in February of 1930, he organized a meeting with several business executives in order to discuss how improvements could be made, although not much came of the effort. He also proposed a tax equalization measure, and wanted to work toward helping troubled children have a better chance at life.

In the 1930 campaign for governor, Norblad came in second in the primary, but soon after, the primary winner, George W. Joseph, died. However, although Norblad would have been next in line to run in the general election, took himself out of the running, deciding to concentrate on the remainder of his term. Wanting to meet the economic crisis head-on, he established a labor commission and put himself at the head of it. Out of that organization came two million dollars earmarked for the construction of State highways, which in turn, provided jobs for nearly 5,000 people. Norblad also created a State Pardons Board, taking a hands-on approach by visiting the penitentiary and speaking with the inmates himself.

Norblad stepped down from office on January 12, 1931. He was married to Edna Lyle Cates, and the couple had two children. He died on April 17, 1960.

MEIER, JULIUS L. (1874-1937), fifteenth governor of Oregon (1931-1935), was born on December 31, 1874 in Portland, Oregon.

Meier attended the University of Oregon Law School, graduating in 1895. Meier partnered with George W. Joseph in a law practice, then joined his father in the family business, the largest department store in Oregon at that time. Starting out as the general manager in 1910, he held that position until 1930, when he was named president. During World War I, Meier led several Liberty Loan drives, and was named regional director of the Council of National Defense. Later, he was overseer of San Francisco's Oregon Commission of the Pan-Pacific International Exposition.

Although politically active, Meier didn't run for office until 1930, after the death of his former law partner, George W. Joseph, who had won the Republican gubernatorial primary. A major issue concerned the development of hydroelectric power along the Columbia River, with the debate centering on whether it should be privately developed or State-run. Agreeing with his late friend that it should be the latter, Meier decided to run for the governorship as an independent. Both parties were at extreme odds on the issue, and managed to cancel each other out, with Meier winning the election and taking office on January 12, 1931. The issue was ultimately moot when the federal government stepped in and decided to develop the Columbia River instead.

However, Meier still made his mark as governor. After Oregon voters approved a State income tax initiative in 1930, he made some budget cuts, and eventually under his guidance, the State's budget was balanced. In addition, Meier supported the Knox Law, which placed regulations on the alcohol industry, and oversaw the creation of both the State Unemployment Commission and the State Board of Agriculture. Also, working in tandem with General Smedley Butler, Meier organized the Oregon State Police.

While in office Meier declined offers to run for the United States Senate, and in 1934, also turned down both political parties who requested he run for their gubernatorial primaries. Meier stepped down from office on January 14, 1935. He was married to Grace Mayer, with whom he had three children; he died on July 14, 1937.

MARTIN, CHARLES HENRY (1863-1946), sixteenth governor of Oregon (1935-1939), was born on October 1, 1863 in White County, Illinois.

Martin studied at Ewing College for a year then received an appointment to West Point. After graduating in 1887, Martin was initially assigned to Fort Vancouver in Washington, then later stationed at various locations throughout the world, including Mexico, Panama, China, France, Germany, and the Philippines. By the time of his retirement in 1927, he had achieved the rank of Major General. Throughout his years of travel, Martin had kept a home in Oregon.

Always politically active, Martin had been registered as a Republican for several years, but after 1930, served two terms as a Democratic Oregon Congressman. In 1934 he ran for the Oregon governorship on the Democratic ticket, defeating Republican candidate, Joe E. Dunn, and the independent challenger, Peter Zimmerman, taking office on January 14, 1935. Not a supporter of the New Deal, Martin was vocal in his derision of its policies and programs. Instead, he was a strident "law and order" leader, and was unsympathetic to the social and economic suffering of Oregon's citizens, often refusing to allow the federal government to step in and help. His methods led to a bitter division in the Democratic Party, and ultimately proved to be his downfall in his bid for reelection, with a defeat in the 1938 primary by Henry L. Hess. He stepped down from office on January 9, 1939.

Martin was married to Louise J. Hughes, and the couple had four children. He died on September 22, 1946.

SPRAGUE, CHARLES ARTHUR (1887-1969), seventeenth governor of Oregon (1939-1943), was born on November 12, 1887 in Lawrence, Kansas.

While he was a young boy, Sprague moved with his family to Iowa. He later attended Monmouth College in Illinois, where he earned an A.B. degree in 1910, then returned to Iowa to work as a schoolteacher. Later in 1910 Sprague moved to Washington State, settling in Waitsburg, where he served as Superintendent of Schools until 1913. Between 1913 and 1915 he was Assistant Superintendent of Public Instruction. In the latter year Sprague became publisher and editor of the *Journal-Times*, working there for a decade, then from 1925 until 1937, he was the business manager of the *Gazette-Times*, a Corvallis, Oregon daily newspaper. He purchased a controlling interest in the Salem *Oregon Statesman* in 1929, where he was manager and editor, then in 1939, attained sole ownership. Through his newspaper work he became known as a respected editorialist.

Although registered as a Republican, Sprague maintained a progressive stance on many issues, which often differed with that of Republican Party leaders. In the 1938 gubernatorial election, when the Democrats were bitterly divided between the anti-New Deal incumbent, Charles Martin, and New Deal supporters, Sprague secured the nomination from his party for governor, and went on to win that office, defeating his challenger, Henry L. Hess. He took office on January 9, 1939. Although the Republicans swept both houses of the State Legislature, Sprague's progressive ideas and unwillingness to bow to special interest legislation prompted his opponents to make a recall attempt that was ultimately unsuccessful.

During his tenure, Sprague created several State employment services, and also helped bring a reduction of over 12 million dollars to the State debt. In addition, he made the protection of Oregon's forests a high priority, and insisted on the regulation of logging companies. After the start of World War II, Sprague made sure that Oregon was involved in the war effort by establishing civilian defense units.

In the 1942 race for governor, Sprague was defeated by Oregon's Secretary of State, Earl Snell, and stepped down on January 11, 1943. Along with continuing his publishing ventures, Sprague, in 1952, served as an alternate delegate to the United Nations. He was married to Blanche Chamberlain, and the couple had two children. Sprague died on March 13, 1969.

SNELL, EARL WILCOX (1895-1947), eighteenth governor of Oregon (1943-1947), was born in Gilliam County, Oregon on July 11, 1895.

Snell attended the Oregon Institute of Technology in Portland. After a short stint at newspaper work, Snell engaged in the automobile business, and between 1915 and 1945, he and a partner ran a highly successful auto dealership. Later business ventures included banking and wheat farming. His entry into political life was a seat on the Arlington City Council.

A Republican, Snell served from 1927 to 1933 in the Oregon House of Representatives. In 1934 he was elected as Secretary of State, serving until 1943. Snell next ran for the Oregon governorship on the Republican ticket, defeating the incumbent governor, Republican Charles A. Sprague in the primary, and going on to win the general election over the Democratic challenger, Lew Wallace. He took office on January 11, 1943 then won a second term in 1946, defeating Democrat Carl C. Donough.

During his tenure, Sprague experienced a high rate of success with the mostly Republican State Legislature. During that time many of Oregon's voters supported some of the federal government's New Deal programs, and Snell was able to steer the Legislature toward making small changes that served those citizens. In addition, he created a number of measures that would directly benefit returning World War II veterans, and asked for legislation that supported such important economic industries as wood and its various products. He also sought out federal assistance whenever possible for such State needs as the expansion of Oregon's highway system.

During his second term, on October 28, 1947, Snell died in an airplane crash, along with Secretary of State Robert S. Farrell, Jr. and Marshall E. Cornett, the President of the State Senate. He was married to Edith Welshons, and the couple had one son.

HALL, JOHN HUBERT (1899-1970), acting governor of Oregon (1947-1949), was born on February 7, 1899 in Portland, Oregon.

During World War I Hall served on the troop transport ship, *Florida*, as a naval medical corpsman. After returning home he studied business administration at Oregon State College, earning a degree in 1923, then studied law at Portland's Northwestern College of Law. After passing the Oregon Bar in 1926, Hall practiced at his father's law firm, then later became a member of Jay Bowerman's firm.

Hall's entry into politics began with his election to the Oregon House of Representatives, a body to which he was reelected four additional times. In 1947 he was named Speaker of the House, and upon the death of the incumbent governor, Earl Snell, succeeded to the governorship on October 30, 1947. Although not that familiar to Oregon voters, Hall soon made his presence felt when he asked for the resignation of the Oregon Liquor Control Commission.

In the May, 1948 gubernatorial race, Hall ran against Republican State Senator Douglas McKay, who had strong backing, both as a friend of the late governor and as a highly successful businessman. Due to the short time Hall was governor he was not able to garner a solid support base from voters, and although he still made a strong showing at the primary, it wasn't enough to keep him in office. Because of his subsequent victory in the general election over Democrat Lew Wallace, Douglas McKay served out the rest of Snell's unexpired term.

After stepping down on January 10, 1949, Hall settled in Lincoln County and returned to his law practice, later serving one term as District Court judge. He was married twice: to Elizabeth Walch, who died in 1937, and with whom he had two children; and Alyce Johnson, with whom he had one daughter. Hall died on November 14, 1970.

MCKAY, JAMES DOUGLAS (1893-1959), nineteenth governor of Oregon (1949-1952), was born in Portland, Oregon on June 24, 1893.

After losing his father at an early age, McKay helped support his mother and younger sister. He attended Oregon Agricultural College, earning a B.S. degree in 1917. He fought in World War I, and after sustaining an injury, was discharged due to being severely disabled. McKay subsequently became an insurance salesman, then sold automobiles, establishing a highly successful dealership in Salem between 1927 and 1955. In 1933 he began serving as Salem's mayor, a post he held until 1935, when he became an Oregon State Senator, being reelected again in 1938. During his two terms, he served as Chairman of both the Road and Highways Committee, and the Willamette Basin Project Committee. After the start of World War II, he served for over three years in the United States Army, at Camp Adair in Oregon, and after his discharge, was once again elected to the State Senate in 1946.

Upon the death of incumbent Governor Earl Snell in 1947, State Speaker of the House John Hall succeeded to the governorship. In May of 1948, with the strong backing of his business connections, McKay defeated Hall in the Oregon gubernatorial primary, and went on to win the general election over Democrat Lew Wallace. Due to his victory, Hall stepped down and McKay served out the rest of the late Governor Snell's unexpired term. McKay won a full term in the 1950 race, defeating Democrat Austin F. Flegel. During his tenure the State budget was in solid shape, and when it came time to build more highways or support State schools, McKay refused to touch the treasury funds, and instead adopted a pay-as-you-go policy, and when it was necessary, asked for help from the federal government.

After the election of Dwight D. Eisenhower for the presidency in 1952, he named Douglas McKay as his Secretary of the Interior, making him overseer of 50,000 employees; McKay stepped down from the governorship on December 27, 1952. In 1956 he made an unsuccessful attempt for a seat in the United States Senate, and later was named by President Eisenhower as Chairman of the United States Section of the International Joint Commission.

McKay was married to Mabel Christine Hill, and the couple had three children. He died on July 22, 1959.

PATTERSON, PAUL LINTON (1900-1956), acting and twentieth governor of Oregon (1952-1955, 1955-1956), was born on July 18, 1900 in Kent, Ohio.

While a young boy Patterson moved with his family to Portland, Oregon. During World War I Patterson served a brief stint in the United States Army, then studied business administration at the University of Oregon, earning a degree in 1923. Deciding to pursue a law career, he received a LL.B. degree in 1926. Later that year he was named Deputy District Attorney for Washington County, serving in that post until 1933, then subsequently served as City Attorney for Hillsboro.

A Republican, Patterson entered politics in 1944 when he successfully ran for the Oregon State Senate, serving from 1945 to 1952. He also served as president of that body, and as such, was sworn in as governor after the resignation of incumbent Douglas McKay, taking office on December 27, 1952. Although his name was not familiar to most of Oregon's population, he became a popular leader, and in the 1954 race for the governorship, defeated his Democratic challenger, Joseph K. Carson, Jr. During his tenure, Patterson kept tight control over the State budget, often turning to the federal government for needed funding whenever possible. He pushed for continued construction of State highways, and helped organize the Water Resources Board.

Only two days after announcing his candidacy for the United States Senate, Patterson died, on January 31, 1956. He was married to Georgia Searle Benson, and the couple had three children.

SMITH, ELMO EVERETT (1909-1968), acting governor of Oregon (1956-1957), was born on November 19, 1909 near Grand Junction, Colorado.

While still a young boy Smith's mother and father died, three years apart, and he went to live with an uncle on a ranch near Wilder, Idaho. Smith attended the College of Idaho, earning a B.A. in History in 1932. He then migrated to Ontario, Oregon, where he purchased and ran a newspaper. He subsequently served as Mayor of Ontario, then during World War II, enlisted in the United States Navy, serving in the South Pacific. Upon returning home, Smith was again elected Mayor. Having sold his other newspaper, he purchased a new one, the John Day *Blue-Mountain Eagle*. In 1948 he successfully ran for the Oregon State Senate.

Having been chosen President of the Senate in 1955, Smith succeeded to the governor's chair the following year, on February 1, 1956, after the death of Governor Paul Patterson. A campaign for the governorship took place soon after, and although he secured the Republican primary, Smith lost the general election to the Democratic challenger, Robert Holmes. After stepping down from office on January 14, 1957, Smith continued to add to his publishing empire, buying the Albany *Democrat-Herald*, along with several other smaller papers. After making an unsuccessful bid for the United States Senate, he was chosen to serve as State Chairman of the Republican Party in 1964.

Smith was married to Dorothy Leininger, and the couple had two children. He died on July 15, 1968.

HOLMES, ROBERT DENISON (1909-1976), twenty-first governor of Oregon (1957-1959), was born in Canisteo, New York on May 11, 1909.

Upon his finishing high school, Holmes and his family moved to Oregon, where he attended the University of Oregon, graduating in 1932. A few years later, Holmes settled in Clatsop County, where he worked in radio and advertising. Between 1943 and 1957 Holmes served as manager of KAST radio station in Astoria.

Originally a Republican, Holmes switched to the Democratic Party, and in 1948, was elected to the State Senate, then reelected in 1952. Interested in a strong and viable education system, Holmes was appointed Chairman of the Education Committee by Governor Paul Patterson. Ultimately, Holmes was also instrumental for not only strengthening the Democratic Party, but also turning it from a "tool of conservative patriarchs" to a party with a more liberal viewpoint. Upon the death of the governor, Holmes declared his candidacy on the Democratic ticket, and in the general election, defeated Elmo Smith by a very small margin, taking office on January 14, 1957.

During his tenure, Holmes was determined to improve and streamline the State government. He organized the first Department for Economic Planning, reduced State taxes, and pushed for the adoption of legislation earmarked for education and social welfare, along with better wages for workers. However, he also angered a lot of voters by some of his decisions. In his opposition to capital punishment, he commuted the death sentences of three convicts to life imprisonment. This, along with campaign smears against him, caused him to lose the subsequent gubernatorial election to the Republican challenger, Mark O. Hatfield.

After stepping down from office on January 12, 1959, Holmes did consulting with public relations work and was moderator for the Portland television program, "Let's Face It." He was later appointed to serve on the State Board of Higher Education, but eventually resigned to protest what he perceived as too much interference into educational matters by the State Legislature.

Holmes was married to Marie Hoy. He died on June 6, 1976.

HATFIELD, MARK O. (1922-), twenty-second governor of Oregon (1959-1967), was born on July 12, 1922 in The Dalles, Oregon.

Hatfield attended Willamette University, earning an A.B. degree in 1943, then studied at Stanford University where he garnered an M.A. degree in 1948. Between 1943 and 1946, Hatfield served in the United States Naval Reserve. During 1949 he was an instructor at Willamette University, then the following year, was named associate professor of political science, as well as dean of students at that facility, teaching until 1956.

A Republican, Hatfield's entry into politics was his election to the Oregon House of Representatives in 1951; then in 1955 he began serving a two-year term in the Oregon State Senate. Between 1957 and 1959, he was Oregon's Secretary of State. In 1958 Hatfield ran for the Oregon governorship on the Republican ticket, defeating his Democratic challenger, the incumbent governor, Robert D. Holmes, taking office on January 12, 1959. In 1962, Hatfield was elected to a second term.

During Hatfield's tenure, legislation for the reduction of State taxes was passed in 1959, capital punishment was abolished, and a State-funded birth control system was organized. In addition, during that time the State of Oregon endured a number of damaging earthquakes, and many of Oregon's citizens were vocal in their dissatisfaction with such issues as the Vietnam War and racial inequality.

Deciding not to run for a third term, Hatfield stepped down from office on January 9, 1967, and later that year was elected to the United States Senate. He is the author of several books, including *Not Quite So Simple*, 1967; *Conflict and Conscience*, 1971; *Between A Rock and A Hard Place*, 1976; and *How You Can Help Prevent Nuclear War*, 1982; among others.

Hatfield is married to Antoinette Kuzmanich, and the couple has four children.

MCCALL, THOMAS LAWSON (1913-1983), twenty-third governor of Oregon (1967-1975), was born on March 22, 1913 in Egypt, Massachusetts.

McCall attended the University of Oregon, earning a B.A. degree in 1936. Between 1944 and 1964, McCall worked as a journalist and political analyst in Portland, and from 1949 to 1952, he served as administrative assistant to Governor Douglas McKay. During 1965-66, McCall was Oregon's Secretary of State.

In 1966 McCall was elected to the Oregon governorship on the Republican ticket, defeating his Democratic challenger, Robert W. Straub, and taking office on January 9, 1967. In 1970 he was reelected to a second term. A passionate environmentalist, one of his first decisions was to appoint himself as chairman of the State Sanitary Authority in order to implement a massive clean-up of the polluted Willamette River, a successful venture that ultimately saw the return of the salmon. He continued his battle by fighting against the encroachment of companies settling in the State without stringent pollution guidelines. Also, in order to investigate new ways of conserving energy, McCall organized the State Office of Energy Research and Planning in 1971.

Deciding not to run for a third term, McCall stepped down from office on January 13, 1975, and subsequently taught journalism at Oregon State University in Corvallis. He married Audrey Owen and the couple has two children. McCall died January 8, 1983.

STRAUB, ROBERT WILLIAM (1920-), twenty-fourth governor of Oregon (1975-1979), was born in San Francisco, California on May 6, 1920.

Straub attended Dartmouth, earning a B.A. degree in 1943, and a M.B.A. degree in 1947. Between 1947 and 1950, Straub was an executive with the Weyerhaeuser Timber Corporation in Springfield, Oregon, then from the latter year until 1953, was a building contractor. From 1955 to 1959 he served as Commissioner of Lane County, Oregon.

In 1959 Straub was elected to the Oregon State Senate, serving until 1963, then was State Treasurer between 1964 and 1972. Straub, a Democrat, ran unsuccessfully for the governorship in 1966 and 1970, then in his third try, won the election over his Republican opponent, Victor Atiyeh, taking office on January 13, 1975. During his tenure he paid special attention to the often ignored rights of Oregon's Native American population, and also offered a number of State agency appointments to minorities, women, and handicapped people. In addition, due to his influence, the unemployment rate in the State dropped significantly, from twelve percent to five, which was below the national average. Straub also supported a reduction in utility rates for seniors, State funding for Oregon's entire grade and high school system, and the establishment of several new industries that brought hundreds of jobs to the State.

In the 1978 gubernatorial race, Straub lost to his former challenger, Victor Atiyeh, and stepped down from office on January 8, 1979. Straub is married to Patricia S. Stroud, and the couple has six children.

ATIYEH, VICTOR G. (1923-), twenty-fifth governor of Oregon (1979-1987), was born in Portland, Oregon on February 20, 1923.

Atiyeh studied at the University of Oregon for two years; then joined the family business, Atiyeh Brothers, a Portland Carpet Company founded by his father. His entry into politics was when he was elected to the Oregon House of Representatives in 1959. He held that post until 1964, when he was elected to the Oregon State Senate, where he served until 1978. He made an attempt at the Oregon governorship in 1974, but was defeated by Robert Straub. However, the situation was reversed in the 1978 race, with Atiyeh winning, and taking office on January 8, 1979.

During Atiyeh's tenure, both worker's compensation and welfare were revamped, the State government was streamlined, and he continued to back measures that supported the environment. In addition, in an effort to balance the State budget, Atiyeh reduced his own salary three times. Although national observers counted him out for the next gubernatorial election in 1982, citing the downward turn in the economy, Atiyeh won nearly sixty-two percent of the vote over his Democratic challenger, Ted Kulongowski, and then went on to win one more term before stepping down on January 12, 1987.

Atiyeh is married to Dolores Atiyeh, and the couple has two children.

GOLDSCHMIDT, NEIL E. (1940-), twenty-sixth governor of Oregon (1987-1991), was born in Eugene, Oregon on June 16, 1940.

Goldschmidt attended the University of Oregon, earning a B.A. degree in 1963, and continued his education at the University of California's Boalt School of Law, receiving his law degree in 1967. Between 1967 and 1969, he worked as a legal aid attorney in Portland; then in 1971, was named City Commissioner, serving in that post until 1973. In that year he was elected Mayor of Portland on the Democratic ticket, making him the youngest mayor of a major U.S. city at that time. Goldschmidt resigned in 1979 after President Jimmy Carter appointed him U.S. Secretary of Transportation, a post he held until 1981, when Carter stepped down from office. After Goldschmidt returned home he was hired by the Nike, working at their main headquarters in Oregon from 1981 to 1985, when he was named head of their subsidiary, Nike Canada.

Goldschmidt ran for the Oregon governorship on the Democratic ticket, defeating his challenger, Republican Norma Paulus, in a very close race, and taking office on January 12, 1987. During his tenure he stressed the importance of economic growth, asking for "an activist State role in the economy." He also disagreed with the closing of schools due to exorbitant property tax levies placed on them.

Goldschmidt stepped down from office on January 14, 1991. He is married to Margaret Wood, and the couple has two children.

ROBERTS, BARBARA K. (1936-), twenty-seventh governor of Oregon (1991-1995), was born on December 21, 1936 in Corvallis, Oregon.

Roberts attended Portland State University between 1961 and 1964, then much later, in 1989, studied at Harvard University's John F. Kennedy School of Government. Because of her experience with an autistic son, Roberts' entry into public life in 1969 was an advocate for handicapped youth, working as an unpaid lobbyist. In 1981 she was elected to the Oregon House of Representatives, and was appointed the State's first woman House majority leader in her second term. When she was elected as Oregon's Secretary of State in 1984, she created another new record as the first Democrat to hold that office in over 100 years; she was reelected to a second term in 1988.

In 1990 Roberts ran for the Oregon governorship on the Democratic ticket, defeating Republican Dave Frohnmeyer and the Independent candidate, Al Mobley. During her tenure, she was intent on making the State government run more efficiently. She also stressed the importance of improving public education, and was a vocal supporter of human rights, especially in the area of gay and lesbian rights. In addition, Roberts created an opinion-based survey for Oregon voters called "A Conversation With Oregon," in which citizens were able to voice their concerns about State government and taxes. The results of the project helped Roberts in her efforts to streamline Oregon's government on several levels.

Other contributions by Roberts included her working in tandem with the Clinton Administration in order to secure funding for the Oregon Health Plan; being responsible for the increase of the number of children participating in the Head Start program; securing funding for several units of low-cost housing; and her support for programs designed to help welfare recipients find employment.

Roberts stepped down from office on January 9, 1995, and was subsequently hired to an administrative post with the John F. Kennedy School of Government at Harvard University. Also, in September of 1995, Roberts joined the board of governors of The Human Rights Campaign Fund (HRCF), an organization that works to abolish discrimination against gays and lesbians.

Roberts was married to Oregon Senator Frank Roberts, who died in 1993. She has two sons from a previous marriage.

KITZHABER, JOHN (1947-), twenty-eighth governor of Oregon, Kitzhaber, John (1995-), was born in Colfax, Washington on March 5, 1947. He attended Dartmouth College, earning a bachelor's degree in 1969. Kitzhaber then studied at the University of Oregon Medical School where he received a medical degree in

1973, and for the next thirteen years, practiced emergency medicine in the town of Roseburg, Oregon.

Deciding to enter politics, Kitzhaber, a Democrat, ran for and won a seat in the Oregon House of Representatives, serving one term. In 1980 he was voted into the Oregon Senate, where he served for three terms. Between 1985 and 1993, Kitzhaber served as President of the Senate. In that capacity, Kitzhaber guided three major bills through the State Senate, including the Oregon Forest Practices Act, the Oregon Education Act for the 21st Century, and the Oregon Health Plan, the latter of which he authored. His efforts in support of health care garnered him the Dr. Nathan Davis Award from the American Medical Association.

While serving in the Senate, Kitzhaber also held a faculty post at the Estes Park Institute, and was a clinical professor at Oregon Health Sciences University. In 1994, Kitzhaber ran for and won the Oregon governorship on the Democratic ticket, taking office in January of 1995. He was reelected to a second term in 1998.

Kitzhaber is married to Sharon LaCroix, and the couple has one child.

DICTIONARY OF PLACES

Population figures and demographic information are official U.S. Census Bureau finals for 1990. When two figures are shown, separated by a slash, the first figure is the 1990 and the second is the U.S. Census Bureau 1999 estimate—the most recent available. Year 2000 census supplements will be available in the Fall of 2001.

ADAIR VILLAGE, City; Benton County; Pop, 589 / 549; The town is named after the former U.S. Army base camp Adair. Lieutenant Henry Adair was a World War I era military hero.

ADAMS, City; Umatilla County; Pop. 240 / 256; Zip Code 97810; Elev. 1513; Lat. 45-46-03 N, Long. 118-33-41 W; The town's name remembers original settler John F. Adams.

ADRIAN, City; Malheur County; Pop. 162 / 134; Zip Code 97901; Lat. 43-44-27 N, Long. 117-04-15 W; The town was founded in the early 1900's and named after sheepman James Adrian.

ALBANY, City; Benton & Linn Counties; Linn County Seat; Pop. 26,546 / 38,773; Zip Code 97321; Elev. 212; Lat. 44-38-12 N, Long. 123-06-17 W; Founded in 1848 and named after Albany, New York.

AMITY, City; Yamhill County; Pop. 1,092 / 1,225; Zip Code 97101; Lat. 45-06-57 N, Long. 123-12-22 W; Settled in the mid-1800s and named for an amicable settlement of a local school dispute.

ANTELOPE, City; Wasco County; Pop. 39 / 39; Zip Code 97001; Elev. 2632. Lat. 44-54-39 N, Long. 120-43-18 W; Descriptively named for the abundant antelope of pioneer days.

ARLINGTON, City; Gilliam County; Pop. 521 / 540; Zip Code 97812; Elev. 2851; Lat. 45-43-01 N, Long. 120-11-59 W; Established in 1881 and named for the famous Virginia home of Robert E. Lee.

ASHLAND, City; Jackson County; Pop. 14,943 / 18,659; Zip Code 97520; Elev. 1951; Lat. 42-11-41 N, Long. 122-42-30 W; Named in 1852 for Henry Clay's birthplace near Ashland, Kentucky.

ASTORIA, City; Clatsop County Seat; Pop. 9,998 / 10,012; Zip Code 97103; Elev. 18; Lat. 46-11-17 N, Long. 123-49-48W; The city was founded in 1813 and named in honor of fur trade magnate John Jacob Astor.

ATHENA, City; Umatilla County; Pop. 965 / 1,116; Zip Code 97813; Elev. 1710; Lat. 45-48-43 N, Long. 118-29-22 W; Originally Centerville, the name was changed in 1889 to the more romantic Athena. Athena was the Greek goddess of war and industry.

AUMSVILLE, City; Marion County; Pop. 1,432 / 2,335; Zip Code 97325; Elev. 363; Lat. 44-50-28 N, Long. 122-52-11 W; Aumus was the nickname of early settler Amos M. Davis. The town was named in his honor.

AURORA, City; Marion County; Pop. 523 / 697; Zip Code 97002; Elev. 133; Lat. 45-13-52 N, Long. 122-45-17 W; Settled in 1857 and later named Aurora, the Roman goddess of dawn.

BAKER CITY, City; Baker County Seat; Pop. 9,471 / 9,735; Zip Code 97814; Elev. 3443; Lat. 44-46-42 N, Long. 117-49-42 W; The town's name honors Edward D. Baker, U.S. Senator from Oregon and Civil War hero.

BANDON, City; Coos County; Pop. 2,311 / 2,580; Zip Code 97411; Elev. 67; Lat. 43-07-09 N, Long. 124-24-26 W; Settled in the 1870s and named by an Irish settler for Bandon, Ireland.

BANKS, City; Washington County; Pop. 489 / 712; Zip Code 971+; Lat. 45-37-08 N, Long. 123-06-47 W; Banks is named in honor of pioneer resident Robert.

BARLOW, City; Clackamas County; Pop. 105 / 111; Elev. 101; Lat. 45-15-07 N, Long. 122-43-10 W; The town is named after pioneer settler William Barlow.

BAY CITY, City; Tillamook County; Pop. 986 / 1,102; Zip Code 97107; Elev. 18; Lat. 45-31-22 N, Long. 123-53-17 W; Established in 1888 and named after Bay City, Michigan.

BEAVERTON, City; Washington County; Pop. 30,582 / 64,563; Zip Code 970+; Elev. 189; Lat. 45-29-14 N, Long. 122-48-09 W; Settled in 1869 and named for the many beaver once in the area.

BEND, City; Deschutes County Seat; Pop. 17,263 / 36,210; Zip Code 977+; Elev. 3629; Lat. 44-03-30 N, Long. 121-18-51 W; Descriptively named for its location on a bend of the Deschutes River.

BOARDMAN, City; Morrow County; Pop. 1,261 / 2,220; Zip Code 97818; Lat. 45-50-24 N, Long. 119-41-58 W; Settled in 1916 and named for town founder Sam Boardman.

BONANZA, Town; Klamath County; Pop. 270 / 380; Zip Code 97623; Elev. 4116; Lat. 42-11-56 N, Long. 121-24-18 W; Bonanza is Spanish for "prosperity." Well-developed irrigation water supplies suggested this name to its early settlers.

BROOKINGS, City; Curry County; Pop. 3,384 / 5,174; Zip Code 97415; Lat. 42-03-10 N, Long. 124-16-58 W; Settled at the beginning of the 20th century and named in honor of lumberman Robert S. Brookings.

BROWNSVILLE, City; Linn County; Pop. 1,261 / 1,352; Zip Code 97327; Elev. 356; Lat. 44-23-37 N, Long. 122-59-01 W; The city was established in 1853 and named for Hugh Brown, who started a store in the area.

BURNS, City; Harney County Seat; Pop. 3,579 / 2,981; Zip Code 977+; Elev. 4148; Lat. 43-35-11 N, Long. 119-03-11 W; Pioneer George McGowan named the town after poet Robert Burns.

BUTTE FALLS, Town; Jackson County; Pop. 428 / 269; Zip Code 97522; Elev. 2536; Las. 42-32-36 N, Long. 122-33-52 W; Descriptively named for the town's location on the falls of Big Butte Creek.

CANBY, City; Clackamas County; Pop. 7,659 / 12,339; Zip Code 97013; Elev. 153; Lat. 45-15-47 N, Long. 122-41-29 W; The town's name honors General Edward Canby who was killed by Modoc Indians on April 11, 1873.

CANNON BEACH, City; Clatsop County; Pop. 1,187 / 1,386; Zip Code 971+; Lat. 45-53-31 N, Long. 123-57-37 W; In 1846 the U.S. Navy Schooner Shark was wrecked near the Columbia River shore. An iron cannon from the wreck named the beach, and later the town.

CANYON CITY, Town; Grant County Seat; Pop. 639 / 613; Zip Code 97820; Elev. 3198; Lat. 44-23-23 N, Long. 118-56-57 W; Descriptively named for its location in a canyon.

CANYONVILLE, City; Douglas County; Pop. 1,288 / 1,165; Zip Code 97417; Elev. 785; Lat. 42-55-39 N, Long. 123-16-48 W; Situated at the end of Canyon Creek Canyon, and thus descriptively named.

CARLTON, City; Yarnhill County; Pop. 1,302 / 1,324; Zip Code 97111; Elev. 199; Lat. 45-17-40 N, Long. 123-10-31 W; Established in 1874 and named for early settler John Carl.

CASCADE LOCKS, City; Hood River County; Pop. 838 / 1,034; Zip Code 97014; Lat. 45-40-12 N, Long. 121-53-22 W; Named for the cascade locks constructed in 1888.

CAVE JUNCTION, City; Josephine County; Pop. 1,023 / 1,369; Zip Code 97523; Elev. 1295; Lat. 42-09-47 N, Long. 123-38-49 W; Named for its location on the highway which branches to the Oregon caves.

CENTRAL POINT, City; Jackson County; Pop. 6,357 / 11,134; Zip Code 97502; Elev. 1278; Lat. 42-22-34 N, Long. 122-54-55 W; Descriptively named for the cross of two pioneer wagon trails of the Rogue River valley.

CHILOQUIN, City; Klamath County; Pop. 778 / 722; Zip Code 97604; Elev. 4179; Lat. 42-34-40 N, Long. 121-51-54 W; The name of a Klamath Indian chief Chaloquin.

CITY OF THE DALLES, City; Wasco County; Pop. 10,820 / 11,388; Zip Code 97058. Dalles is a French word meaning "flag stone," which was applied to the narrows of the Columbia River. The town's name reflects its location on the river.

CLATSKANIE, City; Columbia County; Pop. 1,648 / 1,704; Zip Code 97016; Elev. 33; Lat. 46-06-05 N, Long. 123-12-20 W; An old Indian place named for a spot in the Nehalem Valley. White settlers named the river for it, and the town also.

COBURG, City; Lane County; Pop. 699 / 845; Zip Code 97401; Elev. 400; Lat. 44-08-14 N, Long. 123-03-55 W; Blacksmith Thomas Kane named the town for a well-known local stallion.

COLUMBIA CITY, City; Columbia County; Pop. 678 / 1,497; Zip Code 97018; Elev. 24; Lat. 45-53-25 N, Long. 122-48-21 W; Founded in 1867 and named after the Columbia River.

CONDON, City; Gilliam County Seat; Pop. 783 / 752; Zip Code 97823; Elev. 2844; Lat. 45-14-04 N, Long. 120-11-02 W; Condon was established in 1884 and named for lawyer Harvey C. Condon.

COOS BAY, City; Coos County; Pop. 14,424 / 15,340; Zip Code 97420; Elev. 11; Lat. 43-22-05 N, Long. 124-12-57 W; The city is named after its bay on the Pacific. The Coos Indians named the bay.

COQUILLE, City; Coos County Seat; Pop. 4,481 / 3,900; Zip Code 97423; Elev. 50; Lat. 43-10-38 N, Long. 124-11-11 W; Once the home of the Ku-kwil-tunne Indians, French trappers translated this name as Coquille.

CORNELIUS, City; Washington County; Pop. 4,055 / 7,774; Zip Code 97113; Elev. 179; Lat. 45-31-12 N, Long. 123-03-31 W; Named for pioneer Colonel T.A. Cornelius who came to Oregon in 1845.

CORVALLIS, City; Benton County Seat; Pop. 40,960 / 50,340; Zip Code 9733+; Elev. 225; Lat. 44-33-53 N, Long. 123-15-39 W; Named by pioneer Joseph Avery in 1853, the name is a Latin compound word meaning "heart of the valley."

COTTAGE GROVE, City; Lane County; Pop. 7,148 / 7,762; Zip Code 97424: Elev. 641; Lat. 43-47-52 N, Long. 123-03-30 W; The first postmaster, G.C. Pearce, had his home in a nearby oak grove and so named the settlement Cottage Grove.

COVE, City; Union County; Pop. 451 / 603; Zip Code 97824; Lat. 45-17-48 N, Long. 117-48-25 W; Descriptively named for its location where Mill Creek flows from the Wallowa Mountains.

CRESWELL, City; Lane County; Pop. 1,770 / 2,924; Zip Code 97426; Elev. 547; Lat. 43-55-05 N, Long. 123-01-24 W; The town's name honors John A. Creswell, U.S. Postmaster General from 1869-74.

CULVER, City; Jefferson County; Pop. 514 / 609; Zip Code 97734; Elev. 2636; Lat. 44-31-33 N, Long. 121-12-43 W; The town took the ancestral name of its first postmaster O.G. Collver as its name.

DALLAS, City; Polk County Seat; Pop. 8,530 / 12,465; Zip Code 97338; Elev. 326; Lat. 44-55-10 N, Long. 123-18-57 W; The city is named after U.S. Vice-President George Dalles who served from 1845-49.

DAYTON, City; Yamhill County; Pop. 1,409 / 1,894; Zip Code 97114; Lat. 45-13-15 N, Long. 123-04-30 W; Settled in 1848 and named after Dayton, Ohio.

DAYVILLE, Town; Grant County; Pop. 199 / 139; Zip Code 97825; Lat. 44-28-06 N, Long. 119-32-05 W; The town is named after the John Day River. John Day was an explorer with the Astor expedition.

DEPOE BAY, City; Lincoln County; Pop. 723 / 1,107; Zip Code 97341; Elev. 58; Lat. 44-48-31 N, Long. 124-03-43 W; An Indian associated with an early army supply depot acquired the nick name "Depot," and this later became Depoe.

DETROIT, City; Marion County; Pop. 367 / 362; Zip Code 97342; Lat. 44-44-03 N, Long. 122-08-55 W; Established in 1891 and named after Detroit, Michigan.

DONALD, City; Marion County; Pop. 267 / 655; Zip Code 97020; Elev. 195; Lat. 45-13-21 N, Long. 122-50-17 W; Donald's name remembers R.L. Donald, a railroad construction official.

DRAIN, City; Douglas County; Pop. 1,148 / 1,063; Zip Code 97435; Elev. 292; Lat. 43-39-32 N, Long. 123-19-03 W; The city was named after pioneer-settler, Charles Drain.

DUFUR, Town; Wasco County; Pop. 560 / 560; Zip Code 97021; Elev. 1320; Lat. 45-27-12 N, Long. 121-07-46 W; Founded in 1878 and named in honor of Andrew and Burnham Dufur, local farmers.

DUNDEE, City; Yamhill County; Pop. 1,223 / 2,844; Zip Code 97115; Elev. 190: Lat. 45-16-42 N, Long. 123-00-35 W; Named after Dundee, Scotland by pioneer William Reid.

DURHAM, City; Washington County; Pop. 707 / 1,442; Elev. 142; Lat. 45-24-08 N, Long. 122-45-06 W; Durham's name remembers pioneer lumberman Albert A. Durham.

EAGLE POINT, City; Jackson County; Pop. 2,764 / 4,034; Zip Code 97524; Elev. 1305; Lat. 42-28-22 N, Long. 122-48-06 W; Settled in 1872 and named for nearby rocky cliffs, the nesting place of many eagles.

EASTSIDE, City; Coos County; Pop. 1,601; Zip Code 97420; Elev. 61; Lat. 43-21-49 N, Long. 124-11-30 W; On the eastside of Coos Bay, and so descriptively named.

ECHO, City; Umatilla County; Pop. 624 / 588; Zip Code 97826; Elev. 638; Lat. 45-44-33 N, Long. 119-11-40 W; The town is named in honor of Echo Koontz, the daughter of a pioneer family.

ELGIN, City; Union County; Pop. 1,701 / 1,731; Zip Code 97827; Elev. 2716; Lat. 45-33-54 N, Long. 117-54-59 W; Once called Fishtrap, the first postmaster named the town for a song about the "wreck of the Lady Elgin."

ELKTON, City; Douglas County; Pop. 155 / 191; Zip Code 97436; Elev. 149; Lat. 43-38-16 N, Long. 123-34-01 W; Settled in 1850 and descriptively named for its location on Elk Creek.

ENTERPRISE, City; Wallowa County Seat; Pop. 2,003 / 2,046; Zip Code 97828; Elev. 3756; Lat. 45-25-35 N, Long. 117-16-40 W; Named in 1887 after the pioneer virtue.

ESTACADA, City; Clackamas County; Pop. 1,419 / 2,136; Zip Code 97023; Lat. 45-17-23 N, Long. 122-19-57 W; A Spanish word meaning "staked out, or marked off."

EUGENE, City; Lane County Seat; Pop. 105,624 / 130,501; Zip Code 974+; Elev. 419; Lat. 44-03-08 N, Long. 123-05-08 W; Eugene Skinner claimed this land in 1847. The city is named after him.

FAIRVIEW, City; Multnomah County; Pop. 1,749 / 6,064; Zip Code 97024; Elev. 125; Lat. 43-13-01 N, Long. 124-04-21 W; Settled in the 1850s and given the name of a Methodist Church.

FALLS CITY, City; Polk County; Pop. 804 / 899; Zip Code 97344; Elev. 370; Lat. 44-51-59 N, Long. 123-26-05 W; Descriptively named for the nearby falls on the Little Luckiamute River.

FLORENCE, City; Lane County; Pop. 4,411 / 6,745; Zip Code 97439; Elev. 23; Lat. 43-58-58 N, Long. 124-05-55 W; Florence is named in honor of early Oregon State Senator, A.B. Florence.

FOREST GROVE, City; Washington County; Pop. 11,499 / 15,463; Zip Code 9711+; Lat. 45-31-12 N, Long. 123-06-34 W; Named in 1851 for the homestead of pioneer settler J.O. Thornton.

FOSSIL, City; Wheeler County Seat; Pop. 535 / 420; Zip Code 97830; Elev. 2654; Lat. 44-59-54 N, Long. 120-12-54 W; Founded in the 1870s and named after the numerous fossils in the area.

GARIBALDI, City; Tillamook County; Pop. 999 / 940; Zip Code 97118; Elev. 10; Lat. 45-33-36 N, Long. 123-54-35 W; Pioneer Daniel Bayley settled here in the 1860s and named the town for the great Italian patriot, Giuseppe Garibaldi.

GASTON, City; Washington County; Pop. 471 / 685; Zip Code 97119; Lat. 45-26-11 N, Long. 123-08-18 W; The town's name remembers Joseph Gaston, pioneer railroad promoter.

GATES, City; Linn and Marion Counties; Pop. 455 / 575; Zip Code 97346; Elev. 942; Lat. 44-45-23 N, Long. 122-24-56 W; Settled in 1882 and named after Mrs. Gates, one of the oldest pioneer settlers.

GEARHART, City; Clatsop County; Pop. 967 / 1,224; Zip Code 97138; Elev. 16; Lat. 46-01-28 N, Long. 123-54-36 W; The town is named after pioneer Philip Gearhart.

GERVAIS, City; Marion County; Pop. 1,144 / 1,529; Zip Code 97026; Elev. 184; Lat. 45-06-30 N, Long. 122-53-47 W; French trapper Joseph Gervais came to Oregon in 1811. The town is named for him.

GLADSTONE, City; Clackamas County; Pop. 9,500 / 11,697; Zip Code 97027; Lat. 45-22-51 N, Long. 122-35-37 W; Established in 1890 and named for British statesman William E. Gladstone.

GLENDALE, City; Douglas County; Pop. 712 / 747; Zip Code 97442; Elev. 1423; Lat. 42-44-11 N, Long. 123-25-20 W; Settled in the 1880s and named for either Glendale, Massachusetts, or Glendale, Scotland.

GOLD BEACH, City; Curry County Seat; Pop. 1,515 / 1,825; Zip Code 97444; Elev. 51; Lat. 42-24-27 N, Long. 124-25-14 W; The city is named after the placer gold operations conducted here in the 1850s.

GOLD HILL, City; Jackson County; Pop. 904 / 996; Zip Code 97525; Gold Hill was the site of a gold discovery in Southern Oregon and was so named.

GRANITE, City; Grant County; Pop. 17 / 7; Elev. 4689; Lat. 44-48-34 N, Long. 182-25-00 W; Descriptively named for the abundant granite rocks in the region.

GRANTS PASS, City; Josephine County Seat; Pop. 14,997 / 22,717; Zip Code 975+; Elev. 948; Lat. 42-26-21 N, Long. 123-19-38 W; Founded in the 1860s and named in honor of U.S. Grant.

GRASS VALLEY, City; Sherman County; Pop. 164 / 146; Zip Code 97029; Elev. 2252; Lat. 45-21-37 N, Long. 120-47-04 W; Incorporated in 1900.

GREENHORN, City; Baker and Grant Counties; Lat. 44-42-29 N, Long. 118-29-25 W; The town is named for the many amateur miners who came to the area in the 1860s gold rush.

GRESHAM, City; Multnomah County; Pop. 33,005 / 87,106; Zip Code 97030; Elev. 323; Lat. 45-29-54 N, Long. 122-25-49 W; Gresham's name honors Civil War General Walter Q. Gresham.

HAINES, City; Multnomoh County; Pop. 440; Zip Code 97833; Elev. 3333; Lat. 44-54-42 N, Long. 117-56-16 W; Founded in 1884 and named for "Judge" I.D. Haines, who was the original landowner.

HALFWAY, City; Baker County; Pop. 380 / 440; Zip Code 97834; Elev. 2663; Lat. 44-52-51 N, Long. 117-06-49 W; Founded in 1887 and descriptively named for its location between Pine and Cornucopia.

HAMMOND, Town; Clatsop County; Pop. 516; Zip Code 97121; Elev. 9; Lat. 46-12-01 N, Long. 123-57-01 W; Hammond is named for Pacific Coast businessman Andrew H. Hammond.

HAPPY VALLEY, City; Clackamas County; Pop. 1,499 / 3,646; Lat. 45-26-49 N, Long. 122-31-45 W; An early settler named the town for its hospitable and happy residents.

HARRISBURG, City; Linn County; Pop. 1,881 / 2,807; Zip Code 97446; Elev. 309; Lat. 44-16-27 N, Long. 123-10-10 W; Incorporated in 1866 and named for Harrisburg, Pennsylvania.

HELIX, City; Umatilla County; Pop. 155 / 166; Zip Code 97835; Elev. 1754; Lat. 45-50-59 N, Long. 118-39-21 W; An early resident suffered an infection of the helix of the ear about the time the town was being named.

HEPPNER, City; Morrow County Seat; Pop. 1,498 / 1,774; Zip Code 97836; Elev. 1955; Lat. 45-21-12 N, Long. 119-33-24 W; The town is named after Henry Heppner, who opened the first store here in 1873.

HERMISTON, City; Umatilla County; Pop. 9,408 / 12,366; Zip Code 97838; Elev. 457; Lat. 45-50-26 N, Long. 119-17-18 W; Pioneer Colonel F. McNaught named the town after an unfinished novel by Robert Louis Stevenson, *Wier of Hermiston*.

HILLSBORO, City; Washington County Seat; Pop. 27,664 / 65,835; Zip Code 9712+; Lat. 45-31-23 N, Long. 122-59-19 W; The city is named after David Hill, who settled in Oregon in 1842.

HINES, City; Harney County; Pop. 1,632 / 1,399; Zip Code 97738; Elev. 4157; Lat. 43-33-51 N, Long. 119-04-48 W; Hines is named after the Edward Hines Lumber Company.

HOOD RIVER, City; Hood River County Seat; Pop. 4,329 / 5,384; Zip Code 97031; Lat. 45-42-20 N, Long. 121-31-13 W; The city is named for the nearby Hood River.

HUBBARD, City; Marion County; Pop. 1,640 / 2,120; Zip Code 97032; Elev. 182; Lat. 45-10-57 N, Long. 122-48-24 W; Named in honor of pioneer settler Charles Hubbard who came to Oregon in 1847.

HUNTINGTON, City; Baker County; Pop. 539 / 550; Zip Code 97907; Elev. 2108; Lat. 44-21-05 N, Long. 117-15-56 W; The town's name remembers the Huntington brothers who settled here in 1882.

IDANHA, City; Linn and Marion Counties; Pop. 319 / 321; Zip Code 97350; Elev. 1718; Lat. 44-42-10 N, Long. 122-04-39 W; Incorporated in 1895 and located on the North Santiam River. Named by an early settler.

IMBLER, City; Union County; Pop. 292 / 315; Zip Code 97841; Elev. 2731; Lat. 45-27-35 N, Long. 117-57-40 W; Settled in the 19th century and named for the Imblers, a pioneer family.

INDEPENDENCE, City; Polk County; Pop. 4,024 / 6,338; Zip Code 97351; Elev. 168; Lat. 44-51-05 N, Long. 123-11-08 W; Settler E.A. Thorp came to Oregon in 1845. He named Independence after Independence, Missouri.

IONE, City; Morrow County; Pop. 345 / 329; Zip Code 97843; Elev. 1085; Lat. 45-30-05 N, Long. 119-49-25 W; Pioneer E.G. Sperry named the town for Ione Arthur.

IRRIGON, City; Morrow County; Pop. 700 / 1,230; Zip Code 97844; Elev. 297; Lat. 45-53-45 N, Long. 119-29-25 W; Settled around 1900 and named by combining the words "irrigation," and "Oregon."

ISLAND CITY, City; Union County; Pop. 477 / 851; Lat. 45-20-28 N, Long. 118-02-37 W; Descriptively named for its location on an island formed by a slough of the Grande Ronde River.

JACKSONVILLE, City; Jackson County; Pop. 2,030 / 2,020; Zip Code 97530; Elev. 1569; Lat. 42-18-49 N, Long. 122-57-57 W; The city is named for its location on Jackson Creek.

JEFFERSON, City; Marion County; Pop. 1,702 / 1,995; Zip Code 9735+; Elev. 230; Lat. 44-43-11 N, Long. 123-00-33 W; The town is named for President Thomas Jefferson.

JOHN DAY, City; Grant County; Pop. 2,012 / 1,895; Zip Code 97845; Elev. 3084; Lat. 44-24-58 N, Long. 118-57-07 W; The town is named after the John Day River. John Day was an explorer and trapper with the Astor expedition in 1811.

JOHNSON CITY, City; Clackamas County; Pop. 378 / 849; Lat. 43-08-23 N, Long. 124-10-42 W; The town is named after its developer, Delbert Johnson.

JORDAN VALLEY, Town; Malheur County; Pop. 473 / 446; Zip Code 97910; Elev. 4389; Lat. 42-58-27 N, Long. 117-03-12 W; Established in the 1870s and named for the Biblical Jordan Valley.

JOSEPH, City; Wallowa County; Pop. 999 / 1,211; Zip Code 97846; Elev. 4190; Lat. 45-21-16 N, Long. 117-13-43 W; The town's name remembers Chief Joseph who fought a war here with the U.S. in the nineteenth century.

JUNCTION CITY, City; Lane County; Pop. 3,320 / 4,409; Zip Code 97448; Elev. 327; Lat. 44-13-10 N, Long. 123-12-16 W; Descriptively named as the site of the joining of two main railroad lines.

KING CITY, City; Washington County; Pop. 1,853 / 1,967; Zip Code 97224. A recent community, its developers gave it a "royalty" theme, and hence the name.

KLAMATH FALLS, City; Klamath County Seat; Pop. 16,661 / 18,561; Zip Code 976+; Lat. 42-13-30 N, Long. 121-46-50 W; On the falls of the Link River in Klamath County, the town is thus named. Klamath was the name of the local Indian tribe when the Europeans came.

LAFAYETTE, City; Yamhill County; Pop. 1,215 / 1,923; Zip Code 97127; Lat. 45-14-40 N, Long. 123-06-49 W; Founded in 1846 and named after Lafayette, Indiana.

LA GRANDE, City; Union County Seat; Pop. 11,354 / 12,249; Zip Code 972+; Elev. 2771; Lat. 45-19-29 N, Long. 118-05-12 W; Settled in the 1860s and given the name "the grand" to reflect the surrounding Grande Ronde Valley and its impressive views.

LAKE OSWEGO, City; Clackamas, Multnomah and Washington Counties; Pop. 22,868 / 34,952; Zip Code 97034; Elev. 100; Lat. 45-25-15 N, Long. 122-40-10 W; Descriptively named for its position on Lake Oswego. The lake is named after Oswego, New York.

LAKESIDE, City; Coos County; Pop. 1,453 / 1,602; Zip Code 97449; Elev. 29; Lat. 43-34-33 N, Long. 124-10-26 W; Located on Tenmile Lake and so descriptively named.

LAKEVIEW, Town; Lake County Seat; Pop. 2,770 / 2,329; Zip Code 97630; Elev. 4798; Lat. 42-11-20 N, Long. 120-20-41 W; The town's name was chosen for its view of Goose Lake.

LEBANON, City; Linn County; Pop. 10,413 / 12,797; Zip Code 97355; Lat. 44-32-12 N, Long. 122-54-21 W; Named by early settlers for Lebanon, Tennessee.

LEXINGTON, Town; Morrow County; Pop. 307 / 372; Zip Code 97839; Lat. 45-26-43 N, Long. 119-41-00 W; Prominent pioneer William Penland named the town for his former home in Lexington, Kentucky.

LINCOLN CITY, City; Lincoln County; Pop. 5,469 / 6,699; Zip Code 97367; Lat. 44-57-30 N, Long. 124-01-00 W; In 1964 three local communities combined under the name of Lincoln. Lincoln is the county name and honors Abraham Lincoln.

LONEROCK, City; Gilliam County; Pop. 26 / 13; Descriptively named for a 100 ft. high rock landmark near the center of the community.

LONG CREEK, City; Grant County; Pop. 252 / 252; Zip Code 97856; Elev. 3772; Lat. 44-42-51 N, Long. 119-06-11 W; Descriptively named for a long creek in Grant County.

LOSTINE, City; Wallowa County; Pop. 250 / 251; Zip Code 97857; Lat. 45-30-14 N, Long. 117-25-23 W; Named by a pioneer for Lostine, Kansas, probably his former home.

LOWELL, City; Lane County; Pop. 661 / 816; Zip Code 97438; Elev. 741; Lat. 43-55-07 N, Long. 122-46-57 W; Settled in the 1850s and named for Lowell, Maine.

LYONS, City; Linn County; Pop. 877 / 1,111; Zip Code 97352; Elev. 659; Lat. 44-46-29 N, Long. 122-36-50 W; The town is named after the pioneer family that established the town.

MADRAS, City; Jefferson County Seat; Pop. 2,235 / 4,229; Zip Code 97741; Lat. 44-38-01 N, Long. 121-07-42 W; Named by an early merchant for cotton cloth from Madras, India.

MALIN, City; Klamath County; Pop. 539 / 724; Zip Code 97632; Lat. 42-00-46 N, Long. 121-24-27 W; Named by Czechoslovakian settlers who founded the community in 1909, after their former home town in Czechoslovakia.

MANZANITA, City; Tillamook County; Pop. 443 / 710; Zip Code 97130; Elev. 111; Lat. 45-43-07 N, Long. 123-56-02 W.

MAUPIN, City; Wasco County; Pop. 495 / 496; Zip Code 97037; Elev. 1041; Lat. 45-10-31 N, Long. 121-04-49 W; The town's name remembers central Oregon pioneer Howard Maupin.

MAYWOOD PARK, City; Multnomoh County; Pop. 1,083 / 933; Incorporated in 1967 and named by the developer's family for the beautiful woods during May.

MCMINNVILLE, City; Yamhill County Seat; Pop. 14,080 / 24,440; Zip Code 97128; Elev. 160; Lat. 45-12-37 N, Long. 123-11-51 W; Pioneer William Newby named the town for his birthplace in McMinnville, Tennessee.

MEDFORD, City; Jackson County Seat; Pop. 39,603 / 59,937; Zip Code 975+; Elev. 383; Lat. 42-19-36 N, Long. 122-52-28 W; Named by railroad engineer David Loring for the town's location on the middle ford of Bear Creek.

MERRILL, City; Klamath County; Pop. 809 / 894; Zip Code 97633; Elev. 4067; Lat. 42-01-31 N, Long. 121-35-58 W; The town is named for early pioneer Nathan S. Merrill.

METOLIUS, City; Jefferson County; Pop. 451 / 1,020; Zip Code 97741; Elev. 2530; Lat. 44-35-12 N, Long. 121-10-38 W; Named after a tributary of the Deschutes River, it is an Indian word meaning "salmon water."

MILL CITY, City; Linn & Marion Counties; Pop. 1,565 / 1,605; Zip Code 97360; Elev. 827; Lat. 44-45-15 N, Long. 122-28-37 W; Located on the North Santiam River, and named for an early sawmill.

MILLERSBURG, City; Linn County; Pop. 562 / 782; Elev. 242; Lat. 44-40-52 N, Long. 123-03-37 W; Named for the pioneer Miller family who have lived there for more than a hundred years.

MILTON-FREEWATER, City; Umatilla County; Pop. 5,086 / 6,093; Zip Code 97862; Elev. 1033: Lat. 45-55-58 N, Long. 118-23-12 W; Milton and Freewater merged in 1951 and thereafter had a joint name.

MILWAUKIE, City; Clackamas and Multnomah Counties; Pop. 17,931 / 19,770; Zip Code 97222; Lat. 45-26-47 N, Long. 122-38-17 W; Settled in 1847 and named for Milwaukee, Wisconsin.

MITCHELL, City; Wheeler County; Pop. 183 / 179; Zip Code 97750; Elev. 748; Lat. 44-18-20 N, Long. 122-41-20 W; Mitchell's name honors U.S. Senator J.H. Mitchell who served Oregon in the years 1873-79.

MOLALLA, City; Clackamas County; Pop. 2,992 / 5,042; Zip Code 97038; Elev. 373; Lat. 45-08-51 N, Long. 122-34-33 W.

MONMOUTH, City; Polk County; Pop. 5,594 / 7,927; Zip Code 97361; Elev. 201; Lat. 44-50-55 N, Long. 123-13-58 W; Settled in 1853 and named for Monmouth, Illinois.

MONROE, City; Benton County; Pop. 412 / 408; Zip Code 97456; Elev. 288; Lat. 44-18-51 N, Long. 123-17-44 W; Founded in 1853 and named in honor of James Monroe, fifth President of the United States.

MONUMENT, City; Grant County; Pop. 192 / 159; Zip Code 97864; Elev. 2008; Lat. 44-49-10 N, Long. 119-25-12 W; Settled in the 1870s and named for a nearby mountain that resembles a monument.

MORO, City; Sherman County Seat; Pop. 336 / 264; Zip Code 97039; Elev. 1808; Lat. 45-29-03 N, Long. 120-43-48 W; The town was founded in the late 1860s and named after Moro, Illinois.

MOSIER, City; Wasco County; Pop. 340 / 272; Zip Code 97040; Elev. 121; Lat. 45-41-01 N, Long. 121-23-46 W; The town's name remembers pioneer-founder J.H. Mosier, who began the community in 1853.

MOUNT ANGEL, City; Marion County; Pop. 2,876 / 2,9049; Zip Code 97362; Elev. 168; Lat. 45-04-05 N, Long. 122-47-56 W; Named in 1883 after Engelberg, Switzerland. Angel is anglicized Engle.

MOUNT VERNON, City; Grant County; Pop. 569 / 601; Zip Code 97865; Elev. 2871; Lat. 44-25-04 N, Long. 119-06-45 W; The town is named for a well-known black stallion of the 1870s.

MYRTLE CREEK, City; Douglas County; Pop. 3,365 / 3,231; Zip Code 97457; Elev. 640; Lat. 43-01-13 N, Long. 123-17-31 W; Myrtle Creek was descriptively named for the groves of Oregon Myrtle in the area.

MYRTLE POINT, City; Coos County; Pop. 2,859 / 2,633; Zip Code 97458; Elev. 90; Lat. 43-03-54 N, Long. 124-08-16 W; The town is named for the abundance of Oregon Myrtle.

NEHALEM, City; Tillamook County; Pop. 258 / 243; Zip Code 97131; Lat. 45-43-13 N, Long. 123-53-34 W; Nehalem's name remembers the Nehalem Indians who lived there before the Europeans arrived.

NEWBERG, City; Yamhill County; Pop. 10,394 / 17,847; Zip Code 97132; Elev. 176; Lat. 45-18-01 N, Long. 122-58-19 W; The first postmaster, Sebastian Brutscher, named the town after Newberg, Germany.

NEWPORT, City; Lincoln County; Pop. 7,519 / 10,142; Zip Code 97365; Elev. 177; Lat. 44-38-13 N, Long. 124-03-08 W; Named in 1868 after Newport, Rhode Island.

NORTH BEND, City; Coos County; Pop. 9,779 / 9,685; Zip Code 97459; Elev. 23; Lat. 43-24-24 N, Long. 124-13-23 W; Captain A.M. Simpson named the town descriptively for its location near Coos Bay in 1856.

NORTH PLAINS, City; Union County; Pop. 430 / 1,677; Zip Code 97133; Lat. 45-35-50 N, Long. 122-59-32 W; The name in use since pioneer days whose original designation is uncertain.

NORTH POWDER, City; Union County; Pop. 430 / 468; Zip Code 97867; Elev. 3256; Lat. 45-01-43 N, Long. 117-55-08 W; The city was named descriptively for its location on the North Powder River.

NYSSA, City; Malheur County; Pop. 2,862 / 2,834; Zip Code 97913; Elev. 2177; Lat. 43-52-37 N, Long. 116-59-38 W; Named by a Greek section hand for a mythological nymph who reared the infant Bacchus.

OAKLAND, City; Douglas County; Pop. 886 / 905; Zip Code 97462; Elev. 430; Lat. 43-25-20 N, Long. 123-17-50 W; Descriptively named for the oak trees around the original townsite.

OAKRIDGE, City; Lane County; Pop. 3,729 / 3,107; Zip Code 97463; Elev. 1209; Lat. 43-44-48 N, Long. 122-27-38 W; Established in 1912 and named for the oak-covered ridge forming part of the town.

ONTARIO, City; Malheur County; Pop. 8,814 / 10,777; Zip Code 979+; Elev. 2154; Lat. 44-01-36 N, Long. 116-57-43 W; Pioneer James Virtue named it after his birthplace, the province of Ontario, Canada.

OREGON CITY, City; Clackamas County Seat; Pop. 14,673 / 24,417; Zip Code 97045; Lat. 45-21-27 N, Long. 122-36-20 W; Founded in 1842 and named for the state.

PAISLEY, City; Lake County; Pop. 343 / 353; Zip Code 97636; Elev. 4369; Lat. 42-41-38 N, Long. 120-32-42 W; Named by early Scottish settlers for Paisley, Scotland.

PORTLAND, City; Clackamas, Multnomah and Washington Counties; Multnomah County Seat; Pop. 366,383 / 503,637; Zip Code 972+; Elev. 77; The largest city and principle port of Oregon. Portland was founded in 1845 and incorporated in 1851. It

was named for the city in Maine. During the 1860s and 1870s it was a supply center for the gold rushes of the Northwest.

POWERS, City; Coos County; Pop. 819 / 687; Zip Code 97466; Lat. 45-54-43 N, Long. 119-18-10 W; The town was named for lumber businessman A.H. Powers in 1914.

PRAIRIE CITY, City; Grant County; Pop. 1,106 / 1,121; Zip Code 978+; Lat. 44-27-48 N, Long. 118-42-32 W; Descriptively named by early miners for the surrounding locale.

PRESCOTT, City; Columbia County; Pop. 73 / 79; Elev. 25; Lat. 46-02-57 N, Long. 122-53-10 W; The city was named for the owners of the local sawmill.

PRINEVILLE, City; Crook County Seat; Pop. 5,276 / 6,471; Zip Code 97754; Elev. 2952; Lat. 44-18-45 N, Long. 121-09-47 W; Barney Prine, the town's first merchant, had the town named after him.

RAINIER, City; Columbia County; Pop. 1,655 / 1,742; Zip Code 97048; Elev. 24; Lat. 46-05-21 N, Long. 122-56-05 W; Named after Mount Rainier. Peter Rainier was a Rear Admiral in the Royal Navy.

REDMOND, City; Deschutes County; Pop. 6,452 / 12,408; Zip Code 97756; Elev. 2997; Lat. 44-16-22 N, Long. 121-10-22 W; The town's name remembers pioneer Frank Redmond who settled in the area in 1905.

REEDSPORT, City; Douglas County; Pop. 4,984 / 4,874; Zip Code 97467; Elev. 10; Lat. 43-42-09 N, Long. 124-05-44 W; Reedsport honors Alfred Reed, an early pioneer in the area.

RICHLAND, Town; Baker County; Pop. 181 / 180; Zip Code 97870; Lat. 44-46-09 N, Long. 117-10-03 W; The land's fertile soil led to this descriptive name.

RIDDLE, City; Douglas County; Pop. 1,265 / 1,082; Zip Code 97469; Elev. 705; Lat. 42-57-04 N, Long. 123-21-47 W; Riddle is named after pioneer William Riddle who settled here in 1851.

RIVERGROVE, City; Clackamas & Washington Counties; Pop. 314 / 280; Lat. 45-23-29 N, Long. 122-43-56 W; Incorporated in 1971 and named by combining the names Tualatin River and Lake Grove.

ROCKAWAY BEACH, City; Tillamook County; Pop. 906 / 1,076; Zip Code 97136; Elev. 16; Lat. 45-36-49 N, Long. 123-56-31 W; The city is named after the rockaway summer resorts in Rockaway, Long Island.

ROGUE RIVER, City; Jackson County; Pop. 1,308 / 2,090; Zip Code 97537; Elev. 1001; Lat. 42-26-10 N, Long. 123-10-15 W; Named after the Rogue River Indians.

ROSEBURG, City; Douglas County Seat; Pop. 16,644 / 19,874; Zip Code 97470; Elev. 459; Lat. 43-13-00 N, Long. 123-20-26 W; Aaron Rose settled here in 1851. The town is named in his honor.

RUFUS, City; Sherman County; Pop. 352 / 307; Zip Code 97050; Elev. 206; Lat. 45-41-42 N, Long. 120-44-05 W; Rufus is named after the original settler Rufus C. Wallis.

ST. HELENS, City; Columbia County Seat; Pop. 7,064 / 9,133; Zip Code 9705+; Elev. 73; Lat. 45-51-51 N, Long. 122-48-19 W; Descriptively named for its location near Mount St. Helens.

ST. PAUL, City; Marion County; Pop. 312 / 386; Zip Code 97137; Elev. 170; Lat. 45-12-41 N, Long. 122-58-32 W; The town is named after the Saint Paul Mission established here in 1839.

SALEM, City; Marion & Polk Counties; Marion County Seat; Capitol of Oregon; Pop. 89,233 / 129,650; Settled in 1840 by a group of Methodist ministers on a site known as *Chemetka*, Indian for "place of peace." This was translated to the Biblical name of Salem.

SANDY, City; Clackamas County; Pop. 2,905 / 5,243; Zip Code 97055; Lat. 45-23-51 N, Long. 122-15-37 W; The city is near the Sandy River and so descriptively named.

SCAPPOOSE, City; Columbia County; Pop. 3,213 / 4,878; Zip Code 97056; Elev. 61; Lat. 45-45-16 N, Long. 122-52-35 W; *Scappoose* is an Indian word meaning "gravel plain."

SCIO, City; Linn County; Pop. 579 / 633; Zip Code 97374; Elev. 317; Lat. 44-42-18 N, Long. 122-50-53 W; The city is named after Scio, Ohio. Scia, or Chios, is an island off Turkey.

SCOTTS MILLS, City; Marion County; Pop. 249 / 313; Zip Code 97375; Lat. 45-02-35 N, Long. 122-40-02 W; Pioneers Robert and Thomas Scott ran a sawmill here in the 1860s. The town is named after this operation.

SEASIDE, City; Clatsop County; Pop. 5,193 / 5,914; Zip Code 97138; Lat. 45-59-36 N, Long. 123-55-17 W; The city is named after a well-known hotel and resort, the Seaside House.

SENECA, City; Grant County; Pop. 285 / 182; Zip Code 97873; Elev. 4666; Lat. 44-08-05 N, Long. 118-58-14 W; The town is named after Judge Seneca Smith of Portland.

SHADY COVE, City; Jackson County; Pop. 1,097 / 1,892; Zip Code 97539. The town is on the Rogue River and is descriptive of a little nook on the river bank.

SHANIKO, City; Wasco County; Pop. 30 / 26; Zip Code 97057; Elev. 3341; Lat. 45-00-14 N, Long. 120-45-04 W; Pioneer rancher August Scherneckau settled in Oregon after the Civil War. The Indians mispronounced the name Shoniko.

SHERIDAN, City; Yamhill County; Pop. 2,249 / 4,384; Zip Code 97378; Lat. 45-05-58 N, Long. 123-23-37 W; The town is named after Philip Henry Sheridan, soldier and Civil War hero.

SHERWOOD, City; Washington County; Pop. 2,386 / 9,479; Elev. 205; Lat. 45-21-24 N, Long. 122-50-20 W; Originally Smockville, the name was changed in 1891 to Sherwood, after Sherwood, Michigan, or possibly England's Sherwood Forest.

SILETZ, City; Lincoln County; Pop. 1,001 / 1,138; Zip Code 97357; Elev. 131; Lat. 44-43-19 N, Long. 123-55-08 W; The city is named after the Siletz River, itself named for the Siletz Indians.

SILVERTON, City; Marion County; Pop, 5,168 / 6,886; Zip Code 97381; Elev. 249; Lat. 45-00-19 N, Long. 122-46-55 W; Settled in the 1840s and named for its location on Silver Creek.

SISTERS, City; Deschutes County; Pop. 696 / 868; Zip Code 97759; Elev. 3186; Lat. 44-17-28 N, Long. 121-32-53 W; The city is east of the Cascades, and descriptively named for the nearby three sister peaks.

SODAVILLE, City; Linn County; Pop. 171 / 230; Lat. 44-29-05 N, Long. 122-52-14 W; The town is descriptively named for a nearby mineral springs.

SPRAY, Town; Wheeler County; Pop. 155 / 172; Zip Code 97874; Elev. 1798; Lat. 44-50-04 N, Long. 119-47-36 W; John Spray came to Oregon in 1864. He founded Spray in 1900. The town is named in his honor.

SPRINGFIELD, City; Lane County; Pop. 41,621 / 50,744; Zip Code 974+; Elev. 456; Lat. 44-02-47 N, Long. 123-01-15 W; Settled in 1849 and named for a natural spring on the site.

STANFIELD, City; Umatilla County; Pop. 1,568 / 1,773; Zip Code 97875; Lat. 45-46-50 N, Long. 119-12-58 W; Founded in the 1880s and named after U.S. Senator Robert N. Stanfield.

STAYTON, City; Marion County; Pop. 4,396 / 6,485; Zip Code 9738+; Elev. 457; Lat. 44-48-03 N, Long. 122-47-36 W; Established in 1872 and named after Drury S. Stayton, who founded the town.

SUBLIMITY, City; Marion County; Pop. 1,077 / 2,431; Zip Code 97385; Elev. 548; Lat. 44-49-47 N, Long. 122-47-36 W; Sublimity was founded in 1852 and descriptively named for the "sublime" scenery in the adjacent vicinity.

SUMMERVILLE, Town; Union County; Pop. 132 / 152; Zip Code 97876; Lat. 45-29-19 N, Long. 118-00-07 W; Settled in 1865 and named for pioneer Alexander Sommerville.

SUTHERLIN, City; Douglas County; Pop. 4,560 / 5,919; Zip Code 97479; Elev. 540; Lat. 43-23-25 N, Long. 123-18-41 W; The city's name honors pioneer horticulturist Fendel Sutherlin.

SWEET HOME, City; Linn County; Pop. 6,921 / 7,592; Zip Code 97386; Elev. 525; Lat. 44-23-52 N, Long. 122-44-06 W; An early pioneer named the "sweet home valley," the name was taken for the town.

TALENT, City; Jackson County; Pop. 2,577 / 3,842; Zip Code 97540; Elev. 1635; Lat. 42-14-45 N, Long. 122-47-15 W; A.P. Talent founded the town in the 1880's. It is named after him.

TANGENT, City; Linn County; Pop. 478 / 726; Zip Code 97389; Elev. 246; Lat. 44-32-29 N, Long. 123-06-25 W; The town is on a straight 20 mile segment of the Southern Pacific Railroad Line, and so suggested "a tangent."

TIGARD, City; Washington County; Pop. 14,286 / 38,212; Zip Code 97223; Elev. 166; Lat. 45-25-53 N, Long. 122-46-13 W; Wilson M. Tigard came to Oregon in 1852. The town is named after him.

TILLAMOOK, City; Tillamook County Seat; Pop. 3,981 / 4,341; Zip Code 971+; Elev. 16; Lat. 45-27-23 N, Long. 123-50-34 W; Tillamook was the name of a tribe of Salish Indians who lived in the area.

TOLEDO, City; Lincoln County Seat; Pop. 3,151 / 3,244; Zip Code 97391; Elev. 59; Lat. 44-37-18 N, Long. 123-56-14 W; Settled in 1868 and named by a homesick pioneer after Toledo, Ohio.

TROUTDALE, City; Multnomah County; Pop. 5,908 / 13,621; Zip Code 97060; Elev. 73; Lat. 45-32-22 N, Long. 122-23-10 W; Originally Sandy, the name was changed to describe a nearby pond stocked with trout.

TUALATIN, City; Clackamas & Washington Counties; Pop. 7,348 / 20,321; Zip Code 97062; Elev. 123; Lat. 45-23-03 N, Long. 122-45-46 W; An Indian word meaning "sluggish" and referring to the Tualatin River.

TURNER, City; Marion County; Pop. 1,116 / 1,374; Zip Code 97392; Lat. 44-50-36 N, Long. 122-57-06 W; The city's name honors pioneer Henry L. Turner.

UKIAH, City; Umatilla County; Pop. 249 / 293; Zip Code 97880; Elev. 3353; Lat. 45-08-03 N, Long. 118-55-53 W; Settled in 1890 and named for Ukiah, California.

UMATILLA, City; Umatilla County; Pop. 3,199 / 3,540; Zip Code 97882; Elev. 296; Lat. 45-55-03 N, Long. 119-20-29 W; The Umatilla were among the original Indians in the area.

UNION, City; Union County; Pop. 2,062 / 1,961; Zip Code 97883; Elev. 2788; Lat. 45-12-31 N, Long. 117-51-51 W; Founded in 1862 and named by patriotic citizens for the embattled "union."

UNITY, City; Baker County; Pop. 115 / 97; Zip Code 97884; Lat. 44-26-15 N, Long. 118-11-30 W; The original town post office was moved after a "unity" meeting concerning its location. The name stuck on the new site.

VALE, City; Malheur County Seat; Pop. 1,558 / 1,573; Zip Code 97918; Lat. 43-58-56 N, Long. 117-14-14 W; Named by early settlers for a vale, or valley.

VENETA, City; Lone County; Pop. 2,449 / 2,762; Zip Code 97487; Lat. 44-02-56 N, Long. 123-20-59 W; Founded in 1913 by E.E. Hunter, and named for his daughter, Veneta Hunter.

VERNONIA, City; Columbia County; Pop. 1,785 / 2,245; Zip Code 97064; Elev. 621; Lat. 45-51-32 N, Long. 123-11-30 W; Ozias Cherrington was one of the town's founders. The town is named after his daughter Vernonia.

WALDPORT, City; Lincoln County; Pop. 1,274 / 1,940; Zip Code 97376; Elev. 11; Lat. 44-25-37 N, Long. 124-04-03 W; Named in the 1880s by combining the German word *wald*, or forest, with the English word "port."

WALLOWA, City; Wallowa County; Pop. 847 / 825; Zip Code 97885; Elev. 2948; Lat. 45-34-13 N, Long. 117-31-38 W; Wallowa is a Nez Perce Indian word describing a structure of stakes for catching fish.

WARRENTON, City; Clatsop County; Pop. 2,493 / 4,433; Zip Code 97146; Lat. 46-09-55 N, Long. 123-55-21 W; The city is named in honor of D.K. Warrenton, an early settler.

WASCO, City; Sherman County; Pop. 415 / 354; Zip Code 97065; Elev. 1270; Lat. 45-35-31 N, Long. 120-41-49 W; Named after the Wasco Indians who once lived on the Columbia River.

WATERLOO, Town; Linn County; Pop. 221 / 223; Lat. 44-29-39 N, Long. 122-49-27 W; Named after the famous battle that led to Napoleon's downfall.

WESTFIR, City; Lane County; Pop. 312 / 278; Zip Code 97492; Lat. 43-45-27 N, Long. 122-29-43 W; Named for the great quantity of Douglas fir in the area.

WEST LINN, City; Clackamas County; Pop. 12,956 / 22,432; Zip Code 97068; Elev. 128; Lat. 45-21-57 N, Long. 122-36-40 W; settled in the 1840's and named for U.S. Senator Lewis Linn of Missouri, who urged the American settlement of Oregon.

WESTON, City; Umatilla County; Pop. 719 / 646; Zip Code 97886; Elev. 1838; Lat. 45-48-50 N, Long. 118-25-25 W; Established in the 1860s and named for Weston, Missouri.

WHEELER, City; Tillamook County; Pop. 319 / 364; Zip Code 97147; Elev. 18; Lat. 45-41-21 N, Long. 123-52-46 W; Prominent Portland lumberman C.H. Wheeler had the town named in his honor.

WILLAMINA, City; Polk and Yamhill Counties; Pop. 1,749 / 2,005; Zip Code 97396; Elev. 225; Lat. 45-04-44 N, Long. 123-29-05 W; The city is named after Willamina Creek. The creek is named after the first white woman in the area, Mrs. Willamina Williams.

WILSONVILLE, City; Clackamas and Washington Counties; Pop. 2,920 / 13,703; Zip Code 97070; Lat. 45-18-00 N, Long. 122-46-21 W; Settled in the 1870s and named after pioneer Charles Wilson.

WINSTON, City; Douglas County; Pop. 3,359 / 4,037; Zip Code 97496; Elev. 534; Lat. 43-07-21 N, Long. 123-24-41 W. Founded in 1893 and named for its first postmaster, Elijah Winston.

WOODBURN, City; Marion County; Pop. 11,196 / 15,713; Zip Code 97071; Elev. 183; Lat. 45-08-38 N, Long. 122-51-15 W. Descriptively named for the main energy source of its settlers.

WOOD VILLAGE, City; Multnomah County; Pop. 2,253 / 3,085; Lat. 45-32-04 N, Long. 122-25-03 W. Founded in World War II and named in honor of Portland Real Estate Agent, Lester J. Wood.

YAMHILL, City; Yamhill County; Pop. 690 / 941; Zip Code 97148; Lat. 45-20-30 N, Long. 123-11-10 W. The town is named for the nearby river, itself named for the Yamel Indians.

YONCALLA, City; Douglas County; Pop. 805 / 999; Zip Code 97499; Lat. 43-35-55 N, Long. 123-16-56 W. The town is named for a nearby mountain. Yoncalla is an Indian word meaning "eagle."

PENNSYLVANIA
The Keystone State

Civil War reenactment - Gettysburg

Pittsburgh skyline

GOVERNOR
Tom Ridge

Waterfall in the
Pocono Mountains

Pocono International Raceway

Penn State
Blue Band Drum

Amish Country

INTRODUCTION

PENNSYLVANIA, THE KEYSTONE STATE

Pennsylvania, with its coal mines, oil wells, and steel mills, is a state unto itself. Although it is one of the original thirteen colonies, it is not a New England state. Although it touches on Lake Erie, it is not one of the Great Lakes or Midwest states. And, in spite of the fact that tobacco is grown on the farmlands around Lancaster, Pennsylvania has never been a Southern state. Yet it connects all of the regions that surround it, and the history of the nation has almost always been paralleled by the events taking place in Pennsylvania.

This is the nation's factory land; other states have much more land and many more resources. Yet historically, Pennsylvania will always be known as the place where urban-industrial America was born. Here, Thomas Edison and George Westinghouse perfected their electrical appliances, and here John D. Rockefeller and others controlled the railroads and the oil that powered them to carry the nation's goods. It was also in Pennsylvania that the first Bessemer steel was produced, revolutionizing all aspects of industry. And it was in Pittsburgh and other city factories that workers first joined hands in order to get a fair shake of the new wealth.

Pennsylvania was William Penn's Promised Land. His Society of Friends envisioned a Utopia, but received instead an imperfect Commonwealth. Today, the "Peaceable Kingdom" is often torn with dissension among various groups for various reasons. Problems of unemployment, racial strife, and aging cities have caused many people to leave. Still, many programs have been created to help poor and minority groups, and many older urban neighborhoods have undergone renovations.

State government officials continue to have hopes of a brighter, more technological future for Pennsylvania. The city of Pittsburgh looks better today than it did a few decades ago as a result of this visionary outlook, and many people have found non-farming ways to live in the less populated countryside of the State. The future of Pennsylvania continues to be a subject of study in the new millennium. The outward appearances of the State may have changed dramatically, but to get a picture of the heart of the Commonwealth, one cannot overlook the symbols created during its history.

THE STATE NAME

Pennsylvania means "Penn's woods." King Charles II named it in honor of William Penn's father, who had served in a high rank in King James' court.

On March 14, 1681, when Charles signed the land grant making William Penn the leader of a vast tract of land in America, Penn wrote to his friend Robert Turner: "This day my country was confirmed to meet under the Great Seal of England, with large powers and privileges, by the name of Pennsylvania; a name the king would give it in honor of my father. I chose New Wales, being, as it is, a pretty hilly country, but Penn being Welsh for a head, as Penn in Buckinghamshire, the highest land in England, (they) called this Pennsylvania." Penn maintained afterward that the province's name meant simply, the "high or head woodlands," and tried to downplay his role in the naming. "I much opposed it," he said. "And went to the king to have it struck out and altered, he said it was past. Nor could 20 guineas move the under secretary to vary the name."

Penn's reference to the "head woodlands" comes from a combination of two words from two different languages. *Penn* is an old Celtic term, meaning "a head" or "a headland," and *Sylvania* is a Neo-Latin term meaning "relating to a forest," derived from the Latin feminine place name Sylva, denoting "a wood forest." The founder originally suggested Sylvania because of the forestland he found in the province, but the King prefixed it with Penn, much to the latter's embarrassment. In any case, Penn returned to his Quaker settlement soon afterwards, and no one ever tried to change the name to his suggestion of "New Wales."

Pennsylvania, along with Virginia, Kentucky, and Massachusetts, has the designation of "Commonwealth." The word is of English derivation, and refers to the common "weal" or well being of the public. It is a traditional, official designation used in referring to the State, and all legal processes use the name of the Commonwealth. In 1776, the first State constitution referred to Pennsylvania as both the "Commonwealth" and the "State." The pattern of usage was continued in the 1790, 1838, and 1874 constitutions, as well as in revisions in 1968. Today, both designations are used interchangeably. The distinction between them has been held to have no legal significance.

STATE NICKNAMES

Five nicknames have been used in reference to Pennsylvania. They include the Coal State, the Oil State, the Steel State, the Quaker State, and the Keystone State. However, the currently established nickname remains the Keystone State.

The Coal State, the Oil State, and the Steel State are all suggestive of the three largest commodities produced in Pennsylvania. The nickname of the Quaker State commemorates the fact that William Penn and his Society of Quakers were the first white settlers in this region; from 1680, Penn was instrumental as a Quaker leader in attracting many more Friends to settle here.

The Keystone State is the more official sobriquet, probably because it relates to the first American government in Pennsylvania. The name is accounted for in several different ways. First, when the government was moved to Washington, D.C. in 1790, and the Pennsylvania Avenue Bridge over Rock Creek to the old city of Georgetown was built, the initials of the name of the State of Pennsylvania were put on the thirteenth, or key stone, of the arch. Second, Pennsylvania was in a central position among the states when the first U.S. Constitution was adopted, and when Pennsylvania delegate, John Morton, became the thirteenth signer of the Declaration of Independence, he made the State "the keystone" in the Federal arch. The term may also have been used to refer to the State's geographical location in the original thirteen colonies that straddled the Atlantic Ocean.

One of the earliest ways in which Pennsylvania was seen as the Keystone State is displayed in the American Philosophical Society's halls in Philadelphia. There, a drawing of a stone arch representing the thirteen states show Pennsylvania in the keystone position.

THE STATE SEAL

When the Commonwealth was still a province of England, its seals were those of the Penn family. In 1776, at the State Constitutional Convention, a State seal was directed to be used by "all State commissions;" it was approved in 1791. By 1778, a seal similar to the present one was in use. In 1809, a new die was cut.

The seal depicts a shield upon which are displayed a sailing ship, a plough, and three sheaves of wheat. These three symbols originated in county seals: the ship was the crest of Philadelphia County;

the plough was the crest of Chester County; and the sheaf of wheat was the crest of Sussex County (which is now in Delaware).

To the left of the shield is a stalk of Indian corn, and to the right, an olive branch. An eagle is centered above the shield. "And on the wreath of its colours a bald eagle—proper, perched, wings extended for the crest." Encircling the design is the inscription: "Seal of the State of Pennsylvania." The reverse of the seal shows a woman representing Liberty trampling a lion representing Tyranny. The woman holds a wand topped by a liberty cap, another traditional symbol of freedom. This design is encircled with "Both Can't Survive," meaning Liberty and Tyranny.

Although the seal was modified by the introduction of scrollwork to the bottom of the circular seal in 1868, the essential symbols of the Commonwealth remained. The present seal was officially adopted in 1893.

THE STATE FLAG

The State flag of Pennsylvania was approved in 1907. The first flag bearing the State coat of arms was authorized by the General Assembly in 1799. In 1871, Governor Curtin procured regimental flags bearing the arms of the Commonwealth. During the Civil War, many Pennsylvanian regiments carried flags modeled after the U.S. flag, but placed the State's coat of arms on the blue field in the place of the stars.

The description of the State flag is as follows: "The flag shall be of blue, same color as the blue field in the flag of the United States, and of the following dimensions and design; to wit, The length, or height of the staff to be nine feet, including brass spearhead and ferrule; the fly of the said flag to be six feet two inches, and to be four feet six inches on the staff; in the center of the flag there shall be embroidered in silk the same on both sides of the flag the coat of arms of the commonwealth of Pennsylvania, in proportionate size; the edges to be trimmed with knotted fringe of yellow silk, two and one-half inches wide; a cord, with tassels, to be attached to the staff, at the spearhead, to be eight feet six inches long, and composed of white and blue silk strands."

THE STATE MOTTO

Pennsylvania's State Motto is "Virtue, Liberty, and Independence." This motto was included in the State coat of arms designed in 1778 by Caleb Lownes of Philadelphia. It was approved in 1875.

"Virtue" is a long-time tradition of Pennsylvania, dating from the time when the province passed out of the hands of the profligate Charles II of England into the possession of the great humanitarian, William Penn. Pennsylvania has always been active in the struggle for freedom, hence the motto "liberty and independence."

THE STATE BIRD

In 1931, the State Legislature adopted the official State bird, the ruffled grouse, (*Bonasa umbellus*). Pennsylvania has the only game bird designated as the State bird.

The ruffled grouse is fifteen to nineteen inches in length, and its tail length is five to six inches. Its habitat is wooded areas in North America. It is a medium size wood grouse. Underparts are buff or whitish, broken by broad bars of brownish; the lower half of the tarsus is nude and scale like. The tail is nearly as long as the wing, and has from eighteen to twenty tail feathers, gray or rusty in color, with numerous zigzag narrow bars of blackish and a broad subterminal band of black or dark brown. Crown feathers are distinctly elongated, forming a crest. In summer, the male has a bright orange or red naked space above the eye.

In mating season, the ruffled grouse makes an ear-splitting drumming noise by either the wild flapping of the wings against the sides or by the sheer force of the wings against the air. The bird is primarily a fruit and vegetable eater; insects account for approximately ten percent of its diet. The grouse is tame by nature, and some have even become pets. In areas where the grouse is hunted, however, they are much more cautious of humans and take evasive actions. A popular game bird, the grouse is also called a pheasant in the South and a partridge in northern states. Its enemies include raccoons, skunks, weasels, and opossum. Disease and parasites take a heavy toll on the population of the grouse.

THE STATE FLOWER

The State flower of Pennsylvania is the mountain laurel (*Kalmia latifolia*). It was adopted by the Legislature in 1933. In June when it blooms into a soft, pink flower, Tioga County holds an annual laurel festival to celebrate its beauty.

THE STATE TREE

In 1931, the hemlock tree, (*Tsuga canadensis,*) was adopted as the State tree of Pennsylvania.

The hemlock is also called the Eastern hemlock, Canadian hemlock, spruce pine, hemlock spruce, New England hemlock, and spruce. It is native to the Northeastern United States, adjacent Canada, and the Appalachian Mountain region of north Alabama and Georgia.

The hemlock is a medium-sized to large tree. Its brown or purplish bark is deeply furrowed into broad, scaly ridges. Needles are from 3/8 to 5/8 inches long, short stalked, flat, soft, and blunt pointed; they are shiny dark green above and lighter beneath, and appear in two rows. Cones are brownish, and from 5/8 to 3/4 inch long.

THE STATE SONG

The official State song of the Commonwealth of Pennsylvania is "Pennsylvania." Adopted on November 29, 1990 and signed into law by Governor Robert P. Casey, it was written and composed by Eddie Khoury and Ronnie Bonner.

The lyrics to the State song are as follows:

PENNSYLVANIA

Pennsylvania, Pennsylvania,
Mighty is your name.
Steeped in glory and tradition,
Object of acclaim.
Where brave men fought the foe of freedom,
Tyranny decried
'Til the bell of independence
Filled the countryside.

Chorus:
Pennsylvania, Pennsylvania,
May your future be
filled with honor everlasting
as your history.

Pennsylvania, Pennsylvania,
Blessed by God's own hand,
Birthplace of a mighty nation,
Keystone of the land.
Where first our country's flag unfolded,
Freedom to proclaim,
May the voices of tomorrow
glorify your name.

Chorus:
Pennsylvania, Pennsylvania,
May your future be,
filled with honor everlasting
as your history.

THE STATE LICENSE PLATE

The State of Pennsylvania began to issue statewide license plates in 1906. The first plate, made of porcelain, had white lettering on a deep blue background. A number of color combinations were used on the plates until 1924, when yellow and deep blue were chosen. These two colors were used in different shades and alternating combinations for background and lettering until the 2000 issue plate.

The 1976 plate for Pennsylvania was yellow on deep blue. In 1979, deep blue on a yellow plate was valid. In 1985, the plate was again yellow on deep blue. The latest plate is the 2000 issue, which has a deep blue border at the top with the word PENNSYLVANIA lettered across, a yellow border at the bottom with the State's Internet address: WWW.STATE.PA.US lettered across, and a white centered background with dark blue letters and numbers. Although older series plates will still be valid, they began being phased out in 2000.

THE STATE POSTAGE STAMP

To commemorate the bicentennial of the ratification of the U.S. Constitution in 1788, the United States Postal Service issued thirteen stamps, one to represent each of the original thirteen states. The stamp for the Commonwealth of Pennsylvania was the second of the series issued, as the State was the second to ratify the Constitution. Issued on August 26, 1987, the twenty-two-cent stamp was designed by Richard D. Sheaff.

Depicted on Pennsylvania's stamp is Independence Hall in Philadelphia, the birthplace of American independence. Below the building is the date of the Commonwealth's ratification: De-cember 12, 1787. Below this is printed the name of the State. The stamp is multi-colored on a blue background.

OTHER STATE DESIGNATIONS

A number of additional symbols have been added to the Commonwealth of Pennsylvania's official list. The State animal (1959) is the white-tailed deer; the State dog (1965) is the Great Dane; the Brook trout (*Salvenlinus fontinalis*) is the official State fish (1970); the firefly (*Lampyridae*) is the State insect (1974); milk is designated as the State beverage (1982); and the Penngift crownvetch (*Coronilla varia L. penngift*) is the State's beautification and conservation plant (1982).

THE STATE CAPITOL

Philadelphia was the state's capital city from 1683 to 1799. From 1799 to 1810, Lancaster was made the capital. The General Assembly passed a law in 1810 which made Harrisburg the State's capital city after 1812. Authorization was given for construction of a capitol building in 1816; it became occupied in 1821. An addition was authorized in 1864. The main building was destroyed by fire in 1897.

By an act of April 14, 1897, supplemented by an act on July 18, 1901, authorization was given for erection of the present capitol building, which was rapidly constructed and dedicated by President Theodore Roosevelt on October 4, 1906. The architect, commissioned in 1902, was Joseph M. Huston of Philadelphia. Designed in the classic style adopted from the architecture of the Italian Renaissance, the five-story capitol is 520 feet long and 254 feet wide. The dome is 272 feet in height and is topped by a symbolic figure of the Commonwealth.

The capitol covers thirteen acres of ground, and within its one-half mile circumference are 415 rooms. The exterior is of Vermont slate. Throughout the interior, the capitol is furnished in marble, mahogany, bronze, and tiling. It is adorned with appropriate decorations, including mural paintings by such well-known artists as Violet Oakley. According to State records, the Capitol Building cost over ten million dollars, exclusive of furnishings.

Barnard Group of Statuary. Flanking the sides of the front entrance, facing west, are two heroic groups of statuary by the Pennsylvania-born sculptor, George Grey Barnard. To the right as one faces this entrance is a group of men and women in attitudes representing the spiritual burdens carried by humans; a group to the left represents "work" and "brotherhood."

At the center of the entrance are huge bronze doors, enriched with sculptured relief. These doors depict historic events in the State's life and recall Ghiberti's doors in the Baptistry at Florence, Italy. The leaves of this central door weigh one ton each and were cast in one piece.

Rotunda. The size and immense space within the Rotunda below the dome, the sweep of the grand staircase, and the rich ornamentation of the walls and ceiling add to the monumental and inspiring effect of this focal point of the government of the Commonwealth. Appropriately placed around this great rotunda, just under the main cornice, are the famous words of William Penn which outline his hopes for the new experiment in democratic government he was founding: "There may be room there for such a Holy Experiment, for the nations want a precedent. And my God will make it the seed of a nation, that an example may be set up to the nations, that we may do the thing that is truly wise and just."

In the recessed arches and circular panels are paintings by the Pennsylvania artist, Edwin Austin Abbey, which commemorate the spiritual, intellectual, and economic advances of the Commonwealth.

Around the rotunda are six glass cases containing flags carried by Pennsylvania soldiers in the Civil and Spanish-American wars, and an Honor Roll list of State employees in World War II.

The Main Corridor. Extending to the north and south are wide corridors. In the south corridor, to the right as one faces the staircase, are mural paintings by W. B. Van Ingen, a noted Pennsylvania artist. The works represent various phases of the religious influences that are a part of Pennsylvania's history. Carved on the gilded capitals along these corridors are heads representing outstanding individuals of the many nationalities that have contributed to the growth of Pennsylvania.

The Senate Chamber. North of the rotunda, off the second floor balcony is the Senate Chamber, which is richly furnished and conveys a feeling of quiet dignity. In this room are paintings by Violet Oakley, one of Pennsylvania's most outstanding artists and a member of the Brandywine School of Artists. The paintings in front and to the left of the central niche represent *The Creation of the Union.* One painting portrays Washington and his troops marching through Philadelphia on their way to Brandywine in 1777, and a second shows Washington presiding over the Constitutional Convention at Independence Hall in Philadelphia in 1787.

To the right are paintings representing *The Preservation of the Union,* which depict General Meade and his troops in camp before Gettysburg in 1863, and President Lincoln at the dedication of the National Cemetery at Gettysburg in 1863. The panel above represents William Penn's vision of *International Understanding.* At the rear of the room are two other paintings by Violet Oakley, representing two old Quaker legends: one, the Open Latch String, and the other, the Friend who purchased and set free a boatload of slaves.

Just below the ceiling are circular stained glass windows by W.B. Van Ingen, symbolizing subjects such as Weaving, Temperance, Glass Blowing, Peace, Railroads, Militia, Legislature, History, Foundries, and Architecture.

The House of Representatives Chamber. South of the rotunda and off the second floor balcony is the richly decorated Chamber of the House of Representatives. This room is ornamented with a wealth of architectural detail and with stained glass windows and paintings. The windows, by W. B. Van Ingen, depict outstanding Pennsylvania activities. The paintings in this room are by Edwin Austin Abbey. The largest is the *Apotheosis,* directly above the Speaker's platform, which portrays those prominent in the Commonwealth's early history. To the left is a picture of *Penn's Treaty With the Indians,* while to the right is shown the *Reading of the Declaration of Independence* at Independence Hall. To the rear of the chamber between the two entrances is Abbey's picture of *Valley Forge,* showing Baron Von Steuben instructing recruits. In the circular panel in the ceiling of the House is *The Passage of the Hours,* another striking example of Abbey's symbolic art.

The Appellate Courtroom. This room on the fourth floor is used by the Supreme Court and the Superior Court. It is approached by a corridor extending east from the rotunda. In this room of quiet dignity are displayed sixteen panels by Violet Oakley, portraying the evolution of law through the ages.

The Governor's Suite. This suite of richly furnished rooms is on the second floor of the south wing. The public reception room, paneled in English crotched oak, is enhanced by a series of mural paintings by Violet Oakley. These paintings portray events in the history of religious liberty in England, and in the rise of the Society of Friends. In addition, they show dramatic moments in the life of William Penn, culminating with his arrival in America on the ship, *Welcome.*

The Lieutenant Governor's Suite. In the front of the building and off the second floor balcony over the main entrance is the lieutenant governor's suite. The public reception room is of considerable interest because of its wainscoting of mahogany and the decorative leather surfacing the walls.

Planning of the Capitol. Long ago it became apparent that grounds were needed for a proper setting of the capitol, as well as additional buildings. The original park, a four-acre grant from John Harris, was increased to fifteen acres by 1873 at a cost of 36,400 dollars. Between the years of 1912-1919, the park area was enlarged to 45 acres through the purchase of the area between the capitol and the railroad and between Walnut Street and North Street. This area included 537 properties, and with the removal of the buildings, was acquired at a cost of over two million dollars.

In 1916, architect Arnold W. Brunner and landscape architect Warren H. Manning were commissioned to prepare comprehensive plans for the future development of this area. In 1941, surveys and studies were made for the acquisition of more property to the north, to provide space and a setting for additional buildings necessary to an expanded sphere of State services.

In the early 1940s, the General Assembly established a Capital Park Extension Commission to examine and approve all acquisition proceedings involved in purchasing the north section of the capital to Forster Street between Third and the railroad. The former Department of Property and Supplies was directed to acquire this property, and three million dollars were appropriated for this purpose. In 1945, an additional six million dollars were allocated to acquire more land for the Capitol complex, and plans were begun for construction of the State Archives and Museum Building as a memorial to William Penn.

OTHER FACTS ABOUT PENNSYLVANIA

Total area: 46,058 square miles
Land area: 44,820 square miles
Water area: 1,239 square miles
Rank in total area: 33
Average elevation: 1,100 feet
Highest point: Mount Davis, 3,213 feet
Lowest point: Delaware River, sea level
Highest temperature: 111 degrees Fahrenheit, July 10, 1936
Lowest temperature: -42 degrees Fahrenheit, January 5, 1904, Smeth Point
Population in 1990: 11,881,643
Population density in 1990: 265.10 persons per square mile
Population 1980-1990: +0.1 percent change
Population in 2000: 12,281,054
Population density in 1999: 267.6 persons per square mile
Population 1990-2000: +3.4 percent change
Population difference 1990-2000: 399,411 persons
Black population in 1990: 1,089,795
Hispanic population in 1990: 232,262
Native American population in 1990: 14,733
White population in 1990: 10,520,201
Per capita income 1998: $27,469
Per capita income 1999 est.: $28,676
Resident: Pennsylvanian
Capital: Harrisburg
Admitted to Union: December 12, 1787
Order of Statehood: 2
Electoral votes: 23

CHRONOLOGY

200,000 B.C. Glaciers are laid over entire Great Lakes region, including Lake Erie and western Pennsylvania.

18,000 B.C. Ice begins to melt slowly.

8,000-6,000 B.C. Ancestors of Delaware and Iroquois, Archaic Indians, arrive in Middle Atlantic states after long trek over Bering Strait land-bridge from Asia.

200 A.D. Woodland Culture of Paleo-Indians dominates Pennsylvania; culture evolves from subsistence-hunting level to highly organized farming and religiously artistic level.

to 1608 Mound builders build effigy earthworks in Pennsylvania, especially near rivers.
– Susquehannock and Iroquoian Indian cultures develop.

1608 Captain John Smith journeys to Susquehanna River from Virginia; he visits Susquehannock tribes, who are in control of that territory.

1609 Henry Hudson sails into Delaware Bay and River, meeting Algonquin Indians who worship him as religious figure.
– Dutch claim area is explored by Hudson for East India Company.

1615 Etienne Brule explores Susquehanna from headwaters to mouth.

1616 Hendrick Christiansen and Adrien Block, Dutchmen, explore Delaware Bay, reaching Schuylkill River.

1634 Virginia voyagers sail up Delaware River and establish small fort at mouth of Schuylkill River near Philadelphia.

1638 First expedition to colonize New Sweden sets out.
– Fort Christina is built at site of present Wilmington, Delaware.

1641 Sixty English Puritans from Connecticut make unsuccessful settlement at mouth of Schuylkill River.

1643 John Printz leads group of Swedes and establishes first European permanent settlement at Tinicum Island; local government and court system is planned at site within present Pennsylvania borders.

1645 Dutch in Manhattan send expedition to Schuylkill to erect Fort Beversrede.
– Trouble begins to develop between Dutch and Swedish settlers.

1655 Dutch Governor, Peter Stuyvesant, seizes New Sweden to make it part of New Netherlands colony.

1664 Charles II grants to his brother, Duke of York, "all the land west of the Connecticut River to the east side of the Delaware Bay."
– Colonel Richard Nicolls carries out king's order to seize area from Dutch and establish English rule.

1673-74 Dutch regain control of Delaware area for short period, but English claim is made formal by Treaty of Westminster.

1681 William Penn, friend of Duke of York, asks King Charles II for land grant between Lord Baltimore's province of Maryland and Duke's province of New York.
– Charles II signs Charter of Pennsylvania on March 4, named in honor of Penn's father.
– Penn sends his cousin, William Markham, to take possession of territory he hopes will be haven and "holy experiment" for his ideal Quaker society.

1682 Penn arrives in Pennsylvania, after sending Thomas Holmes to survey town of Philadelphia.
– Penn establishes three original counties and unites three "lower counties" by calling together first meeting of general assembly at Chester.
– Assembly passes Act of Union and Naturalization as well as "Great Law," a humanitarian code providing for religious freedom, which becomes foundation of Pennsylvania law.
– Penn helps make treaties with Indians that promotes good relations with them for 70 years.

1683 Penn's "Frame of Government" is accepted by council and assembly.
– First witchcraft trial is held in February.
– First glass factory is built at Frankford, now part of Philadelphia.
– Town of Germantown is founded by Francis D. Pastorius.

1684 Penn sails to England to settle boundary disputes with Lord Baltimore, leaving established Quaker province.

1685 Penn's rights to Lower Counties are confirmed by King James; he remains in London as James' advisor.

1687 Malt liquor is brewed for first time for commercial sale by Anthony Morris.

1688 Quakers begin to fight black slavery in Germantown.
– "Glorious Revolution" overthrows King James and causes Penn to be arrested and jailed twice for treason; known as "Penn the Traitor and Penn the Jacobite," he is blamed for power conflicts that begin to develop in his American colony.
– Penn names John Blackwell deputy governor of province, but Quakers join forces against him when he arrives in Philadelphia.

1689 Blackwell resigns.

1690 America's first paper mill is built by William Rittenhouse in Philadelphia.

1692 King William and Queen Mary remove Penn's claim to Pennsylvania, re-annexing territory to New York.

1694 Appealing to Queen Mary alone, Penn is able to regain proprietorship over Pennsylvania.

1699-1701 Penn returns to Pennsylvania; facing need for new constitution, with provisions for power of assembly, he accepts assembly's "Charter of Privileges."
– Penn deals with conflicting land claims and, with Legislature, forms "Bill of Proprieties."
– Political divisions between aristocratic and back-country Quakers leads to formation of Propriety Party and Popular Party.

1701 Penn issues Charter of Privileges.
– Penn returns to London after hearing rumors that colonies might be consolidated.
– Philadelphia is chartered as city.

1703 Although Delaware withdraws from Quaker Province and forms own assembly, governor of Pennsylvania will continue to serve Delaware.

1708 Unable to pay his debts, Penn mortgages Province for 6,600 pounds.

1710 Attracted by Quakers' religious tolerance, a number of Germans, Scotch-Irish, and French Huguenots immigrate and settle in province.

1712 Penn suffers paralytic stroke in England, just before he is to sign documents handing over Province to Queen; his wife, Hannah Penn, takes over his duties.

1714 Amish, branch of Swiss Mennonite religion, begins settlements in Berks County.

1716 Thomas Rutter, German immigrant, builds first iron forge near Pottstown.

1718 Penn dies in England.

1723 Benjamin Franklin arrives in Philadelphia from Boston.
– First paper money is issued in Philadelphia.

1724 Carpenter's Company is organized in Philadelphia.

1727 Hannah Penn dies, leaving proprietorship to her sons John, Tom, and Richard Penn, who are not Quakers.
– Benjamin Franklin founds Junto, group that opposes slavery, in Philadelphia.

1729 Franklin becomes publisher of Pennsylvania Gazette and writes "Modest Enquiry into the Nature and Necessity of a Paper Currency."

1731 Franklin originates Library Company of Philadelphia.

1732 First steel is forged by Samuel Nutt at Chester County's Coventry Forge.
– Governor James Logan's plan to consolidate Iroquois Indians as leaders of all tribes resident in Pennsylvania is agreed upon in treaty with principal chief, John Shickellamy, enabling Pennsylvania government to negotiate for Indian land with centralized representative.

1736 German population grows to 40,000.

1737 Gov. Logan stages infamous "Walking Purchase" of Delaware Indian lands.

1740 Estimated population is 200,000.
– University of Pennsylvania is established in Philadelphia.

1742 Henry M. Muhlenburg arrives in Pennsylvania to found large German-Lutheran settlement.

1744 Benjamin Franklin perfects stove that bears his name.

1746 First nail factory is built by John Taylor at Chester Creek.
– John Penn dies.

1747 Benjamin Franklin establishes public lottery to provide funds for Commonwealth's defense.

1751 Bell is ordered from England to celebrate 50th anniversary of Commonwealth; it becomes "Liberty Bell."

1753 French build string of forts on Lake Erie and headwaters of Ohio River; Indians, impressed with these forts, begin to side with French rather than English.
– George Washington is sent to interview French commander at Fort Le Boeuf; he warns him to leave territory.

1754 Governor Dinwiddie of Virginia sends militia to build fort at Ohio River Forks, but French seize it before completion and call it Fort Duquesne.
– Washington builds Fort Necessity near Uniontown.
– Washington's troops attack French party at Great Meadows; ten die and rest surrender.
– French and Indian War officially begins, as Washington is attacked in return by French at Fort Necessity.

1755 Gen. Braddock's troops are trapped and captured by French on Monongahela.
– Shawnees and Delawares avenge loss of their homeland by attacking settlers west of Susquehanna.

1756 Pennsylvania assembly declares war on Indians, despite Quakers' pacifist beliefs.
– Britain formally declares war on France.

1758 Grand council with Iroquois, and subsequently Delawares at Easton, ends in peace agreement.
– British General John Forbes captures Fort Duquesne from French and renames it Fort Pitt.

1760 French surrender at Montreal, September 8.

1762 Anthracite is found in Wyoming Valley.

1763 Treaty of Paris is signed in February.
– Indians rise up against British in Pontiac's War, destroying Forts Presque Isle, Le Boeuf, and Venango before Col. Henry Bouquet leads them to defeat at Bushy Run.
– Paxton Boys murder peaceful Indians at Lancaster.
– William Henry of Lancaster builds first steamboat in America.
– War ends with British victory; Pennsylvania region is completely under British rule.

1764 Col. Bouquet forces Indians at Muskingum, Ohio to sue for peace.
– Grassroots Anti-Propriety party urges King to purchase Pennsylvania from Penn family.

1765 Stamp Act is passed in March, amid bitter opposition in province.
– William Steigel opens glass factory in Lancaster County.

1766 Stamp Act is repealed, ending much political excitement.

1767 Townshend Acts to tax imported glass, lead, paint, paper, and tea goes into effect; Philadelphia leaders urge opposition.
– Charles Mason and Jeremiah Dixon complete laying of boundary line for Pennsylvania and Maryland.

1768 Assembly opposes Stamp Act and Townshend Acts as "taxation without representation."
– Indian grievances are settled with Fort Stanwix Treaty.

1769 Philadelphia merchants join in non-importation agreement.

1770 British repeal all Townshend Acts except tax on tea.

1773 Philadelphia citizens declare a boycott on tea, threatening lives of river pilots who would dare bring tea ships up Delaware.

1774 First Continental Congress meets in Philadelphia.
– Inter-colonial boycott of imported tea is resolved.

1775 American Revolution begins.
– Delegates from all province's counties meet.
– Second Continental Congress meets in Philadelphia.

– George Washington is appointed commander of Continental Army, and six companies of Pennsylvania riflemen are sent to Boston for battle.
– "Twelve United Colonies" is referred to for first time.
– Pennsylvania Abolition Society is formed.

1776 Pennsylvania is third largest colony in America, with 275,000 inhabitants and 11 counties.
– Provincial delegates agree to accept Declaration of Independence.
– Declaration of Independence is signed at Philadelphia by Second Continental Congress on July 4; new constitution is prepared by provisional government.
– Pennsylvania assembly passes new Constitution, providing for one-house assembly and executive council instead of governor.
– Pennsylvania Navy forces retreat of two British warships.
– Gen. Washington crosses Delaware to defeat British at Trenton, December 26.

1777 June 14. Congress adopts United States Flag design in Philadelphia.
September 11. Battle of Brandywine is fought; George Washington is defeated by British General William Howe.
September 26. British occupy Philadelphia after second attempt by General Howe's troops.
– Liberty Bell is secreted in Allentown during British occupation of Philadelphia.
September 30. American forces are defeated in Battle of Paoli.
November 10. American troops are driven from Fort Mifflin by British.
December 19. General Washington moves to winter quarters at Valley Forge, protecting inner Pennsylvania from invasion.

1778 Radicals in Congress pass law that no Tory can vote or hold office, and anyone who has not made oath of allegiance to Commonwealth can have his property confiscated.
June 18. British are forced out of Philadelphia; Congress again convenes there on July 2.
– British and Indians join forces against frontier settlers in Wyoming Valley.
November 15. Articles of Confederation are adopted in Philadelphia.

1779 Radical party passes act to take over public lands owned by Penn family.
– Mob attack on Republicans by Radicals in Philadelphia leads to unorthodox party's downfall.

1780 Pennsylvania passes first law for abolition of slavery.
– Commonwealth of Pennsylvania contributes $6 million to Congress and loans large sums to Continental Army, more than any other colony.

1781 American Revolution ends.

1782 Bank of North America is established by wealthy Pennsylvanians to support government finances.

1783 Treaty of Paris ends American Revolution.
– Three thousand Pennsylvania troops march on Congress in Philadelphia to obtain "prompt settlement of their accounts."

1784 Pennsylvania gains remaining lands in province from Indians by treaty.

1787 Constitutional Convention for U.S. meets in Philadelphia.
– On December 12, Pennsylvania becomes second state to ratify Constitution.

1788 U.S. Constitution is ratified June 21.

1789 Forty-two degrees latitude for Pennsylvania-New York boundary is formally established.

1790 New State Constitution for Pennsylvania is adopted.
– Thomas Mifflin takes seat as first governor.
– Congress establishes Philadelphia as seat of federal government.
– State population is 434,373.

1791 Bank of U.S. is established in Philadelphia.
– City carpenters go on strike for 12-hour workday.

1792 U.S. Mint is founded in Philadelphia.
– Government purchases "Erie Triangle" to complete present land holdings in State.
– First American labor union is organized by shoemakers in Philadelphia.
– Excise tax on distilled liquor is imposed by Congress.
– Yellow fever epidemic kills 4,000 in Philadelphia.

1794 Pennsylvanians burn home of Inspector General John Neville in rebellion of new federal tax on whiskey; "Whiskey Rebellion" is suppressed by Governor Mifflin's army.

1799 State capital is moved to Lancaster from Philadelphia.
– Fries Rebellion takes place among homeowners, and is suppressed by State militia.

1800 Congress moves national capital from Philadelphia to Washington, D.C.
– Population is 602,364.

1802 First law for free public schools is enacted.

1804 First bank in western Pennsylvania is opened in Pittsburgh.
– Western Pennsylvania bituminous coal is first shipped to east coast cities.
– Expansion of turnpike and stage routes begins in State.

1804-1806 President Thomas Jefferson orders expedition to explore Louisiana Territory; Lewis and Clark, with Indian woman guide named Sacajawea, become first travelers to Pacific Northwest.

1808 First ocean-going steamboat arrives in Philadelphia from New York.

1811 First steamboat to operate on Ohio and Mississippi rivers is launched from Pittsburgh.

1812 War of 1812 begins.

– After war is declared, government asks for 4,000 volunteers from Pennsylvania to fight in effort.
– Stephen Girard, Albert Gallatin, and Alexander J. Dallas, Pennsylvania entrepreneurs, provide U.S. army with funds to pay for American army.
– State capital is moved to permanent home in Harrisburg.
– Anthracite is used commercially for first time at Falls of Schuylkill.

1813 Oliver H. Perry's fleet wins Battle of Lake Erie.
– Ships are built by native Pennsylvanian, Daniel Dobbins.
– Legislature passes law to charter 41 new banks.

1814 War of 1812 ends.
– Treaty of Ghent is signed in favor of Americans.

1819 First Pennsylvania savings bank is founded.

1820 Many anthracite coal mining companies are established.
– Canal and turnpike expansion continues.
– Population is 1,040,458.

1823 Monroe Doctrine declares that U.S. and rest of Americas are not open to future colonization or interference by European powers.

1825 Early coal railroads in western Pennsylvania begin.

1828 Workingman's party is formed in Philadelphia.

1830-34 Over 300 miles of rail lines are constructed out of Philadelphia.
– Baldwin locomotive works is established in city.

1834 Free School Act is passed, beginning large-scale construction of public schools.

1836 Natural gas is first used for public energy in Philadelphia.

1837 Anthracite is first used in smelting iron ore at Mauch Chunk.

1838 New State Constitution is passed, reducing governor's appointive power and shortening terms of office.

1840 Population is 1,724,033.
– State debt, caused by over expenditures on public works, leads to financial crash and bank closures.

1841 Pennsylvania Legislature passes act forbidding use of State jails to detain fugitive slaves.

1845 Steel rails are first manufactured at Danville.

1846 War with Mexico is declared by Congress.
– State militia is organized to fight.
– First telegraphic communication between Harrisburg and Lancaster is completed.
– First telegraph message is sent over Alleghenies.
– Pennsylvania railroad is organized.

1848 First miner's union is organized.
– Mexican War begins; Mexican-claimed Texas territory is seized by General Zachary Taylor; U.S. declares war after border clashes.

1849 First miner's strike occurs in May.

1851 Christiana riot breaks out in Lancaster County when man refuses to return fugitive slaves to their former owner.

1854 Bill is approved to consolidate city and county of Philadelphia into single body.

1855 First horsecars operate in Philadelphia.
– Pennsylvania State University is established.

1856 First Republican National Convention is held at Philadelphia.

1857 In Dred Scott Decision, Supreme Court rules that slave does not become free when brought into free state, that Congress cannot restrict slavery from territory and that blacks cannot be citizens; ruling begins chain of events that leads to Civil War.

1859 Nation's first successful oil well is drilled by E.L. Drake at Titusville.
– Several trade unions are formed.

1860 Population is 2,906,215.
– Several million tons of anthracite coal are produced from western mines.

1861 Civil War begins.
– Governor Curtin pledges Pennsylvania's support for Union cause in his inaugural address; he is State's first Republican governor.
– Lincoln speaks at Independence Hall; State sends 25 regiments of soldiers after Lincoln's call for volunteers; Pennsylvania delegation is first to reach Washington, April 18.

1862 -Curtin calls conference of northern governors, held at old Logan House in Altoona.
– Stuart's raid on Chambersburg results in loss of Union supplies and horses.
– Bethlehem Iron Company is founded.

1863 Battle of Gettysburg constitutes major invasion of Pennsylvania.
– In bitterly fought three-day engagement, July 1-3, Union army throws back Confederate forces.
– President Abraham Lincoln delivers Gettysburg Address.
– Decreed by President Lincoln, Emancipation Proclamation abolishes slavery in rebel states.

1864 Chambersburg is burned by Confederate army.

1865 Civil War ends.
– President Abraham Lincoln is assassinated.

1866 National Labor Union is founded, a coalition of a number of craft unions.

1867 First practical Bessemer steel is produced at Steelton.

1869 Pennsylvania Railroad, recently acquired by Jay Gould, stretches as far west as Columbus, Ohio.

1870 First open-hearth method of steel production is used, making possible large-scale, inexpensive steelmaking; Pittsburgh is nation's center of steel industry.

1873 Philadelphia bank, owned by Jay Cooke, fails; financial panic follows.
– Legislature passes law for iron and steel industry incorporation, limiting liability and allowing for loans through bond issues.

1874 Fourth State Constitution takes effect, providing for more elected officers.

1876 Philadelphia hosts U.S. Centennial Exhibition; Alexander Graham Bell demonstrates his new telephone at event.
– New typewriter is exhibited.
– Ten thousand American newspapers are displayed.
– Twenty-four buildings representing various states are erected.

1877 Pittsburgh citizens unite against Pennsylvania Railroad Company in Trainmen's Union strike.
– Twenty-six workers are killed by Philadelphia militia.

1880 State's first elevated railroad is built in Philadelphia.
– Population is 4,282,891.

1881 Labor leaders meet in Pittsburgh to form Federation of Organized Trade and Labor Unions, which becomes American Federation of Labor (AFL) in 1886.

1885 State Board of Health is established.

1887 Bethlehem Iron Company gains first American contract for U.S. Navy's armor plate.

1889 South Fork Dam breaks, pouring 20 million tons of water on Johnstown and killing 2,209.

1891 Various labor strikes, especially at Carnegie's steel plants, break out in State.

1892 Spartansburg dam bursts, killing 100.
– Workers at Carnegie's steel plant at Homestead protest violently against unfair wages and working conditions.

1895 State Department of Agriculture is formed.

1897 Twenty die in labor riots at Luzerne.
– Fire destroys Capitol building at Harrisburg.
– Three million dollars in damage is reported after fire in Pittsburgh.

1898 Cornerstone of new State Capitol is laid.
– Spanish-American War; fought between U.S. and Spain over treatment of American interests in Cuba, battleship *Maine* is blown up in Havana; Treaty of Paris cedes Guam, Phillipines, and Puerto Rico to U.S.

1900 Population is 6,302,115.
– Pennsylvania has 300 public high schools and 27,412 students; only two in 1,000 of population are college students.

1901 Charles M. Schwab becomes president of U.S. Steel Corporation.

1905 Child Labor Act raises minimum age of factory and mine workers in State to 14.
– First all-motion picture theater opens in Pittsburgh.

1908 Capitol building is completed, but Governor Berry discovers graft involved in construction.

1914 World War I begins.

1915 Police block doors of theater where conscientious objectors have planned anti-draft meeting.

1917 World War I soldiers march in gala Philadelphia parade.
– Twenty-eighth Division lands in France.
– State's factories and mills produce steel and other materials in war effort.

1918 Peak coal production reaches 99,612,000 tons in State.
– World War I ends; one million American troops have fought in effort.

1919 Treaty of Versailles is signed.

1920 Pioneer radio station, KDKA, broadcasts first message from Pittsburgh; it becomes first permanent commercial broadcasting station in world.
– Population is 8,720,071.
– Ratification of 19th Amendment gives women voting rights in all elections.

1921 Edmonds Act is passed, an attempt to streamline and equalize State education.

1923 At Governor Pinchot's insistence, Legislature passes law closing licensed saloons.

1926 Sesqui-Centennial International Exposition is held in Philadelphia.

1927 State Department of Revenue is created.
– Rapid development of macadam and concrete roads begins.

1929 Stock Market Crash leads to Great Depression.

1930 Population is 9,631,350.

1932 Industrial production slides to less than half of 1929 level.
– Talbot Law is enacted, allotting $10 million for unemployment relief.

1933 State Emergency Relief Board is formed by Legislature; $45 million is appropriated for unemployed.
– Pennsylvania Historical Association is organized.

1935 Governor George Earle takes office; he is first Democrat to do so in 45 years.

1936 Earle's "Little New Deal" begins, with special legislative session allotting huge sums for relief, as well as levying emergency taxes.
– Floods plague State.
– Franklin D. Roosevelt is renominated at Democratic National Convention held in Philadelphia.

1937 Little Wagner Act protects labor's right to organize and creates State Labor Relations Board.
– Fifty million-dollar bond issue for flood control is approved by assembly.
– One hundred fiftieth anniversary of U.S. Constitution is celebrated at Philadelphia.

1939 World War II begins; war stimulates return to high productions in State's coal and steel industries.

1940 Republicans return to Pennsylvania politics with election of Governor Arthur James.
– Republican convention is held in Philadelphia.
– First section of Pennsylvania Turnpike is completed from Harrisburg to Pittsburgh; it is later extended to meet Delaware River and western boundary of State.

1941 Communist Party members are arrested and jailed for distributing party election petitions in Allegheny County.
– Pennsylvania regiment is inducted into U.S. Army.
– Japanese attack Pearl Harbor.

1942 Eighty-five liquor stores close, as CIO workers walk out because of wage disputes with Liquor Control Board.
– Battle of Midway turns tide of war.

1943 Women's employment with Pennsylvania Railroad Company reaches all time high.
– First female "brakemen" are hired and trained.

1945 World War II ends; over one million Pennsylvanians have served in armed forces.
– Governor Martin reports surplus in State budget.
– American Labor Party is accused of fraudulent handling of nomination petitions in Philadelphia during county elections.
– State Supreme Court rejects Democrats petitions to bar American Labor Party from ballot.

1947 State's birth rate sets new high.
– Population increases by three percent since 1940.
– University of Pennsylvania researchers are sent to find traces of Delaware Indians.
– Truman Doctrine is first serious effort toward containing communist expansion; it becomes basis for U.S. Cold War policy.

1948 State industrial output is valued at $18.6 billion.
– Pennsylvania Turnpike is expanded to reach Philadelphia.

1950 Korean War begins; United Nations forces are sent to South Korea to repel North Korean attack (aided by USSR).
– Population is 10,435,965.

1951 Quakers meet in Philadelphia, oppose loyalty oath bill for public employees.
– Legislature passes proposal to outlaw Communist Party.
– Pennsylvania Railroad Company's Bayhead Junction-bound commuter train plunges off temporary wooden trestle; 84 are killed and 320 injured in Woodbridge, New Jersey; grand jury charges company with manslaughter for neglect.

1952 Governor Fine leads State employees in taking loyalty oath; several State employees are dismissed for refusing to pledge loyalty to State.
– First blacks are hired to State police.

1953 Armistice is signed to end Korean War; no peace treaty is signed.

1954 Supreme Court upholds State Loyalty Act as constitutional.
– First Democratic governor in 20 years, Sen. George M. Leader, wins election over Republican Lt. Governor.
– Brown vs. Board of Education; Supreme Court rejects concept of "separate but equal" and rules unanimously that racial segregation in schools violates 14th Amendment that guarantees equal protection under law.

1955 Seventeen-month legislative session ends, after many of Gov. Leader's social and industrial development measures are passed.
– Fair Employment Practices Commission is established.
– Natural gas fields in northern Pennsylvania are expanded by new wells.

1956 One hundred sixteen University of Pennsylvania students are held, after May 3 riot against old-fashioned school policies.
– Philadelphia Crime Commission holds conference to try to bar further student disorders.
– First commercial nickel refinery begins operations at Crum Lynne.

1957 Nation's first full-scale nuclear power reactor for civilian purposes begins operations at Shippingport.

1958 Judge Alpern is named attorney general; she is first woman to serve in the post.
– Copper refinery east of Mississippi River begins production near Reading; it is first built in more than 50 years.

1959 Old governor's mansion at Harrisburg is sold to Insurance Co.

1961 University of Pennsylvania's student newspaper admits women to staff for first time.

1962 Major research laboratory to study use of coal is established at Monroeville.
– Cuban Missile Crisis begins when reconnaissance photos show long-range missile construction sites in Cuba; President John Kennedy orders naval blockade of Soviet ships until construction is halted and missiles are withdrawn.

1963 President John F. Kennedy is assassinated in motorcade in Dallas; Lee Harvey Oswald is arrested for his murder.

– Nightclub owner Jack Ruby kills assassination suspect Lee Harvey Oswald.
– Vice President Lyndon B. Johnson becomes president.

1964 Race riots break out in black neighborhoods of Chester and North Philadelphia.
– Unemployment rate, which was second highest in nation, drops below national level.

1966 Democrats in Legislature demonstrate against Republican Gov. Scranton's political policies and appointments.
– Philadelphia County employee is dismissed for wearing beard; Civil Service Commission orders his reinstatement.
– Atomic power station begins operations at Peach Bottom.

1967 Student newspaper urges President Harnwell's resignation from University of Pennsylvania, claiming he is "old man who has allowed the generation gap to arise on campus."
– About 150 demonstrators protest Vietnam involvement and CIA recruitment on campus.
– Steel haulers begin violent and lengthy strike; economy of western Pennsylvania is disrupted.

1968 Constitutional Convention is called, and new document allows governor to serve for two successive terms; guidelines for local government is seen as model for nation.
– Martin Luther King is assassinated in Memphis, Tennessee Civil Rights rally; James Earl Ray pleads guilty to murder and is sentenced to 99 years in prison.

1969 Apollo 11 spacecraft lands on moon; Commander Neil Armstrong is first man to walk on moon.

1970 Population is 11,793,909.

1971 Democratic Governor Shapp takes office.
– State Supreme Court declares income tax unconstitutional, throwing Shapp's administration into quandary, since $135 million has already been collected and mostly spent.
– Three hundred and fifty University of Pennsylvania women file complaint with State government over alleged biases in university hiring, admissions, salary, and promotion practices.

1972 Tropical storm Agnes plagues much of State, causing worst floods in U.S. history; fifty are killed and 250,000 left homeless.

1973 Former State police commission and six others are charged with wiretapping telephones at secret headquarters of State Crime Commission.
– More than a decade after U.S. troops invade Vietnam, peace treaty is signed to end Vietnam war; over 550,000 troops have been involved in effort.
– Arab oil-producing nations impose oil embargo on U.S. following U.S. support to Israel during Yom Kippur War.

1974 Milton Shapp is reelected, becoming first governor to succeed himself in Pennsylvania in twentieth century.
– After severe gas shortages and rationing, oil embargo ban is lifted.

1975 Three State troopers charge government discrimination against whites in hiring of State policemen.
– Harrisburg experiences severe flooding.

1976 Two Pennsylvania congressmen admit receiving illegal campaign contributions from Gulf Oil Corporation.
– Bicentennial of United States is celebrated in Philadelphia.

1977 Governor Shapp orders all State building thermostats to be set at 62 degrees in January because of gas shortage.
– Eight thousand State workers stage "sick-in" when pay is suspended during funding crisis; Legislature subsequently approves new State budget.
– Unemployment figures in many depressed areas of State falls to lowest levels in six to ten years.

1978 Census Bureau predicts that shifting population might cause State to lose one Congressional representative after 1980 census.
– Governorship is returned to Republicans, with election of Richard Thornburgh.

1979 Nation's first large nuclear power accident occurs at Three Mile Island power station in Middletown after closing of reactor leads to release of radiation; "above normal" levels of radiation are registered, and nearby residents are evacuated; congressional task force blames faulty design and valves.
– Nuclear Regulatory Commission (NRC) announces that hydrogen bubble trapped in reactor vessel has been eliminated.
– Cold shutdown of Three Mile Island begins.
– Polio epidemic begins among Pennsylvania's 18,000 Amish.
– Iranian revolutionaries take over U.S. Embassy in Teheran to protest aid to former Shah of Iran; ninety U.S. hostages are taken, 63 are Americans.

1980 World Series baseball games are played in Philadelphia; Phillies win pennant over Kansas City.
– Fort Indiantown Gap is pressed into service as processing center for some 19,000 Cuban refugees.
– Population is 11,828,095.

1981 Democratic Representative Eugene V. Atkinson announces decision to switch parties and run as Republican in next election; President Ronald Reagan hails switch as "historic occasion."
March 14. Commonwealth of Pennsylvania begins celebration of tercentenary of its founding.
– Three Mile Island radioactive clean-up will cost $1 billion.
December. Nuclear Regulatory Commission decides that undamaged portions of Three Mile Island power station may resume operation in 1982.
– American hostages taken from U.S. Embassy in Teheran in 1979 are released.

1982 New plans for "renaissance" of downtown Pittsburgh are under construction.
– Unemployment in State reaches post-Depression levels; many steel plants close.

1983 Blizzard strikes middle Atlantic and northeastern states with as much as 35 inches of snow, drifts up to nine feet; Philadelphia is severely crippled by storm; other Pennsylvania cities set all-time records in snow accumulation.

– Four engineers involved in cleanup project at Three Mile Island nuclear power plant accuse officials of inefficiency, mismanagement, and waste; estimates of cleanup costs are revised; total of $339 million has already been spent on effort.

1984 Storm dumps about two feet of snow in parts of State; widespread flooding, hurricane-force winds, and power outages also result.

1985 Republican National Committee Chairman, Frank J. Fahrenkopf Jr. announces party drive to persuade 100,000 registered Democrats to switch to Republican registration in next 100 days; Pennsylvania is among four states targeted in effort.
May. Philadelphia police bomb rowhouse occupied by radical group called MOVE; resulting fire destroys 61 homes; eleven members of group are killed, among them four children.
– Commission appointed by Philadelphia Mayor Wilson Goode holds hearings on police bombing of MOVE rowhouse; FBI is also probing into disaster.
– Although figures fall short of goal, Republican Party officials claim success in 100-day, four-state effort to persuade Democrats to switch parties; some political analysts speculate realignment of voter loyalties, but skeptics argue that loyalties have become so weak that party identification no longer has much meaning.
April. *Philadelphia Inquirer* wins Pulitzer Prize for investigative reporting and photography; *Newsday* wins Pulitzer for international reporting and commentary.
October. A 46-day newspaper strike by *Philadelphia Inquirer* and *Daily News* ends with approval of four-year contract by 4,100 employees; Philadelphia Chamber of Commerce estimates business losses from strike as high as $7 million per day.
– Series of tornadoes, with winds up to 200 mph in some areas, strike Pennsylvania and two other states; more than 700 injured, and 64 dead in northwest part of State; damages reported at about $225 million.
– Despite objections from anti-nuclear groups and State government, NRC approves restarting of undamaged nuclear reactor at Three Mile Island.

1986 Lieutenant Governor William W. Scranton III, son of former Governor William Scranton, announces candidacy for State governor.
– High temperatures and severe drought cause major crop damage and death for many southern U.S. cities; temperatures in Pennsylvania top 100 degrees Fahrenheit.
– State Treasurer R. Budd Dwyer and Republican ex-Chairman Robert B. Asher are convicted of 11 counts of bribery in attempt to steer $4.8 million State computer contract to company in California; Dwyer is described as highest-ranking Pennsylvania official ever convicted in twentieth century.
– More that 20,000 municipal and private employees strike after contracts expire.
– U.S. space shuttle *Challenger* explodes 74 seconds after liftoff from Cape Canaveral in Florida; entire crew of seven killed.

1987 R. Budd Dwyer, State treasurer convicted of bribery, calls press conference day before sentencing; after reading statement asserting innocence, he pulls out pistol, puts it to his mouth, and kills himself.
– Festivities celebrate 200-year anniversary of Constitutional Convention in Pennsylvania; Independence Mall ceremony includes speeches by Vice President George Bush, former Chief Justice Warren E. Burger, and Philadelphia Mayor W. Wilson Goode.

– Federal Communications Commission adopts new restrictions on broadcasting obscene and offensive material; three stations are warned, including Infinity Broadcasting Corporation's WYSP-FM in Philadelphia, which broadcasts call-in show hosted by Howard Stern that has received complaints from local listeners.

– Cleanup of Three Mile Island is extended into 1989; original plan called for completion by late 1988, but some work in reducing radiation levels and disposing of radiation contaminated water is taking longer than expected, according to GPU Nuclear Corp. spokesman.

1988 Bess Myerson pleads guilty to shoplifting $44.07 in merchandise from South Williamsport department store; she is fined $100 plus $48.50 in court costs.

– Pittsburgh District Court Judge Hubert Teitelbaum reprimands attorney Barbara Wolvovitz, threatens her with jail when she insists on using maiden name and honorific "Ms." in court; Teitelbaum later apologizes.

– Philadelphia jury convicts Gary Heidnik, sentences him to death for murder of two of six women he abducted and kept shackled in basement of his North Philadelphia home.

1989 Pittsburgh *Post-Gazette* pays nearly $2.8 million to Richard DiSalle, former judge who says he was defamed by article suggesting he may have conspired to alter terms of disputed will; DiSalle sued the newspaper after 1979 article suggesting he had conspired to alter terms of will in order to favor woman with whom he had been having an affair while he was private attorney.

1990 Singer Gloria Estefan is injured in highway accident in eastern Pennsylvania, after truck runs into tour bus in which she and other members of Miami Sound Machine group are traveling; Estefan's recovery is estimated to take from three to six months.

– Philadelphia Mayor W. Wilson Goode, in effort to forestall impending bankruptcy of city, announces plan that will reschedule payment of $25 million court settlement over real-estate transfer taxes, freeze city hiring, and defer $90 million in pension payments; other proposals include allowing city to borrow at least $250 million from banks, State, and city pension plans as well as sell $90 million in assets and raise $125 million in new taxes.

– Seven people, including Senator John Heinz, are killed when helicopter collides with Heinz's chartered plane over Philadelphia suburb of Lower Merion Township; two children die after two aircraft crash onto Merion Elementary School grounds; five other children and adults are also injured by falling debris.

– Fire rages through One Meridan Plaza, a 38-story office building in downtown Philadelphia located next to City Hall; three firefighters die in blaze, which burns for more than 18 hours before being brought under control.

– Governor Robert B. Casey announces appointment of his secretary of labor and industry, Harris Wofford, to succeed late Senator John Heinz; Wofford was previously special assistant on civil rights in administration of President John F. Kennedy and founder of Peace Corps.

– Appointed Senator Harris Wofford (D) defeats former U.S. Attorney General Richard L. Thornburgh (R) in Senate race; political analysts regard results as major upset.

1991 Persian Gulf War; multi-national coalition, led by U.S., launches air strikes against Iraq following Iraqi refusal to leave Kuwait after 1990 takeover; six-week ground assault, known as Desert Storm, ends war.

1992 Representative Joseph M. McDade is indicted on federal charges of bribery, racketeering, and conspiracy for allegedly accepting over $100,000 in bribes and illegal gifts from military contractors.

– Department of Housing and Urban Development (HUD) seizes control of day-to-day operations of Philadelphia Housing Authority (PHA), on grounds that pervasive corruption has rendered local bureau unable to function.

– FCC levies $600,000 fine against company that employs controversial disc jockey, Howard Stern, for allegedly indecent comments made on Stern's syndicated radio show; 1991 shows were aired on stations in Philadelphia and three other major cities.

1993 Pennsylvania Governor Robert P. Casey undergoes rare heart-liver transplant at University of Pittsburgh Medical Center; Lieutenant Governor Mark Singel takes over gubernatorial duties pending Casey's recovery.

1994 U.S. District Judge Clarence C. Newcomer of Philadelphia overturns November 1993 election of Pennsylvania State Senator William G. Stinson (D), citing "massive absentee ballot fraud" by supporters to secure victory; Stinson's opponent, Bruce S. Marks (R), is installed in his place, a move that will give control of State Senate to GOP.

– Supreme Court Justice David H. Souter declines to issue emergency order to prevent State law limiting women's access to obtaining abortions from going into effect; six Pennsylvania abortion clinics requested that legislation be restrained pending renewed court challenges to law.

– Governor Robert P. Casey strongly objects to Federal efforts to override Pennsylvania State law allowing abortion funding only in rape or incest cases that are documented "promptly" by local law-enforcement or health officials.

– Wheeling-Pittsburgh Steel Corp. and United Steelworkers of America agree on new contract after two-day strike; agreement includes life and health insurance coverage for retired employees, additional holidays, improved pension plan, and raises and bonuses for workers.

– Swarthmore College officials offer to pay one semester's tuition for male student accused of sexual harassment; after case against Ewart Yearwood ends in a committee deadlock, President Alfred H. Bloom gives offer on grounds that Yearwood attend another college; he may return to Swarthmore after one semester if he agrees to undergo counseling.

– Commonwealth Court judge rejects most of Philadelphia school district's plan to overhaul racially divided schools; Judge Doris A. Smith says that schools need to utilize proven strategies not detailed in district plan.

1995 One hundred fifty inmates break out of dining hall at Federal prison in Allenwood; one staff member is injured; some speculate that riots may have been prompted by inmate displeasure over House's passage of bill to give stiffer prison penalties for individuals convicted of crack cocaine offenses than those convicted of similar offenses involving powdered cocaine.

– Democrat Ed Rendell wins second term as mayor of Philadelphia; during first term, he cut city's income tax, is credited with saving city from bankruptcy.

– Two neo-Nazi skinhead brothers are accused of killing parents and another brother in Salisbury Township; Brian and David Freeman are charged with stabbing and beating parents and younger brother to death, then fleeing in family car; Nelson Birdwell III is charged as accessory after fact; trio are arraigned in Midland, Michigan.

1996 Blizzard shuts down Philadelphia airport for two days; record 31 inches of snow falls in some parts of State.

– Flooding results from heavy rains and melting snow from earlier blizzard; President Clinton declares State federal disaster area; local officials estimate losses of $700 million.

– Philadelphia jury convicts three youths of murder and three others of lesser charges in 1994 beating death of 16-year old boy on steps of church in Fox Chase neighborhood; case gained national attention due to accusations that 911 emergency operators mishandled calls regarding beating.

– Philadelphia jury convicts Daniel J. Carr and Gerald Laarz of violating Solid Waste Management Act through mismanagement of large tire dump that catches fire, causing more than $6 million in damage to surrounding area, and forcing stretch of Interstate 95 to be temporarily closed; duo reportedly ignored warnings from State regulators that dump's accumulation of some 300,000 tires was hazardous.

1997 University of Pennsylvania researchers say vaccine containing genetic material from HIV virus that causes AIDS has successfully protected two chimpanzees from infection of virus; it is not yet known how vaccine worked in experiment.

– Eden Jacobowitz, charged in 1993 with racial harassment, settles emotional-distress suit he filed against University of Pennsylvania while he was student; Jacobowitz claimed that school and five students conspired to bring false charges against him; under settlement, university admits no wrongdoing and pays only for legal fees.

– Philadelphia is one of three cities (in nation's ten largest) to lose population between 1990 and 1996.

– Philadelphia District Judge Edmund V. Ludwig sentences John G. Bennett Jr. to 12 years imprisonment for defrauding charity organizations of millions of dollars; Bennett was founder of New Era Philanthropy, which filed for bankruptcy in 1995.

– Philadelphia Flyers hockey team fires coach Terry Murray because of problems between him and players.

– Pittsburgh Penguins hockey team hires Kevin Constantine as new coach; he will take over duties assumed by General Manager Craig Patrick after firing of former coach Eddie Johnson.

– Philadelphia district attorney's office releases 10-year-old tape in which former prosecutor, Jack McMahon, explains to young colleagues how to exclude blacks from juries.

– One-year-old Melissa Ann Bruch is killed while riding in front seat of her mother's car when air bag inflates after car is hit by pickup truck; accident accelerates controversy over safety of air bags.

1998 Supreme Court agrees to consider whether inmates in State prisons are protected by Americans with Disabilities Act; case is brought by prisoner denied placement in boot camp program because of hypertension; Philadelphia appeals court previously upheld prisoner's complaint, but other lower courts dismissed such complaints in similar cases.

– Governor Ridge signs bill addressing need to improve manner in which domestic violence victims seeking medical treatment are identified and referred for further care, including training hospital workers and doctors to identify signs of domestic violence.

– State Board of Education approves stricter academic standards for reading, writing, and mathematics; measurable standards will outline what students should know at grades three, five, eight, and eleven.

– Program of 27 grants, $3.7 million will aid planning, acquisition, and protection of critical habitat and open space in Commonwealth; funded through Keystone Recreation, Park and Conservation Fund Act, grants will acquire more than 9,200 acres of habitat and open space areas.

1999 State unveils new offender-identification system in Lower Allen Township Police Department central booking; new system combines electronic fingerprinting, digitalized photo-imaging network and video arraignment to aid in police investigations and increase public safety.

– Twenty-seven State colleges and universities will receive $349,500 grant to help disadvantaged secondary-school students considering higher education and strengthen existing services for disadvantaged college students.

– Governor Ridge announces findings of State's annual School Violence and Weapons Possession Report; results show slight decline in violence and weapons possessions in 1997-1998 school year; fifty-four districts will receive about $1 million to further develop local violence and substance-abuse prevention programs.

– Independent poll shows State voters favor school vouchers that allow parents to send children to school of choice, receive tuition discount at chosen school.

2000 Grants of $1.4 million will integrate county criminal and juvenile justice record-keeping systems with Justice Network (JNET); funds will further aid law enforcement community to obtain timely information on offenders.

– Governor Ridge signs Education Empowerment Act to help children in State's lowest performing schools receive quality education through $25 million funding and potent new management tools for improvements.

– SAT report for 2000 shows that State students are more technologically literate; report shows dramatic increase in classroom computer literacy and Internet activity, average increase in mathematics scores, and steady verbal scores.

– More than $1 million is earmarked for grants in counties and municipalities to fund startup of recycling projects; fund will ensure that State reduces amount of waste sent to landfills and incinerators, thereby creating greener environment.

DIRECTORY OF STATE SERVICES

OFFICE OF THE GOVERNOR
222 Main Capitol Bldg., Room 225
Harrisburg, PA 17120
Fax: 717-772-8284
Governor: 717-787-2500
http://www.state.pa.us/PA_Exec/Governor/overview/html

Administrative Office
207 Finance Bldg.
Harrisburg, PA 17120
Fax: 717-783-4374
Secretary: 717-787-9945

Budget Office
238 Main Capitol
Harrisburg, PA 17120
Fax: 717-787-4590
Secretary: 717-787-4472

Washington, DC Office
444 N. Capitol St., Suite 700
Washington, DC 20001
Fax: 202-624-7831
Director: 202-624-7828

OFFICE OF THE LIEUTENANT GOVERNOR
200 Main Capitol Bldg.
Harrisburg, PA 17120
Fax: 717-783-0150
Lieutenant Governor: 717-787-3300
http://www.state.pa.us//PA_Exec.State/

Pardons Board
Harristown II 15th Floor
333 Market St.
Harrisburg, PA 17126
Fax: 717-772-3135
Secretary: 717-787-2596

SECRETARY OF COMMONWEALTH (State Department)
North Office Building, Room 302
Harrisburg, PA 17120
Fax: 717-787-1734
Secretary of Commonwealth: 717-787-7630

OFFICE OF THE ATTORNEY GENERAL
16th Floor, Strawberry Square
Harrisburg, PA 17120
Fax: 717-787-8242
Attorney General: 717-787-3391
http://www.attorneygeneral.gov/

Civil Law Office
15th Floor, Strawberry Square
Harrisburg, PA 17120
Fax: 717-772-4526
Executive Deputy Attorney General: 717-787-1100

Criminal Law Division
16th Floor, Strawberry Square
Harrisburg, PA 17120
Fax: 717-783-5431
Executive Deputy Attorney General: 717-787-2100

Management Services Office
14th Floor, Strawberry Square
Harrisburg, PA 17120
Fax: 717-787-1190
Director: 717-787-4499

Public Protection Office
14th Floor, Strawberry Square
Harrisburg, PA 17120
Fax: 717-787-1190
Consumer Advocate Fax: 717-783-7152
Executive Deputy Attorney General: 717-787-9716

TREASURER (TREASURY DEPARTMENT)
129 Finance Bldg.
Harrisburg, PA 17120
Fax: 717-783-9760
State Treasurer: 717-787-2465

AUDITOR GENERAL
229 Finance Bldg.
Harrisburg, PA 17120
Fax: 717-783-4407
Auditor General: 717-787-2543
http://www.auditorgen.state.pa.us/

DEPARTMENTS

AGING DEPARTMENT
Rachel Carson Office Bldg.
400 Market St.
MSSOB 6th Floor
Harrisburg, PA 17120-1919
Fax: 717-772-6842
Secretary: 717-783-1550
http://www.state.pa.us/PA_Exec/Aging/overview.html

AGRICULTURE DEPARTMENT
2301 N. Cameron St.
Harrisburg, PA 17110-9408
Fax: 717-772-9709
Secretary: 717-772-2853
http://www.state.pa.us/PA_Exec/Agriculture/index.htm

BANKING DEPARTMENT
333 Market St., 16th Floor
Harrisburg, PA 17101-2290
Fax: 717-787-8773 or 717-783-8427
Secretary: 717-787-6991
http://www.state.pa.us/PA_Exec/Banking/overview.html

COMMUNITY AND ECONOMIC DEVELOPMENT DEPARTMENT
433 Forum Bldg.
Harrisburg, PA 17120
Fax: 717-787-6866
Secretary: 717-787-3003
http://www.DCED.state.pa.us/PA_Exec/Commerce/overview.html

Industrial Development Authority
480 Forum Building
Harrisburg, PA 17120
Fax: 717-772-2890
Executive Director: 717-787-6245

CONSERVATION AND NATURAL RESOURCES DEPARTMENT
P.O. Box 8767
Harrisburg, PA 17120
Fax: 717-772-9106
Secretary: 717-787-2869
http://www.dcnr.state.pa.us/

CORRECTIONS DEPARTMENT
P.O. Box 598
Camp Hill, PA 17011-0598
Fax: 717-787-0132
Commissioner: 717-975-4860
http://www.state.pa.us/PA_Exec/Corrections/overview.html

EDUCATION DEPARTMENT
333 Market St.
Harrisburg, PA 17126-0333
Fax: 717-783-4517
Secretary: 717-787-5820
http://www.cas.psu.edu/pde.html

Administration Office
333 Market St.
Harrisburg, PA 17126-0333
Fax: 717-787-7222
Chief of Staff: 717-787-9744

Elementary and Secondary Education Office
333 Market St.
Harrisburg, PA 17126-0333
Fax: 717-783-6802
Commissioner: 717-787-2127

Postsecondary and Higher Education Office
333 Market St.
Harrisburg, PA 17126-0333
Fax: 717-783-0583
Commissioner: 717-787-5041

ENVIRONMENTAL PROTECTION DEPARTMENT
P.O. Box 2063
Harrisburg, PA 17105-2063
Fax: 717-705-4980
Secretary: 717-787-2814
http://www.dep.state.pa.us/

Air, Recycling, and Radiation Management
P.O. Box 2063
Harrisburg, PA 17105-2063
Fax: 717-787-8885
Deputy Secretary: 717-772-2724

Chief Counsel
P.O. Box 2063
Harrisburg, PA 17105-2063
Fax: 717-783-8926
Chief Counsel: 717-787-4449

Management and Technical Services
P.O. Box 2063
Harrisburg, PA 17105-2063
Fax: 717-772-5996
Deputy Secretary: 717-787-7116

Mineral Resources Management
P.O. Box 2063
Harrisburg, PA 17105-2063
Fax: 717-783-0930
Deputy Secretary: 717-783-5338

Pollution Prevention and Compliance Assistance
P.O. Box 2063
Harrisburg, PA 17105-2063
Fax: 717-783-8926
Deputy Secretary: 717-783-0540

Water Management
P.O. Box 2063
Harrisburg, PA 17105-2063
Fax: 717-772-5996
Deputy Secretary: 717-787-4686

GENERAL SERVICES DEPARTMENT
Room 515, North Office Bldg.
Harrisburg, PA 17125

Fax: 717-772-2026
Secretary: 717-787-5996
http://www.dgs.state.pa.us/

Administration
Room 515, North Office Bldg.
Harrisburg, PA 17125
Fax: 717-772-2026
Deputy Secretary: 717-783-8720

Central Services
Room 503, North Office Bldg.
Harrisburg, PA 17125
Fax: 717-772-5317
Deputy Secretary: 717-783-5028

Procurement
Room 414, North Office Bldg.
Harrisburg, PA 17125
Fax: 717-783-6241
Deputy Secretary: 717-787-5295

Public Works
18th & Herr Sts., Room 100
Harrisburg, PA 17125
Fax: 717-772-3473
Deputy Secretary: 717-787-7095

HEALTH DEPARTMENT
P.O. Box 90
Harrisburg, PA 17108
Fax: 717-772-6959
Secretary: 717-787-6436
http://www.health.state.pa.us/

Administration and Management
P.O. Box 90
Harrisburg, PA 17108
Fax: 717-772-6959
Executive Deputy Secretary: 717-783-0296

Public Health Programs
P.O. Box 90
Harrisburg, PA 17108
Fax: 717-772-6959
Deputy Secretary: 717-787-9857

Health Planning & Assessment
P.O. Box 90
Harrisburg, PA 17108
Fax: 717-772-6959
Deputy Secretary: 717-787-8804

Laboratories Bureau
P.O. Box 500
Exton, PA 19341-0500
Fax: 610-436-3346
Director: 610-363-8500

Quality Assurance
P.O. Box 90
Harrisburg, PA 17108
Fax: 717-772-6959
Deputy Secretary: 717-783-1078

INSURANCE DEPARTMENT

1326 Strawberry Square
Harrisburg, PA 17120
Fax: 717-783-1969
Insurance Commissioner: 717-783-0442
http://www.state.pa.us/PA_Exec/Insurance/overview.html

Erie Regional Office

P.O. Box 6142
Erie, PA 16512
Fax: 814-871-4888
Regional Manager: 814-871-4466

Philadelphia Regional Office

1400 Spring Garden St.
State Office Bldg., Room 1701
Philadelphia, PA 19130
Fax: 215-560-2648
Regional Manager: 215-560-2630

Pittsburgh Regional Office

300 Liberty Ave.
304 State Office Bldg.
Pittsburgh, PA 15222
Main Phone: 412-565-7648
Regional Manager: 412-565-5020

LABOR AND INDUSTRY DEPARTMENT

Seventh & Forster Streets
Harrisburg, PA 17120
Fax: 717-783-5225
Secretary: 717-787-3756
http://www.li.state.pa.us/

Administration

Labor & Industry Bldg.
Harrisburg, PA 17120
Fax: 717-772-1461
Deputy Secretary: 717-787-8667

Compensation & Insurance

Labor & Industry Bldg.
Harrisburg, PA 17120
Fax: 717-787-8826
Deputy Secretary: 717-787-9948

Unemployment Insurance Programs

Labor & Industry Bldg.
Harrisburg, PA 17120
Fax: 717-787-8826
Deputy Secretary: 717-787-13907

Labor and Management Relations

Labor & Industry Bldg., 17th Fl.
Harrisburg, PA 17120
Fax: 717-787-8826
Deputy Secretary: 717-787-7882

Workforce Development and Safety

Labor & Industry Bldg., Room 1720
Harrisburg, PA 17120
Fax: 717-772-1461
Deputy Secretary: 717-787-8665

MILITARY AND VETERANS AFFAIRS DEPARTMENT

Fort Indiantown Gap
Annville, PA 17003
Fax: 717-861-8481
Adjutant General: 717-861-8500
http://www.state.pa.us/PA_Exec/Military_Affairs/

PUBLIC WELFARE DEPARTMENT

Box 2675
Harrisburg, PA 17105
Fax: 717-772-2062
Secretary: 717-787-2600
http://www.state.pa.us/PA_Exec/Public_Welfare/overview.html

REVENUE DEPARTMENT

11th Floor, Strawberry Square
Harrisburg, PA 17128-1100
Fax: 717-787-3990
Secretary: 717-783-3680

State Lottery

2850 Turnpike Industrial Dr.
Middletown, PA 17057
Fax: 717-986-4767
Executive Director: 717-986-4759

TRANSPORTATION DEPARTMENT

555 Walnut St., 9th Fl.
Forum Place
Harrisburg, PA 17101-1900
Fax: 717-787-1738
Secretary: 717-787-2838
http://www.state.ppt.psu.edu/

Administration

555 Walnut St., 9th Fl.
Forum Place
Harrisburg, PA 17101-1900
Fax: 717-787-1738
Deputy Secretary: 717-787-5628

Aviation

555 Walnut St., 9th Fl.
Forum Place
Harrisburg, PA 17101-1900
Fax: 717-787-1738
Deputy Secretary: 717-783-2026

Highway Administration

555 Walnut St., 9th Fl.
Forum Place
Harrisburg, PA 17101-1900
Fax: 717-787-1738
Deputy Secretary: 717-787-6875

Local and Area Transportation

555 Walnut St., 9th Fl.
Forum Place
Harrisburg, PA 17101-1900
Fax: 717-787-1738
Deputy Secretary: 717-787-8197

Planning
555 Walnut St., 9th Fl.
Forum Place
Harrisburg, PA 17101-1900
Fax: 717-787-1738
Deputy Secretary: 717-787-3154

Safety Administration
555 Walnut St., 9th Fl.
Forum Place
Harrisburg, PA 17101-1900
Fax: 717-705-1046
Deputy Secretary: 717-787-3928

BOARDS AND COMMISSIONS

ARCHITECTURE LICENSURE BOARD
P.O. Box 2649
Harrisburg, PA 17105
Fax: 717-787-7769
President: 717-783-4866

ARTS COUNCIL
216 Finance Bldg.
Harrisburg, PA 71720
Fax: 717-783-2538
Executive Director: 717-787-6883

CLAIMS BOARD
200 N 3rd St., Suite 700
Harrisburg, PA 17101-1501
Fax: 717-787-0415
Chairman: 717-787-3325

CIVIL SERVICE COMMISSION
P.O. Box 569
Harrisburg, PA 17108-0569
Fax: 717-772-5120
Chairman: 717-787-3094
http://www.scsc.state.pa.us/

DELAWARE RIVER PORT AUTHORITY
2 Riverside Dr.
P.O. Box 1949
One Port Center
Camden, NJ 08101
Fax: 609-968-2000
Executive Director: 609-968-2000

EDUCATION BOARD
333 Market St.
Harrisburg, PA 17126-0333
Fax: 717-787-7306
Executive Director: 717-787-3787

EMERGENCY MANAGEMENT AGENCY
P.O. Box 3321
Harrisburg, PA 17105-3321
Fax: 717-651-2021
Director: 717-651-2001

ENVIRONMENTAL HEARING BOARD
P.O. Box 8457
Harrisburg, PA 17105-8457

Fax: 717-783-4738
Chairman: 717-787-3483

ETHICS COMMISSION
309 Finance Bldg.
P.O. Box 11470
Harrisburg, PA 17108-1470
Fax: 717-787-0806
Executive Director: 717-783-1610

FISH AND BOAT COMMISSION
P.O. Box 67000
Harrisburg, PA 17106-7000
Fax: 717-657-4033
Executive Director: 717-657-4515
http://www.state.pa.us/PA_Exec/Fish-Boat/pfbchom2.html

GAME COMMISSION
2001 Elmerton Ave.
Harrisburg, PA 17110-9797
Fax: 717-772-0502
Executive Director: 717-787-3633
http://www.state.pa.us/PA_Exec/PGC/index.htm

GENERAL STATE AUTHORITY
North Office Bldg., Room 515
Harrisburg, PA 17125
Fax: 717-720-3902
Executive Director: 717-787-5996

HIGHER EDUCATION ASSISTANCE AGENCY
1200 N. 7th St.
Harrisburg, PA 17102-1444
Fax: 717-720-3902
President & CEO: 717-720-2860

HIGHER EDUCATIONAL FACILITIES AUTHORITY
P.O. Box 990
Camp Hill, PA 17001-0900
Fax: 717-975-2215
Executive Director: 717-975-2200

HISTORICAL AND MUSEUM COMMISSION
P.O. Box 1026
Harrisburg, PA 17108-1026
Fax: 717-705-0482
Executive Director: 717-787-2891
http://www.state.pa.us/PA_Exec/Historical_Museum/overview.html

HOUSING FINANCE AGENCY
2101 N Front St.
P.O. Box 8029
Harrisburg, PA 17105
Fax: 717-780-3905
Executive Director: 717-780-3911

HUMAN RELATIONS COMMISSION
P.O. Box 3145
Harrisburg, PA 17105-3145
Fax: 717-787-0420
Executive Director: 717-787-4410

LIQUOR CONTROL BOARD
Northwest Office Bldg.
Harrisburg, PA 17124-0001
Fax: 717-772-3714
Chairman: 717-787-5230
http://www.lcb.state.pa.us/

MILK MARKETING BOARD
2301 N. Cameron St., Room 110
Harrisburg, PA 17110-9408
Fax: 717-783-6492
Chairman: 717-787-4786
http://www.state.pa.us/PA_Exec/Milk/

MUNICIPAL RETIREMENT SYSTEM
P.O. Box 1165
Harrisburg, PA 17108
Fax: 717-783-8363
Secretary: 717-783-8124

PROBATION AND PAROLE BOARD
P.O. Box 1661
1101 N. Front St.
Harrisburg, PA 17104-2517
Fax: 717-772-2157
Chairman: 717-787-5100

PUBLIC SCHOOL EMPLOYEES RETIREMENT SYSTEM
P.O. Box 125
Harrisburg, PA 17108
Fax: 717-772-5372
Executive Director: 717-787-8540

PUBLIC TELEVISION NETWORK COMMISSION
P.O. Box 397
Hershey, PA 17033
Fax: 717-533-4236
General Manager: 717-533-6010
http://www.pall.org/

PUBLIC UTILITY COMMISSION
North Office Bldg.
P.O. Box 3265
Harrisburg, PA 17105-3265
Fax: 717-787-5813
Chairman: 717-783-7349
http://www.state.pa.us/PA_Exex/Public_Utility/

SECURITIES COMMISSION
1010 N. 7th St., 2nd Floor
Harrisburg, PA 17102-1410
Fax: 717-783-5122
Chairman: 717-787-6828
http://www.psc.state.pa.us/

Chief Counsel
1109 State Office Bldg.
Philadelphia, PA 19130
Fax: 215-560-3977
Chief Counsel: 215-560-2088

Enforcement and Litigation Office
806 State Office Bldg.
Pittsburgh, PA 15222-1210

Fax: 412-565-7646
Assistant Director: 412-565-5083

STATE EMPLOYEES CREDIT UNION
P.O. Box 67013
Harrisburg, PA 17106-7013
Fax: 717-772-9251
Chairman: 717-234-8484

STATE EMPLOYEES RETIREMENT SYSTEM
P.O. Box 1147
Harrisburg, PA 17108-1147
Fax: 717-783-7300
Executive Director: 717-787-9657

STATE POLICE
1800 Elmerton Ave.
Harrisburg, PA 17110
Fax: 717-787-2948
Commissioner: 717-772-6924
http://www.state.pa.us/PA_Exec/State_Police/

STATE PUBLIC SCHOOL BUILDING AUTHORITY
Box 990
Camp Hill, PA 17001-0990
Fax: 717-975-2215
Executive Director: 717-975-2200

STATE TAX EQUALIZATION BOARD
705 Transportation & Safety Bldg.
Harrisburg, PA 17120-0909
Fax: 717-787-3860
Chairman: 717-787-5950

TURNPIKE COMMISSION
P.O. Box 67676
Harrisburg, PA 17106-7676
Fax: 717-986-9649
Chairman: 717-939-9551
http://www.state.paturnpike.com/

MEMBERS OF CONGRESS

SENATE

SEN. ARLEN SPECTER (R) (b. 1930); 4th Term;
Phone: 202-224-4254; Fax: 202-228-1229;
E-mail: senator_specter@specter.senate.gov.

www.senate.gov/~specter/

SEN. RICK SANTORUM (R) (b. 1958); 1st Term;
Phone: 202-2254-6324; Fax: 202-228-0604;
E-mail: pennstater@santorum.senate.gov.

www.santorum.senate.gov

HOUSE

ROBERT A. BRADY (D-1st) (b. 1945); 2nd Term;
Phone: 202-225-4731; Fax: 202-225-0088;
E-mail: robert.brady@mail.house.gov.

www.house.gov/robertbrady/

CHAKA FATTAH (D-2nd) (b. 1956); 3rd Term;
Phone: 202-225-4001; Fax: 202-225-5392;
E-mail: pa02@legislators.com.

www.house.gov/fattah/

ROBERT A. BORSKI (D-3rd) (b. 1948); 9th Term;
Phone: 202-225-8251; Fax: 202-225-4628;
E-mail: robert.borski@mail.house.gov.

www.house.gov/borski/

RON KLINK (D-4th) (b. 1951); 4th Term;
Phone: 202-225-2565; Fax: 202-2256-2274

JOHN E. PETERSON (R-5th) (b. 1938); 2nd Term;
Phone: 202-225-5121; Fax: 202-225-5796;
E-mail: pa05@legislators.com.

www.house.gov/johnpeterson/

TIM HOLDEN (D-6th) (b. 1957); 4th Term;
Phone: 202-225-5546; Fax: 202-226-0996;
E-mail: pa06@legislators.com.

www.house.gov/holden/

CURT WELDON (R-7th) (b. 1947); 7th Term;
Phone: 202-225-2011; Fax: 202-225-8137;
E-mail: curtpa07@mail.house.gov.

www.house.gov/curtweldon

JIM GREENWOOD (R-8th) (b. 1951); 4th Term;
Phone: 202-225-4276; Fax: 202-225-9511

www.house.gov/greenwood/

BUD SHUSTER (R-9th) (b. 1932); 14th Term;
Phone: 202-225-2431; Fax: 202-225-2486; E-mail: (None).

www.house.gov/shuster/

DON SHERWOOD (R-10th) (b. 1941); 1st Term;
Phone: 202-225-3731; Fax: 202-225-9594;
E-mail: pa10@legislators.com.

www.house.gov/sherwood

PAUL E. KANJORSKI (D-11th) (b. 1937); 8th Term;
Phone: 202-225-6511; Fax: (None);
E-mail: paul.kanjorski@mail.house.gov.

www.house.gov/kanjorski

JOHN P. MURTHA (D-12th) (b. 1932); 14th Term;
Phone: 202-225-2065; Fax: 202-225-5709;
E-mail: murtha@mail.house.gov.

www.house.gov/murtha/

JOSEPH M. HOEFFEL III (D-13th) (b. 1950); 1st Term;
Phone: 202-225-6111; Fax: 202-226-0611;
E-mail: pa13@legislators.com.

www.house.gov/hoeffel/

WILLIAM J. COYNE (D-14th) (b. 1936); 10th Term;
Phone: 202-225-2301; Fax: 202-225-1844;
E-mail: pa14@legislators.com.

www.house.gov/coyne

PAT TOOMEY (R-15th) (b. 1961); 1st Term;
Phone: 202-225-6411; Fax: 202-2256-0778;
E-mail: pa15@legislators.com.

www.house.gov/toomey

JOSEPH R. PITTS (R-16th) (b. 1939); 2nd Term;
Phone: 202-225-2411; Fax: 202-225-2013;
E-mail: pitts.PA16@mail.house.gov.

www.house.gov/pitts/

GEORGE W. GEKAS (R-17th) (b. 1930); 9th Term;
Phone: 202-225-4315; Fax: 202-225-8440;
E-mail: gwgwebsite@mail.house.gov.

www.house.gov/gekas/

MIKE DOYLE (D-18th) (b. 1953); 3rd Term;
Phone: 202-225-2135; Fax: 202-225-3084;
E-mail: rep.doyle@mail.house.gov.

www.house.gov/doyle/

WILLIAM F. GOODLING (R-19th) (b. 1927); 13th Term;
 Phone: 202-225-5836; Fax: 202-226-1000;
E-mail: pa19@legislators.com.

www.house.gov/goodling/

FRANK R. MASCARA (D-20th) (b. 1930); 3rd Term;
Phone: 202-225-4665; Fax: 202-225-3377;
E-mail: pa20@legislators.com.

www.house.gov/mascara

PHILIP S. ENGLISH (R-21st) (b. 1956); 3rd Term;
Phone: 202-225-5406; Fax: 202-225-3103;
E-mail: pa21@legislators.com.

www.house.gov/english/

TWENTIETH CENTURY GOVERNORS

STONE, WILLIAM A. (1846-1920), twenty-third governor of Pennsylvania (1899-1903), was born in Delmar, Pennsylvania, the son of Israel and Amanda Howe Stone, who were farmers. He was reared on a farm and attended local public schools, as well as a normal school before he enlisted, at the age of seventeen, in the Union Army during the Civil War. His father forced him to return home because he was underage, but the determined young man re-enlisted a year later and served until the close of the war.

Afterwards, Stone once again studied at the State Normal School, and supported himself by farming and teaching. In 1868 he began reading law, and gained admittance to the bar two years later. He practiced law in Wellsboro and entered public life in 1874 as Tioga County District Attorney. In 1877 he moved to Pittsburgh, and was appointed U.S. District Attorney for western Pennsylvania, under the administrations of Presidents Hayes, Garfield, Arthur, and Cleveland.

President Cleveland had forbidden officials of the Federal Government from taking any active part in politics, and when Stone publicly supported Governor Beaver's reelection campaign, he was promptly fired from his long-held position.

Stone was elected to the U.S. Congress in 1891, serving until 1898, when he ran for Governor. In office, he balanced the State budget. However, his appointment of Republican Party leader, Matthew S. Quay, to the U.S. Senate at a time when Quay was being charged with misappropriation of State funds, cost him much public esteem.

At the end of his term, Stone retired to private law practice with his son, Stephen, for many years. He eventually served as Prothonotary of the Supreme Court in 1915, and of the Superior Court in 1916.

Stone was married to Ellen Stevens in 1870, with whom he had six children. He died in Philadelphia in 1920.

PENNYPACKER, SAMUEL W. (1843-1916), twenty-fourth governor of Pennsylvania (1903-07), was born at Phoenixville, Chester County, Pennsylvania, the son of Isaac, a physician, and Anna Whitaker Pennypacker. He was educated at the Grovemont Seminary in Phoenixville and at the West Philadelphia Institute.

Pennypacker was preparing to enter Yale College when the Civil War effort called him away, and he went to the front in 1863 as a member of the 26th Pennsylvania Regiment, which met the first onslaught of forces at Gettysburg. After the war, he read law with Peter McCall, and at the University of Pennsylvania, and he was admitted to the bar in 1866, beginning his law practice soon afterwards.

Two years later, Pennypacker's scholarly approach to law led to his election as president of the Law Academy of Philadelphia. He co-edited the *Digest of the English Common Law Reports*, and wrote his own *Pennypacker's Supreme Court Cases*, a four-volume set, as well as a volume of Pennsylvania colonial cases. He became active with the Board of Public Education in the State in 1886, acting as controller of public schools in the 29th ward until 1889. At that time, Governor Beaver appointed him to the Court of Common Pleas, where he served for eleven years.

Pennypacker researched the early history of Philadelphia and the vicinity, and was the author of thirty-seven books and papers on related subjects, several of which were translated into Dutch and German. He was also a trustee of the University of Pennsylvania and a commissioner for the Valley Forge Reservation.

In 1902, Pennypacker ran on the Republican ticket for Governor and won. His aim was to reform the politics in Harrisburg, as evidenced by a bill requiring personal voter registration, penalties for election violations, and requirements for civil service examinations for some State offices, all of which he forced through the Legislature in a special session. He also encouraged the institution of a Pennsylvania State police force to guard against abuses by coal and iron companies' security forces.

After leaving office, Pennypacker returned to Pennsylvania, where he died in 1916.

STUART, EDWIN SYDNEY (1853-1937), twenty-fifth governor of Pennsylvania (1907-11), was the son of Hugh and Anna Newman Stuart, small farmers outside of Philadelphia. After attending public schools, he worked in Leary's bookstore in Philadelphia as a clerk. In time, he rose to the post of head clerk, and eventually bought out the Leary enterprise.

Stuart was well liked by his staunch Republican friends in the city and was president of the Young Republicans in 1880. Two years later, he was elected president of the State party, a post he held until 1891. The State League of Republican Clubs also elected him president in 1884. He was on the Philadelphia Select Council in 1886; in 1891, was elected mayor of that city. His term was highlighted by his investigation of a city trustee and other members of his own party who had embezzled large sums of money from the city.

Stuart's continued favor with the Republican Party led to his nomination for governor in 1906, and he won by a 40,000 margin over his Democratic opponent. During his administration, acts relating to public health and pure food, as well as child labor, were passed. When his State treasurer discovered that the State Capitol Building should have cost much less than its thirteen million dollars, he also found that the State had been misled by a number of officials who had padded the actual cost when reporting it to the State auditors. The scandal caused Stuart political embarrassment, although he indicted the guilty parties. As a result, a law requiring specific legislative authority for disbursement of State funds was passed, and a legislative reference bureau was created.

Stuart was also instrumental in starting a State campaign against tuberculosis, encouraging the Legislature to appropriate one million dollar to the Department of Health to help stop the spread of the disease. He also encouraged large appropriations for common schools in the State.

Stuart returned to his business interests in Philadelphia after his term ended; he died in that city in 1937, after many years of retirement.

TENER, JOHN K. (1863-1946), twenty-sixth governor of Pennsylvania (1911-15), was born in County Tyrone, Ireland, the son of George Evans and Susan Wallis Tener, who moved the family to Pittsburgh in 1873. He was educated in public schools before getting a job as a clerk with Oliver Brothers and Phillips in 1881.

Tener then worked as an officer in the Chartiers Valley Gas Company from 1887 until 1891, when he moved to Charleroi, Pennsylvania. There, he served as president of the First National Bank, becoming prominent in the city's financial community.

Tener was also increasingly active in politics with the Republican Party. He was elected to the U.S. Congress in 1908, where he represented his community until 1911. At that time, he took over the Governor's seat after a tight battle against the Democratic and Keystone Party candidates. When the automobile boom began in the nation, Tener started to update the State highway system in Pennsylvania. He also set new controls on public utilities, and he created a department of labor and industries. A new school code for vocational training was introduced during his term, and he also supported prison reforms. The Pennsylvania Historical Commission was also approved, as was a plan to expand the capital area.

Tener left gubernatorial office in 1915. His early years as a professional baseball player for the Pittsburgh National League club, as well for clubs in Baltimore and Chicago, earned him a position as president of the National Baseball League. He was also head of an insurance company and another financial institution in Pittsburgh.

Tener was married to Harriet Day in 1889; she died in 1935. He had a second marriage in 1936 to Leone Evans. He died in Charleroi in 1946.

BRUMBAUGH, MARTIN G. (1862-1930), twenty-seventh governor of Pennsylvania (1915-19), was born in Huntingdon County, the son of George Boyer and Martha Peightal Brumbaugh, German immigrant farmers. After attending local public schools, he studied at Juniata College in Huntingdon, where he graduated in 1881. He studied higher mathematics at the State Normal School in Millersville in 1882 then did postgraduate studies at both Harvard University (1891-92), and the University of Pennsylvania (1892-94), receiving an A.D. degree in 1893 and a Ph.D. in 1894.

Brumbaugh worked as a professor for one year, and was also a superintendent of schools in his home county during 1884-90. After receiving his doctorate, he was chosen to take the Chair of Pedagogy at the University of Pennsylvania in 1894, and then studied at the University of Jena, Germany, in 1895. In 1898 he was elected president of the Pennsylvania State Teacher's Association, and among other activities, was a member of the Pennsylvania Historical Society and the Pennsylvania German Society.

In addition, Brumbaugh was for several years an appointed minister in the church of the Christian Brethren, or "Dunkers," and wrote the *Juniata Bible Lectures* in 1890, as well as the *History of the Church of the German Baptists Brethren* in 1895. He was also the author of several books on secular history and pedagogy; *Stories of Pennsylvania* (1893) and *The Making of a Teacher* (1905) are two examples. During 1900-02, he was First Commissioner of Education for Puerto Rico.

After several years of study and teaching, he was supported by three parties (Republican, Keystone and Liberty) for Governor of the State in 1914, and was elected despite President Roosevelt's support for the Democratic candidate. Brumbaugh, a conservative scholar, led an administration characterized by its libertarian ideals. He vetoed hundreds of bills such as those dealing with child labor, conservation, and labor interests. He did, however, organize Council of Defense when World War I broke out.

Brumbaugh returned to a quiet life after the governorship with his wife, the former Anna Konigmacher, and his two children until his death in 1930.

SPROUL, WILLIAM C. (1870-1928), twenty-eighth governor of Pennsylvania (1919-23), was born in Octorary, Pennsylvania to William Hall and Deborah Slokom Sproul, Quaker farmers. He attended Swarthmore College, obtaining a B.S. degree in 1891, and soon afterwards, bought a half interest in the *Chester Times* newspaper. For several years, he was active in the newspaper business, subsequently becoming the sole proprietor of the *Times* and also the Chester Morning Republican.

In Chester, Sproul also became interested in shipbuilding as director of the Roach Shipyards, and in 1900 he organized the Seaboard Steel Casting Company to manufacture steel castings for ship and locomotive building. Sproul soon gained more influence in a variety of businesses, such as a traction company, an in-terstate railway, a brick manufacturing company, and several financial institutions.

Sproul's public career began in 1896 when he was elected to the Pennsylvania State Senate as a Republican; through successive reelections, he served in that body for a total of twenty-two years. Together with all of his business holdings, he became one of the most powerful political leaders in the State, and in 1918, he was elected by a wide margin for the governorship.

Sproul's commitment to building a State highway system had begun when he was in the Senate, and while he was Governor, the State spent 125 million dollars on highway building and improvement, more than the total amount spent for constructing railroads, canals, public institutions, and the State capital during the previous 100 years. Sproul's progressive term also brought about a reorganization of the public school system and relief measures for disabled veterans of World War I.

In 1921, Sproul created a new department of public welfare. He was also involved in quelling the steel and coal strikes in the State, calling out the State National Guard when violence broke out, and a fuel commission to deal with the situation peacefully. He was a Presidential contender in the 1920 Republican National Convention, but withdrew his name after several ballots. Deeply interested in State history, he was chairman of the Historical Commission from its creation in 1913 (by an act of which he was the author) until 1919.

Sproul built and endowed the Sproul Observatory at Swarthmore College, which contained at that time one of the largest telescopes in the world. During his professional life, he received honorary LL.D. degrees from nine educational institutions. After leaving office, he returned to his business interests in Chester.

Sproul was married to Emeline Roach in 1892; the couple had two children. He died in 1928.

PINCHOT, GIFFORD (1865-1946), twenty-ninth and thirty-first governor of Pennsylvania (1923-27 and 1931-35), was born to James and Mary Eno Pinchot in Simsbury, Connecticut. His father was a New York City merchant as well as a city official on the executive committee in charge of the erection of the Statue of Liberty.

Pinchot attended Phillips Exeter Academy and received his B.A. from Yale University in 1889. At first, he considered working as a forester, since his father was the founder of the Yale School of Forestry and conducted summer school courses in the woods near his Milford, Pennsylvania estate. However, forestry had not become a bona fide profession as yet in the United States, and after a visit to the English Forest School and the Ecole National Forestiere in France, he studied forestry in the French Alps and the Vosges.

After Pinchot's return to the U.S. in 1891, he made a survey of the forest lands for the Phelps-Dodge Company in Pennsylvania and Arizona, and in 1892, began the first systematic forest work done in the nation on the estate of George W. Vanderbilt in North Carolina. He became a consulting forester when he opened an office in New York City at the end of these studies, and from 1893 to 1895, he continued to work for the Vanderbilt's as well as for the State of New Jersey.

In 1895, Pinchot encouraged the creation of a National Forest Commission as part of the Federal Government, and a year later was a member of the commission, being appointed by the U.S. Secretary of Agriculture to become chief of the division two years later. He held that post until 1905, when the division was placed directly under the Department of Agriculture and the Forest Reserves became the National Forests. Thereafter the practice of forestry sanctioned by the government grew by leaps and bounds; the aggregate area of national forest lands increased from forty-one million acres to 120 million acres. Stringent regulations were placed on all commercial uses of forestlands to insure stream protection and the prevention of hazardous industrial waste at a time when much of the nation's former forest land had been decimated by loggers, miners, and ranchers.

As a result of his dealings in Washington, Pinchot became increasingly involved in politics. In 1912, he took an active role in the organization of the Progressive Party, and when Theodore Roosevelt failed to win the Republican nomination for President in 1912, Pinchot helped draft the new party's platform, becoming one of the main Progressive leaders.

Pinchot continued to work as a member of the National Conservation Commission, and in 1920, he was appointed Forester of the State of Pennsylvania. Two years later, he won the Republican nomination for Governor of the State in a contest with the "Old Guard" of the party, and won the election, serving for four years.

During his term, Pinchot reorganized the State government into a more efficient group of departments, and tightened the budget to relieve a thirty million dollar deficit. He also backed legislation providing for care and treatment of mentally ill persons, as well as a system of annuities for retired State employees.

Under the constitution at the time, Pinchot could not succeed himself; he left political life for the next four years, but in 1930 was reelected Governor (also a revolt against the "Old Guard"). His second term brought new problems, since the Depression had just begun to take its toll on the State. He advocated new banking, corporation, and building and loan association laws. He also approved 20,000 miles of road improvements, and laws to stop unfair use of labor injunctions. Utility rates were reduced during his term, and he sponsored a pension fund for the blind. After his second term, Pinchot continued to battle for conservation of the world's natural resources.

Only a few days before Pinchot's his death in New York City, President Harry S. Truman submitted to the Economic and Social Council of the United Nations a plan for a world conservation conference that Pinchot had been urging for thirty-seven years.

Pinchot was married to Cornelia Elizabeth Bruce in 1914. He died in 1946.

FISHER, JOHN S. (1867-1940), thirtieth governor of Pennsylvania (1927-31), was born in South Mahoning Township, Pennsylvania, the son of Samuel Royer and Maria McGaughey Fisher, who were farmers. In between his chores on the farm, he attended local public schools and later worked his way through the Pennsylvania State Normal School, from which he graduated in 1886. For seven years, he taught school, and then was the principal of the Plumville School as well as the public schools in Indiana, Pennsylvania.

In the meantime, Fisher began to study law in the office of Samuel Cunningham. After admittance to the bar in 1893, he began a partnership with Cunningham that lasted until 1927. At the same time, he was interested in development of the State, and became president of the Beech Creek Railroad Company and other coal and land companies.

Fisher's political career began when he was elected to the State Senate, serving from 1901 to 1909. During one of his terms, he was chair of an investigating committee that exposed frauds in connection with the construction of the new State Capitol Building in Harrisburg. He was a delegate to the Republican National Convention in 1916, and State Commissioner of Banking from 1919 to 1922. He was also a member of the Commission on Constitutional Revision.

Fisher defeated his Democratic opponent in the 1926 gubernatorial election by more than 700,000 votes. His administration was characterized by a concern for a tight fiscal policy, elimination of voting fraud, and more highway construction. He created a State Department of Revenue in 1929, the year of the Wall Street stock market crash. In that year, he also approved a motor vehicle code providing for an annual inspection of all autos, among other things. He also supervised an extensive building program that included a new mental hospital; another State normal school, State office buildings, and a farm show building. About 450,000 acres were added to the State parklands while he was in office.

When Gifford Pinchot won his second term in 1930, Fisher returned to law practice with his son, Robert, and pursued new business interests. He was chairman of the board of the National Union Fire Insurance Company in Pittsburgh, and was director of Forbes National Bank until his death in that city.

Fisher was married to Hapsie Miller. He died in 1940.

EARLE, GEORGE H. (1890-1974), thirty-second governor of Pennsylvania (1935-39), was born in Devon, Pennsylvania, the son of George H. and Catherine French Earle, prominent members of the community. After finishing his early education, he attended Harvard University during 1909-11, and then continued his education at Temple University, where he received his LL.B. degree in 1915.

During World War I, Earle served as commander of a submarine chaser, and was a second lieutenant in the skirmishes along the Mexican border in 1917. He also served in the Navy during World War II. He worked with his father in his Pennsylvania Sugar Company, but later broke away to found his own Flamingo Sugar Company in Philadelphia.

Earle was U.S. Minister to Austria in 1933-34, and returned home to accept the nomination for Governor of Pennsylvania by the Democratic Party. He received his LL.D. and LH.D. from Waynesburg College in 1935, the year he took office.

After forty years of exile, the Democrats were again in control at Harrisburg. During Earle's administration, additional revenues were provided to cover a deficit incurred by unemployment relief, and these, with substantial Federal appropriations, met the emergency. An act against old Sunday blue laws legalized Sunday sports, and municipalities were allowed to hold referendums to decide whether or not to show movies after 2 p.m. on Sundays. Laws further restricting child labor was signed, and a forty-four-hour work week was established.

Earle also created a Department of Public Assistance to take care of the unemployed, the aged, the blind, and poor mothers. Revenue for this was derived from liquor and other taxes. Floods ravaged the State during his term, further dwindling the supply of money as relief was sent out, and flood control structures were built. Earle also signed a bill which permitted the Pennsylvania Turnpike plans to begin.

"Pennsylvania's Little New Deal," as his administration was called, did not last very long, since the State's voters returned to the traditional party in the next election. Earle returned to his sugar business and was U.S. Minister to Bulgaria in 1940. He was also Assistant Governor of Samoa in 1945 before retiring to private life completely.

Earle was married Huberta Potter in 1916, with whom he had four children; he had a second marriage to Jacqueline Sacre in 1945. He died in 1974.

JAMES, ARTHUR H. (1883-1973), thirty-third governor of Pennsylvania (1939-43), was born in Plymouth, Pennsylvania to Rachel Edwards and James David, a coal miner. He studied at the local public schools and began working in his youth in the anthracite mines near home as a breaker boy.

In 1904, James completed his law studies at Dickinson College in Carlisle, and began to practice law in his hometown. The next year, he opened another office in Wilkes-Barre and soon became active in politics.

James was elected district attorney of Luzerne County in 1919, a position he held until 1926 when he was elected Lieutenant Governor of the State. After 1932, he was elected Superior Court Judge of the State. While in that office, he led a campaign against Democratic Governor Earle, pointing to the extravagance of his administration and attacking his alleged coercion of steel and coal workers into the Congress of Industrial Organizations. Other charges of graft and corruption in the State government allowed for an easy Republican victory in 1938, with James winning the governorship.

During his tenure, James cut the State administration drastically, and eliminated political expenditures and graft as much as possible. He created a State Department of Commerce, and provided funds to extend the Pennsylvania Turnpike. Despite harsh criticism from "New Dealers" and other liberals, James signed a bill banning sit-down strikes. The State liquor laws were also reinforced through limitation of the number of licenses. Despite heavy demands for relief, his administration was able to balance the budget. When World War II broke out, he created a bipartisan council of defense in the State as well as a Selective Service Board. He also organized the Citizens' Defense Corps to guard civilians against air raids.

When James left office, he returned to his private law practice in Wilkes-Barre. He was twice married, first to Ada Morris, with whom he had two children, and then to Emily Radcliffe. He died in 1973.

MARTIN, EDWARD (1879-1967), thirty-fourth governor of Pennsylvania (1943-47), was born in Washington Township, Pennsylvania, the son of Joseph T. and Hannah Bristor Martin, who were farmers. He attended local public schools and was studying at Waynesburg College when the Spanish-American War broke out, and he left school to join the army. Later, as a corporal, he fought alongside fellow Pennsylvanians in the Philippines. In 1899, the nineteen-year-old sergeant was honorably discharged, but he returned home to join the National Guard at the same rank.

Martin finished his studies at Waynesburg in 1901, and continued his military career, working up to the position of major by 1910. Six years later, he guarded the Mexican border from Villa's forces. During World War I, he went to France as a major, but was promoted to lieutenant colonel by 1918. He was wounded in battle and demonstrated enough heroism to merit a Distinguished Service Cross and a Purple Heart decorated with an Oak Leaf Cluster.

Martin continued moving up the military ranks to brigadier-general in 1922. In 1939, he was promoted to command the Pennsylvania National Guard, and when that body was federalized two years later, he was sent to lead in training maneuvers. However, his advancing age forced him to retire from active military work, and he decided to pursue his Republican political interests full time. He had been chair of the party's State Committee from 1928 to 1934, and adjutant-general of Pennsylvania between 1939 and 1943, except when he fought in 1941-42.

In 1942, Martin was offered a chance at the governorship. His campaign slogan was "Pennsylvania needs a governor familiar with the terror and tumult of war," which apparently struck a chord in the hearts of Pennsylvanians. But he did not run the State like the army. He supported liberal reforms such as increased funds for the unemployed, occupational insurance, and inspec-

tions of coalmines and industrial plants. In 1944, he advocated a jump in Pennsylvania oil prices to "stimulate production and keep the industry healthy by insuring good wages to employees." Some of these measures surprised fellow Republicans. However, in 1945 he returned to the party line when he vetoed a bill to further increase unemployment compensation.

Martin resigned from gubernatorial office to take a seat in the U.S. Senate in 1947, where he served until 1959. He was married in 1908 to Charity Scott, and their two children survived him when he died in 1967.

BELL, JOHN C. (1892-1974), thirty-fifth governor (temporary) of Pennsylvania (1947), was born in Philadelphia to Fleuretta DeBenneville Myers and John Cromwell Bell. His father was Attorney General of the State while he was a boy, and he decided to follow in his father's footsteps by studying law at the University of Pennsylvania, graduating with an LL.D. degree in 1917. He was admitted to the State bar that same year.

From 1919 to 1922, Bell was assistant solicitor for the City of Philadelphia, and was then appointed assistant to the local district attorney (1922-25). Governor Arthur James chose him as State Secretary of Banking in 1938, and four years later he was elected Lieutenant Governor of Pennsylvania. In the latter position, he held a key role in the State Senate and acted as chair of the State Board of Pardons.

When Governor Martin resigned office early to take a seat in the U.S. Senate, Bell automatically took over and filled out the term until the James Duff's term began. The new governor appointed him to the State Supreme Court in 1950, where he eventually became Chief Justice. Upon his retirement in 1972, Bell worked as a special consultant to the district attorney until his death.

Bell was married to Sarah A. Baker in 1918, and the couple had three sons and two daughters. He died at Wynnewood, Pennsylvania in 1974.

DUFF, JAMES H. (1883-1970), thirty-sixth governor of Pennsylvania (1947-51), was born in Mansfield (now Carnegie), Pennsylvania, the son of Joseph Miller, a minister, and Margaret Morgan Duff. After graduation from the town's high school, he studied at Princeton University, where he received an A.B. degree in 1904. He also studied at the University of Pennsylvania Law School and at the University of Pittsburgh, which awarded him an LL.B. degree in 1907. For many years afterwards, he practiced in partnership with two other lawyers in Pittsburgh. Duff owned a number of oil wells in East Pennsylvania, but lost most of his profits during the Depression.

A Republican, he was a delegate to the national conventions in 1932, 1936, and 1940. Governor Martin appointed him Attorney General of the State in 1943. It was in this office that he first took measures to curb industrial pollutants in the lakes and streams of the State, where he loved to fish. He continued to advocate controls on industry when he took over the governorship, reinstating and raising taxes to provide funds for conservation and public health. He also encouraged development of the Philadelphia port and new bridges along the Delaware River.

Ridding the rivers of contamination, expanding overcrowded mental hospitals, and increasing teachers' pay were high on Duff's priority list. Throughout his term, he was able to work independently of the strong Republican political machine directed by manufacturer, Joseph Grundy. He also helped women's rights by approving "equal pay for equal work," despite union opposition.

Duff left office to serve in the U.S. Senate for six years. He married Jean Taylor in 1909; they had no children. He died in 1970.

FINE, JOHN S. (1893-1978), thirty-seventh governor of Pennsylvania (1951-55), was a native of Luzerne County, Pennsylvania, near the town of Nanticoke. His parents were Margaret Croop and Jacob W. Fine, a coalminer. He went to local public schools and from the age of eight, earned money by milking and plowing on a coal company farm. While still a teenager, he worked as a news reporter for the Wilkes-Barre *Record*, earning money to study at the Dickinson School of Law during 1911-14.

Fine began his law practice in Wilkes-Barre, but soon afterward, World War I broke out and he served as a sergeant from 1917-19. After the Armistice, he was in Ireland and decided to attend Trinity University in Dublin for postgraduate study while awaiting his formal discharge.

Fine resumed his law practice when he returned home, and also became increasingly involved in politics. He was secretary of the Luzerne County Republican Committee in 1920, attending the Republican National Convention in Chicago as an alternative delegate that same year. In 1922-23, he was the county's Republican chairman. He had campaigned for Gifford Pinchot in 1926, and the following year, Pinchot appointed him a judge of the Court of Common Pleas in his home county; he served in that post until 1947.

Governor Duff appointed him to fill a vacant seat in the State Superior Court in 1947, which gave Fine enough notoriety to try for the governor's seat in 1950. Despite his opponents' charges that he tolerated corruption and vice and that he ran a "political machine," Fine, who had been vice-president of the Pennsylvania Council of Churches for two years, stood up with a testimonial signed by 117 clergymen of all faiths as to his "high moral character."

During his administration, Fine was an advocate of "belt tightening and strict Spartan living." The State was in debt over one billion dollars for the first two years, and he tried to get a one percent income tax approved to offset it. The Assembly opposed it, but did eventually pass sales and use taxes. He also reorganized the State government structures, including the Department of Health, and was also concerned with expanding the State highways and purifying the State's rivers and streams.

When Fine left office, he returned to Nanticoke, where he was director of the First National Bank. He was married to Helene Pennebecker Morgan, and was the father of two sons. He died in Wilkes-Barre in 1978.

LEADER, GEORGE M. (1918-), thirty-eighth governor of Pennsylvania (1955-59), was the son of Guy Alvin and Beulah Boyer Leader, poultry breeders in York County, Pennsylvania. He attended public schools in York and the York Collegiate Institute in 1934-35 then graduated with a B.S. degree from the University of Pennsylvania in 1939, majoring in education. Later, he did graduate work there at the Wharton School of Finance (1942).

Leader was secretary-treasurer in his father's firm for a time, but World War II led him to the U.S. Navy as an Ensign in 1942. In 1946, he left that post, after surviving as a supply officer on the aircraft carrier, *Randolph*. He then returned to his father's business.

In 1949, Leader opened his own hatchery, Willow Brook Farm, in Dover, Pennsylvania. He also became increasingly active in the Democratic Party; he was chairman of the York County Democratic Committee when he was elected State Senator in 1950. In the latter year, he was elected Governor, one of two Democrats to have been voted into that office in fifty years.

The State budget for Leader's first two years was over one billion dollars, and to meet these expenses, he levied new taxes while increasing the old ones. He modernized the business procedures

in the administration by installing uniform accounting methods in all departments and the first electronic computing system.

Leader was concerned with expanding educational and public assistance in the State; he stressed a focus on the cure rather than the custody in dealing with mental patients, for the first time in history. The Health Department was reorganized to deal with problems posed by narcotic and alcoholic addiction, and he approved new programs to deal with increasing juvenile delinquency in a changing society.

Leader created an Office of Administration to make the State government operate more efficiently, and was also concerned about conservation and urban renewal.

Leader returned to his hatchery interests after leaving office. He married Mary Jane Strickler Leader, with whom he had four children.

LAWRENCE, DAVID LEO (1889-1966), thirty-ninth governor of Pennsylvania (1959-63), was the son of Catherine Conwell and Charles B. Lawrence, a teamster leader. He grew up in a working class neighborhood in Pittsburgh, and was early exposed to a liberal political environment through his father, who held a county job in the city. He attended Catholic schools and then a commercial high school for a two-year business course. At the age of fourteen, Lawrence worked for Democratic Party leader William J. Brennan as an office boy, which, after several years, led to a job as a ward worker for the party.

In 1912, Lawrence worked as a pageboy for Woodrow Wilson at the Democratic National Convention; after that, he served in an official capacity at most of the party's conventions. He was a registrar for Pittsburgh in 1914-24, and was appointed Collector of Internal Revenue for the Western District of Pennsylvania under President Roosevelt in 1933-34. Afterwards, he was chair of the Democratic State Committee until he was elected Secretary of the Commonwealth under Governor Earle (1935-39).

For a time, Lawrence headed an insurance company in Pittsburgh and continued as the city's party leader. He had been accused of graft and corruption for passing out illegal contracts while serving in Harrisburg, but was acquitted after lengthy trials. In 1945, the cloud from that scandal had dissipated enough to allow him to be elected mayor of Pittsburgh. He served an unprecedented four terms, until 1958, when he tried successfully for the governorship.

Lawrence's programs to clean Pittsburgh's air quality were continued statewide. He also tried to lead the State out of a recession. "Pennsylvania's problems are not political. They are economic," he said at the beginning of his term. He increased sales taxes to balance a debt-ridden budget, but continued with most of former Governor Leader's programs and personnel. He also encouraged the building of such projects as the William Penn Memorial Museum and Archives Building in the State capital.

After leaving Harrisburg, Lawrence returned to his hometown with his wife, the former Alice Golden, and three children (two of his sons had died in an auto accident in 1942). After pursuing private business interests for three years, he died in 1966.

SCRANTON, WILLIAM WARREN (1917-), fortieth governor of Pennsylvania (1963-67), was born in Madison, Connecticut, the son of Worthington and Marion Warren Scranton, controllers of a large gas and water company, and descendants of the family for which Scranton, Pennsylvania was named. Both his parents were active in the city's commercial and community affairs, and Scranton was exposed early to State politics, especially the powerful Pennsylvania Republican Party leaders.

Scranton was sent to the private Fessenden School in Massachusetts, and prepared for college at the Hotchkiss School in Connecticut. In 1939, he received an A.B. degree in history from Yale University then completed his law studies there in 1946. His studies were interrupted for a time by World War II, when he served as a lieutenant in the Air Force.

Scranton practiced law in Scranton with the firm of O'Malley, Harris, Warren & Hill for a short time in 1947, but was soon involved in industry and business rather than his profession. He attempted to revitalize Pennsylvania's industries by branching out into new endeavors. One of the new industries he brought to the city was a million-dollar Chrysler plant, which provided thousands of jobs. He was also director of the Scranton-Lackawanna Trust Co. from 1952 until 1956.

Meanwhile, Scranton was following in his family's footsteps by becoming active in the Republican Party. Calling himself a "liberal on civil rights, a conservative on fiscal policy," he served on the staff of both John F. Dulles and Christian Herter in 1959-60. In the latter year, he was elected a U.S. Representative. His congressional record was indicative of his beliefs in easing unemployment and poverty by supporting big industries. He served on the House Bank and Finance Committee, approving foreign aid and the Peace Corps support through that body. He also supported a Democratic-sponsored bill to redevelop areas of urban blight and poverty.

In 1962, former President Eisenhower prompted Scranton to run for Pennsylvania Governor, and he received unanimous support from both his party and the State's voters. In office, Scranton called for a reorganization of the State's legislative districts, and created a Department of Mental Health as well as a State Board of Education. His main purpose, however, was to continue revitalizing the State's economy through support to industry. To that end, he funded the Pennsylvania Industrial Development Authority, and began a campaign to encourage foreign investment in the State. He also supported a search for new markets and uses for coal.

After leaving office, Scranton continued his public life in Washington as a member of the President's Price Commission (1971-72), General Advisory Commission on Arms Control and Disarmament (1972-76), and consultant to President Ford during his entire term. He was also an Ambassador to the United Nations.

Scranton married Mary Lowe Chamberlain in 1942; the couple had four children. His son, William Worthington Scranton, has been Pennsylvania's Lieutenant Governor.

SHAFER, RAYMOND P. (1917-), forty-first governor of Pennsylvania (1967-71), was a native of New Castle, Pennsylvania, and son of David and Mina Belle Miles Shafer, who were farmers. He attended local schools before studying at Allegheny College, where he received an A.B. degree cum laude in 1938. He then studied law at Yale University, earning his LL.B. degree in 1941.

After passing both the New York and Pennsylvania bar exams, Shafer settled in New York City to join the firm of Winthrop, Stimson, Putnam & Roberts, while holding another office in Meadville, Pennsylvania. He served as an officer for the Navy from 1942-45, working on P.T. boats in the Pacific. The Republican lawyer soon became active in politics and was appointed District Attorney of Crawford County (1948-56), where he served until election to the State Senate. He was Lieutenant Governor under William Scranton.

In 1966, Shafer was elected by fifty-two percent of voters to become Governor of the State. As with Scranton, Shafer encouraged foreign investors in the State's industries, and approved of cutting back on regulations for business. Targeted as a "moderate Republican," and one of the "favored sons" of the party, he often sided with Richard Nixon's policies, especially his efforts to end the Vietnam War "with honor."

After Shafer finished his term, he returned to his private law practice and activities with the native Pennsylvanian religious organization, the Disciples of Christ. He is a past chair of the National Commission on Marijuana and Drug Abuse and the Board of Trustees at Allegheny College. He resides in Crawford County, Pennsylvania.

Shafer married Jane Harris Davies in 1941; he is the father of three children.

SHAPP, MILTON J. (1912-1988), forty-second governor of Pennsylvania (1971-79), is a native of Cleveland, Ohio and the son of Eva Smelsey and Aaron Shapiro, a hardware wholesaler. He studied at public schools in Cleveland and then attended Case Institute of Technology, where he received a B.S. in electrical engineering in 1933. Despite his education, he was forced to work as a truck driver and salesman during the Great Depression.

When World War II broke out, Shapp signed up with the army. He also changed his name legally to Shapp. By 1946, he had risen through the military ranks to captain.

After Shapp's discharge, he founded the Jerrold Electronics Corporation and became active with a number of organizations as a consultant, including the Peace Corps, Department of Commerce, and the National Public Advisory Committee on Area Redevelopment. His work under President Kennedy's administration gave him the support to run for governor in 1966, but he lost against the Republican candidate.

Four years later, however, Shapp won the gubernatorial chair. A campaign staffer blamed his earlier failure on his lack of "charisma." Shapp was also described as a man of "single-minded intensity," ill at ease among political back-slappers. "Milt knows more about the subject he's talking about than anybody I've ever worked with, including Jack Kennedy," Shapp's campaign manager said after his success. "Of course, Kennedy had national problems and was a very smart guy. But Shapp knows *his* subject, the State of Pennsylvania, better."

During his administration, Shapp pushed for improved low-cost hospitalization and life insurance in the State through regulations. He also instituted a State lottery, which has helped to bring in a large portion of the State's budget money each year. Thirty percent of lottery revenues go to lowering the property taxes for elderly citizens.

After Pennsylvania's State law prohibiting a governor from succeeding himself was repealed, Shapp was able to be reelected in 1974. He served until 1979, when a Republican resurgence took over State politics.

Shapp, a multimillionaire from the electronics corporation he sold in 1970, returned to private life in Philadelphia after his last term. He has been the recipient of numerous awards, including B'nai B'rith's Reuben J. Miller award, Pennsylvania AFL-CIO's "Man of the Year" award in 1963, and awards from the National Business League and Pennsylvania State Baptist Convention. In 1973, he was elected chair of the Mid-Atlantic Governor's Conference, an alliance aimed at gaining more Federal assistance for social welfare.

Shapp played the violin; his 1970 campaign song, "Stand Up and Fight for the Things You Stand For" came from one of his two unproduced musical comedies.

Shapp died on November 24, 1988.

THORNBURGH, RICHARD (1932-), forty-third governor of Pennsylvania (1979-1987), was born in Pittsburgh, Pennsylvania, the son of Charles G. and Alice Sanborn Thornburgh. He studied engineering at Yale University, obtaining a B.E. degree in 1954. Soon afterwards, he decided to pursue a law degree at the University of Pittsburgh, receiving an LL.D. with high honors in 1957.

For more than a decade, Thornburgh was active in the private sector as a business attorney and advisor. He worked for the Aluminum Company of America from 1957 to 1959, and with the Pittsburgh law firm of Kirkpatrick, Lockhart, Johnson & Hutchinson for ten years thereafter. He rejoined that firm after his return from Washington, D.C. in 1977.

A U.S. District Attorney for Western Pennsylvania from 1969 to 1975, Thornburgh gained acclaim for his attack on organized crime and official corruption. He created the first special grand jury in the nation to investigate racketeering and corruption under the Organized Crime Control Act of 1970, attempting to root out corruption at all levels of government, and obtaining indictments and convictions of nearly fifty persons for abuse of public office.

Thornburgh also probed the growing interstate pornography industry and its ties to organized crime, and prosecuted industrial polluters and more than one-hundred narcotics dealers. Never personally losing a case, he kept the office success rate at ninety percent. Much of his drive for social causes came out of a personal tragedy, according to Thornburgh. In 1960, his first wife was killed, and a son suffered brain damage as a result of an auto accident. "That's a jolt. It made me think about what I wanted to do with my life, what I could contribute to the world."

Thornburgh's contributions led President Ford to appoint him Assistant U.S. Attorney General in 1975. In the Department of Justice in Washington, he helped restore morale and reduce bureaucracy, instituting a Public Integrity Department to combat official corruption on a statewide basis.

Thornburgh got his first close look at the workings of State government in 1967-68, when he was a part of the historic Constitutional Convention. Later, he served on the Pittsburgh Home Rule Charter Advisory Committee. His successes led to favor from the Republican Party, and when he tried for the governorship in 1978, he stood out as a shining underdog against Governor Shapp's administration, which had been riddled by indictments and resignations within the staff. He beat the Democratic candidate by more than 200,000 votes with his "big time crime buster image."

Upon taking office, Thornburgh promised to substitute a merit system for patronage in State government and to limit spending and curb scandals. In 1979, he had to deal with his first big crisis when the nuclear accident at Three Mile Island in central Pennsylvania occurred. Keeping cool under pressure, Thornburgh tried to reassure the State when he himself was not sure of the facts surrounding the accident. "There isn't any Republican or Democratic way to deal with a nuclear crisis. Nobody has ever had to deal with this kind of accident before. You just do what you can for people." His handling of the situation was praised by President Jimmy Carter when he visited the area.

Thornburgh was reelected to a second term in 1982, serving until 1987. He has won numerous awards, including "Man of the Year," from the City of Pittsburgh in 1975, and a Special Medallion from the Federal Drug Enforcement Administration in 1973, for "significant personal efforts to help eliminate drug abuse."

Thornburgh married Virginia Judson, a former New York schoolteacher, in 1963; the couple has four sons.

CASEY, ROBERT P. (1932-), forty-fourth governor of Pennsylvania (1987-1994) was born in Jackson Heights, New York on January 9, 1932, the son of Alphonsus and Marie Casey. His family moved to Scranton while he was still young. In 1949, he graduated from Scranton Preparatory School. He attended Holy Cross College in Worcester, Massachusetts on a basketball scholarship, and received his B.A. in English in 1953.

In 1956, Casey received his J.D. from George Washington University Law School. He worked as an associate for the Washington, D.C. firm of Covington & Burling for two years, then returned to Scranton and began his own law practice. In 1963, he was elected to the State Senate, where he distinguished himself as an environmentalist. He served as First Vice President of the Pennsylvania State Constitutional Convention in 1967. From 1969 to 1977, he was Pennsylvania Auditor General. After leaving this office, he returned to his law practice.

Casey was elected Governor of Pennsylvania in 1986. After taking office, his administration focused efforts on several vital issues, including creating jobs and economic opportunity, cleaning the environment, fighting drug abuse, and improvements in the schools.

Casey established the Pennsylvania Economic Development Partnership in 1987. Composed of business executives, college presidents, labor leaders, and local officials, the group sought to create new jobs and new investment in the State. At the core of the group was the "Governor's Response Team," which created and saved many jobs in large companies that included Ford Electronics in Montgomery County, PPG Industries in Allegheny County, and Prudential Asset Management in Lackawanna County. The Partnership also gave support to nine Industrial Resource Centers in the State to assist small and medium-sized businesses in putting new technologies into practice that would enhance productivity and create new jobs.

Casey enacted a new program to rebuild Pennsylvania's local water and sewage systems. Called "PENNVEST," the program's twenty-five year, two-and-a- half billion-dollar plan sought to help communities replace water and sewage treatment facilities that failed health and safety standards, or were too small to support new economic growth. Also included in the plan were a statewide recycling program and some of the toughest environmental enforcement actions in the nation.

Casey's leadership in the area of environmental protection earned him honor in such organizations as the Pennsylvania Resources Council, the Audubon Council of Pennsylvania, the Pennsylvania Environmental Council, and the National Recreation and Parks Association.

Casey also created a comprehensive program to combat the drug crisis in the State. Called PENNFREE," the plan of 90 million dollars was geared toward doubling Pennsylvania's anti-drug efforts, including massive support for State and local law enforcement, expansion of school and community-based drug education and prevention programs, and treatment and solutions of problems created by drug abuse, such as child abuse, homelessness, domestic violence, and AIDS.

Other innovative projects initiated and supported by Casey included a program to expand prenatal and neonatal care; increased funding for child nutrition, special education, and child protection; a commitment of State dollars for the Women, Infants, and Children nutrition program; appointment of an advisor on child care policy and the creation of model child care centers in State facilities; and a program to provide home health care for the elderly and support for caregivers of elderly relatives in their homes.

Casey's administrative cabinet had twice as many women and Blacks than any previous governor; he also named the first Black State police chief in the nation and the first Black woman in U.S. history to sit on the Supreme Court.

Casey stepped down from his position as Pennsylvania's chief executive at the end of his second term in January 1994, upon election of Republican candidate, Tom Ridge.

Casey was married to Ellen Theresa Harding in 1953. The couple have eight children and eighteen grandchildren.

RIDGE, TOM (1945-), forty-fifth Governor of Pennsylvania (1995-), was born in Munhall, Pennsylvania to a working-class family. After completing his early education, he received an academic scholarship to Harvard. In 1967, he graduated with honors and earned a degree in government studies.

Ridge was drafted into the U.S. Army in 1969 and served for two years as an infantry staff sergeant. He received the Bronze Star for Valor, the Vietnamese Cross of Gallantry, and the Combat Infantry Badge. After returning home, he began studying law and completed his law education at Dickinson Law School in 1972.

Ridge was an Erie County Assistant District Attorney before election to the U.S. House of Representatives in 1982. He represented four counties, and won reelection five times during his years of representing Pennsylvania in Washington. He supported laws to expand economic development, encourage economic revitalization of inner cities, and provide affordable housing. Laws passed during his tenure included the Bank Enterprise Law, the Neighborhood Mortgage Lenders Accountability Law, the Community Enterprise Revitalization Law, the Stewart B. McKinney Homeless Assistance Block Grant Law, and the John Heinz Neighborhood Development Program Law.

In February 1993, Ridge announced his candidacy for Governor of Pennsylvania. He was well endorsed by Republicans in the State, and was the favored candidate by such newspapers as the *Pittsburgh Post Gazette*, the *Williamsport Sun Gazette*, the *Erie Daily Times/Morning News*, the *Centre Daily Times*, and the *Warren Times Observer*. After winning the primary, he went on to become successful in the November election against incumbent Democrat, Robert Casey.

Ridge is married to the former Michele Moore, who is Executive Director of the Erie County Library System. The couple has two children.

DICTIONARY OF PLACES

Population figures and demographic information are official U.S. Census Bureau finals for 1990. When two figures are shown, separated by a slash, the first figure is the 1990 and the second is the U.S. Census Bureau 1999 estimate—the most recent available. Year 2000 census supplements will be available in the Fall of 2001.

AARONSBURG, Village; Centre County; Pop. 500; Zip Code 16820; Elev. 1200; Lat. 40-53-59 N, Long. 077-27-13 W; NW of Lewisburg in central Pennsylvania; Settled in 1775; Named for Aaron Levy, who founded the town in 1786.

ABBOTTSTOWN, Borough; Adams County; Pop. 689 / 639; Zip Code 17301; Elev. 544; Lat. 39-53-11 N, Long. 076-59-06 W; S Pennsylvania; on Beaver Creek.

ABINGTON, Township; Montgomery County; Pop. 59,084; Zip Code 19001; Elev. 350; Lat. 40-07-14 N, Long. 075-07-06 W; SE Pennsylvania; Founded in 1714, when the Abington Presbyterian Church was built.

ACMETONIA, Village; Allegheny County; Pop. 1,200; Zip Code 15024; located near Pittsburgh in W Pennsylvania.

ACOSTA, Village; Somerset County; Pop. 500; Zip Code 15520; Elev. 1,880; Lat. 40-06-37 N, Long. 079-04-09 W; S Pennsylvania.

ADAH (alt. ANTRAM), Village; Fayette County; Pop. 600; Zip Code 15410; Elev. 920; Lat. 39-53-47 N, Long. 079-55-20 W; SW Pennsylvania.

ADAMSTOWN, Borough; Berks and Lancaster Counties; Pop. 1,119 / 1,167; Zip Code 19501; Elev. 500; Lat. 40-14-28 N, Long. 076-03-24 W; SE Pennsylvania. William Bird, an ironmaster, obtained a patent for 356 acres here in 1739.

AKRON, Borough; Lancaster County; Pop. 3,471 / 3,952; Zip Code 17501; Elev. 400; Lat. 40-09-24 N, Long. 076-12-09 W; SE Pennsylvania; Was settled by Germans in the 1800s and was incorporated as a borough in 884.

ALBA, Borough; Bradford County; Pop. 222 / 171; Zip Code 16910; Elev. 1,340; Lat. 41-42-18 N, Long. 076-49-43 W; N Pennsylvania.

ALBANY, Village; Berks County; Pop. 1,109; Zip Code 19529; Lat. 40-02-16 N, Long. 079-52-18 W; SE Pennsylvania; Named for James II, whose Scottish title was Duke of Albany.

ALBION, Borough; Erie County; Pop. 1,818 / 3,401; Zip Code 16401; Elev. 904; Lat. 41-53-26 N, Long. 080-22-00 W; NW Pennsylvania; Was settled in 1815. First known as Jackson Cross Roads.

ALBURTIS, Borough; Lehigh County; Pop. 1,428 / 2,113; Zip Code 18011; Elev. 440; Lat. 40-30-39 N, Long. 075-36-12 W; Near Allentown in E Pennsylvania.

ALDAN, Borough; Delaware County; Pop. 4,671 / 4,556; Elev. 120; Lat. 39-55-17 N, Long. 075-17-18 W; suburb of Chester in SE Pennsylvania.

ALDEN, Village; Luzerne County; Pop. 800; Zip Code 18634; Lat. 41-10-55 N, Long. 076-00-46 W; E central Pennsylvania; Suburb of Nanticoke and Wilkes-Barre.

ALIQUIPPA, Borough; Beaver County; Pop. 17,094 / 12,320; Zip Code 15001; Elev. 725; Lat. 40-38-12 N, Long. 080-14-25 W; W Pennsylvania. It was named for Iroquois Indian Queen Aliquippa, who is said to have lived on the site of McKeesport in the 1750s. Her name may mean 'hat' in Iroquois. Aliquippa was called "Queen of the Delaware," although she was probably Mohawk.

ALLEGHENY, Village; Allegheny County; Pop. 650; Zip Code 15076; W central Pennsylvania; Unincorporated suburb of Pittsburgh.

ALLEN, Township; Northampton County; Pop. 1,856; Zip Code 18067; Named for William Allen, who was Chief Justice of Pennsylvania (1750-74) and received 3,000 acres here in 1748.

ALLENPORT, Borough; Washington County; Pop. 735 / 541; Zip Code 15412; Lat. 40-05-53 N, Long. 079-50-57 W; SW Pennsylvania.

ALLENTOWN, City; Seat of Lehigh County; Pop. 103,758 / 100,160; Zip Code 181+; Elev. 364; Near Bethlehem and Easton in E Pennsylvania; Incorporated as a borough in 1811 and as a city in 1867. Originally known as Northampton Town, the city was first settled by German immigrants in the 1720s.

ALLISON, Village; Fayette County; Pop. 1,040; Zip Code 15413; Elev. 1,060; Lat. 39-59-20 N, Long. 079-51-54 W; SW Pennsylvania.

ALLISON PARK, Borough; Allegheny County; Pop. 5,600; Zip Code 15101; Elev. 861; W Pennsylvania; Suburb of Pittsburgh.

ALTOONA, City; Blair County; Pop. 57,078; Zip Code 166+; Elev. 1,171; Lat. 40-31-07 N, Long. 078-23-42 W; S central Pennsylvania.

ALUTA, Village; Northampton County; Pop. 700; Zip Code 18064; Lat. 40-46-15 N, Long. 075-19-02 W; E Pennsylvania.

ALVERDA, Village; Indiana County; Pop. 700; Zip Code 15710; Elev. 1,917; Lat. 40-37-49 N, Long. 078-51-26 W; 25 mi. N of Johnstown in W central Pennsylvania; Name means "all green."

AMBLER, Borough; Montgomery County; Pop. 6,628 / 6,437; Zip Code 19002; Lat. 40-09-16 N, Long. 075-13-19 W; SE Pennsylvania. Named for a prominent family of early settlers one of whom, Joseph Amber, settled here in 1723.

AMBRIDGE, Borough; Beaver County; Pop. 9,575 / 7,207; Zip Code 15003; Elev. 775; Lat. 40-35-21 N, Long. 080-13-31 W; W Pennsylvania. It was named for the American Bridge Company, which brought the community called Harmony Society here in 1901.

AMBRIDGE HEIGHTS, Village; Beaver County; Pop. 2,000; Zip Code 15003; Elev. 751; Lat. 40-35-30 N, Long. 080-12-43 W; Suburb of Ambridge in Pittsburgh area, in W Pennsylvania.

ANCIENT OAKS, Village; Lehigh County; Pop. 1,800; Zip Code 18062; Lat. 40-32-50 N, Long. 075-35-23 W; E central Pennsylvania; Suburb of Allentown.

ANDALUSIA, City; Bucks County; Pop. 4,500; Zip Code 19020; Elev. 37; Lat. 40-04-10 N, Long. 074-58-18 W; Near Philadelphia in SE Pennsylvania; On the Delaware River, named for 95-acre estate of Charles T. Biddle, which he named for the southern region of Spain.

ANITA, Village; Jefferson County; Pop. 600; Zip Code 15711; Elev. 1500; Lat. 41-00-05 N, Long. 078-57-48 W; Near Punsatavney in mountainous region in W central Pennsylvania.

ANNVILLE, Elev. 420; Lat. 40-19-46 N, Long. 076-30-56 W; on Quitapahilla Creek; Was formerly called Millerstown for Abraham Miller, who laid it out in 1762, but the name was changed at Millers suggestion to honor his wife Ann.

APOLLO, Borough; Armstrong County; Pop. 2,212 / 1,758; Zip Code 15613; Elev. 809; Lat. 40-34-53 N, Long. 079-34-00 W; W Pennsylvania; Once known as Warren for an Indian trader who of-

ten stopped here, it was renamed in 1848 by Dr. Robert Mckisson, physician, poet, and student of the classics.

ARCHBALD, Borough; Lackawanna County; Pop. 6,295 / 6,277; Zip Code 18403; Elev. 919; Lat. 40-48-31 N, Long. 079-31-19 W; NE Pennsylvania. It was called White Oak Run until 1846 when the Delaware and Hudson Canal Company began exploiting its coal deposits and named it for James Archbald, a company engineer.

ASHLAND, Borough; Schuylkill County; Pop. 4,737 / 3,598; Zip Code 17921; Elev. 885; Lat. 40-46-54 N, Long. 076-20-46 W; E central Pennsylvania. Named for Henry Clay's estate in Lexington, Kentucky by Samuel Lewis in 1847.

ASHLEY, Borough; Luzerne County; Pop. 3,512 / 2,941; Zip Code 18706; Elev. 643; Lat. 41-12-37 N, Long. 075-53-49 W; E Pennsylvania. Town was known as Scrabbletown, Coalville, Skunktown, Peestone, Hightown, Newton, Hendricksburg, Nanticoke Junction and Alberta since it was settled in 1810. Current name was adopted in 1871 for a prominent family of coal operators including Herbert Henry Ashley of Wilkes-Barre.

ASPINWALL, Borough; Allegheny County; Pop. 3,284 / 2,221; Zip Code 15215; Elev. 800; Lat. 40-29-29 N, Long. 079-54-18 W; SW Pennsylvania; On Allegheny River. Founded in 1796 and named for the Aspinwall family, early landowners.

ASTON, Borough and Township; Delaware County; Pop. 6,900 (Township 13,704); Zip Code 19014; Elev. 200; Suburb of Philadelphia near Delaware state line and Delaware River.

ASYLUM, Township; Bradford County; Pop. 843; Lat. 41-42-47 N, Long. 076-20-02 W; Towanda area. Colony was originally established in 1794 for refugees of the French Revolution, promoted by Robert Morris and John Nicholson.

ATGLEN, Borough; Chester County; Pop. 669 / 1,061; Zip Code 19310; Elev. 504; Lat. 39-56-57 N, Long. 075-58-26 W; SE Pennsylvania.

ATHENS, Borough; Bradford County; Pop. 3,662 / 3,317; Zip Code 18810; Elev. 772; Lat. 41-57-26 N, Long. 076-31-06 W; N Pennsylvania. Athens took the name of the township, founded in 1786, and named for the capital of Greece, probably because the ring of hills surrounding the city resembles the Greek metropolis.

ATLAS, Village; Northumberland County; Pop. 1,527; Zip Code 17851; Elev. 1,160; Lat. 40-47-59 N, Long. 076-25-41 W; Near Mt. Carmel and Kulpmont in E central Pennsylvania.

ATLASBURG, Village; Washington County; Pop. 550; Zip Code 15004; Elev. 1,120; Lat. 40-20-28 N, Long. 080-22-59 W; SW Pennsylvania.

AUBURN, Borough; Schuylkill County; Pop. 999; Zip Code 17922; Elev. 500; Lat. 40-35-54 N, Long. 076-05-37 W; E central Pennsylvania.

AUDUBON, Montgomery County; Pop. 4,400; Zip Code 19407; Elev. 200; Lat. 40-54-38 N, Long. 075-59-31 W; SE Pennsylvania; Unincorporated suburb of Norristown and Philadelphia. Located on the Perkiomen Creek, this borough is nearby the former estate of John James Audubon, the ornithologist for whom it was named.

AVALON, Borough; Allegheny County; Pop. 6,240 / 5,197; Elev. 727; Lat. 41-50-20 N, Long. 076-52-27 W; SW Pennsylvania. First settled in late 1700s by Irish trader James Taylor. Originally known as Birmingham for Captain John Birmingham, who purchased land from Taylor. In 1874, it was incorporated as West Bellevue, and in 1894 the name was changed to Avalon, a Celtic word meaning "orchard," or "land of apples."

AVELLA, Village; Washington County; Pop. 1,109; Zip Code 15312; Elev. 960; Lat. 40-16-30 N, Long. 080-27-39 W; Approx. 25 mi. SW of Pittsburgh in W Pennsylvania.

AVIS, Borough; Clinton County; Pop. 1,718 / 1,488; Zip Code 17721; Elev. 600; Lat. 41-11-05 N, Long. 077-18-51 W; Central Pennsylvania; Named for Avis Cochran, daughter of one of the chief promoters of the town in the early 20th century.

AVOCA, Borough; Luzerne County; Pop. 3,536 / 2,537; Zip Code 18641; Elev. 660; Lat. 41-20-23 N, Long. 075-44-12 W; E Pennsylvania; At the junction of the Lackawanna and Wyoming Valleys, was originally named Pleasant Valley.

AVON, Village; Lebanon County; Pop. 1,271; Zip Code 17042; Lat. 40-20-44 N, Long. 076-23-25 W; SE central Pennsylvania; suburb of Lebanon.

AVONDALE, Borough; Chester County; Pop. 891 / 1,040; Zip Code 19311; Elev. 227; Lat. 39-49-24 N, Long. 075-47-01 W; on White Clay Creek in SE Pennsylvania; In agricultural area, mainly producing mushrooms.

AVONMORE, Borough; Westmoreland County; Pop. 1,234 / 1,030; Zip Code 15618; Elev. 880; Lat. 40-31-44 N, Long. 079-27-42 W; SW Pennsylvania.

BADEN, Borough; Beaver County; Pop. 5,318 / 4,719; Zip Code 15005; Elev. 673; Lat. 40-38-06 N, Long. 080-13-42 W; On Ohio River, just N of Ambridge in W Pennsylvania; Residential; Incorporated as a borough 1866.

BAEDERWOOD, Borough; Montgomery County; Pop. 1,300; Zip Code 19046; Lat. 40-06-24 N, Long. 075-08-33 W; Residential suburb of Philadelphia.

BAIDLAND, Village; Washington County; Pop. 800; Zip Code 15063; Lat. 40-11-41 N, Long. 079-58-16 W; W Pennsylvania.

BAINBRIDGE, Village; Lancaster County; Pop. 650; Zip Code 17502; Elev. 320; Lat. 40-05-27 N, Long. 076-40-04 W; on Susquehanna River in SE Pennsylvania; Named for Commander William Bainbridge in 1817.

BAIRDFORD. Village; Allegheny County; Pop. 950; Zip Code 15006; Elev. 900; Lat. 40-25-57 N, Long. 079-16-45 W; 15 mi. NE of Pittsburgh in SE Pennsylvania.

BAKERSTOWN, Village; Allegheny County; Pop. 1,000; Zip Code 15007; Elev. 1,107; Lat. 40-39-03 N, Long. 079-56-12 W; 20 mi. NE of Pittsburgh in W Pennsylvania.

BALA-CYNWYD, Borough; Montgomery County; Pop. 8,600; Zip Code 19004; Elev. 304; Lat. 40-00-27 N, Long. 075-14-04 W; SE Pennsylvania; NW suburb of Philadelphia.

BALD EAGLE, Township; Clinton County; Pop. 1,282; Lat. 40-43-19 N, Long. 078-11-08 W; Named for Indian Chief who once lived here.

BALDWIN, Borough; Allegheny County; Pop. 24,598 / 20,031; Lat. 10-20-17 N, Long. 079-58-45 W; SW Pennsylvania; S suburb of Pittsburgh; Named for locomotive originator Mathics Bladwin.

BALLY, Borough; Berks County; Pop. 1,051; Zip Code 19503; Elev. 480; Lat. 40-24-08 N, Long. 075-35-15 W; SE Pennsylvania. It was laid out in 1742 on ground owned by the Society of Jesus, was later named for the Reverend Augustin Bally, S.J.

BANGOR, Borough; Northampton County; Pop. 5,006; Zip Code 18013; Elev. 514; Lat. 40-51-56 N, Long. 075-12-25 W; E Pennsylvania. It was founded in 1773 and named for a slate producing city in Wales, is the center of Pennsylvania's slate quarrying area.

BARESVILLE, Village; York County; Pop. 1,700; Zip Code 17331; Near Hanover in S Pennsylvania.

BAREVILLE, Village; Lancaster County; Pop. 800; Zip Code 17540; Lat. 40-05-32 N, Long. 076-09-22 W; NE of Lancaster in SE Pennsylvania.

BARNESBORO, Borough; Cambria County; Pop. 2,741; Zip Code 15714; Elev. 1,446; Lat. 40-39-45 N, Long. 078-46-49 W; SW central Pennsylvania. Thomas Barnes, a coal mine operator, laid out the town in 1891 after first coal was discovered.

BATH, Borough; Northampton County; Pop. 1,952 / 2,529; Zip Code 18014; Lat. 40-43-32 N, Long. 075-23-40 W; E Pennsylvania.

BATH ADDITION, Village; Bucks County; Pop. 800; Zip Code 19007; Lat. 40-06-27 N, Long. 074-51-56 W; SE Pennsylvania; Suburb of Philadelphia included with Bristol.

BAUERSTOWN, Village; Allegheny County; Pop. 2,700; Zip Code 15209; Lat. 40-29-45 N, Long. 079-58-36 W; W Pennsylvania; Suburb of Pittsburgh.

BEALSVILLE, Borough; Washington County; Pop. 588 / 511; Zip Code 15313; Elev. 1,136; Lat. 40-03-55 N, Long. 080-01-26 W; SW Pennsylvania.

BEAR CREEK, Village and Township; Luzerne County; Pop. 200 / 204 (township, 2,450); Zip Code 18602; Elev. 1,670; Lat. 41-10-43 N, Long. 075-45-24 W; Near Wilkes-Barre in NE Pennsylvania; on W bank of Bear Creek. Named for numerous bears in region when it was first settled.

BEAR ROCKS, Village; Fayette County; Pop. 500; Zip Code 15610; Lat. 40-07-22 N, Long. 079-27-43 W; In Chestnut Ridge region in SW Pennsylvania.

BEAVER, Borough; Seat of Beaver County; Pop. 5,441 / 4,753; Zip Code 15009; Elev. 723; Lat. 40-41-43 N, Long. 080-18-18 W; 25 mi. NW of Pittsburgh in W Pennsylvania.

BEAVERDALE, Village; Cambria County; Pop. 1,579; Zip Code 15921; Elev. 1,929; 80 mi. W of Pittsburgh in W central Pennsylvania.

BEAVER FALLS, City; Beaver County; Pop. 12,525 / 10,075; Zip Code 15010; Elev. 758; Lat. 40-45-07 N, Long. 080-19-10 W; 30 mi. NW of Pittsburgh in W Pennsylvania; On W bank of Beaver River where it forms falls. Laid out in 1806, the town was called Brighton by the Constable brothers of Brighton, England. However, after New Brighton was founded, the name was changed to Beaver Falls in 1866 by members of the Harmony Society.

BEAVER MEADOWS, Borough; Carbon County; Pop. 1,078 / 961; Zip Code 18216; Elev. 1,355; Lat. 40-55-41 N, Long. 075-54-45 W; Near Hazelton in E Pennsylvania; Named for nearby Beaver Creek.

BEAVERSPRINGS, Village; Snyder County; Pop. 725; Zip Code 17812; Elev. 591; Lat. 40-44-46 N, Long. 077-12-35 W; Near Beavertown in central Pennsylvania.

BEAVERTOWN, Borough; Snyder County; Pop. 853 / 869; Zip Code 17813; Elev. 651; 8 mi. W of Middleburg in central Pennsylvania; Clothing is important industry; Named for beaver colonies once numerous here.

BECCARIA, Village and Township; Clearfield County; Pop. 200 (township, 1,877); Zip Code 16616; Lat. 40-46-12 N, Long. 078-26-54 W; Central Pennsylvania; Named for Italian publicist and philosopher Cesare the Marquis of Beccaria (1735-94).

BECHTELSVILLE, Borough; Berks County; Pop. 832 / 947; Zip Code 19505; Elev. 420; Lat. 40-22-24 N, Long. 075-37-46 W; SE Pennsylvania.

BEDFORD, Borough; Seat of Bedford County; Pop. 3,326; Zip Code 15522; Elev. 1,060; Lat. 40-01-07 N, Long. 078-30-15 W; S Pennsylvania; Was settled about 1750 and first named Raystown for a Scottish trader named John Wray who had a post here.

BEDMINSTER, Village and Township; Bucks County; Pop. 350 (township, 3,252); Zip Code 18910; Elev. 440; Lat. 40-25-33 N, Long. 075-10-46 W; Approximately 35 mi. N of Philadelphia in SE Pennsylvania.

BEECH CREEK, Borough; Clinton County; Pop. 760 / 689; Zip Code 16822; Elev. 617; Lat. 41-04-33 N, Long. 077-35-20 W; on E bank of Beech Creek in central Pennsylvania; Near Lock Haven.

BELLEFONTE, Borough; Seat of Centre County; Pop. 6,300; Zip Code 16823; Elev. 749; Lat. 40-54-48 N, Long. 077-46-43 W; Central Pennsylvania. Bellefonte (French, beautiful fountain), was surveyed in 1769 and settled shortly afterward. It occupies seven hills at the southeastern base of Bald Eagle Mountain, The name is attributed, in story, to Talleyrand's exclamation of pleasure upon seeing the Big Spring here during his exile from France in 1794-95

BELLEVUE, Borough; Allegheny County; Pop. 10,128; Zip Code 15202; Elev. 727; Lat. 40-29-38 N, Long. 080-03-07 W; SW Pennsylvania; Suburb of Pittsburgh; On Ohio River. Name means "beautiful view" in French, given for the sight obtained from a nearby hill. In colonial times Bellevue was a Delaware Indian hunting ground under Chief Killbuck.

BELMONT, Borough; Cambria County; Pop. 1,800; Zip Code 15904; Lat. 40-17-14 N, Long. 078-53-23 W; W central Pennsylvania; Suburb of Johnstown.

BELMONT HILLS, Borough; Bucks County; Pop. 1,300; Zip Code 19020; Lat. 40-02-03 N, Long. 075-15-29 W; Unincorporated suburb of Philadelphia near Trevoze in SE Pennsylvania.

BEN AVON, Borough; Allegheny County; Pop. 2,134 / 1,899; Elev. 727; Lat. 40-30-29 N, Long. 080-05-00 W; Suburb to NW of Pittsburgh in SW Pennsylvania; Incorporated borough in 1891; Name is Scottish for "hill by the waters."

BENDERSVILLE, Borough; Adams County; Pop. 533 / 618; Zip Code 17306; Elev. 740; Lat. 39-58-57 N, Long. 077-14-59 W; S Pennsylvania.

BENS CREEK, Village; Cambria and Somerset Counties; Pop. 500; Zip Code 15905; Lat. 40-16-57 N, Long. 078-56-12 W; S central Pennsylvania.

BENTLEYVILLE, Borough; Washington County; Pop. 2,525 / 2,500; Zip Code 15314; Elev. 960; Lat. 40-07-00 N, Long. 080-00-31 W; Approx. 25 mi. S of Pittsburgh in SW Pennsylvania; Named for Sheshbazzar Bentley, Jr., who laid out the town in 1816.

BENTON, Borough; Columbia County; Pop. 981 / 883; Zip Code 17814; Elev. 760; Lat. 41-11-42 N, Long. 076-23-02 W; 15 mi. N of Bloomsburg in E central Pennsylvania; Named in honor of Colonel Thomas H. Benton, popular U.S. Senator from Missouri; Incorporated in 1850.

BERKELEY HILLS, Borough; Allegheny County; Pop. 3,700; Zip Code 15237; Lat. 40-31-54 N, Long. 080-00-14 W; Unincorporated suburb of Pittsburgh in W Pennsylvania.

BERLIN, Borough; Somerset County; Pop. 1,999 / 2,164; Zip Code 15530; Elev. 1,163; Lat. 39-55-14 N, Long. 078-57-29 W; 40 mi. S of Johnstown in S Pennsylvania; On a ridge in Brothers Valley; Named by Germans who settled here in 1769; Coal mining and farming region.

BERWICK, Borough; Columbia County; Pop. 12,189 / 10,283; Zip Code 18603; Elev. 505; Lat. 41-03-16 N, Long. 076-14-01 W; E central Pennsylvania. It is named for Berwick upon Tweed, an English town on the Scottish border.

BERWYN, Borough; Chester County; Pop. 9,300; Zip Code 19312; Elev. 500; Lat. 40-02-41 N, Long. 075-26-21 W; Residential suburb W of Philadelphia in SE Pennsylvania.

BESSEMER. Borough; Lawrence County; Pop. 1,293 / 1,104; Zip Code 16112; Elev. 1100; Lat. 40-23-40 N, Long. 079-51-16 W; 10 mi. W of New Castle in W Pennsylvania; Named for Sir Henry Bessermer, inventor of an economical process to make steel that revolutionized the industry.

BETHEL, Village and Township; Berks County; Pop. 600 (township 2,600); Zip Code 19501; Elev. 525; 40 mi. E of Harrisburg in SE Pennsylvania.

BETHEL PARK, Borough; Allegheny County; Pop. 34,755 / 32,627; Zip Code 15102; Elev. 1,200; SW Pennsylvania; suburb of Pittsburgh.

BETHLEHEM, City; Lehigh and Northampton Counties; Pop. 70,419 / 69,522; Zip Code 180+; Elev. 237; Lat. 40-51-42 N, Long. 078-43-50 W; Borders on Allentown in E Pennsylvania; On the Lehigh River. Founded in 1741 by the Moravian Brethren. Bethlehem was named on Christmas Eve that year when the congregation and their leader, Count Nicholas Ludwig, sang an old German hymn meaning "Bethlehem gave us that which makes life rich."

BEVERLY ESTATES, Borough; Lancaster County; Pop. 500; Zip Code 17601; Lat. 40-04-27 N, Long. 076-18-08 W; Suburb of Lancaster in SE central Pennsylvania.

BIGLERVILLE. Borough; Adams County; Pop. 991 / 1,097; Zip Code 17307; Elev. 649; Lat. 39-55-49 N, Long. 077-14-54 W; 7 mi. N of Gettysburg in S Pennsylvania; Surveyed in 1817, the town is the center of a fruit growing region.

BIG RUN, Borough; Jefferson County; Pop. 822 / 702; Zip Code 15715; Elev. 1,286; Lat. 41-04-53 N, Long. 077-40-05 W; 7 mi. N of Punxsutawney in W central Pennsylvania; Founded in 1822 and named for a stream that flows into Stump Creek here; Coal mining and farming area.

BIRD IN HAND, Village; Lancaster County; Pop. 700; Zip Code 17505; Elev. 355; Lat. 40-02-19 N, Long. 076-10-57 W; Named for an early inn that displayed a sign reading "a bird in the hand is worth two in the bush." Tavern was rebuilt three times over original 18th century site.

BIRDSBORO, Borough; Berks County; Pop. 3,481 / 4,852; Zip Code 19508; Elev. 190; Lat. 40-15-52 N, Long. 075-48-16 W; 11 mi. W of Pottstown in SE Pennsylvania; On Schuylkill River; Founded in 1740; Named for ironmaster William Bird.

BLACK LICK, Village; Indiana County; Pop. 1,074; Zip Code 15716; Elev. 967; Lat. 40-28-45 N, Long. 079-12-00 W; Near Blainsville on Conemaugh River Reservoir in W central Pennsylvania. Settled in 1807 and laid out in 1860, this town was named for a nearby coal-black creek, which once contained a salt lick.

BLAINE HILL, Village; Allegheny County; Pop. 1,300; Zip Code 15037; Lat. 40-16-25 N, Long. 079-52-31 W; SE suburb of Pittsburgh in W Pennsylvania.

BLAIRSVILLE, Borough; Indiana County; Pop. 4,166 / 3,321; Zip Code 15717; Elev. 1,012; Lat. 40-25-52 N, Long. 079-15-40 W; W central Pennsylvania. Located on the Conemaugh River, Blairsville was settled in 1792 and named for Captain John Blair, of Blairs Gap, who was among the first promoters of the turnpike and canal portage system.

BLAKELY, Borough; Lackawanna County; Pop. 7,438 / 6,650; Zip Code 18447; Elev. 872; Lat. 41-28-51 N, Long. 075-35-42 W; NE Pennsylvania; suburb of Scranton; on Lackawanna River; Named for Captain Johnston Blakely, naval commander during the War of 1812.

BLANCHARD, Village; Centre County; Pop. 750; Zip Code 16826; Elev. 650; Lat. 40-39-26 N, Long. 079-49-43 W; Central Pennsylvania.

BLANDBURG, Village; Cambria County; Pop. 775; Zip Code 16619; Elev. 2,047; Lat. 40-41-13 N, Long. 078-24-40 W; In Allegheny Mountain Range in W central Pennsylvania.

BLANDON, Village; Berks County; Pop. 1,113; Zip Code 19510; Elev. 400; Lat. 40-26-28 N, Long. 075-53-14 W; Suburb of Reading in SE central Pennsylvania.

BLOOMFIELD, Borough; Seat of Perry County; Pop. 1,109 / 1,089; Zip Code 152+; Lat. 40-27-39 N, Long. 079-57-04 W; S central Pennsylvania.

BLOOMINGDALE, Village; Lancaster County; Pop. 1,200; Zip Code 17601; Lat. 40-49-29 N, Long. 075-51-02 W; suburb of Lancaster in SE Pennsylvania.

BLOOMSBURG, Town; Seat of Columbia County; Pop. 11,717 / 12,355; Zip Code 17815; Elev. 482; Lat. 40-25-46 N, Long. 076-00-49 W; E central Pennsylvania. It lies at the foot of Spectator Bluff, and on Fishing Creek. Ludwig Eyer laid it out in 1802, and the name was chosen in honor of Samuel Bloom, who had been a county commissioner when the old Bloom Township was organized in 1797.

BLOSSBURG, Borough; Tioga County; Pop. 1,757 / 1,531; Zip Code 16912; Elev. 1,348; Lat. 41-40-46 N, Long. 077-03-51 W; N Pennsylvania. First known as Peters Camp; Renamed for Aaron Bloss, who opened a tavern here in 1802.

BLOSSOM HILL, Village; Lancaster County; Pop. 1,300; Zip Code 17601; Lat. 39-44-45 N, Long. 079-53-50 W; Suburb of Lancaster in SE Pennsylvania.

BLUE BALL, Village; Lancaster County; Pop. 700; Zip Code 17506; Elev. 469; Lat. 40-07-07 N, Long. 076-02-51 W; 45 mi. W of Chester in SE Pennsylvania; Founded in 1766 by Robert Wallace, who opened an inn and tavern here called the "Blue Ball," which was a favorite stopping place for marketing farmers.

BLUE BELL, Village; Montgomery County; Pop. 1,600; Zip Code 19422; Elev. 360; Lat. 40-09-08 N, Long. 075-16-00 W; Northern suburb of Philadelphia in SE Pennsylvania.

BOALSBURG, Village; Centre County; Pop. 950; Zip Code 16827; Elev. 1,100; Lat. 40-46-32 N, Long. 077-47-34 W; Near State College in central Pennsylvania. Laid out in 1810, this village was named for Capt. David Boal, a native Irishman who settled here in 1798.

BOBTOWN, Village; Greene County; Pop. 1,055; Zip Code 15315; Lat. 39-45-40 N, Long. 079-58-54 W; Near Dunkard Creek in SW Pennsylvania.

BOILING SPRINGS, Village; Cumberland County; Pop. 1,521; Zip Code 17007; Lat. 40-08-59 N, Long. 077-07-43 W; 15 mi. SW of Harrisburg; Rural.

BOOTHWYN, Borough; Delaware County; Pop. 7,100; Zip Code 19061; Elev. 100; Lat. 39-49-48 N, Long. 075-26-31 W; Suburb of Philadelphia in SE Pennsylvania; Residential.

BOSTON, Borough; Allegheny County; Pop. 1,200; Zip Code 15135; Elev. 760; Lat. 40-18-43 N, Long. 079-49-24 W; Suburb of Pittsburgh to SE.

BOSWELL, Borough; Somerset County; Pop. 1,480 / 1,405; Zip Code 15531; Lat. 40-09-41 N, Long. 079-01-45 W; S Pennsylvania.

BOWMANSTOWN, Borough; Carbon County; Pop. 1,078 / 860; Zip Code 18030; Elev. 437; E Pennsylvania. Founded in 1796. It occupies the flat center of a large mountain-rimmed bowl.

BOYERTOWN, Borough; Berks County; Pop. 4,428 / 3,811; Zip Code 19512; Elev. 386; Lat. 40-20-01 N, Long. 075-38-16 W; 25 mi. S of Allentown in SE central Pennsylvania. First settled in 1720 and founded in 1834, this town was named for Henry Boyer, early settler.

BRACKENRIDGE, Borough; Allegheny County; Pop. 4,297 / 3,340; Zip Code 15014; Elev. 757; Lat. 40-36-29 N, Long. 079-44-29 W; N suburb of Pittsburgh in SW Pennsylvania; Named for Brackenridge family, prominent in the area during the nineteenth century; Incorporated as a borough in 1901.

BRADDOCK, Borough; Allegheny County; Pop. 5,634 / 4,041; Zip Code 15104; Elev. 700; Lat. 40-24-12 N, Long. 079-52-07 W; 10 mi. E of Pittsburgh in SW Pennsylvania; Incorporated as a borough in 1867 and named for Gen. Edward Braddock, who was fatally wounded nearby in a battle with the French and Indians in 1755; An important steel and cool manufacturing center around the turn of the century.

BRADENVILLE, Village; Westmoreland County; Pop. 1,200; Zip Code 15620; Elev. 1,100; Lat. 40-19-17 N, Long. 079-20-25 W; Near Latrobe in W central Pennsylvania.

BRADFORD, City; McKean County; Pop. 11,211 / 9,297; Zip Code 16701; Elev. 1,443; Lat. 41-57-21 N, Long. 078-38-39 W; 4 mi. S of New York state line in N Pennsylvania. First known as Littleton for the county's first landowner Colonel L.C. Little of Boston, the name was changed to honor William Bradford when Daniel Kingsbury purchased the land in 1850.

BRENTWOOD, Borough; Allegheny County; Pop. 11,907 / 9,830; Zip Code 15227; Elev. 884; Lat. 40-22-14 N, Long. 079-58-30 W; SW Pennsylvania. It was incorporated in 1915 with the merger of the villages of Brentwood, Whitehall, and Point View.

BRIAR CREEK, Borough; Columbia County; Pop. 637 / 629; Lat. 41-02-45 N, Long. 076-16-57 W; E central Pennsylvania.

BRIDGEPORT, Borough; Montgomery County; Pop. 4,843 / 4,233; Zip Code 19405; Lat. 39-55-56 N, Long. 077-18-43 W; SE Pennsylvania.

BRIDGEVILLE, Borough; Allegheny County; Pop. 6,154 / 5,071; Zip Code 15017; Lat. 40-21-22 N, Long. 080-06-37 W; SW Pennsylvania.

BRIDGEWATER, Borough; Beaver County; Pop. 879 / 799; Elev. 710; W Pennsylvania. Bridgewater, across the Beaver River from Rochester, was consolidated with Sharon in 1868. Seventy

years later Major Robert Darragh erected the first building and opened the first store.

BRISTOL, Borough; Bucks County; Pop. 10,867 / 10,101; Zip Code 19007; Elev. 21; Lat. 40-06-02 N, Long. 074-51-08 W; 20 mi. NE of Philadelphia in SE Pennsylvania, on the Delaware River. First settled in 1697 and designated as Bucks County Seat in 1705. Named for the western seaport in England, where some of William Penn's ancestors lived.

BROCKTON, Village; Schuylkill County; Pop. 550; Zip Code 17925; Elev. 700; Lat. 40-44-54 N, Long. 076-04-08 W; 10 mi. N of Pottsville in E central Pennsylvania.

BROCKWAY, Borough; Jefferson County; Pop. 2,376 / 2,154; Zip Code 15824; Elev. 1,445; Lat. 41-14-57 N, Long. 078-47-59 W; W central Pennsylvania. First settled in 1822 by Alonzo and Chauncey Brockway, they named the town for themselves fourteen years later.

BRODHEADSVILLE, Village; Monroe County; Pop. 500; Zip Code 18322; Elev. 675; Lat. 40-55-28 N, Long. 075-23-39 W; 20 mi. NW of Easton in E Pennsylvania; Near Weir Mountain range and ski resorts; Named for David Brodhead, who established a Moravian mission nearby in 1739.

BROOKHAVEN, Borough; Delaware County; Pop. 7,912 / 8,197; Zip Code 19015; Elev. 119; Lat. 39-52-09 N, Long. 075-22-58 W; SE Pennsylvania.

BROOKSIDE, Borough; Erie County; Pop. 1,800; Zip Code 16510; Lat. 40-19-55 N, Long. 080-03-20 W; 2 mi. W of Lake Erie shore and the city of Erie in NW Pennsylvania; Residential.

BROOKVILLE, Borough; Seat of Jefferson County; Pop. 4,568 / 4,224; Zip Code 15825; Elev. 1,269; Lat. 41-09-40 N, Long. 079-05-00 W; Approx. 80 mi. NW of Pittsburgh in W central Pennsylvania; on Red Bank Creek and three of its tributaries. First settled in 1801, but not laid out and named until 1830, when it became the county seat and was christened for the various brooks flowing in and around town.

BROOMALL, Borough; Delaware County; Pop. 25,040; Zip Code 19008; Elev. 350; Lat. 39-58-53 N, Long. 075-21-25 W; 15 mi. NW of Philadelphia in SE Pennsylvania; Residential; Incorporated as the township of Marple.

BROWNSTOWN. Village; Lancaster County; Pop. 800 / 876; Zip Code 17508; Elev. 320; Lat. 40-32-54 N, Long. 079-30-48 W; NE suburb of Lancaster in S Pennsylvania; Near airport.

BROWNSVILLE, Borough; Fayette County; Pop. 4,043 / 3,091; Zip Code 15417; Elev. 900; Lat. 40-22-01 N, Long. 076-04-35 W; SW Pennsylvania. Combined with South Brownsville borough since 1933.

BRYN GWELED, Village; Bucks County; Pop. 500; Zip Code 18966; N of Philadelphia and near Southampton in SE Pennsylvania; Residential suburb.

BRYN MAWR, Unincorporated town; Montgomery and Delaware Counties; Pop. 9,500 (including college); Zip Code 19010; Elev. 413; Lat. 40-18-14 N, Long. 080-05-13 W; NW suburb of Philadelphia in SE Pennsylvania. Name means "great hill" in Welsh.

BUCKINGHAM, Village and Township; Bucks County; Pop. 500; Zip Code 18912; Elev. 217; Lat. 40-19-25 W, Long. 075-03-37 W; N suburb of Philadelphia in SE Pennsylvania; Founded in 1702.

BURGETTSTOWN, Borough; Washington County; Pop. 1,867 / 1,541; Zip Code 15021; Elev. 989; Lat. 40-22-55 N, Long. 080-23-35 W; 20 mi. W of Pittsburgh in SW Pennsylvania; Named for Fort Burgett, which was erected here during the Revolutionary War by Sebastian Burgett, a native of Germany. His son, George Burgett, laid out the town in 1795.

BURNHAM, Borough; Mifflin County; Pop. 2,457 / 2,150; Zip Code 17009; Elev. 520; Lat. 40-38-19 N, Long. 077-34-08 W; Central Pennsylvania. First known as Freedom Forge and later as Logan, the town was renamed in 1911 for William Burnham, official of a local steel plant.

BUSHKILL, Pop. 500 (summer 1,000); Elev. 641; Lat. 41-05-36 N, Long. 075-00-08 W; Name means "little river" in Dutch; Was settled in 1812.

BUTLER, City; Seat of Butler County; Pop. 17,026 / 14,778; Zip Code 16001; Elev. 1,011; Lat. 40-51-40 N, Long. 079-53-44 W; 33 mi. N of Pittsburgh in W Pennsylvania. Built on rolling hills originally owned by Robert Morris of Philadelphia, financier of the American Revolution; Was laid out in 1803, and named for Richard Butler of York County, a lieutenant colonel with Morgan's Rifles in 1777, an Indian agent in Ohio in 1787, and a major general in the St. Clair expedition of 1791, in which he was killed. The city is bisected by Conoquenessing Creek.

CALIFORNIA, Borough; Washington County; Pop. 5,703 / 5,207; Zip Code 15419; Elev. 800; Lat. 40-28-32 N, Long. 075-20-51 W; 40 mi. S of Pittsburgh in SW Pennsylvania; Annexed to E Pike Run Township in 1954; Site of California State College. It was laid out in 1849, shortly after the discovery of gold in California, when this alluring name was in everyone's mouth.

CALUMET, Village; Westmoreland County; Pop. 800; Zip Code 15621; Elev. 1,080; Lat. 40-12-39 N, Long. 079-29-08 W; E suburb of Pittsburgh in W central Pennsylvania.

CAMBELLTOWN, Village; Lebanon County; Pop. 1,355; Zip Code 17010; Elev. 440; Lat. 40-16-39 N, Long. 076-35-08 W; 20 mi. E of Harrisburg and near Hershey in SE central Pennsylvania.

CAMBRIA HEIGHTS, Village; Cambria County; Pop. 500; Zip Code 15906; In the hills near Johnstown in S Pennsylvania; Name is derived from the old poetic word for Wales, "Cymry."

CAMBRIDGE SPRINGS, Borough; Crawford County; Pop. 2,102 / 1,811; Zip Code 16403; Elev. 1,181; Lat. 41-48-13 N, Long. 080-03-24 W; NW Pennsylvania. It is on French Creek. Dr. John H. Gray found a mineral spring herein 1884 while prospecting for oil.

CANONSBURG, Borough; Washington County; Pop. 10,459 / 8,504; Zip Code 15317; Elev. 931; Lat. 40-15-45 N, Long. 080-11-15 W; 17 mi. SW of Pittsburgh in SW Pennsylvania. It was settled about 1773 and laid out in 1787 by Colonel John Canon, militia officer and member of the State assembly.

CANTON, Borough; Bradford County; Pop. 1,959 / 1,913; Zip Code 17724; Elev. 1,255; Lat. 41-39-23 N, Long. 076-51-13 W; 30 mi. NE of Williamsport in N Pennsylvania. It was founded in 1800 and named for the Connecticut town by early settlers.

CARBONDALE, City; Lackawanna County; Pop. 11,255 / 9,569; Zip Code 18407; Elev. 1,078; Lat. 41-34-25 N, Long. 075-30-08 W; on Lackawanna River, 16 mi. NE of Scranton in NE Pennsylvania. It had been an anthracite town since 1814, when William Wurts, a Philadelphia merchant, owner of large tracts in the vicinity, and David Nobles, a hunter who knew the region, opened veins and obtained coal for exhibition and appraisal in New York and Philadelphia.

CARLISLE, Borough; Seat of Cumberland County; Pop. 18,314 / 17,504; Zip Code 17013; Elev. 478; Lat. 40-12-05 N, Long. 077-11-21 W; 15 mi. W of Harrisburg in S Pennsylvania. Molly Pitcher, the famous Revolutionary War fighter and nurse, died and was buried here. The Carlisle Barracks (Civil War) have been preserved nearby.

CARNEGIE, Borough; Allegheny County; Pop. 10,099 / 8,298; Zip Code 15106; Elev. 769; Lat. 40-24-31 N, Long. 080-05-01 W; 6 mi. W of Pittsburgh in SW Pennsylvania. The community was named for Andrew Carnegie.

CARNOT, Village; Allegheny County; Pop. 4,000; Zip Code 15108; Lat. 40-31-10 N, Long. 080-13-18 W; NW suburb of Pittsburgh in SW Pennsylvania; Near Coraopolis in a hilly area.

CARROLLTOWN, Borough; Cambria County; Pop. 1,395 / 1,177; Zip Code 15722; Elev. 2,140; Lat. 40-36-10 N, Long. 078-42-32 W; SW central Pennsylvania. It was laid out in 1840, was named by Prince Demetrius Gallitzin for John Carroll who, in 1788, became the first Roman Catholic Bishop in the United States and 20 years later was Archbishop of Baltimore. His cousin, Charles Caroll, signed the Declaration of Independence, and later resided here.

CASTLE SHANNON, Borough; Allegheny County; Pop. 10,164 / 8,284; Zip Code 15234; Elev. 1,040; Lat. 40-21-53 N, Long. 080-01-21 W; 8 mi. S of Pittsburgh in SW Pennsylvania; On Saw Mill Run; Suburban area.

CATASAUQUA. Borough; Lehigh County; Pop. 7,944 / 6,343; Zip Code 18032; Elev. 320; Lat. 40-39-17 N, Long. 075-28-30 W; On Lehigh River, N of Allentown in E Pennsylvania. Site of Allentown Bethlehem-Easton Airport. In 1853 the growing town was incorporated as Catasauqua, for the creek flowing nearby. A name corrupted from the Delaware Indian phrase *gotto-shacki*, "burnt ground," "parched land," or "the earth thirsts."

CATAWISSA, Borough; Columbia County; Pop. 1,568 / 1,586; Zip Code 17820; Lat. 40-57-07 N, Long. 076-27-36 W; E central Pennsylvania; On Susquehanna River near a group of "growing fat." The Indian hunters may have killed a deer along the stream in the season when deer fatten. Catawissa was laid out in 1787 by William Hughes, a Berks County Quaker.

CENTERVILLE, Borough; Washington County; Pop. 4,207; Zip Code 15301; Elev. 1,160; Lat. 40-10-53 N, Long. 080-15-52 W. First settled in 1766, Centerville was laid out in 1821 as a pike town and was named for its position between Uniontown and Washington.

CENTRAL CITY, Borough; Somerset County; Pop. 1,496 / 1,221; Zip Code 15926; Lat. 40-05-11 N, Long. 078-50-15 W. Terminal of the Penn Central rail line is here.

CENTRALIA, Borough; Columbia County; Pop. 1,017 / 64; Zip Code 17927; Elev. 1,484; Lat. 40-48-17 N, Long. 076-20-32 W. Founded in 1826 and named for its then strategic commercial situation.

CENTRE HALL, Borough; Centre County; Pop. 1,233 / 1,184; Pop. 814; Zip Code 16828; Elev. 1,320; Lat. 40-50-51 N, Long. 077-41-11 W; Central Pennsylvania. Named for its central position in Penn's Valley, one of the state's finest hunting and fishing sections.

CHALFANT, Borough; Allegheny County; Pop. 1,119 / 881; Eastern suburb of Pittsburgh in a low density residential area.

CHALFONT, Borough; Bucks County; Pop. 2,802 / 3,943; Zip Code 18914; Elev. 225; Lat. 40-24-31 N, Long. 079-50-21 W; SE Pennsylvania. Chalfont, originally Butlers Mill, was renamed for Chalfont St. Giles, an English parish where William Penn is buried.

CHAMBERSBURG, Borough; Seat of Franklin County; Pop. 16,174 / 17,760; Zip Code 17201; Elev. 620; Lat. 39-56-15 N, Long. 077-39-41 W; 50 mi. SW of Harrisburg in S Pennsylvania. Benjamin Chambers settled on this tract as miller, sawyer, trader, physician, militia colonel, judge and arbitrator. The town was formally laid out in 1764.

CHARLEROI, Borough; Washington County; Pop. 5,717 / 4,692; Zip Code 15022; Elev. 761; Lat. 40-08-16 N, Long. 079-53-54 W; S of Pittsburgh in SW Pennsylvania. It is the trading center of this glass manufacturing region. It was laid out in 1890 as the site of a large glass plant, and named Charleroi for an industrial town of that name in Belgium.

CHELTENHAM, Village; Montgomery County; Pop. 6,500; Zip Code 19012; Elev. 130; Lat. 40-03-39 N, Long. 075-05-40 W; N suburb of Philadelphia in SE Pennsylvania; Seat of a large township by the same name.

CHERRY CITY, Village (unincorporated); Allegheny County; Pop. 4,000; Zip Code 15223; Lat. 40-29-41 N, Long. 079-57-47 W; NE suburb of Pittsburgh that grew substantially after World War II; On the Allegheny River.

CHERRY TREE. Borough; Indiana County; Pop. 520 / 396; Zip Code 15724; Elev. 1,365; Lat. 40-43-35 N, Long. 078-46-25 W; W central Pennsylvania. Known to the Indians as Canoe Place, it was renamed for the cherry tree that was used to determine one of the boundaries of the territory conveyed to the Pennsylvania Proprietary by the Fort Stonwix Treaty of 1768.

CHESTER, City; Delaware County seat; Pop. 45,705 / 40,148; Zip Code 19013; Elev. 23; Lat. 39-50-58 N, Long. 075-21-22 W; 15 mi. SW of Philadelphia on the Delaware River. It is the second oldest settlement in Pennsylvania. The city, center of en industrial area and the second port of Pennsylvania, was named by William Penn allegedly in honor of Lord Chester.

CHESTER HEIGHTS, Borough; Delaware County; Pop. 1,302; Zip Code 19017; Elev. 340; Lat. 39-53-24 N, Long. 075-28-33 W; SE Pennsylvania.

CHESTER HILL, Borough; Clearfield County; Pop. 1,054 / 926; Zip Code 16866; Elev. 1,440; Lat. 40-53-23 N, Long. 078-13-43 W; On the Moshannon Creek near Phillipsburg in W Pennsylvania.

CHESWICK, Borough; Allegheny County; Pop. 2,336 / 1,820; Zip Code 15024; Lat. 40-32-30 N, Long. 079-47-58 W; 12 mi. NE of Pittsburgh in an industrial-mining area in SW Pennsylvania; on Allegheny River.

CHICORA, Borough; Butler County; Pop. 1,192 / 1,047; Zip Code 16025; Elev. 1,247; Lat. 40-56-53 N, Long. 079-44-35 W; 10 mi. NE of Butler in W Pennsylvania; on B&O Railroad line; Name was changed from Millerstown in 1956.

CHRISTIANA, Borough; Lancaster County; Pop. 1,183 / 989; Zip Code 17509; Elev. 494; Lat. 39-57-17 N, Long. 075-59-50 W; SE Pennsylvania. Christiana was not named, as has often been asserted, for King Christian and Queen Christiana of Sweden, but for Christiana, the first wife of William Noble, who built the first house and started a machine-shop here in 1833.

CHURCHILL, Borough; Allegheny County; Pop. 4,285 / 3,557; Zip Code 15221; Elev. 1,100; Lat. 40-26-18 N, Long. 079-50-36 W; E suburb of Pittsburgh in SW Pennsylvania.

CHURCHVILLE, Village; Bucks County; Pop. 2,600; Zip Code 18966; Lat. 40-09-53 N, Long. 078-30-45 W; Near Southampton in SE Pennsylvania; N suburb of Philadelphia.

CLAIRTON, City; Allegheny County; Pop. 12,188 / 8,572; Zip Code 15025; Elev. 960; Lat. 40-17-32 N, Long. 079-52-55 W; SW Pennsylvania. The origin of the city's name is not certain. One can be fairly sure the name Clairton has been made by adding the locative suffix ton ("town") to Clair ("clear, bright, or illustrious"), the second syllable of the surname St. Clair or its variant form, Sinclair. The current traditional explanation is that the name Clairton is derived from the name of Samuel Sinclair, who once owned a tract of 215 acres of land on which part of the present city is built.

CLARION, Borough; Seat of Clarion County; Pop. 6,664 / 6,469; Zip Code 16214; Elev. 1,491; Lat. 41-12-53 N, Long. 079-23-08 W; 28 mi. SE of Oil City in W Pennsylvania.

CLARKS SUMMIT, Borough; Lackawanna County; Pop. 5,272 / 5,222; Zip Code 18411; Elev. 1,240; Lat. 41-29-19 N, Long. 075-42-32 W; 5 mi. NW of Scranton in NE Pennsylvania; Residential. Clarks Summit has strong ties with Clarks Green, the adjacent borough. Both were named for Deacon William Clark who in 1799 cleared the triangular "Green." The "Summit" was the peak of a grade on the Legett's Gap Railroad, northern division of the Lackawanna and Western.

CLAYSBURG, Village (unincorporated); Blair County; Pop. 1,516; Zip Code 16625; Elev. 1,148; Lat. 40-17-48 N, Long. 078-27-00 W; Claysburg is a narrow town set on a mountainside, and threaded by the Frankstown branch of the Juniata River; The town was founded in 1804 by John Ulrich Zeth.

CLAYSVILLE, Borough; Washington County; Pop. 1,029 / 213; Zip Code 15323; Elev. 1,001; 38 mi. SW of Pittsburgh in SW Pennsylvania. It was named by its founder for Henry Clay, probably because he championed both the National Highway and a protective tariff on coal, once the community's chief support.

CLEARFIELD, Borough; Seat of Clearfield County; Pop. 7,580 / 6,468; Zip Code 16830; Elev. 1,112; Lat. 41-01-38 N, Long. 078-26-22 W; 50 mi. N of Altoona in W central Pennsylvania. It is named for nearby Clearfield Creek, so called because buffalo are supposed to have cleared the undergrowth from large tracts along the creek "so as to give them the appearance of cleared fields."

CLEARVIEW, Village; Lancaster County; Pop. 1,200; Zip Code 17601; 2 mi. N of Lancaster in SE central Pennsylvania; Residential.

CLEONA, Borough; Lebanon County; Pop. 2,003 / 2,253; Zip Code 17042; Elev. 460; Lat. 40-20-14 N, Long. 076-28-33 W; W of Lebanon in SE central Pennsylvania; Residential.

CLIFTON HEIGHTS, Borough; Delaware County; Pop. 7,320 / 6,956; Zip Code 19018; Elev. 109 Lat. 39-55-45 N, Long. 075-17-48 W; SE Pennsylvania; Settled in the last decade of the eighteenth century and incorporated as a borough in 1885.

CLYMER, Borough; Indiana County; Pop. 1,761 / 1,377; Zip Code 15728; Elev. 1,218; Lat. 40-40-05 N, Long. 079-00-43 W; 10 mi. NE of Indiana in W central Pennsylvania; On Two Lick Creek. Clymer was laid out in 1905 by the Dixon Run Land Company, which chose this name in honor of George Clymer, a Pennsylvania signer of the Declaration of Independence and one of the framers of the Constitution of the United States.

COALDALE, Borough; Schuylkill County; Pop. 2,762 / 2,277; Zip Code 18218; Elev. 1,040; 15 mi. SE of Hazelton in E central Pennsylvania; On Highway 209. Incorporated in 1906, it owes its existence and its name to a dale containing rich deposits of anthracite coal.

COATESVILLE, City; Chester County; Pop. 10,698 / 12,945; Zip Code 19320; Elev. 381; 38 mi. W of Philadelphia in SE Pennsylvania. It became a post-office in 1812; Its first postmaster was Moses Coates, who owned a large tract of land now occupied by the town.

COCHRANTON, Borough; Crawford County; Pop. 1,240 / 1,138; Zip Code 16314; Elev. 582; Lat. 41-31-12 W, Long. 080-02-55 W; Approx. 10 mi. SE of Meadville in NW Pennsylvania; On French Creek; Residential.

COLLEGEVILLE, Borough; Montgomery County; Pop. 3,406; Zip Code 19426; Elev. 200; Lat. 40-11-08 N, Long. 075-27-07 W; 20 mi. NW of Philadelphia in SE Pennsylvania. Originally known as Perkiomen Bridge and then as Freeland.

COLONIAL PARK, Village; Dauphin County; Pop. 9,000; Zip Code 17109; Lat. 40-18-02 N, Long. 076-48-36 W; NE suburb of Harrisburg in SE central Pennsylvania; home of many city workers.

COLUMBIA, Borough; Lancaster County; Pop. 10,466 / 10,492; Zip Code 17512; Elev. 255; Lat. 40-02-01 N, Long. 076-30-17 W; 12 mi. W of Lancaster in SE Pennsylvania. Received its name at the time it was being considered as one of many possible sites for the national capital.

COLUMBUS, Village; Warren County; Pop. 500; Zip Code 16405; Elev. 1,425; Lat. 41-56-27 N, Long. 079-34-55 W; NW Pennsylvania; Named for the legendary discoverer of North America.

COLWYN, Borough; Delaware County; Pop. 2,851 / 2,494; Zip Code 19023; Elev. 50; Lat. 39-54-44 N, Long. 075-15-15 W; 10 mi. SW of downtown Philadelphia on Cobbs Creek (the city boundary) in SE Pennsylvania.

CONNELLSVILLE, City; Fayette County; Pop. 10,319 / 8,546; Zip Code 15425; Elev. 890; Lat. 40-01-04 N, Long. 079-35-23 W; 47 mi. SE of Pittsburgh in SW Pennsylvania. Occupies the site of an early Shawnee village. Zechariah Connell and several other pioneers came to this vicinity in 1770 about the time coal was discovered here, and 23 years later Connell laid out a village.

CONSHOHOCKEN, Borough; Montgomery County; Pop. 8,475 / 8,141; Zip Code 19428; Elev. 220; Lat. 40-04-45 N, Long. 075-18-07 W; 11 mi. NW of Philadelphia on the Schuylkill River in SE Pennsylvania; Suburban. *"Conshohocken"* is an Indian name meaning "pleasant valley."

CONWAY, Borough; Beaver County; Pop. 2,747 / 2,289; Zip Code 15027; Elev. 760; Lat. 40-39-35 N, Long. 080-14-22 W; 19 mi. NW of Pittsburgh on E bank of the Ohio River in W Pennsylvania; Suburban-industrial community.

CONYNGHAM, Borough; Luzerne County; Pop. 2,242 / 1,977; Zip Code 18219; Elev. 940; Lat. 40-59-31 N, Long. 076-03-25 W; 5 mi. W of Hazleton in an old mining area in E Pennsylvania.

COOPERSBURG, Borough; Lehigh County; Pop. 2,595 / 2,590; Zip Code 18036, Elev. 539 Lat. 40-30-41 N, Long. 075-23-27 W; 10 mi. S of Allentown in E Pennsylvania; Founded in 1780.

COPLAY, Borough; Lehigh County; Pop. 3,130 / 3,222; Zip Code 18037; Elev. 380; Lat. 40-40-12 N, Long. 075-29-45 W; On Lehigh River; N of Allentown in E Pennsylvania; Suburban; Name is Indian for "smooth running stream."

CORAOPOLIS, Borough; Allegheny County; Pop. 7,308 / 6,100; Zip Code 15108; Elev. 730; Lat. 40-31-06 N, Long. 080-10-01 W; 10 mi. NW of Pittsburgh in SW Pennsylvania; Was settled about 1760. According to some, the name comes from the Greek *Koreopolis*, "maiden city," but others hold that it was named for Cora Watson, daughter of an influential citizen.

CORNWALL, Borough; Lebanon County; Pop. 2,653 / 3,255; Zip Code 17016; Elev. 680; Lat. 40-16-25 N, Long. 076-24-23 W; SE central Pennsylvania; Served by major rail lines heading to and from Lebanon, 3 mi. north. Site of the old Cornwall Blast Furnace. Named for a region in England.

CORNWELLS HEIGHTS, Village; Bucks County; Pop. 8,200; Zip Code 19020; Elev. 60; Lat. 40-04-36 N, Long. 074-56-57 W; 12 mi. NE of downtown Philadelphia in SE Pennsylvania; On the Delaware River.

CORRY, City; Erie County; Pop. 7,149 / 6,715; Zip Code 16407; Elev. 1,429; Lat. 41-55-13 N, Long. 079-38-26 W; 28 mi. SE of Erie in NW Pennsylvania; on S branch of the French Creek. Born in 1861 when the rights of way of two railroads intersected on Hiram Corry's farm, was nursed on the oil discovered by Drake at Titusville, some 25 miles to the south.

COUDERSPORT, Borough; Seat of Potter County; Pop. 2,791 / 2,864; Zip Code 16915; Elev. 1,650; Lat. 41-46-29 N, Long. 078-01-15 W; N Pennsylvania, near the New York state line. Coudersport was named for Jean Samuel Couderc, of the Amsterdam banking firm that had managed the interests of those exiled Frenchmen of Asylum who had invested in the Ceres Land Company. The final letter in M. Couderc's name was dropped for the sake of euphony.

CRAFTON, Borough; Allegheny County; Pop. 7,623 / 6,482; Zip Code 15205; Elev. 880; Lat. 40-26-06 N, Long. 080-03-59 W; SE suburb of Pittsburgh in SW Pennsylvania; On Chartiers Creek; It was laid out about 1870 by Charles C. Craft, and named in honor of his father, James S. Craft, a prominent Pittsburgh lawyer, from whom he inherited the land on which the town is built.

CREIGHTON, Village; Allegheny County; Pop. 2,081; Zip Code 15030; Elev. 800; Lat. 40-35-14 N, Long. 079-46-43 W; Suburb of Pittsburgh. It grew up about a tavern erected here in 1792.

CRESSONA, Borough; Schuylkill County; Pop. 1,810 / 1,536; Zip Code 17929; Elev. 600; Lat. 40-37-36 N, Long. 076-11-35 W; E central Pennsylvania. It was named for John Chapman Cresson, who laid out the town. He was a civil engineer in Philadelphia, manager of the Schuylkill Navigation Company, president of the Mine Hill and Schuylkill Haven Railroad Company, and chief engineer of Fairmount Park in Philadelphia.

CROYDON, Village; Bucks County; Pop. 9,800; Zip Code 19020; Lat. 40-05-14 N, Long. 074-54-14 W; 10 mi. NE of downtown Philadelphia in SE Pennsylvania; On Neshaminy Creek; Named for a suburb of London, England.

CRUM LYNNE, Village; Delaware County; Pop. 3,700; Zip Code 19022; Elev. 20; Lat. 39-52-20 N, Long. 075-19-42 W; SW suburb of Philadelphia near Chester, in SE Pennsylvania.

CURWENSVILLE, Borough; Clearfield County; Pop. 3,116 / 2,937; Zip Code 16833; Elev. 1,167; Lat. 40-58-32 N, Long. 078-31-31 W; W central Pennsylvania. The first settlement occurred in 1812, 14 years after John Curwen obtained title to the tract. Curwen never resided here, however. Curwensville State Park is nearby.

DALE, Borough; Cambria County; Pop. 1,906 / 1,454; Zip Code 15902; Elev. 1250; Lat. 40-24-58 N, Long. 075-36-58 W; Suburb of Johnstown in a hilly area in SW central Pennsylvania.

DALLAS, Borough; Luzerne County; Pop. 2,679 / 2,837; Zip Code 18612; Elev. 1,128; Lat. 41-20-10 N, Long. 075-57-49 W; 10 mi. NW of Wilkes-Barre in E Pennsylvania. It took its name from the Philadelphia author, lawyer, statesman, and financier, Alexander James Dallas, who won fame by his efficient administration as Secretary of the Treasury in 1814-17.

DALLASTOWN, Borough; York County; Pop. 3,949 / 3,923; Zip Code 17313; Elev. 880; Lat. 39-53-58 N, Long. 076-38-26 W; Named in honor of George Mifflin Dallas of Philadelphia, who served as United States Senator from Pennsylvania in 1831, as Vice President of the United States during Polk's administration, and as minister to Great Britain from 1856 to 1861. George M. Dallas was the son of Alexander J. Dallas.

DARBY, Borough; Delaware County; Pop. 11,513 / 10,360; Zip Code 19023; Elev. 50; Lat. 39-55-06 N, Long. 075-15-34 W; SW of downtown Philadelphia in SE Pennsylvania; In a residential area along Derby Creek. It was so called for appearing as "Derbytown" in 1699. Three centuries ago the form Darby was used quite as frequently as Derby.

DAVIDSON HEIGHTS, Village; Beaver County; Pop. 2,000; Zip Code 15001; Suburb of Aliquippa in W Pennsylvania.

DENVER, Borough; Lancaster County; Pop. 2,018 / 3,131; Zip Code 17517; Elev. 380; Lat. 40-13-59 N, Long. 076-08-15 W; 15 mi. NE of Lancaster in SE Pennsylvania.

DERRY, Borough; Westmoreland County; Pop. 3,072 / 2,815; Zip Code 15627; Elev. 1050; Lat. 41-11-18 N, Long. 076-27-42 W; 35 mi. E of Pittsburgh in SW Pennsylvania. It was named for the Northern Irish town that was known as Derry before the British took control end renamed it Londonderry.

DEVON, Village; Chester County; Pop. 4,500; Zip Code 19333; Elev. 495; Lat. 40-02-57 N, Long. 075-25-46 W; 10 mi. NW of Philadelphia in SE Pennsylvania; Devereux Foundation is located here.

DICKSON CITY, Borough; Lackawanna County; Pop. 6,699 / 5,676; Zip Code 18519; Elev. 752; Lat. 41-28-17 N, Long. 075-36-29 W; NE Pennsylvania. It was named for Thomas Dickson, president of the Delaware end Hudson Canal Company (1869-84), merges with Blakely on one side and Scranton on the other, William M. Richmond, of Scranton, opened coal drifts here in 1859; the following year the first breaker was erected.

DILLSBURG, Borough; York County; Pop. 1,733 / 2,010; Zip Code 17019; Elev. 580; Lat. 40-06-39 N, Long. 077-02-07 W; 15 mi. S of Harrisburg in S Pennsylvania; reached by U.S. Highway 15, where a roadside picnic area marks the outskirts of town.

DONORA, Borough; Washington County; Pop. 7,524 / 5,498; Zip Code 15033; Elev. 780; Lat. 40-10-24 N, Long. 079-51-28 W; SW Pennsylvania. It was en important industrial town founded in 1900 on the west bank of the Monongahela River. It is named for William H. Donner, president of the town's developing company, and Nora Mellon, wife of Andrew W. Mellon.

DORMONT, Borough; Allegheny County; Pop. 11,275 / 8,714; Zip Code 15216; Elev. 1,220; Lat. 40-23-45 N, Long. 080-02-00 W; S suburb of Pittsburgh in SW Pennsylvania; Population declined in the 1970s. The ornate and somewhat pretentious name Dormant, from the French *d'or mont*, "mount of gold," was suggested by Gilbert M. Brown, who became the first burgess of Dormont. The name refers to the beautiful hills on which the town is built and to the wonderful opportunities that they offered.

DOVER, Borough; York County; Pop. 1,910 / 8,832; Zip Code 17315; Elev. 431; Lat. 40-00-06 N, Long. 076-51-02 W; S Pennsylvania; on Fox Run Creek at the foot of the Conewago Mountains; Residential town named for the English port city.

DOWNINGTOWN, Borough; Chester County; Pop. 7,650 / 7,483; Zip Code 19335; Elev. 264; Lat. 40-00-23 N, Long. 075-42-13 W; SE Pennsylvania. It is on the East Branch of Brandywine Creek, was settled by emigrants from Birmingham, England. First known as Milltown, it was renamed for Thomas Downing, who purchased a mill here in 1739, and was incorporated as a borough in 1859.

DOYLESTOWN, Borough; Seat of Bucks County; Pop. 8,717 / 8,467; Zip Code 18901; Elev. 355; Lat. 40-18-36 N, Long. 075-07-49 W; 25 mi. N of Philadelphia in SE Pennsylvania. It was settled in 1735 by William Doyle, was once an overnight stop of stage travelers between Easton end Philadelphia.

DRAVOSBURG, Borough; Allegheny County; Pop. 2,511 / 2,161; Zip Code 15034; Elev. 800; Lat. 40-21-02 N, Long. 079-53-11 W; SE suburb of Pittsburgh, on the Mongahela River in SW Pennsylvania; Bordered by the Allegheny County Airport. The town was named for John F. Drava, pioneer coal operator.

DREXEL HILL, Village; Delaware County; Pop. 30,000; Zip Code 19026; Elev. 210; Lat. 39-56-49 N, Long. 075-17-33 W; A residential area 6 mi. W of Philadelphia, along the Darby Creek in SE Pennsylvania.

DUBLIN, Borough; Bucks County; Pop. 1,565 / 1,975; Zip Code 18917; Lat. 40-22-18 N, Long. 075-12-07 W; SE Pennsylvania.

DUBOIS, City; Clearfield County; Pop. 9,290 / 8,006; Zip Code 15801; Elev. 1339; Lat. 41-07-09 N, Long. 078-45-37 W; 100 mi. N of Pittsburgh in W central Pennsylvania. It is bisected by Sandy Lick Creek, and lies in a narrow basin at the lowest pass in the Alleghenies. In 1880 the town was incorporated under the name of DuBois, given in honor of John DuBois, its most important citizen.

DUNBAR, Borough; Fayette County; Pop. 1,369; Zip Code 15431; Elev. 1,000; Lat. 39-58-40 N, Long. 079-36-53 W; 7 mi. NE of Uniontown in a farming area in SW Pennsylvania. Colonel Thomas Dunbar was defeated by a French and Indian army here in 1755. His name was given to the new town shortly afterwards.

DUNCANNON, Borough; Perry County; Pop. 1,645 / 1,387; Zip Code 17020; Elev. 260; Lat. 40-23-53 N; N of Harrisburg on the Susquehanna River, in S central Pennsylvania.

DUNCANSVILLE, Borough; Blair County; Pop. 1,355 / 1,156; Zip Code 16635; Elev. 1,020; Lat. 40-25-24 N, Long. 078-26-03 W; 4 mi. SW of Lekemont in S central Pennsylvania. It was founded by Samuel Duncan. At the same time Jacob Walter owned a site to the east called Welterstown. The two met on a bridge spanning Blair Creek and tossed a penny to decide what the common name should be.

DUNMORE, Borough; Lackawanna County; Pop. 16,781 / 13,983; Zip Code 18512; Elev. 939; Lat. 41-25-11 N, Long. 075-37-58 W; NE Pennsylvania. It was settled in 1783 by William Allsworth, a convivial shoemaker. Called Buckstown until 1840, it was renamed for the second son of the fifth Earl of Dunmore.

DUPONT, Borough; Luzerne County; Pop. 3,460 / 3,159; Zip Code 18641; Elev. 701; Lat. 41-19-30 N, Long. 075-44-45 W; E Pennsylvania. Set in a hollow, it was founded in 1917 and named for the Dupont's, operators of a nearby powder plant.

DUQUESNE, City; Allegheny County; Pop. 10,094 / 7,618; Zip Code 15110; Elev. 841; Lat. 40-22-53 N, Long. 079-51-36 W; SW Pennsylvania. It was incorporated in 1891. The name came from old Fort Duquesne, which was built at the forks of the Ohio in 1754, and named in honor of the Marquis Duquesne de Menneville, then governor of New France.

DURYEA, Borough; Luzerne County; Pop. 5,415 / 4,669; Zip Code 18642; Elev. 589; Lat. 41-20-38 N, Long. 075-44-20 W; E Pennsylvania. It was named for Abram Duryea, who opened coal mines here in 1845. For a time the settlement was known as Babyton because of the mixture of tongues occasioned by the influx of immigrant miners. Duryea was a colonel with the fifth New York Infantry in the Civil War.

EAST BERLIN, Borough; Adams County; Pop. 1,054 / 1,307; Zip Code 17316; Elev. 430; Lat. 39-56-15 N, Long. 076-58-44 W; Along the Conewago Creek in S Pennsylvania; Named by German settlers.

EAST BRADY, Borough; Clarion County; Pop. 1,153 / 999; Zip Code 16028; Elev. 1,080; Lat. 40-59-09 N, Long. 079-36-48 W; on Brady's Bend of the Allegheny River in W Pennsylvania. It was laid out in 1866 and named for Captain Brady. During the Revolutionary War, Captain Brady's father and brother were killed by Indians. The captain swore vengeance and for many years led expeditions against his enemies.

EAST CONEMAUGH, Borough; Cambria County; Pop. 2,128 / 1,365; Zip Code 15909; Elev. 1,240; Lat. 40-20-55 N, Long. 078-53-02 W; One mi. N of Johnstown in SW central Pennsylvania. It dates back to a time when it was necessary to use the prefix East to distinguish this town from the older borough of Conemaugh, which was consolidated with Johnstown about 130 years ago. The Conemaugh River, which became famous at the time of the Johnstown flood in 1889, has given its name to East Conemaugh. The name is derived from the Indian Connernach, which signifies "otter creek."

EAST FAXON, Village; Lycoming County; Pop. 4,000; Zip Code 17706; 1 mi. E of Williamsport along the Susquehanna River in E central Pennsylvania; Residential suburb.

EAST GREENVILLE, Borough; Montgomery County; Pop. 2,456 / 3,083; Zip Code 18041; Elev. 415; Lat. 40-24-23 N, Long. 075-30-08 W; 20 mi. In SE Pennsylvania S of Allentown on the main rail lines between that city and Philadelphia, near Perkiomen Creek.

EAST LANSDOWNE, Borough; Delaware County; Pop. 2,806 / 2,526; Zip Code 19050; Elev. 130; Lat. 39-56-44 N, Long. 075-15-42 W; 5 mi. W of downtown Philadelphia along Cobbs Creek in SE Pennsylvania.

EAST LAWN, Village; Northampton County; Pop. 18,064; Zip Code 18064; Lat. 40-45-01 N, Long. 075-17-41 W; Suburb of Easton and Allentown-Bethlehem in E Pennsylvania.

EAST MCKEESPORT, Borough; Allegheny County; Pop. 2,940 / 2,364; Zip Code 15035; Elev. 1,200; Lat. 40-22-59 N, Long. 079-48-24 W; Near McKeesport in SW Pennsylvania; Incorporated about 1895. Site of the Bliss Speedway, near State Highway 48.

EAST NORRITON, Village; Montgomery County; Pop. 11,837; Zip Code 19401; Near Norristown in SE Pennsylvania; Residential.

EAST PETERSBURG, Borough; Lancaster County; Pop. 3,600 / 4,404; Zip Code 17520; Elev. 380; Lat. 40-06-00 N, Long. 076-21-16 W; 5 mi. N of Lancaster in SE Pennsylvania.

EAST PITTSBURGH, Borough; Allegheny County; Pop. 2,493 / 2,036; Zip Code 15112; Elev. 1,000; Lat. 40-23-44 N, Long. 079-50-20 W; Adjacent to Pittsburgh in SW Pennsylvania, near Monongahela River in a residential area.

EAST STROUDSBURG, Borough; Monroe County; Pop. 8,039 / 10,341; Zip Code 18301; Elev. 430; Lat. 40-59-58 N, Long. 075-10-54 W; E Pennsylvania. Originally just an extension of Stroudsburg, it is almost as large and important today as the older town.

EAST WASHINGTON. Borough; Washington County; Pop. 2,241 / 1,926; Zip Code 15301; Elev. 1,220; Lat. 40-10-25 N, Long. 080-14-16 W; Adjacent to Washington in SW Pennsylvania. The historic Lemoyne House is located here.

EASTON, City; Northampton County seat; Pop. 26,069 / 25,292; Zip Code 18042; Elev. 271; Lat. 41-07-38 N, Long. 079-32-28 W; on Delaware River, E of Allentown in E Pennsylvania; Near Phillipsburg, New Jersey. The town was named Easton, at the proprietor's wish, for the Northemptonshire estate (Easton Weston) of Lord Pomfret, Penn's father-in-law.

EBENSBURG. Borough; Seat of Cambria County; Pop. 4,096 / 3,674; Zip Code 15931; Elev. 2,022; Lat. 40-29-06 N, Long. 078-43-30 W; 18 mi. NE of Johnstown in SW central Pennsylvania; On N branch of Conemaugh Creek. It was founded in the early 1800s by the Reverend Rees Lloyd, a religious dissenter and leader of Welsh immigrants. Rev. Lloyd named the town for his son, Eber, who died in childhood.

ECONOMY, Borough; Beaver County; Pop. 9,538 / 9,731; Zip Code 15005; Elev. 1,180; W Pennsylvania; Incorporated in 1958. In 1825 the Harmony Society moved into Pennsylvania, bought about three thousand acres of land, and founded the town and the township of Economy.

EDDYSTONE, Borough; Delaware County; Pop. 2,555 / 2,239; Zip Code 19013; Elev. 20; Lat. 39-51-36 N, Long. 075-20-41 W; 15 mi. SW of Philadelphia in SW Pennsylvania, on the Delaware River; Port facilities along the riverfront.

EDGEWOOD, Borough; Allegheny County; Pop. 4,382 / 3,223; Zip Code 15218; Elev. 920; Lat. 40-25-55 N, Long. 079-52-54 W; E suburb of Pittsburgh in SW Pennsylvania.

EDGEWORTH, Borough; Allegheny County; Pop. 1,738 / 1,498; Zip Code 15143; Elev. 723; Lat. 40-33-04 N, Long. 080-11-35 W; NW of Pittsburgh in SW Pennsylvania, on Ohio River.

EDINBORO, Borough; Erie County; Pop. 6,324 / 6,787; Zip Code 16412, Elev. 1,210; Lat. 41-52-27 N, Long. 080-07-55 W; 20 mi. S of Lake Erie Shore in NW Pennsylvania; Named for city in Scotland.

EDWARDSVILLE, Borough; Luzerne County; Pop. 5,729 / 4,951; Zip Code 18704; Elev. 760; Lat. 41-16-10 N, Long. 075-55-00 W; 3 mi. NW of Wilkes-Barre in E Pennsylvania. It was incorporated in 1884, was named for Daniel Edwards, superintendent of the Kingston Coal Company, whose mining operations opened here soon after the borough was incorporated.

ELIZABETH, Borough; Allegheny County; Pop. 1,892 / 1,450; Zip Code 15037; Elev. 731; Lat. 40-16-09 N, Long. 079-53-24 W; SE suburb of Pittsburgh in SW Pennsylvania. It was laid out in 1787 by Stephen Bayard and named in honor of his bride, Elizabeth Mackay Bayard, daughter of Colonel Aeneas Mackay, once commandant at Fort Pitt.

ELIZABETHTOWN, Borough; Lancaster County; Pop. 8,233 / 10,739; Zip Code 17022; Elev. 462; Lat. 40-09-10 N, Long. 076-36-11 W; 15 mi. SE of Harrisburg in SE Pennsylvania. It was named for the wife of Captain Barnabas Hughes who purchased the tavern and the original Harris tract in 1750.

ELKLAND, Borough; Tioga County; Pop. 1,974 / 1,765; Zip Code 16920; Elev. 1,130; Lat. 41-59-10 N, Long. 077-18-40 W; just S of New York state line in N Pennsylvania.

ELLSWORTH, Borough; Washington County; Pop. 1,228 / 1,269; Zip Code 15331; Elev. 1,060; Lat. 40-06-43 N, Long. 080-01-03 W; 30 mi. S of Pittsburgh in SW Pennsylvania, in an old coal mining region.

ELLWOOD CITY, Borough; Beaver and Lawrence Counties; Pop. 9,998 / 8,364; Zip Code 16117; Elev. 900; 10 mi. N of Beaver Falls in W Pennsylvania, on the Shenango River. It was laid out in 1890 by the Pittsburgh Company and was named in honor of Colonel I.L. Ellwood of Indiana, who pioneered the manufacturing of wire fencing.

EMMAUS, Borough; Lehigh County; Pop. 11,001 / 11,558; Zip Code 18049; Elev. 433; Lat. 40-32-22 N, Long. 075-29-50 W; 5 mi. S of Allentown in E Pennsylvania. It was founded shortly after 1740 by the Moravians, was called successively Maguntchi (Ind. "place of the bears") and Salrburg. Not until 1761, when Bishop August Spangenberg, founder of the Moravian Church in America, conducted a feast here, was it named for the biblical town of Emmaus. In the succeeding years one "m" was dropped from the name, but in 1939 the earlier spelling was officially restored.

EMPORIUM, Borough; Seat of Cameron County; Pop. 2,837 / 2,302; Zip Code 15834; Elev. 1,031; Lat. 41-30-44 N, Long. 078-14-07 W; on Bucktail Trail, near New York state line in N central Pennsylvania. Emporium is the Latin form of the Greek word for "market, " or "centre of trade." The name Emporium, which was assumed by the county seat at the time of its incorporation in 1864.

ENOLA, Village; Cumberland County; Pop. 7,000; Zip Code 17025; Elev. 400; Lat. 40-17-24 N, Long. 076-56-03 W; Across the Susquehanna River from Harrisburg in S Pennsylvania; The erroneous popular explanation of this peculiar name is that the call for the lonely telegraph tower which once stood across the river from Harrisburg was the word alone, and that the name Enola was suggested by spelling this word backward. In point of fact, the name Enola has been traced to Amanda Gingrich Underwood who once lived in Mechanicsburg, Pennsylvania.

EPHRATA, Borough; Lancaster County; Pop. 11,095 / 13,341; Zip Code 17522; Elev. 380; Lat. 40-10-47 N, Long. 076-10-45 W; 12 mi. NE of Lancaster in SE Pennsylvania; Site of the historic Ephrata Cloister along a scenic route. The German Seventh-Day Adventists established a monastic community here in 1735.

ERIE, City; Erie County seat; Pop. 118,964 / 101,474; Zip Code 165+; Elev. 709; Lat. 42-07-45 N, Long. 080-05-07 W; on Lake Erie, 90 mi. W of Buffalo, New York in NW Pennsylvania. Erie's first known inhabitants were Indians of the Eriez nation, from which the lake and later the city received their names. They were exterminated by the Seneca about 1654, and for decades thereafter the region remained under control of the Iroquois Confederacy.

ETNA, Borough; Allegheny County; Pop. 4,534 / 3,713; Zip Code 15223; Elev. 750; Lat. 40-30-15 N, Long. 079-56-57 W; SW Pennsylvania. Etna, appropriately named for Sicily's famed volcano, is a town of flaming furnaces, iron works, and steel mills. Etna's history as an industrial town dates form 1832 when an iron making establishment was set up here. It became a borough in 1868.

EVANS CITY, Borough; Butler County; Pop. 2,299 / 2,006; Zip Code 16033; Elev. 940; Lat. 40-46-09 N, Long. 080-03-47 W; W Pennsylvania. Evans City was settled in 1796 by Robert Boggs, who exchanged a mare for a 400-acre tract on which he built a cabin and a mill. In 1836, Thomas B. Evans laid out the village, after buying half of Bogg's land.

EVERETT, Borough; Bedford County; Pop. 1,828 / 1,722; Zip Code 15537; Elev. 1,106; Lat. 40-00-41 N, Long. 078-22-25 W; 42 mi. S of Altoona in S Pennsylvania; In the Tussey Mountains.

EXETER, Borough; Luzerne County; Pop. 5,493 / 5,809; Zip Code 18643; Elev. 591; Lat. 41-19-14 N, Long. 075-49-10 W; E Pennsylvania. Exeter was named for Exeter Township, organized in 1790 by settlers from Exeter, Rhode Island.

EXTON, Village; Chester County; Pop. 2,000; Zip Code 19341; Elev. 370; Lat. 40-01-44 N, Long. 075-37-16 W; A suburban area 25 mi. NW of Philadelphia in SE Pennsylvania.

FAIRCHANCE, Borough; Fayette County; Pop. 2,106 / 1,899; Zip Code 15436; Lat. 39-49-29 N, Long. 079-45-17 W; 6 mi. S of Uniontown in a rural area of SW Pennsylvania.

FAIRFIELD, Borough; Adams County; Pop. 591 / 619; Zip Code 17320; Elev. 608; Lat. 39-47-14 N, Long. 077-22-08 W; A hilly, densely forested area 8 mi. SW of Gettysburg in S Pennsylvania.

FAIRHOPE, Village; Fayette County; Pop. 2,500; Zip Code 15012; Lat. 39-50-24 N, Long. 078-47-32 W; 2 mi. E of Belle Vernon along the Monongahela River in SW Pennsylvania.

FAIRLESS HILLS, Village; Bucks County; Pop. 12,500; Zip Code 19030; Elev. 100; Lat. 40-10-46 N, Long. 074-51-20 W; NE suburb of Philadelphia in SE Pennsylvania; A residential area extending from Levittown.

FARRELL, City; Mercer County; Pop. 8,645 / 6,383; Zip Code 16121; Elev. 853; Lat. 41-12-44 N, Long. 080-29-49 W; W Pennsylvania. Farrell was incorporated as South Sharon In 1901. It was renamed in 1911 to honor James A. Farrell, president of the United States Steel Corporation.

FAYETTEVILLE, Village; Franklin County; Pop. 2,400; Zip Code 17222; Elev. 800; Lat. 40-26-20 N, Long. 080-12-50 W; 7 mi. SE of Chambersburg in S Pennsylvania; Named for General La Fayette.

FERNDALE, Borough; Cambria County; Pop. 2,204 / 1,784; Zip Code 18921; Lat. 40-32-01 N, Long. 075-10-45 W; S suburb of Johnstown in SW central Pennsylvania; Residential.

FLEETWOOD, Borough; Berks County; Pop. 3,422 / 3,975; Zip Code 19522; Elev. 440; Lat. 40-27-14 N, Long. 075-49-06 W; 15 mi. NE of Reading in SE Pennsylvania. In 1859, the growing settlement took the name of Fleetwood after a prominent English capitalist, who encouraged the construction of the railroad.

FLEMINGTON. Borough; Clinton County; Pop. 1,416 / 1,288; Zip Code 19522; Elev. 440; Lat. 41-07-35 N, Long. 077-28-19 W; Central Pennsylvania; Named for John Fleming, an associate justice in Lycoming County (1798), who once owned this site.

FLOURTOWN, Village; Montgomery County; Pop. 5,000; Zip Code 19031; Elev. 169; Lat. 40-06-12 N, Long. 075-12-46 W; SE Pennsylvania. Flourtown, founded in 1743, was once noted for its flour trade. Farmers came to buy supplies and have their wheat ground by the millers along the Wissahickon River.

FOLCROFT, Borough; Delaware County; Pop. 8,231 / 7,200; Zip Code 19032; Elev. 70; Lat. 39-53-27 N, Long. 075-17-03 W; SW suburb of Philadelphia in SE Pennsylvania.

FORD CITY, Borough; Armstrong County; Pop. 3,923 / 3,298; Zip Code 16226; Elev. 785; Lat. 40-46-20 N, Long. 079-31-48 W; W Pennsylvania. Ford City, off U.S. Highway 422 on the Allegheny River, was named for Captain John B. Ford, "father of the plate glass industry in America," who erected a factory here in 1887.

FOREST CITY, Borough; Susquehanna County; Pop. 1,924 / 1,980; Zip Code 18421; Elev. 1,480; Lat. 41-39-05 N, Long. 075-28-01 W; 20 mi. NE of Scranton in NE Pennsylvania.

FOREST HILLS, Borough; Allegheny County; Pop. 8,198 / 6,881; Zip Code 15221; Elev. 1,080; Lat. 40-58-28 N, Long. 077-02-59 W; E suburb of Pittsburgh, off U.S. Highway 30 in SW Pennsylvania.

FORT LOUDON, Village; Franklin County; Pop. 900; Zip Code 17224; Elev. 641; Lat. 39-54-53 N, Long. 077-54-18 W.

FORT WASHINGTON, Village; Montgomery County; Pop. 4,000; Zip Code 19034; Elev. 174; Lat. 40-08-30 N, Long. 075-12-34 W; 18 mi. N of Philadelphia. Fort Washington was named for General Washington's encampment.

FORTY FORT, Borough; Luzerne County; Pop. 5,590 / 4,369; Zip Code 18704; Elev. 554; Lat. 41-16-44 N, Long. 075-52-43 W; E Pennsylvania; Named for the first 40 settlers who came to the valley.

FOUNTAIN HILL, Borough; Lehigh County; Pop. 4,805 / 4,437; Zip Code 18015; Elev. 360; Lat. 40-36-05 N, Long. 075-23-44 W; In a residential area 1 mi. W of Bethlehem in E Pennsylvania.

FOX CHAPEL, Borough; Allegheny County; Pop. 5,049 / 5,153; Zip Code 15238; Elev. 980; NE suburb of Pittsburgh in SW Pennsylvania.

FRACKVILLE, Borough; Schuylkill County; Pop. 5,308 / 6,388; Zip Code 17931; Elev. 1,476; Lat. 40-47-02 N, Long. 076-13-50 W; 20 mi. SW of Hazleton in E central Pennsylvania.

FRANKLIN, City; Seat of Venango County; Pop. 8,146 / 6,783; Zip Code 16323; Elev. 1,017; Lat. 40-20-32 N, Long. 078-53-06 W; 70 mi. N of Pittsburgh in NW Pennsylvania. The town was laid out for the county seat in 1795 on a tract of 1,000 acres belonging to the state and took its name from Fort Franklin.

FREDERICKTOWN, Village; Washington County; Pop. 1,000; Zip Code 15333; Elev. 790; Lat. 40-00-09 N, Long. 079-59-54 W; SW Pennsylvania. The town was named for its founder Frederick Wise, in 1790.

FREEDOM, Borough; Beaver County; Pop. 2,272 / 1,761; Zip Code 15042; Elev. 703; Lat. 40-45-47 N, Long. 076-56-23 W; On bend of Ohio River in W Pennsylvania.

FREELAND, Borough; Luzerne County; Pop. 4,285 / 3,490; Zip Code 18224; Elev. 1,880; Lat. 41-01-00 N, Long. 075-53-51 W; 10 mi. NE of Hazelton in E Pennsylvania. The Donop plot became generally known as "free land," that is, land that could be purchased, as distinguished from the coal companies land, which was not for sale. Mr. Donop preferred to name his new town Freehold, a name that it retained until the establishment of a post office in 1874. The postal authorities objected to this name because of the nearness and importance of Freehold in New Jersey, so the townspeople then adopted the nickname Freeland.

FREEPORT, Borough; Armstrong County; Pop. 2,381 / 1,915; Zip Code 16229; Elev. 775; Lat. 40-40-26 N, Long. 079-41-06 W; W Pennsylvania. Freeport, at the confluence of the Allegheny and Kiskiminetas Rivers and Buffalo Creek, in a fertile farming country with valuable orchard and dairy interests, was laid out in 1796 by William and David Todd as a free port for river craft.

GALETON, Borough; Potter County; Pop. 1,462 / 1,314; Zip Code 16922; Elev. 1315; Lat. 41-43-59 N, Long. 077-38-32 W; At the forks of Pine Creek, near Lyman Run State Park in N Pennsylvania.

GALLITZIN, Borough; Cambria County; Pop. 2,315 / 1,789; Zip Code 16641; Elev. 2,167; Lat. 40-28-56 N, Long. 078-33-07 W; 10 mi. W of Altoona in SW central Pennsylvania; On a scenic route, Gallitzin bears the name of the priest, Prince Demetrius Augustine Gallitzin, one of the pioneers of Cambria County. Prince Gallitzin, the son of a Russian diplomat and the scion of on ancient and noble family, moved to Baltimore on his *wanderiahr* in 1792 at the age of 22.

GEISTOWN, Borough; Cambria County; Pop. 3,304 / 2,625; Zip Code 15904; Elev. 1,900; 6 mi. SE of Johnstown in SW central Pennsylvania.

GETTYSBURG, Borough; Seat of Adams County; Pop. 7,194 / 7,589; Zip Code 17325; Lat. 03-49-51 N, Long. 077-13-53 W; S Pennsylvania. About ten years before Adams County was organized, James Gettys, who has been described as "a man of brains, force of character, and resources," scenting the certainty of a new county and the possibility of securing an eligible site for the county-seat, bought a tract of land and laid out a village, which he called Gettystown. The name of the little town which he planned and plotted was destined to become famous throughout the world and memorable in history as the name of a bloody battlefield, on which the great Rebellion was to be checked and the fate of the Union decided.

GIRARD, Borough; Erie County; Pop. 2,615 / 3,004; Zip Code 16417; Elev. 831; Lat. 42-00-01 N, Long. 080-19-06 W; 10 mi. SW of Erie on Elk Creek in NW Pennsylvania. Settlement occurred prior to 800; Named for Stephen Girard, a Philadelphia merchant who owned land in the vicinity, it was incorporated as a borough in 1846.

GLASSPORT, Borough; Allegheny County; Pop. 6,242 / 5,033; Zip Code 15045; Elev. 755; Lat. 40-19-29 N, Long. 079-53-33 W; SW Pennsylvania on the east bank of the Monongahela; Named in 1888 when the United States Glass Company established a plant here. The borough was incorporated in 1902.

GLEN ROCK, Borough; York County; Pop. 1,662 / 1,836; Zip Code 17327; Elev. 560; Lat. 39-47-35 N, Long. 076-43-50 W; 15 mi. S of York in a farming region in S Pennsylvania.

GLENOLDEN, Borough; Delaware County; Pop. 7,633 / 7,002; Zip Code 19036; Elev. 90; 5 mi. SW of central Philadelphia in SE Pennsylvania; Residential.

GLENSHAW, Village; Allegheny County; Pop. 18,000; Zip Code 15116; Elev. 1,060; Lat. 40-31-58 N, Long. 079-58-04 W; NW suburb of Pittsburgh in SW Pennsylvania; Pine Creek flows through this hilly residential community.

GLENSIDE, Village; Montgomery County; Pop. 17,000; Zip Code 19038; Elev. 260; Lat. 40-06-08 N, Long. 075-09-09 W; One of the largest suburbs N of Philadelphia in SE Pennsylvania.

GRATERFORD, Village; Montgomery County; Pop. 800; Zip Code 19426; Elev. 140; Lat. 40-13-32 N, Long. 075-27-18; 10 mi. E of Pottstown; Founded in 1756 and named for Jacob Kreater.

GREEN TREE, Borough; Allegheny County; Pop. 5,722 / 4,484; Zip Code 15242; Elev. 1,100; Lat. 40-24-42 N, Long. 080-02-45 W; S suburb of Pittsburgh which includes Mann Oak and Parkway Center; SW Pennsylvania.

GREENCASTLE, Borough; Franklin County; Pop. 3,679 / 3,850; Zip Code 17225; Elev. 580; S of Chambersburg in S Pennsylvania; On a scenic route (181); Laid out in 1782 by Colonel John Allison and named for his native town, a tiny seaport in County Donegal, Ireland.

GREENSBURG, City; Seat of Westmoreland County; Pop. 17,558 / 15,357; Zip Code 15601; Elev. 1,110; Lat. 340-18-05 N, Long. 079-32-21 W; 30 mi. E of Pittsburgh in SE Pennsylvania. About this time a town was laid out on the land of Christopher Truby, and named Greensburg in honor of General Nathaniel Greene (1742-86), under whom had fought many a Scotch-Irish soldier from Westmoreland.

GREENVILLE, Borough; Mercer County; Pop. 7,730 / 6,283; Zip Code 16125; Elev. 963; Lat. 41-00-38 N, Long. 078-36-16 W; 70 mi. N of Pittsburgh in W Pennsylvania. The town, which was long called West Greenville, is generally believed to have been named for General Nathaniel Greene. No other plausible or authoritative explanation has ever been given.

GROVE CITY, Borough; Mercer County; Pop. 8,162 / 8,132; Zip Code 16127; Elev. 1,246; Lat. 41-09-28 N, Long. 080-05-20 W; 55 mi. N of Pittsburgh in W Pennsylvania; Site of Grove City College.

HALLAM, Borough; York County; Pop. 1,428 / 1,343; Zip Code 17406; Elev. 380; Lat. 40-00-17 N, Long. 076-36-16 W; 5 mi. NE of York along a scenic route; Named by early settler Samuel Blunston for his native town of Upper Hallam in Yorkshire, England.

HALLSTEAD, Borough; Susquehanna County; Pop. 1,280 / 1,355; Zip Code 18822; Elev. 884; Lat. 41-57-40 N, Long. 075-44-37 W; on N branch of Susquehanna River in NE Pennsylvania; Named for William F. Hallstead, an official of the Lackawanna Railroad.

HAMBURG, Borough; Berks County; Pop. 4,011 / 4,179; Zip Code 19526; Elev. 387; Lat. 40-33-20 N, Long. 075-58-56 W; 17 mi. N of Reading in SE Pennsylvania on the east bank of the Schuylkill. Founded in 1779.

HANOVER, Borough; York County; Pop. 14,890 / 14,478; Zip Code 17331; Elev. 599; Lat. 41-11-08 N, Long. 075-58-57 W; 8 mi. N of Massachusetts state line in S Pennsylvania. To please the German settlers, the town was, at the suggestion of Michael Danner, who owned a large tract of land southeast of the site, formally christened Hanover for his native Hanover in Germany.

HARMONY, Borough; Butler County; Pop. 1,334 / 1,003; Zip Code 16037; Elev. 913; Lat. 40-48-05 N, Long. 080-07-39 W; W Pennsylvania. Harmony is the site of the first settlement of the Harmony Society, organized in 1805 by George Rapp, for more than 40 years the religious and industrial leader of the Harmony Society.

HARRISBURG, City. Dauphin County seat and capital of Pennsylvania; Pop. 53,113 / 48,618; Zip Code 171; Elev. 374; Lat. 40-16-25 N, Long. 076-53-05 W; 100 mi. W of Philadelphia lying on the east bank of the Susquehanna River in S central Pennsylvania. John Harris, a Yorkshireman, licensed in 1705 as an Indian trader, settled at Paxtang about 1712 and established a trading post and ferry. The town is named for him.

HARVEY'S LAKE, Borough; Luzerne County; Pop. 2,318 / 2,597; Zip Code 18618; Elev. 1,287; Lat. 41-23-00 N, Long. 076-01-30 W; N of Wilkes-Barre in E Pennsylvania.

HATFIELD, Borough; Montgomery County; Pop. 2,533 / 2,580; Zip Code 19440; Elev. 340; Lat. 39-52-40 N, Long. 079-44-22 W; N suburb of Philadelphia, 10 mi. W of Dylestown in SE Pennsylvania.

HAVERTOWN, Village; Delaware County; Pop. 35,000; Zip Code 19083; Lat. 39-58-51 N, Long. 075-18-32 W; NW suburb of Philadelphia in SE Pennsylvania; A large bedroom community for city commuters.

HAWLEY, Borough; Wayne County; Pop. 1,181 / 1,323; Zip Code 18428; Elev. 896; Lat. 41-28-33 N, Long. 075-10-57 W; 25 mi. E of Scranton in NE Pennsylvania.

HAWTHORN, Borough; Clarion County; Pop. 547 / 496; Zip Code 16230; Elev. 1,000; Lat. 41-01-12 N, Long. 079-16-29 W; On Red Bank Creek in W Pennsylvanian a rural area.

HAZLETON, City; Luzerne County; Pop. 27,318 / 22,981; Zip Code 18201; Elev. 1,624; Lat. 40-57-30 N, Long. 075-58-30 W; E Pennsylvania. Hazleton is named for Hazel Creek.

HEIDELBERG, Borough; Allegheny County; Pop. 1,606 / 1,149; Zip Code 15106; Elev. 820; Lat. 40-23-32 N, Long. 080-05-28 W; 4 mi. S of Central Pittsburgh in SW Pennsylvania; Named by German founders for the medieval city in their native land. A large racetrack is located here.

HERSHEY, Village (Unincorporated); Zip Code 17033; Elev. 400; Lat. 40-17-09 N, Long. 076-39-02 W; 15 mi. E of Harrisburg. Hershey is the privately owned and planned community of M.S. Hershey, a former Lancaster caramel manufacturer, who bought a cornfield here in 1903 and created a chocolate manufacturing center.

HIGHSPIRE, Borough; Dauphin County; Pop. 2,959 / 2,633, Zip Code 17034; Elev. 299; Lat. 40-12-39 N, Long. 076-47-29 W; 5 mi. SE of Harrisburg in SE central Pennsylvania. It is said to have been named for the old church spire here that served as a landmark for Susquehanna River boatmen.

HOLLIDAYSBURG, Borough; Seat of Blair County; Pop. 5,897 / 5,364; Zip Code 16648; Elev. 953; Lat. 40-25-38 N, Long. 078-23-21 W; 5 mi. S of Altoona in W central Pennsylvania. The settlement was founded in 1768 by Adam and William Holliday, Irish immigrants, at a time when Indians were still fighting white encroachment.

HOKENDAUQUA, Village; Lehigh County; Pop. 2,000; Zip Code 18052; Lat. 40-39-43 N, Long. 075-29-29 W; N suburb of Allentown along the Lehigh River in E Pennsylvania; Name is Indian for "searching for land," which probably came about as tribesmen observed the first white land surveyors here.

HOMER CITY, Borough; Indiana County; Pop. 2,248 / 1,735; Zip Code 15748; Elev. 1,023; Lat. 40-32-36 N, Long. 079-09-45 W; 7 mi. S of the town Indiana in W central Pennsylvania; Founded in 1854.

HOMESTEAD, Borough; Allegheny County; Pop. 5,092 / 3,721; Zip Code 15120; Elev. 852; Lat. 40-24-21 N, Long. 079-54-44 W; Adjoining Pittsburgh in SW Pennsylvania. Homestead was originally Amity Homestead, and renamed when incorporated as a borough in 1880. The settlement was laid out in 1871 by a Pittsburgh corporation called the Homestead Bank and Life Insurance Company. The town took its name from this company. It happened, however, that one of the farms which the company bought belonged to Abdiel McClure, who lived in a fine old farmhouse locally known as "the McClure homestead," embowered in a clump of trees. Many believe that this stately old homestead suggested the name of the town.

HONESDALE, Borough; Seat of Wayne County; Pop. 5,128 / 5,254; Zip Code 18431; Elev. 982; Lat. 41-34-36 N, Long.

075-15-33 W; 24 mi. NE of Scranton in NE Pennsylvania. In 1826, Philip Hone, mayor of New York City, later president of the Delaware & Hudson Canal Company, came to the settlement to push construction of a canal that would divert the flow of coal to his city.

HOUSTON, Borough; Washington County; Pop. 1,568 / 1,409; Zip Code 15342; Elev. 960; Lat. 40-14-47 N, Long. 080-12-42 W; 18 mi. SW of Pittsburgh in SW Pennsylvania.

HOUTZDALE, Borough; Clearfield County; Pop. 1,222 / 1,177; Zip Code 16651; Elev. 1,518; Lat. 40-49-30 N, Long. 078-21-05 W; 30 mi. NE of Altoona in W central Pennsylvania. Town was named for Dr. Daniel Houtz, who owned the land upon which it was built in 1870.

HUGHESTOWN, Borough; Luzerne County; Pop. 1,783 / 1,572; Elev. 760; Lat. 41-19-37 N, Long. 075-46-25 W; Residential suburb of Wilkes-Barre in E Pennsylvania, just NE of Pittston.

HUGHESVILLE, Borough; Lycoming County; Pop. 2,174 / 2,055; Zip Code 17737; Elev. 483; Lat. 41-14-28 N, Long. 076-43-27 W; 15 mi. E of Williamsport in N central Pennsylvania. Hughesville was laid out in 1816 by Jeptha Hughes, who called it Hughesburg. In 1827, when the post office was established, the name was changed to Hughesville.

HULMEVILLE, Borough; Bucks County; Pop. 1,014 / 971; Zip Code 19047; Elev. 40; Lat. 40-06-35 N, Long. 074-54-41 W; NE suburb of Philadelphia in SE Pennsylvania.

HUMMELSTOWN, Borough; Dauphin County; Pop. 4,267 / 4,001; Zip Code 17036; Elev. 370; Lat. 40-15-55 N, Long. 076-42-31 W; SE central Pennsylvania. Hummelstown was founded about 1740 by Frederick Hummel and known as Frederickstown until his death in 1780. During the Revolution Hummelstown was an important depot of arms and munitions for garrisons and forts situated to the west and the north.

HUNTINGDON, Borough; Seat of Huntingdon County; Pop. 7,042 / 7,154; Zip Code 16652; Elev. 630; Lat. 40-29-05 N, Long. 078-00-38 W; 35 mi. E of Altoona in S central Pennsylvania. Huntingdon was originally called Standing Stone. The settlement was laid out in 1767 by Dr. William Smith, first Provost of the University of Pennsylvania, and named for Selina Hastings, Countess of Huntingdon, who had responded liberally to Smith's appeal for funds to aid the university.

HYNDMAN, Borough; Bedford County; Pop. 1,106 / 1,043; Zip Code 15545; Elev. 934; Lat. 39-49-23 N, Long. 078-43-06 W; On Wills Creek, 50 mi. SW of Altoona in S Pennsylvania. Hyndman was first called Bridgeport, for which, at the time of its incorporation in 1877, the name Hyndman was substituted, in honor of E.K. Hyndman, president of the Pittsburgh and Western Railroad.

IMPERIAL, Village; Allegheny County; Pop. 2,000; Zip Code 15126; Elev. 940; Lat. 40-26-58 N, Long. 080-14-41 W; NW suburb of Pittsburgh in SW Pennsylvania. The town was laid out by the Imperial Coal Company in 1879, and was named for their Imperial Mine.

INDIANA, Borough; Seat of Indiana County; Pop. 16,051 / 14,674; Zip Code 15701; Elev. 1,310; Lat. 40-37-17 N, Long. 079-09-10 W; 46 mi. NE of Pittsburgh in W central Pennsylvania.

Indiana, founded in 1805 when George Clymer of Philadelphia, one of the signers of the Declaration of Independence, donated 250 acres for county buildings. It was probably named for the Territory of Indiana, which Congress formed from the Northwest Territory in 1800.

INDUSTRY, Borough; Beaver County; Pop. 2,417 / 2,027; Zip Code 15052; Elev. 695; Lat. 40-38-40 N, Long. 080-24-59 W; W Pennsylvania.

INGRAM, Borough; Allegheny County; Pop. 4,346 / 3,604; Zip Code 15205; Elev. 880; Lat. 40-26-46 N, Long. 080-04-04 W; S suburb of Pittsburgh in SW Pennsylvania.

IRWIN, Borough; Westmoreland County; Pop. 4,995 / 4,320; Zip Code 15642; Elev. 879; Lat. 40-19-28 N, Long. 079-42-05 W; 20 mi. SE of Pittsburgh in SW Pennsylvania.

JACOBUS, Borough; York County; Pop. 1,396 / 1,409; Zip Code 17407; 10 mi. S of York in S Pennsylvania.

JEANNETTE, City; Westmoreland County; Pop. 13,106 / 10,280; Zip Code 15644; Elev. 1,040; Lat. 40-19-41 N, Long. 079-36-56 W; 23 mi. SE of Pittsburgh in SW Pennsylvania; Named for the wife of H. Sellers McKee, who in 1889 helped to establish a glass works that led to the transformation of a farm site into an industrial city.

JEFFERSON, Borough; Allegheny County; Pop. 8,643 / 9,616; Zip Code 15025; Elev. 780; Lat. 41-12-21 N, Long. 079-23-19 W; SE suburb of Pittsburgh in SW Pennsylvania; Incorporated in 1950 as a residential subdivision; Named for Thomas Jefferson.

JENKINTOWN, Borough; Montgomery County; Pop. 4,942 / 4,263; Zip Code 19046; Elev. 250; Lat. 40-05-45 N, Long. 075-07-32 W; In a suburb of Philadelphia in SE Pennsylvania; Low density houses and country clubs are in vicinity. Jenkintown was named for the Welsh pioneer, William Jenkins, who settled here before 1697. The place was called Jenkintown as early as 1759.

JERMYN, Borough; Lackawanna County; Pop. 2,411 / 2,176; Zip Code 18433; Elev. 952; Lat. 41-31-51 N, Long. 075-32-45 W; NE Pennsylvania. Jermyn, which with Mayfield forms the so-called "twin boroughs," was named by the Delaware and Hudson Canal Company for John Jermyn, a wealthy English merchant, and much of the subsequent immigration was from Great Britain.

JERSEY SHORE, Borough; Lycoming County; Pop. 4,631 / 3,977; Zip Code 17740; Elev. 603; 16 mi. W of Williamsport on Susquehanna River in N central Pennsylvania. Jersey Shore, settled in 1785 by several families from New Jersey, was named by settlers on the opposite shore of the river.

JESSUP (alt. Winton), Borough; Lackawanna County; Pop. 4,974 / 4,414; Zip Code 18434; Elev. 872; Lat. 41-28-07 N, Long. 075-33-45 W; NE Pennsylvania. This community, settled in 1849, was successively called Saymour, and Mount Vernon; When William W. Winton established a coal breaker and laid out some semblance of a town in 1074, the townsmen named it for him.

JOHNSONBURG, Borough; Elk County; Pop. 3,938 / 3,153; Zip Code 15845; Elev. 1,453; Lat. 41-29-26 N, Long. 078-40-31 W; 100 mi. NE of Pittsburgh in NW central Pennsylvania. Johnsonburg, at the forks of the Clarion River, was laid out in 1888. It is said to have received its name from John Johnson, the traditional pioneer settler in that region, who about 50 years before the town was laid out, occupied a small cabin at the junction of the east and west branches of the Clarion River, near the center of the present town.

JOHNSTOWN, City; Cambria County; Pop. 35,496 / 24,998; Zip Code 159+; Elev. 1,184; Lat. 40-19-36 N, Long. 078-55-20 W; 75 mi. E of Pittsburgh in SW central Pennsylvania. Johnstown is squeezed firmly between narrow valley walls. The city was named for Joseph Johns, Jahns, or Yahns (as the name was variously spelled) a native Switzerland, who came to America in 1769, at the age of 19. First named Conemaugh in 1831, and three years later the legislature formally changed its name to Johnstown.

JOSEPHINE, Village; Indiana County; Pop. 500; Zip Code 15750; Elev. 1020; Lat. 39-43-42 N, Long. 080-19-19 W; Founded in 1905 and named for the wife of a partner in a local steel company. An exodus occurred after this plant suspended operations about 1926.

KANE, Borough; McKean County; Pop. 4,916 / 4,162; Zip Code 16735; Elev. 2,000; Lat. 41-39-46 N, Long. 078-48-41 W; On E border of the Allegheny National Forest in N Pennsylvania.

KENHORST, Borough; Berks County; Pop. 3,187 / 2,722; Zip Code 19607; Elev. 310; Lat. 40-18-38 N, Long. 075-56-23 W; Residential suburb of Reading in SE Pennsylvania.

KENNETT SQUARE, Borough; Chester County; Pop. 4,715 / 5,274; Zip Code 19348; Elev. 268; Lat. 39-50-48 N, Long. 075-42-43 W; 12 mi. NW of Wilmington, Delaware in SE Pennsylvania. Kennett Square, settled in 1686 by Francis Smith, who had come from Kennett, a village in Wiltshire, England. A major shipping center for fresh mushrooms, it also has a large mushroom cannery.

KENSINGTON, Residential village; Philadelphia County; Pop. (incl. with Philadelphia); Zip Code 19125; SE Pennsylvania. Incorporated as Kensington, after the English village, which is now a part of London.

KING OF PRUSSIA (Brandywine Village), Village; Montgomery County; Pop. 11,000; Zip Code 19406; Elev. 190. Lat. 40-05-21 N, Long. 075-23-47 W; King of Prussia had its nucleus in the King of Prussia Inn, which the first proprietor, a native of Prussia, named for the Brandenburg prince, who in 1701 transformed Prussia from a duchy into a kingdom, taking the title of King Frederick I.

KINGSTON, Borough; Luzerne County; Pop. 15,681 / 13,216; Zip Code 18704; E Pennsylvania. The name of Kingston was borrowed from Kingston in Rhode Island, from which some of the "first 40" of the early settlers had migrated.

KITTANNING, Borough; Set of Armstrong County; Pop. 5,432 / 4,838; Zip Code 16201; Elev. 807; Lat. 40-48-59-N, Long. 079-31-20 W; 43 mi. NE of Pittsburgh in W Pennsylvania; On Allegheny River. Kittanning stretches along the eastern bank of the

Allegheny. Kittanning was laid out in 1803 by Judge George Rose. From this place a famous Indian trail known as "the Kittanning Path" led across the mountains to Standing Stone, now Huntingdon.

KNOX, Borough; Clarion County; Pop. 1,364 / 1,136; Zip Code 16232; Elev. 1,400; Lat. 41-14-04 N, Long. 079-32-15 W; 20 mi. SE of Oil City in W Pennsylvania.

KNOXVILLE, Borough; Tioga County; Pop. 650 / 565; Zip Code 16928; Elev. 1,241; Lat. 40-25-11 N, Long. 079-59-42 W; At the foot of 2,200 ft. Fork Hilt in N Pennsylvania.

KOPPEL, Borough; Beaver County; Pop. 1,146 / 947; Zip Code 16136; Elev. 890; Lat. 40-50-03 N, Long. 080-19-21 W; W Pennsylvania. Koppel was named for Arthur Koppel of Germany, who established a freight car factory here a few years before World War I.

KULPMONT, Borough; Northumberland County; Pop. 3,675 / 2,977; Zip Code 17834; Elev. 900; Lat. 40-47-36 N, Long. 076-28-22 W; E central Pennsylvania; Founded in 1875 and incorporated as a borough in 1914.

KUTZTOWN, Borough; Berks County; Pop. 4,040 / 4,719; Zip Code 19530; Elev. 450; Lat. 40-23-55 N, Long. 076-19-20 W; 18 mi. N of Reading in SE Pennsylvania. Kutztown was founded in 1771 and named for George Kutz, who laid it out.

LACKAWAXEN. Village; Pike County; Pop. 500; Elev. 647; Lat. 41-28-55 N, Long. 074-59-11 W; Lackawaxen (Ind. "swift waters" or "where the way forks") was founded in 1770.

LAFAYETTE HILL, Village; Montgomery County; Pop. 5,500; Suburb of Philadelphia; Also known as Barren Hill.

LAFLIN, Borough; Luzerne County; Pop. 1,650 / 1,485; Elev. 727; Lat. 41-17-20 N, Long. 075-48-21 W; 4 mi. N of Wilkes-Barre in E Pennsylvania on Gardner's Creek.

LAKE CITY, Borough; Erie County; Pop. 2,384 / 2,272; Zip Code 16423; Elev. 721; Lat. 41-21-53 N, Long. 078-53-09 W; NW Pennsylvania. Name changed from North Girard in 1954. Located on Lake Erie shore. 15 mi. SE of Erie.

LANCASTER, City; Lancaster County Seat; Pop. 54,632 / 52,712; Zip Code 176+; Lat. 40-02-16 N, Long. 076-18-21 W; 64 mi. W of Philadelphia in SE Pennsylvania; Near the Susquehanna River. Both county and town were named by John Wright, chief magistrate, for his home shire of Lancaster, England.

LANDISVILLE, Village; Lancaster County; Pop. 2,000 Zip Code 17538; Elev. 403; Lat. 40-20-57 N, Long. 075-06-49 W; German residential town, was laid out in 1808.

LANGHORNE, Borough; Bucks County; Pop. 1,697 / 1,322; Zip Code 19047; Elev. 220; Lat. 40-10-28 N, Long. 074-55-23 W; SE Pennsylvania. Named for early settler Jeremiah Langhorne, chief justice of the province in 1739-43. Today it is a suburb of Philadelphia, mainly residential.

LANGHORNE MANOR, Borough; Bucks County; Pop. 1,103 / 783; Zip Code 19047; Elev. 200; Lat. 40-10-01 N, Long. 074-55-05 W; 1 mi. N of Langhorne in SE Pennsylvania; Also a suburb of Philadelphia.

LANDSDALE, Borough; Montgomery County; Pop. 16,526 / 15,768; Zip Code 19446 Lat. 40-14-29 N, Long. 075-17-03 W; 24 mi. NW of Philadelphia in a suburban area in SE Pennsylvania.

LANSDOWNE. Borough; Delaware County; Pop. 11,891 / 11,037; Zip Code 19050; Elev. 205; Lat. 39-56-17 N, Long. 075-16-20 W; SE Pennsylvania; Was probably named for Lord Lansdowne.

LANDSFORD, Borough; Carbon County; Pop. 4,466 / 4,326; Zip Code 18232; Elev. 1,100; Lat. 40-49-54 N, Long. 075-52-58 W; E Pennsylvania; Founded in 1846 and named for Asa Lansford Foster, mining engineer, coal operator, and early champion of the public school system.

LARKSVILLE, Borough; Luzerne County; Pop. 4,410 / 4,502; Elev. 940; Lat. 41-14-42 N, Long. 075-55-52 W; E suburb of Wilkes-Barre in E Pennsylvania; A mining borough originally called Blidtown, was renamed in 1895 in honor of Peggy Lark, who had owned the village site and died here at the reputed age of 106.

LATROBE, Borough; Westmoreland County; Pop. 10,799 / 9,216; Zip Code 15650; Elev. 1,006; Lat. 40-19-16 N, Long. 079-22-47 W; 41 mi. SE of Pittsburgh in SW Pennsylvania. Latrobe, on Loyalhanna Creek, was named for Benjamin Henry Lotrobe, Jr., son of the father of architecture in the United States.

LAUGHLINTOWN, Village; Westmoreland County; Pop. 750; Zip Code 15655; Elev. 1,274; Lat. 40-12-43 N, Long. 079-11-53 W; At the base of Laurel Hill, was founded in 1797 by Robert Laughlin.

LAUREL RUN, Borough; Luzerne County; Pop. 715 / 603; Elev. 900; Lat. 41-13-20 N, Long. 075-51-48 W; Suburb of Wilkes-Barr in E Pennsylvania.

LAURELDALE, Borough; Berks County; Pop. 4,047 / 3,651; Zip Code 19605; Elev. 380; N suburb of Reading in SE Pennsylvania.

LEBANON, City; Seat of Lebanon County; Pop. 25,711 / 23,463; Zip Code 17042; Elev. 468; Lat. 40-20-27 N, Long. 076-24-42 W, 80 mi. NW of Philadelphia in SE central Pennsylvania. Lebanon lies on a branch of Quitapahilla (Ind. "spring which flows from among pines") Creek between the South and Blue Mountains. Laid out in 1756 by George Steitz, the settlement was first known as Steitztown. Cedar trees growing in the vicinity may have reminded the Moravian settlers of the Biblical "cedars of Lebanon," and thus inspired its name.

LEECHBURG, Borough; Armstrong County; Pop. 2,612 / 2,364; Zip Code 15656; Elev. 789 W Pennsylvania; Lat. 40-30-16 N, Long. 079-45-49 W; Leechburg, on the Kiskiminetas, was laid out in 1828 by David Leech, a native of Mercer County.

LEESPORT, Borough; Berks County; Pop. 1,258 / 1,982; Zip Code 19533; Elev. 340; Lat. 40-26-49 N, Long. 075-58-00 W; SE Pennsylvania; Name changed from West Leesport in 1950.

LEETSDALE, Borough; Allegheny County; Pop. 1,604 / 1,237; Zip Code 15056; Elev. 714; Lat. 40-33-47 N, Long. 080-12-31 W; suburb of Pittsburgh in SE Pennsylvania; settled by William Leet in 1796.

LEHIGHTON, Borough; Carbon County; Pop. 5,826 / 5,768; Zip Code 18235; Elev. 478; Lat. 40-50-01 N, Long. 075-42-51 W; 26 mi. NW of Allentown in E Pennsylvania. Lehighton is on a plateau overlooking river and valley. The town was laid out in 1794 by Colonel Jacob Weiss and William Henry, and took its name from the Lehigh River, on which it is situated.

LEVITT, Unincorporated village; Bucks County; Pop. 7,200; Zip Code 19053; Elev. 60; 25 mi. NE of Philadelphia in SE Pennsylvania. Levitt is a large residential area. Community was planned by the Levitt brothers in the 1950s, who also developed a Levittown on Long Island, N.Y.

LEWISBURG, Borough; Seat of Union County; Pop. 5,407 / 5,856; Zip Code 17837; Elev. 461; Lat. 40-57-52 N, Long. 076-53-05 W; 10 mi. NW of Sunbury in central Pennsylvania, on Susquehanna River. Laid out in 1785, the settlement was named for Ludwig (Lewis) Doerr, storekeeper and early settler.

LEWIS RUN, Borough; McKean County; Pop. 677 / 575; Zip Code 16738; Elev. 1,551; Lat. 41-52-15 N, Long. 078-39-42 W; N Pennsylvania. Lewis Run is on a plain at the southern edge of the Bradford oil field, and bisected by the stream for which it is named.

LEWISTOWN, Borough; Seat of Mifflin County; Pop. 9,830 / 9,229; Zip Code 17044; Elev. 495; Lat. 40-35-57 N, Long. 077-34-18 W; Lewistown, near the western end of Lewistown Narrows, was laid out in 1790, and named Lewistown in honor of William Lewis, an ironmaster, who then owned and operated Hope Furnace, which was situated in old Derry Township, a few miles west of the new town.

LIBERTY, Borough; Allegheny County; Pop. 3,112 / 184; Elev. 1,648; Lat. 40-19-31 N, Long. 079-51-23 W; Liberty began its history as a blockhouse. In the village center is the site of the Liberty Blockhouse erected as a provision station and refuge in 1792 during construction of Blockhouse or Williamson Road, between Northumberland and Canoe Camp.

LIGONIER, Borough; Westmoreland County; Pop. 1,917 / 1,576; Zip Code 15658; Elev. 1,200; Lat. 40-14-35 N, Long. 079-14-16 W; Laid out in 1816 and named for Fort Ligonier, erected in 1758 by Colonel Henry Bouquet and named for a noted English soldier of French extraction, Field Marshal Sir John Louis Ligonier, who was raised to an earldom in 1766.

LILLY, Borough; Cambria County; Pop. 1,462 / 1,140; Zip Code 15938; Elev. 1,904; Lat. 40-25-33 N, Long. 078-37-13 W; Hilly area 20 mi. SW of Altoona in SW central Pennsylvania.

LINCOLN, Borough; Allegheny County; Pop. 1,428 / 1,139; Elev. 1,100; Lat. 40-11-47 N, Long. 076-12-05 W; In 1958 from Lincoln Township; suburb of Pittsburgh in SW Pennsylvania.

LINESVILLE, Borough; Zip Code 16424; Elev. 1,050; Lat. 41-39-22 N, Long. 080-25-27 W; Received its name from Amos Line, who was employed as a surveyor by the Pennsylvania Population Company, and who laid out the town about 1825.

LITITZ, Borough; Lancaster County; Pop. 7,590; Zip Code 17543; Elev. 360; Lat. 40-09-26 N, Long. 076-18-26 W; of Lancaster in SE Pennsylvania. Lititz was laid out in 1757 by Moravian missionaries from Bethlehem and named for a barony in Moravia.

LITTLESTOWN, Borough; Adams County; Pop. 2,870 / 3,206; Zip Code 17340; Elev. 640; Lat. 40-31-13 N, Long. 079-01-34 W; S Pennsylvania. Adam Klein, a German immigrant, began this settlement in 1765. Early on, the village was known both as Petersburg and Kleine-staedtel. Finally the latter name stuck, and was translated into "Littlestown."

LOCK HAVEN, City; Seat of Clinton County; Pop. 9,617 / 8,931; Zip Code 17745; Elev. 579; Lat. 41-08-13 N, Long. 077-26-50 W; On the Susquehanna River in the Bald Eagle Mountains in central Pennsylvania. Lock Haven was christened because the canal had a lock here, and the river furnished an excellent harbor, or haven, for rafts.

LOGANVILLE, Borough; Zip Code 17342; Elev. 782 / 909; Lat. 39-51-20 N, Long. 076-42-28 W; Loganville was laid out about 1820 and named for Colonel Henry Logan, York County representative in Congress.

LORETTO, Borough; Cambria County; Pop. 1,395 / 1,302; Zip Code 15940; Elev. 2,102; Lat. 40-30-11 N, Long. 078-37-50 W; SW of Altoona in SW central Pennsylvania. Loretta was named for the celebrated religious shrine in Italy near the Adriatic Sea by the priest Demetrius Gollatzin.

LOWER BURRELL, City; Westmoreland County; Pop. 13,200 / 12,165; Zip Code 15068; Elev. 760; Lat. 40-33-11 N, Long. 079-45-27 W; N suburb of Pittsburgh in SE Pennsylvania.

LUZERNE, Borough; Luzerne County; Pop. 3,703 / 3,174; Zip Code 18709; Elev. 570; Lat. 39-59-57 N, Long. 079-57-47 W; suburb of Wilkes-Barre in E Pennsylvania.

LYKENS, Borough; Dauphin County; Pop. 2,181 / 1,861; Zip Code 17048; Elev. 677; Lat. 40-34-00 N, Long. 076-42-03 W; central Pennsylvania; Founded in 1826, one year after the discovery of anthracite at the lower end of Short Mountain. It is named for Andrew Lycon, or Lykens, who had settled here in 1732.

MACUNGIE, Borough; Lehigh County; Pop. 1,899 / 3,142; Zip Code 18062; Elev. 380; Lat. 40-30-57 N, Long. 075-33-20 W; of Allentown on Swope Creek in E Pennsylvania; Indian name means "feeding place of the bears."

MAHAFFEY, Borough; Clearfield County; Pop. 513 / 331; Zip Code 15757; Elev. 1,323; Lat. 40-52-22 N, Long. 078-42-38 W; On west branch of the Susquehanna River in W central Pennsylvania.

MAHANOY CITY, Borough; Schuylkill County; Pop. 6,167 / 5,012; Zip Code 17948; Elev. 1,256; Lat. 40-48-45 N, Long. 076-08-31 W; Mahanoy was derived from the language of the Delaware. The word *mahoni* meaning a "lick," a term used in pioneer days to denote saline deposits where deer congregate.

MALVERN, Borough; Chester County; Pop. 2,999 / 3,199; Zip Code 19355; Elev. 550; Lat. 40-02-10 N, Long. 075-30-51 W; Suburb of Philadelphia near Pool, in SE Pennsylvania; Residential area.

MANCHESTER, Borough; York County; Pop. 2,027 / 1,928; Zip Code 17345; Elev. 500; Lat. 40-27-18 N, Long. 080-01-12 W; Named for the large industrial city in England, Manchester in Pennsylvania has a few industries of its own.

MANHEIM, Borough; Lancaster County; Pop. 5,015 / 4,841; Zip Code 17545; Elev. 339; Lat. 40-09-48 N, Long. 076-23-43 W; SE Pennsylvania.

MANOR, Borough; Westmoreland County; Pop. 2,235 / 2,826; Zip Code 15665; Elev. 1,000; Lat. 40-37-57 N, Long. 078-59-02 W; Named for one of the manors owned by the Penn family, which once stood here.

MANSFIELD, Borough; Tioga County; Pop. 3,322 / 3,165; Zip Code 16933; Elev. 1,174; Lat. 41-48-26 N, Long. 077-04-40 W; SW of Elmira, New York in N Pennsylvania. Named in 1824 for Asa Mann, an early settler.

MARIETTA, Borough; Lancaster County; Pop. 2,740 / 2,605; Zip Code 17547; Elev. 261; Lat. 40-03-25 N, Long. 076-33-09 W; 22 mi. SE of Harrisburg on Susquehanna River in SE Pennsylvania. The town was originally two distinct settlements, New Haven, laid out by David Cook in 1803, and Waterford laid out at "Andersons Ferry" by James Anderson in 1804. In 1812 the two villages were incorporated under one charter as Marietta, a name said to have been compounded of Mary and Etta, the first names of Mrs. Cook and Mrs. Anderson, the wives of the two founders.

MARS, Borough; Butler County; Pop. 1,803 / 1,713; Zip Code 16046; Elev. 1,031; Lat. 40-41-45 N, Long. 080-00-43 W; In W Pennsylvania.

MARTINSBURG. Borough; Blair County; Pop. 2,231 / 2,120; Zip Code 16662; Elev. 1,407; Lat. 40-18-40 N, Long. 078-19-28 W.

MARYSVILLE, Borough; Perry County; Pop. 2,452 / 2,423; Zip Code 17053; Elev. 460; N of Harrisburg, on Susquehanna River in S central Pennsylvania.

MASONTOWN, Borough; Fayette County; Pop. 4,909 / 3,707; Zip Code 15461; Elev. 1,050; Lat. 40-11-28 N, Long. 078-15-33 W; Settled in 1796.

MASTHOPE, Village; Pike County; Pop. 500; Name is an Anglicization of an Indian word meaning "glass beads." Today it is a ski resort.

MATAMORAS, Borough; Pike County; Pop. 2,111 / 2,496; Zip Code 18336; Elev. 868; Lat. 40-26-24 N, Long. 076-56-01 W; Delaware River, near New York and New Jersey state lines in NE Pennsylvania.

MAYFIELD, Borough; Lackawanna County; Pop. 1,812; Zip Code 18433; Elev. 952; Lat. 41-32-27 N, Long. 075-32-11 W; NE Pennsylvania; Was developed prior to 1840 by John Gibson, who sold out in 1874 to the Delaware and Hudson Canal Company.

MCADOO, Borough; Schuylkill County; Pop. 2,940 / 2,214; Zip Code 18237; Elev. 1,836; Lat. 40-54-36 N, Long. 075-59-30 W; In 1880 and later named by postal authorities for William Gibbs McAdoo.

MCCLURE, Borough; Snyder County; Pop. 1,024 / 1,026; Zip Code 17841; Elev. 700; Lat. 40-06-14 N, Long. 079-33-15 W; Was founded in 1367 and named for Alexander Kelley McClure (1828-1909), journalist, politician, and author. McClure was one of the founders of the Republican Party. The town was formerly called Stricktown for a noted Indian fighter.

MCCONNELLSBURG, Borough; Seat of Fulton County; Pop. 1,178 / 1,223; Zip Code 17233; Elev. 955; Lat. 39-55-57 N, Long. 077-59-57 W.

MCDONALD, Borough; Allegheny and Washington Counties; Pop. 2,772 / 2,180; Zip Code 15057; Elev. 1,020; Lat. 40-22-15 N, Long. 080-14-06 W; McDonald was laid out in 1781 and took its name from old Fort McDonald, which was built during the Revolutionary War on the land of John McDonald, who settled here in 1775.

MCKEESPORT. City; Allegheny County; Pop. 31,012 / 22,698; Zip Code 151+; Elev. 750; Lat. 40-20-52 N, Long. 079-51-52 W; McKeesport is at the junction of the Youghiogheny and Monongahela Rivers. David McKee, a north country Irishman who settled here in 1755, acquired title to 844 acres and in 1755 obtained ferry privileges from Colonial authorities. The town is named after his family.

MCSHERRYSTOWN, Borough; Adams County; Pop. 2,764 / 3,075; Zip Code 17344; Elev. 571; Lat. 39-48-26 N, Long. 077-00-42 W; Named after settler Patrick McSherry, who came here in 1765.

MEADVILLE, City; Seat of Crawford County; Pop. 15,544 / 13,900; Zip Code 16335; Elev. 1,078; Lat. 41-38-29 N, Long. 080-09-06 W; On French Creek, Meadville is in the western foothills of the Alleghenies, and was settled in 1788 by David Mead, his brothers, and other pioneers from Sunburgh, who made the first white settlement in Northwestern Pennsylvania.

MECHANICSBURG, Borough; Cumberland County; Pop. 9,487 / 8,943; Zip Code 17055; Elev. 460; Lat. 40-33-42 N, Long. 080-24-11 W; Named for the large number of mechanics who worked in the foundries and machine shops here.

MEYERSDALE, Borough; Somerset County; Pop. 2,581 / 2,453; Zip Code 15552; Elev. 1,975; Lat. 39-48-49 N, Long. 079-01-30 W; NW of Cumberland, Maryland in S Pennsylvania; Was laid out in a valley in 1844 and named for Peter Meyers, an early settler who converted his farm into building lots.

MIDDLETOWN, Borough; Dauphin County; Pop. 10,122 / 8,679; Zip Code 7057; Elev. 355; Lat. 41-55-38 N, Long. 076-41-57 W; 8 mi. SE of Harrisburg in SE central Pennsylvania, on the Susquehanna River. Middletown, halfway between Lancaster and Carlisle, was founded in 1755.

MIDLAND, Borough; Beaver County; Pop. 4,310 / 3,040; Zip Code 15059; Elev. 750; Lat. 40-37-57 N, Long. 030-26-48 W; 7 mi. E of East Liverpool, Ohio in W Pennsylvania. Midland, on the north bank of the Ohio River, is a smoky steel-producing center named for the Midland Steel Company.

MIDWAY, Borough; Washington County; Pop. 1,187 / 1,003; Zip Code 15060; Elev. 1,120; Lat. 39-48-30 N, Long. 077-00-11 W; SW Pennsylvania; So named because it is located between Pittsburgh and Steubenville, Ohio.

MILESBURG, Borough; Centre County; Pop. 1,309 / 1,150; Zip Code 16853; Elev. 700; Lat. 40-56-39 N, Long. 077-47-07 W;

Central Pennsylvania; Founded in 1793 by General Samuel Miles, Indian fighter, patriot, landowner, iron manufacturer, and onetime mayor of Philadelphia (1790).

MILLERSBURG, Borough; Dauphin County; Pop. 2,770 / 2,731; Zip Code 17061; Elev. 397; 28 mi. N of Harrisburg in SE central Pennsylvania, on the Susquehanna River. Settlement was made in 1790 by Daniel and John Miller, brothers, who owned 400 acres here.

MILLERSVILLE, Borough; Lancaster County; Pop. 7,668 / 7,808; Zip Code 17551; Elev. 360; Suburb of Lancaster in SE Pennsylvania; Site of Millersville State College, with 4,700 students.

MILLVALE, Borough; Allegheny County; Pop. 4,754 / 4,149; Zip Code 15209; Elev. 900; SW Pennsylvania.

MILTON, Borough; Northumberland County; Pop. 6,730 / 6,749; Zip Code 17847; Elev. 473; Lat. 40-54-35 N, Long. 079-13-01 W; 23 mi. SE of Williamsport in E central Pennsylvania, on the Susquehanna River.

MINERSVILLE, Borough; Schuylkill County; Pop. 5,635 / 4,748; Zip Code 17954; Elev. 820; Lat. 40-20-32 N, Long. 078-55-33 W; E central Pennsylvania. Named for the fact that a large number of its people have from the beginning been coal miners.

MONACA, Borough; Beaver County; Pop. 7,661 / 6,376; Zip Code 15061; Elev. 720; Lat. 40-41-14 N, Long. 080-16-18 W; 2 mi. S of Beaver in W Pennsylvania.

MONESSEN, City; Westmoreland County; Pop. 11,928 / 8,944; Zip Code 15062; Elev. 756; Lat. 40-08-54 N, Long. 079-53-17 W; 22 mi. S of Pittsburgh in SW Pennsylvania, on Monongahela River. The name Monessen is a curious hybrid compound, formed by combining the first syllable of Monongahela with Essen, the name of the greatest iron town in Germany, the home of the famous Krupp works. The original meaning of the name Essen has been lost. It has no connection with *Eisen*, the German word for iron.

MONONGAHELA, City; Washington County; Pop. 5,950 / 4,513; Zip Code 15063; Elev. 754; Lat. 40-12-11 N, Long. 079-55-35 W; 18 mi. S of Pittsburgh in SW Pennsylvania on Monongahela River. The name "Monongahela" is a form of the Indian *Menaun-gehilla*, meaning "river with the sliding banks."

MONSOEVILLE, Borough; Allegheny County; Pop. 30,977; Zip Code 15146; Elev. 1,980; 13 mi. E of Pittsburgh in SW Pennsylvania; Residential suburb.

MONTOURSVILLE, Borough; Lycoming County; Pop. 5,403 / 4,594; Zip Code 17754; Elev. 525; Lat. 41-15-15 N, Long. 076-55-15 W; Near Williamsport in N central Pennsylvania, on Susquehanna River. The site, once occupied by the Indian village of Otzinachson, was given in 1768 to Andrew Montour, a half-breed Indian interpreter, for his loyalty to the provincial government.

MOOSIC, Borough; Lackawanna County; Pop. 6,068 / 5,422; Zip Code 18507; Elev. 650; Lat. 41-21-12 N, Long. 075-44-19 W; NE Pennsylvania; Named for the great herds of moose that once roamed the Lackawanna River Valley. Suburb of Scranton.

MORTON, Borough; Delaware County; Pop. 2,412 / 2,869; Zip Code 19070; Elev. 130; Lat. 39-54-35 N, Long. 075-19-26 W; SW suburb of Philadelphia in SE of Pennsylvania. Named for John Morton, who may have cast the deciding vote from Pennsylvania in favor of the Declaration of Independence, and who signed the historic document.

MOSCOW, Borough; Lackawanna County; Pop. 1,536 / 1,785; Zip Code 18444; Elev. 1,600; Lat. 41-20-12 N, Long. 075-31-08 W; 12 mi. SE of Scranton in NE Pennsylvania.

MOUNT OLIVER, Borough; Allegheny County; Pop. 4,576 / 3,685; Zip Code 15210; Elev. 1,100; Lat. 40-24-51 N, Long. 079-59-17 W; SW Pennsylvania. The origin of the name "Oliver" is not definitely known, although some think the name is derived from Oliver Ormsby, who owned several hundred acres of land here in 1840. The next year it was apportioned among his eight children.

MOUNTVILLE, Borough; Lancaster County; Pop. 1,505 / 2,350; Zip Code 17554; Elev. 440; Lat. 40-02-21 N, Long. 076-25-52 W; SE Pennsylvania.

MUNCY, Borough; Zip Code 17756; Pop. 497 / 2,646; Lat. 41-12-20 N, Long. 076-47-09 W; 12 mi. E of Williamsport on the Susquehanna River in N central Pennsylvania. Muncy was laid out in 1797 and named for the Munsee Indians.

MYERSTOWN, Borough; Pop. 3,236 / 3,418; Zip Code 17067; Elev. 472; Lat. 40-02-37 N, Long. 077-11-23 W; 8 mi. E of Lebanon in SE central Pennsylvania.

NANTICOKE, City; Luzerne County; Pop. 13,044 / 11,393; Zip Code 18634; Elev. 640; Lat. 41-12-19 N, Long. 076-00-19 W; Suburb of Wilkes-Barr, on Susquehanna River. Nanticoke received its name from a tribe of Indians.

NARBETH, Borough; Montgomery County; Pop. 4,496 / 4,111; Zip Code 19072; Elev. 285; Lat. 40-00-30 N, Long. 075-15-39 W; NW suburb of Philadelphia in SE Pennsylvania.

NAZARETH, Borough; Northampton County; Pop. 5,443 / 5,398; Zip Code 18064; Elev. 485; Lat. 40-44-25 N, Long. 075-18-36 W; 13 mi. NE of Allentown in E Pennsylvania; Nazareth was the second Moravian settlement in Pennsylvania.

NESQUEHONING, Borough; Carbon County; Pop. 3,346 / 3,317; Zip Code 18240; Elev. 801; Lat. 40-51-52 N, Long. 075-48-41 W; 28 mi. S of Wilkes-Barre in E Pennsylvania. Nesquehoning is an Indian term meaning "at the black lick," or "narrow valley."

NEW BEAVER, Borough; Lawrence County; Pop. 1,885 / 1,810; Suburb of Beaver Falls in W Pennsylvania; Incorporated in 1960 from Big Beaver Township.

NEW BETHLEHEM, Borough; Clarion County; Pop. 1,441 / 1,072; Zip Code 16242; Elev. 1,075; Lat. 41-00-06 N, Long. 079-19-54 W; 36 mi. SE of Oil City in W Pennsylvania.

NEW BRIGHTON, Borough; Beaver County; Pop. 7,364 / 6,187; Zip Code 15066; Elev. 750; Lat. 40-43-49 N, Long. 080-18-37 W; Just S of Beaver Falls in W Pennsylvania. Named for the great English sea resort.

NEW BRITAIN, Borough; Bucks County; Pop. 2,519 / 2,504; Zip Code 18901; Elev. 300; Lat. 40-17-56 N, Long. 075-10-53 W; N suburb of Philadelphia in SE Pennsylvania; Named for the industrial city in Connecticut by west-moving pioneers.

NEW CASTLE, City; Seat of Lawrence County; Pop. 33,621 / 25,841; Zip Code 161+; Elev. 806; Lat. 41-00-13 N, Long. 080-20-50 W; 44 mi. NW of Pittsburgh in W Pennsylvania, on the Shenango River. Named the spot for Newcastle upon Tyne, the English industrial city.

NEW CUMBERLAND, Borough; Cumberland County; Pop. 8,051 / 7,199; Zip Code 17070; Elev. 308; Lat. 40-13-56 N, Long. 076-53-06 W; Suburb of Harrisburg in S Pennsylvania, on the Susquehanna River. It was named for the county in which it sits, which is Welsh for "land of compatriots."

NEW EAGLE, Borough; Washington County; Pop. 2,617 / 2,265; Zip Code 15067; Elev. 840; Lat. 40-12-28 N, Long. 079-56-50 W; 16 mi. S of Pittsburgh in SW Pennsylvania, on Monongahela River.

NEW GALILEE, Borough; Beaver County; Pop. 596 / 597; Zip Code 16141; Elev. 960; Lat. 40-50-08 N, Long. 080-23-59 W; Suburb of Pittsburgh and Beaver Falls in W Pennsylvania; Named by religious settlers for Jesus' homeland.

NEW HOLLAND, Borough; Lancaster County; Pop. 4,147 / 4,731; Zip Code 17557; Elev. 495; Lat. 40-06-06 N, Long. 076-05-08 W; 13 mi. NE of Lancaster in a tobacco and corn farming region.

NEW KENSINGTON, City; Westmoreland County; Pop. 17,660 / 14,703; Zip Code 15068; Elev. 614; Lat. 40-34-11 N, Long. 079-45-54 W; 16 mi. NE of Pittsburgh in SW Pennsylvania, on the Allegheny River. New Kensington probably took its name from the London district of Kensington.

NEW OXFORD, Borough; Adams County; Pop. 1,921 / 1,804; Zip Code 17350; Elev. 560; Lat. 39-51-49 N, Long. 077-03-22 W; S Pennsylvania; Was laid out in 1792. The name was inspired by the English medieval university town.

NEW STANTON, Borough; Westmoreland County; Pop. 2,600 / 2,028; Zip Code 15672; Elev. 980; Lat. 40-13-09 N, Long. 079-36-35 W; SW Pennsylvania.

NEWTOWN, Borough; Bucks County; Pop. 2,419 / 2,523; Zip Code 18940; Elev. 150; Lat. 40-50-57 N, Long. 078-15-42 W; 22 mi. NE of Philadelphia.

NEW WILMINGTON, Borough; Lawrence County; Pop. 2,774 / 2,521; Zip Code 16142; Elev. 950; Lat. 41-07-20 N, Long. 080-19-59 W; 9 mi. N of New Castle in W Pennsylvania on Little Neshannock Creek, was incorporated from Wilmington Township in 1863.

NEWELL, Borough; Fayette County; Pop. 629 / 504; Zip Code 15466; Elev. 800; SE Pennsylvania; Incorporated in 1952 from Jefferson Township.

NORRISTOWN, Borough; Seat of Montgomery County; Pop. 34,648 / 29,276; Zip Code 194+; Elev. 83; Lat. 40-07-17 N, Long. 075-20-25 W; Located on the Schuylkill River 15 miles NW of

Philadelphia in SE Pennsylvania in a fertile rolling section of the Schuylkill Valley. On October 7, 1704, Isaac Norris and William Trent purchased the land now occupied by the borough for 50 cents an acre. The town is named for Norris.

NORTHAMPTON, Borough; Northampton County; Pop. 8,240 / 8,949; Zip Code 18067; Elev. 320; 5 miles N of Allentown in E Pennsylvania. This borough is named for the county of the same name.

NORTH APOLLO, Borough; Armstrong County; Pop. 1,487 / 1,368; Zip Code 15673; Elev. 900; Lat. 40-35-46 N, Long. 079-33-21 W; W Pennsylvania.

NORTH BELLE VERNON, Borough; Westmoreland County; Pop. 2,425 / 1,959; Zip Code rural; Elev. 900; Lat. 40-07-45 N, Long. 079-52-06 W; SW Pennsylvania.

NORTH BRADDOCK, Borough; Allegheny County; Pop. 8,711 / 6,430; Elev. 1,220; Lat. 40-23-56 N, Long. 079-50-28 W; 10 miles E of Pittsburgh in SW Pennsylvania; Incorporated in 1897 and named for its southern neighbor, Braddock. Metal products are manufactured.

NORTH EAST, Borough; Erie County; Pop. 4,568 / 4,271; Zip Code 16428; Elev. 800; Lat. 42-12-56 N, Long. 079-50-04 W; 15 miles NE of Erie in NW Pennsylvania on Lake Erie; The town is named for North East Township, which occupies the northeast corner of the Erie Triangle, a wedge-shaped slice of land once claimed by New York, Massachusetts, and Connecticut.

NORTH IRWIN, Borough; Westmoreland County; Pop. 1,016 / 955; Elev. 1,104; Lat. 40-20-15 N, Long. 079-42-49 W; E suburb of Pittsburgh in SW Pennsylvania.

NORTH WALES, Borough; Montgomery County; Pop. 3,391 / 3,786; Zip Code 19454; Elev. 380; Lat. 40-12-39 N, Long. 075-16-43 W; 20 miles N of Philadelphia in SE Pennsylvania.

NORTH YORK, Borough; York County; Pop. 1,755 / 1,587; Zip Code 17371; Elev. 380; Lat. 39-58-41 N, Long. 076-44-00 W; Just N of the city of York in S Pennsylvania.

NORTHUMBERLAND, Borough; Northumberland County; Pop. 3,636 / 3,634; Zip Code 17857; Elev. 452; Lat. 40-53-30 N, Long. 076-47-52 W; 28 miles SE of Williamsport in E central Pennsylvania; On the Susquehanna River; Was laid out in 1772 on a wedge of land formed by the junction of the two branches of the Susquehanna River, and was named for the newly-formed county it sits in.

NORVELT, Village; Westmoreland County; Pop. 1,800; Zip Code 15674; Elev. 1,040; Lat. 40-12-29 N, Long. 079-29-52 W; SW Pennsylvania; Norvelt was named by combining the final syllables of Mrs. Eleanor Roosevelt's first and last names.

NORWOOD, Borough; Delaware County; Pop. 6,647 / 6,093; Zip Code 19074; Elev. 50; Lat. 39-53-30 N, Long. 075-18-00 W; 9 miles SW of Philadelphia in SE Pennsylvania.

OAKDALE, Borough; Allegheny County; Pop. 1,955; Zip Code 15071; Elev. 900; Lat. 40-59-31 N, Long. 075-55-14 W; S suburb of Susquehanna in SW Pennsylvania.

OAKMONT, Borough; Allegheny County; Pop. 7,939 / 6,593; Zip Code 15139; Elev. 840; Lat. 40-31-18 N, Long. 079-50-33 W; 11 miles NE of Pittsburgh.

OBERLIN, Village; Dauphin County; Pop. 3,500; Zip Code 17713; Lat. 40-14-29 N, Long. 076-48-54 W; Suburb of Harrisburg near Steelton. Named for the preacher, Jean F. Oberlin, who was a preacher in the Alsace-Lorraine region of France.

OGONTZ, Village; Montgomery County; Pop. (incl. with Elkins Park); Named for an Indian chief who converted to Christianity and became a missionary to his people. A campus of Pennsylvania State University is here.

OHIOVILLE, Borough; Beaver County; Pop. 4,217 / 3,792; Elev. 1,100; Lat. 40-40-45 N, Long. 080-29-42 W; 25 miles SW of New Castle in W Pennsylvania; Incorporated in the early 1960s.

OIL CITY, City; Venango County; Pop. 13,888 / 11,159; Zip Code 16301; Elev. 1,029; Lat. 40-24-08 N tong. 078-38-25 W; 90 miles N of Pittsburgh in NW Pennsylvania; on the Allegheny River at the mouth of Oil Creek, and once the site of a Seneca village, emerged in 1860 as an important oil center. It owes its name to the rise and growth of the petroleum business.

OLD FORGE, Borough; Lackawanna County; Pop. 9,304 / 8,566; Zip Code 185+; 6 miles SW of Scranton in NE Pennsylvania; Founded in 1789 when a forge was built by Dr. William Hooker Smith, the pioneer physician of this region.

OLEONA, Village; Elev. 1,250; Lat. 41-33-22 N, Long. 077-42-07 W; Was the principal site of the colony established in 1852 by the Norwegian violin virtuoso, Ole Borneman Bull, who wished "to found a New Norway, consecrated to liberty. baptized with independence, and protected by the Unions mighty flag."

OLYPHANT, Borough; Lackawanna County; Pop. 5,204 / 4,847; Zip Code 18447; Elev. 790; Lat. 41-28-06 N, Long. 075-36-12 W; 5 miles NE of Scranton in NE Pennsylvania; James Ferris erected the first house here in 1789. Olyphant was named in honor of George Talbot Olyphant of New York, who became president of the Delaware and Hudson Canal Company in 1858.

ORANGEVILLE, Borough; Columbia County; Pop. 507 / 476; Zip Code 17859; Elev. 580; Lat. 41-04-41 N, Long. 076-24-53 W; E central Pennsylvania; Named by early settlers for Orange County, New York.

ORBISONIA, Borough; Huntingdon County; Pop. 506 / 443; Zip Code 17243; Elev. 628; Lat. 40-14-34 N, Long. 077-53-36 W; S central Pennsylvania; Was founded in 1760 and named for Thomas E. Orbison, early landowner.

ORWIGSBURG, Borough; Schuylkill County; Pop. 2,700 / 2,820; Zip Code 17961; Elev. 640; Lat. 40-39-17 N, Long. 076-06-04 W; 5 miles SE of Pottsville in E central Pennsylvania; Laid out and named by Peter Orwig in 1796. It was Schuylkill County seat from 1811 to 1851, when the seat was moved to Pottsville.

OXFORD, Borough; Chester County; Pop. 3,633 / 3,888; Zip Code 19363; Elev. 507; Lat. 39-47-07 N, Long. 075-58-45 W; SE Pennsylvania; Founded in 1801 and was named for the English university town.

PAINT, Borough; Somerset County; Pop. 1,177 / 1,044; Lat. 40-14-37 N, Long. 078-50-57 W; in S Pennsylvania.

PALMERTON, Borough; Carbon County; Pop. 5,455 / 5,209; Zip Code 18071; Elev. 420; Lat. 40-48-05 N, Long. 075-36-38 W; 15 miles NW of Allenton in E Pennsylvania; Laid out in 1898 by the New Jersey Zinc Company and named for Stephen J. Palmer, company president, was incorporated at a borough in 913.

PALMYRA, Borough; Lebanon County; Pop. 7,228 / 7,299; Zip Code 17078; Elev. 450; Lat. 40-18-32 N, Long. 076-35-37 W; 15 miles E of Harrisburg in SE central Pennsylvania; Settled by John Palm, who came to America from Germany in 1749. Palm called his settlement Palmstown, but several years later the place was re-named for the ancient Syrian city.

PAOLI, Village; Chester County; Pop. 5,335; Zip Code 19301; Elev. 452; Lat. 40-02-31 N, Long. 075-23-36 W; 15 miles NW of Philadelphia; Took its name from the General Pool Tavern, de-stroyed by fire in 1906, which had been named for General Pasquale Paoli, the Corsican patriot.

PARKESBURG. Borough; Chester County; Pop. 2,578 / 3,088; Zip Code 19365; Elev. 539; Lat. 39-57-31 N, Long. 075-55-11 W; In SE Pennsylvania; Named for the old and influential Parkes family. Wooden and metal skids are made in Parkesburg.

PARKSIDE, Borough; Delaware County; Pop. 2,464 / 2,238; Elev. 100; Lat. 39-51-51 N, Long. 075-22-44 W; SW suburb of Philadelphia in SE Pennsylvania.

PATTON, Borough; Cambria County; Pop. 2,441 / 1,972; Zip Code 16668; Elev. 1,750; Lat. 40-38-02 N, Long. 078-39-02 W; 20 miles NW of Altoona in SW central Pennsylvania; Named for Colonel John Patton of Curwensville; The seldom seen Valley Mine is near town, where mining history is preserved and dis-played.

PAXTANG, Borough; Dauphin County; Pop. 1,646; Zip Code 17111; Elev. 400; Lat. 40-15-32 N, Long. 076-49-56 W; SE cen-tral Pennsylvania.

PEN ARGYL, Borough; Northampton County; Pop. 3,388 / 3,399; Zip Code 18072; Elev. 831; Lat. 40-52-07 N, Long. 075-15-19 W; 20 miles NE of Allentown in E Pennsylvania.

PENBROOK, Borough; Dauphin County; Pop. 1,006 / 2,676; Zip Code 17103; Elev. 490; Lat. 40-16-31 N, Long. 076-50-54 W; 5 miles NE of Harrisburg in SE central Pennsylvania.

PENN, Borough; Westmoreland County; Pop. 619 / 468; Zip Code 15675; Elev. 930; Lat. 40-19-44 N, Long. 079-38-29 W; E suburb of Pittsburgh in SW Pennsylvania; Named for William Penn.

PENNDEL, Borough; Bucks County; Pop. 2,703 / 2,799; Zip Code 19047; Elev. 100; Suburb of Philadelphia in Pennsylvania; Named for William Penn.

PENNSBURG, Borough; Montgomery County; Pop. 2,339 / 2,582; Zip Code 18073; Lat. 40-23-27 N, Long. 075-29-33 W; 40 miles N of Philadelphia in SE Pennsylvania.

PERKASIE, Borough; Bucks County; Pop. 5,241 / 8,460; Zip Code 18944; Elev. 400; Lat. 40-22-19 N, Long. 075-17-35 W; 20 miles SE of Allentown in SE Pennsylvania.

PERRYOPOLIS, Borough; Fayette County; Pop. 2,139 / 1,825; Zip Code 15473; Elev. 741; Lat. 40-05-13 N, Long. 079-45-03 W; In SW Pennsylvania; Was laid out in 1814 and named for the naval hero, Oliver Hazard Perry.

PHILADELPHIA, City; Philadelphia County Seat; Pop. 1,681,185 / 1,417,601; Elev. 110; Lat. 39-57-03 N, Long. 075-09-51 W; Fourth largest of American cities, it is long-recognized as the birthplace of the nation. It was also the first citadel of high finance in the New World and for a time its largest settlement. William Penn and his early settlers would not recognize the sprawling commercial and industrial giant Philadel-phia has become today. Penn's former "greene country towne" now covers over 130 square miles and while Penn wasn't able to see his city grow, he was able to plan it. He had soured on Eng-land's rigidity and crooked streets, and today the central part of Philadelphia is a neat network of straight north-south and east-west thoroughfares. Only after the Quaker colonizer had ac-quired the Pennsylvania grant from Charles II in 1681 did the "City of brotherly love" come into existence.

PHILIPSBURG, Borough; Centre County; Pop. 3,464 / 2,875; Zip Code 16866; Elev. 1,433; Lat. 40-53-47 N, Long. 078-13-15 W; 28 miles NE of Altoona in central Pennsylvania; Was founded in 1797 by two Englishmen, Henry and James Phillips.

PHOENIXVILLE, Borough; Chester County; Pop. 14,165 / 15,425; Zip Code 19460; Elev. 127; Lat. 40-07-49 N, Long. 075-30-55 W; 10 miles W of Norristown on the Schuylkill River in SE Pennsylvania.

PINE GROVE, Borough; Schuylkill County; Pop. 2,244 / 2,053; Zip Code 17963; Elev. 540; Lat. 40-29-07 N, Long. 078-37-15 W; In E central Pennsylvania.

PITCAIRN, Borough; Allegheny County; Pop. 4,175 / 3,660; Zip Code 15140; Elev. 880; Lat. 40-24-11 N, Long. 079-46-42 W; 13 miles E of Pittsburgh in SW Pennsylvania; The town was incorpo-rated under the name of Pitcairn in honor of Robert Pitcairn, then superintendent of the Pittsburgh division of the Pennsylvania Railroad. Pitcairn means "cairn-croft."

PITTSBURGH, City; Allegheny County Seat; Pop. 424,205 / 336,882; Zip Code 152+; Elev. 744; Lat. 40-26-26 N, Long. 079-59-46 W; Pennsylvania's second city of importance and one of the greatest steel centers of the world embraces the forks where the Monongahela and Allegheny Rivers unite to form the Ohio. Named for the great British statesman, the elder William Pitt, this city in western Pennsylvania had its origin in a cluster of log cab-ins built near Fort Pitt after 1758.

PITTSTON, City; Luzerne County; Pop. 9,930 / 9,079; Zip Code 186+; Elev. 570; Lat. 41-19-33 N, Long. 075-47-23 W; 10 miles NE of Wilkes-Barre on the Susquehanna River in E Pennsylvania; Was named for the elder William Pitt, British statesman and friend of the Colonies.

PLYMOUTH, Borough; Luzerne County; Pop. 7,605 / 6,264; Zip Code 18651; Elev. 540; Lat. 41-14-25 N, Long. 075-56-42 W; W suburb of Wilkes-Barre on the Susquehanna River in E Pennsylvania; Named and incorporated from Plymouth Township, one of the five townships formed by the Susquehanna Company on December 28, 1768. Its name was derived from Plymouth in Litchfield County, Connecticut. The Connecticut town was doubtless named for Plymouth in Massachusetts, the oldest settlement in New England. The Pilgrim Fathers called their town Plymouth because the Mayflower had sailed from Plymouth in Devonshire, which lies at the mouth of the River Plym.

POINT MARION, Borough; Fayette County; Pop. 1,642 / 1,309; Zip Code 15474; Elev. 815; Lat. 39-44-20 N, Long. 079-53-56 W; 20 miles SW of Uniontown in SW Pennsylvania; At the confluence of the Cheat and Monongahela Rivers, was laid out in 1842, and named for General Francis Marion, the "Swamp Fox" of the Revolution.

POLK, Borough; Venango County; Pop. 1,884 / 1,078; Zip Code 16342; Elev. 1,116; Lat. 41-22-01 N, Long. 079-55-46 W; 15 miles SW of Oil City in NW Pennsylvania; Settled about 1798. Took form in 1839 when Aaron McKissick purchased the site and laid auto village. When incorporated in 1886, it was named for President James K. Polk.

PORT ALLEGANY, Borough; McKean County; Pop. 2,593 / 2,248; Zip Code 16743; Elev. 1,484; Lat. 41-48-39 N, Long. 078-16-48 W; 20 miles SE of Olean, New York on the Allegheny River in N Pennsylvania; Was the center of the tremendous lumbering operations along the Allegheny River that reached their peak between 1830 and 1840.

PORTAGE, Borough; Cambria County; Pop. 3,510 / 2,829; Zip Code 15946; Elev. 1,700; 20 miles NE of Johnstown in a coal mining region in SW central Pennsylvania; Named for the old Portage Railroad, which once extended from Hollidaysburg to Johnstown.

PORTLAND, Borough; Northampton County; Pop. 540 / 580; Zip Code 18351; Elev. 293; Lat. 40-55-23 N, Long. 075-05-49 W; In E Pennsylvania; Was founded in 1845 by Captain James Ginn, of Portland, Maine.

POTTSTOWN, Borough; Montgomery County; Pop. 22,729 / 21,236; Zip Code 19464; Elev. 138; Lat. 40-14-43 N, Long. 075-39-00 W; 15 miles SE of Reading in SE Pennsylvania, at the junction of Manatawny (Ind. "place where we drink") Creek and the Schuylkill River. About 1754, John Potts, a prominent iron master whose father had been associated with Rutter, laid out a town, and in 1815 the place was incorporated as the borough of Pottstown.

PRINGLE, Borough; Luzerne County; Pop. 1,221 / 1,050; Zip Code 18704; Elev. 660; Lat. 41-16-41 N, Long. 075-53-51 W; Near Wilkes Barre in E Pennsylvania.

PROSPECT, Borough; Butler County; Pop. 1,016 / 1,264; Zip Code 16052; Elev. 1369; Lat. 40-54-16 N, Long. 080-02-48 W; In W Pennsylvania; In an early agricultural section, first settled in 1796. Today it is a residential suburb of Butler.

PUNXSUTAWNEY, Borough; Jefferson County; Pop. 7,479 / 6,738; Zip Code 15767; Elev. 1,236; Lat. 40-56-37 N, Long. 078-58-16 W; 80 miles NE of Pittsburgh on Mahoning Creek in W central Pennsylvania. Shawnee wigwam villages once occupied the site. Swarms of gnats plagued early settlers and their livestock. Indians called the insects *ponkies* (living dust and ashes),

and the village was called *Ponkis Utenink* ("land of the ponkies"), from which the present name evolved.

QUAKERTOWN, Borough; Bucks County; Pop. 8,867 / 8,784; Zip Code 18951; Elev. 499; Lat. 40-26-30 N, Long. 075-20-31 W; 15 miles SE of Allentown in SE Pennsylvania; Was founded by Quakers from Gwynedd, Wales in 1715.

RADNOR, Urban Township; Delaware County; Elev. 250; Lat. 40-02-46 N, Long. 075-21-37 W; In W Pennsylvania; Residential suburb. Settled and named in 1683 by Quakers from Radnorshire, Wales.

RAMEY, Borough; Clearfield County; Pop. 568 / 510; Zip Code 6671; Elev. 1,610; Lat. 40-47-53 N, Long. 078-23-51 W; In W central Pennsylvania.

RANKIN, Borough; Allegheny County; Pop. 2,892 / 2,204; Zip Code 15104; Elev. 747; Lat. 40-24-45 N, Long. 079-52-46 W; 5 miles E of Pittsburgh, on the Monongahela River in SW Pennsylvania. About 1870 a man named Thomas Rankin bought a farm, built a house, and lived where the town now stands. At that time Rankin's house was the only one in sight, and the Baltimore and Ohio Railroad made it a stopping place, calling the station Rankin.

READING, City; Seat of Berks County; Pop. 78,582 / 73,778; Zip Code 196+; Elev. 264; Lat. 40-20-08 N, Long. 075-55-38 W; 70 miles NW of Philadelphia on the Schuylkill River in SE Pennsylvania; On the Schuylkill River's bank in southeastern Penn named it for the seat of Berkshire, England, the name of which was derived from the Saxon words rhedin, a fern, and meaning, a meadow.

RED LION, Borough; York County; Pop. 5,824 / 6,377; Zip Code 17356; Elev. 910; Lat. 40-28-50 N, Long. 075-36-59 W; 10 miles SE of York in S Pennsylvania; Named for a tavern built here in colonial times, which had a lion pointed red as its emblem.

RENOVO, Borough; Clinton County; Pop. 1,812 / 1,329; Zip Code 17764; Elev. 668; Lat. 41-19-35 N, Long. 077-45-04 W; 60 miles NW of Williamsport in central Pennsylvania; Located on the Susquehanna River in a soft coal mining region; Takes its name from the Latin verb renovo, "I renew."

RICHLAND, Borough; Lebanon County; Pop. 1,470 / 1,530; Zip Code 17087; Elev. 490; Lat. 40-35-48 N, Long. 078-29-09 W; In SE central Pennsylvania.

RICHLANDTOWN, Borough; Bucks County; Pop. 180 / 1,324; Zip Code 18955; Elev. 520; Lat. 40-28-12 N, Long. 075-19-15 W; In SE Pennsylvania.

RIDGWAY, Borough; Seat of Elk County; Pop. 5,604 / 4,423; Zip Code 15853; Elev. 1,381; Lat. 41-25-13 N, Long. 078-43-44 W; 20 miles N of DuBois in NW central Pennsylvania; In a crook of the Clarion River at the mouth of Elk Creek, occupies part of an 80,000 acre tract purchased in 1817 by Jacob Ridgway, a prominent Philadelphia Quaker merchant.

RIMERSBURG, Borough; Clarion County; Pop. 1,096 / 996; Zip Code 16248; Elev. 1,450; Lat. 41-02-29 N, Long. 079-30-12 W; in W Pennsylvania; John Rimer settled here in 1829 and later opened a tavern.

RIVERSIDE, Borough; Northumberland County; Pop. 2,266 / 1,859; Zip Code 17868; Elev. 500; Lat. 40-17-00 N, Long. 078-55-21 W; In E central Pennsylvania; Annexed to Gearheart township in 1950.

ROBESONIA, Borough; Berks County; Pop. 1,748 / 2,018; Zip Code 19551; Elev. 453; Lat. 40-21-06 N, Long. 076-08-05 W; In SE Pennsylvania; Was founded in 1855 and named for an early settler, Andrew Robeson. Robeson was an immigrant from Sweden who eventually became wealthy and powerful in his community.

ROCHESTER, Borough; Beaver County; Pop. 4,759 / 3,829; Zip Code 15074; Elev. 707; Lat. 40-42-08 N, Long. 080-17-12 W; In W Pennsylvania; At the confluence of the Beaver and Ohio Rivers, where the latter turns southwestward. The name Rochester was not used until 1838, when Ovid Pinney named it for his native Rochester, New York.

ROCKLEDGE, Borough; Montgomery County; Pop. 2,538 / 2,582; Zip Code 19111; Elev. 200; Lat. 40-04-52 N, Long. 075-05-24 W; 10 miles NE of Philadelphia in SE Pennsylvania; A large shopping mall graces this residential suburb.

ROME, Borough; Bradford County; Pop. 426 / 948; Zip Code 18837; Elev. 830; Lat. 41-51-30 N, Long. 076-20-28 W; In N Pennsylvania; Named for the city in New York by the first settlers.

ROSETO, Borough; Northampton County; Pop. 1,484 / 1,701; Zip Code 18013; Elev. 720; Lat. 40-52-50 N, Long. 075-12-54 W; Near Bangor in E Pennsylvania.

ROSE VALLEY, Borough; Delaware County; Pop. 1,038 / 950; Elev. 150; SW suburb of Philadelphia in SE Pennsylvania.

ROYALTON, Borough; Dauphin County; Pop. 981 / 1,062; Zip Code 17101; Elev. 300; Lat. 40-11-14 N, Long. 076-43-39 W; Suburb of Harrisburg in SE central Pennsylvania.

ROYERSFORD, Borough; Montgomery County; Pop. 4,243 / 4,331; Zip Code 19468; Elev. 180; Lat. 40-11-03 N, Long. 075-32-18 W; 5 miles N of Phoenixville in a residential area in SE Pennsylvania.

RURAL VALLEY, Borough; Armstrong County; Pop. 1,033 / 912; Zip Code 16249; Elev. 1,111; Lat. 40-11-13 N, Long. 080-20-56 W; In W Pennsylvania.

RUSSELL, Village; Warren County; Pop. 800; Elev. 1,233; Lat. 41-56-29 N, Long. 079-08-07 W; 5 miles S of New York state line in NW Pennsylvania; Was laid out in 1843 on part of an extensive tract owned by Robert Russell.

RUTLEDGE, Borough; Delaware County; Pop. 934 / 912; Zip Code 19070; Elev. 130; Lat. 39-54-06 N, Long. 075-19-44 W; SW suburb of Philadelphia in SE Pennsylvania.

SAEGERTOWN, Borough; Crawford County; Pop. 942 / 1,041; Zip Code 16433; Elev. 1,120; Lat. 41-43-08 N, Long. 080-08-52 W; In NW Pennsylvania.

ST. CLAIR, Borough; Schuylkill County; Pop. 4,037 / 3,184; Zip Code 17970; Elev. 749; Lat. 40-24-59 N, Long. 079-58-18 W; 5 miles NW of Pottsville in E central Pennsylvania; Was founded in 1831. Saint Clair took the name of St. Clair Nichols, who owned the farm on which the town was built.

ST. LAWRENCE, Borough; Berks County; Pop. 1,376 / 1,849; Elev. 360; Lat. 40-19-37 N, Long. 075-52-20 W; In SE Pennsylvania.

ST. MARYS, City; Elk County; Pop. 6,417 / 13,830; Zip Code 15857; Elev. 1,702; Lat. 41-25-40 N, Long. 078-33-40 W; Near New York state line in NW central Pennsylvania; In 1842 Philadelphia and Baltimore German Catholics, who had fled the "Know Nothing" persecution, settled on land owned by the German Catholic Brotherhood. As the date of settlement was the feast of the Immaculate Conception of the Virgin Mary, and as the name of the first white woman who set foot on the new town was also Mary, the settlers called the place Saint Mary's.

SALTSBURG, Borough; Indiana County; Pop. 964 / 941; Zip Code 15681; Elev. 852; Lat. 40-29-11 N, Long. 079-27-06 W; 30 miles NE of Pittsburgh in W central Pennsylvania. Tradition credits a Mrs. Deemer with the discovery of salt deposits here when she found the food she cooked in water that trickled from rocks along the Conemaugh had a salty taste.

SAXONBURG, Borough; Butler County; Pop. 1,336 / 1,396; Zip Code 16056; Elev. 1,300; Lat. 40-45-14 N, Long. 079-48-37 W; NE suburb of Pittsburgh in W Pennsylvania; Is all that now remains of on ambitious German colony, named for their former home in Old Saxony. The founder of this colony, John A. Roebling, afterward became a civil engineer and a builder of suspension bridges.

SAYRE, Borough; Bradford County; Pop. 6,951 / 5,558; Zip Code 18840; Elev. 772; Lat. 41-58-44 N, Long. 076-30-57 W; 20 miles SE of Elmire, New York in N Pennsylvania; Was a small railway settlement until the Lehigh Valley Railroad constructed a roundhouse and shops here in 1871 and named the place for Robert H. Sayre, superintendent of the road.

SCALP LEVEL, Borough; Cambria County; Pop. 1,186 / 1,026; Elev. 1,840; Lat. 40-14-59 N, Long. 078-50-57 W; in SW central Pennsylvania.

SCHUYLKILL HAVEN, Borough; Schuylkill County; Pop. 5,977 / 5,420; Zip Code 17972; Elev. 526; Lat. 40-37-50 N, Long. 076-10-17 W; 5 miles S of Pottsville in E central Pennsylvania; The completion in 1825 of the Schuylkill Canal between Philadelphia and a point just north of Schuylkill Haven gave the town its name and its principal support for six decades.

SCOTTDALE, Borough; Westmoreland County; Pop. 5,833 / 4,833; Zip Code 15683; Elev. 1,061; Lat. 40-06-01 N, Long. 079-35-14 W; 15 miles NE of Uniontown in a coal mining and agricultural area in SW Pennsylvania on Jacobs Creek; Originally named Fountain Mills, was renamed for Thomas A. Scott, president of the Pennsylvania Railroad, after a spur was extended to the town in 1873.

SCRANTON, City; Lackawanna County seat; Pop. 87,378 / 73,766; Zip Code 185+; Elev. 741; Lat. 41-24-32 N, Long. 075-39-46 W; In 1840 two brothers, George W. and Selden T. Scranton came to the settlement from New Jersey. At that time it was a community of five weather-beaten old houses. Attracted by the abundance of iron ore and anthracite nearby, the Scrantons and their partners William Henry, Sanford Grant, and Philip Mattes organized the firm of Scranton, Grant, and Company, and built a forge here. This firm was the nucleus of the Lackawanna Iron and Steel Company. Despite a lot of discouragement, they finally succeeded in manufacturing iron with anthracite as a fuel. In 1845 the Scrantons named the place Harrison in honor of President William Henry Harrison. The post office at Scranton was established in 1850. Less than a year later the name of the town and post office was simplified as Scranton.

SELINSGROVE, Borough; Snyder County; Pop. 5,227 / 5,403; Zip Code 17870; Elev. 445; Lat. 40-47-56 N, Long. 076-51-45 W; 5 miles S of Sunbury on the W banks of the Susquehanna River in central Pennsylvania; Was laid out in 1790 by Anthony Selin, a Swiss soldier of fortune who accompanied Lafayette to America.

SELLERSVILLE, Borough; Bucks County; Pop. 3,143 / 4,739; Zip Code 18960; Elev. 336; Lat. 40-21-14 N, Long. 075-18-19 W; 20 miles SE of Allentown in SE Pennsylvania; A narrow town founded in 1738. Samuel Sellers operated Old Sellers Tavern, a three-story stucco stone building that served as an early stage stop along the road to Allentown.

SEWARD, Borough; Westmoreland County; Pop. 675 / 526; Zip Code 15954; Elev. 1,140; Lat. 40-24-51 N, Long. 079-01-13 W; In SW Pennsylvania.

SEWICKLEY, Borough; Allegheny County; Pop. 4,778 / 3,706; Zip Code 15143; Elev. 720; Lat. 40-32-11 N, Long. 080-11-05 W; 10 miles NW of Pittsburgh on the Ohio River in SW Pennsylvania; Named for an Indian tribe.

SHAMOKIN, City; Northumberland County; Pop. 10,357 / 8,135; Zip Code 17872; Elev. 730; In E central Pennsylvania; Was laid out in 1835 and named from the old Indian village that once stood at its mouth. On the present site of Sunbury, 18 miles west of the borough of Shamokin. The Delaware called this village *Schachamekhon*, which signifies "eel stream." Another form of the name was *Schahamokink*, or "the place of eels."

SHARON, City; Mercer County; Pop. 19,057 / 16,154; Zip Code 16416; Elev. 853; Lat. 41-13-59 N, Long. 080-29-37 W; 15 miles NE of Youngstown, Ohio on the Ohio River in W Pennsylvania; Named, probably, by some Bible-reading pioneer who likened its flat topography to the plain of Sharon in Palestine.

SHARON HILL, Borough; Delaware County; Pop. 6,221 / 5,492; Zip Code 19079; In SE Pennsylvania.

SHARPSBURG, Borough; Allegheny County; Pop. 4,351 / 3,670; Zip Code 15215; Elev. 741; Lat. 39-54-23 N, Long. 075-16-19 W; 5 miles NE of Pittsburgh on the Allegheny River in SW Pennsylvania; In this community, founded in 1826 by James Sharp and incorporated as a borough in 1841, the eight-year-old Howard I, Heinz began his billion dollar business by selling the produce of his mothers garden patch. James Sharp kept a temperance hotel here until his death in 1861.

SHARPSVILLE, Borough; Mercer County; Pop. 5,375 / 4,358; Zip Code 16150; Elev. 950; Lat. 41-15-33 N, Long. 080-28-20 W; 20 miles NW of New Castle in an industrial area in W Pennsylvania; Named for James Sharp, one of the original owners of the town site.

SHEFFIELD, Village; Warren County; Pop. 1,500; Elev. 1,336; Lat. 41-42-14 N, Long. 079-02-09 W; 10 miles SE of Warren in NW Pennsylvania.

SHENANDOAH, Borough; Schuylkill County; Pop. 7,589 / 5,793; Zip Code 17976; Elev. 1,300; Lat. 40-49-13 N, Long. 076-12-04 W; 10 miles N of Pottsville in E central Pennsylvania; Was first settled in 1835; Mining on a large scale began in 1862 when a land company laid out the town.

SHICKSHINNY, Borough; Luzerne County; Pop. 1,192 / 962; Zip Code 18655; Elev. 520; Lat. 41-09-11 N, Long. 076-09-02 W; E Pennsylvania; Indian word meaning "five mountains."

SHILLINGTON, Borough; Berks County; Pop. 5,601 / 5,053; Zip Code 19607; Elev. 350; Lat. 40-18-28 N, Long. 075-57-57 W; 5 miles SW of Reading in SE Pennsylvania. Samuel Shilling laid out this town in 1860 when he decided to locate his 130-acre farm. The town was also named after this earlier farmer a very short time after he settled here.

SHINGLEHOUSE, Borough; Potter County; Pop. 3,310 / 1,205; Zip Code 16748; Elev. 1,490; Lat. 41-57-49 N, Long. 078-11-28 W; Located in N Pennsylvania; Named for an old English pioneer clapboard house with shingles belonging to a French immigrant named Jaudrie about 1806.

SHIPPENSBURG, Borough; Cumberland and Franklin Counties; Pop. 5,261 / 5,633; Zip Code 17257; Elev. 649; Lat. 40-03-02 N, Long. 077-31-14 W; Is located 10 miles N of Chambersburg in S Pennsylvania. Shippensburg is the oldest town in Pennsylvania, with the exception of York that is W of the Susquehanna River. It was founded in 1730 by Edward Shippen, who in 1737 was said to have had been the biggest person, the biggest house, and the biggest coach in Philadelphia.

SHIPPENVILLE, Borough; Clarion County; Pop. 558 / 462; Zip Code 16254; Elev. 1,208; Lat. 41-15-01 N, long 079-27-35 W; W Pennsylvania; Was laid out by Henry Shippen. In its early years was known as an iron center.

SHREWSBURY, Borough; York County; Pop. 2,668 / 3,096; Zip Code 17361; Elev. 735; Lat. 39-46-07 N, Long. 076-40-48 W; Founded in 1739 by immigrants from Shrewsbury, England.

SINKING SPRING, Borough; Berks County; Pop. 2,617 / 2,484; Zip Code 19608; Elev. 345; Lat. 40-19-38 N, Long. 076-00-41 W; 5 miles W of Reading in a red brick residential area in SE Pennsylvania; Was founded in 1793 and named for the Sinking Spring at 402 Penn Ave., which fills in each February when water begins to ooze from the frost-packed ground but dries up before summer.

SLATINGTON. Borough; Lehigh County; Pop. 4,277 / 4,622; Zip Code 18080; Elev. 367; Lat. 40-44-54 N, Long. 075-36-44 W; 15 miles NW of Allentown in E Pennsylvania; Is a slate center where quarrying began in 1845.

SLIGO, Borough; Clarion County; Pop. 798 / 673; Zip Code 16255; Elev. 769; Lat. 40-38-36 N, Long. 079-41-31 W; In W Pennsylvania, bisected by Big Licking and Little Licking Creeks. Sligo Furnace, built in 1845 by four men from Sligo, Ireland, was shut down after the panic of 1873.

SLIPPERY ROCK, Borough; Butler County; Pop. 3,047 / 3,110; Zip Code 16057; Elev. 1,302; Lat. 41-03-50 N, Long. 080-03-24 W; 10 miles NW of Butler in W Pennsylvania; Was called Ginger Hill by early settlers, from the local tavern keeper's practice of giving away plenty of ginger with the whiskey he sold.

SMETHPORT, Borough; Seat of McKean County; Pop. 1,797 / 1,683; Zip Code 16749; Elev. 1,486; Lat. 41-48-40 N, Long. 078-26-42 W; 20 miles S of Bradford in N Pennsylvania; Was named for Raymond and Theodore de Smeth. Dutch bankers and business agents of the exiled French nobility in their dealings with the Ceres Land Company.

SMITHFIELD, Borough; Fayette County; Pop. 1,084 / 995; Zip Code 25478; Elev. 986; Lat. 39-48-11 N, Long. 079-48-29 W; In SW Pennsylvania; Was laid out in 1799.

SNOW SHOE, Borough; Centre County; Pop. 852 / 806; Zip Code 16874; Elev. 1,572; Lat. 41-01-51 N, Long. 077-56-59 W; S of Clarence in central Pennsylvania; Was named for "Snow Shoe Camp Survey," so called, it is supposed, because the surveyor found snowshoes at a deserted Indian camp here in 1773.

SOMERSET, Borough; Seat of Somerset County; Pop. 6,474 / 6,287; Zip Code 15501; Elev. 2,250; Lat. 40-00-30 N, Long. 079-04-42 W; 30 miles S of Johnstown in S Pennsylvania; Was originally called Brunerstown, after Ulrich Bruner, who arrived in 1787.

SOUDERTON, Borough; Montgomery County; Pop. 6,657 / 6,433; Zip Code 18964; Elev. 428; Lat. 40-18-42 N, Long. 075-19-32 W; 5 miles N of Lansdale in SE Pennsylvania; Was founded in 1676 but much older in settlement.

SPANGLER, Borough; Cambria County; Pop. 2,399 / 1,882; Zip Code 15775; Elev. 1,470; Lat. 40-38-34 N, Long. 078-46-23 W; 20 miles NW of Altoona in a coal mining region in SW Pennsylvania; When it was incorporated in 1893, Spangler was named for Colonel J.L. Spangler of Bellefonte.

SPEERS, Borough; Washington County; Pop. 1,425 / 1,262; Zip Cede 15012; Elev. 767; Lat. 40-07-28 N, Long. 079-52-48 W; W of Belle Vernon in SW Pennsylvania on the west bank of the Monongahela River, named for Apollos Speers, and closely identified with the early development of the Monongahela Valley.

SPRING CITY, Borough; Chester County; Pop. 3,389 / 3,388; Zip Code 19475; Elev. 150; Lat. 40-10-36 N, Long. 075-32-53 W; 30 miles NW of Philadelphia on the Schuylkill River in SE Pennsylvania; It was at first called Springville from a large spring situated at the corner of Yost and Main Streets. About 1872, when the post office was established and the town incorporated, the name was changed to Spring City because there was already one Springville in Pennsylvania.

SPRINGDALE, Borough; Allegheny County; Pop. 4,418 / 3,621; Zip Code 15144; Elev. 801; Lat. 40-32-27 N, Long. 079-47-043 W; 15 miles NE of Pittsburgh on the Allegheny River in SW Pennsylvania along a sweeping curve of the Allegheny River. Settled in 1795, it was later named for springs in a nearby hollow.

SPRINGFIELD, Urban Village and Township; Delaware County; Pop. 29,000; Zip Code 19064; Elev. 220; Lat. 41-50-57 N, Long. 076-44-46 W; 15 miles W of Philadelphia in a residential area in SE Pennsylvania; Probably named for Springfield, Massachusetts.

SPRING MILLS, Village; Centre County; Pop. 600; Zip Code 16875; Elev. 52; Lat. 40-51-12 N, Long. 077-34-04 W; In central Pennsylvania on Penns Creek. Was part of the "Manor of Succoth," held by the Penns until 1791.

STATE COLLEGE, Borough; Seat of Centre County; Pop. 36,082 / 39,017; Zip Code 16801; Elev. 1,191; Lat. 40-47-36 N, Long. 077-51-37 W; 50 miles NE of Altoona in central Pennsylvania; Located in the Nittany Valley between the Bald Eagle Ridge (NW) and the Seven Mountains (SE).

STEELTON, Borough; Dauphin County; Pop. 6,484 / 4,918; Zip Code 17113; Elev. 306; Lat. 40-14-07 N, Long. 076-50-30 W; In SE central Pennsylvania; Rudolph and Henry Kelker, who owned land adjoining the steel works, first called the town Baldwin in honor of Matthew Baldwin, a large stockholder in the steel company. The post office renamed it Steel Works in 1871, and nine years later steel works superintendent Luther Bent suggested its present name.

STOCKDALE, Borough; Washington County; Pop. 641 / 603; Zip Code 15483; Elev. 765; Lat. 40-05-00 N, Long. 079-50-54 W; In SW Pennsylvania; Named for the dairy cows that have grazed on the land here.

STOCKERTON, Borough; Northampton County; Pop. 661 / 630; Zip Colt 18083; Elev. 374; in E Pennsylvania; Bisected by Schuylkill Creek. Was named for Andrew Stocker, who laid out the village in 1774.

STRASBURG, Borough; Lancaster County; Pop. 1,999 / 2,634; Zip Code 17579; Elev. 480; Lat. 39-58-59 N, Long. 076-11-04 W; 10 miles SE of Lancaster in SE Pennsylvania; The LeFevres, or Ferrees, and other French immigrants settled this town in 1733.

STROUDSBURG. Borough; Seat of Monroe County; Pop. 5,148 / 5,888; Zip Code 18360; Elev. 420; Lat. 40-59-12 N, Long. 075-11-42 W; 30 miles N of Easton in E Pennsylvania; Lies among the Pocono foothills at the confluence of McMichaels, Pocono and Brodhead Creeks. In 1776 Colonel Jacob Stroud, a veteran of the French and Indian War, erected a stockade house here and called it Fort Penn.

SUGAR NOTCH, Borough; Luzerne County; Pop. 1,191 / 999; Zip Code 18706; Elev. 740; Lat. 41-11-49 N, Long. 075-55-43 W; In E Pennsylvania; Named for the mountain gap nearby, covered in sugar maples.

SUGARCREEK, Borough; Venango County; Pop. 5,954 / 5,363; Zip Code 16301; Lat. 41-25-17 N, Long. 079-52-53 W; 10 miles W of Oil Creek in NW Pennsylvania; Incorporated in 1968.

SUMMERHILL, Borough; Cambria County; Pop. 725 / 550; Zip Code 15958; Elev. 1,540; Lat. 40-22-41 N, Long. 078-45-39 W; In SW central Pennsylvania; Originally named Somerhill for Joseph and David Somer, two landowners in the area.

SUMMIT HILL, Borough; Carbon County; Pop. 3,418 / 3,211; Zip Code 18250; Elev. 1,410; Lat. 40-50-27 N, Long. 075-52-31 W; In E Pennsylvania; so named because it is at the summit of Sharp Mountain.

SUNBURY, City; Seat of Northumberland County; Pop. 12,292 / 10,337; Zip Code 17801; Elev. 450; Lat. 40-51-45 N, Long.

076-47-41 W; 50 miles N of Harrisburg on the Susquehanna River in E central Pennsylvania; Is bounded roughly by the Shamokin Creek and the Susquehanna River. Etymologically Sunbury signifies "the city of the sun."

SUSQUEHANNA DEPOT, Borough; Susquehanna County; Pop. 1,994 / 1,868; Elev. 920; Lat. 41-56-36 N, Long. 075-36-00 W; In NE Pennsylvania; Named for the county and river flowing through it. Near New York state line in a farming region.

SUTERSVILLE, Borough; Westmoreland County; Pop. 863 / 712; Zip Code 15083; Elev. 800; Lat. 40-14-10 N, Long. 079-47-58 W; In SW Pennsylvania.

SWARTHMORE, Borough; Delaware County; Pop. 5,950 / 5,900; Zip Code 19081; Elev. 190; Lat. 39-54-07 N, Long. 075-21-01 W; 10 miles SW of Philadelphia in SE Pennsylvania; Named for Swarthmore Hall, home of George Fox (1624-91), founder of the Society of Friends.

SWISSVALE, Borough; Allegheny County; Pop. 11,345 / 9,495; Zip Code 15218; Elev. 920; Lat. 40-25-25 N, Long. 079-52-59 W; 5 miles E of Pittsburgh in SW Pennsylvania; Was built upon the farm of James Swisshelm, who inherited it from his father, John. The name Swissvale is said to have been invented by Jane Gray Swisshelm, the wife of the proprietor.

SWOYERSVILLE, Borough; Luzerne County; Pop. 5,795 / 4,978; Zip Code 18704; Elev. 840; Lat. 41-17-30 N, Long. 075-52-30 W; 5 miles N of Wilkes-Barre in E Pennsylvania; Named for Henry Swoyer, early coal operator.

SYKESVILLE, Borough; Jefferson County; Pop. 1,537 / 1,381; Zip Code 15865; Elev. 1,352; Lat. 41-03-01 N, Long. 078-49-21 W; 5 miles SW of DuBois in a farming area in W central Pennsylvania; Settled in 1861 and named for Jacob Sykes, sawmill owner of the 1880s.

TAMAQUA, Borough; Schuylkill County; Pop. 8,843 / 7,275; Zip Code 18252; Elev. 805; Lat. 40-47-50 N, Long. 075-58-11 W; 15 miles NE of Pottsville in E central Pennsylvania; Laid out in 1829 by the Lehigh Coal and Navigation Company, Tomaqua was named for the creek flowing by. Tamaque is a Delaware Indian word meaning "beaver."

TARENTUM, Borough; Allegheny County; Pop. 6,419 / 5,078; Zip Code 15084; Elev. 737; Lat. 40-36-05 N, Long. 079-45-36 W; In SW Pennsylvania; Settled in the last decade of the eighteenth century when a gristmill was erected on Bull Creek. Was laid out in 1829 by Judge Henry Marie Brackenridge, and given this classical name for the town. He was a scholar and a student of ancient history and the classical languages, and he may have been attracted by the name of the ancient city in southern Italy which the Romans called Tarentum, and which the Greeks had previously named Taras from the small stream on which the old Greek colony was planted.

TAYLOR, Borough, Lackawanna County; Pop. 7,246 / 6,519; Elev. 680; Lat. 41-23-41 N, Long. 075-42-25 W; 5 miles SW of Scranton in NE Pennsylvania; Was named for the late Moses Taylor, a prominent New York merchant and capitalist, who had extensive business interests in the place that now bears his name.

TELFORD, Borough; Bucks and Montgomery Counties; Pop. 3,507 / 4,486; Zip Code 18969; Elev. 420; Lat. 40-19-19 N, Long. 075-19-42 W; 25 miles E of Reading in SE Pennsylvania.

TEMPLE, Borough; Berks County; Pop. 1,486; Zip Code 19560; Elev. 380; Lat. 40-24-31 N, Long. 075-55-19 W; In SE Pennsylvania, Near Reading; Named for an old hotel sign that bore the words, "Stop at Solomon's Temple." Solomon was the innkeeper's name.

THROOP, Borough; Lackawanna County; Pop. 4,166 / 3,639; Zip Code 18512; Elev. 860; Lat. 41-27-05 N, Long. 075-36-44 W; 5 miles NE of Scranton in NE Pennsylvania; Was named in honor of Dr. Benjamin Henry Throop, the pioneer physician of Scranton, Doctor Throop.

TITUSVILLE, Borough; Crawford County; Pop. 6,884 / 6,226; Zip Code 16354; 15 miles N of Oil City in an agricultural region in NW Pennsylvania on Oil Creek.

TOPTON, Borough; Berks County; Pop. 1,818 / 2,045; Zip Code 19562; Elev. 480; Lat. 40-30-12 N, Long. 075-42-06 W; In SE Pennsylvania.

TOBYHANNA, Village; Monroe County; Pop. 900; Zip Code 18466; Elev. 1,940; Lat. 41-10-38 N, Long. 075-25-02 W; In E Pennsylvania; Name means "older stream," from an Indian word.

TOWANDA, Borough; Seat of Bradford County; Pop. 3,526 / 3,320; Zip Code 18848; Elev. 837; Lat. 41-46-03 N, Long. 076-26-35 W; 50 miles NW of Wilkes-Barre in a mountainous resort area in N Pennsylvania; (Ind. "where we bury the dead"). Occupies a slope on the west shore of the Susquehanna, at the convergence of three valleys.

TOWER CITY, Borough; Schuylkill County; Pop. 1,667 / 1,449; Zip Code 17980; Elev. 800; Lat. 40-35-21 N, Long. 076-33-10 W; 25 miles W of Pottsville in E central Pennsylvania; Was built on reclaimed marsh lands in 1868 by Charlemagne Tower.

TRAFFORD, Borough; Allegheny and Westmoreland Counties; Pop. 3,662 / 3,207; Zip Code 15085; Elev. 820; Lat. 40-23-08 N, Long. 079-45-33 W; E suburb of Pittsburgh in SW Pennsylvania.

TRAINER, Borough; Delaware County; Pop. 2,056 / 2,292; Elev. 29; Lat. 39-49-39 N, Long. 075-24-53 W; SW suburb of Philadelphia in SE Pennsylvania; Grew up around grist and sawmills established by David Trainer.

TRAPPE, Borough; Montgomery County; Pop. 1,800 / 2,669; Elev. 300; Lat. 40-11-56 N, Long. 075-28-36 W; In SE Pennsylvania; The origin of the name is uncertain, though many historians declare than an early taverns high stoop caused it to be called *treppe* (steps) by the German settlers, and that a corrupted form of the word came into popular use as the village name. Another explanation is that the tavern's high steps often became a "trap" for the unsteady feet of steady patrons.

TREMONT, Borough; Schuylkill County; Pop. 1,796 / 2,100; Zip Code 17981; Elev. 760; Lat. 40-37-42 N, Long. 076-23-15 W; In E central Pennsylvania.

TULLYTOWN, Borough; Bucks County; Pop. 2,277 / 2,291; Zip Code 19007; Elev. 20; Lat. 40-08-21 N, Long. 074-48-54 W; E suburb of Philadelphia in SE Pennsylvania.

TUNKHANNOCK, Borough; Seat of Wyoming County; Pop. 2,144 / 2,187; Zip Code 18657; Elev. 613; Lat. 41-32-19 N, Long. 075-56-49 W; 20 miles NW of Scranton in NE Pennsylvania, at the confluence of Tunkhannock Creek and the Susquehanna's North Branch The township and the village of Tunkhannock were named for the Tunkhannock Creek. This name is a corruption of *tank-hanne*, "a small stream." The earliest form of the name was *Tenkghanacke*, which may be identified with *Tagh-ka-nick*, an Indian name in New York, and with *Toconic* in Massachusetts and Connecticut. *Tenkghanacke*, *Taghkanick*, and *Taconic* are all apparently the same Algonquin word in different forms. The common interpretation of this name is "forest," or "wilderness."

TURTLE CREEK, Borough; Allegheny County; Pop. 6,959 / 5,894; Zip Code 15145; Elev. 900; Lat. 40-24-21 N, Long. 079-49-31 W; In SW Pennsylvania; Was settled about 1765. The settlement grew into a pleasant suburban community, stimulated by the laying of the Greensburg turnpike, and was incorporated in 1892.

TYRONE, Borough; Blair County; Pop. 6,346 / 5,570; Zip Code 16686; Elev. 909; Lat. 40-40-14 N, Long. 078-14-20 W; 15 miles NE of Altoona in S central Pennsylvania; (Irish, the land of Owen). Was settled in 1850, but emigrants from North Ireland had penetrated the region earlier. They named the place for their native county of Tyrone.

UNION CITY, Borough; Erie County; Pop. 3,263 / 3,543; Zip Code 16438; Elev. 1,300; Lat. 41-53-58 N, Long. 079-50-44 W; 20 miles SE of Erie in NW Pennsylvania.

UNIONTOWN, City; Seat of Fayette County; Pop. 14,023 / 11,263; Zip Code 15401; Elev. 1,023; Lat. 40-42-17 N, Long. 078-49-51 W; 45 miles SE of Pittsburgh in SW Pennsylvania.

UPLAND, Borough; Delaware County; Pop. 3,458 / 3,195; Elev. 60; Lat. 39-51-09 N, Long. 075-22-5 W; SW suburb of Philadelphia, near Chester in SE Pennsylvania.

VANDERBILT, Borough; Fayette County; Pop. 689 / 534; Zip Code 15486; Elev. 900; Lat. 40-01-59 N, Long. 079-39-42 W; In SW Pennsylvania.

VANDERGRIFT, Borough; Westmoreland County; Pop. 6,823 / 5,345; Zip Code 15690; Elev. 860; Lat. 40-36-10 N, Long. 079-33-54 W; 30 miles NE of Pittsburgh in SW Pennsylvania; Steel milling and coal mining are the major industries.

VANDLING, Borough; Lackawanna County; Pop. 557 / 635; Zip Code 18421; Elev. 1,600; Lat. 41-37-59 N, Long. 075-28-15 W; Near Forest City in NE Pennsylvania.

VANPORT, Village; Beaver County; Suburb of Beaver Falls in W Pennsylvania; Named for Martin Van Buren during his 1836 presidential campaign.

VERONA, Borough; Allegheny County; Pop. 3,179 / 3,069; Zip Code 15147; Elev. 860; Lat. 40-30-23 N, Long. 079-50-36 W; In SW Pennsylvania; Named for the Northern Italian city.

VERSAILLES, Borough; Allegheny County; Pop. 2,150 / 1,654; Elev. 850; Lat. 40-18-56 N, Long. 079-49-53 W; 15 miles SE of Pittsburgh on the Youghiogheny River in SW Pennsylvania; Named for the palace of French kings to commemorate the earliest settlers of western Pennsylvania.

VILLANOVA, Urban Village; Delaware County; Pop. 5,000; Zip Code 19085; Elev. 430; Lat. 40-02-14 N, Long. 075-20-58 W; 10 miles NW of Philadelphia in a residential area in SE Pennsylvania; Villanova University, with about 8,000 students, is located here. The village name means "new town."

WALLINGFORD, Urban Village; Delaware County; Pop. 4,000; Elev. 160; Lat. 39-53-27 N, Long. 075-21-48 W; SW suburb of Philadelphia in SE Pennsylvania; Residential; Named for town in Connecticut.

WALNUTPORT, Borough; Northampton County; Pop. 2,007 / 2,148; Zip Code 18088; Elev. 380; Lat. 40-45-15 N, Long. 075-35-57 W; In E Pennsylvania.

WAMPUM, Borough; Lawrence County; Pop. 851 / 614; Zip Code 16157; Elev. 783; Lat. 40-53-17 N, Long. 080-20-18 W; In W Pennsylvania; Settled in 1796 on the Beaver River and was incorporated as a borough in 1876. The name is a contraction of *Wampumpeak* (Indian, meaning "a string of shell beads").

WARMINSTER, Urban Village; Bucks County; Pop. 37,200; Zip Code 18974; Elev. 310; Lat. 40-12-24 N, Long. 075-06-00 W; 20 miles NE of Philadelphia in a residential area in SE Pennsylvania; Burpee Seed Company has its national headquarters here, as does the Society for Individual Liberty.

WARREN, City; Seat of Warren County; Pop. 12,146 / 10,175; Zip Code 16365; Elev. 1,185; Lat. 41-50-38 N, Long. 079-08-43 W; 20 miles S of Jamestown, New York in NW Pennsylvania; Near the mouth of the Conewago Creek, on the Allegheny River.

WASHINGTON, City; Seat of Washington County; Pop. 18,363 / 14,727; Zip Code 15301; Elev. 1,039; Lat. 40-12-08 N, Long. 077-28-42 W; 30 miles SW of Pittsburgh in SW Pennsylvania; The site, once known as Catfish's Camp, was a Delaware Indian village, the headquarters of Chief Tingoocqua. A town laid out in 1781 shortly became the county seat of newly created Washington County. Incorporated as a borough in 1810, Washington was chartered as a city in 1924.

WATSONTOWN, Borough; Northumberland County; Pop. 2,311 / 2,235; Zip Code 17777; Elev. 500; Lat. 41-05-04 N, Long. 076-51-51 W; In E central Pennsylvania; Named for John Watson, who bought 610 acres here in 1792, and two years later laid out the town.

WAYMART, Borough; Wayne County; Pop. 1,248 / 1,500; Zip Code 18472; Elev. 1,400; Lat. 41-34-49 N, Long. 075-24-31 W; In NE Pennsylvania.

WAYNESBORO, Borough; Franklin County; Pop. 9,726 / 10,007; Zip Code 17268; Elev. 713; Lat. 39-45-21 N, Long. 077-34-41 W; 10 miles NE of Hagerstawn, Maryland in S Pennsylvania; Set in a natural hollow and laid out in 1797 by John Wallace, who had served under General Anthony Wayne.

WAYNESBURG, Borough; Seat of Greene County; Pop. 4,482 / 5,797; Zip Code 15370; Elev. 1,035; Lat. 39-53-47 N, Long. 080-10-46 W; 50 miles S of Pittsburgh in SW Pennsylvania; Was laid out in 1796 and named for General Anthony Wayne, whose Indian battles allowed for extensive settlement of western Pennsylvania in the early 1800s.

WEATHERLY, Borough; Carbon County; Pop. 2,891 / 2,653; Zip Code 16255; Elev. 1,095; 10 miles E of Hazleton in E Pennsylvania; The town was settled in 1840 and named for the clockmaker, David Weatherly.

WELLSBORO, Borough; Seat of Tioga County; Pop. 3,085 / 3,329; Zip Code 16901; Elev. 1,308; Lat. 41-44-55 N, Long. 077-18-03 W; 440 miles SW of Elmira, New York in N Pennsylvania; The town was laid out in 1806 by Benjamin W. Morris, a land agent who arrived in 1799 and gave the settlement his wife's maiden name. Mary Wells Morris and her brothers promoted their town to be the seat of the new county of Tioga in 1806.

WESLEYVILLE, Borough; Erie County; Pop. 3,998 / 3,487; Zip Code 165+; Elev. 730; Lat. 42-08-25 N, Long. 080-00-55 W; In NW Pennsylvania; Was laid out by John Shadduck in 1828 and named for John Wesley, founder of Methodism.

WEST CHESTER, Borough; Seat of Chester County; Pop. 17,435 / 17,858; Zip Code 19380; Elev. 455; Lat. 39-57-38 N, Long. 075-36-21 W; 25 miles W of Philadelphia in SE Pennsylvania; is within cannon sound of Brandywine, Paoli, Valley Forge, and other hallowed places of the Revolution.

WESTFIELD. Borough; Tioga County; Pop. 1,268 / 1,093; Zip Code 16950; Elev. 1,370; 50 miles SW of Elmira, New York in N Pennsylvania; Named for Westfield, Massachusetts by Henry Trowbridge, who established a woolen mill here in the early 1800s.

WEST GROVE, Borough; Chester County; Pop. 1,820 / 2,401; Zip Code 19390; Elev. 400; Lat. 39-49-19 N, Long. 075-49-40 W; Residential suburb of Philadelphia in SE Pennsylvania.

WEST HAZLETON, Borough; Luzerne County; Pop. 4,871 / 3,023; Zip Code 18201; Elev. 1,700; Lat. 40-57-31 N, Long. 075-59-47 W; Adjacent to Hazleton in E Pennsylvania; Residential.

WEST HOMESTEAD, Borough; Allegheny County; Pop. 3,128; Zip Code 15120; Elev. 1,000; Lat. 40-23-38 N, Long. 079-54-44 W; SE suburb of Pittsburgh, adjacent to Homestead in SW Pennsylvania on the Monongahela River.

WEST KITTANNING, Borough; Armstrong County; Pop. 1,591 / 1,055; Zip Code 16201; Elev. 980; Lat. 40-48-37 N, Long. 079-31-47 W; W of Kittanning in W Pennsylvania.

WEST MIFFLIN, Borough; Allegheny County; Pop. 26,279 / 22,024; Zip Code 15122; Elev. 1,000; Lat. 40-46-48 N, Long. 080-20-19 W; SE suburb of Pittsburgh in SW Pennsylvania.

WEST READING, Borough; Berks County; Pop. 4,507 / 3,969; Zip Code 19611; Elev. 320; Lat. 40-20-01 N, Long. 075-56-52 W; On Schuylkill River, across from Reading in SE Pennsylvania; Laid out in 1873 and incorporated in 1907.

WEST YORK, Borough; York County; Pop. 4,526 / 3,993; Zip Code 174+; Elev. 400; Lat. 39-57-09 N, Long. 076-45-06 W; 5 miles W of York in S Pennsylvania; Includes in its 320 acres the 160-acre farm of Henry Ebert, for whose ancestors the town was originally named Eberton.

WESTMONT, Borough; Cambria County; Pop. 6,113 / 5,317; Zip Code 16603; Elev. 1,795; Near Altoona in a highlands area in SW central Pennsylvania.

WHEATLAND, Borough; Mercer County; Pop. 1,132 / 718; Zip Code 16161; Elev. 900; Lat. 40-02-22 N, Long. 076-21-05 W; In W Pennsylvania; Laid out about 1865 by James Wood, a Philadelphia Democrat who named the town for President James Buchanan's Lancaster County estate.

WHITEHALL, Borough; Allegheny County; Pop. 15,206 / 13,540; Zip Code 18052; Elev. 1,200; Lat. 41-06-59 N, Long. 076-37-55 W; S suburb of Pittsburgh in SW Pennsylvania.

WHITE OAK, Borough; Allegheny County; Pop. 9,480 / 8,165; Zip Code 15131; Elev. 1,100; Lat. 40-20-15 N, Long. 079-48-34 W; S suburb of Pittsburgh in SW Pennsylvania.

WHITEMARSH, Township and Village; Montgomery County; Pop. 15,886; Elev. 203; 15 miles N of Philadelphia on the Wissahocken Creek in SE Pennsylvania.

WILKES-BARRE, City; Seat of Luzerne County; Pop. 51,117 / 42,358; Zip Code 187+; Elev. 575; Lat. 41-14-45 N, Long. 075-52-54 W; 20 miles SW of Scranton in NE Pennsylvania.

WILKINSBURG, Borough; Allegheny County; Pop. 23,669 / 18,736; Zip Code 15221; Elev. 922; Lat. 40-26-30 N, Long. 079-52-56 W; 10 miles E of Pittsburgh in SW Pennsylvania; Settled in 1780 and known successively as McNairsville and Rippeysville, was incorporated in 1887. Its name was changed to honor Judge William Wilkins, Minister to Russia and President Tyler's Secretary of War.

WILLIAMSBURG, Borough; Blair County; Pop. 1,400 / 1,355; Zip Code 16693; Elev. 885; Lat. 40-27-43 N, Long. 078-12-00 W; In S central Pennsylvania.

WILLIAMSPORT, City; Seat of Lycoming County; Pop. 33,401 / 29,922; Zip Code 17701; In N central Pennsylvania.

WILLOW GROVE, Urban Village; Montgomery County; Pop. 21,000; Zip Code 19090; Elev. 284; Lat. 40-57-12 N, Long. 080-22-59 W; 15 miles N of Philadelphia in SE Pennsylvania.

WILMERDING, Borough; Allegheny County; Pop. 2,421 / 2,151; Zip Code 15148; Elev. 900; Lat. 40-23-27 N, Long. 079-48-37 W; 10 miles E of Pittsburgh in SW Pennsylvania; Was first a railroad station, built about 1885, on land originally owned by Major William B. Negley. The name Wilmerding was suggested by Robert Pitcairn, then superintendent of the Pittsburgh division of the Pennsylvania Railroad, in honor of Negley's wife, Joanna Wilmerding Negley. Wilmerding was the family name of her mother.

WILSON, Borough; Northampton County; Pop. 7,564 / 7,471; Zip Code 15025; Near Easton in an industrial area in E Pennsylvania.

WINDBER, Borough; Somerset County; Pop. 5,585 / 4,422; Zip Code 15963; Elev. 1,600; Lat. 40-14-23 N, Long. 078-50-07 W; In S Pennsylvania; Was selected by the Pennsylvania Railroad Company in 1897 for its new station at this point. This name, which was suggested by E.J. Berwind, the chief stockholder in the Berwind White Coal company. Was formed by transposing the two syllables of the family name Berwind.

WIND GAP, Borough; Northampton County; Pop. 2,651 / 2,909; Zip Code 18091; Elev. 841; In E Pennsylvania; Incorporated as a borough in 1893 and named for the Wind Gap to the north.

WINDSOR, Borough; York County; Pop. 1,205 / 1,373; Zip Code 17366; Elev. 660; Lat. 39-54-58 N, Long. 076-35-05 W; In S Pennsylvania; Named for Windsor, England by Thomas Armor, who was Justice of the township in the 1750s.

WOMELSDORF, Borough; Berks County; Pop. 1,827 / 2,918; Zip Code 19567; Elev. 434; Lat. 40-21-42 N, Long. 076-11-04 W; In SE Pennsylvania; Founded by Germans in 1723. Was called Middletown until 1762, when it was renamed for John Womelsdorf, leader of emigrants from the German Palatinate.

WORMLEYSBURG, Borough; Cumberland County; Pop. 2,772 / 2,539; Zip Code 17043; Elev. 320; Lat. 40-15-46 N, Long. 076-54-51 W; Suburb of Harrisburg in S Pennsylvania.

WYOMING, Borough; Luzerne County; Pop. 3,655 / 2,960; Zip Code 18644; Elev. 557; Lat. 41-18-42 N, Long. 075-50-16 W; 5 miles NE of Wilkes-Barre on the Susquehanna River in E Pennsylvania; The site of the Battle of Wyoming, where valley settlers fought an invading party of Tories known as Butlers Rangers and a band of Iroquois on July 3, 1778.

WYOMISSING, Borough; Berks County; Pop. 6,551 / 7,808; Zip Code 19610; Elev. 320; Lat. 40-19-46 N, Long. 075-57-56 W; 45 miles W of Reading in SE Pennsylvania; Residential suburb; Name is derived from an Indian phrase which means "place of flats."

YEADON, Borough; Delaware County; Pop. 11,727 / 11,344; Zip Code 19050; Elev. 100; Lat. 39-56-20 N, Long. 075-15-21 W; 5 miles SW of Philadelphia in SE Pennsylvania; Residential.

YORK, City; Seat of York County; Pop. 44,619 / 39,704; Zip Code 174+; 10 miles WSW of the Susquehanna River in SE Pennsylvania. Named by Richard, Thomas and John Penn, probably to honor their royal patron and benefactor of their family, the Duke of York, but possibly in memory of the ancient English city of York.

YOUNGSVILLE, Borough; Warren Borough; Pop. 2,006 / 1,715; Zip Code 16371; Elev. 1,211; 10 miles W of Warren in NW Pennsylvania; Settled in 1795 by John Mckinney, and named for Matthew Young, who taught school from his tent here beginning in 1796.

YOUNGWOOD, Borough; Westmoreland County; Pop. 3,749 / 3,157; Zip Code 15697; Elev. 976; 30 miles E of Pittsburgh in an industrial area in SW Pennsylvania.

ZELIENOPLE, Borough; Butler County; Pop. 3,502 / 4,241; Zip Code 16063; Elev. 906; 30 miles NW of Pittsburgh; Was laid out an Connoquenessing Creek in 1802 by Baron Dettmar Basse, who later sold half of his 10,000 acre tract to Father Rapp for the latter's harmony colony. The Baron named the settlement for his daughter, nicknamed Zelie.

RHODE ISLAND
The Ocean State

International Tennis Hall of Fame - Newport

Museum of Yachting - Newport

GOVERNOR
Lincoln Almond

Newport waterfront

Downtown Providence

Block Island

North Lighthouse - Block Island

INTRODUCTION

Rhode Island is one of the six New England states as well as one of the original thirteen states. Early in its history, it made a considerable contribution to the forming of the new nation and its concept of liberty, and it also had a great amount of influence on the country's industrial development.

Rhode Island is bounded on the north and east by Massachusetts, on the west by Connecticut, and on the south by Rhode Island Sound. The smallest state in the Union in area, it is also one of the most densely populated. Its large population, economic activity, and compactness of area have helped it to develop and maintain strong ties with its neighboring states.

STATE NAME

Rhode Island's name is attributed to Dutch explorer Adrian Block, who named this island with red clay shores in his native language, calling it *Roodt Eylandt*, which is translated to mean "red island." Under English rule, the name was later anglicized into the current spelling.

STATE NICKNAME

There are several nicknames for Rhode Island. They include the Smallest State, Little Rhody, the Land of Roger Williams, the Plantation State, and the Ocean State.

The first two nicknames were given because Rhode Island is the smallest state in the Union. The Land of Roger Williams is a sobriquet used to honor Roger Williams, who founded Providence Plantation in 1636. The State's full name is The State of Rhode Island and Providence Plantations, and it is for this reason that it is called the Plantation State. The nickname of the Ocean State is used to promote tourism.

STATE SEAL

The official State seal was designated in 1875. However, the anchor on the seal was adopted by the assembly on the 1647 seal. The law reads as follows: "There shall continue to be one (1) seal for the public use of the state; the form of an anchor shall be engraven thereon; the motto thereof shall be the word Hope; and in a circle around the same shall be engraven the words, Seal of the State of Rhode Island and Providence Plantations, 1636."

The arms on the flag are described as follows: "The arms of the state are a golden anchor on a blue field, and the motto thereof is the word Hope."

STATE FLAG

The original act to designate the State flag for Rhode Island was passed in 1897. Although it has been amended, the flag is essentially unchanged. It is described as follows: "The flag of the state shall be white, five (5) feet and six (6) inches fly and four (4) feet and (10) inches deep on the pike, bearing on each side in the centre a gold anchor, twenty-two (22) inches high, and underneath it a blue ribbon twenty-four (24) inches long and five (5) inches wide, or in these proportions, with the motto 'Hope' in golden letters thereon, the whole surrounded by thirteen (13) golden stars in a circle. The flag to be edged with yellow fringe. The pike shall be surmounted by a spearhead and the length of the pike shall be nine (9) feet, not including the spearhead, provided, however, that on the 29th day of August, 1978 the flag of the Rhode Island first regiment shall be flown as the official state flag for that day."

The law also provided for a flag and pennant of the governor as follows: "The flag and pennant of the governor shall be white bearing on each side the following: A gold anchor on a shield with a blue field and gold border; above the shield a gold scroll bearing the words in blue letters 'State of Rhode Island;' below the shield a gold scroll bearing in blue letters the word 'Hope'; the shield and scrolls to be surrounded by four (4) blue stars, both the flag and pennant to be edged with yellow fringe."

STATE MOTTO

The official motto of Rhode Island is "Hope." It was added to the seal in 1644, after the colony received a new, more liberal charter. The symbol of hope is the anchor, which was the colonial seal at the beginning of settlement in the State.

STATE BIRD

The bird called Rhode Island Red was designated as the official State bird by the legislature in 1954. It is a well-known American breed of domesticated fowl. Weighing from 6½ to 8½ pounds, it has yellow skin beneath brownish red feathers. A single rose-colored comb extends from the base of the beak to the upper back of the head. Brown eggs are laid by the hen.

STATE FLOWER

The violet, *Viola* palmata, was adopted as the official State flower of Rhode Island in 1968. It is also called the early blue violet and Johnny-jump-up. The flower grows from Massachusetts to Minnesota and south to Florida. Flowers are colored violet-purple.

STATE TREE

The official State tree of Rhode Island is the red maple, *Acer rubrum*, adopted in 1964. Also called the soft maple, shoe-peg maple, water maple, scarlet maple, white maple, swamp maple, and erable, it is native to the eastern half of the United States and adjacent Canada, and west to the Dakotas, Texas, and Nebraska.

STATE SONG

The State legislature declared the song, "Rhode Island" to be the official song of Rhode Island in 1946. It was composed and written by T. Clarke Brown.

STATE LICENSE PLATE

The State of Rhode Island first began issuing license plates in 1904. The first plate was white on black. A series of black and white combinations continued through the current issue, except for the year 1946, when a black and aluminum plate was used.

The State's current plate is blue on white. The slogan "Ocean State" is lettered at the bottom center, and an anchor is depicted to its left. The slogan first appeared on the plate for 1973. The anchor, however, is a familiar symbol for Rhode Island, and has been used on all colonial and state seals since 1647. The words "Rhode Island" are lettered at the top of the plate. Through the middle of the plate a gray wave extends lengthwise across the plate.

STATE POSTAGE STAMP

The Rhode Island Tercentenary Commemorative stamp was issued on May 4, 1936 in Providence. Designed by A.R. Meissner, the stamp depicts the statue of Roger Williams, State founder, which still stands in Roger Williams Park in the capital city. The tercentenary dates 1636-1936 are lettered at each side near the top. The State seal is depicted on the lower left and the three-cent denomination is shown on the lower right in a circular shield. The vignette was engraved by L.C. Kauffmann, F. Pauling, and C.T. Arlt. The lettering was engraved by W.B. Wells and D.R. McLeod. A total of 67,127,650 of the stamp were printed.

OTHER STATE DESIGNATIONS

Over the years, the Rhode Island legislature has adopted a number of additional symbols to officially represent the State. Included are the State mineral as bowenite (1966); the State rock as cumberlandite (1966); the State shell as quahaug (1987), and the State fruit as Rhode Island greening apple (1991).

STATE CAPITOL

In 1895, the capital city of Providence held a ground-breaking ceremony for a new statehouse. The capitol building was designed by Charles Follen McKim in the Greek Renaissance tradition, with exterior walls of white Georgia marble. The building is 333 feet in length and 180 feet wide at the center. The dome, one of only four unsupported marble domes in the world, is topped by an eleven-foot high, gold leaf statue of the "Independent Man." Some offices were in use as early as 1900. However, the grounds and building were not fully completed until 1904. Total cost of the building, including furnishings, was 3,018,416 dollars.

OTHER FACTS ABOUT RHODE ISLAND

Total area: 1,212 square miles
Land area: 1,055 square miles
Water area: 158 square miles
Average elevation: 200 feet
Highest point: Jerimoth Hill, 812 feet
Lowest point: Atlantic Ocean, sea level
Highest temperature: 104 degrees Fahrenheit
Lowest temperature: -23 degrees Fahrenheit
Population in 1990: 1,003,464
Population density in 1990: 960.26 persons per square mile
Population 1980-1990: +5.9 percent change
Population projected for year 2000: 1,049,000
Asian/Pacific Islander population in 1990: 18,325
Black population in 1990: 38,861
Hispanic population in 1990: 45,752
Native American population in 1990: 4,071
White population in 1990: 917,375
Capital: Providence
Admitted to Union: May 29, 1790
Order of Statehood: 13
Electoral votes: 4

CHRONOLOGY

1524 April 21-May 5. Verrazzano, Florentine navigator, visits Narragansett Bay.

1614 Captain Adriaen Block visits Block Island.

1635 William Blackstone settles at Study Hill, considered part of Massachusetts (it is now part of Cumberland, Rhode Island).

1636 June. Roger Williams settles at Providence.

1638 March 7. Aquidneck Island is occupied by William Coddington, John Clarke, and others; Coddington is chosen as judge.
March 24. Date of first known written deed, in which Canonicus and Miantonomi sell land to Williams.
– William Coddington, others purchase Aquidneck from Indians and found Pocasset (Portsmouth).
November 12. First militia muster in Rhode Island is held at Portsmouth.

1639 March. First Baptist Church in America is organized at Providence.
April. Settlement on Aquidneck, first called Pocasset, is divided into towns of Portsmouth and Newport.
May. William Coddington, John Clarke, and others found Newport.

1640 March 12. Governments of Newport and Portsmouth are combined into one government.
August. Newport allots land for support of public school, the Rev. Robert Lenthal being called by vote to open it.

1641 Benedict Arnold purchases land at Pawtuxet from Miantonomi.
March. General Assembly asserts Rhode Island to be democracy.
September. Robert Jeffreys is authorized by Newport to "exercise the function of Chirurgerie."

1642 October. Samuel Gorton purchases Shawomet (Warwick) from Miantonomi.

1643 Narragansett sachem, Miantonomi, dies.
– Gorton is seized by soldiers from Massachusetts Bay, taken to Boston to stand trial for heresy.
– Newman Congregational Church is founded in Rumford.
– Roger Williams goes to England, applies for Patent of Incorporation for Providence, Portsmouth, and Newport.
– Roger Williams's *Key Into the Language of America* is published in London.

1644 March 13. Name of 'Aquidneck' is ordered to be changed to 'Rhode Island.'
March 14. English Parliamentary Commission, headed by Earl of Warwick, grants Rhode Island its first charter, sometimes called 'Charter of 1643.'
April 19. Gorton secures submission of Narragansett sachems to authority of English Crown.

1645 Christinas Ludowic publishes The New England Almanac for 1645; it is first almanac by Rhode Islander.

1647 May 19-21. First General Assembly convenes at Portsmouth, and adopts code of laws and colony seal.
– Narragansett sachem, Canonicus, dies.

1651 Coddington "usurpation" causes separation between Portsmouth and Newport on one side, and Providence and Warwick on other.
October. Roger Williams, agent of Providence to obtain confirmation of charter, and Dr. John Clarke, agent of Portsmouth and Newport to obtain repeal of Coddington's commission, sail for England.

1653 February 18. William Dyer, secretary of province and husband of Mary Dyer (later put to death in Boston as Quaker), arrives from England with news of repeal of Coddington's commission.

1654 First naval commission issued by united Rhode Island Colony is granted to Newport vessel.
August 31. Four original towns reunite, partly due to efforts of Roger Williams, who is president from September 1654 to May 1657.

1657 Conanicut Island is purchased by Benedict Arnold and William Coddington from sachem, Cashanaquoont.
– First Quakers come to Rhode Island.

1657-58 Pettaquamscutt Purchase, large tract of land running west from Narragansett to Charlestown, is made.

1658 About fifteen Jewish families arrive in Newport from Holland.
May 26. Pawtuxet men withdraw allegiance to Massachusetts, given in 1642, and transfer it to Rhode Island.
October 19. Block Island is granted to Governor Endicott and three others, "for public services;" they sell it in 1660 to Simeon Ray and eight associates, who begin settlement in 1661.
October 22. Massachusetts relinquishes jurisdiction over Pawtuxet and Shawomet.

1660 William Vaughan, other Newport men purchase from Niantic chief, Socho, Misquamicut tract on east side of Pawcatuck River.

1661 Settlement of Misquamicut, now Westerly, begins.

1663 May. Providence sets aside lands for maintenance of school.
July 8. King Charles II grants Rhode Island second charter.

1664 May 4. Block Island becomes part of Rhode Island Colony.

1665 March. Royal Commissioners set aside Narragansett Country, in dispute between Rhode Island and Connecticut, as King's Province.

1669 Vaughan purchase is incorporated as town of Westerly.

1671 Joseph Jencks, Jr. sets up forge, sawmill, and carpenter shop at Pawtucket Falls.

1672 Block Island is incorporated, and its name changed to New Shoreham.
July. George Fox, English Quaker leader, visits Rhode Island.

1674 First settlement is made in Little Compton by Captain Benjamin Church.
– Part of Pettaquamscutt settlement is incorporated as Kings Towne.

1675 August 1. Important peace pact is made between Capt. Benjamin Church and Awashonks, squaw-sachem of Sakonnet Indians.
– King Philip's War begins.
December 19. Great Swamp Fight takes place in South Kingstown.

1676 Benedict Arnold conveys Coaster's Harbor Island and Goat Island to Newport.
March 16. Warwick is destroyed by Indians.
March 26. Capt. Michael Pierce's company is routed in Pawtucket and Cumberland.
March 30. Indians burn many houses in Providence and vicinity.
July 3. Massacre near Warwick leaves 171 Indians dead.
August 12. Capt. Benjamin Church's company captures and kills King Philip at Mount Hope, Bristol, ending King Philip's War.

1680 First wharf and warehouse are built in Providence.

1681 April 1. Customhouse is established at Newport to enforce Navigation Acts.

1683 Roger Williams dies (some time between January 16 and March 15).

1686 June 3. Sir Edmund Andros is commissioned as governor of Dominion of New England (including Rhode Island).
December. Andros assumes government of Rhode Island, setting aside Charter of 1663.

1687 Courthouses are ordered to be built in Newport and Rochester (or Kings Towne).
November. Governor Andros, stopping at Newport, demands Rhode Island Charter; foiled by Governor Clarke, he destroys seal of Colony and departs.

1689 April. Andros is deposed at Boston.
May 1. Rhode Island, learning of accession of William and Mary, resumes government under Charter of 1663.
August 3. Sir Edmund Andros, after fleeing to Rhode Island from Boston, is captured at Newport and returned to Massachusetts authorities.

1690 Beginning of King William's War between England and France.

1693 June. Massachusetts establishes first postal route between Boston and Rhode Island.

1694 Privateers are authorized for King William's War.
– Tiverton is incorporated by Massachusetts.

1695 First ferry connecting Jamestown with Newport is established.

1696 May 6. General Assembly is separated into two houses.

1697 End of King William's War.

1702 Beginning of Queen Anne's War between England and France.

1703 May. Commissioners representing Rhode Island and Connecticut agree on boundary, but line is not settled until 1727.
June 22. Counties of Providence and Newport are organized.

1704 First Trinity Church building is erected in Newport.

1707 Saint Paul's, or Old Narragansett Church, is erected in North Kingstown.

1708 December. Rhode Island's first census shows population of 7,181.

1710 July. Colony authorizes first issue of paper money or bills of credit (5,000 pounds).

1711 Latin school is opened in Newport by Mr. Galloway.
– First quarantine act is made against smallpox.

1713 End of Queen Anne's War.

1715 General Assembly appropriates funds towards paving streets of Newport; it is first instance of street paving within Colony.

1719 First digest of Colony laws is printed.

1723 February 26. South Kingstown is incorporated as town.
July. First almshouse in Rhode Island is erected at Newport.
July 19. Twenty-six pirates are executed at Gravelly Point, Newport.

1724 February 18. Property qualification for suffrage is established at 'freehold of value of 100 pounds, or annual income of 2 pounds.'

1725 Second building for First Trinity Church is erected in Newport.

1727 First Rhode Island printing press is established at Newport by James Franklin.
February 8. Boundary line with Connecticut is settled by royal decree.

1729 June 16. Washington County is organized.

1730 Colony population is 17,935.
May. Assembly passes Act for Relief of Poor Sailors; act levies sixpence per month from wages of all Rhode Island seamen.

1731 Old Colony House at Providence is completed.
February 20. Glocester, Scituate, and Smithfield are incorporated as towns.

1732 September 27. Colony's first newspaper, *Rhode Island Gazette*, is issued at Newport by James Franklin.

1733 Lottery system makes first appearance, but is suppressed by severe penalty.
June. Sloop Pelican, first whaling vessel from Rhode Island, arrives at Newport with cargo.

1735 Redwood Library is formed at Newport.

1738 Courthouse in Newport is removed to Prison Lane, and made dwelling.
August 22. Charlestown is incorporated as town.

1739 Old Colony House at Newport is built by Richard Munday (building still stands next to modern Newport County Courthouse).
October. "War of Jenkins Ear" begins between England and Spain.

1741 April 6. West Greenwich is incorporated as town.
August 21. Coventry is incorporated as town.

1742 February 1. Newport Artillery is incorporated.

1743 March 8. Exeter is incorporated as town.
June 16. Middletown is made separate town from Newport, and is incorporated.

1744 Colony sloop, *Tartar*, is built.
– Beginning of King George's War between England and France.

1746 Royal Decree gives Rhode Island towns of Warren, Bristol, Tiverton, Little Compton, and Cumberland (they were previously claimed by Massachusetts).

1747 Bristol, Cumberland, Little Compton, Tiverton, and Warren are incorporated as towns.
February 17. Bristol County is organized.
August 18. Richmond is incorporated as town.
– Redwood Library is chartered.

1748 End of King George's War.

1750 June 11. Kent County is organized.

1752 September. Great Britain adopts "New Style" or Gregorian calendar; eleven days are omitted from current month; September 3 becomes September 14, and subsequent years will begin January 1 instead of March 25, as formerly.

1754 February 25. Providence Library Association is chartered.
June. Stephen Hopkins and Martin Howard, Jr. are sent as commissioners to intercolonial Congress at Albany, N.Y.
June 14. Cranston is taken from Providence and is incorporated as town.
– Beginning of last French and Indian War.

1757 March 19. Hopkinton is incorporated as town.

1758 James Franklin, Jr., founds Newport Mercury.
December 24. Old Colony House at Providence is burned.

1759 March 6. Johnston is incorporated as town.
June 11. Masonic Society in Newport is incorporated.

1761 September 7. First Rhode Island dramatic performance is held in Newport.

1762 October 20. William Goddard sets up first printing press in Providence; he publishes Providence Gazette and Country Journal.

1763 Spermaceti trust is formed.
– End of last French and Indian War.
March 4. Rhode Island College is incorporated.
December 2. Touro Synagogue is dedicated in Newport.

1765 Governor Samuel Ward refuses oath to enforce Stamp Act.
June 4. British vessel, Maidstone, impresses seamen in Newport Harbor; 500 sailors and boys seize one of her boats, drag it to Commons, and burn it.
June 13. North Providence is incorporated as town.
September. General Assembly adopts resolutions opposing Stamp Act, and appoints Metcalf Bowler and Henry Ward commissioners to Stamp Act Congress at New York City.

1766 March 4. "Daughters of Liberty" society is organized by 18 young women at Dr. Ephraim Bowen's house in Providence.

1769 July 19. Newporters destroy British revenue sloop, Liberty.
– First commencement is held at Rhode Island College.

1770 June 16. Barrington is separated from Warren and incorporated as town.

1772 First equestrian performance (circus) in Rhode Island occurs at Newport.
June 9. British revenue schooner, Gaspee, is burned while aground in Warwick, by expedition from Providence.

1773 August. Revs. Samuel Hopkins and Ezra Stiles of Newport invite subscriptions to colonize free blacks on western coast of Africa. (This was inception of American Colonization Society of 19th century.)

1774 Colony population is 58,221, including 3,768 blacks.
June. Rhode Island prohibits further importation of slaves.
June 15. Stephen Hopkins and Samuel Ward are elected delegates to First Continental Congress at Philadelphia.

1775 April 19. American Revolution begins at Lexington and Concord, Massachusetts.
April 20. More than one thousand Rhode Islanders, armed and disciplined soldiers, mobilize overnight and march toward Boston.
April 22. Over protest by Governor Joseph Wanton, General Assembly approves levy of 1,500 troops for war.
June. Rhode Island postal system is organized.
June 15. Capt. Abraham Whipple captures armed tender belonging to British frigate, Rose, on shore of Conanicut Island.
October 7. Bristol is bombarded by British expedition under Capt. James Wallace.
November 5. Congress appoints Esek Hopkins Commander-in-Chief of Continental Navy.

1776 April 5. General Washington visits Providence.
May 4. Rhode Island General Assembly formally renounces allegiance to Great Britain; Rhode Island is "the first colony to declare, by solemn act, her absolute independence of the Crown."
July 18. General Assembly approves Congressional Declaration of Independence, and votes that title of government shall be "State of Rhode Island and Providence Plantations."
December 8. British forces under Sir Henry Clinton take possession of Newport.

1777 July 9. Colonel Barton captures British General Prescott in Overing House at Portsmouth.

1778 February 9. Articles of Confederation are adopted by Rhode Island.
May 25. British pillage Bristol and Warren.
July 9. Articles of Confederation are signed by William Ellery, Henry Merchant, and John Collins.
July 29. French fleet arrives off Newport.
August 29. Battle of Rhode Island is fought in Portsmouth.

1779 October 25. Newport is evacuated by British.

1780 July 10. Count Rochambeau arrives at Newport with 6,500 French troops.

1781 March 6. Public reception is held for General Washington in Newport.
August 24. Foster is incorporated as town.

1783 February. General Assembly repeals statute denying franchise to Roman Catholics.

1784 February 23. Emancipation Act provides for gradual abolition of slavery.
June 1. Newport is incorporated as city.

1786 Emission of bills of credit 100,000 pounds; legal tender at par. (Repealed October 12, 1789.)
September. Paper-money case, *Trevett v. Weeden*, is settled at Newport.
– State's first jewelry business is established by Seril and Nehemiah Dodge, and Jabez Gorham, in Providence.

1787 Population of State is 52,391.
– First spinning jenny in United States is constructed and put into operation by Daniel Jackson of Providence.
March 27. City Charter of Newport is repealed.
October 29. African slave trade is forbidden in Rhode Island.

1789 September. First Methodist service is held by Jesse Lee in Charlestown.

1790 Population of State (first Federal census) is 68,825.
– Calico printing from wooden blocks begins at East Greenwich.
May 29. Rhode Island ratifies Federal Constitution.
December. Cotton factory is put into operation at Pawtucket by Samuel Slater.

1791 Providence Bank opens.

1792 Elijah Ormsbee makes successful trip on Providence River in steamboat, Experiment.

1793 Second Almy, Brown, and Slater cotton mill is built in Pawtucket (this mill still stands on bank of Blackstone River).

1794 May 8. Bristol sloop, Nautilus, is accused at Newport of impressing American sailors.

1796 Samuel Slater of Pawtucket provides Sunday School instruction for mill children.

1800 Statewide free school law is enacted; it is carried into effect only by Providence.
– Population of State is 69,122.
– Saint Paul's, or Old Narragansett Church, is moved from North Kingston to Wickford.

1802 Kent Academy is founded (now East Greenwich Academy).

1803 Free school law is repealed, except in Providence.

1804 Rhode Island College becomes Brown University.

1805 Line of packet ships is established between Newport and Charlestown.

1806 Lighting by "hydrogenous gas or inflammable air produced from pit coal" is introduced by David Melville at Newport.
October 29. Burrillville is incorporated as town.

1810 Broadcloth is manufactured by Bellefonte Company at Cranston.

1812 June. Beginning of second war with Great Britain.

1813 British occupy Block Island.
September 10. Commodore Oliver Hazard Perry of Rhode Island defeats British in naval engagement on Lake Erie.

1814 "Heroes of the Lake," drama celebrating Perry's victory, is played in Providence.
December. End of second war with Great Britain.
– Rhode Island is represented by four delegates at Hartford, Connecticut Convention.

1815 September 22-23. Great Gale devastates Providence.

1816 Rowland Hazard installs power-looms at Peace Dale woolen mills.

1817 May. Steamboat, Firefly, from New York, makes first trip between Providence and Newport, inaugurating steam navigation in Narragansett Bay.

1819 Moses Brown School opens in Providence.

1821 Streets of Providence are first to be publicly lighted.

1823 June. Blackstone Canal Company is incorporated.

1824 August 23. Lafayette visits Providence.

1827 April. First public temperance meeting is held in Providence.

1828 Permanent School Fund is established.
– Blackstone Canal (Providence to Worcester) is opened for traffic.
January. Act is passed establishing public schools throughout State.
April 14. First public Roman Catholic service is held in Providence.

1831 Franklin Lyceum is founded (it remains active until 1906).
– Providence is incorporated as city.
September 21-24. Race riots take place in Providence, between seamen and blacks.
December. New England Association of Farmers, Mechanics, and Other Workmen is founded at Providence.

1833 Antislavery movement gets underway.
June 19. Andrew Jackson, President of United States, visits Newport.

1834 New England Association of Farmers, Mechanics, and Other Workmen at Providence is disbanded.

1835 June 2. First railroad train operates between Boston and Providence.

1836 Henry Wheaton publishes first edition of Elements of International Law.

1837 November 10. Railroad connecting Rhode Island with Stonington, Connecticut, is opened.

1841 October-December. "People's Constitution" is framed and voted upon.

1842 Permanent garrison is established at Fort Adams.
February-March. "Landholders Constitution" is framed and rejected.
April. Thomas Wilson Dorr is elected governor on "People's Constitution" ticket.
June 28. Dorr's forces are routed at Acote Hill in Chepachet.
November 5-23. Present State Constitution is framed and adopted.

1843 Survey of public schools is undertaken by Henry Barnard.

1845 "Barnard School Law" is passed; it is foundation for State's modern public school system.
June. Persons convicted of treason for participation in Dorr War are freed.

1847 September 27. First passenger train travels over Providence-Worcester railroad.

1850 Population of State is 147,545.
– Sockanosset School (reform) for boys is founded.

1852 Capital punishment is abolished in State.
– Normal school opens in Providence.
– Prohibitory liquor law is passed.

1853 Survey of Providence Harbor is made by Lieut. William A. Rosecrans.
May 20. Newport is reincorporated as city.

1854 Normal school in Providence becomes State institution; it later becomes Rhode Island College of Education.

1861 Controversy with Massachusetts over eastern boundary of Rhode Island is settled.
April 18. First Rhode Island troops leave for Civil War.

1862 March 1. East Providence is incorporated as town.

1863 Bryant and Stratton Business School is founded.
– Prohibitory liquor law is repealed.

1864 First train runs to Newport from Boston.

1865 Civil War ends.

1866 David Wallis Reeves becomes head of American Brass Band in Providence.

1867 January 31. Woonsocket is incorporated as town.

1868 Providence Board of Trade is organized.

1869 United States Naval Torpedo Station is established at Goat Island.

1870 State Board of Education is created.
– Legislature abolishes imprisonment for debt.

1871 Betsey Williams dies; she bequeaths Roger Williams Park to City of Providence.
– LaSalle Academy in Providence is founded.
March 8. Lincoln and North Smithfield are incorporated as towns.

1872 Providence Opera House is built.

1873 Steamboat ferries are put into operation between Jamestown and Newport.

1876 Corliss engine, designed by George H. Corliss of Providence, is set in motion at Centennial Exhibition in Philadelphia; President Grant is present.

1877 Rhode Island Institute for Deaf is founded.
– Rhode Island School of Design is founded.

1880 Tribal authority of Narragansett Indians ends.
December. Coaster's Harbor Island is ceded to United States government by citizens of Newport, for purpose of establishing training school for United States Navy.

1882 Electric carbon lights are used for street lighting in Providence.

1883 Coaster's Harbor Island is designated by Navy Department as permanent naval training station.
– Northern boundary line of Rhode Island is settled.

1884 Lincoln School is founded in Providence.
– Naval War College is founded at Newport.

1885 Prohibition amendment is added to State Constitution.
March 27. Pawtucket is incorporated as city.

1887 Compulsory Education Act is passed.
– State Agricultural School opens at Kingston.
– Talma Dramatic Club is founded.
April. Western boundary of Rhode Island is settled.

1888 First electric street railway in Rhode Island is opened in Woonsocket.
June. Woonsocket is incorporated as city.

1889 Mary C. Wheeler School is founded in Providence.
– Old Providence Cove is filled in.
– Prohibition amendment is repealed.

1890 September 29-October 4. Cotton Centenary is celebrated at Pawtucket.

1892 Women's College in Brown University is founded; it is renamed Pembroke College in 1928.
October 21. Columbus Day is first celebrated in State.
– Agricultural School at Kingston becomes Rhode Island College of Agriculture and Mechanic Arts.
– First electric street railway line in Providence begins operating.

1893 St. Andrew's Industrial School is founded at Barrington.

1895 "Rhode Island Red" hen is officially recognized as new breed.
– Verdandi Male Chorus is founded.
February 21. Central Falls is incorporated as city.

1896 St. George's School is founded at Middletown.

1897 May 19. New State Flag is adopted.

1898 Rhode Island Textile School is founded.
– Spanish-American War begins.

1899 June 3. Eastern boundary between Rhode Island and Massachusetts is finally established.

1900 Population of State is 428,556.

1901 January 1. General Assembly holds first session in new State House at Providence.
March 28. Narragansett is incorporated as town.

1902 Incandescent lamps are introduced for house lighting.
– Rhode Island College of Pharmacy and Allied Sciences is founded in Providence.
June. Street railway strike results in rioting in Pawtucket.

1903 Wireless telegraph is introduced into State.

1907 Exeter School is founded.

1909 Rhode Island College of Agriculture and Mechanic Arts becomes Rhode Island State College.
– Players Dramatic Club is organized.

1910 March 10. Cranston is incorporated as city.
– State population is 542,610.

1911 University Glee Club is founded in Providence.

1912 April 29. First Workmen's Compensation Act is passed.

1913 March 14. West Warwick is incorporated as town.
April. Naval Hospital is commissioned at Newport.
September 10. Perry Day honors one-hundred-year anniversary of Battle of Lake Erie.

1914 Car-tunnel is constructed under College Hill in Providence.
– Providence Lodge of Sons of Italy is organized.
– Providence Board of Trade becomes Providence Chamber of Commerce.
– World War I begins.

1915 April 16. Nelson W. Aldrich, United States Senator from Rhode Island from 1881 to 1911, dies.
April 23. Farm Bureaus of Rhode Island is organized.
September 11. William Sprague II, Civil War Governor of State, dies.

1917 Providence College is founded.

– Pulitzer Prize is awarded to Maud Howe Elliott for biography of Julia Ward Howe.
July 25. Rhode Island National Guard musters into service of United States for World War I fight against Germany.
September 5. State's first draft quota of troops in World War I leaves for training camp.

1918 Explosion at Newport Naval Torpedo Station results in 14 deaths.
November 11. Armistice Day marks end of World War I.

1919 State population is 604,397.
July 1. First registration day for women voters for presidential election.

1920 State rejects ratification of national prohibition amendment.
– Rhode Island ratifies 19th Amendment giving suffrage to women; on November 2. Women vote for first time in national election.

1922 Radio broadcasting begins over stations WEAN and WJAR.
January-September. Textile strike affects 18,000 local workers.

1923 Watchman Industrial School is opened.
– Administration creates Department of State Police.

1924 Percy Marks publishes The Plastics Age.

1925 April. Department of State Police is created.

1928 Oliver Hazard Perry statue at State House is dedicated.
– Mount St. Charles Academy is founded in Cumberland.

1929 Pulitzer Prize is awarded to Oliver La Farge for "Laughing Boy."
October 24. Mount Hope Toll Bridge between Bristol and Portsmouth is dedicated, opened to traffic.

1930 Population of State is 687,497.
September 25. New Washington Bridge is opened between Providence and East Providence.

1931 State pier on Providence River burns down.
April 21. Warwick is incorporated as city.
September 27. State airport at Hillsgrove is dedicated (it is later closed for reconstruction, and opened again on May 30, 1936).
– Providence Opera House is demolished.
– Statue of General Nathanael Greene is dedicated at State House.

1932 Providence Symphony Orchestra (city's fifth) is founded.
March. Independent Textile Union is founded at Woonsocket.
May. New State Pier No. 1, constructed on Providence River to replace burned pier, is completed.
September 16. Remains of Roger Williams are placed in vault in North Burial Ground.

1933 State voters approve 21st Amendment repealing prohibition.

1934 **May 18**. Horse racing and pari-mutuel betting are legalized.
August 1. Narragansett Park opens.
September. National Guard is called out for strike duty in Saylesville.

1935 **January 1**. General Assembly begins reorganization of State government; offices of Supreme Court are declared vacant, and five new judges are elected.
May. State Department of Labor is established.
July 31. Rhode Island inaugurates police teletype system in 29 police departments and law-enforcing agencies within State through central sending and receiving station at State House.
November 1. Earthquake shakes northern section of United States and eastern Canada, jarring Rhode Island for 30 seconds at 1:07 A.M.
– Bryant and Stratton Business School becomes Bryant College.

1936 State population is 680,712.
– Rhode Island observes 300th anniversary of its founding and settlement.
March 10. Proposal to call constitutional convention is defeated at special election.
June. In case of *City of Newport v. Newport Water Corporation*, Superior Court renders decision that city has right to acquire water works.

1938 Hurricane and tidal wave hit State, causing more than 300 deaths, property damage in excess of $100 million.

1939 World War II begins.

1941 Providence bans showing of Two-Faced Woman, starring Greta Garbo, after Legion of Decency denounces it as "immoral."
– Providence shipyards build 64 cargo and combat ships.

1946 Law is passed which requires employers to pay women equal wages to that of men.

1949 Governor John Pastore names attorney Edward Leahy to complete Senate term of Howard McGrath, newly-appointed Attorney General.

1954 Two disastrous hurricanes cause great damage in State.

1955 Major flooding results in Rhode Island being declared major disaster area.

1956 Bond issues for Korean War veteran's bonus is approved by State voters.

1962 Rhode Island is one of 10 states in which federal and state courts have intervened on apportionment questions this year.

1963 Supreme Court rules 8-1 that Rhode Island Commission to Encourage Morality went "far beyond" its constitutional rights in drive against obscene literature.

1969 Newport Bridge is completed across Narragansett Bay; it has 1,600-foot suspension.

1971 Governor Frank Licht signs bill approving State income tax.

1972 Brown University announces expansion of medical program; Brown becomes first full medical school in State.
– Equal Rights Amendment (ERA) is ratified.

1973 Riot breaks out at State prison; reform-oriented warden resigns.
– Providence teachers accept new contract, ending nine-day strike.
– In effort to save fuel, President Nixon signs bill to put most of U.S. on year-round daylight savings time for two years; only Alaska and Hawaii are exempted.

1974 Rhode Island adopts voluntary gasoline distribution plan.
– Governor Philip W. Noel is reelected.
– Attorney General William B. Saxbe tells representatives of Rhode Island, 12 other states that he will seek permanent injunctions against state lotteries unless they obtain Congressional exemption from federal anti-lottery laws within 90 days.

1975 U.S. Labor Department announces that number of unemployed receiving benefits in week ending February 22 rose to 300,000; State is one of five in which unemployment compensation funds have already been exhausted.
– State borrows $30.4 million from federal fund to pay unemployment insurance for April.
– Teachers' strikes affect some 22,300 pupils in State.

1976 U.S. government halts swine-flu inoculation program after 58 cases of paralysis, known as Guillain-Barre syndrome, is reported in 18 states, including Rhode Island.
– "Operation Sail" armada of square riggers is brought to Newport, then to New York City to honor Rhode Island's U.S. Bicentennial celebration.

1977 Worst blizzard in decades paralyzes State for more than week.
– Providence holds skiing contests on city streets.

1978 John Joseph Garrahy (D) is elected governor.
– State sales tax has increased one percent since 1967.

1979 Nationwide gasoline shortage causes energy crisis.
– At meeting of Coalition of Northeast Governors, Energy Secretary Charles W. Duncan Jr. reassures Governor Garrahy, and governors of eight other states, that region will be supplied with enough heating fuel for winter, and that federal subsidy will help to pay for it.
– As summer tourist season ends, fuel supplies increase; governor announces end to odd-even restrictions on gasoline sales.

1980 U.S. Census Bureau reports population total of 947,154 in 1980; State will have two representatives in 98th Congress in 1982.
– Rhode Island is one of 12 states reporting widespread influenza outbreaks; number of deaths in U.S. during three-week period of January- February is about 300 higher than normal.

1981 In address to legislature, Governor Garrahy reports substantial achievement in attracting new industry to State, bringing jobless rate below seven percent in past four years.

1982 Newport jury charges Claus Von Bulow on two counts of assault with intent to murder wife, Martha, by twice injecting her with high doses of insulin; trial attracts widespread publicity after decision to allow closed-circuit television cameras in courtroom.

1983 State's economy improves steadily.

1984 Former Roman Catholic nun, Arlene Violet, wins election as State attorney general; she is first woman in history to win election to attorney general's office in any state.
– Rhode Island is only state remaining to set governor's term at two years.
– Voters approve measure calling for constitutional convention to amend State Constitution.

1985 School bond issue passes in State.

1986 Incumbent Edward D. PiPrete (R) is governor.

1987 EPA asks for delay in implementing clean air deadlines to reduce carbon monoxide and ozone pollution; Rhode Island is among six Northeast states to question whether EPA has legislative authority to delay clean air deadlines; Thomas Jorling, Department of Environmental Protection commissioner, requests cooperative action at federal level to help meet air pollution standards.

1988 Senator John H. Chafee defeats challenge by Frank H. Murkowski (Alaska) as Republican Conference chairman.
– Governor DiPrete wins reelection by narrow margin.
– Rhode Island holds VJ Day celebration on second Monday in August; Rhode Island is only state that still celebrates victory over Japan during World War II.

1989 Environmental officials from Rhode Island, seven other Northeast states agree to restrict toxic emissions from cars and light trucks beginning in 1993 model year; rules patterned from California code will lessen emissions for several pollutants, require anti-pollution devices that will last 100,000 instead of current 50,000 miles.

1990 Broadcasting executive Bruce Sundlun wins race against incumbent Governor DiPrete with 74 percent of vote; State's troubled economy and alleged corruption in DiPrete's administration were major issues in campaign.

1991 Population totals 1,003,464; figure is 5.9 percent higher than in 1980.
– In attempt to shrink $222 million budget deficit, State government closes down for one day; plan calls for having most State employees stay home one workday every two weeks until end of fiscal year in order to reduce payroll by 10 percent; State workers gather at Providence State house to protest forced furlough.
– Vartan Gregorian, president of Brown University, upholds student Douglas Hann's expulsion for using racial slurs on campus; Hann is also charged with violating campus rules against excessive drinking.

– Under current system, Rhode Island is one of four states where long-term unemployed residents qualify for extended benefits.
– U.S. Coast Guard announces Providence port as one of four New England ports scheduled to receive new equipment for cleaning up oil spills.

1992 State voters reelect Governor Bruce Sundlun to second term.

1993 Rhode Island is one of 14 states in U.S. without capital punishment.

1994 State Senator defeats incumbent Bruce G. Sundlun in Democratic gubernatorial primary.
– U.S. Commerce Secretary Ronald H. Brown approves plan to reduce fishing of some species off New England coast over next five to seven years; restrictions are created to increase stock of ground fish that have been over-fished in recent years; Brown also proposes economic aid to Rhode Island and two other states where new rules are expected to severely affect fishing industry workers.
– Republican Lincoln Almond becomes governor.

1995 Cornell University research team incubates and hatches 330-year-old zooplankton eggs; oldest eggs ever hatched were found in dormant state (called diapause) at bottom of Rhode Island pond.

1996 Democrats retain Senate seat they have held for last 60 years after victory by Representative Jack Reed over Republican State Treasurer Nancy J. Mayer.

1997 Judge Dominic Cresto, citing misconduct by prosecutors, dismisses charges of racketeering, bribery, and extortion against former governor Edward D. DiPrete.

1998 Governor Almond wins reelection.

1999 Republican Senator John Chafee announces he will not seek reelection in 2000, opening up chance for Democrats to pick up Senate seat; Democratic Representative Bob Weygand announces candidacy for Chafee's seat.

DIRECTORY OF STATE SERVICES

OFFICE OF THE GOVERNOR
State House
Providence, RI 02903
Governor: 401-277-2080
Fax: 401-272-5729

Commission of Women
260 E Exchange St.
Providence, RI 02903
Director: 401-277-6105
Fax: 401-861-0131

LIEUTENANT GOVERNOR
State House, Rm. 317
Providence, RI 02903
Lieutenant Governor: 401-277-2371
Fax: 401-277-2012

ATTORNEY GENERAL
72 Pine St.
Providence, RI 02903
Attorney General: 401-274-4400
Fax: 401-277-1331

SECRETARY OR STATE
State House, Rm. 218
Providence, RI 02903
Secretary of State: 401-277-2357
Fax: 401-277-1356

TREASURER (TREASURY DEPARTMENT)
107 State House
Providence, RI 02903
General Treasurer: 401-277-2397
Fax: 401-277-6140

Retirement
40 Fountain St.
Providence, RI 02903
Executive Director: 401-277-2203

ADJUTANT GENERAL
1050 N Main St.
Providence, RI 02904
Adjutant General: 401-457-4100
Fax: 401-457-4338

ADMINISTRATION DEPARTMENT
1 Capitol Hill
Providence, RI 02908-5890
Director: 401-277-2280

Accounts and Control Office
1 Capitol Hill
Providence, RI 02908-5883
State Controller: 401-277-2271
Fax: 401-277-6437

Human Resources Office
1 Capitol Hill
Providence, RI 02908-5868
Associate Director: 401-277-2155
Fax: 401-277-6378

Purchases Office
1 Capitol Hill
Providence, RI 02908-5855
Associate Dir./Purchasing Agent: 401-277-2321
Fax: 401-277-6387

State Building Code Commission
1 Capitol Hill
Providence, RI 02908-5859
Commissioner: 401-277-3033
Fax: 401-277-2599

State Employee Workers Compensation
1 Capitol Hill
Providence, RI 02908-5866
Administrator: 401-277-6465
Fax: 401-277-6378

Taxation Office
1 Capitol Hill
Providence, RI 02908-5800
Administration Assoc. Dir./Tax Adm.: 401-277-3050
Fax: 401-277-6006

BUSINESS REGULATIONS DEPARTMENT
233 Richmond St.
Providence, RI 02903-6098
Director: 401-277-2246
Fax: 401-277-6098

CHILDREN, YOUTH, AND THEIR FAMILIES DEPARTMENT
610 Mt. Pleasant Ave.
Providence, RI 02908-1935
Director: 401-457-4708
Fax: 401-457-5363

CORRECTIONS DEPARTMENT
40 Howard Ave.
Cramston, RI 02920
Director: 401-464-2611
Fax: 401-464-2630

Parole Board
250 Benefit St.
Providence, RI 02903
Chairperson: 401-277-3262
Fax: 401-277-1418

Elementary and Secondary Office
22 Hayes St.
Providence, RI 02908
Commissioner: 401-277-2031
Fax: 401-277-6178

Career & Vocational Education Office
22 Hayes St.
Providence, RI 02908
Director: 401-227-2691
Fax: 401-277-2537

Higher Education Office
301 Promenade St.
Providence, RI 02908-5089
Commissioner: 401-277-6560
Fax: 401-277-6111

ELDERLY AFFAIRS DEPARTMENT
160 Pine St.
Providence, RI 02903
Director: 401-277-2894
Fax: 401-277-1490

EMPLOYMENT AND TRAINING DEPARTMENT
101 Friendship St.
Providence, RI 02903
Director: 401-277-3732
Fax: 401-277-1473

Air, Solid Waste and Hazardous Waste Office
291 Promenade St.
Providence, RI 02908

Assistant Director: 401-277-2234
Fax: 401-277-2017

ENVIRONMENTAL MANAGEMENT DEPARTMENT
9 Hayes St.
Providence, RI 02908
Director: 401-277-2771

Natural Resources
22 Hayes St.
Providence, RI 02908
Associate Director: 401-277-6605

Planning and Development Services
83 Park St.
Providence, RI 02903
Associate Director: 401-277-2776
Fax: 401-277-1181

Employee Relations Office
22 Hayes St.
Providence, RI 02908
Chief: 401-277-2774

Water Quality Management
291 Promenade St.
Providence, RI 02908
Associate Director: 401-277-3961
Fax: 401-521-4230

HEALTH DEPARTMENT
3 Capitol Hill
Providence, RI 02908-5097
Director: 401-277-2231
Fax: 401-277-6548

Environmental Health Services
3 Capitol Hill
Providence, RI 02908-5097
Associate Director: 401-277-3118
Fax: 401-277-6953

Family Health
3 Capitol Hill
Providence, RI 02908-5097
Medical Director: 401-277-2312
Fax: 401-277-1442

Health Services Regulations
3 Capitol Hill
Providence, RI 02908-5097
Associate Director: 401-277-6015
Fax: 401-277-4350

State Medical Examiners
48 Orms St.
Providence, RI 02904
State Medical Examiner: 401-277-1333
Fax: 401-277-6197

HUMAN SERVICES DEPARTMENT
600 New London Ave.
Cranston, RI 02920
Director: 401-464-2121

Fax: 401-464-3677

Community Services
600 New London Ave.
Cranston, RI 02920
Associate Director: 401-464-2423
Fax: 401-464-3677

Economic and Social Services
600 New London Ave.
Cranston, RI 02920
Associate Director: 401-464-2371
Fax: 401-464-3677

Management Services
600 New London Ave.
Cranston, RI 02920
Associate Director: 401-464-2421
Fax: 401-464-3677

Medical Services
600 New London Ave.
Cranston, RI 02920
Associate Director: 401-464-3575
Fax: 401-464-3677

LABOR DEPARTMENT
610 Manton Ave.
Providence, RI 02907
Director: 401-457-1701

Labor Relations Board
610 Manton Ave.
Providence, RI 02909
Supervisor: 401-457-1820
Fax: 401-457-1821

Rehabilitation Center
249 Blackstone Blvd.
Providence, RI 02906
Administrator: 401-277-3994
Fax: 401-277-3887

Workers Compensation Unit
610 Mantun Ave.
Providence, RI 02909
Director: 401-457-1701
Fax: 401-277-2127

**MENTAL HEALTH RETARDATION AND HOSPITALS
DEPARTMENT**
600 New London Ave.
Cranston, RI 02920
Director: 401-464-3201
Fax: 401-464-3570

STATE LIBRARY SERVICES DEPARTMENT
300 Richmond St.
Providence, RI 02903-4222
Director: 401-277-2726
Fax: 401-831-1131

SUBSTANCE ABUSE DEPARTMENT
Access Rd, P.O. Box 20363
Cranston, RI 02920
Director: 401-464-2091
Fax: 401-464-2089

TRANSPORTATION DEPARTMENT
210 State Office Bldg.
Providence, RI 02903
Director: 401-277-2481

Administrative Adjudication
345 Harris Ave.
Providence, RI 02909
Assistant Director: 401-277-2251

Highway Operations
210 State Office Bldg.
Providence, RI 02903
Chief Engineer: 401-277-2492

Maintenance Division
90 Calverly St.
Providence, RI 02908
Assistant Director: 401-277-2378

Motor Vehicle Division
210 State Office Building
Providence, RI 02903
Director: 401:277-2970

Motor Vehicle Safety & Emission Control
1310 Pontiac Ave.
Cranston, RI 02920
Chief: 401-277-2970
Fax: 401-277-3886

Program Support
210 State Office Bldg.
Providence, RI 02903
Administrator: 401-277-2481

RHODE ISLAND AIRPORTS CORPORATION
Theodore Francis Green Airport
Warwick, RI 02886
Director: 401-737-4000

BOARD OF ELECTIONS
50 Branch Ave.
Providence, RI 02904
Chairman: 401-277-2345
Fax: 401-621-3255

ECONOMIC DEVELOPMENT
7 Jackson Walkway
Providence, RI 02903
Executive Director: 401-277-2601
Fax: 401-277-2102

Industrial-Recreation Building Authority
7 Jackson Walkway
Providence, RI 02903
Manager: 401-277-2601
Fax: 401-277-2102

Industrial Facilities Corporation
7 Jackson Walkway
Providence, RI 02903
Manager: 401-277-2601
Fax: 401-277-2102

ETHICS COMMISSION
43 Jefferson Blvd.
Warwick, RI 02888-1080
Executive Director: 401-277-3790
Fax: 401-461-7049

FIRE MARSHAL
272 W Exchange St.
Providence, RI 02903
Fire Marshal: 401-277-2331
Fax: 401-273-1222

HEALTH AND EDUCATION BUILDING CORPORATION
400 Westminister St.
Providence, RI 02903
Executive Director: 401-831-3770
Fax: 401-421-3910

HIGHER EDUCATION ASSISTANCE AUTHORITY
560 Jefferson Blvd.
Warrick, RI 02886
Executive Director: 401-736-1100
Fax: 401-732-3541

HISTORIC PRESERVATION COMMISSION
150 Benefit St.
Providence, RI 02903
Chairperson: 401-277-2678
Fax: 401-277-2968

HOUSING AND MORTGAGE FINANCE CORPORATION
60 Eddy St.
Providence, RI 02903
Executive Director: 401-751-5566
Fax: 401-272-8956

HOUSING, ENERGY AND INTERGOVERNMENTAL RELATIONS OFFICE
State House, Rm. 112
Providence, RI 02903-5872
Director: 401-277-2850
Fax: 401-273-5301

HUMAN RIGHTS COMMISSION
10 Abbott Park Place
Providence, RI 02903-3768
Chair: 401-277-2661
Fax: 401-277-2615

PUBLIC BUILDINGS AUTHORITY
260 W Exchange St.
Providence, RI 02903
Executive Director: 401-421-2932
Fax: 401-421-6530

PUBLIC UTILITIES COMMISSION
100 Orange St.
Providence, RI 02903

Chairman: 401-277-3500
Fax: 401-277-6850

STATE COUNCIL ON THE ARTS
95 Cedar St.
Providence, RI 02903-1034
Executive Director: 401-277-3880
Fax: 401-521-1351

STATE INVESTMENT COMMISSION
102 State House
Providence, RI 02903
Chairman: 401-277-2287
Fax: 401-277-6140

STATE LOTTERY
1425 Pontiac Ave.
Cranston, RI 02920
Executive Director: 401-463-6500
Fax: 401-463-5669

STATE POLICE
311 Danielson Pike
North Scituate, RI 02857
Superintendent: 401-444-1000
Fax: 401-444-1105 or 1133

TURNPIKE AND BRIDGE AUTHORITY
PO Box 437
Jamestown, RI 02835
Director: 401-423-0800
Fax: 401-423-0830

TWENTIETH CENTURY GOVERNORS

DYER, ELISHA, JR. (1839-1906), thirty-eighth governor of Rhode Island (1897-1900), was born in Providence, Rhode Island, on November 29, 1839, the son of former Rhode Island governor, Elisha Dyer, Sr. He studied chemistry at Brown University for two years, then in 1860, earned a Ph.D. from the University of Giessen, in Germany. After returning home, he worked as a chemist. In 1856 Dyer joined the State militia, serving in the First Light Infantry Company, then after the start of the Civil War, was a part of the Rhode Island Light Artillery. In 1862 Governor Sprague appointed him to the rank of major. From 1882 to 1895, Dyer was Adjutant General of Rhode Island, during which time he updated and completed the records from the Civil War, and also revamped the State militia.

Dyer entered politics in 1877 when he was elected to the Rhode Island Senate, then in 1878, he was appointed to the State Board of Health, where he served for five years. During 1880-81, he served in the State General Assembly, then during 1890-91, was an Alderman. Between 1888 and 1897, Dyer served on the Providence School Committee.

In 1897 Dyer was a successful candidate for the Rhode Island governorship on the Republican ticket, and went on to win two more terms. During his tenure, the voters approved an 800,000-dollar bond issue for the Statehouse, plus the State's eastern boundary line was set. A proposition to amend the State Constitution was presented twice, and voted down both times, and the State flag was adopted. Dyer stepped down from office in 1900. He returned to politics in 1904 when he won a seat in the State Senate, then the following year, became Mayor of Providence.

He was married to Nancy Anthony Viall, and the couple had four children, one of whom died in infancy. Dyer died on November 29, 1906.

GREGORY, WILLIAM (1849-1901), thirty-ninth governor of Rhode Island (1900-1901), was born in Astoria, New York, on August 3, 1849. He attended day and night classes, the latter in Moosup, Connecticut, where he supported himself by working in mills. Relocating to Westerly, Rhode Island, he graduated high school there in 1864. After his schooling, he found employment as a mill superintendent. In the late 1870s Gregory moved to New York City, and served as manager and agent for A.T. Stewart & Co. In 1880, he purchased a mill, and bought another in 1894. He next served as president and director of Wickford National Bank, and was later Chairman of the Board of State Charities and Corrections.

Active in Republican politics, in 1888 Gregory won a seat in the State House of Representatives, then in 1894, was elected State Senator, and went on to win another two terms. Starting in 1898, Gregory served two terms as Rhode Island's Lieutenant Governor.

In 1900 and 1901, Gregory won the Rhode Island governorship on the Republican ticket. During his tenure, the State capital was relocated from Newport to Providence, where a new marble Statehouse was also constructed, with Gregory becoming the first governor to reside there. In addition, the State's Constitution was amended so that the General Assembly was allowed to hold annual sessions.

Gregory was married to Harriet Vaughan, and the couple had two children. He died on December 16, 1901.

KIMBALL, CHARLES DEAN, (1859-1930), fortieth governor of Rhode Island (1901-1903), was born in Providence, Rhode Island, on September 13, 1859. Receiving a public school education, he afterward found employment at the Kimball & Colwell Company, co-owned by his father. In 1892, Kimball bought his father's interest in the firm, where he subsequently served as treasurer and secretary.

In 1894 Kimball, a Republican, entered politics with his election to the State General Assembly, serving for several terms, then beginning in 1900, he was Rhode Island's Lieutenant Governor. On December 16, 1901, the incumbent governor, William Gregory, died in office, and on January 7, 1902, Kimball assumed the governorship.

During his tenure, Kimball sought several changes, which included a State tax law revision, having annual State elections instead of biennial, and the power of veto by the governor's office, all of which were eventually adopted by the State Legislature. Also during that time, in 1902, there was a railroad strike, prompting Kimball to call on the militia for help. The issue in question was the refusal by the railroad workers to accept a ten-hour work day, and after the strike was quelled, Kimball requested a special session of the General Assembly, the result being the repeal of the ten-hour statute. In 1902 Kimball lost his reelection bid for the governorship, and stepped down from office. He subsequently served on the Board of Managers of the Rhode Island College of Agriculture and Mechanic Arts. In his later years, during 1925-26, Kimball was a colonel with the Providence First Light Infantry Veterans.

Kimball was married to Gertrude Greenhalgh, and the couple had one child. He died on December 8, 1930.

GARVIN, LUCIUS FAYETTE CLARK (1841-1922), forty-first governor of Rhode Island (1903-1905), was born in Knoxville, Tennessee on November 13, 1841. He attended Amherst College, graduating in 1858. At the start of the Civil War, Garvin served in North Carolina with the Massachusetts Volunteers, receiving his discharge in 1863 and subsequently worked as a schoolteacher for a year in Massachusetts. He then relocated to Pawtucket, Rhode Island, where he studied medicine under a doctor's tutelage, then attended Harvard Medical School, earning his degree in 1867. Garvin engaged in his own medical practice soon after.

Politically active, Garvin was initially a Republican, but switched to the Democratic Party around 1876. Between 1883 and 1888, Garvin served in the Rhode Island House of Representatives, and then again between 1895 and 1903. In the interim, from 1889 to 1892, he was a member of the State Senate. Starting in 1894, he ran unsuccessfully for the United States Congress on five different occasions.

In 1901 Garvin made his first bid for the Rhode Island governorship, but was defeated. He was successful in his second attempt the following year, and in 1903, won another term as well. While in office, Garvin sought a number of reforms, but often had to fight the mostly Republican State Legislature. He recognized how important the State's individual towns and cities were in regard to reform, feeling that the federal government was too big and complex an entity to accomplish what was needed. He also strongly supported equal rights, and voting rights for immigrants.

Garvin lost his bid for reelection in 1904 and again in 1905, and subsequently returned to his medical career. For a short time in 1912, he was a member of the Progressive Party, but in 1916, returned to the Democratic Party. In 1921 Garvin became a member of the Rhode Island State Senate.

Garvin was married twice: to Lucy Waterman Southmayd and after her death, to Sarah E. Tomlinson. He had three children from his first union, and two from his second. Garvin died on October 2, 1922.

UTTER, GEORGE HERBERT (1854-1912), forty-second governor of Rhode Island (1905-1907), was born in Plainfield, New Jersey on July 24, 1854. He attended Amherst College, graduating in 1877. Utter subsequently joined his father in a printing venture, and in 1893, founded the *Westerly Sun*, a daily newspaper that became a prominent and influential publication.

Utter's political career began when he worked as an aide to Governor Bourn between 1883 and 1885. In the latter year, Utter, a Republican, was elected to the Rhode Island House of Representatives, serving in that post until 1889. Between 1891 and 1894, he served as Secretary of State, then in 1903, he was Rhode Island's Lieutenant Governor. In 1904 he successfully ran for the Rhode Island governorship, and won a second term the following year. During his tenure, he implemented the practice of having the Lieutenant Governor officiate the proceedings of the State Senate. Utter was widely admired as a serious and dedicated leader, who was also a proficient debater, and an eloquent orator. However, those attributes were not enough to garner him another term. After losing his reelection bid, Utter stepped down from office and returned to his publishing ventures. In 1910 he successfully ran for a seat in the United States Congress, serving one term.

Utter was married to Elizabeth L. Brown, and the couple had four children. He died on November 12, 1912.

HIGGINS, JAMES HENRY (1876-1927), forty-third governor of Rhode Island (1907-1909), was born in Lincoln, Rhode Island, on January 22, 1876. He graduated from Brown University in 1898, then earned a law degree in 1900 from Georgetown University Law School. Higgins subsequently partnered in the law firm of Fitzgerald and Higgins. In 1901 Higgins, a Democrat, was elected to one term in the Rhode Island House of Representatives, then from 1902 to 1907, served as Mayor of Pawtucket.

In 1906 Higgins ran for and won the Rhode Island governorship on the Democratic ticket, securing a second term the following year. During his tenure, he followed his party's platform of major reform in several areas, including women's voting rights, and other women's issues, plus child welfare. However, he was continually at odds with the mostly-Republican State Legislature. Intent on fighting corruption, he attempted to have the Republican Party boss ousted from the sheriff's office when it was surmised that the man was conducting personal business on State time. Although Higgins was not successful, he let it be known that he would not tolerate such abuse of power.

Deciding not to seek a third term, Higgins stepped down from office, and returned to his law work. He later served as a director of the Industrial Trust Company. Married to Ellen Frances McGuire, the couple had two children. He died on September 16, 1927.

POTHIER, ARAM (1854-1928), forty-fourth and forty-eighth governor of Rhode Island (1909-1915, 1924-1928), was born in Philimene, Quebec, Canada on July 26, 1854. After graduating from Nicolet College in Quebec in 1872, he relocated to Woonsocket, Rhode Island. In 1875 he found employment as a clerk with the Woonsocket Institute for Savings. In 1889 and 1900 Pothier was asked to represent the State of Rhode Island at the Paris Exhibitions.

Pothier's launch into politics started when he was elected to the Woonsocket School Committee, a post he held from 1885 to 1889. In 1887 he was elected to the Rhode Island Legislature, then in 1889, he was elected City Auditor of Woonsocket. In 1894 he began serving two terms as that city's Mayor. In 1897 Pothier served as Rhode Island's Lieutenant Governor, then subsequently left public office for a time. He came back in 1907 when he was elected to the State Board of Education.

Pothier ran for and won the Rhode Island governorship on the Republican ticket in 1908, plus he secured four more terms, the last under the new two-year term period. During his tenure, labor laws affecting women and children were revised, workmen's compensation was created, the State Superior Court was expanded, and the State Board of Tax Commissioners was organized. Also, several amendments to the State Constitution were adopted, which included allowing the governor veto power, and State officials being elected biennially.

After stepping down from office in 1915, Pothier returned to his banking interests, serving as president of both the Woonsocket Institute for Savings and the Providence Union Trust Company. In 1924 Pothier once again made a bid for the governorship after being drafted by the Republican Party and won the election, as well as another term in 1926. During this administration, Pothier gave the State Legislature less control of the State budget, and took more responsibility himself in putting the State's finances in order. In addition, the Rhode Island State Police force was organized, plus the offices of State Commissioner of Finance, and State Comptroller, were both established. Some of the constitutional amendments he supported were adopted after his death, including the reorganization of the State Senate, and biennial voting registration.

Pothier was married to Francoise de Charmigny; the couple had no children. He died on February 4, 1928.

BEECKMAN, ROBERT LIVINGSTON (1866-1935), forty-fifth governor of Rhode Island (1915-1921), was born in New York City on April 15, 1866. After his family relocated to Newport, Rhode Island, he received both public and private schooling there. He quit school at the age of sixteen to work as a messenger at the H.R. Hollins Company. At twenty-one he became one of the youngest people to ever buy a seat on the New York Stock Exchange. Remaining in New York City, Beeckman went to work for the family firm, Lapsley Beeckman & Co., where he stayed until 1906.

Eventually returning to Rhode Island, Beeckman entered politics with his seat in the State House of Representatives, serving from 1902 to 1912, then between 1912 and 1914, he served in the State Senate. In the latter year he successfully ran for the Rhode Island governorship on the Republican ticket, and went on to win two more terms.

During his administration, Beeckman successfully sought a number of reforms, including for such State institutions as hospitals, prisons, and insane asylums. Also, an inheritance tax law was adopted, and the State Parole Board was organized. In addition, with World War I taking place during those years, Beeckman helped prepare the needed State resources for the war effort, and went so far as to travel to France to visit soldiers from Rhode Island. At the end of his third term, Beeckman stepped down from office and returned to his various business enterprises. In 1922 he made an unsuccessful bid for the United States Senate.

Beeckman was married twice: to Eleanor Thomas, then after her death, to Edna Marston Burke. He had no children. Beeckman died on January 21, 1935.

SAN SOUCI, EMERY J. (1857-1936), forty-sixth governor of Rhode Island (1921-1923), was born on July 24, 1857. Receiving a rudimentary education, he started working at the age of eleven, as a machinist's apprentice. In 1875 he became a shoe salesman, and from 1877 to 1888, sold his product as a traveling salesperson. San Souci later joined his brothers in a highly successful men's clothing enterprise in Providence, Rhode Island, of which he served as secretary and treasurer from 1909 to 1919.

In 1901 San Souci ran successfully for the Providence Common Council, a post he held until 1907. Between 1909 and 1915, he was a staff member with Governor Pothier's administration, and from 1915 to 1919, served as Rhode Island's Lieutenant Governor.

In 1920 San Souci ran for and won the Rhode Island governorship on the Republican ticket. Part of his victory came from the vote of women, who were allowed to participate in State elections for the first time. During his tenure, several social reforms were established, which included more stringent laws regarding the pasteurization of milk, rehabilitation programs for the disabled, welfare for veterans who had been hurt during the war, and an increase in workmen's compensation benefits. In 1922 San Souci had to deal with a massive textile strike, calling out the State militia in order to help subdue rioters. It was his handling of this matter that caused the Republican Party to withhold the nomination for another term. After stepping down from office, San Souci was appointed Collector of the Port of Providence in 1923, by President Warren G. Harding. Three subsequent presidents, Coolidge, Hoover and Roosevelt, named him to that post as well, with San Souci finally retiring in 1935.

He was married to Minnie A.J. Duffy, and the couple had two children. He died on August 10, 1936.

FLYNN, WILLIAM SMITH (1855-1966), forty-seventh governor of Rhode Island (1923-1925), was born in Providence, Rhode Island, on August 14, 1885. He attended the College of the Holy Cross in Worcester, Massachusetts, graduating in 1907, then studied at Georgetown University Law School, earning his degree in 1910. He subsequently had his own law practice in Providence.

In 1912 Flynn, a Democrat, was elected to the Rhode Island House of Representatives, a post he held until 1923. In 1922 he successfully ran for the Rhode Island governorship on the Democratic ticket, a feat during that time, because Republicans filled most of the public offices. During his tenure, several of the young Democrats in the State Senate held all night filibusters, demanding that the more seasoned Republican members agree to a resolution to establish a Constitutional Convention. The hostilities reached a fever pitch, causing several of the Republicans to flee to Massachusetts.

In 1924 Flynn ran for the United States Senate, but was defeated. He then stepped down from the governorship, and during 1933-34, served as Chairman of the Advisory Board for the Public Works Administration. During 1942-43, Flynn was Division Director for Providence Civilian Defense.

Flynn was married to Virginia W. Goodwin; the couple had no children. He died on April 13, 1966.

CASE, NORMAN STANLEY (1888-1967), forty-ninth governor of Rhode Island (1928-1933), was born in Providence, Rhode Island on October 11, 1888. He attended Brown University, graduating in 1908, studied at Harvard University Law School for a time, then earned his degree at Boston University Law School in 1912.

While maintaining his own law practice, Case pursued political office, and was elected to the Providence City Council. In 1920 he served on the Soldiers' Bonus Board, then the following year, President Warren G. Harding appointed him to serve as United States District Attorney for Rhode Island. Case, a Republican, left that post in 1926 when he successfully sought the office of Lieutenant Governor. A few days after the death of the incumbent, Governor Aram Pothier, Case assumed the governorship, on February 9, 1928. He ran for two subsequent terms, winning both times. During his tenure, Case often found his attempts at decision-making thwarted by the two men who wielded the real power in the State of Rhode Island—financial czar Fred Peck, and Republican State Chairman, William C. Pelkey. After the Great Depression hit, Case sought to have the towns and cities of the state take more responsibility in helping the needy. As such, Case later supported a law by which the towns and cities could borrow from the State budget, with a three-percent interest rate.

Case lost his 1932 bid for reelection and stepped down from office. In 1934 he was appointed by President Franklin Roosevelt to serve with the Federal Communications Commission. Case left that position in 1945, subsequently becoming a partner in the Washington, D.C. law firm of Case and Wozencraft.

Case was married to Emma Louise Arnold, and the couple had three children. He died on October 9, 1967.

GREEN, THEODORE FRANCIS (1867-1966), fiftieth governor of Rhode Island (1933-1937), was born on October 2, 1867, in Providence, Rhode Island. He attended Brown University, earning an A.B. degree in 1887, and an A.M. degree in 1890. From the latter year until 1892, Green was a student at Harvard Law School, and passed the Rhode Island bar soon after. Later in 1892, Green relocated in Europe, studying at two German universities, then in 1894, returned to Rhode Island to teach Roman Law at Brown University until 1897. Also in 1894, Green partnered with his father in a law practice. In 1906 he headed his own firm of Green, Hinckley and Allen, until 1923, then did the same with Green, Curran and Hart, until 1926. He continued practicing law for several years thereafter.

Green, a Democrat, entered politics with his 1907 election to the Rhode Island House of Representatives. In 1912 he made an unsuccessful bid for the Rhode Island governorship and in 1930, lost in his second attempt as well. He also lost a 1920 run for the United States Congress.

In 1932 Green was finally successful in his attempt for the governorship and also won his reelection bid in 1934. During his administration, Rhode Island, like the rest of the country, was still reeling from the Great Depression, and his main concern was to provide economic relief to the State's citizens. As such, Green adopted a number of the federal government's public works projects, including the upgrading of State institutions, the development of land near the shore for beaches, plus reforestation. Also during that time, Green was forced to declare the Riot Act and call out the National Guard during a labor dispute. In addition, power was shifted from the legislative to the executive branch of Rhode Island's State government. Stepping down after his second term in 1937, Green was elected to the United States Senate in 1936, where he served until 1961.

Green never married. He died on May 20, 1966.

QUINN, ROBERT EMMET (1894-1975), fifty-first governor of Rhode Island (1937-1939), was born in West Warwick, Rhode Island on April 2, 1894. He attended Brown University, graduating in 1915, then studied at Harvard University Law School, taking his degree in 1918. During World War I, Quinn served in England and France as a member of the United States Intelligence Service. After returning home, he became a partner in the law firm of Quinn, Kernan and Quinn, in Providence.

Quinn, a Democrat, won a seat in the Rhode Island State Senate, serving from 1922 to 1925. He made an unsuccessful bid for Lieutenant Governor in 1924, but won reelection to the Senate in 1928, holding that post until 1933. In 1932 he won the office of Lieutenant Governor and served until 1937. During his tenure, he managed to launch a "Bloodless Revolution," when he appointed a committee to recount the ballots from an earlier State Senate election. This led to proof that Republicans from three districts had committed fraud to get their party members elected, and that Democrats had, in fact, won those districts. The aftermath of the situation provided the Democrats the opportunity to reorganize the State government.

Quinn won the Rhode Island governorship on the Democratic ticket in 1936. During his tenure he sought a number of major changes, including the implementation of State income taxes and a Civil Service System, plus the exemption of the State's more indigent citizens from real estate taxes. In addition, Quinn made a name for himself when he took on racetrack boss, Walter O'Hara. Legal horse racing was brand new in the State and Quinn would not tolerate any form of fraudulence. He was determined to remove O'Hara from his post, and although the latter tried to defy him, Quinn won that battle, garnering him the moniker "Fighting Bob."

In 1938, although nominated once again by his party, Quinn lost his reelection bid and stepped down from office. In 1941 he was named a Superior Court Judge, but left soon after to accept the post of Commander in the United States Navy's legal branch. While there, he was overseer of the processing method regarding court martial trials. By the end of his four-year tenure, Quinn had attained the rank of Captain, and subsequently returned to his judgeship. Quinn was appointed Chief Judge to the newly organized United State Court of Military Appeals, serving in that seat from 1951 to 1975.

Quinn was married to Mary I. Carter, and the couple had five children. He died on May 19, 1975.

VANDERBILT, WILLIAM HENRY (1901-1981), fifty-second governor of Rhode Island (1939-1941), was born in New York City on November 24, 1901. He was a descendant of industrialist Cornelius Vanderbilt, and the son of Alfred Gwynne Vanderbilt, who lost his life during the sinking of the *Titanic*. During World War I, Vanderbilt served in the United States Navy from 1917 to 1919. After his discharge, he attended Princeton University during 1920-21. He was first employed as a messenger at the banking house of Lee Higginson, Co., then in 1925 he founded the Automotive Transportation Company.

In 1929 Vanderbilt, a Republican, entered politics with his election to the Rhode Island State Senate, a post he held until 1935. The following year he made an unsuccessful run for the governorship, but secured that office in 1938. Vanderbilt immediately set out to trim the State budget, and his first decision was to eliminate over 400 State governmental jobs. Considered to be a man of integrity, he would not even accept the complimentary racetrack passes normally proffered to State officials. Also during his tenure, he continued the fight begun by his predecessor to implement a Civil Service Act for State employees, which was ultimately passed by the General Assembly. In addition, he authorized a bidding system for work paid for by the State government. His sense of fairness intact, Vanderbilt managed to anger members of his own party when he reappointed Democrats to posts, due to their hard work and efficiency. It was surmised that this was one of the main reasons he lost his reelection bid in 1940.

After stepping down from office, Vanderbilt reenlisted in the United States Navy during World War II. After his discharge, he served on the board of directors of the New York Central Railroad Company, which was owned by the Vanderbilt family. In 1963 he chaired the United States Naval Academy Board of Visitors.

Vanderbilt was married three times: to Emily O'Neil Davies, Anne Gordon Colby, and Helen Cummings Cook. He had one child from his first union, and three from his second. He died on October 14, 1981.

MCGRATH, JAMES HOWARD (1903-1966), fifty-third governor of Rhode Island (1941-1945), was born in Woonsocket, Rhode Island on November 28, 1903. He attended Providence College, graduating in 1926, then studied at Boston University Law School, earning his degree in 1929.

Politically active in Democratic politics, in 1932 McGrath led the delegation at the Democratic National Convention that nominated Franklin D. Roosevelt for president. Between 1930 and 1934, he served as City Solicitor for Central Falls, then from 1934 to 1940, he served as United States Attorney for Rhode Island. In 1940 he was elected to the State governorship on the Democratic ticket, and went on to win two more terms.

During McGrath's administration, an illness benefits law went into effect, plus a juvenile court was created. In addition, he headed Rhode Island's first Constitutional Convention to revamp the State's general law. When he seconded the vice presidential nomination of Harry S. Truman in 1944, Truman returned the favor after he became president by naming McGrath United States Solicitor General. McGrath stepped down from the governorship to accept the post.

In 1946 McGrath successfully ran for the United States Senate, and in 1947, he was named Democratic National Chairman by President Truman. In that post, McGrath deftly guided the defeat of Thomas E. Dewey by Harry Truman in the 1948 election. In 1949 Truman named McGrath to serve as United States Attorney General. He resigned from that post three years later after the Justice Department was accused of pulling back from a tax investigation at the urging of top government officials.

McGrath remained in Washington, D.C., where he had a law practice, but often came back to Rhode Island to pursue his various business interests. McGrath established the First Federal Savings and Loan Association of Providence, plus he was director of the Mortgage Title and Guarantee Company, and president of the Rhode Island League of Savings and Loans Associations.

McGrath was married to Estelle A. Cadorette, and the couple had one child. He died on September 2, 1966.

PASTORE, JOHN ORLANDO (1907-), fifty-fourth governor of Rhode Island (1945-1950), was born in Providence, Rhode Island on March 17, 1907. He attended night school at Northeastern University, where he earned a law degree in 1931 and subsequently had a private law practice in Providence.

Pastore, a Democrat, pursued a political career when he won a seat in the State House of Representatives, serving between 1935 and 1937. In the latter year he was appointed Assistant Attorney General of Rhode Island, serving until 1938, then later served in that post again from 1940 to 1944.

In 1944 Pastore served as Rhode Island's Lieutenant Governor, and the following year, assumed the governorship upon the resignation of the incumbent, James Howard McGrath. He successfully ran for the office in 1946 and 1948, making him the first Italian-American to hold a governorship in U.S. history.

During Pastore's tenure, laws passed included a one-percent sales tax, a corporate income tax, and Rhode Island's first primary election law. In addition, World War II veterans divided a twenty million-dollar bonus, and funding in the amount of five million dollars was earmarked to prevent water pollution.

When James McGrath resigned from the United States Senate, Pastore initially named someone to fill the post, then ran for that seat himself in 1950 for the unexpired term, winning the race. His win made him the first person of Italian ancestry to serve in that body. Pastore ran for reelection to the Senate for a full term in 1952, and won three more terms, in 1958, 1964, and 1970. Interested in the possible uses of atomic energy, in 1957 Pastore was a member of the first conference held by the International Atomic Energy Agency, and for three years, 1955, 1958 and 1961, he served as a delegate to the Geneva Conferences on Peaceful Uses of Atomic Energy. Also while in the Senate, he was successful in his push for ratification of the Limited Nuclear Test Ban Treaty in 1963, and the Nuclear Non-Proliferation Treaty in 1969.

Pastore stepped down from the United States Senate in 1976. He is married to Elena E. Caito, and the couple has three children.

MCKIERNAN, JOHN SAMMON (1911-), acting governor of Rhode Island (1950-1951), was born in Providence, Rhode Island on October 15, 1911. He attended Notre Dame University, graduating in 1934, then studied at Boston University Law School, earning his degree in 1937. McKiernan subsequently had a private law practice in Providence. During 1941 he served as a legal advisor to the Civil Service Commission, Chairman of the Fair Rents Committee, and first Assistant City Solicitor, all for the City of Providence, plus he was a roving clerk in the General Assembly. During World War II, McKiernan served in the United States Army between 1942 and 1946.

When incumbent Governor John O. Pastore resigned from office, McKiernan, as presiding officer of the Rhode Island Senate, succeeded to the governorship, taking office on December 19, 1950. As Acting Governor, he had a very short tenure, and stepped down from the post on January 2, 1951, after the inauguration of the new governor, Dennis J. Roberts. McKiernan then returned to the office Lieutenant Governor. He resigned that position in 1956 after being named an Associate Justice of the State Superior Court.

McKiernan is married to Elizabeth St. Pierre.

ROBERTS, DENNIS JOSEPH (1903-1994), fifty-fifth governor of Rhode Island (1951-1959), was born in Providence, Rhode Island, on April 8, 1903. He attended Fordham University, from where he graduated in 1927, then studied at Boston University Law School, earning his degree in 1930, subsequently engaging in private law practice.

Roberts entered politics when he won a seat in the State Senate in 1934, serving until 1939. In 1940 he secured the office of Mayor of Providence, serving until 1951. In 1950 Roberts successfully ran for the Rhode Island governorship on the Democratic ticket, and went on to win three more terms. There was some question concerning his win in 1956, with his securing the election only after 5,000 absentee and shut-in ballots were disqualified by the State Supreme Court, which had ruled that all of the votes in question needed to be cast on the actual day of the election.

During Roberts's tenure, the State had begun to grow at a rapid pace. Roberts organized the Department of Administration, a sort of clearinghouse for potential problems and issues within the State government, a program which other states later adopted. Also, the Rhode Island Development Council was created in order to boost the State's economic development, plus the Department of Social Welfare was reorganized.

Roberts lost his 1958 bid for reelection, and stepped down from office, then subsequently lost in his attempt to run for the United States Senate. In 1964 he was chosen to chair the State Constitutional Convention, and caused some dissent when he proposed a unicameral State Legislature.

Roberts, who never married, ultimately returned to his private law practice. He died on June 3, 1994 while in surgery for a ruptured aneurysm.

DEL SESTO, CHRISTOPHER (1907-1973), fifty-sixth governor of Rhode Island (1959-1961), was born in Providence, Rhode Island, on March 10, 1907. He attended Boston University, graduating in 1928, then studied at Georgetown University Law School, earning his degree in 1938. Del Sesto also took additional classes at New York University and the University of Miami.

Del Sesto worked both as an attorney and a certified public accountant after finishing his schooling. Later, he taught at Boston University and Northeastern University.

In 1935 Del Sesto entered public office with his position as State Budget Officer. Between 1938 and 1940 he served as Special Assistant to the United States Attorney General, and from 1940 to 1942, was director of the State Finance Department. Between 1942 and 1945 Del Sesto was State Director for the Office of Price Administration. During his time in these posts, some of his reforms were later adopted by other State governments in the U.S.

Del Sesto had an unsuccessful campaign in 1952 for Mayor of Providence. In 1958 he ran for and won the Rhode Island governorship on the Republican ticket, the first governor from that party to be elected in twenty years. During his tenure Del Sesto was a colorful figure, who was outspoken and innovative in his approach to leading the State. In those years an extensive plan was launched for the construction of interstate highways, plus educational funding for towns and cities was expanded, and a State scholarship program was established.

Del Sesto lost his 1960 bid for reelection, and stepped down from office, returning to his law work. In 1966 Governor John H. Chafee appointed him Associate Justice of the State Superior Court, where he served until 1973.

He married Lola Elda Faraone, with whom he had three children. Del Sesto died on September 27, 1973.

NOTTE, JOHN A. (1909-1983), fifty-seventh governor of Rhode Island (1961-1963), was born in Providence, Rhode Island, on May 3, 1909. He attended Providence College, graduating in 1931, then studied at Cornell University during 1931-32. Notte subsequently entered Boston University Law School, earning his degree in 1935. Notte engaged in his own law practice, and in 1937, was named Town Solicitor of North Providence. From 1943 to 1946, Notte served at the rank of Lieutenant in the United States Navy. In 1947 Notte was asked to chair the Rhode Island Veterans Bonus Board.

In 1948, Notte began serving on the staff of Senator Theodore Francis Green, then resigned in 1956 to run for Secretary of State. Winning the election, Notte served in that post until 1959. From that year until 1961, Notte was Rhode Island's Lieutenant Governor. In 1960 Notte successfully ran for the governorship on the Democratic ticket. During his tenure, both the Democratic and Republican parties instituted the new "one-day, one-place" primaries. In addition, a family court was established.

Notte eventually lost the support of labor leaders, who were unhappy when he backed off from his initial support of a State income tax, and refused to back him when he ran for reelection in 1962. He ultimately lost the race, albeit by a small margin. He returned to his law work for a time, and had an unsuccessful run for the United States Congress in 1967.

Notte married Marie J. Huerth, and the couple had two children. He died on March 7, 1983.

CHAFEE, JOHN HUBBARD (1922-1999), fifty-eighth governor of Rhode Island (1963-1969), was born in Providence, Rhode Island, on October 22, 1922. He served in the United States Marine Corps during World War II, and fought in Guadalcanal. After his discharge, he attended Yale University, graduating in 1947, then studied at Harvard Law School, earning his degree in 1950. During the Korean War, Chafee was recalled to active duty.

After returning home to Providence, Chafee entered into his own law practice. Chafee engaged in politics in 1956 when he won a seat in the State House of Representatives, where he served for three terms. In 1962 he successfully ran for the Rhode Island governorship on the Republican ticket, and went on to secure two more terms.

During his administration, although most of the State was Democratic, Chafee was a popular leader. However, he had a harder time with the mostly Democratic State Legislature, who, in April of 1963, overrode one of his vetoes. Also, when Chafee signed a law that offered funding to private and parochial schools for textbooks, the decision raised some protest. Despite this, during Chafee's time in office, the State Medicare Program for seniors was initiated, the first Fair Housing Law in the State was passed, and a State-run junior college was established, plus he implemented what he called the Green Acres Program, which was established to set aside land for beaches and State parks.

In 1968 Chafee lost his bid for reelection, and stepped down from office. The following year he was appointed Secretary of the Navy in Washington, D.C, a post he served in until 1972, when he returned to Providence and resumed his law work. Later in 1972 he ran unsuccessfully for the United States Senate, but won a seat in that body in 1976. During his tenure, he served on the National Ocean Policy Study Committee, and the National Transportation Policy Study Commission.

Chafee married to Virginia Coates, and the couple had five children; a sixth is deceased. Chafee died of heart failure on October 24, 1999 in National Naval Medical Center, Bethesda, Maryland.

LICHT, FRANK (1916-), fifty-ninth governor of Rhode Island (1969-1973), was born in Providence, Rhode Island on March 3, 1916. He attended Brown University, graduating in 1938, then studied at Harvard University Law School, receiving his degree in 1941. Between 1943 and 1956, Licht was a member of the law firm of Letts and Quinn.

Entering the political arena, Licht, a Democrat, successfully ran for the Rhode Island State Senate, serving from 1949 to 1956. In the latter year he was named to the State Superior Court as an Associate Justice, then left that post in 1968 to run for the Rhode Island governorship. Winning the race, he went on to secure a second term in 1970.

During his tenure, Licht reneged on his campaign promise to not implement a State income tax. Two years into his administration, he called for a more comprehensive tax on personal income, which the State Legislature backed him on. Also during that time, Licht organized the Board of Regents, whose nine members were chosen to supervise the State's public education system, plus he reorganized both the district court and the social service systems, the latter of which included the establishment of the Department of Mental Health, Retardation and Hospitals, and the Department of Social Rehabilitation Service. In addition, the Department of Transportation was organized. Licht, throughout his two terms, also had to handle a number of strikes from several different factions, including teachers, truck drivers, and meat-cutters. It was also the time of student protests against President Nixon's Vietnam War policies.

Licht decided to step down from office after his second term, and returned to his Providence law practice. In June of 1965, he was co-author of "Trial Judges' Code," an article published in the *Massachusetts Law Quarterly*. In 1969, Licht was honored with the Herbert H. Lehman Ethics Award by the Jewish Theological Seminary of America.

Licht is married to Dorothy Shirlee Krauss, and the couple has three children.

NOEL, PHILIP WILLIAM (1931-), sixtieth governor of Rhode Island (1973-1977), was born in Warwick, Rhode Island, on June 6, 1931. He attended Brown University, graduating in 1954, then studied at Georgetown University Law School, earning his degree in 1957. He subsequently engaged in his own law practice. His entry into politics was in 1958, when he served as clerk of the Rhode Island Constitutional Convention. From 1961 to 1967 Noel, a Democrat, was a member of the Warwick City Council, and served as Mayor from 1967 to 1973.

In 1972 Noel ran for and won the Rhode Island governorship on the Democratic ticket, and in the 1974 election, won his second term by a landslide. During his administration, one of Noel's priorities was to lure industry to Rhode Island. Part of that came from the closing of the Quonset Point naval base, which had been a severe blow to the State's economy. His answer was to form the Economic Renewal Coordinating Center, and call upon leaders from industry, labor and government to offer their expertise in how to alleviate the crisis. During that time he pushed his economic development legislation through the General Assembly, and upgraded the taxation system regarding businesses. Also during that time, he organized the Rhode Island Port Authority and the Economic Development Corporation. In addition, a bill was passed in 1974 for the creation of Rhode Island's first State lottery.

Noel's administration was tarnished somewhat in 1976 when some derogatory comments he made about African-Americans were printed in an article. At the time he had been nominated to serve as chairman of the National Democratic Platform Committee, but after the quotes were made public, Noel withdrew his name from the running.

Eschewing a third term, Noel stepped down from office in 1977. The previous year he made an unsuccessful run for the United States Senate, and subsequently returned to his law practice.

Noel is married to Joyce Sandberg, and the couple has five children.

GARRAHY, JOHN JOSEPH (1930-), sixty-first governor of Rhode Island (1977-1985), was born in Providence, Rhode Island, on November 26, 1930. In 1952 Garrahy studied at the University of Buffalo, then the following year, attended the University of Rhode Island. Between 1953 and 1955 he served in the United States Air Force.

A Democrat, Garrahy successfully ran for the State Senate in 1962, holding that post until 1968, when he was elected Lieutenant Governor. In 1976 Garrahy secured the Rhode Island governorship on the Democratic ticket, taking office on January 4, 1977, and went on to win three more terms.

During his tenure, Garrahy sought to erase the long-held image about the State as "Poor Little Rhode Island." Also, 1,800 acres of land, alleged to have been stolen from the Narragansett Indians, were returned to the tribe, Interstate Highway 84 was approved for construction, and a bill was adopted by the State Legislature banning the sale of spray paint to minors. In addition, in 1979 Garrahy joined several other state governors on a trip to Russia for a summit regarding strategic arms limitation.

Garrahy stepped down from office in 1985. He is the author of such publications as: *Rhode Island in the Year 1975*; *Campaign Spending and Practices—A Direction to Pursue*; and *Financial Aid Information—A Guide for Rhode Island High School Students*.

Garrahy is married to Margherite De Pietro, and the couple has five children.

DI PRETE, EDWARD DANIEL (1934-), sixty-second governor of Rhode Island (1985-1991), was born in Cranston, Rhode Island on July 8, 1934. He attended Holy Cross College in Massachusetts, earning a B.S. degree in 1955.

Di Prete began his political career as a member of the Cranston School Committee between 1970 and 1974, serving as chairman the last two years, then between 1974 and 1978 he was councilman-at-large for the Cranston City Council. From 1979 to 1984 Di Prete served as mayor of Cranston, and also during that time, between 1979 and 1985, he was a member of the Rhode Island State Representatives Executive Committee. In 1984 he was elected to the Rhode Island governorship on the Republican ticket.

For a number of years Di Prete has also pursued his business interests, serving as vice president of Frank A. Di Prete Realty from 1959 to 1978, and returning to that post after stepping down from the governor's chair in 1991. He has also served as director of the Independent Insurance Agency of Rhode Island.

Di Prete has received a number of honors, including the Tree of Life Award; Man of the Year from the Holy Cross Club of Rhode Island; and an award from the Sons of Italy. He is married to Patricia Hines, and the couple has seven children.

SUNDLUN, BRUCE (1920-), sixty-third governor of Rhode Island (1991-1995), was born in Providence, Rhode Island on January 19, 1920. He attended college for a time, then between 1942 and 1945, during World War II, Sundlun served as a captain in the Army Air Corps. Stationed in Europe, he flew with the 384th Bomb Squadron. After the war he finished his education at Williams College, where he earned a B.A. degree in 1946, then attended Harvard Law School, taking his LL.B. degree in 1949.

Sundlun entered the political arena that same year when he was named to the post of Assistant United States Attorney, serving in Washington, D.C. until 1951. He was subsequently named special assistant to the United States Attorney General in the U.S. Department of Justice's Civil Division, serving from 1951 to 1954.

In 1961, and again in 1965, Sundlun was chairman of the Inaugural Medal Commission, and in the former year, served as vice chairman of the Inaugural Parade Commission. For over twenty years Sundlun served on a number of Democratic Party committees, and as a delegate at several Democratic conventions. Between 1987 and 1990, he chaired the Providence Housing Authority. In 1990 Sundlun successfully ran for the governorship of Rhode Island, serving through 1994.

Along with his political activities, Sundlun has been involved in various business ventures. Starting in 1963 he served as incorporator and director at Communications Satellite Corporation in Washington, D.C., and from 1972 to 1990, was director at Quest Tech Inc. in McLean, Virginia. Between 1970 and 1976, Sundlun was president of Executive Jet Aviation, Inc. in Columbus, Ohio, and served in the same capacity for Outlet Communications Inc. in Providence, Rhode Island from 1976 to 1984. From the latter year to 1988, he was CEO of that firm. In 1988 Sundlun began serving as chairman of Sundlun and Company in Providence.

Sundlun is married to Marjorie Lee and the couple has five children.

ALMOND, LINCOLN (1936-), sixty-fourth governor of Rhode Island (1995-), was born in Central Falls, Rhode Island, on June 16, 1936. He attended the University of Rhode Island, earning a B.S. degree in 1958, then studied at Boston University Law School where he took his J.D. degree in 1961. In 1963 he was named Town Administrator for Lincoln, serving until 1969, when he became United States Attorney for Rhode Island. He held that post until 1978, then again between 1981 to 1993.

For several years, Almond was president of the Blackstone Valley Development Foundation, Inc., a land development firm. He resigned his post in 1994 when he successfully ran for the Rhode Island governorship on the Republican ticket, and went on to win another term in 1998. An early decision in his administration was the privatization of the Rhode Island Department of Economic Development, which was revamped into the semi-public Economic Development Corporation. In its new guise, it offered State employers suggestions on how to keep their companies competitive. In addition, Almond put together the Economic Policy Council, an impartial group hired to conduct research, then provide a breakdown of its findings, which would then be offered to State officials as a recommendation for improvements regarding the economy of the State.

Almond did his part to help eliminate the budget deficit by slashing several State departments, and cutting down the governmental workforce. All of these decisions ultimately led to a first-time surplus in the State budget, a huge drop in the unemployment rate, and a stronger public education sys0tem. Almond, during his two terms, also implemented extensive welfare reform.

In 1992, Almond was inducted into the Historic Central Falls Hall of Fame, plus the National Conference of Christians and Jews bestowed their Brotherhood Award on him.

Almond is married to Marilyn Johnson, and the couple has two children. His current term expires in 2003.

DICTIONARY OF PLACES

Population figures and demographic information are official U.S. Census Bureau finals for 1990. When two figures are shown, separated by a slash, the first figure is the 1990 and the second is the Census Bureau 1999 estimate – the most recent available. Year 2000 census supplements will be available in the fall of 2001.

BARRINGTON, Town; Bristol County; Pop. 16,174; Zip Code 02806; Lat. 41-43-44 N, Long. 071-18-38 W. Settled in 1677, incorporated by Massachusetts in 1717, then by Rhode Island in 1770, the town was named in honor of English theologian Lord Barrington, an advocate of religious toleration.

BRISTOL, Town; Bristol County Seat; Pop. 20,128; Zip Code 02809; Lat. 41-40-52 N, Long. 071-16-00 W. Named for Bristol, England.

BURRILLVILLE, Town; Providence County; Pop. 13,164. Named for James Burrill, Jr. Attorney-General of the state who later became a chief justice and U.S. Senator.

CENTRAL FALLS, City; Providence County; Pop, 16,995 / 16,390; Lat. 41-53-26 N, Long. 071-23-34 W. Descriptively named for its location.

CHARLESTOWN, Town; Washington County; Pop. 4,800; Zip Code 02813; Lat. 41-22-46 N, Long. 071-44-44 W. Incorporated in 1738 and named for King Charles II, who had granted Rhode Island its charter in 1663.

COVENTRY, Town; Kent County; Pop. 27,065; Zip Code 02816; Lat. 41-41-26 N, Long. 071-34-00 W. Named for Coventry, England.

CRANSTON, City; Providence County; Pop, 71,992 / 75,009; Lat. 41-46-47 N, Long. 071-26-16 W. Named after an early settler. Cranston was incorporated in 1910. The primary economic venture of the city has always been farming. Acquired from the Pawtuxet Indians in the Pawtuxet Purchase, Cranston was first settled in the 1600s by William Arnold, a proprietor from Providence.

CUMBERLAND, Town; Providence County; Pop. 27,069; Zip Code 02864; Lat. 41-54-32 N, Long. 071-23-32 W. Previously known as Attleboro Gore, the name was changed to honor Prince William, Duke of Cumberland.

EAST GREENWICH, Town; Kent County Seat; Pop. 10,211; Zip Code 02818; Lat. 41-39-48 N, Long. 071-27-33 W. The name is derived from a district of London in Kent County, England.

EAST PROVIDENCE, City; Providence County; Pop, 50,980 / 47,835; Elev. 59; Lat. 41-48-49 N, Long. 071-22-14 W. Named by Roger Williams in 1636 for "God's merciful providence."

EXETER, Town; Washington County; Pop. 4,453; Zip Code 02822; Lat. 41-34-37 N, Long. 071-32-21 W. The town is named for Exeter, England.

FOSTER, Town; Providence County; Pop. 3,370; Zip Code 02825; Lat. 41-51-10 N, Long. 071-45-39 W. Incorporated in 1781 and named for Theodore Foster, a U.S. Senator who owned property in the town.

GLOCESTER, Town; Providence County; Pop. 7,550. Named for Gloucester, England.

HOPKINTON, Town; Washington County; Pop. 6,406; Zip Code 02833; Lat. 41-27-41 N, Long. 071-46-40 W. Named in 1757 for Governor Stephen Hopkins.

JAMESTOWN, Town; Newport County; Pop. 4,040; Zip Code 02835; Lat. 41-29-22 N, Long. 071-21-51 W. Named in honor of James II, Duke of York and Albany.

JOHNSTON, Town; Providence County; Pop. 24,907; Zip Code 02919; Lat. 41-49-18 N, Long. 071-29-44 W. Incorporated in 1759 and named for Augustus Johnston, Attorney-General of the colony from 1757-1765.

LINCOLN, Town; Providence County; Pop. 16,949; Zip Code 02865; Lat. 41-53-47 N, Long. 071-24-55 W. Named for President Abraham Lincoln in 1871.

LITTLE COMPTON, Town; Newport County; Pop. 3,085; Zip Code 02837; Lat. 41-30-28 N, Long. 071-10-25 W. Named for the town in England.

MIDDLETOWN, Town; Newport County; Pop. 17,216; Zip Code 02840; Lat. 41-32-44 N, Long. 071-17-31 W. Named for its central location on the island of Rhode Island.

NARRAGANSETT, Town; Washington County; Pop. 12,088; Zip Code 02882; Lat. 41-23-24 N, Long. 071-28-24 W. The town takes its name from the Indian tribe that at one time lived in this territory.

NEWPORT, City; Newport County Seat; Pop. 29,259 / 24,232; Zip Code 02840; Lat. 41-29-32 N, Long. 071-18-45 W; Settled and named in 1639 after several English towns.

NEW SHOREHAM, Town; Washington County; Pop. 620. Incorporated in 1672 and named for a place in England.

NORTH KINGSTOWN, Town; Washington County; Pop. 21,938; Zip Code 02852; Lat. 41-37-35 N, Long. 071-27-17. Incorporated as King's Towne in 1674, the name was changed to Rochester in 1686, then changed back to its original name in 1689. In 1723 the town was divided into North and South Kingstown.

NORTH PROVIDENCE, Town; Providence County; Pop. 29,188. Named for its location, north of Providence.

NORTH SMITHFIELD, Town; Providence County; Pop. 9,972. The name indicates the town's geographical location north of Smithfield.

PAWTUCKET, City; Providence County; Pop, 71,204 / 67,662; Zip Code 02860; Lat. 41-52-32 N, Long. 071-22-53 W. An Algonquin Indian word meaning "falls-in-the-river."

PORTSMOUTH, Town; Newport County; Pop. 14,257; Zip Code 02871; Lat. 41-36-03 N, Long. 071-15-00 W. Founded in 1638 by colonists from Massachusetts Bay Colony and named for Portsmouth, England.

PROVIDENCE, City; Providence County Seat; Pop. 156,804 / 149,887; Zip Code 029+; Lat. 41-49-24 N, Long. 071-25-32 W. A thankful reference by the state's early settlers to "divine providence." It was acquired from the Pawtuxet Indians in the "Grand Purchase" of Providence, 1636, by Roger Williams.

RICHMOND, Town; Washington County; Pop. 4,018. Probably named for Edward Richmond, attorney-general of the colony from 1677-1680.

SCITUATE, Town; Providence County; Pop. 8,405. Settlers from Scituate, Massachusetts came here in 1710 and named the town for their former home.

SMITHFIELD, Town; Providence County; Pop 16,886. The origin of the town's name is uncertain; however, the land on which the Quaker Meeting House was built was deeded by a party named Smith, and the town may have been named in his honor.

SOUTH KINGSTOWN, Town; Washington County; Pop. 20,414. Formerly part of Kingstown, which was divided in 1723 into North and South Kingstown.

TIVERTON, Town; Newport County; Pop. 13,526; Zip Code 02878; Lat. 41-37-31 N, Long. 071-12-27 W. Named for Tiverton, England, the town was previously known as Pocasset, for the Pocasset Indians from whom the land was purchased.

WARREN, Town; Bristol County; Pop. 10,640; Zip Code 02885; Lat. 41-43-30 N. long. 071-16-10 W. Incorporated in 1747 and named for Sir Peter Warren, a British Navy admiral.

WARWICK, City; Kent County; Pop, 87,123 / 83,994; Zip Code 028+; Elev. 64; Lat. 41-43-00 N, Long. 071-26-22 W. Named for the town and county in England.

WEST KINGSTON, Washington County Seat; Zip Code 02892; Lat. 41-28-55 N, Long. 071-49-40 W. The name refers to the town's location.

WEST WARWICK, Town; Kent County; Pop. 27,026; Zip Code 02893; Lat. 41-42-08 N, Long. 071-30-14 W. Named in honor of the Earl of Warwick, who had been appointed Governor-in-Chief and Lord High Admiral in the Colonies.

WESTERLY, Town; Washington County; Pop. 18,580; Zip Code 02891; Lat. 41-22-29 N, Long. 071-49-40 W. Named for its location in the most westerly part of the state.

WOONSOCKET, City; Providence County; Pop. 45,914 / 41,409; Zip Code 02895; Elev. 162; Lat. 42-00-07 N, Long. 071-30-25 W. An Algonquian Indian word meaning "steep descent."

SOUTH CAROLINA
The Palmetto State

Magnolia Plantation includes the country's oldest garden

The Carolina Opry - Myrtle Beach

GOVERNOR
Jim Hodges

Lighthouse
Morris Island

Charleston's marina

Hunting Island State Park

Boone Hall is still a working plantation
Charleston

INTRODUCTION

South Carolina, the Palmetto State, is the least written about and the least understood of all the States that have played an important part in our history.

The South Carolinian is a product of many conflicts, as well as of great unifying forces. Incongruities and contrasts abound in his environment. With some of the most beautiful gardens in the world, the State has a variety of pleasure resorts from mountains to seacoast.

South Carolina is roughly a triangle covering 30,989 square miles, 494 of which consist of water area. From the northwest corner a jagged man-made line, running east and southeast for 333 miles to Little River Inlet, marks the boundary between the two Carolinas; the Savannah River, with its tributaries, the Tugaloo and the Chattooga, extending southeast from the same corner for 238 miles to Tybee Sound, separates the State from Georgia; while the Atlantic shore line stretches for approximately 190 miles, between Little River Inlet and Tybee Sound.

The Blue Ridge Mountains occupy an area of about 500 square miles in the northwestern part of the State. The Highest point, Sassafras Mountain (alt. 3,548 ft.), is almost on the North Carolina boundary. Outcroppings of granite are not uncommon, and at Table Rock and Caesar's Head are vertical cliffs of gneiss. From this mountainous border the land drops successively to the Piedmont Plateau, the Sand Hills, the Coastal Plain, and sea level, over a distance of about 235 miles. The mean altitude of the State in general is estimated at 350 feet.

STATE NAME

Two different forms of the name of the Carolinas have been used. This territory was first called *Carolina* by Jean Ribaut; but under the control of King Charles I, it was named *Carolana*, and from the time of King Charles II, it has been called *Carolina*.

Thwaits gives the following account of the naming of the Carolinas: While on an exploring expedition in 1562, Jean Ribaut left colonists on Lemon Island at Port Royal, and called this territory Carolina in honor of Charles IX, the boy-king of France, under whose auspices he went out.

In the grant of 1629 to Sir Robert Heath, his attorney general, King Charles I called this country *Carolana*, or the *Province of Carolana*. In 1663 King Charles II gave *Carolina* to eight Lords Proprietors.

It is definitely stated in *A Sketch of North Carolina* that King Charles I named after himself the territory granted to Sir Robert Heath:

"In 1629, a charter was granted by King Charles I of England to Sir Robert Heath of the Southern part of Virginia, latitudes thirty-one degrees to thirty-six degrees, under the name, in honor of that king, of Carolina. As Heath did nothing under it, a renewal was granted in 1663 to eight Lords Proprietors, and an enlargement to thirty-six degrees, under the name, in honor of that king, of Carolina. As Heath did nothing under it, a renewal was granted in 1663 to eight Lords Proprietors, and an enlargement to 36 degrees thirty seconds and twenty-nine degrees, two years afterwards."

This assertion is also borne out by Ashe in his quotation from Sir Robert Heath's patent, dated October 30, 1629, which granted the territory "between thirty-one and thirty-six degrees of north latitude" to Heath, and says: "'Know that we do erect and incorporate them into a Province, and name the same *Carolana*, or the *Province of Carolana*'"

"The fixing of the name Carolana upon the coast and interior regions between the 31st and 36th degrees of north latitude dates from the charter granted by Charles I of England to Sir Robert Heath, his attorney general, on October 30, 1629. Afterward Carolina came to be applied to the coastal domain, and Carolana to the interior as far as the Mississippi."

The territory was divided into North and South Carolina by the Lords Proprietors in 1665, yet this division corresponded roughly to the two districts previously colonized; one by colonists from the English community on the island of Barbados, settling at Clarendon in 1664.

As to the meaning of the word *Carolina*, W. Robertson's Dictionary says that the word *Carolina* (*Carlina*) is a Latin feminine noun meaning "the Chameleon or the white thistle."

The *New English Dictionary* derives the term *Carline*, said to be the same word as *Carolina*, from the expression *Carolus Magnus*, the Latin name of *Charlemagne*. It also gives Carline as a noun denoting "a genus of composite plants closely allied to the thistles," and hence generally called the *Carline Thistle*.

Murray further states the *Caroline* used as an adjective may mean of or pertaining to Charles; of Charles the Great (Charlemagne); and of Charles I and II of England, or their periods.

The English name *Charles* is derived from the Latin term *Carolus* that is the latinized form of the German word *Carl*, meaning "strong, stout, courageous, and valiant."

STATE NICKNAMES

The sobriquets of South Carolina are: the *Iodine State*, the *Keystone of the South Atlantic Seaboard*, the *Palmetto State*, the *Rice State*, the *Sand-lapper State*, and the *Swamp State*.

South Carolina is designated as the *Iodine State* from the fact that the plants are grown in this State contain a great percentage of iodine.

The fact that South Carolina is wedge shaped and that it is located so that the point of its wedge extends into the Appalachian Mountains and its base extends to the Atlantic Ocean has caused it to be called *The Keystone of the South Atlantic Seaboard*.

The palmetto grows abundantly in South Carolina, especially along the coast, and is pictured on her coat of arms; consequently it has given the nickname, the *Palmetto State*, to the State.

South Carolina is also called the *Rice State* from the enormous quantities of rice it produces and handles each year.

The *Sand-lapper State* is given as a nickname to South Carolina, probably, from the fact that some of its poorer inhabitants live on the sandy ridges which are covered with scrubby pine forests, it being humorously said that they lap up sand for sustenance.

The *Swamp State* is applied to South Carolina in reference to the lands where the rice is grown and other swampy lands.

The South Carolinians have six nicknames; namely, *Clay-eaters*, *Palmettoes*, *Rice-birds*, *Sand-hillers*, *Sand-lappers*, and *Weasels*. These are mostly derogatory terms given to the classes of poorer white people. *Clay-eaters* refers to the fact that certain classes of poor white people living in some of the remoter districts are said to have eaten abundantly of the white, aluminous clay found in these parts of the State when they could get no more substantial food. For the origin and the significance of the sobriquets, *Palmettoes* and *Sand-lappers*, see the previous narrative dealing with the nicknames, the *Palmetto State* and the *Sand-lapper State*. *Rice-birds* is a nickname given to the well-to-do rice planters and those people living in the rich rice sections of the State. The country surrounding Beaufort, South Carolina, "embraces the best rice fields of the South, so proverbially so indeed that the irrelevant 'up country' are accustomed to call the aristocratic inhabitants of the region rice-birds." *Sand-hillers* was applied especially to the poor descendants of the laboring white people who were driven out of the pine woods on the sandy hills of South Carolina when slave labor was introduced, and there became skinny and cadaverous-looking. They are said to have skins the color of the sand of their habitat. The name might have been derived from the sand-hill crane (*Grus canadensis*), a long-legged species found commonly in the sections of the country in which these people live. *Sand-lappers* is a jesting nickname given to those people living in the Pine Barrens, whom William Gilmore Simms calls a "Sand-lapper or a Clay-eater." The Sand-lappers are generally described as being little, dried up, and jaundiced. Simms in *The Forayers* speaks of a woman as being "the fattest and yellowest sandlapper of a woman I ever saw." The people living in the out-of-the-way sections of the State are called *Weasels*.

GREAT SEAL

The South Carolina Constitution of 1895 says "the seal of the State now in use shall be used by the Governor officially, and shall be called 'The Great seal of the State of South Carolina."

The Great Assembly of the Provincial Congress of South Carolina on April 2, 1776, authorized the designing and making of the Great Seal of South Carolina. The designing of this seal is as follows:

"ARMS: A Palmetto-tree growing on the sea-shore, erect; at its base, a toryn up Oak-tree, its branches lopped off, prostrate; *both proper*. Just below the branches of the Palmetto, two shields, pendent; one of them on the dexter side is inscribed March 26-the other on the sinister size July 4. Twelve Spears, *proper*, are bound crosswise to the stem of the Palmetto, their points raised; the band uniting them together, bearing the inscription QUIS SEPARABIT. Under the prostrate Oak, is inscribed MELIOREM LAPSA LOCAVIT; below which appears in large figures 1776. At the Summit of the Exergue, are the words SOUTH CAROLINA and at the bottom of the same, ANIMIS OPIBUSQUE PARATI.

"REVERSE: A Woman walking on the Sea-shore, over swords and daggers; she holds in her dexter hand, a laurel branch-and in her sinister, the folds of her robe: she looks towards the sun, just rising above the sea; *all proper*. On the upper part, is the sky azure. At the summit of the Exergue, are the words DUM SPIRO SPERO: and within the field below the figure, is inscribed the word SPES. The Seal is in the form of a circle, four inches in diameter; and four-tenths of an inch thick."

STATE FLAG

The flag of South Carolina consists of a blue field upon the center of which is imaged a palmetto tree. Near the upper corner, next to the staff, is pictured a crescent pointing toward the center. This, the flag of the State as a member of the Southern Confederacy, was adopted by action of the State legislature January 28, 1861.

STATE MOTTO

South Carolina is credited with two mottoes: (1) *Animis Opibusque Parati*, meaning *Ready in soul and resource*, found in Virgil's *Aeneid*, Book II, line 799, and (2) *Dum Spiro, Spero*, signifying *While I breath, I hope*, was the motto of the Irish Viscounts Dillion. The latter motto refers to the figure of Hope on the State seal. Two more Latin mottoes appear on the State seal: (1) *Quis Separabit?* meaning "Who shall separate us?," and (2) *Meliorem Lapsa Locavit*, was a Latin inscription on the Seal of the Northwest Territory. He says that it with the coiled snake, the boats, the rising sun, the felled forest tree, and the apple tree laden with fruit, "all combine forcibly to express the idea that the wild and savage condition is to be superseded by a higher and better organization."

STATE FLOWER

The State legislature of South Carolina passed a concurrent resolution on March 14, 1923, to appoint a commission to select a suitable State flower. This commission was to consist of "two members from the House of Representatives, to be appointed by the Speaker, and one member from the senate, to be appointed by the President of the Senate."

The Legislative Manual of South Carolina, 1927, says that upon "the report of a select legislative commission consisting of Senator T.B. Butler, of Gaffney, and Representatives G.B. Ellison, of Columbia, and T.S. Heyward, of Buffton," the General Assembly on February 1, 1924, adopted as the State flower the yellow jessamine, called also the Carolina jessamine (*Gelsemium sempervirens*).

STATE SONG

On February 11, 1911, the South Carolina General Assembly adopted as the State Song the song *Carolina*, written by Henry Timrod and music composed by Anne Curtis Burgess.

The Senate concurrent resolution adopting this song says:

"WHEREAS, The Daughters of the American Revolution have memorialized the General Assembly to adopt as a State Song the beautiful poem written by the gifted Timrod, and set to music by Miss Curtis, a daughter of South Carolina; therefore,

"Be it resolved by the Senate, the House of Representatives concurring, that the song 'Carolina' be accepted as and declared to be the State Song of South Carolina.

"On immediate consideration the Concurrent Resolution was adopted. Ordered sent to the House for concurrence." The members of the House approved the resolution on the date given above.

STATE BIRD

In 1931 the South Carolina Federated Women's Clubs adopted as their State bird the Carolina wren.

The Carolina wren (*Thryothorus ludovicianus*) is about 5 ½ inches in length. Its habitation is the southern part of the United

States, extending as far north as Connecticut. Its color is a bright rusty brown. It has a white throat and a white line extending from the bill through the eyes. Its food consists of bugs, worms, and small insects.

STATE LICENSE PLATE

The current license plate issued in 1998 displays the motto "Smiling Faces, Beautiful Places" across the top in blue letters. The background of the plate shows the hillsides in dark blue and fades to light blue towards the middle down to the bottom. The center of the plate has black letters and numerals with a palmetto tree in the center. On the bottom center of the plate "South Carolina" is displayed in blue letters.

CAPITOL BUILDING

The Statehouse of South Carolina, located at Columbia, was begun in 1851 and completed in 1904. The original architect was Major John R. Niernsee who died before the building was completed. The succeeding architects were J. Crawford Neilson, J. Frank Niernsee, Frank P. Milburn, and Charles C. Wilson. This structure was built of local granite. It represents a rather free style of the Corinthian type of Roman architecture. The building from start to finish cost more than three million, five hundred forty thousand dollars.

CHRONOLOGY

1525 Spaniards from San Domingo, sent out by Lucas Vasquez de Ayllon and others, skirt coast almost as far north as River Jordan (probably Cape Fear River), carrying away 150 natives as slaves.
– Hilton Head is discovered on St. Helen's Day by Pedro de Quexos, who names it Punta de Santa Elena—the last two words by which the adjacent harbor and country are long known.

1526 First settlement is made by Spaniards under Vasquez de Ayllon (abandoned after a few months), probably on Winyah Bay.

1562 French Huguenots under Jean Ribaut unsuccessfully attempts to settle on what is now Parris Island at Santa Elena, or Port Royal.

1566-87 Spaniards settle at Santa Elena (maintained about 20 years).

1629 Charles I to Attorney General Sir Robert Heath from sea to sea grants Territory between 31st and 36th parallels and extending; it is named *Carolana*.

1663 Territory is granted by Charles II to eight Lords Proprietors, who renamed it *Carolina* (limits extending in 1665 from 29 degrees to 36 degrees 30').
– Exploration of coast, which extends through two years, is begun by order of Lords Proprietors, as aid to future settlements.

1669 John Locke writes Fundamental Constitutions, or 'Grand Model,' for Proprietors, who adopt it as feudal system for Carolina.

1670 First permanent settlement, Charles Town, is located on southern bank of Ashley River, ten miles from its mouth.

1680 Charles Town is moved from Albemarle Point to Oyster Point, at confluence of Ashley and Cooper Rivers.
– Charles I authorizes transportation for French Protestant immigrants in H.M.S. *Richmond*.

1682 Province is divided into three counties: Berkeley, Craven, and Colleton.

1685 Rice becomes South Carolina's staple crop, continuing as such until 1850.

1687 Huguenot Church is organized in Charles Town.

1696 Act is passed making all alien inhabitants freemen on petition of governor swearing allegiance to king, and granting liberty on conscience to all Christians except Papists.

1697 Congregationalists from Massachusetts, with Reverend Joseph Lord, settle at Dorchester near head of Ashley River.

1698 Thomas Welch, South Carolina Indian trader, crosses Mississippi into northern part of present State of Arkansas.
– Free liberty is established for province.

1700 Estimated population of province is more than 5,000.

1702 Carolina land and sea forces, under Moore and Daniell, besiege St. Augustine in September; they burn town but fail to capture fort; Carolinians retire upon arrival of Spanish men-of- war.

1703 Province issues first paper money: $6,000 in bills of credit to pay war expenses.

1706 French-Spanish expedition against Charles Town fails.
– Church of England becomes established church; province is divided into twelve parishes.

1712-13 -Colonel John Barnwell, with force of South Carolinians and 500 friendly Indians, helps defeat Tuscarora in North Carolina.
– Colonel James Moore captures Fort Nahucke, North Carolina, garrisoned by 800 Tuscarora.

1715 Yamasee War is fought; four hundred colonists are killed; Indians are defeated and driven out.
– Territory is considered safe for new settlers.

1718 Governor Robert Johnson and Colonel William Rhett rid Carolina coast of pirates.

1719 Colonists who set up temporary government and ask king to make Carolina a royal province overthrow proprietary government.

1721 Crown appoints Sir Francis Nicholson as provincial governor.

1729 Crown purchases property rights of Proprietors.

1730 Robert Johnson becomes first Royal Governor of South Carolina.
– Nine townships are laid out to extend settlement and provide better defense for colony.
– First attempt is made to define boundary line between North and South Carolina; issue is not settled until 1815.

1732 Thomas Whitmarch founds *South-Carolina Gazette*; first issue is published January 8.

1735 Friendly Society for the Mutual Insuring of Houses Against Fire is organized.
– First theater is erected in Charles Town; The *Orphan* is presented following February 12.

1739 Twenty-one whites are killed in Stono slave insurrection; 44 blacks are killed or executed.

1740 Shipbuilding begins at Charles Town and Beaufort.
– Nearly half of Charles Town is destroyed by fire.

1744 Eliza Lucas, after three years of experimentation, brings good crop of indigo seed to maturity; she distributes indigo seeds and persuades a number of neighbors to join in raising plant, thereby beginning commercial production in South Carolina.

1747 More than 100,000 pounds of indigo are exported to England.

1753 Governor Glen secures several thousand acres from Cherokee on Keowee River, and erects Fort Prince George.

1755 Governor Glen makes treaty with Old Hop, Cherokee Chief, at Saluda Old Town, whereby Cherokees cede land later included in Ninety Six District (ten of present counties).

1760 Cherokee War begins, lasting into following year.

1762 St. Cecelia Society is founded as musical organization.

1765 Stamped paper is stored in Fort Johnson by order of Governor Bull.
– Thomas Lynch, John Rutledge, and Christopher Gadsden attend Stamp Act Congress in New York.

1769 Association of "Regulators" forms in inland settlements to suppress horse stealing, arson, etc., and leads to law establishing circuit courts of justice throughout province rather than in Charles Town alone.

– Province becomes divided into districts: Charles Town, Georgetown, Beaufort, Orangeburg, Cheraw, Camden, and Ninety Six, with circuit courts in each.

1773 Cargoes of tea sent to South Carolina are stored, and consignees are restrained from offering it for sale.
– Charles Town Chamber of Commerce is organized.

1774-75 Delegates Christopher Gadsden, Thomas Lynch, Henry Middleton, and Edward and John Rutledge attend Continental Congress; Middleton serves as president last six days of session of 1775.

1775 Estimated population of province is 140,000, including 60,000 whites, 80,000 blacks.
– First Provincial Congress meets (January 11), appoints Secret Committee, and seizes public arms and ammunition.
– Council of Safety is appointed on June 4 to manage all affairs of colony.
– Royal administration ends September 15, when Governor Campbell dissolves assembly and flees to man-of-war in Charles Town harbor.
– First bloodshed of American Revolution takes place at Ninety Six in September.

1776 Independent government is set up, with constitution, on March 26. John Rutledge is president, Henry Laurens is vice president, and William Henry Drayton is chief justice.
June 28. British fleet of eleven warships under Admiral Parker is repulsed at Charles Town by Colonel William Moultrie from fort of palmetto logs on Sullivan's Island.
July 4. Thomas Heyward, Jr., Thomas Lynch, Jr., Arthur Middleton, and Edward Rutledge agree to sign Declaration of Independence.

1777 May 20. Cherokee Nation cedes to South Carolina all its land except small strip to northwest.
June 14. General La Fayette and Baron De Kalb land on North Island, Georgetown.
November 1. Henry Laurens is elected president of Continental Congress.

1778 Second State Constitution is adopted by general assembly March 19; it disestablishes the Anglican Church.

1780 British win at Old Moncks Corner April 14.
– Charles Town surrenders to British May 12, after two-month siege.
– Americans win Battle of Hanging Rock July 30 and August 6.
– British win Battle of Camden August 15 and 16.
– Americans win Battle of Kings Mountain October 7, and Blackstock November 20.

1781 Americans win Battle of Cowpens January 17.
– British win at Hobkirk's Hill April 25.
May 12, Americans capture British post at Motte's.
– Indecisive Battle of Eutaw Springs occurs September 8.
– Several engagements take place at British posts of Fort Watson and Wright's Bluff; Maham log tower, an unusual strategy, is employed at former.

1782 Charles Town is evacuated by British December 14.

1783 Name of Charles Town is changed to Charleston August 13.

1786 Legislature provides for removing capital from Charleston to point near center of State, resulting in founding of Columbia.

1788 Constitution of United States is ratified by State May 23.

1790 Third constitution is adopted by State.
– Census gives population as 249,000; 140,000 whites, 109,000 blacks.

1800 Population (U.S. Census) is 345,500; 196,200 whites, 149,300 blacks.
– Santee Canal is completed, connecting Charleston with Santee River system.

1801 South Carolina College is chartered by State, and opens at Columbia in January 1805; it later became University of South Carolina.
– Legislature pays Miller and Whitney $50,000 to allow South Carolinians to manufacture cotton gins after their patented models for use within State.

1808 Amendment is adopted to State Constitution basing representation on white population and taxable wealth.

1811 Suffrage is extended to all white men.
– Census gives population as 415,000: 214,000 whites, 201,000 blacks.

1811 Free school system is instituted, mainly for benefit of indigent children.

1812 State Bank of South Carolina is incorporated.
– John C. Calhoun, Langdon Cheves, David R. Williams, and William Lowndes take lead in bringing about declaration of war with England; Calhoun writes bill.
– Paul Hamilton of South Carolina becomes Secretary of War.

1813 *Decatur*, Charleston privateer commanded by Captain Diron, captures British ship *Dominicia*, with 15 guns and 80 men; shortly afterwards, he takes *London Trader*, also having valuable cargo.

1817 President Monroe appoints John C. Calhoun as Secretary of War.

1820 Census gives population of 502,000; 237,000 whites, 265,000 blacks.

1822 Denmark Vesey, a free black man, leads suppression of slave conspiracy.

1828 Andrew Jackson, native South Carolinian, is elected President of United States; John C. Calhoun is elected Vice President.

1830 Census gives population of 581,000; 258,000 whites, 323,000 blacks.
– Public meeting on States' rights is held in Columbia September 20.
– Governor Hamilton advises legislature to pass Nullification Act.

– Famous States' rights debate takes place in Congress between Robert Y. Hayne and Daniel Webster.

1832 Legislature passes Ordinance of Nullification on November 20, forbidding enforcement of Federal tariff act after February 1 of following year. (Ordinance is repealed March 11, 1833, after Clay Compromise.)

1833 Charleston-Harburg railroad line of 136 miles is completed; it is longest steam railroad in world at the time.

1837 President Van Buren appoints Joel R. Poinsett Secretary of War.

1840 Census gives population of 594,000; 259,000 whites, 335,000 blacks.

1841 President Tyler appoints Hugh S. Legare United States Attorney General.

1845 Charter is granted William Gregg's cotton factory and factory village at Graniteville.

1847 Palmetto Regiment, made up of 1,100 volunteers under Colonel Pierce M. Butler, plays conspicuous part in winning Mexican War; regiment's flag is first to fly over captured Mexico City.

1850 John C. Calhoun dies March 31 and is buried in St. Philip's churchyard, Charleston.
– Population (U.S. Census) is 668,500.

1852 State convention declares right of State to secede.

1860 Population (U.S. Census) is 703,500.
– South Carolina secedes from Union December 20.

1861 **January 2**. Fort Johnson, Charleston, is occupied by State troops.
January 9. *Star of the West* retires when fired upon by batteries on Morris Island and Fort Moultrie.
January 11. Governor Pickens demands surrender of Fort Sumter.
April 12. Civil War begins; Howitzer batteries on James Island fire on Fort Sumter; Fort Sumter is surrendered by Major Anderson.

1861-65 With a voting population of only 47,000, South Carolina furnishes about 60,000 to confederate armies during Civil War.

1865 Sherman marches across State from January to March; he burns Columbia.
April 9. War ends, with surrender of Lee at Appomattox.
June 30. President Johnson appoints Benjamin F. Perry provisional governor.

1868 **January 14**. Constitutional convention, made up of 34 whites and 63 blacks, meets at Charleston.
March 17. Draft of new constitution is completed.
– Constitution is ratified April 14-16.
June 25. State is readmitted to Union; blacks, carpetbaggers, and scalawags begin eight-year rule.

1870 Population is 706,500.

1876 General Wade Hampton is elected governor; whites regain control of State.

1880 Population is 995,500.
— Cotton mill industry begins rapid expansion (next three decades show increase from 14 mills with less than $3,000,000 capital to 160 mills with capital of more than 100,000,000).

1886 August 31. Ninety-two persons are killed in earthquake centering at Charleston; property losses total approximately $8,000,000.

1889 Clemson Agricultural and Mechanical College is established.

1890 Population is 1,151,000.
— The Farmers' Movement, led by Benjamin R. Tillman, triumphs in State election; Tillman is elected governor.

1892 General assembly establishes State Dispensary for sale and control of liquor.

1893 Clemson Agricultural and Mechanical College is formally opened.
— Hurricane sweeps State, causing great property damage and loss of 1,000 lives along the coast.

1894 Winthrop College, State college for women, opens at Rock Hill.

1895 South Carolina adopts sixth constitution, providing some limitations to suffrage and nomination of State officials by direct primary.

1896 First direct primary election is held, in which state officials and members of Congress are nominated.

1898 South Carolina furnishes two regiments, independent battalion of infantry, and body of naval reserves for Spanish-American War; M.C. Butler is commissioned Major General in United States Volunteer Army; Major Micah Jenkins and Lieutenant Victor Blue are cited for heroism.

1900 Census gives population of 1,340,316; 557,807 whites, 782,321 blacks, 188 others.

1901-02 Interstate and West Indian Exposition held at Charleston.

1907 Dispensary law is repealed.

1910 Population is 1,515,000.

1913 National Corn Show is held in Columbia.

1915 Five-year movement begins for establishment of social welfare agencies, including State Board of Charities (later State Board of Public Welfare), Girls' Industrial School, and State Training School for Feeble-minded.
— Statewide prohibition law is enacted.

1917-18 South Carolina furnishes about 62,300 soldiers for World War I; of this total, about 57,000 serve in Army; about 5,000 in Navy; and about 300 in Marine Corps.
— Contributions to benevolent agencies total $3,012,740; purchase of government securities totals $94,211,740.
— Six of 78 Congressional Medals are won by South Carolinians; only New York and Illinois receive greater number.
— Camp Jackson, National Army camp, is located at Columbia; National Guard camps are established at Greenville and Spartanburg, and Navy Yard is located at Charleston.

1920 Census gives population of 1,684,000; 818,000 whites, 884,500 blacks, 500 others.

1924 New school law provides more nearly equal educational opportunities for rich and poor school districts.

1929 State Highway Department begins statewide highway-building program.

1930 Census gives population of 1,738,000; 944,000 whites, 793,000 blacks, 1,000 others; whites predominate in population for first time since 1810.
— Dreher Shoals Dam and powerhouse on Saluda River near Columbia are completed; capacity is 200,000 h.p.

1934 Prohibition is repealed; State regulates sale of liquor.

1936 Constitutional amendment allows participation in national social security program.

1938 Forty-hour law for textile industry is enacted by legislature, but is superseded in few months by national 44-hour Fair Labor Standards Act.
— Total of 286 mills, operating 5,753,779 spindles and 144,296 looms, have invested capital of $198,987,588.
September 20. Two tornadoes strike Charleston; 29 are killed, property damage is estimated at more than $2,000,000.

1940 Population (U.S. Census) is 1,905,500.
— In June, Camp Jackson is made permanent Army Post and renamed Fort Jackson; Eighth Division, and later Thirtieth Division, are stationed here.
— On August 12, hurricane lashes coast; Beaufort, Edisto Island, and Charleston are hardest hit; about 40 are killed, and property damage totals nearly $5,000,000; damage to crops over State is estimated at $5,000,000.

1941 South Carolina Senator Byrnes is named to U.S. Supreme Court.

1942 Governor Harley dies while in office.
— University library will house State historical data.

1943 SEC approves merger of South Carolina Electrical & Gas Co. with Lexington Water Power Co.

1944 State legislature holds extraordinary session to keep Democratic primaries "pure white" by blocking black voting.

1945 University of South Carolina establishes college clinic to help World War II servicemen plan their education.

1946 Legislature defeats bill to abolish poll tax.

1947 NAACP sponsors test lawsuit against the State's White primary law.

1948 U.S. Supreme Court refuses to reverse lower courts' ruling permitting blacks to vote in Democratic primaries.

1949 Judge Waring receives National Lawyer's Guild award for opening Democratic primaries to blacks.
– Population is 2,117,000.

1950 South Carolina reports 212 percent rise in per capita income between 1929 and 1949.

1951 Governor-elect Byrnes urges legislative approval of poll tax abolition amendment.
– Savannah River Plant of U.S. Atomic Energy Commission is constructed for manufacture of plutonium for nuclear weapons.

1952 Governor Byrnes urges defeat of white politicians allied with NAACP.
– Supreme Court upholds segregation; decision is reaffirmed by three-judge federal court.

1953 University of South Carolina increases advanced degree offerings in sciences.
– Republican Bryson dies.

1954 Strom Thurmond is elected to Senate by write-in vote, the first senator so elected.
– Supreme Court bars school segregation.

1955 University Dean Travelstead resigns after criticizing public school segregation.

1956 Legislature passes law barring NAACP members from public employment.

1957 Black teachers urge U.S. Supreme Court to void law barring public employment of NAACP members.

1958 Lieutenant-Governor Hollings leads fight against racial integration in public schools, and is elected governor.

1959 Governor Hollings travels to New York to attract industry to South Carolina.
– Population is 2,383,000.

1960 Justice Department investigates McCormick County voting records; although blacks outnumber whites in county, there is no record of black voters.

1961 Legislature considers resolution attacking Dr. Graham of Winthrop College for backing black civil rights demonstrations.

1962 Governor Hollings works to attract new industry to State and avoid turmoil over racial integration.

– Corinne Boyd Riley (D), 68, widow of Republican John Riley, is elected in unopposed special election to South Carolina 2nd Congressional district seat left vacant by her husband.

1963 Supreme Court reverses conviction of 187 blacks on breach of peace charges for demonstrating on State Capitol grounds in Columbia, South Carolina; all are freed on bail; decision is based on First Amendment.
– Black student, Harvey B. Gantt, enrolls in Clemson College, challenging State's segregation policies.

1964 Republican Party offers eleven person slates in Greenville County, only second time in history Republicans have run for every office on South Carolina slate.
– Schools in South Carolina desegregate without incident; State is last to adopt integration policies.

1965 Colonial town of Dorchester is restored.
– Olin DeWitt Johnston, Senator serving since 1945, dies of pneumonia.
– Harvey S. Gantt, 22, graduates from Clemson University; he is first black to attend previously all-white State supported school in State.

1966 South Carolina senator is one of nine senators who write letter to President Johnson protesting school desegregation guidelines.
– Ernest Hollings and Strom Thurmond are elected to U.S. Senate.

1967 Black leaders criticize Senator Hollings for voting against confirmation of Supreme Court Justice Thurgood Marshall.

1968 Black voter registration drive results in 60,000 new voters on State rolls.
– South Carolina College suspends classes after violence and rioting against segregation at local bowling alley in Orangeburg; National Guard seals off deserted campus.

1969 University of South Carolina students and faculty protest trustee's plan to expand football stadium before needs of law and nursing schools are met.
– Population is 2,591,000.

1970 Governor-elect West names black to major post in his administration; it is first time a black is appointed since Reconstruction.
– Woodlands cover 62 percent of land in South Carolina.

1971 J.C. West is inaugurated as governor; he pledges to eliminate any vestige of discrimination from government.
– Lower court ruling says South Carolina does not discriminate against men by maintaining Winthrop College (Rock Hill) as all-female institution, since the State also maintains all male and coeducational institutions.
– South Carolina is one of twelve states left, which bans sale of alcohol by the drink on Sundays.
– Twenty-two whites are indicted on riot charges from 1970 incident in which they overturned two school buses carrying black students.

1972 U.S. Senator Strom Thurmond is reelected by 5 to 1 margin over challenger.

1973 South Carolina adds 500 million dollars of industrial development.
– President Nixon addresses South Carolina Assembly in Columbia, S.C. on Vietnam War settlement; Nixon says peace with honor was attained in Vietnam.
– Tornado hits State.

1974 Vice President Ford has mixed reaction to Watergate transcript material, and gives renewed support for President Nixon; Ford says transcripts "do not exactly confer sainthood on anyone concerned," but he has not lost faith in Nixon's capability to do great job.
– Kiawah Island off the South Carolina coast is sold to Kurwait's Sea Pines Co., to develop large vacation resort.

1975 Vice President Nelson A. Rockefeller speaks conservatively during two-day swing through Alabama and South Carolina; he advocates states' rights and a balanced budget, and scorns government bureaucracy, fiscal profligacy, and welfare 'cheats.'
– James B. Edwards becomes first Republican governor of State since 1876.

1976 Federal Law Enforcement Assistance Administration warns South Carolina Highway Patrol to end discrimination against women or lose federal funds.

1977 Native American tribes in South Carolina press claims for land.
– Surveys show widespread poverty and disease still plague rural South Carolina counties.

1978 U.S. government files suit to block primary elections in Chester and Sumter counties on grounds that the at-large voting system discriminates against blacks.
– Anti-nuclear energy activists begin three-day protest.

1979 Sheriff James Metts of Lexington County is only sheriff in the U.S. to hold Ph.D. degree.
– Kennedy visits Charleston, speaks out against Carter's "silence" on crime and law enforcement, and his unwillingness to tackle difficult, complex side of crime in respectable way.
– Reagan campaigns in Columbia; in speech to reporters regarding federal financing of elections, he says, "I don't believe in government funding. I'd like to see us return to the candidates raising their own funds and not have government money in it."
– Population is 3,122,000.

1980 U.S. Assistant Attorney General Drew sends letter to South Carolina Governor Riley informing him that present method of electing State senators violates Voting Rights Act of 1965.

1981 U.S. Department of Justice rejects State's House Reapportionment Plan.
– President Reagan reverses ban on commercial reprocessing of spent nuclear fuel, put into effect by President Carter.

1982 Widespread fiscal mismanagement is discovered in South Carolina's Technical Education System.

1983 Rev. I. DeQuincey is elected to State Senate; he is first black senator elected in twentieth century.

1984 Senator Strom Thurmond, at age 81, is elected to Senate for sixth term.
– Hurricane Diana hits coast, causing relatively mild damage.
– Tornadoes cut path of destruction through North Carolina and South Carolina, killing 61, injuring 1000 or more; in Bennettsville, entire shopping center is leveled.

1985 Justice Department files suit against at-large voting practices of Darlington County as discriminatory against blacks.

1986 South Carolina House of Representatives votes to bar women in slacks and men without ties from House Chamber.
– Ernest Hollings is reelected to Senate.

1987 Bitter struggle rages between supporters of George Bush and evangelical supporters of presidential candidate Rev. Pat Robertson.
– Mayor Joseph P. Riley of Charleston is reelected with 81 percent of vote.
– Pope John Paul visits South Carolina to meet evangelical Christians on home ground; he delivers prayer service at University of South Carolina; South Carolina has smallest percentage of Catholics of any State.

1988 Presidential campaign is described as most negative in memory; voter turnout in South Carolina is at all time low, below 40 percent.
– Charlotte Observer wins two Pulitzer prizes.
– Savannah River nuclear weapons fuel plant shuts down after 25 workers are exposed to radiation.

1989 Hurricane Hugo hits; seven counties are designated federal disaster areas by President Bush; five others are added to list in September; National Hurricane Center reports Hugo as 10th worst hurricane (out of 137) to hit U.S. in 20th century.
– Treasure hunters report raising hundreds of millions of dollars in gold bars and coins from wreck of 19th century steamer that sunk off coast of South Carolina; total gold & treasure valued at one billion dollars.
– Population is 3,486,700.

1990 State Senator Theo Mitchell, 16-year veteran of legislature, earns Democratic nomination for governor; Mitchell seeks to become first black governor of State.
– Treasure hunters who discovered gold from shipwrecked *Central America* are awarded ownership; it is largest treasure in U.S. history, and first time individuals rather than nations are given deep-sea salvage rights in international waters; it is also believed to be first time treasure hunters were permitted to stake claim to wreck using remote video cameras and robots to find and recover treasure, rather than diving to site themselves.
– State's high school dropout rate has more than doubled since 1986.

1991 James Brown, soul singer, is paroled from prison near Aiken after serving two years of six-year sentence for aggravated assault and eluding police; Brown is ordered by parole board to enroll in substance-abuse program and to undergo drug testing.

– Scandals are exposed in State's largest university, most powerful law firm, largest newspaper, and State Legislature.

1992 U.S. Supreme Court rules property owners can demand government compensation when land-use regulations deprive their land of economic value; ruling challenges Beachfront Management Act, which bars construction on some coastal lands if considered fragile by environmental regulations.

– The Citadel Military Academy in Charleston ends program that allows male military veterans to take courses at school; decision follows sex-bias suit filed against academy by three female Navy veterans denied entrance to program in 1991.

1993 State Legislature is ordered by federal judges to draw up new State and federal legislative districts before elections in November 1994; federal court in 1992 drew up temporary short-term plan for districting after Democratic Legislature and Republican governor failed to agree on district plan of their own.

– U.S. Court of Appeals rules that The Citadel must permit Shannon R. Faulkner to attend classes while it hears challenge to male-only admissions policy; lower court will decide whether Faulkner will join Citadel's corps of cadets as full member in 1994.

1994 Hilton Head is site of march that supports keeping Confederate States of America flag flying above State capitol building in Columbia; rally is attended by 400 whites bearing Confederate flag, in response to march one day earlier in which National Association for the Advancement of Colored People (NAACP) maintained flag is symbol of slavery and racism; defenders say flag represents southern heritage.

– George Bell Timmerman, Jr., segregationist governor of State (1955-1959) dies at age 82; Timmerman fought 1954 Supreme Court decision declaring segregated schools unconstitutional, and led Southern opposition movement at 1956 Democratic National Convention that attacked what he considered radical legislation and platform planks for civil rights.

– Republican candidate, David Beasley, wins gubernatorial race in November election.

1995 Supreme Court declines hearing appeal from The Citadel, after U.S. 4th Circuit Court of Appeals rules school's exclusion of female students is unconstitutional; Citadel seeks appeal on grounds that military program for women at Converse College in Spartanburg provides equal educational opportunities for women.

– Susan Smith, mother who confessed to drowning two young sons in John D. Long Lake near Union, escapes death penalty for crimes; Smith was convicted of first-degree murder in July.

1996 Savannah River nuclear facility is one of several sites across United States scheduled to disclose inventory of plutonium, in report entitled *Plutonium: the First 50 Years*; report marks first public disclosure of atomic data by any nation possessing nuclear weapons.

– In ruling that affects The Citadel's admissions policies, U.S. Supreme Court votes in *U.S. v Virginia* that state-supported Virginia Military Institute's all-male admissions policy is violation of women's equal protection rights; school is ordered to admit women; The Citadel is nation's only other state-supported all-male academy, and also will be ordered to admit women.

– The Citadel admits four women candidates to educational program; several compromises, including pregnancy circumstances and locks on barracks doors, are included in new admissions policies.

– Attorney General Janet Reno announces investigation into series of fires at churches in South Carolina and four other southern states; although arson is suspected to be racially-motivated, top officials later find no evidence linking fires to national or regional conspiracy.

– Senator Strom Thurmond is reelected to seventh full term, defeating Democrat Elliott Close; voters also approve referendum on victims' rights to keep victims informed about developments in their cases, allowing them to gain restitution and protect right to be treated fairly.

– Two former Ku Klux Klan members plead guilty in Charleston federal court to four conspiracy counts related to burning predominantly black church and migrant labor camp; federal indictment accuses Arthur Haley and Hubert Rowell of providing flammable liquid to burn facilities.

1997 Charleston judge David W. Norton sentences former KKK members Gary C. Cox and Timothy A. Welch to at least 18 years in prison for burning of two predominantly black churches in 1995; men plead guilty to civil rights charges in arson of churches.

– Two of four women attending The Citadel announce they have dropped out of formerly all-male institution; Kim Messer and Jeanie Mentavlos cite acts of harassment and abuse suffered at hands of upperclassmen as reason for decision.

1998 Singer James Brown is picked up at Beech Island home after calls from concerned family members; he is admitted to hospital for treatment of addiction to painkilling medications.

– Series of tornadoes sweeps through South Carolina and three other southern states; two people die, and at least 20 are injured.

– Incumbent Governor David Beasley wins 72 percent of vote in GOP gubernatorial primary; he will face former Democrat State legislator Jim Hodges in November election; Senate primary results in nomination of Bob Inglis as GOP candidate to challenge Democrat Ernest Hollings.

– Hurricane Bonnie threatens coastal areas of South Carolina and several other southeastern states.

– Hodges wins gubernatorial election.

1999 Four largest tobacco companies in U.S. announce plans to establish $5.15 billion fund to aid tobacco farmers who face reduced market following industry settlement of states' tobacco-related lawsuits; details will affect South Carolina and 11 other states.

– U.S. 4th Circuit Court of Appeals rules 2-1 that prosecutors can use suspect's voluntary confession even if he/she has not been read Miranda rights; ruling was previously binding only in federal cases, but appeal now affects South Carolina and four other states within court's jurisdiction.

DIRECTORY OF STATE SERVICES

OFFICE OF THE GOVERNOR
P.O. Box 11369
Columbia, SC 29211
Fax: 803-734-1598
Governor: 803-734-9818

Commission on Women
2221 Devine St., Ste. 408
Columbia, SC 29205
Fax: 803-734-9109
Chairperson: 803-734-9143

Washington, DC Office
444 N. Capitol St. NW, Ste. 203
Washington, DC 20001
Fax: 202-624-7800
Director: 202-624-7784

LIEUTENANT GOVERNOR
Box 142
Columbia, SC 29202
Fax: 803-734-2082
Lieutenant Governor: 803-734-2080

ATTORNEY GENERAL
P.O. Box 11549
Columbia, SC 29211
Fax: 803-253-6283
Attorney General: 803-734-3970

SECRETARY OF STATE
P.O. Box 11350
Columbia, SC 29211
Fax: 803-734-2164
Secretary of State: 803-734-2155

TREASURER
P.O. Box 11778
Columbia, SC 29211
Fax: 803-734-2039
Treasurer: 803-734-2101

DEPARTMENTS

ADJUTANT GENERAL
1 National Guard Rd.
Columbia, SC 29201
Fax: 803-748-4329
Adjutant General: 803-748-4217

AGRICULTURE DEPARTMENT
P.O. Box 11280
Columbia, SC 29211-1280
Fax: 803-734-2192
Commissioner: 803-734-2210

Administration Division
P.O. Box 11280
Columbia, SC 29211-1280
Fax: 803-734-2192
Assistant Commissioner: 803-734-2210

Consumer Services Division
1101 Williams St.
Columbia, SC 29211
Fax: 803-734-2192
Assistant Commissioner: 803-737-2080

Laboratories Division
1101 Williams St.
Columbia, SC 29211
Fax: 803-734-2192
Assistant Commissioner: 803-734-2070

Market and Promotion Division
P.O. Box 11280
Columbia, SC 29211-1280
Fax: 803-734-2192
Director: 803-723-2200

Commodity Boards
Fax: 803-734-2192

Market Services Division
P.O. Box 11280
Columbia, SC 29211-1280
Fax: 803-734-2192
Director: 803-734-2200

Grain Inspection Services
P.O. Box 5286
North Charleston, SC 29406
Fax: 803-747-4284
Director: 803-554-1311

State Farmers Market & Commodity Inspection
Bluff Road
90 Box 13504
Columbia, SC 29201
Fax: 803-253-4039
Manager: 803-253-4041

ALCOHOL AND OTHER DRUG ABUSE SERVICES DEPARTMENT
3700 Forest Dr., Ste. 300
Columbia, SC 29204
Fax: 803-734-9663
Director: 803-734-9520

ARCHIVES AND HISTORY DEPARTMENT
P.O. Box 11669
Columbia, SC 29211
Fax: 803-734-8820
Director: 803-734-8577

COMMERCE DEPARTMENT
P.O. Box 927
Columbia, SC 29202
Fax: 803-737-0418
Secretary: 803-737-0400

Public Railways Division
P.O. Box 279
Charleston, SC 29402
Fax: 803-727-2005
Director: 803-727-2067

Aeronautics Division
P.O. Box 280068
Columbia, SC 29228-0068
Fax: 803-822-8002
Director: 803-822-5400

COMPTROLLER GENERAL
P.O. Box 11228
Columbia, SC 29211
Fax: 803-734-2064
Comptroller General: 803-734-2121

CONSUMER AFFAIRS DEPARTMENT
P.O. Box 5757
Columbia, SC 29250
Fax: 803-734-9365
Administrator: 803-734-9458

CORRECTIONS DEPARTMENT
P.O. Box 21787
Columbia, SC 29221-1787
Fax: 803-896-1220
Director: 803-896-8555

Administration
P.O. Box 21787
Columbia, SC 29328-1787
Fax: 803-896-1220
Deputy Director: 803-896-8515

Operations
P.O. Box 21787
Columbia, SC 29221-1787
Fax: 803-896-1218
Deputy Director: 803-896-8540

Program Services
P.O. Box 21787
Columbia, SC 29221-1787
Fax: 803-896-1220
Deputy Director: 803-896-8550

DISABILITIES AND SPECIAL NEEDS DEPARTMENT
P.O. Box 4706
Columbia, SC 29240
Fax: 803-737-6323
Director: 803-737-6444

EDUCATION DEPARTMENT
1429 Senate St.
Columbia, SC 29201
Fax: 803-734-8624
State Superintendent: 803-734-8492

Business Division
1429 Senate St.
Columbia, SC 29201
Fax: 803-734-8624
Senior Executive Assistant: 803-734-8122

Collaboration Division
1429 Senate St.
Columbia, SC 29201
Fax: 803-734-8624

Senior Executive Assistant: 803-734-8071

Curriculum Division
1429 Senate
Columbia, SC 29201
Fax: 803-734-8624
Senior Executive Assistant: 803-734-8396

Development Division
1429 Senate St.
Columbia, SC 29201
Fax: 803-734-8624
Senior Executive Assistant: 803-734-8559

Educational Initiatives Division
1429 Senate St.
Columbia, SC 29201
Fax: 803-734-8624
Senior Executive Assistant: 803-734-8258

Internal Administration Division
1429 Senate St.
Columbia, SC 29201
Fax: 803-734-8624
Senior Executive Assistant: 803-734-8092

Regional Services and Partnership Division
1429 Senate St.
Columbia, SC 29201
Fax: 803-734-8624
Senior Executive Assistant: 803-734-8562

Support Services Division
1429 Senate St.
Columbia, SC 29201
Fax: 803-734-8624
Senior Executive Assistant: 803-734-8244

HEALTH AND ENVIRONMENTAL CONTROL DEPARTMENT
2600 Bull St.
Columbia, SC 29201
Fax: 803-734-4620
Commissioner: 803-734-4880

Administrative Services Division
2600 Bull St.
Columbia, SC 29201
Fax: 803-734-4620
Deputy Commissioner: 803-734-4900

Environmental Quality Control Division
2600 Bull St.
Columbia, SC 29201
Fax: 803-734-5407
Deputy Commissioner: 803-734-5360

Health Regulation Division
2600 Bull St.
Columbia, SC 29201
Fax: 803-737-7212
Deputy Commissioner: 803-737-7200

Health Services Office
2600 Bull St.
Columbia, SC 29201
Fax: 803-737-3946
Deputy Commissioner: 803-737-3900

INSURANCE DEPARTMENT
P.O. Box 100105
Columbia, SC 29202-3105
Fax: 803-737-6205
Chief Commissioner: 803-737-6160

JUVENILE JUSTICE DEPARTMENT
P.O. Box 21069
Columbia, SC 29221-1069
Fax: 803-737-7445
Director: 803-737-8221

LABOR, LICENSING AND REGULATION DEPARTMENT
P.O. Box 11329
Columbia, SC 29211-1329
Fax: 803-734-9716
Director: 803-734-9594

Fire Safety Division
141 Monticello Trail
Columbia, SC 29203
Fax: 803-896-9806
Director: 803-896-9802

Architectural Examiners Board
3710 Landmark Dr., Ste. 206
Columbia, SC 29204
Fax: 803-734-9731
Executive Director: 803-734-9750

Auctioneer's Commission
P.O. Box 11329
Columbia, SC 29211-1329
Fax: 803-734-4284
Chairman: 803-734-4233

Accountancy Board
P.O. Box 11329
Columbia, SC 29211-1329
Fax: 803-734-4284
Administrator: 803-734-4228

Engineering and Land Surveyors Registration Board
P.O. Box 50408
Columbia, SC 29250-0408
Fax: 803-734-9364
Executive Director: 803-734-9166

Medical Examiners Board
101 Executive Center Dr.
Columbia, SC 29210
Fax: 803-731-1660
Director: 803-731-1650

Pharmacy Board
P.O. Box 11927
Columbia, SC 29211
Fax: 803-734-1552

Administrator: 803-734-1010

Real Estate Commission
1201 Main St., Ste. 1500
Columbia, SC 29201
Fax: 803-737-0848
Executive Director: 803-737-0700

Residential Home Builders Board
2221 Devine St., Ste. 530
Columbia, SC 29205
Fax: 803-734-9290
Chairman: 803-734-9174

LAW ENFORCEMENT DEPARTMENT
P.O. Box 21398
Columbia, SC 29221
Fax: 803-896-7041
Director: 803-737-9000

MENTAL HEALTH DEPARTMENT
P.O. Box 485
Columbia, SC 29202
Fax: 803-734-7879
Director: 803-734-7780

NATURAL RESOURCES DEPARTMENT
P.O. Box 167
Columbia, SC 29202
Fax: 803-734-6310
Director: 803-734-4007

PARKS, RECREATION AND TOURISM DEPARTMENT
1205 Pendleton St., Ste. 248
Columbia, SC 29201
Fax: 803-734-1409
Director: 803-734-0166

PROBATION, PAROLE AND PARDON SERVICES DEPARTMENT
P.O. Box 50666
Columbia, SC 29250
Fax: 803-734-9369
Director: 803-734-9278

PUBLIC SAFETY DEPARTMENT
5410 Broad River Rd.
Columbia, SC 29210
Fax: 803-896-7881
Director: 803-896-7839

REVENUE AND TAXATION DEPARTMENT
P.O. Box 125
Columbia, SC 29214
Fax: 803-737-9881
Executive Director: 803-737-9840

Motor Vehicle Division
P.O. Box 1498
Columbia, SC 29216
Director: 803-737-1135

SOCIAL SERVICES DEPARTMENT
P.O. Box 1520
Columbia, SC 29202-1520
Fax: 803-734-5597
Director: 803-734-5760

TRANSPORTATION DEPARTMENT
P.O. Box 191
Columbia, SC 29202
Fax: 803-737-1719
Director: 803-737-1302

VOCATIONAL REHABILITATION DEPARTMENT
P.O. Box 15
W. Columbia, SC 29171-0015
Fax: 803-822-5386
Commissioner: 803-822-5303

BOARDS AND COMMISSIONS

ARTS COMMISSION
1800 Gervais St.
Columbia, SC 29201
Fax: 803-734-8526
Executive Director: 803-734-8696

BUDGET AND CONTROL BOARD
P.O. Box 12444
Columbia, SC 29211
Fax: 803-734-2117
Executive Director: 803-734-2320

Auditor
P.O. Box 11333
Columbia, SC 29211
Fax: 803-343-0723
State Auditor: 803-253-4160

Economic Advisory Board
1000 Assembly St., Ste. 442
Columbia, SC 29201
Fax: 803-734-4719
Director: 803-734-3805

Energy Research & Development Center
Clemson University
386-2 College Ave.
Clemson, SC 29634-0929
Fax: 803-656-0142
Director: 803-656-2267

General Services Division
1201 Main St., Ste. 420
Columbia, SC 29201
Fax: 803-737-0952
Director: 803-737-3880

Human Resource Management Division
1201 Main St., Ste. 1000
Columbia, SC 29201
Fax: 803-737-0968
Director: 803-737-0900

Information Resource Management Division
1202 Main St., Ste. 930
Columbia, SC 29201
Fax: 803-737-0069
Director: 803-737-0077

Insurance Services Division
P.O. Box 11696
Columbia, SC 29211
Fax: 803-737-3832
Director: 803-737-0022

Research and Statistical Services Division
1000 Assembly St., Rm. 425
Columbia, SC 29201
Fax: 803-734-3619
Director: 803-734-3793

Retirement System Division
P.O. Box 11960
Columbia, SC 29211
Fax: 803-737-6810
Director: 803-737-6934

COMMISSION FOR THE BLIND
1430 Confederate Ave.
Columbia, SC 29201
Fax: 803-734-7885
Commissioner: 803-734-7522

EDUCATION ASSISTANCE AUTHORITY
P.O. Box 210219
Columbia, SC 29221
Fax: 803-772-9410
Commissioner: 803-798-7960

EDUCATIONAL TELEVISION NETWORK
1101 George Rogers Blvd.
Columbia, SC 29201
Fax: 803-737-3526
President & General Manager: 803-737-3240

ELECTION COMMISSION
P.O. Box 5987
Columbia, SC 29250
Fax: 803-734-9366
Executive Director: 803-734-9060

EMPLOYMENT SECURITY COMMISSION
P.O. Box 995
Columbia, SC 29202
Fax: 803-737-2642
Chairman: 803-737-2655

ETHICS COMMISSION
P.O. Box 11926
Columbia, SC 29211
Fax: 803-253-7539
Executive Director: 803-253-4192

FINANCIAL INSTITUTIONS BOARD
P.O. Box 11194
Columbia, SC 29211
Fax: 803-734-2039

Chairman/State Treasurer: 803-734-2688

Examining Division
1015 Sumter St., Rm. 309
Columbia, SC 29201
Fax: 803-734-2013
Banking Commissioner: 803-734-2001

Consumer Finance Division
P.O. Box 11905
Columbia, SC 29211
Fax: 803-734-2025
Director: 803-734-2020

FORESTRY COMMISSION
P.O. Box 21707
Columbia, SC 29221
Fax: 803-798-8097
State Forester: 803-896-8800

**HEALTH AND HUMAN SERVICES FINANCE
COMMISSION**
P.O. Box 8206
Columbia, SC 29202-8206
Fax: 803-253-4137
Executive Director: 803-253-6100

HIGHER EDUCATION COMMISSION
1333 Main St., Ste. 200
Columbia, SC 29201
Fax: 803-737-2297
Chief Executive Officer: 803-737-2260

HOUSING FINANCE AND DEVELOPMENT AUTHORITY
919 Bluff Rd.
Columbia, SC 29201
Fax: 803-734-2356
Executive Director: 803-734-2000

HUMAN AFFAIRS COMMISSION
P.O. Box 4490
Columbia, SC 29240
Fax: 803-253-4191
Commissioner: 803-253-6336

MUSEUM COMMISSION
P.O. Box 100107
Columbia, SC 29202-3107
Fax: 803-737-4969
Director: 803-737-4921

PORTS AUTHORITY
P.O. Box 817
Charleston, SC 29402
Fax: 803-577-8616
Executive Director: 803-577-8600

PUBLIC SERVICE AUTHORITY
P.O. Box 2946101
Moncks Corner, SC 29461-2901
Fax: 803-761-7037
President & Chief Executive Officer: 803-761-7024

PUBLIC SERVICE COMMISSION
P.O. Drawer 11649
Columbia, SC 29211
Fax: 803-737-5199
Executive Director: 803-737-5120

REORGANIZATION COMMISSION
1105 Pendleton St., Ste. 228
Columbia, SC 29201
Fax: 803-734-3163
Director: 803-734-3152

SCHOOL FOR THE DEAF AND BLIND
355 Cedar Spring Rd.
Spartanburg, SC 29302-4699
Fax: 803-585-3555
President: 803-585-7711

STATE ACCIDENT FUND
P.O. Box 102100
Columbia, SC 29221-5000
Fax: 803-731-1428
Director: 803-737-8100

STATE ARCHAEOLOGIST
1321 Pendleton St.
Columbia, SC 29208
Fax: 803-254-1338
State Archaeologist: 803-777-8170

STATE LIBRARY
P.O. Box 11469
Columbia, SC 29211
Fax: 803-734-8676
Librarian: 803-734-8666

**TECHNICAL AND COMPREHENSIVE EDUCATION
BOARD**
111 Executive Center Dr.
Columbia, SC 29210
Fax: 803-737-9343
Executive Director: 803-737-9320

WORKERS COMPENSATION COMMISSION
P.O. Box 1715
Columbia, SC 29202-1715
Fax: 803-737-5768
Executive Director: 803-737-5744

MEMBERS OF CONGRESS

SENATE

SEN. STROM THURMOND (R) (b. 1902); 8th Term;
Phone: 202-224-5972; Fax: 202-224-1300;
E-mail: senator@thurmond.senate.gov.

www.senate.gov/~thurmond/

SEN. ERNEST F. HOLLINGS (D) (b. 1922); 7th Term;
Phone: 202-224-6121; Fax: 202-224-4293; E-mail: (None).

www.senate.gov/~hollngs/

HOUSE

MARK SANFORD, Jr. (R-1st) (b. 1960); 3rd Term;
Phone: 202-225-3176; Fax: 202-225-3407;
E-mail: sanford@mail.house.gov.

www.house.gov/sanford/

FLOYD SPENCE (R-2nd) (b. 1928); 15th Term;
Phone: 202-225-2452; Fax: 202-225-2455;
E-mail: sc02@legislators.com.

www.house.gov/spence

LINDSEY GRAHAM (R-3rd) (b. 1955); 3rd Term;
Phone: 202-225-5301; Fax: 202-225-3216;
E-mail: sc03@legislators.com.

www.house.gov/graham/

JIM DeMINT (R-4th) (b. 1951); 1st Term;
Phone: 202-225-6030; Fax: 202-226-1177;
E-mail: jim.demint@mail.house.gov.

www.demint.house.gov

JOHN M. SPRATT, Jr. (D-5th) (b. 1942); 9th Term;
Phone: 202-225-5501; Fax: 202-225-0464; E-mail: (None).

www.house.gov/spratt/

JAMES CLYBURN (D-6th) (b. 1940); 4th Term;
Phone: 202-225-3315; Fax: 202-225-2313;
E-mail: jclyburn@mail.house.gov.

www.house.gov/clyburn/

TWENTIETH CENTURY GOVERNORS

MCSWEENEY, MILES BENJAMIN (1855-1921), sixtieth governor of South Carolina (1899-1903), was born in Charleston, the son of Mary and Miles McSweeney.

McSweeney's father died when he was four years old and he was forced to work at an early age. He was a newsboy, then a clerk in a bookstore. He was the corresponding secretary of the Columbia Typographical Union and, later, was also its president.

McSweeney attended evening school, and earned the Typographical Union of Charleston Scholarship to attend Washington and Lee University in Lexington, Virginia. However, he was unable to complete his studies there because of lack of funds.

McSweeney served in the State militia, first as a staff officer holding the rank of major, and later, as a lieutenant colonel. He began publishing the *Guardian* in Ninety-six, South Carolina in 1877 and published the *Hampton County Guardian* in 1879.

McSweeney was a delegate to the Democratic National Convention in 1888, 1896, and 1900 and was chairman of the Hampton County Democratic Committee for ten years. He was elected to the South Carolina House of Representatives in 1894 and was elected lieutenant governor of South Carolina, 1897-1899.

After the death of Governor William H. Ellerbe on June 2, 1899, McSweeney became his successor, serving the remainder of Ellerbe's term. McSweeney was elected to gubernatorial office in

his own right in November 1900. During his administration, the Interstate and West Indian Exposition opened, which was held to promote Charleston's status as a major seaport. Also during his tenure, William D. Crum, a black, was appointed postmaster of Charleston. A controversy surrounded the appointment.

McSweeney left office in January 1903. He died on June 4, 1921 in Charleston, South Carolina.

HEYWARD, DUNCAN CLINCH (1864-1943), sixty-first governor of South Carolina (1903-1907), was born in Richland County, South Carolina on June 24, 1864, the son of Edward Barnwell and Catherine (Clinch) Heyward. His parents died when he was six years old. He attended Cheltenham Academy in Pennsylvania, then went on to Washington and Lee University in Virginia from 1882 to 1885. He was married the following year to Mary Elizabeth Campbell. They had four children.

Heyward served as captain in the cavalry based in Colleton County. In subsequent years, he worked in business and as a rice planter. He was president of Standard Warehouse Company; president of Columbia Savings Bank and Trust Company; and special agent of the Group Division of the Protective Life Insurance Company. He was elected Governor of South Carolina in 1902, running as a Democrat with no opposition. Developments during his administration included passage of the Brice Act, which enabled counties to vote out the liquor dispensary system if they desired. Heyward was vocal about the lack of gubernatorial power, declaring in 1905 that the "governor is practically powerless where the details of the enforcement of law are concerned." He was elected to a second term in 1904 in an unopposed election.

Since the constitution limited the governor to serve no more than two terms, Heyward left office in 1907. In 1913, he was appointed Collector of Federal Internal Revenue Taxes for South Carolina. He was the author of the book, *Seed of Madagascar* (1937). Heyward died on January 23, 1943 in Columbia.

ANSEL, MARTIN FREDERICK (1850-1945), sixty-second governor of South Carolina (1907-1911), was born in Charleston on December 12, 1850, the son of John and Frederika (Bowers) Ansel. He studied law under James H. Whitner and was admitted to the South Carolina Bar in 1870. He began a law office in Franklin, North Carolina and worked there for about four years. In 1876, he moved his practice to Greenville, South Carolina. He was married in 1878 to Ophelia Spreight, who lived until 1895. Three years after that, in 1898, he married Mrs. Addie (Hollingsworth) Harris. He was the father of three children.

Ansel was elected to the State House of Representatives and served from 1882-1888. He was solicitor of the Eighth Judicial District of South Carolina from 1888 to 1901. He ran for the Democratic gubernatorial nomination in 1902, but was defeated. Four years later, in 1906, he ran again and not only received the nomination, but also won in the general election, running unopposed. During his tenure in office, the state liquor dispensary system was abolished in favor of a statewide prohibition giving counties the option of retaining dispensaries on a local level. Also during his administration, state funding was provided for high schools, a Confederate Veterans Home was founded, as well as the State Health Office, the State Insurance Department, and the Audubon Society. Ansel was reelected to the governorship in 1908. He retired from office in 1911 and returned to practice law in Greenville, where he died on August 23, 1945.

BLEASE, COLEMAN LIVINGSTON (1868-1942), sixty-third governor of South Carolina (1911-1915), was born near Newberry, South Carolina on October 8, 1868, the son of Henry and Mary Ann (Livingston) Blease. He attended Newberry College, the University of South Carolina, and Georgetown University where he received his LL.B. degree in 1889. He was admitted to the South Carolina Bar that same year and went into private practice with his brother in Newberry. In 1890, he married Lillie Sumners.

Blease was a member of the South Carolina House of Representatives from 1890 to 1894 and again from 1899 to 1900. During that time, from 1891 to 1892, he was Speaker Pro Tempore of the House. He was a presidential elector in 1896 and 1900. From 1901 to 1902, he served as city attorney of Newberry. He was elected to the State Senate and served from 1904 to 1908, acting as President Pro Tempore from 1907 to 1908. In 1910, he was Mayor of Newberry. That same year, he ran for governor of South Carolina as a Democrat and won in an uncontested election. He was reelected in 1912.

Blease was at odds with the Legislature during much of his administration, and as a consequence many of his vetoes were overridden. Even so, a number of state institutions were established during this time. These included the State Tuberculosis Sanitarium, the University of South Carolina Press, and the Medical College of Charleston, which came under state funding. In response to complaints from the federal government about inefficiency in the South Carolina militia, Blease decided to dismiss the militia entirely. He resigned his office one week later on January 14, 1915, just five days before the end of his second term.

After leaving office Blease continued to participate in Democratic Party politics. He was a U.S. senator from South Carolina from 1925 to 1931. He was also a delegate to numerous state conventions; was a member of the State Executive Committee for eighteen years; was president of the 1926 State Convention; and served as a delegate to the Democratic National Convention of 1936. He was married to Mrs. Caroline Floyd Hoyt in 1937, his first wife having died in 1934. In 1941, he was elected to serve on the State Unemployment Commission. He died on January 19, 1942.

SMITH, CHARLES A. (1861-1916),
sixty-fourth (acting) governor of South Carolina (1915), was born in Hertford County, North Carolina on January 22, 1861, the son of Joseph and Eva Smith. He attended Wake Forest University and graduated in 1882. In 1884, he married Fannie Byrd. They had eight children.

Smith worked for many years in the mercantile business and was the owner of the Charles A. Smith Company in Timmonsville. He also worked for the Smith-Williams Company of Lake City; was president of Citizens Bank of Timmonsville; president of the Bank of Lynchburg; and president of the Peoples' Bank of Lamar. In addition he served as president of the Board of Trustees of Furman University, and trustee of Greenville Women's College. He was a member of the State House of Representatives in 1910, and from 1911 to 1915, served as South Carolina's Lieutenant Governor. On January 14, 1915, when Governor Blease resigned his office just five days before the end of his term, Smith became the new State Governor. He served out Blease's term, leaving office on January 19, 1915. The following year, on April 1, Smith died in Baltimore.

MANNING, RICHARD IRVINE, III (1859-1931),
sixty-fifth governor of South Carolina (1915-1919), was born on Holmesley Plantation in what is now Sumter County, South Carolina, on August 15, 1859, the son of Richard and Elizabeth (Sinkler) Manning. He received his education at Kenmore University High School in Amherst, Virginia and the University of Virginia. He was captain of the Red Shirts in 1876, and an adjutant and captain

in the Volunteer State Troops in 1878. In 1881, he married Lelia Bernard Meredith. They had six sons.

In the years that followed, Manning made a name for himself in business, banking, and cotton farming. He was president of the American Products Export and Import Corporation; president of the Bank of Maysville, South Carolina; president of the National Bank of Sumter, South Carolina; president of the Cotton Warehouse Company; president of the South Carolina Land and Settlement Association; director of Sumter Telephone Company; director of the Telephone Manufacturing Company; director of Palmetto Fire Insurance Company; director of Magneto Manufacturing Company; and chairman of the board of the Peoples' State Bank of South Carolina. In addition, he served as a trustee for Clemson College and the University of South Carolina.

Manning became interested in politics and attended every Democratic state convention from 1884. In 1892 he was elected to the South Carolina House of Representatives, and served until 1896. Two years later, he entered the State Senate where he remained until 1906, acting as President Pro Tempore in 1905. In 1914, he ran for governor as a Democrat and was unopposed in the general election. He was reelected in 1916. His administration saw the creation of the State Highway Department and the State Board of Charities and Corrections. With the coming of World War I, nearly 62,000 South Carolinians joined the armed forces, and a number of army camps were set up around the state. Manning left office in 1919 at the end of his second term and moved to Charleston. Later that year, he served on the U.S. Peace Committee. He died on September 11, 1931.

COOPER, ROBERT ARCHER (1874-1953),
sixty-sixth governor of South Carolina (1919-1922), was born in Laurens County, South Carolina on June 12, 1874, the son of Henry and Elizabeth (Jones) Cooper. He studied law at the Polytechnic Institute in San German, Puerto Rico, and was admitted to the South Carolina Bar in 1898. He started a law practice in Laurens, South Carolina and was magistrate in that town from 1899 to 1900. In 1899, he married Mamie Machen. She died in 1914, and three years later he married Dorcas Calmes. He was the father of two children.

Cooper was a member of the State House of Representatives from 1900 to 1904. In 1905, 1908 and 1912, he was elected solicitor for the Eighth Judicial District of South Carolina. Also during this time, he served as a trustee for Anderson College, and Furman University. He ran for governor in 1918 on the Democratic ticket, and won in an unopposed general election. He was reelected in 1920, again without opposition. Accomplishments during his terms included increases to teachers' salaries; imposition of a seven month school term and a compulsory school attendance law; funding for road construction and increased public health services; legislation which limited working hours in textile mills to fifty-five hours a week or ten hours a day; and stricter enforcement of tax laws.

Cooper resigned the governorship in 1922 to take a position with the Federal Farm Loan Board. He remained there until 1927. From 1929 to 1932, he served as assistant to the chairman of the Executive Committee of the Democratic National Committee. He was the U.S. District Judge for Puerto Rico from 1934 to 1947. Cooper died on August 7, 1953.

HARVEY, WILSON GODFREY (1866-1932),
sixty-seventh governor of South Carolina (1922-1923), was born in Charleston on September 8, 1866, the son of Wilson and Cornelia (Elbridge) Harvey. He attended Charleston High School until age sixteen, then went to work as a clerk for the Charleston *New Courier*.

Within five years, he had become manager of the *World and Budget* newspaper in Charleston. He was named state manager for Bradstreet Company (later Dun and Bradstreet, Inc.) in 1892. In 1894, he married Mary Franklin. They had three children.

Harvey continued his way up the ladders of business, helping to organize and becoming cashier for the Enterprise Bank of Charleston in 1894. Ten years later, he was president of the Enterprise Bank. In addition, he became interested in politics and in 1903 was elected to the Charleston Board of Aldermen. He served until 1911. In 1910, he was Mayor Pro Tempore of Charleston; from 1916 to 1920 he served as chairman of the Sanitary and Drainage Commission of Charleston County. He was president of the South Carolina Bankers' Association in 1911; president of the Charleston Chamber of Commerce from 1912 to 1914; and president of the Charleston Clearing House Association from 1913 to 1914. After his first wife died in 1911, he remarried Margaret Waring on June 24, 1914.

Harvey was elected Lieutenant Governor of South Carolina and served from 1921 to 1922. When Governor Cooper resigned in the latter year, Harvey succeeded him in office. As governor, he sought to establish higher standards within the state school system and promoted the construction of concrete highways. He served only eight months, to complete Governor Cooper's remaining term, and left office on January 16, 1923. In the years that followed, he worked in Greenville as an agent for the Carolina Life Insurance Company, and later in Columbia as state manager for that same company. In January 1932 he moved to Tampa, Florida, as the Florida state manager of the Carolina Life Insurance Company. He died there on October 7, 1932.

McLEOD, THOMAS GORDON (1868-1932), sixty-eighth governor of South Carolina (1923-1927), was born in Lynchburg, South Carolina on December 17, 1868, the son of William and Amanda (Rogers) McLeod. He attended Wofford College and the University of Virginia where he studied law. He was admitted to the South Carolina Bar in 1896. He then taught for two years. In 1902, he married Elizabeth Alford. They had one child.

In 1903, McLeod started a law practice in Bishopville. He also served as a trustee to Winthrop College, Emory University, and Columbia College. He was elected to the South Carolina House of Representatives and served from 1900 to 1902, and then in the Senate from 1902 to 1906. In 1904 and 1924, he was a delegate to the Democratic National Convention. He served as Lieutenant Governor of South Carolina from 1907 to 1911. He was State legal advisor for a time, and served on occasion as a special judge. In 1912, he was president of the Democratic State Convention. Running as a Democrat in an unopposed general election, McLeod won the governorship in 1922. He was reelected in 1924.

McLeod entered office at a time when South Carolina was in an agricultural depression. As governor, he worked for tax reform and called a tax convention in 1925, which formed a "Committee of Seventeen" to make recommendations to the Legislature on specific tax reforms. He also supported education, and worked to establish a more systematic state administration. During the last year of his second term the State Constitution was amended to allow a four year term for governors, but made them ineligible to succeed themselves in office.

McLeod left office in 1927 and went to Nashville, Tennessee as the district manager of the Life and Casualty Insurance Company. He later became president of the Bishopville Telephone Company, and director of the Bishopville National Bank. He died on December 11, 1932.

RICHARDS, JOHN GARDINER (1864-1941), sixty-ninth governor of South Carolina (1927-1931), was born in Liberty Hill, South Carolina on September 11, 1864, the son of Rev. John and Sophie (Edwards) Richards. He attended Bingham Military Institute and was a captain in the Liberty Hill Rifles for fourteen years. He was also member of the South Carolina Military Board for four years, and was a major in the South Carolina Militia, retiring as a lieutenant colonel. He married Elizabeth Coates Workman in 1888. They had eleven children.

Concurrent with his military career, Richards worked as a farmer and was active in railroad business. He was chairman of the Executive National Association of Railways, and president of the Southeastern Association of Railroad Commissioners. Richards served as magistrate from 1892 to 1900. In 1898 he was elected to the South Carolina House of Representatives. He remained there until 1910, serving for ten years on the Ways and Means Committee, part of that time as chairman. After leaving the House, he became South Carolina Railroad Commissioner. He held that post from 1910 to 1918, and from 1922 to 1926. He was also chairman of the board for the South Carolina Railroad Commission for four years. Richards ran for governor in 1910, 1914 and 1918, but was unsuccessful in each campaign. He was elected twice to the Democratic National Committee. During World War I, he served on the South Carolina Council of Defense. Later, he was South Carolina Tax Commissioner.

In 1926, Richards tried again for the Democratic gubernatorial nomination and was successful. He went on to win in the general election, running without opposition. He was the first governor in South Carolina elected to a four-year term, and his administration ended as the Great Depression took hold. Before the stock market crash however, new funding was voted for the construction of state highways. Since he was constitutionally ineligible to seek a second consecutive term, Richards left office in 1931. In the years that followed, he served as chairman of the South Carolina Natural Resources Commission. He died on October 9, 1941.

BLACKWOOD, IRBA CHARLES (1878-1936), seventieth governor of South Carolina (1931-1935), was born in Blackwood, South Carolina on November 21, 1878, the son of Charles and Louvenia (Burns) Blackwood. He attended Furman University, and Wofford College where he graduated in 1898. He studied law privately and in 1902 was admitted to the South Carolina Bar. He established a law practice in Spartanburg, meanwhile serving as a member of the South Carolina House of Representatives from 1902 to 1906. He was married to Margaret Hodges on October 4, 1915.

From 1914 to 1916, Blackwood was a U.S. Revenue Agent. Following that, from 1916 to 1930, he was a solicitor for the Seventh Judicial Circuit of South Carolina. He ran for the Democratic gubernatorial nomination in 1926, but was unsuccessful. Four years later, he won both the nomination and the general election. As governor, he worked for judicial reform, recommending changes to criminal court procedure and simplification of the system for selecting petty jurors. Also during his term, the South Carolina Public Service Authority was established; Prohibition was repealed and the State took on the task of regulating liquor. In 1934, more than half of South Carolina's 80,000 textile workers went on strike, and in Honea Path, the protest became violent and seven strikers were shot and killed by deputies.

After leaving office in 1935, Blackwood returned to his law practice in Spartanburg. He died in Spartanburg the following year, on February 12.

JOHNSTON, OLIN DEWITH TALMADGE (1896-1965), seventy-first and seventy-fifth governor of South Carolina (1935-1939 and 1943- 1945), was born near Honea Path, South Carolina on November 18, 1896, the son of Edward and Leila (Webb) Johnston. He served as a sergeant in the U.S. Army during World War I. On his return, he attended Wofford College (A.B.), and the University of South Carolina (M.A. and LL.B.) After graduation in 1924, he was admitted to the South Carolina Bar and he established a law practice in Spartanburg. In 1923, he married Gladys Atkinson. They had three children.

Johnston moved to Columbia and became a partner in the legal firm, Johnston and Williams. He was elected to the State House of Representatives and served from 1923 to 1924 and from 1927 to 1930. From 1934 to 1940 and again between 1944 and 1948, he was a member of the Democratic National Committee. He won the state governorship in 1934 in an unopposed general election. During his term, he ordered the National Guard to occupy the offices of the State Highway Department because of alleged violations, which proved to be unfounded. Also, during this time, the South Carolina Public Welfare Act and Alcoholic Beverage Control bill were both passed into law.

Since he was constitutionally ineligible to succeed himself in office, Johnston left the governorship in 1939. After a time had elapsed however, he ran again, and in 1942, was elected to a second term in office. His second administration was concerned with World War II and with keeping South Carolina on a wartime status. He resigned the governorship in 1945 to take a seat in the U.S. Senate, where he served for the next twenty years. He died on April 18, 1965.

MAYBANK, BURNET RHETT (1899-1954), seventy-second governor of South Carolina (1939-1941), was born in Charleston on March 7, 1899, the son of Joseph and Harriet (Rhett) Maybank. He attended Porter Military Academy and the College of Charleston. During World War I, he served in the South Carolina Naval Militia and the U.S. Naval Reserve. He married Elizabeth de Rossett in 1923. They had three children.

From 1920 to 1938, Maybank worked in the cotton export business. He was an alderman in Charleston from 1927 to 1931, and for a short time, in 1930, served as Mayor Pro Tempore for the city. Elected in his own right, he was Mayor of Charleston from 1931 to 1938. During that time, he also was a member of the South Carolina State Advisory Board of the Federal Administration of Public Works, and chairman of the South Carolina Public Service Authority. He ran as a Democrat for governor in 1938, and won in an uncontested election. During his term, construction began on the Santee-Cooper dams and power stations; President Roosevelt made Fort Jackson a permanent army post; and the palmetto was selected as the state tree. Maybank resigned his office in 1941 to take a seat in the U.S. Senate. His wife, Elizabeth died in 1947, and he remarried a year later to Mary Randolph Piezer. He was a member of the American Battle Monuments Commission from 1947 to 1954. Maybank continued to serve in the U.S. Senate up until the time of his death, on September 1, 1954.

HARLEY, JOSEPH EMILE (1880-1942), seventy-third governor of South Carolina (1941-1942), was born in Williston, South Carolina on September 14, 1880, the son of Lunsford and Mary (Hummel) Harley. He received his education at South Carolina Co-Educational Institute and the University of South Carolina. During the Spanish-American War, he was a sergeant in the First South Carolina Volunteers. He was later captain of the South Carolina National Guard, eventually rising to the rank of colonel and serving on the staff of Governor Thomas G. McLeod. He was married to Sarah Richardson and had three children.

For several years, Harley had a private law practice in Barnwell. In 1905, he became a member of the State House of Representatives. He served until 1906, and again from 1927 to 1930. In 1908, 1920, and 1938 he was a delegate to the Democratic National Convention. Meanwhile, from 1912 to 1922, he was Mayor of Barnwell. The South Carolina Supreme Court appointed him in 1924 as a special judge. In 1934, he became Lieutenant Governor of South Carolina. He remained at that post until November 1941 when Governor Maybank resigned to take a seat in the U.S. Senate. Harley succeeded to the governorship but served only four months. His short time in office was mainly concerned with putting the state on a wartime footing as the country entered World War II. He died in office on February 27, 1942.

JEFFRIES, RICHARD MANNING (1889-1964), seventy-fourth governor of South Carolina (1942-1943), was born in Union County (now Cherokee County), South Carolina on February 27, 1889, the son of John and Mary Jeffries. He studied law at the University of South Carolina and was admitted to the South Carolina Bar in 1912. Soon after, he started a private law practice in Walterboro. He was married to Annie Keith Savage in 1911.

Jeffries was Superintendent of Jasper County in 1912. He also served on the South Carolina Democratic Executive Committee that same year. From 1913 to 1927, he was the Master in Equity and Probate Judge for Colleton County. He was elected to the State Senate and was a member from 1926 to 1958, serving as President Pro Tempore of the Senate from 1941 to 1942. Always active in Democratic politics, he was a delegate to the Democratic State Convention for more than thirty years, and he attended the Democratic National Convention in 1924, 1928, 1932, 1936, 1940, 1944, 1956, and 1960.

In 1941, when Governor Maybank resigned his office, Lieutenant Governor Joseph Harley took over as governor. When he died after just four months in office, the governorship devolved upon Jeffries who was President Pro Tempore of the State Senate. He entered office on March 2, 1942 just as the state had begun to organize its World War II effort, which included major shifts in the economy, and legislation to allow South Carolina citizens serving in the military to vote by absentee ballot. In 1942, German submarines mined the harbor in Charleston. Jeffries left office in January 1943 when the newly elected, Olin Johnston, was inaugurated.

After leaving the governorship, Jeffries returned to the State House of Representatives. He continued to work for the war effort as chairman of the South Carolina War Fund from 1943 to 1946, and director of the National War Fund from 1944 to 1945. He was general manager of the South Carolina Public Service Authority from 1944 to 1964. In addition, he served on the South Carolina Tax Study Commission and the Democratic National Platform Committee. He died on April 20, 1964.

WILLIAMS, RANSOME JUDSON (1892-1970), seventy-sixth governor of South Carolina (1945-1947), was born in Cope, South Carolina on January 4, 1892, the son of Theophilus and Ida (Williams) Williams. He attended the Medical College of South Carolina. In 1916, he married Virginia Allen. They had two children.

Williams was president of the Delta Drug Company of Myrtle Beach, South Carolina, and later, part owner of a drug store in Mullens. He also worked as a manager for the Jefferson Standard Life Insurance Company in Florence. He began his political career with his election as Mayor of Mullens. From there he went on to become a member of the South Carolina House of Representatives. He was elected Lieutenant Governor and served from 1943 to 1945. In January of the latter year, when Governor Johnston resigned to take a seat in the U.S. Senate, Williams succeeded to the governorship. During his administration, the Forest Fire Protection Act was passed, as was legislation to control the standard weights of containers, to continue the poll tax, and to lower the voting age for registered Democrats. Other developments included establishment of a retirement system for state, county, and city employees, and the formation of a Department of Research, Planning and Development. Williams left office in 1947. He was a trustee of Coker College in Hartsville; chairman of the Board of Trustees of the Medical College of South Carolina; trustee of the University of South Carolina, Columbia; and trustee of the Citadel. He died on January 7, 1970.

THURMOND, JAMES STROM (1902-), seventy-seventh governor of South Carolina (1947-1951), was born in Edgefield, South Carolina on December 5, 1902, the son of John and Eleanor (Strom) Thurmond. He attended Clemson College, studied law through the South Carolina law course, and was admitted to the South Carolina Bar in 1930. He taught school in Edgefield from 1923 to 1929, and was the Superintendent of Education from 1930 to 1938. Also during that time, he served as city and county attorney for Edgefield. He was elected to the South Carolina Senate and served from 1933 to 1938. From 1938 to 1942 and again in 1946, he was a circuit judge. He was a delegate to the Democratic National Convention in 1932, 1936, 1948, 1952, 1956, and 1960.

During World War II, Thurmond served in the U.S. Army in Europe and the Pacific. He achieved the rank of lieutenant colonel and received numerous awards, including: the Purple Heart, Legion of Merit, Bronze Star with V, Bronze Arrowhead, Distinguished Unit Citation with five battle stars, Croix de Guerre from France, and the cross of the Order of the Crown of Belgium. Returning from service, he married Jean Crouce in November 1947. They had six children. In 1946, Thurmond was elected governor, running without opposition in the general election. During his term in office, the state constitution was amended to allow divorces in South Carolina. A suit was presented to federal court asking that school segregation be made unconstitutional, and in a separate court ruling, blacks were allowed to take part in Democratic Party primaries. Thurmond ran for president of the United States in 1948 on the States' Rights ticket, but was not elected. He was also unsuccessful in a bid for the U.S. Senate in 1950.

Thurmond left the governorship in 1951 and practiced law in Aiken, South Carolina for the next four years. Also during that time, he was president of the Aiken Federal Savings and Loan Association. In 1954, he won election to the U.S. Senate. He resigned the following year in April, but then decided to run again, and was reelected in November 1956. He has remained in the Senate since that time and has changed his affiliation to the Republican Party. He was a delegate to the Republican National Convention in 1968 and 1972. After the death of his first wife, Jean, he remarried in 1968 to Nancy Moore. Thurmond is the author of the book, *The Faith We Have Not Kept*.

BYRNES, JAMES FRANCIS (1879-1972), seventy-eighth governor of South Carolina (1951-1955), was born in Charleston, South Carolina on May 2, 1879, the son of James and Elizabeth (McSweeney) Byrnes. He attended school until age fourteen, when he was forced to quit due to family finances. Later however, he studied law and was admitted to the South Carolina Bar in 1903. He worked as a court reporter in the Second Circuit Court of South Carolina from 1900 to 1908. In 1906, he married Maude Busche.

Byrnes established a law practice in Aiken, South Carolina and from 1908 to 1910 was a solicitor for the Second Circuit Court. Also around this time, he became owner and editor of the Aiken *Review and Journal*. He was elected to the U.S. House of Representatives and served from 1911 to 1925. He made an unsuccessful bid for the U.S. Senate in 1924. In 1930, he was elected to the Senate and served until 1941 when he became a member of the U.S. Supreme Court. He remained on the court only until the following year. With the coming of World War II, he served as director of Economic Stabilization of the United States (1942-43) and director of the U.S. War Mobilization Board (1943-45.) He was with President Roosevelt at the Yalta Conference in 1945.

After the war, Byrnes returned to his law practice. He served as U.S. Secretary of State from 1945 to 1947, and was present with President Truman at the Potsdam Conference. In 1946, he was a senior delegate to the U.N. General Assembly. Four years later, he ran for governor of South Carolina as a Democrat in an unopposed election and won easily. He entered office in January 1951. During his term the U.S. Supreme Court ruled in the case of *Brown vs. Board of Education of Topeka*, *Kansas* that school segregation was unconstitutional. The South Carolina Legislature appropriated 75 million dollars to upgrade black schools to the level of white public schools, and instituted a three percent sales tax to provide the funds. Byrnes left office at the end of his term in January 1955. He died on April 4, 1972.

TIMMERMAN, GEORGE BELL (1912-1994), seventy-ninth governor of South Carolina (1955-1959), was born in Anderson, South Carolina on August 11, 1912, the son of George and Mary (Sullivan) Timmerman. He received his education at The Citadel and at the University of South Carolina where he graduated with an LL.B. degree in 1937. He was admitted to the South Carolina Bar that same year and began a law practice in Lexington, South Carolina. In 1936, he married Helen Miller DuPre.

Timmerman served in the U.S. Naval Reserve during World War II. He was the assistant chief trial attorney for the South Carolina Public Service Authority in 1941. From 1947 to 1955, he was Lieutenant Governor of the State. He was active in Democratic politics, and in 1954, running on the Democratic Party ticket, he won election as governor of South Carolina. He was governor during a time when the Civil Rights Movement began to be felt. The Interstate Commerce Commission came out against segregation on public transportation, the National Association for the Advancement of Colored People (NAACP) threatened to sue for desegregation, and the South Carolina bus segregation law was finally struck down. Timmerman left the governorship in 1959 at the end of his term. He subsequently was chairman of the South Carolina delegation to the Democratic National Convention of 1956, and in 1964, he served as a Democratic presidential elector.

Timmerman died on August 11, 1994.

HOLLINGS, ERNEST FREDERICK (1922-), eightieth governor of South Carolina (1959-1963), was born in Charleston on January 1, 1922, the son of Adolph and Wilhelmine (Meyer) Hollings. He attended The Citadel and the University of South Carolina, and was admitted to the South Carolina Bar in 1947. During World War II, he served in the U.S. Army, attaining the rank of captain. He was married in 1946 to Martha Patricia Salley. They had four children.

Hollings maintained a private law office in Charleston, beginning in 1947. He was a member of the South Carolina House of Representatives from 1948 to 1954, serving as Speaker Pro Tempore of the House from 1950 to 1954. In 1955, he was appointed to the Federal Commission on Organization of the Executive Branch. That same year, he became Lieutenant Governor of South Carolina, remaining at that post until 1959 when he became Governor of the State. He was elected as a Democrat, running without opposition in the general election. The Civil Rights Movement gained momentum during Governor Holling's administration. Anti-segregationists marched on the State Capitol, and blacks began to hold sit-ins in defiance of segregation rules.

As governor, Hollings was active on the Federal Advisory Commission on Intergovernmental Relations and the Regional Advisory Council on Nuclear Energy of the Southern Governors' Conference. He left office in 1963 and returned to his law practice for three years. In 1966, he became a U.S. Senator. He has remained in the Senate since that time. Hollings was married in 1971 to Rita Liddy.

RUSSELL, DONALD STUART (1906-1998), eighty-first governor of South Carolina (1963-1965), was born in Lafayette Springs, Mississippi on February 22, 1906, the son of Jesse and Lula (Russell) Russell. He attended the University of South Carolina and the University of Michigan in Ann Arbor, and was admitted to the South Carolina Bar in 1928. The following year, he married Virginia Utsey. They had four children.

Russell moved to Spartanburg, South Carolina and established a law practice there in 1930. During World War II, he was a member of the Price Adjustment Board for the U.S. War Department (1942). He was the assistant to the director of War Mobilization in 1943. In 1944 he served in the U.S. Army as a major in the Supreme Headquarters of the Allied Forces in Europe. The following year he was deputy director for the Office of War Mobilization Reconversion. He was the assistant to the U.S. Secretary of State from 1945 to 1947, and a member of the Committee on the Reorganization of the U.S. Foreign Service in 1954. From 1951 to 1957, he was president of the University of South Carolina.

Russell ran for governor of South Carolina in 1962, and won as an unopposed Democrat in the general election. Desegregation progressed during his term, and the first black students entered Clemson College and the University of South Carolina. When Senator Olin Johnston died in April 1965, Russell resigned the governorship to fill his seat in the U.S. Senate. He remained in the Senate until 1966. From 1967 to 1971, he was a U.S. District Judge. He was appointed a U.S. Circuit Court Judge in 1971.

Russell died on February 22, 1998.

McNAIR, ROBERT EVANDER (1923-), eighty-second governor of South Carolina (1965-1971), was born in Cades, South Carolina on December 14, 1923, the son of Daniel and Claudia (Crawford) McNair. During World War II, he served in the U.S. Naval Reserve. He graduated from the University of South Carolina in 1948 with an LL.B. degree and was admitted to the bar that same year. In 1944, he married Josephine Robinson. They had four children.

Following graduation, McNair moved to Allendale, South Carolina and began a private law practice there. He was also active in business, and served as president of Investors Heritage Life Insurance; director of the Southern Railway System, Georgia-Pacific Corporation; director of AIRCO Incorporated; and director of R.L. Ryan Company. He was elected to the South Carolina House of Representatives and served from 1951 to 1962. From 1962 to 1965, he was Lieutenant Governor of South Carolina. When Governor Russell resigned in April of the latter year, McNair took over as governor. In the 1966 election, he ran for the office on the Democratic ticket and won in an uncontested race.

Civil Rights continued to be a major issue during this time. As governor, McNair saw graduation of the first black student from Clemson College and the election of four blacks to the State Legislature. But as the struggle for rights continued, three black students were killed during a riot at South Carolina College in Orangeburg, and actions were begun in the courts to force compliance with desegregation laws. In other developments, approval was given to begin a hydroelectric project on the Cooper River. McNair served as chairman of the Southern Regional Educational Board; vice-chairman of the Committee of Southern Governors' Conference; and vice-chairman of the Democratic National Committee. He left the governorship in January 1971 and became a senior partner in the law firm of McNair, Konduros and Corley.

WEST, JOHN CARL (1922-), eighty-third governor of South Carolina (1971-1975), was born in Camden, South Carolina on August 27, 1922, the son of Sheldon and Mattie (Ratterree) West. He attended The Citadel, where he received his A.B. degree in 1942, and the University of South Carolina where he graduated magna cum laude with an LL.B. degree in 1948. He was admitted to the South Carolina Bar in the latter year. During World War II, he served in the U.S. Army, attaining the rank of major. He married Lois Rhome in 1942. They have three children.

From 1946 to 1948, West worked as a part-time instructor of political science at the University of South Carolina. He also began a law practice in Camden, later forming the firm of West, Holland and Furman, with which he remained from 1948 to 1970. In addition, he served on the South Carolina Highway Commission from 1948 to 1952, and in the South Carolina Senate from 1954 to 1966. In 1966, he became Lieutenant Governor. He served until 1970 when he was elected Governor of South Carolina, running on the Democratic ticket. During his administration, some of the racial unrest of the previous years began to diminish. At the University of South Carolina, a black was elected student president for the first time. The Methodist Church, which had segregated congregations, united the black and white services. Other developments included prohibition of the sale of rare and endangered animal species and the State ratification of the Twenty-sixth amendment to the U.S. Constitution. At the end of his term, in 1975 West returned to practice law with the firm of West, Cooper, Bowen and Quinn.

EDWARDS, JAMES BURROWS (1927-), eighty-fourth governor of South Carolina (1975-1979), was born in Hawthorne, Florida on June 24, 1927, the son of O. Morton and Bertie (Hieronymus) Edwards. He attended the College of Charleston, the University of Louisville and the University of Pennsylvania where he studied dentistry. He was a resident at Henry Ford Hospital in Detroit from 1958 to 1960. From 1944 to 1947, he was in the U.S. Maritime Service, and from 1955 to 1957, he served in the U.S. Naval Reserve. He was married in 1951 to Ann Norris Darlington. They have two children.

Edwards moved to Charleston and began a dental practice in 1960. He was a consultant for the U.S. Public Health Service in 1964. In 1966, he became vice-president of the East Cooper Private School Corporation in Mount Pleasant, South Carolina. Two years later, he was named clinical associate in oral surgery at the Medical University of South Carolina.

Edwards was also active in politics during this time. From 1964 to 1969, he was chairman of the South Carolina Republican Committee in Charleston County. He was a delegate to the Republican National Convention in 1968; a member of the Steering Committee of the Charleston County Republican Committee, 1969 to 1972; and a member of the Steering Committee of the

South Carolina Republican Committee, 1969 to 1970. He ran for the U.S. House of Representatives in 1971, but was unsuccessful. In 1972, however, he was elected to the State Senate. Two years later he ran for governor and won, becoming the first Republican elected in South Carolina in almost a century. His victory was attributed in part to poor organization and infighting within the Democratic Party.

Edwards entered office on January 21, 1975. During his administration, new oil sites were discovered offshore, and the U.S. Marine base at Parris Island was investigated. Also, the Legislature passed a bill requiring malpractice insurance for doctors. A proponent of nuclear energy, Edwards established the South Carolina Energy Research Institute to study the energy problem, and he urged the reopening of the nuclear reprocessing plant in Barnwell, which had been closed as part of President Carter's nuclear nonproliferation policy. He also alienated many of the State's blacks when he ran a campaign to cut down on allegedly wasteful practices within the Welfare Department. Ineligible constitutionally to seek a second term, Edwards returned to his dental practice in 1979. In 1981, President Reagan named him Secretary of the Department of Energy. He remained at that post until 1982, when he became president of the Medical University of South Carolina.

RILEY, RICHARD WILSON (1933-), eighty-fifth governor of South Carolina (1979-1987), was born in Greenville, South Carolina on January 2, 1933, the son of Edward and Martha (Dixon) Riley. He attended Furman University and received his A.B. degree in 1954. From 1954 to 1956, he served in the U.S. Navy as an operations officer on board a minesweep control ship. After service, he returned to school and studied law at the University of South Carolina. He was married in 1957 to Ann Yarborough. They have four children.

Riley became legal counsel for the U.S. Senate's Judiciary Subcommittee in 1959. In 1963, he was elected to the South Carolina House of Representatives. He became a member of the State Senate in 1967, resigning in 1975 to manage Jimmy Carter's presidential campaign in South Carolina. In 1978, he ran for governor on the Democratic ticket and won over Republican Edward Young. He entered office in January 1979. As governor, Riley supported environmental issues, refusing, to allow the Three Mile Island nuclear power plant to dump radioactive waste from their accident in South Carolina. Instead he encouraged a federal solution to the problem, and in 1980, President Carter appointed him to the Nuclear Waste Disposal Council to study the question. Also during his term, the State Constitution was amended to allow governors to run for consecutive terms. Riley therefore ran and was reelected to a second term. During his second administration, he continued the environmental work begun previously. He left office in January 1987.

CAMPBELL, CARROLL A., JR. (1940-), eighty-sixth governor of South Carolina (1987-1994), was born in Greenville, South Carolina on July 24, 1940, the son of Carroll and Anne (Williams) Campbell. He was educated in the Greenville public schools and graduated from McCallie School. He was unable to attend college full-time for financial reasons. Instead, he went to work and studied when he could. At age nineteen he was working in the real estate business when he and a partner established Handy Park Company, a chain of parking facilities. In 1967, he helped found Rex Enterprises, which developed a chain of Burger King Restaurants. He married Iris Rhodes. They have two sons.

Campbell became interested in Republican politics about 1960 and for many years managed campaigns, including the cam-

paign that elected the first Republican mayor of Greenville. Campaigning for himself in 1970, he was elected to the South Carolina House of Representatives where he remained until 1974, serving during that time as Assistant Minority Leader. He ran for lieutenant governor in 1974, but lost in a close race. In 1975, he was executive assistant to Governor Edwards, and in 1976, he won election to the South Carolina Senate. Two years later, he was elected to the U.S. Congress, where he served for eight years. While in Congress, he continued his formal education and earned his M.A. in political science. He was the South Carolina campaign chairman for Ronald Reagan's presidential race in 1980 and 1984.

In 1986, Campbell ran for governor of South Carolina and won, becoming only the second Republican elected to that office within the century. Campbell became prominent in State politics for his position on fiscal responsibility and as a supporter of rights for the handicapped. He was reelected to a second term in 1990.

BEASLEY, DAVID M. (1957-), eighty-seventh Governor of South Carolina (1995-1999) was born in Lamar, South Carolina on February 26, 1957. After graduating from Lamar High School in 1975, he went on to Capitol Page School in Washington D.C. the same year. He studied at Clemson University in 1976-78, and at the International Institute of Human Rights in Strasburg, France and the European Summer Program of the Simon Greenleaf School of Law. In 1983, he earned his law degree at the University of South Carolina School of Law.

Beasley served in the State House from 1979-1991, and was Speaker Pro Tempore in 1991-1992. He was Chairman of the South Carolina Mining Council in 1985-1986; Vice Chairman of the Joint Legislative Committee on Children, and Chairman of the Joint Legislative Committee on Education in 1987; Majority Leader in 1987-1988; Chairman of House Education and Public Works Committee in 1989-1990; member of the Board of Trustees at University of South Carolina in 1990-1991, and at the Marion College in 1988- 1991. He received a Doctorate of Law from the University of South Carolina and the Citadel in May 1995.

Beasley was elected Governor of South Carolina on November 8, 1994. After being defeated in a reelection bid in 1998, he stepped down from the executive office in January 1999 and accepted a five-month fellowship at Harvard University's John F. Kennedy School of Government to teach and participate in Harvard Institute of Politics activities. He is married to the former Mary Wood Payne and is the father of four children.

HODGES, JIM (1956-), eighty-eighth Governor of South Carolina (1999-), was born on November 19, 1956 in Lancaster, South Carolina. After attending Davidson College, he graduated from the University of South Carolina with a bachelor's degree in Business Administration in 1979. He attended the University of South Carolina School of Law and received his law degree in 1982.

Hodges represented Lancaster County in the State legislature for eleven years, and in 1993 was named Legislator of the Year by the South Carolina Chamber of Commerce. From 1992 to 1994, he served as chair of the State House Judiciary Committee, and was elected the Democratic leader in 1994.

During his tenure in the State House, Hodges also served as general counsel to the Springs Company, a business with interests in financial services, real estate, railroads, insurance, machine tools, and other enterprises. He also served on the Board of the Springs Company as well as several related businesses. In 1996, he was honored by the National Federation of Independent Business as a "Guardian of Small Business."

In 1994, Hodges was awarded the Complete Lawyer Silver Medallion by the University of South Carolina School of Law. He was elected to the executive office in South Carolina in the November 1998 election, and began serving his term as Governor in January 1999. Hodges is married and has two children.

DICTIONARY OF PLACES

Population figures and demographic information are official U.S. Census Bureau finals for 1990. When two figures are shown, separated by a slash, the first figure is the 1990 and the second is the U.S. Census Bureau 1999 estimate—the most recent available. Year 2000 census supplements will be available in the Fall of 2001.

ABBEVILLE, City; Abbeville County Seat; Pop. 5,863 / 5,762; Zip Code 29620; Elev. 597; Lat. 34-10-42 N, Long. 082-22-39.

AIKEN, City; Aiken County Seat; Pop. 14,978 / 23,849; Zip Code 298+; Lat. 33-33-56 N, Long. 081-44-01 W.

ALLENDALE, Town; Allendale County Seat; Pop. 4,400 / 4,047; Zip Code 29810; Elev. 191; Lat. 33-00-22 N, Long. 081-18-12 W.

ANDERSON, City; Anderson County Seat; Pop. 27,313 / 26,166; Zip Code 29621; Elev. 771; Lat. 34-30-42 N, Long. 082-38-58 W.

ANDREWS, Town; Georgetown & Williamsburg Counties; Pop. 3,129 / 3,014; Zip Code 29510; Elev. 37; Lat. 33-27-12 N, Long. 079-34-42 W.

ARCADIA LAKES, Town; Richland County; Pop. 611 / 879; Zip Code 29320; Lat. 34-57-48 N, Long. 081-59-15 W; Arcadia is an old English name for the ideal garden-like environment. The town's beautiful surroundings suggested the name.

AYNOR, Town; Horry County; Pop. 643 / 462; Zip Code 29511; Elev. 104; Lat. 33-59-55 N, Long. 079-11-57 W; Named after an early settler.

BAMBERG, Town; Bamberg County Seat; Pop. 3,672 / 3,573; Zip Code 29003; Elev. 168; The town, as well as the county, are named in honor of the prominent Bamberg family.

BARNWELL, City; Barnwell County Seat; Pop. 5,572 / 5,573; Zip Code 29812; Lat. 33-14-41 N, Long. 081-21-42 W; The town's name honors Revolutionary War hero General John Barnwell.

BATESRURG, Town; Lexington and Saluda Counties; Pop. 4,023 / 6,116; Zip Code 29006; Elev. 649; Named after Captain Tom Bates, a Civil War captain and prominent citizen.

BEAUFORT, City; Beaufort County Seat; Pop. 8,634 / 10,193; Zip Code 29902; Elev. 11; Founded in 1710 and named in honor of the Duke of Beaufort.

BELTON, City; Anderson County; Pop. 5,312 / 4,208; Zip Code 29627; Elev. 885; Lat. 34-31-24 N, Long. 082-29-36 W; Judge John Belton was a lawyer, railroad president, and historian. The town is named in his honor.

BENNETSVILLE, City; Marlboro County Seat; Pop. 8,774 / 9,765; Zip Code 29512; Lat. 34-36-51 N, Long. 079-41-28 W; The city's name honors Thomas Bennet, governor of South Carolina in 1820.

BETHUNE, Town; Kershaw County; Pop. 481 / 376; Zip Code 29009; Elev. 283; Named in 1899 for a prominent citizen.

BISHOPVILLE, Town; Lee County Seat; Pop. 3,429 / 3,574; Zip Code 29010; Elev. 226; The town is named after Dr. Jacob Bishop, who owned land and ran a store in the area.

BLACKSBURG, Town; Cherokee County; Pop. 1,873 / 2,203; Zip Code 29702; Elev. 768; Originally Stark's Folly, the town was later renamed to honor the Black family, who were well-to-do landowners.

BLACKVILLE, Town; Barnwell County; Pop. 2,840 / 2,609; Zip Code 29817; Let. 33-21-03 N, Long. 081-16-04 W; Railroad developer Alexander Black helped establish the South Carolina railroad. The town is named in his honor.

BLENHEIM, Town; Marlboro County; Pop. 202 / 190; Zip Code 29516; Elev. 120; Lat. 34-30-36 N, Long. 079-39-08 W; The town is named for the famous Blenheim Castle in England.

BLUFFTON, Town; Beaufort County; Pop. 541 / 1,048; Zip Code 29910; Elev. 25; Lat. 32-14-19 N, Long. 080-51-50 W; Descriptively named for its location on the May River.

BLYTHEWOOD, Town; Richland County; Pop. 92 / 250; Zip Code 29016; Elev. 504; Named for the nearby Blythewood Academy following the Civil War.

BONNEAU, Town; Berkeley County; Pop. 401 / 378; Zip Code 29431; Elev. 62; Lat. 33-18-26 N, Long. 079-56-20 W; The town is named for the Bonneau family, who were Huguenot pioneers.

BOWMAN, Town; Orangeburg County; Pop. 1,137 / 1,265; Zip Code 29018; Elev. 39; The town's name honors the Bowman family, who were large landowners.

BRANCHVILLE, Town; Orangeburg County; Pop. 1,769 / 1,262; Zip Code 29432; Elev. 125; Lat. 33-15-10 N, Long. 080-46-56 W; Descriptively named for a branch of the South Carolina railway.

BRUNSON, Town; Hampton County; Pop. 590 / 587; Zip Code 29911; Elev. 138; Let. 32-55-30 N, Long. 081-11-21 W; Named for an early settler.

BURNETTOWN, Town; Aiken County; Pop. 359 / 2,670; Burnettown's name remembers an early settler.

CALHOUN FALLS, Town; Abbeville County; Pop. 2,491 / 2,345; Zip Code 29828; Lat. 34-05-27 N, Long. 082-35-52 W; Originally Terryville, the town was renamed to honor Colonel J.E. Calhoun.

CAMDEN, City; Kershaw County Seat; Pop. 7,462 / 6,973; Zip Code 29020; Settled in 1733 and named in honor of Lord Camden, who defended the colonies in Parliament.

CAMERON, Town; Calhoun County; Pop. 536 / 426; Zip Code 29030; Lat. 33-33-33 N, Long. 080-42-41 W; Cameron is a Scotch clan name bestowed by early settlers.

CAMPOBELLO, Town; Spartanburg County; Pop. 472 / 504; Zip Code 29322; Elev. 848; Lat. 35-06-57 N, Long. 082-08-44 W; Incorporated in 1881 and named Campa Bella, or "beautiful fields."

CARLISLE, Town; Union County; Pop. 503 / 490; Zip Code 29031; Lat. 34-35-31 N, Long. 081-27-58 W; Originally Fish Dam, the name was later changed to honor Methodist minister, Coleman Carlisle.

CAYCE, City; Lexington County; Pop. 11,701 / 12,641; Zip Code 29033; Lat. 33-58-02 N, Long. 081-04-31 W; The town's name remembers John Cayce, whose house figured in local Revolutionary War history.

CENTRAL, Town; Pickens County; Pop. 1,914 / 2,514; Zip Code 29630; Elev. 910; Lat. 34-43-23 N, Long. 082-46-45 W; Descriptively named for its location between Atlanta and Charlotte.

CHAPIN, Town; Lexington County; Pop. 311 / 421; Zip Code 29036; Lat. 34-09-55 N, Long. 081-21-08 W; Named in honor of early settler Tom Chapin.

CHARLESTON, City; Charleston County Seat; Pop. 69,510 / 89,063; Zip Code 29401; Elev. 118; Lat. 32-46-30 N, Long. 079-56-23 W; Settled in 1670 and named in honor of King Charles II.

CHERAW, Town; Chesterfield County; Pop. 5,654 / 5,742; Zip Code 29520; Elev. 157; Lat. 34-41-51 N, Long. 079-53-18 W; The town was settled in 1752 and named after the local Cheraw Indians.

CHESNEE, City; Spartanburg County; Pop. 1,069 / 1,364; Zip Code 29323; Elev. 913; Lat. 35-08-52 N, Long. 081-51-45 W; The Chesnee family settled in the area in the 1750s and held large land grants. The town is named after them.

CHESTER, City; Chester County Seat; Pop. 6,200 / 7,176; Zip Code 29706; Elev. 549; Lat. 34-42-32 N, Long. 081-12-52 W; Settlers from Chester, Pennsylvania came to the area in 1785. They named their new home after the old.

CHESTERFIELD, Town; Chesterfield County Seat; Pop. 1,432 / 1,335; Zip Code 29709; Lat. 34-44-11 N, Long. 080-05-08 W; Settled in the late 1700s and named in honor of the Earl of Chesterfield.

CLEMSON, City; Anderson & Pickens Counties; Pop. 8,118 / 12,529; Zip Code 29631; Lat. 34-40-58 N, Long. 082-48-06 W; The town is named after Clemson College, that name honoring its founder Thomas Clemson.

CLINTON, City; Laurens County; Pop. 8,596 / 9,622; Zip Code 29325; Elev. 676; Lat. 34-28-15 N, Long. 081-52-43 W; Founded in 1850 and named for lawyer Colonel Henry Clinton Young.

CLIO, Town; Marlboro County; Pop. 1,031 / 860; Zip Code 29525; Lat. 34-35-08 N, Long. 079-32-29 W; Originally Ivy's Cross Roads, the name was changed to a coined word created by placing together initials of circulars signed by English writer Addison in the Spectator: Chelsea, London, Islington, and Office.

CLOVER, Town; York County; Pop. 3,451 / 3,665; Zip Code 29710; Elev. 814; Lat. 35-06-39 N, Long. 081-13-40 W; Early settlers found white clover growing abundantly in the area. They named the town after this clover.

COLUMBIA, City; Richland County Seat; Pop. 99,296 / 111,821; Zip Code 292+; Lat. 34-00-36 N, Long. 081-00-08 w; Founded in 1786 and given the patriotic name for America.

CONWAY, City; Horry County Seat; Pop. 10,240 / 10,152; Zip Code 29526; Lat. 33-50-42 N, Long. 079-03-26 W; Settled as Kingston, but renamed in 1801 in honor of Revolutionary War hero, General Robert Conway.

COPE, Town; Orangeburg County; Pop. 167 / 130; Zip Code 29038; Lat. 33-22-48 N, Long. 081-00-24 W; Named for an early settler.

CORDOVA, Town; Orangeburg County; Pop. 202 / 127; Zip Code 29039; Elev. 252; Lat. 33-26-14 N, Long. 080-55-01 W; Originally Smoaks, the name was later changed to the better sounding Cordova by Atlantic Coast Railroad Company.

COTTAGEVILLE, Town; Colleton County; Pop. 371 / 619; Zip Code 29435; Lat. 32-58-26 N, Long. 080-29-30 W; The widow of Methodist minister, Mrs. H.H. Durant, needed a home, which the community built. It was subsequently named for that "cottage."

COWARD, Town; Florence County; Pop. 428 / 669; Zip Code 29530; Lat. 33-58-20 N, Long. 079-44-55 W; Named for an early settler.

COWPENS, Town; Spartanburg County; Pop. 2,023 / 2,254; Zip Code 29330; Lat. 35-01-20 N, Long. 081-48-14 W; Cattle were raised in the area prior to the Revolutionary War. The name was later adopted.

CROSS HILL, Town; Laurens County; Pop. 604 / 545; Zip Code 29332; Elev. 587; Lat. 34-18-16 N, Long. 081-59-00 W; Descriptively named by its settlers.

DARLINGTON, City; Darlington County Seat; Pop. 7,989 / 7,572; Zip Code 295+; Lat. 34-18-24 N, Long. 079-52-32 W; Founded in 1798 and either named after Darlington, England, or Colonel Darlington of the Revolutionary War.

DENMARK, City; Bamberg County; Pop. 4,434 / 3,709; Zip Code 29042; Elev. 244; Lat. 33-19-19 N, Long. 081-08-30 W; Originally Graham's Turnout, it was renamed to honor the Denmark family, who promoted the railroad.

DILLON, City; Dillon County Seat; Pop. 7,042 / 6,971; Zip Code 29536; Elev. 113; Lat. 34-25-05 N, Long. 079-22-14 W; Named in honor of prominent Irish settler, J.W. Dillion, who helped build the railroad in the county.

DONALDS, Town; Abbeville County; Pop. 1,366 / 334; Zip Code 29638; Elev. 762; Lat. 34-22-41 N, Long. 082-20-42 W; Named for an early settler.

DUE WEST, Town; Abbeville County; Pop. 1,366 / 1,197; Zip Code 29639; Lat. 34-19-57 N, Long. 082-23-16 W; Originally called Duett's Corner, the present name is a corruption.

DUNCAN, Town; Spartanburg County; Pop, 1,259 / 2,583; Zip Code 29334; Lat. 34-56-11 N, Long. 082-08-11 W; Founded as Vernon, but renamed in 1876 as Duncan, after a local settler.

EASLEY, City; Pickens County; Pop 14,264 / 17,998; Zip Code 29640; Elev. 1091; Lat. 34-50-12 N, Long. 082-37-12 W; Easley is named after prominent railroad attorney, William K. Easley.

EASTOVER, Town; Richland County; Pop. 899 / 1,051; Zip Code 29044; Elev. 190; Lat. 33-52-44 N, Long. 080-41-22 W; Descriptively named by its early settlers.

EDGEFIELD, Town; Edgefield County Seat; Pop, 2,713 / 2,809; Zip Code 29824; Lat. 33-47-15 N, Long. 081-55-49 W; Founded in 1798 and descriptively named as the "edge" of South Carolina at that time.

EDISTO BEACH, Town; Colleton County; Pop. 193 / 378; The town's name recalls early Indians, the Adusta, also the name of their Chief.

EHRHARDT, Town; Bamberg County; Pop. 353 / 546; Zip Code 29081; Elev. 146; Lat. 33-05-49 N, Long. 081-00-44 W; Named for an early settler.

ELGIN, Town; Kershaw County; Pop. 595 / 718; Zip Code 29045; Elev. 420; Lat. 34-10-22 N, Long. 080-47-43 W; Once called St. Luke's, the railroad changed the name in 1895.

FAIRFAX, Town; Allendale & Hampton Counties; Pop. 2,154 / 2,411; Zip Code 29827; Elev. 136; Lat. 32-57-09 N, Long. 081-13-58 W; Settled in 1872 and named after historic Lord Fairfax of Virginia.

FLORENCE, City; Florence County Seat; Pap. 30,062 / 30,053; Zip Code 29501; Elev. 149, Lat. 34-12-18 N, Long. 079-45-05 W; Settled in 1888 and named in honor of a railroad president's daughter, Miss Florence Harllee.

FOLLY BEACH, City; Charleston County; Pop. 1,478 / 1,708; Zip Code 29439; Lat. 32-39-23 N, Long. 079-56-09 W; Named for particular incidents in the town's history.

FOREST ACRES, City; Richland County; Pop, 6,033 / 9,562; Descriptively named for the once abundant forests.

FORT LAWN, Town; Chester County; Pop. 471 / 833; Zip Code 29714; Elev. 556; Lat. 34-41-48 N, Long. 080-53-53 W; The town is named after an early fort.

FORT MILL, Town; York County; Pop. 4,162 / 6,333; Zip Code 29715; Elev. 668; Lat. 35-00-32 N, Long. 080-56-35 W; A fort for the Catawba Indians was founded in 1796 near a mill. The name followed from this fact.

FOUNTAIN INN, City; Greenville & Laurens Counties; Pop. 4,226 / 5,613; Zip Code 29644; Elev. 872; Lat. 34-41-18 N, Long. 082-11-23 W; An overnight stop during stagecoach days, the spot was named for a fountain near the station.

FURMAN, Town; Hampton County; Pop. 13,453 / 276; Zip Code 29921; Elev. 112; Lat. 32-41-01 N, Long. 081-11-27 W; The town was established in 1901 and was named for a black woman, Mum Lizzie Furman.

GAFFNEY, City; Cherokee County Seat; Pop. 13,453 / 13,665; Zip Code 29340; Elev. 769; Lat. 35-04-25 N, Long. 081-38-17 W; Captain Michael Gaffney settled in the area in 1804 and started the town. It is named after him.

GASTON, Town; Lexington County; Pop. 960 / 1,263; Zip Code 29053; Lat. 33-49-08 N, Long. 081-05-19 W; Named for an early settler.

GEORGETOWN, City; Georgetown County Seat; Pop. 10,144 / 9,201; Zip Code 294+; Elev. 18; Lat. 33-22-06 N, Long. 079-17-24 W; Founded in the 1760s and named in honor of King George II.

GIFFORD, Town; Hampton County; Pop. 385 / 332; Zip Code 29923; Elev. 139; Lat. 32-51-33 N, Long. 081-14-10 W; Gifford is named after an early settler.

GILBERT, Town; Lexington County; Pop. 211 / 441; Zip Code 29054; Elev. 529; Lat. 33-55-25 N, Long. 081-23-28 W; Named after a prominent early settler.

GOOSE CREEK, City; Berkeley County; Pop. 17,811 / 28,818; Zip Code 29445; Lat. 32-59-430 N, Long. 080-02-32 W; Descriptively named by wealthy planters for the winding creek which reminded them of a goose's neck.

GRAY COURT, Town; Laurens County; Pop. 988 / 991; Zip Code 29645; Lat. 34-36-39 N, Long. 082-06-54 W; Originally Dorran's, the name was later changed to honor the Grey family, prominent plantation owners.

GREAT FALLS, Town; Chester County; Pop. 2,601 / 2,238; Zip Code 29055; Elev. 467; Lat. 34-34-25 N, Long. 080-54-04 W; Descriptively named for its location on the falls of the Catawba River.

GREELEYVILLE, Town; Williamsburg County; Pop. 593 / 443; Zip Code 29056; Elev. 79; Lat. 33-34-55 N, Long. 079-59-25 W; Legend has it that the town is named for famous newspaperman, Horace Greeley.

GREENVILLE, City; Greenville County Seat; Pop. 58,242 / 56,873; Zip Code 29601; Lat. 34-50-56 N, Long. 082-24-08 W; Settled in the 1780s and named in honor of Revolutionary War hero, General Nathaniel Greene.

GREENWOOD, City; Greenwood County Seat; Pop. 21,613 / 19,278; Zip Code 29646; Elev. 665; Lat. 34-11-34 N, Long. 082-09-02 W; Originally Woodville, the name was changed in 1850 to "Greenwood," after the nearby home of Judge John McGehee.

GRIER, City; Greenville and Spartanburg Counties; Pop. 10,525 / 15,222; Zip Code 29651; Elev. 1016; Lat. 34-56-21 N, Long. 082-13-01 W; Incorporated in 1875 and named after a local family.

HAMPTON, Town; Hampton County Seat; Pop. 3,143 / 3,189; Zip Code 29913; Elev. 95; Lat. 32-55-04 N, Long. 081-04-45 W; The town is named in honor of Governor Wade Hampton, who was in office from 1876 to 1879.

HARDEEVILLE, Town; Jasper County; Pop. 1,250 / 1,538; Zip Code 29927; Elev. 20; Lat. 32-16-43 N, Long. 081-04-22 W; Hardeeville is named for an early settler.

HARLEYVILLE, Town; Dorchester County; Pop. 606 / 653; Zip Code 29448; Elev. 92; Lat. 33-12-52 N, Long. 080-26-56 W; Named for an early settler.

HARTSVILLE, City; Darlington County; Pop. 7,631 / 8,535; Zip Code 29550; Lat. 34-22-57 N, Long. 080-04-31 W; Incorporated in 1891 and named after the Hart family.

HEATH SPRINGS, Town; Lancaster County; Pop. 979 / 941; Zip Code 29058; Elev. 687; Lat. 34-35-49 N, Long. 080-40-10 W; Descriptively named after nearby Heath's Spring, a mineral spring.

HEMINGWAY, Town; Williamsburg County; Pop. 853 / 743; Zip Code 29554; Elev. 53; Lat. 33-44-28 N, Long. 079-28-42 W; Once called Lamberts, it was renamed in 1908 for the Hemingway family, who were prominent English planters.

HICKORY GROVE, Town; York County; Pop. 344 / 335; Zip Code 29717; Elev. 485; Lat. 34-58-45 N, Long. 081-24-53 W; Descriptively named for the many hickory groves in the area.

HODGES, Town; Greenwood County; Pop. 154 / 128; Zip Code 296+; Lat. 34-17-24 N, Long. 082-14-48 W; Named after an early pioneer family.

HOLLY HILL, Town; Orangeburg County; Pop. 1,785 / 1,472; Zip Code 29059; Elev. 108; Lat. 33-19-33 N, Long. 080-24-37 W; Descriptively named for a nearby hill covered with holly.

HOLLYWOOD, Town; Charleston County; Pop. 729; Zip Code 29449; Lat. 32-44-02 N, Long. 080-14-24 W; Originally Cross Roads, it was renamed to reflect the many holly trees in the area.

HONEA PATH, Town; Abbeville & Anderson Counties; Pop. 4,114 / 4,326; Zip Code 296+; Lat. 34-29-48 N, Long. 082-17-07 W; An Indian name meaning "great path."

INMAN, City; Spartanburg County; Pop. 1,554 / 1,966; Zip Code 29349; Elev. 986; Lat. 35-02-43 N, Long. 082-05-28 W; The town's name honors Southern Railway official, Samuel M. Inman.

IRMO, Town; Lexington and Richland Counties; Pop. 3,957 / 10,882; Zip Code 29063; Lat. 34-05-21 N, Long. 081-11-12 W; Named for an early settler.

ISLE OF PALMS, City; Charleston County; Pop. 3,421 / 4,514; Zip Code 29451; Lat. 32-47-33 N, Long. 079-46-34 W; Descriptively named for the many palms in the area.

IVA, Town; Anderson County; Pop. 1,369 / 1,208; Zip Code 29655; Lat. 34-18-12 N, Long. 082-39-51 W; The town's name honors Iva Cook, daughter of a pioneer family.

JACKSON, Town; Aiken County; Pop. 1,771 / 1,911; Zip Code 29831; Elev. 204; Lat. 33-19-53 N, Long. 081-47-32 W; Named after President Andrew Jackson.

JAMESTOWN, Town; Berkeley County; Pop. 193 / 91; Zip Code 29453; Elev. 40; Lat. 33-17-04 N, Long. 079-41-45 W; The town's name remembers an early Huguenot settlement on the Santee River, named for King James of England.

JOHNSONVILLE, City; Florence County; Pop. 1,421; Zip Code 29555; Elev. 94; Lat. 33-48-58 N, Long. 079-27-03 W; Named for an early settler.

JOHNSTON, Town; Edgefield County; Pop. 2,624 / 2,609; Zip Code 29832; Elev. 661; Lat. 33-49-46 N, Long. 081-42-03 W; Johnston's name honors W.P. Johnston, president of the Southern Railway Company.

JONESVILLE, Town; Union County; Pop. 1,188 / 1,208; Zip Code 29353; Elev. 682; Lat. 34-50-07 N, Long. 081-40-54 W; The town remembers Charlie Jones, an early settler.

KERSHAW, Town; Lancaster County; Pop. 1,993 / 1,747; Zip Code 29067; Elev. 522; Lat. 34-32-48 N, Long. 080-34-51 W; The town's name honors Colonel Joseph Kershaw, a Revolutionary War hero.

KINGSTREE, Town; Williamsburg County Seat; Pop. 4,147 / 3,596; Zip Code 29556; Lat. 33-40-12 N, Long. 079-49-50 W; In colonial days, trees marked with an arrow sign were reserved for the royal Navy's sailing ships. The town was named for a large white pine on the Black River so marked.

KLINE, Town; Barnwell County; Pop. 315 / 295; Named for an early settler.

LAKE CITY, City; Florence County; Pop. 5,636 / 6,877; Zip Code 29560; Elev. 77; Lat. 33-52-01 N, Long. 079-45-27 W; Named either for its location near Lake Swamp or after the Lake family, who were pioneer settlers.

LAKE VIEW, Town; Dillon County; Pop. 939 / 1,055; Zip Code 29563; Lat. 34-20-34 N, Long. 079-10-06 W; An early mill created an artificial lake and cause the site to be named "Lake View."

LAMAR, Town; Darlington County; Pop. 1,333 / 1,129; Zip Code 29069; Lat. 34-10-08 N, Long. 080-03-55 W; Once known as Devil's Woodyard, its name was changed in 1880 to honor J.Q. Lamar, a member of President Cleveland's cabinet.

LANCASTER, City; Lancaster County Seat; Pop. 9,603 / 9,285; Zip Code 29720; Lat. 34-42-17 N, Long. 080-47-15 W; Settled in the 1790s and named for Lancaster, Pennsylvania, the former home of many early settlers.

LANDRUM, City; Spartanburg County; Pop. 2,141 / 2,611; Zip Code 29356; Lat. 35-10-43 N, Long. 082-10-56 W; The first house in the village was built by Reverend John Landrum. The city is named in his honor.

LANE, Town; Williamsburg County; Pop. 554 / 534; Zip Code 29564; Elev. 70; Lat. 33-31-18 N, Long. 079-52-52 W; Named for an early settler.

LATTA, Town; Dillon County; Pop. 1,804 / 1,596; Zip Code 29565; Lat. 34-20-13 N, Long. 079-25-54 W; Founded in 1888 and named for an official of the Atlantic Coast Line Railroad.

LAURENS, City; Laurens County Seat; Pop. 10,587 / 9,718; Zip Code 29360; Lat. 34-30-31 N, Long. 082-00-18 W; Established in 1798 and named in honor of statesman and member of the Continental Congress, Henry Laurens.

LEESVILLE, Town; Lexington County; Pop. 2,296; Zip Code 29070; Elev. 656; Lat. 33-55-16 N, Long. 081-28-02 W; The town is named in honor of Colonel John Lee, a prominent citizen.

LEXINGTON, Town; Lexington County Seat; Pop. 2,131 / 7,830; Zip Code 29072; Elev. 392; Lat. 33-59-01 N, Long. 081-14-16 W; The town's names the Battle of Lexington in the early part of the Revolutionary War.

LIBERTY, Town; Pickens County; Pop. 3,167 / 3,775; Zip Code 29657; Elev. 1005; Lat. 34-47-04 N, Long. 082-41-56; Once called Salubrity, the name was changed during the Revolution to Liberty.

LINCOLNVILLE, Town; Charleston County; Pop. 808; Settled by blacks after the Civil War and named in honor of President Abraham Lincoln.

LITTLE MOUNTAIN, Town; Newberry County; Pop. 282 / 308; Zip Code 29075; Lat. 34-11-40 N, Long. 081-24-33 W; Named for a nearby hill called Little Mountain.

LIVINGSTON, Town; Orangeburg County; Pop. 166 / 176; Mrs. Lavinia Livingston donated land to the town and had it named in her honor.

LODGE, Town; Colleton County; Pop. 145 / 145; Zip Code 29052; Elev. 111; Lat. 33-04-22 N, Long. 080-56-25 W; The town is named after Hope Masonic Lodge No. 122.

LORIS, City; Horry County; Pop. 2,193 / 2,195; Zip Code 29569; Elev. 99; Lat. 34-03-20 N, Long. 078-53-07 W; Loris is probably named after an early settler.

LOWNDESVILLE, Town; Abbeville County; Pop. 197 / 2167; Zip Code 29659; Lat. 34-12-37 N, Long. 082-38-54 W; Lowings is named after an early settler.

LOWRYS, Town; Chester County; Pop. 225 / 206; The Lowry family settled in the area in the 1750s. The town is named after them.

LURAY, Town; Hampton County; Pop. 149 / 108; Zip Code 29932; Elev. 140; Lat. 32-48-53 N, Long. 081-14-21 W; Founded in 1893 and named after Luray Caverns in Virginia.

LYMAN, Town; Spartanburg County; Pop. 1,067 / 2,625; Zip Code 29365; Lat. 34-56-47 N, Long. 082-07-27 W; Originally called Lyman, the town's name was changed to honor Arthur Lyman, who directed a large textile mill in the area.

LYNCHBURG, Town; Lee County; Pop. 534 / 485; Zip Code 29080; Lat. 34-03-44 N, Long. 080-04-38 W; Descriptively named for its location on the Lynch River.

MANNING, City; Clarendon County Seat; Pop. 4,746 / 4,434; Zip Code 29102; Lat. 33-42-56 N, Long. 080-17-18 W; Manning's name honors Richard Manning, who was governor from 1824-26.

MARION, City; Marion County Seat; Pop. 7,700 / 7,594; Zip Code 29571; Elev. 77; Lat. 34-10-39 N, Long. 079-23-55 W; Founded in 1800 and named in honor of Revolutionary War hero, General Francis Marion.

MAULDIN, City; Greenville County; Pop. 8,245 / 14,911; Zip Code 29662; Elev. 942; Lat. 34-46-51 N, Long. 082-18-20 W; Named for an early settler.

MAYESVILLE, Town; Sumter County; Pop. 663 / 630; Zip Code 29104; Elev. 326; Lat. 33-59-12 N, Long. 080-12-33 W; Mayesville is named after a pioneer settler.

MCBEE, Town; Chesterfield County; Pop. 774 / 683; Zip Code 29101; Lat. 34-28-14 N, Long. 080-15-27 W; Named by railroad officials in 1900 in honor of Bunch McBee.

MCCLELLANYILLE, Town; Charleston County; Pop. 436 / 359; Zip Code 29458; Elev. 9; Lat. 33-05-11 N, Long. 079-27-44 W; The town's name remembers a prominent colonial family, the McClellans.

MCCOLL, Town; Marlboro County; Pop. 2,677 / 2,722; Zip Code 29570; Elev. 185; Lat. 34-40-09 N, Long. 079-32-35 W; Settled in 1759 and later named for D.D. McCall, president of a local railroad.

MCCONNELLS, Town; York County; Pop. 171 / 321; Zip Code 29726; Elev. 698; Lat. 34-52-19 N, Long. 081-13-39 W; The town is named for an early settler.

MCCORMICK, Town; McCormick County Seat; Pop. 1,725 / 1,638; Zip Code 29835; Lat. 33-54-44 N, Long. 082-17-39 W; The town's name honors Cyrus McCormick, the inventor of the McCormick reaper.

MEGGETT, Town; Charleston County; Pop. 249 / 980; Zip Code 29460; Lat. 32-43-03 N, Long. 080-14-18 W; Meggett's name remembers original landowner William Meggett, who was also a prosperous cotton planter.

MONCKS CORNER, Town; Berkeley County Seat; Pop. 3,699 / 6,259; Zip Code 29461; Elev. 56; Lat. 33-11-39 N, Long. 080-00-53 W; Thomas Monck purchased the townsite as part of a plantation in 1735. The town is named after him.

MONETTA, Town; Aiken & Saluda Counties; Pop. 108 / 275; Zip Cole 29105; Elev. 634; Lat. 33-51-16 N, Long. 081-36-39 W; Founded in 1888 and according to legend named for an Indian princess buried nearby.

MOUNT CARMEL, Town; McCormick County; Pop. 182; Zip Code 29840; Elev. 546; Lat. 34-00-14 N, Long. 082-36-01 W; Given this biblical name by early settlers.

MOUNT CROGHAN, Town; Chesterfield County; Pop. 146 / 136; Zip Code 29727; Elev. 449; Lat. 34-46-14 N, Long. 080-13-37 W; The town's name remembers French Revolutionary War soldier Major Croghan.

MOUNT PLEASANT, Town; Charleston County; Pop. 13,838 / 44,785; Zip Code 29464; Elev. 24; Lat. 32-48-17 N, Long. 079-51-46 W; Originally Haddrell's Point, the name was later changed to reflect the site's "pleasant" location.

MULLINS, City; Marion County; Pop. 6,068 / 5,390; Zip Code 29574; Elev. 101; Lat. 34-12-22 N, Long. 079-15-21 W; Incorporated in 1872 and named in honor of railroad president William Mullins.

MYRTLE BEACH, City; Horry County; Pop. 18,758 / 25,495; Zip Code 29577; Elev. 30; Lat. 33-39-22 N, Long. 078-55-59 W; Descriptively named for the Myrtle business found in the area.

NEESES, Town; Orangeburg County; Pop. 557 / 425; Zip Code 29107; Lat. 33-31-58 N, Long. 081-07-30 W; Founded in 1890 by J.W. Neece and named in his honor.

NEWBERRY, Town; Newberry County Seat; Pop. 9,866 / 10,074; Zip Code 29108; Elev. 503; Lat. 34-16-31 N, Long. 081-36-54 W; Established in 1789 and named in honor of Revolutionary War hero, Captain John Newberry.

NEW ELLENTON, Town; Aiken County; Pop. 2,628 / 2,723; Zip Code 29809; Lat. 33-25-13 N, Long. 081-41-13 W; Named for the wife of an early pioneer.

NICHOLS, Town; Marion County; Pop. 606 / 478; Zip Code 29581; Elev. 61; Lat. 34-13-56 N, Long. 079-08-52 W; Named in honor of prominent businessman A.B. Nichols, who helped develop the community in the 1850s.

NINETY SIX, Town; Greenwood County; Pop. 2,249 / 2,369; Zip Code 29666; Lat. 34-10-22 N, Long. 082-01-13 W; Founded in 1730 and named after the distance from Charleston to Keowee.

NORRIS, Town; Pickens County; Pop. 903 / 1,150; Zip Code 29667; Elev. 999; Lat. 34-45-51 N, Long. 082-45-46 W; The town grew around the Norris Cotton Mill and took its name.

NORTH, Town; Orangeburg County; Pop. 1,304 / 733; Zip Code 29076; Lat. 33-33-10 N, Long. 081-07-12 W; Captain John North was an early settler and prominent landowner. He contributed land to the town and its settlers named it in his honor.

NORTH AUGUSTA, City; Aiken County; Pop. 13,593 / 16,369; Zip Code 29841; Lat. 33-30-41 N, Long. 081-56-29 W.

OLANTA, Town; Florence County; Pop. 699 / 687; Zip Code 29114; Elev. 118; Lat. 33-56-04 N, Long. 079-55-50 W; Originally called Bealah, the name was changed in 1909 by the U.S. Post Office.

OLAR, Town; Bamberg County; Pop. 381 / 350; Zip Code 29843; Elev. 381; Lat. 33-12-00 N, Long. 081-10-51 W; Named for an early settler.

ORANGEBURG, City; Orangeburg County Seat; Pop. 14,933 / 13,463; Zip Code 29115; Elev. 245; Lat. 33-29-56 N, Long. 080-51-44 W; Founded in 1768 and named for William of Orange, son-in-law of King George II.

PACOLET, Town; Spartanburg County; Pop. 1,556 / 2,915; Zip Code 29372; Lat. 34-54-06 N, Long. 081-45-32 W; The town is named after the Pacolet River.

PACOLET MILLS, Town; Spartanburg County; Pop. 686; Zip Code 29373; Lat. 34-54-58 N, Long. 081-44-45 W; Named for the Pacolet River.

PAGELAND, Town; Chesterfield County; Pop. 2,720 / 2,804; Zip Code 29728; Elev. 654; Lat. 34-46-29 N, Long. 080-23-23 W; Established in 1904 and named for an early resident.

PAMPLICO, Town; Florence County; Pop. 1,213 / 1,188; Zip Code 29583; Lat. 33-59-42 N, Long. 079-34-14 W; The origin of the town's name is uncertain.

PARKSVILLE, Town; McCormick County; Pop. 157 / 214; Zip Code 29844; Elev. 348; Lat. 33-46-58 N, Long. 082-12-55 W; settled in 1758 and named for Indian trader Anthony Park.

PATRICK, Town; Chesterfield County; Pop. 375 / 391; Zip Code 29584; Elev. 223; Lat. 34-34-25 N, Long. 080-02-41 W; Founded in 1902 and named for railroad agent John T. Patrick.

PEAK, Town; Newberry County; Pop. 82 / 88; Zip Code 29122; Lat. 34-14-13 N, Long. 081-19-22 W; The town is named for H.T. Peak, the first superintendent of the Columbia and Greenville Railway Company.

PELION, Town; Lexington County; Pop. 213 / 375; Zip Code 29123; Elev. 390; Lat. 33-45-54 N, Long. 081-14-29 W; Named after an early settler.

PELZER, Town; Anderson County; Pop. 130 / 71; Zip Code 29669; Lat. 34-38-41 N, Long. 082-27-42 W; The town was founded by Francis J. Pelzer and named in his honor.

PENDLETON, Town; Anderson County; Pop. 3,154 / 3,527; Zip Code 29670; Elev. 859; Lat. 34-39-12 N, Long. 082-46-53 W; The town was settled in 1790 and named for Virginia Jurist Henry Pendleton.

PERRY, Town; Aiken County; Pop. 273 / 257; Zip Code 29124; Lat. 33-37-30 N, Long. 081-18-27 W; Perry is named after an early settler.

PICKENS, Town; Pickens County Seat; Pop. 3,199 / 3,735; Zip Code 29671; Elev. 1110; Lat. 34-53-02 N, Long. 082-42-18 W; Pickens is named in honor of Revolutionary War hero General Andrew Pickens.

PINE RIDGE, Town; Lexington County; Pop. 1,287 / 2,317; Descriptively named for the white pine forests in the area.

PINEWOOD, Town; Sumter County; Pop. 689 / 567; Zip Code 29125; Lat. 33-44-20 N, Long. 080-27-48 W; Descriptively named for the many pine trees in the region.

PLUM BRANCH, Town; McCormick County; Pop. 73 / 105; Zip Code 29845; Elev. 471; Lat. 33-51-00 N, Long. 082-15-30 W; Plums grow in the region and gave the town its descriptive name.

POMARIA, Town; Newberry County; Pop. 271 / 224; Zip Code 29126; Elev. 404; Lat. 34-15-54 N, Long. 081-24-58 W; Pomaria is Latin for fruit and describes the region's horticultural production.

PORT ROYAL, Town; Beaufort County; Pop. 2,977 / 3,400; Zip Code 29935; Lat. 32-22-40 N, Long. 080-41-16 W; The town was named by French explorer Jean Ribaut in 1562 for its good harbor.

PROSPERITY, Town; Newberry County; Pop. 672 / 1,181; Zip Code 29127; Elev. 541; Lat. 34-00-33 N, Long. 080-17-07 W; Originally called Frog Level, the name was changed by majority petition to the more positive "prosperity."

RAVENEL, Town; Charleston County; Pop. 1,655 / 863; Zip Code 29470; Elev. 38; Lat. 32-46-43 N, Long. 080-14-21 W; The town is named for an early settler.

REEVESVILLE, Town; Dorchester County; Pop. 241 / 230; Zip Code 2947; Elev. 12; Lat. 33-12-15 N, Long. 080-38-41 W; Reevesville's name honors an early settler.

RIDGELAND, Town; Jasper County Seat; Pop. 1,143 / 1,094; Zip Code 29912; Elev. 62; Lat. 32-35-19 N, Long. 080-55-31 W; Situated on a high ridge and so descriptively named.

RIDGE SPRING, Town; Saluda County; Pop. 969 / 881; Zip Code 29129; Lat. 33-50-43 N, Long. 081-39-46 W; The town is founded on a ridge with a nearby spring and so named.

RIDGEVILLE, Town; Dorchester County; Pop. 603 / 1,566; Zip Code 29472; Elev. 75; Lat. 33-05-55 N, Long. 080-19-02 W; Originally called Timothy Creek, but later renamed to reflect its location on a ridge.

RIDGEWAY, Town; Fairfield County; Pop. 343 / 407; Zip Code 29130; Elev. 34-18-16 N, Long. 080-57-34 W; Located on the watershed of Fairfield County and so descriptively named for its topography.

ROCK HILL, City; York County; Pop. 35,344 / 48,474; Zip Code 29730; Elev. 667; Lat. 34-55-52 N, Long. 081-11-23 W; Railroad construction crews here blasted a roadbed through the hill, which gave it a descriptive name.

ROWESVILLE, Town; Orangeburg County; Pop. 388 / 314; Zip Code 29123; Elev. 166; Lat. 33-22-22 N, Long. 080-50-02 W; The Rowe family settled in the area in 1740. The town is named after them.

RUBY, Town; Chesterfield County; Pop. 256 / 310; Zip Code 29741; Elev. 381; Lat. 34-44-33 N, Long. 080-11-06 W; Called Flint Hill when settled in 1875. In 1890 the name Ruby was chosen by contest to replace the old title.

ST. GEORGE, Town; Dorchester County Seat; Pop. 2,134 / 1,932; Zip Code 29477; Elev. 102; Lat. 33-11-11 N, Long. 080-34-33 W; During colonial times the area was part of St. George Parish and ultimately so named when settled.

ST. MATTHEWS, Town; Calhoun County Seat; Pop. 2,496 / 2,098; Zip Code 29135; Lat. 33-39-55 N, Long. 080-46-46 W; Once called Lewisburg, the name was later changed in honor of St. Matthews Parish.

SALEM, Town; Oconee County; Pop. 194 / 297; Zip Code 29676; Elev. 1061; Lat. 34-53-33 N, Long. 082-58-30 W; Salem is named after Salem, Massachusetts.

SALLEY, Town; Aiken County; Pop. 584 / 519; Zip Code 29137; Lat. 33-33-44 N, Long. 081-18-18 W; The town is named in honor of prominent early settler, D.H. Salley.

SALUDA, Town; Saluda County Seat; Pop. 2,752 / 3,005; Zip Code 29138; Lat. 34-00-12 N, Long. 081-46 03 W; The city and the river are named after the Indian tribe that once occupied the area.

SANTEE, Town; Orangeburg County; Pop. 612 / 646; Zip Code 29142; Lat. 33-29-05 N, Long. 080-28-38 W; The town is named after the Santee River. *Santee* is an Indian word meaning "haven."

SCRANTON, Town; Florence County; Pop. 861 / 886; Zip Cede 29591; Elev. 95; Lat. 33-55-05 N, Long. 079-44-48 W; Scranton is named after the city in Pennsylvania.

SELLERS, Town; Marion County; Pop. 388 / 376; Zip Code 29592; Lat. 34-16-53 N, Long. 079-28-43 W; John Seller was a prominent farmer in the community. The town is named in his honor.

SENECA, Town; Oconee County; Pop. 7,436 / 8,170; Zip Code 29678; Elev. 950; Lat. 34-40-52 N, Long. 082-56-22 W; The town is named after a pre-colonial Cherokee Indian town of Sinica.

SHARON, Town; York County; Pop. 323 / 312; Zip Code 29742; Elev. 652; Lat. 34-57-04 N, Long. 081-20-22 W; The town is named after the Sharon Church.

SILVERSTREET, Town; Newberry County; Pop. 200 / 153; Zip Code 29145; Lat. 34-13-08 N, Long. 081-42-40 W; Silvery-looking plants once lined the motor street and gave the town its name.

SIMPSONVILLE, Town; Greenville County; Pop. 9,037 / 11,909; Zip Code 29681; Elev. 865; Lat. 34-43-26 N, Long. 082-18-17 W; Named for an early settler named Simpson.

SIX MILE, Town; Pickens County; Pop. 470 / 612; Zip Code 29682; Elev. 1027; Lat. 34-48-23 N, Long. 082-49-15 W; The town is six miles from Charlestown and so named.

SMOAKS, Town; Colleton County; Pop. 165 / 138; Zip Code 29481; Lat. 33-05-24 N, Long. 080-48-31 W; Named for an early settler.

SMYRNA, Town; York County; Pop. 47 / 60; Zip Code 29743; Elev. 520; Lat. 35-02-25 N, Long. 081-24-24 W; The name of the Presbyterian Church formed in 1843, the name was adopted for the town.

SOCIETY HILL, Town; Darlington County; Pop. 848 / 696; Zip Code 29593; Elev. 166; Lat. 34-30-38 N, Long. 079-51-00 W; Originally Long Bluff, the name was later changed to note the academy founded on the site by the St. David's Society.

SOUTH CONGAREE, Town; Lexington; Pop. 2,113 / 3,208; Named by Irish settlers for a place in the old country.

SPARTANBURG, City; Spartanburg County Seat; Pop. 43,968 / 40,704; Zip Code 293+; Elev. 816; Lat. 34-56-37 N, Long. 081-57-44 W; The Spartan militia was formed in the area in 1776 and fought honorably throughout the American Revolution. The town is named in their honor.

SPRINGDALE, Town; Lexington County; Pop. 2,985 / 3,714; Descriptively named for the verdant countryside.

SPRINGFIELD, Town; Orangeburg County; Pop. 604 / 513; Zip Code 29146; Elev. 300; Lat. 33-29-50 N, Long. 081-16-52 W; Settled in 1756 and finally named for an early settler, a Mr. Spring.

STARR, Town; Anderson County; Pop. 241 / 179; Zip Code 29684; Elev. 771; Lat. 34-22-40 N, Long. 082-41-41 W; The town is named in honor of a C&WC Railroad official.

STUCKEY, Town; Williamsburg County; Pop. 222 / 328; The town is named after an early settler.

SULLIVAN'S ISLAND, Town; Charleston County; Pop. 1,867 / 1,718; Zip Code 29482; Lat. 32-45-43 N, Long. 079-50-31 W; Sullivan was an early settler, and the town is named after him.

SUMMERTON, Town; Clarendon County; Pop. 1,173 / 1,037; Zip Code 29148; Lat. 33-36-32 N, Long. 080-21-08 W; A summer resort before the Civil War, it was noted for its warm, balmy weather, and descriptively named.

SUMMERVILLE, Town; Charleston and Dorchester Counties; Pop. 6,368 / 24,875; Zip Code 29483; Elev. 75; Lat. 33-00-57 N, Long. 080-10-36 W; The town was used by rich planters and given a resort name.

SUMTER, City; Sumter County Seat; Pop. 24,890 / 46,111; Zip Code 29150; Elev. 169; Lat. 33-54-40 N, Long. 080-20-52 W; Incorporated in 1798 and named in honor of Revolutionary War soldier, General Thomas Sumter.

SURFSIDE BEACH, Town; Horry County; Pop. 2,522 / 4,656; The town is descriptively named for its location.

SWANSEA, Town; Lexington County; Pop, 888 / 497; Zip Code 29160; Lat. 33-44-19 N, Long. 081-05-57 W; The town is named after Swansea, the city in England.

SYCAMORE, Town; Allendale County; Pop. 261 / 196; Zip Code 29846; Elev. 153; Lat. 33-02-12 N, Long. 081-13-19 W; Sycamore trees grow abundantly in the area, so the townspeople gave their community this descriptive name.

TATUM, Town; Marlboro County; Pop. 101 / 42; Zip Code 29594; Elev. 199; Lat. 34-38-39 N, Long. 079-35-10 W; Originally called Mount Washington, the name was changed to Tatum after an early settler.

TIMMONSVILLE, Town; Florence County; Pop. 2,112 / 2,313; Zip Code 29161; Elev. 150; Lat. 34-08-03 N, Long. 079-56-32 W; The Timmons family were early settlers in the community, and the town is named after them.

TRAVELERS REST, City; Greenville County; Pop. 3,107 / 3,759; Zip Code 29690; Lat. 34-58-17 N, Long. 082-26-15 W; An old stage coach stop, the town was named for its function as an overnight rest stop.

TRENTON, Town; Edgefield County; Pop. 404 / 834; Zip Code 29847; Elev. 621; Lat. 33-44-30 N, Long. 081-50-26 W; Once called Pine House, the city was renamed for Trenton, New Jersey.

TROY, Town; Greenwood County; Pop. 705 / 155; Zip Code 29848; Lat. 33-59-16 N, Long. 082-17-37 W; Troy is named after Troy, New York.

TURBEVILLE, Town; Clarendon County; Pop. 549 / 760 Zip Code 29162; Elev. 131; Lat. 33-53-19 N, Long. 080-01-04 W; The town's name recalls on early settler.

ULMER, Town; Allendale County; Pop. 91 / 81; Zip Code 29849; Elev. 164; Lat. 33-03-27 N, Long. 081-16-14 W; Ulmer is named after one of its original settlers.

UNION, City; Union County Seat; Pop. 10,523 / 9,399; Zip Code 29379; Elev. 639; Lat. 34-43-08 N, Long. 081-36-33 W; The city was founded in 1765 and named after a multi-denominational church.

VANCE, Town; Orangeburg County; Pop. 89 / 217; Zip Code 29163; Lat. 33-26-16 N, Long. 080-25-09 W; Vance is named for an early settler.

VARNVILLE, Town; Hampton County; Pop. 1,948 / 1,939; Zip Code 29944; Elev. 111; Lat. 32-51-16 N, Long. 081-04-59 W; Established in 1873 and named in honor of Methodist minister Berry Varn.

WAGENER, Town; Aiken County; Pop. 903 / 856; Zip Code 29164; Lat. 33-38-55 N, Long. 081-21-42 W; The town's name honors C.G. Wagener, a well-known early pioneer.

WALHALLA, Town; Oconee County Seat; Pop. 3,977 / 4,272; Zip Code 29691; Elev. 1027; Lat. 34-46-05 N, Long. 083-03-49 W; Named by the German colonization society in 1850, the word is the English "valhall," or garden of the gods.

WALTERBORO, City; Colleton County; Pop. 6,036 / 5,325; Zip Code 29488; Elev. 69; Lat. 32-57-01 N, Long. 080-39-37 W; Once called Ireland Creek, the name was changed to honor an early citizen named Walter.

WARD, Town; Saluda County; Pop. 98 / 133; Zip Code 29166; Elev. 672; Lat. 33-51-33 N, Long. 081-43-57 W; The Ward family emigrated from England in 1819 and later operated a stagecoach in the South.

WARE SHOALS, Town; Abbeville, Greenwood and Laurens Counties; Pop. 2,370 / 2,704; Zip Code 29692; Elev. 642; Lat. 34-24-11 N, Long. 082-15-06 W; A shortened version of the descriptive "beware shoals."

WATERLOO, Town; Laurens County Seat; Pop. 200 / 145; Zip Code 29384; Lat. 34-21-44 N, Long. 082-03-18 W; Named after the great Battle of the Napoleon Wars.

WELLFORD, City; Spartanburg County; Pop. 2,143 / 2,493; Zip Code 29385; Lat. 34-57-19 N, Long. 082-06-09 W; Incorporated in 1882 and named in honor of Southern Railway Director P.A. Wellford.

WEST COLUMBIA, City; Lexington County; Pop. 10,409 / 12,583; Formerly Brookland, the name was changed to West Columbia in 1938.

WESTMINSTER, Town; Oconee County; Pop. 3,114 / 3,576; Zip Code 29693; Elev. 935; Lat. 34-39-57 N, Long. 083-05-38 W; The town is named for the Westminster Union Church.

WEST UNION, Town; Oconee County; Pop. 300 / 286; Zip Code 29696; Lat. 34-45-25 N, Long. 083-02-31 W; Temperance leader Joseph Greshman named the town "West of Temperance Union" which was shortened to West Union.

WHITMIRE, Town; Newberry County; Pop. 2,038 / 1,689; Zip Code 29178; Lat. 34-30-14 N, Long. 081-36-51 W; The town's name honors settler and trader George Whitmire.

WILLIAMS, Town; Colleton County; Pop. 205 / 194; Zip Code 29493; Lat. 33-02-52 N, Long. 080-50-05 W; Williams is named after an early settler.

WILLIAMSTON, Town; Anderson County; Pop. 4,310 / 3,911; Zip Code 29697; Elev. 826; Lat. 34-37-02 N, Long. 082-28-44 W; Named in memory of its founder, W.A. Williams.

WILLISTON, Town; Barnwell County; Pop. 3,173 / 3,179; Zip Code 29853; Elev. 353; Lat. 33-24-06 N, Long. 081-25-22 W; An early settler, Willis, gave his name to the town.

WINDSOR, Town; Aiken County; Pop. 55 / 227; Zip Code 29856; Elev. 391; Lat. 33-29-04 N, Long. 081-29-08 W; Named before the American Revolution for Windsor, England.

WINNSBORO, Town; Fairfield County Seat; Pop. 2,919 / 3,720; Zip Code 29180; Lat. 34-22-06 N, Long. 081-05-05 W; Incorporated in 1785 and named for Colonel Richard Winn, an officer in the Revolutionary War.

WOODRUFF, Town; Spartanburg County; Pop. 5,171 / 4,242; Zip Code 99388; Elev. 189; Lat. 34-44-21 N, Long. 082-02-04 W; Thomas Woodruff was the town's first settler. It was named in his honor.

YEMASSEE, Town; Beaufort and Hampton Counties; Pop. 1,048 / 801; Zip Code 29945; Elev. 25; Lat. 32-41-17 N, Long. 080-50-53 W. The town is named for the Yemassee Indians.

YORK, City; York County Seat; Pop. 6,412 / 7,833; Zip Code 29745; Elev. 756; Lat. 34-59-37 N, Long. 081-14-19 W. Named for the town in England.

SOUTH DAKOTA
The Mount Rushmore State

Crazy Horse Statue and Memorial

Annual Motorcycle Rally - Sturgis

GOVERNOR
William J. Janklow

Sitting Bull's Grave
near Mobridge

Mount Rushmore - Black Hills

The Badlands

Devil's Tower
Black Hills

South Dakota is bordered on the north by North Dakota, on the south by Nebraska, on the east by Minnesota, and on the west by Montana and Wyoming. It is a Great Plains state whose area is split by the upper Missouri River valley into "east river" and "west river" regions.

South Dakota is primarily a rural state with a highly diverse population. Thirteen tribes of Native American Sioux Indians total almost one-tenth of residents. More than twenty other ethnic and religious groups reside here as well, including Norwegians, Swedes, Danes, Dutch, German-Russians, Irish, Mennonites, Hutterites, "Plain" Germans, English, Welsh, and Czechs.

STATE NAME

The entire Dakota Territory was named for the Dakota tribe that lived in the region earlier in history. In 1889, the territory became separated into north and south divisions, and South Dakota became the fortieth state of the Union. The name Dakota was retained; it is a Sioux Indian word that means "friends" or "allies."

STATE NICKNAME

South Dakota has several nicknames. They include the Sunshine State, the Coyote State, the Blizzard State, and the Artesian State.

The first sobriquet is used to promote tourism and is often used in State publications for this purpose. The Coyote State is given because of the large population of the animal in South Dakota. The Blizzard State is given for the severe winter weather here. South Dakota is called the Artesian State because of its artesian wells.

STATE SEAL

South Dakota's State seal was set out in the constitutions of 1885 and 1889. In 1961, the legislature changed the law slightly to specify the colors to be used, although the design remained the same. It is described here: "The design of the colored seal of the state of South Dakota shall be as follows: An inner circle, whose diameter shall be five-sevenths of the diameter of the outer circle of any seal produced in conformity herewith: within which inner circle shall appear; in the left foreground on the left bank of a river, a rust-colored smelting furnace from which grey smoke spirals upward and adjacent to which on the left are a rust-colored hoist house and mill, and to the left a grey dump; these three structures being set in a yellow field and above and back of a light green grove on the left bank of the river. In the left background is a series of three ranges of hills, the nearer range being a darker green than the said grove, the intermediate range of a blue-green and the higher range of blue-black coloration.

"In the right foreground is a farmer with black hat, red shirt, navy-blue trousers and black boots, holding a black and silver breaking plow, drawn by a matched team of brown horses with a black harness. In the right background and above the horses in a pasture of grey-green, a herd of rust-colored cattle graze in front of a field of yellow-brown corn, part in shock and part in cut rows to the rear and above which are blue and purple hills forming a low background and receding into the distance. Between the right and left foregrounds and backgrounds is a light blue river merging in the distance into a sky-blue and cloudless sky. Moving upstream on the river is a white steamboat with a single black funnel from which grey smoke spirals upward. Green shrubbery appears on the near bank of the river, in the left foreground and on the right bank of the river near the pasture is a yellow field. The farmer is turning black-brown furrows, which reach across the circle and in his foreground is a field of brown-green-yellow.

"Near the upper edge of the inner circle at the top on a golden quarter circle which is one-fifth in width the distance between the innermost and the outermost circles that compose the seal, shall appear in black, the state motto: 'Under God the People Rule.' This innermost circle is circumscribed by a golden band one-fourth as wide as the above-described quarter circle, which inner border, shall be circumscribed by a deep blue circle four and one-half times as wide as the above quarter circle, on which in golden letters one-third its width, in height, shall appear at the top the words, 'State of South Dakota.' In the lower half of the deep blue circle shall appear in words of equal height 'Great' and 'Seal' between which shall be the numerals '1889.' Between the above-stated names and on either side shall appear a golden star one-half in size the width of the deep blue circle. Circumscribing this deep blue circle shall be a band of gold of the same width as of the inner golden band.

"Outside of this outer golden band shall be a serrated or saw-toothed edge of small triangles whose base shall be of the same width as the above quarter circle."

STATE FLAG

There are two official State flags that represent South Dakota. The first was adopted in 1909; it depicts the sun on the obverse and the seal on the reverse. However, it was determined that manufacturing a flag with two emblems had too high a cost, and in 1963, a second flag was designed with a single emblem. The new flag is described as follows: "The state flag or banner shall consist of a field of sky-blue one and two-thirds as long as it is wide. Centered on such field shall be the great seal of South Dakota made in conformity with the terms of the Constitution, which shall be four-ninths the width of the said flag in diameter; such seal shall be on a white background with the seal outlined in dark blue thereon, or, in the alternative shall be on a sky-blue background with the seal outlined in dark blue thereon; surrounding the seal in gold shall be a serrated sun whose extreme width shall be five-ninths the width of the said flag. The words 'South Dakota' symmetrically arranged to conform to the circle of the sun and seal shall appear in gold letters one-eighteenth the width of the said field above said sun and seal and the words 'The Sunshine State' in like-sized gold letters and in like arrangement shall appear below the said sun and seal. Flags designed of such material as may be provident for outdoor use need have no fringe but flags for indoor and display usage shall have a golden fringe one-eighteenth the width of said flag on the three sides other than the hoist. All state flags made in conformity with state law prior to March 11, 1963 shall remain official state flags but the creation of a state flag from and after said date, other than in conformity with S 1-6-4, is prohibited."

In 1987, the legislature adopted an official pledge to the State flag as follows: "I pledge loyalty and support to the flag and state of South Dakota, land of sunshine, land of infinite variety."

STATE MOTTO

The official State motto for South Dakota is "Under God the People Rule." The motto was adopted in the 1885 and 1889 constitutions for South Dakota at the suggestion of Dr. Joseph Ward, who is the founder of Yankton College.

STATE BIRD

The legislature of South Dakota adopted the ring-necked pheasant, *Phasianus colchicus*, as the official State bird in 1943. This pheasant is native to eastern China, and has now become well established in the northern half of the United States, southern Canada, Hawaii, and Europe.

The total length of the ring-necked pheasant is twenty to twenty-seven inches, with a tail proportionately long, from eighteen inches for the male to ten inches for the female.

The head, crown, and neck of the male are colored a variety of shades of glossy green, from Roman green to bottle green and dark zinc green. The nape of the neck is tinged with a glossy dark violet blue that also predominates along the sides of the neck. There are erectile tufts of iridescent blue-green blackish feathers on each side towards the back of the crown. A white collar is around the neck. Exposed interscapulars are bright yellow with a white triangular space at the base. Upperparts are light neutral gray or brown tinged with pale olive buff and broadly edged with russet or black. The lower back region is yellow-green to deep lichen green. The dark coppery breast is broadly glossed with magenta purple. The bare skin on the side of the head is bright red. The tail is brown or dark olive buff, with black transverse markings.

The female pheasant is brownish and buffy, variegated with black. Interscapulars are bright hazel to tawny russet. The central area terminates in a brownish gray or black distally pointed V. Scapulars and upper wing feathers are brown to tawny olive, and are edged and tipped with pale buffy. Back and upper tail feathers are brownish black, broadly edged with pale pinkish buff. Tail feathers are light pinkish hazel, transversely blotched with black. The chin, upper breast, and abdomen are white to buffy.

The female's muted earth tone colorings are effective as a camouflage, and make it possible for potential intruders to invade within a few feet without noticing her in the nest. Females have no scent, and this makes her even more secure against attack. She lays ten to twelve eggs in a set. After the brownish olive eggs hatch, newborn chicks follow her while she teaches them how to scavenge for food and protect themselves from predators.

Part of the pheasant's diet consists of harmful insects. However, they also eat farm and garden crops of corn, tomatoes, and beans, which can cause serious damage for farmers. If they are trapped by trees or buildings, they escape from danger by making rapid vertical movements. They make noise by fluttering their wings and croaking loudly in alarm.

The ring-neck pheasant was originally introduced in the United States in 1881 in Oregon by Judge O.N. Denny, American consul general of Shanghai.

STATE FLOWER

The legislature of South Dakota designated the American pasque flower (*Pulsatilla hirsutissima*) in 1903. It is also called the May Day flower, the wild crocus, the rock lily, the badger, the April-fools, and the wind flower. Its lavender flowers bloom in early spring. It grows best in arid prairie soil in South Dakota and other midwestern states north to British Columbia.

STATE TREE

In 1947, the Black Hills spruce (*Picea glauca densata*) was adopted as the official State tree of South Dakota. It is also called the white spruce, single spruce, bog spruce, cat spruce, skunk spruce, spruce, pine, and double spruce. It is native to the northeastern United States, the Black Hills, Canada, and Alaska.

The Black Hills spruce is medium-sized, with thin and scaly gray or brown bark. Blue-green needles are four-angled, about one-half to three-quarter inches long. Cones are slender, from 1½ to two inches long. They are pale brown and shiny, with thin, flexible, and rounded scales that have smooth margins.

STATE SONG

In 1943, the legislature designated "Hail! South Dakota" as the official State song, with words and music by Descort Hammitt.

STATE LICENSE PLATE

The State of South Dakota first began registering vehicles in 1905. The first registration on record is by James F. Biglow of Flandreau, who received a small disk stamped "No. 1" when he registered his Oldsmobile. From that date to 1912, 17,692 State residents received stamped disks. In 1913, two plates were issued for each vehicle, and annual issues also began. On the 1939 plate, Mount Rushmore began to be depicted on the plate. In 1952, it became a permanent feature and was authorized as such by the legislature. The current graphic plate has the figures carved on Mount Rushmore (Washington, Jefferson, Theodore Roosevelt, and Lincoln) in the top right background. At the bottom left appears 'South Dakota' in red script lettering. The slogan 'Great Faces. Great Places' appears at the bottom right. The plate's background tan color moves from dark to light from top to bottom.

The current plate issued as the 2000 series is a tri-colored plate. Across the middle of the top appears 'South Dakota' in white letters on a red background; the middle of the plate is white with raised numerals in dark blue. The bottom center of the plate displays Mount Rushmore with a blue landscape to both sides.

STATE POSTAGE STAMP

In 1952, when the Mount Rushmore Memorial had its twenty-fifth anniversary, the US Post Service issued a three-cent stamp to commemorate the event. Designed by William K. Schrage, the green stamp is dominated by the figures of Washington, Jefferson, Theodore Roosevelt, and Lincoln. At the lower right of the stamp are a woman and child, seated and looking up at the mountain. In front of them, a sign reads "Mount Rushmore National Memorial 1927-1952." At the lower left is lettered "Black Hills South Dakota." A total of 116,255,000 of the stamp were printed.

OTHER STATE DESIGNATIONS

Over the years, the legislature has adopted a number of additional symbols to officially represent the State. Included are the State animal as the coyote (1949); the State fish as walleye (1982); the State fossil as Triceratops (1988); the State gem as fairburn agate (1966); the State insect as the honeybee (1978); the State jewelry as Black Hills gold (1988); and the State mineral as rose quartz (1966).

STATE CAPITOL

When South Dakota became part of the Union in 1889, Pierre became the temporary capital city. Then in 1904, an election was held, and Pierre was adopted the permanent State capital. In 1907, construction was begun on the capitol building. It was completed in 1910.

Designed by C.E. Bell of Minneapolis, the capitol was patterned after the capitol building in Montana. The exterior is constructed from limestone. The rotunda has marble, scagliola pillars, and mosaic floors. The inner dome, made of leaded stained glass, rises ninety-six feet. The outer dome rises 159 feet. Some 40,000 pounds of copper adorn the outer dome.

In 1932, an annex was added to the original building. Total cost for original construction of the capitol was one million dollars.

OTHER FACTS ABOUT SOUTH DAKOTA

Total area: 77,116 square miles
Land area: 75,952 square miles
Water area: 1,164 square miles
Average elevation: 2,200 feet
Highest point: Harney Peak, 7,242 feet
Lowest point: Big Stone Lake, 966 feet
Highest temperature: 120 degrees Fahrenheit
Lowest temperature: -58 degrees Fahrenheit
Population in 1990: 696,004
Population density in 1990: 9.17 persons per square mile
Population 1980-1990: +0.8 percent change
Population projected for year 2000: 714,000
Asian/Pacific Islander population in 1990: 3,123
Black population in 1990: 3,258
Hispanic population in 1990: 5,252
Native American population in 1990: 50,575
European American population in 1990: 637,515
Capital: Pierre
Admitted to Union: November 2, 1889
Order of Statehood: 40
Electoral votes: 3

CHRONOLOGY

1743 March 30. Two sons of explorer Pierre Gaultier de Varennes, Sieur de La Verendrye, bury inscribed lead plate near present-day Pierre; seeking a water route to Pacific Ocean, they follow Missouri River downstream.

1775 French Canadian explorer, Pierre Dorion of St. Louis, arrives at a Yankton Sioux (Dakota) village on lower James River; he marries into tribe, thereby becoming first white resident of what is later South Dakota.

1794-1796 Jean Baptiste Truteau builds winter quarters on Missouri River near subsequent site of Fort Randall.

1804 August 22. Traveling upstream from St. Louis on expedition to Pacific Ocean, Meriwether Lewis and William Clark enter South Dakota and spend 54 days exploring.

1806 Lewis and Clark return to South Dakota.

1815-1850 Heyday of upper Missouri fur trade; traders buy pelts of beaver, muskrat, otter, buffalo hides, deerskins from Indians.

1831 June 19. *Yellowstone*, first steamboat on Missouri, reaches Fort Tecumseh (present-day Fort Pierre) from St. Louis; among passengers is artist George Catlin.

1851 Indians cede to United States all lands east of Big Sioux River in present South Dakota.

1857 Group of Iowa businessmen lay out Sioux Falls.

1858 Yankton Sioux sell fourteen million acres of land between Big Sioux and Missouri rivers for twelve cents per acre.

1861 March 2. Dakota Territory is organized, including what later become North Dakota and South Dakota.
– Population totals 2,402 white inhabitants.
– First federal land office opens at Vermillion.

1862 Yankton becomes territorial capital; it will remains so until 1883.

1868 Fort Laramie Treaty sets aside what is now South Dakota west of Missouri River as Indian reservation.

1873 Dakota Southern Railroad reaches Yankton from Sioux City, Iowa.

1874 Gold is discovered in Black Hills, in Indian Territory.

1876 As part of campaign to force Indian bands onto reservations, George A. Custer leads federal cavalrymen into Montana, where they are annihilated at Battle of Little Big Horn on June 25; later in year, Sioux agree to cede Black Hills region.
August 2. Wild Bill Hickok is shot to death in Black Hills mining town of Deadwood while holding aces over eights ("dead man's hand"); Calamity Jane is later buried next to him.
– There are about 10,000 Europeans in area.

1877 George Hearst buys Homestake Mine claim for 70,000 dollars; By 1935, mine will produce 301 million dollars worth of gold bullion: eighty-four percent of total taken from the Black Hills region.

1880 Railroad lines reach Missouri at Pierre and Chamberlain.

1881 Sioux leader, Sitting Bull, returns to western South Dakota after five years in Canada following Battle of Little Big Horn.

1882 University of South Dakota is founded at Vermillion.

1883 Peak of land boom; filings at public land offices in southern Dakota total 5,410,687 acres, about twenty-three percent of national total.

1885 Population of southern Dakota has risen to 248,569 from 81,781 in 1880.

1889 Great Sioux Reservation is reduced by about nine million acres and broken up into five smaller reservations.
November 2. North Dakota and South Dakota enter Union as 39th and 40th states, respectively; Pierre becomes capital of South Dakota.

1890 Indian messianic movement featuring "ghost" dances alarms whites.
December 15. Sitting Bull is killed.
December 29. Federal cavalry massacre 146 Indians at Wounded Knee Creek in southwestern South Dakota; thirty-one soldiers also are killed.

1897 State prohibition of liquor is repealed by popular referendum.

1904-1913 Series of agreements with Teton Sioux make over four million acres of reservation lands available for purchase by whites;

1909 John Morrell & Company opens meatpacking plant at Sioux Falls; meatpacking gradually replaces flour milling as chief industry.

1910 Population of western half of State has increased from 57,575 in 1905 to 137,687.

1917 Legislation permits State to extend loans to farmers; program ends in 1928 due to mismanagement and corruption.

1918 Ostracized for failing to support World War I, all but one of 17 Hutterite communities emigrate to Canada; they later return.

1919 Legislature votes to establish State hail insurance, State-owned coal mine and cement plant; all enterprises except cement plant at Rapid City prove uneconomical and will be liquidated in 1930s.

1930 Agricultural depression during 1920s results in fifty-percent price drop for farmland since 1921.

1932 Farm foreclosures hit high of 3,864.

– For first time in history of South Dakota, Democrats win all State electoral offices, and gain major control over legislature.

1935 State approves taxes on net income, retail sales; four-percent tax hike on gold ore provides one-third of State budget.

1939 World War II begins.

1941 Mount Rushmore National Memorial is completed.
– US enters war.

1943 State income tax is repealed.

1945 Republican governor M.Q. Sharpe signs bill to end closed shop in State.

1946 Closed shop is outlawed, following adoption of right-to-work constitutional amendment.

1948 Governor of South Dakota, three other states, end Des Moines conference by voting to form Midwestern Governors Conference with 12 states.

1949 State becomes 22nd to ratify proposed constitutional amendment to limit president to two terms.

1951 Winds up to 100 mph hit South Dakota, two other states; thirteen die, extensive property damage results.

1953 State's first commercial oil well is drilled at Harding County.

1955 Law is passed prohibiting formation of new Hutterite communities or expansion of existing ones.

1956 Fort Randall Dam is completed; it is first of four dams to be built in State on Missouri River for flood control, irrigation, power.

1958 Sioux Falls Stock Yards hit tenth place among country's livestock markets; sales total 1,522,415 head.

1962 George McGovern (D) announces plans to run for Senate seat currently held by Francis Case (R).

1963 At Wall, 150 Minutemen intercontinental ballistic missiles are put into place.

1964 Oahe Dam, largest of four Missouri River dams in State, is completed.

1970 With about twenty-two percent of residents working on farms; State has higher proportion of agricultural workers than any other state.

1972 Flash flood hits Rapid City and other communities on eastern edge of Black Hills; about 236 people die in disaster.
– For first time since 1936, Democrats win control of both legislative houses.

– Senator George McGovern, born in Mitchell, is Democratic candidate for president; he fails to carry South Dakota.
– Equal Rights Amendment (ERA) is ratified.

1973 State ranks fourth in nation in hog production, fifth in sheep, eighth in cattle.
– Members and supporters of American Indian Movement seize Wounded Knee, holding it to dramatize demands for reform in Indian tribal government; two are killed.
– AIM leaders, federal representatives sign agreement ending thirty-seven-day armed confrontation at Wounded Knee; agreement provides for preliminary talks in Washington to set up Presidential commission on Sioux treaty rights.
– About one hundred cattle producers protest low beef prices, high production costs, federal farm policies via "cross country beef-in;" livestock caravan travels from Bison to Washington D.C. Agriculture Department headquarters.
– In effort to save fuel, President Nixon signs bill to put most of US on year-round daylight savings time for two years; only Alaska and Hawaii are exempted.

1974 Democrat Richard Kneip wins unprecedented third term as governor.
– State ranks first in nation in rye production, second in flaxseed, third in oats and durum wheat.
– Average farm size in State is 1,046 acres, compared to 439 acres in 1935.
– Gasoline shortage situation worsens; federal allocations are reduced in South Dakota, nine other states.

1975 Russell Means, leader in AIM, is charged with murder in shooting death of Martin Montileaux of Kyle; also charged is AIM member Richard Marshall.

1976 Of State's Native American tribes, enrolled population totals 46,350, of which 29,750 are on reservations.
– Supreme Court approves coal strip mining in South Dakota, three other states; approval rejects Sierra Club's request for delay until regional environmental impact study is completed.

1977 Severe snowstorm sweeps through Midwest; more than 100 miles of Interstate 90 are blocked in State.

1978 State leads nation in gold production for last time.
– William J. Janklow (R) is elected governor.
– U.S. government reports 8.5 million-dollar payment to Sioux Indians for over 100,000 acres of State land.
– California Governor Edmund Brown Jr. formally refuses South Dakota extradition for Dennis Banks, American Indian Movement (AIM) leader convicted of assault in Wounded Knee 1973 occupation.

1979 Interior Department announces proposal to protect forty-seven of nation's most primitive and historic areas from air pollution; Badlands is listed in plan.
– South Dakota is one of thirteen states to pass law authorizing arbitration of medical malpractice claims.
– Sioux tribes win 105 million-dollar award over 102 years for forced cession of Black Hills region.

1980 U.S. Census Bureau reports population total of 690,178 in 1980; State will have one representative in 98th Congress in 1982.

1981 In address to legislature, Governor William Janklow reports that State was confronted with a variety of hardships and problems in 1980, but says economic development has been best ever.

1982 Republicans are left with majorities in State house and senate.
– Unemployment on Indian reservations is seventy-five to ninety percent after federal funding housing and job training cuts.
– Citicorp, nation's largest bank holding company, moves credit-card operations to Sioux Falls.

1983 Supreme Court votes to strike down life sentence imposed under State's "Habitual offender" law; it is first time high court has invalidated prison term as violation of Eighth Amendment on cruel and unusual punishment; ruling affects case of Jerry Helm, on basis that life in prison sentence was too harsh for seventh nonviolent felony.

1984 South Dakota is one of five states showing highest increases in per capita income.

1985 Farm Credit System settles plan to bail out Omaha Intermediate Credit Bank.
– Wildfires spread through South Dakota, ten other Western states; more than one million acres burn.
– Grasshopper plague results from dry hot weather in South Dakota, ten other Western states.

1986 Republican George Mickelson is voted into governor's office.

1987 Supreme Court upholds Congressional authority requiring states to raise drinking age to twenty-one or lose federal highway aid; South Dakota is one of eight states to challenge law on basis that states should make drinking age decision.

1988 Senator Thomas A. Daschle is elected co-chairman of Democratic Policy Committee.

1989 Deadwood voters approve measure to legalize poker, blackjack, and slot machine gambling.

1990 Governor Mickelson wins reelection.

1991 Population totals 696,004; figure is eight percent higher than 1980.
– Senate defeats bill containing strict restrictions on abortion; defeated measure would have prohibited all abortions except in cases of rape reported to police within seven days, incest, threat to physical health of woman, or cases where fetus is severely handicapped.
– State is one of ten in which poor pay highest rate of taxes as compared with rich.
– Arlette Schweitzer becomes first woman in US to give birth to own grandchildren; she was impregnated with daughter's eggs fertilized by daughter's husband's sperm; Schweitzer delivers twins by cesarean section.

1992 Federal government seizes priceless Tyrannosaurus skeleton from fossil collectors; government claims skeleton was illegally removed from US land.
– Census Bureau reports that Shannon County is poorest in nation; about 16,000 Sioux Indians are residents.

1993 South Dakota is one of thirty-six states with capital punishment.

1994 William Janklow is elected governor.

1995 Democrat Senate Minority Leader Thomas A. Daschle releases thirty-one-page report rebutting allegations that he intervened improperly with federal aviation inspectors to benefit air-charter company owner and friend of Daschle.

1996 Truck transporting two nuclear bombs to Ellsworth Air Force Base in Rapid City slides off I-83 highway in western Nebraska; it is first accident involving transportation of "sensitive nuclear materials" in thirteen years.
– State voters approve initiative requiring candidates who do not support term limits to be identified on ballot; voters also approve ballot initiative requiring voter approval or two-thirds approval in State legislature for tax increases or new taxes

1997 Supreme Court declares unconstitutional 1984 federal law barring American Indians from passing reservation land to heirs; ruling affects small parcels of land sought by heirs of William Youpee in South Dakota and two other states.

1998 Former governor William Janklow is again elected to executive office.
– Corporate hog farmers are ordered to institute air pollution measures.
– Voters reject measure to prevent property taxes being applied to educational expenses.

1999 Facilities in Rapid City and Sioux Falls are targeted in anthrax threats hoax in fourteen letters sent to abortion and Planned Parenthood centers across nation.
October 25. Payne Stewart, a professional golfer, is killed with two agents and two pilots when their Lear Jet crashes near Mina, South Dakota. The plane flies for hours on autopilot before it crashes.

DIRECTORY OF STATE SERVICES

OFFICE OF THE GOVERNOR
500 East Capitol Ave.
Pierre, SD 57501
Governor: 605-773-3212
Fax: 605-773-4711

LIEUTENANT GOVERNOR
209 S Phillips Ave.
Sioux Falls, SD 57102
Lieutenant Governor: 605-330-6120
Fax: 605-334-1218

ATTORNEY GENERAL
500 E. Capitol
Pierre, SD 57501-5070
Attorney General: 605-773-3215
Fax: 605-773-4106

SECRETARY OF STATE
500 E. Capitol, Ste 204
Pierre, SD 57501-5077

Secretary of State: 605-773-3537
Fax: 605-773-6580

TREASURER
500 E. Capitol, 2nd Fl
Pierre, SD 57501
State Treasurer: 605-773-3378
Fax: 605-773-3115

DEPARTMENTS

ADMINISTRATION DEPARTMENT
500 E. Capitol
Pierre, SD 57501
Commissioner: 605-773-3688
Fax: 605-773-3887

AGRICULTURE DEPARTMENT
523 E. Capitol, Foss Bldg.
Pierre, SD 57501
Secretary: 605-773-3375
Fax: 605-773-5926

AUDITOR
500 East Capitol
Pierre, SD 57501
Auditor: 605-773-3341
Fax: 605-773-5929

COMMERCE AND REGULATIONS DEPARTMENT
500 E. Capitol
Pierre, SD 57501
Secretary: 605-773-3177
Fax: 605-773-5369

CORRECTIONS DEPARTMENT
115 E Dakota
Pierre, SD 57501
Secretary: 605-773-3478
Fax: 605-773-3194

Lamont Youth Development Program
P.O. Box 410
Redfield, SD 57469
Director: 605-472-2400
Fax: 605-472-0922

Springfield Correctional Facility
P.O. Box 322
Springfield, SD 57062
Warden: 605-369-2201
Fax: 605-369-2813

State Penitentiary
Box 911
Sioux Falls, SD 57117-0911
Warden: 605-339-6762
Fax: 605-339-2971

State Training School
Box 70
Plankinton, SD 57368
Superintendent: 605-942-7704
Fax: 605-942-7707

Youth Forestry Camp
Box 151
Custer, SD 57730
Director: 605-255-4524
Fax: 605-255-4526

EDUCATION AND CULTURAL AFFAIRS DEPARTMENT
700 Governors Drive
Pierre, SD 57501-2291
Secretary: 605-773-3134
Fax: 605-773-6139

Arts Council
230 S. Phillips Ave.
Sioux Falls, SD 57102-0720
Director: 605-367-5678
Fax: 605-332-7965

Education Division
700 Governors Dr.
Pierre, SD 57501-2291
Secretary: 605-773-3134
Fax: 605-773-6139

State Archives
900 Governors Dr.
Pierre, SD 57501-2217
State Archivist: 605-773-3804
Fax: 605-773-6041

ENVIRONMENT AND NATURAL RESOURCES DEPARTMENT
Foss Bldg, 523 E. Capitol Ave.
Pierre, SD 57501
Secretary: 605-773-3151
Fax: 605-773-6035

GAME, FISH AND PARKS DEPARTMENT
523 E. Capitol
Pierre, SD 57501
Secretary: 605-773-3387
Fax: 605-773-6245

HEALTH DEPARTMENT
445 E. Capitol
Pierre, SD 57501-3185
Secretary: 605-773-3361
Fax: 605-773-5683

State Health Laboratory
500 E. Capitol
Pierre, SD 57501
Director: 605-773-3368
Fax: 605-773-6129

HUMAN SERVICES DEPARTMENT
500 E. Capitol Ave.
Pierre, SD 57501
Secretary: 605-773-5990
Fax: 605-773-5483

Custer Development Center
Rural Route 1
Custer, SD 57730

Administrator: 605-673-2521
Fax: 605-673-5489

Human Services Center
P.O. Box 76
Yankton, SD 57078-0076
Director: 605-668-3102
Fax: 605-668-3460

Redfield Development Center
Box 410
Redfield, SD 57469
Superintendent: 605-472-2400
Fax: 605-472-0922

INFORMATION AND TELECOMMUNICATIONS BUREAU
700 Governors Dr.
Pierre, SD 57501
Commissioner: 605-773-3116
Fax: 605-773-3741

Public Broadcasting
P.O. Box 500
Vermillion, SD 57069
Director: 605-677-5861
Fax: 605-677-5010

LABOR DEPARTMENT
700 Governors Dr.
Pierre, SD 57501
Secretary: 605-773-3101
Fax: 605-773-4211

Aberdeen Office
P.O. Box 4730
Aberdeen, SD 57402-4730
Job Service Div.: 605-626-2452
Fax: 605-626-2322

MILITARY AND VETERANS AFFAIRS DEPARTMENT
2823 W. Main
Rapids City, SD 57702-8186
Adjutant General: 605-399-6702
Fax: 605-399-6677

Emergency and Disaster Services Division
500 E Capitol
Pierre, SD 57501
Director: 605-773-3231
Fax: 605-773-5380

State Veterans Home
2500 Minnekahta Ave.
Hot Springs, SD 57747-1199
Superintendent: 605-745-5127
Fax: 605-745-5547

Veterans Affairs Division
500 E Capitol
Pierre, SD 57501-3182
Director: 605-773-3269
Fax: 605-773-5380

REVENUE DEPARTMENT

700 Governors Dr.
Pierre, SD 57501-2291
Secretary: 605-773-3311
Fax: 605-773-5129

SOCIAL SERVICES DEPARTMENT

700 Governors Dr.
Pierre, SD 57501
Secretary: 605-773-3165
Fax: 605-773-4855

TOURISM DEPARTMENT

711 E Wells Ave.
Pierre, SD 57501
Secretary: 605-773-3301
Fax: 605-773-5632

TRANSPORTATION DEPARTMENT

700 Broadway Avenue E
Pierre, SD 57501-2586
Secretary: 605-773-3265
Fax: 605-773-3921

BOARDS AND COMMISSIONS

ANIMAL INDUSTRY BOARD

411 S. Fort St.
Pierre, SD 57501
Executive Secretary & State Veterinarian: 605-773-3321
Fax: 605-773-5459

ARCHITECTURAL AND ENGINEERING EXAMINERS COMMISSION

2040 W. Main St., Ste 304
Rapid City, SD 57702-2447
Executive Director: 605-394-2510
Fax: 605-394-2509

ECONOMIC DEVELOPMENT AND TOURISM OFFICE

711 Wells Avenue
Pierre, SD 57501-3369
Commissioner: 605-773-5032
Fax: 605-773-3256

FINANCE AND MANAGEMENT BUREAU

500 E Capitol Ave.
Pierre, SD 57501
Commissioner: 605-773-3411
Fax: 605-773-4711

HOUSING DEVELOPMENT AUTHORITY

221 S Central, P.O. Box 1237
Pierre, SD 57501-1237
Executive Director: 605-773-3181
Fax: 605-773-5154

INVESTMENT OFFICE

4009 W 49th St., Ste 300
Sioux Falls, SD 57601
Investment Officer: 605-367-5850

OAHE STATE AND FEDERAL CREDIT UNION

Box 818
Pierre, SD 57501
Manager: 605-224-6264
Fax: 605-224-7332

PAROLE AND PARDONS BOARD

P.O. Box 5911
Sioux Falls, SD 57117-5911
Executive Director: 605-367-5040
Fax: 605-367-5025

PERSONNEL BUREAU

500 E. Capitol
Pierre, SD 57501
Commissioner: 605-773-3148
Fax: 605-773-4344

PHARMACY BOARD

500 E. Capitol
Pierre, SD 57501
Commissioner: 605-773-3148
Fax: 605-773-4344

SCHOOL AND PUBLIC LANDS OFFICE

500 E Capitol
Pierre, SD 57501
Commissioner: 605-773-3303
Fax: 605-773-5520

STATE FAIR

P.O. Box 1275
Huron, SD 57350
Manager: 605-353-7340
Fax: 605-353-7348

STATE LOTTERY

207 E. Capitol Avenue
Pierre, SD 57501
Executive Director: 605-773-5770
Fax: 605-773-5786

STUDENT LOAN FINANCE CORPORATION

105 1st Avenue SW
Aberdeen, SD 57401
President & Director: 605-229-5918
Fax: 605-662-4547

TWENTIETH CENTURY GOVERNORS

LEE, ANDREW ERICSON (1847-1934), third governor of South Dakota (1897-1901), was born in Bergen, Norway, on March 18, 1847. His family immigrated to Wisconsin in 1851, where he attended public schools. Before engaging in politics, Lee farmed and bred livestock and was also a merchant. Eventually he made his way to South Dakota, where he served on the City Council of Vermillion during 1892-93. In the latter year he became Mayor of that city, a post he held until 1896, when he ran for the South Dakota governorship as a candidate of the People's Party. Inaugurated first on January 5, 1897, he also won a second term in 1898, this time with the Fusion Party.

During Lee's tenure, he sought to make the State government more efficient, and also asked the State Legislature for more autonomy over such businesses as the railroads, on which the State's farmers heavily depended for their livelihoods. Although his administration did not see his programs passed, they came to fruition in later administrations. Lee decided to step down from office after his second term, and returned to his business interests. He made another bid for the governorship in 1908 on the Democratic ticket, but was unsuccessful.

Lee was married to Annie M. Chapell, and the couple had one child. Lee died on March 19, 1934.

HERREID, CHARLES N. (1857-1928), fourth governor of
South Dakota (1901-1905), was born in Dane County, Wisconsin on October 20, 1857. Between 1874 and 1878 he attended Galesville University, then studied at the University of Wisconsin from 1880 to 1882. In 1883 Herreid relocated to McPherson County, South Dakota. His career path included time spent as an attorney and a businessman. He served as director of the Western Mutual Life Insurance Company, and was vice-president of the Citizens Trust and Savings Bank. Herreid was also Federal Food Administrator for South Dakota. From 1888 to 1891, he was Judge of McPherson County Court, and between 1892 and 1896, was South Dakota's Lieutenant Governor. Beginning in 1898, he served for two years as Chairman of the Republican State Central Committee.

In 1900 Herreid was a successful candidate for the South Dakota governorship on the Republican ticket, taking office on January 8, 1901, and went on to secure a second term in 1902. During his tenure, he sought to revamp South Dakota's penal code, and the struggle of the State's farmers was alleviated somewhat after railroad rates were reduced. Herreid guided the State's big business interests with a firm hand and also managed to keep the powerful political machines in check. Herreid stepped down from office after his second term, and returned to his law work.

Herreid was married to Jeanette Slye, with whom he had one child. Herreid died on July 6, 1928.

ELROD, SAMUEL HARRISON (1856-1935), fifth governor
of South Dakota (1905-1907), was born in Coatesville, Indiana on May 1, 1856. He attended De Paul University, graduating in 1882 and eventually made his way to South Dakota. He went into the field of law and in 1884, began serving as Clark County Attorney. Between 1885 and 1887, Elrod was Postmaster of Clark, South Dakota and from the latter year until 1897, served as State's Attorney. From 1892 to 1900, Elrod was the Disbursing Agent for the United States Bureau of Indian Affairs.

In 1904 Elrod successfully ran for the South Dakota governorship on the Republican ticket, taking office on January 3, 1905. Like his predecessor, Governor Charles Herreid, Elrod made sure the power of the State's political machines was kept to a minimum. In addition, direct primary elections were implemented and campaign contributions from corporations were outlawed. The Anti-Lobbying Law was adopted as well.

Elrod decided to serve only the one term and stepped down from office in 1907. He married Mary Ellen Masten, with whom he had two children. Elrod died on July 13, 1935.

CRAWFORD, CORIE ISAAC (1858-1944), sixth governor of
South Dakota (1907-1909), was born in Volney, Iowa on January 14, 1858. He studied at the University of Iowa between 1878 and 1882. Pursuing a career in law, Crawford moved to Hughes County in Dakota Territory, where he was State's Attorney from 1886 to 1888. From 1888 to 1889, Crawford served on the Dakota

Territory Legislative Council, and from 1889 to 1890 Crawford held a seat in the South Dakota House of Representatives. In 1896 and 1904, he made unsuccessful bids for the United States Congress.

In 1906 Crawford ran for and won the South Dakota governorship on the Republican ticket, taking office on January 8, 1907. A progressive administrator, rather than control the State's "machine" politics like his predecessors, he sought to disassemble them entirely. Some of the political legislation adopted during his tenure included the installation of primary elections, the mandatory revelation of all campaign contributions, and the control of lobbyists. Crawford stepped down from office on January 5, 1909, and later that year, he successfully ran for the United States Senate, serving until 1915.

Crawford was married twice: to May Robinson, and after her death, he married her sister, Lavinia Robinson. He had five children from his second union. Crawford died on April 25, 1944.

VESSEY, ROBERT SCADDEN (1858-1960), seventh governor of South Dakota (1909-1913), was born in Winnebago County, Wisconsin on May 16, 1858. He received a public school education, and also studied at Daggett Commercial School in Oshkosh, Wisconsin. He was a sheep rancher for a time, then entered a mercantile career, owning and operating Vessey Brothers Merchandise Store. From 1899 to 1908, he served as president of the Wessington Springs State Bank.

Pursuing politics, Vessey served in the South Dakota State Senate between 1905 and 1909. In 1908 he successfully ran for the South Dakota governorship on the Republican ticket, taking office on January 5, 1909 and winning another term in 1910. During his tenure, discord reigned between the progressives and the conservatives, but Vessey still managed to secure the revision of several bills that concerned railroad, banking, and insurance statutes.

Vessey stepped down from the governorship on January 7, 1913, and returned to his business interests. Married to Florence Albert, the couple had four children. He died on January 25, 1960.

BYRNE, FRANK M. (1858-1927), eighth governor of South
Dakota (1913-1917), was born in Volney, Iowa on October 23, 1858. Receiving a public school education, he made his living as a farmer, and also sold real estate. He eventually pursued politics, holding a seat in the South Dakota State Senate from 1891 to 1893, then again from 1907 to 1909. From the latter year until 1913, he was South Dakota's Lieutenant Governor.

In 1912 Byrne successfully secured the State governorship on the Republican ticket, taking office on January 7, 1913 and going on to win a second term in 1914. During his tenure, the progressive and conservative factions were even more divided than in the previous administration, and the State Legislature deadlocked on almost every issue. The only decision agreed upon was the consolidation of some of the smaller State governmental departments.

Byrne stepped down from office on January 2, 1917, and returned to his various business interests. He was named Commissioner of the State Department of Agriculture in 1922.

Byrne was married to Emma Beaver, and the couple had six children. He died on December 25, 1927.

NORBECK, PETER (1870-1936), ninth governor of South Dakota (1917-1921), was born on August 27, 1870 in Vermillion, South Dakota. He studied at the University of South Dakota between 1890 and 1894. He subsequently worked as a businessman, serving as president of the Norbeck Drilling Company, and also sold real estate.

Entering politics, Norbeck held a seat in the South Dakota State Senate between 1901 and 1907, and from 1909 to 1911, he was South Dakota's Lieutenant Governor. In 1916 Norbeck successfully sought the governorship on the Republican ticket, and was inaugurated on January 2, 1917. A progressive administrator, 376 new laws were adopted by the State Legislature in his first year of office, plus the State's citizenry voted affirmatively on a number of constitutional amendments. They included the establishment of State grain elevators and warehouses, hail insurance, and permission for the upgrading of State governmental operations. In addition, during his time in office, the progressive Nonpartisan League was established in South Dakota. In 1917, during World War I, Norbeck was instrumental in guiding South Dakota's involvement toward the war effort, which included his overseeing the Red Cross Blood Drive.

Norbeck decided to leave office after his second term, and stepped down on January 4, 1921. In 1920 he secured a seat in the United States Senate, and was reelected in 1926 and 1932.

Norbeck was married to Lydia Anderson, with whom he had one child. He died on December 20, 1936.

MCMASTER, WILLIAM HENRY (1877-1968), tenth governor of South Dakota (1921-1925), was born in Ticonic, Iowa on May 10, 1877. Between 1895 and 1899, he studied at Beloit College in Wisconsin. McMaster made his living as a farmer, and in the banking business. After moving to South Dakota, he served as Cashier of the Security State Bank in Gayville between 1901 and 1910, and from the latter year until 1923, was president of a banking chain in the State.

McMaster entered politics in 1911 with a seat in the South Dakota House of Representatives, serving until 1913, and from that year until 1917, he served in the State Senate. Between 1917 and 1921, he was South Dakota's Lieutenant Governor.

In 1920 McMaster ran for the South Dakota governorship on the Republican ticket, and won the election, taking office on January 4, 1921, then went on to secure a second term in 1922. During his administration he was supportive of the plight of the State's farmers and pushed for laws that would alleviate some of their hardship, including State guaranteed credit and revamped tax levies. He was also successful in his rollback of gasoline prices.

Eschewing a third term, McMaster stepped down from office on January 6, 1925, to immediately occupy the United States Senate seat he'd won, serving until 1931.

McMaster was married to Harriett Louise Renstle, with whom he had two children. He died on September 16, 1968.

GUNDERSON, CARL (1864-1933), eleventh governor of South Dakota (1925-1927), was born on June 6, 1864 in Clay County, Dakota Territory. His uncle, Andrew E. Lee, was South Dakota's third governor. Gunderson attended the University of South Dakota between 1886 and 1890, then studied at Cornell University in 1892. He subsequently engaged in an engineering career, working as a surveyor, as well as in farming.

Gunderson entered politics in 1893 with a seat in the South Dakota House of Representatives, serving until 1895, then served an additional two terms from 1897 to 1903 and from 1917 to 1919. Between 1904 and 1911, Gunderson was the Alloting Agent for the Standing Rock, Rosebud and Cheyenne River Indian Reservations and from 1921 to 1925, was South Dakota's Lieutenant Governor. In 1924 he successfully sought the South Dakota governorship on the Republican ticket, taking office on January 6, 1925. During his tenure, the State Department of Agriculture was established, the Executive Budget Law was adopted, plus the Standard Cooperative Law was passed. In addition, a number of

State agencies were consolidated into three main departments: Finance, Agriculture and Rural Credit.

Gunderson lost his bid for a second term, and stepped down from office on January 2, 1927, returning to his farming interests. He made two more attempts to win his former office in 1930 and 1932 but lost in the nominating process. He was married to Gertrude Bertlesen, and the couple had four children. Gunderson died on February 26, 1933.

BULOW, WILLIAM JOHN (1869-1931), twelfth governor of South Dakota (1927-1931), was born in Moscow, Ohio on January 13, 1869. He attended the University of Michigan between 1887 and 1893, where he earned a law degree. Bulow subsequently made his way to South Dakota, settling in Beresford in 1894, where he kept a law office until 1927. From 1899 to 1901 he served as a member of the South Dakota State Senate, and between 1902 and 1912, he was City Attorney for Beresford, holding that post again from 1913 to 1927. In 1918, he was County Judge for Beresford.

In 1926 Bulow was a successful candidate for the South Dakota governorship on the Democratic ticket, taking office on January 2, 1927, and went on to secure another term in 1929. During his second administration, the Great Depression began, and he helped guide South Dakota through that especially hard time. Farmers were offered guaranteed loans for their planting, and other citizens were given the basics for living. Bulow was not nominated by his party for a third term in 1930, and he stepped down from office on January 6, 1931.

Bulow was married twice: to Katherine Reedy and after her death, to Sarah Johnson Farrand. He had three children. Bulow died on February 26, 1960.

GREEN, WARREN EVERETT (1870-1945), thirteenth governor of South Dakota (1931-1933), was born on March 10, 1870, in Jackson County, Wisconsin. In 1881 he moved with his family to Hamlin County, South Dakota, where he received his public schooling. Beginning in 1895, Green pursued farming and livestock raising.

Entering politics, Green served in the South Dakota State Senate from 1907 to 1909, and again later from 1923 to 1927. In the interim, from 1913 to 1919, he served on the State Board of Charities and Corrections. In 1930 Green successfully sought the South Dakota governorship on the Republican ticket, taking office on January 6, 1931. During his tenure, South Dakota, like the rest of the nation, was still reeling from the Great Depression, a situation compounded by the drought the State was experiencing. In order to help alleviate some of the suffering, Green streamlined the operations of the State government and oversaw the organization and running of South Dakota's relief agencies.

Green lost his bid for a third term, and stepped down from the governorship in January of 1933. He continued his involvement in Republican politics for a time, then returned to his farming interests.

Green was married to Elizabeth Jane Parliament, with whom he had four children. He died on April 27, 1945.

BERRY, THOMAS MATTHEW (1879-1951), fourteenth governor of South Dakota (1933-1937), was born on April 23, 1879 in Paddock, Nebraska. He received a public school education. In 1897 Berry relocated to South Dakota, where he engaged in ranching and livestock raising.

Berry entered the political arena in 1922 when he was elected to the South Dakota House of Representatives, where he served three terms. Between 1927 and 1931, Berry was a member of the

Custer State Park Board. In 1932 he ran for the South Dakota governorship on the Democratic ticket, and riding the wave of the Roosevelt landslide, won the election, also securing a second term in 1934.

During his tenure, Berry guided the State through the remnants of the Great Depression. One of his first decisions was to secure federal aid for South Dakota's citizens, and during 1935-36, he served as Federal Relief Administrator. Berry was able to drastically reduce the State debt. On two occasions he requested a special session of the State Legislature, for the passage of an unemployment compensation bill under the Federal Social Security Act, as well as for the legalization of a certain type of beer.

Berry lost his bid for a third term in 1936 and stepped down from office in January of the following year. Between 1942 and 1947 he served as director of the Farm Credit Administration for the Omaha District. In 1942, he made an unsuccessful run for the United States Senate.

Berry was married to Lorena McLain, and the couple had four children. He died on October 30, 1951.

JENSEN, LESLIE (1892-1964), fifteenth governor of South Dakota (1937-1939), was born on September 15, 1892 in Hot Springs, South Dakota. He attended Culver Military Academy. Between 1913 and 1916, Jensen was employed as a lineman and during 1916-17, served in the United States Army. From 1917 to 1919, he served at the rank of captain with the American Expeditionary Force. Jensen was a collector for the Internal Revenue Service between 1922 and 1934 and later was named president and general manager of the People's Telephone and Telegraph Company.

In 1936 Jensen successfully sought the South Dakota governorship on the Republican ticket. During his administration, the effects of the Great Depression continued to be an issue, and he oversaw the relief efforts. Amazingly, during that time he also managed to pay off a twenty-year-old debt, as well as significantly reduce the State debt. Also, in 1937 the State Legislature organized a new governmental department to execute the new federal Social Security Act.

Near the end of his term, Jensen made a run for the United States Senate, but was defeated. He stepped down from the governorship in 1939. During World War II, Jensen served at the rank of colonel in the United States Armed Forces from 1941 and 1945.

Jensen was married to Elizabeth Ward, and the couple had three children. He died on December 14, 1964.

BUSHFIELD, HARLAN JOHN (1882-1948), sixteenth governor of South Dakota (1939-1943), was born on August 6, 1882 in Atlantic, Iowa. He attended Dakota Wesleyan University between 1899 and 1901. Bushfield then studied at the University of Minnesota, earning an LL.B. degree in 1904, and started his own law practice soon after, in Miller, South Dakota.

Politically active, Bushfield served as Chairman of the South Dakota State Republican Committee in 1936. Two years later he ran for the South Dakota governorship on the Republican ticket, taking office in January of 1939, and also won a second term in 1940. During his tenure, the State property tax was eliminated, income taxes were reduced, and the State's budget was slashed significantly.

In 1942 Bushfield secured a seat in the United States Senate, and stepped down from the governorship in 1943. While in the Senate, he was a vocal opponent of the United Nations, and was also against President Roosevelt's reciprocal trade agreement policy.

Bushfield was married to Vera Cahalan, and the couple had three children. He died on September 27, 1948.

SHARPE, MERRELL QUENTIN (1888-1962), seventeenth governor of South Dakota (1943-1947), was born in Marysville, Kansas on January 11, 1888. Receiving a public school education, Sharpe was a schoolteacher from 1905 to 1907. In the latter year he entered the United States Navy, and after his discharge, he began study at the Night School of Law in Kansas City, Missouri. He then attended the University of South Dakota, where he earned an LL.B. degree in 1914. Sharpe subsequently settled in Cachoma, South Dakota, where he farmed and had his own private law practice. From 1916 to 1920, he served as State's Attorney for Lyman County, and in 1929 he was elected to two terms as South Dakota's Attorney General, serving between 1929 and 1933. Sharpe chaired the South Dakota Code Commission from 1937 to 1939 and in that post, oversaw the revision of a number of State laws.

In 1942 Sharpe secured the South Dakota governorship on the Republican ticket, taking office in January of 1943 and went on to win a second term in 1944. During his tenure attention was focused on World War II, and he worked hard to guide South Dakota's contribution to the war effort. Education was also a priority for Sharpe, and by the time he left office, the State's educational system had been upgraded and streamlined. He also sought to promote tourism in the State. A dedicated conservationist, Sharpe created the Natural Resources Commission and also helped organize the Missouri River States Committee, in an effort to develop that body of water.

In 1946 Sharpe lost his bid for a third term and stepped down from office in January of 1947, returning to his law work. He was married to Emily Auld, with whom he had one child. Sharpe died on January 22, 1962.

MICKELSON, GEORGE THEODORE (1903-1965), eighteenth governor of South Dakota (1947-1951), was born on July 23, 1903 in Selby, South Dakota. He attended the University of South Dakota, earning an LL.B. degree in 1927. He subsequently entered the law firm of Smith and Mickelson, and in 1933 he left in order to practice law on his own. Also in 1933, he was named State's Attorney for Walworth County, a post he held until 1936, at which point he secured a seat in the South Dakota House of Representatives. He left the House in 1947 to run for the South Dakota governorship on the Republican ticket, and won that election, as well as the subsequent race in 1948.

During his administration, Mickelson's main objective was to reduce the State's bond debt. In addition, he sought to promote the construction of more public institutions and State highways, while simultaneously seeking to protect South Dakota's natural resources. With his persuasion, several conservation measures were passed by the State Legislature. He also continued the work of his predecessor in overseeing the development of the Missouri River. Mickelson also directed the distribution of bonuses given to World War II veterans.

Eschewing a third term, Mickelson stepped down from office in January of 1951. The following year, he headed the South Dakota presidential campaign of Dwight D. Eisenhower. He was appointed a United States District Judge in 1953, where many of his decisions concerned tribal issues of Native Americans.

Mickelson was married to Madge Turner, and the couple had four children. He died on February 28, 1965.

ANDERSON, SIGURD (1904-1990), nineteenth governor of South Dakota (1951-1955), was born on January 22, 1904, in Arendal, Norway. When he was two years old, his family immigrated to the United States, and in 1912, he became a U.S. citizen. The family settled in South Dakota, where he attended South Dakota State College during 1925-26. He subsequently studied at the University of South Dakota, where he earned a B.A. degree in 1931 and an LL.B. degree in 1937. While attending college, Anderson made his living as a high school teacher. After he was admitted to the South Dakota bar, he went into private law practice.

Anderson became State's Attorney for Day County in 1939, serving in that post until 1941, then served as Assistant Attorney General of South Dakota from 1939 to 1941. Between 1943 and 1946, during World War II, Anderson served in the United States Navy. After his discharge, he became South Dakota's Attorney General, a post he held from 1947 to 1951.

In 1950 Anderson ran for the South Dakota governorship on the Republican ticket, winning the election, and won again in 1952. During his tenure, Korean War veterans began receiving pension benefits, and State employees had their salaries increased. The State sales tax was reduced, and a State highway construction program was launched. Anderson also sought to develop South Dakota's natural resources, and chaired the Missouri River States Committee. By 1954, the rural credit debt was eliminated.

Anderson stepped down after his second term, and soon after, served on the Federal Trade Commission. In 1964 he reestablished his law practice in Webster, South Dakota, and in 1967, he accepted the judgeship of the Fifth Judicial Circuit of South Dakota.

Anderson married Vivian Walz, and the couple had one child. He died on December 21, 1990.

FOSS, JOSEPH JACOB (1915-), twentieth governor of South Dakota (1955-1959), was born on April 17, 1915 in Sioux Falls, South Dakota. He first studied at Sioux Falls College and Augustana College, then attended the University of South Dakota, earning a B.A. degree in 1940. At the start of World War II, Foss enlisted in the United States Marine Corps and was stationed in the Pacific Theater. As a fighter pilot, he shot down twenty-six enemy planes and was highly decorated for his efforts, receiving the Bronze and Silver stars, as well as the Purple Heart. In addition, he was awarded the Congressional Medal of Honor by President Franklin Roosevelt. After his return to South Dakota, Foss launched his own flying service, and in 1953 he started the Foss Motor Company.

Foss became politically active in 1948, securing a seat in the State House of Representatives for two terms. He made an unsuccessful run for the South Dakota governorship in 1950, but won the 1954 election, as well as the 1956 race. During his tenure, funding for the State's educational system was increased, and several school statutes were revised. In addition, the 1957 State Legislature passed a substantial State budget, and veterans of the Korean War received bonuses.

In 1958 Foss ran unsuccessfully for the United States House of Representatives. After stepping down from the governorship, he returned to his aviation interests. In 1960 Foss was appointed Commissioner of the American Football League, a post he held until 1966.

Foss is married to June Shakstad, and the couple has three children.

HERSETH, RALPH (1909-1969), twenty-first governor of South Dakota (1959-1961), was born in Houghton, South Dakota on July 2, 1909. He studied for two years at North Dakota State College in Fargo, and subsequently made his living as a farmer and rancher. In 1935 he was appointed Civilian Superintendent of the Civilian Conservation Corps, serving at Sand Lake, South Da-

kota until 1939. For several years after that, he was in the mercantile trade, selling implements.

Herseth entered politics with a seat in the State House of Representatives during 1951-52, then again during 1957-58. In the latter year he successfully sought the South Dakota governorship on the Democratic ticket. During his administration, State taxes were a big issue, and Herseth organized a Citizens Tax Study Commission in order to implement tax reform. Also, construction on the Big Bend Dam began during that time. In 1959 South Dakota suffered several natural disasters, causing complicated issues within the State government, a situation that perhaps cost Herseth a second term in the governorship in 1960. He later lost his 1962 bid as well.

Herseth married Lorna Buntrock, and the couple had three children. He died on January 24, 1969.

GUBBRUD, ARCHIE (1910-), twenty-second governor of South Dakota (1961-1965), was born on December 31, 1910 in Lincoln County, South Dakota. He graduated from Augustana Academy in 1929. Gubbrud took up farming in 1934, and that same year he began serving as Clerk of Norway Township, until 1950. From 1946 to 1951, he was a member of the Alcester School Board and from 1949 to 1969, was director of the State Bank of Alcester.

In 1950 Gubbrud began serving several terms in the South Dakota House of Representatives. During that time, between 1955 and 1957, he also served as a member of the South Dakota Legislative Research Council. In 1960 Gubbrud ran for the South Dakota governorship on the Republican ticket, winning the election and securing a second term in 1962.

During Gubbrud's tenure, funding for education was increased substantially, and the State's welfare laws were revamped. In addition, Gubbrud organized a Centennial Commission to plan a big celebration for the centennial anniversary of the founding of Dakota Territory.

In the 1964 gubernatorial race, Gubbrud was replaced by another candidate on the Republican ticket. After stepping down from office, he was appointed Chairman of the Board of Beefland, International, and also served as director of the South Dakota Farmers Home Administration.

Gubbrud married Florence Dexter, with whom he has two children.

BOE, NILS ANDREAS (1913-), twenty-third governor of South Dakota (1965-1969), was born on September 10, 1913, in Baltic, South Dakota. He attended the University of Wisconsin, earning a B.A. degree in 1935, and an LL.B. degree in 1937. Passing the State bar soon after, he began his own law practice. During World War II, between 1942 and 1945, Boe served in the United States Navy. After his discharge, Boe returned to his law work.

Entering politics in 1950, Boe served several terms in the South Dakota House of Representatives. In 1963 Boe began serving a two-year term as South Dakota's Lieutenant Governor, then in 1964 he was a successful candidate for the South Dakota governorship on the Republican ticket and won a second term in 1966.

During Boe's tenure, State employees were given a retirement plan, and the State's educational system received substantial funding. In an effort to lure new industry to the State, a training program for workers was implemented. In addition, laws affecting women were passed that included equal pay for equal work and an employment anti-discrimination bill. His administration also saw a number of natural disasters and severe weather conditions, all of which took a heavy toll on the State.

Boe stepped down from office after his second term and in 1969, was appointed Director of the Office of Intergovernmental Affairs in the Executive Office of the President, a post he held until 1971. In that year he was named Chief Judge of the United States Customs Court.

FARRAR, FRANK LEROY (1929-), twenty-fourth governor of South Dakota (1969-1971), was born on April 2, 1929 in Britton, South Dakota. He studied at the University of South Dakota, earning a B.S. degree in 1951, and an LL.B. degree in 1953. Between 1955 and 1957, Farrar served as an Internal Revenue Agent; in 1958 he was a Marshall County Judge, and the following year, was named State's Attorney for Marshall County. In 1962 he left that post after being elected South Dakota Attorney General, where he served until 1969.

Farrar successfully sought the South Dakota governorship on the Republican ticket in 1968. During his tenure, relentless weather conditions continued to devastate South Dakota, creating floods so bad as to cause twenty-six counties to be declared disaster areas. In addition, long-simmering hostilities between Native Americans and white citizens escalated during that time.

Farrar lost his bid for reelection in 1970, and stepped down from office. He is married to Patricia Jean Henley, and the couple has five children.

KNEIP, RICHARD FRANCIS (1933-1987), twenty-fifth governor of South Dakota (1971-1978), was born on January 7, 1933, in Tyler, Minnesota. He served in the United States Air Force between 1951 and 1955, after which he studied at South Dakota State University, then at Minnesota's St. John's University. In 1962 he returned to South Dakota and launched his own business, selling dairy equipment.

Kneip entered politics in 1964 with a seat in the South Dakota Senate, where he served until 1971. In 1970 he successfully ran for the South Dakota governorship on the Democratic ticket, and was reelected to that office twice more, in 1972 and 1974. His last win made him the first governor to be elected to the newly-instituted four-year term. Kneip's administration saw the infamous hostilities at Wounded Knee on the Pine Ridge Indian Reservation, which brought South Dakota national attention. Kneip tried to diffuse the volatile situation by working in tandem with a task force to keep the lines of communication open between the tribal leaders and the State government. In addition, during that time he streamlined South Dakota's governmental operations by consolidating 160 agencies and boards into sixteen departments. He also tried to raise taxes in order to help reduce State expenditures, but his measure was defeated by the State Legislature.

While in his last term, Kneip was appointed by President Jimmy Carter to serve as United States Ambassador to Singapore, and left office in 1978, serving in his new post until 1980.

Kneip married Nancy Lou Pankey, and the couple had eight children. He died on March 9, 1987.

WOLLMAN, HARVEY (1935-), twenty-sixth governor of South Dakota (1978-1979), was born in Frankfort, South Dakota on May 14, 1935. He first attended Bethel College in St. Paul, Minnesota, then returned to South Dakota to study at Huron College, from which he earned a B.A. degree in 1961. During this time, from 1958 to 1960, he served in the United States Army. Wollman worked as a high school teacher from 1961 to 1965 and later settled in Hitchcock, South Dakota, near the James River, where he farmed. Also during this time, he returned to school to do his graduate work at the University of South Dakota.

Wollman entered the political arena in 1968 when he won a seat in the South Dakota Senate, and also won an additional two terms, in 1970 and 1972. In the latter year, he chaired the Midwest Conference of the Council of State Governments and in 1973 was elected to the National Executive Board of that organization. Also in 1972, Lieutenant Governor Bill Dougherty appointed Wollman to serve on the South Dakota Constitutional Revision Commission, and during 1973-74, he was Chairman of the Executive Board of the Legislative Research Council. Also during his Senate tenure, Wollman was the key sponsor of the Developmental Disabilities Act, and was in the forefront of the organization of the South Dakota Housing Development Authority.

In 1974, Wollman, a Democrat, won the Lieutenant Governor's post alongside the gubernatorial candidate, Richard F. Kneip. On July 24, 1978, Kneip stepped down from office to accept an ambassadorship, and Wollman assumed the governorship. However, it was a short tenure of six months, as he had lost his bid for the Democratic nomination in June of that year. Admitting that his contribution would be "very, very limited," Wollman still had a great deal of plans he wanted to implement for the State. The main ones included the securing of more water resources for South Dakota and the protection of those resources from those who sought to limit the State's rights to them, and he wanted to establish a mutually agreed upon compact concerning the water issue with the State's Native American population. Wollman also wanted to have personal property taxes abolished, as well as serious consideration given to alternative energy sources.

Wollman stepped down from office on January 6, 1979. Married to Anne Geigel, the couple has three children.

MICKELSON, GEORGE S. (1941-1993), twenty-eighth governor of South Dakota (1987-1993), was born on January 31, 1941 in Mobridge, South Dakota. His father, George Theodore Mickelson, served as South Dakota's eighteenth governor between 1947 and 1951. He first attended the University of South Dakota, Vermillion, from which he graduated in 1963, then studied at the University of South Dakota School of Law, earning his degree in 1965. That same year he enlisted in the United States Army and served several tours, including one in Vietnam. Discharged in 1967, the following year he entered a private law practice, and in 1970, was named Brookings County State's Attorney, serving in that post until 1974. Between 1975 and 1980, Mickelson served in the South Dakota House of Representatives. During that time he also chaired the State Board of Pardons and Paroles.

In 1986 Mickelson ran for the South Dakota governorship on the Republican ticket, winning that election, as well as a second one in 1990. During his tenure, he pushed for increased economic development. He also sought to hike up the State's sales tax, wanting to raise 4.7 million dollars to proffer to the State's universities for research projects, and use some of it to give raises to faculty members. Mickelson also supported the expansion of vocational education programs. Also during his time in office, he served as Chairman of both the Western Governors' Association, and the National Governors' Association Committee on Agriculture and Rural Development.

Mickelson died while in office, on April 19, 1993. He was married to Linda McCahren, and the couple had three children.

MILLER, WALTER D. (1925-), twenty-ninth governor of South Dakota (1993-1995), was born in Viewfield, South Dakota, on October 5, 1925. After graduating high school, he studied at the South Dakota School of Mines and Technology. A businessman, Miller served as President of the Dakota National Life Insurance Co., as well as the Dakota Allied Business Corp. He later purchased a 7,000 acre ranch in Meade County, South Dakota, which he operates with his son.

Active in Republican Party politics, Miller held a seat in the South Dakota House of Representatives from 1967 to 1986. In the latter year he was elected to serve as South Dakota's Lieutenant Governor, and was reelected to that office in 1990. During that time, he was named an advisory committee member of the Export-Import Bank of the United States, and in 1992, was chairman-elect of the National Conference of Lieutenant Governors. On April 19, 1993, the incumbent, Governor, George S. Mickelson, died, and the following day, Miller was sworn in as Governor of South Dakota.

Miller stepped down from office in 1995 and returned to his business interests. He is married to Patricia Caldwell, with whom he has four children.

JANKLOW, WILLIAM JOHN (1939-), twenty-seventh and thirtieth governor of South Dakota (1979-1987, 1994-current), was born in Chicago, Illinois, on September 13, 1939. He enlisted in the United States Marine Corps in 1956, during which time he was stationed in Southeast Asia, then was discharged in 1959. After returning to the United States he began his studies at the University of South Dakota, from where he earned a B.S. degree in 1964 and two years later, earned a J.D. degree from the University of South Dakota Law School. Janklow subsequently became an attorney for the South Dakota Legal Services System and was appointed chief officer for the Rosebud Indian Reservation, serving in that post between 1966 and 1973. In the latter year he was named Chief Prosecutor for the Attorney General's Office of South Dakota. During his tenure in this post, the State was experiencing its most tumultuous period regarding its large Native American population.

During the Wounded Knee battle in 1973, Janklow adopted a tough law and order position, especially with several members of the American Indian Movement, prosecuting a number of them. Eventually dubbed the "premier anti-Indian politician in the State," due to his opposition to AIM's land claims, his immovable stance pleased much of South Dakota's constituency, while making enemies of Indian leaders and passionate Native American supporters.

In 1974 Janklow, a Republican, was elected South Dakota's Attorney General, and was the first person in that post to argue and win two cases before the United States Supreme Court. In 1978 he successfully sought the South Dakota governorship on the Republican ticket, and resoundingly won a second term in 1982. Known as a conservative with populist leanings, Janklow managed to run a balanced State budget without raising taxes for several years. Continuing to be a controversial figure, Janklow stirred up trouble when he allowed an energy company in San Francisco to draw water from Lake Oahe and pipe it to Wyoming's coal fields at the Powder River Basin. The fallout from that decision was immediate and formidable, with everyone from Native Americans and conservationists, to several officials from other states, reacting with anger and lawsuits. Another controversy erupted during Janklow's efforts to lure businesses to South Dakota. Due to Minnesota's high tax rate, nearly sixty business firms from that state moved to South Dakota, causing a highly public feud between Janklow and Minnesota's chief executive, Rudy Perpich.

Janklow stepped down from office in 1987, and returned to private life for eight years. He ran again for the governorship in 1994 and was reelected. He once again concentrated on the lowering of taxes, convincing the State Legislature to approve a sub-

stantial tax decrease, the largest tax drop in the history of the State. He also lowered State government expenditures. In addition, Janklow helped implement a prison inmate work program, in which prisoners constructed affordable housing for senior citizens. Children were another priority for Janklow, with his bringing computers to the State's schools, expanding the immunization program, and seeking to replace long-term foster care with more adoptions. For all the controversy surrounding him, Janklow had many admirers of his accomplishments in office, the latter of which have included: joint agreements with the State's Native Americans, with the intent being tribal autonomy over their own affairs; the passing of stringent banking laws; the development of tourism; and the saving of millions of dollars after the refurbishing of a small college campus into a prison. In addition, efficient management of the State government and its agencies by Janklow netted over fifty million dollars for the State treasury.

Janklow was elected to another term in 1998, making him the first Governor of the State to win that post four times. He married Dean Thom, with whom he had three children. His current term expires in 2003.

DICTIONARY OF PLACES

Population figures and demographic information are official U.S. Census Bureau finals for 1990. When two figures are shown, separated by a slash, the first figure is the 1990 and the second is the Census Bureau 1999 estimate – the most recent available. Year 2000 census supplements will be available in the fall of 2001.

ABERDEEN, City; Brown County Seat; Pop. 25,956 / 25,019; Zip Code 57401; Elev. 1304; Lat. 45-27-46 N, Long. 098-28-47 W; Founded in 1881 and named by railroad officials for Aberdeen, Scotland.

AGAR, Town; Sully County; Pop. 139 / 78; Zip Code 57520; Elev. 1851; Lat. 44-50-15 N, Long. 100-04-19 W; The town was founded in 1910 and named in honor of county commissioner Charles Agar.

AKASKA, Town; Walworth County; Pop. 49 / 55; Zip Code 57420; Elev. 3505; Lat. 45-19-35 N, Long. 100-07-00 W; A Sioux Indian word meaning "a woman who lives with several men."

ALBEE, Town; Grant County; Pop. 23 / 10; Zip Code 57210; Elev. 1768; Lat. 45-03-06 N, Long. 096-33-04 W; Albee's name remembers early train dispatcher W. C. Albee.

ALCESTER, City; Union County; Pop. 885 / 1,094; Zip Code 57001; Lat. 43-01-24 N, Long. 096-37-36 W; The town was founded in 1879 and named for a colonel in the British Army.

ALEXANDRIA, City; Hanson County Seat; Pop. 588 / 523; Zip Code 57311; Lat. 43-39-06 N, Long. 097-46-40 W; The town's name honors Alexander Mitchell, one time president of the Milwaukee Railroad.

ALPENA, Town; Jerauld County; Pop. 288 / 228; Zip Code 57312; Lat. 44-10-54 N, Long. 098-21-58 W; The town was platted in 1883 and named for Alpena, Michigan by local railroad officials.

ALATMONT, Town; Deuel County; Pop. 58 / 48; Founded in the 1880s and named for the highest point in the county.

ANDOVER, Town; Day County; Pop. 139 / 93; Zip Code 57422; Elev. 1482; Lat. 45-24-27 N, Long. 097-54-04 W; Andover is named after Andover, Massachusetts.

ARDMORE, Town; Fall River County; Pop. 16; Established in 1889 and named for the town's schoolteacher, Dora Moore; The name evolved to "Ardmore."

ARLINGTON, City; Brookings & Kingsbury Counties; Pop. 991 / 928; The town is named after Arlington, Virginia.

ARMOUR, City; Douglas County Seat; Pop. 819 / 828; Zip Code 57313; Elev. 1523; Lat. 43-19-03 N, Long. 098-21-04 W; Founded in 1886 and named in honor of Phillip D. Armour, industrialist and railroad director.

ARTAS, Town; Campbell County; Pop. 43 / 26; Zip Code 57423; Elev. 1813; Lat. 45-53-09 N, Long. 099-48-28 W; Artas was established in 1901 and given a Greek name "artos" or "bread." A descriptive name referring to the region's wheat growing virtues.

ARTESIAN, Town; Sanborn County; Pop. 227 / 204; Zip Code 57314; Elev. 1317; Lat. 44-00-30 N, Long. 097-55-09 W; Originally called Dianna, but later changed to Artesian for its location in a great artesian basin.

ASHTON, City; Spink County; Pop. 154 / 141; Zip Code 57524; Elev. 1291; Lat. 44-59-24 N, Long. 098-29-53 W; Founded in 1879 and named by early settlers for the groves of ash trees.

ASTORIA, Town; Deuel County; Pop. 154 / 136; Zip Code 57213; Lat. 44-33-21 N, Long. 096-32-24 W; Established in 1900 and named for Astoria, Oregon.

AURORA, Town; Brookings County; Pop. 507 / 590; Zip Code 57002; Lat. 44-17-03 N, Long. 096-41-05 W; At its founding in 1880 its first settlers gave the town the name of the Roman gods of dawn.

AVON, City; Bon Homme County; Pop. 576 / 578; Zip Code 57315; Elev. 1608; Lat. 43-00-09 N, Long. 098-03-28 W; The post office was founded in 1879 and named by the first postmaster for Shakespeare's Avon.

BADGER, Town; Kingsbury County; Pop. 99 / 112; Zip Code 57214; Lat. 44-29-09 N, Long. 097-12-25 W; Badger was founded in 1906 and named for the nearby lake.

BALTIC, Town; Minnehaha County; Pop. 679 / 725; Zip Code 57003; Elev. 1510; Lat. 43-45-33 N, Long. 096-44-05 W; Founded in 1881 and named for the Baltic Sea.

BANCROFT, Town; Kingsbury County; Pop. 41 / 29; Zip Code 57316; Lat. 44-29-34 N, Long. 097-45-04 W; L.L. Bancroft started a newspaper in the town in 1884. The town later took his name.

BATESLAND, Town; Shannon County; Pop. 163 / 161; Zip Code 57716; Lat. 43-07-44 N, Long. 102-06-04 W; The town is named for C.A. Bates, the government surveyor who plotted the area.

BELLE FOURCHE, City; Butte County Seat; Pop. 4,692 / 4,924; Zip Code 57717; Elev. 3023; Lat. 44-39-49 N, Long. 103-50-50 W; Situated on the Belle Fourche River and thus descriptively named.

BELVIDERE, Town; Jackson County; Pop. 80 / 62; Zip Code 57521; Lat. 43-49-57 N, Long. 101-17-29 W; Settlers from Belvidere, Illinois named the town for their former home.

BERESFORD, City; Lincoln & Union Counties; Pop. 1,865 / 1,894; Zip Code 57004; Elev. 1498; Lat. 43-04-59 N, Long. 096-46-30 W; Originally called Paris, but later changed to Beresford after Admiral Lord Charles Beresford who had a financial interest in the local railroad.

BIG STONE CITY, City; Grant County; Pop. 672 / 620; Zip Code 57216; Elev. 977; Lat. 45-17-34 N, Long. 096-28-07 W; Located on Big Stone Lake and descriptively named.

BISON, Town; Perkins County Seat; Pop. 457 / 418; Zip Code 57620; Elev. 2460; Lat. 45-31-21 N, Long. 102-27-57 W; Founded in 1907 and named for the American Bison, commonly called the Buffalo.

BLUNT, City; Hughes County; Pop. 424 / 317; Zip Code 57522; Elev. 1619; Lat. 44-30-15 N, Long. 099-59-20 W; Settled in 1882 and named in honor of John Blunt, Chief Engineer of the North Western Railroad.

BONESTEEL, City; Gregory County; Pop. 358 / 286; Zip Code 57317; Elev. 1963; Lat. 43-04-28 N, Long. 098-56-43 W; Pioneer H.E. Bonesteel settled in the territory in 1872. He later started a well-known freight company.

BOWDLE, City; Edmunds County; Pop. 644 / 573; Zip Code 57428; Elev. 2004; Lat. 45-27-07 N, Long. 099-39-20 W; Laid out in 1886 and named in honor of C.C. Bowdle, pioneer banker.

BOX ELDER, City; Pennington County; Pop. 3,186 / 3,024; Zip Code 57719; Elev. 3030; Lat. 44-06-59 N, Long. 103-03-46 W; The town is named after Box Elder Creek.

BRADLEY, Town; Clark County; Pop. 135 / 109; Zip Code 57217; Elev. 1795; Lat. 45-05-32 N, Long. 097-38-38 W; E.R. Bradley broke up a fight between a railroad official and a group of laborers. Grateful railroad officials named the town for him.

BRANDON CITY, City; Minnehaha County; Pop. 2,589 / 5,392; Zip Code 57005; Elev. 1357; Lat. 43-35-25 N, Long. 096-33-32 W; The town is named after Brandon, Vermont.

BRANDT, Town; Deuel County; Pop. 129 / 126; Zip Code 57218; Elev. 1851; Lat. 44-39-52 N, Long. 096-37-27 W; Founded in 1884 and named after the Reverend P.O. Brandt.

BRENTFORD, Town; Spink County; Pop. 91 / 61; Zip Code 57429; Lat. 45-09-32 N, Long. 098-19-06 W; Established in 1905 and named after Brentford, England.

BRIDGEWATER, City; McCook County; Pop. 653 / 491; Zip Code 57319; Lat. 43-32-57 N, Long. 097-29-48 W; Originally called Nation, railroad workers carrying their drinking water across a bridge led to the new name.

BRISTOL, City; Day County; Pop. 445 / 408; Zip Code 57219; Elev. 1790; Lat. 45-20-32 N, Long. 097-44-51 W; Founded in 1881 and named for Bristol, England.

BRITTON, City; Marshall County Seat; Pop. 1,590 / 1,251; Zip Code 57430; Elev. 1358; Lat. 45-47-42 N, Long. 097-45-08 W; Plotted in 1881 and named for Colonel Issac Britton, the general manager of the Dakota and Great Southern Railroad.

BROOKINGS, City; Brookings County Seat; Pop. 14,951 / 17,286; Zip Code 57006; Elev. 1623; Lat. 44-18-51 N, Long. 096-47-01 W; Platted in 1879 as Ada, the name was changed to honor Judge Wilmot Brookings, a prominent early pioneer.

BRUCE, City; Brookings County; Pop. 254 / 227; Zip Code 57220; Elev. 1620; Lat. 44-26-14 N, Long. 096-53-28 W; Founded in 1881 and renamed for B.K. Bruce, a well-known black statesman.

BRYANT, City; Hamlin County; Pop. 388 / 383; Zip Code 57221; Lat. 44-25-20 N, Long. 097-28-06 W; Plotted in 1887 and named for an official of the Milwaukee land company.

BUFFALO, Town; Harding County Seat; Pop. 453 / 429; Zip Code 57720; Elev. 2877; Lat. 45-34-51 N, Long. 103-32-37 W; The town is named after the once numerous buffalo herds.

BUFFALO GAP, Town; Custer County; Pop. 186 / 208; Zip Code 57722; Elev. 3260; Lat. 43-29-32 N, Long. 103-18-41 W; Named for the large buffalo herds once found in the area.

BURKE, City; Gregory County Seat; Pop. 859 / 739; Zip Code 57523; Elev. 1745; Lat. 43-10-48 N, Long. 099-17-32 W; Founded in 1904 and named in honor of state legislator Charles Burke.

BUSHNELL, Town; Brookings County; Pop. 76 / 75; Frank Bushnell owned the land upon which the town was founded. It is named in his honor.

BUTLER, Town; Day County; Pop. 22 / 9; Zip Code 57222; Elev. 1822; Lat. 45-15-11 N, Long. 097-42-41 W; Established in 1887 and named after Harrison Butler, who deeded the land to the town.

CAMP CROOK, Town; Harding County; Pop. 100 / 134; Zip Code 57724; Lat. 45-33-08 N, Long. 103-58-31 W; Founded in 1884 and named for General George Crook, a well-known Indian fighter in the 1870s.

CANISTOTA, City; McCook County; Pop. 626 / 596; Zip Code 57012; Elev. 1549; Lat. 43-35-39 N, Long. 097-17-30 W; Founded in 1883 and given an Indian name meaning "board on the water."

CANOVA, Town; Miner County; Pop. 194 / 142; Zip Code 57321; Lat. 43-52-46 N, Long. 097-30-10 W; Settled in 1883 and named for Antonio Canova, a famous Italian sculptor.

CANTON, City; Lincoln County Seat; Pop. 2,886 / 3,390; Zip Code 57013; Lat. 43-18-05 N, Long. 096-35-33 W; Canton is named after Canton, China. Early settlers thought their town apposite that great Chinese city.

CARTER, Town; Tripp County; Pop. 7; Zip Code 57526; Lat. 43-23-27 N, Long. 100-12-14 W; The town was platted in 1909 and named in honor of Jervis Carter, who was a local U.S. land office registrar.

CARTHAGE, City; Miner County; Pop. 274 / 177; Zip Code 57323; Lat. 44-10-16 N, Long. 097-42-53 W; Established in the early 1880s and named after Carthage, New York.

CASTLEWOOD, City; Hamlin County; Pop. 557 / 641; Zip Code 57223; Lat. 44-43-30 N, Long. 097-01-45 W; Named after "Castlewood," the home of hero Henry Esmond in Thackery's novel.

CAVOUR, Town; Beadle County; Pop. 117 / 158; Zip Code 57324; Elev. 1310; Lat. 44-22-15 N, Long. 098-02-28 W; Named in 1880 to honor Carriello Benno, Count Cavour, Italian statesman and patriot.

CENTERVILLE, City; Turner County; Pop. 892 / 882; Zip Code 57014; Elev. 1226; Lat. 43-07-10 N, Long. 096-57-45 W; Named in 1872 for its location between Swan Lake and Vermilion.

CENTRAL CITY, City; Lawrence County; Pop. 232 / 114; Founded in 1877 and named for its location between lead and deadwood.

CHAMBERLAIN, City; Brule County Seat; Pop. 2,258 / 2,489; Zip Code 57325; Elev. 1465; Lat. 43-48-26 N, Long. 099-19-33 W; Milwaukee Railroad director Selah Chamberlain gave his name to the town when it was founded in 1881.

CHANCELLOR, Town; Turner County; Pop. 257 / 311; Zip Code 57015; Elev. 1367; Lat. 43-22-19 N, Long. 096-59-10 W; Early German farmers / settlers named the town after Otto Bismarck, Germany's "Iran Chancellor."

CHELSEA, Town; Faulk County; Pop. 41 / 33; The local town development company named the town after Chelsea, England in 1907.

CLAIRE CITY, Town; Roberts County; Pop. 87 / 83; Zip Code 57224; Lat. 45-51-23 N, Long. 097-06-13 W; Town founder A. Feeney named the town for his wife Claire. It was established in 1913.

CLAREMONT, Town; Brown County; Pop. 180 / 128; Zip Code 57432; Lat. 45-40-21 N, Long. 098-00-50 W; The Great Northern Railway founded the town in 1886 and named it for Claremont, New Hampshire.

CLARK, City; Clark County Seat; Pop. 1,351 / 1,293; Zip Code 57225; Elev. 1845; Lat. 44-52-44 N, Long. 097-44-02 W; Founded in 1882 and named in honor of territorial legislator Newton Clark.

CLEAR LAKE, City; Deuel County Seat; Pop. 1,310 / 1,188; Zip Code 57226; Elev. 1800; Lat. 44-45-05 N, Long. 096-41-04 W; Settled in 1884 and descriptively named for the nearby "clear lake."

COLMAN, City; Moody County; Pop. 501 / 530; Zip Code 57017; Lat. 43-59-04 N, Long. 096-49-00 W; Originally called Sankey, the name was changed to honor the Colman Lumber Company.

COLOME, City; Tripp County; Pop. 361 / 287; Zip Code 57528; Elev. 2268; Lat. 43-15-35 N, Long. 099-43-01 W; Founded in 1905 and named for the Colome brothers who established the town.

COLTON, City; Minnehaha County; Pop. 757 / 635; Zip Code 57018; Elev. 1304; Lat. 43-47-16 N, Long. 096-56-03 W; Railroad builder J.E. Colton had the town named after him in 1898 after donating a park to the community.

COLUMBIA, City; Brown County; Pop. 161 / 124; Zip Code 57433; Elev. 2479; Lat. 45-36-59 N, Long. 098-18-34 W; Originally Richmond, the name was changed due to a postal conflict to the patriotic "Columbia."

CONDE, City; Spink County; Pop. 259 / 186; Zip Code 57434; Elev. 1314; Lat. 45-09-32 N, Long. 098-05-32 W; French settlers named the town in 1886 after the famous French Conde family.

CORONA, Town; Roberts County; Pop. 126 / 111; Zip Code 57227; Lat. 45-20-11 N, Long. 096-46-12 W; Named by its early settlers for Corona, New York.

CORSICA, City; Douglas County; Pop. 644 / 666; Zip Code 57328; Lat. 43-25-18 N, Long. 098-24-34 W; Many Corsicans helped build the railroad in the area. The town was named in their honor in 1905.

COTTONWOOD, Town; Jackson County; Pop. 4 / 16; Originally called Ingham after an early settler, the name was later changed to the descriptive Cottonwood for the nearby Cottonwood Creek.

CRESBARD, Town; Faulk County; Pop. 221 / 175; Zip Code 57435; Lat. 45-10-05 N, Long. 098-56-47 W; Founded in 1906 and given a coined name made by combining the names of two early settlers, John Cressey and Fred Baird.

CROOKS, Town; Minnehaha County; Pop. 594 / 706; Zip Code 57020; Lat. 43-39-45 N, Long. 096-48-40 W; The town's name honors W.A. Crooks, the town's first postmaster.

CUSTER, City; Custer County Seat; Pop. 1,830 / 1,853; Zip Code 57730; Elev. 5318; Lat. 43-45-54 N, Long. 103-35-35 W; Established in 1875 and named in honor of George Armstrong Custer, who was killed fighting the Sioux Indians the following year.

DALLAS, Town; Gregory County; Pop. 199 / 140; Named for Dallas, Texas in 1907. G.M. Dallas was Vice-President of the United States in 1844.

DANTE, Town; Charles Mix County; Pop. 83 / 93; Zip Code 57329; Lat. 43-02-21 N, Long. 098-11-03 W; Dante was founded in 1908 and named after the great Italian author and poet.

DAVIS, Town; Turner County; Pop. 100 / 85; Zip Code 57021; Elev. 1250; Lat. 43-15-28 N, Long. 096-59-39 W; The town began in 1893 and was named for Jackson Davis, the original landowner.

DE SMET, City; Kingsbury County Seat; Pop. 1,237; Zip Code 57231; Elev. 1905; Lat. 44-23-13 N, Long. 097-32-59 W; Incorporated in 1883 and named in honor of Father Peter John De Smet, who spent his life ministering to the Indians in the nineteenth century.

DEADWOOD, City; Lawrence County Seat; Pop. 2,035 / 1,628; Zip Code 57732; Elev. 4537; Lat. 44-22-41 N, Long. 103-43-36 W; Descriptively named in 1876 for its location in Deadwood Gulch.

DELL RAPIDS, City; Minnehaha County; Pop. 2,389 / 2,878; Zip Code 57022; Elev. 1498; Lat. 43-49-31 N, Long. 096-42-28 W; Incorporated in 1871.

DELMONT, City; Douglas County; Pop. 290 / 214; Zip Code 57330; Lat. 43-15-57 N, Long. 098-09-58 W; Delmont was founded in 1886 and named for an official of the Milwaukee Railroad Company.

DIMOCK, Town; Hutchinson County; Pop. 140 / 147; Zip Code 57331; Lat. 43-28-33 N, Long. 097-59-42 W; A surveyor named Dimock charted the railroad link in 1885. Railroad officials named the town for him in 1910.

DOLAND, City; Spink County; Pop. 381 / 275; Zip Code 57436; Elev. 1358; Lat. 44-53-56 N, Long. 098-05-47 W; Settled in 1882 and named in honor of F.H. Doland, who was a director of the North Western Railroad, and a local landowner.

DOLTON, Town; Turner County; Pop. 47 / 42; Zip Code 57023; Lat. 43-29-32 N, Long. 097-23-06 W; Incorporated in 1907 and named after a director of the townsite development company.

DRAPER, Town; Jones County; Pop. 138 / 112; Zip Code 57531; Elev. 2257; Lat. 43-55-36 N, Long. 100-31-53 W; Established in 1906 and named for Milwaukee Railroad conductor, C.A. Draper.

DUPREE, City; Ziebach County Seat; Pop. 562 / 448; Zip Code 57622; Lat. 44-36-18 N, Long. 101-29-56 W; Settled in 1910 and named after early rancher and trader, Fred Dupris.

EAGLE BUTTE, Town; Dewey County; Pop. 435 / 865; Zip Code 57625; Lat. 45-00-00 N, Long. 101-12-54 W; Founded in 1910 and descriptively named for nearby Eagle Butte.

EGAN, City; Moody County; Pop. 248 / 238; Zip Code 57024; Lat. 44-00-00 N, Long. 096-39-00 W; Settled in 1880 and named for a Milwaukee railroad official.

ELK POINT, City; Union County Seat; Pop. 1,661 / 1,687; Zip Code 57025; Elev. 1127; Lat. 42-41-05 N, Long. 096-40-51 W; The town is descriptively named after nearby Elk Point on the Missouri River.

ELKTON, City; Brookings County; Pop. 632 / 575; Zip Code 57026; Elev. 1751; Lat. 44-14-34 N, Long. 096-28-58 W; Plotted in the 1880s and named after Elkton, Maryland.

EMERY, City; Hanson County; Pop. 399 / 416; Zip Code 57332; Elev. 1382; Lat. 43-36-02 N, Long. 097-37-13 W; First settled in 1881 and named in honor of original landowner S.M. Emery.

ERWIN, Town; Kingsbury County; Pop. 66 / 38; Zip Code 57233; Lat. 44-29-23 N, Long. 097-26-28 W; The town's name honors its first postmaster, James Erwin Hollister.

ESTELLINE, City; Hamlin County; Pop. 719 / 708; Zip Code 57234; Lat. 44-34-30 N, Long. 096-53-58 W; The town's name remembers the daughter of the original landowner, D.J. Spalding.

ETHAN, Town; Davison County; Pop. 351 / 307; Zip Code 57334; Elev. 1344; Lat. 43-32-49 N, Long. 097-59-06 W; The town was plotted in 1883, and named for Revolutionary War patriot Ethan Allen.

EUREKA, City; McPherson County; Pop. 1,360 / 992; Zip Code 57434; Elev. 1891; Lat. 45-46-08 N, Long. 099-37-22 W; Settled in 1887 by enthusiastic Russo-German homesteaders who suggested the Greek word *Eureka*, or "I have found it," as the town's name.

FAIRBURN, Town; Custer County; Pop. 41 / 69; Zip Code 57738; Elev. 3289; Lat. 43-41-03 N, Long. 103-11-51 W; Located on an attractive creek, the town's name means "fair," "burn," or Scotch for "fair stream."

FAIRFAX, Town; Gregory County; Pop. 225 / 142; Zip Code 57335; Elev. 1932; Lat. 43-01-25 N, Long. 098-53-21 W; Established in 1890 and named after Fairfax County, Virginia.

FAIRVIEW, Town; Lincoln County; Pop. 90 / 95; Zip Code 57027; Elev. 1213; Lat. 43-13-16 N, Long. 096-28-49 W; Located on the beautiful Sioux River Valley, and so descriptively named.

FAITH, City; Meade County; Pop. 576 / 447; Zip Code 57626; Lat. 45-01-11 N, Long. 102-02-21 W; The town is believed to be named in honor of Faith Rockefeller, wife of an important Milwaukee Railroad stockholder.

FARMER, Town; Hanson County; Pop. 27 / 23; Zip Code 57336; Elev. 1394; Lat. 43-43-16 N, Long. 097-41-16 W; A fertile landscape inspired early settler Joseph Altenhofer to describe the area as a "farmers paradise." The name stuck to the town.

FAULKTON, City; Faulk County Seat; Pop. 981 / 668; Zip Code 57438; Elev. 1589; Lat. 45-02-01 N, Long. 099-07-23 W; The city was plotted in 1886 and named in honor of Andrew Faulk, third governor of the Dakota Territory.

FLANDREAU, City; Moody County Seat; Pop. 2,114 / 2,257; Zip Code 57028; Elev. 1570; Lat. 44-02-50 N, Long. 096-35-21 W; Settled in 1857 and named in honor of Judge Charles Flandreau of St. Paul, Minnesota.

FLORENCE, Town; Codington County; Pop. 192 / 190; Zip Code 57235; Lat. 45-03-18 N, Long. 097-20-00 W; Named by North Western Railroad officials for the wife of a personal friend.

FORT PIERRE, City; Stanley County Seat; Pop. 1,789 / 2,166; Zip Code 57532; Lat. 44-21-17 N, Long. 100-22-17 W; One of the oldest white settlements in South Dakota, the town is named after the old fort.

FRANKFORT, City; Spink County; Pop. 209 / 180; Zip Code 57440; Elev. 5336; Lat. 44-52-27 N, Long. 098-18-21 W; Settled in 1882 and named for the famous German city.

FREDERICK, Town; Brown County; Pop. 307 / 223; Zip Code 57441; Lat. 45-50-06 N, Long. 098-30-25 W; Established in 1882 and named for the son of a Milwaukee railroad official.

FREEMAN, City; Hutchinson County; Pop. 1,462 / 1,345; Zip Code 57029; Lat. 43-20-57 N, Long. 097-26-07 W; The site of a large settlement of Mennonites, the town is named for an early settler.

FRUITDALE, Town; Butte County; Pop. 88 / 48; Founded in 1910 and named by original landowner, Henry Stearns, for the many fruit varieties growing in the area.

FULTON, Town; Hanson County; Pop. 108 / 70; Zip Code 57340; Elev. 1328; Lat. 43-43-35 N, Long. 097-49-21 W; The town is named in honor of inventor Robert Fulton.

GARDEN CITY, Town; Clark County; Pop. 104 / 91; Zip Code 57236; Lat. 44-57-37 N, Long. 097-34-49 W; Settled in 1889 and given this descriptive name for its picturesque surroundings.

GARRETSON, City; Minnehaha County; Pop. 963 / 1,005; Zip Code 57030; Elev. 1481; Lat. 43-42-59 N, Long. 096-29-13 W; Incorporated in 1891 and named for Sioux City banker, A.S. Garretson.

GARY, City; Deuel County; Pop. 354 / 248; Zip Code 57237; Elev. 1483; Lat. 44-47-38 N, Long. 096-26-39 W; Established in 1877 and named in honor of II.B. Gary, an early day mail agent.

GAYVILLE, Town; Yankton County; Pop. 407 / 414; Zip Code 57031; Elev. 1165; Lat. 42-53-26 N, Long. 097-10-18 W; The post office was established in 1872 and named after the first postmaster, Elkanah Gay.

GEDDES, City; Charles Mix County; Pop. 303 / 280; Zip Code 57342; Elev. 1620; Lat. 43-15-17 N, Long. 098-41-43 W; Founded in 1900 and named after Milwaukee railroad official, D.C. Geddes.

GETTYSBURG, City; Patter County Seat; Pop. 1,623 / 1,285; Zip Code 57442; Elev. 2061; Lat. 45-00-48 N, Long. 099-56-56 W; Settled in the 1880s by Civil War veterans who named the town after the great Civil War battle.

GLENHAM, Town; Walworth County; Pop. 169 / 132; Zip Code 57631; Elev. 1709; Lat. 45-32-05 N, Long. 100-16-18 W; Established in 1900 and descriptively named for its location in a glen.

GOODWIN, Town; Deuel County; Pop. 139 / 135; Zip Code 57238; Lat. 44-52-40 N, Long. 096-51-23 W; Originally known as Prairie Siding, the name was later changed to Goodwin after local railroad official George Goodwin.

GREGORY, City; Gregory County; Pop. 1,503 / 1,168; Zip Code 575+; Elev. 2166; Settled in 1904 and named after Gregory County.

GRENVILLE, Town; Day County; Pop. 119 / 75; Zip Code 57239; Lat. 45-27-46 N, Long. 097-23-17 W; Incorporated in 1918 and descriptively named for the grass-covered hills nearby.

GROTON, City; Brown County; Pop. 1,230 / 1,185; Zip Code 57439; Elev. 1308; Lat. 45-19-52 N, Long. 098-05-57 W; The city is named after Groton, Massachusetts.

HARRISSURG, Town; Lincoln County; Pop. 558 / 1,139; Zip Code 57032; Elev. 1425; Lat. 43-25-47 N, Long. 096-41-47 W; The town was named for its first postmaster in 1873.

HARROLD, Town; Hughes County; Pop. 196 / 153; Zip Code 57536; Elev. 1796; Lat. 44-31-30 N, Long. 099-44-20 W; Settled in 1881 and named for railroad official Harrold McCullough.

HARTFORD, City; Minnehaha County; Pop. 1,207 / 1,790; Zip Code 57033; Elev. 1568; Lat. 43-37-15 N, Long. 096-57-08 W; Early settlers from Connecticut named the town in 1881 for their former home.

HAYTI, Town; Hamlin County Seat; Pop. 371 / 396; Zip Code 57241; Lat. 44-39-38 N, Long. 097-12-18 W; Meeting to discuss the town's name, early settlers tied some hay together for fuel and decided on that name as an inspiration.

HAZEL, Town; Hamlin County; Pop. 94 / 204; Zip Code 57242; Elev. 1766; Lat. 44-45-39 N, Long. 097-23-02 W; Founded in 1888 on land owned by pioneer C.A. Bowley, and named for his daughter Hazel.

HECLA, City; Brown County; Pop. 435 / 379; Zip Code 57446; Elev. 1299; Lat. 45-53-02 N, Long. 098-09-04 W; The town was settled in 1886 and named for a volcano in Iceland.

HENRY, Town; Codington County; Pop. 217 / 210; Zip Code 57243; Lat. 44-52-58 N, Long. 097-28-00 W; Henry is named in honor of its first settler, J.E. Henry.

HERMOSA, Town; Custer County; Pop. 251 / 282; Zip Code 57744; Elev. 3303; Lat. 43-50-16 N, Long. 103-10-53 W; Founded in 1886 and given the Spanish name meaning "beautiful."

HERREID, City; Campbell County; Pop. 570 / 438; Zip Code 57632; Elev. 1682; Lat. 45-49-42 N, Long. 100-04-16 W; The town's name honors Charles Herreid, Governor of South Dakota in 1907.

HERRICK, Town; Gregory County; Pop. 115 / 136; Zip Code 57538; Elev. 2155; Lat. 43-06-39 N, Long. 099-11-15 W; Town founder Samuel Herrick left his name on the town.

HETLAND, Town; Kingsbury County; Pop. 66 / 49; Zip Code 57244; Elev. 1733; Lat. 44-22-34 N, Long. 097-13-50 W; Established in 1880 and named for pioneer homesteader, John Hetland.

HIGHMORE, City; Hyde County Seat; Pop. 1,055 / 783; Zip Code 57345; Elev. 1888; Lat. 44-31-14 N, Long. 099-26-16 W; Originally called Siding No. 5., the name was changed to reflect its position on high ground in the area.

HILL CITY, Town; Pennington County; Pop. 535 / 774; Zip Code 57745; Elev. 4979; Lat. 43-55-44 N, Long. 103-34-21 W; Settled during the gold rush of 1876 and named for its location in the Black Hills.

HITCHCOCK, Town; Beadle County; Pop. 132 / 110; Zip Code 57348; Lat. 44-37-33 N, Long. 098-24-33 W; Called Clarkesville in the beginning, railroad officials later changed it to honor an early settler named Hitchcock.

HOSMER, City; Edmunds County; Pop. 385 / 289; Zip Code 57448; Elev. 1906; Lat. 45-34-48 N, Long. 099-29-08 W; Named in 1887 after the maiden name of the wife of a settler named Arnold.

HOT SPRINGS, City; Fall River County Seat; Pop. 4,742 / 3,891; Zip Code 57747; Elev. 3464; Lat. 43-26-14 N, Long. 103-28-22 W; Located on a hot springs used by the Indians, the first settlers gave it a descriptive name.

HOVEN, Town; Potter County; Pop. 615 / 429; Zip Code 57450; Elev. 1902; Lat. 45-14-39 N, Long. 099-46-28 W; Founded in 1883 and named after townsite landowners Peter and Matt Hoven.

HOWARD, City; Miner County Seat; Pop. 1,169 / 963; Zip Code 57349; Elev. 1572; Lat. 44-00-46 N, Long. 097-31-28 W; Howard's name remembers the son of Judge J.D. Farmer, the original townsite owner, who died while a young man.

HUDSON, Town; Lincoln County; Pop. 388 / 446; Zip Code 57034; Elev. 1221; Lat. 43-07-41 N, Long. 096-27-16 W; Settled in 1868 and named by early settlers for their former home in Hudson, Iowa.

HUMBOLDT, Town; Minnehaha County; Pop. 487 / 479; Zip Code 57035; Elev. 1308; Lat. 43-38-33 N, Long. 097-05-07 W; Founded in the 1880s and named for Baron Alexander van Humboldt, the famous German naturalist.

HURLEY, City; Turner County; Pop. 419 / 373; Zip Code 57036; Elev. 1293; Lat. 43-16-51 N, Long. 097-05-21 W; Plotted in 1883 and named after R.E. Hurley, Chief Engineer of the North Western Railroad.

HURON, City; Beadle County Seat; Pop. 13,000 / 11,742; Zip Code 57350; Lat. 44-21-23 N, Long. 098-13-00 W; Settled in 1880 and named after the Huron Indians.

INTERIOR, Town; Jackson County; Pop. 62 / 77; Zip Code 57750; Elev. 2378; Lat. 43-43-38 N, Long. 101-59-02 W; Descriptively named for its position inside the Badland's Wall.

IPSWICH, City; Edmunds County Seat; Pop. 1,153 / 969; Zip Code 57451; Lat. 45-26-55 N, Long. 099-01-42 W; Settled in 1883 and named after Ipswich, England.

IRENE, Town; Clay, Turner & Yankton Counties; Pop. 523 / 461; Zip Code 57037; Elev. 1364; Lat. 43-04-58 N, Long. 097-09-31 W; The town's name honors Irene Fry, the daughter of the original landowner.

IROQUOIS, City; Beadle & Kingsbury Counties; Pop. 348 / 295; Zip Code 57353; Elev. 1398; Lat. 44-22-00 N, Long. 097-51-04 W; Founded in the 1880s and named for the Iroquois Indians.

ISABEL, City; Dewey County; Pop. 332 / 335; Zip Code 57633; Lat. 45-23-24 N, Long. 101-24-36 W; The city's name honors a daughter of a Milwaukee railroad official.

JAVA, City; Walworth County; Pop. 261 / 138; Zip Code 57452; Elev. 2079; Lat. 45-30-16 N, Long. 099-52-54 W; Milwaukee Railroad officials named the town after "Java" coffee.

JEFFERSON, Town; Union County; Pop. 592 / 554; Zip Code 57038; Elev. 1119; Lat. 42-36-12 N, Long. 096-33-36 W; The town is named in honor of Thomas Jefferson.

KADOKA, City; Jackson County Seat; Pop. 832 / 746; Zip Code 57543; Elev. 2458; Lat. 43-50-06 N, Long. 101-35-29 W; Founded in 1906 and named a Sioux word meaning "opening" and referring to the town's location along the Badland's wall.

KENNEBEC, Town; Lyman County Seat; Pop. 334 / 292; Zip Code 57544; Elev. 1690; Lat. 43-54-13 N, Long. 099-51-42 W; Established in 1905 and named by Milwaukee railroad officials.

KEYSTONE, Town; Pennington County; Pop. 295 / 236; Zip Code 57751; Elev. 4323; Lat. 43-53-48 N, Long. 103-25-07 W; The town was founded in 1891 and named after a nearby mine.

KIMBALL, City; Brute County; Pop. 752 / 727; Zip Code 57355; Elev. 1788; Lat. 43-44-47 N, Long. 098-57-18 W; Incorporated in 1883 and named in honor of surveyor J.W. Kimball.

KRANZBURG, Town; Codington County; Pop. 136 / 147; Zip Code 57245; Lat. 44-53-35 N, Long. 096-54-54 W; Platted in 1879 and named after the four Kranz brothers, who were pioneer settlers.

LA BOLT, Town; Grant County; Pop. 94 / 81; Zip Code 57246; Elev. 1392; Lat. 45-02-55 N, Long. 096-40-30 W; The town's name remembers Alfred La Bolt, an early landowner.

LAKE ANDES, City; Charles Mix County Seat; Pop. 1,029 / 840; Zip Code 573+; Lat. 43-09-28 N, Long. 098-32-10; Founded in 1904 and named for nearby Lake Andes.

LAKE CITY, Town; Marshall County; Pop. 46 / 42; Zip Code 57247; Elev. 1466; Lat. 45-43-34 N, Long. 097-24-40 W; Established in 1914 and descriptively named for its location in South Dakota's lake region.

LAKE NORDEN, City; Hamlin County; Pop. 417 / 450; Zip Code 57248; Elev. 1864; Lat. 44-34-50 N, Long. 097-12-24 W; Platted in 1908 and named for nearby Lake Norden.

LAKE PRESTON, City; Kingsbury County; Pop. 789 / 634; Zip Code 57249; Lat. 44-21-48 N, Long. 097-22-29 W; Nearby Lake Preston gave its name to the town in 1881.

LANE, Town; Jerauld County; Pop. 83 / 66; Zip Code 57358; Elev. 2882; Lat. 44-04-05 N, Long. 098-25-14 W; The town's name remembers T.W. Lane, who was the original landowner.

LANGFORD, Town; Marshall County; Pop. 307 / 275; Zip Code 57454; Elev. 1376; Lat. 45-36-13 N, Long. 097-49-46 W; Langford is named after original landowner Sam Langford.

LEAD, City; Lawrence County; Pop. 4,330 / 3,376; Zip Code 57754; Lat. 44-20-54 N, Long. 103-45-58 W; Founded as Washington in 1876 and renamed "lead," or gold-bearing vein, in 1877.

LEBANON, Town; Patter County; Pop. 129 / 100; Zip Code 57455; Lat. 45-04-08 N, Long. 099-45-48 W; Plotted in 1887 and named for the country in the Middle East.

LEMMON, City; Perkins County; Pop. 1,871 / 1,339; Zip Code 57638; Elev. 1698; Lat. 45-56-08 N, Long. 102-09-30 W; The town's name honors G.E. Lemmon, a well-known early cowboy.

LENNOX, City; Lincoln County; Pop. 1,827 / 2,319; Zip Code 57039; Elev. 2577; Lat. 43-21-21 N, Long. 096-53-32 W; Settled in 1879 and named for Milwaukee railroad official, Ben Lennox.

LEOLA, City; McPherson County Seat; Pop. 645 / 432; Zip Code 57456; Elev. 1596; Lat. 45-43-13 N, Long. 098-56-11 W; The city is named in honor of Leala Hayes, the daughter of an early pioneer family.

LESTERVILLE, Town; Yankton County; Pop. 156 / 182; Zip Code 57040; Elev. 1380; Lat. 43-02-09 N, Long. 097-35-23 W;

Originally called Moscow, the town's first postmaster, A.S. Duning, had the town renamed Lester for his first grandson.

LETCHER, Town; Sanborn County; Pop. 221 / 189; Zip Code 57359; Elev. 1308; Lat. 43-53-51 N, Long. 098-08-15 W; The town is named after original landowner O.T. Letcher.

LILY, Town; Day County; Pop. 38 / 21; Zip Code 57250; Elev. 1845; Lat. 45-10-36 N, Long. 097-40-52 W; Settled in 1887 and named for the first postmaster's sister, Lily.

LONG LAKE, Town; McPherson County; Pop. 117 / 55; Zip Code 57457; Lat. 45-51-20 N, Long. 099-12-21 W; The town is named for a nearby lake.

LOYALTON, Town; Edmunds County; Pop. 6; Civil War veterans from New Hampshire settled the area in 1887, and gave the town this complimentary name.

MARION, City; Turner County; Pop. 830 / 878; Zip Code 57043; Lat. 43-25-25 N, Long. 097-15-34 W; Established in 1879 and named after the daughter of a Milwaukee railroad official.

MARTIN, City; Bennett County Seat; Pop. 1,018 / 1,267; Zip Code 57551; Lat. 43-10-31 N, Long. 101-43-54 W; The town's name honors US Congressman Eben Martin, who represented South Dakota in 1908-12.

MARVIN, Town; Grant County; Pop. 52 / 36; Zip Code 57251; Lat. 45-15-39 N, Long. 096-54-50 W; Founded as Grant's Siding and named after a Marvin Safe Company vault in the town.

MCINTOSH, City; Carson County Seat; Pop. 418 / 294; Zip Code 57641; Elev. 2301; Lat. 45-55-20 N, Long. 101-18-54 W; McIntosh takes its name from the McIntosh Construction company, who worked here on the Milwaukee Railroad in 1909.

MELLETTE, City; Spink County; Pop. 192 / 180; Zip Code 57461; Elev. 1296; Lat. 45-09-12 N, Long. 098-30-02 W; Settled in 1878 and named in honor of the first governor of South Dakota, Arthur Melette.

MENNO, City; Hutchinson County; Pop. 793 / 737; Zip Code 57045; Elev. 1326; Lat. 43-14-10 N, Long. 097-34-52 W; Founded in 1879 and named for a large colony of Mennonites in the area.

MIDLAND, Town; Hoakan County; Pop. 277 / 210; Zip Code 57552; Elev. 1879; Lat. 44-04-09 N, Long. 101-09-07 W; Established in 1890 and descriptively named for its location halfway between the Missouri and Cheyenne Rivers.

MILBANK, City; Grant County Seat; Pop. 4,120 / 3,730; Zip Code 57252; Elev. 1150; Lat. 45-13-07 N, Long. 096-38-06 W; Railroad director Jeremiah Milbank donated a 15,000-dollar church to the new town, and had it named in his honor.

MILLER, City; Hand County Seat; Pop. 1,931 / 1,642; Zip Code 57362; Elev. 1578; Lat. 44-31-17 N, Long. 098-59-14 W.

MISSION, City; Todd County; Pop. 748 / 974; Zip Code 57555; Elev. 2581; Lat. 43-18-21 N, Long. 100-39-24 W; S.J. Kimmel founded the town in 1915 and descriptively named it for the many churches in the area.

MISSION HILL, Yankton County; Pop. 197 / 193; Zip Code 57046; Lat. 42-55-18 N, Long. 097-16-50 W; Reverend C.B. Nichols named the town for a nearby hill in 1894.

MITCHELL, City; Davison County Seat; Pop. 13,916 / 14,232; Zip Code 57301; Lat. 43-42-34 N, Long. 098-01-35 W; The town's name honors Alexander Mitchell, President of the Milwaukee Railroad in 1879.

MOBRIDGE, City; Walworth County; Pop. 4,174 / 3,501; Zip Code 57601; Elev. 1676; Lat. 45-32-20 N, Long. 100-26-03 W; Established in 1906 and named for a railroad bridge across the Missouri River.

MONTROSE, City; McCook County; Pop. 396 / 427; Zip Code 57048; Elev. 1480; Lat. 43-41-53 N, Long. 097-10-56 W; Settled in 1880 and named after a Walter Scott novel Legend of Montrose.

MORRISTOWN, Town; Carson County; Pop. 127 / 58; Zip Code 57645; Lat. 45-56-12 N, Long. 101-43-02 W; Named after prominent rancher Nets P. Morris, whose cattle drives led to the founding of the town.

MOUND CITY, Town; Campbell County Seat; Pop. 111 / 84; Zip Code 57646; Elev. 1722; Lat. 45-43-24 N, Long. 100-04-10 W; Nearby Indian mounds gave the town its descriptive name.

MOUNT VERNON, City; Davison County; Pop. 402 / 358; Zip Code 57363; Elev. 1411; Lat. 43-42-39 N, Long. 098-15-28 W; Founded in the 1880s and named for George Washington's estate, Mount Vernon.

MURDO, City; Jones County Seat; Pop. 723 / 602; Zip Code 57559; Elev. 2326; Lat. 43-53-10 N, Long. 100-42-20 W; Murdo's name honors early cattleman Murdo McKenzie.

NEW EFFINGTON, Town; Roberts County; Pop. 261 / 208; Zip Code 57255; Elev. 1108; Lat. 45-51-19 N, Long. 096-55-21 W; Effington was moved in 1913 and became New Effington. It had been named for the first girl born in the town.

NEWELL, City; Butte County; Pop. 638 / 713; Zip Code 57760; Elev. 2853; Lat. 44-42-56 N, Long. 103-24-46 W; Founded in 1910 and named in honor of reclamation engineer, F.H. Newell.

NEW UNDERWOOD, Town; Pennington County; Pop. 517 / 575; Zip Code 57761; Elev. 2839; Lat. 44-05-32 N, Long. 102-50-10 W; Established in 1906 and named for Johnny Underwood, the partner of the original landowner.

NEW WITTEN, Town; Tripp County; Pop. 134 / 82; Settled in 1910 and named for a local government land agent.

NISLAND, Town; Butte County; Pop. 216 / 202; Zip Code 57762; Elev. 2857; Lat. 44-40-20 N, Long. 103-32-51 W; The town was founded in 1909 as the land of pioneer Nils Sorenson. It is named in his honor.

NORTH SIOUX CITY, City; Union County; Pop. 1,992 / 2,474; Zip Code 57049; Elev. 1100; Lat. 42-31-37 N, Long. 096-28-56 W; Named after the Sioux Indians.

NORTHVILLE, Town; Spink County; Pop. 138 / 96; Zip Code 57465; Elev. 1279; Lat. 45-09-12 N, Long. 098-35-08 W; Platted in 1881 and given a descriptive name as the northern point of North Western Railroad.

NUNDA, Town; Lake County; Pop. 60 / 45; Zip Code 57050; Lat. 44-09-33 N, Long. 097-01-04 W; Pioneer settler John Fleming named the township for his farmer home in Nunda, Vermont.

OACOMA, Town; Lyman County; Pop. 289 / 396; Zip Code 57365; Elev. 1390; Lat. 43-48-01 N, Long. 099-23-23 W; Founded in 1890 and given a Sioux Indian name meaning "a place between." The name refers to the town's location between the Missouri River and its bluffs.

OELRICHS, Town; Fall River County; Pop. 124 / 144; Zip Code 57763; Lat. 43-10-43 N, Long. 103-13-47 W; Established in 1885 and named in honor of prominent rancher Harry Oelrichs.

OLDHAM, City; Kingsbury County; Pop. 222 / 174; Zip Code 57051; Lat. 44-13-38 N, Long. 097-18-08 W; Originally Huffman, the name was changed by Milwaukee railroad officials to honor Oldham Carrot, a farmer who granted the right-of-way to the railroad.

OLIVET, Town; Hutchinson County; Pop. 96 / 70; Zip Code 57052; Elev. 1220; Lat. 43-14-34 N, Long. 097-40-38 W; Two early settlers named the town after their former home in Olivet, Michigan.

ONAKA, Town; Faulk County; Pop. 70 / 52; Zip Code 57466; Lat. 45-11-29 N, Long. 099-27-48 W; A Sioux Indian word meaning "places."

ONIDA, City; Sully County Seat; Pop. 851 / 698; Zip Code 57564; Lat. 44-42-11 N, Long. 100-03-59 W; New York settlers founded the place in 1883 and named it after Oneida, New York.

ORIENT, Town; Faulk County; Pop. 87 / 54; Zip Code 57467; Lat. 44-54-05 N, Long. 099-05-09 W; Started in 1887 and named by Milwaukee railroad officials for the for east.

ORTLEY, Town; Roberts County; Pop. 80 / 59; Originally Anderson, but later renamed after an Indian who lived in the area.

PARKER, City; Turner County Seat; Pop. 999 / 1,032; Zip Code 57053; Elev. 1372; Lat. 43-23-53 N, Long. 097-08-16 W; Settled in 1879 and named after railroad official Kimball Parker.

PARKSTON, City; Hutchinson County; Pop. 1,545 / 1,629; Zip Code 57366; Elev. 1396; Lat. 43-23-36 N, Long. 097-59-12 W; Parkston's name recalls the original landowner, R.S. Parke.

PEEVER, Town; Roberts County; Pop. 232 / 197; Zip Code 57257; Lat. 45-32-25 N, Long. 096-57-22 W; Landowner, T.H. Peever named the town after himself.

PHILIP, City; Haakon County Seat; Pop. 1,088 / 898; Zip Code 57567; Elev. 2162; Lat. 44-02-17 N, Long. 101-39-36 W; Cattleman James Philip had the town named in his honor in 1907.

PIERPONT, Town; Day County; Pop. 184 / 145; Zip Code 57468; Lat. 45-29-39 N, Long. 097-49-49 W; Settled in 1883 and named after a Milwaukee railroad official.

PIERRE, City; Hughes County Seat; Capital of South Dakota; Pop. 11,973 / 13,357; Zip Code 57501; Elev. 1484; Lat. 44-22-03 N, Long. 100-20-14 W; Settled in 1878 and named for Fort Pierre just across the Missouri River.

PLANKINTON, City; Aurora County Seat; Pop. 644 / 547; Zip Code 57368; Elev. 1525; Lat. 43-42-59 N, Long. 098-29-09 W; Organized in 1881 and named after Milwaukee Railroad Director, John H. Plankinton.

PLATTE, City; Charles Mix County; Pop. 1,334 / 1,365; Zip Code 57369; Elev. 1612; Lat. 43-23-16 N, Long. 098-50-30 W; Dutch settlers named the town for nearby Platte Creek in 1882.

POLLOCK, Town; Campbell County; Pop. 355 / 339; Zip Code 57648; Elev. 1665; Lat. 45-53-54 N, Long. 100-17-51 W; Originally called Harba but renamed to honor pioneer settler James Pollock.

PRESHO, City; Lyman County; Pop. 760 / 720; Zip Code 57568; Lat. 43-54-20 N, Long. 100-03-29 W; Settled in 1905 and named for J.S. Presho, an early trader.

PRINGLE, Town; Custer County; Pop. 105 / 108; Zip Code 57773; Lat. 43-36-31 N, Long. 103-35-47 W; Rancher W.H. Pringle owned the local water rights, and wound up with the town named for him.

PUKWANA, Town; Brute County; Pop. 234 / 271; Zip Code 57370; Elev. 1549; Lat. 43-46-41 N, Long. 099-11-06 W; Founded in 1881 and given an "Indian" name from Longfellow's poem *Hiawatha*.

QUINN, Town; Pennington County; Pop. 80 / 79; Zip Code 57775; Elev. 2606; Lat. 43-59-11 N, Long. 102-07-24 W; Established in 1907 and named for pioneer rancher Michael Quinn.

RAMONA, Town; Lake County; Pop. 241 / 193; Zip Code 57054; Elev. 1800; Lat. 44-07-08 N, Long. 097-12-51 W; Platted in 1886 and named after a Swiss settler family, the Ramons.

RAPID CITY, City; Pennington County Seat; Pop. 46,492 / 58,268; Zip Code 57701; Elev. 3247; Lat. 44-06-00 N, Long. 103-09-07 W; Settled in 1876 and named for Rapid Creek, which flows through the town.

RAYMOND Town; Clark County; Pop. 106 / 94; Zip Code 57258; Elev. 1456; Lat. 44-54-41 N, Long. 097-56-12 W; North Western Railroad Engineer had the town named for him in 1909.

REDFIELD, City; Spink County Seat; Pop. 3,027 / 2,635; Zip Code 57469; Elev. 1303; Lat. 44-52-12 N, Long. 098-30-59 W; Redfield was named in honor of North Western Railroad official J.B. Redfield.

REE HEIGHTS, Town; Hand County; Pop. 88 / 120; Zip Code 57371; Elev. 1729; Lat. 44-31-01 N, Long. 099-12-00 W; Descriptively named for its location near the Arikara hills.

RELIANCE, Town; Lyman County; Pop. 190 / 180; Zip Code 57569; Elev. 1796; Lat. 43-52-54 N, Long. 099-36-00 W; Settled in 1905 and given this popular name by the local townsite officials.

REVILLO, Town; Grant County; Pop. 168 / 158; Zip Code 57259; Elev. 3059; Lat. 44-00-52 N, Long. 096-34-12 W; His name was spelled backward, but the town is named for popular railroad man, J.S. Oliver.

ROCKHAM, Town; Faulk County; Pop. 52 / 46; Zip Code 57470; Elev. 1396; Lat. 44-54-14 N, Long. 098-48-57 W; Named for Rockham, Australia in 1886.

ROSCOE, City; Edmunds County; Pop. 370 / 352; Zip Code 57471; Elev. 1830; Lat. 45-27-03 N, Long. 099-20-01 W; Founded in 1877.

ROSLYN, Town; Day County; Pop. 261; Zip Code 57261; Elev. 1865; Lat. 45-29-23 N, Long. 097-29-16 W; The town's name is a coined word made by Roscoe Conkling of New York.

ROSHOLT, Town; Roberts County; Pop. 4 combining the names of nearby Lakes Rosholt and Linn.

ROSWELL, Town; Miner County; Pop. 19 / 16; Milwaukee Railroad President Roswell Miller had the town named in his honor in 1883.

ST. FRANCIS, Town; Todd County; Pop. 766 / 922; Zip Code 57572; Lat. 43-08-38 N, Long. 100-54-04 W; The town is named after the nearby St. Francis Indian School.

ST. LAWRENCE, Town; Hand County; Pop. 223 / 209; Zip Code 57373; Lat. 44-30-54 N, Long. 098-56-07 W; Settled in 1881 and named for the St. Lawrence.

SALEM, City; McCook County Seat; Pop. 1,486 / 1,315; Zip Code 57058; Elev. 1527; Lat. 43-43-34 N, Long. 097-23-14 W; The first postmaster, O.S. Pender, named the town for his farmer home in Salem, Massachusetts.

SCOTLAND, City; Bon Homme County; Pop. 1,022 / 910; Zip Code 57059; Elev. 1348; Lat. 43-08-42 N, Long. 097-43-09 W; Plotted in 1879 and named by Scottish settlers for their former home.

SELBY, City; Walworth County Seat; Pop. 884 / 647; Zip Code 57472; Elev. 1912; Lat. 45-30-18 N, Long. 100-01-54 W; Founded in 1899 and named after a local railroad official.

SENECA, Town; Faulk County; Pop. 103 / 78; Zip Code 57473; Elev. 1907; Lat. 45-03-41 N, Long. 099-30-42 W; Named by its founders after Seneca, New York.

SHERMAN, Town; Minnehaha County; Pop. 100 / 84; Zip Code 57060; Lat. 43-45-24 N, Long. 096-27-42 W; Territorial banker, E.A. Sherman had the town named in his honor in 1888.

SINAI, Town; Brookings County; Pop. 129 / 116; Zip Code 57061; Lat. 44-14-46 N, Long. 097-02-38 W; Named in 1907 for nearby Lake Sinai.

SIOUX FALLS, City; Lincoln & Minnehaha Counties; Minnehaha County Seat; Pop. 81,343 / 116,720; Zip Code 570+, 571+; Elev. 1442; Lat. 43-31-11 N, Long. 096-33-23 W; Settled in 1857 and descriptively named for its location an the falls of the Big Sioux River.

SISSETON, City; Roberts County Seat; Pop. 2,789 / 2,190; Zip Code 57262; Elev. 1204; Lat. 45-39-49 N, Long. 097-02-58 W; Settled in the late 1860s and named after Fort Sisseton.

SOUTH SHORE, Town; Codington County; Pop. 241 / 258; Zip Code 57263; Elev. 1862; Lat. 45-06-14 N, Long. 096-55-53 W; Named for its location in the South shore of Punished Woman Lake.

SPEARFISH, City; Lawrence County; Pop. 5,251 / 8,332; Zip Code 57783; Elev. 3643; The city was founded in 1876 and after nearby Spearfish Creek.

SPENCER, City; McCook County; Pop. 380 / 304; Zip Code 57374; Elev. 1381; Lat. 43-43-43 N, Long. 097-35-36 W; Settled in the 1880s and named for Omaha Railfard official Hugh Spencer.

SPRINGFIELD, City; Ban Homme County; Pop. 1,377 / 1,147; Zip Code 57062; Elev. 1275; Lat. 42-51-07 N, Long. 097-53-43 W; Incorporated in 1879 and descriptively named for the many springs in the area.

STICKNEY, Town; Aurora County; Pop. 409 / 283; Zip Code 57375; Lat. 43-35-28 N, Long. 098-27-21 W; Plotted in 1905 and named after Milwaukee Railway official, J.B. Stickney.

STOCKHOLM, Town; Grant County; Pop. 95 / 85; Zip Code 57264; Lat. 45-05-59 N, Long. 096-47-50 W; Founded in 1896 by Swedish settlers and named for the capital of Sweden.

STRANDBURG, Town; Grant County; Pop. 79 / 69; Zip Code 57265; Lat. 45-02-39 N, Long. 096-45-31 W; John Strandburg, the first postmaster, left his name on the town.

STRATFORD, Town; Brown County; Pop. 82 / 79; Zip Code 57474; Lat. 45-18-58 N, Long. 098-18-15 W; The name was chosen by officials of the Minneapolis and St. Louis Railway.

STURGIS, City; Meade County Seat; Pop. 5,184 / 5,449; Zip Code 57784; Elev. 3440; The town's name honors Lieutenant J.G. Sturgis, who was killed in 1876 in the Custer massacre.

SUMMIT, Town; Roberts County; Pop. 290 / 261; Zip Code 57266; Lat. 45-18-15 N, Long. 097-02-14 W; Descriptively named for the town's 2000-foot altitude.

TABOR, Town; Ban Homme County; Pop. 460 / 366; Zip Code 57063; Elev. 1364; Lat. 42-56-37 N, Long. 097-39-39 W; Settled in 1872 by Czech emigrants who named the town for a city in Bohemia.

TEA, Town; Lincoln County; Pop. 729 / 1,868; Zip Code 57064; Elev. 1486; Lat. 43-26-49 N, Long. 096-50-05 W; Originally called Bryan, a postal conflict required a town meeting that went on to "tea time." The settlers promptly adopted the name.

TIMBER LAKE, City; Dewey County Seat; Pop. 660 / 532; Zip Code 57656; Lat. 45-25-01 N, Long. 101-04-30 W; The town is named for the nearby lake.

TOLSTOY, Town; Patter County; Pop. 97 / 59; Zip Code 57475; Elev. 1997; Lat. 45-12-32 N, Long. 099-36-23 W; Founded in 1907 and named for the great Russian writer.

TORONTO, Town; Deuel County; Pop. 236 / 201; Zip Code 57268; Lat. 44-34-08 N, Long. 096-38-16 W; Established in 1884 by Daniel McCraney, a settler from Canada.

TRENT, Town; Moody County; Pop. 197 / 239; Zip Code 57065; Elev. 1531; Lat. 43-54-25 N, Long. 096-39-27 W; Founded as Brookfield, but later renamed by railroad officials.

TRIPP, City; Hutchinson County; Pop. 804 / 650; Zip Code 57376; Lat. 43-13-22 N, Long. 097-58-05 W; Barlett Tripp served as territorial chief justice in 1886 when the town was founded. It is named in his honor.

TULARE, Town; Spink County; Pop. 238 / 224; Zip Code 57476; Elev. 1322; Lat. 44-44-05 N, Long. 098-30-37 W; Descriptively named as a marshy region with abundant reeds.

TYNDALL, City; Ban Homme County Seat; Pop. 1,253 / 1,104; Zip Code 57066; Elev. 1422; Lat. 42-59-09 N, Long. 097-51-55 W; Incorporated in 1887 and named in honor of British scientist, John Tyndall.

UTICA, Town; Yankton County; Pop. 100 / 119; Zip Code 57067; Lat. 42-58-48 N, Long. 097-29-45 W; Named after Utica, New York.

VALLEY SPRINGS, City; Minnehaha County; Pop. 801 / 742; Zip Code 57068; Elev. 1392; Lat. 43-34-54 N, Long. 096-26-52 W; Settled in 1872 and named for the many springs in the area.

VEBLEN, City; Marshall County; Pop. 368 / 306; Zip Code 57270; Lat. 45-51-40 N, Long. 097-17-07 W; Founded in 1900 and named for the first homesteader J.E. Veblen.

VERDON, Town; Brown County; Pop. 7 / 7; A misspelling of the French town of Verdun, for which it was named in 1886.

VERMILLION, City; Clay County Seat; Pop. 9,582 / 10,066; Zip Code 57069; Elev. 1931; Lat. 42-45-30 N, Long. 096-54-59 W; Founded in 1859 and named for the adjacent Vermillion River.

VIBORG, City; Turner County; Pop. 812 / 777; Zip Code 57070; Elev. 1304; Lat. 43-10-13 N, Long. 097-04-48 W; Settled in 1886 and named by Danish settlers for a city in Denmark.

VIENNA, Town; Clark County; Pop. 93 / 90; Originally named Stusted, the name was changed in 1888 in honor of the great European city.

VILAS, Town; Miner County; Pop. 28 / 23; Established in 1883 and named in honor of Postmaster General of the United States, W.F. Vilas.

VIRGIL, Town; Beadle County; Pop. 37 / 29; Zip Code 57379; Lat. 44-17-29 N, Long. 098-25-46 W; The town began in the 1880s and was named for the Latin poet Virgil.

VOLGA, City; Brookings County; Pop. 1,221 / 1,350; Zip Code 57071; Elev. 1634; Lat. 44-19-29 N, Long. 096-55-29 W; Settled in the 1880s and named for the great river in Russia.

VOLIN, Town; Yankton County; Pop. 156 / 177; Zip Code 57072; Elev. 1185; Lat. 42-57-29 N, Long. 097-10-51 W; The town is named for pioneer settler, Henry Volin.

WAGNER, City; Charles Mix County; Pop 1,453 / 1,546; Zip Code 57380; Elev. 1448; Lat. 43-04-29 N, Long. 098-17-52 W; Laid out in 1900 and named in honor of postmaster Walt Wagner.

WAKONDA, Town; Clay County; Pop. 383 / 326; Zip Code 57073; Elev. 1377; Lat. 43-00-36 N, Long. 097-06-11 W; Plotted in 1888 and given a Sioux name meaning "holy."

WALL, Town; Pennington County; Pop. 542 / 836; Zip Code 57729; Elev. 2818; Lat. 44-15-19 N, Long. 102-12-29 W; Founded in 1907 near the Badlands National Monument wall and descriptively named for its location.

WALLACE, Town; Codington County; Pop. 90 / 88; Zip Code 57272; Lat. 45-04-58 N, Long. 097-28-45 W; Named for the original landowner.

WARD, Town; Moody County; Pop. 43 / 33; Zip Code 57074; Lat. 44-09-16 N, Long. 096-27-54 W; Settled in the 1880s and named after Dakota railroad promoter, James A. Word.

WARNER, Town; Brown County; Pop. 322 / 415; Zip Code 57479; Elev. 1298; Lat. 45-19-28 N, Long. 098-29-59 W; Warner is named for early settler, Warren Tarbox.

WASTA, Town; Pennington County; Pop. 99 / 90; Zip Code 57791; Elev. 2313; A Sioux Indian word meaning "good."

WATERTOWN, City; Codington County Seat; Pop. 15,649 / 20,063; Zip Code 57201; Elev. 1739; Lat. 44-54-13 N, Long. 097-07-02 W; The city was founded in 1875 and named for Watertown, New York.

WAUBAY, City; Day County; Pop. 675 / 584; Zip Code 57256; Elev. 1814; Lat. 45-20-10 N, Long. 097-12-24 W; The city was named in 1885 for nearby Waubay Lake.

WEBSTER, City; Day County Seat; Pop. 2,417 / 1,847; Zip Code 57274; Elev. 1847; Lat. 45-19-56 N, Long. 097-31-07 W; Plotted in 1881 and named for the first settler, J.B. Webster.

WENTWORTH, Village; Lake County; Pop. 193 / 181; Zip Code 57075; Lat. 43-59-47 N, Long. 096-57-43 W; Founded in 1879 and named for the first settler, George Wentworth.

WESSINGTON, City; Beadle County; Pop. 304 / 222; Zip Code 57381; Elev. 1415; Lat. 44-27-28 N, Long. 098-41-56 W; Settled in 1880 and named for the nearby Wessington Hills.

WESSINGTON SPRINGS, City; Jerauld County Seat; Pop. 1,203 / 911; Zip Code 57382; Elev. 1687; Lat. 44-04-48 N, Long. 098-34-03 W; So named because the town's springs arise from the Wessington Hills.

WESTPORT, Town; Brown County; Pop. 122 / 109; Zip Code 57481; Lat. 45-38-58 N, Long. 098-29-58 W; The town was named for a Milwaukee railroad official.

WHITE, City; Brookings County; Pop. 474 / 528; Zip Code 57276; Elev. 1777; Lat. 44-26-09 N, Long. 096-38-33 W; Plotted in 1884 and named for the original settler, W.H. White.

WHITE LAKE, City; Aurora County; Pop. 419 / 414; Zip Code 57383; Lat. 43-43-42 N, Long. 098-42-51 W; First known as Siding 36, it was later named for nearby White Lake.

WHITE RIVER, City; Mellette County Seat; Pop. 561 / 547; Zip Code 57579; Lat. 43-34-04 N, Long. 100-44-34 W; Founded in 1911 and named after the adjacent White River.

WHITE ROCK, Town; Roberts County; Pop. 10 / 7; Descriptively named for a large gray rock landmark near the town.

WHITEWOOD, City; Lawrence County; Pop. 821 / 903; Zip Code 57793; Elev. 3748; Plotted in 1888 and named for the numerous birch and aspen trees in the area.

WILLOW LAKE, City; Clark County; Pop. 375 / 312; Zip Code 57271; Lat. 44-42-23 N, Long. 097-29-55 W; Settled in 1882 and named for a nearby lake.

WILMOT, City; Roberts County; Pop. 507 / 553; Zip Code 57279; Lat. 45-24-32 N, Long. 096-51-34 W; The town is named in honor of distinguished Judge Wilmot Brookings, a well-known early pioneer.

WINFRED, Town; Lake County; Pop. 81; Zip Code 57076; Elev. 1710; Lat. 43-59-49 N, Long. 097-21-40 W; Founded in 1882 and named for the daughter of an early settler.

WINNER, City; Tripp County Seat; Pop. 3,472 / 3,284; Zip Code 57580; Lat. 43-22-26 N, Long. 099-51-39 W; Named as the winner of the railroad right-of-way contest in the area.

WOLSEY, Town; Beadle County; Pop. 437 / 396; Zip Code 57384; Lat. 44-24-32 N, Long. 098-28-24 W; Settled in 1882 and named after Cardinal Thomas Wolsey, a 16th century British prelate.

WOOD, Town; Mellette County; Pop. 134 / 69; Zip Code 57585; Lat. 43-29-39 N, Long. 100-28-45 W; A. K. Wood founded the town in 1910. It is named in his honor.

WOONSOCKET, City; Sanborn County Seat; Pop. 799 / 724; Zip Code 57385; Elev. 1307; Lat. 44-03-18 N, Long. 098-16-16 W; Settled in 1883 and named after Woonsocket, Rhode Island.

YANKTON, City; Yankton County Seat; Pop. 12,011 / 14,079; Zip Code 57079. The name comes from the Sioux Indian name *Ihanktonwan*, meaning "end village."

TENNESSEE
The Volunteer State

The Cherokee National Forest

Davy Crockett Birthplace State Park - Limestone

GOVERNOR
Don Sundquist

National Civil Rights
Museum - Memphis

Knoxville skyline

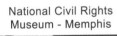

The District at Night - Nashville

Jack Daniel Distillery - Lynchburg

INTRODUCTION

Tennessee is primarily an agricultural state. Thus, the culture of its people has grown out of their struggle with the earth. This is true despite the rapid growth of industry, for even urban areas continue to be dominated by the traditions of farm life. With few exceptions, the cities largely retain the flavor of country towns.

East, middle, and west Tennessee, the three geographical divisions, are in many ways like separate states. Although the people are alike in heritage and in general attitude, there are striking sectional differences fostered by the lay of the land. West Tennesseans may differ as much from East Tennesseans in manners and customs as the people of the Appalachian Mountain regions differ from those of the Mississippi Delta.

A noted Tennessee orator used to declare: "Our great State is the *multum in parvo* of all the lands lying between the ramparts of the Alleghenies and the majestic currents of the mighty Mississippi. Within its borders flourished every shape of beast and bug, every variety of tree and flower found from the blue waters of the Gulf to the somber snow laden forests of Canada."

Stated in less sweeping language, this would not be the exaggeration it seems. A relief map shows Tennessee as a succession of mountain slopes, the worn-down remnant of the towering Appalachian chain of remote geologic time. From the crest of the Great Smokies, the land drops westward in a series of lower ridge and plateau systems to the Mississippi bottoms.

Roughly a parallelogram in shape, with an east-west length of 432 miles and a width of 106 miles, Tennessee is bounded on the north by Kentucky and Virginia; on the east by North Carolina; on the south by Georgia, Alabama, and Mississippi; and on the west by the Mississippi River, which separates it from Arkansas and Missouri. Of its total area of 42,144 square miles, 989 are water surface.

STATE NAME

From the time Tennessee was discovered until the time it was admitted as a State into the Union, the region had a long and checkered career. First, it was a part of the original territory granted by King Charles II to the Lords Proprietors of Carolina in 1665. It was known as the Washington District from 1775 to 1776. It was formed into the State of Franklin on August 23, 1784, and existed as such until 1788. It was then formed into the Territory South of the Ohio.

As is true in many other states, the name *Tennessee* is derived from the American Indian dialect; however, it cannot be definitely traced to any specific parent Indian word, since there are several Indian words from which historians claim it originated. But the consensus of critical opinion seems to be that the State name is derived from the Indian word *Tenasee, Tanasi, Tanassee, or Tansi,* the name of the ancient capital of the Cherokee tribe which dwelt "on the west bank of the present Little Tennessee River, a few miles above the mouth of Tellico, and afterwards gave the name to the Tennessee River and to the State." It is speculated that the river was named after the villages and the region was named after the river.

Some historians say that the first mention of the name Tennessee (*Tanassee*) was by Alexander Cummings, who, in 1730, "had been sent by Great Britain to meet the chiefs of all the Cherokee towns at Nequasse, near the present town of Franklin in North Carolina." Some fanciful derivations of the original name are river with a big bend and a curved spoon.

When the matter of naming the State came up, several names were suggested. One name was *Cherake*, the old Indian name for what is now the Tennessee River. The river, however, had been called the *Tennessee* for a long time, and the whole Southwest Territory was often called the Tennessee country; therefore Tennessee was adopted as the name of the State.

STATE NICKNAMES

The following are nicknames for Tennessee: the Big Bend State, the Hog and Hominy State, the Mother of South-western Statesmen, and the Volunteer State.

The first of these, no doubt, originated in the expression "The River with the Big Bend," which is the Indian name for the Tennessee River. Tennessee received the nickname of the Hog and Hominy State because corn and pork products of Tennessee reached such great proportions between 1800 and 1840. The name eventually became obsolete and is today not used.

Because Tennessee furnished the United States with three presidents and a number of distinguished statesmen, it came to be designated as The Mother of South-western Statesmen.

With regard to the sobriquet, the Volunteer State, Governor Brown on May 26, 1847, called for three regiments of soldiers to serve in the Mexican War. Thirty thousand volunteered at once; consequently Tennessee was nicknamed the Volunteer State.

Tennesseans have been nicknamed Big-benders, Butter-nuts, and Mudheads. The first nickname is derived from the fact that the Tennessee River is called the river with a big bend, referring in all probability to the Moccasin bend at the foot of Lookout Mountain at Chattanooga. The name Butter-nuts was first given to the soldiers of Tennessee during the Civil War from the tan color of their uniforms, and later it came to be applied to the people of the entire State. Mudheads was given as a nickname to Tennesseans by more than one early writer, but its origin and significance are not explained.

THE GREAT SEAL

Tennessee has no officially designated seal. However, the seal in use today is essentially the same as the one recommended in 1801 by a special committee.

Each of the three constitutions of Tennessee said that "there shall be a seal of this state, which shall be kept by the governor, and used by him officially, and shall be called the 'Great Seal of the State of Tennessee.'"

John Trotwood Moore, late State Librarian and Archivist, said "there is no evidence that any action was taken relative to procuring a great seal until April 29, 1796, when the General Assembly passed an act authorizing the governor to procure a seal for the use of the state."

A committee was appointed by the legislative bodies of Tennessee to devise and report on a suitable State seal on September 26, 1801. The report of this committee was made and adopted on November 14, 1801, which provided the following: "the said seal shall be a circle, two inches and a quarter in diameter, that the circumference contain the words THE GREAT SEAL OF TENNESSEE, that in the lower part of said circumference be inserted Feb. 6th 1796, the date of the constitution of this State; that in the inside of the upper part of said circle, be set in numerical letters XVI, the number of the state in chronological order; that under the base of the upper semicircle, there be the word AGRICULTURE; that above said base, there be the figure of a plough, sheaf of wheat and cotton plant; that in the lower part of the lower semicircle, there be the word COMMERCE, and said lower semicircle shall also contain the figure of a boat and boatman."

The above seal was used until 1829, when a second seal came into use, and was used until 1865. The so-called Brownlow Seal was used in 1865, and afterward two new seals came into use. The seal used today is the larger of the two new seals, and differs from the original 1801 seal in that the boat is a different design, and it is pointed in the opposite direction. Also, the month and day were dropped from the date.

STATE FLAG

The State flag of Tennessee was designed by LeRoy Reeves and was approved by an act of the legislature on April 17, 1905. The description is as follows: "The flag or banner of the state of Tennessee shall be of the following design, colors, and proportions, to wit, an oblong flag or banner in length one and two thirds (1 2/3) times its width, the principal field of same to be of color red, but said flag or banner ending at its free or outer end in a perpendicular bar of blue, of uniform width, running from side to side, that is to say, from top to bottom of said flag or banner, and separated from the red field by a narrow margin or stripe of white of uniform width; the width of the white stripe to be one fifth (1/5) that of the blue bar; and the total width of the bar and stripe together to be equal to one eighth (1/8) of the width of the flag. In the center of the red field shall be a smaller circular field of blue, separated from the surrounding red field by a circular margin or stripe of white of uniform width and of the same width as the straight margin or stripe first mentioned. The breadth or diameter of the circular blue field, exclusive of the white margin, shall be equal to one half (½) of the width of the flag. Inside the circular blue field shall be three (3) five-pointed stars of white distributed at equal intervals around a point, the center of the blue field, and of such size and arrangement that one (1) point of each star shall approach as closely as practicable without actually touching one (1) point of each of the other two (2) around the center point of the field; and the two (2) outer points of each star shall approach as nearly as practicable without actually touching the periphery of the blue field. The arrangement of the three (3) stars shall be such that the centers of no two (2) stars shall be in a line parallel to either the side or end of the flag, but intermediate between same; and the highest star shall be the one nearest the upper confined corner of the flag."

STATE MOTTO

The State motto of Tennessee, *Agriculture and Commerce*, was officially adopted in 1987, although it was used on the State seal since 1801. Agriculture denotes "that the first reliance of the state should be upon products of the soil...," and Commerce indicates "that the prosperity of all may be promoted through this means."

The legislature also has a state slogan, *Tennessee—America at Its Best*, which was adopted in 1965.

STATE BIRD

Tennessee, by Senate Joint Resolution Number 51 on April 19, 1933, adopted the mockingbird, *Mimus polyglottos*, as the official State bird.

The resolution is as follows: "WHEREAS, forty-five of the forty-eight States of the Union have chosen an official bird for their commonwealth, and

"WHEREAS, the State of Tennessee did not, until this year, determine to choose the State Bird, and

"WHEREAS, the Tennessee Ornithological Society, aided by the Garden Clubs, the Parent Teacher Associations, the Superintendents of Schools, the State Department of Education, the State Department of Agriculture and the Division of Game and Fish, has just conducted a campaign of education in connection with the state-wide choice of an official bird, and

"WHEREAS, an election has just been concluded in which every person within the confines of the State has been afforded an opportunity of expressing a preference for a State bird, and

"WHEREAS, the Mocking Bird received more votes, according to the official count of the ballots, made by the Department of Game and Fish, now

"THEREFORE, be it resolved, that the Mocking Bird is hereby declared the official State bird of Tennessee."

The *Nashville Banner* says that on April 11, 1933 the mockingbird was selected as the State bird of Tennessee by popular vote, that the Tennessee Ornithological Society planned a state-wide ballot for the selection of the official bird, and that there was a total of 72,031 votes cast, distributed as follows: the mockingbird, 15,553; the robin, 15,073; the cardinal, 13,969; the bobwhite, 10,460; the bluebird, 9,125; and others, 8,751.

The mockingbird ranges in the eastern United States and southern Canada, along the Gulf coast to Texas, and on the Bahaman Islands. It is 8 ½ to nine inches in length, with a tail length of four to 4 ½ inches.

The bird is mostly plain gray or brownish gray from the top of the head over most of the back region. Lateral tail feathers are white; the wings and tail are dull blackish slate; the middle and greater wing coverts are tipped with dull or grayish white. Primary coverts are white with a subterminal dusky spot or streak. The auricular region is gray, and the area beneath the eye and along the side of the head is dull white transversely flecked with gray or dusky. The chin and throat are dull white margined along each side by a distinct dusky streak. The chest is pale smoke gray turning to white on the center of the breast and abdomen. Feathers under the tail are pale buff or buff white. When the mockingbird is in flight, the broad white spots above can easily be seen against the slate black of the upper wings.

The mockingbird is a sturdy creature that builds a nest that may last several seasons. From the time the nest is completed to the time when fledglings take flight is from three to four weeks. Eggs range in color from bright blue to bluish green or greenish blue spotted with hazel or cinnamon. Both sexes build the nests, and both also care for the young.

In personality, mockingbirds are feisty creatures who fight among themselves as well as tormenting dogs and cats. The bird is also a masterful imitator, and is considered one of the most versatile and beautiful songsters; it may sometimes change tunes as much as thirty times within a ten-minute period. The diet of the bird consists of insects and wild fruit.

STATE FLOWER

Tennessee has experienced a curious situation in that it has officially adopted two State flowers—a wildflower and a cultivated flower. The reasons are as follows:

The General Assembly of the State of Tennessee by Senate Joint Resolution Number 13, on January 23, 1919, resolved:

"That the Governor of the State be authorized and requested to name a commission of five distinguished citizens of the State, who shall serve without compensation, which commission shall be headed by the State Superintendent of Public Instruction, to name a date on which the school children of the state may have the right and opportunity of voting on a State flower for the State of Tennessee," also

"That the flower which shall be named by the school children and certified by said commission shall be the recognized State flower."

The flower selected was the passion flower, genus *Passiflora*, also called the wild apricot, the may-pop, and the ocoee. From this flower the Indians took the names of the Ocoee valley and river, and they prized it as the most abundant and beautiful of all their flowers.

Then, by Senate Joint Resolution Number 53 approved on April 19, 1933, Tennessee adopted the Iris, genus *Iridaceae*, as the State flower.

"WHEREAS, the Iris is one of the most beautiful and one of the most popular flowers in the State, its profusion and beauty attracting many visitors to the State, now, therefore,

"Be it resolved by the Sixty-eighth General Assembly of the State of Tennessee, the Senate and House concurring, that the Iris be adopted as the State flower of Tennessee."

The law adopting the Iris as the State flower of Tennessee did not abolish the act of 1919 adopting the passion flower selected by the school children of the state. Because of this, an act in 1973 gave Tennessee two official state flowers. Today, the State wildflower is the passion flower, and the State cultivated flower is the iris.

STATE TREE

In 1947, the legislature selected the tulip poplar, *Liriodendron tulipifera*, as the official State tree of Tennessee. The tree is plentiful throughout the State, and early settlers found it to be particularly useful for dwelling and barn construction.

The tulip poplar is also commonly called the yellow poplar, blue poplar, hickory poplar, basswood, cucumber tree, tulipwood, whitewood, white poplar, poplar, and oldwife's shirt-tree. It is native to the eastern third of the United States and southern Ontario.

The tulip tree is the tallest of the eastern hardwoods. Its bark is brown, becoming thick and deeply furrowed. The unusually shaped leaves are square-like with a broad, slightly notched or nearly straight apex and two or three lobes on each side. Leaves are from three to six inches long, shiny dark green above and pale green underneath. Flowers are large and tulip shaped, from 1 ½ to two inches in diameter, and is usually green except in the spring, when they are orange. The fruit is cone-like; from 2 ½ to three inches long, and ½ inch thick.

STATE SONG

The State of Tennessee has five official songs. The reason for this is that, while the legislature has designated new official songs, it has never repealed formerly designated songs.

The first official song, "My Homeland, Tennessee," by Nell Grayson Taylor and Roy Lamont Smith, was adopted in 1925. In 1935, the legislature adopted "When It's Iris Time in Tennessee," by Willa Mae Waid as the State's second official song. In 1955, "My Tennessee," by Francis Hannah Tranum was adopted as the third song. "The Tennessee Waltz" by Redd Stewart and Pee Wee King became the fourth officially adopted song in 1965. The fifth song is "Rocky Top," by Boudleaux and Felice Bryant, adopted in 1982.

STATE LICENSE PLATE

The State of Tennessee first required motor vehicle registrations in 1905. However, it was not until 1915 that the State supplied the license plates. Before this, owners were required to make their own plates, which were usually fashioned from leather or enamel. In 1915, the plate had white numerals on a blue background. Annual issues of plates took place until 1943, when a corner tab was used on the 1942 plate. Plates were again issued annually until 1962. Between 1956 and 1976, plates were either black on white or white on black. From 1977 through 1987, the plate was white with blue numerals. The most current plate, issued on 1988, has the state name in blue at the top, the name of the country in white on a blue background strip on the bottom, and numerals in red. The tri-star symbol that bisects the license plate number in the center is a reproduction of the emblem on the State flag, which was designed in 1905.

The current plate is the 2000 series with "TENNESSEE" in all capital letters printed in blue letters across the center of the top; the background of the plate is white. Across the center of the plate are black numerals with a yellow sun rising over the top of the state of Tennessee; the slogan "Volunteer State" appears under the state. Each plate denotes the county in which the owner lives.

STATE POSTAGE STAMP

Tennessee issued a purple three-cent Tennessee Statehood Commemorative stamp in Nashville on June 1, 1946. It was designed by V.S. McCloskey, Jr., and engraved by C.A. Brooks, C.T. Arlt, and A.W. Christensen.

A design of the State capitol, reminiscent of and Ionic temple is at the center of the stamp. To the upper left, on an oval panel, is a portrait of Andrew Jackson. On the upper right, on a symmetrical panel, is a portrait of John Sevier, early governor and founding father of the State. The stamp commemorates the 150th anniversary of Tennessee statehood and identifies Tennessee as the Volunteer State. A total of 132,274,500 of the stamp were printed.

OTHER STATE DESIGNATIONS

The legislature of Tennessee has officially adopted additional symbols to represent the State through the years. They include the official game bird (1988) as the Bobwhite quail; the official gem (1979) as the Tennessee pearl; the official rock (1979) as limestone; and the official insects (1975) as the firefly and ladybug.

CAPITOL BUILDING

In 1843, forty-seven years after joining the Union, a bitter debate was ended when Nashville became the permanent capital city of Tennessee. An area known as Campbell's Hill, purchased by the city in 1843 for 30,000 dollars, was given to the State for the capitol site. The cornerstone of the capitol building in Nashville was laid on July 4, 1845, but the structure was not completed until 1855. William Strickland of Philadelphia, Pennsylvania, was the architect who designed it. This building "follows the lines of a Greek Ionic Temple, with the tower rising 205 feet from the ground, patterned after Demosthenes' Lantern of Athens."

The structure, built in the form of a parallelogram, is 239 feet and three inches long, 112 feet and five inches wide, and 191 feet and seven inches high from the ground to the top of the tower. It was built from stratified limestone embedded with fossils, which was quarried about a half mile west of the building. Exterior restoration took place in 1956, and interior restoration and repair were done in 1958. In 1969-70, additional restoration work was undertaken in the assembly chambers and in various other offices and meeting rooms of the capitol.

OTHER FACTS ABOUT TENNESSEE

Total area: 42,144 square miles
Land area: 41,155 square miles
Water area: 989 square miles
Average elevation: 900 feet
Highest point: Clingmans Dome, 6,643 feet
Lowest point: Mississippi River: 178 feet
Highest temperature: 113 degrees Fahrenheit
Lowest temperature: -32 degrees Fahrenheit
Population in 1990: 4,877,185
Population density in 1990: 118.32 persons per square mile
Population 1980-1990: +6.2 percent change
Population projected for year 2000: 5,266,000
Black population in 1990: 778,035
Hispanic population in 1990: 32,741
Native American population in 1990: 10,039
White population in 1990: 4,048,068
Capital: Nashville
Admitted to Union: June 1, 1796
Order of Statehood: 16
Electoral votes: 11

CHRONOLOGY

1541 De Soto crosses Mississippi at or near Fourth Chickasaw Bluff, where Memphis now stands.

1673 Needham and Arthur enter East Tennessee.
– Joliet and Marquette descend Mississippi from Wisconsin River to 34 N Latitude and stop at Chickasaw Bluffs.

1682 La Salle builds Fort Prud'homme on First Chickasaw Bluff near mouth of Hatchie River.

1692 Martin Chartier, one of La Salle's men, after some years' stay with Shawnee of Cumberland Valley, travels from French Lick up Cumberland River and overland to Virginia.

1711 Eleazer Wiggan, English trader, establishes trade with Overhill Cherokee.

1714 Charleville, French trader, operates trading post at Great French Lick, where Nashville now stands.

1730 Sir Alexander Cuming negotiates first treaty between English and Cherokee; group of chiefs go with him to England.

1736 Christian Priber reaches Cherokee town of Great Tellico; he makes plans to establish "Kingdom of Paradise."
May 20. D'Artaguette is defeated by Chickasaw and English traders.
May 26. Bienville's forces are defeated by Chickasaw.

1748 Dr. Thomas Walker of Virginia explores vicinity of present Kingsport.

1750 Walker and party explore upper East Tennessee and pass through Cumberland Gap into Kentucky; Walker is first explorer to record discovery of what he later names Cumberland Gap.

1756 Major Andrew Lewis builds Virginia fort near Chota, Cherokee capital.

1757 Fort Loudoun, near Virginia fort, is completed; it is first Anglo-American fort in Tennessee to be garrisoned.

1758 Presbyterian Mission is established at Fort Loudoun by Rev. John Martin.

1760 War is fought between English and Cherokee; Indians take Fort Loudoun.
– Daniel Boone is commissioned by Henderson and Co. to scout East Tennessee.

1761 Peace is made between English and Cherokee.
– Ensign Henry Timberlake and Sergeant Thomas Sumter travel through Overhill Cherokee country.
– Elijah Walden, with party of Long Hunters, explores East Tennessee and Cumberland Valley.
– Fort Robinson is built by Col. Adam Stephen near Long Island of Holston River, site of modern Kingsport.

1763 Ensign Timberlake, Sergeant Sumter, Ostenaco, and two warriors visit England.

1764 Henry Scaggs (Scoggins) explores Tennessee region as representative of Henderson & Co.

1766 Col. James Smith leads exploring party that discovers Stone's River, named for Uriah Stone, a member of party.

1768 Treaty of Hard Labour between English and Cherokee is signed.

1769 William Bean, supposed to have been first permanent settler in Tennessee, builds cabin on Boone's Creek near junction with Watauga River.

1772 Watauga Association is formed; first independent government is established in America by native white Americans.

1775 Washington District supersedes Watauga Association.
March 17. Richard Henderson and Co. buys Cherokee land between Kentucky and Cumberland rivers.

1776 July 20. Battle of Island Flats is fought between settlers and Cherokee.
July 31. Indians attack Fort Coswell.

1777 Washington District becomes Washington County, with boundaries co-extensive with present State of Tennessee.
July 20. Commissioners of Virginia and North Carolina negotiate Treaty of Long Island with Cherokee.

1779 Jonesboro, first town in Tennessee, is established.
– Col. Evan Shelby defeats hostile Chickamauga near present site of Chattanooga.
– James Robertson, "Father of Tennessee," reaches Cumberland Settlement.
– John Donelson begins voyage on flatboat *Adventure*.
– Commissioners of Virginia and North Carolina run separate boundary lines called, respectively, "Walker's Line" and "Henderson's Line."

1780 Rev. Samuel Doak, pioneer evangelist, preaches at Salem.
– Martin Academy (Doak's school) is established at Monette; it is first institution of higher learning in Mississippi Valley (chartered in 1783).
April 24. John Donelson and party reach Nashborough (Nashville).
– Cherokee towns are destroyed by Sevier.
May 1. Cumberland Compact is signed by Cumberland settlers.
October 7. Battle of King's Mountain is fought; Tennessee troops participate.

1781 January 15. Battle of Freeland Station is fought between settlers and hostile Cherokee and Creek.
April 2. Battle of the Bluffs is fought between Cumberland settlers and Chickamauga.

1782 John Sevier defeats Chickamauga and burns their towns.

1783 June 1. McGillivray, Creek chief, forms alliance with Spanish.
– Indians raid Cumberland settlements.
– Davidson County is organized.

1784 June 2. North Carolina cedes western lands to U.S., but repeals act in same year.
December 14. State of Franklin is established; constitution is adopted.
– Nashville is incorporated to succeed Nashborough.

1785 Davidson Academy, forerunner of University of Nashville, and George Peabody College for Teachers, are chartered.
March. First Franklin Legislature meets at Greeneville.
– John Sevier is elected governor.
– Four new counties are established.
November. Hopewell Treaty is signed by U.S. Commissioners and Cherokee Chiefs; Cherokee title to Tennessee lands is recognized by U.S.

1786 Treaty of Hopewell between U.S. and Chickasaw is signed; Chickasaw title to West Tennessee is recognized by U.S. Franklin and North Carolina both claim jurisdiction in East Tennessee.
– Capt. James White and James Connor settle on site of Knoxville.

1787 Franklin Legislature meets at Greeneville for last time.
– Robertson conducts Coldwater Expedition against Creek Indians near Muscle Shoals.

1788 Peter Avery blazes Avery's Trace from East Tennessee across Cumberland Plateau to Nashville.
March. Government of Franklin collapses.
– Spanish agents intrigue against colonists.
April. Bishop Francis Asbury holds first Methodist Conference west of Alleghenies at Half-Acres in East Tennessee.

1789 John Sevier is elected first Representative to U.S. Congress from Washington District.
– District of Mero is established in Middle Tennessee.
December 22. North Carolina cedes western lands to U.S.

1790 Territorial U.S. Census population is 35,691.
May 26. Congress passes act for government of "Territory of the United States South of the River Ohio," including Tennessee.
– William Blount, appointed Territorial Governor, takes oath on September 20 and organizes Washington County on October 22.

1791 William Blount, Governor of the Territory South of the River Ohio, establishes headquarters at White's Fort (Knoxville); Knoxville is platted.
July 2. Treaty of Holston, between U.S. and Cherokee, is signed; Indian land cession is secured, new boundaries are agreed upon, and Cherokee come under protection of government.
November 5. Knoxville *Gazette*, weekly newspaper, is established at Rogersville.

1792 September 10. Andrew Jackson receives his first military appointment, "Judge Advocate for Davidson Regiment."
September 30. Buchanan's Station is attacked by Indians.

1793 September 25. Cavett's Station is destroyed by Indians.

1794 September 10. Blount College, forerunner of University of Tennessee, is chartered (opened 1795).
September 13. James Ore destroys Chickamauga towns of Nickajack and Running Water.

1795 Walton Road is completed from Knoxville to Nashville across Cumberland Plateau.

1796 February 6. First State constitution is adopted.

March 29. First General Assembly meets at Knoxville.

March 30. First State Governor, John Sevier, is inaugurated; he serves until 1801, and again from 1803 to 1809.

March 31. William Blount and William Cocke are elected first United States senators; they are reelected four months later.

June 1. Tennessee is admitted into Union as sixteenth state.

November 12. Jackson is first Representative in Congress from Tennessee; he takes seat December 5.

1797 Jackson succeeds William Cocke as U.S. Senator.

January 23. Thomas Embree, in Knoxville *Gazette* article, urges organization of an abolition society.

July 8. William Blount is expelled from U.S. Senate.

1798 Jackson resigns as U.S. senator and is appointed judge of State Superior Court.

1800 Population is 105,602.

– Great religious revival sweeps State.

1802 Jackson is elected major general of militia in contest with John Sevier and James Winchester.

1803 General Wilkinson builds Fort Pickering at Memphis.

1805 Aaron Burr visits Nashville on way to Mississippi territory.

1806 May 30. Jackson kills Charles Dickinson in duel in Logan, Kentucky.

April 18. Congress grants 1,000 acres to be sold for support of county academies, and 1,000 acres more for two colleges, Blount in east and Cumberland in west.

1807 Nashville Bank, first in Tennessee, is chartered.

1810 Population is 261,727.

February 4. Cumberland Presbyterian Church is organized in Dickson County.

1811 Bank of the State of Tennessee is established.

1812 September 12. Legislature convenes in Nashville for first time.

1813 September 4. Jackson is seriously wounded by Bentons at Talbot (afterward City) Hotel, Nashville.

September 7. Jackson mobilizes troops at Fayetteville for Creek War.

1814 March 27. Jackson defeats Creeks at Battle of Tohopeka, ending Creek War.

April 20. Treaty of Fort Jackson is made with Creeks.

1815 Manumission Society of Tennessee is organized at Lost Creek, Jefferson County.

January 8. Jackson defeats British forces at New Orleans.

September. John Sevier dies near Fort Decatur, Alabama.

1818 January-May. Jackson is ordered to direct campaign against Seminoles; he drives Spanish garrison from Pensacola.

October 19. Jackson and Isaac Shelby, Governor of Kentucky, as U.S. Commissioners, make treaty with Chickasaw, who cede to U.S. all territory claimed by them east of Mississippi River and north of 35 latitude.

1819 First steamboat arrives at Nashville.

– W.L. Brown and Felix Grundy are appointed commissioners for Tennessee to determine (with Kentucky commissioners) line between Tennessee and Kentucky.

– John Overton, with collaboration of Jackson and James Winchester, lays out city of Memphis.

– *Manumission Intelligencer*, later *Emancipator*, first anti-slavery paper in United States, is published at Jonesboro.

1820 Population is 422,823.

– Madison County is organized and Jackson is settled.

1821 Jackson is appointed Territorial Governor of Florida.

1823 *Pioneer*, first newspaper in West Tennessee, is established at Jackson.

– Jackson is elected U.S. Senator to succeed Col. John Williams.

1825 Nashoba, Fanny Wright's colony for freed slaves, is established.

May 4. Lafayette visits Nashville.

1826 Memphis *Advocate* is established; it is first newspaper in Memphis.

– Duel is fought between Sam Houston and Gen. William White.

– Davy Crockett is elected to U.S. Congress.

1827 Davidson Academy becomes University of Nashville.

August. Sam Houston is elected governor.

– Jackson defeats John Quincy Adams for president of the United States.

– First steamboat reaches Knoxville.

1829 April. Governor Houston resigns governorship, and goes into voluntary exile among Cherokee in Arkansas.

March 9. John H. Eaton is appointed Secretary of War by President Jackson.

1830 Population is 681,904.

1831 *Railroad Advocate*, one of first newspapers devoted to railroad promotion, is published at Rogersville.

1833 Epidemic of Asiatic cholera sweeps over Tennessee; large cities are paralyzed, and many small towns are almost depopulated.

1834 New State constitution is adopted.

1835 James K. Polk becomes Speaker of national House of Representatives.

March 5 and 6. New constitution is ratified by people.

1836 Sam Houston and other Tennesseans lead Texans in war for independence from Mexico.

– First superintendent of public instruction is appointed.

1837 Uniform system of public schools in State is established by law.

1838 Great Removal of Cherokee from Tennessee begins.
– James K. Polk is elected governor, serving from 1839-41.

1840 Population is 829,210.

1842 First train in Tennessee makes exhibition run over LaGrange and Memphis Railroad.
– Cumberland University at Lebanon is chartered and opened.

1843 Nashville becomes State capital.

1844 November. James K. Polk becomes President-elect.

1845 January 1. Work begins on State capitol.
July 4. Great "Western and Southwestern Convention" is held in Memphis to promote railroad connection between Tennessee and other southern states.
June 8. Andrew Jackson dies at Hermitage, at age 78.

1847 New Orleans and Ohio Telegraph Company is chartered; it is first company of its kind in Tennessee.
May 26. Governor Brown calls for volunteers for Mexican War; Tennessee's quota is 2,800, but 30,000 respond, and Tennessee becomes nicknamed "Volunteer State."

1849 Tennessee Historical Society is founded.
June 5. James K. Polk dies at Nashville, at age 54 years.
December. Memphis is given city charter.

1850 Population is 1,002,717.
June 3. Southern Convention opens nine-day session at Nashville to discuss slavery question.

1851 Col. John Pope wins first prize in cotton exhibit at World's Fair in London.
April 13. Nashville & Chattanooga Railroad, first railroad successfully operated in Tennessee, begins service.

1853 Andrew Johnson is elected governor, serving 1853-57.
– State Library is founded.

1854 February 28. Governor Andrew Johnson's recommendation for tax to provide public schools becomes law.
– State agricultural bureau is established and county agricultural societies are organized.

1855 State capitol is completed.
– First Biennial State Fair, forerunner of present annual State Fair, is held in Nashville.
– Nashville Academy of Music and Fine Arts is incorporated.

1860 Population is 1,109,801.

1861 May 6. Tennessee, by legislative act, secedes from Union.
June 24. Governor Harris proclaims Tennessee's secession from Union.
September. Gen. Albert Sidney Johnston prepares State military defense.

1862 February 6. Confederate Fort Henry surrenders.
February 16. Confederate Fort Donelson surrenders.
February 20. Seat of State government is removed to Memphis.
March 3. Andrew Johnson is appointed military governor of Tennessee.
April 6-7. Battle of Shiloh is fought.
July-September. Gen. Nathan Bedford Forrest raids Federal troops in Middle Tennessee.
August 16. General Bragg begins Tennessee campaign at Chattanooga; General Forrest raids Federal troops in West Tennessee.

1863 On December 31 (1862), January 1 and 2, Battle of Stone's River is fought.
June 20-July 7. Confederate army under Bragg retires to Tullahoma, blocking way to Chattanooga.
September 19-20. Battle of Chickamauga is fought.
November 24-25. Battle of Chattanooga (Missionary Ridge and Lookout Mountain) fought; Bragg, outnumbered, retreats to Georgia.

1864 September 4. Gen. John H. Morgan is killed at Greeneville, East Tennessee.
November 4. Gov. Andrew Johnson becomes Vice-President elect.
November 30. Battle of Franklin is fought.
December 15-16. Battle of Nashville is fought.

1865 Reconstruction begins.
March 4. William G. Parson Brownlow is elected Governor.
April 5. Legislature ratifies 13th amendment.
April 15. Andrew Johnson becomes president of United States.

1866 July 19. Tennessee ratifies Fourteenth amendment to U.S. Constitution.
July 24. Tennessee is restored to Union.
– Fisk University (for blacks) opened at Nashville (chartered 1867).

1867 Gen. John H. Eaton, Jr., former Union officer, is elected State superintendent of public instruction.
– Legislature passes law providing separate schools for blacks at State's expense.

1868 Ku Klux Klan is organized at Pulaski.

1869 March. Ku Klux Klan is disbanded by Gen. Nathan Bedford Forrest, "Grand Cyclops."
– Gen. John Eaton publishes *Reports of School Conditions in Tennessee.*
– DeWitt C. Senter is appointed governor.

1870 Population is 1,258,521.
– Third constitution is adopted.

1873 Educational law is passed, establishing uniform system of free public schools.

1875 First State Board of Education is created.
– Bill abolishing office of county superintendent of public schools is pushed through legislature, but is vetoed.
July 31. Andrew Johnson, former President, dies near Jonesboro.

1877 State Board of Health is created.

1878 Worst yellow fever epidemic in history of U.S. strikes Memphis; of 6,000 white population, 4,204 die; of 14,000 blacks, 946 die.

1880 Population is 1,542,359.
– Centennial celebration of Nashville settlement takes place.

1882 Julia Doak is appointed State superintendent of education; she is first woman in U.S. to hold such office.

1886 "The War of the Roses" is fought; Robert L. Taylor, Democratic candidate for Governor, defeats his brother, Alfred A. Taylor, Republican candidate.

1890 Population is 1,767,518.

1891 July 21. First major strike in Tennessee history is called by miners at Coal Creek.

1892 Steel cantilever bridge over Mississippi at Memphis is opened.

1895 Chickamauga and Chattanooga National Military Park is dedicated.

1897 May 1-November 1. Tennessee Centennial Exposition is held at Nashville.

1898 Tennessee furnishes four regiments for war with Spain.

1899 County courts are given power to establish county high schools and provide for their support and supervision.

1900 Population is 2,020,616.

1907 Local option law is extended to include all cities and towns.

1908 State militia stops activities of night riders at Reelfoot Lake.

1909 General education bill is enacted.
January. Statewide prohibition law is passed; it becomes effective July 1.
– Francis Joseph Campbell, blind educator, is knighted by King Edward VII for his services to blind.

1910 Population is 2,184,789.
– Independents elect candidates for judiciary.

1913 One-third of gross revenue of State is appropriated for education.
– Highway improvement begins.
– Workmen's compensation law is passed.

1917 April 6. U.S. declares war against Germany; many Tennesseans volunteer; First Liberty Loan is oversubscribed in Tennessee.

1918 Sergeant Alvin C. York, with small squad and armed only with pistol and rifle, takes Hill 223 in Argonne Forest.
December. Col. Luke Lea of Nashville leads party of commissioned and non-commissioned officers on daring unofficial raid into Holland to capture Kaiser; attempt fails.

1919 State agrees to furnish $1,000,000, City of Nashville $600,000, and Davidson County $400,000, for memorial building in honor of soldiers of World War I.
January 13. Eighteenth amendment (prohibition) to Federal Constitution is ratified.

1920 Population is 2,337,885.
August 18. Nineteenth amendment (woman's suffrage) is ratified.

1923 Gov. Austin Peay (1923-1927) puts all activities of State under eight major departments, abolishing some fifty bureaus and departments.

1925 Scopes evolution trial is held at Dayton; William Jennings Bryan and Clarence Darrow are opposing counsel.

1929 By agreement with North Carolina, land for Great Smoky Mountains National Park is offered to Federal government and accepted.
March. Heavy rains cause floods, with loss of life and property.

1930 Population is 2,616,556.
– State has $6,000,000 in closed banks.

1931 Legislature investigating committee votes against impeachment of Governor Horton.
July 21. Tennessee votes for repeal of 18th amendment to Constitution.

1932 Coal miners strike at Wilder.

1932 August 31. Tennessee Valley Authority is created by an Act of Congress to develop natural resources of territory within Tennessee River watershed.
November. Construction of Norris Dam begins.

1934 Barnard Astronomical Association is founded as memorial to Dr. Edward Emerson Barnard, Nashville astronomer.

1935 Rural Electrification Act is passed by legislature regulating operation of TVA in State.

1936 January. Convict lease law is repealed.
January. Construction of Chickamauga Dam begins.
March 4. Norris Dam, first Unit of TVA, is completed.
December. Coal miners strike at Jamestown; State militia is called out.
December. Unemployment compensation law is enacted at special session of legislature.

1937 January. Floods cause much property damage.
May 18. Strike closes fabricating plant of Aluminum Company of America at Alcoa.

November 5. Governor Gordon Browning's unit bill for proportional suffrage among counties is passed at special session of Legislature.

1938 County unit bill is invalidated by Tennessee Supreme Court.

1939 State legislature overrides Governor's veto of act to permit, or forbid at county's option, package sales of alcoholic liquor.

1940 Population is 2,916,000.
– U.S. Supreme Court rules in favor of Tennessee in boundary dispute with Arkansas.
September. Chickamauga Dam is dedicated.

1941 Senate approves appropriation for F. Loudon Dam construction.

1942 Most of Kentucky-Tennessee Light & Power Company properties are transferred to TVA.

1943 State legislature passes permanent registration bill.

1944 Representative J. McCord is elected governor.

1945 D.E. Lilienthal is reappointed chairman of TVA in controversial campaign.

1946 Stamp is planned to commemorate Tennessee statehood.
– Lilienthal resigns chairmanship of TVA; G.R. Clapp is appointed.

1947 University of Tennessee opens graduate school at Oak Ridge as part of Oak Ridge Nuclear Studies Institute.

1948 Blacks receive letters warning them to stay away from polls; some are signed by Ku Klux Klan.

1949 Engineers blast mountain at Elizabethtown for construction of Holston Dam.

1950 Population is 3,292,000.
– Governor Browning is reelected.

1951 Federal District Court rules Tennessee University must admit four blacks to its professional schools; court denies plea to ban segregated classes.

1952 Clement is elected governor.
– Tennessee-Tombigbee Canal is projected.

1953 State constitution is amended to extend governor's term to four years.

1954 Governor Clement is reelected; Clapp leaves post as chairman of TVA; General Vogel is confirmed as new chairman.
– Mrs. L.D. Jenkins is first black to receive graduate degree from Tennessee University.

1955 July. AFL strike halts work on secret Oak Ridge Atomic Energy Plant.

1956 Governor Clement orders National Guard to Clinton in racial integration dispute; pro-segregationists urge Clement's impeachment.
– State Supreme Court rules school segregation laws are 'unenforceable,' barring trial in state courts of any suit to prevent integration.

1957 A.R. Jones is appointed to TVA board of directors.
– Tennessee Education Board approves desegregation of six State-operated colleges.
– Capitol building is renovated.

1958 Ellington is elected Governor.
– Judge Schoolfield faces impeachment proceedings.

1959 Democratic executive committee and election officials are charged with barring blacks from voting in primary election.

1960 Population is 3,567,000.
April. 2000 blacks march on City Hall to protest bombing of Nashville home of black Councilman Looby.
– Judge Schoolfield is impeached.
– Whites use economic pressure to prevent blacks from registering to vote.

1961 Hundreds of black tenant farmers and sharecroppers are evicted for registering to vote.

1962 U.S. Supreme Court rules that Tennessee Legislature apportionment is subject to constitutional scrutiny of Federal courts.
– U.S. Justice Department bars 74 Fayette County land owners from interfering with black sharecroppers' right to vote.

1963 Governor Clement is inaugurated for third term.
– Senator Estes Kefauver dies; H.S. Walters is appointed to his seat.

1964 Black voter registration is met with threats and intimidation from whites.
– Tennessee University Dental School accepts first black student.

1965 Bills are signed to redistrict Congress and reapportion Legislature; they are upheld by Federal court.

1966 Baker is elected Senator; he becomes first Republican in State to be elected to Senate by popular vote.

1967 Mrs. Lyndon B. "Lady Bird Johnson embarks upon Appalachia tour to see "the people behind the statistics" in education programs to help poor children; tour includes visits to schools in Charleston, West Virginia.
– Ellington is sworn in as governor.

1968 Legislature attempts to ban strikes after Memphis garbage collectors' walkout.

1969 Former Governor Clement is killed in auto accident.

1970 Population is 3,926,000.
– 2,000 students demonstrate at University of Tennessee over selection of new president, Dr. E. Boling.

1971 W.C. Dunn is sworn in as governor; he works on Tennessee-Tombigbee waterway halted by court order until ecological damage can be assessed.

1972 U.S. Supreme Court rules that Tennessee law requiring citizens to have three months residence in county and one year in State before registering to vote is unconstitutional.
December. Construction begins on Tennessee-Tombigbee Waterway after Judge Keady dissolves court order that it be halted for environmental reasons.

1973 Senator Baker reveals source of 185,000 dollars campaign contributions in wake of Watergate scandal.

1974 Ray Blanton is elected governor.

1975 Federal Appeals Court rules on Tennessee law minimizing theory of evolution in school textbooks.

1976 Army Corp. of Engineers begins to cut canal linking Tennessee River with the Tombigbee River.

1977 Federal District Judge Frank Gray Jr. orders merger of University of Tennessee's Nashville campus and Tennessee State University as means to end racial segregation.

1978 Governor Blanton is called before grand jury investigation of extortion and scandal within his administration; Blanton decides not to run for reelection.
– Supreme Court rules against completion of Tellico Dam in order to protect snail darters, an endangered species.

1979 Governor Blanton grants clemency to fifty-two convicts just before the end of his term; action draws protests.
– Governor-elect Alexander, in emergency ceremony, is sworn in three days early.
– President Carter signs legislation "with regret" allowing completion of Tellico Dam.

1980 Population is 4,591,000.
– Tennessee House expels Representative Robert Fisher, convicted of asking for bribes.

1981 Former Governor Blanton is convicted of extortion, conspiracy and mail fraud; he is sentenced to three years in prison; ruling is appealed.

1982 TVA halts construction of three nuclear reactors because of high costs.
May 1. President Reagan opens World Fair in Knoxville.

1983 Tennessee Valley Authority celebrates fifty-year anniversary.

1984 Former Governor Blanton enters Federal prison to begin three-year term after his conviction is upheld.

1985 Tennessee-Tombigbee Waterway opens to commercial traffic.

1986 Richard Freeman, one of three members of TVA board of directors, resigns unexpectedly.
– Blanton is released from halfway house after serving two years for conspiracy.

1987 Victor Ashe is elected mayor of Knoxville, with fifty-four percent of vote.
– On 10th anniversary of death of singer Elvis Presley, thousands of fans gather at Memphis State University for three- hour memorial service.
– Mail fraud charges against former Memphis State basketball coach, Dana Kirk, are dropped.
– Dickye Baggett, forty-two year old Tennessee woman, becomes first American treated for Parkinson's disease with transplant of adrenal gland tissue to brain; experimental surgery, pioneered in Mexico, is performed April 9 by team led by Dr. George Allen at Vanderbilt University, Nashville.

1988 Tennessee receives less than 25 percent of normal rainfall, and is severely affected by drought; Agriculture Department says it is driest spring since dust bowl year of 1934.
December 6. Roy Orbison, 52, singer and songwriter, one of world's most popular recording artists in early 1960s, dies of heart attack.
December 19. Country music singer Johnny Cash undergoes heart bypass surgery in Nashville; his cardiologist says operation convinces Cash, 56, to give up smoking.

1989 September 7. Energy Department announces closing of three- year-old, 176 million-dollar uranium plant because it is not needed.

1990 Tennessee Court of Appeals awards joint custody of several frozen embryos to divorced couple; decision overturns 1989 ruling.

1993 U.S. District Court in Nashville signs order ending Federal supervision of Tennessee State prison system; system has been overseen since 1982, when Federal court found that overcrowding violated inmates' constitutional rights; State has since constructed new jails and improved prison conditions overall.
– Shelby County officials file Nashville lawsuit to undertake another investigation into circumstances surrounding death of singer Elvis Presley; although official report lists cause of death as heart attack, Charles Thompson, author of 1991 book, *The Death of Elvis: What Really Happened*, claims that Presley died of drug overdose.
– Study in *New England Journal of Medicine* finds that likelihood of being killed in household that keeps guns is 2.7 times higher than in homes without guns; three counties, including one near Memphis, were used in study.

1994 U.S. District Court in Memphis gives prison sentence to Milpitas, California married couple earlier convicted of distributing pornographic pictures via their computer; case marks first time bulletin board operators have been tried in state where material was received rather than state from which it was transmitted.
– Knoxville police arrest and charge newspaper reporter, Michael Frazier, with attempted murder of man he had written about in award-winning article; Frazier of *Oak Ridger* wrote article about

Lisa Whedbee and husband John Whedbee, and their struggles to raise young, mentally retarded daughter; Frazier and Lisa Whedbee were allegedly lovers, and attempted to kill John Whedbee with butcher knife while he slept.

1995 Senate Judiciary Committee holds hearing on reports that active and retired ATF agents attended or helped organize annual racist camp-out for law enforcement officers; "Good Old Boys Roundup," held annually since 1980, took place in Ocoee with more than 300 participants; event allegedly featured sale of racial slur shirts and performance of racist skits, among other racially-motivated activities.
– St. Jude Children's Research Hospital in Memphis receives one million dollar donation in form of winning ticket from game sponsored by McDonald's fast food restaurants; donor does not reveal identity, but sends ticket anonymously via U.S. Postal Service from Dallas, Texas.

1996 Series of 17 suspicious fires in churches in Tennessee and four other southern states spurs announcement by Attorney General Janet Reno that civil-rights investigation will be undertaken; racially motivated arson is suspected.
– U.S. Navy F-14A Tomcat fighter jet crashes in suburb of Luna Heights, killing two crew members and three bystanders.

1997 Tennessee becomes last state in Union to ratify 15th Amendment, which guarantees U.S. citizens voting rights without regard to "race, color, or previous condition of servitude" (amendment was approved in 1869, and was incorporated into U.S. Constitution in 1870); impetus for ratification results after constitutional scholar, Gregory Watson, explains that State never officially adopted measure; other states that approved amendment after formal ratification are Delaware (1901), Oregon (1959), California (1962), Maryland (1973), and Kentucky (1976).
– Overflow of Ohio River causes thirty deaths in Tennessee and four other states; tens of thousands of Ohio River Valley residents are affected by flood conditions.
– Memphis officials announce recovery of stolen Chevrolet Suburban truck and high-power weapons; truck is burned, and twelve of thirteen weapons are recovered in raid near place where truck was stolen; truck and weapons were property of FBI assault team from Little Rock in Memphis for training exercises.

1998 Spring Hill Saturn automobile plant workers vote to retain current labor contract; in voting to keep contract, they decline opportunity to lobby for UAW's national contract agreement with GM, but are guaranteed security in event of plant layoffs; contract prohibits company from laying off employees except in case of "catastrophic events and severe economic conditions.")
– Authorities announce agreement to drop pornography charges against Barnes & Noble, Inc. after bookstore chain promises to keep explicit photography books out of reach of youths.
– Tornadoes hit Tennessee and two other states, killing ten people; storm in Nashville causes more than 100 injuries and widespread property damage; 300 homes in East Nashville are damaged.

1999 Four largest tobacco companies in U.S. announce plans to establish 5.15 billion dollar fund to aid tobacco farmers who face reduced market following industry settlement of states' tobacco-related lawsuits; details will affect Tennessee and eleven other states.

– Chain of tornadoes kill nine and injure at least one hundred in western Tennessee; second chain kills eight more and causes about one billion dollars in destruction; more than 1,000 Little Rock buildings and homes are damaged in what meteorologists announce as highest number of tornadoes in one state on one day ever recorded.

DIRECTORY OF STATE SERVICES

OFFICE OF THE GOVERNOR
State Capitol Bldg.
Nashville, TN 37243-0001
Fax: 615-741-1416
Governor: 615-741-2001

LIEUTENANT GOVERNOR
Legislative Plaza, Ste. #1
Nashville, TN 37243-0026
Fax: 615-741-9349
Lieutenant Governor: 615-741-2368

ATTORNEY GENERAL
450 James Robertson Pkwy.
Nashville, TN 37243-0485
Fax: 615-741-2009
Attorney General: 615-741-6474

SECRETARY OF STATE
State Capitol, 1st Fl.
Nashville, TN 37243-0305
Fax: 615-741-5962
Secretary of State: 615-741-2817

State Library and Archives Division
403 7th Ave. N
Nashville, TN 37243-0312
Fax: 615-741-7328
State Librarian/Archivist: 615-741-7996

TREASURER (TREASURY DEPARTMENT)
State Capitol, 1st Fl.
Nashville, TN 37243-0225
Fax: 615-741-7328
State Treasurer: 615-741-2956

DEPARTMENTS

AGRICULTURE DEPARTMENT
P.O. Box 40627
Nashville, TN 37204
Fax: 615-360-0333
Commissioner: 615-360-0100

COMMERCE AND INSURANCE DEPARTMENT
500 James Robertson Pkwy.
Nashville, TN 37243-0565
Fax: 615-741-4000
Commissioner: 615-741-2241

Regulatory Boards
500 James Robertson Pkwy.
Nashville, TN 37243-0565
Fax: 615-741-6470
Assistant Commissioner: 615-741-3449

Claims Commission
500 James Robertson Pkwy., #620
Nashville, TN 37243-0576
Fax: 615-532-1146
Administrative Clerk: 615-741-0741

COMPTROLLER OF THE TREASURY
State Capitol
Nashville, TN 37243-0260
Fax: 615-741-7328
Comptroller: 615-741-2501

CORRECTIONS DEPARTMENT
320 6th Ave. N, 4th Fl.
Nashville, TN 37243-0465
Fax: 615-741-4605
Commissioner: 615-741-2071

Administrative Services
320 6th Ave. N, 4th Fl.
Nashville, TN 37243-0465
Fax: 615-741-4605
Assistant Commissioner: 615-741-3720

Adult Institutions
320 6th Ave. N, 4th Fl.
Nashville, TN 37243-0465
Fax: 615-741-4605
Assistant Commissioner: 615-741-2192

Community Services
320 6th Ave. N, 4th Fl.
Nashville, TN 37243-0465
Fax: 615-741-4605
Assistant Commissioner: 615-741-5752

ECONOMIC AND COMMUNITY DEVELOPMENT DEPARTMENT
320 6th Ave. N, 8th Fl.
Nashville, TN 37243-0405
Fax: 615-741-7306
Commissioner: 615-741-1888

EDUCATION DEPARTMENT
Gateway Plaza, 6th Fl.
710 James Robertson Pkwy.
Nashville, TN 37243-0375
Fax: 615-741-6236
Commissioner: 615-741-2731

Accountability Division
Gateway Plaza, 6th Fl.
710 James Robertson Pkwy.
Nashville, TN 37243-0375
Fax: 615-523-7860
Assistant Commissioner: 615-523-4703

Curriculum & Instruction Division
Gateway Plaza, 6th Fl.
710 James Robertson Pkwy.
Nashville, TN 37243-0375
Fax: 615-532-8536
Assistant Commissioner: 615-532-6291

Finance and Administration Division
Gateway Plaza, 6th Fl.
710 James Robertson Pkwy.
Nashville, TN 37243-0375
Fax: 615-741-6236
Assistant Commissioner: 615-532-1650

Special Education Division
Gateway Plaza, 6th Fl.
710 James Robertson Pkwy.
Nashville, TN 37243-0375
Fax: 615-741-6236
Assistant Commissioner: 615-741-2851

Vocational Education Division
Gateway Plaza, 6th Fl.
710 James Robertson Pkwy.
Nashville, TN 37243-0375
Fax: 615-532-8226
Assistant Commissioner: 615-532-2815

EMPLOYMENT SECURITY DEPARTMENT
Volunteer Plaza Bldg., 12th Fl.
Nashville, TN 37245-0001
Fax: 615-741-3203
Commissioner: 615-741-2131

ENVIRONMENT AND CONSERVATION DEPARTMENT
401 Church St., 21st Fl.
Nashville, TN 37243-0435
Fax: 615-532-0120
Commissioner: 615-532-0109

Environmental Bureau
401 Church St., 21st Fl.
Nashville, TN 37248-0438
Fax: 615-532-0120
Assistant Commissioner: 615-532-0220

Resource Management Bureau
401 Church St., 21st Fl.
Nashville, TN 37248-0438
Fax: 615-532-0231
Assistant Commissioner: 615-532-0736

FINANCE AND ADMINISTRATION DEPARTMENT
State Capitol, 1st Fl.
Nashville, TN 37243-0285
Fax: 615-741-9872
Commissioner: 615-741-2401

Accounts Division
Andrew Jackson Bldg., 3rd Fl.
Nashville, TN 37219
Fax: 615-741-0684
Chief: 615-741-0320

Administration Division
304 John Sevier Bldg.
Nashville, TN 37219
Fax: 615-532-8532
Assistant Commissioner: 615-741-0320

Budget Division
304 John Sevier Bldg.
Nashville, TN 37219
Fax: 615-741-4390
Assistant Commissioner: 615-741-0320

Facilities Management Division
Nashville City Ctr., 7th Fl.
Nashville, TN 37243-0287
Fax: 615-641-7599
Director: 615-741-6311

FINANCIAL INSTITUTIONS DEPARTMENT
500 Charlotte Ave., 4th Fl.
Nashville, TN 37243-0705
Fax: 615-741-2883
Commissioner: 615-741-2236

GENERAL SERVICES DEPARTMENT
312 8th Ave. N, 9th Fl.
Nashville, TN 37243-0530
Fax: 615-741-8408
Commissioner: 615-741-9263

HEALTH DEPARTMENT
312 8th Ave. N, 9th Fl.
Nashville, TN 37247-0101
Fax: 615-741-2491
Commissioner: 615-741-3111

Administrative Services Bureau
312 8th Ave. N, 9th Fl.
Nashville, TN 37247-0101
Fax: 615-741-2491
Director: 615-741-3824

Alcohol and Drug Abuse Services Bureau
312 8th Ave. N, 12th Fl.
Nashville, TN 37247-0101
Fax: 615-532-2286
Director: 615-741-1921

Health Services Bureau
312 8th Ave. N, 11th Fl.
Nashville, TN 37247-4501
Fax: 615-532-2286
Director: 615-741-7305

Health Systems Development Bureau
312 8th Ave. N, 11th Fl.
Nashville, TN 37247-4501
Fax: 615-741-1063
Director: 615-741-7308

Manpower and Facilities Bureau
283 Plus Park Blvd.
Nashville, TN 37247-0501
Fax: 615-367-6397
Director: 615-367-6204

Tenncare
729 Church St.
Nashville, TN 37219-5406
Fax: 615-741-0882

Assistant Commissioner: 615-741-0213

HUMAN SERVICES DEPARTMENT
400 Deaderick St.
Nashville, TN 37248-0003
Fax: 615-741-4165
Commissioner: 615-741-3241

Administrative Services
400 Deaderick St.
Nashville, TN 37248-0001
Fax: 615-741-4165
Assistant Commissioner: 615-741-6982

Family Assistance
400 Deaderick St.
Nashville, TN 37248-0001
Fax: 615-741-4165
Assistant Commissioner: 615-741-5463

Rehabilitation Services
400 Deaderick St.
Nashville, TN 37248-0001
Fax: 615-741-4165
Assistant Commissioner: 516-741-2019

LABOR DEPARTMENT
710 James Robertson Pkwy., 2nd Fl.
Nashville, TN 37243-0655
Fax: 615-741-5078
Commissioner: 615-741-2582

MENTAL HEALTH AND MENTAL RETARDATION DEPARTMENT
710 James Robertson Pkwy.
Nashville, TN 37243-0675
Fax: 615-532-6514
Commissioner: 615-532-6500

Administrative Services Division
706 Church St.
Nashville, TN 37243-0675
Fax: 615-532-6514
Assistant Commissioner: 615-532-6670

Mental Health Services Division
706 Church St.
Nashville, TN 37243-0675
Fax: 615-532-6514
Assistant Commissioner: 615-532-6767

Mental Retardation Services Division
706 Church St.
Nashville, TN 37243-0675
Fax: 615-532-6964
Assistant Commissioner: 615-532-6530

MILITARY DEPARTMENT
P.O. Box 41502
Nashville, TN 37204-1502
Fax: 615-532-3419
Adjutant General: 615-532-3001

PERSONNEL DEPARTMENT
James K Polk Bldg., 2nd Fl.
Nashville, TN 37243-0635
Fax: 615-641-6985
Commissioner: 615-741-2598

REVENUE DEPARTMENT
1200 Andrew Jackson Bldg.
Nashville, TN 37242
Fax: 615-741-0682
Commissioner: 615-741-2461

SAFETY DEPARTMENT
1150 Foster Ave., Rm. 292
Nashville, TN 37249-1000
Fax: 615-251-5144
Commissioner: 615-251-5166

TOURIST DEVELOPMENT DEPARTMENT
P.O. Box 23170
Nashville, TN, 37202
Fax: 615-741-7225
Commissioner: 615-741-9001

TRANSPORTATION DEPARTMENT
700 James K Polk Bldg.
Nashville, TN 37243-0349
Fax: 615-741-2502
Commissioner: 615-641-2848

Operations Bureau
700 James K Polk Bldg.
Nashville, TN 37243-0349
Fax: 615-741-2508
Executive Director: 615-741-5374

Planning and Development Bureau
700 James K Polk Bldg.
Nashville, TN 37243-0349
Fax: 615-741-2508
Executive Director: 615-741-0791

Region I Office
711 Concord St.
P.O. Box 58
Knoxville, TN 37901
Fax: 615-594-6104
Civil Engineering Director: 615-594-6300

Region II Office
Cromwell Rd.
P.O. Box 22368
Chattanooga, TN 37422-2368
Fax: 615-899-1636
Civil Engineering Director: 615-892-3430

Region III Office
6601 Centennial Blvd.
Nashville, TN 37209
Fax: 615-350-4396
 Civil Engineering Director: 615-350-4300

Region IV Office
120 State St.
P.O. Box 429
Jackson, TN 38301
Fax: 615-423-6586
Civil Engineering Director: 615-423-6644

VETERANS AFFAIRS DEPARTMENT
215 8th Ave. N.
Nashville, TN 37243-1010
Fax: 615-532-4785
Commissioner: 615-741-2930

YOUTH DEVELOPMENT DEPARTMENT
710 James Robertson Pkwy., 9th Fl.
Nashville, TN 37243-1290
Fax: 615-532-7531
Commissioner: 615-741-7250

BOARDS AND COMMISSIONS

AGING COMMISSION
500 Veaderic St., 9th Fl.
Nashville, TN 37243-0860
Fax: 615-741-3309
Executive Director: 615-741-2056

ALCOHOLIC BEVERAGE COMMISSION
226 Capitol Blvd., Ste. 300
Nashville, TN 37243-0755
Fax: 615-741-0847
Chairman: 615-741-3602

ARTS COMMISSION
404 James Robertson Pkwy., Ste. 160
Nashville, TN 37243-0780
Fax: 615-741-8559
Executive Director: 615-741-1701

CHILDREN AND YOUTH COMMISSION
710 James Robertson Pkwy., 1st Fl.
Nashville, TN 37243-0800
Fax: 615-741-5956
Executive Director: 615-741-2633

FISCAL REVIEW COMMITTEE
G-19 War Memorial Bldg.
Nashville, TN 37243-0057
Fax: 615-741-1146
Executive Director: 615-741-2564

HIGHER EDUCATION COMMISSION
404 James Robertson Pkwy., Ste. 1900
Nashville, TN 37243-0830
Fax: 615-741-6230
Executive Director: 615-741-7562

HOUSING DEVELOPMENT AGENCY
404 James Robertson Pkwy., Ste. 1114
Nashville, TN 37243-0900
Fax: 615-741-9634
Executive Director: 615-741-2473

HUMAN RIGHTS COMMISSION
530 Church St., Ste. 400
Nashville, TN 37243-0745
Fax: 615-532-2197
Executive Director: 615-741-5825

PUBLIC SERVICE COMMISSION
460 James Robertson Pkwy.
Nashville, TN 37243-0505
Fax: 615-741-5015
Chairman: 615-741-0917

RACING COMMISSION
500 James Robertson Pkwy., Ste. 635
Nashville, TN 37243-1138
Fax: 615-532-2965
Executive Secretary: 615-741-1952

TENNESSEE BUREAU OF INVESTIGATIONS
1148 Foster Ave.
Nashville, TN 37210
Mail to: P.O. Box 1000940
Nashville, TN 37224-0940
Fax: 615-741-4788
Director: 615-741-0430

WILDLIFE RESOURCES AGENCY
P.O. Box 40747
Nashville, TN 37204
Fax: 615-741-4606
Executive Director: 615-781-6552

MEMBERS OF CONGRESS

SENATE

SEN. FRED THOMPSON (R) (b. 1942); 2nd Term;
Phone: 202-224-4944; Fax: 202-228-3679;
E-mail: senator_thompson@thompson.senate.gov.

www.senate.gov/~thompson/

SEN. BILL FRIST (R) (b. 1952); 1st Term;
Phone: 202-224-3344; Fax: 202-228-1264;
E-mail: senator_frist@frist.senate.gov.

www.senate.gov/~frist/

HOUSE

WILLIAM "BILL" L. JENKINS (R-1st) (b. 1936); 2nd Term;
Phone: 202-225-6356; Fax: 202-225-5714;
E-mail: tn01@legislators.com.

www.house.gov/jenkins

JOHN J. DUNCAN, Jr. (R-2nd) (b. 1947); 7th Term;
Phone: 202-225-5435; Fax: 202-225-6440;
E-mail: tn02@legislators.com.

www.house.gov/duncan/

ZACH WAMP (R-3rd) (b. 1957); 3rd Term;
Phone: 202-225-3271; Fax: 202-225-3494;
E-mail: tn03@legislators.com.

www.house.gov/wamp/

VAN HILLEARY (R-4th) (b. 1959); 3rd Term;
Phone: 202-225-6831; Fax: 202-225-3272;
E-mail: tn04@legislators.com.

www.house.gov/hilleary/

BOB CLEMENT (D-5th) (b. 1943); 7th Term;
Phone: 202-225-4311; Fax: 202-226-1035;
E-mail: tn05@legislators.com.

www.house.gov/clement/

BART GORDON (D-6th) (b. 1949); 8th Term;
Phone: 202-225-4231; Fax: 202-225-6887;
E-mail: bart.gordon@mail.house.gov.

www.house.gov/gordon/

ED BRYANT (R-7th) (b. 1948); 3rd Term;
Phone: 202-225-2811; Fax: 202-225-2989;
E-mail: tn07@legislators.com.

www.house.gov/bryant/

JOHN S. TANNER (D-8th) (b. 1944); 6th Term;
Phone: 202-225-4714; Fax: 202-225-1765;
E-mail: john.tanner@mail.house.gov.

www.house.gov/tanner/index.htm

HAROLD E. FORD, Jr. **(D-9th)** (b. 1970); 2nd Term;
Phone: 202-225-3265; Fax: 202-225-5663;
E-mail: rep.harold.ford.jr@mal.house.gov.

www.house.gov/ford/

TWENTIETH CENTURY GOVERNORS

McMILLIN, BENTON (1845-1933), thirty-first governor of Tennessee (1899-1903), was born September 11, 1845 in Monroe County, Kentucky, the son of John and Willette (Black) McMillin. He attended Philomath Academy and Kentucky University and studied law. He was admitted to the Tennessee Bar in 1871 and began to practice in Celina. About that time, he married Marie Brown. They had one child.

McMillin was elected to the Tennessee Legislature and served from 1875-77. He moved to Carthage, where he practiced law and was involved in various business enterprises. In 1875, Governor Porter appointed him to negotiate the purchase of land from Kentucky. The following year, he served as a presidential elector on the Tilden-Hendricks ticket. He became Special Judge of the 5th Judicial Circuit in 1877, and in 1879 he was elected to the U.S. House of Representatives, where he served for twenty years as a Democrat. In 1897, he married Lucille Foster. They had one daughter.

McMillin ran an unsuccessful race for the U.S. Senate in 1897. The following year, he tried for the governorship of Tennessee and won. He was reelected in 1900. As governor, McMillin worked to create a sinking fund to reduce the state debt. He also sponsored educational reform bills, including a uniform textbook system for state schools. After leaving office, he was a presidential elector on the Bryan-Kern ticket in 1908. He ran for the U.S. Senate again in 1911, but lost. He also tried for the Tennessee governorship once again in 1912, but was defeated by Ben Hooper in the general election. In 1913, he was appointed Ambassador to Peru, and later, Minister to Guatemala, where he spent eight years. He ran for Governor of Tennessee in 1922, but was again defeated. In 1928, he became Democratic National Committeeman. He also entered the U.S. Senate race that year, but withdrew before the primary. His last political office was that of pre-convention manager in Tennessee for Franklin D. Roosevelt. He was eighty-seven years old at the time. McMillin died in Nashville on January 8, 1933.

FRAZIER, JAMES BERIAH (1856-1937), thirty-second governor of Tennessee (1903-1905), was born in Pikeville, Tennessee on October 18, 1856, the son of Thomas and Margaret (McReynolds) Frazier. He was educated at Franklin College and the University of Tennessee. After graduation in 1878, he worked as a schoolteacher. He studied law on the side, was admitted to the bar in 1880, and began to practice in Chattanooga. In 1883, he married Louise Douglas Keith. They had four children.

While in Chattanooga, Frazier was appointed a special judge on various occasions. He became a presidential elector-at-large in 1900. In 1902, he ran for governor on the Democratic ticket and won. His administration was characterized by its economic restraint. During his years of service, Frazier reduced the state debt by a significant amount. He was a strong advocate of public education, especially in rural areas. He also worked for improved mining conditions, state temperance, and effective law enforcement. He was reelected in 1904, but cut short his second term to take the Senate seat of the recently deceased, William Bate. Frazier served in the Senate until 1911. Then he retired to his law practice in Chattanooga. He was a prominent speaker throughout the state for many years. He died in Chattanooga on March 28, 1937.

COX, JOHN ISAAC (1855-1946), thirty-third governor of Tennessee (1905-1907), was born in Blountville, Tennessee on November 23, 1855, the son of Henry and Martha (Smith) Cox. His father died in the Civil War, and from the age of thirteen, John provided the sole support for his mother and three brothers and sisters. He worked at various jobs, including that of farmer and mail carrier, and although he had little time for school, he managed to attend the Blountville Academy for two terms. He later studied law under Judge William Van Dyke Deaderick. He married the judge's daughter, Laura Lee Deaderick. They had one son.

In 1889, Cox moved to Bristol where he started a law practice. At the age of twenty-two, he was elected Justice of the Peace. Ten years later, he became Judge of Sullivan County. He also served for a time as Alderman, Bristol City Attorney, and State Revenue Agent. Cox was elected to the Tennessee House, and served from 1893 to 1895. Six years later, he was voted in as State Senator, and served for three terms. He was Speaker of the 54th Assembly, and, when Governor James Frazier resigned in 1905, he succeeded him in the office. As governor, Cox handled routine matters and made recommendations on legislation proposed under Governor Frazier. He ran for the governorship in 1906, hoping to be elected in his own right, but lost the nomination to Malcolm R. Patterson.

Cox was reelected to the State Senate that same year, and won additional terms in 1908 and 1910. He returned to the Tennessee House in 1913 for a single term. From 1914 to 1922, he was Postmaster of Bristol. He retired from his law practice in 1913, and spent much of his time managing his 600-acre farm near Bristol. He married a second time, to Lorena Butler, and had two children by that union. Cox died on September 5, 1946.

PATTERSON, MALCOLM RICE (1861-1935), thirty-forth governor of Tennessee (1907-1911), was born in Somerville, Alabama on June 7, 1861, the son of Josiah and Josephine (Rice) Patterson. He attended Christian Brothers College in Memphis and Vanderbilt University where he studied law. He was admitted to the bar in 1883, and began to practice law in Memphis. In 1894, he became an Attorney General in the Criminal Court, a post he held until 1900. He was subsequently elected to the U.S. House of Representatives and served from 1901-1907. In the latter year, he married Mary Russell Gardner. They had four children.

Patterson ran for governor in 1906, and won against Republican H. Clay Evans. He was reelected in 1908. During his administration, Patterson banned public executions, put down raids by "Night Riders" in western Tennessee, and supported measures to improve public health, labor, and agriculture. He also attempted to reorganize the public school system. Patterson's time in office was marred by controversy over the Prohibition issue. He opposed Prohibition. The controversy came to a head when Edward Ward Carmack, Patterson's political opponent, was shot by Duncan Cooper, an old Patterson ally. Shortly after Cooper was convicted, Patterson pardoned him, causing public outrage that eventually brought about the adoption of state prohibition in 1909. Patterson was destroyed politically. He ran for governor again in 1910, but was accused of attempting to intimidate the State Supreme Court, and withdrew from the campaign.

Patterson returned to his home in Memphis, where he eventually switched alliances and became a spokesman for the cause of Prohibition. He lectured for the Anti-Saloon League. In 1915, he ran for the U.S. Senate, but lost the nomination. He was appointed to the Circuit Court bench in Memphis by Governor Peay in 1923, and was later elected to the post. For several years, Patterson wrote a column for the Memphis *Commercial Appeal*. He ran for governor again in 1932, but lost the nomination. He died in Sarasota, Florida on March 8, 1935.

HOOPER, BEN WALTER (1870-1957), thirty-fifth governor of Tennessee (1911-1915), was born on Big Pigeon River, Tennessee on October 13, 1870, the son of Dr. L.W. Hooper and Sarah Walker. He lived with his mother in various parts of East Tennessee until age eight when he was placed in St. John's Orphanage in Knoxville. His father took him from the orphanage the following year, and brought him up in Newport. Ben Hooper attended Carson-Newman College, then studied law under Horace Nelson Cate. He was admitted to the bar in 1894, and began to practice in Newport.

In 1893, Hooper was elected to the Lower House of the Tennessee General Assembly, and served until 1897. He married Anna Bell Jones in September 1901. They had six children. During the Spanish-American War, Hooper entered the U.S. Volunteer Infantry and served as captain. From 1906 to 1910, he was Assistant Attorney General for the Eastern Division of Puerto Rico. He returned to Tennessee, where in 1910, he was nominated for governor on the Republican ticket. He won easily, and was reelected in 1912. As governor, Hooper reorganized state government and created a Banking Department, Auditing Department, Department of Shop and Factory Inspection, and Insurance Department. He was active in the passage of legislation that included a compulsory school law, increases to the public school fund, a parole and indeterminate sentence law, wage and hour laws, mining safety guidelines, prison reforms, anti-narcotics laws, and measures to regulate public utilities.

Despite poor health and declines in his business affairs, Hooper yielded to pressure from Republicans and Independents and ran for a third term in 1914. He lost the election. In 1916, he ran for the U.S. Senate unsuccessfully. He became Judge of the 15th Chancery Division in 1920, but resigned when President Warren Harding appointed him to the United States Railroad Labor Board, where he served as chairman from 1922 to 1925. He next served as commissioner on the Tennessee board in charge of acquisition and development for Great Smoky Mountains Park. Hooper became a director and associate editor of the *Knoxville Times* in 1932, and wrote a daily column for the paper. In 1953, he was the Vice-President of the Tennessee Constitutional Convention. He died on April 18, 1957 in Newport.

RYE, THOMAS CLARKE (1863-1953), thirty-sixth governor of Tennessee (1915-1919), was born on June 2, 1863 in Camden, Tennessee, the son of Wayne and Elizabeth (Atchison) Rye. He attended local schools, then studied law with his uncle, Colonel Tom Morris, and was admitted to the Tennessee Bar in 1884. He began to practice law in Benton, and he became Master of Chancery Court in Camden for three years. In 1887, he married Bettie Arnold. They had two children.

Rye served for four years as division chief of the Pension Bureau in Washington, D.C. In 1897, he moved with his family to Paris, Tennessee where he practiced law. He was elected Attorney General of the 13th Judicial District in 1908, and served until 1914 when he ran for governor. Running on a platform that sought to maintain prohibition in the state, he defeated incumbent, Ben Hooper. Rye's administration was concerned with cleaning up government. He pushed for the enactment of laws to give the courts power to remove derelict officials, and to make city government responsible for enforcing state laws. He also promoted legislation to regulate soft drink stands and night clubs, outlaw liquor advertising, and stop the shipment of liquor. Rye was reelected in 1916. His second term was noted for improvements to education and public roads. The 18th Amendment to the U.S. Constitution was submitted for ratification during this time, but he refused to call a special session of the Legislature.

In 1919, Rye retired to his law practice. He was elected Chancellor of the 8th Chancery Court of Tennessee in 1922. He lived in Paris, Tennessee until his death on September 12, 1953.

ROBERTS, ALBERT HOUSTON (1868-1946), thirty-seventh governor of Tennessee (1919-1921), was born in Overton County, Tennessee on July 4, 1868, the son of John and Sarah (Carlock) Roberts. He attended Hiwassee College then studied law under Captain Jesse Barnes. From 1892 to 1894, he taught school in Nettle Carrier, where he was Superintendent of Schools for two terms. In 1888, he married Nora Deane Bowden.

Roberts was admitted to the Tennessee Bar, and practiced in Overton County from 1894 to 1910. For the next eight years, he was Chancellor of the 4th Judicial District. In 1918, he ran for governor on the Democratic ticket. He won in the primary against Austin Peay, largely due to interference from the city "bosses." Roberts went on to win in the general election. As governor, he promoted a widespread tax reform, but was largely unsuccessful because of divisions in his party. The women's suffrage amendment was ratified during his term. He was criticized for his handling of labor strikes. Consequently, his 1920 campaign for

reelection was marred by mud slinging and scandalmongers, and he lost to Republican Alfred A. Taylor.

Roberts retired to his law practice in Nashville. In 1935, he was married to a Miss Edwards. Roberts was the father of four children. He died on June 25, 1946.

TAYLOR, ALFRED ALEXANDER (1848-1931), thirty-eighth governor of Tennessee (1921-1923), was born in Happy Valley, Tennessee on August 6, 1848, the son of Nathaniel and Emma (Haynes) Taylor. He attended Pennington Seminary, and the Buffalo Institute (Milligan College), then studied law. He was admitted to the Tennessee Bar, and practiced law in Jonesboro, and later in Johnson City. In 1875, he was elected to the Tennessee House, where he served until 1877. He was married to Jennie Anderson in 1881. They had ten children.

Taylor was a presidential elector for Hayes and Wheeler in 1876, for Garfield and Arthur in 1880, and for Hughes and Fairbanks in 1916. In 1886, he ran for governor of Tennessee, on the Republican ticket, against his brother, Democratic nominee, Robert Love Taylor. The campaign was known as the "War of Roses," and in the end, Alfred was defeated. He returned to his law practice. In 1888, he was a delegate to the Republican National Convention. He was also elected to the U.S. House of Representatives, where he served until 1895. He toured the United States as a lecturer with his brother, Robert. In 1920, he ran for governor again, and won over incumbent Albert H. Roberts.

As governor, Taylor helped create an office of the state tax commissioner. He also signed legislation, which expanded the power of the Railroad, and Public Utilities Commission, created the Tennessee Historical Commission, and restored Andrew Johnson's tailor shop as a historic point of interest. Taylor ran for a second term in 1922, but was defeated by Austin Peay. Taylor then retired to his residence in Johnson City, where he died on November 25, 1931.

PEAY, AUSTIN, III (1876-1927), thirty-ninth governor of Tennessee (1923-1927), was born near Hopkinsville, Kentucky on June 1, 1876, the son of Austin and Cornelia (Leavell) Peay. He was educated at Washington and Lee University, and Center College where he received his LL.B. degree in 1895. He was admitted to the bar and began to practice law in Hopkinsville. Around that time, he married Sallie Hurst, and they had two children. They moved to Clarksville, and he began a law practice there.

In 1901, Peay was elected to the Tennessee House, and remained there until 1905. In 1905, he was also chairman of the State Democratic Committee. He managed the gubernatorial campaign of Malcolm R. Patterson in 1908. In 1922, he ran for the office himself, and won against incumbent Governor Alfred A. Taylor. During his administration, Peay attempted to provide an equitable revenue system for both agriculture and business. He signed into law the Reorganization Act of 1923, which consolidated the executive branch of state government into eight departments. Through careful fiscal management, he turned the state's deficit into a surplus, and for the first time in fifteen years made payments on the state debt. He also made dramatic strides in the areas of transportation, conservation and education. Notable accomplishments during his term were the Education Act of 1925, which reorganized the public school system; the development of a state highway system; and the establishment of Great Smoky Mountain National Park, and of Reelfoot Lake, as wildlife preserves.

Peay was reelected easily in 1924. He ran again in 1926, in a more difficult campaign, and was also reelected. However, shortly after the beginning of his third term, on October 2, 1927, he suffered a cerebral hemorrhage and died at the Executive Mansion in Nashville.

HORTON, HENRY HOLLIS (1866-1934), fortieth governor of Tennessee (1927-1933), was born in Princeton, Alabama on February 17, 1866, the son of Henry and Anne (Moore) Horton. He attended the University of the South in Sewanee from 1891-92. Horton worked as a schoolteacher for several years, then as a lawyer in Winchester, and as director and general counsel for the Home Bank of Winchester. In 1896, he married Adeline Wilhoit. They had one son.

Horton was elected to the Tennessee House in 1907, and served until 1909. He subsequently worked as a public school director in Franklin County, a member of the high school board, a member of the election commission, and chairman of the Board of Mayor and Aldermen in Winchester. He moved to Marshall County where he ran a large farm and continued his law practice. In 1927, he was elected to the State Senate, and was named Speaker. He served for ten months then was inaugurated governor to fill the office left open by the death of Austin Peay. The following year, Horton ran for governor in the general election, and with backing from publisher Luke Lea, and the Caldwell and Company investment bank, he won. He was reelected in 1930 with the same support.

The day after the 1930 election, however, Caldwell and Company failed and went into receivership with over six million dollars of Tennessee funds invested in it. An investigating committee indicted Horton's backers, Lea and Caldwell. By 1931, impeachment proceedings had begun against the governor. But, the House voted against impeachment by a margin of fifty-eight to forty-one. Horton survived the scandal, but it destroyed Luke Lea's political power, and made way for the political influence of Edward Crump of Memphis. Also, in response to the scandal, the Legislature instituted tighter rules to regulate the deposit of state funds in investment banks.

At the end of his second term, Horton retired to his home near Chapel Hill. He died there on July 2, 1934.

McALISTER, HARRY HILL (1875-1959), forty-first governor of Tennessee (1933-1937), was born in Nashville, Tennessee on July 15, 1875, the son of William and Laura (Dortch) McAlister, and a descendant of Willie Blount, and Aaron V. Brown, two former state governors. He attended Vanderbilt University where he received his LL.B. degree in 1897, then began to practice law in Nashville. In 1901, he married Louise Jackson. They had two daughters.

McAlister was the Assistant City Attorney for Nashville in 1901. From 1904 to 1910, he was City Attorney. He was elected to the Tennessee Senate where he served from 1911-15. He later became State Treasurer, a post he held from 1919-27 and from 1931-33. In addition, he was a presidential elector for Wilson and Marshall in 1916, a member of the State Democratic Executive Committee from 1918-1920, a delegate to the Democratic National Convention of 1920, and State Chairman of the Democratic Victory Drive in 1932. He ran for governor in 1926 and 1928, but did not receive his party's nomination. In 1932, with backing from political "Boss" Edward Crump, he ran again and won the nomination and the general election.

McAlister entered office in the midst of the Great Depression. He supported Roosevelt's policies, and took an active part in establishing New Deal programs in Tennessee. As a consequence, the federal government had great influence in state affairs. McAlister was elected to a second term in 1932. During this administration, he split with "Boss" Crump when he proposed a sales tax to reduce the state debt. The political quarrel with Crump grew to such an extent that the Legislature failed to enact a new revenue bill, and the governor had to call an extra session of the Assembly.

McAlister decided not to seek a third term in 1936. He returned home to Nashville, where in 1940 he became a federal referee in bankruptcy cases. He also served for short periods as Special Judge on the State Supreme Court, and as Special Circuit Court Judge in Davidson County. He died on October 30, 1959.

BROWNING, GORDON (1889-1976), forty-second and forty-fifth governor of Tennessee (1937-1939; 1949-1953), was born in Carroll County, Tennessee on November 22, 1889, the son of James and Melissa (Brooks) Browning. He attended Valparaiso University and Cumberland University Law School. After graduation in 1915, he started a law practice in Huntingdon. He served in World War I as a captain, and in World War II as a colonel. In 1920, he married Ida Leach. That same year, he ran for the U.S. House of Representatives, but was defeated by Republican Lon A. Scott. He won against Scott, however, two years later, and served in Congress from 1923 to 1935.

Browning made an unsuccessful bid for the U.S. Senate in 1934. In 1936, he ran for governor of Tennessee, supported by Memphis political boss Ed Crump, and won. During his administration, Browning was largely successful in securing larger appropriations for public education, establishing a merit system for state employees, requiring licensing for automobiles and drivers, improving roads, balancing the budget, reorganizing state government, and continuing work on the Tennessee Valley Authority. By the end of his term, Browning had come to disagree with Crump on many issues. In the 1940 election, Crump backed William Cooper for governor, and Browning was not reelected.

After leaving office, Browning served as Chancellor of the 8th Judicial District and as an official of the military government of Germany. He ran for Tennessee governor again in 1946 and 1948. He was elected in the latter year, and entered the Executive Mansion for a second term. During this administration, Browning worked to improve education and provide roads in rural areas. He was elected governor for a third time in 1950. However, in his fourth bid for office in 1952, he was charged with fraud and mismanagement in regard to the state purchase of a hotel in Nashville, and lost the primary.

Following the end of his third term, Browning retired to Huntingdon. He was president of the Tennessee Valley Insurance Company, and a member of the Tennessee Historical Commission. During his final years Browning was partially disabled due to Parkinson's disease. He died on May 23, 1976.

COOPER, WILLIAM PRENTICE (1895-1969), forty-third governor of Tennessee (1939-1945), was born in Shelbyville, Tennessee on September 28, 1895, the son of William and Argentine (Shofner) Cooper. He attended Vanderbilt University and Princeton University, where he graduated in 1917. He served as a second lieutenant in World War I, and after his return in 1919, studied law at Harvard University. He was admitted to the Tennessee Bar in 1922, and practiced law in Shelbyville and Lewisburg. He also was City Attorney in each of the two cities. From 1923 to 1925, he was a Representative for the 63rd district in Tennessee's General Assembly. He then served as Attorney General of the 8th Judicial Circuit from 1925 to 1927, and from 1937 to 1939, he was a State Senator in the 70th General Assembly. He was also the state commander of the American Legion. In 1938, backed by Boss Ed Crump of Memphis, Cooper challenged incumbent Governor Gordon Browning and won. He was reelected in 1940 and 1942, becoming the first governor of Tennessee since the Civil War to hold three consecutive terms.

During Cooper's administrations, the U.S. was involved in World War II. On a state level, Cooper was successful in reducing

Tennessee indebtedness, while increasing aid to public education. He also helped institute a system of tuberculosis hospitals, and aided in conservation efforts through the establishment of 341,000 new acres of park and forestland. From 1943-44, Cooper was president of the Southern Governors' Conference.

After leaving office, Cooper went to Peru, where from 1946 to 1948, he was U.S. Ambassador. He married Hortense Powell in 1950, and they had three children. In 1953, Cooper was president of the Tennessee Constitutional Convention. He died on May 18, 1969 in Rochester, Minnesota.

McCORD, JIM NANCE (1879-1968), forty-fourth governor of Tennessee (1945-1949), was born in Unionville, Tennessee on March 17, 1879, the son of Thomas and Iva (Steele) McCord. He was educated in Bedford County public schools, and at age seventeen became a traveling salesman. He married Vera Kercheval in 1903.

In 1910, McCord was made a co-partner of the *Marshall Gazette*, and two years later, became its owner and publisher. For twenty-seven years, from 1915 to 1942, he was a member of the Marshall County Court. He was elected Mayor of Lewisburg in 1917, and held the post until 1942. During these years, he also worked as an auctioneer of real estate and livestock. He was an elector for the state-at-large in the 1932 Roosevelt presidential race, and a delegate to the Democratic National Convention in 1940. In 1942, he was elected without opposition to the U.S. House of Representatives. Two years later, he defeated Republican John W. Kilgore, in a bid for the governorship of Tennessee.

As governor, McCord secured increased public school funding, and instituted a two-percent state sales tax. He also helped establish a retirement law for teachers and other state employees. McCord was reelected in 1946, but was defeated when he ran for a third term in 1948. He left office in 1949. Four years later, he became a member of the State Constitutional Convention. He also served as Commissioner of Conservation. His wife Vera died in 1953, and the following year he married Mrs. Lula (Tatum) Sheeley.

McCord ran for governor again in 1958, as an Independent, but was defeated. In 1967, he married for a third time, to the former Mrs. T. Howard Estes. McCord died in Nashville on September 2, 1968.

CLEMENT, FRANK GOAD (1920-1969), forty-sixth and forty-eighth governor of Tennessee (1953-1959; 1963-1967), was born in Dickson, Tennessee on June 2, 1920, the son of Robert and Maybelle (Goad) Clement. He attended Cumberland University, and Vanderbilt University where he received his LL.B. degree in 1942. In 1940, he married Lucille Christianson. They had three children.

After graduation, Clement became a special agent for the Federal Bureau of Investigation. He entered the army in 1943, and reached the rank of first lieutenant. After the war, he returned to Dickson and practiced law. He was named General Counsel for the Public Utilities Commission in 1946, and held that post for four years. Then he formed a law partnership with his father until 1950, when he was recalled to the army. He spent sixteen months at Camp Gordon, Georgia as an instructor. In 1952, he ran for governor of Tennessee, with the political backing of Boss Ed Crump. He defeated incumbent Governor Gordon Browning in the primary, and went on to win the general election.

As governor, Clement sought a bond issue to provide free textbooks to public schools. He also helped establish a revised mental health program, and created the Industrial Development Division within the Department of Conservation. He was reelected in

1954, to a four-year term. During this administration, he began gradual moves toward the integration of schools, and increased the state sales tax to make more monies available for education. Not allowed by law to succeed himself in office, in 1959 Clement returned to his legal practice. However, in 1962, he ran for a third term as governor, and was elected. Once in office, he extended the state sales tax to include utility bills, and allowed counties to collect a one-percent sales tax.

Clement ran for the U.S. Senate twice while still governor, but was defeated in both races. He left office in 1967 and returned to his Nashville law practice. Two years later, on November 4, 1969, he died in an automobile accident in the city.

ELLINGTON, EARL BUFORD (1907-1972), forty-seventh and forty-ninth governor of Tennessee (1959-1963; 1967-1971), was born near Lexington, Mississippi on July 27, 1907, the son of Abner and Cora (Grantham) Ellington. He received his education at Milsaps College, and after graduation went to work as a newspaper editor in Durant. In 1929, he married Catherine Cheek. They had two children.

Ellington moved to Tennessee in 1931, and worked as a salesman for International Harvester Company for eight years. He subsequently bought a general store and a farm near Verona, Tennessee. He was director of the Marshall County Farm Bureau for eight years. From 1948 to 1952, he worked as a field representative for the Tennessee Farm Bureau Insurance Service Program. He was also manager of the insurance service during that time.

Ellington entered politics about 1945, when he managed Joe L. Evins' campaign for U.S. Congress. Ellington ran for state representative in 1949, and was elected to the Tennessee House. He served until 1951. The following year, he was the state manager for Frank G. Clement's gubernatorial campaign. He was also elected chairman of the Democratic State Executive Committee in 1952. In 1953, Governor Clement appointed him Commissioner of Agriculture, a post he held until 1958. He founded the Ellington Agricultural Center, and also served as chairman of the Southern Agricultural Commissioners, a member of the National Organization of Agricultural Commissioners, and president of the Southern States Agricultural Association. He was Governor Clement's choice as successor, since the governor was ineligible to run for re-election. Ellington was elected by a wide margin.

As governor, Ellington supported educational improvements, social welfare, and the extension of the state highway system. He also reorganized state government by streamlining seventy agencies into just eighteen. He left office in 1963, and became vice-president of the L&N Railroad. In 1965, President Lyndon B. Johnson appointed him Director of the U.S. Office of Emergency Planning. He held this position for a year, resigning in 1966 to enter the Tennessee gubernatorial race again. He was elected to a second term as governor and was inaugurated January 16, 1967. During his second administration, he continued to work for improvements to education and the state highway system. Legislation during this term included a revision of the 1939 system of liquor regulation, repeal of the 1925 anti-evolution law, and the creation of a state commission for higher education and race relations.

Ellington left office in 1971, and returned to his home in Nashville. The following year, on April 3, 1972, he died in Boca Raton, Florida.

DUNN, BRYANT WINFIELD CULBERSON (1927-), fiftieth governor of Tennessee (1971-1975), was born in Meridian, Mississippi on July 1, 1927, the son of Aubert and Dorothy (Crum) Dunn. He attended the University of Mississippi where he earned a degree in business administration. After graduation, he worked for an insurance agency, then became interested in dentistry and enrolled in the University of Tennessee to study dental surgery. He started a dental practice in Memphis. In 1950, he married Betty Jean Prichard. They had three children.

While in Memphis, Dunn became interested in politics. He worked at the precincts, and also as a campaign manager, and as chairman of the Shelby County Republican Executive Committee. He was a spokesman for the Eisenhower-Nixon ticket in 1952, and in 1964, he was state leader of the Barry Goldwater presidential campaign. He ran for the Tennessee House in 1962, but was defeated. He remained politically visible, however, in the campaigns of Senator Howard Baker, Representative Dan Kuykendall, and President Richard Nixon.

In 1970, Dunn ran for governor of Tennessee, and won over Democrat John J. Hooker in a close election, thus becoming the first Republican governor of the state in fifty years. Before entering office, Dunn organized a group of businessmen and industrialists into a Committee on Cost Control, to study ways of providing more efficient and more economical government. As governor, Dunn was known for his energetic approach to state affairs. He was elected twice to the Executive Committee of the National Governors' Conference. In 1973, he was vice-chairman, and in 1974, chairman, of the Republican Governors' Association. He also served on the National Education Commission of the States, and was chairman of the Tennessee-Tombigbee Waterway Development Authority. At the end of his term in 1975, Dunn became an executive with the Hospital Corporation of America. He lives in Nashville.

BLANTON, RAY (1930-1996), fifty-first governor of Tennessee (1975-1979), was born in Hardin County, Tennessee on April 30, 1930, the son of Leonard and Ovie (DeLaney) Blanton. He attended the University of Tennessee and received a B.S. in agriculture in 1951. He is married to Betty Littlefield. They have four children.

Upon graduation, Blanton taught agriculture at a high school in Indiana for a year, then returned to Tennessee and started B&B Construction Company. In 1964, he was elected to the Tennessee House. He ran for U.S. Congress in 1966 and won. He was re-elected to two additional terms. While in Congress, he served on the Interstate and Foreign Commerce Committee, the House Subcommittee on Commerce and Finance, the House District of Columbia Committee, and the Special Subcommittee on Investigations. He ran for the Senate in 1972, but lost in the Republican landslide that year, to Howard Baker.

Two years later, Blanton entered the race for Tennessee governor and won with fifty-six percent of the vote. As governor, Blanton called for controlled state spending and more efficient government. He also sought to promote tourism in Tennessee, develop international trade, increase public service jobs for the unemployed, improve education, reorganize state government, and augment highway construction.

Blanton's term, however, was marred by political controversy. Blanton was accused of corruption, and came under scrutiny for his policies of providing pardons to many convicted criminals. In 1978, three of his aides were arrested for selling pardons and commutations of prison sentences. Near the end of his term, Blanton was called on to resign, but in the midst of the controversy, he granted clemency to fifty-two prisoners, including the son of a friend. There was a strong public outcry. To avoid further pardons, possibly to persons involved in the pardon-selling scandal, Governor-elect Lamar Alexander was quickly sworn into office three days early in an emergency cere-

mony on January 17, 1979. Even after Alexander's inauguration, Blanton attempted to pardon thirty more prisoners, before law enforcement officials and the new governor took over the Capitol.

After leaving office, a federal probe unveiled information showing Blanton to have had one of the most corrupt administrations in Tennessee history. Four Blanton aides were indicted in March 1979, and in 1981, Blanton himself was convicted of eleven counts of mail fraud, extortion, and conspiracy in the issuance of liquor licenses. He was sentenced to three years in prison, and in July 1984, he entered Maxwell Air Force Base Federal Prison to serve his sentence.

Blanton died on November 22, 1996.

ALEXANDER, LAMAR (1940-   ), fifty-second governor of Tennessee (1979-1987), was born in Blount County, Tennessee on July 3, 1940, the son of Andrew and Flo Alexander. He attended Vanderbilt University, and graduated with a law degree in 1965. He practiced law in Knoxville for a short time, then became a clerk for Judge John Minor Wisdom of the U.S. Fifth Circuit Court of Appeals. In 1966, he worked as a campaign aide for Howard Baker, and when Baker was elected to the Senate, Alexander became his legislative aide. In 1969, he married Leslee Kathryn Buhler. They have four children.

Also that same year, Alexander became executive assistant to President Nixon's Congressional Relations Advisor, Bruce Harlow. In 1970, Alexander managed Winfield Dunn's campaign for Tennessee governor. He returned to his law practice for the next four years, and in 1974 made a run for governor, but was defeated by Democrat Ray Blanton, partly due to public reaction to the Watergate scandal. He worked as a political commentator for WSM television in Nashville, and in 1977 became special counsel to Howard Baker, who had just been named Minority Leader.

Alexander ran for governor in 1978 and won over the Democratic opposition due to pardon-selling scandals in Governor Blanton's administration. The scandal came to a head in January 1979, five days before the end of Blanton's term. When the Governor pardoned fifty-two convicts, including twenty-four murderers, the public reacted angrily. In an emergency move to prevent further pardons, Alexander was sworn in three days early, on January 17, 1979.

State government was in disarray, and Alexander spent much of his first term dealing with repercussions caused by scandals of the Blanton administration. Apart from the scandals, the state saw the opening of the World's Fair in Knoxville in 1982, with moderate success. Alexander was reelected governor that same year. In 1983, he helped celebrate the golden anniversary of the Tennessee Valley Authority. Alexander's second term ended in January 1987.

McWHERTER, NED R. (1930-   ), fifty-third governor of Tennessee (1987-1994), was born in Palmersville, Weakly County, Tennessee, the son of Lucille Golden Smith and Harmon Ray McWherter.

McWherter's political career began in 1968 when he won a seat in the Tennessee House of Representatives. In 1973, after two terms, he was elected Speaker of the House. In this position, McWherter helped to reestablish the General Assembly as an independent branch of Tennessee government. He worked closely with four governors to find creative solutions to issues facing the State. He also opened the legislative process to participation from all Tennesseans by insisting that House proceedings be open to the public and the press. He also selected the first black committee chairman in the South, and appointed women in the State to legislative leadership positions. McWherter was Speaker of the

House for seven consecutive terms, a record in Tennessee history. In his eighteen years as a representative, McWherter was also chairman of the Calendar and Rules Committee, a member of the Finance, Ways and Means Committee, the General Welfare Committee, and the Joint Fiscal Review Committee.

In 1886, McWherter became a candidate for governorship of the State. Running on a platform that stressed the importance of jobs, education, economic development, transportation, health care, housing, and protection of the environment, McWherter won the election by more than 100,000 votes. He was reelected again in 1990 with only minor opposition.

During his administration, McWherter stressed strict financial management and elimination of bureaucratic red tape. He brought an innovative management style to State government, allowing him to expand services to the public, make new investments in education and economic development, and keep the State's budget balanced. Magazines that have rated fiscal management in all the states consistently rated Tennessee among the best; in 1992, Tennessee was ranked No. 1 by *City and State Magazine*.

McWherter pioneered the concept of open government in Tennessee. His philosophy was that the public's business should always be transacted in public. He established a comprehensive system of public integrity and disclosure requirements for ranking officials in his administration. His open-door policy gave all citizens access to their governor.

McWherter made a strong commitment to the State's educational needs. He helped enact the revolutionary 21st Century Schools education reform policy in 1992, with the goal of renewing Tennessee's position of national leadership in education reform in such areas as accountability, performance standards, and the equalization of funds between rich and poor regions of the State. The program also provided major new financial support for all schools, from kindergarten through higher education institutions.

McWherter accomplished high levels of economic growth and development for Tennessee. His support of a new program to recruit new industry from other nations as well as maintaining and encouraging industry nationally and locally helped Tennessee to become known throughout the world as a premier business location.

Also among McWherter's priorities was a program designed to expand the State's development equally across all ninety-five counties. With a large road-building budget, he opened up the potential for building new communities and creating new jobs. He also gave his support to economically depressed communities by creating a State-funded program to build needed facilities to attract industry and jobs.

McWherter initiated the first State-financed program for low-income housing, started community-based Drug Free Tennessee organizations to attack the problems of drug and alcohol abuse, and encouraged innovative solutions to the issue of available and affordable health care in the State.

McWherter was reelected to a second term in 1990. He was married to the late Bette Jean Beck. The couple has two children.

SUNDQUIST, DON (1936-), fifty-fourth Governor of Tennessee (1994-), was born on March 15, 1936 in Moline, Illinois. He earned his bachelor's degree from Augustana College in 1957, and served in the U.S. Navy until 1959.

After working in several management and corporate positions at Josten's, a company that makes class rings and other graduation related products, Sundquist started his own printing and advertising firm. He was also co-founder of the first Red, Hot, and Blue barbecue restaurant.

Sundquist began his public service career in the U.S. House of Representatives. A fiscal conservative, he retained his seat for six terms. He was elected to the executive office of Tennessee in 1994. As Governor, he created the Families First welfare reform program, and reduced the number of employable adults on welfare by sixty percent.

Also during Sundquist's tenure, Tennessee became the first state in the nation to offer universal health insurance that assures coverage for every child through age eighteen who would not otherwise be eligible to receive coverage. Through the ConnecTen project created during his term, Tennessee became the first state to connect all of its public schools and libraries to the Internet. And in 1998, the State attracted a record 5.2 billion dollars in new capital investment.

Sundquist was reelected to a second term in November 1998. He is married and has three children.

DICTIONARY OF PLACES

Population figures and demographic information are official U.S. Census Bureau finals for 1990. When two figures are shown, separated by a slash, the first figure is the 1990 and the second is the U.S. Census Bureau 1999 estimate—the most recent available. Year 2000 census supplements will be available in the Fall of 2001.

ADAMS, Town; Robertson County; Pop. 600 / 645; Zip Code 37010; Elev. 560; Lat. 36-34-41 N, Long. 087-04-02; Adams is named after the sixth president of the United States, John Quincy Adams.

ADAMSVILLE, Town; McNairy County; Pop. 1,453 / 1,824; Zip Code 38310; Elev. 518; Lat. 35-14-24 N, Long. 088-22-28 W; Named after an early pioneer.

ALAMO, Town; Crockett County Seat; Pop. 2,615 / 2,379; Zip Code 38001; Elev. 367; Lat. 35-47-03 N, Long. 089-06-59 W; The towns name commemorates the Texas battle.

ALCOA, City; Blount County; Pop. 6,870 / 10,153; Zip Code 37701; Lat. 35-47-02 N, Long. 083-59-02 W; Named after the Alcoa Aluminum Company.

ALEXANDRIA, Town; Dekalb County; Pop. 689 / 789; Zip Code 37,012; Elev. 709; 36-04-36 N, Long. 086-02-07 W; Named after the Egyptian city.

ALLARDT, City; Fentress County; Pop. 654 / 666; Zip Code 38504 Lat. 36-22-44 N, Long. 084-52-58 W; A personal name from an early landowner.

ALTAMONT, Town; Grundy County Seat; Pop. 679 / 809; Zip Code 37301; Long. 1,870; Lat. 35-26-00 N, Long. 085-43-24 W; A Spanish word meaning High Mountain.

ARDMORE, City; Giles County; Pop. 835 / 1,103; Zip Code 384+; Lat. 34-59-23 N, Long. 086-50-39 W; Named after Ardmore, Ireland.

ARLINGTON, Town; Shelby County; Pop. 1,778 / 1,451; Zip Code 38002; Lat. 35-16-51 N, Long. 089-39-46 W; The town is named for Arlington, Virginia.

ASHLAND CITY, Town; Cheatham County Scot; Pop. 2,329 / 3,688; Zip Code 37013; Elev. 438; Lat. 36-16-16 N, Long. 087-03-34 W; Named after Henry Clay's Kentucky home.

ATHENS, City; McMinn County; Pop. 12,080 / 13,949; Zip Code 37303; Elev. 867; Lat. 35-26-39 N, Long. 084-36-01 W; Named after the famous Greek city of classical times.

ATOKA, Town; Tipton County; Pop. 691 / 3,641; Zip Code 38004; Elev. 434; Lat. 35-26-10 N, Long. 089-46-430 W; An Indian name of uncertain meaning.

ATWOOD, Town; Carroll County; Pop. 1,143; Zip Code 38220; Elev. 448; Lat. 35-58-19 N, Long. 088-40-43 W; Atwood's name honors an early settler.

AUBURNTOWN, Town; Cannon County; Pop. 204 / 399; Zip Code 37016; Elev. 679; Lat. 35-56-39 N, Long. 086-05-46 W; The town is named after Auburn, New York.

BIG SANDY, Town; Benton County; Pop. 650 / 583; Zip Code 38,221; Lat. 36-14-01 N, Long. 088-04-51 W; Named after local soil conditions.

BAXTER, Town; Putnam County; Pop. 1,411 / 1,656; Zip Code 38544; Elev. 1,031; Lat. 36-09-14 N, Long. 085-38-21 W; Baxter's name recoils an early landowner.

BELLE MEADE, City; Davidson County; Pop. 3,182 / 2,875; the city's name means "Beautiful Meadow."

BELL BUCKLE, Town; Bedford County; Pop. 450 / 364; Zip Code 37020; Elev. 837; Lat. 35-35-26 N, Long. 086-21-04 W; Descriptively named for an historical incident in the town's beginnings.

BELLS, City; Crockett County; Pop. 1,371 / 1,841; Zip Code 38006; Lat. 35-42-53 N, Long. 089-05-11 W; Descriptively named alter local church bells.

BERRY HILL, City; Davidson County; Pop. 1,113 / 775; Descriptively named for the wild berries growing in the area.

BERSHEBA SPRINGS, Town; Grundy County; Pop. 643; Zip Code 37303; Elev. 1,845; Lat. 35-27-43 N, Long. 085-39-51 W; Given a biblical name by its early settler.

BETHEL SPRINGS, Town; McNairy County; Pop. 873 / 1,015; Zip Code 38315; Elev. 462; Lat. 25-13-57 N, Long. 088-36-21 W; Bethel is a biblical term meaning "Hope."

BENTON, Town; Polk County Seat; Pop. 1,115 / 1,841; Zip Code 37307; Elev. 748; Lat. 35-10-32 N, Long. 084-39-04 W; Benton's name recalls a pioneer.

BLAINE, City; Grainger County; Pop. 1,147 / 1,594; Zip Code 37709; Elev. 937; Lat. 36-09-20 N, Long. 083-42-08 W; Named after a prominent politician.

BLUFF CITY, City; Sullivan County; Pop. 1,121 / 1,403; Zip Code, 37618; Elev. 1,429; Lat. 36-27-48 N, Long. 082-15-26 W; Descriptively named for its topography.

BOLIVAR, City; Hardeman County Seat; Pop. 6,597 / 6,115; Zip Code 38008; Elev. 453; Lat. 35-15-31 N, Long. 088-59-55 W; The city's name honors the great South American liberator.

BRADEN, Town; Fayette County; Pop. 293 / 354; Zip Code 38010; Elev. 315; Lat. 35-22-47 N, Long. 089-33-58 W; The city is named after a prominent citizen.

BRADFORD, Town; Gibson County; Pop. 1,146 / 1,165; Zip Code 38316; Elev. 366; Lat. 36-04-29 N, Long. 088-48-39 W; Bradford was an early settler in the area.

BRIGHTON, Town; Tipton County; Pop. 976 / 1,424; Zip Code 38011; Lat. 35-29-00 N, Long. 089-43-22 W; The town is named after the English resort city.

BRENTWOOD, City; Williamson County; Pop. 9,431 24,159; Zip Code 37027; Elev. 725; Lat. 36-01-41 N, Long. 086-47-14 W; Named from famous English estate.

BRISTOL, City; Sullivan County; Pop. 23,986 / 24,564; Zip Code 37620; Lat. 36-34-35 N, Long. 082-11-21 W; The city is named offer Bristol England.

BROWNSVILLE, City; Haywood County Seat; Pop. 9,307 / 10,358; Zip Code 38012; Elev. 390; Lat. 35-35-36 N, Long. 089-15-37 W; Named for an early pioneer

BRUCETON, Town; Carroll County; Pop. 1,579 / 1,581; Zip Code 38317; Elev. 412; Lat. 36-02-05 N, Long. 088-44-37 W; Bruce was a pioneer settler who left his name on the town.

BULLS GAP, Town; Hawkins County; Pop. 821 / 792; Zip Code 37711; Elev. 1,153; Lat. 36-15-15 N, Long. 083-04-57 W; Descriptively named for a local topographic feature.

BURLISON, Town; Tipton County; Pop. 386 / 661; Zip Code 38015; Lat. 35-33-11 N, Long. 089-47-47 W; Named after a pioneer.

BURNS, Town; Dickson County; Pop. 777 / 1,560; Zip Code 37029; Elev. 794; Lat. 36-03-10 N, Long. 087-18-47 W; Burns is named after the Scottish poet Robert Burns.

BYRDSTOWN, Town; Pickett County Seat; Pop. 884 / 990; Zip Code 38549; Elev. 1,037; Lat. 36-34-13 N, Long. 085-07-49 W; Possibly a descriptive name.

CALHOUN, Town; McMinn County; Pop. 590 / 584; Zip Code 37309; Lat. 35-17-45 N, Long. 084-44-43 W; Calhoun's name honors the prominent 19th century southern politician.

CAMDEN, City; Benton County Seat; Pop. 3,279 / 4,526; Zip Code 38320; Elev. 460; Lat. 36-03-32 N, Long. 088-05-50 W; The town is named after the city in New Jersey, site of a revolutionary war battle.

CARTHAGE, Town; Smith County Seat; Pop. 2,672 / 2,855; Zip Code 37030; Elev. 515; Lat. 36-14-37 N, Long. 085-56-53 W; Named after the ancient North African city.

CARYVILLE, Town; Campbell County; Pop. 2,039 / 1,081; Zip Code 37714; Elev. 1,095; Lat. 36-17-35 N, Long. 084-12-49 W; Cary was the family name of an early settler.

CEDAR HILL, Town; Robertson County; Pop. 420 / 428; Zip Code 37032; Lat. 36-33-07 N, Long. 087-00-00 W; The town is named descriptively for the cedar trees originally found in the area.

CELINA, City; Clay County Seat; Pop. 1,580 / 1,468; Zip Code 38551; Elev. 562; Lat. 36-32-54 N, Long. 085-30-08 W; Celina is named after the wife of a pioneer.

CENTERVILLE, Town; Hickman County Seat; Pop. 2,824 / 5,045; Zip Code 37033; Elev. 634; Lat. 35-47-35 N, Long. 087-26-58 W; Named for its location to other towns in the area.

CHAPEL HILL, Town; Marshall County; Pop. 861 / 1,049; Zip Code 37034; Lat. 35-37-46 N, Long. 086-41-43 W; Originally the site of a chapel on a hill and so named.

CHARLESTON, City; Bradley County; Pop. 756 / 631; Zip Code 37310; Elev. 688; Lat. 35-17-14 N, Long. 084-45-30 W; The town is named after the city in South Carolina.

CHARLOTTE, Town; Dickson County Seat; Pop. 788 / 1,032; Zip Code 37036; Elev. 631; Lat. 36-10-42 N, Long. 087-20-24 W; Named after Charlotte Robertson, the wife of Richard Napier.

CHATTANOOGA, City; Hamilton County Seat; Pop. 169,565 / 147,110; Zip Code 37400; Elev. 685; Lat. 35-00-24 N, Long. 085-12-09 W; A Creek Indian word meaning "Rock Rising to a Paint."

CHURCH HILL, Town; Hawkins County; Pop. 4,110 / 6,412; Zip Code 37642; Elev. 1,249; Lat. 36-32-19 N, Long. 082-40-47 W; Descriptively named for a local church on a hill.

CLARKSBURG, Town; Carroll County; Pop. 400 / 436; Zip Code 38324; Lat. 35-52-39 N, Long. 088-24-06 W; Clark was an early landowner.

CLARKSVILLE, City; Montgomery County Seat; Pop. 54,777 / 99,049; Zip Code 37040; Lat. 36-31-53 N, Long. 087-21-31 W; Named in honor of General George Rogers Clark.

CLEVELAND, City; Bradley County Seat; Pop. 26,415 / 36,138; Zip Code 373+; Lat. 35-08-55 N, Long. 084-52-00 W; Named after Cleveland, Ohio.

CLIFTON, City; Wayne County; Pop. 773 / 805; Zip Code 38425; Elev. 403; Lat. 35-23-02 N, Long. 087-59-40 W; Descriptively named for the local topography.

CLINTON, City; Anderson County Seat; Pop. 5,245 / 9,755; Zip Code 37716; Lat. 36-05-22 N, Long. 084-08-15 W; Named in honor of Erie Canal builder DeWitt Clinton.

COALMONT, City; Grundy County; Pop. 625 / 847; Zip Code 37313; Lat. 35-20-19 N, Long. 085-42-32 W; Descriptively named for the coal deposits in the area.

COLLEGEDALE, City; Hamilton County; Pop. 4,607 / 6,531; Zip Code 37315; Lat. 35-02-42 N, Long. 085-02-54 W; The city is named after a local college.

COLLIERVILLE, Town; Shelby County; Pop. 7,839 / 25,629; Zip Code 38017; Elev. 387; Lat. 35-02-37 N, Long. 089-39-47 W; Descriptively named for the coal operations in the area.

COLLINWOOD, City; Wayne County; Pop. 1,064 / 1,036; Zip Code 38450; Elev. 1,056; Lat. 35-10-18 N, Long. 087-44-21 W; The city is named for an early settler.

COLUMBIA, City; Maury County Seat; Pop. 25,767 / 32,308; Zip Code 38401; Lat. 35-36-45 N, Long. 087-02-29 W; The city is named after Columbia, South America.

COOKEVILLE, City; Putnam County Seat; Pop. 20,350 / 26,071; Zip Code 38501; Elev. 118; Lat. 36-10-52 N, Long. 085-28-28 W; Cookeville's name honors Major Richard Cooke who fought in the Mexican-American war.

COPPERHILL, City; Polk County; Pop. 418 / 515; Zip Code 37317; Elev. 1,476; Lat. 34-59-20 N, Long. 084-22-13 W; Named for a local copper deposit.

CORNERSVILLE, Town; Marshall County; Pop. 722 / 838; Zip Code 37047; Elev. 893; Lat. 35-21-34 N, Long. 086-50-19 W; The town is named as the site of an early crossroads.

COTTAGE GROVE, Town; Henry County; Pop. 117 / 82; Zip Code 38224; Lat. 36-22-40 N, Long. 088-28-38 W; Named for an early cottage on the site in a grove of trees.

COVINGTON, City; Tipton County Seat; Pop. 6,065 / 8,932; Zip Code 38019; Elev. 339; Lat. 35-34-28 N, Long. 089-41-57 W; Leonard W. Covington was a general in the War of 1812. The town is named for them.

COWAN, City; Franklin County; Pop. 1,790 / 1,632; Zip Code 37318; Lat. 36-15-39 N, Long. 086-39-03 W; The city is named for a pioneer family.

CRAB ORCHARD, City; Cumberland County; Pop. 1,065 / 1,100; Zip Code 37723; Elev. 1,671; Lat. 35-54-34 N, Long. 084-52-40 W; The site of a crab apple orchard and, hence, so named.

CROSS PLAINS, City; Robertson County; Pop. 655 / 1,566; Zip Code 37049; Elev. 749; Lat. 36-33-00 N, Long. 086-41-01; Descriptively named for the areas role as a pioneer route.

CROSSVILLE, City; Cumberland County Seat; Pop. 6,394 / 10,366; Zip Code 38555; Elev. 1,863; Lat. 35-56-46 N, Long. 085-01-30 W; Named for its location at the junction of the Nashville-Knoxville Road and the Kentucky-Chattanooga Stock Road.

CUMBERLAND CITY, Town; Stewart County; Pop. 276 / 364; Zip Code 37050; Elev. 390; Lat. 36-23-10 N, Long. 087-37-55 W; The town is named for Cumberland County, England.

CUMBERLAND GAP, Town; Claiborne County; Pop. 263 / 219; Zip Code 37724; Elev. 1,302; Lat. 36-35-45 N, Long. 083-39-53 W; The town is named for the local geographic feature.

DANDRIDGE, Town; Jefferson County Seat; Pop. 1,383 / 1,998; Zip Code 37725; Elev. 1,000; Lat. 36-01-00 N, Long. 083-24-55 W; Named for the city in Kentucky, itself named after Martha Dandridge Curtis, George Washington's wife.

DAYTON, City; Rhea County Seat; Pop. 5,913 / 6,403; Zip Code 37321; Elev. 694; Lat. 35-01-10 N, Long. 085-10-54 W; The City is named for Dayton, Ohio.

DECATUR, Town; Meigs County Seat; Pop. 1,069 / 1,671; Zip Code 37322; Elev. 788; Lat. 35-30-53 N, Long. 084-47-24 W; Named after War of 1812 naval hero Stephen Decatur.

DECATURVILLE, Town; Decatur County Seat; Pop. 1,004 / 874; Zip Code 38329; Elev. 517; Lat. 35-34-51 N, Long. 088-07-09 W; The town's name honors War of 1812 naval hero Stephen Decatur.

DECHERD, Town; Franklin County; Pop. 2,233 / 2,366; Zip Code 37324; Elev. 960; Lat. 35-12-36 N, Long. 086-04-55 W; Decherd was an early settler.

DENMARK, Town; Madison County; Pop. 51; Zip Code 38391; Elev. 466; Lat. 35-31-30 N, Long. 089-00-15 W; The town is named for the country in Europe.

DICKSON, City; Dickson County; Pop. 7,040 / 12,564; Zip Code 37055; Elev. 794; Lat. 36-04-33 N, Long. 087-22-38 W; Dickson's name honors an early pioneer.

DOVER, City; Stewart County Seat; Pop. 1,197 / 1,639; Zip Code 37058; Elev. 400; Lat. 36-29-12 N, Long. 087-50-27 W; Named after the English city.

DOWELLTOWN, Town; Dekalb County; Pop. 341 / 328; Zip Code 37059; Lat. 36-00-53 N, Long. 085-56-39 W; Dowelltown is named after an early settler.

DOYLE, Town; White County; Pop. 344 / 494; Zip Code 38559; Elev. 965; Lat. 35-51-06 N, Long. 085-30-43 W; The city is named after an Irish settler.

DRESDEN, Town; Weakley County Seat; Pop. 2,256 / 2,518; Zip Code 38225; Elev. 425; Lat. 36-17-05 N, Long. 088-42-26 W; The town is named after the famous German city.

DUCKTOWN, City; Polk County; Pop. 583 / 422; Zip Code 37326; Lat. 35-04-32 N, Long. 084-27-16 W; Named for the many wild ducks in the area.

DUNLAP, City; Sequatchie County Seat; Pop. 3,681 / 4,688; Zip Code 37327; Elev. 722; Lat. 35-22-17 N, Long. 085-23-21 W; Dunlap was a pioneer.

DYER, City; Gibson County; Pop. 2,419 / 2,227; Zip Code 38330; Elev. 360; Lat. 36-04-02 N, Long. 088-59-38 W; Robert Dyer was a famous Indian fighter. The town is named for him.

DYERSBURG, City; Dyer County Seat; Pop. 15,856 / 16,939; Zip Code 38024; Lat. 36-02-12 N, Long. 089-22-59 W; Named in honor of Indian fighter Robert Dyer.

ELKTON, Town; Giles County; Pop. 540 / 517; Zip Code 38455; Lat. 35-03-06 N, Long. 086-53-14 W; The town is named after the once plentiful elk herds in the area.

ENGLEWOOD, Town; McMinn County; Pop. 1,840 / 1,760; Zip Code 37329; Elev. 869; Lat. 35-25-20 N, Long. 084-29-11 W; Named after the English village.

ENVILLE, Town; Chester & McNairy Counties; Pop. 287 / 200; Zip Code 38332; Elev. 427; Lat. 35-23-11 N, Long. 088-25-47 W; The origin of the town's name are uncertain.

ERIN, City; Houston County Seat; Pop. 1,614 / 1,697; Zip Code 37061; Lat. 36-19-05 N, Long. 087-41-48 W; Named by an Irish settler for his homeland.

ERWIN, City; Unicoi County Seat; Pop. 4,739 / 5,790; Zip Code 37650; Elev. 1,675; Lat. 36-08-09 N, Long. 082-24-48 W; Named in honor of Dr. J.N. Erwin, who donated land to the community.

ESTILL SPRINGS, Town; Franklin County; Pop. 1,324 / 1,641; Zip Code 37330; Elev. 945; Lat. 35-15-44 N, Long. 086-07-41 W; James Estill was a famous Indian fighter. The town is named for him.

ETHRIDGE, Town; Lawrence County; Pop. 548 / 911; Zip Code 38456; Lat. 35-19-26 N, Long. 087-18-17 W; Named by combining a personal name with a local geographical feature.

ETOWAH, City; McMinn County; Pop. 3,758 / 3,804; Zip Code 37331; Elev. 807; Lat. 35-19-35 N, Long. 084-31-40 W; A Creek Indian word meaning "Village."

FAIRVIEW, City; Williamson County; Pop. 3,648 / 3,804; Zip Code 37062; Elev. 1,002; Lat. 35-59-14 N, Long. 087-06-56 W; Descriptively named for its view.

FAYETTEVILLE, City; Lincoln County Seat; Pop. 7,559 / 7,475; Zip Code 37334; Elev. 71; Lat. 35-09-05 N, Long. 086-34-34 W; Named in honor of revolutionary war hero General Marquis Lafayette.

FINGER, City; McNairy County; Pop. 245 / 302; Zip Code 38334; Elev. 431; Lat. 35-21-35 N, Long. 088-35-49 W; Descriptively named for a long and thin geographical feature.

FRANKLIN, City; Williamson County Seat; Pop. 12,407 / 33,656; Zip Code 37064; Elev. 648; Lat. 35-56-57 N, Long. 086-52-34 W; The city is named after Benjamin Franklin.

FRIENDSHIP, City; Crockett County; Pop. 763 / 511; Zip Code 38034; Elev. 403; Lat. 35-54-29 N, Long. 089-14-55 W; Named by its settlers after the virtue.

FRIENDSVILLE, City; Blount County; Pop. 694 / 995; Zip Code 37737; Lat. 35-45-40 N, Long. 084-08-25 W; Named by its settlers for friendship.

GADSDEN, Town; Crockett County; Pop. 683 / 483; Zip Code 38337; Elev. 422; Lat. 35-46-35 N, Long. 088-59-31 W; Gadsen is named in honor of South Carolina soldier and diplomat James Gadsen.

GAINESBORO, Town; Jackson County Seat; Pop. 1,119 / 1,104; Zip Code 38562; Elev. 565; Lat. 36-21-15 N, Long. 085-39-28 W; Named for Edmund P. Gaines.

GALLATIN, City; Sumner County Seat; Pop. 17,191 / 22,125; Zip Code 37066; Elev. 526; Lat. 36-23-08 N, Long. 086-26-18 W; The city's name honors Albert Gallatin, Secretary of the Treasury, under Presidents John Adams and Thomas Jefferson.

GALLAWAY, City; Fayette County; Pop. 804 / 870; Zip Code 38036; Elev. 285; Lat. 35-19-40 N, Long. 089-37-07 W; Gallaway owned land here in the early 1800s. The town is named for him.

GARLAND, Town; Tipton County; Pop. 301 / 538; Named for U.S. Senator Augustus Hill.

GATLINBURG, City; Sevier County; Pop. 3,210 / 4,967; Zip Code 37738; Elev. 1,289; Lat. 35-42-52 N, Long. 083-30-34 W; Named for a pioneer.

GERMANTOWN, City; Shelby County; Pop. 20,459 / 37,781; Named for the ethnic origin of the area's early settlers.

GIBSON, Town; Gibson County; Pop. 458 / 348; Zip Code 38338; Lat. 35-52-32 N, Long. 088-50-38 W; John Gibson served under Andrew Jackson in the War of 1812. The town is named for him.

GLEASON, Town; Weakley County; Pop. 1,335 / 1,435; Zip Code 38229; Lat. 36-13-12 N, Long. 088-36-41 W; Gleason was an early settler.

GORDONSVILLE, Town; Smith County; Pop. 893 / 1,258; Zip Code 38563; Lat. 36-10-44 N, Long. 085-55-50 W; Named for a pioneer family.

GRAND JUNCTION, City; Hardman County; Pop. 360 / 356; Zip Code 38039; Elev. 575; Lat. 35-02-57 N, Long. 089-11-01 W; Descriptively named as a crossroads.

GRAYSVILLE, Town; Rhea County; Pop. 1,380 / 1,538; Zip Code 37338; Elev. 725; Lat. 35-26-45 N, Long. 085-04-57 W; Gray was an early settler.

GREENBACK, City; Loudon County; Pop. 546 / 684; Zip Code 37742; Elev. 902; Lat. 35-39-32 N, Long. 084-10-14 W; Probably descriptive of the local vegetation.

GREENBRIER, Town; Robertson County; Pop. 3,180 / 4,768; Zip Code 37073; Elev. 664; Lat. 36-25-43 N, Long. 086-48-17 W; Named for the local thorny vine, *Smilax Rotundifolia*.

GREENEVILLE, Town; Greene County Seat; Pop. 14,097 / 15,657; Zip Code 37743; Elev. 1,531; Lat. 36-13-18 N, Long. 082-48-13 W; The town is named in honor of Revolutionary War General Nathaniel Greene.

GREENFIELD, City; Weakley County; Pop. 2,109 / 2,027; Zip Code 38230; Elev. 433; Lat. 36-09-28 N, Long. 088-48-03 W; The town is named for its lush agriculture.

HALLS, Town; Lauderdale County; Pop. 2,444 / 2,254; Zip Code 38040; Lat. 35-52-36 N, Long. 089-23-46 W; Halls is named after a local settler.

HARRIMAN, City; Roane County; Pop. 8,303 / 6,970; Zip Code 37748; Lat. 35-56-09 N, Long. 084-32-56 W; The city is named in honor of General Walter Harriman, a former Governor of New Hampshire.

HARTSVILLE, Town; Trousdale County Seat; Pop. 2,674 / 2,431; Zip Code 37074; Elev. 474; Lat. 36-23-18 N, Long. 086-09-30 W; James Hart was an early settler. The town is named for him.

HENDERSON, City; Chester County Seat; Pop. 4,449 / 6,111; Zip Code 38340; Elev. 462; Lat. 35-26-22 N, Long. 088-38-47 W; Named for James Henderson who fought in the War of 1812.

HENDERSONVILLE, City; Sumner County; Pop. 26,561 / 39,728; Zip Code 37075; Elev. 459; The city is named after War of 1812 Soldier James Henderson.

HENNING, Town; Lauderdale County; Pop. 638 / 957; Zip Code 38041; Elev. 293; Lat. 35-40-27 N, Long. 089-34-21 W; The town is named after a pioneer.

HENRY, Town; Henry County; Pop. 295 / 351; Zip Code 38231; Elev. 547; Lat. 36-12-17 N, Long. 088-25-00 W; Henry is named for an early landowner.

HICKORY VALLEY, Town; Hardeman County; Pop. 252 / 160; Zip Code 38042; Elev. 564; Lat. 35-09-16 N, Long. 089-07-26 W; Descriptively named for the Hickory trees in the surrounding valley.

HOHENWALD, City; Lewis County Seat; Pop. 3,922 / 4,621; Zip Code 38462; Elev. 976; Lat. 35-32-52 N, Long. 087-33-34 W; Swiss settlers gave the town a German name meaning "High Forest."

HOLLOW ROCK, Town; Carroll County; Pop. 955 / 965; Zip Code 38342; Elev. 424; Lat. 36-02-11 N, Long. 088-16-22 W; Named after local geological oddity.

HORNBEAK, Town; Obion County; Pop. 452 / 416; Zip Code 38232; Elev. 474; Lat. 36-19-53 N, Long. 089-17-35 W; The town is named after a local geographical feature.

HORNSBY, Town; Hardeman County; Pop. 401 / 252; Zip Code 38044; Lat. 35-13-34 N, Long. 088-49-57 W; Hornsby was a prominent pioneer.

HUMBOLDT, City; Gibson County Seat; Pop. 10,209 / 9,718; Zip Code 38343; Elev. 357; Lat. 35-49-32 N, Long. 088-54-40 W; The city's name honors the great German naturalist Alexander Humboldt.

HUNTINGDON, Town; Carroll County Seat; Pop. 3,962 / 4,877; Zip Code 38344; Lat. 36-00-21 N, Long. 088-25-05 W; Named for the great hunting the first settlers found in the area.

HUNTLAND, Town; Franklin County; Pop. 983 / 911; Zip Code 37345; Lat. 35-03-00 N, Long. 086-15-54 W; Descriptively named for the area's excellent hunting.

HUNTSVILLE, Town; Scott County Seat; Pop. 519 / 901; Zip Code 37756; Lat. 36-24-33 N, Long. 084-29-07 W; Hunting formed an important part of pioneer life in the area. The name recalls that time.

IRON CITY, City; Lawrence County; Pop. 482 / 465; Zip Code 38463; Elev. 559; Lat. 35-02-08 N, Long. 087-30-20 W; The city is named after a local iron foundry.

JACKSBORO, Town; Campbell County Seat; Pop. 1,620 / 1,912; Zip Code 37757; Elev. 1,070; Lat. 36-19-32 N, Long. 084-11-16 W; Jacksboro is named in honor of John F. Jack, early Tennessee legislator and judge.

JACKSON, City; Madison County Seat; Pop. 49,131 / 54,036; Zip Code 38301; Elev. 401; Lat. 35-39-19 N, Long. 088-52-30 W; Jackson's name honors President Andrew Jackson.

JAMESTOWN, City; Fentress County Seat; Pop. 2,364 / 2,087; Zip Code 38556; Elev. 1,716; Lat. 36-26-19 N, Long. 084-55-51 W; Named after the city in Virginia.

JASPER, Town; Marion County Seat; Pop. 2,633 / 2,862; Zip Code 37347; Elev. 622; Lat. 35-03-38 N, Long. 085-39-24 W; The town's name honors Sgt. William Jasper, who fought in the Revolutionary War.

JEFFERSON CITY, City; Jefferson County; Pop. 5,612 / 8,765; Zip Code 37760; Lat. 36-07-15 N, Long. 083-29-31 W; Named in honor of President Thomas Jefferson.

JELLICO, City; Campbell County; Pop. 2,798 / 2,671; Zip Code 37762; Elev. 982; Lat. 36-34-39 N, Long. 084-07-47 W; Originally Jerrico, but subsequently misspelled to Jellico.

JOHNSON CITY, City; Carter & Washington Counties; Washington County Seat; Pop. 39,753 / 59,160; Zip Code 376+; Elev. 1,635; Lat. 36-18-57 N, Long. 082-21-16 W; Named for President Andrew Johnson.

JONESBORO, Town; Washington County Seat; Pop. 2,829 / 4,220; Zip Code 37659; Elev. 1,692; Lat. 36-17-46 N, Long. 082-27-58 W; Jonesboro's name honors North Carolina politician Willie Jones.

KENTON, Town; Gibson & Obion Counties; Pop. 1,551 / 1,377; Zip Code 38233; Lat. 36-12-03 N, Long. 089-00-39 W; Named for Simon Kenton, a famous Indian fighter of the early 1800s.

KINGSPORT, City; Hawkins & Sullivan Counties; Pop. 32,027 / 42,769; Zip Code 376+; Lat. 36-33-30 N, Long. 082-32-47 W; Colonel James King built a mill here. The town is named for him.

KINGSTON SPRINGS, Town; Cheatham County; Pop. 1,017 / 2,741; Zip Code 37082; Lat. 36-05-50 N, Long. 087-06-50 W; The town is named after the springs.

KINGSTON, City; Roane County Seat; Pop. 4,441 / 5,398; Zip Code 37763; Lat. 35-52-20 N, Long. 084-30-45 W; Kingston is named in honor of Major Roger King, Revolutionary War soldier.

KNOXVILLE, City; Knox County Seat; Pop. 183,139 / 174,860; Zip Code 37900; Lat. 35-58-39 N, Long. 083-56-05 W; The city is named in honor of Revolutionary War General Henry Knox.

LA FAYETTE, City; Macon County Seat; Pop. 3,808 / 5,564; The city is named for the French American Revolutionary War hero.

LA FOLLETTE, City; Campbell County; Pop. 8,176 / 8,034; Zip Code 37766; Lat. 36-22-37 N, Long. 084-07-06 W; The city is named after Harvey La Follette, president of the La Follette iron and coal company.

LA GRANGE, Town; Fayette County; Pop. 185 / 162; Zip Code 38046; Lat. 35-02-45 N, Long. 089-14-21 W; Named for the country estate of the Marquis de Lafayette.

LA VERGNE, City; Rutherford County; Pop. 5,495 / 16,137; Zip Code 37086; Lat. 36-00-58 N, Long. 086-33-53 W; Given a French name by its settlers.

LAKE CITY, Town; Anderson County; Pop. 2,335 / 2,086; Zip Code 37769; Elev. 855; Lat. 36-13-10 N, Long. 084-09-28 W; Descriptively named for a nearby lake.

LAWRENCEBURG, City; Lawrence County Seat; Pop. 10,175 / 11,538; Zip Code 38464; Lat. 35-14-48 N, Long. 087-19-37 W; Lawrenceburg is named in honor of Captain James Lawrence, a naval hero in the War of 1812.

LEBANON, City; Wilson County Seat; Pop. 11,872 / 19,781; Zip Code 37087; Elev. 507; Lat. 36-12-29 N, Long. 086-18-02 W; The community was named after biblical Lebanon.

LOBELVILLE, City; Perry County; Pop. 993 / 958; Zip Code 37097; Elev. 501; Lat. 35-45-33 N, Long. 087-47-02 W; Lobel was an early settler. The town is named for him.

LOOKOUT MOUNTAIN, Town; Hamilton County; Pop. 1,886 / 958; Zip Code 37350; Lat. 34-58-41 N, Long. 085-21-08 W; Descriptively named for a local mountain.

LORETTO, City; Lawrence County; Pop. 1,612 / 1,689; Zip Code 38469; Elev. 833; Lat. 35-04-25 N, Long. 087-26-25 W; Founded in 1872 and named after the area in Italy.

LOUDON, Town; Loudon County Seat; Pop. 3,940 / 4,653; Zip Code 37774; Lat. 35-44-01 N, Long. 084-20-36 W; The town is named for British soldier John Campbell, 4th Earl of Loudon, who commanded British armies during the early port of the French Indian War.

LUTTRELL, Town; Union County; Pop. 962 / 1,018; Zip Code 37779; Elev. 1,065; Lat. 36-12-15 N, Long. 083-44-40 W; Named for a prominent pioneer.

LYNCHBURG, Town; Moore County Seat; Pop. 668 / 5,140; Zip Code 37352; Lat. 35-16-58 N, Long. 086-22-29 W; Descriptively named for a nearly famous beech tree that was used for hanging criminals.

LYNNVILLE, Town; Giles County; Pop. 383 / 369; Zip Code 38472; Elev. 755; Lat. 35-22-45 N, Long. 087-00-10 W; Named after the town in Massachusetts.

MADISONVILLE, Town; Monroe County Seat; Pop. 2,884 / 3,635; Zip Code 37354; Elev. 968; Lat. 35-31-16 N, Long. 084-21-34 W; The town is named after President James Madison.

MANCHESTER, City; Coffee County Seat; Pop. 7,250 / 9,888; Zip Code 37355; Elev. 1,063; Lat. 35-28-21 N, Long. 086-04-59 W; The town is named after Manchester, England.

MARTIN, City; Weakley County; Pop. 8,898 / 9,998; Zip Code 38237; Elev. 413; Lat. 36-20-30 N, Long. 088-51-13 W; Named for a pioneer.

MARYVILLE, City; Blount County Seat; Pop. 17,480 / 24,906; Zip Code 37801; Elev. 940; Lat. 35-46-17 N, Long. 083-57-59 W; Maryville's name honors Mary Grainger Blount, the wife of Governor William Blount.

MASON, Town; Tipton County; Pop. 471 / 382; Zip Code 38049; Lat. 35-24-42 N, Long. 089-31-49 W; Named for a pioneer family.

MAURY CITY, Town; Crockett County; Pop. 989 / 859; Zip Code 38050; Elev. 346; Lat. 35-48-56 N, Long. 089-13-36 W; The town is named for Abram Maury, a U.S. Congressman from Tennessee in the 1830s.

MAYNARDVILLE, City; Union County Seat; Pop. 924 / 1,507; Zip Code 37807; Lat. 36-14-35 N, Long. 083-48-11 W; The city is named for Congressman Horace Maynard who served the area during the Civil War.

MCEWEN, City; Humphreys County; Pop. 1,352 / 1,552; Zip Code 37101; Elev. 836; Lat. 36-06-22 N, Long. 087-37-55 W; The town's name honors a prominent local family.

MCKENZIE, City; Corral, Henry & Weakley Counties; Pop. 5,405 / 5,444; Zip Code 38201; Elev. 495; Lat. 36-08-12 N, Long. 088-31-25 W; Named after a pioneer.

MCLEMORESVILLE, Town; Carroll County; Pop. 311 / 406; Zip Code 38235; Lat. 35-59-08 N, Long. 088-34-45 W; The town's name recalls a prominent settler.

MCMINNVILLE, City; Warren County Seat; Pop. 10,683 / 13,454; Zip Code 37110; Lat. 35-42-12 N, Long. 085-45-43 W; Named after an early settler.

MEDINA, City; Gibson County; Pop. 687 / 669; Zip Code 38355; Elev. 505; Lat. 35-48-20 N, Long. 088-46-13 W; Medina is named for the famous Arabian city.

MEDON, City; Madison County; Pop. 162 / 173; Zip Code 38356; Elev. 478; Lat. 35-27-22 N, Long. 088-51-45 W; Medon is named after an early landowner.

MEMPHIS, City; Shelby County Seat; Pop. 646,356 / 606,109; Zip Code 37501; Named after the ancient capital of lower Egypt.

MICHIE, Town; McNairy County; Pop. 530 / 890; Zip Code 38357; Lat. 35-03-44 N, Long. 088-24-38 W; Mitchie's name remembers an early landowner.

MIDDLETON, Town; Hardeman County; Pop. 596 / 567; Zip Code 38052; Elev. 409; Lat. 35-03-49 N, Long. 088-53-22 W; Descriptively named for its location in the area.

MILAN, City; Gibson County; Pop. 8,083 / 7,501; Zip Code 38358; Elev. 420; Lat. 35-55-10 N, Long. 088-45-35 W; The city takes its name from the famous Italian town.

MILLEDGEVILLE, Town; Chester, Hardin & McNairy Counties; Pop. 392 / 424; Zip Code 38359; Elev. 118; Lat. 35-22-35 N, Long. 088-21-54 W; The town is named for Revolutionary War hero John Milledge.

MONTEAGLE, Town; Grundy County; Pop. 680 / 1,234; Zip Code 37356; Lat. 35-14-24 N, Long. 085-49-53 W; Named after the nearby mountain.

MONTEREY, Town; Putnam County; Pop. 2,610 / 3,115; Zip Code 38574; Elev. 1,875; Lat. 36-08-41 N, Long. 085-15-56 W; Named after the battle in the Mexican-American War.

MORRISON, Town; Warren County; Pop. 587 / 633; Zip Code 37357; Elev. 1,076; Lat. 35-35-42 N, Long. 085-49-29 W; The town is named for one of its founders.

MORRISTOWN, City; Hamblen County Seat; Pop. 19,683 / 23,299; Zip Code 37814; Lat. 36-13-02 N, Long. 083-17-29 W; Named for the three Morris brothers who settled here in 1783.

MOSCOW, Town; Fayette County; Pop. 499 / 395; Zip Code 38057; Elev. 356; Lat. 35-03-34 N, Long. 089-24-00 W; Moscow is named after the famous city in Russia.

MOSHEIM, Town; Greene County; Pop. 1,539 / 1,944; Zip Code 37818; Elev. 1,298; Lat. 36-11-24 N, Long. 082-57-26 W; Mosheim is named for a local settler.

MOUNT PLEASANT, City; Maury County; Pop. 3,375 / 4,722; Zip Code 38474; Elev. 675; Lat. 35-32-08 N, Long. 087-12-23 W; Descriptively named from the local geography and scenery.

MOUNTAIN CITY, Town; Johnson County Seat; Pop. 2,125 / 2,791; Zip Code 37683; Elev. 2,429; Lat. 36-28-42 N, Long. 081-48-11 W; Descriptively named for its location in a valley surrounded by mountains.

MURFREESBORO, City; Rutherford County Seat; Pop. 32,845 / 61,177; Zip Code 37130; Elev. 619; Lat. 35-50-56 N, Long. 086-22-43 W; The city is named for Revolutionary War hero Col. Hardy Murfree.

NASHVILLE, City; Davidson County Seat and Capital of Tennessee; Pop. 455,651 / 506,385; Zip Code 372+; Elev. 440. Founded in 1779 by James Robertson and John Donelson on land formerly serving as a French trading post. It originally was occupied by Shawnee Indians. Named Fort Nashborough for Gen. Francis Nash and renamed in 1784 to its present name.

NEW JOHNSONVILLE, City; Humphreys County; Pop. 1,824 / 2,099; Zip Code 37134; Elev. 429; Lat. 36-00-55 N, Long. 087-57-49 W; Named after an early settler.

NEW MARKET, Town; Jefferson County; Pop. 1,216 / 1,397; Zip Code 37820; Lat. 36-06-08 N, Long. 083-32-38 W; Descriptively named for the town's commerce.

NEW TAZEWELL, Town; Claiborne County; Pop. 1,677 / 2,058; Zip Code 37825; Lat. 36-26-06 N, Long. 083-36-03 W; New Tazewell's name honors Littleton W. Tazewell, a U.S. Senator from Virginia in 1824.

NEWBERN, Town; Dyer County; Pop. 2,794 / 2,995; Zip Code 38059; Elev. 376; Lat. 36-06-50 N, Long. 089-15-47 W; The town is named after the city in Switzerland.

NEWPORT, City; Cooke County Seat; Pop. 7,580 / 1,397; Zip Code 37821; Elev. 1,055; Lat. 35-57-45 N, Long. 083-11-10 W; Descriptively named for its location on the bank of the French Broad River.

NORRIS, City; Anderson County; Pop. 1,374 / 126; Zip Code 37828; Lat. 36-12-59 N, Long. 084-03-49 W; George Norris, a U.S. Senator from Nebraska, helped bring the Tennessee valley authority project. The town is named after him.

OAK HILL, City; Davidson County; Pop. 4,609 / 4,251; Descriptively named for the oaks in the vicinity.

OAK RIDGE, City; Anderson & Roane Counties; Pop. 27,662 / 26,788; Zip Code 37830; Lat. 35-58-34 N, Long. 084-18-03 W; Descriptively named after the area's oak covered ridge.

OAKLAND, Town; Fayette County; Pop. 472 / 552; Zip Code 38060; Elev. 382; Lat. 35-13-34 N, Long. 089-30-52 W; The town is named for the oak trees in the area.

OBION, Town; Obion County; Pop. 1,282 / 1,224; Zip Code 38240; Elev. 290; Lat. 36-15-40 N, Long. 089-11-08 W; An Indian word meaning "Many Forks."

OLIVER SPRINGS, Town; Anderson, Morgan & Roane Counties; Pop. 3,659 / 3,450; Zip Code 37840; Elev. 785; Lat. 36-02-29 N, Long. 084-20-27 W; The town is named after the nearby springs.

ONEIDA, Town; Scott County; Pop. 3,029 / 3,450; Zip Code 37841; Lat. 36-30-08 N, Long. 084-30-33 W; The town is named after the Indian tribe.

ORLINDA, Town; Robertson County; Pop. 382 / 623; Zip Code 37141; Elev. 720; Lat. 36-35-57 N, Long. 086-42-50 W; Named for the wife of an early settler.

PALMER, Town; Grundy County; Pop. 1,027 / 801; Zip Code 37365; Elev. 1810; Lat. 35-21-21 N, Long. 085-33-38 W; Palmer was a 19th century landowner.

PARIS, City; Henry County Seat; Pop. 10,728 / 11,635; Zip Code 38242; Elev. 519; Lat. 36-18-01 N, Long. 088-19-03 W; The city is named for the French capitol.

PARROTTSVILLE, Town; Cooke County; Pop. 118 / 269; Zip Code 37843; Lat. 36-00-23 N, Long. 083-05-30 W; Parrottsville's name honors the town's founders.

PARSONS, Town; Decatur County; Pop. 2,422 / 2,430; Zip Code 38363; Elev. 497; Lat. 35-38-53 N, Long. 088-07-22 W; Named after a local farmer.

PEGRAM, Town; Cheatham County; Pop. 1,081 / 1,951; Zip Code 37143; Elev. 549; Lat. 36-06-05 N, Long. 087-03-00 W; The town took the name of a pioneer.

PETERSBURG, Town; Lincoln & Marshall Counties; Pop. 681 / 501; Zip Code 37144; Elev. 747; Lat. 35-18-57 N, Long. 086-38-17 W; Peters was a prominent local citizen.

PHILADELPHIA, City; Loudon County; Pop. 507 / 600; Zip Code 37846; Elev. 863; Lat. 35-40-27 N, Long. 084-24-10 W; The city is named after the metropolis in Pennsylvania.

PIGEON FORGE, City; Sevier County; Pop. 1,822 / 5,424; Named for an iron foundry on the Little Pigeon River.

PIKEVILLE, City; Bledsoe County Seat; Pop. 2,085 / 1,969; Zip Code 37367; Elev. 865; Lat. 35-36-19 N, Long. 085-11-23 W; The town is named after an early road.

PLEASANT HILL, Town; Cumberland County; Pop. 371 / 687; Zip Code 38578; Elev. 1,902; Lat. 35-58-27 N, Long. 085-11-43 W; Descriptively named by its settlers after the garden-like setting.

RIDGELY, Town; take County; Pop. 1,932 / 1,726; Zip Code 38080; Elev. 280; Lat. 36-15-49 N, Long. 089-29-01 W; located on a ridge and so named.

RIDGETOP, Town; Davidson & Robertson Counties; Pop. 1,225 / 1,214; Zip Code 37152; Lat. 36-16-43 N, Long. 086-46-16 W; Descriptively named for its location.

RIPLEY, City; Lauderdale County Seat; Pop. 6,366 / 7,282; Zip Code 38063; Elev. 459; Lat. 35-44-32 N, Long. 089-31-50 W; Named in honor of War of 1812 General Eleazer W. Ripley.

RIVES, Town; Obion County; Pop. 386 / 358; Zip Code 38253; Elev. 300; Lat. 36-21-18 N, Long. 089-02-52 W; Rives was an early settler.

ROCKWOOD, City; Roane County; Pop. 5,767 / 5,956; Zip Code 37854; Lat. 35-52-08 N, Long. 084-40-56 W; Descriptive of the rugged, wooded area.

ROCKFORD, City; Blount County; Pop. 567 / 873; Zip Code 37853; Lat. 35-49-58 N, Long. 083-56-29 W; Descriptively named for a Rocky Ford.

ROGERSVILLE, Town; Hawkins County Seat; Pop. 4,368 / 4,779; Zip Code 37857; Elev. 1,294; Lat. 36-24-06 N, Long. 083-00-16 W; Named after Joseph Rogers who settled in the area in 1785.

ROSSVILLE, Town; Fayette County; Pop. 379 / 384; Zip Code 38066; Elev. 313; Lat. 35-02-39 N, Long. 089-32-40 W; Given an early settler's name.

RUTHERFORD, Town; Gibson County; Pop. 1,378 / 1,285; Zip Code 38369; Lat. 36-07-38 N, Long. 088-59-21 W; Named after American Revolutionary War General Griffith Rutherford.

RUTLEDGE, Town; Grainger County Seat; Pop. 1,058 / 1,175; Zip Code 37861; Elev. 1,015; Lat. 36-16-39 N, Long. 083-31-08 W; Named in honor of General George Rutledge.

SALTILLO, Town; Hardin County; Pop. 434 / 449; Zip Code 38370; Lat. 35-22-55 N, Long. 088-12-40 W; Named for a nearby salt lick.

SAMBURG, Town; Obion County; Pop. 465 / 404; Zip Code 38254; Lat. 36-22-52 N, Long. 089-21-04 W; Samburg is named after a local resident.

SARDIS, Town; Henderson County; Pop. 301 / 427; Zip Code 38371; Lat. 35-26-38 N, Long. 088-17-33 W; Given a biblical name by its settlers.

SAULSBURY, Town; Hardeman County; Pop. 156 / 149; Zip Code 38067; Lat. 35-02-52 N, Long. 089-05-12 W; The town is named after a pioneer.

SAVANNAH, City; Hardin County Seat; Pop. 6,992 / 6,588; Zip Code 38372; Lat. 35-13-31 N, Long. 088-14-18 W; Savannah is named for the port city in Georgia.

SCOTTS HILL, Town; Decatur & Henderson Counties; Pop. 668 / 859; Zip Code 38374; Elev. 519; Lat. 35-30-49 N, Long. 088-14-28 W; Descriptively named for a local hill.

SELMER, Town; McNairy County Seat; Pop. 3,979 / 4,854; Zip Code 38375; Elev. 442; Lat. 35-10-07 N, Long. 088-35-16 W; Named after Selma, Alabama, but miss-spelled.

SEVIERVILLE, Town; Sevier County Seat; Pop. 4,566 / 11,627; Zip Code 37862; Elev. 903; Lat. 35-49-22 N, Long. 083-33-23 W; The town's name honors Tennessee's first Governor, John Sevier.

SHARON, Town; Weakley County; Pop. 1,134 / 1,005; Zip Code 38255; Elev. 414; Lat. 36-14-11 N, Long. 088-49-38 W; The town is named for a pioneer's wife.

SHELBYVILLE, City; Bedford County Seat; Pop. 13,530 / 17,003; Zip Code 37160; Elev. 765; Lat. 35-29-03 N, Long. 086-27-08 W; Shelbyville's name honors Revolutionary War hero Colonel Isaac Shelby.

SIGNAL MOUNTAIN, Town; Hamilton County; Pop. 5,818 / 6,914; Zip Code 37377; Lat. 35-07-31 N, Long. 085-19-27 W; Descriptively named for its function during pioneer days.

SILERTON, Town; Chester County; Pop. 2 / 61; Zip Code 38377; Lat. 35-20-28 N, Long. 088-47-47 W.

SLAYDEN, Town; Dickson County; Pop. 69 / 139; Zip Code 37165; Lat. 36-17-38 N, Long. 087-28-14 W; Slayden is named after an early landowner.

SMITHVILLE, Town; De Kolb County Seat; Pop. 3,839 / 4,496; Zip Code 37166; Elev. 1,032; Lat. 35-57-13 N, Long. 085-49-02 W; The town is named after a prominent settler family.

SMYRNA, Town; Rutherford County; Pop. 8,839 / 25,162; Zip Code 37167; Elev. 1,030; Lat. 35-59-13 N, Long. 086-30-57 W; Named after an ancient Greek seaport.

SNEEDVILLE, Town; Hancock County Seat; Pop. 1,110 / 1,634; Zip Code 37869; Elev. 1,169; Lat. 36-32-03 N, Long. 083-12-45 W; William H. Sneed served as a congressman in 1855. The town is named for him.

SODDY-DAISY, City; Hamilton County; Pop. 8,388 / 10,986; Zip Code 37379; Lat. 35-15-48 N, Long. 085-10-34 W; A combined name created by the union of two towns.

SOMERVILLE, Town; Fayette County Seat; Pop. 2,264 / 2,918; Zip Code 38068; Lat. 35-14-25 N, Long. 089-20-59 W; The town's name honors a Lieutenant Somerville who was killed during the Creek Indian War.

SOUTH FULTON, City; Obion County; Pop. 2,735 / 2,600; Named after the inventor of the steamboat.

SOUTH PITTSBURG, City; Marion County; Pop. 3,636 / 3,103; Zip Code 37380; Elev. 624; Lat. 35-01-16 N, Long. 085-42-40 W; Named after the city in Pennsylvania.

SPARTA, City; White County Seat; Pop. 4,864 / 5,121; Zip Code 38583; Elev. 885; Lat. 35-55-58 N, Long. 085-28-06 W; Sparta is named after the ancient Greek city.

SPENCER, Town; Van Buren County Seat; Pop. 1,126 / 1,162; Zip Code 38585; Elev. 1,820; Lat. 35-44-45 N, Long. 085-27-23 W; Named after the Spencer family who were early settlers.

SPRING HILL, Town; Maury & Williamson Counties; Pop. 989 / 5,968; Zip Code 37174; Elev. 438; Lat. 35-45-13 N, Long. 086-55-29 W; Descriptively named after a local spring.

SPRINGFIELD, City; Robertson County Seat; Pop. 10,814 / 14,182; Zip Code 37172; Elev. 677; Lat. 36-30-02 N, Long. 086-52-58 W; Named after a spring in the area.

ST. JOSEPH, City; Lawrence County; Pop. 897 / 1,088; Zip Code 38481; Lat. 35-02-08 N, Long. 087-30-20 W; The city is named after the biblical Joseph, husband of Virgin Mary.

STANTON, Town; Haywood County; Pop. 540 / 496; Zip Code 38069; Elev. 314; Lat. 35-27-44 N, Long. 089-24-00 W; Stanton is probably named after a pioneer settler.

STANTONVILLE, Town; McNairy County; Pop. 271 / 304; Zip Code 38379; Lat. 35-09-30 N, Long. 088-25-36 W; Named after a pioneer settler.

SURGOINSVILLE, Town; Hawkins County; Pop. 1,536 / 1,677; Zip Code 37873; Elev. 1,136; Lat. 36-28-02 N, Long. 082-51-24 W.

SWEETWATER, City; Monroe County; Pop. 4,725 / 5,745; Zip Code 37874; Elev. 917; Lat. 35-36-18 N, Long. 084-27-51 W; The city is named for its location in the Sweetwater Valley.

TAZEWELL, Town; Claiborne County Seat; Pop. 2,090 / 2,424; Zip Code 37879; Lat. 36-27-07 N, Long. 083-34-14 W; The town's name honors 19th century U.S. Senator Henry Tazewell.

TELICO PLAINS, Town; Monroe County; Pop. 698 / 758; Zip Code 37385; Lat. 35-21-39 N, Long. 084-17-44 W; The origin of the town's name is uncertain.

TENNESSEE RIDGE, City; Houston & Stewart Counties; Pop. 1,325 / 1,421; Zip Code 37178; Elev. 742; Lat. 36-19-02 N, Long. 087-45-59 W; Given a combination of the state's name with a local geographical feature.

TIPTONVILLE, Town; Lake County Seat; Pop. 2,438 / 2,113; Zip Code 38079; Elev. 301; Lat. 36-22-31 N, Long. 089-28-44 W; Named in honor of Indian fighter Jacob Tipton.

TOONE, Town; Hardeman County; Pop. 355 / 288; Zip Code 38381; Elev. 395; Lat. 35-21-06 N, Long. 088-57-02 W; Toone is named after a 19th century settler.

TRACY CITY, Town; Grundy County; Pop. 1,356 / 1,623; Zip Code 37387; Elev. 1,829; Lat. 35-15-38 N, Long. 085-44-09 W; Named after a prominent settler.

TRENTON, City; Gibson County Seat; Pop. 4,601 / 4,972; Zip Code 38382; Elev. 338; Lat. 35-58-23 N, Long. 088-56-30 W; The city's name honors the site of an important Revolutionary War battle.

TREZEVANT, Town; Carroll County; Pop. 921 / 919; Zip Code 38258; Elev. 464; Lat. 36-00-42 N, Long. 088-37-14 W; A name made by combining Trezevant and Levant.

TRIMBLE, Town; Dyer & Obion Counties; Pop. 722 / 806; Zip Code 38259; Elev. 293; Lat. 36-12-09 N, Long. 089-11-06 W; The town's name honors U.S. Supreme Court Justice Robert Trimble.

TROY, Town; Obion County; Pop. 1,093 / 1,098; Zip Code 38260; Elev. 378; Lat. 36-20-09 N, Long. 089-09-31 W; Troy is named after the famous Homeric City.

TULLAHOMA, City; Coffee & Franklin Counties; Pop. 15,800 / 2,314; Zip Code 37388; Elev. 1,071; Lat. 35-21-12 N, Long. 086-12-17 W; A Muskogee Indian term meaning "Red Town."

UNION CITY, City; Obion County Seat; Pop. 10,436 / 10,409; Zip Code 38261; Elev. 337; Lat. 36-25-21 N, Long. 089-02-41 W; Named after the union of the United States.

VANLEER, Town; Dickson County; Pop. 401 / 453; Zip Code 37181; Elev. 849; Lat. 36-14-04 N, Long. 087-26-35 W; The town is named for a prominent settler.

VIOLA, Town; Warren County; Pop. 149 / 128; Zip Code 37394; Elev. 995; Lat. 35-31-59 N, Long. 085-46-21 W; Viola is named for a pioneer's wife.

VONORE, Town; Monroe County; Pop. 528 / 938; Zip Code 37885; Elev. 852; Lat. 35-35-21 N, Long. 084-14-33 W; Given the name of an early pioneer.

WARTBURG, City; Morgan County Seat; Pop. 761 / 906; Zip Code 37887; Lat. 36-06-01 N, Long. 084-35-47 W; Named for Wartburg, Germany.

WARTRACE, Town; Bedford County; Pop. 540 / 537; Zip Code 37183; Elev. 824; Lat. 35-31-33 N, Long. 086-20-03 W; Descriptively named for a path through the forest used by Indian War parties.

WATAUGA, City; Carter County; Pop. 376 / 465; Zip Code 37694; Elev. 1,451; Lat. 36-21-54 N, Long. 082-17-28 W; A Cherokee Indian word meaning "Beautiful River."

WATERTOWN, City; Wilson County; Pop. 1,300 / 1,315; Zip Code 37184; Elev. 667; Lat. 36-06-00 N, Long. 086-08-08 W; Named after a nearby body of water.

WAVERLY, City; Humphreys County Seat; Pop. 4,405 / 4,436; Zip Code 37185; Elev. 546; Lat. 36-05-04 N, Long. 087-47-21 W; The city is named after a popular Sir Walter Scott novel.

WAYNESBORO, City; Wayne County Seat; Pop. 2,109 / 1,950; Zip Code 38485; Lat. 35-18-50 N, Long. 087-45-38 W; The city is named in honor of Revolutionary War hero General Anthony Wayne.

WESTMORELAND, Town; Sumner County; Pop. 1,754 / 1,844; Zip Code 37186; Lat. 36-33-58 N, Long. 086-14-54 W; Named after a county in England.

WHITE BLUFF, Town; Dickson County; Pop. 2,055 / 2,532; Zip Code 37187; Elev. 819; Lat. 36-06-25 N, Long. 087-13-17 W; The town is named for its local geographic feature.

WHITE HOUSE, City; Robertson & Sumner Counties; Pop. 2,225 / 6,622; Zip Code 37188; Elev. 862; Lat. 36-28-14 N, Long. 086-39-10 W; Named for a local landmark.

WHITE PINE, Town; Jefferson County; Pop. 1,900 / 2,606; Zip Code 37890; Elev. 1,140; Lat. 36-06-23 N, Long. 083-17-10 W; Descriptively named for the White Pine groves in the area.

WHITEVILLE, Town; Hardeman County; Pop. 1,270 / 1,224; Zip Code 38075; Lat. 35-19-33 N, Long. 089-08-44 W; A pioneer named White gave his name to the town.

WHITWELL, City; Marion County; Pop. 1,783 / 1,523; Zip Code 37397; Lat. 35-12-11 N, Long. 085-30-59 W; Whitwell was an early settler.

WINCHESTER, City; Franklin County Seat; Pop. 5,821 / 7,410; Zip Code 37398; Elev. 965; Lat. 35-11-09 N, Long. 086-06-33 W; The city is named in honor of General James Winchester, pioneer Indian fighter and legislator.

WOODBURY, Town; Cannon County Seat; Pop. 2,160 / 2,748; Zip Code 37190; Elev. 735; Lat. 35-49-19 N, Long. 086-04-06 W; Originally Danville, the name was changed to reflect the forested areas nearby.

WOODLAND MILLS, City; Obion County; Pop. 526 / 376; Zip Code 38271; Elev. 368; Lat. 36-30-13 N, Long. 089-03-56 W; Descriptively named for a local mill and the surrounding forests.

YORKVILLE, City; Gibson County; Pop. 272 / 367; Zip Code 38389; Lat. 36-06-00 N, Long. 089-07-12 W; The city is named in honor of World War I infantry hero Alvin C. York.

TEXAS
The Lonestar State

Austin Skyline

The Alamo - San Antonio

GOVERNOR
Rick Perry

San Jacinto Monument
at Final Battle Site

Downtown Dallas

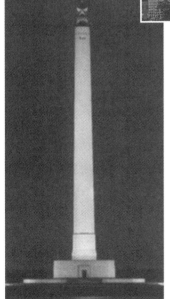

Galveston Bay

Permian Basin Petroleum Museum
Midland

INTRODUCTION

THE LONE STAR STATE

The history of Texas was begun long before the first English settlers arrived on the eastern coast of America. In Texas, it was the Spanish *padres* and *conquistadors* who began colonization of this vast territory in the sixteenth century. Few reminders of the early Spanish days remain in Texas; most outsiders now think of the State in terms of its newness and vast area, which all but hides its history.

In the early 1900s, oil was first drilled at Spindletop, marking the path for the State's great petroleum industries, Cattle ranches and farmers have supplied the demands for much of the U.S. beef And the cities of Dallas, Houston, and San Antonio remain near the top in American cities.

Perhaps all of this growth was built on the unusual history of Texas. It was a much-disputed territory between Spain, Mexico, France, and the United States, and is the only State to have been its own nation before entering the Union. Its land area is so vast that for a long period of time there seemed no end to possibilities for expansion. Perhaps this is why Texas is known for its friendliness to outsiders, and its pride and expansive outlook on the world.

THE STATE NAME

While the name of Texas has several possible origins, it is generally agreed that the name was solidly established in 1690, when the Spanish called their first mission "St. Francis of the Texas."

Texas was a republic from March 2, 1836, until Anson Jones, the last President of the Republic of Texas, turned over executive authority of the republic to James Pinkney Henderson, newly elected Governor of the State of Texas on February 19, 1846.

It is speculated that the name of Texas was derived from the Spanish form of "tejas," signifying allies, friends, or confederates, and was commonly applied to the Indian tribes that allied themselves together for mutual protection. It also may have been derived from the Spaniards who were survivors of the expedition of Don Hernando De Soto when they reached the Rio Grande in search of land and gold. They called the new country by various names, including *Amichel*, the New Philippines, and finally *Tejas* from the Indians.

A second possible origin of the State name was given by J. Morphis, who said that "at an early day some Spaniards traveling the Camino del Rey, between San Antonio and the Hondo, camped on the Neches, and their commander, in the morning, beholding many spider-webs between himself and the rising sun, all spangled with dew drops and glittering like diamonds, joyfully exclaimed: 'Mira las tejas!'—that is to say, 'look at the spider webs!'—and named the land Texas."

A third possible origin is that the name is derived from the word *teysha*, which in the Caddo Indian language means "hello friend." The Spanish may have used this term to refer to the friendly tribes throughout the area of Louisiana, Oklahoma, and eastern Texas. The tribes of the Caddo confederacy who lived in Louisiana and eastern Texas came to be called "the kingdom of the Texas."

STATE NICKNAMES

The State of Texas has been designated as: the Banner State, the Beef State, the Blizzard State, the Jumbo State, and the Lone Star State.

The sobriquet of Banner State is applied to Texas, probably from the fact that it polls a large vote in national elections. Historian Charles Norton says that under the name Banner State: "the state, county, town, or other political subdivision that gives the largest vote for a party candidate is termed the banner state ..." It is a term commonly used to signify a leading position.

The sobriquet of Beef State is attributed to Texas in commemoration of the fact that it has been, and still is, noted for its cattle production and its position as one of the largest cattle-raising areas of the United States.

The nickname of the Blizzard State was given to Texas undoubtedly because of the frequent windstorms that sweep over the State.

The origin of the sobriquet the Jumbo State is as follows: "Barnum and Bailey bought the largest African elephant ever kept in captivity and brought him from London to America to be used in their circus. The fact that this elephant's name was Jumbo has caused all unusually large things to be called Jumbo. Texas is the largest state in the Union; therefore it acquired the nickname the Jumbo State."

Texas is called the Lone Star State because after it was a province of Mexico, it became an independent republic; it bore a single star in its coat of arms, and was for a time left alone to struggle unaided against the whole power of its formidable enemy. The lone star on the State flag also connotes this history.

Texans are called Beef-heads, Blizzards, Cowboys, and Rangers. The appellation of Beef-heads is easily accounted for by the fact that Texas is a great cattle-raising country, and this fact gives an insight into the origin of the nicknames Cowboys and Rangers. Texans are called Blizzards for the same reason the State is nicknamed the Blizzard State.

STATE SEAL

In 1839, an act of the Legislature adopted a National Seal for the Republic of Texas as follows:

"Be it enacted that from and after the passage of this act the national arms of the Republic of Texas be and the same is hereby declared to be a white star of five points on an azure ground, encircled by an olive and live oak branches."

When Texas became a State in 1845, the word "Republic" was changed to "State." The Texas Constitution of 1876 provided for a State seal of the same design as the Republic seal as follows:

"There shall be a Seal of the State which shall be kept by the Secretary of State, and used by him officially under the direction of the Governor. The Seal of the State shall be a star *of* five points encircled by olive and live oak branches, and the words 'The State of Texas.'"

STATE FLAG

The flag of the Republic of Texas, approved by the Republic of Texas on January 25, 1839, became the official State flag in 1845 when Texas became the 28th state in the Union. The flag was officially adopted in the State Constitution in 1876.

In March 1933, the Legislature of the State of Texas passed "an act for the purpose of making plain the salute to the Texas flag and giving uniformity to the salute; providing a clear description of the flag to the end that pupils in the lower grades of the elementary school will be able to draw or make the flag; providing for the standardization of the star in the blue stripe in the dimensions used and its position in the stripe so that uniformity shall be the result hereafter in the making of Texas flags; describing the method of construction of the star in language that is definite and clear; and outlining rules for correct use and display of the Texas flag and declaring an emergency."

The act reads: "Be it enacted by the legislature of the state of Texas:

"Section 1. This act of the legislature is not a substitute for any previous legislation pertaining to the Lone Star Flag of Texas, which may have been passed by either the Republic of Texas or the legislature of this state, but the sole purpose of this act is to clarify the description of the Texas flag, to standardize the star in the blue field, and to outline some important rules to govern the correct use of the Texas flag.

"Section 2. A drawing of the Texas flag to illustrate the general outline of the three stripes, and the star in the blue stripe:

"Section 3. Salute to the Texas flag: 'Honor the Texas flag of 1836; I pledge allegiance to thee, Texas, one and indivisible.'

"Section 4. Description of the Texas flag: The Texas flag is an emblem of four sides, and four angles of 90 degrees each. It is a rectangle having its width equal to two-thirds of its length. The flag is divided into three equivalent parts, called bars or stripes, one stripe being blood red, one white, and the other azure blue. These stripes are rectangles, also, and they are exact duplicates of one another in every respect. The width of each stripe is equal to one-half of its length, or one-third of the length of the flag, while the length of each stripe is equal to the width of the flag, or two-thirds of the length of the emblem.

"One end of the flag is blue, and it is called flag's right. This stripe is a perpendicular bar next to the staff or the halyard, and it is attached by means of a heading made of strong and very durable material. The remaining two-thirds of the flag is made up of two horizontal bars of equal width, one being white and the other red, and this end of the emblem is called the flag's left. Each one of the stripes is perpendicular to the blue stripe, and when the flag is displayed on a flagpole or staff, or flat on a plane surface, the white stripe should always be at the top of the flag, with the red stripe directly underneath it. Thus, each stripe of the Texas flag touches each of the other stripes, which signifies that the three colors are mutually dependent upon one another in imparting the lessons of the flag: bravery, loyalty, and purity.

"Section 5. Description of the star: In the center of the blue stripe is a white star of five points. One point of this star is always at the top, and in vertical line drawn from one end of the blue stripe to the other, and midway between its side. This line is the vertical axis of the blue stripe, and it is perpendicular to the horizontal axis at the central point of the stripe. The two lowest points of the star are in a line parallel to the horizontal axis, and the distance from the topmost point of the star to the line through these two points is equal to approximately one-third of the length of the blue stripe, or one-third of the width of the flag. The center of the star is at the point of intersection of the horizontal axis with the vertical axis, or at the central point of the blue stripe. The other two points of the star are above the horizontal axis, and near the sides of the blue stripe.

"Section 7. The fact that the Texas flag represents all the people of this state, and stands for the Alamo and Goliad and San Jacinto and all the glorious history of the past, as well as the living present and the matchless future possibilities; and, in view of the fact that there is much confusion and doubt in the minds of the citizenry concerning the description, meaning, and use of the Texas flag, and that all minds should be clear in this matter creates an emergency and an imperative need requiring that the constitutional rules that bills be read on three separate days shall be suspended and that this law shall go into effect from and after its passage, and such rule is hereby suspended, and this law shall take effect from and after its passage, and it is so enacted."

STATE MOTTO

The official motto of the State, derived from the earliest meaning of its name, is "Friendship." It was adopted in 1930 for three reasons: (1) the Indian (Spanish) word *tejas* from which the name of Texas may have been taken meant friendship; (2) it is emblematic of the universal spirit existing in Texas; and (3) it reflects the spirit that has at all times influenced the people of Texas.

STATE BIRD

The mockingbird (*Mimus polyglottos*), was selected as the state Bird of Texas by an act of the Legislature approved January 31, 1927. The mockingbird was selected because (1) "it is found in all parts of the state;" (2) Texas "ornithologists, musicians, educators and Texans in all walks of life unite in proclaiming the mockingbird the most appropriate species for the state bird of Texas;" (3) it "is a singer of distinctive type, a fighter for the protection of his home, falling if need be, in its defense, like any true Texan;" (4) the Texas Federation of Women's Clubs named the mockingbird as the state bird of Texas, and asked the fortieth Legislature to adopt it.

The mockingbird is 8 ½ to nine inches long; its tail length is four to 4 ½ inches. It is native to the eastern United States, southern Canada, along the Gulf Coast to Texas, and the Bahaman Islands.

The bird is mostly plain gray or brownish gray from the top of the head and over most of the back region. Lateral tail feathers are white. The wings and tail are dull, blackish slate. Middle and greater wing coverts are tipped with dull or grayish white. The primary coverts are white with a subterminal dusky spot or streak; the auricular region is gray; the area beneath the eye and along the side of the head is dull white transversely flecked with gray or dusky; the chin and throat are dull white, margined along each side by a distinct dusky streak; the chest is pale smoke gray turning to white on the center of the breast and abdomen; feathers under the tail are pale buff or buffy white. When the bird is in flight, broad white spots above can easily be seen against the slate black of the upper wings.

The mockingbird is a sturdy creature, which often builds its nest to last several seasons. From the time the nest is completed to the time when fledglings take flight is usually from three to four weeks. Eggs range from bright blue to bluish green or greenish blue spotted with hazel or cinnamon. Both sexes not only build nests, but also care for their young. They are lively and bellicose, fighting among themselves as well as tormenting cats and dogs. The bird is a master imitator, and is considered one of the most versatile and beautiful songsters, sometimes changing tunes as often as thirty times in a ten-minute period. The mockingbird's diet consists mostly of insects and wild fruit.

STATE FLOWER

In 1901, the bluebonnet, (*Lupinus subcarnvsis*), was adopted by the Legislature as the State flower of Texas. The bluebonnet is a member of the pea family, and is one of over 100 species of a mostly herbaceous family.

STATE TREE

In 1919, the Legislature adopted the pecan as the State tree. On March 25, 1927, the Legislature passed an amendment making it the duty of the State Board of Control and the State Park Board "to give due consideration to the pecan tree when planning beautification of the state parks or other public property belonging to the state."

The scientific name for the Texas State tree is *Carya illinoensis*. It is also known as the pecan nut, pecanier, and pecan hickory. It is native to the Mississippi valley region, Texas, and Mexico.

The pecan is a large tree, with deeply and irregularly furrowed and cracked light brown or gray bark. The compound leaves are from twelve to twenty inches in length. Leaflets number from eleven to seventeen; they are short-stalked, lance-shaped, and slightly sickle-shaped, and from two to seven inches long, long pointed, finely toothed, smooth, and slightly hairy. The nuts are slightly four winged, oblong, and pointed; from one to two inches long, they have thin husks, and are sweet and edible.

STATE SONG

Texas, by a Senate concurrent resolution, approved "Texas, Our Texas" as the State song in 1928. The lyrics were written by Gladys Yoakum Wright and William J. Marsh; Marsh also composed the music. Contests were held for the State song in each senatorial district throughout the State, and in a final contest in Dallas that year, Texas, Our Texas "sung itself into the hearts of the people." A legislative committee also chose it twice following the contest. The song was copyrighted by W.J. Marsh in 1925. The lyrics are as follows:

Texas, our Texas! All hail the mighty state!
Texas, our Texas: So wonderful, So great!
Boldest and grandest, withstanding every test;
O empire wide and glorious, you stand
supremely blest.

Chorus
God Bless you, Texas! And keep you brave and strong.
That you may grow in power and worth, throughout the ages long.

Refrain
Texas, O Texas! Your freeborn single star,
Sends out its radiance to nations near and far.
Emblem of freedom! It sets our hearts aglow.
With thoughts of San Jacinto and glorious Alamo.
Texas, dear Texas! From tyrant grip now free,
Shines forth in splendor your star of destiny!
Mother of heroes! We come your children true.
Proclaiming our allegiance, our faith, our love for you.

In 1933, the Legislature also designated a song to represent the State flower. The song, *Bluebonnets,* has lyrics by Julia D. Booth and music by Lora C. Crockett.

STATE LICENSE PLATE

The State of Texas began to require vehicle registration by county clerks in 1907. However, statewide plates were not issued until 1917, when the State Highway Department was created. The first plates were good for as long as the vehicle was in operation, but the State also issued radiator seals in different colors for different years that validated the registration on an annual basis. The 1917 plate was white on black, and the round seal was white on red. When a new plate was issued in 1920, it was again white on black, but smaller in size than the first plate, and the validation disc was changed to a seal. A third white on black plate was issued in 1923; the last validation seal was used in 1924.

In 1925, annual license plates began to be issued, except for the years 1943 and 1944. Multi-year plates were introduced in 1975. A number of color combinations were used over the years. However, black and gold combinations were used from 1941 to 1945 and from 1948 to 1956; black and white combinations were issued in 1917, 1920, 1923, 1931, 1947, and from 1957 to 1968; and black and silver combinations were used in 1969, 1971, 1973, 1975, 1977, 1978, and 1983.

The 1992 plate issued for the State of Texas was red, white and blue. A depiction of the State flag was displayed on the top left in all three colors; next to the flag was the word "Texas" in dark blue. At the bottom was the slogan "The Lone Star State," also in blue. An outline of Texas in red divided the dark blue letters and numbers in the center of the plate. The background color was white.

In 2000, a new plate was designed with a light blue background. Dark blue letters and numbers are again separated by an outline of the State in red. The word "TEXAS" is lettered across the top in red, and centered across the bottom is a depiction of a cowboy on a horse riding on a field of dark blue terrain.

STATE POSTAGE STAMP

The Texas Statehood stamp was issued in Austin on December 29, 1945. The stamp commemorated the centennial anniversary of the admission of Texas to the Union. Designed by James B. Winn and engraved by ER. Grove and E.H. Helmuth, depicted on the stamp are the flags of the United States and Texas; a ray of light from the 28th star on the U.S. flag illuminates the single star on the State flag, showing that Texas was the 28th state to join the Union. Beneath the U.S. flag is printed "Statehood 1845-1945." A border on the left is printed with the State name. A total of 170,640,000 of the three-cent stamps were printed in multi-shaded blue.

OTHER STATE DESIGNATIONS

Through the years, the legislature has added a number of additional symbols to define Texas as a state. They include the State dish as chili; the State fruit as red grapefruit; the State musical instrument as the guitar; the State sport as rodeo; the State stone as petrified palmwood; the State small mammal as the armadillo; the State large mammal as the longhorn; the State reptile as the horned lizard; and the State vegetable as sweet Texas onion.

THE STATE CAPITOL

Few reminders remain of the early buildings in which the seat of government was housed. The Spanish Governors' palace still stands in San Antonio, and the one-story frame building, which served as the capitol, has been restored. The former capitols at Houston and Austin no longer exist.

Austin was chosen as the permanent capital of the Republic of Texas in 1839, and it remained the capital after Texas joined the Union in 1845.

Construction of the present capitol was begun in 1882 to replace an 1852 structure that burned down in 1881. A temporary building was constructed in 1881 and was used until completion of the new Capitol in 1888. The temporary structure burned down in 1889.

The Capitol building is of Classical Renaissance design; E.E. Meyers of Detroit, Michigan was the architect. The statehouse is 585 feet, ten inches in length, and 229 feet, ten inches in width. It is 309 feet, eight inches from the basement floor to the top of the five-pointed star held by the sixteen foot statue of the Goddess of Liberty, which surmounts the dome, patterned after St. Peter's in Rome. The exterior walls are of Texas pink granite. The interior and dome walls are of Texas limestone. The structure has 273,799 feet of usable space, and is built on three million acres of land in the Texas Panhandle that were given to the builders as payment for constructing the Capitol. It was built at a cost of about 3.7 million dollars, and was formally opened on May 16, 1888.

OTHER FACTS ABOUT TEXAS

Total area: 268,608 square miles
Land area: 261,914 square miles
Water area: 6,687 square miles
Rank in total area: 2
Average elevation: 1,700 feet
Highest point: Guadalupe Peak, 8,749 feet
Lowest point: Gulf of Mexico, sea level
Highest temperature: 120 degrees Fahrenheit, August 12, 1936, Semour
Lowest temperature: -23 degrees Fahrenheit, February 8, 1933, Seminole
Population in 1990: 16,986,510

Population density in 1990: 64.86 persons per square mile
Population 1980-1990: +19.4 percent change
Population in 2000: 20,851,820
Population density in 2000: 76.5 persons per square mile
Population 1990-2000: +22.8 percent change
Population difference 1990-2000: 3,865,310 persons
Black population in 1990: 2,021,632
Hispanic population in 1990: 4,339,905
Native American population in 1990: 65,877
White population in 1990: 12,774,762
Per capita income 1998: $25,369
Per capita income 1999 est.: $26,525
Capital: Austin
Admitted to Union: December 29, 1845
Order of Statehood: 28th
Electoral votes: 32
Resident: Texan

CHRONOLOGY

10,000 B.C. Early Llano People inhabit Texas region and hunt great elephant that later becomes extinct.

8,000 B.C. Folsom Culture begins to transform human life in Texas region; people become skilled in stone work, and kill bison instead of elephants for meat.

5,000 B.C. End of Ice Age; elephants disappear and new way of life begins.
– Agriculture begins with planting of seeds and corn.

2500 B.C. Corn farming becomes more developed, and pottery is made from clay.
– Evidence is found of more permanent homes.

1519 Cortez defeats Aztecs.
– Alonzo Alvarez de Pineda explores and maps coast of Texas, occupying mouth of Rio Grande for 40 days (first known European visit).

1528 Alvar Nunez Cabeza de Vaca and others of Narvaez expedition are shipwrecked on Texas coast near Galveston Island; De Vaca and black man wander interior of Texas until 1536.

1541 Francisco Vazquez de Coronado, after searching for mythic seven Cities of Cibola, marches across Llano Estacado to locate Gran Quivira; he meets Querechos, ancestors of Apaches, on West Texas plains.

1542 Luis De Moscoso leads survivors of De Soto's expedition on High Plains of Texas (De Soto died earlier on Mississippi River).

1598 Juan de Onato establishes first Spanish settlement on Rio Grande near Santa Fe.

1609 Santa Fe is founded near Onato's settlement.

1629 Father Juan de Salas joins Jumano Indians, who move from mission in New Mexico region to village on Pecos or Concho River.

1659 Mission Nuestra Senora de Guadalupe de El Paso is founded on present site of Juarez, Mexico.

1680 Spaniards and Indians establish Mission Corpus Christi de la Isleta near El Paso (site of present Ysleta).

1682 Robert Cavalier, Sieur de La Salle descends Mississippi River to its mouth, claiming region for France.
– Settlements are founded at Seneca, San Lorenzo, and Socorro, along Rio Grande, by Spaniards.

1684 Capt. Juan de Mendoza and Father Nicolas Lopez establish chapel and ford called San Clemente near present-day Menard on San Saba River.

1685 La Salle lands on shore of Matagorda Bay and establishes Fort St. Louis on Garcitas Creek. (La Salle is later murdered by his own men, spelling failure of French colony.)

1690 First Spanish missionaries meet Hasinai tribe; first mission in East Texas—Mission San Francisco de los Tejasis—is founded on their territory.

1691 Texas officially becomes Spanish province.
– More missions are founded, although many die within first year.

1713 Captain Luis Juchereau de St. Denis establishes storehouse and Indian trading post on Red River near Natchitoches.

1714 St. Denis crosses into Texas at San Juan Bautista on Rio Grande, alarming Spaniards.

1716 East Texas is settled through establishment of six missions.
– Mission San Francisco is reestablished and named Nuestro Padre San Francisco de los Tejas.

1718 Mission San Antonio de Valero (later the Alamo) is founded on San Antonio River.
– Presidio and villa of San Antonio de Bexar are established.

1719 French and Spanish fight over Adaes Mission in "Chicken War."
– French step up invasions of Tejas lands.

1721 Marquis de San Miguel de Aguayo establishes presidio of Nuestra Senora del Pilar at Los Adaes mission.

1722 Aguayo and his soldiers descend on La Salle's Fort St. Louis, and rebuild it as Mission Nuestra Senora del Espiritu Santo Zuniga, also known as La Bahia; France never again challenges Spain's claim to Texas.

1731 Group of Canary Islanders reach San Antonio de Bexar to establish first municipality for civilians.

1744 Estimated population (exclusive of Indians) is 1,500.

1746 Definite western boundary for Texas is established; Medina River separates it from Spanish province of Nuevo Santander.

1749 Goliad is founded.

1756 Spanish occupy many missions, including Gulf region, and expansion continues with little conflict.
– Seven Year War breaks out in Europe among England, Spain and France.

1759 Taovayas Indians, along with Comanches and Wichitas, defeat Colonel Diego Ortiz Parrilla and his men near Red River.

1762 Spain acquires Louisiana Territory.

1767 Marquis de Rubi sets out to explore region from Gulf of California to Louisiana; he visits El Canon, San Saba, San Antonio, Nacogdoches, Los Adaes, and La Bahia on his long journey.

1772 Rubi's reports on his journey results in treatise, "Regulation for the Presidio" from Spanish King, which follows former's recommendations.

1779 Nacogdoches is founded as town.

1788-89 Pedro Vial travels from Santa Fe to Natchitoches, and to San Antonio, where he discovers 700 inhabitants.

1800 Napoleon of France convinces Spanish King to cede Louisiana back to France.

1801 Adventurer Philip Nolan is killed in Texas by Spanish, and men in his expedition are held hostage.

1803 Napoleon sells Louisiana Territory to United States, increasing threat of invasion by British.

1806 General James Wilkinson of U.S. Army makes Neutral Ground Agreement with Spanish General Herrera for region east of Arroyo Hondo.

1811 Juan Bautista de las Casas proclaims himself governor of Texas after seizing Spanish leaders.

1812-13 Gutierrez-Magee expedition invades Texas and is defeated on Medina River by Arredondo.

1813 First Texas newspaper, *El Mejicano,* is published in Nacogdoches.

1817-21 Jean Lafitte, a pirate, operates on Galveston Island.

1819 Florida Purchase Treaty is signed by United States, which gives Florida to Spain and relinquishes American claim to Texas territory.

1819-21 Dr. James Long, filibuster, leads expeditions into Texas.

1820 Moses Austin secures permission to colonize 300 Anglo-American families.

1821 Augustin de Iturbide and Vicente Guerrero sign Plan of Iguala, proclaiming constitutional monarchy and racial equality in New Spain.
– First Anglo-American colony in Texas is founded by Stephen F. Austin.
– Mexico gains freedom from Spain, and Texas becomes Mexican state.

1824-32 Mexico grants colonization contracts to empresarios.
– Towns of Victoria and Gonzales are founded.

1826 Hayden Edwards, empresario, proclaims to head "The Republic of Fredonia," but is ousted by Mexicans.

1827 Juan Maria Ponce de Leon builds first home on site of El Paso.

1828 Two thousand and twenty Anglo-Americans populate Texas.

1830 Mexico passes law to slow down further immigration of English-speaking Americans into Texas.

1831 Population (exclusive of Indians) is 20,000.

1832 Biegel, a German settlement, is founded near Cummins Creek in present Fayette County.
– Texans and Mexicans clash at Velasco and American.
– At convention in San Felipe, attendees petition for political separation of Texas from Coahuila.

1834 Stephen F. Austin is imprisoned in Mexico after he encourages more Anglo-American settlement in Texas.

1835 Mexican troops are driven from America, June 30.
October 2. Settlers win Battle of Gonzales, first battle of Texas Revolution.
October 9. Texans capture Goliad.
October 12. Volunteer Texan Army, under Stephen Austin, marches on San Antonio, Mexican stronghold.
October 28. Battle of Concepcion is won by Texans.
November 3. Provisional government is created.
December 5-9. Final siege is waged against San Antonio, with Ben Milam leading attack on city.
December 10. Mexican General Cos surrenders.
December 14. General Cos and 1,100 men depart, and Texas is freed of Mexico.

1836 February 23. Vanguard of General Santa Anna's Mexican army arrive at San Antonio to lay siege to Alamo.
February 27. Colonel Frank W. Johnson's command is captured in San Patricio.
– Declaration of independence is issued at Washington-on-the-Brazos from provisional government.
March 2. Dr. Grant's command is annihilated at Agua Dulce.
March 6. Alamo falls.
March 13. General Sam Houston, leading Texas army, begins retreat eastward; Gonzales is burned.

March 17. Texas Constitution is adopted at Washington-on-the-Brazos, and interim national officials are selected.
March 20. Battle of the Coleto ends in surrender of Colonel James Fannin, with his men.
March 27. Fannin and his men are killed at Goliad.
April 21. General Houston defeats Mexican army under Santa Anna at San Jacinto, thus winning Texas Revolution and ending Spanish domination.
May 14. Treaty of Velasco is signed by Texas officials and Santa Anna.
– Sam Houston is elected first President of Texas Republic.
– Texas Congress meets at Columbia.
– Stephen F. Austin dies.

1837 United States recognizes Texas' independence.
– General Land Office is established.

1838 Vincente Cordova, inciting Indians and Mexicans, threatens revolt against Texas.

1839 Homestead Law and first educational law are passed.
– Cherokees are expelled from East Texas.
– Austin is established as Capital of Texas.
– President Lamar's commission selects site, "the town of Waterloo," and names it for Revolutionary hero.

1841 Santa Fe expedition, bent on conquest of New Mexico, fails.
– John Neely Bryan builds first trading post on site of present-day Dallas.
– Government grants land to immigrant agents.

1842 Invading Mexican troops capture Goliad, Refugio, San Antonio, and Victoria.
– Battle of Salado results in withdrawal of Woll, Mexican general, and annihilation of Dawson's command.
– Mier expedition invades Mexico and is captured.
– Texans are forced to draw beans in lottery of death.
– Austin citizens are fired on by troops sent to remove archives.

1843 Hostilities between Texans and Mexico die down.

1844 Henry Castro establishes Alsatian colony at Castroville.

1845 Texas' annexation to United States is voted on by U.S. Congress and Texas Convention.
– New Braunfels is founded with about 200 German immigrants.
– Norwegians move into Henderson County.
December 29. Texas is admitted as twenty-eighth State of Union.

1846 Annexation is completed.
– First State legislature convenes in Austin.
– J.P. Henderson is inaugurated first governor of State of Texas.
– First battle of Mexican War is won by General Zachary Taylor at Palo Alto.

1847 Baron Ottfried Hans Von Meusebach explores Indian territory, following treaty with Comanches to allow German settlement.
– "The Forty," German fraternity of students and two professors, form commune on north bank of Llano River, and call it Bettina.

1848 Rio Grande is accepted by Mexico as Texas State boundary in Treaty of Guadalupe Hidalgo.
– Sven Swenson and 25 Swedish people begin settlement in Texas.
– Santa Fe County is formed.
– Texas lays claim to 100,000 square miles outside present State.

1849 Brevet Major Ripley Arnold establishes Camp Worth, later Fort Worth.
– "The Forty" organizes another commune named Tusculum, later town of Boerne.

1850 Texas accepts $10 million from Federal government for disputed territory; western State boundary is fixed on present lines.
– Population is 212,592; twenty percent of white population is German.

1851 Construction begins on first railroad.

1852 Sixteen Czechoslovakian families move into Austin County to start town in what was formerly German territory.

1853 U.S. Congress approves surveys for new rail line to Pacific.
– Captain John Pope surveys route, formerly Marcy Trail, through Texas.
– Two Indian reservations are established.
– German abolitionist movement gains momentum.
– First State Capitol is built at Austin.

1854 Victor Considerant's French colony is settled near Dallas.
– Texas legislature sets aside $2,000,000 for public education.
– Norwegian immigrants buy land in Bosque County.
– Polish settlers are brought by Father Leopold Moczygemba and Johann Twohig to Cibolo and San Antonio River region.

1855 Carl Burkli leads Swiss immigrants to region of La Reunion, but new settlers soon move to section of Dallas.

1856 Jefferson Davis, U.S. Secretary of War, sends 75 camels to Texas to aid military, but by time of Civil War, these animals are no longer used for transportation.

1857 San Antonio and San Diego Overland Mail, as well as Southern Overland Mail, operate for first time.
– Galveston paves streets with seashells.

1859 Bandit Juan Cortinas terrorizes lower region of Rio Grande.
– First Jewish congregation is organized in Houston.
– Thirty thousand copies of *Texas Almanac* are published.

1860 Population is 604,215, almost 300 percent increase over 1850; one-third of population is black.
– Illiteracy rate is only four percent among men, and five percent among women.
– San Antonio city officials install gas street lights.
– Texas Legislature rebels against U.S. Congress' opposition to slavery, claiming State is "sovereign and independent nation."

1861 Ordinance of Secession is passed on February 1.

– Sam Houston is deposed as Governor for refusing to take oath of allegiance to Confederacy.
– Federal troops still in Texas are held as prisoners of war after April 12.

1862 Galveston is captured by Federal forces.
– Homestead Act is passed.
– Antiwar sentiment increases in northwest Texas, and a few of 58,533 Texas cavalry members try to desert after entering service.

1863 Confederates recapture Galveston.
– Sam Houston dies at Huntsville.
September 8. Lieutenant Dick Dowling repulses Federal attack on Sabine Pass.

1865 Last battle of the Civil War is fought in May at Palmito Hill.
June 19. Texas slaves are declared free.
– 50,000 Federal soldiers occupy Texas to push through Reconstruction reforms.
– Thousands of refugees of war flee to wide-open spaces of Texas; confusion prevails in back country.

1866 Constitutional Convention is held at Austin.
– First Texas cattle are driven north to market.

1869 Reconstruction Convention frames new constitution, and Republicans control State government.

1870 Texas is readmitted to Union.
– Population is 818,579.
– "All Civil authority" is remitted to State government by Reconstructionist leaders.

1871 Wagon team is massacred at Salt Creek by vengeful Indians.
– "Radical Republicans" declare martial law in order to enforce Reconstruction policy in State.

1872 Democrats regain control of Legislature.
– First extensive railroad lines connect Texas with other states.

1873 "Financial panic" causes banks to close.
– State school system is decentralized by Democratic Legislature.

1874 Radical rule is completely overthrown, and Reconstruction period ends.
– Battle at Adobe Walls is fought.

1875 Indian raids into Texas decrease.
– State Legislature is composed mainly of old Democrats, with six African-Americans out of 90 members.

1876 Present State Constitution is framed and adopted.
– Agricultural and Mechanical College opens.
– Barbed wire is first used by cattle ranchers.
– Sam Houston Normal School and Prairie View Normal School open, as does Industrial College for Negroes.

1877 Stock Raisers' Association is organized.

– Greenbackers begin campaign against gold standard, and advocate income tax in Texas.

1878 Outlaw Sam Bass is killed.
– Railroad lands are sold, and settlement of West Texas is encouraged.
– Many Swedes move into older settlements.
– Over 100,000 buffalo hides are taken from Texas range; it is peak of hunting of that animal.

1879 State debts reach $5.5 million.
– George Arrington is sent to Panhandle to control spreading crime, feuding, and vigilante activities.

1880 Buffalo population is depleted from Texas prairies.
– Better irrigation brings German farmers to West Texas.
– Population is 1,591,749.

1881 First African-American state senator is elected.
– State Capitol Building is destroyed by fire.

1883 Minimum prices are set for land sales, and limits are set on amount of land sold at one time.
– University of Texas is established at Austin.

1884 First windmills appear on Texas plains.

1885-87 Severe winters and dry summers lower cattle population.

1886 Indianola is destroyed by storm.

1887 First home for orphans in Texas is opened at Corsicana.

1888 New State Capitol is completed and dedicated.

1890 Population is 2,235,527.

1891 State has 8,710 miles of rail lines, and State Railroad Commission is created.
– Oil refinery at Corsicana begins operation with out-of-state oil.

1893 Financial panic of New York banks affects both ranchers and businessmen in Texas.

1896 Greer County case is settled by Supreme Court, awarding Oklahoma land claimed by Texas.

1898 With Spanish-American War in full force, Theodore Roosevelt trains "Rough Riders" in San Antonio.

1900 Six thousand are killed in Galveston hurricane; many Gulf Coast towns are devastated.
– Population is 3,048,710.

1901 Oil is discovered in large quantities at Spindletop field.
– Commission form of government is developed at Galveston.
– Construction of sea wall is begun at Galveston.

1902 Lucas' fields produce more than 12,000,000 barrels of oil.

1904 Texas has more miles of railroad than any other state.

1905 Terrell Election Law is passed.

1906 Port Arthur becomes port of entry.
– African-American soldiers of 25th Infantry mutiny and riot in Brownsville.

1909 President Theodore Roosevelt signs bill authorizing completion of Sabine Neches Canal.
– Most of Fort Worth is destroyed by fire.

1910 First citrus orchards are planted near Rio Grande.
– Pipeline of natural gas is connected to supply Fort Worth and all of Texas.
– First official airplane flight of U.S. Army takes place at Fort Sam Houston.
– Population is 3,896,542.

1911 Texas border is occupied by U.S. troops because of Mexican revolutions.

1912 Sulfur is first produced in State.

1914 World War I begins in Europe.

1915 Compulsory education law is passed.
– Houston ship channel is opened.
– Mennonites establish colony near Littlefield.

1917 Race riots occur in Houston.

1917-18 Droughts plague farmers and ranchers.

1918 Women are granted vote in Texas; many push for Prohibition.
– By the end of World War I, 197,389 Texans have served in Europe, and 5,000 of those have died.
– Free textbooks are provided for all public school students.

1919 Dallas city charter is amended to provide for City Planning Commission, pursuant to remodeling of city.
– Five hundred Texans die during Mexican border conflicts.
– Prohibition goes into effect.

1920 Population is 4,663,228; urban population will increase by 48 percent during 1920s.

1921 San Antonio River flood takes 50 lives.
– Ku Klux Klan appears on political scene.

1923 Miriam Ferguson is first woman to serve as Governor of State; Edith Williams is State's first woman legislator.

1926 Ship channel and deep port are completed at Corpus Christi.

1928 Texas tops list in U.S. oil production.
– Construction of Randolph Field, "West Point of the Air," begins.

1929 Stock Market crashes in New York.
– Prices for Texas produce and cattle begin to drop.

1930 East Texas oil field is discovered.
– Population is 3,824,715

1931 Governor Rose Sterling, attempting to enforce proration of East Texas oil, calls out National Guard.

1932 One-half of street lights in Houston are shut off because of lack of funds to keep them on.
– Texas cotton prices fall to only five cents per pound, compared to 18 cents in 1928.
– Miriam Ferguson is reelected, bringing new taxes and relief measures.

1933 Banks close in March.
– Unemployment reaches 105,045, or 13 percent of Texas work force.
– Treaty is signed between United States and Mexico, empowering International Boundary Commission to direct and inspect construction of Rio Grande Rectification Project.
– State votes $20,000 in bonds for economic relief.

1934 Longshoremen's strike in Houston is called "waterfront reign of terror."
– Intracoastal Canal, from Sabine River to Galveston Bay, is opened.

1935 Texas commission is organized to plan construction projects in State.
– Yount-Lee Oil Company is sold to Stanolind Company for $41.6 million in cash, an impressive cash transaction in the history of American business.
– Big Bend National Park is planned.
– State prohibition is repealed.

1936 Texas celebrates centennial of its independence from Mexico.
– Port of Brownsville is opened.

1937 New London school disaster takes lives of more than 290 children and teachers.
– Bill legalizing para-mutuel betting on horse races is repealed.

1938 The $2,750,000 Port Arthur-Orange Bridge, which spans across Neches River, is completed.
– U.S. Housing Authority reports it made commitments totaling $16,236,000 to Texas cities for slum clearance.
– New Galveston Causeway, over 8,000 feet long and costing $2,500,000, is completed.

1939 Scientists attend dedication of McDonald Observatory on Mount Locke, near Fort Davis; it is second largest observatory in world.
– Governor O'Daniel's plans for economy meet with resistance, especially subscription plan to repay bank loans for old age pensions.
– More than 80,000 Texas oil wells are shut down for 15 days in August by order of State Railroad Commission, in the face of crude oil price collapse; two days later, six other states order similar shutdowns, cutting off 70 percent of U.S. oil supply.

– Texas sets new record for building, with total of over $75.3 million—an increase of $10.7 million over 1938.
– Texas Company stock is admitted to Chicago Stock Exchange, and Texas Corporation stock soon follows.

1940 Gubernatorial candidates use super power Mexican radio stations, which have no wattage restrictions, to beam campaign promises across Texas.
– Population is 6,414,824.

1942 Dr. E.P. Schock, at University of Texas at Austin, receives State funds to research synthetic rubber processing.

1943 At Texas company, employees give a penny to Red Cross for each Japanese plane shot down.
– U.S. Supreme Court orders State courts to resume discussion of African-Americans' voting rights in Democratic primaries, despite party ban.
– Lone Star flag is flown over aircraft carrier *San Jacinto.*

1944 When State assistant attorney general defends ban on African-American voting in Democratic primaries in Texas, U.S. Supreme Court once again declares action unconstitutional under Fifteenth Amendment; Mexican-Americans also barred in primary voting.

1945 For first time in years, there is a surplus in State funds.
– Statehood centennial is celebrated.

1946 After heavy rains, Houston voters are forced to row to and from polling places during November elections.
– Three amendments to State Constitution are proposed.
– African-American student, H.M. Sweat, tries to enter Texas University Law School at Austin; court stalls action as plans for African-American law school are begun.

1947 Strikes are outlawed in State and unions must adhere to new anti-trust laws.
– Legislators vote against inviting any pro-liberal representative to speak before House.
– State gains ownership of all submerged lands off Gulf Coast after years of dispute with Federal government.
– Refusing to enter "Negro school" planned by State, H.M. Sweat continues efforts to enter Texas University Law School; however, he is once again barred from that institution.
– Texas City suffers severe damage from series of offshore chain explosions, coming from Monsanto Company freighter, *Grandcamp*, which was being loaded with ammonium nitrate; 408 die and almost 2,000 are injured in fiery catastrophe.

1948 Industrial growth exceeds population growth.
– Lyndon B. Johnson wins U.S. Senate seat amid controversy over close vote.

1950 Population is 7,711,194.

1951 Communist Party members are denied right to hold office; loyalty oaths are required of all State officials.

1952 Five African-Americans protest exclusion from Democratic primaries in Jaybird; case eventually reaches U.S. Supreme Court.

– Students at Texas University are not allowed to smoke or drink soda in classrooms.

1953 President and Mrs. Eisenhower attend Independence Day festivities in Washington, Texas.
– Texas farmers suffer from Statewide drought.

1954 Democratic Party leader G.B. Parr fears members of Texas Rangers, and asks for Federal Court protection, but is refused; later in year, Ranger Captain Allee is tried on charges of attempting to kill Parr.
– State police are trained to recognize "signs of Communism."
– More votes are reported from Harris County election than number of voters registered in that area; governor calls commission to investigate.

1955 Governor Shivers is sworn in for unprecedented fourth term.
– Senator Phillips holds floor for 23 hours and 35 minutes, a U.S. record for filibustering.

1956 Rockefellers invest in 5,000-acre industrial park near Fort Worth-Dallas.
– Regents at Texas University urge tighter control over student newspapers after unfavorable editorials are published on State's natural gas bill; in response, *Daily Texan* editor charges that administration is against free press.

1958 U.S. government claims rights to some tidelands past three-mile limit of State ownership.

1959 Twenty-three percent of African-Americans are registered voters in Texas; although somewhat small amount, it is increase over last decade.

1960 Lyndon Johnson is made U.S. Vice President, serving with newly-elected President John F. Kennedy.
– Census figures show small towns are losing population and dying, while total population has increased 24 percent since 1950.
– Population is 9,579,677.

1961 Mexican-American wins Texas U.S. Congressional seat with support of both President Kennedy and Vice President Johnson.

1962 John Connally is elected Governor of Texas.
– Increasing conservative movement in State aids Republican Party, but Democrats still reign in politics.

1963 President John F. Kennedy is assassinated while riding in motorcade through Dallas; Governor Connally is also hit by gunfire.

1964 Senator Yarborough is charged with accepting $50,000 bribe from Billie S. Estes, multimillionaire businessman and real estate investor.

1965 Plans are made to exhibit Lyndon B. Johnson Library at Texas University at Austin.
– Visiting professor H. M. Jones resigns because he refuses to take Texas University oath of loyalty.

1966 Texas moves from sixth place to fifth in State population.
– President Johnson is host of television special on central Texas.
– Ku Klux Klan leader is barred from Texas University campus.
– Honor student C.J. Whitman kills 16 persons and wounds 29 others when he shoots indiscriminately from tower at Texas University; he is slain by police.

1967 Hurricane Beulah destroys much of southern Texas near Rio Grande.
– Democrats begin drive to register more African-Americans and Hispanics for 1968 election.

1968 Free registration replaces poll tax system of voting.

1969 State economy is in good shape as oil development booms.
– Lyndon B. Johnson School of Public Affairs is founded at University of Texas at Austin.

1970 Because of pacifist beliefs, University of Texas's Professor Dean refuses to teach Army Major.
– Texas Rangers are seen as threat to civil rights of citizens by some groups, but they are not disbanded.
– Population is encouraged in rural areas.
– State economy is on downswing.
– Population is 11,196,730.

1971 Ex-governor Sharp is charged in fraudulent stock scandal.
– State employees receive wage increases despite President Nixon's national wage-price freeze; however, Justice Department bars increases before checks are sent out.
– Lyndon Baines Johnson Library is dedicated.

1972 La Raza Unida, Hispanic political party, organizes for statewide elections for first time.

1973 Minimum voting age is lowered to 18.
– Texas legislators are allowed to wear turtlenecks and sport shirts without ties for first time.
– State mourns former-President Johnson's death.
– Texas Democrats accuse six Republicans of "smear" campaign in 1972.
– Texas is fourth most populous State in U.S., with 11,800,000 residents.

1974 Public Safety Department closely investigates pilot Robert Pomeroy, leader of group opposed to nuclear power plant in Glen Rose; department official later apologizes for incident, and promises to destroy all "dossiers" on Pomeroy and other activists.
– State Constitutional Convention deliberates, and then defeats, new document.

1975 Texas Legislature moves to assure minority voting rights. Southwest Bell Telephone Company is investigated for falsifying records to gain rate increases, and is charged with wiretapping of State officials' phones.
– Texas voters reject new amendments to Constitution.
– Lorene Rogers is named president of University of Texas at Austin; she is first woman to hold the position.

1977 Texas is acknowledged as leader in U.S. cattle production.

1978 William Clements is elected governor, first Republican in 105 years to attain the office.

1979 Wide income disparity is noted in Texas, where wealthy oil barons contrast sharply with poor immigrant farm workers.

1980 Texas House Speaker William Clayton is implicated in Federal bribery investigation, with FBI possessing tapes of him receiving money for political maneuvering; Clayton is later found "not guilty."
– Population is 14,173,876.
– Texas is ranked third most populous State in nation.

1981 Texas gains three more seats in U.S. House of Representatives.
– Heat wave scorches State, causing over 100 deaths and substantial loss in farm revenues.

1982 Recession hits Texas belatedly, with eight percent unemployment reported in larger cities in July; unemployed workers from other parts of U.S. arrive in Texas cities seeking jobs; when none can be found, many camp out in State parks, having nowhere else to go.
– Democrats once again gain power in State elections.
March 6. Twelve people die and 28 are injured in one-room fire at Westchase Hilton Hotel in Houston.
– A 1906 Pablo Picasso painting, *Nude Combing Her Hair,* is purchased from Norton Simon Foundation by Kimbell Art Museum in Fort Worth for $4 million.

1983 After leaving U.S. Congress as Democrat on January 5, Phil Gramm reenters that body as Republican on February 12 upon winning special election in State's Sixth Congressional District; switch is prompted by his not being allowed to sit on House Budget Committee due to strong backing of President Reagan's economic program.
March 25. Exxon Corp. is ordered by Federal judge to refund $1.49 billion to all 50 state governments, after company has received several "notices of probable violation" by Energy Department due to overcharging of crude oil customers between 1975 and 1981; Hawkins Field in Wood County, Texas is one area involved.
May 18. Delegates at United Automobile Workers Convention in Dallas elect Owen Bieber as organization president.
– Houston is one of several towns in Gulf Coast area ravaged by tornadoes and storms between May 18-23, with 11 deaths reported and 1,000 people losing homes.
June 14. Fort Worth Ramada Inn is scene of early-morning fire in which 5 people are killed, 33 injured.
August 23. Long-time Republican Texas Senator, John Tower, announces he will not seek another Senate term in 1984, after having served 22 years.
November 15. Convicted con man, Billie Sol Estes, is released from Federal Penitentiary in Big Spring, Texas, several years earlier than his 1998 release date; jailed since 1963, Estes, known as friend and financial backer of Lyndon B. Johnson, was convicted for selling nonexistent fertilizer tanks.
– Two companies, Ciba-Geigy Corp. and McGregor Chemical Corp., former owners of property acquired by Naval Weapons Industrial Reserve Plant in McGregor, Texas, are sued in order to secure major cleanup operation or $400,000 to cover same.

1984 March 31. At Texas State Penitentiary in Huntsville, Ronald Clark O'Bryan, 39, known as "Candy Man" killer, is executed by lethal injection; convicted murderer acquired nickname after poisoning his 8-year old son's Halloween candy in 1974 in order to collect huge insurance stipend.
June 8. Four Harris County disposal sites are focal point of lawsuit filed in Houston Federal District Court by group of environmental lawyers; some of large companies named in suit include Arco Chemical Corp., Exxon Corp., Shell Oil Co., U.S. Steel Corp., and Houston Lighting and Power Co., all accused of indiscriminate toxic chemical dumping.
July 13. Governor Mark White signs $4.8 billion, 3-year tax increase bill, largest tax hike in Texas history; money is earmarked for public education reform.

1985 January 19. In single-issue election, ordinance that opposes hiring discrimination against homosexuals in workplace is soundly rejected by Houston voters, as is ordinance proposing inclusion of gays in city affirmative action programs.
April 6. Democratic San Antonio mayor, Henry Cisneros, is reelected to third term.
July 2. Corpus Christi is chosen as new home base for *Wisconsin* battleship, as well as *Lexington,* a training aircraft carrier.
– Nelson Bunker Hunt and W. Herbert Hunt, of wealthy Texas Hunt family, are forced to begin divesting massive holdings in silver market; acquiring about 59 million ounces in late 1970s, they sell 90 percent of cache, leaving them with roughly 6 million ounces, worth around $38 million.
– Nobel prizes are awarded to molecular geneticists Michael S. Brown and Joseph L. Goodstein, researchers at University of Texas Health Science Center in Dallas, who are honored for work in field of cholesterol metabolism.
November. Massive oil-well accident causes 6.3 million gallon oil spill off coast of Texas.
November 5. Mayor of Houston, Democrat Kathy Whitmire, is reelected to third term, defeating former Republican mayor, Louie Welch.
– Proposal for funds in amount of $1.4 billion to improve water systems in several Texas cities is overwhelmingly approved by Texas voters; money is earmarked for construction of new pipelines, reservoirs, and treatment plants.
December 6. A 47-year old convicted murderer, Carroll E. Cole, is executed by lethal injection for killing five women in Texas and Nevada.

1986 Pioneer Corp., company in Amarillo that processes oil and natural gas, is purchased by Mesa Limited Partnership for approximately $800 million; in 1985, revenues for Pioneer were over $300 million.
April 16. In Huntsville, 28-year old Jeffrey Allen Barney is executed by lethal injection for 1981 rape and murder of minister's wife; the next month, lethal injection is also used in execution of Jay Kelly Pinkerton, 24, for rape and murder of two Amarillo women.
June 24. Nelson Bunker Hunt and brothers, Lamar and Herbert, sue 23 banks from whom they borrowed money; asking $4.8 billion in damages; brothers accuse banks of "deception and fraud in a conspiracy to destroy" after banks refuse to restructure loans the brothers were late in paying.
September 30. New bill is unveiled by Texas Legislature and immediately signed by Governor Mark White; bill increases taxes and cuts spending in order to help balance budget.

– Lomas & Nettleton Financial Corporation makes $300 million deal with MCorp., Texas bank in financial crisis, to acquire latter's lucrative mortgage banking and credit card operations; Lomas & Nettleton pay 100 million of amount in cash.

1987 February 17. A 21-year old Miss Texas, Michelle Renee Royer, wins title of Miss USA; victory automatically qualifies her for competition in Miss Universe pageant; she is third consecutive winner from Texas to capture Miss USA crown.

– Under aegis of Superfund Law, several companies reach agreement with Environmental Protection Agency to cover costs for cleanup of La Marque, Texas, toxic waste dump; firms are required to clean up toxins they are responsible for, and government agrees to clean up remainder.

July 31. John B. Connally, former Secretary of U.S. Treasury, files Chapter 11 bankruptcy in order to restructure personal finances; he also files Chapter 7 bankruptcy to dissolve Barnes-Connally Partnership, real estate company he co-owned with Ben F. Barnes.

1988 April 28. Congressional Gold Medal, first ever to be awarded to former First Lady, is given to Lady Bird Johnson, 75, in Washington, D.C., for her extensive humanitarian and environmental work.

May 4 is final day of United States amnesty program for illegal aliens; over a million people apply for permanent status, with 17 percent of that number coming from Texas.

– Texas is chosen over several other states as home base for Superconducting Super Collider (SSC), largest and costliest atom smasher in world, for use in massive project.

1989 Major political battle is won by San Antonio's mayor, Henry Cisneros, after city voters approve small tax increase for construction of 65,000-seat Alamodome; Cisneros once again confirms his plan to leave politics at end of mayoral term to establish Hispanic-owned asset firm.

– T. Boone Pickens Jr., corporate raider from Amarillo, becomes largest shareholder of Japan-based firm, Koito Manufacturing Co., after acquiring 20.2 percent of their stock.

June 23. Galveston Bay is inundated with 250,000 gallons of heavy crude oil after freighter from Panama, *Rachel B.,* and barge carrying oil, collide in Houston Ship Channel; within a few days, large amount of oil has been cleaned up.

– United States Justice Department, at request of Environmental Protection Agency, files suit against four U.S. cities, including San Antonio and El Paso, under Clean Water Act, for dumping untreated industrial toxins into public sewer systems; first to settle is San Antonio, who pays $225,000 penalty and promises to create better enforcement procedures.

– After 29-year fight, Texas Instruments Inc. is finally awarded Japanese patent for integrated circuits that it has been seeking.

December 18. New York's Mayor-elect, David N. Dinkins, names Houston Police Chief Lee P. Brown Police Commissioner of New York, making Brown second African-American to hold the office.

1990 March 29. Ruling by U.S. District Court Judge Lucius Bunton stipulates that both Japan's Hitachi Ltd. and America's Motorola Inc., are guilty of patent infringement, a charge each has leveled at other; they are ordered to pay fines and to stop selling their microprocessors; the next day, however, the judge allows room for the two companies to negotiate.

July 28. Texas Gulf Coast sustains another massive oil spill when two oil-carrying barges collide with Greek tanker in Galveston Bay; after it is estimated that 500,000 gallons of oil have spilled, Governor William P. Clements declares region a disaster area.

– According to Anita Collins of U.S. Department of Agriculture's Honey Bee Research Laboratory in Weslaco, Texas, first U.S. sighting and subsequent trapping of Africanized honeybees, widely known as "killer bees," is documented near Hidalgo, Texas.

1991 January 19. Corpus Christi voters, by substantial margin, strike down proposed "Human Family Amendment" to city's charter, which states that "human life begins at conception and continues until natural death."

April 5. Long-time Republican Texas Senator, John Goodwin Tower, dies; he served in U.S. Senate between 1961 and 1984, and headed Senate Armed Services Committee from 1981-1984; in 1989, Tower was nominated by President George Bush as Secretary of Defense; however, his strong ties with military contractors, coupled with allegations of drinking and womanizing, caused much heated debate in Senate, which eventually rejected his nomination.

– Three Texas military bases are among 24 to close in 15 states, a move decided by the Defense Base Closure and Realignment Commission; they include Bergstrom Air Force Base, Carswell Air Force Base, and Chase Field Naval Air Station.

November 5. Houston is one of three areas to approve measure limiting number of terms a municipal official can serve in their city.

November 7. Constitutional amendment allowing creation of State lottery is approved by Texas voters.

1992 According to *New York Times*, Texas billionaire Ross Perot has only donated $500,000 to help support presidential library of former President Ronald Reagan, an amount that falls substantially short of $2.5 million he had originally pledged.

– Fort Worth plant of General Dynamics Corp. is earmarked for major layoffs by end of 1994, with up to 5,800 workers scheduled to lose their jobs.

November 10. At Sotheby's auction, Matisse painting, *Asia,* created in 1946, is purchased for $11 million by Kimbell Art Museum in Fort Worth.

1993 February 28. Two Branch Davidian cult members and four agents of the U.S. Bureau of Alcohol, Tobacco, and Firearms lose lives in gun battle after abortive raid on cult compound near Waco.

April 8. Day 40 of intense standoff between religious cult leader, David Koresh, and law-enforcement officials in Waco; more than 90 followers, including 17 children, are barricaded in compound.

In annual Toxic Release Inventory Report published by Environmental Protection Agency on May 25, Texas is one of two states that have expelled most chemical waste into environment during 1991; other is Louisiana.

– In special election held to fill Senate seat of Lloyd M. Bentsen, newly-chosen Clinton appointee for Secretary of Treasury, Republican Texas State Treasurer Kay Bailey Hutchison defeats Democratic interim Senator Bob Krueger by two-to-one margin.

April 19. Using tanks and tear gas, law enforcement officials carry out attack on Branch Davidian compound; building is burned to ground shortly after, in what FBI calls "mass suicide;" David Koresh and about 80 cult members die in blaze.

June 24. U.S. Supreme Court upholds Texas law that would allow juries to ask for death penalty in cases where teen is convicted of murder.

– Dallas and Fort Worth are two of several U.S. cities targeted by anti-abortion group, Operation Rescue, during July 9-18 in Cities of Refuge campaign, in which they hold protests at several abortion clinics.

July 30. Florida businessman, Les Alexander, purchases Houston Rockets basketball team for $85 million.

November 7. Texas businessman and independent presidential candidate, Ross Perot, tells supporters at Tampa, Florida anti-NAFTA rally that he was informed by FBI of plot to kill him.

November 9. At Houston rally, George W. Bush, oldest son of former President and managing partner of Texas Rangers baseball team, announces he will run for governor of Texas on Republican ticket in 1994 race.

November 9. Vice President Al Gore and independent presidential candidate Ross Perot appear on Larry King's CNN talk show and enter into somewhat combative debate over controversial North American Free Trade Agreement (NAFTA) proposal.

– After two-year battle in which funding was sought for construction of Superconducting Supercollider (SSC) in State of Texas, project is shelved; for two years in question, costs exceeded $2 billion, and were estimated to rise to $11 billion by the time project was completed.

November 22. On 30th anniversary of assassination of President John F. Kennedy, Dealey Plaza in Dallas is dedicated as national historical landmark.

1994 January. Senator Kay Bailey Hutchison is accused of using State employees of Texas State Treasury, as well as State equipment and time, to help with her special Senate election campaign.

January 30. In Super Bowl XXVIII, with a 30-13 score, Dallas Cowboys secure second consecutive National Football League championship, defeating Buffalo Bills.

February 11. State Court jury in Fort Worth is directed by Presiding Judge, John F. Onion Jr., to find Hutchison "not guilty" on all five counts of misconduct; ruling comes after clash between Onion and Travis County District Attorney prosecutor, Ronnie Earle; Earle claims judge will not rule on evidence reportedly taken without search warrant, and refuses to pursue his case against Hutchison.

February 26. Eleven members of Branch Davidian cult are acquitted of murder and conspiracy charges concerning deaths of four Federal agents in February 1993 at Waco, Texas Davidian compound; seven other cult members are convicted on lesser charges.

March 8. Democratic Texas Governor Ann Richards and Republican George W. Bush each secure overwhelming victory in their respective gubernatorial primary races.

November. Republican George W. Bush wins Texas gubernatorial race.

1995 U.S. Customs Department agents raid 44 U.S. stores selling electronic surveillance equipment; San Antonio's Spy Factory chain, with 16 retail outlets, heads list of distributors selling illegal devices.

– Western Texas hit by earthquake measuring 5.6 on Richter scale; epicenter in Marathon causes major damage in Alpine, located 20 miles north-northwest.

– Texas district judge Samuel C. Kiser orders Mexican-American woman to speak English to her five-year-old daughter at home; Kiser's comment sparks controversy after criticism of woman during child custody hearing, on grounds of her "relegating her (child) to the position of housemaid" by speaking Spanish rather than English in home.

– U.S. Attorney in Houston, Gaynelle Griffin Jones, says no retrial will be held for Dale Brown, defendant who pled not guilty in indictment against 13 for bribery and kickbacks involving NASA contracts; Brown was sole defendant to plead not guilty; his first trial ended in hung jury.

1996 Supreme Court lets stand previous ruling against race-based admissions policy at University of Texas School of Law in Austin; policy had been implemented to boost number of Mexican-American students, but lower court ruling took strong stance against race-based admissions policies.

– Supreme Court rules unanimously to uphold rules governing implementation of capital punishment in armed services; ruling comes after Dwight J. Loving fights death sentence order received in 1988 case at Fort Hood, where he was found guilty of murdering two taxi cab drivers.

– Baylor University in Waco holds on-campus dance for first time in 151-year history; unwritten ban on dancing at Baptist university was based on consideration that dancing was violation of religious tenets and potential precursor to premarital sex.

– University of Houston study estimates that 3,200 undocumented aliens drowned from 1985 to 1994 while attempting to enter U.S. by crossing Rio Grande River; high death toll is considered result of stricter border enforcement by U.S.

– Senator Phil Gramm steps down from presidential nomination race after poor results in Iowa caucuses.

1997 Three-judge panel upholds boundaries it had redrawn in August 1996 for three districts declared unconstitutional and for ten other affected districts; special elections were held in all 13 districts in 1996.

– Houston grand jury returns 11-count indictment against five current and former Houston officials accused of bribery in FBI sting operation; indicted include two current council city members, Michael J. Yarbrough and John Castillo; former council members, Ben Reyes and John Peavy Jr.; and former commissioner, Elizabeth Maldonado.

– At least six tornadoes sweep through central part of State, killing 30 and causing widespread damage; twenty-seven deaths occur in Jarell, where tornado runs through Double Creek housing subdivision.

– Houston Intercontinental Airport changes name to George Bush Intercontinental/Houston Airport.

1998 Five people plead guilty in Lubbock to charges of visa fraud and alien smuggling; felons lured about 500 nurses from Philippines and South Korea into U.S. to work in hospitals and nursing homes for substandard wages.

– Karla Faye Tucker, convicted for 1983 pickax murder of Jerry Lynn Dean, is executed by lethal injection in Huntsville; she is first woman to be executed in State since 1863.

– Federal court upholds State law that makes Health Maintenance Organizations (HMOs) liable for decisions having impact on quality of health care to providers.

1999 Texas Natural Resource Conservation Commission (TNRCC) and 13 charter members of Clean Industries Plus make commitment to pollution prevention program; leading industries in State will work with local communities to make large environmental reductions in hazardous waste and other pollutants.

– Attorney General John Cornyn receives $50,000 federal grant to prevent expansion and development of colonias along Texas-Mexico border; grant will aid fund for education and outreach, compliance investigation, and enforcement components of anti-colonias efforts.

– State earmarks over $10 million for aiding Texas Education Agency's after-school programs in 71 school districts; funds set to reduce risky behavior among middle-school students.

U.S. Environmental Protection Agency releases figures showing State has lower overall rating among states for release of toxic industrial emissions.

2000 Widespread forest and marsh grass fires in southeast Texas result in smoke pollution in some sections; conditions cause health risks for children and elderly with respiratory or heart conditions; prevailing winds expected to dissipate smoke, but fires could flare up again.

– State attorney general sues two online pharmacies for misleading consumers and threatening health by selling dangerous drugs and controlled substances over Internet without protective safeguards.

– Attorney General Cornyn announces that child support collections exceed $1 billion, an increase of $161 million from 1999 and $111 million from 1998; contributing to higher numbers are better calling system and web information site.

– Voluntary Workforce Training program is launched; program will help high school students earn on-the-job experience and build trust fund for college expenses; program also allows internships to continue while students pursue associates or bachelor's higher education programs.

– TNRCC announces it is taking steps to control use of addictive methyl tertiary butyl ether (MTBE) in gasoline sold in Texas; reduction efforts will aid air quality.

DIRECTORY OF STATE SERVICES

OFFICE OF THE GOVERNOR
P.O. Box 12428
State Capitol
Austin, TX 78711
Fax: 512-463-1849
Governor: 512-463-2000

OFFICE OF THE LIEUTENANT GOVERNOR
Box 12068
Austin, TX 78711
Fax: 512-463-0356
Lieutenant Governor: 512-463-0001

OFFICE OF THE ATTORNEY GENERAL
P.O. Box 12548
Austin, TX 78711
Fax: 512-463-2063
Attorney General: 512-463-2191

OFFICE OF THE SECRETARY OF STATE
P.O. Box 12697
Austin, TX 78711
Fax: 512-475-2761
Secretary of State: 512-463-5770

DEPARTMENT OF TREASURY
P.O. Box 12608

Austin, TX 78711
Fax: 512-463-6315
State Treasurer: 512-463-5944

ADJUTANT GENERAL
P.O. Box 5128
Austin, TX 78763
Fax: 512-465-5578
Adjutant General: 512-465-5006

AGING DEPARTMENT
Box 12786
Austin, TX 78763
Fax: 512-465-5578
Executive Director: 512-444-2727

AGRICULTURE DEPARTMENT
P.O. Box 12847
Austin, TX 78711
Fax: 512-463-1104
Commissioner: 512-463-7435

AUDITOR
P.O. Box 12067
Austin, TX 78711
Fax: 512-479-4884
Auditor: 512-479-4700

BANKING DEPARTMENT
2601 N. Lamar Blvd.
Austin, TX 78705
Fax: 512-475-1313
Executive Director: 512-472-5059

COMMERCE DEPARTMENT
P.O. Box 12728
Austin, TX 78712
Fax: 512-936-0303
Executive Director: 512-472-5059

COMPTROLLER OF PUBLIC ACCOUNTS
111 E. 17th St.
Austin, TX 78774
Fax: 512-463-4965
Comptroller: 512-463-4000

CRIMINAL JUSTICE DEPARTMENT
P.O. Box 99
Huntsville, TX 77342
Fax: 409-294-2123
Executive Director: 409-294-2101

Administrative Services
P.O. Box 99
Huntsville, TX 77342
Fax: 409-294-6996
Director: 409-294-2107

Community Justice Assistance Division
P.O. Box 13084
Capital Station
Austin, TX 78711
Fax: 512-305-9370
Director: 512-305-9305

Data Services
P.O. Box 99
Huntsville, TX 77342
Fax: 409-294-2918
Director: 409-305-1304

Engineering Directorate
P.O. Box 99
Huntsville, TX 77342
Fax: 409-294-6951
Director: 409-305-6916

Health Services
P.O. Box 99
Huntsville, TX 77342
Fax: 409-294-2911
Director: 409-305-2932

Institutional Division
P.O. Box 99
Huntsville, TX 77342
Fax: 409-294-6325
Director: 409-294-2169

Pardons and Paroles Division
Capital Station
Box 13401
Austin, TX 78711
Fax: 512-406-5858
Director: 512-406-5200

State Jails
P.O. Box 13084
Capitol Station
Austin, TX 78711
Fax: 512-463-7728
Director: 512-463-9988

HEALTH DEPARTMENT
1100 West 49th St.
Austin, TX 78756
Fax: 512-458-7477
Commissioner: 512-458-7375

Administration
1100 West 49th St.
Austin, TX 78756
Fax: 512-458-7477
Deputy Commissioner: 512-458-7378

Human Resources and Support
1100 West 49th St.
Austin, TX 78756
Fax: 512-458-7694
Associate Commissioner: 512-458-7738

Information Resources Management
1100 West 49th St.
Austin, TX 78756
Fax: 512-458-7477
Associate Commissioner: 512-465-7793

Programs
1100 West 49th St.
Austin, TX 78756
Deputy Commissioner: 512-458-7378

Health Care Delivery
1100 West 49th St.
Austin, TX 78756
Associate Commissioner: 512-458-7321

Disease Control and Prevention
1100 West 49th St.
Austin, TX 78756
Fax: 512-458-7249
Associate Commissioner: 512-458-7234

Environmental and Consumer Health
1100 West 49th St.
Austin, TX 78756
Fax: 512-458-7686
Associate Commissioner: 512-458-7541

Health Care Financing
1100 West 49th St.
Austin, TX 78756
Fax: 512-338-6945
Associate Commissioner: 512-338-6501

Health Care Quality and Standards
1100 West 49th St.
Austin, TX 78756
Fax: 512-458-7477
Associate Commissioner: 512-834-8634

HOUSING AND COMMUNITY AFFAIRS DEPARTMENT
P.O. Box 13941
Austin, TX 78711
Fax: 512-469-9606
Executive Director: 512-475-3934

HUMAN SERVICES DEPARTMENT
P.O. Box 149030
Austin, TX 78714
Fax: 512-450-4220
Commissioner: 512-450-3030

INFORMATION RESOURCES DEPARTMENT
P.O. Box 13564
Austin, TX 78711
Fax: 512-475-4759
Executive Director: 512-475-4700

INSURANCE DEPARTMENT
P.O. Box 149104
Austin, TX 78714
Fax: 512-475-2205
Insurance Commissioner: 512-463-6464

Administrative Services
P.O. Box 149104
Austin, TX 78714
Fax: 512-322-2272
Chief Financial Officer: 512-475-1753

Consumer Protection
P.O. Box 149104
Austin, TX 78714
Fax: 512-475-1771
Deputy Commissioner: 512-463-6652

Financial Affairs
P.O. Box 149104
Austin, TX 78714
Fax: 512-322-5074
Deputy Commissioner: 512-322-5040

Human Resources
P.O. Box 149104
Austin, TX 78714
Fax: 512-475-1864
Deputy Commissioner: 512-463-6578

Information Services
P.O. Box 149104
Austin, TX 78714
Fax: 512-475-1919
Deputy Commissioner: 512-463-6530

Legal and Compliance Services
P.O. Box 149104
Austin, TX 78714
Fax: 512-475-1843
Senior Associate Commissioner: 512-463-6119

Regulation and Safety
P.O. Box 149104
Austin, TX 78714
Fax: 512-322-4296
Senior Associate Commissioner: 512-305-7342

LICENSING AND REGULATION DEPARTMENT
P.O. Box 12157
Austin, TX 78711
Fax: 512-475-2854
Executive Director: 512-463-3173

MENTAL HEALTH AND MENTAL RETARDATION DEPARTMENT
P.O. Box 12668
Austin, TX 78711
Fax: 512-206-4560
Commissioner: 512-206-4588

PARKS AND WILDLIFE DEPARTMENT
4200 Smith School Rd.
Austin, TX 78744
Fax: 512-389-4814
Chairman: 512-389-4802

PUBLIC SAFETY DEPARTMENT
P.O. Box 4087
Austin, TX 78773
Fax: 512-483-5708
Director: 512-465-2000

SAVINGS AND LOAN DEPARTMENT
2601 N. Lamar
Suite 201
Austin, TX 78705
Fax: 512-475-1360
Commissioner: 512-475-1350

TRANSPORTATION DEPARTMENT
11th & Brazos
Austin, TX 78701
Fax: 512-305-9567
Executive Director: 512-463-8616

ALCOHOL AND DRUG ABUSE COMMISSION
710 Brazos
Austin, TX 78701
Fax: 512-474-6675
Executive Director: 512-867-8700

ALCOHOLIC BEVERAGE COMMISSION
Box 13127
Austin, TX 78711
Fax: 512-206-3350
Administrator: 512-458-2500

ANIMAL HEALTH COMMISSION
P.O. Box 12966
Austin, TX 78711
Fax: 512-719-0719
Executive Director: 512-719-0700

ARCHITECTURAL EXAMINERS BOARD
8213 Shoal Creek Blvd.
Suite 107
Austin, TX 78757
Fax: 512-458-1375
Executive Director: 512-458-1363

ARTS COMMISSION
Box 13406
Austin, TX 78711
Fax: 512-475-2699
Executive Director: 512-463-5535

BRAZOS RIVER AUTHORITY
P.O. Box 7555
Waco, TX 76714
Fax: 817-772-5780
General Manager: 817-776-1441

COMMISSION FOR THE BLIND
Box 12866
Austin, TX 78711
Fax: 512-459-2685
Executive Director: 512-459-2500

COMMISSION FOR THE DEAF AND HEARING IMPAIRED
Box 12904
Austin, TX 78711
Fax: 512-451-9316
Executive Director: 512-451-8494

CONSUMER CREDIT COMMISSION
2601 N. Lamar Blvd.
2nd Floor
Austin, TX 78705
Fax: 512-479-1293
Commissioner: 512-479-1280

DEVELOPMENT DISABILITIES PLANNING COUNCIL
4900 N. Lamar St.
Austin, TX 78751
Fax: 512-483-4097
Executive Director: 512-483-4080

ECONOMIC GEOLOGY BUREAU
University of Texas
University Station, Box X
Austin, TX 78713
Fax: 512-471-0140
Director: 512-471-1534

EDUCATION AGENCY
1701 N. Congress Ave.
Austin, TX 78701
Fax: 512-463-9008
Commissioner: 512-463-8985

EMPLOYEES' RETIREMENT SYSTEM
P.O. Box 13207
Austin, TX 78711
Fax: 512-867-3334
Executive Director: 512-476-6431

EMPLOYMENT COMMISSION
101 E. 15th St.
Austin, TX 78778
Fax: 512-463-1289
Chairman: 512-463-2800

FIRE PROTECTION COMMISSION
P.O. Box 2286
Austin, TX 78768
Fax: 512-918-7107
Executive Director: 512-918-7100

GENERAL LAND OFFICE
1700 Congress
Austin, TX 78701
Fax: 512-475-1558
Commissioner: 512-463-5256

GENERAL SERVICES COMMISSION
P.O. Box 13047
Austin, TX 78711
Fax: 512-463-3311
Chairman: 512-463-3446

GUARANTEED STUDENT LOAN CORPORATION
P.O. Box 201725
Austin, TX 78720
Fax: 512-219-4803
President: 512-219-5700

HIGHER EDUCATION COORDINATING BOARD
P.O. Box 12788

Austin, TX 78711
Fax: 512-483-6127
Commissioner: 512-483-6160

HISTORICAL COMMISSION
P.O. Box 12276
Austin, TX 78711
Fax: 512-475-4872
Executive Director: 512-463-6100

HUMANITIES COMMITTEE
3809 S. 2nd St., Suite A
Austin, TX 78704
Fax: 512-440-0115
Executive Director: 512-440-1991

JAIL STANDARDS COMMISSION
P.O. Box 12985
Austin, TX 78711
Fax: 512-463-3185
Executive Director: 512-463-5505

LIBRARY AND ARCHIVES
P.O. Box 12927
Austin, TX 78711
Fax: 512-463-5436
Director: 512-463-5460

LOWER COLORADO RIVER AUTHORITY
P.O. Box 220
Austin, TX 78767
Fax: 512-473-3298
General Manager: 512-473-3200

MOTOR VEHICLE COMMISSION
P.O. Box 2293
Austin, TX 78768
Fax: 512-476-8042
Executive Director: 512-476-3587

MUNICIPAL POWER AGENCY
P.O. Box 7000
Bryan, TX 77805
Fax: 409-873-2676
General Manager: 409-873-2013

NATURAL RESOURCE CONSERVATION COMMISSION
P.O. Box 13087
Austin, TX 78711
Fax: 512-239-0077
Chairman: 512-239-5505

Administrative Services Office
P.O. Box 13087
Austin, TX 78711
Fax: 512-239-0077
Deputy Director: 512-239-0590

Air Quality Office
P.O. Box 13087
Austin, TX 78711
Fax: 512-239-1123
Deputy Director: 512-239-1117

Legal and Regulatory Services Office
P.O. Box 13087
Austin, TX 78711
Fax: 512-239-0606
Deputy Director: 512-239-5100

Policy and Regulatory Development Office
P.O. Box 13087
Austin, TX 78711
Deputy Director: 512-239-3900

Waste Management Office
P.O. Box 13087
Austin, TX 78711
Fax: 512-239-2177
Deputy Director: 512-239-2104

Water Resources Management Office
P.O. Box 13087
Austin, TX 78711
Fax: 512-239-4303
Deputy Director: 512-239-4300

NUECES RIVER AUTHORITY
P.O. Box 349
Uvalde, TX 78802
Fax: 210-278-2025
Executive Director: 210-278-6810

PROTECTIVE AND REGULATORY SERVICES AGENCY
P.O. Box 149030
Austin, TX 78711
Fax: 512-450-3525
Executive Director: 512-450-4778

PUBLIC UTILITY COMMISSION
7800 Shoal Creek Blvd.
Austin, TX 78757
Chairman: 512-458-0295

RAILROAD COMMISSION
P.O. Drawer 12967
Austin, TX 78711
Fax: 512-463-7161
Chairman: 512-463-7131

REAL ESTATE COMMISSION
P.O. Box 12188
Austin, TX 78711
Fax: 512-465-3910
Administrator: 512-465-3900

REHABILITATION COMMISSION
4900 N. Lamar Blvd.
Austin, TX 78751
Fax: 512-483-4012
Commissioner: 512-483-4001

SABINE RIVER AUTHORITY
P.O. Box 579
Orange, TX 77631
Fax: 409-746-3780
General Manager: 409-746-2192

SAN ANTONIO RIVER AUTHORITY
P.O. Box 830027
San Antonio, TX 77631
Fax: 409-746-3780
General Manager: 409-746-2192

SAN JACINTO RIVER AUTHORITY
P.O. Box 329
Conroe, TX 77305
Fax: 409-588-3043
General Manager: 409-588-1111

SECURITIES BOARD
P.O. Box 13167
Austin, TX 78711
Fax: 512-305-8310
Commissioner: 512-305-8300

SOIL AND WATER CONSERVATION BOARD
P.O. Box 658
Temple, TX 76503
Fax: 817-773-3311
Executive Director: 817-773-2250

SOUTH TEXAS HIGHER EDUCATION AUTHORITY
P.O. Box 6500
McAllen, TX 78502
Fax: 210-682-9853
President: 210-682-6371

TEACHER RETIREMENT SYSTEM
1000 Red River
Austin, TX 78701
Fax: 512-370-0585
Executive Director: 512-397-6400

TRINITY RIVER AUTHORITY
P.O. Box 60
Arlington, TX 76004
Fax: 512-465-0970
General Manager: 817-467-4343

VETERANS AFFAIRS COMMISSION
P.O. Box 12277
Austin, TX 78711
Fax: 512-475-2395
Chairman: 512-463-5538

WATER DEVELOPMENT BOARD
P.O. Box 13231
Austin, TX 78711
Fax: 512-475-2053
Executive Administrator: 512-463-7847

YOUTH COMMISSION
P.O. Box 4260
Austin, TX 78765
Fax: 512-483-5010
Executive Director: 512-483-5001

MEMBERS OF CONGRESS

SENATE

SEN. PHIL GRAMM (R) (b. 1942); 3rd Term;
Phone: 202-224-2934; Fax: 202-228-2856;
E-mail: phil_gramm@gramm.senate.gov.

www.senate.gov/~gramm

SEN. KAY BAILEY HUTCHISON (R) (b. 1949); 1st
Term; Phone: 202-224-2353; Fax: 202-228-3973;
E-mail: senator.hutchinson@hutchinson.senate.gov.

www.senate.gov/~hutchinson

HOUSE

MAX A. SANDLIN (D-1st) (b. 1952); 2nd Term;
Phone: 202-225-3035; Fax: 202-225-5866;
E-mail: tx01@legislators.com.

www.house.gov/sandlin/

JIM TURNER (D-2nd) (b. 1946); 2nd Term;
Phone: 202-225-2401; Fax: 202-225-5955;
E-mail: tx02@legislators.com.

www.house.gov/turner

SAM JOHNSON (R-3rd) (b. 1930); 5th Term;
Phone: 202-225-4201; Fax: 202-225-1485; E-mail: (None)

www.house.gov/samjohnson

RALPH M. HALL (D-4th) (b. 1923); 10th Term;
Phone: 202-225-6673; Fax: 202-225-3332;
E-mail: tx04@legislators.com.

www.house.gov/ralphhall

PETE SESSIONS (R-5th) (b. 1955); 2nd Term;
Phone: 202-225-2231; Fax: 202-225-5878;
E-mail: petes@mail.house.gov.

www.house.gov/sessions/

JOE BARTON (R-6th) (b. 1949); 8th Term;
Phone: 202-225-2002; Fax: 202-225-3052; E-mail: (None).

www.house.gov/barton/

BILL ARCHER (R-7th) (b. 1928); 15th Term;
Phone: 202-225-2571; Fax: 202-225-4381;
E-mail: tx07@legislators.com.

www.house.gov/archer/

KEVIN P. BRADY (D-8th) (b. 1955); 2nd Term;
Phone: 202-225-4901; Fax: 202-225-5524;
E-mail: rep.brady@mail.house.gov.

www.house.gov/brady

NICHOLAS V. LAMPSON (D-9th) (b. 1945); 2nd Term;
Phone: 202-225-6565; Fax: 202-225-5547;
E-mail: b. 1958); 3rd Term; Phone: 202-225-3706;
Fax: 202-225-3486; E-mail: nick.lampson@mail.house.gov

www.house.gov/thornberry/

RON E. PAUL (R-14th) (b. 1935); 6th Term;
Phone: 202-225-2831; Fax: 202-226-4871;
E-mail: rep.paul@mail.house.gov.

www.house.gov/paul/

RUBEN E. HINOJOSA (D-15th) (b. 1940); 2nd Term;
Phone: 202-225-2531; Fax: 202-225-5688;
E-mail: tx15@legislators.com.

www.house.gov/hinojosa

SILVESTRE REYES (D-16th) (b. 1944); 2nd Term;
Phone: 202-225-4831; Fax: 202-225-2016;
E-mail: tx16@legislators.com.

www.house.gov/reyes/

CHARLES W. STENHOLM (D-17th) (b. 1938); 11th Term;
Phone: 202-225-6605; Fax: 202-225-2234;
E-mail: tx17@legislators.com.

www.house.gov/stenholm/

SHEILA JACKSON LEE (D-18th) (b. 1950); 3rd Term;
Phone: 202-225-3816; Fax: 202-225-3317;
E-mail: tx18@legislators.com.

www.house.gov/jacksonlee/

LARRY COMBEST (R-19th) (b. 1945); 8th Term;
Phone: 202-225-4005; Fax: 202-225-9615;
E-mail: tx19@legislators.com.

www.house.gov/combest/

CHARLES A. GONZALEZ (D-20th) (b. 1945); 1st Term;
Phone: 202-225-3236; Fax: 202-225-1915;
E-mail: tx20@legislators.com.

www.house.gov/gonzalez

LAMAR S. SMITH (R-21st) (b. 1947); 7th Term;
Phone: 202-225-4236; Fax: 202-225-8628;
E-mail: tx21@legislators.com.

www.house.gov/lamarsmith/

TOM DeLAY (R-22nd) (b. 1947); 8th Term;
Phone: 202-225-5951; Fax: 202-225-5241;
E-mail: tx22@legislators.com.

www.tomdelay.house.gov/

HENRY BONILLA (R-23rd) (b. 1954); 4th Term;
Phone: 202-225-4511; Fax: 202-225-2237;
E-mail: tx23@legislators.com.

www.house.gov/bonilla

MARTIN FROST (D-24th) (b. 1942); 11th Term; Phone: 202-225-3605; Fax: 202-225-4951; E-mail: tx24@legislators.com.

www.house.gov/frost/

KEN BENTSEN (D-25th) (b. 1959); 3rd Term; Phone: 202-225-7508; Fax: 202-225-2947; E-mail: tx25@legislators.com.

www.house.gov/bentsen

RICHARD K. ARMEY (R-26th) (b. 1940); 8th Term; Phone: 202-225-7772; Fax: 202-226-2028; E-mail: tx26@legislators.com.

www.armey.house.gov

SOLOMON P. ORTIZ (D-27th) (b. 1937); 9th Term; Phone: 202-225-7742; Fax: 202-226-1134; E-mail: (None).

www.house.gov/ortiz

CIRO D. RODRIGUEZ (D-28th) (b. 1946); 2nd Term; Phone: 202-225-1640; Fax: 202-225-1641; E-mail: tx28@legislators.com.

www.house.gov/rodriquez

GENE GREEN (D-29th) (b. 1947); 4th Term; Phone: 202-225-1688; Fax: 202-225-9903; E-mail: ask.gene@mail.house.gov.

www.house.gov/green/

EDDIE BERNICE JOHNSON (D-30th) (b. 1935); 4th Term; Phone: 202-225-8885; Fax: 202-226-1477; E-mail: rep.e.b.johnson@mail.house.gov.

www.house.gov/ebjohnson/

TWENTIETH CENTURY GOVERNORS

SAYERS, JOSEPH D. (1841-1929), twenty-first Governor of Texas (1899-1903), was born in Grenada, Mississippi, the son of Mary Peete and David Sayers. His father, a physician, moved to Texas in 1851 and settled the family in Bastrop County. Joseph studied at the Bastrop Military Institute, but his studies were interrupted when the Civil War broke out and he joined the Confederate Army. He taught school for a while after the defeat, and studied law so that he was admitted to the bar in 1866.

In 1873, Sayers was elected to the State Senate, and in 1875-78 he served as chair of the Democratic State Executive Committee. In 1879, he was elected lieutenant Governor and then was elected to U.S. Congress in 1885. After several terms, Sayers was elected Governor of Texas in 1898. He was considered well-versed in Texas history as well as its economy and agriculture, but he was not prepared for the natural disasters that plagued his two terms of office. A State penitentiary was destroyed by fire in 1899, and floods damaged large areas of the State later in the year, most especially Galveston.

Sayers was respected for his support of higher education in the State. After his terms as Governor, Sayers defended the Univer-

sity of Texas as a regent against Governor James Ferguson. Sayers continued to practice law and was chair of the Industrial Accident Board of Texas in 1922-26. He was on the State Board of Legal Examiners at the time of his death at San Antonio in 1929.

LANHAM, SAMUEL W.T. (1846-1908), twenty-second Governor of Texas (1903-07), was born in Spartanburg, South Carolina to Louisa Tucker and James M. Lanham. He studied at public schools until the Civil War interrupted his education, when he signed with the Third South Carolina regiment.

After the war, Lanham moved to Texas and began to study law and teach school. He was admitted to the Texas bar in 1869 and opened an office in Red River County. In 1883, he was elected to the U.S. House of Representatives, and served until 1893, and again in 1897-1903. He left Washington to become Governor of Texas, the last Civil War veteran to take that seat.

Lanham was concerned with the State election codes of the time, and he helped lay the foundation for Texas' present election laws during his administration, providing for primary elections and filing of candidates' campaign expenditures, among other measures. A major oil field was unplugged while Lanham was Governor, and so he witnessed the birth of Texas' future economy.

After his second term, Lanham retired to Weathertop, Texas, where he died in 1908. He was married to Sarah Meng and had five children.

CAMPBELL, THOMAS MITCHELL (1856-1923), twenty-third Governor of Texas (1907-11), was born in Rusk, Texas. He was the second Governor who was a native Texan. His parents were Rachel Moore and Thomas Duncan Campbell. After studying at local public schools, he attended the Rusk Masonic Institute and the Trinity University at Tehuacana.

Campbell began work at the county clerk's office at Longview, and studied law at night until he was admitted to the bar in 1878. He was soon regarded as one of the top lawyers in the growing State, and in 1889 was appointed master in chancery in an International and Great Northern Railroad Company receivership case. In 1891, the rail company hired him as its private counsel, and two years later he was manager of the improved railroad.

Campbell resumed his law practice at Palestine in 1897, and became increasingly active in Democratic Party activities. It wasn't until 1907, however, that he ran for public office. He was elected Governor by a healthy margin and immediately undertook reform measures in Texas government.

Campbell's bold and progressive policies woke the opposition of certain wealthy and influential businessmen. However, he saw that immense corporate properties were wholly escaping taxation, so he helped institute a new gross receipts law and an intangible assets law to bring more money into the depleted State budget. Funds were then provided to keep public schools open for at least six months out of the year, and money went to improve all educational facilities in the State. Instead of crippling legitimate enterprises and preventing an influx of capital and population, as many had predicted, business became more prosperous than ever before.

Campbell also created new State departments to deal with the new issues and problems of the booming State. Departments of insurance and banking, agriculture, labor, taxes, and libraries were instituted. He also insured that leasing of prisoners would no longer be allowed in Texas. The Governor tried to bring about many other reforms, such as the simplification of the court procedure and cheaper railroad fares, but was prevented by strong business and government opposition.

Campbell won easily in 1908 for a second term, and continued working on reforms. He moved back to Palestine, Texas in 1911, and never held elective office again, although he tried in 1916 for a U.S. Senate seat. He was on the Exemption Board during World War I. Campbell died in Galveston in 1923, and was buried in his hometown.

COLQUITT, OSCAR B. (1861-1940), twenty-fourth Governor of Texas (1911-15), was born in Camilla, Georgia, the son of Ann Burkhalter and Thomas J. Colquitt. He lived on the family plantation until his father went bankrupt in 1878, and moved the family to Texas to work as tenant farmers. He then worked as a railroad station porter and later turned it into a furniture factory.

Colquitt attended public school in Daingerfield, Texas, and a private academy in town. After deciding to learn the printer's trade, Colquitt obtained a job at the Morris County *Banner* newspaper. In 1884, he founded his own paper, the Pittsburg (Texas) *Gazette*. Two years later, he sold this paper to a younger brother and purchased the Terrell (Texas) *Star*. During these years in journalism, he also had a share in establishing the first cottonseed mill in Texas, erected at Pittsburgh in 1885. In 1888 he founded the First National flank of Terrell.

Colquitt's interest in politics was stimulated by his editorial work, and in 1890 he was made chair of the Kaufman County Democratic organization. He was elected to the State Senate in 1895, and was a State Revenue Agent for eight months in 1898. In 1899-1900, after his Senate term was up, he was on the State Tax Commission. He had sold his newspaper in 1897 and became active in oil development in the Corsicana area.

In 1902, Colquitt was elected to the State Railroad Commission; he was reelected in 1908. His reorganization of the State transportation system led to his election as Governor, Colquitt continued the reforms initiated by Campbell in the State prison system. He refused to submit the question of prohibition to the Legislature, and brought the wrath of the Methodist church on himself. There was also strong opposition to his support of Germany in the early stages of World War I. However, he was reelected in 1912.

In his second term, Colquitt approved a parole system and created a Bureau of Child and Animal Protection. He was forced to call out the Texas National Guard on several occasions to patrol the Mexican border as the Revolution erupted there. He left Austin to try to win a U.S. Senate seat, but was unsuccessful. He resumed his oil business and worked his farm near Dallas.

In 1928, Colquitt headed the anti-Smith faction of the Democratic Party in Texas, and was President Hoover's appointee to the U.S. Board of Mediation, where he served until 1933. After that, he was a member of the railway division of the Reconstruction Finance Corporation, holding that post until he died in Dallas in 1940.

FERGUSON, JAMES E. (1871-1944), twenty-fifth Governor of Texas (1915-17), was born in Temple, Bell County, Texas on his family's farm. His parents were Fannie Fitzpatrick and James Edward Ferguson, who operated a gristmill on Salado Creek. He was only four years old when his father died, so he was not able to receive a formal education.

When Ferguson was sixteen, he left home to travel west, looking for work. He was a grape picker in California, a teamster on some large ranches, and a placer miner in the Rocky Mountains. He also worked in a San Francisco wire factory and as a lumber cutter in Washington State before returning to Texas to work on construction of bridges. He also began to farm and study law. He was admitted to the bar in 1897. He opened an office in Belton,

Texas, and opened a small bank there as well. In Temple, Texas he organized another bank, which evolved into a major institution.

Ferguson was campaign manager for R.L. Henry in 1902, and for R.V. Davidson in 1910. When he ran for Governor in 1914 on an anti-prohibition platform, he won by one of the greatest majorities ever received by a gubernatorial candidate in Texas. He pushed for State aid to common schools and compulsory education in the State. He was reelected in 1916, but his popularity had waned. He was accused of misuse of State funds, although the charges were acquitted.

Ferguson continued to raise a public storm when he attacked the University of Texas; he disliked several of the school's faculty members, and demanded their discharge. When university officials refused to do so, he tried to stop funding to the school. As a result, his opponents brought new charges against him, one of embezzlement of State funds. When he called a special session of the Legislature to deal with the University of Texas, the meeting turned instead to a call for Ferguson's impeachment.

Rather than waiting to be fired, Ferguson resigned his office, calling the proceedings against him a "kangaroo court." He tried again for the Governorship in 1918, but his reputation had fallen greatly. He ran for President on the Know-Nothing ticket in 1920, and took a last stab at gaining political office in 1922 for U.S. Senator. After that, he concentrated on his wife's career, and helped her win the 1924 and 1932 gubernatorial elections. The two retired in 1940, at Austin, where he lived until his death there in 1944.

HOBBY, WILLIAM P. (1878-1964), twenty-sixth Governor of Texas (1917-21), was born in Moscow, Texas, the son of Eudora Pettus and Edwin F. Hobby. He attended Houston High School and studied with private tutors until he was seventeen and became a reporter with the Houston *Post*. In 1905, he was made managing editor of that newspaper; two years later, he owned two papers himself in Beaumont, which he managed until 1930. In 1916-17, he was director of the Federal Land flank of Houston.

Early on, Hobby became an active Democrat; he was elected lieutenant Governor under James Ferguson in 1914 and 1916. When Ferguson resigned, Hobby automatically became Governor. He was elected in his own right in 1918 for a full term.

As war Governor of Texas, Hobby immediately enacted special military measures to support the federal government. He was forced to declare martial law and occupy the port of Galveston when strikers kept freighters from unloading there. He also provided for relief of drought victims in western Texas as well as those whose possessions were lost in hurricanes in Corpus Christi. He approved spending limits on political campaigns and increased the State highways budget.

Hobby left office to become president of the Houston *Post*, and in 1924 brought about a merger between that paper and the *Dispatch*. He also built up the circulation from 35,855 in 1921 to 155,317 in 1946. In 1939, he and his wife, Oveta Culp Hobby purchased the *Post-Dispatch*, He also continued his ownership of the Beaumont papers until 1930. In the 1950s he acquired Houston's KPRC radio station as well as KPRC-TV. Hobby died and was buried in his hometown in 1964.

NEFF, PAT M. (1871-1952), twenty-seventh Governor of Texas (1921-25), was born in McGregor, Texas, the son of Isabel Shepherd and Noah Neff, ranchers. He attended public school in Eagle Springs and then graduated from Baylor University in 1894. He received his M.A. in 1898.

The University of Texas granted Neff an L.L.B. degree in 1897, and soon he was admitted to the bar and was practicing law at Waco. He was elected to the State Legislature in 1901 and in 1903 became Speaker of the House. He was county attorney in McLennan County in 1906-12, trying over 400 cases. He was the first prosecutor in Texas to convict a man for allowing gambling and drinking in a prohibition area.

A Democrat, Neff was elected Governor after defeating political strongman Joseph Baily in the primary. He founded the Texas Technological College, now Texas Tech. University and the South Texas State Teachers College, now Texas A & M University. In 1924, he set up the planning for Texas' Centennial Celebration, twelve years in advance of the event. He also abolished the Texas State Pardon Board. Riotous railroad strikes caused Neff to call martial law to Mexia as well as Limestone and Freestone Counties.

Neff resumed his private law practice in 1925. Two years later, President Coolidge appointed him to the National Board of Mediation. He was also on the Texas Railroad Commission in 1929-31. In 1932-47, Neff was President of Baylor University. He died of a heart attack in Waco in 1962.

FERGUSON, MIRIAM A. (1875-1961), twenty-eighth and thirty-first Governor of Texas (1925-27 and 1933-35), was a native of Bell County Texas, the daughter of Eliza Garrison and Joseph L. Wallace. She was educated at Salado (Texas) College and at Baylor College for Women. She gained recognition when her husband became Governor, and even more so after he was nearly impeached. He resigned instead, and Mrs. "Ma" Ferguson defended him in the next election, but to no avail.

In 1924, failing to get her husband's name on the ballot, Ferguson entered the contest herself. She was elected easily, becoming the first woman Governor of Texas, and the second woman Governor in U.S. history. Her platform was anti-Ku Klux Klan, and one of her most important actions was to pass a law prohibiting the wearing of masks in public. She also succeeded in balancing the budget, and sought enforcement of the State liquor law, being a staunch prohibitionist.

Ferguson differed from her husband in that she favored large appropriations for the University of Texas and all other State educational institutions. She also granted large numbers of paroles, pardons, and proclamations of clemency during her term, which gave her a kindly reputation. However, her husband's shadow followed her, and charges were soon made against her administration's use of funds. Political considerations, including underlying trouble of the division of gubernatorial authority between an elected wife and her husband, and the influence of the Ku Klux Klan, led to her declining popularity.

Ferguson lost her re-nomination for Governor in 1926, and returned to political actions to clear her husband's reputation. However, Miriam was the favored Ferguson, and deep into the Great Depression, Texas voters returned to her again. Her second term was quiet; she maintained a conservative fiscal policy and continued to grant reprieves to worthy prisoners, going as far as to commute the sentences of several persons on Death Row.

Ferguson did not seek reelection in 1934, but retired for a time in Austin, She did attempt a third term in 1940, but was defeated by W. Lee Daniel. When her husband died, Mrs. Ferguson lived privately in Austin until her death of a heart attack in 1961. She was buried next to her husband. She was married to James E. Ferguson; the couple had two daughters.

MOODY, DANIEL (1893-1966), twenty-ninth Governor of Texas (1927-31), was a native of Taylor, Texas, and the son of Nannie Robertson and Daniel Moody; his father was first mayor of Taylor He attended the local high school before being admitted

to the University of Texas. After graduation from the University in 1914, with a degree in law, he opened his own law office in Taylor in partnership with Harris Melasky.

When World War I broke out, Moody volunteered for service with the aviation section of the Army. He was commissioned second lieutenant with the Texas National Guard instead, and was stationed at Camp Pike, Arkansas. After the war, he worked as an attorney in Taylor, and in 1920 was named County Attorney for Williamson County. In 1922-25, he was the District Attorney in his region, and in 1925 he was elected Attorney General of Texas. In that office, he conducted an investigation of Governor James Ferguson, which resulted in a recovery of over one million dollars from two contractors. He also defended Texas in boundary disputes with neighboring states at the U.S. Supreme Court.

In 1926, Moody defeated incumbent Miriam Ferguson, and in 1927 he was the youngest person ever to assume Texas Governorship. He concentrated on reforms during his term; he approved a process of auditing State budgets, and reorganized the highway system and prison administration in the State. He was reelected for a second term, in which he proved to be one of the most progressive Governors in Texas history.

Moody did not try for a third term, but returned to law at an office in Austin. He wanted to prevent Texas from repealing prohibition, but was unsuccessful, He was a special assistant to the U.S. Attorney General in the mid-1930s, but was never again an elected official. In 1948, he was not able to keep Lyndon B. Johnson off the Texas senatorial ballot, although the primary elections were questionable.

Moody lived in Austin until his death there in 1966. He was married to Mildred Paxton.

STERLING, ROSS S. (1875-1949), thirtieth Governor of Texas (1931-1933), was born in Anahuac, Texas to Mary Jane Bryan and Benjamin Franklin Sterling. He attended local public schools home and worked on the family farm. After 1896, he entered his own business, freighting produce from the farm area to Galveston, Texas. He also owned a general store in Chambers County, and soon had a chain of feed stores in several rural towns.

Sterling established a bank in Batso and soon became interested in the new oil fields. In 1910, he founded Humble Oil and Refining Company with two flowing wells. He built the Dayton-Goose Creek Railroad in 1917, and after 1925 he was active in real estate development as well as newspapers in Houston. In 1926 in Houston he built the *Post-Dispatch* building, where he also housed the first radio station there, KPRC. That building became the Shell Building in 1930.

In 1927, Sterling was appointed chair of the State Highway Commission, where he did much to take politics out of the department. He campaigned for good roads in 1930, and was elected Governor by a large majority. The Depression had hit, and he provided a relief fund for the unemployed as well as a new child welfare board. In order to control oil production, Sterling invoked martial law in East Texas for six months. He also sought to decrease the amount of cotton grown in order to increase prices.

Sterling lost his bid for renomination in 1932. He returned to his own oil business, the Sterling Oil and Refining Corporation, and was chairman of the board from 1946 until his death. In his lifetime, he was also president of American Maid Flour Mills and an investment company, as well as chairman of the board of the Houston National Bank. He died in Fort Worth, Texas in 1949.

ALLRED, JAMES V. (1889-1959), thirty-second Governor of Texas (193 5-39), was born in Bowie, Texas, the son of Mary Hinson and Renne Allred. He attended public school, and received an L.L.B. from Cumberland University in 1921, after a brief term at the Rice Institute, He joined the U.S. Navy during World War I, but returned to his hometown to practice law after the War.

Allred was elected district attorney for his area in 1923, and then returned to a private practice in 1926. Five years later, he was elected Attorney General of Texas. When Governor Ferguson decided not to run for a third term, he was easily nominated and elected to her seat.

Allred took office in January 1935, at a time when the Depression had already wrought large changes in the State government. Voters and the Legislature continued to approve new programs to help the needy, including unemployment insurance, old age assistance, and farm relief; however, no new taxes were approved. Twelve new boards and commissions had been created to carry out the relief programs, but no new money was coming in to meet continued payments.

When Allred sought reelection in 1936, pensions and taxes were the key issues of the day, and the Governor advocated pensions only for elderly persons who really needed it, while asking for few new taxes. A large majority reelected him. However, he was forced to appeal to the Legislature for additional revenue. The lawmakers refused to raise taxes on oil, gas, and sulfur, and they repealed a law allowing betting on horseracing, which had been a rich source of revenue since 1933. However, liquor taxes helped the State make its pension obligations, and the Federal government provided some assistance. In 1936, he presided over the Texas centennial celebrations, which were held at Dallas and various historical places in the State.

After Allred left office, he was appointed by President Roosevelt to become a federal district judge. He resigned in 1942 when he ran for U.S. Senator, but was unsuccessful. President Truman reappointed Allred to his former judgeship in 1949, and he served there until his death in 1959. His grave is in Wichita Falls.

O'DANIEL, WILBER LEE (1890-1969), thirty-third Governor of Texas (1939-41), was born in Malta, Ohio to Alice Thompson and William Barnes O'Daniel. He attended public schools after the family moved to Arlington, Kansas, and he studied at a business college in Hutchinson.

O'Daniel became involved with a flour-milling company, eventually rising to executive levels. He was most known for his radio work in Texas; he gave a noontime music and humor show with the "Light Crust Doughboys." Although this may have been a ploy to sell more of his company's flour, his humor and down-home advice brought in many listeners in Texas. He also wrote "Beautiful Texas," now the State song.

Although O'Daniel was not an active politician, he entered the Democratic primary for Governor in 1938. Soon, people took notice of his promises of better old-age pensions and an accessible administration. O'Daniel did retain his "down-home" demeanor in office but wasn't able to increase in old-age funds. His inexperience in government made him less than effectual at times. However, he had strong support from the public, who saw him as someone who had beaten the odds and defied the powerful rich.

O'Daniel's reputation as a shrewd businessman and a good actor gained him favor by the voters, and he was reelected by a large majority in 1940. When Morris Sheppard died and his U.S. Senate seat was empty, O'Daniel successfully ran to take his place. He resigned the Governorship in August 1941.

After a second Senate term that ended in 1949, O'Daniel returned to Austin and remained a public figure despite his failure to win the Governor's seat in 1956 and 1958. He died at Austin in 1969.

STEVENSON, COKE R. (1888-1975), thirty-fourth Governor of Texas (1941-47), was born in Mason County Texas on a farm. His parents were Virginia Hurley and Robert Milton Stevenson; his father was the county surveyor. He received no formal education, but worked on ranches until 1904 and drove a freight team until 1906. Then he moved to Junction, Texas to work as a cashier at the First State Bank. In the meantime, he studied law and was admitted to the Texas bar in 1913.

In 1914, Stevenson resigned from his bank work and began a position as county attorney of Kimble County. In 1918-21 he was county judge there, and gained a reputation for fairness. He returned to Junction and became president of the First National Bank in 1921, serving until his campaign for the State Legislature in 1927. He served in 1928-38, representing his district in Austin, and in 1933-37 was Speaker of the House.

Stevenson was elected lieutenant Governor under O'Daniel in 1938, and served in that capacity until the Governor resigned to take a seat on the U.S. Senate. Stevenson immediately took over his duties, and the next year won the office in his own right without opposition. He was a conservative Democrat who believed in keeping State spending down; this fact, combined with the new abundance after World War II, led to a surplus in the State budget. Some of these funds were turned over to the State highway system as well as the State colleges and universities. Stevenson was reelected in 1944, but did not try for another term and left office after serving the longest amount of time of any Texas Governor.

Stevenson managed his ranch near Junction afterwards, and held no other elective office. He did try for U.S. Senator in 1948, but lost by a disputed eighty votes against Lyndon B. Johnson. He died in San Angelo in 1975 and was buried on his ranch.

JESTER, BEAUFORT H. (1893-1949), thirty-fifth Governor of Texas (1947-49), was born in Corsicana, Texas, the son of Frances Gordon and George Taylor Jester. He attended public schools in town, and in 1916 finished his education at the University of Texas. He served as a captain with the U.S. Army for a time before attending law school (L.L.B., 1920).

Jester opened a general practice in Corsicana in 1920, and eventually represented large Texas oil companies in the region. He also served on the Board of Regents of the University of Texas after 1929. By 1940, he was prominent enough to become the director of the State Bar Association.

Jester was elected to the State Railroad Commission in 1942, remaining in that position until he became a candidate for Governor in 1946.

Once elected, Jester maintained the conservative attitude against new taxes. However, the economy was on his side, and he was able to approve more funding for State hospitals and other public institutions with the excess money. He also advocated some new regulations on labor unions, and generally opposed New Deal programs and approaches. He approved the founding of a Texas university for Blacks, and reorganized public education, with a new Youth Development Council for mobilizing and coordinating services for the young.

Jester easily won in the 1948 election, but was unable to fill out his term; he died while traveling to Galveston in July 1949.

SHIVERS, ALLAN (1907-1985), thirty-sixth Governor of Texas (1949-57), was born in Lufkin, Texas, the son of Easter Creasy and Robert Andrew Shivers. He attended public schools in Woodville and Port Arthur, Texas, and completed his studies at the University of Texas in 1931 with an A.B. degree, and in 1933 with an L.L.B. He supported his education by working as a shoe salesman.

Once admitted to the bar, Shivers joined his father's firm in Port Arthur. He joined in partnership with other lawyers from 1935 on. In 1934, he was elected to the Texas Senate and was reelected twice. In that seat, he supported old age pensions, and wrote the law that extended the Texas boundary for twenty-seven miles into the Gulf of Mexico. He served in the U.S. Army in 1943-45, seeing conflicts in North Africa, Italy, France and Germany, before leaving with the rank of major.

Shivers was elected lieutenant Governor in 1946, and when Governor Jester died during his second term, Shivers automatically stepped up to carry his duties. He called for new taxes to pay for the increasing demand for services in the State. For example, facilities for the mentally ill were so inadequate that some patients were housed in jails. More taxes were added in 1951, as the budget grew more complex.

Shivers also faced declining revenue when the Federal government declared the Gulf Coast tidelands belonged to the U.S. rather than Texas. These lands had been under lease for oil and gas development, and President Truman vetoed a Congressional bill giving the State the right to lease them in 1946. This issue was one of the most important of Shivers' administration, and it wasn't until 1953 that the lands were restored to Texas.

Although many opposed the new taxes on gasoline as well as the Governor's program to require safety inspections of cars, Shivers was reelected to serve three full terms. In his last administration, Shivers endorsed a new Commission on Higher Education. He also supported twenty-seven new regulatory laws on the State budget in 1955.

Shivers left office in 1957 and continued his alliance with John H. Shary Enterprises in Mission, Texas, with concerns in agriculture, cattle, banking, real estate, and publishing of the *Mission Times*. He was married to the former Marialice Shary.

Shivers died on January 14, 1985.

DANIEL, MARION PRICE (1910-1988), thirty-seventh Governor of Texas (1957-63), was born in Dayton, Texas, the son of Nannie Partlow and Marion Price Daniels. He studied at public schools at Liberty and Fort Worth, Texas before entering Baylor University. There he received his A.B. in 1931 and his L.L.B. in 1932. He also worked at the Fort Worth *Star-Telegram* as a reporter for a year, and for the Waco *News Tribune* for two years while he was a student.

Once admitted to the bar in 1932, Daniel he left journalism to work as a lawyer in Liberty. In 1938, he was elected to the State Legislature, becoming Speaker of the House in 1943. Soon afterwards, however, he joined the Army to serve in World War II; he enlisted as a private, but was made a captain before his discharge in 1946.

In November 1946, Daniel was elected attorney general of Texas, and soon after moved to Austin. In that position, he succeeded in prosecuting gambling wire service operators and major drug dealers. He also defended the State during the Texas tidelands controversy with the federal government. He published such essays as "Texas Ownership of Submerged Lands," and "Ownership of the Continental Shelf," which made him an expert on legal rights to tidelands.

In 1953, Daniel took his elected seat on the U.S. Senate, where he served until taking office as Governor in 1957. He was a member of the Interstate and Foreign Commerce Committee as well as the Judiciary Committee in the Senate, and continued his fight for Texas rights to lease offshore lands. As Governor, Daniel supported water conservation and irrigation projects; more than forty dams and reservoirs were built during his six-year term. He also signed bills appropriating more money to both elementary and higher education. He created the Texas Youth Council and a Texas Law Enforcement Commission, and encouraged more controls on lobbyists and insurance companies in the State.

During the third term, Daniel approved a State sales tax to offset the costs of all of his new projects. He lost in his attempt for a fourth term in 1962, and returned to his law practice, this time in Austin. After 1971, he was a justice on the Texas Supreme Court, and made his home in Liberty, Texas.

Daniel died on August 25, 1988.

CONNALLY, JOHN BOWDEN (1917-1993), thirty-eighth Governor of Texas (1963-69), was born in son of Lila Wright and John Bowden Connally. His beginnings were poor, but he helped build the family ranch into an 8,000-acre cattle operation that afterward made him a multimillionaire.

Connally graduated from the University of Texas in 1941. He received a law degree and practiced in his hometown until he became president and general manager of KVET Radio in Austin. Senator Lyndon B. Johnson hired him as an assistant in 1949, and at the same time he joined a law partnership in Austin. Oilmen Sid Richardson and Perry Bass hired him as their personal attorney in 1952, where he learned a great deal about making money. He left their Fort Worth operation in 1961 to become President John F. Kennedy's Secretary of the Navy. That position only lasted eleven months, however, since he was elected Governor of Texas in 1962.

Although he was a Democrat, Connally vowed to cut back on funding for the aged, poor, and education. He also promised to cut the State budget by ten percent. However, by the end of his terms, the State budget had increased by sixty-three percent. He also hired more women and minorities than any previous Governor, and reformed the State penal code.

In 1963, Connally was wounded at the scene of President John F. Kennedy's assassination, which heightened voter sympathy in the next election. The Governor continued to increase support for welfare programs in the State, despite his vocal opposition to it. He also created a Texas Tourist Bureau, which helped begin a large immigration to the State.

Connally was elected to two more terms, but declined a fourth. He then joined a law firm in Houston, where he worked for two years until his appointment as President Richard M. Nixon's Secretary of Defense. In 1973, he was made a special advisor to the President. The same year, he switched parties to become a Republican. Before Nixon resigned, Connally returned to Houston to work at his former law firm.

In July 1974, Connally was indicted by a Watergate jury for taking 10,000 dollars from the Associated Milk Producers, Inc., the largest U.S. dairy cooperative, and for covering up the crime, He was acquitted of all charges in 1975, however, and returned to his Houston law office. In 1979, he announced his candidacy for U.S. President, but lost in the Republican primary to Ronald Reagan.

Connally continued to reside in Houston, but visited his Floresville ranch from time to time. He was married to Idanell Brill in 1941; the couple has three children.

Connally died on June 15, 1993.

SMITH, PRESTON (1912-), thirty-ninth Governor of Texas (1969-73), was born in Williamson County, Texas, the son of Effie Mae Strickland and Charles Kirby Smith. He attended local schools before studying at Texas Technological College, graduating with a B.S. in 1934. He also operated a movie theater in his hometown.

Smith become active in the Democratic Party, and was elected to the Texas Legislature in 1944, serving three terms. In 1957, he was elected to the Texas Senate. At the side of John Connally, Smith was then elected lieutenant Governor in 1962, and when Connally declined to run again in 1968, he was able to win by a substantial majority to take his place.

Although there was a growing Republican movement in the State, and the Legislature was sympathetic to business and finance, Smith supported a State minimum wage, and signed appropriations for more vocational training for the poor.

Smith won a second term, but soon after beginning it, rumors of his involvement in a stock fraud caused a major scandal. The "Sharpstown Affair," named for the town bank that was the location of the dealings, led to the allegation that high-ranking State officials had profited by illegal stock transactions. It was disclosed that among others, Governor Smith and his friend Gus Mutscher (Speaker of the House) had amassed profits totaling more than 300,000 dollars. Although he was not impeached or convicted, Smith wasn't reelected for the next term; in fact, most of the incumbents in the 1972 election were not reelected.

Smith returned to his home in Lubbock and continued his business interests there. He was married to Ima Mae Smith; the couple has two children.

BRISCOE, DOLPH (1923-), fortieth Governor of Texas (1973-79), was born in Uvalde, Texas, the son of Georgie and Dolph Sr. Briscoe; his mother was his father's cousin, and had the same last name. He attended public school in town, and then studied at the University of Texas, graduating with an A.B. in 1942. He was an army officer during World War II, and then returned to his home area to work on the family ranch.

Briscoe was voted Outstanding Conservation Rancher of Texas in 1958, He was soon one of the wealthiest ranchers in South Texas, and represented his district in the State Legislature for many years (1949-57). He was an active Democrat, but didn't hold another elected office until he ran against incumbent Governor Smith in 1972. However, he defeated the Republican candidate by only 100,000 votes, or forty-seven percent of the total vote.

Briscoe was an innocuous Governor, which was a relief after the turmoil of Smith's term. He was able to befriend minority groups and labor leaders as well as the rich ranchers and oil company executives in Texas. He brought no new taxes, and supported strong law enforcement, school finances, but did not support the movement for a constitutional convention at that time.

Briscoe was reelected in 1974, this time for a four-year term under the new Constitution. He was not the Democratic candidate in the next election, however. Briscoe subsequently returned to his ranch.

CLEMENTS, WILLIAM P. (1917-), forty-first and forty-third Governor of Texas (1979-1982 and 1987-1990), was born in Dallas, Texas on April 13, 1917. He studied at Southern Methodist University, and after his 1937 graduation, began working as a roughneck and driller in the oil fields of northeast Texas. He gained experience on the rigs, and within ten years, he had the capital to found SEDCO, an offshore drilling platform company that eventually became very successful and made Clements a multimillionaire.

In Democratically dominated Texas, Clements became active in the Republican Party. He was a conservative with a growing income from SEDCO and other involvement with various Texas banks and the Keebler Company. He was also active in the Boy Scouts of America, eventually becoming president of the Circle

Ten Council, and later a member of the National Executive Board of that organization. From 1965 to 1973, he was chairman of the Board of Governors of Southern Methodist University.

Clements' involvement with the Republicans earned him a good reputation within the party, and in 1973, President Gerald Ford named him a Deputy Secretary of Defense, one of the highest-level jobs in Washington. He served four years, receiving a Department of Defense Medal for Distinguished Public Service in 1975, and a Bronze Palm award from the President in 1976. These successes made elements a well-known figure in Texas.

After his term in Washington, Clements began to consider running for Governor. With a large amount of confidence and money (seven million dollars went into his campaign), he won over Democratic favorite, John Hill, in 1978, the first Republican to do so since the Reconstruction. This did much to encourage growth of the Republicans in the State, which was especially evident in 1980, when a fellow southerner, Jimmy Carter, was defeated by the Texans in favor of Republican, Ronald Reagan.

During the 1982 gubernatorial campaign, however, Clements' somewhat abrasive personal style caused many people to become unhappy with him on what became known as the "meanness issue." He described his opponent, Democrat Mark White, as a "bumbling incompetent," and even went so far as to bring up the issue of White's twenty-year old drunk driving arrest. It was a decision that backfired; White took full advantage of Clements' unpopular rancorous image, along with the latter's inability to fulfill all of his campaign promises. Since Clements couldn't have predicted that the recession or falling oil prices would hit Texas as hard as they did, White was able to point out his failings as a leader, and Clements lost the election forty-six percent to fifty-four percent.

Upon his return to civilian life, Clements once again headed his oil drilling equipment company and at the request of President Reagan, served on two national commissions. In the 1986 gubernatorial race, Governor White was the one brought down by the dire economic woes that had befallen Texas. In addition, White infuriated many people when he created and pushed through bills to ban failing students from joining high school sports teams, and required that teachers take competency tests. Due to these factors, Clements was able to reclaim the Governor's chair, winning the election fifty-three percent to forty-six percent.

Soon after Clements' second victory, along with the almost impossible task of trying to balance the State budget, he had to confront personal scandal when it was revealed that while he had served as chairman of the Southern Methodist University Board of Governors, he and other board members had allowed student athletes to receive money to which they were not entitled.

Clements left gubernatorial office at the end of his term. He is married to the former Rita Crocker; the couple has two children.

WHITE, MARK (1940-), forty-second Governor of Texas (1983-1987), was born on March 17, 1940 in Henderson, Texas. He attended Baylor University, where he received a business administration degree in 1961, then went on to take his law degree in 1965.

White aligned himself with the Democratic Party, and began serving as assistant attorney general of the State's Insurance, Banking and Securities Division. While in this post, he was overseer of the State's very first consumer protection cases. He subsequently served as a member of the Houston law firm of Reynolds, Allen and Cook for four years, after which, in 1973, Governor Dolph Briscoe appointed him to serve as Secretary of State. While in that position, White was in charge of the first State-supported voter registration drive, and by 1976, a record 6.3

million voters were registered. In addition, he encouraged free-flowing information between State agencies with the creation of the *Texas Registrar*, and also established a twenty-four hour toll-free telephone operation so that the public could get information on several State government departments.

White's next State post was the elected office of attorney general, which he secured in 1978. While there, he introduced computerization into that division in order to streamline operations, and was also responsible for the increase of minorities and women in high State positions. In the 1982 gubernatorial race, White ran and won against combative Republican candidate William P. Clements, Jr., becoming the youngest person to win the Governorship in almost fifty years.

White faced several tough issues due to the runaway recession, and ultimately had to request a tax increase. In addition, while trying to push through major educational reform, the Governor ran into roadblocks. Along with angering a number of high school teachers by supporting mandatory teacher testing programs, he also he alienated rural Texans by implementing the "no pass, no play" law, which stipulated that failing high school students would not be allowed to play on any sports teams for a six-week period. However, he also reduced teachers' paperwork, raised their salaries, and put a limit on class sizes. His request for a tax increase in the same year he was running for reelection was "highly unpopular," and it contributed to his losing the race to his former nemesis, William Clements, Jr. with a margin of forty-six percent to 52.7 percent.

White is married to Linda Gale and the couple has three children.

RICHARDS, (DOROTHY) ANN (1933-),

forty-third governor of Texas (1991-1994), was born in Lakeview, Texas, the daughter of Ona and Cecil Willis. After graduating from Waco High School in 1950, she attended Baylor University, graduating in 1954 with a major in speech and a minor in political science. She attended graduate school and earned a teaching certificate from the University of Texas. In 1955, she began teaching social studies and history at Fulmore Junior College in Austin.

Richards' became involved in politics while raising her children; she worked on local and statewide campaigns, and supported civil rights and economic justice. In 1976, she earned a seat on the Travis County Commissioners Court, defeating a three-term incumbent; she held her seat for six years. In 1982, she entered the mace for State Treasurer, and became the first woman in more than fifty years to be elected to statewide office. She was reelected in 1986.

As State Treasurer, Richards overhauled the treasury's outdated methods and installed new technology; she also pioneered banking and investment practices that earned more non-tax revenue for taxpayers than all previous treasurers in the history of Texas. She delivered the Keynote Address at the Democratic National Convention in 1988.

Richards became Governor of Texas in the 1990 election, becoming the second woman in history to hold the office of the State's chief executive. (The first was Miriam M. Ferguson.) During her administration, she focused efforts on making State government accountable, accessible, efficient, and inclusive.

In 1993, Richards signed into law a seventy billion dollars budget without any new taxes, making it the lowest budget in the State in thirty years. She also gave strong support to measures against crime. Under her administration, the sentence was tripled for capital murders, early release for violent offenders was cut by two-thirds, and the Texas Penal Code was rewritten to assure that the State's most violent criminals remained behind bars. In an ef-

fort to stop the cycle of crime where it often begins—with drug and alcohol addiction—a prison substance abuse program for repeat offenders was also introduced, resulting in a decline in the crime rate in Texas for the first time in ten years.

Richards' efforts toward education included a site-based management program that allowed parents, teachers, students, and principals to work together in making their schools successful; results of this program included a fifty percent lower drop-out rate, SAT scores higher than they had been in fourteen years, and higher scores on standardized test scores.

Richards' creation of Capital For A Day program took State government out of Austin and into local communities to respond to citizens' concerns and provide on-site State services. She appointed more minorities and women to State posts than the previous two governors combined, and supported efforts to make health care more affordable and accessible by passing a Health Insurance Bill to provide better insurance for small businesses.

Richards stepped down from her gubernatorial position at the end of her term in January 1995, upon the election of Republican George W. Bush, son of former U.S. president, George Bush.

Richards was married to Dave Richards in 1953, The couple has four children. They were divorced in 1984.

BUSH, GEORGE W. (1946-),

forty-fourth Governor of Texas (1995-) was born in New Haven, Connecticut. He received his education at Yale University, earning a B.A. in history in 1968. He went on to complete a masters degree program in business administration at Harvard University in 1975.

Bush was a F-102 fighter pilot in the Texas Air National Guard from 1968-1973. In 1975, he founded and became CEO of Bush Exploration, a Midland-based oil and gas company. In 1983, the company merged with Spectrum 7 Energy Corporation. Bush ran the company until a second merge with Harken Energy Company in 1987.

In 1989, Bush's interest in baseball led him to form a partnership to purchase the Texas Rangers from late owner, Eddie Chiles. As a general partner in the organization, he was instrumental in bringing together the Rangers and the city of Arlington to build a new home for the Rangers, The Ballpark in Arlington.

Bush was nominated for U.S. Congress in 1978, but lost in the general election. He was the Republican nominee for Governor of Texas in 1994, and won in the November 1994 election against incumbent Democrat, Ann Richards. He campaigned on the issues of constructive changes in education, juvenile and criminal justice, and welfare.

Bush is the son of former U.S. President George Bush. In November, 2000, after an historical vote count George W. Bush was elected president of the United States. He is married to the former Laura Welsh. The couple has two children.

DICTIONARY OF PLACES

Population figures and demographic information are official U.S. Census Bureau finals for 1990. When two figures are shown, separated by a slash, the first figure is the 1990 and the second is the U.S. Census Bureau 1999 estimate—the most recent available. Year 2000 census supplements will be available in the Fall of 2001.

ABERNATHY, City; Hale & Lubbock Counties; Pop. 2,904 / 2,771; Zip Code 79311; NW Texas; 19 mi. N of Lubbock.

ABILENE, City; Jones & Taylor Counties; Taylor County Seat; Pop. 98,315 / 108,995; Elev. 1,179; NW central Texas; 150 mi. W of Fort Worth; was named for Abilene, Kansas.

ACAMPO, Village; Shackelford County; N central Texas; Mexican icon immigrants worked on the Missouri, Kansas and Texas Railroad here, and lived in temporary housing known as Acampos. This stock loading station was then named for these shacks.

ADDISON, Town; Dallas County; Pop. 5,506 / 12,320; Zip Code 75001; N suburb of Dallas. Town population has risen 10 times during the 1970s.

ALAMO, City; Hidalgo County; Pop. 5,810 / 12,600; Zip Code 78516; S Texas; 10 mi. E of McAllen. The town was first known as Ebenezer in 1909, when a town was settled here by the Alamo Land and Sugar Company. Later named Swallow but was changed to honor the shrine of Texas Liberty in San Antonio, Alamo is a Spanish word meaning "cottonweed tree."

ALAMO HEIGHTS, City; Bexar County; Pop. 6,243 / 6,851; Zip Code 782+; S central Texas; N residential suburb of San Antonio.

ALBA, Town; Rains & Wood Counties; Pop. 568 / 554; Zip Code 75410; NE Texas; 65 mi. E of Dallas. The town's name means "white" in Latin, which indicates the policy of the early, post-Civil War settlement here which did not admit blacks within its limits.

ALBANY, City; Shackelford County Seat; Pop. 2,453 / 1,841; Zip Code 76430; Elev. 1,429; N central Texas; 35 mi. NE of Abilene. Named for Albany, New York, this city was an early supply point on the Western Trail to Dodge City.

ALEDO, City; Parker County; Pop. 1,028 / 1,893; Zip Code 76008; N Texas; 15 mi. W of Fort Worth.

ALICE, City; Jim Wells County Seat; Pop. 20,853 / 20,833; Zip Code 78332; Elev. 205; S Texas, 43 mi. W of Corpus Christi. The town was founded as a depot for the San Antonio and Aransas Pass Railroad in 1880. It was named for one of the founder's daughters of the King Ranch.

ALLEN, City; Collin County; Pop. 8,303 / 42,075; Zip Code 75002; NE Texas; 30 mi. NE of Dallas; suburban population has increased 800 percent in the 1970s.

ALLRED, Village; Yoakum County; NW Texas; 10 mi. E of New Mexico state line. James V. Allred was governor of Texas when this town was founded (1938) by a (Mr. Young) and his associates.

ALPINE, City; Brewster County Seat; Pop. 5,455 / 5,848; Zip Code 79830; Elev. 4,481; SW Texas. Cradled in a valley between towering mountains, Alpine was founded in 1882 with the coming of the railroad. Originally named Murphyville. Named after a random selection of the zip code directory by early townspeople who picked Alpine. Alabama. "Alpine" seemed apt to Walter Garnett because of the mountainous terrain here.

ALTO, Town; Cherokee County; Pop. 1,200 / 1,008; Zip Code 75925; Elev. 433; E Texas, 50 mi. S of Tyler; on a divide between the Neches and Angelina Rivers. The town's name is a Spanish word meaning "high," given by Captain Henry Berryman in 1849.

ALVARADO, City; Johnson County; Pop. 2,685 / 3,415; Zip Code 76009; N Texas, 28 mi. SW of Dallas.

ALVIN, City; Brazoria County; Pop. 16,110 / 20,551; Zip Code 77611; SE Texas, 25 mi. SE of Houston.

ALVORD, Town; Wise County; Pop. 862 / 1,110; Zip Code 76225; N Texas; 45 mi. NW of Fort Worth.

AMARILLO, City; Potter & Randall Counties; Potter County Seat; Pop. 149,230 / 171,959; Elev. 3,676; NW Texas, 320 mi. NW of Fort Worth. The selection of the name Amarillo (yellow) is said by some to have been due to the nearness of Amarillo Creek, named because of its yellow banks, while others insist that the name resulted from the yellow flowers that blanketed the prairies in spring. At any rate the name so pleased Sanborn who ran the hotel and several business houses, that he had them all painted a bright yellow.

ANAHUAC, City; Chambers County Seat; Pop. 1,860 / 2,062; Zip Code 77514; on Trinity Bay of Galveston Boy in SE Texas; the city is named for the Indian Aztec meaning "plain near the water." Past names Chambersia and Perry's Point (before 1870).

ANDREWS, City; Andrews County Seat; Pop. 11,010 / 10,182; Zip Code 79714; Lat. 32-19-2 N, Long. 102-32 8 W; NW Texas; named after Richard Andrews who was the first soldier to die in the Texas Revolution during the battle of Concepcion.

ANGLETON, City; Brazoria County Seat; Pop. 13,873 / 19,419; Zip Code 77515; SE Texas, 40 mi. S of Houston in a flat coastal wetlands area. Named for G.W. Angle an early developer.

ANTHONY, Town; El Paso County; Pop. 2,644 / 3,605; Zip Code 88021; Elev. 3,800; W Texas, 25 mi. NW of El Paso at New Mexico state line. Anthony was named for Saint Anthony of Paduo by a Spanish-speaking woman named Shrina who owned a chapel in the area. Originally named in 1881 *La Tuna*, meaning "prickly pear cactus" in Spanish.

ANTON, City; Hockley County; Pop. 1,187 / 1,125; Zip Code 79313; NW Texas, 25 mi. NW of Lubbock.

ARANSAS PASS, City; Aransas, Nueces & San Patricia Counties; Pop. 7,173 / 8,673; Zip Code 78336; Elev. 20; 27-59-1 N, Long. 97-09-0 W; S Texas.

ARCADIA, Village; Galveston County; Zip Code 77517; SE Texas, 20 mi. NW of Galveston. Named for the ancient region of Greece, poetically referred to as a tranquil wonderland.

ARCHER CITY, City; Archer County Seat; Pop. 1,859 / 1,741; Zip Code 76351; Elev. 1,041; N Texas, 30 mi. S of Wichita Falls.

ARLINGTON, City; Tarrant County; Pop. 161,192 / 311,962; Elev. 616; N Texas, 13 mi. E of Fort Worth in a residential-industrial suburban area.

ARTHUR CITY, Village; Lamar County; Zip Code 75411; Elev. 426; NE Texas, on Red River, lust S of Oklahoma, Arthur City is at or near the site of one of the French trading posts known to have been established on the Red River.

ASHERTON, City; Dimmit County; Pop. 1,637 / 1,504; Zip Code 78827; S Texas, 43 miles SE of Eagle Pass.

ASPERMONT, Town; Stonewall County Seat; Pop. 1,349 / 1,052; Zip Code 79502; Elev. 1,773; NW Texas; originally called Sunflower Flat by ranchers in the late 1880s. The site was donated by A.L. Rhomberg in 1889 and named it for its descriptive location "rough mountain" from the Latin.

ATHENS, City; Henderson County Seat; Pop. 10,085 11,733; Zip Code 75751; Elev. 490; NE Texas, 70 miles SE of Dallas. Originally named Alvin but later named in 1850 by Mrs. Dull Averitt for Athens, Greece because she thought Athens would be the cultural center of eastern Texas. Interestingly, the town is built on seven hills, as is the ancient Greek city. Some locals would argue that Mrs. Averitt named the town for her native Athens, Georgia. however.

ATLANTA, City; Cass County; Pop. 6,189 / 5,416; Zip Code 75551; Elev. 264; NE Texas, 25 mi. S of Texarkana. Established in 1872 with building of the Texas and Pacific Railroad; the town was named for Atlanta, Georgia by early settlers.

AUBREY, City; Denton County; Pop. 956 / 1,363; Zip Code 76227; N Texas; originally known as Omega, present name was selected randomly by townspeople when the post office opened here in 1881. The man whose choice won in the town lottery is said to have used the name of his girlfriend.

AUSTIN, City; State Capital; Travis & Williamson Counties; Travis County Seat; Pop. 345,496 / 587,873; Zip Code 787; Elev. 650; Central Texas; 85 mi. N of Son Antonio on the Colorado River, which is dammed in seven places here. The town is named for Stephen Austin who was killed at the Alamo.

AZLE, City; Parker & Tarrant Counties; Pop. 5,822 / 10,631; Zip Code 76020; N Texas, 20 mi. NW of Fort Worth.

BAIRD, City; Callahan County Seat; Pop. 1,696 / 1,808; Zip Code 79504; Elev. 1,708; N central Texas, 20 mi. E of Abilene. It was established in 1880 when the Texas and Pacific Railroad was built. This railroad switching point was named for director Matthew Baird, who drove the first Texas and Pacific in 1875.

BALCH SPRINGS, City; Dallas County; Pop. 13,746 / 18,353; Zip Code 75180; NE Texas, E suburb of Dallas.

BALLINGER, City; Runnels County Seat; Pop. 4,207 / 4,041; Zip Code 76821; Elev. 1,637; W central Texas, 35 mi. NE of San Angelo on the Colorado River.

BANDERA, City; Bandera County Seat; Pop. 947 / 1,345; Zip Code 78003; Elev. 1,258; SW central Texas; 50 mi. NW of San Antonio. The name probably comes from General Bandera, a Spanish Indian fighter in San Antonio. The name is also a Spanish word meaning "flag."

BANGS, City; Brown County; Pop. 1,716 / 1,596; Zip Code 76823; Central Texas, 10 mi. W of Brownwood.

BARTLETT, City; Bell & Williamson Counties; Pop. 1,567 / 1,656; Zip Code 76511; central Texas; 20 mi. S of Temple in a rural area.

BASTROP, City; Bastrop County Seat; Pop. 3,789 / 5,736; Zip Code 78602; Elev. 369; S central Texas; on a navigable point in the Colorado River, 30 mi. SE of Austin. Bastrop was founded in the 1830s. In 1837 the town was incorporated. Its name honors the Baron de Bastrop, a friend of Moses Austin, who claimed he was from Holland. However, he was actually born in Dutch Gukyana of ordinary Dutch parents. He had been an accused embezzler in his homeland.

BAY CITY, City; Matagorda County Seat; Pop. 17,837 / 18,896; Zip Code 77414; Elev. 55; on Colorado River, 65 mi. SW of Houston.

BAYTOWN, City; Chambers & Harris Counties; Pop. 56,923 / 69,588; Elev. 26; E Texas. 15 mi. E of Houston on W Galveston Bay.

BEAUMONT, City; Jefferson County Seat; Pop. 118,102 / 109,697; Elev. 21; SE Texas on Neches River, 85 mi. NE of Houston. About 1835, Henry Millard, member of a land-purchasing group known as Thomas B. Huling and Company of Jasper County, purchased fifty acres of land from Noah Trevis, and in October a town was laid out. Of numerous stories regarding its name, one asserts that Millard named it Beaumont for his brother-in-law, Jefferson Beaumont, another, that Beaumont (Fr., "beautiful Hill"), was chosen because of a slight elevation southeast of town.

BEDFORD, City; Tarrant County; Pop. 20,821 / 50,451; Zip Code 76021; N Texas; NE suburb of Fort Worth, near the International Airport. Population doubled during 1970s.

BEEVILLE, City; Bee County Seat; Pop. 14,574 / 13,696; Zip Code 78102; Elev. 214; S Texas, 45 mi. NW of Corpus Christi. Beeville was named for General Barnard E. Bee, who was founder of the Texas Republic Army, and later Secretary of War for the independent nation.

BELLAIRE, City; Harris County; Pop. 14,950 / 15,704; Zip Code 77401; Elev. 41; SE Texas; W suburb of Houston, surrounded by that city's limits.

BELLS, Town; Grayson County; Pop. 846 / 1,105; Zip Code 75414; NE Texas, 12 mi. E of Sherman. The original name here was Gospel Ridge, for the many houses of worship along the hills. On Sundays, the chaotic chiming of all of the church bells caused Texas and Pacific Railroad planners to dub the place "Bells." That name stuck.

BELMONT, Gonzales County; Zip Code 78604; S central Texas; 45 mi. NE of San Antonio. Name is from the French, meaning, "beautiful hill."

BELTON, City; Bell County Seat; Pop. 10,666 / 14,664; Zip Code 76513; Central Texas; 7 mi. W of Temple. Near Belton Lake and Stillhouse Hollow Reservoir; Recreational area.

BENAVIDES, City; Duval County; Pop. 1,978 / 1,757; Zip Code 78341; S Texas; 55 mi. SW of Corpus Christi; Rural.

BERTRAM, City; Burnet County; Pop. 824 / 1,200; Zip Code 78605; Central Texas; 35 mi. NW of Austin.

BESSMAY, Village; Jasper County; Pop. 1,669; E Texas. J.H. Kirby, a lumber mill owner here, around the turn of the century named the place for his daughter.

BEVERLY, McLennan County; Zip Code 76711; Elev. 430; Central Texas; suburb of Waco.

BIG LAKE, City; Reagan County Seat; Pop. 3,404 / 3,195; Zip Code 76932; Elev. 2,678; W Texas; 60 mi. SW of San Angelo on a lake by the same name.

BIG SANDY, Town; Upshur County; Pop. 1,258 / 1,405; Zip Code 75755; NE Texas; 100 mi. E of Dallas on the Sabine River.

BIG SPRING, City; Howard County Seat; Pop. 24,804 / 21,995; Zip Code 79720; Elev. 2,397; NW Texas; 90 mi. W of Abilene on Sulphur Springs Creek. It was named for a large spring, now dry, was formerly a frontier watering place where buffalo hunters and bone gatherers erected their hide and wood huts.

BISHOP, City; Nueces County; Pop. 3,706 / 3,427; Zip Code 78343; S Texas; 6 mi. NE of Kingsville.

BLANCO, City; Blanco County; Pop. 1,179 / 1,769; Zip Code 78606; Elev. 1,350; Central Texas; 50 mi. N of San Antonio, on Blanco River.

BLOSSOM, Town; Lamar County; Pop. 1,487 / 1,607; Zip Code 75416; NE Texas; 10 mi. E of Paris, Texas; Named for wildflowers growing here.

BOERNE, City; Kendall County Seat; Pop. 3,229 / 6,704; Zip Code 78006; Elev. 1,405; S central Texas; 30 mi. NW of San Antonio. Members of the German colony of Bettina founded Boemne in 1849. After two years they moved to the site of the present town, which was named for Ludwig Boerne, a poet who was one of its founders.

BOGATA, Town; Red River County; Pop. 1,508 / 1,318; Zip Code 75417; NE Texas; 25 mi. SE of Paris. Bogata was supposed to be named for the capital of Columbia, Bogotá; but the postmasters embellished handwriting was interpreted as Bogata.

BONHAM, City; Fannin County Seat; Pop. 7,338 / 7,718; Zip Code 75418; Elev. 568; NE Texas; 25 mi. E of Sherman in a residential area. S of Red River. The town was named for Alamo defender James Butler Bonham.

BOOKER, Town; Lipscomb & Ochiltree Counties; Pop. 1,219 / 1,136; Zip Code 79005; NW Texas; 16 mi. NE of Perrytown.

BORGER, City; Hutchinson County; Pop. 15,837 / 14,183; Zip Code 79007; NW Texas; 45 mi. NE of Amarillo, near Lake Meredith.

BOSTON, Village; Bowie County Seat; Pop. included in New Boston; Zip Code 78887; NE Texas; 25 mi. W of Texarkana; Named for Boston, Massachusetts.

BOVINA, City; Parmer County; Pop. 1,499 / 1,671; Zip Code 79009; NW Texas; near New Mexico state line on Running Water Creek. The town was originally known as Bull Town. The newer name also suggests the amount of steers that inhabit the region.

BOWIE, City; Montague County; Pop. 5,610 / 5,641; Zip Code 76230; N Texas; 40 mi. SE of Wichita Falls; Named for James A. Bowie, famous pioneer and maker of a knife that still bears his name.

BOYD, Town; Wise County; Pop. 889 / 1,373; Zip Code 76023; N Texas; 20 mi. NW of Fort Worth along the West Fork of the Trinity River.

BRACKETTVILLE, City; Kinney County Seat; Pop. 1,676 / 1,893; Zip Code 78832; Elev. 1,020; SW Texas; 40 mi. N of Eagle Pass near the Anachacho Mountains.

BRADY, City; McCulloch County Seat; Pop. 5,969 / 5,939; Zip Code 76825; Elev. 1,670; Central Texas; 77 mi. SE of San Angelo.

BRAZORIA, City; Brazoria County; Pop. 3,025 / 3,034; Zip Code 77422; Elev. 32; SE Texas; 50 mi. S of Houston on the Brazos River.

BRECKENRIDGE, City; Stephens County Seat; Pop. 6,921 / 5,717; Zip Code 76024; Elev. 1,200; N central Texas; E of Hubbard Creek Lake, 48 mi. NE of Abilene. The city was named for Buchanan's Vice President, John C. Breckenridge (1857-61).

BREMOND, City; Robertson County; Pop. 1,025 / 1,133; Zip Code 76629; E central Texas; 40 mi. SE of Waco.

BRENHAM, City; Washington County Seat; Pop. 10,966 / 13,833; Zip Code 77833; Elev. 350; SE central Texas.

BRIAR, City; Parker, Tarrant & Wise Counties; Pop. 1,810; N Texas; 20 mi. NW of Fort Worth near Eagle Mountain Lake.

BRIDGE CITY, City; Orange County; Pop. 7,667 / 8,377; Zip Code 77611; E Texas; 5 mi. N of Port Arthur, near Sabine Lake.

BRIDGEPORT, City; Wise County; Pop. 3,737 / 4,513; Zip Code 76026; Elev. 754; N Texas; 35 mi. NW of Fort Worth along the West Fork of the Trinity River, near Lake Bridgeport.

BROADDUS, Town; San Augustine County; Pop. 225 / 4,513; Zip Code 75929; E Texas; On Angelina Bayou of Sam Rayburn Reservoir within the Angelina National Forest.

BROOKSHIRE, City; Waller County; Pop. 2,175 / 3,402; Zip Code 77423; Elev. 168; SE Texas; 35 mi. W of Houston.

BROWNFIELD, City; Terry County Seat; Pop. 10,387 / 8,966; Zip Code 79316; Elev. 3,312; NW Texas; 40 mi. SW of Lubbock.

BROWNSVILLE, City; Cameron County Seat; Pop. 84,997 / 147,701; Elev. 35; S Texas; on Rio Grande River, 145 mi. S of Corpus Christi.

BROWNWOOD, City; Brown County Seat; Pop. 19,203 / 19,711; Zip Code 76801; Elev. 1,342; Central Texas; 100 mi. E of San Angelo, S of Lake Brownwood.

BRUCEVILLE, (alt. Eddy), City; Falls & McLennan Counties; Pop. 1,038 / 1,172; Zip Code 76630; Central Texas; 17 mi. S of Waco.

BRYAN, City; Brazos County Seat; Pop. 44,337 / 58,920; Zip Code 77801; Elev. 367; E central Texas; 100 mi. NE of Austin near the Brazos River.

BUDA, City; Hays County; Pop. 597 / 2,751; Zip Code 78610; S central Texas; 11 mi. SW of Austin. Name is from the Spanish word for widow, viuda, for a women who lived here in the early settlement days. The town may also have been known as "the City of Widows." It was organized in 1887.

BUFFALO, City; Leon County; Pop. 1,507 / 1,839; Zip Code 75831; Elev. 4; E central Texas; 110 mi. SE of Dallas.

BULLARD, Town; Cherokee & Smith Counties; Pop. 681 / 1,166; Zip Code 75757; Elev. 500; NE Texas; 15 mi. S of Tyler.

BUNA, Village; Jasper County; Pop. 1,500; Zip Code 77612; Elev. 76; E Texas; 120 mi. NE of Houston.

BUNKER HILL VILLAGE, City; Harris County; Pop. 3,750 / 3,715; E Texas; W suburb of Houston; Named for the Revolutionary War battle site.

BURKBURNETT, City; Wichita County; Pop. 10,668 / 10,749; Zip Code 76354; Elev. 1,040; N Texas; 11 mi. N of Wichita Falls near the Oklahoma State line. The 6666 Ranch originally encompassed this community, then known as Nesterville. Theodore Roosevelt hunted wolves here in 1905, and stayed with ranch owner Burk Burnett. According to the local story, President Roosevelt personally recommended the town's new name in 1907, remembering the rancher's hospitality.

BURLESON, City; Johnson & Tarrant Counties; Pop. 11,734 / 22,095; Zip Code 76028; N central Texas; 12 mi. S of Fort Worth; Named for Colonel Edward Burleson.

BURNET, Town; Burnet County Seat; Pop. 3,410 / 4,776; Zip Code 78611; Elev. 1,319; Central Texas; 45 mi. NW of Austin near Inks Lake.

CACTUS, City; Moore County; Pop. 898 / 2,004; Zip Code 79013; NW Texas; near Dumas. The presence of the prickly desert plants led to the name of this town. Before the first houses could be built here in the late 1940s, large numbers of cactus had to be removed.

CADDO MILLS, City; Hunt County; Pop. 1,060 / 1,203; Zip Code 75005; NE Texas; 8 mi. SW of Greenville; Named for the Indian tribe that once lived near this site.

CALDWELL, City; Burleson County Seat; Pop. 2,953 / 3,555; Zip Code 77836; Elev. 402; E central Texas; 65 mi. NE of Austin in a resort area. Founded in 1840, Caldwell was once Milam County seat. It was named for Mathew Old Paint Caldwell, a noted Indian fighter and signer of the Texas Declaration of Independence.

CALVERT, City; Robertson County; Pop. 1,732 / 1,499; Zip Code 77837; Elev. 335; E central Texas; 20 mi. NE of Bryan. Most of the town looks much as it did in Victorian times. Named for a descendant of Lord Baltimore, Robert Calvert, a plantation owner who donated the town site.

CAMERON, City; Milam County Seat; Pop. 5,721 / 5,905; Zip Code 76520; Elev. 402; Central Texas; On Little River, 50 mi. S of Waco. Cameron was settled before the Texas Revolution and named for Captain Ewen Cameron, one of the state's first cowboys, whose statue is on the courthouse lawn.

CANADIAN, Town; Hemphill County Seat; Pop. 3,491 / 2,255; Zip Code 79014; Elev. 2,340; NW Texas; 100 mi. NE of Amarillo. Lying in a curve of the Canadian River, Canadian was first known as Hogtown, then as Desperado City.

CANTON, City; Van Zandt County Seat; Pop. 2,845 / 3,536; Zip Code 75103; Elev. 540; NE Texas; 60 mi. SE of Dallas in a farming and livestock raising region. Canton is a French word meaning a "district" or other geographic division, similar to a county.

CANYON, City; Randall County Seat; Pop. 10,724 / 12,584; Zip Code 79015; Elev. 3,566; NW Texas; 15 mi. S of Amarillo. Nearby is the Palo Duro Canyon, for which the city was named.

CARRIZO SPRINGS, City; Dimmit County Seat; Pop. 6,886 / 5,925; Zip Code 78834; Elev. 602; S Texas; 45 mi. E of Eagle Pass.

CARROLLTON, City; Collin, Dallas & Denton Counties; Pop. 40,591 / 103,311; Elev. 500; NE Texas; suburb of Dallas (NW); Population has increased three times here during the 1970s.

CARTHAGE, City; Panola County Seat; Pop. 6,447 / 6,937; Zip Code 75633; Elev. 302; E Texas; 25 mi. S of Marshall. It was named for Carthage, Mississippi by Mr. Major Holland, an early settler.

CASTROVILLE, City; Medina County; Pop. 1,821 / 3,152; Zip Code 78009; Elev. 787; S central Texas; 30 mi. SW of San Antonio, on a bend in the Medina River. Castroville is a bit of old Alsace-Lorraine, uprooted and transplanted beside the Medina River. Castroville was founded in 1844 by a group of colonists under Count Henri de Castro (who, however, signed all papers Henry Castro), and was named in his honor.

CEDAR HILL, City; Dallas & Ellis Counties; Pop. 6,849 / 29,542; Zip Code 75104; NE Texas; 20 mi. SW of Dallas; Residential suburb that is growing rapidly.

CEDAR PARK, City; Williamson County; Pop. 3,474 / 27,115; Zip Code 78613; Central Texas; N suburb of Austin; Incorporated during the 1970s.

CELINA, Town; Collin County; Pop. 1,520 / 2,207; Zip Code 75009; NE Texas; 30 mi. N of Dallas; Named for county; in Ohio.

CENTER, City; Shelby County Seat; Pop. 5,827 / 4,850; Zip Code 75935; Elev. 345; E Texas; 50 mi. S of Longview. Quick to take advantage of this, Jesse Amason donated fifty acres for a town site that was named Center.

CHANDLER, Town; Henderson County; Pop. 1,308 / 2,344; Zip Code 75758; NE Texas; 10 mi. W of Tyler.

CHARLOTTE, City; Atascosa County; Pop. 1,443 / 1,733; Zip Code 78011; Lat. 2-51-8 N, Long. 98-42-5 W; S Texas; 45 mi. S of San Antonio.

CHICO, City; Wise County; Pop. 890 / 1,016; Zip Code 76030; N Texas; 12 mi. NE of Decatur; named for Chico, California. Chico is Spanish for little."

CHILDRESS, City; Childress County Seat; Pop. 5,817 / 5,299; Zip Code 79201; Elev. 1,877; NW Texas; 120 mi. NW of Wichita Falls; It was named for George Campbell Childress, author of the Texas Declaration of Independence.

CHILLICOTHE, City; Hardeman County; Pop. 1,052 / 662; Zip Code 79225; Elev. 1,400; N Texas; 85 mi. NW of Wichita Falls. The name means "big town where we live" in Indian.

CHINA, City; Jefferson County; Pop. 1,351 / 1,269; Zip Code 77613; SE Texas; 11 mi. W of Beaumont; Named for Chinese immigrants that have lived here.

CIBOLO, City; Guadalupe County; Pop. 549 / 3,019; Zip Code 78108; S central Texas; Near Seguin. *Cibolo* is a Spanish word meaning buffalo, itself taken from an Indian word.

CISCO, City; Eastland County; Pop. 4,517 / 3,324; Zip Code 76437; Elev. 1,608; N central Texas; 45 mi. E of Abilene. Cisco was the first town west of Fort Worth to hove two railroads. It was named for J.J. Cisco, leading railroad promoter of the 1860s.

CLARENDON, City; Donley County Seat; Pop. 2,220 / 1,907; Zip Code 79226; Elev. 2,727; NW Texas. It is the offspring of one of the first settlements in the Panhandle. Old Clarendon was founded in 1878 by a Methodist minister, Lewis Carhard, who named the place for his wife, Clara.

CLARKSVILLE, City; Red River County Seat; Pop. 4,917 / 4,048; Zip Code 75426; Elev. 442; Lat. 33-36-6 N, Long. 95-03-1 NW; NE Texas.

CLAUDE, City; Armstrong County Seat; Pop. 1,112 / 1,364; Zip Code 79019; Elev. 3,405; NW Texas; 28 mi. E of Amarillo.

CLEBURNE, City; Johnson County Seat; Pop. 19,218 / 26,198; Zip Code 76031; Elev. 764; N central Texas; 55 mi. SW of Dallas on the West Buffalo Creek in a wooded, hilly area. It was established in 1854 and first known as Camp Henderson. In 1867, the name was changed to honor Confederate General Pat Cleburne.

CLEVELAND, City; Liberty County; Pop. 5,977 / 8,021; Zip Code 77327; E Texas; 45 mi. NE of Houston; Named for Grover Cleveland, twenty-fourth U.S. President.

CLIFTON, City; Basque County; Pop. 3,063 / 3,380; Zip Code 76634; Elev. 670; Central Texas on Basque River, 32 mi. NW of Waco; named for cliffs by the river.

CLINT, Town; El Paso County; Pop. 1,314 / 1,151; Zip Code 79836; Elev. 3,630; W Texas; Suburb of El Paso. Many adobe houses grace this little town.

CLYDE, City; Callahan County; Pop. 2,562 / 2,892; Zip Code 79510; N central Texas; 15 mi. E of Abilene. Robert Clyde established a railroad worker's camp here in 1881.

COAHOMA, Town; Howard County; Pop. 1,069 / 1,165; Zip Code 79511; W Texas; 10 mi. E of Big Spring; Name is Indian for "signal," because of a hill nearby known as Signal Mountain.

COCKRELL HILL, City; Dallas County; Pop. 3,262 / 3,728; Zip Code 75211; NE Texas; Suburb of Dallas; Residential.

COLEMAN, City; Coleman County Seat; Pop. 5,960 / 5,235; Zip Code 76834; Elev. 1,710; Central Texas; 30 mi. W of Brownwood near the geographic center of the state; Named for Robert M. Coleman.

COLLEGE STATION, City; Brazos County; Pop. 37,272 / 61,121; Zip Code 77840; Elev. 308; E central Texas; 4 mi. SE of Bryan. Home of the Texas Agricultural and Mechanical University (commonly called "Texas A&M"), the state's first public institution of higher learning. It was established in 1876 and granted university status in 1963, and has made important contributions to the development of Texas agriculture.

COLLEYVILLE, City; Tarrant County; Pop. 6,700 / 20,747; Zip Code 76034; N Texas; Suburb of Fort Worth.

COLORADO CITY, City; Mitchell County Seat; Pop. 5,405 / 5,587; Zip Code 79512; Elev. 2,067; Zip Code 79512; NW central Texas; on Colorado River, 30 mi. E of Big Springs.

COLUMBUS, City; Colorado County Seat; Pop. 3,923 / 3,627; Zip Code 78934; Elev. 207; SE central Texas; 65 mi. W of Houston.

COMANCHE, City; Comanche County Seat; Pop. 4,075 / 4,155; Zip Code 76442; Elev. 1,358; Central Texas; 33 mi. NE of Brownwood. Established as a trade center for the surrounding ranches in 1858, Comanche was plagued by fighting between colonists and Indians.

COMBES, Town; Cameron County; Pop. 1,441 / 2,605; Zip Code 78535; Lat. 26-15-0 N, Long. 97-44-72 W; S Texas; Suburb of Brownsville.

COMBINE, City; Dallas & Kaufman Counties; Pop. 688 / 1,848; NE Texas.

COMMERCE, City; Hunt County; Pop. 8,136 / 7,392; Zip Code 75428; Elev. 546; NE Texas; 60 mi. NE of Dallas. Commerce is a shipping center for the agricultural "Blacklands Belt" of Texas.

COMFORT, Village; Kendall County; Pop. 1,226; Zip Code 78013; Elev. 1,437; S central Texas; 45 mi. NW of San Antonio on the edge of the Guadalupe River Valley. Comfort was established by German settlers in 1854. Wearied by their journey from New Braunfels, the small group was so happy to see the picturesque site and pure water they named it "Camp Comfort."

CONROE, City; Montgomery County Seat; Pop. 18,034 / 38,517; Elev. 213; E Texas; 35 mi. N of Houston.

COOPER, City; Delta County Seat; Pop. 2,338 / 2,317; Zip Code 75432; Elev. 495; NE Texas; 70 mi. NE of Dallas, between North and South Sulphur Rivers.

COPPELL, City; Dallas & Denton Counties; Pop. 3,826 / 30,620; Zip Code 75019; NE Texas; NW suburb of Dallas, near the International Airport.

COPPERAS COVE, City; Coryell County; Pop. 19,469 / 31,039; Zip Code 76522; Central Texas; on SW border of Fort Hood Military Reservation. Named for the creek flowing nearby, which seeped a mineral that resembled the sulfate copperas.

CORPUS CHRISTI, City; Kleberg, Nueces & San Patricia Counties; Nueces County Seat; Pop. 231,999 / 281,791; Elev. 35; S Texas; 130 mi. SE of San Antonio at Nueces River mouth. Its name was taken from that given the bay by the Spaniard, Alonso Alvarez de Pineda, who, in 1519, claimed the outer island and the land beyond for his king.

COTULLA, City; LaSalle County Seat; Pop. 3,912 / 4,413; Zip Code 78014; Elev. 442; S Texas; On Nueces River, 60 mi. N of Laredo.

CRANDALL, City; Kaufman County; Pop. 831 / 2,899; Zip Code 75114; NE Texas; 25 mi. SE of Dallas.

CRANE, City; Crone County Seat; Pop. 3,622 / 3,228; Zip Code 79731; W Texas; 32 mi. S of Odessa in a ranching region.

CROCKETT, City; Houston County Seat; Pop. 7,405 / 7,442; Zip Code 75835; Elev. 350; E Texas; 33 mi. S of Palestine. It was named for Davy Crockett, who is said to have camped, while on his way to the Alamo, under a large oak near a spring about 500 feet from Crockett Circle.

CROSBYTON, City; Crosby County Seat; Pop. 2,289 / 2,010; Zip Code 79322; Elev. 3,000; NW Texas; At "Crown of Cap Rock."

CROSS PLAINS, Town; Callahan County; Pop. 1,240 / 1,185; Zip Code 76443; N central Texas; 40 mi. SE of Abilene.

CROWELL, City; Ford County Seat; Pop. 1,509 / 985; Zip Code 79227; Elev. 1,463; N Texas; 80 mi. W of Wichita Falls.

CROWLEY, City; Tarrant County; Pop. 5,852 / 7,999; Zip Code 76036; N Texas; S suburb of Fort Worth in a growing residential area.

CRYSTAL CITY, City; Zavala County Seat; Pop. 8,334 / 8,195; Zip Code 78839; Elev. 580; S Texas. The town was named for the clear well water pumped in the vicinity by early settlers. It was founded in 1907 and become county seat 21 years later.

CUERO, City; DeWitt County Seat; Pop. 7,124 / 6,456; Zip Code 77954; Elev. 177; S Texas; On Guadalupe River, 28 mi. NW of Victoria. Cuero received its name from the creek on which it is located. This creek, called *Arroyo del Cuero* (Creek of the Rawhide) by the Spanish as early as 1745, was so named because of the exceedingly baggy banks in which wild cattle and buffaloes, seeking water, became mired and unable to extricate themselves. Mexicans and Indians killed the helpless beasts chiefly for their hides, which were a medium of exchange.

CUT AND SHOOT, Town; Montgomery County; Pop. 568 / 1,591; Zip Code 77302; E Texas; N of Houston in a rural area. The name may have arisen from the cry of revenge from townsmen who discovered the local preacher had been philandering with their wives. Most sources, however, claim it is derived from a dispute over the shape of a church steeple. The town was incorporated during the 1970s.

DAINGERFIELD, Town; Morris County Seat; Pop. 3,030 / 2,695; Zip Code 75638; Elev. 402; NE Texas. The town was named by early settlers (1840s) for Captain London Daingerfield, who was killed in a battle with Indians on this site. It is one of the smallest county seats in Texas.

DAISETTA, City; Liberty County; Pop. 1,177 / 1,044; Zip Code 77533; E Texas; 35 mi. W of Beaumont. Named for two early townswomen, Daisy Barrett and Etta White. It was settled in about 1850, but was not officially founded until 1921, after oil had been drilled nearby.

DALHART, City; Dallam & Hartley Counties; Dallam County Seat; Pop. 6,854 / 7,106; Zip Code 79022; Elev. 3,985; NW Texas; 75 mi. NW of Amarillo. Since this city is located near the line between Dallam and Hartley Counties, early rancher Ora Atkinson suggested its present name. It had also been known as Twist and Denrock, because it grew at the junction of the Denver City and Rock Island railroad lines after 1901.

DALLAS, City; Collin, Dallas, Denton, Kaufman & Rockwall Counties; Dallas County Seat; Pop. 904,078 / 1,076,214; Zip Code 752+; Elev. 512; NE Texas; On Trinity River, 35 mi. E of Fort Worth. The origin of the town s name is uncertain, one group of historians believing it was named for George Mifflin Dallas, a Pennsylvanian who 3 years later became Vice President of the United States; another group say that the name honored Commander Mifflin Dallas; a third that the town was named for Joseph Dallas, a friend of John Neely Bryan who came to the region from Washington County, Arkansas, in 1843, and settled at Cedar Springs, now within the Dallas city limits, in 1852 to Alexander Cockrell for seven thousand dollars.

DANBURY, City; Brazoria County; Pop. 1,357 / 1,547; Zip Code 77534; SE Texas; 25 mi. NW of the Brazosport area.

DAYTON, City; Liberty County; Pop. 4,908 / 6,559; Zip Code 77535; E Texas; 25 mi. NE of Houston; Named for early settler by the name of Day.

DE KALB, Town; Bowie County; Pop. 2,217 / 2,043; Zip Code 75559; Elev. 407; NE Texas; 27 mi. N of Texarkana. DeKalb was founded about a half mile north of its present location, was named in honor of Baron de Kalb (1721-1780), a German general in the American Revolutionary Army.

DE LEON, City; Comanche County; Pop. 2,478 / 2,307; Zip Code 76444; Elev. 1,268; Central Texas; 83 mi. SE of Abilene. Founded in 1881, De Leon was named for the nearby Leon River, which was named for Alonso de Leon, an early Mexican explorer.

DECATUR, City; Wise County Seat; Pop. 4,104 / 5,557; Zip Code 76234; Elev. 1,097; N Texas; 40 mi. NW of Fort Worth. The town was first settled in the 1850s and known as Taylorville but renamed for Stephen Decatur, a War of 1812 naval hero.

DEER PARK, City; Harris County; Pop. 22,648 / 30,804; Zip Code 77536; Elev. 50; SE Texas; Suburb, 17 mi. SE of Houston, near the Galveston Bay along the ship channel.

DEL RIO, City; Val Verde County Seat; Pop. 30,034 / 35,728; Zip Code 78840; Elev. 948; SE Texas; 145 mi. W of San Antonio. The town was named for San Felipe del Rio (Saint Philip of the River).

DENISON, City; Grayson County; Pop. 23,884 / 22,447; Zip Code 75020; Elev. 767; NE Texas; 10 mi. N of Sherman near the Oklahoma state line.

DENTON, City; Denton County Seat; Pop. 48,063 / 79,208; Zip Code 76201; Elev. 620; N Texas; 35 mi. NE of Fart Worth. Named for an early Texas preacher called Denison.

DESOTO, City; Dallas County; Pop. 15,538 / 36,139; Zip Code 75115; NE Texas; 17 mi. SW of Dallas in a residential area that has grown enormously in recent years.

DEVINE, City; Medina County; Pop. 3,756 / 5,237; Zip Code 78016; Elev. 670; S central Texas; 27 mi. SW of San Antonio.

DIBOLL, City; Angelina County; Pop. 5,227 / 5,402; Zip Code 75941; E Texas; 100 mi. NE of Houston, near the Neches River.

DICKINSON, Village; Galveston County; Pop. 7,505 / 16,669; Zip Code 77539; SE Texas; 15 mi. N of Galveston in a residential suburban area.

DILLEY, City; Frio County; Pop. 2,579 / 3,006; Zip Code 78017; S Texas; 65 mi. SW of San Antonio in o rural region; Named for George M. Dilley of the International and Great Northern Railroad, from Palestine, Texas.

DIME BOX, (alt. OLD DIME BOX), Village; Lee County; Pop. 313; Zip Code 77853; Central Texas; 40 mi. NE of Austin. Stagecoach drivers and railroaders carried mail to and from this settlement in early times for a fee of 10 cents. The mail was delivered to a special box erected by the citizens. In 1943, Dime Box received recognition when it "Contributed 100 percent" to the March of Dimes, the first U.S. town to do so.

DIMMITT, City; Castro County Seat; Pop. 5,019 / 4,148; Zip Code 79027; Lat. 34-33-0 N, Long. 102-18-9 W; NW Texas; 60 mi. SW of Amarillo in a ranching region; Named for Philip Dimmit.

DUBLIN, City; Erath County; Pop. 2,723 / 3,516; Zip Code 76446; Elev. 1,450; N central Texas; 50 mi. NE of Brownwood. The name, despite its Celtic sound, has a purely local origin. It was derived from a huge double log cabin erected by early-day citizens as a protection against Indians. "Dublin in" was a term for a retreat to the cabin, and the town became known as Doublin, later contracted to Dublin, an Irish railroad man added to the impression that the town had an Irish origin by giving many of the streets Celtic names.

DUMAS, City; Moore County Seat; Pop. 12,194 / 13,721; Zip Code 79029; Elev. 3,668; NW Texas; 50 mi. N of Amarillo. It was named for Louis Dumas, president of a company that founded this county seat in 1892. Oil was discovered in 1926.

DUNCANVILLE, City; Dallas County; Pop. 27,781 / 35,939; Zip Code 751+; NE Texas; Suburb of Dallas, in a residential area that has doubled in population during the 1970s.

EAGLE PASS, City; Maverick County Seat; Pop. 21,407 / 30,205; Zip Code 78852; Elev. 797; SW Texas; on Rio Grande, 130 mi. SW of San Antonio; Across river from Piedras Negras, Mexico. Eagle Pass is a tourist resort of narrow streets and Mexican border atmosphere, which during the days of the war with Mexico, was the site of a U.S. military encampment at the crossing of the Rio Grande. It was named Camp Eagle Pass from the doily flight of an eagle back and forth cross the river to its nest in a huge cottonwood tree on the Mexican bank.

EARLY, City; Brown County; Pop. 2,313 / 2,732; Zip Code 76801; Central Texas; 1 mi. NE of Brownwood; Residential.

EARTH, City; Lamb County; Pop. 1,512 / 1,146; Zip Code 79031; NW Texas; 40 mi. W of Plainview. Named during a sandstorm, Earth is strung out along U.S. Highway 70.

EASTLAND, City; Eastland County Seat; Pop. 3,747 / 3,750; Zip Code 76448; Elev. 1,421; Lat. 32-23-9 N, Long. 98-49-1 W; N central Texas; 55 mi. E of Abilene.

EDCOUCH, City; Hidalgo County; Pop. 3,092 / 3,398; Zip Code 78538; S Texas; 15 mi. NW of Harlingen in a citrus farming area.

EDEN, City; Concho County; Pop. 1,294 / 1,554; Zip Code 76837; Elev. 2,046; Lat. 31-13-1 N, Long. 99-50-6 W; W central Texas; 45 mi. SE of San Angelo.

EDGEWOOD, Town; Van Zandt County; Pop. 1,413 / 1,466; Zip Code 75117; NE Texas; 35 mi. E of Dallas in a rural area.

EDINBURG, City; Hidalgo County Seat; Pop. 24,075 / 45,454; Zip Code 78539; Elev. 91; S Texas; 55 mi. NW of Brownsville. It was first named Chopin for an early promoter and renamed in 1911.

EDNA, City; Jackson County Seat; Pop. 5,650 / 6,106; Zip Code 77957; Elev. 72; SE Texas; 95 mi. SW of Houston.

EL CAMPO, City; Wharton County; Pop. 10,462 / 11,147; Zip Code 77437; Elev. 110; SE Texas; 70 mi. SW of Houston. When incorporated in 1902, the city fathers used Spanish words for its name.

EL PASO, City; El Paso County Seat; Pop. 425,259 / 612,770; Zip Code 799+; Elev. 3,762; W Texas. El Paso is the lowest natural pass in that region of deserts and mountains where the westernmost tip of Texas touches the borders of Mexico and New Mexico. It was named for the pass of the early Spanish conquistadors.

ELDORADO, Town; Schleicher County Seat; Pop. 2,061 / 2,019; Zip Code 76936; Elev. 2,410; W central Texas; 45 mi. S of San Angelo. First a stage station known as Verand, it was located in Vermont Pasture. The town was moved on top of the divide in 1895 and took its Spanish name, which means "the gilded one."

ELECTRA, City; Wichita County; Pop. 3,755 / 2,956; Zip Code 76360; Elev. 1,229; N Texas; 30 mi. NW of Wichita Falls. Electra was named by W.T. Waggone for his daughter.

ELGIN, City; Bastrop County; Pop. 4,535 / 6,827; Zip Code 78621; S central Texas; 22 mi. E of Austin. It was named for Robert M. Elgin, who was land commissioner for the Houston and Texas Central Railroad after the Civil War.

ELKHART, Town; Anderson County; Pop. 1,317 / 1,082; Zip Code 75839; E Texas; 15 mi. S of Palestine. This town may have been named for a friendly Indian chief, or for an abandoned covered wagon that had an elk carved on it; hence elkhart.

ELSA, City; Hidalgo County; Pop. 5,061 / 6,048; Zip Code 78543; S Texas; 20 mi. W of Harlingen.

EMORY, City; Rains County Seat; Pop. 813 / 1,183; Zip Code 75440; Elev. 464; NE Texas; 30 mi. SE of Greenville. Emory was named for Emory Rains, first settler in the area in 1848.

ENNIS, City; Ellis County; Pop. 12,110 / 16,717; Zip Code 75119; Elev. 548; NE central Texas; 30 mi. SE of Dallas.

EULESS, City; Tarrant County; Pop. 24,002 / 45,911; Zip Code 76039; Lat. 32-50-2 N, 97-05-0 W; N Texas; 15 mi. NE of Fort Worth in a rapidly changing agricultural - residential area.

EVERMAN, City; Tarrant County; Pop. 5,387 / 5,883; Zip Code 76140; N Texas; 5 mi. SE of Fort Worth in a residential area.

FAIRFIELD, City; Freestone County Seat; Pop. 3,505 / 3,256; Zip Code 75840; Elev. 461; E central Texas; 60 mi. E of Waco.

FALFURRIAS, City; Brooks County Seat; Pop. 6,103 / 6,082; Zip Code 78355; Elev. 119; S Texas; 75 mi. SW of Corpus Christi. Falfurrias is Spanish for "Heart's Delight," the name of a local wildflower.

FARMERS BRANCH, City; Dallas County; Pop. 24,863 / 26,375; Zip Code 75234; NE Texas; N suburb of Dallas in a growing residential area; Named because it was once an agricultural village on a large branch of the Trinity River.

FARMERSVILLE, City; Collin County; Pop. 2,360 / 2,795; Zip Code 75031; NE Texas; 15 mi. W of Greenville; so named because of its agricultural character.

FARWELL, City; Parmer County Seat; Pop. 1,354 / 1,449; Zip Code 79325; NW Texas; 90 mi. SW of Amarillo. This city was named for the Farwell brothers, who received a land grant reaching into ten counties, as payment for building the capital at Austin.

FERRIS, City; Dallas & Ellis Counties; Pop. 2,228 / 2,781; Zip Code 75125; NE central Texas; 35 mi. N of Corsicana.

FLATONIA, Town; Fayette County; Pop. 1,070 / 1,465; Zip Code 78941; SE central Texas; 50 mi. SE of Austin. Named for F.W. Flato, an early settler among the early Czech immigrants who first came here.

FLORENCE, Town; Williamson County; Pop. 744 / 1,150; Zip Code 76527; Central Texas; 50 mi. N of Austin in a rural area.

FLORESVILLE, City; Wilson County Seat; Pop. 4,381 / 7,075; Zip Code 78114; Elev. 389; S central Texas; 20 mi. SE of San Antonio. It was named for early rancher, Don Francisco Flares de Abrego, who moved here from Mexico in 1832.

FLOYDADA, City; Floyd County Seat; Pop. 4,193 / 3,810; Zip Code 79235; Elev. 3,137; NW Texas; 40 mi. NE of Lubbock. It is named for Alamo hero Dolphin Floyd.

FORNEY, Town; Kaufman County; Pop. 2,483 / 6,081; Zip Code 75126; NE Texas; 20 mi. E of Dallas near E Fork of the Trinity River.

FORT STOCKTON, City; Pecos County Seat; Pop. 8,688 / 8,393; Zip Code 79735; Elev. 3,052; W Texas; 150 mi. W of San Angelo.

FORT WORTH, City; Tarrant County Seat; Pop. 385,141 / 502,369; Zip Code 761+; Elev. 670; N Texas; 30 mi. W of Dallas. The camp was named Fort Worth in honor of General William Jenkins Worth, Mexican War hero.

FRANKLIN, City; Robertson County Seat; Pop. 1,349 / 1,327; Zip Code 77856; Elev. 450; E central Texas; 30 mi. NW of Bryan in a farming area.

FRANKSTON, Town; Anderson County; Pop. 1,255 / 1,213; Zip Code 75763; Elev. 389; E Texas; 25 mi. SW of Tyler.

FREDERICKSBURG, Town; Gillespie County Seat; Pop. 6,412 / 9,667; Zip Code 78624; Elev. 1,743; Central Texas; 70 mi. NW of San Antonio. It was named Frederick for the Great of Prussia.

FREEPORT, City; Brazoria County; Pop. 13,444 / 11,942; Zip Code 77541; Elev. 5; SE Texas; 60 mi. S of Houston at point where Brazos River flows into the Gulf.

FREER, City; Duval County; Pop. 3,213 / 3,404; Zip Code 78357; S Texas; 60 mi. NE of Laredo.

FRIENDSWOOD, City; Galveston & Harris Counties; Pop. 10,719 / 29,418; Zip Code 77546; SE Texas; Suburb of Galveston.

FRIONA, City; Parmer County; Pop. 3,809 / 3,951; Zip Code 79035; NW Texas; 65 mi. SW of Amarillo, This city was called Frio, for the creek flowing nearby, but since another Texas town had token the name before, the ending was added for the post office records.

FRISCO, City; Collin & Denton Counties; Pop. 3,420 / 32,101; Zip Code 75034; NE Texas; 20 mi. N of Dallas; Probably named for the California city of San Francisco during the great Gold Rush.

FRITCH, City; Hutchinson & Moore Counties; Pop. 2,299 / 2,174; Zip Code 79036; Elev. 3,200; NW Texas; on E shore of Lake Meredith, 33 mi. N of Amarillo.

FULTON, Town; Aransas County; Pop. 725 / 1,024; Zip Code 78358; Elev. 6; S Texas; S of Rockport; Named for the Coleman-Fulton Cattle Company.

GAINESVILLE, City; Cooke County Seat; Pop. 14,081 / 15,125; Zip Code 76240; Elev. 730; N Texas; 35 mi. W of Sherman.

GALENA PARK, City; Harris County; Pop. 9,879 / 10,324; Zip Code 77547; SE Texas; Named for the lead ore found here.

GALVESTON, City; Galveston County Seat; Pop. 61,902 / 59,790; Zip Code 775+; Elev. 6 to 17; SE coastal Texas; 50 mi. SE of Houston. It was named in honor of Count Bernardo de Galvez, Viceroy of Mexico.

GANADO, Town; Jackson County; Pop. 1,770 / 1,758; Zip Code 77962; Elev. 71; SE Texas; 90 mi. SW of Houston. It is the Spanish ward for 'cattle.'

GARLAND, City; Collin, Dallas & Rockwall Counties; Pop. 138,857 / 193,272; Zip Code 750+; Elev. 540; NE Texas; 15 mi. NE of Dallas; Residential suburb.

GARRISON, Town; Nacogdoches County; Pop. 1,059 / 1,104; Zip Code 75946; E Texas; 28 mi. NE of Nacogdoches.

GATESVILLE, City; Coryell County Seat; Pop. 6,260 / 13,010; Zip Code 76528; Elev. 795; Central Texas; 40 mi. W of Waco. It was named for Fort Gates a frontier post established in 1849 as a unit in the earliest line of U.S. Government defenses, behind which settlement of the western part of the country began.

GEORGETOWN, City; Williamson County Seat; Pop. 9,468 / 32,368; Zip Code 78626; Elev. 750; Central Texas; 30 mi. N of Austin.

GEORGE WEST, City; Live Oak County Seat; Pop. 2,627 / 2,716; Zip Code 78022; Elev. 162; S Texas; 60 mi. NW of Corpus Christi. Ranchman George West built this town.

GIDDINGS, City; Lee County Seat; Pop. 3,950 / 4,535; Zip Code 78942; Elev. 520; Central Texas; 50 mi. E of Austin.

GILMER, City; Upshur County Seat; Pop. 5,167 / 5,595; Zip Code 75644; Elev. 370; NE Texas; 110 mi. E of Dallas.

GLADEWATER, City; Gregg & Upshur Counties; Pop. 6,548 / 6,639; Zip Code 75647; Elev. 333; NE Texas. Originally established at a different site and called St. Clair, the town was moved to location on Texas and Pacific Railroad in 1872 and renamed for Glade Creek.

GLEN ROSE, City; Somervell County Seat; Pop. 2,075 / 2,512; Zip Code 76043; Elev. 680; N central Texas; 50 mi. SW of Fort Worth on the Paluxy River.

GOLDTHWAITE, City; Mills County Seat; Pop. 1,783 / 1,694; Zip Code 76844; Elev. 1,580; Central Texas; 88 mi. W of Waco.

GOLIAD, City; Goliad County Seat; Pop. 1,990 / 2,313; Zip Code 77963; Elev. 167; S Texas; 20 mi. SW of Victoria. Goliad grew around a mission and presidio established here by the Spaniards in 1749.

GONZALES, City; Gonzales County Seat; Pop. 7,152 / 6,811; Zip Code 78629; Elev. 301; S central Texas; On both sides of Guadalupe River. 55 mi. SE of Austin. It was named for Don Rafael Gonzales, then provisional governor of the Mexican province of Caohila and Texas.

GORMAN, City; Eastland County; Pop. 1,258 / 1,271; Zip Code 76454; N central Texas; 60 mi. SE of Abilene in a farm region.

GRANBURY, City; Hood County Seat; Pop. 3,332 / 6,615; Zip Code 76048; Elev. 725; N central Texas; 40 mi. SW of Fort Worth along the Brazos River. Picturesquely situated on Lake Granbury. Granbury was settled in 1854 by Thomas Lambert who united it with the settlement called Stockton to form nucleus of Granbury.

GRAND PRAIRIE, City; Dallas, Ellis & Tarrant Counties; Pop. 71,462 / 114,906; Zip Code 750+; Elev. 528; NE Texas; 12 mi. W of Dallas, at E edge of Grand Prairie region of state.

GRAND SALINE, City; Van Zandt County; Pop. 2,709 / 2,857; Zip Code 75140; Elev. 407; NE Texas; 65 mi. E of Dallas. The town is built on a hill surrounded by salt flats.

GRANDVIEW, City; Johnson County; Pop. 1,205 / 1,342; Zip Code 76050; N central Texas; 14 mi. SE of Cleburne in a farming and ranching area; Named for the long vistas of flatlands here.

GRANGER, City; Williamson County; Pop. 1,236 / 1,385; Zip Code 76530; Central Texas; 25 mi. S of Temple; Named for General Gordon Granger.

GRANITE SHOALS, City; Burnet County; Pop. 634 / 1,975; Zip Code 78654; Central Texas; Named for the rock along the Colorado River banks here.

GRAPELAND, City; Houston County; Pop. 1,634 / 1,638; Zip Code 75844; E Texas; 20 mi. S of Palestine.

GRAPEVINE, City; Dallas & Tarrant Counties; Pop. 11,801 / 42,106; Zip Code 76051; N Texas; 20 mi. NE of Fort Worth; An industrial suburb in a rapidly growing area.

GREENVILLE, City; Hunt County Seat; Pop. 22,161 / 24,923; Zip Code 75401; Elev. 554; NE Texas; 50 mi. NE of Dallas.

GREGORY, City; San Patricia County; Pop. 2,739 / 2,584; Zip Code 78359; Elev. 32; S Texas; 11 mi. NE of Corpus Christi, across the bay.

GROESBECK, City; Limestone County Seat; Pop. 3,373 / 3,263; Zip Code 76642; Elev. 477; E central Texas; 35 mi. E of Waco. Groesbeck was dedicated in 1870 as a town site by Houston and Texas Central Railroad and named for one of its directors.

GROVES, City; Jefferson County; Pop. 17,090 / 16,362; Zip Code 77619; SE Texas; S of Port Arthur.

GROVETON, City; Trinity County Seat; Pop. 1,262; Zip Code 75845; E Texas; 40 mi. NE of Huntsville in a lumbering area; large stands of pine gave the place its name.

GRUVER, City; Hansford County; Pop. 1,216 / 1,122; Zip Code 79040; NW Texas; 45 mi. N of Borger in a ranching area.

GUNTER, Town; Grayson County; Pop. 849 / 1,085; Zip Code 75058; N Texas; 20 mi. SW of Sherman.

HALLETTSVILLE, City; Lavaca County Seat; Pop. 2,865 / 2,895; Zip Code 77964; Elev. 232; SE central Texas; 80 mi. SE of Austin on Lavaco River.

HALLSVILLE, City; Harrison County; Pop. 1,556 / 2,530; Zip Code 75650; NE Texas; 12 mi. W of Marshall.

HALTOM CITY, City; Tarrant County; Pop. 29,014 / 37,510; Zip Code 76117; N Texas; 5 mi. NE of Fort Worth in a growing residential area.

HAMILTON, City; Hamilton County Seat; Pop. 3,189 / 2,910; Zip Code 79520; Central Texas; 60 mi. NW of Waco.

HAMILTON, City; Jones County; Pop. 3,189; Zip Code 79520; Elev. 1,750; NW central Texas; 40 mi. NW of Abilene.

HARKER HEIGHTS, City; Bell County; Pop. 7,345 / 17,375; Zip Code 76541; Central Texas; Suburb of Temple; Residential.

HARLINGEN, City; Cameron County; Pop. 43,543 / 57,139; Zip Code 785S0; Elev. 36; S Texas; 26 mi. N of Brownsville in Lower Rio Grande Valley. Named for a city in The Netherlands, Harlingen was incorporated in 1905.

HART, City; Castro County; Pop. 1,008 / 1,124; Zip Code 79043; NW Texas; 25 mi. NW of Plainview; Named for Simeon Hart, early rancher and developer.

HASKELL, City; Haskell County Seat; Pop. 3,782 / 2,603; Zip Code 79521; Elev. 2,553; N Texas; 50 mi. N of Abilene.

HASLET, City; Tarrant County; Pop. 262 / 1,145; Zip Code 76052; N Texas; Near Fort Worth.

HAWKINS, City; Wood County; Pop. 1,302 / 1,498; Zip Code 75765; NE Texas; 25 mi. W of Longview.

HEARNE, City; Robertson County; Pop. 5,418 / 5,051; Zip Code 77859; Elev. 305; E central Texas; 55 mi. SE of Waco.

HEBBRONVILLE, Village; Jim Hogg County Seat; Pop. 4,050; Zip Code 78361; Elev. 550; S Texas; On Noriacitas Creek, 53 mi. E of Laredo in a cattle ranching area.

HEMPHILL, City; Sabine County Seat; Pop. 1,353 / 1,231; Zip Code 75948; Elev. 257; E Texas; 80 mi. N of Beaumont; Named for John Hemphill, a Republic of Texas justice.

HEMPSTEAD, City; Waller County Seat; Pop. 3,456 / 4,327; Zip Code 77445; Elev. 251; SE Texas; 50 mi. W of Houston.

HENDERSON, City; Rusk County Seat; Pop. 11,473 / 11,276; Zip Code 75652; Elev. 505; E Texas; 22 mi. S of Longview.

HENRIETTA, City; Cloy County Seat; Pop. 3,149 / 2,675; Zip Code 7636S; Elev. 886; N Texas.

HEREFORD, City; Deaf Smith County Seat; Pop. 15,853 / 14,654; Zip Code 79045; Elev. 3,806; NW Texas. It was named for early herds of Hereford cattle.

HICO, City; Hamilton County; Pop. 1,375 / 1,284; Zip Code 76457; Central Texas; 70 mi. NW of Waco. Founder J.R. Alford named this town for his native town in Kentucky. It may also come from the name of the local Indian tribe, also spelled Hueco.

HIDALGO, City; Hidalgo County; Pop. 2,288 / 6,160; Zip Code 78557; S Texas; Just N of Renyosa. Mexico on the Rio Grande. This town, named for Mexican Revolutionary leader Miguel Hidalgo (1753-1811), has survived floods, bandit raids and droughts.

HILLSBORO, City; Hill County Seat; Pop. 7,397 / 7,993; Zip Code 76645; Elev. 634; NE central Texas; 35 mi. N of Waco.

HITCHCOCK, City; Galveston County; Pop. 6,655 / 6,270; Zip Code 77563; SE Texas; 6 mi. NW of Galveston; Named for Colonel E.A. Hitchcock, Mexican War soldier.

HOLLAND, Town; Bell County; Pop. 863 / 1,320; Zip Code 76534; Central Texas; 15 mi. S of Temple.

HOLLIDAY, City; Archer County; Pop. 1,349 / 1,501; Zip Code 76366; Elev. 1,055; N Texas; 14 mi. SW of Wichita Falls.

HONDO, City; Medina County Seat; Pop. 6,057 / 7,976; Zip Code 78861; Elev. 887; S central Texas; 40 mi. W of San Antonio. City was named for the Honda River.

HONEY GROVE, City; Fannin County; Pop. 1,973 / 1,905; Zip Code 75446; Elev. 668; NE Texas; 22 mi. W of Paris.

HOOKS, City; Bowie County; Pop. 2,507 / 2,783; Zip Code 75561; Elev. 375; Lat. 33-28-0 N, Long. 94-15-5 W; NE Texas; 15 mi. W of Texarkana. It was named for landowner Warren Hooks.

HOUSTON, City; Fort Bend, Harris & Wailer Counties; Harris County Seat; Pop. 1,594,086 / 1,845,967; Zip Code 770+; Elev. 53; SE Texas; on Buffalo Bayou, 50 mi. NW of Galveston Bay. The founders named the town for Sam Houston.

HOWE, Town; Grayson County; Pop. 2,072 / 2,318; Zip Code 75059; NE Texas; 10 mi. S of Sherman, in a farming area.

HUGHES SPRINGS, City; Cass County; Pop. 2,196 / 1,612; Zip Code 75656; Elev. 378; NE Texas; 60 mi. SW of Texarkana. Situated on site of old Choctaw Indian village, the city was named for Reece Hughes, who visited the area on a buffalo hunt in 1829 and returned in 1839 to settle here.

HUMBLE, City; Harris County; Pop. 6,729 / 13,472; Zip Code 773+; Elev. 92; SE Texas; 20 mi. NE of Houston. It was originally named for the Humble Oil Company, now Exxon Corporation, which in turn was named for town founder P.S. Humble.

HUNTINGTON, City; Angelina County; Pop. 1,672 / 1,868; Zip Code 75949; E Texas; 10 mi. SE of Lufkin; Residential.

HUNTSVILLE, City; Walker County Seat; Pop. 23,936 / 32,148; Zip Code 77340; Elev. 401; E Texas; 70 mi. N of Houston.

HURST, City; Tarrant County; Pop. 31,420 / 37,240; Zip Code 76053; N Texas; NE suburb of Fort Worth; Name is Anglo-Saxon for 'wooded hill.'

HUTCHINS, City; Dallas County; Pop. 2,996 / 3,062; Zip Code 75141; NE Texas; S suburb of Dallas.

HUTTO, City; Williamson County; Pop. 659 / 1,362; Zip Code 78634; Central Texas; 26 mi. NE of Austin.

IDALOU, Town; Lubbock County; Pop. 2,348 / 2,136; Zip Code 79329; NW Texas; 11 mi. NE of Lubbock. Ida Bassett and Lou Bacon, founding mothers of this town, gave it its name.

INGLESIDE, City; San Patricia County; Pop. 5,436 / 10,561; Zip Code 78362; S Texas; across bay from Corpus Christi.

INGRAM, City; Kerr County; Pop. 1,949 / 1,644; Zip Code 78025; Elev. 1,600; Central Texas; 5 mi. W of Kerrville. On north bank of Guadalupe River, city founded 1883 by J.C.W. Ingram, who built a store and conducted church services.

IOWA PARK, Town; Wichita County; Pop. 6,184 / 6,531; Zip Code 76367; N Texas; 11 mi. W of Wichita Falls; a small airport serves this community.

IRAAN, City; Pecos County; Pop. 1,358 / 1,387; Zip Code 79744; Elev. 2,200; W Texas; 95 mi. S of Odessa. Name, chosen in a contest, combines names of the town site owners, Ira and Ann Yates.

IRVING, City; Dallas County; Pop. 109,943 / 179,520; Zip Code 750+; Elev. 460; NE Texas; 9 mi. W of Dallas.

ITALY, Town; Ellis County; Pop. 1,306 / 2,023; Zip Code 76651; Elev. 576; NE central Texas; 45 mi. S of Dallas. Gabriel J. Penn named the town after returning from a visit to Italy and discovering similar weather and terrain in this area.

ITASCA, City; Hill County; Pop. 1,600 / 1,608; Zip Code 7605S; Elev. 704; NE central Texas; 45 mi. S of Fort Worth. It was named by a railroad worker for Lake Itasca, Minnesota, and was formally established in 1881.

JACKSBORO, City; Jack County Seat; Pop. 4,000 / 3,565; Zip Code 76056; Elev. 1,074; N Texas; 60 mi. NW of Fort Worth.

JACKSONVILLE, City; Cherokee County; Pop. 12,264 / 13,880; Zip Code 75766; Elev. 516; E Texas; 30 mi. S of Tyler.

JASPER, City; Jasper County Seat; Pop. 6,959 / 8,841; Zip Code 75951; Elev. 221; E Texas; 80 mi. N of Beaumont. The building of John Bevil's log cabin in 1824 marked the beginning of this settlement, which was named in honor of Sergeant William Jasper, South Carolina hero of the American Revolution.

JEFFERSON, City; Marion County Seat; Pop. 2,643 / 2,457; Zip Code 75657; Elev. 191; NE Texas; 15 mi. N of Marshall on Caddo Lake. It is named in honor of President Thomas Jefferson.

JOHNSON CITY, City; Blanco County Seat; Pop. 872 / 1,461; Zip Code 78636; Elev. 1,197; Central Texas; 50 mi. W of Austin in ragged hills near the Edwards Plateau; Named for pioneer Johnson family, ancestors of Lyndon B. Johnson.

JOSHUA, City; Johnson County; Pop. 1,470 / 4,907; Zip Code 76058; N central Texas; 30 mi. S of Fort Worth in a growing residential area.

JOURDANTON, City; Atascosa County Seat; Pop. 2,743 / 4,331; Zip Code 78026; Elev. 491; S Texas; 50 mi. S of San Antonio.

JUNCTION, City; Kimble County Seat; Pop. 2,593 / 2,796; Zip Code 76849; Elev. 2,180; W central Texas; 100 mi. SE of San Angelo.

JUSTIN, City; Denton County; Pop. 920 / 1,729; Zip Code 76247; N Texas; Suburb of Denton.

KARNES CITY, City; Karnes County Seat; Pop. 3,296 / 2,826; Zip Code 78118; Elev. 404; S Texas; 50 mi. SE of San Antonio. Name honors Henry W. Karnes, Texas Revolutionary figure and Indian fighter.

KATY, City; Fort Bend, Harris & Wailer Counties; Pop. 5,660 / 11,199; Zip Code 774+; SE Texas; Residential area near Houston; Named for 'The Katy,' a common name for the Missouri, Kansas and Texas Railroad.

KAUFMAN, City; Kaufman County Seat; Pop. 4,658 / 6,914; Zip Code 75142; Elev. 440; NE Texas; 30 mi. SE of Dallas.

KEENE, City; Johnson County; Pop. 3,013 / 5,590; Zip Code 76059; Elev. 890; N central Texas; 25 mi. S of Fort Worth. This growing town was named for a leader in the Seventh Day Adventist Church, whose members dominate the community.

KEMAH, City; Galveston County; Pop. 1,304 / 1,687; Zip Code 77565; SE Texas; 12 mi. N of Galveston on the Bay; Name is Indian for "facing the winds," since the place received blusters from Galveston Bay.

KEMP, Town; Kaufman County; Pop. 1,035 / 1,376; Zip Code 75143; Lat. 32-26-4 N, Long. 96-13-.8 W; NE Texas; 45 mi. SE of Dallas in a cattle raising area.

KENDLETON, City; Fort Bend County; Pop. 606 / 687; Zip Code 77451; Elev. 102; SE Texas; 45 mi. S of Houston.

KENEDY, City; Karnes County; Pop. 4,356 / 3,624; Zip Code 78119; Elev. 271; S Texas; 60 mi. SE of San Antonio.

KENNEDALE, City; Tarrant County; Pop. 2,594 / 5,075; Zip Code 76060; N Texas; 8 mi. SE of Fort Worth.

KERENS, City; Navarro County; Pop. 1,582 / 1,650; Zip Code 75144; NE central Texas; 14 mi. E of Corsicana in a farming area; Fertilizers are manufactured.

KERMIT, City; Winkler County Seat; Pop. 8,015 / 6,216; Zip Code 79745; Elev. 2,890; W Texas; 45 mi. W of Odessa. The town was named for President Theodore Roosevelt's twenty-one year old son in 1910.

KERRVILLE, City; Kerr County Seat; Pop. 15,276 / 20,556; Zip Code 78028; SW central Texas; 65 mi. NW of San Antonio on the Guadalupe River.

KILGORE, City; Gregg & Rusk Counties; Pop. 10,968 / 11,574; Zip Code 75662; Elev. 371; NE Texas; 120 mi. E of Dallas.

KILLEEN, City; Bell County; Pop. 46,296 / 81,405; Zip Code 765+; Elev. 833; Central Texas; 30 mi. W of Temple City is edged by 218,000-acre Fort Hood. Named for Frank Kileen, a civil engineer of the Santa Fe Railroad that built across county in 1822.

KINGSLAND, Village; Llano County; Pop. 2,216; Zip Code 78639; Elev. 856; Central Texas; 60 mi. NW of Austin in Highland Lakes area.

KINGSVILLE, City; Kleberg County Seat; Pop. 28,808 / 24,820; Zip Code 78363; S Texas; 30 mi. SW of Corpus Christi. It is named for the local King Ranch.

KIRBYVILLE, City; Jasper County; Pop. 1,972 / 1,982; Zip Code 75956; Elev. 101; E Texas; 40 mi. N of Beaumont. Town was named for sawmill operator John Kirby.

KNOX CITY, City; Knox County; Pop. 1,546 / 1,346; Zip Code 79529; N Texas; 60 mi. N of Abilene. The town is named for General Henry Knox.

KOUNTZE, City; Hardin County Seat; Pop. 2,716 / 2,185; Zip Code 77625; Elev. 85; E central Texas; 40 mi. SE of Tyler.

KRUM, City; Denton County; Pop. 917 / 2,062; Zip Code 76249; N Texas; Suburb of Denton.

KYLE, Town; Hays County; Pop. 2,093 / 4,250; Zip Code 78640; S central Texas; 20 mi. SW of Austin.

LA COSTE, City; Medina County; Pop. 862 / 1,329; Zip Code 78039; S central Texas; 24 mi. W of Son Antonio.

LA FERIA, City; Cameron County; Pop. 3,395 / 5,409; Zip Code 78559; S Texas; 8 mi. W of Harlingen near the Rio Grande in a lush tropical and citrus fruit-growing area.

LA GRANGE, City; Fayette County Seat; Pop. 3,768 / 3,045; Zip Code 78945; Elev. 272; SE central Texas; 65 mi. SE of Austin on the Colorado River.

LA JOYA, City; Hidalgo County; Pop. 2,018 / 3,389; Zip Code 78560; S Texas; Near the Rio Grande; Name is taken from Spanish word for "jewel."

LAKE DALLAS, City; Denton County; Pop. 3,177 / 5,876; Zip Code 75065; Elev. 581; N Texas; N suburb of Dallas.

LAKE JACKSON, City; Brazoria County; Pop. 19,102 / 27,297; Zip Code 77566; SE Texas; 30 mi. SW of Galveston on the Gulf, considered part of the Brazosport area.

LAKE WORTH, City; Tarrant County; Pop. 4,394 / 4,806; Zip Code 76135; N Texas; 9 mi. W of downtown Fort Worth. This village grew around the 5,000-acre reservoir by the same name.

LA MARQUE, City; Galveston County; Pop. 15,372 / 14,693; Zip Code 77568; Elev. 17; SE Texas; 13 mi. W of Galveston in a residential area. This city, once known as Buttermilk Station, became La Marque after the Civil War when post mistress Madame St. Ambrose renamed it. The name is French for "the mark."

LAMESA, City; Dawson County Seat; Pop. 11,790 / 14,693; Zip Code 79331; Elev. 2,975; NW Texas; 65 mi. S of Lubbock. Cotton, cattle, and black-eyed peas are the mainstays of this town. Its position on the plains at the edge of Cap Rock gave La Mesa its name, which makes one ward of the Spanish *la mesa*, "the table."

LAMPASAS, City; Lampasas County Seat; Pop. 6,165 / 8,019; Zip Code 76550; Elev. 1,025; Central Texas; 60 mi. NW of Austin. Named for the Spanish word for water lily.

LANCASTER, City; Dallas County; Pop. 14,807 / 24,606; Zip Code 751+; NE Texas; S suburb of Dallas in a growing residential area.

LANGTRY, Val Verde County; Zip Code 78871; Elev. 1,315; SW Texas; Just N of Mexico border on Rio Grande.

LA PORTE, City; Harris County; Pop. 14,062; Zip Code 77571; Elev. 28; SE Texas; On Galveston Bay, 15 mi. E of Houston. It was given its name, meaning "the door," by French settlers in 1889 when the city was founded on upper Galveston Bay.

LAREDO, City; Webb County Seat; 91,449 / 183,160; Zip Code 780+; Elev. 438; S Texas 140 mi. SW of Son Antonio on the Rio Grande. On May 15, 1755, with three or four families, Thomas Sanchez formally founded the Villa de Laredo.

LA VERNIA, City; Wilson County; Pop. 632 / 1,061; Zip Code 78121; S central Texas; 20 mi. E of San Antonio. Town was settled by William Wiseman and his family in 1850. Originally named "Live Oak Grove," it was changed in 1859 to the Spanish name for the tree," or "the green."

LEAGUE CITY, City; Galveston County; Pop. 16,578 / 44,966; Zip Code 77573; SE Texas; 20 mi. NW of Galveston; Residential.

LEANDER, City; Williamson County; Pop. 2,179 / 9,127; Zip Code 78641; Central Texas; 20 mi. NW of Austin.

LEONARD, City; Fannin County; Pop. 1,421 / 1,851; Zip Code 75452; Elev. 704; NE Texas; 30 mi. SE of Sherman.

LEVELLAND, City; Hockley County Seat; Pop. 13,809 / 13,564; Zip Code 79336; Elev. 3,523; NW Texas; 30 mi. W of Lubbock. Appropriately named for the surrounding terrain.

LEWISVILLE, City; Denton County; Pop. 24,273 / 77,355; Zip Code 24,145; Elev. 484; N Texas; 15 mi. SE of Denton.

LEXINGTON, Town; Lee County; Pop. 1,065 / 1,137; Zip Code 78947; Central Texas; 40 mi. NE of Austin.

LIBERTY, City; Liberty County Seat; Pop. 7,945 / 8,786; Zip Code 77575; Elev. 30; E Texas; 40 mi. NE of Houston. Liberty was first named Atoscosita from its position on a frontier highway, the Atascosita Road. Later called Liberty Town, it sent a delegation to the San Felipe de Austin Convention of 1832, and in 1836 a company from Liberty joined Sam Houston's army in time to fight the Battle of San Jacinto.

LINDALE, Town; Smith County; Pop. 2,180 / 3,117; Zip Code 75771; NE Texas; 80 mi. SE of Dallas.

LINDEN, City; Cass County Seat; Pop. 2,443 / 2,499; Zip Code 75563; Elev. 270; NE Texas; 35 M. N of Marshall. Linden was named for a town in a popular poem by Thomas Campbell.

LITTLE RIVER, City; Bell County; Pop. 1,155; Zip Code 76554; Central Texas; 5 mi. S of Temple on a river by the same name.

LIVINGSTON, Town; Polk County Seat; Pop. 4,928 / 8,169; Zip Code 77351; Elev. 194; E Texas; 70 mi. NE of Houston.

LLANO, City; Llano County Seat; Pop. 3,071 / 3,472; Zip Code 78643; Elev. 1,029; Central Texas; 65 mi. NW of Austin. Name means "level land" in an Indian language.

LOCKHART, City; Caldwell County Seat; Pop. 7,953 / 11,803; Zip Code 78644; Elev. 518; S Central Texas; 30 mi. S of Austin; Named for town site owner and Texas soldier Byrd Lockhart.

LOCKNEY, Town; Floyd County; Pop. 2,334 / 2,178; Zip Code 79241; NW Texas; 20 mi. SE of Plainview in a ranching area.

LOLITA, Village; Jackson County; Pop. 1,200; Zip Code 77971; SE Texas; 30 mi. E of Victoria. The town was named in 1910 for Lolita Reese, who claimed as her ancestors a soldier at the bottle of San Jacinto and a member of the Mier Expedition. The name was nearly changed during the 1950s when the movie Lolita scandalized townspeople.

LONE STAR, Town; Morris County; Pop. 2,036 / 1,639; Zip Code 75668; NE Texas; 40 mi. NW of Marshall. Incorporated in 1948, Lone Star was named for the Lone Star Steel Company, which in turn was taken from the state's nickname.

LONGVIEW, City; Gregg & Harrison Counties; Gregg County Seat; Pop. 62,762 / 75,534; Zip Code 756+; Elev. 339; NE Texas; 65 mi. W of Shreveport, Louisiana.

LORENA, City; McLennan County; Pop. 619 / 1,548; Zip Code 76655; Central Texas; 10 mi. S of Waco.

LORENZO, Town; Crosby County; Pop. 1,394 / 1,165; Zip Code 79343; NW Texas; 25 mi. E of Lubbock.

LOS PRESNOS, City; Cameron County; Pop. 2,173; Zip Code 78566; S Texas; 12 mi. N of Brownsville. Its name is Spanish for "the ash trees."

LUBBOCK, City; Lubbock County Seat; Pop. 173,979 / 190,002; Zip Code 794+; Elev. 3,241; NW Texas; 110 mi. S of Amarillo. Named after Thomas Lubbock, a Confederate leader.

LUFKIN, City; Angelina County Seat; Pop. 28,562 / 33,482; Zip Code 75901; Elev. 326; E Texas; 115 mi. N of Houston.

LULING, City; Caldwell County; Pop. 5,039 / 5,482; Zip Code 78648; Elev. 418; S central Texas; 55 mi. NE of San Antonio.

LUMBERTON, City; Hardin County; Pop. 2,480 / 8,327; Zip Code 77711; E Texas; 20 mi. N of Beaumont in a heavily timbered area.

LYFORD, Town; Willacy County; Pop. 1,618 / 1,854; Zip Code 78569; S Texas; 15 mi. N of Horlingen.

LYONS, Burleson County; Zip Code 77863; E central Texas; 20 mi. SE of Bryan; Named for early shopkeeper WA. Lyon.

LYTLE, City; Atascosa, Bexar & Medina Counties; Pop. 920 / 2,670; Zip Code 78052; S Texas; 20 mi. SW of San Antonio.

MABANK, Town; Kaufman County; Pop. 1,437 / 2,125; Zip Code 75147; NE Texas; 55 mi. SE of Dallas on N shore of Cedar Creek Lake. Dodge Mason and Tom Eubank were early settlers here. Parts of each of their names were used for the name of this town.

MADISONVILLE, City; Madison County Seat; Pop. 3,660 / 3,871; Zip Code 77864; Elev. 278; E central Texas. Named for fourth President of the United States it is today the center for cotton, cattle, and lumber in the region.

MAGNOLIA, Town; Montgomery County; Pop. 867 / 1,266; Zip Code 77355; E Texas; 40 mi. NW of Houston.

MALAKOFF, City; Henderson County; Pop. 2,082 / 2,237; Zip Code 75148; NE Texas; 25 mi. E of Carsicana at S tip of Cedar Creek Lake.

MANOR, City; Travis County; Pop. 1,044 / 1,142; Zip Code 78653; Central Texas; 10 mi. NE of Austin; Residential.

MANSFIELD, City; Johnson & Tarrant Counties; Pop. 8,092 / 24,850; Zip Code 76063; N Texas; 15 mi. SE of Fort Worth; Residential. City was named for early settlers R.S. Mann and Julian Field.

MANVEL, City; Brazoria County; Pop. 3,549 / 3,586; Zip Code 77578; SE Texas; 20 mi. S of Houston.

MARBLE FALLS, City; Burnet County; Pop. 3,252 / 6,066; Zip Code 78654; Elev. 764; Central Texas; On the Colorado River, 40 mi. NW of Austin. This town in the Hill Country was named for nearby Colorado River waterfalls over marble out croppings.

MARFA, City; Presidio County Seat; Pop. 2,466 / 2,781; Zip Code 79843; Elev. 4,668; W Texas; 175 mi. SE of El Paso.

MARION, City; Guadalupe County; Pop. 674 / 1,171; Zip Code 78124; S central Texas; 25 mi. NE of San Antonio; Named for Genera Francis Marion.

MARSHALL, City; Harrison County Seat; Pop. 24,921 / 24,338; Zip Code 75670; Elev. 375; 32-33-0 N, Long. 94-23-0 W; NE Texas; 70 mi. S of Texarkana. Marshall, named for U.S. Chief Justice John Marshall, was established in 1841.

MART, City; McLennan County; Pop. 2,324 / 2,022; Zip Code 76664; Central Texas; 17 mi. E of Waco.

MASON, City; Mason County Seat; Pop. 2,153 / 2,235; Zip Code 76856; Elev. 1,450; Central Texas; 120 mi. NW of San Antonio near the Llano River. Named after Charles H. Mason, who was killed during the Mexican War.

MATADOR, Town; Motley County Seat; Pop. 1,052 / 624; Zip Code 79244; Elev. 2,347; NW Texas; 60 mi. SE of Plainview. Named for its proximity to the great Matador Ranch.

MATHIS, City; San Patricia County; Pop. 5,667 / 5,981; Zip Code 78368; Elev. 161; S Texas; 40 mi. NW of Corpus Christi.

MAUD, City; Bowie County; Pop. 1,059 / 1,090; Zip Code 75567; Elev. 284; NE Texas; 20 mi. SW of Texarkana.

MAYPEARL, City; Ellis county; Pop. 626 / 1,033; Zip Code 76064; NE central Texas; 35 mi. S of Dallas. The town, incorporated in 1914, was named for May Pearl Trammel, wife of a railroad engineer.

MCALLEN, City; Hidalgo County; Pop. 67,042 / 110,292; Zip Code 78501; S Texas; 50 mi. NW of Brownsville, near the Rio Grande.

MCCAMEY, City; Upton County; Pop. 2,436 / 1,785; Zip Code 79752; Elev. 2,241; W Texas; 100 mi. W of San Angelo. Then an oil driller named McCamey hit a gusher. In less than a year, McCamey was brawling boom town of 10,000 housed in tents and hastily constructed buildings.

MCGREGOR, City; McLennan County; Pop. 4,513 / 4,754; Zip Code 76657; Elev. 713; Central Texas; 19 mi. W of Waco.

MCKINNEY, City; Collin County Seat; Pop. 16,249 / 44,807; Zip Code 75069; Elev. 612; NE Texas; 30 mi. S of Sherman. Settled in 1845, city and county were named for Collin McKinney, a signer of the Texas Declaration of Independence and leader in establishment of the Disciples of Christ (Christian Church) in Texas.

MCLEAN, Town; Gray County; Pop. 1,160 / 804; Zip Code 79057; NW Texas; 70 mi. E of Amarillo.

MEMPHIS, City; Hall County Seat; Pop. 3,352 / 2,224; Zip Code 79245; Elev. 2,067; NW Texas.

MENARD, City; Menard County Seat; Pop. 1,697 / 1,628; Zip Code 76859; Elev. 1,960; W central Texas; on the Son Saba River, 65 mi. SE of San Angelo. Named after Michael Branaman Menard, founder of Galveston.

MERCEDES, City; Hidalgo County; Pop. 11,851 / 15,661; Zip Code 78570; Elev. 61; S Texas; 18 mi. W of Harlingen. Had its establishment in 1906, in the early days of the citrus boom, and was named for Mercedes Diaz wife of the then President of Mexico.

MERIDIAN, City; Basque County Seat; Pop. 1,330 / 1,405; Zip Code 76665; Elev. 791; Central Texas; 40 mi. NW of Waco; Named because it lies at the ninety-eighth meridian.

MERKEL, Town; Taylor County; Pop. 2,493 / 2,512; Zip Code 79536; NW central Texas; 15 mi. W of Abilene.

MESQUITE, City; Dallas County; Pop. 67,053 / 116,179; Elev. 491; Zip Code 751+; Lot 32-45-9 N. Long. 96-35-8 W; NE Texas; 10 mi. E of Dallas. Named for nearby Mesquite Creek.

MEXIA, City; Limestone County; Pop. 7,094 / 6,444; Zip Code 76667; Elev. 534; E central Texas; 30 mi. S of Corsicana. Established 1871, named for Mexican General Jose Antonio Mexia, whose family donated town site.

MIDLAND, City; Midland County Seat; Pop. 70,525 / 98,293; Zip Code 797+; Elev. 2,779; W Texas; 20 mi. NE of Odessa. Named for location halfway between Fort Worth and El Paso.

MIDLOTHIAN, City; Ellis County; Pop. 3,219 / 8,287; Zip Code 76065; NE central Texas; 20 mi. SW of Dallas. It was named by a railroad workers for the county in Scotland.

MINEOLA, City; Wood County; Pop. 4,346 / 5,085; Zip Code 75773; NE Texas; 20 mi. N of Tyler.

MINERAL WELLS, City; Palo Pinto & Parker Counties; Pop. 14,468 / 14,923; Zip Code 76067; Elev. 925; N central Texas; 50 mi. W of Fort Worth. Discovery of medicinal qualities in waters made city nationally famous in the nineteenth century.

MISSION, City; Hidalgo County; Pop. 22,589 / 43,947; Zip Code 78572; Elev. 134; S Texas; 6 mi. W of McAllen. Town was laid out on the La Lomita Rancho; property of the Oblate Fathers, who, carrying on the work started by Franciscans 100 years before, founded a chapel in 1824 on the north bank of the Rio Grand., south of town.

MISSOURI CITY, City; Fort Bend & Harris Counties; Pop. 24,533 / 66,341; Zip Code 774+; SE Texas; 10 mi. SW of Houston; Residential. Named because a number of settlers had read advertisements for the townsite in their local newspapers in Missouri.

MONAHANS, City; Ward & Winkler Counties; Ward County Seat; Pop. 8,397 / 6,515; Zip Code 79756; Elev. 2,613; W Texas; 140 mi. W of San Angelo.

MONT BELVIEU, City; Chambers County; Pop. 1,730 / 2,080; Zip Code 77580; SE Texas; 15 mi. N of Baytown; Name means 'Beautiful Old Hill.'

MOODY, Town; McLennan County; Pop. 1,385 / 1,398; Zip Code 76557; Elev. 783; Central Texas; 25 mi. SW of Waco. Renamed in 1881 to honor Col. W.L. Moody, director of the Gulf, Colorado and Santa Fe Railroad, when that line was built through.

MORTON, City; Cochran County Seat; Pop. 2,674 / 2,272; Zip Code 79346; Elev. 3,758; NW Texas; 40 mi. S of Bailey.

MOULTON, Town; Lavaca County; Pop. 1,009 / 929; Zip Code 77975; SE central Texas; 75 mi. NE of San Antonio.

MOUNT PLEASANT, City; Titus County Seat; Pop. 11,003 / 13,130; Zip Code 75455; Elev. 416; NE Texas; 65 mi. SW of Texarkana. The town was named for its pleasant wooded location.

MOUNT VERNON, Town; Franklin County Seat; Pop. 2,025 / 2,882; Zip Code 75457; Elev. 476; NE Texas. The area first settled in 1830 by Joshua T. Johnson, has been known as Keith and Lone Star. In 1875, the new name was chosen, honoring George Washington's plantation.

MUENSTER, City; Cooke County; Pop. 1,408 / 1,560; Zip Code 76252; Elev. 970; N Texas; 60 mi. N of Fort Worth. Founded in 1889 by two brothers, Muenster was named for a city in their fatherland.

MULESHOE, City; Bailey County Seat; Pop. 4,842 / 4,357; Zip Code 79347; Elev. 3,789; NW Texas; 70 mi. NW of Lubbock. Muleshoe is in the center of the Muleshoe Ranch from which it took its name.

MUNDAY, City; Knox County; Pop. 1,738 / 1,136; Zip Code 76371; N Texas; 73 mi. SW of Wichita Falls in a farming region.

NACOGDOCHES, City; Nacogdoches County Seat; Pop. 27,149 / 30,804; Zip Code 75961; Elev. 283; E Texas. The Nacogdoches tribe had a permanent village on the site, and beside on Indian trail the Spaniards built their mission.

NAPLES, Town; Morris County; Pop. 1,908 / 1,470; Zip Code 75568; NE Texas; 65 mi. SW of Texarkana; Named for the Italian city.

NATALIA, City; Medina County; Pop. 1,264 / 1,518; Zip Code 78059; Elev. 686; S central Texas; 25 mi. SW of downtown San Antonio.

NAVASOTA, City; Grimes County; Pop. 5,971 / 8,040; Zip Code 77868; Elev. 215; E central Texas; 60 mi. NW of Houston.

NEDERLAND, City; Jefferson County; Pop. 16,855 / 17,599; Zip Code 77627; Elev. 25; SE Texas; 7 mi. SE of Beaumont. It was founded in 1896 by colonists from The Netherlands. The name means "lowland" in Dutch.

NEEDVILLE, City; Fort Bend County; Pop. 1,428 / 3,316; Zip Code 77461; SE Texas; 38 mi. SW of Houston. The post office was called Needville because the local settlers were needy.

NEW BADEN, Town; Robertson County; Zip Code 77870; Elev. 427; E central Texas. It was established in 1880 by J.G. Meyer, colonizer who worked with a land company that brought in cultured German colonists principally from Baden.

NEW BOSTON, Town; Bowie County; Pop. 4,628 / 5,451; Zip Code 75570; NE Texas; 25 mi. E of Texarkana. Named because it is adjacent to and was founded after the town of Boston.

NEW BRAUNFELS, City; Comal & Guadalupe Counties; Comal County Seat; Pop. 22,402 / 38,281; Zip Code 78130; Elev. 750; S central Texas; 30 mi. NE of San Antonio. Here the quixotic Prince Carl Zum Solms-Braunfels for whom the city is named, established a German settlement in 1845, and, surrounding himself with a retinue of velvet-clad courtiers and soldiers who wore brilliant plumes.

NEW WAVERLY, City; Walker County; Pop. 824 / 1,011; Zip Code 77358; Elev. 362; E Texas; 70 mi. N of Houston in Sam Houston National Forest.

NEWTON, City; Newton County Seat; Pop. 1,620 / 2,024; Zip Code 75966; E Texas. Named after John Newton, a soldier in the American Revolution.

NIXON, City; Gonzales & Wilson Counties; Pop. 2,008 / 2,039; Zip Code 78140; Elev. 396; S central Texas; 45 mi. SE of San Antonio.

NOCONA, City; Montague County; Pop. 2,992 / 2,650; Zip Code 76255; Elev. 988; N Texas; 50 mi. E of Wichita Falls. Nocona was named for Peta Nocona, an Indian chief.

ODEM, City; San Patricia County; Pop. 2,363 / 2,627; Zip Code 78370; S Texas; 18 mi. NW of Corpus Christi in a farming area.

ODESSA, City; Ector County Seat; Pop. 90,027 / 89,293; Zip Code 797+; Elev. 2,890; W Texas. It is said that the name originated from Russian railroad laborers who compared wide, flat prairies with their homeland on steppes of Russia.

O'DONNELL, City; Dawson & Lynn Counties; Pop. 1,200 / 1,073; Zip Code 79351; Elev. 3,000; NW Texas; 43 mi. S of Lubbock.

OLNEY, City; Young County; Pop. 4,060 / 3,302; Zip Code 76374; Elev. 1,184; N Texas; 45 mi. S of Wichita Falls. Named to honor Richard Olney, Secretary of State in Grover Cleveland's cabinet.

OLTON, City; Lomb County Seat; Pop. 2,235 / 2,026; Zip Code 79064; Elev. 3,615; NW Texas; 25 mi. W of Plainview in a ranching region.

ONALASKA, City; Polk County; Pop. 386 / 1,221; Zip Code 77360; E Texas. T.G. Rowe, lumber company owner, named this town for Oonalaska in Thomas Campbell's poem, Pleasures of Hope, in the mid-1800s.

ORANGE, City; Orange County Seat; Pop. 23,628 / 19,754; Zip Code 77630; Elev. 20; E Texas; 20 mi. E of Beaumont on the Sabine River. Named for the wild orange groves along the banks of the Sabine River.

ORANGE GROVE, City; Jim Wells County; Pop. 1,212 / 1,290; Zip Code 78372; S Texas; 30 mi. W of Corpus Christi; Name is descriptive.

ORE CITY, City; Upshur County; Pop. 1,050 / 1,072; Zip Code 75683; NE Texas; 30 mi. NW of Marshall, near Lake Of The Pines.

OVERTON, City; Rusk & Smith Counties; Pop. 2,430 / 2,079; Zip Code 75684; Elev. 507; E Texas; 24 mi. E of Tyler. Laid out in 1873 when Missouri Pacific Railroad was built; named for a pioneer family.

OZONA, Town; Crockett County Seat; Pop. 3,764; Zip Code 76943; W Texas; Elev. 2,348; 70 mi. SE of San Angela in a sage-covered area.

PADUCAH, Town; Cattle County Seat; Pop. 2,216 / 1,514; Zip Code 79248; Elev. 1,886; NW Texas; 100 mi. NW of Wichita Falls. The town's first residents hailed from Paducah, Kentucky, and named their new home for it.

PALACIOS, City; Matagorda County; Pop. 4,667 / 4,408; Zip Code 77465; Elev. 17; SE Texas; 90 mi. SW of Houston. Settled in 1903, in an area named by shipwrecked Spaniards who supposedly saw a vision of *tres palacios* (three palaces).

PALESTINE, City; Anderson County Seat; Pop. 15,948 / 18,789; Zip Code 75801; Elev. 510; E Texas; 45 mi. SW of Tyler; Named for Palestine, Illinois.

PALMER, Town; Ellis County; Pop. 1,187 / 2,149; Zip Code 75152; Elev. 468; NE central Texas; 30 mi. SE of Dallas. It was named for Martin Palmer, a participant in the Battle of San Jacinto.

PAMPA, City; Gray County Seat; Pop. 2,396 / 18,466; Zip Code 79065; Elev. 3,234; NW Texas; 55 mi. NE of Amarillo. Pampa is so named because of the resemblance of the encircling prairies to the Argentine pampas.

PANHANDLE, Town; Carson County Seat; Pop. 2,226 / 2,104; Zip Code 79068; Elev. 3,451; NW Texas; 28 mi. NE of Amarillo. Named for its location in Texas Panhandle, it became the county seat upon organization of Carson County in 1888.

PANTEGO, Town; Tarrant County; Pop. 2,431 / 2,530; Zip Code 760+; N Texas; Suburb of Fort Worth.

PARIS, City; Lamar County Seat; Pop. 25,498 / 26,215; Zip Code 75460; NE Texas; 95 mi. NE of Dallas.

PASADENA, City; Harris County; Pop. 112,560 / 133,660; Zip Code 775+; Elev. 34; SE Texas; 3 mi. E of Houston. Name is Spanish for "Land of Flowers," chosen for blooming meadows along Vince's Bayou.

PEARLAND, City; Brazoria & Harris Counties; Pop. 13,248 / 34,936; Zip Code 775+; SE Texas; 12 mi. S of Houston; Residential.

PEARSALL, City; Frio County Seat; Pop. 7,383 / 7,563; Zip Code 78061; Elev. 641; S Texas. Established on International-Great Northern Railroad in 1880.

PECOS, City; Reeves County Seat; Pop. 12,855 / 10,336; Zip Code 79772; Elev. 2,850; W Texas; 75 mi. SW of Odessa on the Pecos River. One of the country's earliest versions of the popular western spectacle, the rodeo, as today practiced is credited to Pecos.

PERRYTON, City; Ochiltree County Seat; Pop. 7,991 / 7,357; Zip Code 79070; Elev. 2,942; NW Texas; 120 mi. NE of Amarillo, near Oklahoma state line. The town was formed in 1919, largely by citizens of Ochiltree, Texas and Gray, Oklahoma, who moved to the new town site hauling their homes intact, hitched to tractors.

PETERSBURG, City; Hale County; Pop. 1,633 / 1,291; Zip Code 79250; NW Texas; 28 mi. SE of Plainview.

PFLUGERVILLE, City; Travis County; Pop. 11,360; Zip Code 78660; Central Texas; 12 mi. N of Austin.

PHARR, City; Hidalgo County; Pop. 21,381 / 45,844; Zip Code 78577; Elev. 107; S Texas. Established in 1909, named after Henry N. Pharr, a sugar planter from Louisiana.

PILOT POINT, City; Denton County; Pop. 2,211 / 3,267; Zip Code 76258; N Texas; 20 mi. NE of Denton; Named because it is on a high ridge overlooking a forested valley. George Newcomb platted the town in 1853.

PINELAND, City; Sabine County; Pop. 1,111 / 979; Zip Code 75968; Elev. 267; E Texas; 20 mi. N of Jasper in the Sabine Notional Forest. This lumber mill town has its homes spread out amid the piney woods.

PITTSBURG, City; Camp County Seat; Pop. 4,245 / 4,607; Zip Code 75686; Elev. 392; NE Texas; 50 mi. N of Tyler. A heavily timbered area, also a commercial center for farming, poultry and livestock.

PLAINS, Town; Yoakum County Seat; Pop. 1,457 / 1,284; Zip Code 79355; Elev. 3,400; NW Texas; 32 mi. W of Brownfield. First land claim was filled here in 1890s by family who lived in a dugout, but whose possessions included a piano.

PLAINVIEW, City; Hale County Seat; Pop. 22,187 / 23,079; Zip Code 79072; Elev. 3,366; NW Texas; 40 mi. N of Lubbock. Plainview was founded in the 1880s as a dugout town. Named for its magnificent view of plains.

PLANO, City; Collin & Denton Counties; Pop. 72,331 / 232,904; Zip Code 750+; Elev. 655; NE Texas. Town was established as Fillmore in 1848, but changed to the Spanish word for 'plain' due to its location on the broad, level backlands prairies in 1851.

PLEASANTON, City; Atascosa County; Pop. 6,346 / 9,957; Zip Code 78064; Elev. 365; S Texas; 32 mi. S of San Antonio. Settled in the 1850s, Pleasanton was one of the cattle concentration points on the old Western Trail to Dodge City, Kansas.

POINT COMFORT, City; Calhoun County; Pop. 1,125 / 941; Zip Code 77978; S Texas; 5 mi. across Lavaca Bay from Port Lavaca.

PORT ARANSAS, City; Aransas & Nueces Counties; Pop. 1,968 / 2,507; Zip Code 78373; S Texas; 30 mi. NE of Corpus Christi at Aransas Pass to Gulf of Mexico. The city is on Mustang Island, reached by causeway and free, 24-hour ferry service.

PORT ARTHUR, City; Jefferson County; Pop. 61,195 / 56,574; Zip Code 77640; Elev. 4; SE Texas; 90 mi. E of Houston on Sabine Lake. Having fixed upon the Lake Sabine shores as the site of his dream city in 1895 Arthur Stilwell caused a town site to be surveyed which he named Port Arthur in his honor.

PORT ISABEL, City; Cameron County; Pop. 3,769 / 5,500; Zip Code 78578; Elev. 8; S Texas; 120 mi. S of Corpus Christi on the Gulf. This resort and fishing town was settled by Mexican ranchers as early as 1770, but today hotels, motels and boat slips dominate the scene.

PORT LAVACA, City; Calhoun County Seat; Pop. 10,911 / 12,344; Zip Code 77979; Elev. 22; S Texas; 70 mi. NE of Corpus Christi. Founded by the Spanish in 1815, the early town was called *La Vaca* (the cow), the Lavaca River having been thus named by La Salle.

PORT NECHES, City; Jefferson County; Pop. 13,944 / 13,981; Zip Code 77651; SE Texas; 10 mi. NW of Port Arthur on the Neches River.

PORTLAND, City; Nueces & San Patricia Counties; Pop. 12,023 / 15,176; Zip Code 78374; S Texas; 8 mi. N of Corpus Christi across the bay. Oil and gas refining are important in this port town.

POST, City; Garza County Seat; Pop. 3,961 / 3,345; Zip Code 79356; Elev. 2,590; NW Texas; 40 mi. SE of Lubbock. Founded in 1907 by C.W. Post, of Battle Creek, Michigan, a cereal manufacturer and philanthropist, who dreamed of having a model town where agriculture and industry were to round out its civic existence.

POTEET, City; Atascosa County; Pop. 3,086 / 3,574; Zip Code 78065; Elev. 525; S Texas. In center of truck-forming region; coiled the "Strawberry Capital of Texas."

POTH, Town; Wilson County; Pop. 1,461 / 2,082; Zip Code 78147; S central Texas; 30 mi. SE of San Antonio.

POTTSBORO, Town; Grayson County; Pop. 895 / 1,346; Zip Code 75076; NE Texas; 10 mi. NW of Sherman in a rural area.

PRAIRIE VIEW, City; Waller County; Pop. 3,993 / 4,394; Zip Code 77445; Elev. 250; SE Texas. Named for plantation home of Col. Jack Kirby.

PREMONT, City; Jim Wells County; Pop. 2,984 / 3,133; Zip Code 78375; S Texas; 27 mi. S of Alice.

PRESIDIO, City; Presidio County; Pop. 1,720 / 4,701; Zip Code 79845; Elev. 2,594; W Texas; 200 mi. SE of El Paso on the Rio Grand. Spanish priests came here in the late sixteenth century. In 1684, a formal establishment of a group of missions was made under the name La Junta de los Rios ("junction of the rivers"). In 1830, the name was changed to Presidio del Norte, which was eventually shortened.

PROSPER, Town; Collin County; Pop. 675 / 1,761; Zip Code 75078; NE Texas; 6 mi. NW of McKinney.

QUANAH, City; Hardeman County Seat; Pop. 3,890 / 2,866; Zip Code 79252; Elev. 1,568; N Texas; 80 m, NW of Wichita Falls. The city was named for Quanah Parker, one-time war chief of the Comanche.

QUEEN CITY, City; Cass County; Pop. 1,748 / 1,850; Zip Code 75572; NE Texas; 15 mi. S of Texarkana.

QUINLAN, City; Hunt County; Pop. 1,002 / 1,479; Zip Code 75474; NE Texas; 40 mi. E of Dallas near Lake Tawakoni.

QUITMAN, City; Wood County Seat; Pop. 1,893 / 1,953; Zip Code 75783; Elev. 414; NE Texas; 65 mi. NW of Marshall. Quitman is commercial center for farming, livestock, oil, headquarters for electric co-op.

RALLS, City; Crosby County; Pop. 2,422 / 2,065; Zip Code 79357; NW Texas.

RANGER, City; Eastland County; Pop. 3,142 / 2,341; Zip Code 76470; Elev. 1,429; N central Texas; 60 mi. E of Abilene. Founded in 1881 and named for a camp of Texas Rangers near which the tent village of the first citizens took shape.

RAKIN, City; Upton County Seat; Pop. 1,216 / 904; Zip Code 79778; W Texas; 55 mi. SE of Odessa in oil and cattle country.

RAYMONDVILLE, City; Willacy County Seat; Pop. 9,493 / 9,706; Zip Code 78580; Elev. 40; S Texas; 20 mi. N of Harlingen. Raymondville is a commercial center for an irrigated fruit and vegetable area.

RED OAK, City; Ellis County; Pop. 1,882 / 4,914; Zip Code 75154; NE central Texas; 20 mi. S of Dallas.

REFUGIO, Town; Refugio County Seat; Pop. 3,898 / 3,061; Zip Code 78377; Elev. 50; S Texas. Refugio was founded in 1790 when Franciscan monks built Mission Nuestro Senora Del Refugio (Mission of Our Lady of Refuge), which was first destroyed in wars between Karankawas and Comanche, and later bombarded by the Mexican Army in 1836.

RICHARDSON, City; Collin & Dallas Counties; Pop. 72,496 / 87,517; Zip Code 750+; Elev. 630; NE Texas; N suburb of Dallas. The settlement was called Breckenridge before Civil War; renamed for railroad official.

RICHMOND, City; Fort Bend County; Pop. 9,692 / 14,329; Zip Code 77469; Elev. 104; Lat. 29-34-7 N, Long. 95-45-9 W SE Texas; 30 mi. SW of Houston. Richmond was settled in 1822 by Austin's colonists, this is among the oldest Anglo-American towns in the State.

RIO GRANDE CITY, Village; Starr County Seat; Pop. 8,887 / 14,905; Zip Code 78582; Elev. 238; S Texas. Occupied by Spanish settlers of Escandon in 1753 and founded as a town in 1847 by Henry Clay Davis, a soldier of fortune. Long known locally as Rancho Davis, it was for years on important stop for the river steamers plying the Rio Grande.

RIO HONDO, Town; Cameron County; Pop. 1,673 / 2,248; Zip Code 78583; S Texas; Name means "deep river."

RISING STAR, Town; Eastland County; Pop. 1,204 / 846; Zip Code 76471; N central Texas; 28 mi. N of Brownwood. This town was assigned its name by the post office in 1880, after T.W. Anderson made two other suggestions: "Rising Sun" and "Star."

RIVER OAKS, City; Tarrant County; Pop. 6,890 / 6,852; Zip Code 770+; N Texas; suburb of Fort Worth.

ROANOKE, City; Denton County; Pop. 910 / 2,420; Zip Code 76262; N Texas; 20 mi. N of Fort Worth.

ROBERT LEE, City; Coke County Seat; Pop. 1,202 / 1,218; Zip Code 76945; Elev. 1,850; W central Texas. Promoted as town site in 1889 by two Confederate soldiers; name honors Robert E. Lee.

ROBINSON, City; McLennan County; Pop. 6,074 / 8,125; Zip Code 76706; Central Texas; 5 mi. S of Waco.

ROBSTOWN, City; Nueces County; Pop. 12,100 / 12,795; Zip Code 78380; S Texas; 25 mi. W of Corpus Christi. Named for "Rob" Driscoll, Jr., whose father began a large ranch here in 1905.

ROCKDALE, City; Milam County; Pop. 5,611 / 5,794; Elev. 462; Zip Code 76567; Central Texas; 60 mi. NE of Austin. Oil refining and cottonseed processing are important industries.

ROCKPORT, City; Aransas County Seat; Pop. 3,686 / 7,949; Zip Code 78382; Elev. 20; S Texas. Established in 1867 as shipping point for wool, hides, bones and tallow.

ROCKSPRINGS, Town; Edwards County Seat; Pop. 1,317 / 2,185; Zip Code 78880; Elev. 2,450; SW central Texas; 115 mi. SE of San Angelo. Established in 1891, named for springs prized as water source by wagon trains and Indians.

ROCKWALL, City; Rockwall County Seat; Pop. 5,939 / 17,277; Zip Code 75087; Elev. 552; NE Texas; 20 mi. NE of Dallas. It was named because of a curious subterranean geologic formation, which resembles a rock wall of artificial construction.

ROMA, City; Starr County; Pop. 3,384 / 11,714; Zip Code 78584; Elev. 243; S Texas; 88 mi. SE of Laredo on the Rio Grande. Settled in 1765 by Indians occupying the vistas (civil village) of Escandon's colony at Mier. Ranchers took up holdings on the north bank of the river, where gradually a settlement developed.

ROSCOE, City; Nolan County; Pop. 1,628 / 1,355; Zip Code 79545; Elev. 2,391; NW Texas. Grain is the main product shipped from this railroad stop.

ROSEBUD, City; Falls County; Pop. 2,076 / 1,454; Zip Code 76570; Elev. 392; Central Texas; 32 mi. S of Waco. Czechs and Germans settled this area and made its reputation for being filled with rose plants.

ROSENBERG, City; Fort Bend County; Pop. 17,995 / 31,149; Zip Code 77471; Elev. 106; SE Texas. The population is largely of German, Bohemian, and Polish birth descent. Founded in 1883 with the construction of the railroad.

ROTAN, City; Fisher County; Pop. 2,284 / 1,705; Zip Code 79546; NW central Texas; 30 mi. N of Sweetwater.

ROUND ROCK, City; Travis & Williamson Counties; Pop. 11,812 / 67,173; Zip Code 78664; Elev. 709; Central Texas; 15 mi. N of Austin. Established in 1850 and named for a large round rock in bed of Brushy Creek.

ROWLETT, City; Dallas & Rockwall Counties; Pop. 7,522 / 40,223; Zip Code 75088; NE Texas; Suburb of Dallas.

ROYSE CITY, City; Collin & Rockwall Counties; Pop. 1,566 / 2,827; Zip Code 75089; NE Texas; 30 mi. NE of Dallas.

SAN DIEGO, City; Duval & Jim Wells Counties; Duval County Seat; Pop. 5,225 / 5,132; Zip Code 78384; Elev. 312; S Texas; 50 mi. W of Corpus Christi. San Diego was once an important cattle shipping point, which required Ranger detachments to cope with its gun-toting citizens and cowboys and with the bands of rustlers that infested the back country.

SAN SABA, Town; San Saba County Seat; Pop. 2,336 / 3,063; Zip Code 76877; Elev. 1,210; Central Texas; 80 mi. W of Temple. Settled in 1854 and named for scenic river on which it is located.

SANTA ANNA, Town; Coleman County; Pop. 1,535 / 1,199; Zip Code 76878; Elev. 1,743; Central Texas; 80 mi. E of San Angelo. Named for its location at the foot of Santa Anna Mountain.

SANTA ROSA, Town; Cameron County; Pop. 1,535 / 2,348; Zip Code 78593; S Texas; 8 mi. NW of Harlingen.

SCHERTZ, City; Bexar, Comal & Guadalupe Counties; Pop. 7,262 / 17,825; Zip Code 78154; S central Texas; 15 mi. NE of San Antonio.

SCHULENBURG, City; Fayette County; Pop. 2,469 / 2,763; Zip Code 78956; Elev. 344; SE central Texas; 78 mi. SE of Austin. Germans and Bohemians settled this town.

SEABROOK, City; Chambers, Galveston & Harris Counties; Pop. 4,670 / 9,375; Zip Code 77586; SE Texas; Suburb of Houston.

SEADRIFT, City; Calhoun County; Pop. 1,277 / 1,369; Zip Code 77983; S Texas; 30 mi. SE of Victoria on San Antonio Boy.

SEAGOVILLE, City; Dallas & Kaufman Counties; Pop. 7,304 / 11,036; Zip Code 75159; NE Texas; 20 mi. SE of Dallas.

SEAGRAVES, City; Gaines County; Pop. 2,596 / 2,442; Zip Code 79359; NW Texas; 60 mi. SW of Lubbock.

SEGUIN, City; Guadalupe County Seat; Pop. 17,854 / 24,429; Zip Code 78155; Elev. 553; S central Texas; 30 mi. NE of San Antonio. Named in 1839 for Colonel Juan N. Seguin, who commanded the only detachment of Texas-born Mexicans in the Battle of San Jacinto.

SEMINOLE, City; Gaines County Seat; Pop. 6,080 / 6,805; Zip Code 79360; NW Texas; 80 mi. SW of Lubbock in a ranchland area; Named for the Indian tribe native to the area in 1906.

SEYMOUR, City; Baylor County Seat; Pop. 3,657 / 3,054; Zip Code 76380; Elev. 1,290; N Texas; 50 mi. SW of Wichita Falls. Settled in 1878 by a group from Oregon.

SHALLOWATER, City; Lubbock County; Pop. 1,932 / 1,612; Zip Code 79363; Lat. 33-41-3 N. Long. 101-59-7 W; NW Texas; 11 mi. NE of Lubbock; Named because well water was not very far underground.

SHAMROCK, City; Wheeler County; Pop. 2,834 / 1,960; Zip Code 79079; Elev. 2,281; NW Texas; 90 mi. E of Amarillo. In 1883 British noblemen, headed by the Baron of Tweedmouth and the Earl of Aberdeen, purchased land here. The domain was called the Rocking Chair Ranch, from its brand; Texas cowboys dubbed it the Nobility Ranch. When it failed, the noblemen returned to England. leaving the town names of Tweedy, Shamrock, Wellington. Clarendon, and Aberdeen.

SHEPHERD, City; San Jacinto County; Pop. 1,674 / 2,164; Zip Code 77371; E Texas; 53 mi. N of Houston; Named for early settler, B.A. Shepherd.

SHERMAN, City; Grayson County Seat; Pop. 30,413 / 34,105; Zip Code 75090; Elev. 720; NE Texas; 60 mi. N of Dallas. Organized in 1846. First laid out a short distance west of present location, but because of scarce firewood and water, moved to present site in 1848.

SHINER, City; Lavaca County; Pop. 2,213 / 2,036; Zip Code 77984; Elev. 350; SE central Texas; 70 mi. E of San Antonio. Founded in 1887; a trade center for Czech and German farmers.

SILSBEE, City; Hardin County; Pop. 7,684 / 7,166; Zip Code 77656; Elev. 79; E Texas. Established in 1892 around a logging camp of John H. Kirby.

SLATON, City; Lubbock County; Pop. 6,804 / 5,922; Zip Code 79364; Elev. 3,040; NW Texas; 16 mi. SE of Lubbock at a railroad division point.

SMITHVILLE, City; Bastrop County; Pop. 3,470 / 4,290; Zip Code 78957; Elev. 324; S central Texas; 40 mi. SE of Austin in a forested area, rich in varied agriculture.

SNYDER, City; Scurry County Seat; Pop. 12,705 / 11,659; Zip Code 79549; Elev. 2,316; NW central Texas; 90 mi. NW of Abilene. The townsite was laid out in 1882, and the county was organized two years later.

SOMERSET, City; Bexar County; Pop. 1,096 / 1,474; Zip Code 78069; S central Texas; 20 mi. SW of San Antonio.

SOMERVILLE, City; Burleson County; Pop. 1,824 / 1,649; Zip Code 77879; Elev. 250; E central Texas; 30 mi. SW of Bryan; named for early resident Albert Somerville.

SONORA, City; Sutton County Seat; Pop. 3,856 / 3,092; Zip Code 76950; Elev. 2,120; SE central Texas; 60 mi. S of San Angelo. Settled in 1889 on the Dry Fork of the Devil's River. On the western slope of the Edwards Plateau, Sonora began as trading post on Old San Antonio-El Paso Road.

SOUR LAKE, City; Hardin County; Pop. 1,807 / 1,625; Zip Code 77659; E Texas; 14 mi. W of Beaumont near the Big Thicket national preserve.

SOUTH HOUSTON, City; Harris County; Pop. 13,293 / 15,419; Zip Code 77587; Elev. 44; SE Texas; 11 mi. SE of Houston. The town was nearly destroyed by a Gulf storm in 1915.

SOUTHLAKE, City; Denton & Tarrant Counties; Pop. 2,808 / 17,977; Zip Code 76051; N Texas; suburb of Fort Worth.

SOUTH PADRE ISLAND, Town; Cameron County; Pop. 791 / 1,835; Zip Code 78597; Elev. 5; S Texas; incorporated in 1974, small city is on southern tip of storied Padre Island just across Laguna Madre, the body of water separating island from mainland.

SPEARMAN, City; Hansford County Seat; Pop. 3,413 / 2,955; Zip Code 79081; Elev. 3,105; NW Texas; 80 mi. NE of Amarillo, Established in the 1920s when North Texas and Santo Fe Railroad built across Hansford County; named for railroad executive.

SPLENDORA, City; Montgomery County; Pop. 721 / 1,440; Zip Code 77372; E Texas; 40 mi. N of Houston. The first postmaster named this town for its abundance of beautiful wildflowers.

SPRINGTOWN, City; Parker County; Pop. 1,658 / 2,265; Zip Code 76092; N central Texas; 35 mi. NW of Fort Worth; residential.

SPRING VALLEY, City; Harris County; Pop. 3,353 / 3,835; Zip Code 752+; SE Texas; Suburb of Houston.

SPUR, City; Dickens County; Pop. 1,690 / 1,110; Zip Code 79370; Elev. 2,274; NW Texas; 55 mi. E of Lubbock. Founded in 1909 and named for the Old Spur Ranch (Espuela Land and Cattle Company).

STAFFORD, City; Fort Bend & Harris Counties; Pop. 4,755 / 20,270; Zip Code 77477; SE Texas; 20 mi. SW of Houston.

STAMFORD, City; Haskell & Jones Counties; Pop. 4,542 / 3,441; Zip Code 79553; Elev. 1,603; NW central Texas; 40 mi. N of Abilene. Developed in 1899 as project of Texas Central Railroad, named after Connecticut hometown of the railroad president.

STANTON, City; Martin County Seat; Pop. 2,314 / 2,428; Zip Code 79782; Elev. 2,664; NW Texas; 19 mi. NE of Midland. Founded by monks who established a small Roman Catholic colony of German immigrants. It was called Mariensfeld in 1881. The name was changed in 1890 in honor of Abraham Lincoln's Secretary of War. Edwin M. Stanton.

STEPHENVILLE, City; Erath County Seat; Pop. 11,881 / 15,617; Zip Code 86401; Elev. 1,283; N central Texas; 60 mi. SW of Fort Worth. Stephenville began in 1850 with settlement by Stephens brothers in area; one brother, John, donated original town site.

STERLING CITY, City; Sterling County Seat; Pop. 915 / 1,023; Zip Code 76951; Elev. 2,295; W central Texas; 40 mi. NW of San Angelo. The town grew from ranch headquarters of W.S. Sterling. Indian fighter and buffalo hunter in late 1880s.

STINNETT, City; Hutchinson County Seat; Pop. 2,222 / 1,024; Zip Code 79083; Elev. 3,173; NW Texas; 40 mi. N of Amarillo at N Canadian River Valley. Established in 1901, it is a trade center and livestock shipping point in the High Plains.

STOCKDALE, City; Wilson County; Pop. 1,265 / 1,770; Zip Code 78160; S central Texas; named for a Civil War Lieutenant Governor of Texas, Fletcher Stockdale.

STRATFORD, City; Sherman County Seat; Pop. 1,917 / 1,700; Zip Code 79084; Elev. 3,690; NW Texas; 80 mi. NW of Amarillo on Coldwater Creek. Early settler Colonel Walter Cotton named the place for Robert E. Lee's birthplace in Virginia.

SUDAN, City; Lomb County; Pop. 1,091 / 1,043; Zip Code 79371; Elev. 3,752; NW Texas; 50 mi. NW of Lubbock. Named for the grass that is one of the principal crops in the region. It is the center of a large ranching region of yucca-covered prairies.

SUGAR LAND, City; Fort Bend County; Pop. 8,826 / 68,442; Zip Code 774+; Elev. 82; SE Texas; 20 mi. SW of Houston. The Imperial Sugar company once owned one of the largest sugar plantations and refineries in the world here on 12,500 acres of land.

SULPHUR SPRINGS, City; Hopkins County Seat; Pop. 12,804 / 14,547; Zip Code 75482; Elev. 530; NE Texas; 25 mi. E of Greenville. First known as Bright Star, the name was changed in 1871 when mineral springs were advertised.

SUNDOWN, City; Hockley County; Pop. 1,511 / 1,725; Zip Code 79372; NW Texas; Named by early landowner R.L. Slaughter for a movie he had seen being filmed on his property in Mexico.

SUNRAY, City; Moore County; Pop. 1,952 / 1,850; Zip Code 79086; NW Texas; 45 mi. NW of Borger; Named for the Sunray Oil Company in 1931.

SWEENY, City; Brazoria County; Pop. 3,538 / 4,115; Zip Code 77480; Elev. 38; SE Texas; 27 mi. W of Freeport. It was built on the old John Sweeny plantation of the 1830s.

SWEETWATER, City; Nolan County Seat; Pop. 12,242 / 11,702; Zip Code 79556; Elev. 2,164; NW Texas; 40 mi. W of Abilene. Begun in 1877 when a trader, Billy Knight. following the buffalo hunters and Government surveyors, opened a store in a dugout on the banks of Sweet-water Creek.

TAFT, City; San Patricia County; Pop. 3,686 / 3,540; Zip Code 78390; Elev. 54; S Texas; 20 mi. N of Corpus Christi. Named for Charles P. Taft, half-brother of President William H. Taft.

TAHOKA, City; Lynn County Seat; Pop. 3,262 / 2,850; Zip Code 79373; Elev. 3,090; NW Texas; 30 mi. S of Lubbock near Tahoka

Lake. Named for nearby Tahoka Lake, a natural spring-fed lake whose Indian name meant fresh or clear water.

TATUM, City; Panola & Rusk Counties; Pop. 1,339 / 1,370; Zip Code 75691; Elev. 385; E Texas; 17 mi. S of Longview. Established in 1885 when Santa Fe Railroad was built through, town site donated by Tatum family settlers in area.

TAYLOR, City; Williamson County; Pop. 10,619 / 15,278; Zip Code 76574; Elev. 583; Central Texas; 35 mi. NE of Austin. Cotton, oil and dairy farming are important in the vicinity. The town was settled by Germans and Czechs.

TEAGUE, City; Freestone County; Pop. 3,390 / 3,242; Zip Code 75860; Elev. 497; E central Texas; 55 mi. E of Waco. Named for niece of railroad magnate B.F. Yoakum.

TEMPLE, City; Bell County; Pop. 42,483 / 52,154; Zip Code 765+; Elev. 630; Central Texas; 32 mi. S of Waco. Established in 1880. It first grew up as a railroad town on Gulf, Colorado and Santa Fe Railroad, and Missouri, Kansas and Texas lines.

TENAHA, Town; Shelby County; Pop. 1,005 / 1,003; Zip Code 75974; Elev. 351; E Texas; 45 mi. S of Longview. The name is from the Indian word Teneha, meaning muddy water.

TERRELL, City; Kaufman County; Pop. 13,225 / 15,156; Zip Code 75160; Elev. 530; NE Texas. First settled in 1848. The town was organized about 1873 when the railroad was built.

TEXARKANA, City; Bowie County; Pop. 31,271 / 32,285; Zip Code 755+; Elev. 295; NE Texas; on the Texas-Arkansas Line, 20 miles southeast of the Oklahoma border. It is the twin city of Texarkana, Oklahoma. Founded in 1873 when the Texas and Pacific Railway came into the district. Established at the point where the tracks crossed the Texas-Arkansas Line. The place was called Texarkana, a name compounded of the first syllable of Texas, the first two of Arkansas, and the last syllable of Louisiana.

TEXAS CITY, City; Galveston County; Pop. 41,403 / 42,701; Zip Code 775+; Elev. 12; SE Texas; 15 mi. N of Galveston on the bay. Original bay-front community was called Shoal Point.

THORNDALE, City; Milam & Williamson Counties; Pop. 1,300 / 1,174; Zip Code 76577; Elev. 460; Central Texas; 45 mi. S of Temple. Three Spanish missions were built in the area near Thorndale; San Francisco Xavier de Horcasitas (St. Francis Xavier of Horcositas), established in 1748; San Ildefonso (St. Alphonsus), established in 1949, and Nuestra Senora de La Candeloria (Our Lady of Condlemas), built in 1749. They were abandoned in 1755.

THREE RIVERS, City; Live Oak County; Pop. 2,133 / 2,114; Zip Code 78071; Elev. 155; S Texas; At junction of Frio, Atascosa, and Nueces Rivers, for which it was named.

THROCKMORTON, Town; Throckmorton County Seat; Pop. 1,174 / 927; Zip Code 76083; Elev. 1,700; N Texas; 70 mi. SW of Wichita Falls. Established in 1879.

TIMPSON, City; Shelby County; Pop. 1,164 / 1,040; Zip Code 75975; E Texas; 50 mi. S of Longview.

TOMBALL, City; Harris County; Pop. 3,996 / 8,399; Zip Code 77375; SE Texas; Suburb of Houston; Named for Thomas H. Ball, a congressman from Houston.

TRINIDAD, City; Henderson County; Pop. 1,130 / 1,143; Zip Code 75163; NE Texas; 20 mi. E of Corsicana; Name is Spanish for "trinity."

TRINITY, City; Trinity County; Pop. 2,452 / 2,629; Zip Code 75862; Elev. 226; E Texas. The town was settled in 1868 on land of New York and Texas Land Company.

TROUP, City; Cherokee & Smith Counties; Pop. 1,911 / 1,768; Zip Code 75789; NE Texas; 15 mi. SE of Tyler. Named in the 1850s for Georgia Governor George M. Troup.

TROY, Town; Bell County; Pop. 1,353 / 1,482; Zip Code 76579; Central Texas; 15 mi. NE of Temple.

TULIA, City; Swisher County Seat; Pop. 5,033 / 4,849; Zip Code 79088; Elev. 3,501; NW Texas; 45 mi. S of Amarillo. Tulia is a city that began in 1890 when W.G. Connor started a post office on the prairie.

TYE, Town; Taylor County; Pop. 1,378 / 1,207; Zip Code 79563; NW central Texas; 7 mi. NE of Abilene, near Dyess Air Force Base.

TYLER, City; Smith County Seat; Pop. 69,995 / 83,796; Zip Code 757+; Elev. 558; NE Texas. The city founded in the 1840s, was named for John Tyler, tenth president of the United States, who signed the joint resolution under which Texas was admitted to the Union.

UNIVERSAL CITY, City; Bexar County; Pop. 10,720 / 15,862; Zip Code 78148; S central Texas; 12 mi. NE of San Antonio in a residential area.

UVALDE, City; Uvalde County Seat; Pop. 14,178 / 16,596; Zip Code 78801; Elev. 913; SE Texas; 80 mi. SW of Son Antonio. Uvalde was named in honor of Juan de Uvalde (the present spelling being a corruption of his name), a Spanish military leader, who in 1790 defeated the Apaches in what is now Uvalde Canyon.

VALLEY MILLS, City; Basque & McLennan Counties; Pop. 1,236 / 1,075; Zip Code 76689; Central Texas; 21 mi. NW of Waco.

VAN, City; Von Zandt County; Pop. 1,881 / 2,116; Zip Code 75790; NE Texas; 25 mi. NE of Tyler; Named for early settlers Vannie and Henry Vance Tunnell.

VAN ALSTYNE, Town; Grayson County; Pop. 1,860 / 2,245; Zip Code 75095; NE Texas; 15 mi. S of Sherman.

VAN HORN, Town; Culberson County Seat; Pop. 2,772 / 2,599; Zip Code 79855; Elev. 4,010; W Texas; 100 mi. SE of El Paso. Named for Van Horn Wells, a frontier watering place a short distance to the south.

VEGA, City; Oldham County Seat; Pop. 900 / 2,599; Zip Code 79092; Elev. 4,030; NW Texas; 30 mi. W of Amarillo; Cattle and grain are chief export items.

VENUS, Town; Johnson County; Pop. 518 / 1,230; Zip Code 76084; N central Texas; 30 mi. SW of Dallas; Named by a town founder for the natural beauty of the area.

VERNON, City; Wilbarger County Seat; Pop. 12,695 / 11,211; Zip Code 76384; Elev. 1,205; N Texas; 15 mi. W of Oklahoma state line. Founded in 1880, Vernon was an the busy Western Trail, and so its stores carried large amounts of supplies for those crossing the western wilderness, especially cattlemen.

VICTORIA, City; Victoria County Seat; Pop. 50,703 / 61,699; Zip Code 77901; Elev. 93; S Texas; 90 mi. NE of Corpus Christi. Named for General Guadalupe Victoria, later Mexico's first president.

VIDOR, City; Orange County; Pop. 12,117 / 11,453; Zip Code 77662; Elev. 2; E Texas; 7 mi. NE of Beaumont. Named for the Miller-Vidor Lumber Company, which operated here around the turn of the century.

WACO, City; McLennan County Seat; Pop. 101,261 / 108,520; Zip Code 767+; Central Texas; 100 mi. S of Dallas on the Brazos River. A Methodist missionary. Joseph P. Sneed, came to the region in 1849 and preached the first sermon in a log cabin.

WAKE VILLAGE, City; Bowie County; Pop. 3,865 / 5,362; Zip Code 75501; NE Texas; Named during World War II after Battle of Wake Island. It began as a housing project for defense factory workers.

WALLER, City; Harris & Waller Counties; Pop. 1,241 / 1,957; Zip Code 77484; Elev. 250; SE Texas; 40 mi. NW of Houston.

WALLIS, City; Austin County; Pop. 1,138 / 1,290; Zip Code 77485; SE central Texas; 40 mi. W of Houston.

WASKOM, City; Harrison County; Pop. 1,793 / 2,103; Zip Code 75692; Elev. 371; NE Texas; 16 mi. E of Longview; Established in 1850. Originally known as Powellton. Name changed to Waskom Station in 1872 to honor a man who was instrumental in bringing Southern Pacific Railroad through the community.

WATAUGA, City; Tarrant County; Pop. 10,284 / 23,273; Zip Code 76148; N Texas; Name is Cherokee, its meaning unknown.

WAXAHACHIE, City; Ellis County Seat; Pop. 14,624 / 23,059; Zip Code 75165; Elev. 530; NE central Texas; 25 mi. S of Dallas. The name derives from an Indian word meaning "cow (or buffalo) creek."

WEATHERFORD, City; Parker County Seat; Pop. 12,049 / 20,793; Zip Code 76086; Elev. 864; N central Texas; 30 mi. W of Fort Worth. Established in the 1850s and named after Jefferson Weatherford, a member of the Texas Senate.

WEBSTER, City; Harris County; Pop. 2,168 / 5,735; Zip Code 77598; SE Texas; Suburb of Houston.

WEIMAR, City; Colorado County; Zip Code 78962; SE central Texas; 90 mi. W of Houston near the Colorado River. Named by German settlers for their native towns.

WELLINGTON, City; Collingsworth County Seat; Pop. 3,043 / 2,218; Zip Code 79095; Elev. 1,980; NW Texas; 95 mi. SE of Amarillo. Named for the Duke of Wellington.

WESLACO, City; Hidalgo County; Pop. 19,331 / 31,404; Zip Code 78596; Elev. 75; S Texas; 45 mi. NW of Brownsville. The name comes from the initials of W.E. Stewart Land Company that promoted the town site in the irrigated Rio Grand Valley in 1919.

WEST, City; McLennan County; Pop. 2,485 / 2,912; Zip Code 76691; Central Texas; 17 mi. N of Waco in a farming area.

WEST COLUMBIA, City; Brazoria County; Pop. 4,109 / 4,586; Zip Code 77486; Elev. 34; SE Texas; 40 mi. SW of Galveston. In 1826, after he had laid out the town site on the Brazos River, Joseph Bell cleared a two mile long avenue through the prairie, and at its farthest end started this town, which he called Columbia.

WHARTON, City; Wharton County Seat; Pop. 9,033 / 9,461; Zip Code 77488; Elev. 111; SE Texas; 55 mi. SW of Houston. Named for William and John Wharton, brothers prominent during the Texas Revolution.

WHEELER, City; Wheeler County Seat; Pop. 1,584 / 1,286; Zip Code 79096; Elev. 2,520; NW Texas; 107 mi. E of Amarillo. The post office was established when area became "thickly settled" by five families living in dugouts within two-mile radius. The town became seat of Wheeler County in 1906.

WHITE DEER, Town; Carson County; Pop. 1,210 / 1,273; Zip Code 79097; Lat. 35-25-8 N, Long. 101-10-36 W; NW Texas; Named for a nearby creek. Town moved in 1908 to be near Santa Fe rail lines.

WHITE SETTLEMENT, City; Tarrant County; Pop. 13,508 / 16,014; Zip Code 76108; N Texas; W suburb of Fort Worth.

WHITESBORO, City; Grayson County; Pop. 3,197 / 3,878; Zip Code 76273; Elev. 783; NE Texas; 60 mi. N of Dallas.

WHITEWRIGHT, Town; Fannin & Grayson Counties; Pop. 1,757 / 1,886; Zip Code 75491; NE Texas; 50 mi. NE of Dallas.

WHITNEY, Town; Hill County; Pop. 1,631 / 1,740; Zip Code 76692; Elev. 585-57-0 N, Long. 97-19-2 W; NE central Texas; 30 mi. N of Waco. Established in 1879 when the Texas Central Railroad crossed Hill County; named for Charles Whitney of New York, a major railroad stockholder.

WICHITA FALLS, City; Archer & Wichita Counties; Wichita County Seat; Pop. 94,201 / 98,919; Zip Code 763+; Elev. 946; N Texas; 16 miles S of Texas-Oklahoma Line. There are several legends regarding the name "Wichita," but according to the Smithsonian Institution the name is "of uncertain meaning and origin." John Gould, columnist of the Wichita Daily Times, was convinced the name means "men from the north." "Falls" was used in the town's name because of a five-foot waterfall, which in early years, existed in the river.

WILLS POINT, City; Van Zandt County; Pop. 2,631 / 3,592; Zip Code 75169; Elev. 532; NE Texas; 50 mi. E of Dallas; Marketing and shipping center.

WINBERLY, Unincorporated Town; Hays County; Pop. 3,065; Zip Code 78676; Elev. 967; S central Texas; 35 mi. SW of Austin. Established 1848, a center of resort and retirement development in central Texas Hill Country.

WINK, City; Winkler County; Pop. 1,182 / 1,078; Zip Code 79789; Lat. 31-45-3 N. Long. 103-09-4 W; W Texas; 50 mi. W of Odessa; Named for first part of Winkler County.

WINNSBORO, City; Franklin & Wood Counties; Pop. 3,458 / 3,482; Zip Code 75494; Elev. 533; NE Texas; 105 mi. E of Dallas. Founded in 1854 as a trade center at intersection of two main roads, and first known as Crossroads. Name changed to honor early settler, John E. Wynn. Spelling was supposedly changed by a newspaper editor in the 1870s because of a shortage of Ys in his type.

WINTERS, City; Runnels County; Pop. 3,061 / 2,992; Zip Code 79567; W central Texas; 50 mi. NE of San Angelo; Named for early settler, J.N. Winters.

WOLFE CITY, City; Hunt County; Pop. 1,594 / 1,632; Zip Code 75496; NE Texas; 15 mi. N of Greenville.

WOLFFORTH, Town; Lubbock County; Pop. 1,701 / 2,571; Zip Code 79382; NW Texas; 8 mi. SW of Lubbock; Named for early settler George Wolforth, whose name was misspelled on the records.

WOODSBORO, Town; Refugio County; Pop. 1,974 / 1,693; Zip Code 78393; Elev. 48; S Texas; 50 mi. NW of Corpus Christi in a vast ranching area.

WOODVILLE, Town; Tyler County Seat; Pop. 2,821 / 3,995; Zip Code 75979; Elev. 232; E Texas; 55 mi. NW of Beaumont. Named for George T. Wood, second governor of Texas.

WORTHAM, Town; Freestone County; Pop. 1,187 / 972; Zip Code 76693; E central Texas; 25 mi. S of Corsicana.

WYLIE, City; Collin County; Pop. 8,662 / 13,190; Zip Code 75098; NE Texas; 22 mi. NE of Dallas.

YOAKUM, City; De Witt & Lavaca Counties; Pop. 6,148 / 5,485; Zip Code 77995; Elev. 322; SE central Texas; 90 mi. E of San Antonio. Yoakum was founded on a league of land granted to John May of Ireland in 1835. Named after Henderson King Yoakum, pioneer and historian.

YORKTOWN, City; DeWitt County; Pop. 2,498 / 2,050; Zip Code 78164; Elev. 266; S Texas; 65 mi. SE of San Antonio. First settler in 1846 was John York. Road from Indianola to San Antonio, surveyed in 1848, went by way of the York home, and the surveyor, Charles Eckhardt, built a home at the site of Yorktown.

UTAH
The Beehive State

Capitol Reef National Park

Wolfe Ranch - Arches National Park

GOVERNOR
Mike Leavitt

Delicate Arch
Arches National Park

This Is The Place Monument - Heritage Park, Salt Lake City

Salt Lake City

Art Museum
Springville

INTRODUCTION

The State of Utah is located in the western mountain region of the west central United States. It is bounded on the north by Idaho and Wyoming, on the south by Arizona, on the east by Colorado, and on the west by Nevada.

The State is part of three physiographic regions. In the northeast are the Middle Rockies, including the Uinta Mountains, which is the only major east-west mountain range in the United States. In the western third are the Basin and Range provinces, an area of broad, flat, desert-like terrain and an occasional mountain peak; the Great Salt Lake and Great Salt Lake Desert are both in this region. The remainder of Utah lies in the Colorado Plateau.

In prehistoric times, about AD 400, the Pueblo Indian culture dwelled here; their cliff dwellings still dot the State. In about 1250, this culture disappeared and the Shoshone Indians arrived. The area was possessed by the Spanish in the eighteenth century, and was passed to Mexico in 1821. Utah became a part of the United States in 1848, after the end of the Mexican War.

From 1849 to 1887, the Mormons who settled in the Great Salt Valley colonized a large portion of the surrounding area. Although they applied for statehood about six times between 1849 and 1887, Utah did not become a part of the Union until 1896.

STATE NAME

Early in the State's history, the White Mountain Apache referred to the Navajo Indians as *Yuttahih*, meaning one that is higher up. However, European settlers thought that the term referred to the Utes who dwelled further up the mountains from the Navajo. The land of the Ute Indians became known as Utah. When Utah became a territory, and later a state, the name was retained.

STATE NICKNAME

There are several nicknames for Utah. They include the Beehive State, the Mormon State, the Land of the Saints, and the Salt Lake State.

The sobriquet of the Beehive State is given because the beehive is a symbol of industry, and refers to the industrious nature of early settlers. The nicknames of the Mormon State and the Land of the Saints are both due to the Mormons who settled in Utah; the second refers to the official name of the Mormon church: The Church of the Latter-Day Saints. The nickname of the Salt Lake State is because of the Great Salt Lake located here.

STATE SEAL

The State seal was adopted by the legislature in 1896. Designed by Harry Edwards, the symbols on the seal include the American eagle (to symbolize protection in peace and war); the beehive (to symbolize industry) and sego lilies (to symbolize peace). The 1847 date represents the year that Mormons first came to Salt Lake Valley. The year 1896 is the year in which Utah became a state of the Union. The seal is described as follows: "The Great Seal of the state of Utah shall be 2½ inches in diameter, and of the following device: the center a shield and perched thereon an American eagle with outstretching wings; the top of the shield pierced by six arrows crosswise; under the arrows the motto 'Industry': beneath the motto a beehive, on either side growing sego lilies; below the beehive the figures '1847;' and on each side of the shield an American flag; encircling all, near the outer edge of the seal, beginning at the lower left-hand portion, the words 'The Great Seal of the State of Utah,' with the figures '1896' at the base."

STATE FLAG

The legislature of the new state of Utah adopted a State flag in 1896. It was also designated the governor's flag in 1911. The flag was revised in 1933. A description is as follows: "The center a shield; above the shield and thereon an American eagle with outstretched wings; the top of the shield pierced with six arrows arranged crosswise; upon the shield under the arrows the word 'Industry,' and below the word 'Industry' on the center of the shield, a beehive; on each side of the beehive, growing sego lilies; below the beehive and near the bottom of the shield, the word 'Utah,' and below the word 'Utah' and on the bottom of the shield, the figures '1847'; with the appearance of being back of the shield there shall be two American flags on flagstaffs placed crosswise with the flags so draped that they will project beyond each side of the shield, the heads of the flagstaffs appearing in front of the eagle's wings and the bottom of each staff appearing over the face of the draped flag below the shield; below the shield and flags and upon the blue field, the figures '1896;' around the entire design, a narrow circle in gold."

STATE MOTTO

The official motto for the State, adopted in 1896, is "Industry." It recognizes the industrious nature of citizens, and is an appropriate motto for Utah, since another of the official symbols is a beehive, representing industry.

STATE BIRD

The legislature adopted the sea gull, *Larus californicus*, as the official State bird of Utah in 1955. The sea gull ranges in western North America, inland to Nevada, Utah, Kansas, Texas, and Colorado near large lake areas.

The sea gull has a tail length of six inches, and a wing length of 14½ to sixteen inches. The head, neck, upper tail feathers, tail, and all underparts are white. The back, scapulars, and wings are pale to light neutral gray. Wings are tipped with white. The eye ring and rictus are vermilion-red. The subterminal third of the bill is red, immediately preceded by a black spot. Legs and feet are a pale grayish green.

Gulls are aeronautic magicians who make the seemingly impossible appear effortless as they travel through the sky. They can appear motionless in midair when they catch wind currents; they have perfect timing and precision when they position their bodies at just the right angle for riding the currents. They are quiet in behavior, and are usually gentle. They exhibit neither antagonism nor fondness toward man.

California gulls eat crickets, grasshoppers, and even an occasional mouse, which makes them a friend of the farmer, and in fact, this is the primary reason the gull was designated as the State bird. Gulls were credited with saving crops in 1848 when they consumed the insects that endangered the farmers' produce.

STATE FLOWER

The sego lily, *Calochortus nuttalli*, was designated the State flower of Utah by the 1911 legislature. A member of the lily family, the plant has a slender stem and white, blue, or lilac flowers that bloom in midsummer. The flower is native from South Dakota to Nebraska and California.

STATE TREE

The blue spruce (*Picea pungens Engelm*) was designated as the official State tree of Utah in 1933. It is also commonly known as the Colorado blue spruce, balsam, Colorado spruce, white spruce, prickly spruce, silver spruce, and Parry's spruce. It is native to the Rocky Mountain region.

The four-angled needles of the blue spruce are a dull blue green color, from three-quarters to one and one-eighth inches long. The large tree has gray or brown bark, furrowed into scaly ridges. Cones are from 2 ½ to four inches long, light brown, with long, thin, irregularly toothed scales.

STATE SONG

The official State song is "Utah We Love Thee." Written by Evan Stephens, it was adopted in 1937.

STATE LICENSE PLATE

Until 1915, when Utah issued its first plate, motorists made their own plates. The first official plate for the State was dark green and white. A variety of color combinations were used over the years, along with a number of different slogans. In the mid-1940s, "Center Scenic America" was used. In 1947, the plate slogan was "This is the Place." In 1948, plates had "The Friendly State" slogan. In the 1970s, a beehive was depicted on the plate.

The 1986 plate for the state of Utah contains blue and red letters appear on a white background. At the upper right of the plate is the slogan "Ski Utah." A skier in blue is depicted heading down a slope to the left of the slogan. Numerals are in blue. Also in blue is the slogan, "Greatest Snow on Earth," which is lettered at the bottom of the plate.

The 1996 series is the current plate for the state. Across the top of the plate "UTAH" appears in all capital letters, the letters are white with a blue border, the background is light blue. The center background of the plate is light brown with white clouds; blue letters and numerals are raised across the center of the plate. In the bottom left corner the year "1896" appears and the right corner the year "1996", in between these years the word "CENTENNIAL" appears in all capital letters. A picture of an arch is depicted from the bottom to the top of the plate.

STATE POSTAGE STAMP

The purple three-cent stamp for Utah was issued on July 24, 1947 in Salt Lake City. It commemorates the one hundred-year anniversary of settlement in the State. The stamp was designed by E.R. Chickering and engraved by M.D. Fenton and E.H. Helmuth. It depicts a covered wagon of the first settlers arriving at the valley of the Great Salt Lake. Lettered at the top right of the stamp are the words, "This is the place," which are attributed to Brigham Young, leader of the Mormon followers to Utah. Beneath this scene are the dates 1847-1947 on each side of a banner that reads "The Utah Centennial." A total of 131,968,000 of the stamp were printed.

OTHER STATE DESIGNATIONS

Over the years, the legislature has adopted a number of additional symbols to represent officially the State. Included are the State animal as the elk (1971); the State emblem as the beehive (1959); the State fish as the rainbow trout (1971); the State fossil as the *Allosaurus* (1988); the State gem as topaz (1969); and the State insect as the honeybee (1983).

STATE CAPITOL

Although Salt Lake City had long been the capital city of Utah, it was not until 1911 that the legislature authorized a permanent capitol to be constructed in the city. Richard K.A. Kletting designed the capitol building in Renaissance revival style, with Utah granite and Georgia marble. Ground was broken for the building in 1913, and the capitol was completed in 1915. The length of the capitol is 404 feet, and the width is 240 feet. The ceiling of the copper dome is 165 feet above the floor of the rotunda. The dome rises above a pediment and colonnade of twenty-four Corinthian columns. Total cost for construction of the capitol was 2,739,528 dollars.

OTHER FACTS ABOUT UTAH

Total area: 84,899 square miles
Land area: 82,073 square miles
Water area: 2,826 square miles
Average elevation: 6,100 feet
Highest point: Kings Peak, 13,528 feet
Lowest point: Beaverdam Wash, 2,000 feet
Highest temperature: 117 degrees Fahrenheit
Lowest temperature: -69 degrees Fahrenheit
Population in 1990: 1,722,850
Population density in 1990: 20.97 persons per square mile
Population 1980-1990: +17.9 percent change
Population projected for year 2000: 1,991,000
Asian/Pacific Islander population in 1990: 33,371
Black population in 1990: 11,576
Hispanic population in 1990: 84,597
Native American population in 1990: 24,283
White population in 1990: 1,615,845
Capital: Salt Lake City
Admitted to Union: January 4, 1896
Order of Statehood: 45
Electoral votes: 5

CHRONOLOGY

1540 Captain Garcia Lopez de Cardenas approaches Utah at area south of Colorado River.

1776 Father Silvestre Velez de Escalante and Father Francisco Atanasio Dominguez make first comprehensive exploration of Utah.

1813 Old Spanish Trail between Santa Fe and Utah Lake is first used.

1820 Religious revivals on New York frontier lead to first Joseph Smith vision.

1824 General William Henry Ashley's trappers cross South Pass and enter Utah.
– Jim Bridger discovers Great Salt Lake.

1825 Ashley explores Green River.
– First trappers' rendezvous is held on Henry's Fork of Green River.

1826 Trappers circumnavigate Great Salt Lake.
– Jedediah S. Smith makes first American overland journey to California; he traverses Utah en route to Southern California, and returns to Utah in following year; Smith is first white to explore eastward passage of Sierra Nevada Mountains and central Nevada deserts.

1830 Buffalo become virtually extinct in Utah after tremendous winter snows.
– American Fur Company extends operations to intermountain region and institutes bitter ten years' rivalry with Hudson's Bay and Rocky Mountain Fur companies.
– Mormon Church is organized at Fayette, New York.
– Book of Mormon is published.

1832 Antoine Robidoux establishes first fixed European American post in Utah Basin.

1837 Denis Julien makes first known white exploration of lower Green and Colorado canyons.
– Fort Davy Crockett is established in Browns Hole by Philip Thompson and William Craig.
– Latter Day Saints Church begins worldwide proselytizing.

1839 Nauvoo, Illinois is named as gathering-place for harassed Mormons.

1840 Bottom falls out of beaver fur market, dooming mountain fur trade.

1841 Bartleson-Bidwell party, en route to California, brings first emigrant wagons across Utah.

1843 Captain John Charles Fremont explores northern Great Salt Lake; he goes on to Oregon and Southern California, and next year traverses Utah north to Utah Lake, then east through Uintah Basin and Browns Hole.
– Joseph Smith issues revelation on plural marriage at Nauvoo.

1844 Joseph and Hyrum Smith are shot to death by mob at Carthage, Illinois.
– Quorum of Twelve Apostles, headed by Brigham Young, is accepted as presiding authority of Mormon Church.

1844-45 On Ogden site, Miles Goodyear builds first permanent European American post in Utah west of Wasatch Mountains.

1845 Fremont, returning west, circles southern shore of Great Salt Lake and breaks new trail across Salt Desert to California.

1846 Harlan-Young and Donner-Reed emigrant parties break wagon trails across Utah.
– Mormons begin migration from Nauvoo.
– Mormon Battalion enters U.S. Army for service against Mexico.

1847 Advance companies of Mormon pioneers arrive in Great Salt Lake Valley.
– Mormon irrigation begins.
– Brigham Young is named president of Mormon Church.

1848 Mormon Battalion members participate in discovery of gold in California.
– Treaty of Guadalupe Hidalgo ends war with Mexico; Utah area passes under United States sovereignty.
– Ogden is founded as Browns Fort.
– Gulls help destroy marauding crickets.
– First petition is drawn up to Congress for Territorial government.

1849 Colonization begins, with settlements in Utah, Sanpete, and Tooele valleys.
– Gold rush brings thousands west, many through Great Salt Lake City.
– Captain Howard Stansbury commences survey of Great Salt Lake, finishing next year.

– Constitution is adopted for Provisional State of Desert; Brigham Young is named governor.
– Perpetual Emigrating Company is organized to aid poor Latter Day Saints to Utah.

1850 Population of Utah is 11,380.
– General Assembly of Desert charters University of State of Desert; it is first university west of Missouri River, and third west of Mississippi (it is renamed University of Utah in 1892).
– Desert News begins publication; it is first intermountain newspaper.
– Congress creates Territory of Utah to supersede State of Desert.

1851 General Assembly of Desert charters Great Salt Lake City, Ogden, Provo, Manti, and Parowan.
– Brigham Young takes oath of office as governor of Utah Territory.
– First Territorial legislature meets.
– Fillmore is named Territorial capital.
– Colonization continues in Sanpete, Sevier, Little Salt Lake, and northern valleys.

1852 Plural marriage is proclaimed to world as Mormon doctrinal tenet.
– First Utah iron is smelted in Cedar City.

1853 Ground is broken for Mormon Temple in Great Salt Lake City.
– Walker War with Utes begins in Utah Valley; it will continue until following May. Captain John W. Gunnison and seven men are killed by Pahvants on Sevier River.

1854 Grasshopper infestation begins.
– Desert alphabet is originated.

1855 Grasshoppers destroy almost all crops.

1856 Famine conditions prevail.
– Tintic War with Utes is fought in Utah and Cedar valleys.
– "Reformation," initiated by Jedediah M. Grant at Kaysville, results in two years of intense religious feeling.
– Hand-cart migration across plains begin, continuing until 1860; many are lost in first year when they are caught by early snows along Sweetwater River in Wyoming.

1857 Severe winter is followed by best harvest since Mormon arrival in Utah.
– Territorial seat is returned to Great Salt Lake City.
– Government orders army to quell "rebellion" in Utah; army is forced into winter quarters near Fort Bridger.
– Upwards of 120 Arkansas emigrants are slain in Mountain Meadows Massacre.

1858 Territorial seat is moved from Great Salt Lake City to Parowan; it is returned to Great Salt Lake City in following year, although not formally by law.
– Colonel Thomas L. Kane negotiates end of "Utah War"; Mormons return to abandoned homes; Federal troops settle at Camp Floyd in Cedar Valley.

1860 Population of Utah is 40,273.
– Pony Express commences east and west operations through Utah.

1861 Territory of Nevada is created out of western Utah; Colorado Territory is created out of part of eastern Utah.
– Overland Telegraph is completed between Great Salt Lake City and "The States."
– Dixie Mission begins, marking effective colonization of southern Utah.

1862 Salt Lake Theater is dedicated.
– State of Desert "ghost government" is established; it exists until 1870.
– Congress passes Anti-Polygamy bill.
– Colonel Patrick Edward Connor and regiment of California-Nevada volunteers locate Camp Douglas.

1863 Connor crushes Shoshone band at Battle of Bear River.
– George Ogilvie registers first mining claim in Oquirrh Mountains.
– Dry farming begins in Utah.

1865 Congregationalists establish first non-Mormon church in Utah.
– Ute Black Hawk war begins, continuing until 1868.

1866 Utah loses 20,850 square miles to newly-created state of Nevada.
– Desert telegraph line opens between Great Salt Lake City and Ogden; it is subsequently extended up and down Territory.

1867 Grasshoppers begin new series of onslaughts on crops; famine continues for some years.
– Tabernacle is completed in Great Salt Lake City.

1868 Zion's Co-operative Mercantile Institution begins operations in renamed "Salt Lake City."
– Creation of Wyoming Territory cuts Utah to present-day dimensions.

1869 United States land office opens in Salt Lake City, enabling settlers to obtain title to their lands.
– Union Pacific and Central Pacific railroads meet in Golden Spike ceremony at Promontory.
– Major John Wesley Powell commences explorations of Green and Colorado rivers, continuing intermittently until 1872.
– First Utah ore is shipped to California.

1870 Population of Utah is 86,786.
– Utah Central Railroad is completed between Salt Lake City and Ogden.
– Anti-Mormon and Godbeite Mormons organize Liberal political party.
– Large-scale importation of sheep begins.

1871 Utah Northern Railroad is organized to link Ogden and Montana.

1872 First smelting and refining company commences operations in Salt Lake Valley.
– Salt Lake City Gas Works introduces gas as fuel.
– First streetcar system opens in Salt Lake City.

1874 United Order is established in Mormon towns and settlements.

– Congress passes Poland Bill to further the prosecution of polygamists.

1875 Brigham Young Academy is founded by Brigham Young; it will become a university in 1903.

1876 John D. Lee is convicted for participation in Mountain Meadows Massacre; he is shot next year at Mountain Meadows.
– Organization of Pleasant Valley Coal Company marks first important exploitation of Carbon-Emery coals, and beginning of Utah coal industry.

1877 St. George Temple, first completed in Utah, is dedicated by Brigham Young.
– Brigham Young dies in Salt Lake City.

1879 First telephone line is put in at Ogden.

1880 Population of Utah is 143,963.
– John Taylor succeeds Brigham Young as Mormon Church president.
– Electric lighting is instituted in Utah.

1882 Congress passes anti-polygamic Edmunds Law, disfranchising polygamists.

1883 Denver & Rio Grande Western Railroad is completed between Denver and Salt Lake City.

1884 Prosecutions commence under Edmunds Law.

1885 Virtually all grazing lands in Utah are occupied by herds.

1886 First commercial canning begins at Ogden.

1887 Congress passes Edmunds-Tucker Act in continuing war on polygamy.
– John Taylor dies in hiding.
– Utah Supreme Court appoints receiver to take over Mormon Church property confiscated under Edmunds-Tucker Act.

1888 Utah State Agricultural College is established.

1889 Liberal party wins first major victory in Ogden election.
– Wilford Woodruff becomes president of Mormon Church.

1890 Population of Utah is 210,779.
– Liberals carry Salt Lake City for first time.
– Wilford Woodruff issues manifesto advising Church membership to refrain from contracting polygamous marriages.
– Natural gas is transported to Salt Lake City in wooden pipelines from Davis County.
– Free school system is established throughout Territory.

1891 Republican and Democratic parties organize; Mormon People's Party dissolves.
– Lehi opens first successful sugar beet factory in Utah.

1892 First cattlemen's congress in West is held at Ogden.

1893 President Benjamin Harrison issues manifesto of amnesty to polygamists; Mormon Temple is dedicated.
– Congress authorizes return of confiscated property to Mormon Church.
– Liberal party disbands.

1894 Legislature passes eight-hour workday law.

1895 May 8. Seventh constitutional convention signs Constitution of Utah.

1896 January 4. President Grover Cleveland signs proclamation, admitting Utah as 45th State in Union.
January 6. First State legislature convenes.

1897 Uinta Forest Preserve, first "national forest" in Utah, is established.

1898 Park City is largely destroyed in million-dollar fire; it is most disastrous fire in Utah's history.
– Wilford Woodruff dies; he is succeeded in Mormon Church presidency by Lorenzo Snow.

1899 Legislature creates Utah Art Institute to sponsor fine arts.

1900 Population of Utah is 276,749.
– Approximately 200 die in explosion of Winter Quarters coal mine; it is worst Utah mine disaster.

1901 Lorenzo Snow dies; he is succeeded by Joseph F. Smith as Mormon Church president.

1903 Reed Smoot is elected U.S. Senator by State legislature; he begins four-year struggle for his seat.
– Three huge natural bridges are "discovered;" they are included in Natural Bridges National Monument in 1908.
– Lucin Cutoff is completed across Great Salt Lake.

1905 San Pedro, Los Angeles, & Salt Lake Railroad is completed at Caliente, Nevada; it brings Utah into direct rail communication with southern California.
– American Party, new anti-Mormon political organization, carries Salt Lake City election.

1906 Uintah Indian reservation is partially opened to homesteading; it is fully opened in 1914.

1907 First oil wells in Utah are sunk at Virgin.

1908 First junior high school in Utah is instituted at Ogden by John M. Mills.
– Western Pacific Railroad is completed between Salt Lake City and San Francisco.
– Important dinosaur remains are found near Jensen; area is set aside as national monument in 1915; it will be enlarged in 1938.
– Bamberger line, completed between Salt Lake City and Ogden, is first interurban railroad in West; road is electrified in 1911.

1909 Rainbow Bridge is discovered in expedition guided by Nashja-begay; it is made national monument in following year.

– Zion Canyon is set aside as Mukuntuweap National Monument; its status is changed to national park in 1929.

1910 Population of Utah is 373,351.

1911 U.S. Reclamation Service completes Strawberry Reservoir; it is first large reclamation project in Utah to divert water from Colorado basin to Great Basin.
– Three Brigham Young University professors resign in controversy over teaching of evolution.

1913 Legislature establishes first women's minimum wage laws.

1914 Cave-in at Centennial Eureka mine kills eleven, leading to enactment of mine safety laws.

1915 Good-roads agitation reflects increasing importance of automobile transportation.
– Farm Bureau movement begins.
– State Capitol is completed in Salt Lake City.
– Seventeen University of Utah faculty members resign in controversy over free speech.

1917 Utah musters men and capital for World War I.
– Prohibition laws are extended over State.

1918 Joseph F. Smith dies; he is succeeded in presidency of Mormon Church by Heber J. Grant.

1920 Population of Utah is 449,396.
– First commercial airports are instituted.
– Total acreage of Utah farms reaches five million, almost ten percent of State's land area; improved land reaches virtual maximum of 1.7 million acres.
– Sugar beet is State's leading cash crop.

1921 Utah unsuccessfully attempts to prohibit cigarettes; law is repealed in 1923.
– Timpanogos Cave is "discovered," it is made national monument in following year.
– KSL radio station begins broadcasting.

1922 Arches area is "discovered," it is set aside as national monument in 1929.

1923 Floods at Willard and Farmington take nine lives, and cause half million dollars' damage; disaster awakens State legislature to need for watershed control and range conservation.
– Hovenweep prehistoric Indian remains area is declared national monument.

1924 Castle Gate coal mine explosion kills 172 men.

1926 Commercial airlines begin operations in Utah.
– Columbia Steel Company opens plant at Ironton, bringing heavy industry to Utah.

1927 Utah has pari-mutuel horse racing; legislature subsequently passes prohibitory laws.

1928 Bryce Canyon National Park is established; it is enlarged in 1931.

1929 Natural gas is piped into Utah from Wyoming's Baxter Basin; it marks beginning of effectual use of this fuel.

1930 Population is 507,847.
– Legislature adopts taxes on business profits; it also sets up graduated rates on personal and corporate income, uniform rates for all tangible property.

1931 Banks fail; they are restored in 1933 by Federal Deposit Insurance.
– High Uintas "saddleback" is set aside as permanent primitive area.

1932 Mormon Church presents academies to State for junior college purposes.
– State joins in Democratic upheaval; George H. Dern is made Secretary of War in Roosevelt cabinet.
– After twenty-nine years of service, Republican U.S. Senator Reed Smoot is unseated.
– Great Depression causes more than 61,000 persons, comprising 35.8 percent of State's work force, to become unemployed.

1933 Despite Mormon stricture against alcoholic beverages, State voters approve repeal of State prohibition; Utah becomes thirty-sixth to ratify constitutional repeal amendment.
– Cedar Breaks National Monument is established.

1934 Official automobile racing begins on Bonneville Salt Flats.
– Dust storms wreak havoc in Tooele County; government efforts in following years help bring dust storms under some control.
– About twenty-one percent of Utah's population is on government relief.

1935 Legislature passes unemployment insurance laws.

1937 Old age benefits are provided by legislature, through cooperation with Federal Social Security Board.
– Act creating Utah Art Institute is amended to allow cooperation with Federal cultural projects.
– Utah State Institute of Fine Arts is established.
– Capitol Reef National Monument is established.
– Commercial airline accidents in 1937-38 lead to safe-altitude rulings in intermountain area.

1939 World War II begins.

1940 Population of Utah is 550,310.
– Utah State Symphony Orchestra is founded; first concert is given.
– Gregory Natural Bridge discovered by Norman Nevills.

1942-1945 Steel plant is constructed west of Orem; it is later sold to U.S. Steel.
– Utah is site of ten major military bases and army hospital.
– About 49,500 new jobs have opened up in State.
– More than 8,000 Japanese-Americans from Pacific Coast are interned near Delta.

1942 Panel of NWLB recommends one dollar-a-day pay increase for 10,000 copper, lead, and zinc miners in Idaho and Utah.

1943 District Judge Lewis V. Trueman of Ogden, four others are shot to death by Austin Cox, whose wife received divorce in Trueman's courtroom earlier in year.

1944 Fifteen polygamists in Salt Lake City are convicted of "unlawful cohabitation"; all defendants have two to six wives; none offer defense; all announce plans to appeal to U.S. Supreme Court.

1945 Supreme Court dismisses Shoshone Indians' suit for fifteen million dollars in damages from white settlers' occupation of lands in Idaho, Utah, Nevada; judgment is based on grounds that Box Elder Treaty left them no cause for claiming land.

1949 UMW leader halts payments from depleted union welfare fund; eight thousand Utah and Wyoming miners hold strike.

1954 Two days after disclosure of lying about wartime activities, State Representative Douglas Stringfellow (R), withdraws candidacy for reelection; Stringfellow claimed to be last survivor of secret OSS mission behind German lines

1955 Right-to-work law outlaws closed shop.

1958 Utah is second among states in copper, gold, silver, molybdenum, uranium production; third in lead, potash.

1959 President Eisenhower designates drought-stricken sections of State as major disaster areas.

1963 State has more than 17,000 employed in defense industries; defense has become State's single largest manufacturing sector.

1964 Flaming Gorge Dam on Green River is completed.
– More than 10,000 Utah teachers strike to demand more State aid for education.

1973 Federal Trade Commission reports that unfair trade, credit practices by reservation trading posts has worsened poverty of Navajo Indians on 24,000-sq. mi. reservation covering parts of Utah, two other states; most posts are run by white merchants under permits of BIA.
– Interior secretary approves commercial leasing plan for experimental development of oil shale deposits on six federal land tracts in Utah, Wyoming, Colorado.
– Equal Rights Amendment (ERA) is defeated in State.

1974 Research team from University of Utah unearths one-fourth of entire skeleton of prehistoric beast that roamed North America between 40,000-10,000 B.C.; animal weighed about seven tons.
– Bill to lower salinity of Colorado River is approved; bill authorizes construction of desalting plant near Mexico-U.S. border, and four control units in U.S. in Utah (1), Nevada (1), and Colorado (2).
– In effort to save fuel, President Nixon signs bill to put most of U.S. on year-round daylight savings time for two years; only Alaska and Hawaii are exempted.

1975 Supreme Court clears way for construction of six power plants in Four Corners area of Southwest.
– Mormon population comprises about 70 percent of State's total population of 1,219,000.
– State's birth rate is 26 per 1,000 population, almost double national rate of 14.8.
– Oil production hits high of 42 million barrels; Utah ranks ninth in nation in oil production.

1976 U.S. government halts swine-flu inoculation program after report of 58 cases of paralysis, known as Guillain-Barre syndrome, in 18 states including Utah.
– Convicted murderer, Gary Gilmore, is sentenced to death; he pleads for prompt execution by firing squad.
– Gary Gilmore unsuccessfully attempts suicide by overdose of barbiturates.

1977 Utah Supreme Court rules 4-1 that State's death penalty is constitutional.
– Gary Gilmore is executed by firing squad at Utah State Prison; he is first person to suffer death penalty since 1967.

1978 State sales tax has increased one-half percent in last decade.
– Immanuel David, excommunicated Mormon and religious cult leader, commits suicide; his wife, Rachel David, their seven children plunge eleven stories from International Dunes Hotel in downtown Salt Lake City one day later.
– Former Interior Secretary, Stewart Udall, now in private practice, files 100 claims against Energy Department; he seeks up to $232 million in damages for persons who say they or relatives developed cancer or leukemia as result of nuclear weapons testing in Utah, Nevada, and Arizona sites.

1979 Washington Post charges that U.S. Public Health Service commissioned 1965 study, then apparently ignored and withheld findings after results cited definite link between excessive leukemia deaths of Utah residents and radioactive fallout from atomic bomb tests at Nevada Proving Grounds.
– Utah officials claim that AEC refused to investigate 1953 deaths of some 4,300 sheep, and possibility of radiation damage to humans after nuclear bomb tests in Nevada.

1980 U.S. Census Bureau reports population total of 1,461,037 in 1980; State will have three representatives in 98th Congress in 1982.
– Utah is one of 12 states reporting widespread influenza outbreaks; number of deaths in U.S. during three-week period of January-February is about 300 higher than normal.

1981 Glen Canyon is one of five national recreation areas named by Interior Department that will be opened to mineral exploration, oil and gas drilling.

1982 Republicans are left with majorities in State house and senate.

1983 Salt Lake City jury sentences New York woman to life in prison on charge of first degree murder for sending 17-year old son to Utah to murder his millionaire father; Frances Schreuder's son testifies against her, will serve prison term of five years to life for father's death.

1984 Voters defeat proposed ban on pornography on cable television, approve measure guaranteeing right to keep and bear arms.

1985 Great Salt Lake surpasses high-water mark set in 1873; farmlands, highways, lakefront property, and rail causeway are flooded.
– Wildfires spread through parts of Utah, ten other Western states.
– Dry, hot weather causes grasshopper plague in Utah, ten other Western states.

1986 Republican Norman H. Bangerter is governor.

1987 Mine Safety and Health Administration sets record $111,470 in fines against mine owner, Power & Light Co., and Emery Mining Corp., former operator of Wilberg coal mine; fine results from deaths of twenty-seven workers who died in 1984 fire; later investigation uncovered 34 safety violations.

1988 Three tax-cutting ballot initiatives are defeated; proposals sought to cut income, sales, gasoline, and cigarette taxes, limit property taxes.

1989 Panel appointed by U.S. Energy Department concludes scant evidence for cold fusion claims made by two chemists from University of Utah laboratory; panel claims that evidence for discovery of cold fusion process "was not persuasive."

1990 Proposal to reduce State taxes, curb government spending is voted down in Utah, four other states.

1991 Population totals 1,722,850; figure is 17.9 percent higher than 1980.
– University of Utah president, Chase N. Peterson, retires after admission that he secretly transferred $500,000 of university funds to cold fusion research.
– Three rock fans are crushed to death after AC/DC heavy metal group fans surge toward stage at Salt Palace concert; arena officials subsequently announce suspension of "festival seating" (unreserved or open floor) at arena events.
– Governor Bangerter signs bill for some of most strict abortion restrictions in U.S.; law permits abortion only in cases of rape or incest, where pregnancy poses "grave danger" to woman's health, or in cases where fetus suffers "grave defects."
– State legislature votes to clarify abortion ban enacted in January; revision will affect homicide statute, which would charge women who undergo "illegal" abortion, and doctors who perform them with murder.

1992 In response to allegations of massive waste, misappropriations, and theft in his administration, Governor Norman H. Bangerter freezes Navajo trust fund.
– Republican Mike Leavitt wins election to governor's office.

1993 Executions in State since 1976 reinstitution of capital punishment (1976-1993) total four.

1994 Microbiologist Scott R. Woodward at Brigham Young University in Provo claims to have isolated DNA from bone fragments of dinosaurs living in Utah 80 million years ago.
– Utah is one of ten states with fastest growth between 1990-1993.

1995 International Olympic Committee names Salt Lake City as host for 2002 Winter Olympic Games.

1996 Governor Leavitt wins reelection.

1997 Armored car guard, Thomas Wheelock, is arrested for allegedly killing partner, Rodrigo Cortez, stealing 300,000 dollars from vehicle they were in charge of protecting; Wheelock confessed to crime during routine traffic stop, according to police.

1998 Air Force pilot is killed when F-16 jet crashes west of Hill Air Force Base during practice flight; Major Gregory Martineac and plane are not found until next day because of bad weather.

1999 International Olympic Committee votes to expel six members who allegedly took gifts, cash payments, in return for votes to hold 2002 Winter Olympic Games in Salt Lake City; committee sets rules to reform bidding process for games in 2006; new committee will be formed to recommend permanent changes to procedures and structure.
– Rare tornado rips through heart of Salt Lake City; one is dead, another 100 injured; Governor Leavitt declares city in state of emergency.

DIRECTORY OF STATE SERVICES

OFFICE OF THE GOVERNOR
210 State Capitol
Salt Lake City, UT 84114
Governor: 801-538-1000
Fax: 801-538-1528

Planning and Budget Office
116 State Capitol Bldg.
Salt Lake City, UT 84114
Director: 801-538-1027
Fax: 801-538-1547

Washington DC Office
400 N Capitol St. NW, Ste 370
Washington DC 20001
Director: 202-624-7704
Fax: 202-624-7707

LIEUTENANT GOVERNOR
203 State Capitol
Salt Lake City, UT 84114
Lieutenant Governor: 801-538-1040
Fax: 801-538-1557

ATTORNEY GENERAL
236 State Capitol
Salt Lake City, UT 84114
Attorney General: 801-538-1015
Fax: 801-538-1121

TREASURER
215 State Capitol
Salt Lake City, UT 84114
Treasurer: 801-538-1042
Fax: 801-538-1465

ADMINISTRATIVE SERVICES DEPARTMENT
3120 State Office Bldg.
Salt Lake City, UT 84114
Executive Director: 801-538-3010
Fax: 801-538-3844

AGRICULTURAL DEPARTMENT
P.O. Box 146500
Salt Lake City, UT 84114-6500
Commissioner: 801-538-7100
Fax: 801-538-7126

ALCOHOLIC BEVERAGE CONTROL DEPARTMENT
P.O. Box 30408
Salt Lake City, UT 84130-0408
Director: 801-977-6800
Fax: 801-977-6888

AUDITOR
Rm. 211 State Capitol
Salt Lake City, UT 84114
State Auditor: 801-538-1025
Fax: 801-538-1383

COMMERCE DEPARTMENT
P.O. Box 45802
Salt Lake City, UT 84145-0802
Executive Director: 801-530-6701
Fax: 801-530-6650

COMMUNITY AND ECONOMIC DEVELOPMENT DEPARTMENT
324 S State St.
Salt Lake City, UT 84111
Executive Director: 801-538-8700
Fax: 801-538-8888

Job Training for Economic Development Office
324 S State St.
Salt Lake City, UT 84111
Director: 801-538-8700
Fax: 801-538-8888

State Library Division
2150 South, 300 West, Ste. 16
Salt Lake City, UT 84115
Director: 801-466-5888
Fax: 801-533-4657

CORRECTIONS DEPARTMENT
6100 South, 300 East
Murray, UT 84107
Executive Director: 801-265-5500
Fax: 801-265-5670

ENVIRONMENTAL QUALITY DEPARTMENT
P.O. Box 144810
Salt Lake City, UT 84114-4810
Executive Director: 801-536-4402
Fax: 801-536-4401

FINANCIAL INSTITUTIONS DEPARTMENT
P.O. Box 89
Salt Lake City, UT 84110-0089

Commissioner: 801-538-8830
Fax: 801-538-8894

HEALTH DEPARTMENT
P.O. Box 16700
Salt Lake City, UT 84116-0700
Executive Director: 801-538-6111
Fax: 801-538-6694

Community Health Services Division
P.O. Box 16600
Salt Lake City, UT 84116-0600
Director: 801-538-6129
Fax: 801-538-6036

Family Health Services Division
P.O. Box 144100
Salt Lake City, UT 84114-4100
Director: 801-538-6161
Fax: 801-538-6510

Health Care Financing Division
P.O. Box 142851
Salt Lake City, UT 84114-2851
Director: 801-538-6406
Fax: 801-538-6478

Health Systems Improvement Division
P.O. Box 16990
Salt Lake City, UT 84116-0990
Director: 801-538-6107
Fax: 801-538-6387

Medical Examiner's Office
48 N Medical Dr.
Salt Lake City, UT 84113
Medical Examiner: 801-584-8410
Fax: 801-584-8435

State Health Laboratory
46 N Medical Dr.
Salt Lake City, UT 84113
Director: 801-584-8400
Fax: 801-584-8486

HUMAN SERVICES DEPARTMENT
P.O. Box 45500
Salt Lake City, UT 84145-4016
Executive Director: 801-538-3996
Fax: 801-538-4016

INSURANCE DEPARTMENT
3110 State Office Building
Salt Lake City, UT 84114
Commissioner: 801-538-3804
Fax: 801-538-3829

NATURAL RESOURCES DEPARTMENT
1636 W North Temple, Ste. 316
Salt Lake City, UT 84116-3193
Executive Director: 801-538-7200
Fax: 801-538-7315

Energy and Resources Planning Office
355 W North Temple, Ste. 450
Salt Lake City, UT 84180-1204
Director: 801-538-5428
Fax: 801-521-0657

Geological Survey Division
2363 S Foothill Dr.
Salt Lake City, UT 84109-1497
Director: 801-467-7970
Fax: 801-467-4070

Oil, Gas and Mining Division
355 W N Temple, Ste. 350
Salt Lake City, UT 48180-1203
Director: 801-538-5340
Fax: 801-359-3940

Parks and Recreation Division
1636 W North Temple, Rm. 116
Salt Lake City, UT 84116-3193
Director: 801-538-7362
Fax: 801-538-7055

Sovereign Lands and Forestry Division
3 Triad Ctr., Ste 425, 425 W N Temple
Salt Lake City, UT 84180-1204
Director: 801-538-5555
Fax: 801-533-4111

Water Resources Division
1636 W N Temple, Rm. 310
Salt Lake City, UT 84116
Director: 801-538-7230
Fax: 801-538-7279

Water Rights Division
1636 W North Temple, Rm. 220
Salt Lake City, UT 48116
State Engineer: 801-538-7240
Fax: 801-538-7467

Wildlife Resources Division
1596 W North Temple
Salt Lake City, UT 84116
Director: 801-538-4700
Fax: 801-538-4709

PUBLIC SAFETY DEPARTMENT
4501 South, 2700 West
Salt Lake City, UT 84119
Commissioner: 801-965-4461
Fax: 801-965-4756

Peace Officers Standards and Training
4525 S 2700 W
Salt Lake City, UT 84119
Director: 801-965-4595
Fax: 801-965-4756

SCHOOL AND INSTITUTIONAL TRUST LANDS ADMINISTRATION
3 Triad Center, Ste. 400
Salt Lake City, UT 48180-1204

Director: 801-538-5508
Fax: 801-355-0922

TRANSPORTATION DEPARTMENT
4501 South 2700 West
Salt Lake City, UT 84119
Director: 801-965-4113
Fax: 801-965-4338

ASSOCIATED MUNICIPAL POWER SYSTEMS
8722 South 300 West
Sandy, UT 84070
General Manager: 801-566-3933
Fax: 801-561-2687

BOARD OF EDUCATION
250 East 500 South
Salt Lake City, UT 84111
Chairman: 801-538-7510
Fax: 801-538-7521

Education Department
250 East, 500 South
Salt Lake City, UT 84111
Superintendent: 801-538-7510
Fax: 801-538-7512

Rehabilitation Office
250 East, 500 South
Salt Lake City, UT 84111
Executive Director: 801-538-7530
Fax: 801-538-7522

Schools for Deaf and Blind
742 Harrison Blvd.
Ogden, UT 84404
Superintendent: 801-298-3311
Fax: 801-629-4896

DEVELOPMENTAL DISABILITIES COUNCIL
350 East, 500 South, Rm. 201
Salt Lake City, UT 84111
Executive Director: 801-533-4128
Fax: 801-533-5305

HIGHER EDUCATION SYSTEM
355 W North Temple, Ste. 550
Salt Lake City, UT 84180-1205
Commissioner & Chief Executive Officer: 801-321-7100
Fax: 801-321-7199

HOUSING FINANCE AGENCY
544 South, 300 East
Salt Lake City, UT 84111
Executive Director: 801-521-6950
Fax: 801-359-1701

INDUSTRIAL COMMISSION
160 East, 300 South, 3rd Fl.
Salt Lake City, UT 84114-6610
Chairman: 801-530-6880
Fax: 801-530-6804

Employment Security Division
P.O. Box 11249
Salt Lake City, UT 84147
Administrator: 801-538-7401
Fax: 801-536-7420

NATIONAL GUARD
P.O. Box 1776
Draper, UT 84020-1776
Adjutant General: 801-576-3600
Fax: 801-576-3575

PUBLIC EMPLOYEES ASSOCIATION
1000 W Bellwood Lane
Murray, UT 84123-4494
Executive Director: 801-264-8732
Fax: 801-264-8879

RETIREMENT BOARD
540 East 2nd South
Salt Lake City, UT 84102-7734
Executive Director: 801-355-3884
Fax: 801-366-7734

TAX COMMISSION
210 North, 1950 West
Salt Lake City, UT 84134
Chairman: 801-297-2200
Fax: 801-297-3919

TWENTIETH CENTURY GOVERNORS

WELLS, HEBER M. (1859-1938), first governor of Utah (1896-1905), was born in Salt Lake City, Utah, on August 11, 1859. His father, Daniel H. Wells, served as a Second Counselor to Brigham Young between 1857 and 1877, and from that year until 1891, he was Counselor to the Twelve Apostles of the Church of Jesus Christ of Latter-day Saints (Mormons). Before the federal law forbade multiple marriages, Daniel Wells had six wives, and Heber Wells was the son of one of them, Martha Harris Wells.

Wells attended the University of Deseret (later, the University of Utah). Wells was employed as a tax collector for Salt Lake City in 1877, and in 1882, was appointed City Recorder, serving in that post for four terms.

Wells made an unsuccessful bid for the mayorship of Salt Lake City in 1892, but in 1895 he secured the nomination for the Utah governorship on the Republican ticket, and became Utah's first governor. Wells won a second term in 1900. During his tenure, he worked to implement the changeover from the Utah Territory into statehood, and to piece together the necessary elements needed to establish a State government. It was his intention to elevate the new State's economic base, while at the same time, encouraging the conservation of Utah's natural resources. To that end, he promoted the setting aside of forest preserves.

Losing his bid for a third term in 1904, Wells stepped down from office the following year. Soon after, he was named Managing Director of the Utah Savings and Trust Company. During 1913 he served on the Salt Lake City Commission. In 1921, Wells became Assistant Treasurer for the United States Shipping Board Fleet Corporation, and in 1925, was named Treasurer, serving in that post until 1933. Wells was married three times: his first two wives—Mary Elizabeth Beatie and Teresa Clawson—died, and Emily Katz was his third wife. He had three children by his first union, and two from his second. Wells died on March 12, 1938.

CUTLER, JOHN CHRISTOPHER (1846-1928), second governor of Utah (1905-1909), was born in Sheffield, England on February 5, 1846. After his parents converted to the Church of Jesus Christ of Latter-day Saints (Mormon), the family relocated to Utah in 1864. Cutler made his living as a businessman, overseeing the family's dry goods business. In addition, Cutler helmed a number of banks and insurance firms. From 1884 to 1890 he served as Clerk of Salt Lake County.

Politically active in the Republican Party, in 1904 Cutler successfully pursued the Utah governorship. During his tenure, Cutler oversaw the creation of Utah State law. Also, a State juvenile court system was established, the registration process regarding births and deaths was implemented, and jurisdiction of Fort Duchesne and Fort Douglas was ceded to the federal government. In addition, Cutler promoted the construction of a State Capitol building, and pushed for the Uintah Indian Reservation to open its land to white settlement.

In 1908 the Republican Party backed William Spry for the upcoming election, and Cutler supported the new choice, stepping down from office after his term, and returned to his various business interests.

Cutler was married to Sarah Elizabeth Taylor, and the couple had seven children. Having been in failing health for a while, Cutler took his own life on July 30, 1928.

SPRY, WILLIAM (1864-1929), third governor of Utah (1909-1917), was born in Windsor, Berkshire, England on January 11, 1864. His early education was minimal, with his quitting school at the age of thirteen. A Mormon, he served his mission throughout the South, from 1885 to 1891. As a young man he was employed at several jobs, then became involved in ranching.

Spry's first public office was as Tooele County Tax Collector in 1894, then in 1902, he secured a seat in the Utah State Legislature. During 1905 he served as President of the State Land Board, and in 1906 he was appointed U.S. Marshal for the State of Utah. In 1908 Spry, a Republican, ran for the Utah governorship and was elected, also winning his reelection bid in 1912. During his tenure, Spry worked diligently to support the State's needs. He secured substantial funding from the State Legislature for the building of the State Capitol, supported food and drug legislation, and worked to develop Utah's various natural resources. In addition, a number of committees were established for such State needs as irrigation, industrial safety, banking policies, and water rights. During his second administration, he became prominent nationwide when he refused to halt the execution of labor activist Joe Hill, who had been convicted of murder in a Utah trial. Even an appeal from President Woodrow Wilson did not stop Hill from being executed in 1915.

In 1916 Spry lost his bid for a third term in the governorship, and stepped down from office. In 1918 he was unsuccessful in his attempt at a seat in the United States Congress. For a time, Spry was employed by the Western Irrigation Association as their spokesman, then in 1921, he was appointed United States Commissioner of the General Land Office by President Warren G. Harding.

Spry was married to Mary Alice Wrathall, and the couple had three children. He died on April 21, 1929.

BAMBERGER, SIMON (1846-1926), fourth governor of Utah (1917-1921), was born in Eberstadt, Hesse-Darmstadt, Germany on February 27, 1846. At the age of fifteen, Bamberger immigrated to the United States, eventually settling in Utah in 1870.

Not long after, he entered into a number of business ventures that included mining, hotels, railroads, and a resort vacation spot. From 1898 until 1903, Bamberger served on the Salt Lake City Board of Education, then from 1903 until 1907, he served in the Utah State Senate. In 1916 Bamberger secured the Utah governorship on the Democratic ticket.

During Bamberger administration, one of the first pieces of legislation adopted was a prohibition statute. Bamberger actively backed the creation of such departments as the Board of Control, the Public Utilities Commission, the Department of Public Health, plus the establishment of a mental hospital, an industrial school, and a facility for the deaf, dumb, and blind. Bamberger also urged the passage of the Workmen's Compensation Act. In addition, having inherited a State deficit of 400,000 dollars, he managed to create a surplus of two million dollars in the State budget by the time he stepped down from office.

Choosing not to run for another term, after leaving Bamberger continued to helm the Bamberger Railroad, and also served as president of the Salt Lake and Denver Railroad Company.

Bamberger was married to Ida Maas, and the couple had four children. He died on October 6, 1926.

MABEY, CHARLES RENDELL (1877-1959), fifth governor of Utah (1921-1925), was born in Bountiful, Utah on October 4, 1877. In 1896 he earned a teaching certificate from the University of Utah, and subsequently taught school for several years. During the Spanish-American War, Mabey served in the Philippines with the Utah National Guard. A Mormon, Mabey also served his mission in Germany for three years.

Upon his return to Utah, Mabey served as Justice of the Peace, City Councilman, then Mayor of Bountiful. Between 1912 and 1916, he served in the Utah House of Representatives.

In 1920 Mabey ran for the governorship of Utah on the Republican ticket, winning the election. While in office, Mabey's top priority was Utah's educational system, with several new schools being constructed, and teacher certification standards tightened. He also supported highway construction throughout the State, using money from a gasoline sales tax, and urged the Legislature to let Utah join other states in the Colorado River Compact. In addition, he oversaw a comprehensive revamping of the State government.

Since Mabey's highway and education expenditures were not popular with a number of political adversaries, plus several patronage posts were eliminated when Mabey reorganized the governmental structure, both situations probably led to his defeat in the 1924 election. Stepping down in 1925, Mabey returned to his various business interests, such as serving as president of the Bountiful State Bank.

Mabey was married to Afton Rampton, and the couple had four children. He died on April 26, 1959.

DERN, GEORGE HENRY (1872-1936), sixth governor of Utah (1925-1933), was born near Scribner, Nebraska on September 8, 1872. He attended Fremont Normal College, graduating in 1888, then during 1893-94, studied at the University of Nebraska. In the latter year he secured a job as Treasurer of the Mercury Gold Mining and Milling Company. His interest in mining prompted him to co-invent the Holt-Dern ore heating process, a procedure that separates silver from the lower grade of ore.

Deciding to pursue politics, Dern, a Democrat, secured two terms in the Utah State Senate, serving from 1915 to 1923. A forward-minded legislator, Dern had no trouble winning the 1924 election for the Utah governorship as a member of the Progressive Party. Although the majority of the State Legislature was Republican, his liberal stance on many of the issues garnered him a reelection win in 1928.

Dern became known nationwide when he implemented tax laws in Utah that served both middle and lower income citizens, and by his support of unemployment insurance. In addition, he managed to untangle the complicated situation concerning water rights of the states that surrounded the Colorado River and Boulder Dam. Through his persuasion, the federal government acquiesced their jurisdiction of the waters, allowing the states to solve the issue.

Dern stepped down from the governorship in 1933, and immediately accepted a Cabinet post in the War Department offered by President Franklin D. Roosevelt, where Dern served until 1936. Another impressive contribution by Dern was his founding of the Civilian Conservation Corps.

Dern was married to Charlotte Brown, and the couple had seven children. He died on August 27, 1936.

BLOOD, HENRY HOOPER (1872-1942), seventh governor of Utah (1933-1941), was born in Kaysville, Utah on October 1, 1872. He studied at Brigham Young Academy in Provo. Pursuing public office in 1893, he was elected City Recorder of Kaysville, then from 1896 to 1900, was Treasurer of Davis County. In 1901 he was named Minute Clerk of the State Senate. Later that year, Blood began his missionary work for the Mormon Church, serving in England until 1904. After returning, he secured a teaching position at Brigham Young College in Logan. Soon after, he also embarked on a business career, making a name for himself in Utah. Between 1909 and 1918 he was a member of the Davis County School Board, and from 1917 to 1922, he served on the Public Utilities Commission. In the latter year he was named to the State Highway Commission, and in 1925, was made chairman of that group.

In 1932 Blood successfully ran for the Utah governorship on the Democratic ticket, and also won his reelection bid in 1936. During his administration, the entire nation was reeling from the Great Depression, and from the beginning, Blood adopted a "pay-as-you-go" policy. At the start of his term, the State was over twelve million dollars in debt, but due to his perseverance, the debt had been whittled down to less than four million dollars by the time he left. Also, a two-percent sales tax was implemented at that time, the monies of which were intended to help as a welfare measure. Blood was given a large amount of latitude by the federal government in his handling of relief programs for Utah, and through his dedication and powers of persuasion with federal officials, he was able to bring to the State a number of WPA and CCC projects.

Although several of his supporters urged Blood to run for a third term, the Mormon Church requested that he relocate to California to serve as a Mission President, prompting Blood to step down from office at the end of his tenure in 1941.

Blood was married to Minnie A. Barnes, and the couple had four children. He died on June 19, 1942.

MAW, HERBERT BROWN (1893-1990), eighth governor of Utah (1941-1949), was born in Ogden, Utah on March 11, 1893. He attended the University of Utah, where he earned an LL.B. degree in 1916, and a B.S. degree in 1923. He next studied at Northwestern University where he took an M.A. degree in 1926, and a J.D. degree in 1927. In the interim, between 1917 and 1919, he served in the United States Army during World War I.

Maw embarked on a career in law, while at the same time, teaching classes at the University of Utah between 1923 and 1940. From 1928 to 1936, he also served as Dean of Men at that school.

In 1928 Maw secured a seat in the Utah State Senate, where he served until 1938. In 1934 he made an unsuccessful bid for the United States Senate, as well as for the Utah governorship in 1936. The last defeat, which came from Democratic Party leaders who disagreed with his policies, prompted Maw to fight back by sponsoring legislation that abolished the party nomination system, replacing it with the direct primary. It proved to be a smart move, as he won the gubernatorial campaign in 1940.

During his tenure, Maw sought to modernize and streamline the State government, as well as wipe out the State debt, both of which he accomplished. His improvements garnered him another term in office, albeit by a slim margin. Continuing his progressive stance, Maw pushed for legislation that revamped Utah's most prominent utility company, which resulted in utility rates being drastically reduced. In addition, mining companies that had previously used the State as a "minerals colony," with their mining Utah's precious metals and sending them out of state for processing, were slapped with stricter regulations.

In his try for a third term in 1948, Maw found that his progressive ideas in such areas as welfare and labor were being attacked by more conservative politicians, resulting in his loss at the polls. Maw stepped down in 1949 and returned to his law practice.

Maw married Florence Buehler, and the couple had four children. He died on November 17, 1990.

LEE, JOSEPH BRACKEN (1899-1996),

ninth governor of Utah (1949-1957), was born in Price, Utah, on January 7, 1899. Receiving a high school education, Lee served in the United States Army during World War I. In 1921 he engaged in the real estate business, then subsequently in insurance.

Lee's first political office was the mayorship of Price, Utah, a post he held for six terms, from 1936 to 1947. After two unsuccessful campaigns for the U.S. Congress and the Utah governorship, he won the Governor's office on the Republican ticket in 1948 and secured a second term in 1952.

During his tenure, Lee achieved national prominence with his vocal opposition to federal income taxes, and his unique input on the State's economy. With his urging, highway construction and State building programs were escalated, and the State liquor enforcement agency was eliminated, as was the Publicity and Industrial Development Department, the latter being replaced by the more limited Tourist and Publicity Council. Also, a State motor pool was established, gasoline taxes were increased, and individual income taxes were reduced. Through his streamlining of Utah's economic structure, the State remained debt-free for the duration of his administration.

In 1956 the Republican Party refused to back Lee's reelection bid, so he ran on the Independent ticket, but lost the race, stepping down from office in January of 1957. Two months later, Lee was named the National Chairman of "For America," an organization founded to support "constitutional" government, rather than internationalism.

In 1958 Lee made an unsuccessful bid for the United States Senate, and the following year, he purchased the *Utah Statesman*, a Republican weekly, and renamed it *American Statesman*. From 1959 to 1971, Lee served as Mayor of Salt Lake City.

Lee was married twice: to Nellie Amelia Pace, and after her death, to Margaret Ethel Draper. He had one child by his first union, and three by his second. He died on October 20, 1996 and is buried at Mt. Olivet Cemetery.

CLYDE, GEORGE DEWEY (1898-1972),

tenth governor of Utah (1957-1965), was born in Springville, Utah, on July 21, 1898. He attended Utah State Agricultural College, earning a bachelor's degree in agricultural engineering, then studied at the University of California, Berkeley, where he took his master's degree in civil engineering in 1923. Clyde became a faculty member at Utah State Agricultural College, then in 1935, was named Dean of the School of Engineering and Technology. Clyde served in various posts at the United States Soil Conservation Service between 1945 and 1953, then in the latter year, was named director of the Utah Water and Power Board.

Deciding to pursue a political career, Clyde ran for the Utah governorship on the Republican ticket in 1956, winning the election, and also securing another term in 1960. During his tenure, Clyde was instrumental in reorganizing the State government, including replacing "commissions" with professional directors. Also, schools and highways received the funding they needed, and a State parks system was established, as was a State library. In addition, Clyde fought for Utah's right to use water from the Colorado River. During his second administration, the Canyonlands National Park was established by the U.S. Congress in 1964.

Deciding not to run for another term, Clyde stepped down from office in 1965, and returned to his engineering work as an independent consultant. Throughout his professional career, he authored a number of books on water.

Clyde was married to Ora Packard, and the couple had five children. He died on April 2, 1972.

RAMPTON, CALVIN LEWELLYN (1913-),

eleventh governor of Utah (1965-1977), was born in Bountiful, Utah on November 6, 1913. He attended the University of Utah, earning a B.S. degree in 1936. He subsequently studied at George Washington University, then returned to the University of Utah to take his J.D. degree. From 1936 to 1938 Rampton worked for U.S. Congressman J.W. Robinson as an administrative assistant, and during 1939-40, served as Davis County Attorney. During 1941-42, he was Utah's Assistant Attorney General, and served again in that post from 1946 to 1948. In the interim, during World War II, he served in the United States Army, and was stationed in France, Germany and Holland.

In 1964 Rampton successfully ran for the Utah governorship, becoming the first Democrat to hold that office in sixteen years. In 1968, he won a second term, then in 1972, he was elected a third time, the first governor in Utah's history to serve three terms.

During his administration, Rampton was instrumental in the establishment of the Industrial Promotion Council and the Utah Travel Council, the result being that with the subsequent boom in tourism, there were more jobs for Utah residents. Also during those years, the State government was revamped, and through his efforts, there were deficit reductions in the Uniform School Fund and Utah's General Fund. In addition, both the Fair Employment Practice Act and the Public Accommodations Act were strongly enforced, plus the Utah Police Training Academy was founded, as was the Governor's Conference on the Arts.

Although popular enough to win a fourth term, Rampton decided to step down, and left office on January 3, 1977. He is married to Lucybeth Cardon, and the couple has four children.

MATHESON, SCOTT MILNE (1929-1990),

twelfth governor of Utah (1977-1985), was born in Chicago, Illinois on January 8, 1929. He attended the University of Utah, graduating with honors in 1950, then studied law at Stanford University, where he took his degree in 1952.

Matheson entered public office when he secured the post of City Attorney for Parowan, Utah, then Deputy Attorney of Iron County during 1953-54. From 1954 to 1956 Matheson served as a law clerk for a United States District Court Judge in Salt Lake

City, then subsequently went into private law practice. In 1958 Matheson was hired as an attorney for the Union Pacific Railroad, later being named Solicitor General for the firm. He took a break from that company for a short time between 1969 to 1971 to serve as Assistant General Counsel for the Anaconda Copper Company, then returned to Union Pacific Railroad until he resigned in 1976.

In that year, Matheson, a Democrat, ran for the Utah governorship, winning the election, and later securing a second term in 1980. During his tenure, Matheson, the "seventy-hour-a-week" governor was highly respected for his hard work, and wise decisions. With his guidance, the Utah State Legislature passed a one billion-dollar appropriations bill, the highest ever for the State. Also, various sales taxes were reduced, including those for natural gas, electricity, fuel oil, and coal. Matheson, who believed strongly in "full partnership" with the federal government, became prominent outside of Utah for his taking the lead with several western governors in their efforts to work in tandem with federal officials on such core issues as energy development, water conservation, and other concerns. Their goal was to not allow Washington, D.C. complete autonomy regarding decisions that affected their states.

Another serious matter Matheson brought to national attention concerned the highly probable correlation between the government-sanctioned atomic testing in the 1950s, in neighboring Nevada, and the extraordinarily large number of cancer victims in both states.

During 1982-83 Matheson served as Chairman of the National Governors' Association, as well as President of the Council of State Governments. In 1977, Secretary of the Interior, Cecil Andrus, picked Matheson and three other governors to served on the Intergovernmental Task Force on Water Policy. Later, in 1983, President Ronald Reagan named him to the Advisory Council on Intergovernmental Relations.

Although a Democrat in a predominantly conservative Republican state, Matheson was a highly popular administrator, and by all accounts, could have easily won a third term. But, abiding by his own motto, "You get in, you give it your best shot, and then you get out again," he decided to leave office after his second term, stepping down in 1985.

Matheson married Norma Louise Warenski, and the couple had four children. After a bout with cancer, Matheson died on October 7, 1990. He is interred at Parowan City Cemetery, in Parowan, Utah.

BANGERTER, NORMAN H. (1933-), thirteenth governor of Utah (1985-1993), was born on January 4, 1933, in Granger, Utah, the tenth child in a family of eleven children. During the 1970s Bangerter owned and operated a construction company, which specialized in the building of private homes and the development of residential real estate.

Deciding to pursue politics, Bangerter held a seat in the Utah House of Representatives between 1975 and 1985. In 1984 he successfully sought the Utah governorship on the Republican ticket, and also won another term in 1988. Some of the challenges Bangerter faced while in office included the rising of the Great Salt Lake, caused by the heavy rainfall that that region had experienced for a number of years. At a cost of sixty million dollars, Bangerter oversaw the construction of a pumping station that siphoned a large amount of the excess water and pumped it into the desert. With the lake once again at its normal level, the possibility of extensive destruction was alleviated everywhere from the Salt Lake City airport and waste water treatment plants, to the interstate highways. During 1986-87, the State of Utah sustained a recession, caused by falling energy commodity prices. The domino effect included a sixty percent decrease in mining jobs, and a thirty percent drop in construction work, plus some major companies were forced to close for a time, including Kennecott Copper and Geneva Steel.

During this time, Bangerter also had to deal with a dramatic escalation in public school enrollments, which eventually forced him to raise taxes. That situation prompted a number of citizens to form a grassroots tax protest, which resulted in three initiatives being placed on the ballot. However, even with all the press attention surrounding the issue, the initiatives were ultimately defeated in November of 1988. Bangerter stuck to his decision to increase the funding for Utah's educational system in order to upgrade it. Another priority for Bangerter was the boosting of Utah's economic development, which included trade with Europe and Asia.

Eschewing a third term, Bangerter stepped down from office in 1991. He is married to Colleen Monson, with whom he has six children. The couple also raised a foster child.

LEAVITT, MICHAEL O. (1951-), fourteenth governor of Utah (1993-current) was born in Cedar City, Utah, on February 11, 1951. He attended Southern Utah University where he earned a B.A. degree in Business and Economics in 1978. Leavitt eventually got into the insurance business, serving as president and chief executive officer of The Leavitt Group.

Leavitt successfully ran for the Utah governorship in 1992 on the Republican ticket. During his tenure he has guided the State in such issues as education, health care, welfare reform, and the environment. In addition, taxes have been reduced, and highways have been upgraded. Leavitt was a co-founder of Western Governors' University, which offers students a college education through technology. Other educational initiatives proposed by Governor Leavitt include Centennial Schools, which returns autonomy back to the teachers and parents, and Highly Impacted Schools, which offers additional support to disadvantaged children.

Also during this time, *Financial World* magazine named Utah as the most livable state in the nation, and also the best managed. In addition, the 2002 Winter Olympics are scheduled to take place there.

Leavitt is co-author of *Enlibra*, a "commonsense" blueprint for the management and protection of the environment. Due to his longtime states' rights stance, by which the federal government has less input in State decisions, Leavitt was given the Thomas Jefferson Freedom Award by the American Legislative Exchange Council. He was also the recipient of the Nathan Davis Award, given by the American Medical Association for his health care policies.

Leavitt and his wife Jacalyn have five children. His term ends in 2001.

DICTIONARY OF PLACES

Population figures and demographic information are official U.S. Census Bureau finals for 1990. When two figures are shown, separated by a slash, the first figure is the 1990 and the second is the U.S. Census Bureau 1999 estimate—the most recent available. Year 2000 census supplements will be available in the Fall of 2001.

ALPINE, City; Utah County; Pop. 2,649 / 5,743; Descriptively named for its elevated location in the Wasatch Mountains, which provide "alpine" views.

ALTA, Town; Salt Lake County; Pop. 381 / 417; Zip Code 84092; *Alta* is Spanish for "high." At 9,500 feet elevation this ex-mining town evolved to famous ski resort is aptly named.

ALTAMONT, Town; Duchesne County; Pop. 247 / 197; Zip Code 84002; Elev. 6,375; Lat. 40-24-01 N, Long. 110-17-35 W; Descriptively named for its elevation, the name means "high mountain."

AMERICAN FORK, City; Utah County; Pop. 12,417 / 18,893; Zip Code 84003; Lat. 40-21-59 N, Long. 111-47-35 W; Settled in 1850 near the Fork River, the name "American Fork" was chosen to contrast with nearby "Spanish Fork."

ANNABELLA, Town; Sevier County; Pop. 463 / 720; Zip Code 84711; Elev. 5,301; Lat. 38-42-28 N, Long. 112-03-37 W; Named for the wife of an early settler.

AURORA, Town; Sevier County; Pop. 874 / 985; Zip Code 84620; Elev. 5,187; Lat. 38-55-19 N, Long. 111-56-11 W; A Latin word meaning "dawn."

BEAR RIVER CITY, Town; Box Elder County; Pop. 540 / 818; Zip Code 84301; Lat. 41-37-08 N, Long. 112-07-47 W; The town is named after the Bear River, which empties into the Great Salt Lake.

BEAVER, City; Beaver County; Pop. 1,792 / 2,433; Zip Code 84713; Elev. 5,898; Lat. 38-16-45 N, Long. 112-38-21 W; Named after the Beaver River, itself descriptively named for the once plentiful fur bearing animals.

BICKNELL, Town; Wayne County; Pop. 296 / 308; Zip Code 84715; Lat. 38-20-28 N, Long. 111-32-32 W; Bicknell is named for businessman Thomas Bicknell.

BLANDING, City; San Juan County; Pop. 3,118 / 3,600; Zip Code 84510; Elev. 6,105; Lat. 37-12-55 N, Long. 109-11-04 W; First called Red Mesa and later changed to Blanding, the maiden name of Mrs. Thomas Bicknell.

BOUNTIFUL, City; Davis County; Pop. 32,877 / 41,169; Zip Code 84054; Lat. 40-51-29 N, Long. 111-53-52 W; Early settlers gave their town this grateful descriptive name for its fertility.

BRIAN HEAD, Town; Iron County; Pop. 77 / 156; Zip Code 84719; A high point in southwest Utah, the town is named for a member of the U.S. geological survey.

BRIGHAM CITY, City; Box Elder County Seat; Pop. 15,596 / 17,129; Zip Code 84304; Lat. 41-50-12 N, Long. 112-00-20 W; The city's name honors Mormon pioneer Brigham Young. It was originally known as Box Elder, for the Box Elder trees that grew in the area. The city was incorporated in 1869.

CANNONVILLE, Town; Garfield County; Pop. 134 / 130; Zip Code 84718; Named after an early settler.

CASTLE, City; Emery County Seat; Pop. 1,910; Located on the San Rafael River in Cattle Valley and so named.

CEDAR, City; Iron County; Pop. 10,972; Zip Code 84720; Founded in 1851 and named for the abundant scrub cedar in the area.

CEDAR CITY, City; Iron County; Pop. 10,972 / 19,299; Zip Code 84720; Founded in 1851 and named for the abundant scrub cedar in the area.

CEDAR FORT, Town; Utah County; Pop. 269 / 327; Named after the abundant scrub cedar in the area.

CENTERFIELD, Town; Sanpete County; Pop. 653 / 1,006; Zip Code 84622; Lat. 39-07-37 N, Long. 111-49-08 W; Named for its location in the county.

CENTERVILLE, City; Davis County; Pop. 8,069 / 15,899; Zip Code 84014; Lat. 40-54-14 N, Long. 111-53-10 W; Central to the local area and thus given this descriptive name.

CHARLESTON, Town; Wasatch County; Pop. 320 / 463; The town is named after the city in South Carolina.

CIRCLEVILLE, Town; Paiute County; Pop. 445 / 492; Zip Code 84723; Elev. 6,063; Lat. 38-10-19 N, Long. 112-16-16 W; A geographic and descriptive name for the circular contour of the town's valley.

CLARKSTON, Town; Cache County; Pop. 562 / 662; Zip Code 84305; Elev. 4,884; Lat. 41-55-11 N, Long. 112-03-15 W; Named for an early pioneer settler.

CLEARFIELD, City; Davis County; Pop. 17,982 / 27,075; Zip Code 84015; Lat. 41-06-42 N, Long. 112-01-17 W; Descriptively named by the first settlers.

CLEVELAND, Town; Emery County; Pop. 522 / 602; Zip Code 84518; Lat. 39-20-49 N, Long. 110-50-55 W; Named in honor of Grover Cleveland, the 24th President of the United States.

CLINTON, City; Davis County; Pop. 5,777 / 12,082; Clinton is named after the famous governor of New York.

COALVILLE, City; Summit County Seat; Pop. 1,031 / 1,384; Zip Code 84017; Elev. 5,586; Lat. 40-55-09 N, Long. 111-23-37 W; The first coal deposits in Utah were found in the area and gave the town its name.

CORINNE, City; Box Elder County; Pop. 512 / 671; Zip Code 84307; A railroad boom town in the late 1800s, it was named after a town entrepreneur's daughter.

CORNISH, Town; Cache County; Pop. 181 / 234; Zip Code 84308; Named for the local crop.

DELTA, City; Millard County; Pop. 1,930 / 3,132; Zip Code 84624; Lat. 39-21-13 N, Long. 112-34-33 W; The town is located in the dry Sevier Lake in a region of river delta. This geography named the town. The city was established in 1903.

DEWEYVILLE, Town; Box Elder County; Pop. 311 / 328; Zip Code 84309; Named for a prominent early citizen.

DRAPER, City; Salt Lake County; Pop. 5,530 / 18,713; Zip Code 84020; Lat. 40-31-41 N, Long. 111-52-04 W; Draper is named for an early settler.

DUCHESNE, City; Duchesne County Seat; Pop. 1,677 / 1,661; Zip Code 84021; Lat. 40-09-59 N, Long. 110-23-53 W; A French trapper named Du Chesne worked the United Basin in the 1840s and gave his name to the river and the town.

EAST CARBON, City; Carbon County; Pop. 1,942 / 1,230; Zip Code 84520; Lat. 39-32-37 N, Long. 110-24-46 W; Named for the large coal deposits nearby.

EAST LAYTON, City; Davis County; Pop. 3,531; The city is named after an early settler.

ELK RIDGE, Town; Utah County; Pop. 381 / 1,696; Once the home of numerous elk before Europeans arrived, the town's name remembers this heritage.

ELMO, Town; Emery County; Pop. 300 / 350; Zip Code 84521; Elev. 5,694; Lat. 39-23-22 N, Long. 110-48-44 W; Named for an early settler.

ELSINORE, Town; Sevier County; Pop. 612 / 654; Zip Code 84724; Lat. 38-40-58 N, Long. 112-08-59 W; Named by Mormon settlers from Elsinore, Denmark for their former home.

EMERY, Town; Emery County; Pop. 372 / 307; Zip Code 84522; Elev. 6,262; Lat. 38-55-34 N, Long. 111-14-43 W; Named in honor of George Emery, Utah's territorial governor from 1875-1880.

ENOCH, Town; Iron County; Pop. 678 / 3,516; Named by Mormon settlers after Biblical patriarch Enoch.

ENTERPRISE, City; Washington County; Pop. 905 / 1,689; Zip Code 84725; Lat. 37-34-22 N, Long. 113-42-48 W; The site of a major irrigation project in the 1890s, this work led to the town's being labeled enterprise.

EPHRAIM, City; Sanpete County; Pop. 2,810 / 4,333; Zip Code 84627; Lat. 39-21-41 N, Long. 111-35-15 W; A Biblical name given by the Mormon settlers.

ESCALANTE, Town; Garfield County; Pop. 652 / 1,321; Zip Code 84716; Elev. 5812; Lat. 37-55-28 N, Long. 111-25-37 W; The town is named in honor of Spanish explorer Fray Francisco Silvestre De Escalante, who explored the region in 1776.

EUREKA, City; Juab County; Pop. 670 / 670; Zip Code 84628; Elev. 6442; Lat. 39-57-09 N, Long. 112-06-50 W; An historic mining district, the town's name is Greek, meaning "I have found it." The discovery refers to a vein of precious metal.

FAIRVIEW, City; Sanpete County; Pop. 916 / 1,159; Zip Code 84629; Lat. 39-37-42 N, Long. 111-26-19 W; Descriptively named for the city's scenic resources.

FARMINGTON, City; Davis County Seat; Pop. 4,691 / 11,817; Zip Code 84025; Elev. 4,302; Lat. 40-59-06 N, Long. 111-53-13 W; The city's name reflects the area's main economic activity.

FAYETTE, Town; Sanpete County; Pop. 165 / 244; Zip Code 84630; Named by Mormon settlers after Fayette, New York, where Joseph Smith founded the Mormon church in 1830.

FERRON, City; Emery County; Pop. 1,718 / 1,698; Zip Code 84523; Lat. 39-05-23 N, Long. 111-07-40 W; Ferron is named for the original surveyor of Emery and Carbon counties, A.D. Ferron.

FIELDING, Town; Box Elder County; Pop. 325 / 474; Zip Code 84311; Elev. 4,367; Lat. 41-48-42 N, Long. 112-06-50 W; Named for an early settler.

FILLMORE, City; Millard County Seat; Pop. 2,083 / 2,379; Zip Code 84631; Elev. 5,135; Lat. 38-58-12 N, Long. 112-19-51 W; Named in honor of President Millard Fillmore who signed the Utah Territory Act in 1850. The city was first settled in 1859.

FOUNTAIN GREEN, City; Sanpete County; Pop. 578 / 740; Zip Code 84632; Elev. 6025; Lat. 39-37-41 N, Long. 111-38-24 W; A descriptive name for the area's rich agriculture.

GARDEN CITY, Town; Rich County; Pop. 259 / 263; Zip Code 84028; Lat. 41-55-32 N, Long. 111-23-12 W; The city's rich agriculture led to this name.

GARLAND, City; Box Elder County; Pop. 1,405 / 1,887; Zip Code 84312; Elev. 5,273; Lat. 41-44-40 N, Long. 112-09-43 W; Garland is named after an early settler.

GLENDALE, Town; Kane County; Pop. 237 / 347; Zip Code 84710; Elev. 5,824; Lat. 37-26-20 N, Long. 112-28-37 W; A common descriptive name often given to western communities.

GLENWOOD, Town; Sevier County; Pop. 447 / 461; Zip Code 84730; A descriptive name referring to meadow like openings, or glens, in the local forests.

GOSHEN, Town; Utah County; Pop. 582 / 695; Zip Code 84633; Lat. 39-57-01 N, Long, 111-53-55 W; A Biblical name reflecting the area's desirability for farming and ranching.

GRANTSVILLE, City; Tooele County; Pop. 4,419 / 5,787; Zip Code 84029; Lat. 40-35-54 N, Long. 112-27-55 W; Named in honor of General, and later President Ulysses S. Grant.

GREEN RIVER, City; Emery & Grand Counties; Pop. 1,048 / 941; Zip Code 84525; Lat. 38-59-41 N, Long. 110-09-29 W; Named by early Spanish explorers Rio Verde, or Green River, for its characteristic water color.

GUNNISON, City; Sanpete County; Pop. 1,255 / 2,254; Zip Code 84630; Lat. 39-13-30 N, Long. 111-51-23 W; The town's name honors Captain J.W. Gunnison, explorer and surveyor, who was killed by the Ute Indians in 1853.

HARRISVILLE, City; Weber County; Pop. 1,371 / 3,666; The city is named after a local settler.

HATCH, Town; Garfield County; Pop. 121 / 98; Zip Code 84735; Elev. 6917; Lat. 37-38-52 N, Long. 112-25-51 W; Hatch is named after a settler in the area.

HEBER, City; Wasatch County Seat; Pop. 4,362 / 6,603; Zip Code 84032; Elev. 5595; Lat. 40-29-12 N, Long. 111-26-14 W; Heber's name remembers Mormon counselor Heber C. Kimball.

HELPER, City; Dorbon County; Pop. 2,724 / 2,181; Zip Code 84526; Lat. 39-41-14 N, Long. 110-51-07 W; A railroad station on a steep grade, additional "helper" locomotives were added here to cross the mountains. The practice led to this name.

HENEFER, Town; Summit County; Pop. 547 / 692; Zip Code 84033; Lat. 41-01-21 N, Long. 111-29-39 W; Named after a local inhabitant.

HENRIEVILLE, Town; Garfield County; Pop. 167 / 146; Zip Code 84736; Lat. 37-33-44 N, Long. 111-59-42 W; A local settler named Henry gave the town its name.

HIAWATHA, Town; Carbon County; Pop. 249; Zip Code; Named for the legendary Indian hero of Longfellow's famous poem.

HINCKLEY, Town; Millard County; Pop. 464 / 730; Zip Code 84635; Lat. 39-20-00 N, Long. 112-40-24 W; Named for a local settler.

HOLDEN, Town; Millard County; Pop. 364 / 376; Zip Code 84636; Lat. 39-05-59 N, Long. 112-16-34 W; A common personal name recalling a pioneer family.

HONEYVILLE, Town; Box Elder County; Pop. 915 / 1,277; Zip Code 84314; Lat. 41-38-05 N, Long. 112-04-44 W; Descriptively named for the beekeeping activities in the area.

HOWELL, Town; Box Elder County; Pop. 176 / 267; Zip Code 84316; Elev. 4,556; Lat. 41-46-59 N, Long. 112-26-20 W; A common personal name recalling an early settler in the area.

HUNTINGTON, City; Emery County; Pop. 2,316 / 2,089; Zip Code 84528; Elev. 5,791; Lat. 39-19-31 N, Long. 110-57-33 W; Named for a prominent local settler.

HUNTSVILLE, Town; Weber County; Pop. 577 / 656; Zip Code 84317; Elev. 4929; Lat. 41-15-36 N, Long. 111-45-57 W; The town's name honors Captain Jefferson Hunt of the Mormon battalion in the Mexican-American War.

HURRICANE, City; Washington County; Pop. 2,361 / 7,540; Zip Code 84737; Elev. 3,266; Lat. 37-10-29 N, Long. 113-17-15 W; The building of the Hurricane Canal, in the early 1900s, resulted in the settlement of the Hurricane Valley. The early settlers who built the canal saw the potential in the valley if water was harnessed into it.

HYDE PARK, City; Cache County; Pop. 1,495 / 2,947; Zip Code 84318; Lat. 41-47-58 N, Long. 111-49-13 W; Named after the famous residential area of London.

HYRUM, City; Cache County; Pop. 3,952 / 5,631; Zip Code 84319; Lat. 41-37-57 N, Long. 111-51-18 W; The city is named after a Biblical character.

KAMAS, City; Summit County; Pop. 1,064 / 1,646; Zip Code 84036; Lat. 40-37-21 N, Long. 111-16-13 W; The town is named after the edible camossia quomash plant, which resembles a hyacinth.

KANAB, City; Kane County Seat; Pop, 2,148 / 3,943; Zip Code 84741; Kanob is a Ute Indian word for "willow."

KANARRAVILLE, Town; Iron County; Pop. 255 / 255; Zip Code 84742; The town is named after a Paiute Indian Chief, Kanorro.

KANOSH, Town; Millard County; Pop, 435 / 390; Zip Code 84637; Elev. 5015; Lat. 38-48-18 N, Long, 112-26-19 W; Konosh is named after a famous Indian Chief, Konosh.

KINGSTON, Town; Paiute County; Pop. 146 / 158; Zip Code 84743; Named after 19th century geologist Clarence King.

KOOSHAREM, Town; Sevier County; Pop. 183 / 420; Zip Code 84744; Elev. 6914; Lat. 38-30-43 N, Long. 111-52-56 W; A Ute Indian word referring to an edible tuber.

LA VERKIN, Town; Washington County; Pop. 1,174 / 3,488; Zip Code 84745; Lat. 37-12-08 N, Long. 113-16-02 W; A shortened and corrupted version of a nearby stream's name; Rio De La Virgen.

LAKETOWN, Town; Rich County; Pop. 271; Zip Code 84038; Elev. 5,988; Lat. 41-49-13 N, Long. 111-19-00 W; Descriptively named for its lakeside location.

LAYTON, City; Dovis County; Pop. 22,862 / 56,469; Zip Code 84041; Lat. 41-04-27 N, Long. 111-57-26 W; Named for Christopher Layton, who built the "Prairie House" in 1858 to house stagecoach passengers. The first visitors to the area were the Paiute, Ute, and Shoshone Indians. This land was considered "neutral" land to these natives; they would not battle for this land. The first settlers, Ed Phillips, John Green, Elias Adams, and William Kay, arrived in 1850. The town was incorporated in 1937, but at that time, what is now Layton was actually three towns. Two of these areas merged in 1957, and the other joined in 1981. The main economic activity of Layton has always been agriculture.

LEAMINGTON, Town; Millard County; Pop. 113 / 307; Zip Code 84638; Leamington's name recalls one of its early settlers.

LEEDS, Town; Washington County; Pop. 216 / 321; Zip Code 84746; Named after Leeds, England.

LEHI, City; Utah County; Pop. 6,848 / 16,878; Zip Code 84043; Elev. 4,562; Lat. 40-23-31 N, Long. 111-48-51 W; Named after the Book of Mormon colonizer of America.

LEVAN, Town; Juab County; Pop. 453 / 595; Zip Code 84639; Elev. 5,314; Lat. 39-33-24 N, Long. 111-51-40 W; A shortened version of "levant," or "the lands of the sunrise."

LEWISTON, City; Cache County; Pop. 1,438 / 1,580; Zip Code 84308; Elev. 4,506; Lat. 41-58-00 N, Long. 111-57-24 W; Named for an early settler.

LINDON, City; Utah County; Pop. 2,796 / 7,071; Often mistaken by settlers for Linden trees, the name may spring from the cottonwood tree, which is common to the area.

LOA, Town; Wayne County Seat; Pop. 364 / 448; Zip Code 84747; Lat. 38-24-03 N, Long. 111-38-29 W; Loa is a Hawaiian word meaning "long."

LOGAN, City; Cache County Seat; Pop. 26,844 / 40,778; Zip Code 84321; Lat. 41-43-19 N, Long. 111-49-26 W; Logan was originally inhabited by the Shoshone Indians, who lived off the wild foods and game in the Cache Valley. The area was settled in the 1850s by Mormon pioneers, and was named for mountainman Ephraim Logan.

LYNNDYL, Town; Millard County; Pop. 90 / 137; Zip Code 84640; Elev. 4,784; Lat. 39-31-15 N, Long. 112-22-34 W; Named after Lynn, Massachusetts with the euphonious suffix "dyl" added.

MANILA, Town; Doggett County Seat; Pop. 272 / 216; Zip Code 84046; Lat. 40-59-36 N, Long. 109-43-23 W; Named after the city of Manila in the Philippines.

MANTI, City; Sanpete County Seat; Pop. 2,080 / 2,795; Zip Code 84642; Lat. 39-15-49 N, Long. 111-38-13 W; A city mentioned in the Book of Mormon is the source of this town's name.

MAPLETON, City; Utah County; Pop. 2,726 / 4,319; Named after the beloved maple tree.

MARYSVALE, Town; Paiute County; Pop. 359 / 418; Zip Code 84750; Lat. 38-26-56 N, Long. 112-13-38 W; Originally named by the Spanish for the Virgin Mary.

MAYFIELD, Town; Sanpete County; Pop. 397 / 530; Zip Code 84643; Lat. 39-07-07 N, Long. 111-42-30 W; A common name referring to an early settler.

MEADOW, Town; Millard County; Pop. 265 / 246; Zip Code 84644; Lat. 38-53-17 N, Long. 112-24-32 W; Descriptively named for its most prominent feature.

MENDON, City; Cache County; Pop. 663 / 760; Zip Code 84325; Lat. 41-42-29 N, Long. 111-58-51 W; Named after Mendon, Massachusetts, itself named after Mendon, England.

MIDVALE, City; Salt Lake County; Pop. 10,144 / 23,771; Zip Code 84047; Lat. 40-36-59 N, Long. 111-52-47 W; The city is descriptively named for its location in the surrounding valley.

MIDWAY, City; Wasatch County; Pop. 1,194 / 2,400; Zip Code 84049; Lat. 40-31-02 N, Long. 111-28-16 W; Located between two farming areas, the area's settlers called it Midway.

MILFORD, City; Beaver County; Pop. 1,293 / 1,295; Zip Code 84751; Elev. 4957; Lat. 38-23-34 N, Long. 113-00-29 W; The city was named after an ore reduction mill and a nearby river ford.

MILLVILLE, City; Cache County; Pop. 848 / 1,475; Zip Code 84326; Lat. 41-40-49 N, Long. 111-49-36 W; Descriptively named as the site of several mills.

MOAB, City; Grand County Seat; Pop. 5,333 / 4,573; Zip Code 84532; The city is named after the Biblical kingdom of Moab.

MONA, Town; Juab County; Pop. 536 / 952; Zip Code 84645; Elev. 4916; Lat. 39-49-00 N, Long. 111-51-26 W; Possibly named by Welsh immigrants for a county in Wales.

MONROE, City; Sevier County; Pop. 1,476 / 1,823; Zip Code 84739; Lat. 38-37-54 N, Long. 112-13-00 W; The area was originally a fort, built by Mormon settlers to protect against hostile Indians. Nevertheless, Indian wars in the area forced settlers to relocate in the late 1860s. They returned to their fort in 1871 and renamed the area "Monroe," in honor of United States President, James Monroe.

MONTICELLO, City; San Juan County Seat; Pop. 1,929 / 1,879; Zip Code 84535; Elev. 7,066; Lat. 37-52-14 N, Long. 109-20-21 W; *Monticello* means "little mountain." There is a small mountain near the town, and so it is descriptively named.

MORGAN CITY, City; Morgan County Seat; Pop. 1,896 / 2,521; Zip Code 84050; Elev. 5,064; Lat. 41-02-17 N, Long. 111-40-27 W; The city is named after Jedediah Morgan Grant, counselor to Brigham Young.

MORONI, City; Sanpete County; Pop. 1,086 / 1,839; Zip Code 84623; Elev. 5,520; Lat. 39-28-33 N, Long. 111-28-15 W; The Mormons believe the angel Moroni appeared to Joseph Smith and told him to start the Mormon Church.

MOUNT PLEASANT, City; Sanpete County; Pop. 2,049 / 2,766; Zip Code 84647; Elev. 5924; Lat. 39-32-33 N, Long. 111-27-19 W; Descriptively named for the pleasant environment.

MURRAY, City; Salt Lake County; Pop. 25,750 / 32,449; Zip Code 84107; The name honors Utah territorial Governor Eli Murray who governed from 1880-86.

NEPHI, City; Juab County Seat; Pop. 3,285 / 4,635; Zip Code 84648; Elev. 5,133; Lat. 39-42-36 N, Long. 111-49-50 W; Once referred to as "Salt Creek," the area was first settled by the Foote family. They found fertile ground and water in this valley setting. Economic activities since the first settlement have included agriculture, salt, grist mills, and wool. The city is named after the prophet Nephi, on important figure in the *Book of Mormon*.

NEW HARMONY, Town; Washington County; Pop. 117 / 157; Zip Code 84757; Elev. 5,306; Lat. 37-28-39 N, Long. 113-18-11 W; A euphonious name given the place by its settlers.

NEWTON, Town; Cache County; Pop. 623 / 678; Zip Code 84327; Lat. 41-51-37 N, Long. 111-59-31 W; A common English name the town is named after a local settler.

NORTH OGDEN, City; Weber County; Pop. 9,309 / 14,782; Named after Hudson Bay Company's Peter Skene Ogden.

NORTH SALT LAKE, City; Davis County; Pop. 5,548 / 8,692; Zip Code 84054; The city is descriptively named for the Great Salt Lake.

OAK CITY, Town; Millard County; Pop. 389 / 660; Zip Code 84649; Elev. 5105; Lat. 39-22-37 N, Long. 112-20-24 W; The town is descriptively named for the many oaks in the area.

OAKLEY, Town; Summit County; Pop. 470 / 916; Zip Code 84055; Lat. 40-43-34 N, Long. 111-16-50 W; Named after the many local oaks.

OGDEN, City; Weber County Seat; Pop. 64,407 / 68,210; Zip Code 84400; Lat. 41-13-37 N, Long. 111-57-26 W; Peter Ogden was an early Hudson Bay factor in Utah. The city is named after him.

ORANGEVILLE, City; Emery County; Pop. 1,309 / 1,538; Zip Code 84537; The town is named after Orange Seeley, an early pioneer.

ORDERVILLE, Town; Kane County; Pop. 423 / 444; Zip Code 84537; Elev. 5,772; Lat. 39-13-32 N, Long. 111-02-54 W; The name recalls a Mormon economic order established in the pioneering days but later abandoned.

OREM, City; Utah County; Pop. 52,399 / 82,965; Zip Code 84057; Lat. 40-17-08 N, Long. 111-41-25 W; The town is named after an early railway builder.

PANGUITCH, City; Garfield County Seat; Pop. 1,343 / 1,256; Zip Code 84717; Lat. 37-37-44 N, Long. 112-10-06 W; A Paiute Indian word meaning "fish."

PARADISE, Town; Cache County; Pop. 542 / 733; Zip Code 84328; Lat. 41-34-10 N, Long. 111-50-06 W; Descriptively and euphoniously named by the town's settlers.

PARK CITY, City; Summit & Wasatch Counties; Pop. 2,823 / 6,714; Zip Code 84060; Lat. 40-38-52 N, Long. 111-29-26 W; Descriptively named after Parley's Park to the north.

PAROWAN, City; Iron County Seat; Pop. 1,836 / 2,008; Zip Code 84761; A Paiute Indian word meaning "marsh people," and referring to the original local inhabitants.

PAYSON, City; Utah County; Pop. 8,246 / 11,222; Zip Code 84651; Lat. 40-02-17 N, Long. 111-43-50 W; Probably named after a local settler.

PERRY, City; Box Elder County; Pop. 1,084 / 2,401; The town's name honors a prominent early pioneer.

PLAIN CITY, City; Weber County; Pop. 2,379 / 3,371; A descriptive name for the local geography.

PLEASANT GROVE, City; Utah County; Pop. 10,669 / 21,457; Zip Code 84062; Lat. 40-20-55 N, Long. 111-45-15 W; Originally called Battle Creek as a result of Indian-settler frights, later settlers changed it to the more euphonious "Pleasant Grove."

PLEASANT VIEW, City; Weber County; Pop. 3,983 / 5,097; Named after the attractive local environment.

PLYMOUTH, Town; Box Elder County; Pop. 238 / 288; Zip Code 84330; Lat. 41-52-26 N, Long. 112-08-33 W; The town is named after Plymouth, Massachusetts.

PRICE, City; Carbon County Seat; Pop. 9,086 / 9,012; Zip Code 84501; Lat. 39-36-02 N, Long. 110-48-06 W; Both the town and the river are named for pioneer settler, William Price.

PROVIDENCE, City; Cache County; Pop. 2,675 / 4,513; Zip Code 84332; Lat. 41-42-14 N, Long. 111-49-14 W; Named after the city in Rhode Island.

PROVO, City; Utah County Seat; Pop. 73,907 / 110,690; Zip Code 84064; Elev. 4,549; Lat. 41-39-42 N, Long. 111-10-58 W; Provo's name remembers French-Canadian explorer and mountain man, Etienne Provot.

RANDOLPH, City; Rich County Seat; Pop. 659 / 537; The town is named after Randolph Stewart, who was its founder.

REDMOND, Town; Sevier County; Pop. 619 / 727; Zip Code 84652; Lat. 39-00-07 N, Long. 111-51-47 W; Probably a descriptive name for the area's soil or rocks.

RICHFIELD, City; Sevier County Seat; Pop. 5,482 / 6,812; Zip Code 84657; Lat. 38-51-00 N, Long. 111-58-02 W; Ten men settled the area in 1864 and called the area Big Springs or Warm Springs for the springs in the area. It was renamed Richfield for the fertile soil found here. In 1867, the Black Hawk War forced settlers to abandon their homes in Richfield, and resettlement did not occur until the 1970s.

RICHMOND, City; Cache County; Pop. 1,705 / 2,172; Zip Code 84333; Elev. 4,607; Lat. 41-55-16 N, Long. 111-48-24 W; The city is named after one of several similarly named cities on the East Coast of the United States.

RIVERDALE, City; Weber County; Pop. 3,841 / 7,693; A descriptive name for the area's geography.

RIVER HEIGHTS, City; Cache County; Pop. 1,211 / 1,492; A geographic descriptive name for the town's immediate locality.

RIVERTON, City; Salt Lake County; Pop. 7,293 / 21,285; Zip Code 84065; Elev. 4,435; Lat. 40-34-28 N, Long. 111-56-54 W; Named for its location near a local river.

ROOSEVELT, City; Duchesne County; Pop. 3,842 / 4,400; Zip Code 84066; Elev. 5,100; Lat. 40-27-19 N, Long. 110-04-21 W; The city is named after President Theodore Roosevelt. Thousands of years ago, the land was occupied by hunters and gatherers. In more recent times, before the land that is now Roosevelt was opened to homesteaders, it was a reservation for Ute Indians. In 1905-1906, after being held as a Ute Indian Reservation, the land began to be settled by American homesteaders, despite Indian opposition, and the land was sold for $2.25 an acre.

ROY, City; Weber County; Pop. 19,694 / 32,012; Zip Code 84067; Lat. 41-11-14 N, Long. 112-01-10 W; Named after a prominent local settler.

RUSH VALLEY, Town; Tooele County; Pop. 356 / 378; Zip Code 84069; Lat. 40-14-15 N, Long. 112-26-22 W; A descriptive name for the area's local vegetation.

ST. GEORGE City; Washington County Seat; Pop. 11,350 / 47,994; Zip Code 84746; Elev. 2,761; Lat. 37-14-22 N, Long. 113-21-13 W.

SALEM, City; Utah County; Pop. 2,233 / 3,441; Zip Code 84653; Lat. 40-03-03 N, Long. 111-40-08 W; The town has a Biblical name meaning "peace."

SALINA, City; Sevier County; Pop. 1,992 / 2,091; Zip Code 84654; Lat. 38-57-25 N, Long. 111-51-12 W; A Spanish name meaning "salt marsh or pond." It was so named because of the salt deposits nearby. Indian wars forced early settlers out of the area in 1866, and resettlement did not occur for five years. The railroad came through the area in 1891, creating a larger population.

SALT LAKE CITY, City; Salt Lake County Seat and Capital of Utah; Pop. 163,033 / 171,151; Zip Code 84100; Lat. 40-45-26 N, Long. 111-52-29 W; The city is named for the Great Salt Lake near it. The first residents of the area were the Anasazi Indian, pueblo dwellers who occupied the area more than 1,500 years ago. Salt Lake City was founded in 1847 by a group of Mormon settlers, who came in search of a place to practice their religion freely. At the time, the area was part of Mexico. The territory was ceded to the United States in 1848. The Mormon temple at Salt Lake City was built between 1853 and 1892.

SANDY CITY, City; Salt Lake County; Pop. 51,022 / 101,853; Zip Code 84070; Lat. 40-34-52 N, Long. 111-52-24 W; Descriptively named for local soil types.

SANTA CLARA, Town; Washington County; Pop. 1,091 / 4,574; Zip Code 84738; Lat. 37-10-13 N, Long. 113-40-25 W; A Spanish name meaning "Saint Clara."

SANTAQUIN, City; Utah County; Pop. 2,175 / 3,539; Zip Code 84655; Lat. 40-06-16 N, Long. 111-54-30 W; A Paiute Indian chief who found several battles with the Mormons.

SCIPIO, Town; Millard County; Pop. 257 / 294; Zip Code 84656; Mormon settlers named the town after the great Roman general who destroyed Carthage.

SCOFIELD, Town; Carbon County; Pop. 105 / 45; Named after a prominent early settler.

SMITHVILLE, City; Cache County; Pop. 4,993 / 6,979; Zip Code 84335; Elev. 4,595; Lat. 41-50-44 N, Long. 111-52-00 W; Located in N Utah, in an area of livestock and dairy forms.

SOUTH JORDAN, City; Salt Lake County; Pop. 7,492 / 28,009; Named by the pioneers after the Jordan River.

SOUTH OGDEN, City; Weber County; Pop. 11,366 / 14,341; Named in honor of 19th century Hudson Bay factor Peter Ogden.

SOUTH SALT LAKE, City; Salt Lake County; Pop. 10,561 / 9,773; The city is named by its proximity to Salt Lake.

SOUTH WEBER, City; Davis County; Pop. 1,575 / 4,273; Named in honor of early mountain man John Weber.

SPANISH FORK, City; Utah County; Pop. 9,825 / 17,252; Zip Code 84660; Lat. 40-06-37 N, Long. 111-38-42 W; The Fork River comes down here from the Wasatch Mountains. The name "Spanish Fork" honors the observation by Franciscan Friars that the area was "the fairest of all New Spain." The area was settled by a group of pioneers that was sent by Brigham Young.

SPRING CITY, City; Sanpete County; Pop. 671 / 872; Zip Code 84662; Elev. 5826; Lat. 39-28-40 N, Long. 111-29-35 W; Named for the occurrence of local springs.

SPRINGDALE, Town; Washington County; Pop. 258 / 346; Zip Code 84763; Lat. 37-09-40 N, Long. 113-02-26 W; Local springs and the surroundings named the town.

SPRINGVILLE, City; Utah County; Pop. 12,101 / 17,282; Zip Code 84663; Lat. 40-11-04 N, Long. 111-37-02 W; A large spring occurs at the base of the Wasatch Mountains near here. The town

is named for this spring. It was settled by eight families in 1850 and called Hobble Creek, because the first settlers often loosely bound the front feet of their horses, allowing them to graze freely along the stream. If the horses hobbled into the creek, the bindings came off, and so the area gets its name. The towns was renamed in later years, but the stream retains the name "Hobble Creek."

STERLING, Town; Sanpete County; Pop. 199 / 259; Zip Code 84665; Probably a commendatory name, as in a "sterling town."

STOCKTON, Town; Tooele County; Pop. 437 / 528; Zip Code 84071; Lat. 40-27-18 N, Long. 112-21-42 W; The town is named after Stockton, California.

SUNNYSIDE, City; Carbon County; Pop. 611 / 351; Zip Code 84539; Lat. 39-32-58 N, Long. 110-23-09 W; A descriptive name for the town's sunny location.

TABIONA, Town; Duchesne County; Pop. 152 / 139; Zip Code 84072; Elev. 6,517; Lat. 38-16-58 N, Long. 111-28-32 W; A Ute Indian Chief named Tabby organized his tribe into a confederacy. Tabiona is named after him.

TOOELE, City; Tooele County Seat; Pop. 14,335 / 18,460; Zip Code 84074; Lat. 40-31-58 N, Long. 112-17-55 W; An English corruption of the Spanish word "tule," or the common bulrush.

TOQUERVILLE, Town; Washington County; Pop. 277 / 814; Zip Code 84774; Lat. 37-14-28 N, Long. 113-16-54 W; A Paiute word for "black mountain."

TORREY, Town; Wayne County; Pop. 140 / 142; Zip Code 84775; The town is named after a local settler with the family name Torrey.

TREMONTON, City; Box Elder County; Pop. 3,464 / 5,518; Zip Code 84337; Elev. 4,290; Lat. 41-41-59 N, Long. 112-09-11 W; The city was named by French-Canadian trappers who called the area "tres monlan," or "three hills."

TRENTON, Town; Cache County; Pop. 447 / 497; Zip Code 84338; Lat. 41-54-43 N, Long. 111-56-18 W; The town is named after Trenton, New Jersey.

TROPIC, Town; Garfield County; Pop. 338 / 381; Zip Code 84718; Elev. 6,295; Lat. 37-33-50 N, Long. 112-03-15 W; The town's founders gave it this physiogeographic name.

UINTAH, Town; Weber County; Pop. 439 / 1,183; Zip Code 84008; Lat. 39-59-00 N, Long. 109-10-36 W; A branch of the Paiute Indian tribe, the Uintah left their name on the area.

VERNAL, City; Uintah County Seat; Pop. 6,600 / 7,500; Zip Code 84078; Lat. 40-27-22 N, Long. 109-31-39 W; Settled in 1879 and given a name meaning "spring."

VERNON, Town; Tooele County; Pop. 181 / 206; Zip Code 84080; Lat. 40-14-15 N, Long. 112-26-22 W; The town's name honors founder Joseph Vernon.

VIRGIN, Town; Washington County; Pop. 169 / 312; Zip Code 84779; A descriptive name given by its settlers for the area's unspoiled beauty.

WALES, Town; Sanpete County; Pop. 153 / 354; Zip Code 84667; Mormon immigrants from Wales gave their new home the title of their former one.

WALLSBURG, Town; Wasatch County; Pop. 239 / 342; Zip Code 84082; Lat. 40-23-13 N, Long. 111-25-08 W; Descriptively named for canyon-like features nearby.

WASHINGTON, City; Washington County; Pop. 3,092 / 7,108; Zip Code 84780; The city is named after George Washington.

WELLINGTON, City; Carbon County; Pop. 1,406 / 1,699; Zip Code 84542; Elev. 5413; Lat. 39-32-30 N, Long. 110-43-48 W; The city is named in honor of the Great British commander of the Napoleonic Wars.

WELLSVILLE, City; Cache County; Pop. 1,952 / 2,778; Zip Code 84339; Lat. 41-38-02 N, Long. 111-56-15 W; Settled in 1856 and named after Mormon military commander Daniel Wells.

WENDOVER, Town; Tooele County; Pop. 1,099 / 1,259; Zip Code 84034; Lat. 40-02-17 N, Long. 114-59-56 W; A compound word: the verb wend and the adverb over.

WEST BOUNTIFUL, City; Davis County; Pop. 3,556 / 5,107; Named for the assessment the pioneers gave the place.

WEST JORDAN, City; Salt Lake County; Pop. 26,794 / 65,139; Zip Code 84084; Lat. 40-36-07 N, Long. 111-58-22 W. Named for its geographical location and after the Biblical country.

WEST POINT, City; Davis County; Pop. 2,170 / 6,033; The town is named for its geographical features.

WOODS CROSS, City; Davis County; Pop. 4,263 / 6,007; Zip Code 84087; Lat. 40-52-20 N, Long. 11-53-39 W. Descriptively named by its settlers for the local feature.

VERMONT
The Green Mountain State

The village of Peachman

Snow Skiing - Mount Mansfield

GOVERNOR
Howard Dean

Bennington Monument

Cows graze on Vermont Countryside

Sleigh Ride
Sugarbush Mountain

A farmhouse outside of Waitsfield

INTRODUCTION

The State of Vermont is bordered by Quebec, Canada on the north, Massachusetts on the south, and New York on the west. From the Canadian border to the Massachusetts border, the Connecticut River separates the State from New Hampshire on the east, although the river is entirely within the state of New Hampshire.

Vermont is one of the six New England states. Its capital city, Montpelier, is one of the least populous capital cities in the nation. In fact, although millions of tourists visit Vermont each year and many out-of-state residents maintain second homes here, population of the State itself has never been very large.

Vermont is a reminder of an earlier and simpler time in United States history. Most who visit seek the beauty and tranquillity of the State's mountains and valleys. Some also come to experience the sense of our country's past that pervades. From the steeples of the white, wooden churches that rise above small, mountainside towns to the herds of dairy cattle that graze on sloping mountainous pastures, Vermont exudes a strength and sense of continuity that connects the achievements of the past with the purposes of the present.

STATE NAME

In the 1500s, French explorer Samuel de Champlain saw Vermont's Green Mountains from a distance. He designated them as *Verd Mont* or "green mountain" on a map in 1647. The later English naming of Vermont was directly derived from Champlain's original designation on the map.

STATE NICKNAME

Vermont has the nickname of the Green Mountain State. It is given because of the Green Mountains that are located in a north-south pattern across the State.

STATE SEAL

Vermont had an original seal in 1779. In 1821, this seal went into disuse. Until 1937, the State used a number of different seals. Then in 1937, the legislature again adopted the design of the first seal. The current seal is described as follows: "The state seal shall be the great seal of the state, a faithful reproduction, cut larger and deeper, of the original seal, designed by Ira Allen, cut by Reuben Dean of Windsor and accepted by resolution of the general assembly, dated February 20, 1779. The seal shall be kept by the secretary of civil and military affairs."

In 1862, the coat of arms was adopted for Vermont. The description is as follows: "The coat of arms, crest, motto and badge of the state shall be and are described as follows:

"(1)Coat of arms. Green, a landscape occupying half of the shield; on the right and left, in the background, high mountains, blue; the sky, yellow. From near the base and reaching nearly to the top of the shield, arises a pine tree of natural color and between

three erect sheaves, yellow, placed diagonally on the right side and a red cow standing on the left side of the field.

"(2)Motto and badge. On a scroll beneath the shield, the motto: Vermont; Freedom and Unity. The Vermonter's badge: two pine branches of natural color, crossed between the shield and scroll.

"(3)Crest. A buck's head, of natural color, placed on a scroll, blue and yellow."

STATE FLAG

The current State flag for Vermont, adopted in 1923, replaced the previous state flags adopted in 1803 and 1837. The law for the 1923 flag states simply that "the flag of the state shall be blue with the coat of arms of the state thereon."

STATE MOTTO

Vermont's motto is "Freedom and Unity." The motto appeared on the seal designed by Ira Allen in 1778 and was adopted in 1779. It expresses the desire for states to remain free but united.

STATE BIRD

The official State bird of Vermont is the hermit thrush, *Hylocichla guttata faxoni*, adopted by the legislature in 1941. The bird ranges in eastern North America, and has a southern migration pattern to Gulf states.

The hermit thrush has a total length of 6 ½ inches, and a tail length of 2 ½ to three inches. Its upper parts are colored cinnamon brown, and the sides and flanks are buff brown. There is a conspicuous orbital ring of dull white. The ear region is grayish brown streaked with dull whitish; underparts are dull white tinged with pale cream buff. The throat is streaked along each side in a sooty color. The chest has large triangular spots of dusky grayish brown, broader and more rounded on the lower chest. The tail is a dull cinnamon brown. The plumage is brighter in spring and summer months.

The hermit thrush is a hardy bird. It arrives in the early spring and departs in the late fall to migrate southward. The birds travel at night, and they sometimes become so tired and cold that they will lose all natural shyness and feed from the human hand. They have been seen performing a curious act called "anting." This is done by the bird catching ants and placing them in its feathers beneath the wings. It is believed that the formic acid in ants is effective in combating parasitic attacks, or else the ants are hoarded for later consumption during migration.

Hermit thrushes are talented singers, and they sometimes sing in unison and form a harmonious chorus. They have an extraordinary talent for ventriloquism and are capable of completely fooling a listener into thinking they are further away or closer than they actually are. Thrushes are highly protective of their young, and they will fight vigorously against predators so strongly that they are often able to fend off their attackers.

STATE FLOWER

In 1894, the legislature designated the red clover, *Trifolium pratense*, as the official State flower of Vermont. The red clover is not native to Vermont, and was originally brought to the United States from Europe. Also called cowgrass, honeysuckle clover, and sugar plum, the flower is a perennial member of the pea family. It grows wild in meadows and fields.

STATE TREE

The sugar maple was designated the official tree of Vermont in 1949. Its scientific name is *Acer saccharum Marsh*. It is commonly known as the hard maple, rock maple, sugar maple, and black maple.

The sugar maple is native to the eastern half of the United States and Canada. It is a large tree with gray bark, furrowed into irregular ridges or scales. Its leaves are paired, heart-shaped, with three or five lobes, long pointed and sparingly, coarsely toothed; leaves are from three to 5.5 inches in diameter, dark green above, and light green and usually smooth beneath. Leaves turn yellow, orange, or scarlet in the fall.

The stately sugar maple often attains a height of 120 feet. The wavy-grained wood of this tree makes fine furniture, and the sap can be tapped for maple syrup.

STATE SONG

A committee was chosen in 1937 to select an official State song. Over one hundred songs were candidates, and in 1938, "Hail, Vermont" was adopted as the State song. The song was written by Josephine Hovey Perry.

STATE LICENSE PLATE

In December 1904, a law was passed for Vermont drivers to register their automobiles by May 1, 1905. Until 1906, State motorists received a single plate made of enameled iron. The white on blue plate cost two dollars. From 1907 to 1916, black-on-white plates were issued. A variety of colors were used until 1949, including the University of Vermont school colors of yellow and green in 1918 and Norwich University's maroon and tan in 1929. From 1931 to 1942, dark blue and white plates were issued, and black and white plates were used from 1944 to 1947. In 1949, the now familiar Vermont colors of white and green were used. They have been in use since that year.

The current plate for Vermont was issued in 1986. It depicts a maple tree in white at the upper left. The word "Vermont" is in white at the top center of the plate. Numbers are white and are surrounded by a white triangle. The nickname "Green Mountain State" is lettered in white at the bottom of the plate. The background of the plate is solid dark green.

STATE POSTAGE STAMP

On March 4, 1941, a purple three-cent Vermont Statehood Commemorative stamp was issued in Montpelier to celebrate the 150th anniversary of Vermont's entrance into the Union. The stamp was designed by A.R. Meissner. It depicts the State Capitol. A shield at the lower right has thirteen stars that represent the thirteen original states. The star above the shield represents Vermont, the fourteenth state. Engraving for the stamp was done by C.T. Arlt and J.T. Vail. A total of 54,574,550 of the stamp were printed.

OTHER STATE DESIGNATIONS

Over the years, the legislature of Vermont has adopted a number of additional symbols to officially represent the State. Included are the State animal as the Morgan horse (1961); the State beverage as milk (1983); the State gem as grossular garnet (1991); the State insect as the honeybee (1977); the State mineral as talc (1991); the State rocks as marble, granite, and slate (1991); and the State butterfly as the Monarch (1987).

STATE CAPITOL

In 1805, fourteen years after Vermont entered the Union, the legislature designated Montpelier as the permanent capital city. The first capitol was completed in 1808 and was used until 1836. It was then torn down, and a new capitol building was constructed on the site. Created by Ammi B. Young, the new structure was designed after the Greek temple of Theseus. This capitol was destroyed by fire in 1857, and the present statehouse was built in 1859.

The current Vermont capitol was modeled after the building that was burned, excluding the dome and larger wings that were added on the new structure. The exterior is built of Barre granite. The building has six Doric columns and a portico. A fifty-seven-foot high wooden dome, sheathed in copper and covered in gold leaf, rises from the capitol. Originally, a statue of the goddess of agriculture surmounted the dome. In 1938, it was replaced by a statue of Ceres. Total cost for construction of the original capitol was 220,000 dollars.

OTHER FACTS ABOUT VERMONT

Total area: 9,614 square miles
Land area: 9,273 square miles
Water area: 341 square miles
Average elevation: 1,000 feet
Highest point: Mount Mansfield, 4,393 feet
Lowest point: Lake Champlain, 95 feet
Highest temperature: 105 degrees Fahrenheit
Lowest temperature: -50 degrees Fahrenheit
Population in 1990: 562,758
Population 1980-1990: 10 percent change
Population projected for year 2000: 591,000
Asian/Pacific Islander population in 1990: 3,215
Black population in 1990: 1,951
Hispanic population in 1990: 3,661
Native American population in 1990: 1,696
White population in 1990: 555,088
Capital: Montpelier
Admitted to Union: March 4, 1791
Order of Statehood: 14
Electoral votes: 3

CHRONOLOGY

1609 Vermont is discovered by Samuel de Champlain.

1666 Fort and shrine to St. Anne are built on Isle La Motte.

1690 New York outpost is established at Chimney Point (Addison) under Captain Jacobus de Warm.

1704 Indian raid on Deerfield, Massachusetts is made through Vermont.

1724 Pownal is temporarily settled by the Dutch.
– Fort Dummer, first permanent settlement in State, is established near present Brattleboro.

1726 Timothy Dwight is born at Fort Dummer; he is first known white child born on Vermont soil.

1749 Grant of Bennington is made by Governor Wentworth of New Hampshire, which precipitates dispute between New Hampshire and New York.

1752 Maple sugar is first made in State by white settler, Captain Samuel Robinson of Bennington.

1759 St. Francis Indian village in Canada is destroyed in raid made from Crown Point by Rogers' Rangers.

1759-60 Crown Point Military Road is built.

1762 First church is organized in Bennington.

1763 France relinquishes, by treaty, all claims to territory comprising present Vermont.

1764 King George III declares west bank of Connecticut River as boundary between provinces of New Hampshire and New York.

1770 Green Mountain Boys are organized by Ethan Allen.

1775 Rebels engage in armed seizure of courthouse at Westminster; action is sometimes called first engagement of American Revolution.
– Fort Ticonderoga is captured by Ethan Allen.
– Crown Point is captured by Seth Warner.
– Dr. Thomas Young of Philadelphia, in letter to people of Grants, first uses name "Vermont."

1777 Constitution is written and adopted, which creates Vermont as independent republic.
– Battles of Hubbardton and Bennington are fought.

1778 Actual functioning of State government as outlined in Constitution is inaugurated.

1779 Hazen Military Road is built.

1780 First secondary school is incorporated (Clio Hall, at Bennington).

– Royalton is raided and burned; it is most savage of several Indian raids, which take place around this time.

1781 First Vermont newspaper, *The Vermont Gazette*, or *Green Mountain Post Boy*, is issued at Westminster.

1784-85 Toll bridge is built at Bellows Falls; it is first bridge of any sort across Connecticut River from its source to its mouth.

1785 First marble quarry is opened in Dorset.

1788 Vergennes is incorporated; it is oldest and smallest incorporated city in New England and third oldest in country.

1790 Thirty thousand dollars are paid in complete settlement of New York claims to Vermont land.

1791 Vermont is admitted to Union as fourteenth State.
– First library in State is established at Brookfield.

1793 Bennington pottery is first manufactured; it is most famous of early American ceramics.

1795 Justin Morgan, founder of Morgan horses, is brought to Randolph Center.
– Captain Samuel Morey of Fairlee is granted patent for invention of steamboat (it is at least two years since his first successful operation of one).

1805 Montpelier is established as State Capital.
– Joseph Smith, founder of Mormonism, is born in Sharon.

1806 First bank in Vermont, Vermont State Bank, is chartered.

1808 *Vermont*, second regularly operated commercial steamship in world, is launched on Lake Champlain.
– First State House is built at Montpelier.

1809 State Prison is established at Windsor.

1810 Most spectacular natural catastrophe ever to happen in this section of country takes place in Glover when Long Pond, called Runaway Pond, breaks its outlet and runs twenty-seven miles to Lake Memphremagog.
– Merino sheep are first Introduced in State at Weathersfield.

1813 At Salisbury, first glass factory in Vermont begins operations.

1823 First Normal School in America is opened at Concord Corner.
– Champlain Canal opens.

1825 General Lafayette has triumphant tour of State.

1830 Chester A. Arthur is born at Fairfield.
– Thaddeus Fairbanks of St. Johnsbury invents platform scale.

1834 Thomas Davenport invents first electric motor (patented 1837) in Brandon.

1836 Bicameral legislative system is adopted.

1848 Railroad and telegraph are first introduced into State.

1857 Construction begins on new Statehouse.

1864 St. Albans is raided by Confederates.

1866 Fenian Raids occur in Franklin and nearby towns.

1870 Legislature changes from annual to biennial sessions.

1872 Calvin Coolidge is born in Plymouth.

1893 First electric railway in State, Winooski to Burlington, begins operations.

1896 First law providing for absentee voting is made; it is first law of its kind in entire nation.

1909 Champlain Tercentenary is celebrated.

1910 St. Johnsbury is site for first airplane flight in Vermont.

1910-30 Long Trail is built.

1923 After death of President Warren Harding, Calvin Coolidge is inaugurated U.S. president; he is sworn in by father at parents' farmhouse at Plymouth Notch.

1924 Calvin Coolidge is nominated and elected president of U.S.

1927 Great Flood inundates State; 60 are killed; damages total millions of dollars.

1930 First radio station in State, WSYS, begins broadcasts in Rutland.

1931 State income tax is adopted.

1933-34 Woodstock in central region is site of first ski tow operation in U.S.

1938 Severe hurricane causes five deaths, $12 million in damage.

1939 World War II begins.

1941 Legislature defines "armed conflict," declares war on Germany before U.S. does.

1943 George Lansing Fox from Gelman is one of "Four Immortal Chaplains" who lose lives in torpedo bombing of *S. S. Dorchester*.

1944 Lyndon State College is established in north area.

1954 First television station in State, WCAX, begins telecasts from Burlington.

1959 State celebrates 350th anniversary of discovery of Lake Champlain.

1962 Vermont is one of ten states in which federal and state courts have intervened on apportionment questions this year.

1964 For first time in State presidential election, voters favor Democrat, Lyndon Johnson; Democrats also sweep other top State offices.

1972 State Supreme Court rules unanimously that 125-year old abortion law is unconstitutional.
– State establishes stringent laws to regulate pollution sources, such as non-returnable containers.

1973 Extremely heavy rain causes disastrous flooding.

1974 Vermont adopts voluntary gasoline distribution plan.
– Patrick J. Leahy wins Senate seat; he is first Democrat elected since 1854, when Republican Party was founded.

1975 U.S. Labor Department announces that number of unemployed receiving benefits in week ending February 22 rose to 300,000; State is one of five in which unemployment compensation funds have already been exhausted.
– State borrows $12.2 million from federal fund to pay unemployment benefits for April.

1976 Vermont Nuclear Power Corporation closes generating plant in Vernon as safety precaution.

1978 Richard Arkwright Snelling (R) is elected governor.
– Legionnaires' bacterium causes one death, one illness in Burlington.

1979 Rising costs, declining enrollment results in serious fiscal deficits in many of State's small private colleges.
– At meeting of Coalition of Northeast Governors, Energy Secretary Charles W. Duncan Jr. reassures Governor Snelling and governors of eight other states that region will be supplied with enough heating fuel for winter, and that federal subsidy will help to pay for it.
– Vermont is one of 13 states to pass law, authorizing arbitration of medical malpractice claims.
– Survey reports that Vermont is one of three Northeast states in which reliance on wood as primary source of heat has increased from 1 percent to 20 percent in past five years.

1980 U.S. Census Bureau reports population total of 511,456 in 1980; State will have one representative in 98th Congress in 1982.
– Vermont is one of 12 states reporting widespread influenza outbreaks; number of deaths in U.S. during three-week period of January - February is about 300 higher than normal.

1981 Bennington College reports highest total increase in college expenses for 1981-82.

1982 Republicans are left with majorities in State house and senate.

1983 Burlington Socialist mayor, Bernard Sanders, is reelected to second two-year term.
– Vermont has 31 commercial television and radio stations.

1984 Vermont is one of five states showing highest increase in per capita income.
– After November election, Republicans lose control of legislature.

1985 Charges are dropped against member of Island Pond's Northeast Kingdom Community Church; 1984 charge of beating 13-year old girl for over seven hours was part of controversial raid in which state troopers and social workers seized 112 children of sect because of public fear they were being abused.

1986 Incumbent Madeline M. Kunin is governor.

1987 EPA asks for delay in implementing clean air deadlines to reduce carbon monoxide and ozone pollution; Vermont is among six Northeast states to question whether EPA has legislative authority to delay clean air deadlines; Thomas Jorling, Department of Environmental Protection commissioner, requests cooperative action at federal level to help meet air pollution standards.
– Rutland State Fair draws record number of visitors.

1988 Senator Patrick J. Leahy loses to David Pryor in contest for secretary of Democratic caucus.

1989 Environmental officials from Vermont, seven other Northeast states agree to restrict toxic emissions from cars and light trucks beginning 1993 model year; rules patterned from California code will lessen emissions for several pollutants, require anti-pollution devices that will last 100,000 miles instead of current 50,000.

1990 Former Governor Richard A. Snelling wins another gubernatorial term in race with former Senator Peter Welch.

1991 Republican Governor Richard A. Snelling dies from cardiac arrest in his home in Shelburne; Lieutenant Governor Howard Dean (D) steps up to serve remainder of Snelling's term.
– Population is 562,758; figure is 10.0 percent higher than 1980.
– Vermont is one of only two states in which percentage of tax paid generally rises with income.

1992 Montpelier is flooded after ice floes dam Winooski River.
– Vermont Supreme Court rules against Abnaki Indians' claim to 150 square miles in State.

1993 Vermont is one of 14 states in U.S. without capital punishment.
– Attorney David Kelly wins against three other candidates in GOP primary for governor; he will challenge incumbent Howard Dean (D) in November.
– Governor Dean wins another term as governor.

1995 Welfare reform is debated at National Governors' Association meeting; Governor Dean takes stand to continue providing services to poor under current "entitlement" basis.

1996 Governor Howard Dean wins reelection.

1997 After killing four people and wounding four others in shooting spree in Colebrook, New Hampshire, killer Carl Drega crosses state line into Vermont and exchanges fire with police officers for 45 minutes before being fatally wounded.

1998 Conservation Fund agrees to purchase some 300,000 acres of forests and wetlands in Vermont and two other Northeast states; nearly 70 percent of land will remain as working forest; Governor Dean proposes fund for purchase of 39,000 to 48,000 acres in northeastern section near Canadian border for $4.5 million.
February. Bill is passed granting $290 million for Great Lakes marine research; measure in bill gives Lake Champlain status as sixth Great Lake; designation makes Vermont eligible for funds granted states bordering any of Great Lakes.
March. Senate votes unanimously to rescind newfound status of Lake Champlain as sixth Great Lake; under compromise, Vermont will still be allowed to compete for eligible funds under National Sea Grant Program.

1999 Facilities in several Vermont cities are targeted in hoax anthrax threats in 14 letters sent to abortion and Planned Parenthood centers across nation.

DIRECTORY OF STATE SERVICES

OFFICE OF THE GOVERNOR
Pavilion Office Bldg, 109 State St.
Montpelier, VT 05609-0101
Fax: 802-828-3339
Governor: 802-828-3333

LIEUTENANT GOVERNOR
State House
Montpelier, VT 05609-0101
Fax: 802-828-2154
Lieutenant Governor: 802-828-2226

ATTORNEY GENERAL
109 State St.
Montpelier, VT 05609-1001
Fax: 802-828-2154
Attorney General: 802-828-3171

SECRETARY OF STATE
109 State St.
Montpelier, VT 05609-1101
Fax: 802-828-2496
Secretary of State: 802-828-2363

TREASURER
133 State St., 2nd Fl.
Montpelier, VT 05633-6200
Fax: 802-828-2772
State Treasurer: 802-828-2301

ADMINISTRATION AGENCY
Pavilion Office Bldg, 109 State St.
Montpelier, VT 05609-0201
Fax: 802-828-2428
Secretary: 802-828-3322

DEPARTMENTS

Finance and Management Department
Commissioner: 802-828-2376

Buildings Department
2 Governor Aiken Ave.
Montpelier, VT 05602-5633
Fax: 802-828-3533
Commissioner: 802-828-3314

General Services Department
133 State St.
Montpelier, VT 05663-7601
Fax: 802-828-2327
Commissioner: 802-828-3331

Personnel Department
110 State St.
Montpelier, VT 05620-3001
Fax: 802-828-3409
Commissioner: 802-828-3491

Tax Department
109 State St.
Montpelier, VT 05609-0201
Fax: 802-828-2701
Commissioner: 802-828-2505

AGRICULTURE DEPARTMENT
116 State St., Drawer 20
Montpelier, VT 05620-2901
Fax: 802-828-2361
Commissioner: 802-828-2430

AUDITOR OF ACCOUNTS
133 State St.
Montpelier, VT 05633-5101
Fax: 802-828-2198
State Auditor: 802-828-2281

BANKING, INSURANCE, AND SECURITIES DEPARTMENT
89 Main Street, 2nd Fl.
Montpelier, VT 05602
Fax: 802-828-3306
Commissioner: 802-828-3301

DEFENDER GENERAL
State Office Bldg.
Montpelier, VT 05602-3301
Fax: 802-828-3163
Defender General: 802-828-3168

DEVELOPMENT AND COMMUNITY AFFAIRS AGENCY
109 State St.
Montpelier, VT 05609-0501
Fax: 802-828-3383
Secretary: 802-828-3211

Housing and Community Affairs Department
Pavilion Office Bldg.
Montpelier, VT 05609-0501
Fax: 802-828-2928

Commissioner: 802-828-3217

Travel and Tourism Department
134 State St.
Montpelier, VT 05609-0501
Fax: 802-828-3383
Commissioner: 802-828-3236

Vermont Life Magazine
6 Baldwin St.
Montpelier, VT 05602
Fax: 802-828-3383
Editor: 802-828-3241

EDUCATION DEPARTMENT
State Office Bldg.
Montpelier, VT 05620
Fax: 802-828-3140
Commissioner: 802-828-3135

EDUCATIONAL AND HEALTH FINANCING BUILDING AGENCY
2 Spring St.
Montpelier, VT 05602
Fax: 802-229-4709
Executive Director: 802-223-2717

EMPLOYMENT AND TRAINING DEPARTMENT
Green Mt. Dr., P.O. Box 488
Montpelier, VT 05601-0488
Fax: 802-828-4022
Commissioner: 802-299-0311

HOUSING FINANCE AGENCY
P.O. Box 408
Burlington, VT 05402-0408
Fax: 802-334-8266
Chairman: 802-864-5743

HUMAN SERVICES AGENCY
103 S Main St., State Complex
Waterbury, VT 05671-0204
Fax: 802-241-2979
Secretary: 802-241-2220

Child Support Services Office
103 S Main St.
Waterbury, VT 05671-1901
Fax: 802-244-1483
Director: 802-241-2319
Toll Free Number: 800-786-3214

Health Department
P.O. Box 70
Burlington, VT 05402
Fax: 802-863-7425
Commissioner: 802-863-7280

Mental Health Department
103 S Main St.
Waterbury, VT 05671-1601
Fax: 802-241-3052
Commissioner: 802-241-2610

Social and Rehabilitation Services Department
103 S Main St., State Complex
Waterbury, VT 05671-2401
Fax: 802-241-2980
Commissioner: 802-241-2101

Social Welfare Department
State Complex, 103 S Main St.
Waterbury, VT 05671-1201
Fax: 802-241-2830
Commissioner: 802-241-2852

LABOR AND INDUSTRY DEPARTMENT
National Life Insurance Bldg.
Montpelier, VT 05620-3401
Fax: 802-828-2195
Commissioner: 802-828-2286

LIBRARIES DEPARTMENT
109 State St.
Montpelier, VT 05609-0601
Fax: 802-828-2199
State Librarian: 802-828-3265

LIQUOR CONTROL DEPARTMENT
Drawer 20, Green Mountain Dr., State Bldg.
Montpelier, VT 05620-4501
Fax: 802-828-2803
Commissioner: 802-828-2345

MILITARY DEPARTMENT
Green Mt. Armory
Colchester, VT 04406
Fax: 802-654-0425
Adjutant General: 802-654-0000

NATURAL RESOURCES AGENCY
103 S Main St.
Waterbury, VT 05671-0301
Fax: 802-244-1102
Secretary: 802-241-3600

Environmental Conservation Department
103 S Main St.
Waterbury, VT 05671-0301
Fax: 802-244-5141
Commissioner: 802-241-3808

Fish and Wildlife Department
103 S Main St.
Waterbury, VT 05671-0301
Fax: 802-241-0601
Commissioner: 802-241-3700

Forests, Parks and Recreation Department
103 S Main St.
Waterbury, VT 05671-0301
Fax: 802-244-1481
Commissioner: 802-241-3670

PUBLIC SAFETY DEPARTMENT
103 S Main St., State Complex
Waterbury, VT 05671-2101
Fax: 802-244-1106

Commissioner: 802-244-8718

PUBLIC SERVICE DEPARTMENT
120 State St.
Montpelier, VT 05620-2601
Fax: 802-828-2342
Commissioner: 802-828-2321

TRANSPORTATION AGENCY
133 State St.
Montpelier, VT 05633-5001
Fax: 802-828-3522
Secretary: 802-828-2657

Motor Vehicles Department
State Office Bldg.
Montpelier, VT 05633-0001
Commissioner: 802-828-2011

CENTRAL VERMONT COUNCIL ON AGING
18 S Main St.
Barre, VT 05641-4697
Fax: 802-479-4235
Executive Director: 802-479-0531

COMMISSION ON WOMEN
126 State St., Drawer 33
Montpelier, VT 05633-6801
Fax: 802-828-2930
Executive Director: 802-828-3291

COUNCIL ON THE ARTS
136 State St., Drawer 33
Montpelier, VT 05633-6001
Fax: 802-828-3363
Chairman-Board of Trustees: 802-828-3291

VERMONT ECONOMIC INDUSTRIAL DEVELOPMENT AUTHORITY
56 E State St.
Montpelier, VT 05602
Fax: 802-223-4205
Manager: 802-223-7226

LABOR RELATIONS BOARD
133 State St.
Montpelier, VT 05633-6101
Chairman: 802-828-2700

LOTTERY COMMISSION
P.O. Box 420
South Barre, VT 05670-0420
Fax: 802-479-4294
Director: 802-479-5686

PUBLIC POWER SUPPLY AUTHORITY
P.O. Box 298, 100 Stowe Rd.
Waterbury Center, VT 05677
Fax: 802-244-6889
General Manager: 802-244-7678

PUBLIC SERVICE BOARD
89 Main St., 3rd Fl.
Montpelier, VT 05620-2701

Fax: 802-828-3351
Chairman: 802-828-2358

VETERANS AFFAIRS
120 State St.
Montpelier, VT 05620-4401
Fax: 802-828-3381
Director: 802-828-3379

MEMBERS OF CONGRESS

SENATE

SEN. PATRICK J. LEAHY (D) (b. 1940); 5th Term;
Phone: 202-224-4242; Fax: 202-224-3479;
E-mail: senator_leahy@leahy.senate.gov

www.senate.gov/~leahy/

SEN. JIM M. JEFORDS (R) (b. 1934); 2nd Term;
Phone: 202-224-5141; Fax: (None);
E-mail: vermont@jeffords.senate.gov

www.senate.gov/~jeffords/

HOUSE

BERNARD SANDERS (I-At Large) (b. 1941); 5th Term;
Phone: 202-225-4115 Fax: 202-225-6790;
E-mail: bernie@mail.house.gov

www.house.gov/bernie/

TWENTIETH CENTURY GOVERNORS

STICKNEY, WILLIAM W. (1853-1932), forty-eighth governor of Vermont (1900-1902), was born in Plymouth, Vermont, on March 21, 1853. He attended Phillips Exeter Academy. Stickney subsequently studied law, passing the bar in 1878 and establishing the law firm of Stickney, Sargent and Skeels, of which he was president. In addition, he served as president of the Ludlow Savings Bank and Trust Company.

A Republican, between 1882 and 1892 Stickney served as a clerk in the State House of Representatives. Also during that time, from 1882 to 1884, and again from 1890 to 1892, he was State's Attorney. In 1900 Stickney successfully ran for the Vermont governorship on the Republican ticket. During his tenure, Stickney sought to change the statute by which the State Constitution could only be amended once every decade and also asked for the dissolution of the office of Tax Commissioner. In addition, the boundary line between Vermont and Massachusetts was established.

Stickney stepped down from office at the end of his term, and returned to his law and business interests. He was married to Elizabeth Lincoln; the couple had no children. Stickney died on December 15, 1932.

MCCULLOUGH, JOHN GRIFFITH (1835-1915), forty-ninth governor of Vermont (1902-1904), was born near Newark, Delaware, on September 16, 1835. He lost his parents while still a young boy.

McCullough attended Delaware College, graduating in 1855, then studied at the University of Pennsylvania Law School, earning his degree in 1858. He passed the Pennsylvania bar exam in 1869 and entered into a law practice in Philadelphia. Suffering a decline in health, McCullough moved to California for a time and was highly successful in a business career, serving as president of such companies as the Panama Railway, the Chicago and Erie Railroad, and the Bennington and Rutland Railway. He also headed a number of insurance companies and banks. Also while living in California, he was politically active, serving in several public offices.

Eventually settling in Vermont, McCullough served as a delegate to the Republican National Convention for three years, then in 1898, was a member of the Vermont Senate. In 1902 he ran for the Vermont governorship. Since none of the candidates received a majority, the decision was left to the State Legislature, which chose McCullough. During his tenure McCullough sought to separate the State's judicial system from politics and also backed a primary election law. Also during that time, a bill was passed to rein in election corruption; both the health laws and corporation tax laws were revamped and the alcohol statute was revised to allow each individual town or city to decide on the issue of prohibition. In addition, the State Board of Health was organized, and funding was set aside for the formation of local boards of health.

McCullough stepped down from office at the end of his term and returned to his business pursuits. He was married to Eliza Hall Park, and the couple had four children. McCullough died on May 29, 1915.

BELL, CHARLES JAMES (1845-1909), fiftieth governor of Vermont (1904-1906), was born on March 10, 1845, in Walden, Vermont. After receiving a public school education, he joined the Fifteenth Vermont Volunteers during the Civil War and was discharged in 1865 at the rank of corporal. Bell subsequently spent several years farming.

Bell, a Republican, was a member of the State Legislature in 1882, then in 1894, served in the Vermont Senate. From 1894 to 1896 Bell served on the Board of Railroad Commissioners and in 1891 was appointed to the State Board of Agriculture, serving until 1904. Also during that time, between 1898 and 1902, Bell held the post of Secretary for the State Board of Cattle Commissioners.

In 1904 Bell successfully ran for the Vermont governorship on the Republican ticket. During his administration Bell sought to improve State highways and pushed for the building of centralized schools. Also during that time, a law was passed by the State Legislature stating that undeveloped real estate be excluded from any taxation for ten years, and a five percent collateral inheritance tax was approved. In addition, new food and drug inspection legislation was adopted, and a statute was passed that prohibited children from working in factories and mills.

Bell stepped down from office after his term ended and returned to his farming interests. He was married to Mary Louise Perry. Bell died on September 25, 1909.

PROCTOR, FLETCHER DUTTON (1860-1911), fifty-first governor of Vermont (1906-1908), was born in Cavendish, Vermont, on November 17, 1860. He attended Amherst College, graduating in 1882. Soon after, Proctor became an employee of the Vermont Marble Company, and by 1889, he had become president of the firm. He also served as president or director of such enterprises as the New England Telephone and Telegraph Company, Rutland Railroad Company, and the Clarendon and Pittsford Railroad Company.

Proctor's first political appointment was as Secretary of Civil and Military Affairs during the administration of Governor Ormsbee. In 1890, 1900, and 1904 Proctor served in the Vermont State Legislature and in 1892, was elected to the State Senate. In 1906 he secured the Vermont governorship on the Republican ticket. During his tenure Proctor sought to improve both the educational and the prison systems, and as such, he suggested the formation of a committee to research prison and educational facilities. The result of their findings was the organization of the Board of Penal Institutions and to a work program for county jail prisoners. In addition, the judicial system was overhauled, taxation for railroads was increased, and the highway system was upgraded.

Proctor stepped down from office when his term ended. He was married to Minnie E. Robinson, and the couple had three children. Proctor died on September 17, 1911.

PROUTY, GEORGE (1862-1918), fifty-second governor of Vermont (1908-1910), was born in Newport, Vermont, on March 4, 1862. He attended Bryant and Stratton Business College, graduating in 1880 and subsequently went to work for his father in the lumber business.

Prouty, a Republican, entered politics in 1896 when he was elected to the Vermont House of Representatives. In 1904, he secured a seat in the State Senate. Beginning in 1906 he served as Vermont's Lieutenant Governor and in 1908, ran for and won the Vermont governorship on the Republican ticket. During his tenure legislation was passed in which the Railroad Commission would be placed under the aegis of a Public Service Commission, which would oversee other public service organizations as well. Also during that time, the State Supreme Court was revamped, the State Board of Education was organized, and the State Library Commission was created.

Prouty stepped down from office after his term ended and returned to his business pursuits. He was married to Henrietta Allen. Prouty died on August 18, 1918.

MEAD, JOHN ABNER (1841-1920), fifty-third governor of Vermont (1910-1912), was born on April 20, 1841, in Fair Haven, Vermont. He first attended Middlebury College, graduating in 1864, then earned a medical degree in 1868 from the College of Physicians and Surgeons at Columbia University. During the Civil War, Mead served with the Twelfth Vermont Volunteers.

Mead practiced medicine for several years at King's County Hospital in Brooklyn, New York, then relocated to Rutland, Vermont, where he continued as a physician until 1888, when he was named to a chair at the University of Vermont's medical department.

Eventually Mead gave up medicine to engage in his various business interests, including his own firm, the John A. Mead Manufacturing Company. Politics was another interest, and Mead, a Republican, secured a State Senate seat in 1892. In 1893 Governor Fuller named Mead Commissioner to the Colombian Exposition in Chicago, then two years later, he was asked by Governor Woodbury to serve as Commissioner to the Mexican National Exposition. In 1906 he won a seat in the State House of Representatives, then in 1908, began serving as Vermont's Lieutenant Governor.

In 1910 Mead ran for and won the Vermont governorship on the Republican ticket. During his administration, Mead was instrumental in guiding the State Legislature in their reapportionment of Vermont's senatorial districts. In addition, more child labor laws were adopted, new legislation was passed requiring nurses to register with the State, and the State School of Agriculture was created.

Mead stepped down from office after his term ended, but continued his involvement in Republican politics. He was married to Mary M. Sherman, and the couple had one child. Mead died on January 12, 1920.

FLETCHER, ALLEN M. (1853-1922), fifty-fourth governor of Vermont (1912-1915), was born in Indianapolis, Indiana, on September 25, 1853. He studied at two Massachusetts schools: the Swedenborgian School, and Williston Seminary. For a time, Fletcher traveled extensively throughout the United States and other countries. He returned to Indiana and engaged in various business interests, during which time he decided to build a summer home in Vermont. In 1899 he pulled up stakes and relocated to New York City, where he worked for the New York Stock Exchange. He subsequently left that post to settle permanently in Vermont.

Deciding to enter politics, Fletcher, a Republican, began serving in the State House of Representatives in 1902, then two years later, became a member of the State Senate. He returned to the Vermont House in 1906 and was elected to two more terms. In 1912 he ran for the Vermont governorship. None of the candidates received the majority vote, and when the decision was left to the State Legislature, they chose Fletcher to take office.

During his tenure Fletcher sought to make a number of reforms, which included revisions to the State Constitution, the upgrading of the entire school system (including the colleges), and the development of the State's waterpower. Also during that time, the Public Service Commission was given more authority, an office for a State Purchasing Agent was created by vote of the State Legislature, and a woman was named to the Vermont Board of Education for the first time. Fletcher also pushed for an end to capital punishment, but the measure failed to pass in the Legislature.

Fletcher stepped down from office at the end of his term. After an unsuccessful run for the United States Senate in 1916, Fletcher retired from politics. He was married to Mary E. Bence, and the couple had three children. Fletcher died on May 11, 1922.

GATES, CHARLES W. (1856-1927), fifty-fifth governor of Vermont (1915-1917), was born in Franklin, Vermont, on January 12, 1856. He attended Vermont's St. Johnsbury Academy, then subsequently spent several years as a schoolteacher, and later served as principal of Franklin Academy. In 1884 he engaged in mercantile pursuits, and later served as director of the Enosburg Falls Savings Bank and Trust Company.

Gates, a Republican, pursued a political career with his 1898 election to the State Legislature, then won a seat in the Vermont Senate two years later. In 1904 Governor Bell named him State Highway Commissioner, then Governor Proctor reappointed him to that post in 1906, and he served until 1914. In that year Gates ran for and won the Vermont governorship on the Republican ticket.

During his administration several grammar and high schools were established, and a prohibition law was adopted. Also, the Direct Primary law was passed, as was the Employer's Liability Act. In addition, the creation of a vocational education program was approved by the State Legislature.

At the end of his term, Gates stepped down from office. He was married to Mary E. Hayden, and the couple had five children. Gates died on July 1, 1927.

GRAHAM, HORACE FRENCH (1862-1941), fifty-sixth governor of Vermont (1917-1919), was born on February 7, 1862, in Brooklyn, New York. He attended City College of New York, graduating in 1885, then studied at Columbia University Law School, taking his degree in 1888. Along with his own law practice, Graham worked for the firms of Stevens, Graham and Kinney, and Graham and Skinner.

Graham entered politics in 1892 with his election to the State House of Representatives and was elected to a second term in 1900. In 1898 and 1902, he was named State's Attorney and from 1902 to 1916, served as State Auditor of Accounts. Also, in 1913 Governor Fletcher appointed Graham to serve on an educational commission.

Although Graham made his feelings clear that he did not want to run for governor, the Republican Party nominated him for the office in 1918 and he was subsequently elected. During his administration, cognizant that World War I was looming, Graham requested a one million dollar appropriation from the Vermont Legislature, which was given only days before the start of the war. Also during his tenure, female taxpayers were allowed to vote at town meetings, and the Board of Control was organized to oversee the financial records of the various State boards, as well as other State institutions.

Graham had his own financial scandal stemming from his time as the State Auditor, after the books from that time had been examined and determined to be incorrect. Although found guilty of the charges, he was never sentenced, and his successor, Governor Clement, pardoned him, theorizing that the mistakes in question were simple human error, rather than malfeasance.

Graham continued in politics when he secured a seat in the State House of Representatives in 1923, and ten years later, was asked to help draft revisions to a number of State laws.

Graham, who never married, died on November 23, 1941.

CLEMENT, PERCIVAL W. (1846-1927), fifty-seventh governor of Vermont (1919-1921), was born in Rutland, Vermont, on July 7, 1846. He attended Connecticut's Trinity College, graduating in 1868. After college he became an employee at the marble company his father owned, and by 1871, had been made a partner. Having other business interests, Clement served as president of both the Clement National Bank and the Rutland Board of Trade.

Delving into politics, Clement, a Republican, was elected to the State House of Representatives in 1892, and was reelected to four more terms, with an interim term as a member of the Vermont Senate. At various times he served on such organizations as the New England Railroad Conference Commission, the Vermont Education Commission, and the Vermont Committee of Public Safety.

After two unsuccessful attempts at the Vermont governorship, Clement was elected in the 1918 race, on the Republican ticket. During his tenure, a million-dollar appropriation was approved by the State Legislature for weekly paychecks to be distributed to the State's military personnel for their service during World War I. In addition, a bill prohibiting anarchy was adopted, and Vermont joined other states in ratifying the Prohibition Amendment to the United States Constitution.

Clement stepped down from office after his term ended. He was married to Maria H. Goodwin, and the couple had eight children. Clement died on January 9, 1927.

HARTNESS, JAMES (1861-1934), fifty-eighth governor of Vermont (1921-1923), was born on September 3, 1861, in Schenectady, New York. Raised in Cleveland, Ohio, he learned the machinist trade at the age of sixteen.

In 1889 Hartness relocated to Springfield, Vermont, where he became a superintendent at the Jones and Lamson Machine Company, eventually becoming president of the firm. Hartness ultimately made a name for himself as an inventor who, by the end of his life, had applied for almost one hundred patents. His expert engineering skills helped perfect the flat turret lathe, which, in turn, made the city of Springfield, Vermont the principal manufacturer of that product.

After the First World War began, Hartness served as Federal Food Administrator for Vermont, and was also a member of the Inter-Allied Aircraft Standardization Commission. Between 1915 and 1921, at the request of Governor Gates, Hartness served on the State Board of Education.

In 1920 Hartness successfully ran for the Vermont governorship on the Republican ticket. During his tenure he supported both the industrial and agricultural development of the State. He also sought the inclusion of women into the State government, and while he was in office, Vermont saw its first woman elected to Vermont's State House of Representatives. In addition, new amendments to the State Constitution were adopted, including equal rights for women, and the option by accused criminals to waive a trial by jury.

At the end of his term, Hartness stepped down from office and returned to his inventions and other business pursuits. Hartness was married to Lena Sanford Pond, and the couple had two children. He died on February 2, 1934.

PROCTOR, REDFIELD, JR. (1879-1957), fifty-ninth governor of Vermont (1923-1925), was born in Proctor, Vermont, on April 13, 1879. He was the son of the former Governor of Vermont, Redfield Proctor, Sr. He attended the Massachusetts Institute of Technology, earning a mechanical engineering degree in 1902. He subsequently joined his father's firm, the Vermont Marble Company, working first in production, then eventually attaining the vice presidency. Along with that post, Proctor also served as president of the Proctor Trust Company and as director of a number of banks.

Proctor, a Republican, entered politics with his election to the Vermont General Assembly for two terms, beginning in 1912, then in 1917, served in the Vermont State Senate. In 1922 he secured the Vermont governorship on the Republican ticket. During his tenure Proctor sought to protect Vermont from the federal government's attempt to take over the State's responsibilities and also recommended that individual towns and cities should not allow the State government to do the same to them. In addition, he supported the use of the latest scientific advances in agriculture.

At the end of his term, Proctor stepped down from office and returned to oversee the Vermont Marble Company. He was married to Mary Sherwood Hedrick, and the couple had three children. Proctor died on February 5, 1957.

BILLINGS, FRANKLIN SWIFT (1862-1935), sixtieth governor of Vermont (1925-1927), was born in New Bedford, Massachusetts, on May 11, 1862. Billings attended Harvard College, graduating in 1885, then relocated to Kansas where he was supervisor of a sheep ranch. Not long after, he moved again, this time to New York City where he lived for seventeen years, running an import-export business. In 1903 he left New York and settled in Woodstock, Vermont.

Deciding to pursue politics, Billings, a Republican, served as Chief of Staff to Governor Bell between 1904 and 1906. Beginning in 1910 he served two terms in the Vermont House of Representatives, then served another two terms later on, starting in 1921. During 1911-12, he was Commissioner of Conservation of Resources and in 1913, served on the State Board of Education. During 1923-24, Billings was Vermont's Lieutenant Governor and in the latter year, successfully ran for the governorship on the Republican ticket.

During his tenure, State departments that were established included the Bureau of Criminal Identification, and the Motor Vehicle Department. In addition, national forests were designated in Vermont by the federal government.

Billings stepped down from office when his term ended. He was married twice: to Bessie Hewitt Vail, and to Gertrude Curtis. He had one child from each union. Billings died on January 16, 1935.

WEEKS, JOHN ELIAKIM (1853-1949), sixty-first governor of Vermont (1927-1931), was born in Salisbury, Vermont, on June 14, 1853. Receiving a public school education, as an adult he engaged in farming, and also settled estates. He was also involved in other business enterprises, serving as president of the Addison County Trust Company and director of both the National Bank of Middlebury and the Brandon National Bank.

A Republican, Weeks entered politics when he served as assistant doorkeeper for the Vermont Senate in 1884, then in 1888, he became a member of the Vermont State Legislature. Between 1892 and 1894 Weeks was Associate Judge of the Addison County Court and in 1896, secured a seat in the State Senate. Between 1906 and 1917 Weeks served as Chairman of the Vermont Penal Board and in the latter year, was asked to oversee the entire State institutional system. In 1923 he was named Commissioner of Public Welfare, the first person to hold that title in Vermont.

In 1926 Weeks successfully ran for the Vermont governorship on the Republican ticket and won a second term in 1928, making him the first governor since 1868 to serve more than one term. During his tenure Weeks was able to secure over eight million dollars in relief money from the federal government to help alleviate the destruction from the 1927 flood in Vermont. Also, he followed through on his promise to pave several miles of road each year without putting the State budget in debt, and upgraded Vermont's rural schools.

Weeks stepped down from office after his second term ended, then in 1931, was elected to the United States House of Representatives.

Weeks was married to Hattie J. Dyer; the couple had no children. He died on September 10, 1949.

WILSON, STANLEY CALEF (1879-1967), sixty-second governor of Vermont (1931-1935), was born on September 10, 1879, in Orange, Vermont. He attended Tufts College, graduating in 1901. Wilson subsequently studied law, passing the bar in 1904 and engaging in the practice of law at the firm of Gates and Wilson. In the years following, Wilson served as director of several banks and business firms, including the Brocklebank Granite Company, the Orange County Creamery Corporation, and the Hartford Savings Bank, among others.

Deciding to enter politics, Wilson, a Republican, secured the post of State's Attorney in 1908, serving until 1912. Between 1915 and 1917 he served in the Vermont State Legislature, then in the latter year, was elected Superior Court Judge, serving until 1925. In 1927 he won a seat in the State Senate and in 1928, was Vermont's Lieutenant Governor. In 1930 Wilson successfully ran for the Vermont governorship on the Republican ticket and was elected to a second term in 1932.

During Wilson's tenure Vermont's principal highways were put under State jurisdiction, and funding was set aside by the State Legislature to upgrade those roads. Wilson also pushed for money to be spent on a highway beautification program. During those years, Wilson sought to improve the lot of State farmers and saw promise in the youth of Vermont, often accompanying them on visits to industrial firms and other sites. By the end of his administration, Wilson had reduced the State budget by one million dollars.

Wilson stepped down from office after his second term, and retired from public life. He was married to Grace Goodwin Bacon; the couple had no children. Wilson died on October 5, 1967.

SMITH, CHARLES MANLEY (1868-1937), sixty-third governor of Vermont (1935-1937), was born in West Rutland, Vermont, on August 3, 1868. He attended Dartmouth College, graduating in 1891. Smith subsequently engaged in farming for a number of years, then relocated to Rutland in 1901, where he helped manufacture bricks. Also during that time, he served as president of the Vermont Maple Leaf Sugar Company and was named president of the Marble Savings Bank in 1926.

Deciding to enter politics, Smith, a Republican, won two terms in the Vermont State Senate, beginning in 1927, then was elected to the State House of Representatives in 1931. Starting in 1932 he served as Vermont's Lieutenant Governor, then was elected to the governorship on the Republican ticket in 1934. During his tenure the fees for vehicle registration were reduced, and a senior citizen pension law was adopted by the Legislature.

Smith stepped down from office at the end of his term. He was married to Mary Aurelia Stark, and the couple had three children. Smith died on August 12, 1937.

AIKEN, GEORGE D. (1892-1984), sixty-fourth governor of Vermont (1937-1941), was born in Dummerston, Vermont, on August 20, 1892. After high school, Aiken was involved in agricultural pursuits, including fruit farming and overseeing a plant nursery. His special interest was wildflowers, and Aiken became somewhat of an expert at their cultivation, writing the book *Pioneering With Wildflowers* in 1936. Two years later he authored *Speaking From Vermont*. Also during those years, from 1920 to 1937, he was a school director.

Aiken pursued his first political post in 1931 when he successfully ran for the Vermont State House of Representatives. In 1935 he served as Vermont's Lieutenant Governor and the following year, was elected to the Vermont governorship on the Republican ticket, winning a second term in 1938.

During his administration, Aiken teamed up with five other state governors to fight for states' rights when the federal government tried to seize land for flood control by use of intimidation. The governors were ultimately successful in their battle for state autonomy. Aiken promoted the Republican Party as the party of the people, rejecting special interest groups while in office. Also during that time, Aiken stuck to a pay-as-you-go policy with all State expenses.

After his second term, Aiken stepped down from office and immediately took a seat in the United States Senate left vacant by the death of Ernest W. Gibson. Aiken went on to win another five Senate terms, finally retiring in 1975.

Aiken married Beatrice M. Howard, and the couple had four children. He died on November 19, 1984 and is buried at West Hill Cemetery, in Putney Vermont.

WILLS, WILLIAM H. (1882-1946), sixty-fifth governor of Vermont (1941-1945), was born on October 26, 1882, in Chicago, Illinois. He received a public school education and took a number of correspondence courses. When Wills was still a young boy, his father died, and the family subsequently moved to Vermont. After reaching adulthood, Wills launched his own insurance firm, then engaged in the banking and real estate businesses.

A Republican, Wills ran for the State House of Representatives in 1929, winning a seat in that body, then between 1931 and 1935, served in the Vermont State Senate. After one unsuccessful bid for the office of Lieutenant Governor, Wills won that post in 1936 and 1939.

In 1940 Wills ran for the Vermont governorship on the Republican ticket, winning a reelection bid in 1942. During his administration, Wills appeared on the radio frequently, interviewing a number of State government officials. A minimum wage law for schoolteachers was adopted by the State Legislature, as was a bill that implemented a merit system for State employees. Another bill passed that set aside surplus budget funds as bonus money for Vermont's veterans.

After his second term, Wills stepped down from office. The only other post he held was his seat on the Federal Communications Commission. He was married to Hazel McLeod, with whom he had one child. Wills died on May 6, 1946.

PROCTOR, MORTIMER R. (1889-1968), sixty-sixth governor of Vermont (1945-1947), was born on May 30, 1889, in Proctor, Vermont. He attended Yale, graduating in 1912, after which he became an employee of the Vermont Marble Company, the business owned by his family. He also engaged in the insurance and banking industries, serving as vice president of the Proctor Trust Company, and director of the Vermont Mutual Insurance Company. During World War I, Proctor served in the United States Army, then returned home to resume his business interests.

From 1932 to 1934 he served on the Vermont Educational Commission. In 1933 Proctor, a Republican, was elected to the Vermont House of Representatives, serving until 1939. From 1939 to 1941, he was a member of the Vermont State Senate. During the years 1940 to 1944, Proctor served as Vermont's Lieutenant Governor. In 1944 he ran successfully for the governorship on the Republican ticket.

During his tenure, he sought to streamline the State government. One of his decisions was to launch an investigation into a number of governmental agencies such as the Welfare Department, the result being sweeping improvements in several departments. In addition, the State Veterans' Board was established, and the Commission of State Government and Finance was organized. Funding was earmarked for the State's educational system, which included a raise for schoolteachers. Senior citizens also saw their pensions increase. By the end of Proctor's administration, the State debt had been reduced by nearly two million dollars.

In 1946 Proctor was defeated in his bid for a second term, and stepped down from office in 1947. He was married four times: to Margaret Chisholm, her sister Dorothy Chisholm, to Lillian Washburn, and to Geraldine Gates. Proctor died on April 28, 1968.

GIBSON, ERNEST W. (1901-1969), sixty-seventh governor of Vermont (1947-1951), was born in Brattleboro, Vermont, on March 6, 1901. He attended Vermont's Norwich University, graduating in 1923, then relocated to Washington, D.C. to take night classes at George Washington University Law School. Earning his law degree in 1927, he returned to Brattleboro, Vermont, passing the bar later that year and starting a law practice soon after.

Between 1929 and 1933 Gibson served as State's Attorney and from 1931 to 1933, held the post of Assistant Secretary of the State Senate. He subsequently served as Secretary of the Vermont Senate between 1933 and 1940. During 1939-40, Gibson served on the Vermont Railroad Tax Commission. In 1940 Gibson, a Republican, was asked to serve the unexpired United States Senate term left by the death of his father, Senator Ernest Willard Gibson.

During World War II, Gibson served at the rank of Captain in the United States Army and received several medals, including the Purple Heart. In 1945 he was discharged at the rank of Colonel.

After the war he returned home and waged a successful campaign to secure the Vermont governorship. During his tenure Gibson sought to implement a number of economic and social reforms, specifically in the areas of welfare, health, and the State's educational system. In addition, the State's police force was modernized, and the State Highway Department was revamped.

Gibson stepped down before the end of his term after being appointed United States District Judge for the District of Vermont in 1950, a post he held until 1969.

Gibson was married twice: to Dorothy P. Switzer, and after her death, to Ann H. Haag. He died on November 4, 1969.

ARTHUR, HAROLD JOHN (1904-1971), acting governor of Vermont (1950-1951), was born in Whitehall, New York, on February 9, 1904. He attended Albany Business College, then studied at La Salle Extension University, earning an LL.B. degree in 1932, and passing the bar that same year. Between 1928 and 1934 Arthur was superintendent of the U.A. Employment Service.

A Republican, he served as Vermont's Lieutenant Governor, beginning in 1948. When the incumbent governor, Ernest Gibson, stepped down before the end of his term to accept a United States judgeship, Arthur assumed the governorship, serving from January 16, 1950 to January 4, 1951, but refused to run for another term.

In 1958 Arthur made an unsuccessful bid for the United States Congress, and subsequently retired from public life. In 1939 he published the book, *House Precedents*.

Arthur was married to Mary C. Alafat, and the couple had one child. He died on July 19, 1971.

EMERSON, LEE E. (1898-1976), sixty-eighth governor of Vermont (1951-1955), was born in Hardwick, Vermont, on December 19, 1898. He attended Syracuse University, graduating in 1921, then took his law degree from George Washington University Law School in 1926 and passed the Vermont bar the following year.

Pursuing a political career, Emerson was elected to the Vermont House of Representatives, serving between 1939 and 1941, then became a member of the Vermont State Senate in 1943. From 1945 to 1947 Emerson served as Vermont's Lieutenant Governor. In 1950 he secured the Vermont governorship and won a second term in 1952.

During his administration, Emerson supported the launching of a study that would examine whether Vermont would be served by the construction of a natural gas pipeline and also requested another study to determine how much racial discrimination existed in the State.

Emerson sought to have Vermont's veterans of the Korean War receive a stipend, and the "Forest Act" was adopted, which offered funding for Vermont's cities and towns to institute forests. By the time Emerson left office, a large surplus remained in the State treasury.

Emerson stepped down at the end of his second term and returned to his private law practice. He made unsuccessful bids for both the United States House of Representatives and the United States Senate, in 1958 and 1960, respectively.

Emerson was married to Dorcas Ball, with whom he had two children. He died on May 21, 1976.

JOHNSON, JOSEPH BLAINE (1893-1986), sixty-ninth governor of Vermont (1955-1959), was born in Helsingborg, Sweden, on August 29, 1893. He attended the University of Vermont, earning a B.S. degree in mechanical engineering in 1915. Upon graduating, Johnson became an employee of the Bryant Chucking Gear Company, working himself up through the firm as draftsman, designer, chief engineer, then vice president and general manager before leaving the company in 1949.

In 1945 Johnson, a Republican, pursued a political career when he successfully ran for the State House of Representatives in 1945. He subsequently served in the Vermont Senate between 1947 and 1949. From 1950 to 1952, he served as Vermont's Lieutenant Governor, and in 1954 he won the Vermont governorship on the Republican ticket, securing his second term two years later.

During his tenure Johnson sought to have Vermont be a participant in the proposed interstate highway system. In addition, he asked the State Legislature to fund the Vermont Geology Department, and to also earmark additional money for the support of the University of Vermont.

Johnson stepped down from office after his second term ended. He married Virginia F. Slack, and the couple had one child. He died on October 25, 1986.

STAFFORD, ROBERT T. (1913-), seventieth governor of Vermont (1959-1961), was born in Rutland, Vermont on August 8, 1913. He attended Middlebury College, graduating in 1935, then took his law degree at Boston University Law School in 1938, passing the bar the same year. Soon after, he went into partnership at the law firm of Stafford, Abiatell and Stafford.

In 1939 Stafford, a Republican, was named City Prosecutor for Rutland, serving in that post until 1942. During World War II, Stafford served in the United States Navy. After his discharge, he returned home and entered into the law firm of Stafford and La Brake. Between 1947 and 1951 Stafford served as State's Attorney, then during 1953-54, he was Deputy Attorney General. Between 1954 and 1956, Stafford held the office of Vermont's Attorney General, and from 1956 to 1958, he served as Vermont's Lieutenant Governor.

Stafford ran for the governorship in 1958 on the Republican ticket and won the election. During his administration, legislation was adopted by which strict regulations were implemented for cosmetics, food, drugs, and hazardous materials. Also during that time, Stafford sought to boost the State's economy through various projects, while curbing State expenditures in order to keep government costs in line. In addition, the State Legislature adopted a bill that provided the State's college students with scholarships, and approved the establishment of the Vermont Department of Administration.

After his term ended, Stafford stepped down from office and immediately won his bid for the United States House of Representatives and was subsequently reelected to four more terms. He next won a seat in the United States Senate in 1971 and the following year, was elected to serve out a five-year term in the Senate seat vacated by the death of Senator Winston L. Prouty. Stafford was reelected in the 1976 race.

Stafford is married to Helen C. Kelley, and the couple has four children.

KEYSER, F. RAY, JR. (1927-), seventy-first governor of Vermont (1961-1963), was born in Chelsea, Vermont, on August 17, 1927. Keyser served in the United States Navy during World War II. Upon his discharge, he attended Tufts College, graduating in 1949, then earned his law degree from Boston University Law School in 1952. After passing the bar that same year, Keyser became a member of the law firm of Wilson and Keyser.

A Republican, Keyser was elected to two terms in the State House of Representatives, beginning in 1955, and in 1960 he secured the Vermont governorship on the Republican ticket. During his administration, Keyser sought to make improvements throughout Vermont and implemented a state-wide planning program. During that time, the Vermont Industrial Building Author-

ity was established, and the State's Department of Administration was reorganized. In addition, one million dollars was earmarked for the expansion of Vermont's State park system.

Keyser made a bid for reelection in 1962, but was defeated and stepped down from office in 1963. In 1965 he was hired as a company attorney for the Vermont Marble Company, then worked his way up to general counsel and vice president, and ultimately, president of the firm.

Keyser is married to Joan Friedgen, and the couple has three children.

HOFF, PHILIP HENDERSON (1924-), seventy-second governor of Vermont (1963-1969), was born in Greenfield, Massachusetts, on June 29, 1924. He served in the United States Navy during World War II. Upon his discharge, he attended Williams College, graduating in 1948, then earned a law degree from Cornell University Law School in 1951. Later that year he relocated to Vermont, where he passed the bar in 1952. Having worked at the law firm of Black and Wilson as he was studying for his degree, he eventually became a partner, working there until 1963.

A Democrat, Hoff was elected to the State House of Representatives in 1961. In 1962 he won the Vermont governorship, making him the first member of the Democratic Party to ever hold that office. He was reelected two more times, in 1964 and 1966.

During his tenure education was a priority with Hoff, who sought to increase funding for the State's educational system and called for a solid student loan program. Due to his influence, the State Legislature backed the Governor's Committee on Children and Youth and made sure that Vermont became a part of the Interstate Compact on Education. In addition, the State Board of Mental Health was created, and the Department of Social Welfare was given authorization to procure funding from the federal government for Vermont's food stamp program. A housing authority was also established, and the Labor Relations Law was adopted.

At the end of his third term in 1968, Hoff stepped down from office and in 1970, made an unsuccessful bid for the United States Senate. For several years he was a member of the law firm of Hoff, Curtis, Bryan, Quinn and Jenkins.

Hoff is married to Joan P. Brower, and the couple has four children.

DAVIS, DEANE C. (1900-1990), seventy-third governor of Vermont (1969-1973), was born in East Barre, Vermont, on November 7, 1900. He attended Boston University Law School, graduating in 1922 and passing the bar soon after. Initially he opened his own law office, then in 1936, became a member of the Wilson, Carver, Davis and Keyser law firm. He was associated with the National Life Insurance Company, beginning in 1940, when he was general counsel, then was named president in 1950, and chairman in 1965.

Davis, a Republican, entered politics in 1926 when he was elected State's Attorney, serving in that post until 1928. Between 1931 and 1936 he was a Superior Judge for the State. In 1957 he chaired what became known as the "Little Hoover Commission," organized to research the workings of the State government. The Commission eventually became the Vermont Department of Administration.

In 1969 he successfully ran for the Vermont governorship on the Republican ticket and won reelection in the 1970 race. During his tenure, legislation sponsored by Davis was adopted by which regulations were put in place to control both water and land development in the State, with the desired result being environmental protection. In addition, Davis implemented a reorganization of the State government and initiated Vermont's first government cabinet system. During his time in office, he managed to run the government on a balanced budget, and by the time he left office, the huge deficit he had inherited from previous administrations had been eliminated.

Davis stepped down from office after his second term and retired from public life. He was married twice: to Corinne Eastman, and after her death, to Marjorie Smith Conzelman. He had three children by his first union. Davis died on December 8, 1990.

SALMON, THOMAS P. (1932-), seventy-fourth governor of Vermont (1973-1977), was born in Cleveland, Ohio, on August 19, 1932, and raised in Massachusetts. He attended Boston College, graduating in 1954, then studied at Boston College Law School, from which he was graduated in 1957. He went on to earn a Master of Laws degree from New York University Law School. In 1958 Salmon relocated to Vermont, and the following year was named town counsel for the city of Rockingham.

In 1962 Salmon, a Democrat, became Judge of the Bellows Falls Municipal Court, and that same year, secured a seat in the State House of Representatives. In 1965 he resigned his judgeship to serve full time in the Legislature, then stepped down from the latter in 1970.

In 1972 Salmon successfully ran for the Vermont governorship on the Democratic ticket and won a second term in 1974. During his tenure he initiated a reduction on property taxes for everyone from Vermont's seniors to the average citizen. In addition, he upheld the environmental programs initiated by his predecessor.

Salmon stepped down from office in 1976 in order to make a bid for the United States Senate, but lost the race to Robert T. Stafford. Salmon is married to Madeleine G. Savaria and the couple has four children.

SNELLING, RICHARD ARKWRIGHT (1927-1991), seventy-fifth and seventy-seventh governor of Vermont (1977-1985, 1991), was born in Allentown, Pennsylvania on February 18, 1927. After studying at Lehigh University and the University of Havana, Cuba, Snelling earned an A.B. degree cum laude from Harvard University in 1948. During World War II, he served in the United States Army.

Beginning in 1959 Snelling was president of Shelburne Industries, Inc. Between 1961 and 1964 he was president and chairman of the executive committee of the Greater Burlington Industrial Corporation. From 1959 to 1961 he was a participant on the Vermont Development Commission.

A Republican, Snelling ran unsuccessfully for both the Lieutenant Governor's post and the Vermont governorship, in 1964 and 1966, respectively. From 1973 to 1977 Snelling served in the State House of Representatives. In 1976 he was successful in his second bid for the governor's chair, taking office on January 3, 1977, and also won the subsequent two gubernatorial elections in 1978 and 1980.

During his tenure a secession movement was launched by island residents of Lake Champlain, who were outraged that the State Attorney's Office in their county had been eliminated. In addition, Snelling met with officials from the Canadian government to convince them to sell surplus electricity to the New England area from Canada's new hydroelectric plants that were under construction. Snelling vetoed legislation in 1982 that would have increased the drinking age.

Snelling decided to step down after his third term, leaving in 1985, but won the gubernatorial race one more time in 1989 and assumed the governorship in January of 1990. On August 14, 1991, Snelling died of a heart attack while still in office, and was succeeded by Vermont's Lieutenant Governor, Howard Dean.

Snelling was married to Barbara Weil, and the couple had four children.

KUNIN, MADELEINE MAY (1933-), seventy-sixth governor of Vermont (1985-1991), was born on September 28, 1933, in Zurich, Switzerland. In 1940 she immigrated with her widowed mother and her brother to the United States in an attempt to escape from the encroaching Nazi regime. The family settled in Pittsfield, Massachusetts, and Kunin won a scholarship to the University of Massachusetts, from where she graduated in 1956. Kunin subsequently studied at the Columbia School of Journalism, earning a Master's Degree.

Kunin relocated to Vermont and secured a job as reporter and editor of the *Burlington Free Press*. She returned to school at the University of Vermont, where she took her masters degree in English literature in 1967, and in 1969 she was hired as an instructor at Burlington's Trinity College.

Deciding to pursue a political career, Kunin, a Democrat, won a seat in the Vermont House of Representatives in 1971, securing another term three years later. Beginning in 1978 she was Vermont's Lieutenant Governor, serving for two terms in that office. In 1982, Kunin ran unsuccessfully for the governorship and left politics for a time to teach journalism and host a talk show on radio station WJOY.

In 1984 she made another run for the Vermont governorship and with her victory, became the first woman in the State to hold that office. She went on to win two more terms. Kunin made education a priority during her administration, drastically increasing funding for all school districts, and was instrumental in implementing the interactive television educational system. She made sure that pregnant women and children up to six years old were provided with health insurance, and that employers were required to offer unpaid maternity leave for a twelve-week period. During Kunin's tenure, 45,000 new jobs were created throughout the State, more stringent penalties were attached to all hate crimes, drug abuse laws were tightened, a sweeping hazardous waste program was established, and the Vermont Human Rights Commission was organized.

Kunin stepped down from office in 1991 and accepted the post of United States Deputy Secretary of Education. During her tenure she was instrumental in pushing forward President Bill Clinton's education reform program. Working in tandem with President Clinton and Education Secretary Richard W. Riley, several legislative acts were adopted, including the Goals 2000: Educate America Act, the Safe and Drug-Free Schools Act, and the School to Work Opportunities Act. Also during that time, Kunin worked on a number of women's issues and was one of the United States delegates that traveled to Beijing to participate in the Fourth World Conference on Women. In August of 1996, Kunin was appointed ambassador to her homeland of Switzerland by President Clinton.

In 1994 Kunin published a memoir of her years of public service entitled, *Living a Political Life*.

DEAN, HOWARD (1948-), seventy-eighth governor of Vermont (1991-current) was born in New York City on November 17, 1948. He attended Yale University, earning a B.A. degree in 1971. Pursuing a medical career, he studied at the Albert Einstein College of Medicine, taking his M.D. degree in 1978. Dean served his residency in internal medicine at the Medical Center Hospital of Vermont, and subsequently partnered with his wife in an internal medicine practice between 1981 and 1991.

Dean became politically active during his residency, serving as a volunteer for the reelection campaign of President Jimmy Carter. Between 1982 and 1986, he was a member of the Vermont House of Representatives, and then won three terms as Vermont's Lieutenant Governor, in 1986, 1988, and 1990.

On August 14, 1991, incumbent Governor Richard A. Snelling died of a heart attack. Dean received the news while treating someone at his medical clinic, and after completing the patient's appointment, Dean traveled to the State capital to be sworn into office.

During his tenure, one of Dean's first decisions was to slash both the State income tax and the deficit. He also sought to implement welfare reform and upgrade health care. One of his top priorities was children's prevention programs, which resulted in reduced sexual and physical abuse of the State's children and a reduction in teen pregnancies. Health coverage and childhood immunizations were also an important part of Dean's agenda for the care of children.

Under Dean's guidance, Vermont became the first state in the nation to extensively revamp the welfare system. His proposal was based on a welfare time limit: people would receive welfare for limited amounts of time, but would be entitled to job training and child and health care to make the transition easier.

After only one year in the governorship, Dean was asked to chair the National Governors' Association, during which time he launched "The Governors' Campaign for Children." In 1992 Dean won his first complete term, then was reelected to three more terms, in 1994, 1996, and 1998. His current term expires in January 2001.

Dean is married to Judith Steinberg, M.D., and the couple has two children.

DICTIONARY OF PLACES

Population figures and demographic information are official U.S. Census Bureau finals for 1990. When two figures are shown, separated by a slash, the first figure is the 1990 and the second is the U.S. Census Bureau 1999 estimate—the most recent available. Year 2000 census supplements will be available in the Fall of 2001.

ADDISON, Town; Addison County; Pop. 889; The town was named in honor of the great English statesman, Joseph Addison, who died in 1719.

ALBANY, Village; Orleans County; Pop. 705 / 227; Zip Code 05820; Elev. 956; Lat. 44-43-49 N, Long. 072-22-49 W; Originally called Lutterloh, the name was later changed to Albany after that city in New York.

ALBURG, Village; Grand Isle County; Pop. / 386; Zip Code 05440; Elev. 124; Lat. 44-58-31 N, Long. 073-18-05 W; Founded by Ira Allen, the towns name is a contraction of Allenbourg. One of the tow pieces of land I the contiguous United States that does not touch any other piece of land in the United States.

ANDOVER, Town; Windsor County; Pop. 350; Zip Code 05501; The town is named after Andover in Hampshire, England.

ARLINGTON, Town; Bennington County; Pop. 2,184; Zip Code 05250; Lat. 43-04-14 N, Long. 073-09-08; The town is named in honor of Augustus Henry Fitzroy, the fourth Earl of Arlington, and a friend of the American colonies. The town was chartered on July 28, 1761.

ATHENS, Town; Windham County; Pop. 250; Settled in the late 1700s and named for the Greek city.

AVERILL; Town; Essex County; Pop. 7; Lat. 44-56-22 N, Long. 71-39-59 W.

BAKERSFIELD, Town; Franklin County; Pop. 852; Zip Code 05441; Elev. 736; Lat. 44-46-53 N, Long. 072-48-16; Settler Joseph Baker bought the town in 1788 and named it after himself.

BALTIMORE, Town; Windsor County; Pop. 181; Baltimore takes its name from Baltimore, Maryland.

BARNARD, Town; Windsor County; Pop. 790; Zip Code 05031; Elev. 1335; Barnard takes its name from colonial Governor Francis Bernard, who served as Governor of the Massachusetts Bay Colony from 1760-69.

BARNET, Town; Caledonia County; Pop. 1,415; Lat. 44-19-30 N, Long. 72-04-38 W; An early settler of the area named the town for his former home in England.

BARRE, City; Washington County; Pop. 9,824 / 9,106; Zip Code 05641; Elev. 609; Lat. 44-11-56 N, Long. 072-30-08 W; Chartered in 1781 and named after Barre, Massachusetts.

BARTON, Town; Orleans County; Pop. 2,990; Zip Code 05822; Elev. 952; Lat. 44-44-57 N, Long. 072-10-38 W; Settled after the Revolutionary War and named for Colonel William Barton.

BARTON, Village; Orleans County; Pop. 2,990 / 899; Elev. 952; Zip Code 05822; Lat. 44-44-58 N, Long. 72-10-38 W.

BELLOWS FALLS, Village; Windham County; Pop. 3,456 / 3,149; Zip Code 05101, Elev. 299; Named after an early settler and the location of the village.

BELVIDERE, Town; Lamoille County; Pop. 218; Zip Code 05442; Elev. 924; Lat. 44-45-08 N, Long. 072-41-17; Landowner John Kelly named the town after Lake Belvedere in Ireland.

BENNINGTON, Town; Bennington County Seat; Pop. 15,815; Zip Code, 05201; Elev. 681; Lat. 42-52-46 N, Long. 073-11-47; Bennington honors Royal Governor Benning Wentworth, who chartered many areas and towns in Vermont. The first humans in the area of Bennington were here before 3500 BC. The town was chartered in 1749, and was settled in 1761. In the 1800s, the railroad, as well as factories that used waterpower provided in the area, created growth in the town.

BENSON, Town; Rutland County; Pop. 739; The towns name honors Revolutionary War patriot, Egbert Benson.

BERKSHIRE, Town; Franklin County; Pop. 1,116; Settled in 1780 and named after Berkshire County, Massachusetts.

BERLIN, Town; Washington County; Pop. 2,454; Granted in 1763 and named after Berlin, Massachusetts.

BETHEL, Town; Windsor County; Pop. 1,715; Zip Code 05032; Elev. 543; Chartered in 1779 and given the biblical name of Bethel.

BLOOMFIELD, Town; Essex County; Pop. 188; Named in 1830 for its descriptive connotations associated with flowers and blossoms.

BOLTON, Town; Chittenden County; Pop. 715; Named by Governor Wentworth for the Duke of Bolton.

BRADFORD, Town; Orange County; Pop. 2,191; Zip Code 05033; Originally Mooretown, the name was changed after the Revolution to honor early Massachusetts Governor William Bradford.

BRADFORD, Village; Orange County; Pop. 2,191 / 735; Zip Code 05033; Lat. 43-59-38 N, Long. 72-07-41 W.

BRAINTREE, Town; Orange County; Pop. 1,065; Chartered in 1781 and named after Braintree, Massachusetts, itself named after Braintree in Essex, England.

BRANDON, Town; Rutland County; Pop. 4,194; Zip Code 05733; Elev. 431; Lat. 43-47-48 N, Long. 073-05-21 W; Originally named Neshobe and later renamed after Brandon Bay in Ireland.

BRATTLEBORO, Town; Windham County; Pop. 11,886; Zip Code 05301; Elev. 240; Lat. 42-51-06 N, Long. 072-33-52 W; Granted by Benning Wentworth and named for a grantee, Colonel William Brattle. Fort Dummer was built nearby to protect 18th century settlers from Indian attacks. The area was chartered in 1752, after settlers cleared about two hundred acres around the fort. When the Vermont Valley Railroad came through town, population grew as it had been doing for at least a hundred years.

BRIDGEWATER, Town; Windsor County; Pop. 867; Zip Code 05034; Granted in 1761 and named in honor of Francis Egerton, third Duke of Bridgewater, who became famous for his construction of the first canals in Britain.

BRIDPORT, Town; Addison County; Pop. 997; Zip Code 05734; Lat. 43-59-04 N, Long. 073-19-00; The town is named after the English Channel port of Bridport.

BRIGHTON, Town; Essex County; Pop. 1,557; Granted in 1780 and named after the English Resort town.

BRISTOL, Town; Addison County; Pop. 3,293; Zip Code 05443; Elev. 571; Lat. 44-08-16 N, Long. 073-04-54 W; Originally Pocock, the name was changed in 1789 after Bristol, Rhode Island.

BRISTOL, Village; Addison County; Pop. 1,801; Lat. 44-08-11 N, Long. 73-12-38 W.

BROOKFIELD, Town; Orange County; Pop. 959; Zip Code 05036; Elev. 1276; Named after Brookfield, Massachusetts.

BROOKLINE, Town; Windham County; Pop. 310; A grassy brook flows through the town in an almost perfect straight line and gave the town its name.

BROWNINGTON, Town; Orleans County; Pop. 708; Granted in 1782 and named for two Grantees, Daniel and Timothy Brown.

BRUNSWICK, Town; Essex County; Pop. 82; Established in 1761 and named to honor the English Hanover King George III, who was also the Duke of Brunswick-Lungburg.

BUELS GORE, Unincorporated; Chittenden County; Pop. 2; Lat. 44-12-34 N, Long. 72-56-46 W.

BURKE, Town; Caledonia County; Pop. 1,385; The town was named to honor English Statesman Edmund Burke.

BURLINGTON, City; Burlington and Chittenden County Seats; Pop. 37,712 / 38,332; Zip Code 05401; Elev. 113; Lat. 44-29-02 N, Long. 073-13-12 W; Incorporated in 1864, the city was named after the Earl of Burlington in the 18th century.

CABOT, Village; Washington County; Pop. 958 / 341; Zip Code 05647; Elev. 1064; Lat. 44-24-12 N, Long. 072-18-55 W; Chartered in the 1780s and named for the Cabot family.

CALAIS, Town; Washington County; Pop. 1,207; Zip Code 05648; Lat. 44-22-28 N, Long. 072-29-45 W; Granted in 1781 and named for the French Channel port.

CAMBRIDGE, Town; Lamoille County; Pop. 2,019; Zip Code 05444; Elev. 455; Lat. 44-38-39 N, Long. 072-52-37 W; Chartered in 1781 and named for Cambridge, Massachusetts.

CANAAN, Town; Essex County; Pop. 1,196; Zip Code 05901; Lat. 44-59-44 N, Long. 071-42-40 W; Chartered in 1782 and given the biblical name for "the promised land."

CASTLETON, Town; Rutland County; Pop. 3,637; Zip Code 05735; Elev. 439; Lat. 43-36-38 N, Long. 073-10-56 W; Settled in the late 1700s and named after Castleton, England.

CAVENDISH, Town; Windsor County; Pop. 1,355; Zip Code 05142; Elev. 929; The town was named to honor William Cavendish, the fourth Duke of Devonshire (1720-64) and an influential British peer.

CHARLESTON, Town; Orleans County; Pop. 851; The town is named after Charleston, South Carolina, where Commodore Abraham Whipple put up a heroic defense in 1780.

CHARLOTTE, Town; Chittenden County; Pop. 2,561; Zip Code 05445; Elev. 169; Lat. 44-18-55 N, Long. 073-15-17 W; Granted in 1762 and named for Charlotte Sophia of Mecklenburg-Strelitz, the wife of George III.

CHELSEA, Town; Orange County Seat; Pop. 1,091; Zip Code 05038; Originally Turnersburgh, the name was changed in 1794 after Chelsea, Connecticut.

CHESTER, Town; Windsor County; Pop. 2,791; Zip Code 05143; Elev. 623; Originally called New Flamstead. The name changed in 1766 to honor Prince George Augustus Frederick, the eldest son of British Monarch George III.

CHITTENDEN, Town; Rutland County; Pop. 927; Zip Code 05737; Lat. 43-42-27 N, Long. 072-56-59 W; Chittenden was named for Vermont's first Governor, Thomas Chittenden.

CLARENDON, Town; Rutland County; Pop. 2,372; Named by Governor Benning Wentworth for Clarendon in Wiltshire, England.

COLCHESTER, Town; Chittenden County; Pop. 12,629; Zip Code 05446; Lat. 44-32-31 N, Long. 073-08-59 W; Named in 1763 to honor prominent British Nobleman, William Henry Nassau du Zurlostine, Baron of Colchester.

CONCORD, Town; Essex County; Pop. 1,125; Zip Code 05824; Elev. 859; Lat. 44-25-42 N, Long. 071-53-21 W; Founded in 1780 and named after Concord, Massachusetts.

CORINTH, Town; Orange County; Pop. 904; Zip Code 05039; Granted in 1764 by Benning Wentworth and named for the ancient Greek city.

CORNWALL, Town; Addison County; Pop. 993; The town is named for the Maritime County in England.

COVENTRY, Town; Orleans County; Pop. 674; Zip Code 05825; Elev. 718; Lat. 44-51-58 N, Long. 072-16-02 W; Chartered in 1780 and named after Coventry, Connecticut.

CRAFTSBURY, Town; Orleans County; Pop. 844; Zip Code 05826; Lat. 44-38-11 N, Long. 071-37-34 W; Among the original charter members was Colonel Ebenezer Crafts. The town is named for him.

DANBY, Town; Rutland County; Pop. 992; Zip Code 05739; Lat. 43-20-44 N, Long. 072-59-56 W; Named by Benning Wentworth in honor of Basil Fielding, sixth Earl of Denbigh.

DANVILLE, Town; Caledonia County; Pop. 1,705; Zip Code 05828; Lat. 44-24-40 N, Long. 066-08-34 W; Chartered in 1786 and named to honor famous French cartographer Jean Baptiste Bourguignon d'Anville.

DERBY CENTER, Village; Orleans County; Pop. 684 / 726; Elev. 1110; Lat. 44-57-20 N, Long. 72-07-56 W; Also known as Derby, but not coextensive with the town of Derby.

DERBY LINE, Village; Orleans County; Pop. 855 / 993; Elev. 1029; Lat. 45-00-08 N, Long. 72-06-14 W; So named because of its location on the border of Quebec, Canada and Derby, Vermont.

DERBY, Town; Orleans County; Pop. 4,222; Zip Code 05829; Lat. 44-57-22 N, Long. 072-08-13 W. Named for the town and county in England. Chartered just before the end of the Revolutionary War and named after Derby, Connecticut.

DORSET, Town; Bennington County; Pop. 1,648; Zip Code 05251; Elev. 962; Lat. 43-15-13 N, Long. 073-06-02 W; Named in honor of Lionel Sackville, the first Duke of Dorset.

DOVER, Town; Windham County; Pop. 666; Incorporated in 1810 and named after Dover, New Hampshire. First settled by Capt. Abner Perry in 1779. It was primarily an agricultural town.

DUMMERSTON, Town; Windham County; Pop. 1,574; The town is named for an 18th century Lieutenant Governor of Massachusetts, William Dummer.

DUXBURY, Town; Washington County; Pop. 877; Duxbury was granted in 1763 and named after Duxbury, Massachusetts.

EAST HAVEN, Town; Essex County; Pop. 280; Zip Code 05837; Lat. 44-39-52 N, Long. 071-53-14 W; Established in 1790 and named for East Haven, Connecticut.

EAST MONTPELIER, Town; Washington County; Pop. 2,205; Zip Code 05651; Elev. 728; Lat. 44-16-12 N, Long. 072-29-30 W; Originally part of Montpelier and so descriptively named.

EDEN, Town; Lamoille County; Pop. 612; Zip Code 05652; Elev. 1112; Lat. 44-42-22 N, Long. 072-32-50 W; Settled after the Revolutionary War and named for the biblical paradise.

ELMORE, Town; Lamoille County; Pop. 421; Granted to a group of Revolutionary War veterans, among them Colonel Samuel Elmore, for whom the town was named.

ENOSBURG FALLS, Village; Franklin County; Pop. 1,350 / 1,776; Zip Code 05450; Elev. 422; Lat. 72-48-15 W Long. 72-48-15 W; The village is a part of the town of Enosburg.

ENOSBURG, Town; Franklin County; Pop. 2,070; Zip Code 05450; Elev. 422;. Lat. 44-54-10 N, Long. 072-48-14 W; Charted in 1700 and named after the first grantee, General Roger Enos.

ESSEX JUNCTION, Village; Chittenden; Pop. 7,033 / 8,748; Zip Code 05452; Elev. 347; Lat. 44-29-31 N, Long. 073-06-56 W; Granted in 1763 and named after Essex, England.

ESSEX, Town; Chittenden County; Pop. 14,392; Zip Code 05451; Lat. 44-30-42 N, Long. 073-03-36; Named for Essex, England.

FAIR HAVEN, Town; Rutland County; Pop. 2,819; Zip Code 05731; Lat. 43-42-22 N, Long. 073-18-43 W; Settled in the 1780s and given a commendatory name. Colonel Matthew Lyon began an iron works in the area. Other economic ventures of early Fair Haven were quarries, clock companies, and a shirt manufacturing company. Slate from the Fair Haven area was used in the construction of the White House, Lincoln Memorial, and the Pentagon.

FAIRFAX, Town; Franklin County; Pop. 1,805; Zip Code 05454; Lat. 44-39-59 N, Long. 073-00-43 W; Fairfax is named after Thomas Fairfax, the sixth Baron Fairfax, who immigrated to Virginia in 1747.

FAIRFIELD, Town; Franklin County; Pop. 1,493; Zip Code 05455; Lat. 44-48-04 N, Long. 072-56-43 W; The town is named after Fairfield, Connecticut.

FAIRLEE, Town; Orange County; Pop. 770; Zip Code 05045; Settled in the late 1700s and named after a town on the Isle of Wight. The name means "a beautiful meadow."

FAYSTON, Town; Washington County; Pop. 657; The town is named in honor of Vermont's prominent 18th century family. Fayston has the highest average elevation of any town in Vermont. Economic ventures of the area have included lumber and agriculture, specifically potato farming.

FERDINAND, Town; Essex County; Pop. 12; Named by Governor Benning Wentworth in 1761 to honor Prince Karl Wilhelm Ferdinand, a relative of King George III.

FERRISBURG, Town; Addison County; Pop. 2,117; Zip Code 05456; Elev. 218; Lat. 44-12-24 N, Long. 073-14-52 W; Ferrisburg is named after one of its founders, Benjamin Ferris.

FLETCHER, Town; Franklin County; Pop. 626; Chartered in 1781 and named for Revolutionary War General Samuel Fletcher.

FRANKLIN, Town; Franklin County; Pop. 1,006; Zip Code 05457; Elev. 453; Lat. 44-58-57 N, Long. 072-55-07 W; Originally named Huntsburg, the town's name was later changed to honor Statesman Benjamin Franklin.

GEORGIA, Town; Franklin County; Pop. 2,818; Granted in 1763 and named for England's King George III.

GLASTENBURY, Town; Bennington County; Pop. 3; The town was named after Glastonbury in Somerset, England.

GLOVER, Town; Orleans County; Pop. 843; Granted to veterans of the Revolutionary War and named for General John Glover.

GOSHEN, Town; Addison County; Pop. 163; Named after Goshen, Connecticut. Goshen was the biblical land in Egypt where the Israelites lived in exile.

GRAFTON, Town; Windham County; Pop. 604; Zip Code 05146; Elev. 841; Settled in the 1790s and named for Grafton, Massachusetts.

GRANBY, Town; Essex County; Pop. 70; Zip Code 05840; Elev. 1456; Lat. 44-34-13 N, Long. 071-45-15 W; Chartered in 1761 and named in honor of John Manners, the Marquis of Granby, who helped defeat the French in 1759 at the Battle of Minden.

GRAND ISLE, Town; Grand Isle County; Pop. 1,238; Zip Code 05458; Elev. 169; Lat. 44-43-17 N, Long. 073-17-39 W; Descriptively named as the largest island in Lake Champlain. What is believed to be the oldest log cabin standing in the United States is found here.

GRANVILLE, Town; Addison County; Pop. 288; Zip Code 05747; Elev. 1,013; Lat. 43-59-05 N, Long. 072-50-43 W; The town is named after John Carteret (1690-1763), the first Earl of Granville.

GREENSBORO, Town; Orleans County; Pop. 677; Zip Code 05841; Lat. 44-34-34 N, Long. 072-17-50 W; The town was founded in the 1780s and named in honor of printer Timothy Green.

GROTON, Town; Caledonia County; Pop. 667; Zip Code 05046; Chartered in 1789 and named for Groton, Massachusetts, itself named for Groton in Suffolk, England.

GUILDHALL, Town; Essex County Seat; Pop. 202; Zip Code 05905; Elev. 366; Lat. 44-33-57 N, Long. 071-33-36 W; Granted in 1761 and named for London's famous Guildhall.

GUILFORD, Town; Windham County; Pop. 1,532; Granted in 1754 just before the outbreak of the French and Indian War, and named by Benning Wentworth in honor of the Earl of Guilford.

HALIFAX, Town; Windham County; Pop. 488; Halifax's name honors George Montagu-Dunk, the second Earl of Halifax and a prominent colonial administrator.

HANCOCK, Town; Addison County; Pop. 334; Zip Code 05748; Lat. 43-55-34 N, Long. 072-50-33 W; Hancock's name honors revolutionary patriot John Hancock.

HARDWICK, Town; Caledonia County; Pop. 2,613; Zip Code 05843; Elev. 841; Lat. 44-30-19 N, Long. 072-22-06 W; Chartered after the Revolutionary War and named in honor of Philip Yarke, Earl of Hardwicke.

HARTFORD, Town; Windsor County; Pop. 7,963; Zip Code 05047; Granted in 1761 and named for Hartford, Connecticut.

HARTLAND, Town; Windsor County; Pop. 2,396; Zip Code 05048; Elev. 587; Hartland is named after the city in Connecticut and the Hartland in Devonshire, England.

HIGHGATE, Town; Franklin County; Pop. 2,493; Named by Governor Benning Wentworth for Highgate, a well-known suburb of London.

HINESBURG, Town; Chittenden County; Pop. 2,690; Zip Code 05461; Lat. 44-19-37 N, Long. 073-06-45 W; Settled in the 1780s and given the Christian name of the first child born there, Hine.

HOLLAND, Town; Orleans County; Pop. 473; Holland is named for Samuel Holland, who was the Kings Surveyor General of all the colonies north of Virginia.

HUBBARDTON, Town; Rutland County; Pop. 490; Site of the battle of Hubbardtown in 1777; the town was named for a prosperous Boston merchant, Thomas Hubbard.

HUNTINGTON, Town; Chittenden County; Pop. 1,161; Zip Code 05462; Lat. 44-19-45 N, Long. 072-59-04 W; Granted in 1763 and named for the local Hunt family.

HYDE PARK, Village; Lamoille County Seat; Pop. 2,021 / 651; Zip Code 05655; Lat. 44-35-50 N, Long. 072-36-48 W; The town is named after its original grantee, Captain Jedediah Hyde.

IRA, Town; Rutland County; Pop. 354; Granted in 1781 and named for settler Ira Allen.

IRASBURG, Town; Orleans County; Pop. 870; Zip Code 05845; Elev. 814; Lat. 44-48-06 N, Long. 072-16-49 W; Settled in the 1780s and named for pioneer, Ira Allen.

ISLE LA MOTTE, Town; Grand Isle County; Pop. 393; Zip Code 05463; Elev. 188; Lat. 44-53-13 N, Long. 073-20-28 W; Settled by a French army unit in 1666 and named for its Commander Pierre de St. Paul, Sieur de la Matte. Points of interest include the Shrine of St. Anne, which is the site of the first Vermont settlement.

JACKSONVILLE, Village; Windham County; Pop. 252 / 281; Zip Code 05342; Elev. 1334; Lat. 42-47-47 N, Long. 072-49-15 W; Named in honor of President Andrew Jackson.

JAMAICA, Town; Windham County; Pop. 681; Zip Code 05343; Elev. 732; Lat. 43-06-00 N, Long. 072-46-38 W; The towns name is a Natick Indian word meaning "beaver."

JAY, Town; Orleans County; Pop. 302; Chartered in 1792 and named in honor of Statesman John Jay.

JEFFERSONVILLE, Village; Lamoille County; Pop. 491 / 505; Zip Code 05464; Elev. 459; Lat. 44-38-38 N, Long. 072-49-45 W; Named in honor of Thomas Jefferson.

JERICHO, Town; Chittenden County; Pop. 3,575; Zip Code 05465; Elev. 550; Lat. 44-30-24 N, Long. 072-59-41 W; Founded in 1763 and given the Biblical name of Jericho.

JERICHO, Village; Chittenden County; Pop. 3,575 / 1,405; Elev. 550; Lat. 44-30-06 N, Long. 72-59-13 W. Named for the Biblical City of Jericho.

JOHNSON, Village; Lamoille County; Pop. 2,581 / 1,412; Zip Code 05656; Elev. 516; Lat. 44-38-09 N, Long. 072-40-47 W; Granted in 1782 and named for the second grantee, William Samuel Johnson.

KIRBY, Town; Caledonia County; Pop. 282; Incorporated in 1807 and named for Kirby, England. The name means "a village with a church."

LANDGROVE, Town; Bennington County; Pop. 121; Descriptively named by its first settlers for the many trees covering the land.

LEICESTER, Town; Addison County; Pop. 803; Zip Code 05752; Elev. 352; Lat. 43-51-11 N, Long 073-09-13 W; Named for the town of Leicester in England.

LEMINGTON, Town; Essex County; Pop. 108; Settled in the late 1700s and named for Lemington, England.

LEWIS, Town; Essex County; Founded in 1762 and named for early settlers Nathan, Sevignior, and Timothy Lewis.

LINCOLN, Town; Addison County; Pop. 870; Lincoln's name honors Revolutionary War General Benjamin Lincoln.

LONDONDERRY, Town; Windham County; Pop. 1,510; Zip Code 05148; Elev. 1151; Settled in the late 1700s and named after Londonderry, New Hampshire.

LOWELL, Town; Orleans County; Pop. 573; Zip Code 05847; Elev. 996; Lat. 44-48-04 N, Long. 072-26-55 W; Originally Kellyvale, the towns name was later changed to honor John Lowell, a prominent manufacturer.

LUDLOW, Village; Windsor County; Pop. 2,414 / 1,043; Zip Code 05149; Elev. 1067; Granted in 1761 and named in honor of Henry Herbert, Viscount of Ludlow.

LUNENBURG, Town; Essex County; Pop. 1,138; Zip Code 05906; Elev. 1202; Lat. 44-25-42 N, Long. 071-53-21 W; Named in honor of Prince Ferdinand of Brunswick, a relative of England's King George III.

LYNDON, Town; Caledonia County; Pop. 4,924; Zip Code 05849; Elev. 1706; Lat. 44-30-48 N, Long. 072-01-01 W; Chartered in 1780 and named after Josiah Lyndon Arnold, the son of a town founder. Points of interest include tours of the covered bridges.

LYNDONVILLE, Village; Caledonia County; Pop. 1,401 / 1,304; Zip Code 05851; Elev. 714; Lat. 44-32-13 N, Long. 072-00-25 W; Chartered to a group of Revolutionary War soldiers and named in honor of Josiah Lyndon Arnold, son of one of the founders.

MAIDSTONE, Town; Essex County; Pop. 100; Granted in 1761 and named for Maidstone, England.

MANCHESTER, Town; Bennington County Seat; Pop. 561 / 3,261; Zip Code 05254; Elev. 899; Lat. 43-09-43 N, Long. 073-04-25 W; Granted in the 1760s and named after Manchester, England.

MARLBORO, Town; Windham County; Pop. 695; Zip Code 05344; Lat. 42-52-09 N, Long. 072-43-09 W; A popular colonial name, it honored John Churchill, the great 17th century soldier and Duke of Marlborough.

MARSHFIELD, Town; Washington County; Pop. 1,267; Zip Code 05658; Elev. 857; Lat. 44-21-10 Long. 072-21-10 W; Named after Colonel Issac Marsh, an early landowner.

MENDON, Town; Rutland County; Pop. 1,056; Mendon is named after Mendon, Massachusetts.

MIDDLEBURY, Town; Addison County Seat; Pop. 7,574; Zip Code 05753; Elev. 366; Lat. 44-00-52 N, Long. 073-10-07 W; Three towns were chartered in this area at the same time, one north, one south, and between them: Middlebury.

MIDDLESEX, Town; Washington County; Pop. 1,235; Named by Governor Wentworth after Middlesex, England.

MIDDLETOWN SPRINGS, Town; Rutland County; Pop. 603; Zip Code 05757; Elev. 893; Lat. 43-28-57 N, Long. 073-07-18 W; Incorporated in 1784 and named after Middletown, Connecticut and a local mineral springs.

MILTON, Village; Chittenden County; Pop. 1,578 / 6,829; Zip Code 05468; Lat. 44-38-12 N, Long. 073-06-39 W; Named for a relative of Governor Wentworth.

MONKTON, Town; Addison County; Pop. 1,201; Zip Code 05469; Lat. 44-14-12 N, Long. 073-08-48 W; Granted in 1762 and named in honor of British Soldier, General Robert Monckton.

MONTGOMERY, Town; Franklin County; Pop. 681; Zip Code 05470; Elev. 493; Lat. 44-54-05 N, Long. 072-37-40 W; Established in 1789 and named in honor of Revolutionary War hero, General Richard Montgomery.

MONTPELIER, City; State Capital; Washington County Seat; Pop. 8,241 / 7,686; Zip Code 05602; Elev. 525; Lat. 44-15-30 N, Long. 072-34-14 W; Chartered in 1781 and named for Montpelier, France.

MORETOWN, Town; Washington County; Pop. 1,221; Zip Code 05660; Elev. 602; Lat. 44-15-01 N, Long. 072-45-42 W; The area was chartered in 1763, but wasn't settled until the last years of the 18th century.

MORGAN, Town; Orleans County; Pop. 460; Zip Code 05853; Lat. 44-54-40 N, Long. 072-00-56 W; First named Caldersburgh, the towns name was changed in 1801 to honor another landowner, John Morgan.

MORRISTOWN, Town; Lamoille County; Pop. 4,448; The towns name honors the prominent Morris family from New York State.

MORRISVILLE, Village, Lamoille; Pop. 2,074 / 2,306; Zip Code 05657; Elev. 682; Lat. 44-32-30 N, Long. 072-31-27 W; Settled right after the Revolutionary War and named in honor of the Morris family of New York.

MOUNT HOLLY, Town; Rutland County; Pop. 938; Zip Code 05758; Elev. 1558; Lat. 43-27-14 N, Long. 072-49-07 W; Incorporated in 1792 and named after Mount Holly, New Jersey.

MOUNT TABOR, Town; Rutland County; Pop. 211; Granted as Harwich in 1761, but later renamed to honor Revolutionary War veteran Gideon Tabor.

NEW HAVEN, Town; Addison County; Pop. 1,217; Zip Code 05472; Elev. 455; Lat. 44-07-24 N, Long. 073-09-23 W; The town is named after New Haven, Connecticut.

NEWARK, Town; Caledonia County; Pop. 280; Named by its settlers in the 1780s as "New Ark," referring to new settlement, or project.

NEWBURY, Village; Orange County; Pop. 1,699 / 2,306; Zip Code 05051; Granted in 1763 and named after Newbury, Massachusetts.

NEWFANE, Village; Windham County Seat; Pop. 1,129 / 161; Zip Code 05345; Elev. 536; Lat. 42-59-15 N, Long. 072-39-33 W; Named for John Fane, seventh Earl of Westmorland, and a favored relative of Governor Wentworth.

NEWPORT, City; Orleans County Seat; Pop. 4,756 / 4,261; Zip Code 05855; Elev. 723; Lat. 44-56-19 N, Long. 072-12-31 W; Originally Duncansborough, the name was later changed after Newport, Rhode Island.

NORTH BENNINGTON, Village, Bennington County, Pop. 1,685 / 1,263; Zip Code 05257; Lat. 42-55-44 N, Long. 073-14-38 W; Granted by Governor Benning Wentworth and given his first name.

NORTH HERO, Town; Grand Isle County Seat; Pop. 442; Zip Code 05474; Elev. 365; Lat. 44-49-07 N, Long. 073-17-33 W; Chartered by Revolutionary War heroes Ethan Allen and Samuel Herrick and so descriptively named.

NORTH TROY, Village, Orleans County , Pop. 717 / 770; Zip Code; 05859; Lat. 44-59-51 N, Long. 072-24-24 W; Incorporated as Missisquoi, the name was later changed after Troy, New York.

NORTH WESTMINSTER, Village, Windham County, Pop. 310 / 275; Settled in the 1760s and named after Westminster, England.

NORTHFIELD, Village; Washington County; Pop. 2,016 / 5,435; Zip Code 05663; Elev. 7341; Lat. 44-09-01 N, Long. 072-39-29 W; Named after Northfield, Massachusetts.

NORTON, Town; Essex County; Pop. 184; Established in 1779 and named for the Norton family, who were landowners.

NORWICH, Town; Windsor County; Pop. 2,398; Zip Code 05055; Elev. 537; The town is named after Norwich, Connecticut, itself named for Norwich, England.

OLD BENNINGTON, Village; Pop. 279 / 346; Lat. 42-52-59 N, Long. 73-12-49 W; Old Bennington is the oldest part of the town of Bennington.

ORANGE, Town; Orange County; Pop. 752; The town is named after Orange, Connecticut.

ORLEANS, Village; Orleans County; Pop. 983 / 764; Zip Code 05860; Elev. 740; Lat. 44-48-35 N, Long. 072-12-06 W; Named in honor of Louis Phillipe Joseph, the Duke of Orleans, a hero in the French Revolution.

ORWELL, Town; Addison County; Pop. 901; Zip Code 05760; Elev. 379; Lat. 43-48-15 N, Long. 073-17-53 W; Founded in 1763 and named for Francis Vernon, the first Baron Orwell.

PANTON, Town; Addison County; Pop. 537; Panton was named after the English town of Panton in Lincolnshire.

PAWLET, Town; Rutland County; Pop. 1,244; Zip Code 05761; Elev. 681; Lat. 43-20-48 N, Long. 073-10-49 W; Granted in 1761 and named in honor of Charles Paulet, Duke of Bolton.

PEACHAM, Town; Caledonia County; Pop. 531; Zip Code 05862; Elev. 1,310; Lat. 44-19-42 N, Long. 072-10-19 W; The town is named for the popular heroine in John Gays immensely successful 18th century play *The Beggars Opera*.

PERU, Town; Bennington County; Pop. 312; Zip Code 05152; Granted in 1761 as Bromley, but changed in 1804 after the gold-rich South American country.

PITTSFIELD, Town; Rutland County; Pop. 396; Zip Code 05762; Lat. 43-46-14 N, Long. 072-49-01 W; Chartered in 1781 and named after Pittsfield, Massachusetts.

PITTSFORD, Town; Rutland County; Pop. 2,590; Zip Code 05763; Elev. 530; Lat. 43-42-20 N, Long. 073-01-15 W; Settled in 1769 and named in honor of William Pitt, first Earl of Chatham.

PLAINFIELD, Town; Washington County; Pop. 1,249; Zip Code 05667; Elev. 803; Lat. 44-16-43 N, Long. 072-25-21 W; Incorporated in 1797 by John Chapman and named for his home in Plainfield, Connecticut.

PLYMOUTH, Town; Windsor County; Pop. 405; Zip Code 05056; The towns name recalls and honors Plymouth, Massachusetts, site of the first Pilgrim colony.

POMFRET, Town; Windsor County; Pop. 856; Granted in 1761 and named to honor Thomas Fermor, the first Earl of Pomfret.

POULTNEY, Town; Rutland County; Pop. 3,269 / 3,196; Zip Code 05741; Elev. 432; Lat. 43-31,32 N, Long. 073-12-39 W; Granted in the 1760s and named in honor of the first Earl of Bath, William Poultney.

POWNAL, Town; Bennington County; Pop. 3,269; Zip Code 05261; Elev. 553; Lat. 42-46-03 N, Long. 073-14-11 W; John and Thomas Pownal were original characters of the town. It was named for them.

PROCTOR, Town; Rutland County; Pop. 1,998; Zip Code 05765; Elev. 484; Lat. 43-39-44 N, Long. 073-02-03 W; Famous as a marble quarry area, the town was named in 1882 to honor Redfield Proctor, president of the Vermont Marble Company and governor of Vermont.

PROCTORSVILLE, Village; Windsor County; Pop. 481; Zip Code 05153; Named for an early settler.

PUTNEY, Town; Windham County; Pop. 1,850; Zip Code 05346; Lat. 42-58-36 N, Long. 072-31-09 W; Named by Benning Wentworth for Putney, England.

QUECHEE, Unincorporated; Zip Code 05059; Elev. 565; Located in Hartford.

RANDOLPH, Town; Orange County; Pop. 4,689; Zip Code 05060; Elev. 684; Probably named for political advantage to honor Edmund Randolph, the well-known Virginia statesman.

READING, Town; Windsor County; Pop. 647; Zip Code 05062; This Vermont town was named after Reading, Massachusetts, which was named after Reading, England.

READSBORO, Town; Bennington County; Pop. 638; Zip Code 05350; Elev. 1190; Lat. 42-45-35 N, Long. 072-56-53 W; Founded in 1770 and named after the first landowner, John Reade.

RICHFORD, Village; Essex County; Pop. 2,206 / 1,405; Elev. 1477; Zip Code 05476; Lat. 44-59-44 N, Long. 72-40-24 W.

RICHMOND, Town; Chittenden County; Pop. 3,159; Zip Code 05477; Elev. 319; Lat. 44-24-17 N, Long. 072-59-40 W; Incorporated in 1794 and named in honor of Charles Lennox, the third Duke of Richmond.

RIPTON, Town; Addison County; Pop. 327; Ripton is named after Ripton in Huntingdonshire, England.

ROCHESTER, Town; Windsor County; Pop. 1,054; Zip Code 05767; Lat. 43-52-27 N, Long. 072-49-06 W; Chartered in 1781 and named after Rochester, Massachusetts.

ROCKINGHAM, Town; Windham County; Pop. 5,538; The towns name honors Charles Watson-Wentworth, the second Marquis of Rockingham.

ROXBURY, Town; Washington County; Pop. 452; Zip Code 05669; Elev. 1010; Lat. 44-05-45 N, Long. 072-43-53 W; Roxbury is named after Roxbury, Massachusetts.

ROYALTON, Town; Windsor County; Pop. 2,100; Named in 1769 by acting Governor Cadwallader Colden to honor King George III, i.e. Royal Town.

RUPERT, Town; Bennington County; Pop. 605; Zip Code 05768; Elev. 839; Lat. 43-15-33 N, Long. 073-13-29 W; Granted in 1761 and named in honor of Prince Rupert (1619-82) Count Palatine of Rhine and Duke of Cumberland.

RUTLAND, City; Rutland County Seat; Pop. 18,436 / 16,649; Zip Code 05701; Elev. 648; Lat. 43-36-29 N, Long. 072-58-35 W; Named by Governor Wentworth in honor of John Manners, the third Duke of Rutland.

RUTLAND, Town; Rutland County; Pop. 3,781; Lat. 43-7-49 N, Long. 72-58-40 W; Chartered in 1761 and settled in the 1770s.

RYEGATE, Town; Caledonia County; Pop. 1,000; Named after Reigote, England by its settlers in the 1760s and subsequently underwent a spelling corruption.

SALISBURY, Town; Pop. 1,024; Lat. 43-55-00 N, Long. 73-06-46 W; Chartered in 1761.

SANDGATE, Town; Bennington County; Pop. 278; Lat. 43-09-12 N, Long. 73-11-22 W; Named for the town of Sandgate in England.

SAXTONS RIVER, Village; Windham County; Pop. 512; Zip Code 05154; Elev. 528; Named for an early settler and the location of the village.

SEARSBURG, Town; Bennington County; Pop. 72; Searsburg is probably named for Revolutionary War patriot Issac Sears.

SHAFTSBURY, Town; Bennington County; Pop. 3,001; Zip Code 05262; Lat. 43-07-53 N, Long. 073-04-24 W; Shaftsbury is named after Shaftesburg, England.

SHARON, Town; Windsor County; Pop. 828; Zip Code 05065; Elev. 501; The town is named after Sharon, Connecticut.

SHEFFIELD, Town; Caledonia County; Pop. 435; Zip Code 05866; Lat. 44-36-05 N, Long. 072-06-57 W; The town is named after Sheffield, Massachusetts.

SHELBURNE, Town; Chittenden County; Pop. 5,000; Zip Code 05482; Elev. 148; Lat. 44-22-46 N, Long. 073-14-06 W; Granted by Governor Wentworth and named in honor of the Earl of Shelburne.

SHELDON, Town; Franklin County; Pop. 1,618; Zip Code 05483; Elev. 373; Lat. 44-52-59 N, Long. 072-56-33 W; Originally named Hungerford. The town's name was changed in 1792 to honor Revolutionary War veteran Colonel Elisha Sheldon.

SHERBURNE, Town; Rutland County; Pop. 891; Originally named Killington; the name was changed in 1800 to honor one of the first grantees, Colonel Benjamin Sherburne.

SHOREHAM, Town; Addison County; Pop. 972; Zip Code 05770; Elev. 333; Lat. 43-53-36 N, Long. 073-18-47 W; Founded in 1766 and named for Shoreham-by-the-Sea in England.

SHREWSBURY, Town; Rutland County; Pop. 866; Granted in 1761 and named for the Earldom of Shrewsbury.

SOMERSET, Town; Windham County; Pop. 2; Governor Benning Wentworth named the town for the County of Somerset in England.

SOUTH BURLINGTON, City; Chittenden County; Pop. 14,257; Elev. 113; Zip Code 05401; Lat. 44-29-02 N, Long. 073-13-12 W. Incorporated Burlington in 1864 and named after the Earl of Burlington.

SOUTH HERO, Town; Grand Isle County; Pop. 1,188; Zip Code 05486; Elev. 152; Lat. 44-38-43 N, Long. 073-19-00 W; Founded by Revolutionary War hero Ethan Allen and Samuel Herrick and so descriptively named.

SPRINGFIELD, Town; Windsor County; Pop. 10,190; Zip Code 05156; Elev. 410; Chartered in the 1760s and named after Springfield, Massachusetts.

ST. ALBANS, City; Franklin County Seat; Pop. 7,371506; Zip Code 05478; Elev. 429; Lat. 44-48-42 N, Long. 073-05-03 W; Governor Benning Wentworth granted the town in 1763. Named after St. Albans in Hertfordshire, England.

ST. GEORGE, Town; Chittenden County; Pop. 677; St. George was named in honor of England's King George III.

ST. JOHNSBURY, Town; Caledonia County Seat; Pop. 7,938; Zip Code 05819; Elev. 588; Lat. 44-25-15 N, Long. 072-01-14 W; Chartered in 1786 and named to honor author Michel Guillaume St. Jean Creveldeur, who wrote under the pen name Hector St. John. The first settler was Jonathan Arnold, who built a house here in 1787. The town was organized in 1790. Maple sugar production has been one of the most productive industries in the area. Railroads created growth after about 1851.

STAMFORD, Town; Bennington County; Pop. 773; Granted in 1753 and named by Governor Benning Wentworth in honor of Harry Grey, Fourth Earl of Stamford.

STANNARD, Town; Caledonia County; Pop. 142; Originally named Goshen, the name was changed in 1867 to honor Vermont's Civil War hero General George Stannard.

STARKSBORO, Town; Addison County; Pop. 1,336; Zip Code 05487; Elev. 615; Lat. 44-13-41 N, Long. 073-03-38 W; Starksboro is named for Revolutionary War General John Stark.

STOCKBRIDGE, Town; Windsor County; Pop. 508; Zip Code 05772; Elev. 857; Lat. 43-47-02 N, Long. 072-45-16 W; Stockbridge is named after Stockbridge, Massachusetts, itself named after Stockbridge, England.

STOWE, Town; Lamoille County; Pop. 2,991; Zip Code 05672; Elev. 732; Lat. 44-27-54 N, Long. 072-43-05 W; Granted in 1763 and named after Stowe, Massachusetts.

STRAFFORD, Town; Orange County; Pop. 731; Zip Code 05072; The town was named by Governor Benning Wentworth for his family in England, who held the Earldom of Strafford.

STRATTON, Town; Windham County; Pop. 122; The town is named after Stratton in Cornwall, England.

SUDBURY, Town, Rutland County; Pop. 380; Granted by Governor Benning Wentworth in 1763 and named for Sudbury in Middlesex, England.

SUNDERLAND, Town; Bennington County; Pop. 768; Sunderland was named in honor of George Spencer, Sixth Earl of Sunderland.

SUTTON, Town; Caledonia County; Pop. 667; Zip Code 05867; Elev. 1152; Lat. 44-38-00 N, Long. 072-01-42 W; Chartered in 1782 as Billymead but was renamed in the early 1800s after Sutton, Massachusetts.

SWANTON, Town; Franklin County; Pop. 5,141 / 2,732; Zip Code 05488; Elev. 157; Lat. 44-55-09 N, Long. 073-07-13 W; The town's name honors British naval officer William Swanton.

THETFORD, Town; Orange County; Pop. 2,186; Zip Code 05074; The town was named in honor of Augustus Henry Fitzroy, Viscount Thetford.

TINMOUTH, Town; Rutland County; Pop. 406; Granted in 1761 and named after Tynemouth, England.

TOPSHAM, Town; Orange County; Pop. 767; Zip Code 05076; The town is named after Topsham, Maine.

TOWNSHEND, Town; Windham County; Pop. 849; Zip Code 05353; Elev. 574; Lat. 43-02-54 N, Long. 072-40-04 W; Named by Benning Wentworth to honor the prominent British political family.

TROY, Town; Orleans County; Pop. 1,498; Zip Code 05868; Elev. 752; Lat. 44-54-13 N, Long. 072-24-21 W; Incorporated in 1801 and later named after Troy, New York.

TUNBRIDGE, Town; Orange County; Pop. 925; Zip Code 05077; Settled in the late 1700s and named in honor of William Henry Nassau du Zuylestein, Viscount of Tunbridge.

UNDERHILL, Town; Chittenden County; Pop. 2,172; Zip Code 05489; Elev. 706; Lat. 44-31-36 N, Long. 072-56-42 W; Settled in the late 1700s and named after the local Underhill family.

VERGENNES, City; Addison County; Pop. 2,273 / 2,959; Zip Code 05491; Elev. 205; Lat. 44-10-08 N, Long. 073-15-05 W; The third oldest incorporated city in the United States, it is named in honor of Charles Gravier, Comte De Vergennes, who as French foreign affairs minister gave assistance to the colonies in the Revolutionary War.

VERNON, Town; Windham County; Pop. 1,175; Zip Code 05354; Elev. 301; Lat. 42-45-44 N, Long. 072-30-51 W; The towns name recalls Washington's estate, Mount Vernon.

VERSHIRE, Town; Orange County; Pop. 442; Zip Code 05079; Elev. 1268; Chartered in 1791 and given a boundary name, Vermont and New Hampshire.

VICTORY, Town; Essex County; Pop. 56; Founded in 1780 and named for the anticipated victory over the British in the Revolutionary War.

WAITSFIELD, Town; Washington County; Pop. 1,300; Zip Code 05673; Elev. 698; Lat. 44-11-25 N, Long. 072-49-31 W; Chartered in 1782 and named for prominent citizen, Benjamin Wait. Population growth occurred in the late 1800s, due to uses of waterpower from the river, primarily for the mill industry.

WALDEN, Town; Caledonia County; Pop. 575; The towns name remembers original character Samuel Walden.

WALLINGFORD, Town; Rutland County; Pop. 1,893; Zip Code 05773; Lat. 43-28-19 N, Long. 072-58-39 W; Settled in the 1770s and named after Wallingford, Connecticut. The town in Connecticut was named after Wallingford, England.

WALTHAM, Town; Addison County; Pop. 394; The town's founders named it after Waltham, Massachusetts.

WARDSBORO, Town; Windham County; Pop. 505; Zip Code 05355; Elev. 995; Lat. 43-02-27 N, Long. 072-47-29 W; Among the original grantee in 1780 was William Ward. The town is named after him.

WARREN, Town; Washington County; Pop. 956; Zip Code 05674; Lat. 44-06-49 N, Long. 072-51-29 W; Warren was named in honor of Doctor Joseph Warren, revolutionary hero and patriot who was killed at the battle of Bunker Hill. Chartered in 1890, the area was settled primarily for its excellent farmland. Dams and mills were built in the early 1800s, attracting a larger population. During the 1900s, the economy shifted slightly to maple sugar production.

WARRENS GORE, Unincorporated; Essex County; Pop. 2; Lat. 44-54-08 N, Long. 71-52-57 W.

WASHINGTON, Town; Orange County; Pop. 855; Zip Code 05675; Lat. 44-06-24 N, Long. 072-26-10 W; Named, like many other places in the United States, after George Washington.

WATERBURY, Village; Washington County; Pop. 4,465 / 1,694; Zip Code 05676; Elev. 428; Lat. 44-17-37 N, Long. 072-45-20 W; Many early settlers came from Waterbury, Connecticut, so the new town was named after the old.

WATERFORD, Town; Caledonia County; Pop. 882; Waterford is either named descriptively as having a Ford across the Connecticut River within the town, or after Waterford, Ireland.

WATERVILLE, Town; Lamoille County; Pop. 470; Zip Code 05492; Elev. 556; Lat. 44-41-27 N, Long. 072-46-17 W; Incorporated in 1824 and descriptively named for the Lamoille River, which flows through the area.

WELLS RIVER, Village; Orange County; Pop. 396 / 420; Zip Code 05081; Descriptively named for its location.

WELLS, Town; Rutland County; Pop. 815; Zip Code 05774; Lat. 43-24-56 N, Long. 073-12-24 W; Wells was named for Wells in Somerset, England.

WEST BURKE, Village; Caledonia County; Pop. 353 / 366; Lat. 44-38-37 N, Long. 71-58-49 W; Named for its location near Burke.

WEST FAIRLEE, Town; Orange County; Pop. 427; Zip Code 05083; Elev. 741; Created out of the town of Fairlee and so descriptively named.

WEST HAVEN, Town; Rutland County; Pop. 253, Originally port of Fair Haven, it was renamed in 1792.

WEST RUTLAND, Town; Rutland County; Pop. 2,351; Zip Code 05777; Elev. 492; Lat. 43-35-51 N, Long. 073-02-50 W; Incorporated in 1886 from the town of Rutland and so descriptively named.

WESTFIELD, Town; Orleans County; Pop. 418; Zip Code 05874; Elev. 625; Lat. 44-53-30 N, Long. 072-25-45 W; Chartered in the 1760s and named in honor of William West of Rhode Island.

WESTFORD, Town; Chittenden County; Pop. 1,413; Zip Code 05494; Elev. 467; Lat. 44-36-38 N, Long. 073-00-41 W; Granted in 1763 and named as the most westerly of the towns granted at that time.

WESTMINSTER, Village; Windham County; Pop. 2,493 / 417; Zip Code 05158; The town was named after Westminster, England.

WESTMORE, Town; Orleans County; Pop. 257; Founded in the 1780s and named for its location on the then western frontier.

WEYBRIDGE, Town; Addison County; Pop. 667; Weybridge is named after the town in Surrey, England.

WHEELOCK, Town; Caledonia County; Pop. 444; Chartered in 1785 and named for the Reverend Eleazar Wherlock, the founder of Dartmouth College.

WHITING, Town; Addison County; Pop. 379; Zip Code 05778; Elev. 395; Lat. 43-51-47 N, Long. 073-12-07 W; The original settlers included five men with the last name Whiting. The town is named after them.

WHITINGHAM, Town; Windham County; Pop. 1,043; Zip Code 05361; Elev. 1689; Lat. 42-47-19 N, Long. 072-52-52 W; Nathan Whiting was the first grantee. The town is named for him.

WILLIAMSTOWN, Town; Orange County; Pop. 2,284; Zip Code 05679; Lat. 44-07-15 N, Long. 072-32-34 W; Chartered in 1781 and named after Williamstown, Massachusetts.

WILLISTON, Town; Chittenden County; Pop. 3,843; Zip Code 05495; Elev. 501; Lat. 44-26-13 N, Long. 073-04-12 W; The town was granted in 1763 and named for a wealthy Quaker from Long Island, Samuel Willis.

WILMINGTON, Town; Windham County; Pop. 1,808; Zip Code 05363; Lat. 42-52-07 N, Long. 072-52-07 W; Governor Benning Wentworth named the town for an old friend, Spencer Compton, First Earl of Wilmington. It was first settled in the mid-1700s. Population expanded when grist mills were established in the 1760s. Population grew again in 1828 with the construction of a highway, and again when a creamery was built in the 1880s.

WINDHAM, Town; Windham County; Pop. 223; Incorporated in 1795 and named in honor of Charles Wyndham, who had been a close friend of Benning Wentworth.

WINHALL, Town; Bennington County; Pop. 327; Settled after the Revolutionary War and possibly named for Winhall, England.

WINOOSKI, City; Chittenden County; Pop. 6,318 / 6,609; Incorporated in 1921 and named after the adjacent Winooski River.

WOLCOTT, Town, Lamoille County, Pop. 986; Zip Code 05680; Lat. 44-32-44 N, Long. 072-27-26 W; Chartered in 1781 and named in honor of Revolutionary War statesman and soldier, General Oliver Wolcott.

WOODBURY, Town, Washington County; Pop. 573; Zip Code 05681; Elev. 1,164; Lat. 44-26-28 N, Long. 072-24-55 W; Founded in 1781 and named for Colonel Ebeneser Wood.

WOODFORD, Town; Bennington County; Pop. 314; Granted in 1753 and named after Woodford in Essex, England.

WOODSTOCK, Town; Windsor County Seat; Pop. 3,214; Zip Code 05682; Elev. 779; Lat. 44-22-17 N, Long. 072-33-14 W; Governor Benning Wentworth named the town to honor the ancient English city of Woodstock in Oxfordshire, England.

WORCESTER, Town; Washington County; Pop. 727; Zip Code 05682; Elev. 779; Lat. 44-22-17 N, Long. 072-33-14 W; Established in 1763 and named for Worcester, Massachusetts.

VIRGINIA
Old Dominion

American Revolution Reenactment at Yorktown

Bald Eagles in Caledon Natural Area in King George

GOVERNOR
Jim Gilmore

Richmond Skyline

Natural Bridge
near Lexington

The Barter Theatre
Abingdon

Busch Gardens
Williamsburg

INTRODUCTION

Virginia has always been endowed with special historical, cultural, and social significance. Here is an almost perfectly balanced region. Famous men have walked this land; George Washington was born here; Mount Vernon, the most famous home in America, still stands.

The State has five distinctive topographical regions, which include the Tidewater or coastal plain; the Piedmont or Picdmont Plateau; the Blue Ridge Mountains; the ridge and valley region; and the Cumberland Plateau. The last three areas are part of the Appalachian Mountains.

Tidewater is the oldest section of Virginia, and one of the liveliest sections of the State. There are miles and miles of sandy beaches, and years and years of a rich and colorful history. The Eastern Shore area of Tidewater is a seventy-mile peninsula once visited by the notorious pirate, Blackbea Rd. One side of the Eastern Shore is bathed by the Atlantic Ocean, the other by the Chesapeake Bay.

In the Piedmont region, extending southwest from Alexandria in the north, is the heart of early Virginia. It encompasses the spirited old capital city of Richmond, dramatic Civil War battlefields, and many famous historic homes.

Through the Blue Ridge Mountains region is the Shenandoah River, which runs between these mountains and the Appalachians. One of the State's earliest towns was named after the river. Shenandoah, a name famous in legend and song, is an Indian word meaning "daughter of the stars." To follow the Skyline Drive across the highest crests of the Blue Ridge Mountains is literally to ride along the very top of the State. This region is known as Virginia's crowning glory.

The Shenandoah Valley, 200 miles long, is in the ridge and valley section of the State. This section continues to the West Virginia border with a series of hills and valleys that run northeast southwest. In the extreme southwest region of Virginia lies a small part of the Cumberland Plateau of Kentucky.

The outline of the State is roughly the shape of a triangle. The total area of Virginia is 42,769 square miles; of which 3,171 square miles is water surface.

STATE NAME

Historians generally agree that Virginia was named by Queen Elizabeth herself in commemoration of her unmarried state. The name was given about 1584 or 1585 to the woman popularly called the "*Virgin Queen.*"

Thomas Nelson Page says: "Elizabeth graciously accorded the privileges proposed by Raleigh, giving to this new land a name in honor of her maiden state, and it was called Virginia. Raleigh was knighted for his service and given the title of 'Lord and Governor of Virginia.'"

Henry Howe says: "The glowing description given by the adventurers, on their return, of the beauty of the country, the fertility of the soil, and pleasantness of the climate, delighted the queen, and induced her to name the country of which she had taken possession, Virginia, in commemoration of her unmarried life."

The origin of the word Virginia is the feminine form of the Latin word *virginius*.

STATE NICKNAME

Nicknames for Virginia include Old Dominion, Ancient Dominion, Cavalier State, Mother of States, Mother of the Presidents, and the Mother of Statesmen.

The names of Old Dominion and Ancient Dominion are still widely applied to Virginia, having originated in Colonial days. About the year 1663, after Charles Stuart had become King of England, he quartered the Arms of Virginia on his royal shield; thus ranking Virginia along with his other dominions of Scotland, France, and Ireland. Historians say that the new king elevated Virginia to the position of a dominion "by quartering its arms (the old seal of the Virginia Company) on his royal shield with the arms of Scotland and Ireland, and that the burgesses were very proud of this distinction and, remembering that they were the oldest as well as the most faithful of the Stuart settlements in America, adopted the name of 'The Old Dominion.'"

Colonel Richard Lee of the Colony of Virginia is said to have visited Charles Stuart while he was in exile in the city of Brussels about 1658. Charles was proclaimed King Charles II of England on May 8, 1660, and the Virginians accepted him as their king on September the 20th, following his ascension. This pleased King Charles so much that he referred to the people of this colony as "the best of his distant children," and elevated the colony of Virginia to the position of a dominion.

After the restoration of Charles II, a new seal for Virginia, adopted about 1663, had the same motto (*En dat Virginia quintam*), the effect of which was to rank Virginia by the side of his Majesty's other dominions, Scotland, France, and Ireland. It is said that in these circumstances originated the famous epithet 'Old Dominion.'

Virginia's nickname, the Cavalier State, is derived from the name of the Cavaliers who came over and settled there during and shortly after the time of Charles I.

The sobriquet, the Mother of Presidents, alludes to the fact that so many of the early presidents of the United States were native Virginians.

Virginia was called the Mother of States because she was the first of the states to be settled. The original territory of Virginia was split up to make West Virginia, Ohio, Kentucky, Illinois, Indiana, Wisconsin and a part of Minnesota; then she came to be known as the Mother of Statesmen.

Virginians have been nicknamed Beagles or Beadles, Cavaliers, F.F.V.'s, Sorebacks and Tuckahoes. The sobriquet Beadles or Beagles originated during colonial days, due to the fact that Virginians, following the English custom, used beadles in their courts. The second nickname, Cavaliers, alludes to Virginia's English Cavalier settlers. F.F.V.'s stands for the First Families of Virginia, of which the early colonial people of the State were very proud. The abbreviation was of northern origin, and was in common use prior to the Civil War.

Tradition gives two accounts of the origin of the nickname Soreback applied to Virginians. One is that the Virginians were so hospitable that they slapped one another on the backs until their backs become sore. The other is that the people in the southern part of the State grew so much cotton that it made their backs sore to pick it. North Carolinians seemed to be the originators of this account.

The nickname Tuckahoes was originally applied only to the poorer white people living in the lower part of the State. This nickname was often heard during the Civil War because poverty often drove these Virginians to eat tuckahoe (an Old World plant whose rootstocks were used as food by the Indians).

STATE SEAL

The present seal of the Commonwealth of Virginia was adopted by an act of the General Assembly of the State of Virginia, approved March 24, 1930.

The act reads as follows: "The great seal of the Commonwealth of Virginia shall consist of two metallic discs, two and one fourth inches in diameter, with an ornamental border one fourth of an inch wide, with such words and figures engraved there on as will, when used, produce impressions to be described as follows: On the obverse, Virtus, the genius of the Commonwealth, dressed as an Amazon, resting on a spear in her right hand, point downward, touching the earth; and holding in her left hand, a sheathed sword, or parazonium, pointing upward; her head erect and face upturned; her left foot on the form of Tyranny represented by the prostrate body of a man, with his head to her left, his fallen crown nearby, a broken chain in his left hand, and a scourge in his right. Above the group and within the border conforming therewith, shall be the word 'Virginia,' and, in the space below, on a curved line, shall be the motto, 'Sic Semper Tyrannis.' On the reverse, shall be placed a group consisting of Libertas, holding a wand and pileus in her right hand; on her right, Aeternitas, with a globe and phoenix in her right hand; on the left of Libertas, Ceres, with a cornucopia in her left hand, and an ear of wheat in her right; over this device, in a curved line, the word 'Perseverando.'"

The act continues as follows:

"(a) The governor is hereby authorized and directed to cause a new great seal of the Commonwealth to be constructed and engraved, with all reasonable dispatch, in strict conformity with the foregoing description, by artists and engravers of high rank in their profession and under the supervision of the art commission of Virginia, and when completed, to also have constructed end engraved a new lesser seal of the Commonwealth in accordance with section twenty-eight of the Code of Virginia. The governor shall, after said seals shall have been completed, and approved by him, proclaim the same, by such means as he may deem sufficient, to be the true great seal and lesser seal of the Commonwealth.

"(b) The great and lesser seals now in use in the office of the secretary of the Commonwealth are hereby declared to be the true great and lesser seals of the Commonwealth for the time being, and to so continue and be used as such, until the new seals shall be completed and proclaimed as herein provided for, and all official acts done hereunder, in the name of the Commonwealth, are hereby declared to be valid in so far as the affixing of the seal of the State thereto, may have been, or may be, a necessary part of the due execution, or performance thereof.

"(c) Any and all seals now under the care of the secretary of the Commonwealth shall, after the completion and proclamation of the new seals herein provided for, be canceled by quartering the same with two straight lines crossing at right angles at the center of the discs, and cut at least as deep as the figures thereon, which seals so canceled shall be safely kept in the office of the secretary of the Commonwealth and at least three clear impressions thereof filed with the State librarian to be by him duly indexed and safely kept in a suitable place.

"(d) The new, and permanent, seals of the Commonwealth, herein provided for shall, when completed, be kept and used as provided by law, and at least three clear impressions thereof shall be made and filed with the State librarian to be by him kept and displayed in some suitable place in the State library, for public inspection.

"(e) A sum sufficient, not to exceed fifteen hundred dollars, is hereby appropriated, out of any money in the treasury not otherwise appropriated, to meet the necessary expenses of carrying out the provisions of this act."

The Proclamation by the Governor, proclaiming the new seal of the Commonwealth of Virginia, reads as follows:

"Whereas it is provided by section twenty-eight of the Code of Virginia that 'The lesser seal of the Commonwealth shall be one and nine-sixteenth inches in diameter, and have engraved thereon the device and inscriptions contained in the obverse of the great seal,'

"Now, therefore, in conformity with the provisions of section twenty-seven of the Code of Virginia, I do hereby proclaim the first of the said seals, herein above described, to be the great seal of the Commonwealth, and the second of the said seals, to be the lesser seal of the Commonwealth.

"Given under my hand and under the lesser seal of the Commonwealth, at Richmond, this 2nd day of December, in the year of our Lord one thousand, nine hundred and thirty-one, and in the one hundred and fifty-sixth year of the Commonwealth."

This was signed by the Governor, John Garland Pollard, and Peter Saunders, Secretary of the Commonwealth.

STATE FLAG

By an act of the Legislature of Virginia, approved March 24, 1930, the official flag of Virginia was adopted as follows: "The Flag of the Commonwealth shall hereafter be made of bunting or merino. It shall be a deep blue field, with a circular white center of the same material. Upon this circle shall be painted or embroidered, to show on both sides alike, the coat of arms of the State, as described in section twenty-seven of the Code of Virginia, as amended by this act, for the obverse of the great seal of the Commonwealth; and there shall be a white silk fringe on the outer edge, furthest from the flagstaff. This shall be known and respected as the flag of Virginia."

STATE MOTTO

Virginia's motto, Sic *Semper Tyrannis*, is translated to mean "Thus Ever to Tyrants." This is the original motto recommended for the seal of Virginia by George Mason to the Virginia Convention in 1776. It evokes the sentiment for independence among the colonists.

The obverse of the seal of Virginia has Virtus with her foot on a prostrate tyrant, and the motto suggests that all tyrants will meet with such treatment. Robert Hay, in speaking of Virginia's seal, said: "Its motto, Sic semper tyrannis, so appropriate for Richard Henry Lee, had a melancholy fame in connection with the murder of Lincoln."

On the exergon of the reverse of the first seal of Virginia adopted by the convention of delegates held at Williamsburg in July 1776 appeared the motto, *Deus Nobis Pace Ohm Fecit*. This motto is found in Virgil's Eclogues, Book 1, line 6. It means "God gave us this freedom." The motto was changed to *Perseverando* by an act of the General Assembly passed in October 1779.

STATE BIRD

In 1950, the cardinal (*Cardinalis cardinalis*) was designated the official State bird of Virginia by a legislative act. Previous to this, the robin was considered the official State bird.

The cardinal ranges in the eastern United States, west to the Great Plains, southern Arizona, and northwestern Mexico, and south through Georgia to the Gulf States.

Total length of the cardinal is 7½ to eight inches; its tail length is four inches. A member of the finch species, it is crested and thick-billed. Its tail is longer than its short and rounded wings. Adult males are bright red, except for a black patchy band from the eye to the throat on both sides of the bill. The female is brownish above and dull tawny or pale buff below, with a dull grayish patch on the face and throat. The crest, wings, and tail are dull reddish in color, and the under wing feathers are pinkish red.

Cardinal builds their nests in shrubs and bushes, sometimes in areas in close proximity to humans. Eggs are whitish with brown spots; the incubation period lasts between twelve to thirteen days. Both parents attend to the young with frequent feedings of insects. As the young birds mature, they become primarily fruit and grain eaters, although insects still make up a third of their diet. The cardinal is a colorful bird. Its songs are loud, flutelike whistles, the trills lasting about three seconds.

STATE FLOWER

Virginia, by an act of her General Assembly on March 6, 1918, designated the flower of the American dogwood, (*Cornus florida*), to be the official floral emblem of the State. The flowering dogwood is also known as boxwood, white cornel, Indian arrow wood, and nature's mistake.

The dogwood is a small tree or shrub, with greenish yellow flowers and scarlet fruit. It is found from Maine to Florida, and from Minnesota to Texas. In fall, its red leaves brighten the landscape.

The American dogwood was selected as the State flower because it is so prevalent in Virginia, and because it adds beauty to the Virginia landscape, especially in the spring. Although the blossom of the American dogwood may vary in color from white to rose-red, both the white and the pink varieties are found growing in the State. Although the act adopting the Virginia floral emblem does not specify what color it should be, the dogwood with white flowers is more generally found throughout the State.

STATE TREE

The flowering dogwood was designated the official State tree of Virginia in 1956.

The flowering dogwood is also known as the dogwood, boxwood, false box-dogwood, New England boxwood, flowering cornel, and cornel. It is native to the Eastern half of the United States and southern Ontario.

The flowering dogwood is a small tree with dark reddish brown bark, broken into small squares or rounded blocks. Leaves are paired, elliptical or oval, short pointed, and from three to six inches long; their edges appear to be smooth, but are minutely toothed; they are bright green and nearly smooth above, and are whitish and slightly hairy beneath. They turn bright scarlet in the fall. Greenish-brown flowers grow in a dense head with four showy, white, petal-like bracts from 2¼ to four inches in diameter; they bloom in the early spring. The egg-shaped fruits are three-eighths inches long; they are bright scarlet, shiny, fleshy, and have one or two seeds.

STATE SONG

In 1940, the composition entitled "Carry Me Back to Old Virginia," with music composed by James Bland, was adopted by the General Assembly as the official song of the Commonwealth of Virginia. However, in 1970, an attempt was made to repeal the song, as it was determined that the lyrics glorified slavery. In 1997, Virginia's House of Delegates voted to retire the song, after the State Senate had also voted to retire it earlier in the year.

Two other musical compositions have often been used in some parts of the Commonwealth at public gatherings or patriotic occasions. The first is "Call of Virginia," with words written by Lillian Smith and music composed by B.I. Gilmer. This song was published and copyrighted by B.T. Gilmer in 1926. A second popular and widely used song is "Old Virginia," with lyrics by Dr. John W. Wayland, and music by Will H. Ruebush. The song was first published by the Ruebush-Kieffer Company in Dayton, Virginia as a special feature for a collection of State and national songs entitled, *Songs of the People*.

STATE LICENSE PLATE

On June 1, 1906, Carl Leroy Armentrout of Staunton became the first Virginian to register his car, receiving a black and white enamel plate. The State experimented with a variety of materials for the manufacture of plates through the years, including fiber plate in 1925 and fiberboard in 1944. However, both of these plates were apparently appealing to goats, which used them for food. Metal plates became the standard. Aluminum plates have been used since 1973.

The current Virginia plate is a simple blue-on-white plate. "Virginia" is centered at the top in lighter blue than the blue of the license plate number. However, there are several other plates that can be registered, including a "Heritage" plate that depicts a cardinal, the State bird, perched on a branch of the State tree, the flowering dogwood; all are set in a light background with deep blue numerals, and "Virginia" is centered across the bottom. A plate is also issued, and features an ocean scene of blue water, shore, green land, and blue mountains, all on a light blue background with lettering in dark blue.

STATE POSTAGE STAMP

The U.S. Postal Service issued a booklet of fifteen-cent stamps on February 7, 1980 in Lubbock, Texas. The stamps depicted five historic windmills of the United States. An unlimited number of the booklets were printed with the windmills of Illinois, Massachusetts, Rhode Island, Virginia, and the southwestern United States. The Virginia stamp shows the Robertston Windmill in Williamsburg. All the windmill stamps were designed by Ronald C. Sharpe, and engraved by K. Kipperman and A. Saavedra.

OTHER STATE DESIGNATIONS

Over the years, the Legislature has adopted several additional symbols to represent the Commonwealth. They include the official beverage as milk (1982); the official folk dance as square dancing (1991); the insect as the tiger swallowtail butterfly (*Papilio glaucus Linne*) (1991); and the official shell as oyster shell (*Crassoostraea virginica*) (1974).

STATE CAPITOL

The Virginia General Assembly, the oldest law-making body in the Western Hemisphere, held its first official session at Jamestown in 1619. In 1699, the capital was moved to Williamsburg, and in 1779, it was moved permanently to Richmond.

In 1785, Thomas Jefferson was asked to consult an architect for a design for the capitol. Jefferson chose Charles Louis Clerisseau, an architect who shared in his interest of classical buildings. With Jefferson's assistance, Clerisseau modeled the capitol after a Roman temple in France known as "La Maison Carree." The cornerstone was laid in 1785. The central building was completed in 1792; however, the General Assembly first met in the new capitol in 1788. The two-story brick construction is rectangular, with a portico secured by Ionic columns. Wings were added to each side of the original building between 1904 and 1906.

The structure is one hundred and forty-six feet long, eighty-four and one-half feet wide, and fifty-three feet high, not including the added wings. The cost of the original building was about one hundred and twelve thousand dollars. In 1962, extensive renovations and remodeling were approved, and were completed in 1963.

OTHER FACTS ABOUT VIRGINIA

Total area: 40,767 square miles
Land area: 39,704 square miles
Water area: 1,063 square miles
Average elevation: 950 feet
Highest point: Mount Rogers, 5,729 feet
Lowest point: Atlantic Ocean, sea level
Highest temperature: 110 degrees Fahrenheit
Lowest temperature: -30 degrees Fahrenheit
Population in 1990: 6,187,358
Population density in 1990: 156.26 persons per
Population 1980-1990: +15.7 percent change
Population projected for 2000: 6,877,000
Black population in 1990: 1,162,994
Hispanic population in 1990: 160,288
Native American population in 1990: 15,282
White population in 1990: 4,791,739
Capital: Richmond
Admitted to Union: June 25, 1788
Order of Statehood: 10
Electoral votes: 13

CHRONOLOGY

1585 August 17. Sir Walter Raleigh's first settlers reach Roanoke Island in Virginia.

1591 Roanoke Island settlers disappear; colony is abandoned.

1606 April 10. James I grants joint charter to two companies to colonize 'Virginia.'

1607 May 14. First permanent English settlement in New World is established at Jamestown.
August. Colonists of Plymouth Company land at Kennebec (Maine), but make only temporary settlement.
December. Captain John Smith is saved by Pocahontas.

1608 January 12. Arrival of 'First Supply.'
May 23. London Company is granted second charter.

1609-10 'Starving Time;' between September and June, population drops from about 500 to 60.

1610 May 23. Sir Thomas Gates, first governor, arrives at Jamestown.
June 8. Colonists abandon Jamestown, return upon arrival of Thomas West, Lord Delaware, at Point Comfort.

1611 March 12. London Company is granted third chapter.

1612 John Rolfe introduces cultivation of tobacco for export.

1614 April 5. John Rolfe marries Pocahontas at Jamestown.

1619 July 30. First representative legislature in America—House of Burgesses—meets in Jamestown.
August 30. First blacks arrive in Jamestown.
– First foundry in America is established on Falling Creek.

1620 First shipload of 'maids' arrives to become wives of settlers.
December 11. Pilgrims authorized to settle in southern Virginia land at Plymouth, having been thrown off course.

1622 March 22. Indian massacre wipes out about one-third of colonists.

1624 June 16. London Company's charter is revoked by King's Bench; Virginia becomes royal colony.
– Doctrine of no taxation without representation is first asserted in Virginia by burgesses.

1628-29 Population is about 3,000.

1629 October 30. Province of Carolina is carved from Virginia by royal grant to Sir Robert Heath.

1632 Province of Maryland is carved from grant to Lord Baltimore.

1634 First eight counties are formed.

February 12. Syms Free School becomes first educational institution to be endowed; it is oldest free school in United States.

1635 Population is about 5,000.
– Sir John Harvey is 'thrust out' by council and burgesses, who make first assertion of colonists' right to order own government.

1644 April 18. Second Indian massacre kills about 300 colonists.

1649 Virginians assert allegiance to Charles II.

1650 Population is about 20,000.
– Southwest Virginia is explored by Abraham Wood and Edmund Bland.
October. First navigation act is passed by Parliament, banishing Dutch vessels from Virginia.

1651 March 12. Virginia capitulates to Commonwealth.

1652-60 Period of almost complete self-government in Colonial Virginia begins.

1652 May 5. Burgesses declared, "The right of election of all officers of the Colony appertain to the Burgesses."

1659 March 13. Burgesses declare that 'Supreme power of the government' in Virginia rests in them; Berkeley is elected governor.

1660 July 31. Charles II reappoints Berkeley as royal governor.

1670 Population is about 40,000.

1673 Northern Neck of Virginia, granted to Lord Hopton and associates in 1649 by Charles II, actually becomes proprietary when Lord Culpeper assumes control.
– Proprietary right to all Virginia is bestowed upon Lord Arlington and Lord Culpeper.

1675 Susquehannock Indian War begins.

1676 Bacon's Rebellion is fought.

1680 Act for establishment of one town for each county is passed by General Assembly; Charles II suspends its operation.

1682 Tobacco Riots begin.

1691 General Assembly re-enacts law providing for towns, but suspends operation of act in 1693.

1693 February 8. College of William and Mary, second institution of higher learning in America, is founded at Middle Plantation (Williamsburg).

1699 Seat of government is moved to Middle Plantation.
– Act for religious tolerance is passed.
– First group of Huguenots reach Virginia.

1700 Population is about 70,000.

1705 Basis of independence from counties of Virginia's future cities is laid by General Assembly.

1716 First theater in United States is built in Williamsburg.

1722 Williamsburg, capital of colony, becomes first incorporated municipality in Virginia.

1730 Population is 114,000.

1736 August 6. First newspaper in Virginia is founded at Williamsburg.

1749 Five hundred thousand acres are granted to Ohio Company, and 800,000 are given to Loyal Company.
– Christopher Gist explores Ohio tract to falls of Ohio River (present Louisville).

1754 George Washington, with Virginia troops, advances against French in Ohio Valley, precipitating French and Indian War.

1755 March 23. Patrick Henry delivers 'liberty or death' speech at Second Virginia Convention in Richmond.
June 15. Washington is chosen commander in chief of Continental Army.
October 24. First bloodshed of American Revolution occurs in Virginia at Hampton.

1755 July 9. Upon fatal wounding of General Edward Braddock, Washington rallies British regulars and Colonials near Fort Duquesne.

1755-56 Population is 294,000.

1758 November 25. Fort Duquesne is occupied.

1759 General Assembly creates standing committee of correspondence to exchange information with colony's agent in London.

1763 December 1. Patrick Henry flouts British rule in Parsons' Cause.
– French and Indian War ends.
– Royal proclamation forbids further grants west of Alleghenies.

1765 May 29. Patrick Henry, protesting Stamp Act, delivers House of Burgesses 'Caesar-Brutus' speech.

1766 February 27. One hundred and fifteen patriots sign Leedstown Resolutions embodying principles later incorporated in Declaration of Independence.

1769 First 'lunatic asylum' in America is established at Williamsburg.

1773 March 14. Burgesses meet in Raleigh Tavern, call convention, and propose congress of Colonies.
June 1. Virginia observes Fast Day in protest of Boston Port Bill.
August 1. First Virginia Convention meets, chooses delegates to Continental Congress.

September 5. Peyton Randolph of Virginia is elected president of First Continental Congress.
October 10. General Andrew Lewis defeats Shawnee at Point Pleasant (now West Virginia).

1776 May 6-June 29. Fifth Virginia Convention meets in Williamsburg.
– Convention declares Virginia an independent State; instructs Virginia's delegates to Continental Congress to propose independence; adopts George Mason's declaration of rights and first constitution of free and independent state; elects Patrick Henry as first governor of Commonwealth.
June 7. At Continental Congress, Richard Henry Lee offers resolutions for independence, foreign alliances, and form of confederacy.
July 2. Lee's resolutions are adopted by Congress.
July 4. Declaration of Independence, phrased by Thomas Jefferson, is adopted by Congress.
December 5. Phi Beta Kappa Society, first inter-collegiate fraternity in United States, is founded at Williamsburg.
– Kentucky is established as county of Virginia.

1778 July 9. Virginia ratifies Articles of Confederation.

1779 February 25. George Rogers Clark, with Virginia troops, takes Vincennes.
May 9. First formal invasion of Virginia by British, who come by sea.
– First law school in America is established at College of William and Mary; college becomes first American university the same year.

1780 April 30. Governor Jefferson moves executive office to Richmond.
December 30. Benedict Arnold, with 27 ships, arrives in James River.

1781 April 29. La Fayette reaches Richmond.
May 20. Cornwallis reaches Petersburg, takes command of combined British forces.
May 24. La Fayette begins retreat before Cornwallis.
June 4. Warned by Jack Jouette, Jefferson and Virginia Legislature escape Colonel Tarleton, who arrives in Charlottesville.
October 19. Cornwallis surrenders at Yorktown.

1782 Population is 567,114.

1784 March 1. Virginia cedes Northwest Territory to United States.

1785 Virginia Statute for Religious Liberty passes legislature.
March 28. Mt. Vernon Conference, called by Virginia Legislature, results in movement toward Constitutional Convention.

1786 September 11. Annapolis Convention meets at invitation of Virginia Legislature, second step toward Constitutional Convention.

1787 May 25. George Washington is elected president of Constitutional Convention meeting at Philadelphia.
May 29. Governor Edmund Randolph submits to Convention Madison's Virginia Plan basis of deliberations.

1788 June 26. Virginia ratifies Federal Constitution, 89 to 79.

1789 April 30. George Washington is inaugurated first President of United States.
December 3. Virginia cedes to United States part of area for seat of government.

1790 Population is 747,610.
– Virginia Legislature remonstrates against Assumption Bill, first remonstrance of State against Federal Act.

1791 December 15. America's Bill of Rights is added to Constitution, when nine amendments offered by James Madison and tenth by Richard Henry Lee are ratified.

1798 December 21. Legislature adopts 'Virginia Resolutions,' protesting Alien and Sedition laws.

1799 First ship constructed by Federal government, *Chesapeake*, is built at Gosport Navy Yard.

1800 Population is 747,610.

1801 March 4. Thomas Jefferson is inaugurated President.

1803 February 23. Chief Justice John Marshall of Virginia hands down opinion asserting U.S. Supreme Court's Right of Judicial Review.
April 30. James Monroe, Jefferson's emissary, concludes treaty with France for purchase of Louisiana Territory.

1804 May 14. Lewis and Clark, commissioned by Jefferson, begin exploration of Louisiana Territory.

1807 May 22. Trial of Aaron Burr begins in Richmond.
June 22. British frigate, *Leopard*, attacks Chesapeake off Virginia cape.
December 22. Congress passes Jefferson's Embargo Act.

1809 March 4. James Madison is inaugurated president.

1810 Population is 974,600.

1812 June 18. President Madison signs Congressional act declaring war upon England.

1813 British fleet ravages areas contiguous to Virginia waters.

1814 August 24. President and Mrs. Madison flee to Virginia before British enter Washington.

1816 August 19-23. Western Virginians, meeting at Staunton, demand new State constitution equalizing representation.

1817 March 4. James Monroe is inaugurated President.

1819 January 25. University of Virginia is established.
February 22. President Monroe's envoys conclude treaty with Spain for acquisition of Florida.

1820 Population is 1,065,366.

1823 April 24. Stephen F. Austin of Virginia obtains grant of land in Texas from Mexico for colonization.
December 2. President Monroe promulgates 'Monroe Doctrine.'

1825 January 11. President Monroe's signature concludes treaty with Russia establishing Northwest boundary.
March 4. End of 'Virginia Dynasty.'

1829 February 21. Legislature condemns 'Tariff of Abominations' as unconstitutional.

1830 Population is 1,211,405.

1831 August 21. Nat Turner's slave insurrection begins.

1832 Bill to abolish slavery in Virginia loses in house of delegates by vote of 67 to 60.

1835 Edgar Allan Poe becomes editor of *Southern Literary Messenger*, in which his first short stories have already appeared.

1836 October 22. Sam Houston of Virginia is elected first President of Republic of Texas.

1840 Population is 1,239,797.

1841 March 4. William Henry Harrison of Virginia is inaugurated President.
April 4. John Tyler of Virginia is inaugurated President.

1842 January 24. Thomas Walker Gilmer of Virginia moves that Congress censure John Quincy for presenting petition from abolitionists for peaceful dissolution of Union.

1845 March 1. President Tyler signs bill annexing Texas.

1846 May 1. Southern Methodists, meeting in Petersburg, organize Methodist Episcopal Church, South.

1847 September 13. General Winfield Scott of Virginia takes Mexico City.

1849 March 4. Zachary Taylor of Virginia is inaugurated President.

1850 Population is 1,421,661.

1851 October 23-25. New constitution, providing liberal white male franchise, is ratified by large majority.

1859 October 16. John Brown and band seize U.S. Arsenal at Harpers Ferry, are later suppressed by troops under Colonel R.E. Lee.
December 2. John Brown is hanged.

1860 Population is 1,596,300.

1861 February 4. 'Peace Conference,' called by Virginia Legislature, meets in Washington, is attended by representatives of 21 states.
February 13. State Convention (Secession Convention) meets, but refuses to consider secession until peace overtures are exhausted.
– Civil War begins.
April 17. State Convention votes for secession 88 to 55.
April 25. Virginia joins Confederate States.
May 21. Richmond is chosen capital of Confederacy.
July 21. First Battle of Manassas is fought.

1862 March 9. Battle between Monitor and Merrimac in Hampton Roads is fought.
March 23. Battle of Kernstown (beginning of Jackson's Valley Campaign) is fought.
June 26. 'Seven Days' Battles begin around Richmond.
August 29-30. Second Battle of Manassas is fought.
December 13. Battle of Fredericksburg is fought.

1863 May 2-3. Battle of Chancellorsville is fought; Jackson is mortally wounded.
June 20. Virginia is divided; West Virginia is admitted as State.

1864 May 5-6. Battle of Wilderness is fought.
May 8-18. Battle of Spotsylvania Courthouse is fought.
June 3. Second *Battle* of Cold Harbor is fought.
June 15-18. Battle of Petersburg is fought; siege begins.

1865 April 2-3. Confederates evacuate Richmond and Petersburg.
April 9. Lee surrenders at Appomattox.
– Civil War ends.
May 22. Jefferson Davis is imprisoned at Fort Monroe.

1867 March 2. Virginia is designated as Military District No. 1 under Reconstruction Act.
May 13. Jefferson Davis is arraigned in Richmond and indicted for treason.

1869 July 6. New State constitution is ratified.
October 8. Fourteenth and fifteenth amendments to Constitution are ratified.

1870 Population is 1,225,163.
January 26. Virginia is readmitted to Union.

1880 Population is 1,512,565.

1889 April 24. Simpson Dry Dock, largest in world, opens at Newport News.

1890 Population is 1,655,980.

1894 March. Legislative Act provides for secret balloting.

1900 Population is 1,854,184.
May 12. Legislature passes 'Jim Crow' law.

1902 July 10. New State constitution, effective by proclamation, improves public education and governmental efficiency, virtually eliminates black vote through poll tax and 'understanding clause.'

1907 April 26. Jamestown Exposition opens to commemorate 300th anniversary of first landing of English settlers at Cape Henry.
December 16. Atlantic Fleet, commanded by Rear Admiral Robley D. Evans of Virginia, leaves Hampton Roads for World Cruise.

1908 Staunton is first city to adopt city manager form of government.

1910 Population is 2,061,612.

1913 March 4. Woodrow Wilson of Virginia is Inaugurated President.

1914 November 18. Wilson signs Federal Reserve Bank Act, fathered by Congressman Carter Glass of Virginia.

1915 June 14. U.S. Supreme Court decision places upon West Virginia obligation to share Virginia's antebellum State debt.

1917 April 6. President Wilson signs Congressional Act declaring war upon Germany.
– Hampton Roads becomes great naval and military base.

1918 College of William and Mary admits women.
– Budget system, sponsored by Governor Westmoreland Davis, is adopted.

1920 Population is 2,309,187.
– Women are admitted to graduate and professional schools of University of Virginia.
November 2. Virginia women vote, although Virginia votes against ratification of Nineteenth Amendment.

1922 February 27. State Board of Public Welfare evolves from State Board of Charities and Corrections.
March 24. State Highway Commission is created.
March 27. Juvenile and Domestic Relations Court is established.

1924 March 20. Act provides for sterilization of persons committed to State institutions.

1927 April 27. Act for reorganization of State government, sponsored by Governor Harry Flood Byrd, passes General Assembly.

1930 Population is 2,421,851.
March 17. Legislative act exempts new manufactories from taxation for five years under specified conditions.

1936 December 18. Act approved, in conformity with Federal Social Security Act, creates Unemployment Compensation Commission.

1938 March 31. Public newspaper is founded.
– Public Assistance Act is revised and approved, in conformity with Federal Social Security Act, to render old age assistance, aid to dependent children, aid to blind, general relief aid.

1940 Population is 3,967,000.

– Ten new buildings are dedicated at Virginia Polytechnic Institute in Blacksburg.

1942 January 22. C.W. Darden Jr. is sworn in as Governor.
– Students at University of Virginia work for war effort.

1943 City of Richmond proposes using black policemen in black city districts.

1944 July 3. Twenty-fifth anniversary of first meeting of Legislature in Jamestown.
– World War II servicemen are allowed to vote in elections without registering or paying poll tax.

1946 February. Legislature passes bill, prohibiting strikes by State, municipal, or county employees.
December. State of emergency is declared as result of coal strike.

1947 November. W. Lawrence becomes first black elected to County Supervisors Board, Nansemond County.
– 340th anniversary of settlement of Jamestown.

1948 More than 50,000 blacks register to vote in Richmond area.
– Black candidates run for city posts.

1949 Governor Tuck declares state of emergency due to coal strike, orders seizure of mine.

1950 January 19. Population is 3,319,000.
– J.S. Battle is inaugurated as Governor.

1951 U.S. Supreme Court upholds Virginia's poll tax law.
– Seven blacks, one white are executed for rape.

1952 March. Rioting university students burn one building; three students are held in connection with fire.
– School segregation laws are upheld.
– Ex-Governor Peery dies.

1953 Democratic campaign manager Kellam resigns after indictment on Federal income tax charge.

1954 January. T.B. Stanley is inaugurated as Governor.
– Supreme Court Justice Campbell dies.
– Supreme Court rules on racial segregation in schools; State constitution is called into question.

1955 December. State Legislature approves referendum to decide whether Virginia should hold Constitutional Convention to draw up amendment to circumvent U.S. Supreme Court edict on school segregation.
– State is hit by floods; Federal relief is sought.

1956 March. Memorial to World War II and Korean War dead is dedicated in Richmond.
September. Legislative Committee is established to probe racial litigation and public school integration.

1957 November. J.L. Almond, proponent of racial segregation, is elected Governor.

– Norfolk organizers begin drive to increase black voter registration.
– Hampton Roads Bridge-Tunnel is completed.

1958 Governor J.L. Almond closes nine schools rather than accept integration.
– Furor over segregation issue continues; 26 white adults and children sue Governor Almond and State.
– Administration enjoins 'massive resistance' laws against racial integration of public schools.

1959 Coal mine shutdown causes depression in southwestern section of State.
November. Segregation moderates win in most key races for State Legislature.

1960 Population is 3,967,000.

1961 Government is urged to modernize to keep up with shift from rural to urban economy.

1962 January. Harrison is inaugurated as Governor.
October. H.R. Adams becomes first black admitted to University of Virginia, Martinsville.

1963 Republicans make largest gains in century during November elections; resurgence is due in large part to support from black voters.

1964 December. Appeals Court rules Virginia counties must end tuition grants to white students in segregated private schools.
February 13. John Paul, 80, Federal judge from 1931 to 1960 dies; Paul issued first integration order (for Charlottesville public schools in July.

1956 Supreme Court orders opening of Prince Edward County schools, closed since 1959 to avoid racial integration.
– Chesapeake Bay Bridge is completed.
– First atomic-powered aircraft carrier, *U.S.S. Enterprise*, is launched at Newport News.

1965 November. Democrat Mills E. Godwin, Jr. is elected Governor, with strong support from blacks and organized labor.
– Prince Edward Action Group in Prince Edward County, Virginia is granted $90,193 for 3-month remedial reading program for black children who were without schooling from 1959-1964 (county's public school system was abolished during that period to avoid compliance with 1954 Supreme Court school integration ruling; white children had attended private academy).

1966 Business interests expand in State as record number of new manufacturing plants are built.
March. U.S. Supreme Court rules Virginia poll tax is unconstitutional.

1967 Dr. William Ferguson Reid (D), 42, physician, becomes first black elected to General Assembly since 1891.

1968 J.N. Bradby is sheriff, and Mrs. I.W. Adkins is Clerk of Charles City County, becoming first blacks to hold such posts in State.
– Sheriff Bradby found dead in March; death is ruled suicide.

April. Three hundred students at Virginia Union University take over administration building to protest University's system of testing.

1969 November. L. Holton is elected first Republican Governor in 84 years.
– 1500 University of Virginia students protest to demand admission of black assistant admissions dean, and more black coaches and athletes.
– Students demonstrate against U.S. involvement in Vietnam.

1970 Population is 4,651,000.
– Anti-war protests continue on University campuses.
January 13. Governor-elect Linwood Holton announces appointment of William B. Robertson as executive assistant on his staff; he is first black to serve in Virginia governor's office.

1971 Industrial development surges with expansion and establishment of 164 manufacturing plants.

1972 Hurricane Agnes strikes Richmond; area is declared flood disaster area.

1973 November. Former governor Mills E. Godwin, Republican conservative, wins gubernatorial race in close election against independent liberal, H.E. Howell.

1974 June 4. Pope Paul VI creates new diocese at Arlington to end bitter struggle between conservative priests and progressives.

1975 Death penalty is restored.
October 26. Anwar Sadat begins 10-day visit to U.S. to seek economic and military aid for Egypt, and to explain policies to American people; he stays overnight in Williamsburg.

1976 Restored historical buildings are displayed for nation's Bicentennial.

1977 Charles S. Robb, son-in-law of President Lyndon Johnson, is elected Lieutenant Governor.
March 8. Richmond City Council elects Henry L. Marsh III as first black mayor.

1978 November. John W. Warner is elected to Virginia Senate, with campaign help from wife, Elizabeth Taylor.
– Department of Health, Education, and Welfare rejects State plan to desegregate universities and colleges in Virginia.

1979 September 7. Hurricane David causes torrential flood damage.

1980 Population is 5,347,000.
– Legislature proclaims January 16 "Roy Clark Day" in honor of country singer from Maherrin, Virginia.
– Virginia Electric and Power Company consider switching two partially built nuclear power plants to coal due to problems with nuclear power.

1981 John W. Hinckley Jr. is held at U.S. Marine Corps Stockade at Quantico on charges of attempting to assassinate President Reagan.

1982 November. Charles Robb is elected Governor; he is first Democratic governor in twelve years.
- Edwin P. Wilson, former CIA official, is convicted on seven federal counts involving illegal transportation of firearms to Libyan government.
- Federal jury in Alexandria, Virginia finds Wilson guilty of masterminding conspiracy.

1983 Town of Surrey develops plans for emergency evacuation in event of nuclear accident at nearby Virginia Electric and Power Company power plant.

1984 CIA admits having two meetings at agency in Langley, Virginia with Lyndon H. LaRouche in which matters of national security were discussed.

1985 November. L. Douglas Wilder is elected Lieutenant Governor, becoming first black to hold statewide post since Reconstruction.
- Sue Terry becomes first woman Attorney General of Virginia.

1986 April. Hurricane Charley batters Virginia coast, causing deaths, property damage, and over $7 million dollars damage along North Carolina, Virginia and Maryland coasts.

1987 January. Winter storm, with high tides and gale force winds, causes extensive damage along Virginia coast.
February. Grand jury indicts 16 followers of Lyndon LaRouche on charges of securities fraud and other offenses.

1988 August. Virginia Electric & Power Company is fined $100,000 because of "significant weaknesses" in radiation safety at Surry nuclear plant; it is second fine of year.
December. LaRouche and six others are convicted of mail fraud and conspiracy to commit mail fraud; LaRouche is also found guilty of conspiring to defraud IRS.

1989 January 27. Lyndon H. LaRouche Jr. is sentenced in Alexandria to 15 years in Federal prison.
September 21. Hurricane Hugo hits Charleston late in evening; winds of 135 miles per hour set off 17-foot tidal surge that sweeps into Charleston Harbor.
November 27. L. Douglas Wilder is winner of State's gubernatorial election; Wilder wins 897,139 votes, or 50.19 percent; he is first African-American in U.S. history to be elected state governor.

1990 Population is 6,187,358.
August 6-7. President Bush orders deployment of F-15 fighters from Langley Air Force Base for Saudi Arabia; plan is dubbed operation "Desert Shield."
- In speech at Alexandria, President Bush gives first address on AIDS virus since taking office, urging compassion, end of discrimination against individuals infected with virus.

1991 January 9. Governor L. Douglas Wilder asks State Legislature for authority to require furloughs without pay for up to 100,000 State employees.
- Appeals court rules that Jim Bakker be re-sentenced by another judge, since North Carolina judge allowed personal feelings to influence his decision.

1992 Virginia Beach jury rules that local gun store must pay $100,000 to Virginia family after shooting death of schoolteacher by student in 1988; jury decision is first in U.S. to hold gun store liable for injuries inflicted by gun (9 millimeter semiautomatic) purchased in store.
- Federal appeals court in Richmond rules that Virginia Military Academy does not have to admit women; however, ruling specifies that State will have to set up equivalent program for women. Timothy Bunch, convicted of shooting and hanging female acquaintance in 1982, is executed in Jarratt electric chair; Bunch is 17th execution in State since 1976.

1993 Vincent Foster, deputy White House counsel, is found dead of apparent self-inflicted gunshot wound to head in Fort Marcy Park, across Potomac River in northern Virginia; Foster was close friend of President Bill Clinton and wife, Hillary Rodham Clinton, and was partner at Rose law firm where Mrs. Clinton worked.
- Oil pipeline ruptures, releasing more than 350,000 gallons of diesel fuel that flows into tributary of Potomac River; spill kills wildlife and threatens drinking water supplies temporarily.
- Leading State Republicans are alleged to have ridiculed homosexuals and blacks at GOP dinner at Tyson's Corner; accused are Oliver North and State Senator Warren Barry.

1994 Walt Disney Company announces giving up plans to build controversial American history theme park on site in Haymarket, Prince William County; decision is made after historians and environmentalist opponents hold up approval process through protests and legal challenges; Disney spokesperson says another site in Virginia may be chosen.
- Colonial Williamsburg Foundation holds controversial mock slave auction in which employed actors portray slaves and bidders; foundation spokesperson explains that reenactment broadens portrayal of history; critics charge that group recreates painful period in black history for entertainment purposes.
- About 200 vultures attack ducks, dogs, cats, and horses in Stafford County. Federal law protects vultures and residents are forbidden to shoot them; wildlife experts speculate that birds may have become more aggressive because of hard winter and lack of food.

1995 Democrats keep majority in State Legislature; Republicans consider race results setback, after more than $1 million is spent to elect Republican candidates.
- U.S. Supreme Court accepts case involving all male Virginia Military Institute in Lexington; justices will hear sexual-discrimination appeals from two factions.

1999 March 5. A federal appeals court strikes down the 1994 Violence Against Women Act, which lets rape victims, sue for civil-rights violations.

DIRECTORY OF STATE SERVICES

OFFICE OF THE GOVERNOR
Capitol Bldg., 3rd Fl.
Richmond, VA 23219
Fax: 804-371-6351
Governor: 804-786-2211

Washington, DC Office
444 N Capitol St. NW, Ste. 214
Washington, DC 20001
Fax: 202-783-7687
Director: 202-783-1769

LIEUTENANT GOVERNOR
101 N 8th Street, Rm. 104
Richmond, VA 23219
Fax: 804-786-7514
Office: 804-786-2078

ATTORNEY GENERAL'S OFFICE
101 N 8th St.
Richmond, VA 23219
Fax: 804-786-1991
Office: 804-786-2071

SECRETARY OF THE COMMONWEALTH
Old Finance Bldg., Capitol Square
Richmond, VA 23219
Fax: 804-371-0017
Office: 804-786-2441

ADMINISTRATION OFFICE
6th Fl., 9th Street Office Bldg.
Richmond, VA 23219
Fax: 804-371-0088
Secretary: 804-786-1201

Compensation Board
9th Street Office Bldg., Box 710
Richmond, VA 23206-0710
Fax: 804-371-0235
Chairman: 804-786-3886

Elections Board
200 N 9th Street, Ste. 101
Richmond, VA 23219-3497
Secretary: 804-786-6551

Employee Relations Counselors
700 E Franklin St., 700 Center, Suite 910
Richmond, VA 23219-2319
Fax: 804-371-7318
Director: 804-786-6551

General Services Department
202 N 9th Street
Richmond, VA 23219
Fax: 804-371-8305
Director: 804-786-3311

Consolidated Laboratory Services Division
1 North 14th Street
Richmond, VA 23219
Fax: 804-371-7073
Director: 804-786-7905

Engineering & Building Division
805 East Broad St., Room 101
Richmond, VA 23219
Director: 804-786-3263

Facilities Management Bureau
203 Governor Street
Richmond, VA 23219
Director: 804-225-4775

Forensic Science Division
1 North 14th Street
Richmond, VA 23219
Director: 804-786-2281

Purchases & Supplies Division
805 E Broad Street, Box 1199
Richmond, VA 23219
Director: 804-786-3846

Risk Management Division
109 Governor Street
Richmond, VA 23219
Director: 804-786-5968

Human Rights Council
Washington Bldg., 12th Fl.
Richmond, VA 23219
Fax: 804-371-7952
Director: 804-225-2292

Information Management Council
1100 Bank St., 9th Fl.
Richmond, VA 23219
Fax: 804-371-3294
Director: 804-225-3622

Information Technology Department
110 S. 7th Street, 9th Fl.
Richmond, VA 23219
Fax: 804-344-5505
Director: 804-344-5500

Local Government Commission
8th Street Office Bldg., 7th Fl.
Richmond, VA 23219
Fax: 804-371-7999
Director: 804-786-6508

Personnel and Training Department
Monroe Bldg., 12th Fl., 101 N. 14th Street
Richmond, VA 23219
Fax: 804-371-7401
Director: 804-225-2237

Veteran's Affairs Department
P.O. Box 809
Roanoke, VA 24011-2215
Fax: 703-857-7573
Director: 703-857-7104

Virginia Retirement System Office
1200 E Main Street, Box 2500
Richmond, VA 23207
Fax: 804-371-0613
Director: 804-786-3831

AUDITOR OF PUBLIC ACCOUNTS
P.O. Box 1295
Richmond, VA 23210
Fax: 804-225-3357
State Auditor: 804-225-3350

COMMERCE AND TRADE OFFICE
9th Street Office Bldg., Rm. 723
Richmond, VA 23219
Fax: 804-371-0250
Secretary: 804-786-7831

Agriculture and Consumer Services Department
1100 Bank Street, Rm. 210
Richmond, VA 23219
Fax: 804-371-2945
Commissioner: 804-786-3501

Economic Development Department
901 East Byrd Street
Richmond, VA 23219
Mail to: P.O. Box 798
Richmond, VA 23206-0798
Director: 804-371-8106

Employment Commission
703 East Main Street
Richmond, VA 23219
Fax: 804-786-3001
Commissioner: 804-786-3001

Forestry Department
P.O. Box 3758
Charlotteville, VA 22903
Fax: 804-296-2369
State Forester: 804-977-6555

Housing and Community Development Department
Jackson Crt., 501 N. 2nd St.
Richmond, VA 23219-1321
Fax: 804-371-7090
Director: 804-371-7000

Housing Development Authority
601 S Belvedere Street
Richmond, VA 23220-6504
Fax: 804-783-6701
Executive Director: 804-782-1966

Labor and Industry Department
Powers Taylor Bldg., 13 S. 13th St.
Richmond, VA 23219
Commissioner: 804-786-2377

Milk Commission
200 N 9th St., Ste. 1015
Richmond, VA 23219
Fax: 804-786-3779
Administrator: 804-786-2013

Mines, Minerals, and Energy Department
202 N 9th Street, 8th Fl.
Richmond, VA 23219
Fax: 804-692-3238

Director: 804-692-3200

Minority Business Enterprises
11th Fl. 200-202 N. 9th St. Ofc. Bldg.
Richmond, VA 23219
Fax: 804-371-7359
Director: 804-786-5560

Port Authority
600 World Trade Center
Norfolk, VA 23510
Fax: 804-683-8500
Executive Director: 804-683-8000

Professional and Occupational Regulations Department
3600 W Broad St.
Richmond, VA 23230
Fax: 804-367-9537
Director: 804-367-8519

Racing Commission
P.O. Box 1123
Richmond, VA 23206
Fax: 804-371-6127
Executive Director: 804-371-7363

Virginia Resources Authority
P.O. Box 1300
Richmond, VA 23208
Fax: 804-644-3109
Executive Director: 804-644-3100

EDUCATION OFFICE
5th Fl., 9th St. Ofc. Bldg.
Richmond, VA 23219
Fax: 804-371-0154
Secretary: 804-786-3586

Commission for the Arts
223 Governors St.
Richmond, VA 23219
Fax: 804-786-3785
Executive Director: 804-225-3132

Education Department
James Monroe Bldg., 101 N. 14th St.
Richmond, VA 23219
Mail to: P.O. Box 2120
Richmond, VA 23216-2120
Fax: 804-371-2099

Superintendent of Public
Museum of Fine Arts
2800 Grove Ave.
Richmond, VA 23221
Fax: 804-367-2633
Director: 804-367-0800

Science Museum
2500 W. Broad St.
Richmond, VA 23220
Fax: 804-367-9348
Director: 804-367-6799
Education: 804-225-2755

State Council of Higher
James Monroe Bldg., 9th
Richmond, VA 23219
Fax: 804-225-2604
Director: 804-255-2600

State Library and Archives
11th & Capitol Square
Richmond, VA 23219
Fax: 804-786-5855
Librarian: 804-786-2332

Student Assistance Authority
411 E. Franklin St., Ste 300
Richmond, VA 23219
Fax: 804-775-4005
Executive Director: 804-775-4000

FINANCE OFFICE
9th St. Office Bldg., P.O. Box 1475
Richmond, VA 23212

Planning and Budget Department
9th & Grace St., P.O. Box 1422
Richmond, VA 23211
Fax: 804-225-3291
Director: 804-786-5375

Taxation Department
2220 W. Broad St., Box 1880
Richmond, VA 23282
Fax: 804-367-0971
Tax Commissioner: 804-367-8005

Treasury Department
101 N. 14th St., P.O. Box 1879
Richmond, VA 23215-1879
Fax: 804-225-3167
Treasurer: 804-225-2142

HEALTH AND HUMAN RESOURCES DEPARTMENT
9th St. Office Bldg., P.O. Box 1475
Richmond, VA 23212
Fax: 804-371-6984
Secretary: 804-786-7765

Aging Department
700 E Franklin St., 10th Fl.
Richmond, VA 23219-2327
Fax: 804-371-8381
Commissioner: 804-225-2271

Council on Child Daycare/Early Childhood Program
Ste 1116, 1100 Bank
Richmond, VA 23219
Fax: 804-371-6570
Director: 804-371-8603

Deaf and Hard of Hearing Department
Washington Bldg., 12th Fl., 1100 Bank St.
Richmond, VA 23219
Fax: 804-371-7882
Director: 804-225-2570

Department for Rights of Virginians with Disabilities
James Monroe Bldg., 17th Fl., 101 N. 14th St.
Richmond, VA 23219
Fax: 804-225-3221
Director: 804-225-2042

Governor's Employment and Training Department
4615 W Broad St., 3rd Fl.
Richmond, VA 23230
Fax: 804-367-6172
Executive Director: 804-367-9803

Health Department
1500 East Main St.
Richmond, VA 23219
Mail to: P.O. Box 2448
Richmond, VA 23218
Fax: 804-786-4616
State Health Commissioner: 804-786-3561

Administration
1500 East Main St.
Richmond, VA 23219
Fax: 804-786-4616
Deputy Commissioner: 804-786-3561

Public Health Programs
1500 East Main St.
Richmond, VA 23219
Fax: 804-786-4616
Deputy Commissioner: 804-786-3563

Health Cost Review Council
8th St. Ofc. Bldg., 6th Fl.
Richmond, VA 23219
Fax: 804-371-0284
Executive Director: 804-786-6371

Health Professions Department
6606 W Broad St., 4th Fl.
Richmond, VA 23230-1717
Fax: 804-662-9943
Office: 804-662-9920

Medical Assistance Services Department
600 E Broad St., Ste. 1300
Richmond, VA 23219
Fax: 804-225-4512
Director: 804-786-7933

Mental Health, Retardation and Substance Abuse Services Department
P.O. Box 1797
Richmond, VA 23214
Fax: 804-371-6638
Commissioner: 804-786-3921

Pharmacy Board
6606 W Broad St., Ste. 400
Richmond, VA 23230-1717
Fax: 804-662-9313
Director: 804-662-9911

Rehabilitative Services Department
8004 Franklin Farms Dr., P.O. Box K300
Richmond, VA 23238
Fax: 804-662-9532
Commissioner: 804-662-7000

Woodrow Wilson Rehabilitation Center
Fishersville, VA 22939
Director: 703-332-7158

Social Services Department
730 E Broad St.
Richmond, VA 232 19-1849
Fax: 804-692-1949
Commissioner: 804-692-1900

Visually Handicapped Department
397 Azalea Ave.
Richmond, VA 23227
Fax: 804-371-3351
Commissioner: 804-371-3145

NATURAL RESOURCES OFFICE
9th St. Office Bldg., P.O. Box 1475
Richmond, VA 23212
Fax: 804-371-8333
Secretary: 804-786-0044

Conservation and Recreation Department
203 Governors St., Ste. 302
Richmond, VA 23219
Fax: 804-786-6141
Director: 804-786-2121

Environment Quality Department
629 E Main St.
Richmond, VA 23219
Fax: 804-762-4006
Director: 804-762-4020

Abingdon Office
P.O. Box 1190
Abingdon, VA 24210
Regional Director: 703-676-5482

Harrisonburg Office
P.O. Box 268
Bridgewater, VA 22812
Regional Director: 703-828-2595

Richmond Office
4900 Cox Rd.
Glen Allen, VA 23060
Regional Director: 804-527-5020

Roanoke Office
5338 Peters Creek Rd., Ste. D
Roanoke, VA 24019
Regional Director: 703-561-7000

Tidewater Office
287 Pembroke Ofc. Park, Ste. 310
Pembroke, VA 23462
Regional Director: 804-552-1840

Woodbridge Office
1519 Davis Ford Rd., Ste. 14
Woodbridge, VA 22192
Regional Director: 703-490-8922

Game and Inland Fisheries Department
4010 West Broad St.
Richmond, VA 23230
Fax: 804-367-0405
Executive Director: 804-367-1000

Historic Resources Department
221 Governor St.
Richmond, VA 23219
Fax: 804-225-4261
Executive Director: 804-786-3144

Marine Resources Commission
2600 Washington Aye, 3rd Fl.
Newport News, VA 23607-0756
Mail to: P.O. Box 756
Newport News, VA 23607

National Heritage
1500 E Main St., Ste. 312
Richmond VA 23219
Director: 804-786-4554

State Parks Commission
203 Governor St., Ste. 306
Richmond, VA 23219
Fax: 804-786-9294
Director: 804-786-1712

PUBLIC SAFETY OFFICE
202 N 9th Street, Ste. 613
Richmond, VA 23219
Fax: 804-371-6381
Secretary: 804-786-5351

Alcoholic Beverage Control Board
2901 Hermitage Rd., Box 27491
Richmond, VA 23216
Fax: 804-367-0622
Chairman: 804-367-0621

Commonwealth Attorneys Services Council
P.O. Box 3549
Williamsburg, VA 23187
Administrative Coordinator: 804-253-4146

Correctional Education Department
101 N 14th St., 7th Fl.
Richmond, VA 23219-3678
Superintendent: 804-225-3314

Corrections Department
6900 Almore Dr.
Richmond, VA 23225
Fax: 804-674-3509
Director: 804-674-3119

Criminal Justice Services
805 E Broad St., 10th Fl.
Richmond, VA 23229
Fax: 804-371-8981
Director: 804-786-4000

Emergency Services Department
310 Turner Rd.
Richmond, VA 23225
Fax: 804-674-2490
Coordinator: 804-673-2497

Fire Programs
2807 N Parham Rd., Ste. 200
Richmond, VA 23294
Fax: 804-527-4242

Military Affairs Department
600 E Broad St.
Richmond, VA 23219-1832
Fax: 804-775-9151
Adjutant General: 804-775-9100

Parole Board
6900 Atmore Drive
Richmond, VA 23225
Fax: 804-674-3284
Chairman: 804-674-3081

State Police
P.O. Box 27472
Richmond, VA 23261-7472
Fax: 804-674-2132
Superintendent: 804-674-2087

Youth and Family Services
7th & Franklin Sts.
Richmond, VA 23219
Fax: 804-371-0773
Director: 804-371-0700

TRANSPORTATION OFFICE
1401 E Broad St., Rm. 414
Richmond, VA 23219
Fax: 804-786-6683
Secretary: 804-786-8032

Aviation Department
5702 Gulf Stream Rd.
Sanston, VA 23150
Fax: 804-236-3635
Director: 804-236-3624

Motor Vehicles Department
2300 W Broad St.
Richmond, VA 23220
Fax: 804-367-6631
Commissioner: 804-367-6602

Rail and Transportation Department
1401 E Broad St.
Richmond, VA 23219
Fax: 804-786-2940
Commissioner: 804-786-1051

Transportation Department
1401 E Broad St.
Richmond, VA 23219
Fax: 804-786-2940
Commissioner: 804-2701

CHESAPEAKE BAY BRIDGE AND TUNNEL COMMISSION
P.O. Box 111
Cape Charles, VA 23310
Fax: 804-331-4565
Executive Director: 804-331-2960

Financial Institutions Bureau
1300 E Main St., Ste. 800, P.O. Box 640
Richmond, VA 23205-0640
Fax: 804-371-9416
Commissioner: 804-371-9657

Insurance Bureau
P.O. Box 1157
Richmond, VA 23209
Commissioner: 804-371-9741

POLICY PLANNING AND AGRICULTURE DEVELOPMENT
P.O. Box 163
Richmond, VA 23209
Fax: 804-371-7679

Public Defender Commission
1300 E. Main Street
Richmond, VA 23219
Mail to: P.O. Box 1197
Richmond, VA 23209
Fax: 804-371-9376
Commissioner: 804-371-9608

Securities and Retail Franchising Bureau
P.O. Box 1197
Richmond, VA 23209
Fax: 804-371-9911
Director: 804-371-9051

STATE LOTTERY
P.O. Box 4689
Richmond, VA 23220
Fax: 804-367-3116
Director: 804-367-3000

MEMBERS OF CONGRESS

SENATE

SEN. JOHN WARNER (R) (b. 1927); 4th Term;
Phone: 202-224-2023; Fax: 202-224-6295;
E-mail: senator@warner.senate.gov

www.senate.gov/warner

SEN. CHARLES S. ROBB (D) (b. 1939); 2nd Term;
Phone: 202-224-4024; Fax: 202-224-8689;
E-mail: senator@robb.senate.gov

www.senate.gov/robb/

HOUSE

HERBERT H. BATEMAN (R-1st) (b. 1928); 9th Term;
Phone: 202-225-4261; Fax: 202-225-4382;
E-mail: va01@legislators.com

www.house.gov/bateman/

OWEN B. PICKETT (D-2nd) (b. 1930); 7th Term;
Phone: 202-225-4215; Fax: 202-225-4218;
E-mail: owen.pickett@mail.house.gov

www.house.gov/pickett

BOBBY SCOTT (D-3rd) (b. 1947); 4th Term;
Phone: 202-225-8351; Fax: 202-225-8354;
E-mail: va03@legislators.com

www.house.gov/scott/

NORMAN SISISKY (D-4th) (b. 1927); 9th Term;
Phone: 202-225-6365; Fax: 202-226-1170;
E-mail: va04@legislators.com

www.house.gov/sisisky

VIRGIL H. GOODE, Jr. (I-5th) (b. 1946); 2nd Term;
Phone: 202-225-4711; Fax: 202-225-5681;
E-mail: Rep.Goode@mail.house.gov

www.house.gov/goode

BOB GOODLATTE (R-6th) (b. 1952); 4th Term;
Phone: 202-225-5431; Fax: 202-225-9681;
E-mail: va06@legislators.com

www.house.gov/goodlatte

THOMAS J. BLILEY, Jr. (R-7th) (b. 1932); 10th Term;
Phone: 202-225-2815; Fax: 202-225-0011;
E-mail: tom.bliley@mail.houe.gov

www.house.gov/bliley/

JAMES P. MORAN (D-8th) (b. 1945); 5th Term;
Phone: 202-225-4376; Fax: 202-225-0017;
E-mail: jim.moran@mail.house.gov

www.house.gov/moran/

RICK BOUCHER (D-9th) (b. 1946); 9th Term;
Phone: 202-225-3861; Fax: 202-225-0442;
E-mail: ninthnet@mail.house.gov

www.house.gov/boucher

FRANK R. WOLF (R-10th) (b. 1939); 10th Term;
Phone: 202-225-5136; Fax: 202-225-0437;
E-mail: va10@legislators.com

www.house.gov/wolf/

THOMAS M. DAVIS III (R-11th) (b. 1949); 3rd Term;
Phone: 202-225-1492; Fax: 202-225-3071;
E-mail: tom.davis@mail.house.gov

www.house.gov/tomdavis

TWENTIETH CENTURY GOVERNORS

TYLER, JAMES HOGE (1846-1925), forty-fifth governor (1898-1902), was born at Blenheim, Caroline County, Virginia on August 11, 1846, the son of George and Elva (Hoge) Tyler. His mother died giving birth, and James was brought up by his maternal grandparents. When his grandfather died in 1861, he returned to live with his father in Caroline County. He received private education during his early years, and later attended a school run by Franklin Minor in Albemarie County.

Tyler served in the Confederate Army as a private toward the end of the Civil War. After the war, he took up farming. He was married to Sue Montgomery Hammet in 1868. They had seven children.

Tyler served in the Virginia State Senate from 1877 to 1879. In 1889, he was elected Lieutenant Governor, and served from January 1890 to January 1894. He ran for governor in 1893, but was defeated for the Democratic nomination. However in 1897, he gained the nomination and went on to win the governorship from Republican opponent, Patrick H. McCaull. During his administration, funding for public schools was increased, and the state debt was reduced by more than one million dollars. Other accomplishments included establishment of the State Labor Bureau, creation of a conditional parole system, settlement of the dispute of the state's oyster beds, and settlement of the boundary dispute with Tennessee.

Tyler left office in 1902 and moved to East Radford, Virginia, where he resumed farming and other business interests. He was president of the Virginia State Farmers' Institute and the Southwest Virginia Livestock Association, and served as a trustee for the Union Theological Seminary. In 1896, he went to Scotland as a delegate to the Pan-Presbyterian Alliance Convention. He also served as a member of the boards of the Synodical Orphans' Home, and Hampden-Sydney College.

Tyler died in East Radford on January 3, 1925.

MONTAGUE, ANDREW JACKSON (1862-1937), forty-sixth governor (1902-1906), was born near Lynchburg, Virginia on October 3, 1862, the son of Robert and Gay (Eubank) Montague. He attended Richmond College, and after graduation in 1882, worked as a private tutor in Orange County, Virginia. He returned to school in 1884, to study law at the University of Virginia, and received his L.L.B. in 1885. Admitted to the bar that same year, he moved to Danville and began to practice law. In 1889, he married Elizabeth Lynn Hoskins. They had three children.

Montague was appointed U.S. Attorney for the Western District of Virginia in 1893. He remained in that position five years, then served as Attorney General of Virginia from 1898 to 1902. In 1901, he was elected governor on the Democratic ticket. His term as governor was marked by the passage of the Mann Act, which outlined strict licensing regulations for saloons. Other legislation included a law, which made employers liable for job-related injuries, and a primary plan for the nomination of U.S. senators.

After Montague's term expired in 1906, he served as a delegate to the Third Conference of American Republics in Rio de Janeiro. In 1910, he went to Brussels as a delegate to the Third International Conference on Maritime Law. He was also, in 1910, a trustee of the Carnegie Institute, and the Carnegie Endowment for International Peace. He later served as vice president of the Endowment as a member of its executive committee (1911-1935), assistant treasurer (1917-1923), and treasurer (1923-1929). Among his other posts, he was president of the American Society for Judicial Settlement of International Disputes in 1917, president of the American group of the Inter-parliamentary Union from 1930 to 1935, and a member of the council and executive committee of the American Institute of Law.

Montague was elected to the U.S. House of Representatives in 1913, and served in that position until his death on January 24, 1937.

SWANSON, CLAUDE AUGUSTUS (1862-1933), forty-seventh governor (1906-1910), was born in Swansonville, Virginia on March 31, 1862, the son of John and Catherine (Prichett) Swanson. He attended public schools, and worked on his father's farm. From 1878 to 1880, he taught school. Then he enrolled in the Virginia Agricultural and Mechanical College in Blacksburg for a short time. He worked as a clerk in a grocery store for two years, and continued his studies, receiving his A.B. degree in 1885 from Randolph-Macon College, and an LL.B. degree in 1886 from the University of Virginia. He was admitted to the Virginia Bar and began a law practice in Chatham. In 1894, he married Lizzie Deane Lyons.

Swanson entered politics in 1893 when he was elected as a Democrat to the U.S. House of Representatives. He served for seven consecutive terms, resigning in 1906. He ran for governor of Virginia in 1901, but was defeated. Four years later, he ran again, and this time was elected by a vote of 84,235 to Republican challenger, Lunsford L. Lewis' 45,815 votes. During Swanson's term, strides were made in the area of education. Funding for primary schools was increased; two teachers' colleges were created; and low interest loans were made available for the construction of high schools. Other developments included a street ban on cocaine, and the first use of electrocution instead of hanging as a means of capital punishment.

Swanson left office in 1910, and entered the U.S. Senate to fill a position left vacant by the death of John W. Daniel. He was elected to the position in his own right a short time later, and continued to serve until 1933, when he resigned to accept the post of Secretary of the Navy under President Franklin Roosevelt.

Swanson remained in that office until July 7, 1939, when he died while on a visit to a camp in the Blue Ridge Mountains, Madison County, Virginia. Swanson was married a second time in 1923, to Lulie Lyons Hall. The couple had no children.

MANN, WILLIAM HODGES (1843-1927), forty-eighth governor (1910-1914), was born in Williamsburg, Virginia on July 30, 1843, the son of John and Mary (Bowers) Mann. He attended Brownsburg Academy until 1857, then served as deputy clerk for Nottoway County for three years. In 1861, at the beginning of the Civil War, he joined the Virginia Volunteers. He was wounded two years later at the Battle of Seven Pines, and left service and returned to his position as deputy clerk in Nottoway County.

Mann studied law, and was admitted to the Virginia Bar in 1867. In 1869, he married Sallie Fitzgerald. He was elected to serve as the first County Judge of Nottoway County. He held that post from 1870 to 1892. In 1885, after the death of his first wife, he married Etta Donnan. He had two sons.

Mann was elected to the Virginia Senate in 1899, and served until 1910. During that time, he authored the Mann Act, which put strict licensing regulations on bars, and closed about eight hundred saloons in areas where there was no police protection. He was elected Governor of Virginia in 1909. During his administration, he supported Prohibition, but saw a statewide prohibition bill defeated in the State Senate. He also supported aid for public schools. In 1914, at the end of his term, he left office and returned to private life. He served as president of the Bank of Crewe, and president of the Citizens' Bank in Blackstone, Virginia. Mann died on December 12, 1927.

STUART, HENRY CARTER (1855-1933), forty-ninth governor of Virginia (1914-1918), was born in Wytheville, Virginia on January 18, 1855, the son of William and Mary (Carter) Stuart. He attended Emory and Henry College, where he received his A.B. degree in 1874, then studied law for a year at the University of Virginia. After leaving the university, he managed his father's business concerns, and began to farm and to raise livestock. In time, he became well known as the largest livestock breeder east of the Mississippi River. He was married in 1896 to Margaret Bruce Carter. They had one daughter.

In the years that followed, Stuart headed various businesses. He was president of the Stuart Land & Cattle Company of Virginia, president of the Buckhorn Coal Company, president of the First National Bank of Lebanon, Virginia; director of the State Planters' Bank & Trust company. He became involved in politics in 1901, when he served as a member of the State Constitutional Convention. The following year, he was appointed to the State Corporation Commission, a position he held from 1902 to 1908. In 1913, he ran for governor on the Democratic ticket, and was elected. He entered office in February 1914. Serving during World War I, he gave priority to preparing the state's war machinery. He was a member of the price-fixing committee of the War Industries Board. In 1917, President Wilson appointed him chairman of the National Agricultural Advisory Commission.

Stuart left office in 1918 at the end of his term. He subsequently served as a representative to the National Industrial Conference, and was president of the Virginia Pay-as-you-go Association. He was offered a position on the Interstate Commerce Commission in 1920, but declined the appointment. He did, however, serve as chairman of the Emory and Henry College Board of Trustees.

Stuart died in Elk Garden, Virginia on July 24, 1933.

DAVIS, WESTMORELAND (1859-1942), fiftieth governor of Virginia (1918-1922), the son of Thomas and Annie (Morris) Davis, was born on August 21, 1859, while his parents were on board a ship traveling to England. He attended the Virginia Military Institute, graduating in 1877. From there, he went on to study at the University of Virginia, and then at Columbia University, where he received his L.L.B. degree in 1886.

Davis was admitted to the New York Bar that same year, and began to practice law in New York City. In 1892, he married Marguerite Inman. As a practicing attorney in New York for fifteen years, he served as general counsel for the National Standard Insurance Company, the Lafayette Fire Insurance Company, Watson Elevator Company, and the Assurance Company of America. In 1901, he moved to Virginia and took up farming at a large estate in Leesburg. He became interested in studying scientific methods of farming, and in improving agricultural practices throughout the state. From 1908 to 1915, he was president of the Virginia State Farmers' Institute.

In 1912, Davis served as Democratic presidential elector from Virginia's eighth district. He ran for governor in 1917 on the Democratic ticket and was elected. His administration was marked by widespread reforms. He created the executive budget system; overhauled the state prison system; and established the State Industrial Commission to administer worker's compensation. Also during his term, prohibition took effect in the state, and women were given the right to vote.

Davis left office in 1922 and became the editor and publisher of the *Southern Planter*. He remained in that position until his death in 1942. He was also president of the Virginia State Farmers' Institute between 1923-24 and 1941-42, a member of the Virginia Polytechnic Institute Board of Visitors, and president of the Virginia State Fair Association.

He died in Baltimore, Maryland on September 2, 1942.

TRINKLE, ELBERT LEE (1876-1939), fifty-first governor (1922-1926), was born in Wytheville, Virginia on March 12, 1876, the son of Elbert and Letitia (Sexton) Trinkle. He attended Wytheville Military Academy, and then Hampden Sydney College, where he received his A.B. and his B.S. degree in 1896. He went on to the University of Virginia Law School, and received his LL.B. degree in 1898. He was admitted to the Virginia Bar that same year, and began to practice law in Wytheville. In 1910, he married Helen Ball Sexton. They had four children. Trinkle continued to practice in Wytheville until 1921.

Trinkle also served for various years as a partner in the Trinkle Brothers farming company, was vice-president of the Shenandoah Life Insurance Company, director of the United Life & Accident Insurance Company, and vice-president of the American Life Insurance Convention.

Trinkle became involved in politics in 1916, when he served as a Democratic Presidential Elector-at-Large. He ran for governor of Virginia in 1921, and was elected over Republican, Henry Anderson. During his administration, Trinkle supported fiscal conservatism and required state institutions to operate on a pay-as-you-go basis. The Legislature instituted worker's compensation for state and city employees, raised teaching standards for public schools, and amended the Compulsory Education Act to apply to children up to fourteen years old.

Trinkle was active as chairman of the Executive Committee of the Conference of Governors, and was recognized with a medal from the National Committee on Prisons and Prison Labor for his work in establishing an exchange of prison-made goods between states.

Trinkle left office in 1926 and served in various capacities, both public and private, over the next thirteen years. He was president of the Virginia State Boards of Education (1930-39), president of the Children's Home Society of Southwestern Virginia (1935-38); director of Southwestern Virginia, Inc., and a trustee of Hampden-Sydney College.

Trinkle died in Richmond, Virginia on November 25, 1939.

BYRD, HARRY FLOOD (1887-1966), fifty-second governor (1926-1930), was born in Martinsburg, West Virginia on June 10, 1887, the son of Richard Evelyn and Elinor (Flood) Byrd. He attended Shenandoah Valley Academy in Winchester, Virginia.

In 1902, Byrd became manager of the *Winchester Star*. He became owner and publisher of the paper, and in 1907, established his own paper, the Martinsburg Evening Journal. He also founded the Winchester Storage Company. From 1908 to 1918, Byrd was president of the Valley Turnpike Company. He was married in October 1913 to Annie Douglas Beverly. They had four children.

Byrd was elected to the Virginia State Senate, and served from 1915 to 1925. He was also the Virginia Fuel Commissioner in

1918, and was chairman of the Democratic State Committee in 1922. In 1923, he became publisher of the *Harrisonburg Daily News-Record*. Byrd ran for governor in 1925 and won by a wide margin against Republican opponent, S. Harris Hoge. During Byrd's term, the Legislature trimmed government by abolishing over thirty boards, commissions and bureaus, and brought government activities under the control of twelve departments. The Legislature also approved the reform measure known as the "short ballot," which limited the number of elected state officials to three: the governor, lieutenant governor, and attorney general. Also during Byrd's administration, lynching was made an offense against the state, and tax laws were revised.

Since he was constitutionally ineligible to succeed himself, Byrd left the governorship at the end of his term in 1930. In 1933, he was appointed to the U.S. Senate to fill the vacancy left by the resignation of Claude Swanson. Byrd was elected in his own right in the subsequent election, and maintained his Senate seat until 1965. He died on October 20 of the following year in Berryville, Virginia.

POLLARD, JOHN GARLAND (1871-1937), fifty-third governor (1930-1934), was born in King and Queen County, Virginia on August 4, 1871, the son of John and Virginia (Bagby) Pollard. He attended Richmond College and graduated in 1891, then went on to Columbia (later George Washington) University Law School, where he received his LL.B. degree in 1893. He was admitted to the Virginia Bar that same year, and began to practice law in Richmond. In 1898, he married Grace Phillips. They had three children.

Pollard continued his law practice in Richmond for twenty-five years. During that period, he was also president of the Capitol Savings Bank; director of the Bank of Commerce & Trusts; the Peninsula Bank & Trust Company; the National Bank of Virginia, Central National Bank; Old Dominion Trust Company; and vice-president and managing director of the American Terminal Warehouse Corporation.

Pollard was a member of the Virginia Constitutional Convention in 1901. From 1902 to 1907, he served as chairman of the Virginia Commission on Uniform State Laws. He was a Democratic Elector in 1904. From 1913 to 1917, he served as Attorney General of Virginia, and at the same time, was a member of the State Board of Education. He ran for governor, but failing in this effort, decided to go to France and Germany, where he did World War I assistance work from 1918 to 1919. Upon his return, he was chosen as a member of the War Department's Board of Contract Adjustment. From 1920 to 1921, he was a member of the Federal Trade Commission. In 1922, he taught constitutional law and history, and in 1923, he was a professor of government and citizenship at the College of William and Mary. He was made dean of the Marshall Wythe School of Government and Citizenship from 1924 to 1929.

In 1929, running as a Democratic candidate, Pollard was elected Governor of Virginia. His administration was marked by the implementation of economic measures designed to offset the effects of the Great Depression. The measures included reducing his salary by ten percent and establishing a pay-as-you-go program to improve state resources without a tax increase. When violence broke out during a strike of four thousand workers at the Riverside and Dan River textile mills in Danville, Governor Pollard sent in state troops to restore order.

Pollard married Violet McDougall in 1933, his second wife. He left office the following year. During the next three years, he served as chairman of the U.S. Board of Veteran's Appeals. He was the author of several works, including: "The Pamunkey Indians of Virginia" (1894); "Virginia Code, Annotated" (1904); "Virginia Law Register" (1904 and 1906); and "A Connotary" (1935). Pollard died in Washington, D.C. on April 28, 1937.

PEERY, GEORGE CAMPBELL (1873-1952), fifty-fourth governor (1934-1938), was born in Cedar Bluff, Virginia on October 28, 1873, the son of James and Mary (Spotts) Peery. He graduated from Emory and Henry College in 1894 with a B.S. degree. From 1894 to 1896, he was principal of Tazewell High School. He then returned to college, attending Washington and Lee University, and received his LL.B. degree in 1897.

Peery was admitted to the Virginia Bar and began to practice law in Tazewell. In 1899, he went to work for the legal department of the Virginia Iron, Coal & Coke Company. He moved to Wise, Virginia in 1902, and from 1904 to 1915, was a member of the law firm of Vicars & Peery. In 1907, he married Nanie Bane Pendleton. They had three children.

Peery moved back to Tazewell in 1915, and joined the firm of Chapman, Peery & Buchanan, remaining with that practice until 1930. During that time, he also served in various other business capacities, including vice-president and director of Norton Hardware Company; director of Coeburn Home Company, Inc.; secretary and director of Banner Raven Coal Corporation; director of the Buckhorn Coal Company; director of Hazard Coal Corporation; and director of the Richmond, Fredericksburg & Potomac Railroad Company.

Peery became involved in politics in 1916 when he was a Democratic Presidential Elector-at-Large. In 1920 and 1924, he was a delegate to the Democratic National Convention. He was elected to the U.S. House of Representatives in 1923, and served until 1929. In 1928, he was made temporary chairman of the Democratic State Convention. He was a member of the Virginia State Corporation Commission from 1929 to 1933. In the latter year, he ran for governor, and was elected in an easy victory over Republican, Fred McWane.

As governor, Peery supported increased funding for public schools. He also appointed the first members of the State Alcoholic Beverage Control Board, the State Milk Commission, and the Unemployment Compensation Commission.

Other accomplishments during Peery's term included reorganization of the Conservation Commission, and the establishment of the trial justice system in Virginia.

Peery left office in 1938 and retired to his livestock farm near Tazewell. He died in Richlands, Virginia on October 14, 1952.

PRICE, JAMES HUBERT (1878-1943), fifty-fifth governor (1938-1942), was born in Greenbriar County, West Virginia on September 7, 1878, the son of Charles and Nancy (Boone) Price. His family moved to Staunton, Virginia, and he attended Dunsmore Business College there, and later taught at the College for a short time.

Price was secretary-treasurer and director of the insurance firm, W.J. Perry Corporation, before attending law school at Washington and Lee University. He graduated with his LL.B. degree in 1909, was admitted to the Virginia Bar that same year, and began to practice law in Richmond. Shortly thereafter, he became a member of the Richmond Democratic Committee, and served as its chairman for three years.

From 1904 to 1913, Price served in the Virginia National Guard, where he rose to the rank of captain and commissary of the First Infantry. He was a legal advisor to the Richmond local draft boards during World War I. Also, about that time, in October 1918, he married Lillian Martin. They had two children.

Price was elected to the Virginia House of Delegates in 1915, and served until 1928. He was Lieutenant Governor of Virginia from 1930 to 1938, and then went on to the governorship, elected on November 2, 1937 as a Democrat to fill that post. During his administration, the state Social Security Act was adopted and a judicial retirement act was passed. A merit system was also set up for public service work. Other accomplishments included construction of the Supreme Court building, the state library, and a new building for the Medical College of Virginia. Price ended his term in 1942 with a surplus of about fourteen million dollars in the state treasury.

After leaving office, Price became a director of the Central National Bank of Richmond and of the Jefferson Realty Company.

He died in Richmond on November 22, 1943.

DARDEN, COLGATE WHITEHEAD (1897-1981), fifty-sixth governor (1942-1946), was born near Franklin, Virginia on February 11, 1897, the son of Colgate Whitehead and Katherine (Pretlow) Darden. He was educated at the University of Virginia, where he received his B.A. in 1922, and Columbia University, receiving his MA. and LL.B. degrees in 1923. During World War I, he served as en ambulance driver with the French Army, as a member of the American Ambulance Corps, in the aviation branch of the U.S. Navy, and finally as a fighter pilot with the U.S. Marine Corps.

Returning after the war, Darden was admitted to the Virginia Bar in 1922, and began to practice law in Norfolk. In 1923, he received a Carnegie Fellowship to study international law at Oxford University for a year. He was married in 1927 to Constance duPont. They had three children.

Darden was elected to the Virginia House of Delegates, and served from 1930 to 1933. He also served in the U.S. House of Representatives from 1933 to 1937, and again from 1939 to 1941. In the latter year, he ran for governor of Virginia, and was elected by a wide margin over Republican opponent, B. Muse. During his term, strides were made in the area of education, as the state made appropriations to purchase visual aids for public schools, and to assist blacks that wanted to study medicine at Meharry Medical College in Tennessee.

Ineligible constitutionally to succeed himself as governor, Darden left office in 1946 and became chancellor of the College of William and Mary. In addition, he was vice-chairman, and later chairman, of the Navy's *Civilian* Advisory Committee. He became president of the University of Virginia in 1947, remaining until 1959, when he retired into private life.

Darden died on June 1, 1981.

TUCK, WILLIAM MUNFORD (1896-1983), fifty-seventh governor (1946-1950), was born in Halifax County, Virginia on September 28, 1896, the son of Robert and Virginia (Fists) Tuck. He attended the College of William and Mary from 1915 to 1917, and then entered the U.S. Marines as a private during World War I. On his return after the war, he studied law at Washington and Lee University, and graduated with an LL.B. degree in 1921. He was admitted to the Virginia Bar that same year, and began to practice law in South Boston, Virginia. In 1928, he married Eva (Lovelace) Dillard.

Tuck became involved in politics about 1920, when he was a delegate to the Democratic Convention. He was a delegate to numerous subsequent conventions. In 1923, he was elected to the Virginia House of Delegates. He served from 1924 to 1932 then held a seat in the State Senate for ten years. He was a Democratic elector-at-large in 1936. In 1941, he was elected Lieutenant Governor of Virginia, a post he retained from 1942 to 1946.

Tuck ran for governor on the Democratic ticket in 1945, and defeated his Republican opponent, S. Lloyd Landreth, by a vote of more than two to one. During his administration, Tuck sought to limit the power of unions, and secured the passage of legislation, which outlawed the re-employment of any public worker for one year after that employee had gone on strike. He also made it "against public policy" for a public official to bargain with a labor union, and made it illegal to require union membership as a condition of employment. As a means of avoiding a strike at the Virginia Electric and Power Company, Tuck declared 1,600 essential workers from the plant to be part of the state's "unorganized militia." Also during his term, Tuck came out against grants from Congress for most highways, and supported the elimination of the federal gasoline tax in favor of a state gasoline tax.

At the end of his term in 1950, Tuck returned to his law practice. He was a delegate-at-large to the 1948 and 1952 Democratic National Conventions. He was elected to the U.S. House of Representatives in 1953, and remained in Congress until 1969, when he returned to his law practice in South Boston, Virginia.

Tuck died on June 9, 1983.

BATTLE, JOHN STEWART (1890-1972), fifty-eighth governor (1950-1954), was born in New Bern, North Carolina on July 11, 1890, the son of Rev. Dr. Henry and Margaret (Stewart) Battle. He received his education at Wake Forest College and the University of Virginia, where he graduated with an LL.B. degree in 1913. He was admitted to the Virginia Bar that same year, and began to practice law in Charlottesville. During World War I, Battle was a private in the U.S. Army. In 1918, he married Mary Jane Lipscomb. They had two children.

Battle was elected to the Virginia House of Delegates and served from 1930 to 1934. In the latter year, he became a member of the State Senate, where he remained until 1950.

In 1949, Battle ran for governor as a Democrat, and won easily over Republican Walter Johnson. During his administration, Battle supported expansion of local health care programs; funding for mental hospitals; and higher salaries for teachers. At the outbreak of the Korean War, he reinstated the State Council of Defense.

Other developments during Battle's term included new legislation that provided funding for school construction, and gave power to the governor to seize coal mines for state operation in the event it became necessary.

Battle left office at the end of his term in 1954, and joined the law firm of Perkins, Battle and Minor. He was a member of the Civil Rights Commission in 1959. He died in Albernarle County, Virginia on April 9, 1972.

STANLEY, THOMAS BAHNSON (1890-1970), fifty-ninth governor (1954-1958), was born near Spencer, Virginia on July 16, 1890, the son of Crockett and Susan (Walker) Stanley. He attended public schools in Spencer, and then went to work in the coal mines in Maybeury, West Virginia. After a short time, he moved to Poughkeepsie, New York and attended the Eastman National Business College.

After his graduation in 1912, Stanley became a bookkeeper for the R.J. Reynolds Tobacco Company in Winston-Salem, North Carolina for a year. He worked as a clerk for the Bank of Ridgeway, Virginia in 1913; a clerk-bookkeeper for the First National Bank in Martinsville, Virginia from 1914 to 1916; and a cashier for the First National Bank in Rural Retreat, Virginia from 1916 to 1920. In 1918, he married Anne Pocahontas Bassett. They had three children.

Stanley moved to Galax, Virginia and became vice-president of the Vaughan-Bassett Furniture Company from 1921 to 1922. He

was vice-president of the Bassett Furniture Company, Inc. from 1922 to 1924, and then established his own business, the Stanley Furniture Company, Inc. in 1924. He was also president of the Ferrurn Veneer Corporation, and director of Virginia & Forests Inc. for a time. In 1929 he was elected to the Virginia House of Delegates, where he served from 1930 to 1946, acting as speaker from 1942 to 1946. He was subsequently elected to the U.S. House of Representatives, and held that position from 1946 to 1953. In the latter year, he was elected Governor of Virginia, defeating Republican candidate, Ted Dalton.

During his administration, Stanley supported an increased gasoline tax to raise funds for state highways, and advocated higher salaries for teachers. He spoke out in favor of federal funding to maintain interstate highways, and signed legislation to restrict billboards along state roads. He also joined with eight governors from coal-producing states to ask Congress to limit imports of oil and natural gas.

Stanley left office in 1958, and returned to his business interests. In the years that followed, he became president and director of the First National Bank in Bassett, Virginia, and chairman of the Commission on State and Local Revenues and Expenditures. He was also a trustee of Randolph Macon College. He died in Martinsville, Virginia on July 10, 1970.

ALMOND, JAMES LINDSAY (1898-1986), sixtieth governor of Virginia (1958-1962), was born in Charlottesville, Virginia on June 15, 1898, the son of James and Edmonia (Burgess) Almond. He attended the University of Virginia during World War I, and served in the Students' Army Training Corps as a private. In 1923, he received his LL.B. degree from the University of Virginia. Meanwhile, in 1919, he worked as a schoolteacher in Locust Grove, *Virginia*, and from 1921 to 1922, he was principal of Zoar High School.

Almond was admitted to the Virginia Bar in 1921, and began to practice law in Roanoke. In 1925, he married Josephine Katherine Minter. He continued with his Roanoke law practice until 1930, when he became Assistant Commonwealth Attorney of Virginia. He remained at that post until 1933, when he was made judge of the Hustings Court of Roanoke City. In 1945, he was elected to the U.S. House of Representatives, and served from 1946 to 1948. He resigned the House in order to become Attorney General of Virginia, an office he held from 1948 to 1957.

In November of the latter year, Almond ran for governor of Virginia on the Democratic ticket, and won easily over Republican contender, Ted Dalton.

Almond's administration was marked by the controversy over racial integration. The Virginia Legislature attempted to diffuse the federal order for integration of public schools by repealing the compulsory school attendance law. It also offered tuition grants of 250 dollars per year for students who attended private nonsectarian schools. At the same time, it attempted to keep the peace by imposing stiff penalties for bomb threats to houses, schools and other buildings.

Other developments during Almond's term included increases to unemployment benefits and worker's compensation, and pay raise for teachers.

Almond left office in 1962, and soon afterward was appointed interim judge of the U.S. Court of Customs and Patent Appeals. He served as associate judge of that court from 1963 to 1973, when he retired into private life.

HARRISON, ALBERTIS SYDNEY (1907-1995), sixty-first governor of Virginia (1962-1966), was born in Alberta, Virginia on January 11, 1907, the son of Albertis Sydney and Lizzie

(Goodrich) Harrison. He attended the University of Virginia and graduated with an LL.B. degree in 1928. That same year, he was admitted to the Virginia Bar.

In 1930, Harrison was the city attorney for Lawrenceville, Virginia. Also in May of that year, he married Lacey Barkley. They had two children.

Harrison was the commonwealth's attorney for Brunswick County, Virginia from 1932 to 1948, taking time out during World War II to serve as a lieutenant in the U.S. Navy. In 1947, he was elected to the Virginia State Senate, and served from 1948 to 1957, when he was elected State Attorney General. In 1961, he ran for governor on the Democratic ticket, and was elected over Republican H. Clyde Pearson.

During Harrison's administration, funding for public schools was increased, and the daylight savings time bill was enacted. The governor's office took over responsibility for industrial development from the Department of Conservation and Economic Development. Also, the Kerr-Mills hospitalization program for the elderly was established.

Since he was ineligible constitutionally to run for a second term, Harrison left office in 1966. The following year, he was appointed Justice of the Virginia Supreme Court. In 1968, he was a member of the Commission to Revise the Constitution of Virginia. He was also a member of the Board of Visitors of the University of Virginia, and a fellow of the *American College of Trial Lawyers*.

Harrison died on January 23, 1995.

GODWIN, MILLS EDWIN (1914-1999), sixty-second and sixty-fourth governor of Virginia (1966-1970 and 1974-1978), was born in Chuckatuck, Virginia on November 19, 1914 the son of Mills Edwin and Otelia (Darden) Godwin. He attended the College of William and Mary division in Norfolk, and later in Williamsburg, then went on to the University of Virginia where he received his LL.B. degree in 1938. He was admitted to the Virginia Bar, and began to practice law in Suffolk, Virginia. In 1940, he married Katherine Beale. They had one child.

Godwin maintained his Suffolk law practice from 1938 to 1960. During that time he was also a special agent for the Federal Bureau of Investigation from 1942 to 1946; a member of the Virginia House of Delegates from 1947 to 1952; and a member of the State Senate from 1952 to 1961. He was elected Lieutenant Governor of Virginia in the latter year, and served from 1962 to 1966.

In the November 1965 election, Godwin ran for governor on the Democratic ticket and defeated Republican, Linwood Holton and Conservative candidate, William J. Story, Jr. During his administration, Godwin was a strong supporter of education. He became known as "Virginia's Education Governor" for his work to establish a community college system, increases salaries and other benefits for teachers, provide schooling for the handicapped, and fund kindergartens. He also, following programs set down by Gov. Albertis Harrison, promoted industrial development, and attempted to attract new businesses to Virginia.

Since Godwin was ineligible to succeed himself in office, he returned to his business interests in 1970. He was director of the Western Railway Company, director of Standard Brands, Inc. of Norfolk; director of the Union Camp Corporation; director of the Virginia Real Estate Investment Trust; director of Dan River, Inc.; and a member of the Executive Committee and Board of Directors of the Virginia National Bank. He ran for a second term as governor in 1973, this time on the Republican ticket, and was elected in a narrow victory over Independent, Henry Howell.

During Godwin's second term, several bills were defeated, including the Equal Rights Amendment, legislation to permit collective bargaining by public employees, and legislation to allow "death with dignity."

Godwin completed his second term in 1978. During his career, he received numerous awards, including the First Citizen's Award of Suffolk and Nansemond County; the Virginia State Chamber of Commerce's Distinguished Service Award; the Virginia National Guard's Distinguished Citizen's Medal; the Thomas Jefferson Award for Public Service; and honorary degrees from Elon College, the College of William and Mary, Roanoke College, Washington and Lee University, Elmira College, Hampden-Sydney College, the University of Richmond, and Bridgewater College.

Godwin died on January 30, 1999.

HOLTON, ABNER LINWOOD (1923-), sixty-third governor of Virginia (1970-1974), was born in Big Stone Gap, Virginia on September 21, 1923, the son of Abner Linwood and Edith (Van Gorder) Holton. He attended Washington and Lee University and received his B.A. degree in 1944. During World War II, he served as an apprentice seaman in the submarine force of the U.S. Navy.

After the war, Holton entered Harvard University Law School and graduated with an LL.B. degree in 1949. He was admitted to the Virginia Bar, and began to practice law in Roanoke with the firm of Hunter and Fox. He later formed the new firm of Eggleston, Holton, Butler and Glenn with three partners. In 1953, he married Virginia Harrison Rogers. They had four children.

Holton became involved in politics, and during the 1950s was chairman of the Roanoke City Republican Committee. He ran for the House of Delegates in 1955 and 1957, but was defeated in both campaigns. In 1960, he was elected vice-chairman of the Virginia Republican Central Committee. He was also a delegate to the Republican National Conventions of 1960 and 1968, and was a regional coordinator for Richard Nixon's presidential campaign.

Holton ran for governor in 1965, but was defeated by Democratic candidate, Mills Godwin. He ran again in 1969, and this time won the election and was inaugurated on January 17, 1970. During his administration, Holton established the Judicial Inquiry and Review Commission. The Legislature increased corporate, gasoline, and income taxes; provided funding for low cost housing; made appropriations for higher education; lowered the age of majority to eighteen except for liquor purchases and jury duty; reduced penalties for possession of marijuana; and rejected ratification of the Equal Rights Amendment.

Also during Holton's term, the State Constitution was revised and amendments were added to limit the appointive powers of judges, establish yearly legislative sessions, decrease the residency requirement for voting, and bar governmental discrimination based on race, sex, religion or national origin.

Holton left office in 1974, and was soon after named Assistant Secretary of State for Congressional Relations. He served in that position for ten months then went back to practicing law.

DALTON, JOHN NICHOLAS (1931-1986), sixty-fifth governor of Virginia (1978-1982), was born in Emporia, Virginia on July 11, 1931, the son of Ted and Mary (Turner) Dalton. He attended William and Mary College, and received his A.B. degree in 1953. He subsequently served in the U.S. Army from 1954 to 1956, where he attained the rank of first lieutenant.

Dalton returned to school, attending the University of Virginia, and in 1957, graduated with a J.D. degree. He was admitted to the Virginia Bar, and became a partner in the law firm of Dalton and Jebo in Radford, Virginia. In 1956, he married Edwina Panzer. They had four children.

Dalton continued with the law firm of Dalton and Jebo until 1974. Meanwhile, he was also active in various businesses. He was vice-president and director of Meredith and Tate in Pulaski; director of Sutton Development Corporation in Radford; and director of the First Merchant Bank in Radford. He entered politics around 1960, when he served as president of the Young Republican Federation of Virginia. He was treasurer of the Virginia Republican Committee that same year, and from 1961 to 1972, was general counsel for the Virginia Republican Committee. In 1965, he was elected to the Virginia House of Delegates. He remained at that post until 1972 then served a year in the Virginia Senate. From 1974 to 1978, he was Lieutenant Governor of Virginia, and in the following gubernatorial election, he ran as a Republican, and won over Democrat, Henry Howell.

Dalton entered office in January 1978. As governor, he cut federally funded programs for the mentally handicapped, made general reductions to Medicaid payments, and vetoed the use of Medicaid in abortions for rape and incest.

However, in 1981, when the Virginia State Treasury was showing a surplus, Dalton supported restoration of some funding to Medicaid, and salary increases for state employees. He also secured a higher gasoline sales tax to finance highway construction and the Washington, D.C. area subway system, and he created a program to help needy people pay their heating bills. Dalton left office in 1982, and returned to private life.

Dalton died July 30, 1986.

ROBB, CHARLES SPITTAL (1939-)

ROBB, CHARLES SPITTAL (1939-), sixty-sixth governor of Virginia (1982-1986), was born in Phoenix, Arizona on June 26, 1939, the son of James and Frances (Woolley) Robb. He was educated at Cornell University, and at the University of Wisconsin, where he received his B.A.A. degree in 1961. He served in the U.S. Marine Corp during the Vietnam War, and in 1967, married Lynda Bird Johnson, daughter of President Lyndon B. Johnson. They have three children.

After Robb's return from Vietnam in 1970, Robb attended the University of Virginia Law School. While still at law school, he became director of the LBJ Company. He graduated from the University of Virginia in 1973, and was admitted to the Virginia Bar. He served as a law clerk for a short time, then joined the Washington, D.C. law firm of Williams, Connally and Califano in 1974. He also became deputy general counsel and assistant parliamentarian for the Democratic National Committee's Platform Committee.

In 1977, Robb was elected as a Democrat to serve as Lieutenant Governor of Virginia under Republican Governor Dalton. Robb ran for the governorship in 1981 and was elected over J. Marshall Coleman. As governor, Robb came out in favor of budget cuts to alleviate the national deficit, and sought to make Virginia a leader in racial progress. The interest ceiling on credit card transactions was raised during his term, and approval was given for "no-fault" divorces after a waiting period of six months.

Ineligible constitutionally to succeed himself, Robb left office in 1986. In 1985, he helped found the Democratic Leadership Council. He then served as chairman of its board of directors.

BALILES, GERALD L. (1940-)

BALILES, GERALD L. (1940-), sixty-seventh governor of Virginia (1986-1989), was born in Patrick County, Virginia on July 8, 1940. He grew up on his grandparents' farm and attended local public schools. At age fifteen, he left Patrick County to attend Fishburne Military School in Waynesboro, Virginia. He went on to Wesleyan University in Connecticut, where he earned his undergraduate degree in 1963, and then attended the University of Virginia, where he received his law degree in 1967. About that time, he was married to Jeannie Patterson. They have two children.

Between 1967 and 1975, Baliles worked in the Virginia Attorney General's Office as an Assistant Attorney General, and then Deputy Attorney General. In 1975, he was elected to the Virginia House of Delegates, and served until 1982. He became Virginia Attorney General in the latter year, and while in office, served as chairman of the Southern Association of Attorneys General.

In 1985, Baliles ran for governor, and won in a historic Democratic victory that included election of the first black Lieutenant Governor of Virginia and the first woman Attorney General. As governor, Baliles was a strong proponent of environmental issues, and made efforts to end pollution of Chesapeake Bay. Other of his initiatives included a major transportation program to improve roads, seaports, airports, and mass transit; projects to fight illiteracy; and an emphasis on international trade and educational reforms to promote competition in world markets.

WILDER, LAWRENCE DOUGLAS (1931-)

WILDER, LAWRENCE DOUGLAS (1931-), sixty-eighth Governor of Virginia (1990-94), was born in Richmond, Virginia on January 17, 1931. He was the grandson of slaves, and was named after Frederick Douglass and poet Paul Lawrence Dunbar. He attended Virginia Union University, earning a B.S. degree in chemistry in 1951 then continued his studies at Howard University School of Law, where he received a J.D. degree in 1959. That same year, he became a founder of the law firm of Wilder, Gregory and Martin, where he remained a partner until his victory for the governorship.

Wilder's first foray into politics was his successful bid for a Senate seat in 1969 on the Democratic ticket. Wilder was then elected to his post for an additional four terms. During his years in the Senate, he served as chairman on such committees as the Senate Committee on Transportation; Senate Committee on Rehabilitation and Social Services; Senate Committee on Privileges and Elections; Virginia Advisory Legislative Council; and Democratic Steering Committee. A popular political figure, he was consistently named as one of the most effective government officials in an annual survey conducted by the Norfolk Virginian-Pilot.

Some of the major legislation Wilder was directly involved in during his senatorial tenure included prohibiting or regulating the possession, sale or distribution of drug paraphernalia; requiring that the disease of sickle cell anemia be placed under the jurisdiction of the State Health Department; establishing a state holiday in honor of the late Dr. Martin Luther King, Jr. on January 15; requiring detailed investigations concerning discriminatory housing practices; and establishing severe penalties, including additional time, for prisoners that escaped, or who committed capital crimes.

In 1985, Wilder was elected Lieutenant Governor of Virginia. While in that office, he served as chairman of both the National Democratic Lieutenant Governors' Association, and of the National Conference of Lieutenant Governors' Drug Interdiction Task Force.

Wilder was elected Governor of the State of Virginia in the November 1989 race. Immediately before the general election, he was lauded by several newspapers, including the *Washington Post*, whose editor stated: "Mr. Wilder is an uncommon figure in contemporary politics in that he has not ridden the media to his present position but has worked his way up, has served a long, and we believe valuable, apprenticeship." The *Charlottesville Daily Progress* concurred, saying: "Mr. Wilder comes to us after more than nineteen years in public office, where he has proven his mettle and shown, if anything, he is his own man. Wilder's famous eyeball-to-eyeball confrontations with his own party's power structure have inspired respect among friends and political opponents. Like his two predecessors he has a reputation among colleagues as a consensus builder and strong inside player."

Some of the professional organizations of which Wilder has been a member include the American Bar Association; the Virginia State Bar; the American Trial Lawyers Association; and the National Association of Criminal Defense Lawyers. He is also a Permanent Member of the Judicial Conference of the Fourth Circuit (federal), and a Life Member of the National Bar Association.

Governor Wilder served in the United States Army, and was awarded the Bronze Star for heroism in ground combat in Korea. He has three children: Lynn, Lawrence, Jr., and Loren.

ALLEN, GEORGE (1952-), sixty-ninth Governor of Virginia (1994-98), was born on March 8, 1952, the son of Henrietta and the late George H. Allen, who was the former head coach of the Washington Redskins NFL football team.

Allen attended the University of Virginia, graduating in 1974 with a bachelor's degree in history. He earned his Juris Doctorate in 1977. His career in public office began after an election to the Virginia House of Delegates; he kept his seat for nine years. In 1983, he was elected to the General Assembly, and served as assistant minority leader. In a special election in 1991, he was elected to the U.S. House of Representatives for the 7th Congressional District. He received the National Taxpayers' Union's recognition as one of the five "most fiscally responsible members of the 102nd Congress."

In 1993, Allen was elected Virginia's Governor, receiving fifty-eight percent of the vote and becoming the first gubernatorial candidate in the State's history to receive more than one million votes in a general election. Since taking office, Allen has sought to replace the failed welfare system with reforms that promote individual responsibility and the work ethic. He has also abolished the State's lenient parole system and transformed the juvenile justice system; linked higher education spending with high academic standards and a regular testing program to ensure accountability; fostered a pro-growth, pro-opportunity business environment in tax and regulatory policies, leading to unprecedented levels of investments and new jobs; streamlined State government operations to make it less costly and more efficient; and cut taxes.

A further effort of Allen's administration is a nationwide move to restore rights and prerogatives of state and local government and citizens, rather than allowing the federal government to intrude. In this effort, he has proposed the States' Initiative and States' Veto, which would give states enhanced constitutional powers.

Allen's Jeffersonian conservative position has earned him recognition as representing a new generation of principled, creative, and common sense leaders. He chairs the Southern Governors' Association, and is a past chair of the Chesapeake Bay Executive Council. Awards he has received include the Thomas Jefferson Freedom Award from the American Legislative Exchange Council, and honors from other bipartisan national organizations, including the National Federation of Independent Business, National Taxpayers' Union Foundation, and the Council for Citizens Against Government Waste.

Allen is married to the former Susan Brown; the couple has two children.

GILMORE, JIM (1949-), seventieth governor of Virginia (1998-), was born in Richmond on October 6, 1949. He grew up in the Fan District of Richmond. During his high school years, his family moved to the suburbs of Richmond, where he worked as a grocery store cashier to help pay for his education while attending high school and college.

Gilmore graduated from the University of Virginia in 1971. He then volunteered for the U.S. Army, and was assigned to counterintelligence in West Germany. While overseas, he was awarded the Joint Service Commendation Metal for service to NATO. Upon completing his military tour, Gilmore returned to his home state and entered the University of Virginia Law School, where he graduated in 1977. As an attorney and small businessman, Gilmore became actively involved in civic and community efforts.

In 1987, Gilmore was elected the Commonwealth's Attorney for Henrico County, and was reelected by an overwhelming margin in 1991. His leadership efforts in fighting crime helped him to achieve a solid record as a prosecutor determined to protect Virginia's citizens from violent criminals, corrupt officials, and drug dealers.

In 1993, Gilmore was elected Attorney General of the Commonwealth. During his tenure, he earned even more respect from Virginians by his decisive leadership and accomplishments in such areas as education, public safety, consumer protection, and the environment.

Gilmore was elected Virginia's governor in 1997 and was inaugurated in January 1998. His efforts as chief executive of Virginia have included such issues as quality education and tax reform.

Gilmore is married to Roxane Gatling, who teaches at Randolph-Macon College in Ashland. They are members of the River Road Methodist Church; they have two children.

DICTIONARY OF PLACES

Population figures and demographic information are official U.S. Census Bureau finals for 1990. When two figures are shown, separated by a slash, the first figure is the 1990 and the second is the U.S. Census Bureau 1999 estimate—the most recent available. Year 2000 census supplements will be available in the Fall of 2001.

ABINGDON, Town; Washington County Seat; Pop. 7,003; Zip Code 24210; Elev. 2069; 15 mi. NE of Bristol; Lat. 36-42-57 N, Long. 081-58-07 W; Settled in the 1760s and named either for Lord Abingdon or Mary Washington's home town.

ALEXANDRIA, City; Pop. 111,183; Zip Code 22300; 6 mi. S of Washington D.C.; Lat. 38-47-05 N, Long. 077-00-51 W; The town is named after colonial settler John Alexander, who came to the area in 1669.

ALTAVISTA, Town; Campbell County; Pop. 3,686; Zip Code 24517; Elev. 596; 23 mi. S of Lynchburg; Lat. 37-06-59 N, Long. 079-17-28 W; The town is named for a farm owner, settler Henry Lane.

APPALACHIA, Town; Wise County; Pop. 1,994; Zip Code 24216; Elev. 1651; 40 mi. WNW of Bristol; Lat. 36-57-52 N, Long. 082-46-49 W; The town is named after the Appalachia Mountains.

ASHLAND, Town; Hanover County; Pop. 5,864; Zip Code 23005; 16 mi. N of Richmond; Lat. 37-45-28 N, Long. 077-28-57 W; The town is named for the Kentucky home of statesman Henry Clay.

BEDFORD, City; Pop. 6,073; Zip Code 24523; 22 mi. WSW of Lychburg; Lat. 37-20-20 N, Long. 079-31-15 W; Originally named Liberty, the name was changed in 1896 after the county name.

BELLE HAVEN, Town; Accomack & Northhampton Counties; Pop. 526; Zip Code 23306; Elev. 36; 53 mi. NNE of Norfolk; Lat. 37-31-53 N, Long. 075-52-04 W; A pioneer named Bell had a large oven in the area, so the place became Bell's Oven. In 1762 this was changed to Bell's Haven.

BERRYVILLE, Town; Clarke County Seat; Pop. 3,097; Zip Code 22611; Elev. 575; 13 mi. E of Winchester; Lat. 39-09-04 N, Long. 077-59-08 W; In 1798 the town was laid out on land belonging to settler Benjamin Berry who divided the area into town lots.

BIG STONE GAP, Town; Wise County; Pop. 4,748; Zip Code 24219; 40 mi. WNW of Bristol; Lat. 36-56-09 N, Long. 082-46-35 W; Descriptively named for the gap in the mountains nearby through which the Powell River emerges.

BLACKSBURG, Town; Montgomery County; Pop. 34,590; Zip Code 24060; Elev. 2080; 28 mi. W of Roanoke; Lat. 37-13-48 N, Long. 080-24-35 W; The town's name honors William Black who donated land for the town.

BLACKSTONE, Town; Nottoway County; Pop. 3,497; Zip Code 23824; Elev. 427; 36 mi. WSW of Petersburg; Lat. 37-04-44 N, Long. 077-59-50 W; Incorporated in 1888 and named for the famous English jurist, Sir William Blackstone.

BLUEFIELD, Town; Tazewell County; Pop. 5,363; Zip Code 24605; Elev. 2389; 32 mi. WNW of Pulaski; Descriptively named for the blue-grass valley in which it lies.

BRIDGEWATER, Town; Rockingham County; Pop. 3,918; Zip Code 22812; 7 mi. SW of Harrisonburg; Lat. 38-22-59 N, Long. 078-58-34 W; Once the site of a ferry across the North River, ultimately a bridge was built and the town so named.

CAPE CHARLES, Town; Northampton County; Pop. 1,512 / 1,312; Zip Code 23310; Lat. 37-16-18 N, Long. 076-00-05 W; The town is named after the Cape. Cape Charles honored Charles, Duke of York.

CAPRON, Town; Southampton County; Pop. 238 / 137; Zip Code 23829; Lat. 36-42-39 N, Long. 077-12-00 W; Originally called Princeton, the name was later changed to Capron, who was a general passenger agent of the railroad.

CEDAR BLUFF, Town; Tazewell County; Pop. 1,550 / 1,784; Zip Code 24609; Descriptively named for the cedar trees covering the bluff.

CHARLOTTE COURT HOUSE, Town; Charlotte County Seat; Pop. 568 / 564; Zip Code 23923; Elev. 596; Lat. 37-03-29 N, Long. 078-38-30 W; The town had a series of names, but was renamed in 1901 after the county. Charlotte was the wife of King George III.

CHARLOTTESVILLE, City; Pop. 45,010 / 36,815; Zip Code 229+; Elev. 594; Lat. 38-02-12 N, Long. 078-29-06 W; Founded in 1762 and named for Princess Charlotte, wife of King George III.

CHASE CITY, Town; Mecklenburg County; Pop. 2,749 / 2,371; Zip Code 23924; Elev. 546; Lat. 36-47-55 N, Long. 078-27-34 W; The town's name honors U.S. Supreme Court Justice Chase.

CHATHAM, Town; Pittsylvania, County Seat; Pop. 1,390 / 1,260; Zip Code 24531; Lat. 36-49-30 N, Long. 079-24-03 W; The town was renamed in 1874 to honor William Pitt, Earl of Chatham.

CHERITON, Town; Northampton County; Pop. 695 / 491; Zip Code 23316; Lat. 37-17-18 N, Long. 075-58-13 W; Called at one time Cherry Stones, Dr. William Stockley shortened this to "Cheriton."

CHESAPEAKE, City; Pop. 114,226 / 202,759; Zip Code 23320; Lat. 36-41-47 N, Long. 076-03-25 W; An Indian word meaning "great salt water."

CHILHOWIE, Town; Smyth County; Pop. 1,269 / 1,997; Zip Code 24319; Elev. 1950; Lat. 36-47-58 N, Long. 081-41-06 W; Settled in 1750 and named after an Indian phrase meaning "valley of many deer."

CHINCOTEAGUE, Town; Accomack County; Pop. 1,607 / 3,600; Zip Code 233+; Lat. 37-55-59 N, Long. 075-22-20 W; The town takes its name from the Chinco-Teague Indians. The name means "beautiful land across the water."

CHRISTIANSBURG, Town; Montgomery County Seat; Pop. 10,345 / 16,615; Zip Code 240+; Lat. 37-08-02 N, Long. 080-24-24 W; Founded in 1792 and later named in honor of colonial Indian fighter, William Christian.

CLAREMONT, Town; Surry County; Pop. 380 / 359; Zip Code 23899; Elev. 112; Lat. 37-13-38 N, Long. 076-57-56 W; The town is named after "Claremont," a royal home in Surrey, England.

CLARKSVILLE, Town; Mecklenburg County; Pop. 1,468 / 1,261; Zip Code 23927; Elev. 91; Lat. 36-37-17 N, Long. 078-33-44 W; The town takes its name from an early property owner on the Roanoke River.

CLEVELAND, Town; Russell County; Pop. 360 / 202; Zip Code 24225; Elev. 1534; Lat. 36-56-36 N, Long. 082-09-13 W; Established in 1890 and named in honor of President Grover Cleveland.

CLIFTON, Town; Fairfax County; Pop. 170 / 198; Zip Code 22024; Lat. 38-46-58 N, Long. 077-23-09 W; The town is named after the Wyckliffe family of England, who were large property owners in colonial times.

CLIFTON FORGE, City; Pop. 5,046 / 4,205; Zip Code 24422; Lat. 37-49-01 N, Long. 079-49-30 W; Incorporated in 1884 and named after James Clifton's iron furnace.

CLINTWOOD, Town; Dickenson County Seat; Pop. 1,369 / 1,400; Zip Code 24228; Lat. 37-08-59 N, Long. 082-27-09 W; The town's name honors Senator Henry Clinton Wood.

CLOVER, Town; Halifax County; Pop. 215 / 186; Zip Code 24534; Elev. 502; Lat. 36-50-09 N, Long. 078-44-07 W; The town is named for clover Creek.

COEBURN, Town; Wise County; Pop. 2,625 / 2,143; Zip Code 24230; Elev. 1992; Lat. 36-59-38 N, Long. 082-28-03 W; Settled in the 1770s, and later renamed for chief railroad engineer. W.W. Coe.

COLONIAL BEACH, Town; Westmoreland County; Pop. 2,474 / 3,183; Zip Code 22443; Lat. 38-15-12 N, Long. 076-57-59 W; Called White Beach from colonial days, it was renamed by a developer in the 1880s to Colonial Beach.

COLONIAL HEIGHTS, City; Pop. 16,509 / 16,235; Zip Code 23834; Lat. 37-00-03 N, Long. 076-40-07 W; Incorporated in 1926 and named for the general heritage of the area.

COLUMBIA, Town; Fluvanna County; Pop. 111 / 89; Zip Code 23038; Lat. 37-45-10 N, Long. 078-09-33 W; Settled in the 18th century and given the popular name for America in 1897.

COURTLAND, Town; Southampton County Seat; Pop. 976 / 1,099; Zip Code 23837; Elev. 32; Lat. 36-42-58 N, Long. 077-03-45 W; Settled in 1750 and renamed Courtland in 1788.

COVINGTON, City; Pop. 9,063 / 6,846; Zip Code 24426; Lat. 37-46-56 N, Long. 079-59-22 W; Incorporated in 1833 and named for Prince Edward Covington.

CRAIGSVILLE, Town; Augusta County; Pop. 845 / 912; Zip Code 24430; Elev. 23; Lat. 38-05-02 N, Long. 079-23-00 W; The town is named for an early settler.

CREWE, Town; Nottoway County; Pop. 2,325 / 2,188; Zip Code 23930; Lat. 37-10-46 N, Long. 078-07-28 W; Founded in 1886 as a rail center, and named for the English railway town, Crewe.

CULPEPER, Town; Culpeper County Seat; Pop. 6,621 / 9,168; Zip Code 22701; Elev. 430; Lat. 38-28-24 N, Long. 077-59-39 W; The town is named for the county. Culpeper honors Lord Culpeper, Governor of Virginia 1680-1683.

DAMASCUS, Town; Washington County; Pop. 1,330 / 969; Zip Code 24236; Elev. 1928; Lat. 36-38-29 N, Long. 081-46-50 W; The town is named after the ancient Syrian city.

DANVILLE, City; Pop. 45,642 / 50,795; Zip Code 245+; Lat. 36-35-12 N, Long. 079-23-09 W; Descriptively named for its location on the Dan River.

DAYTON, Town; Rockingham County; Pop. 1,017 / 947; Zip Code 22821; Lat. 38-24-51 N, Long. 078-56-33 W; Dayton may be named in honor of Jonathan Dayton, a ratifier of the Constitution.

DENDRON, Town; Surry County; Pop. 307 / 298; Zip Code 23839; Lat. 37-02-21 N, Long. 076-55-40 W; Founded in the 1880s and given a Greek name meaning tree, referring to the town's lumber industry.

DILLWYN, Town; Buckingham County; Pop. 637 / 479; Zip Code 239+; Lat. 37-28-09 N, Long. 078-33-52 W; Named for an early settler.

DRAKES BRANCH, Town; Charlotte County; Pop. 617 / 591; Zip Code 23937; Elev. 383; Lat. 36-59-40 N, Long. 078-36-12 W; Named for the stream, Drakes Branch, that flows through town.

DUBLIN, Town; Pulaski County; Pop. 2,368 / 2,026; Zip Code 24084; Lat. 37-06-09 N, Long. 080-41-17 W; The first settler, Irishman William Christian, named the town for Dublin, Ireland.

DUFFIELD, Town; Scott County; Pop. 148 / 51; Zip Code 24244; Elev. 1365; Lat. 36-43-11 N, Long. 082-47-37 W; The town is named for the Duff family who were early settlers.

DUMFRIES, Town; Prince William County; Pop. 3,214 / 4,837; Zip Code 22026; Lat. 38-35-47 N, Long. 077-19-02 W; An early settler, John Graham named the town for his home in Scotland.

DUNGANNON, Town; Scott County; Pop. 339 / 240; Zip Code 24245; Elev. 1311; Lat. 36-49-52 N, Long. 082-28-07 W; Pioneer Captain Patrick Hogan named the town for his former home in Ireland.

EASTVILLE, Town; Northampton County Seat; Pop. 238 / 171; Zip Code 23347; Lat. 37-21-09 N, Long. 075-56-17 W; Descriptively named for its relative location east of other nearby towns.

EDINBURG, Town; Shenandoah County; Pop. 752 / 931; Zip Code 22824; Lat. 38-49-26 N, Long. 078-33-48 W; Incorporated in 1852 as Edinburg, even though it was described as a "Garden of Eden" and Edenburg suggested.

ELKTON, Town; Rockingham County; Pop. 1,520 / 2,129; Zip Code 22827; Lat. 38-24-29 N, Long. 078-37-06 W; The town takes its name for Elk Run stream, which flows through the town.

EMPORIA, City; Pop. 4,840 / Zip Code 23847; Elev. 119 / 5,662; Lat. 36-41-24 N, Long. 077-32-27 W; Settled as two villages in the 1780s divided by the Meherrin River; the towns merged in 1887 and took the name Emporia. The name means "center of trade."

EXMORE, Town; Northampton County; Pop. 1,300 / 1,099; Zip Code 23350; Elev. 41; Lat. 37-26-56 N, Long. 075-54-56 W; So named because it was the tenth (X) railroad station to the south of Delaware.

FAIRFAX, City; Pop. 19,390 / 20,697; Zip Code 22021; Elev. 447; Lat. 38-53-44 N, Long. 077-25-59 W; The city is named for Lord Fairfax, one of the early great landowners.

FALLS CHURCH, City; Pop. 9,515 / 9,944; Zip Code 22040; Lat. 38-53-03 N, Long. 077-10-38 W; Descriptively named for the town's location on the falls of the Potomac and an Episcopal Church built in 1734.

FARMVILLE, Town; Cumberland & Prince Edward Counties; Prince Edward County Seat; Pop. 6,067 / 7,321; Zip Code 23901; Lat. 37-18-02 N, Long. 078-23-29 W; The town is a distribution point for agricultural produce and so was named Farmville.

FINCASTLE, Town; Botetourt County Seat; Pop. 282 / 328; Zip Code 24090; Lat. 37-30-00 N, Long. 079-52-39 W; The town was founded in 1772 and named for Lord Fincastle.

FLOYD, Town; Floyd County Seat; Pop. 411 / 429; Zip Code 24091; Elev. 2496; Lat. 36-54-25 N, Long. 080-15-30 W; The town was named in honor of a prominent local citizen.

FRANKLIN, City; Pop. 7,308 / 8,139; Zip Code 23851; Lat. 36-40-38 N, Long. 076-55-46 W; The city's name honors patriot Benjamin Franklin.

FREDERICKSBURG, City; Pop. 15,322 / 18,826; Zip Code 224+; Lat. 38-22-39 N, Long. 077-27-23 W; Founded in 1727 and named in honor of Frederic, Prince of Wales.

FRIES, Town; Grayson County; Pop. 758 / 645; Zip Code 24330; Elev. 2180; Lat. 36-42-59 N, Long. 080-58-40 W; The town is named for a local resident.

FRONT ROYAL, Town; Warren County Seat; Pop. 11,126 / 13,677; Zip Code 22630; Elev. 567; Lat. 38-55-21 N, Long. 078-11-37 W; A "royal" oak stood in the village square. During the Revolutionary War a drill sergeant addressed his troops "front the royal oak." The name stuck on the town.

GALAX, City; Pop. 6,524 / 6,484; Zip Code 24333; Elev. 2382; Lat. 36-39-55 N, Long. 080-54-52 W; The town is named for the decorative mountain evergreen plant.

GATE CITY, Town; Scott County Seat; Pop. 2,494 / 2,094; Zip Code 24251; Elev. 1304; Lat. 36-37-43 N, Long. 082-34-06 W; Descriptively named for nearby Moccasin Gap, which was a gateway to western coal fields.

GLADE SPRING, Town; Washington County; Pop. 1,722 / 1,502; Zip Code 24340; Elev. 2084; Lat. 36-47-51 N, Long. 081-46-03 W; The town is descriptively named for the spring found in a glade by the first settlers.

GLASGOW, Town; Rockbridge County; Pop. 1,259 / 1,237; Zip Code 24555; Lat. 37-37-51 N, Long. 079-26-52 W; The town was developed on the Glasgow homestead and so named.

GLEN LYN, Town; Giles County; Pop. 235 / 104; Zip Code 24093; Elev. 1537; Lat. 37-22-18 N, Long. 080-51-59 W; Settled in 1750 and named Montreal, the name was changed to Glen Lyn, or lovely glen, in 1883.

GORDONSVILLE, Town; Orange County; Pop. 1,175 / 1,659; Zip Code 22942; Elev. 493; Lat. 078-11-21 W; Early settler Nathaniel Garden purchased 1300 acres here in 1787. The town is named after him.

GOSHEN, Town; Rockbridge County; Pop. 134 / 388; Zip Code 24439; Lat. 37-59-28 N, Long. 079-29-55 W; The town's name is a biblical synonym of fruitfulness and fertility.

GRETNA, Town; Pittsylvania County; Pop. 1,255 / 1,418; Zip Code 24557; Elev. 844; Lat. 36-57-20 N, Long. 079-21-52 W; Called Franklin Junction until 1916 when the name was changed to Gretna.

GROTTOES, Town; Augusta & Rockingham Counties; Pop. 1,369 / 1,835; Zip Code 24441; Lat. 38-15-43 N, Long. 078-49-23 W; Descriptively named for the many grottoes, or caves, in the nearby Shenandoah Mountains.

GRUNDY, Town; Buchanan County Seat; Pop. 1,699 / 1,094; Zip Code 24614; Elev. 1050; Founded in the 1850s and named for a U.S. Senator from Texas in that era.

HALIFAX, Town; Halifax County Seat; Pop. 772 / 718; Zip Code 24558; Lat. 36-45-50 N, Long. 078-55-57 W; Founded in 1752 and named for George Dunk, Earl of Halifax.

HALLWOOD, Town; Accomack County; Pop. 243 / 226; Zip Code 23359; Lat. 37-52-38 N, Long. 075-35-16 W; Although not incorporated until 1958 the town is named after on old colonial family the Halls.

HAMILTON, Town; Loudoun County; Pop. 598 / 1,260; Zip Code 22068; Elev. 275; Lat. 39-08-05 N, Long. 077-39-46 W; Established in 1829 and named after the town's first postmaster, Charles Hamilton.

HAMPTON, City; Pop. 122,617 / 137,193; Zip Code 236+; The city was founded in 1680 and named in honor of the Earl of Southampton.

HARRISONBURG, City; Pop. 19,671 / 34,129; Zip Code 22801; Elev. 1352; Lat. 38-26-46 N, Long. 078-52-15 W; Founded in 1780 and named for the Harrison family, who were among the earliest settlers.

HAYMARKET, Town; Prince William County; Pop. 230 / 656; Zip Code 22069; Lat. 38-40-12 N, Long. 077-29-26 W; Pioneer William Skinner named the town for the famous race track in London.

HAYSI, Town; Dickenson County; Pop. 371 / 201; Zip Code 24256; Elev. 1266; Lat. 37-12-21 N, Long. 082-17-40 W; General store merchants Charles Hay and Mr. Sypher had their last names combined for the town's name.

HERNDON, Town; Fairfax County; Pop. 11,449 / 19,195; Zip Code 22070; Lat. 38-57-56 N, Long. 077-21-37 W; The town's names commemorates Captain William Herndon, who was lost at sea in 1857.

HILLSBORO, Town; Loudoun County; Pop. 94 / 127; The town is descriptively named for its location on Short Hill Mountain.

HILLSVILLE, Town; Carroll County Seat; Pop. 2,123 / 2,617; Zip Code 24343; Elev. 2557; Lat. 36-45-40 N, Long. 080-44-03 W; The town was named after the Hill family who were early Quaker settlers.

HONAKER, Town; Russell County; Pop. 1,475 / 1,013; Zip Code 24260; Elev. 1860; Lat. 37-01-07 N, Long. 081-58-39 W; The town was named in honor of Squire Harve Honaker, a one-time postmaster.

HOPEWELL, City; Pop. 23,397 / 22,663; Zip Code 23860; Lat. 37-17-29 N, Long. 077-18-11 W; The city is named after the Quaker Hopewell meeting established in 1734.

HURT, Town; Pittsylvania County; Pop. 1,481 / 1,300; Zip Code 24563; Elev. 736; Lat. 37-05-50 N, Long. 079-18-09 W; The town's name honors John L. Hurt, who helped develop the city.

INDEPENDENCE, Town; Grayson County Seat; Pop. 1,112 / 992; Zip Code 24348; Elev. 2,698; Lat. 36-37-15 N, Long. 081-09-06 W; A group of settlers living here in 1849 refused to take sides over where the county seat would be located. As a result the county seat was located here and named independence.

IRON GATE, Town; Alleghany County; Pop. 620 / 380; Zip Code 24448; Lat. 37-47-51 N, Long. 079-47-30 W; Named for the "Iron Gate" gap where the Jackson River cuts through the White Mountain.

IRVINGTON, Town; Lancaster County; Pop. 567 / 491; Zip Code 22480; Elev. 1006; Lat. 37-39-48 N, Long. 076-25-08 W; Incorporated in 1891 and named for an early pioneer family, the Irvings.

IVOR, Town; Southampton County; Pop. 403 / 335; Zip Code 23866; Lat. 36-54-23 N, Long. 076-53-46 W; The town's name comes from a Walter Scott novel.

JARRATT, Town; Greensville & Sussex Counties; Pop. 614 / 528; Zip Code 23867; Lat. 36-49-56 N, Long. 077-28-18 W; The Jarratt family settled in the county in 1652. The town was named in their honor.

JONESVILLE, Town; Lee County Seat; Pop. 874 / 985; Zip Code 24263; Elev. 1530; Lat. 36-40-16 N, Long. 083-06-51 W; The town is named for pioneer Frederick Jones who donated the land for the townsite.

KELLER, Town; Accomack County; Pop. 236 / 221; Zip Code 23401; Elev. 42; Lat. 37-14-06 N, Long. 075-55-52 W; The town's name honors the contractor who built the local railroad.

KENBRIDGE, Town; Lunenburg County; Pop. 1,352 / 1,173; Zip Code 23944; Lat. 36-57-38 N, Long. 078-07-29 W; The town was built on the Kennedy and Bridgeforth family farms. The town's name was coined from the two names.

KEYSVILLE, Town; Charlotte County; Pop. 704 / 695; Zip Code 23947; Elev. 642; Lat. 37-02-20 N, Long. 078-28-54 W; The town was named after early settler and tavern owner, John Keys.

KILMARNOCK, Town; Lancaster & Northumberland Counties; Pop. 945 / 1,242; Zip Code 22482; Lat. 37-42-40 N, Long. 076-23-18 W; Early settlers named the town for the city in Scotland.

LA CROSSE, Town; Mecklenburg County; Pop. 734 / 533; Zip Code 23950; Lat. 36-41-47 N, Long. 078-05-39 W; The town is named after the game of La Crosse.

LAWRENCEVILLE, Town; Brunswick County Seat; Pop. 1,484 / 1,436; Zip Code 23868; Lat. 36-45-33 N, Long. 077-50-55 W; Established in 1783 and named in honor of Captain James Lawrence.

LEBANON, Town; Russell County Seat; Pop. 3,206 / 3,354; Zip Code 24266; Lat. 36-59-46 N, Long. 081-58-32 W; Founded in 1819 and named after Biblical Lebanon for the many cedar trees in the area.

LEESBURG, Town; Loudoun County Seat; Pop. 8,357 / 26,820; Zip Code 22075; Elev. 352; Lat. 39-06-46 N, Long. 077-33-49 W; The town was founded in 1758 and named after Francis Lightfoot Lee.

LEXINGTON, City; Pop. 7,292 / 7,359; Zip Code 24450; Elev. 1084; Lat. 37-47-01 N, Long. 079-26-28 W; The town was named during the Revolutionary War in honor of the Battle of Lexington.

LOUISA, Town; Louisa County Seat; Pop. 932 / 1,270; Zip Code 23093; Elev. 468; Lat. 38-01-39 N, Long. 078-00-10 W; Founded in the 18th century and named for a local settler's wife.

LOVETTSVILLE, Town; Loudoun County; Pop. 613 / 1,368; Zip Code 22080; Lat. 39-16-24 N, Long. 077-38-22 W; The town was established in 1820 on David Lovett's land. It is named in his honor.

LURAY, Town; Page County Seat; Pop. 3,584 / 4,919; Zip Code 22835; Elev. 789; Lat. 38-40-02 N, Long. 078-27-25 W; The town is named either for early Blacksmith Lewis Ray, or after Lorraine (Luray), France.

LYNCHBURG, City; Pop. 66,743 / 63,926; Zip Code 24501; Elev. 818; Lat. 37-24-25 N, Long. 079-09-36 W; The town grew up around John Lynch's ferry, which he built in 1756. The town is named after him.

MADISON, Town; Madison County Seat; Pop. 267 / 319; Zip Code 22719; Elev. 589; Lat. 38-31-45 N, Long. 078-15-38 W; Founded in 1801 and named in honor of James Madison.

MANASSAS, City; Pop. 15,438 / 33,498; Zip Code 22110; Lat. 38-46-37 N, Long. 077-27-54 W; Early settlers named the town for the Biblical Manasseh.

MARION, Town; Smyth County Seat; Pop. 7,029 / 6,696; Zip Code 24354; Elev. 2178; Lat. 36-50-26 N, Long. 081-31-03 W; Founded in the early 1800s and named for Revolutionary War hero, General Francis Marion.

MARTINSVILLE, City; Pop. 18,149 / 14,996; Zip Code 241+; Lat. 36-40-20 N, Long. 079-51-58 W; The city was founded in 1791 and named after pioneer settler Joseph Martin.

MCKENNEY, Town; Dinwiddie County; Pop. 473 / 434; Zip Code 23872; Lat. 36-59-07 N, Long. 077-43-17 W; The town's name honors large area landowner William R. McKenney.

MELFA, Town; Accomack County; Pop. 391 / 417; Zip Code 23410; Lat. 37-39-05 N, Long. 075-44-22 W; The town was named for an official of the Pennsylvania Railroad Company.

MIDDLEBURG, Town; Loudoun County; Pop. 619 / 656; Zip Code 22117; Elev. 492; Lat. 38-58-05 N, Long. 077-44-22 W; Once called Chinn, the name was later changed to reflect its "middle position" between Alexandria and Winchester.

MIDDLETOWN, Town; Frederick County; Pop. 841 / 1,312; Zip Code 22645; Lat. 39-01-38 N, Long. 078-16-39 W; Founded in 1796 as Senseny, the name was later changed to Middletown for its location between Winchester and Woodstock.

MINERAL, Town; Louisa County; Pop. 399 / 536; Zip Code 23117; Lat. 38-00-37 N, Long. 077-54-02 W; Established around 1800 and descriptively named for the mineral deposits in the area.

MONTEREY, Town; Highland County Seat; Pop. 247 / 211; Zip Code 24465; Elev. 2881; Lat. 38-24-42 N, Long. 079-34-54 W; The name was changed to Monterey to honor President Zachary Taylor's victory during the Mexican-American War.

MONTROSS, Town; Westmoreland County Seat; Pop. 456 / 371; Zip Code 22520; Lat. 38-05-36 N, Long. 076-49-38 W; The town was named for an early settler.

MOUNT CRAWFORD, Town; Rockingham County; Pop. 315 / 227; Zip Code 22841; Lat. 38-21-17 N, Long. 078-56-26 W; The town is named after an early settler.

MOUNT JACKSON, Town; Shenandoah County; Pop. 1,419 / 1,756; Zip Code 22842; Lat. 38-44-54 N, Long. 078-38-39 W; The town's name honors President Andrew Jackson.

NARROWS, Town; Gil's County; Pop. 2,516 / 1,917; Zip Code 24124; Lat. 37-20-08 N, Long. 080-48-27 W; The New River cuts a deep gorge, or narrows, through the Alleghenies at this point. The town is named for this feature.

NASSAWADOX, Town; Northampton County; Pop. 630 / 553; Zip Code 23413; Elev. 38; Lat. 37-28-35 N, Long. 075-53-23 W; Settled in 1656 and given an Indian name meaning "a Stream between two Streams."

NEW CASTLE, Town; Craig County Seat; Pop. 213 / 169; Zip Code 24127; Lat. 37-29-45 N, Long. 080-06-45 W; Founded as New Fincastle in 1756, but later changed to New Castle.

NEW MARKET, Town; Shenandoah County; Pop. 1,118 / 1,632; Zip Code 22844; Lat. 38-38-54 N, Long. 078-40-20 W; Founded in 1784 and named for the famous racing town in England.

NEWPORT NEWS, City; Pop. 144,903 / 179,138; Zip Code 23600; Lat. 37-03-15 N, Long. 076-28-36 W; Founded in 1619 and named for Sir Christopher Newport and Sir William Newce, or gradually Newport News.

NEWSOMS, Town; Southampton County; Pop. 368 / 338; Zip Code 23874; Elev. 92; Lat. 36-37-40 N, Long. 077-07-28 W; The town is named after pioneer merchant, Thomas Newsoms.

NICKELSVILLE, Town; Scott County; Pop. 464 / 413; Zip Code 24271; The town is named for an early settler.

NORFOLK, City; Pop. 266,979 / 225,875; Zip Code 23500; Lat. 36-40-40 N, Long. 075-48-43 W; Established in 1682 and named for county Norfolk in England.

NORTON, City; Pop. 4,757 / 4,008; Zip Code 24273; Elev. 2141; Lat. 36-59-19 N, Long. 082-37-31 W; The town is named in honor of Eckstein Norton, who was L & N Railroad president from 1886-1891.

OCCOQUAN, Town; Fairfax & Prince William Counties; Pop. 512 / 593; Zip Code 22125; Lat. 38-40-56 N, Long. 077-15-39 W; The town's name is an Indian word meaning "at the river's end."

ONANCOCK, Town; Accomack County; Pop. 1,461 / 1,317; Zip Code 23417; Lat. 37-42-41 N, Long. 075-44-25 W; Founded in 1680 and eventually given on Indian name meaning "foggy place."

ONLEY, Town; Accomack County; Pop. 526 / 525; Zip Code 23418; Lat. 37-41-33 N, Long. 075-42-57 W; The town was named for the estate of Virginia Governor Henry Wise.

ORANGE, Town; Orange County Seat; Pop. 2,631 / 4,223; Zip Code 22960; Elev. 521; Lat. 38-13-19 N, Long. 078-06-17 W; The town is named for the county. The county is named for the Prince of Orange who married King George II's daughter.

PAINTER, Town; Accomack County; Pop. 321 / 254; Zip Code 23420; Elev. 37; Lat. 37-35-19 N, Long. 075-47-05 W; The town was named for an official of the Pennsylvania Railroad at the time the Station was opened.

PARKSLEY, Town; Accomack County; Pop. 979 / 751; Zip Code 23421; Lat. 37-47-12 N, Long. 075-39-07 W; Founded on land owned by Edmund Parkes in 1742. Originally called Matomkin but later changed to Parksley.

PEARISBURG, Town; Giles County; Pop. 2,128 / 2,709; Zip Code 24134; Elev. 1804; Lat. 37-19-47 N, Long. 080-43-44 W; The town was founded in 1808 and named in honor of Captain George Pearis.

PEMBROKE, Town; Giles County; Pop. 1,302 / 1,056; Zip Code 24136; Lat. 37-19-30 N, Long. 080-38-08 W; The town was named after Pembroke in Wales.

PENNINGTON GAP, Town; Lee County; Pop. 1,716 / 1,874; Zip Code 24277; Elev. 1377; Lat. 36-45-35 N, Long. 083-01-55 W; An early family named Pennington settled near the mountain gap, and gave the town their name.

PETERSBURG, City; Pop. 41,055 / 34,398; Zip Code 23801; Lat. 37-14-40 N, Long. 077-20-02 W; Founded in 1646 and later named for trader Peter Jones.

PHENIX, Town; Charlotte County; Pop. 250 / 271; Zip Code 23959; Elev. 462; Lat. 37-05-03 N, Long. 078-44-48 W; The town was named after the "phenix" legend, where it arose from its own ashes.

POCAHONTAS, Town; Tazewell County; Pop. 708 / 454; Zip Code 24635; Named for the famous Indian princess, the name means "stream between two hills."

PORT ROYAL, Town; Caroline County; Pop. 291 / 214; Zip Code 22535; Lat. 38-10-09 N, Long. 077-11-32 W; Named by Thomas Roy and called Port Roy for its shipping activity. The name evolved to Port Royal.

PORTSMOUTH, City; Pop. 104,577 / 98,305; Zip Code 23700; Lat. 36-49-34 N, Long. 076-20-33 W; Established in 1752 and named for the city in England.

POUND, Town; Wise County; Pop. 1,086 / 976; Zip Code 24279; Lat. 37-08-02 N, Long. 082-36-13 W; Site of an early pioneer mill, settlers brought grain to be milled or "pounded," and gave the town its name.

PULASKI, Town; Pulaski County Seat; Pop. 10,106 / 9,466; Zip Code 24301; Lat. 37-03-38 N, Long. 080-46-34 W; The town was founded in 1839 and named in honor of Polish-American Revolutionary War hero Count Casimir Pulaski.

PURCELLVILLE, Town; Loudoun County; Pop. 1,567 / 2,812; Zip Code 22078; Elev. 576; Lat. 39-06-54 N, Long. 077-41-42 W; The Purcell family opened the first store and post office in 1832. The town is named after them.

QUANTICO, Town; Prince William County; Pop. 621 / 838; Zip Code 22134; Lat. 38-31-15 N, Long. 077-17-43 W; An Indian word meaning "place of dancing."

RADFORD, City; Pop. 13,225 / 15,668; Zip Code 24141; Elev. 1023; Lat. 37-08-04 N, Long. 080-34-18 W; The city takes its name from the original landowner, Dr. John Bane Radford.

REMINGTON, Town; Fauquier County; Pop. 425 / 563; Zip Code 22734; Lat. 38-32-09 N, Long. 077-48-32 W; Originally called Millview, the name was changed in 1890 to Remington.

RICH CREEK, Town; Giles County; Pop. 746 / 710; Zip Code 24147; Lat. 37-23-09 N, Long. 080-49-15 W; A large, cool set of creeks run through the town. Water is bottled from one stream because of its medicinal effects. This business named the town.

RICHLANDS, Town; Tazewell County; Pop. 5,796 / 4,630; Zip Code 24641; Elev. 1967; The high-quality pastures in the area gave the town its name.

RICHMOND, City; Pop. 219,214 / 189,700; Zip Code 230+; Lat. 37-17-55 N, Long. 076-50-26 W; Founded in 1742 and named for Richmond on Thames in England.

RIDGEWAY, Town; Henry County; Pop. 858 / 814; Zip Code 24148; Elev. 638; Lat. 36-32-55 N, Long. 079-51-27 W; Early settler Samuel Sheffield descriptively named the town.

ROANOKE, City; Pop. 100,427 / 93,357; Zip Code 24001; Lat. 37-16-36 N, Long. 079-57-23 W; The city's name is from an Indian word meaning "swell money."

ROCKY MOUNT, Town; Franklin County Seat; Pop. 4,198 / 4,539; Zip Code 24151; Lat. 36-59-58 N, Long. 079-53-23 W; Settled in 1760 and descriptively named for an abrupt precipice in the area.

ROUND HILL, Town; Loudoun County; Pop. 510 / 607; Zip Code 22141; Elev. 97; Lat. 39-08-03 N, Long. 077-46-09 W; The town was settled in 1735 and named for a prominent "round hill" landmark nearby.

RURAL RETREAT, Town; Wythe County; Pop. 1,083 / 992; Zip Code 24368; Elev. 2510; Lat. 36-53-43 N, Long. 081-16-27 W; Named after an early inn on the stage route that was a "retreat" for weary travelers.

ST. CHARLES, Town; Lee County; Pop. 241 / 184; Zip Code 24282; Lat. 36-49-01 N, Long. 083-03-28 W; The town was named in honor of early coal developer Charles Bondurant.

ST. PAUL, Town; Russell & Wise Counties; Pop. 973 / 925; Zip Code 24283; Elev. 1492; Lat. 36-58-04 N, Long. 082-18-28 W; Originally Estonoa, the town had a wave of development in 1885 by promoters from St. Paul, Minnesota. The name was changed at that time to St. Paul.

SALEM, City; Pop. 23,958 / 24,037; Zip Code 24153; Elev. 1060; Lat. 37-16-49 N, Long. 080-03-01 W; The town was laid out in 1802 and named for Salem, New Jersey.

SALTVILLE, Town; Smyth & Washington Counties; Pop. 2,376 / 2,235; Zip Code 24370; Elev. 1718; Lat. 36-52-41 N, Long. 081-46-10 W; Incorporated in 1896 and named for its two century old salt production industry.

SAXIS, Town; Accomack County; Pop. 415 / 369; Zip Code 23427; Lat. 37-55-35 N, Long. 075-43-12 W; The name is a corruption of seventeenth century settler Robert Sike's name.

SCOTTSBURG, Town; Halifax County; Pop. 335 / 153; Zip Code 24589; Elev. 380; Lat. 36-45-28 N, Long. 078-47-28 W; The town's name honors John Scott, a Revolutionary War soldier and officer.

SCOTTSVILLE, Town; Albemarle & Fluvanna Counties; Pop. 250 / 592; Zip Code 24562; Lat. 37-43-53 N, Long. 078-39-32 W; The town is named after the Scott family, who were prominent early settlers.

SHENANDOAH, Town; Page County; Pop. 1,861 / 2,289; Zip Code 22849; Lat. 38-29-14 N, Long. 078-37-19 W; Incorporated in 1884 and given an Indian name meaning "beautiful daughter of the stars."

SMITHFIELD, Town; Isle of Wight County; Pop. 3,649 / 5,545; Zip Code 23430; Elev. 45; Lat. 36-59-20 N, Long. 076-37-49 W; Founded in 1662 on land owned by settler Arthur Smith, and so named.

SOUTH BOSTON, City; Pop. 7,093 / 7,043; Zip Code 24592; Lat. 36-42-30 N, Long. 078-54-17 W; Originally slated to be called Boston, post office objections forced a name change to South Boston.

SOUTH HILL, Town; Mecklenburg County; Pop. 4,347 / 4,584; Zip Code 23970; Elev. 440; Lat. 36-43-45 N, Long. 078-07-25 W; The town is south of a large hill, and was so descriptively named.

STANARDSVILLE, Town; Greene County Seat; Pop. 284 / 895; Zip Code 22973; Lat. 38-17-53 N, Long. 078-26-17 W; The name honors Robert Standards, who donated the land for the courthouse.

STUART, Town; Patrick County Seat; Pop. 1,131 / 1,008; Zip Code 24171; Lat. 36-38-16 N, Long., 080-16-00 W; Founded in the 1700s and later named in honor of General J.E.B. Stuart, Confederate War hero.

SURRY, Town; Surry County Seat; Pop. 237 / 367; Zip Code 23883; Lat. 37-08-10 N, Long. 076-49-56 W; Founded in the later 1700s and named after an area in England.

TANGIER, Town; Accomack County; Pop. 771 / 663; Zip Code 23440; Lat. 37-49-29 N, Long. 075-59-34 W; Settled in 1680 and named for small clay bowls, or tango, which reminded the colonists of similar products of North Africa.

TAPPAHANNOCK, Town; Essex County Seat; Pop. 1,821 / 1,697; Zip Code 22560; Elev. 22; Lat. 37-55-27 N, Long. 076-51-39 W; An Indian name meaning "on the running water."

TAZEWELL, Town; Tazewell County Seat; Pop. 4,468 / 4,144; Zip Code 246+; Elev. 2519; The town is named for Henry Tazewell, a U. S. Senator from 1794-1799.

THE PLAINS, Town; Fauquier County; Pop. 382 / 229; Zip Code 22171; Lat. 38-51-52 N, Long. 077-46-22 W; Formerly White Plains, the name was shortened to avoid confusion with a similarly named city in New York.

TIMBERVILLE, Town; Rockingham County; Pop. 1,510 / 1,757; Zip Code 22853; Lat. 38-38-09 N, Long. 078-46-24 W; Established in the late 1700s and named for the abundant timber nearby.

TOMS BROOK, Town; Shenandoah County; Pop. 226 / 278; Zip Code 22660; Lat. 38-56-50 N, Long. 078-26-28 W; An early settler's cabin named a local stream "Tom's Creek;" this was later changed to Tom's Brook and given to the town.

TROUTDALE, Town; Grayson County; Pop. 248 / 194; Zip Code 24378; Lat. 36-42-05 N, Long. 081-26-23 W; Excellent trout fishing in nearby Fox Creek gave the town its name.

TROUTVILLE, Town; Botetourt County; Pop. 496 / 519; Zip Code 24175; Lat. 37-24-54 N, Long. 079-52-46 W; The town was named in honor of the Trout family.

URBANNA, Town; Middlesex County; Pop. 518 / 569; Zip Code 23175; Lat. 37-38-28 N, Long. 076-34-22 W; Founded in 1705 and named in honor of Queen Anne, or Urb-Anna.

VICTORIA, Town; Lunenburg County; Pop. 2,004 / 1,617; Zip Code 23974; Lat. 36-59-28 N, Long. 078-13-34 W; The town's name honors Great Britain's Queen Victoria.

VIENNA, Town; Fairfax County; Pop. 15,469 / 17,226; Zip Code 22027; Lat. 38-53-26 N, Long. 077-13-39 W; The town was named after Vienna, New York.

VINTON, Town; Roanoke County; Pop. 8,027 / 7,115; Zip Code 24179; Lat. 37-22-35 N, Long. 079-48-36 W; Founded in 1794 as Gish's Mill, but later given a coined name combining pioneer names Vineyard and Preston, or Vinton.

VIRGILINA, Town; Halifax County; Pop. 212 / 156; Zip Code 24598; Elev. 534; The town is situated on the Virginia-North Carolina boundary. The name is derived from a combination of the two state names.

VIRGINIA BEACH, City; Pop. 262,199 / 433,461; Zip Code 234+; Lat. 36-50-51 N, Long. 076-05-52 W; Descriptively named for the state and its ocean location.

WACHAPREAGUE, Town; Accomack County; Pop. 404 / 274; Zip Code 23480; Lat. 37-36-29 N, Long. 075-41-18 W; Incorporated in 1902 and given an Indian name meaning "little city by the sea."

WAKEFIELD, Town; Sussex County; Pop. 1,355 / 1,068; Zip Code 23888; Lat. 36-58-12 N, Long. 076-58-44 W; Incorporated in 1902 and given the name of a place in a Walter Scott novel.

WARRENTON, Town; Fauquier County Seat; Pop. 3,907 / 6,239; Zip Code 22186; Lat. 38-44-02 N, Long. 077-44-18 W; The town was named in honor of Revolutionary War hero, Dr. Joseph Warren.

WARSAW, Town; Richmond County Seat; Pop. 771 / 971; Zip Code 22572; Lat. 37-57-33 N, Long. 076-45-30 W; Originally Richmond Courthouse, renamed in honor of the Polish capitol in 1846.

WASHINGTON, Town; Rappahannock County Seat; Pop. 247 / 206; Zip Code 22747; Lat. 38-42-47 N, Long. 078-09-35 W; Established by George Washington in 1749, and named for him by Lord Fairfax.

WAVERLY, Town; Sussex County; Pop. 2,284 / 2,142; Zip Code 23890; Lat. 37-02-06 N, Long. 077-06-54 W; Incorporated in 1879 and given the name from a Walter Scott novel.

WAYNESBORO, City; Pop. 15,329 / 19,274; Zip Code 22980; Lat. 38-04-27 N, Long. 078-53-34 W; The city was named to honor the Great Revolutionary War General, Anthony Wayne.

WEBER CITY, Town; Scott County; Pop. 1,543 / 1,366; The town's name is copied from radio era show "Amos and Andy" who lived in mythical "Weber City."

WEST POINT, Town; King William County; Pop. 2,726 / 3,422; Zip Code 230+; Lat. 37-31-48 N, Long. 076-41-19 W; Called "The Point" in the 18th century and later given the additional name west for a pioneer family.

WHITE STONE, Lancaster County; Pop. 409 / 383; Zip Code 22578; Elev. 51; Lat. 37-38-42 N, Long. 076-23-20 W; The town is descriptively named for White Stone Beach.

WILLIAMSBURG, City; Pop. 9,870 / 12,495; Zip Code 23081; Elev. 86; Lat. 37-12-28 N, Long. 076-46-29 W; Settled in 1632 and named in honor of William III of England.

WINCHESTER, City; Pop. 20,217 / 22,477; Zip Code 22601; Elev. 720; Lat. 39-11-02 N, Long. 078-09-32 W; The city was settled in 1738 and named for Winchester, England.

WINDSOR, Town; Isle of Wight County; Pop. 985 / 1,004; Zip Code 23487; Lat. 36-48-37 N, Long. 076-44-46 W; The town is named after the location in one of Walter Scott's novels.

WISE, Town; Wise County Seat; Pop. 3,894 / 3,209; Zip Code 24923; Elev. 2,454; Lat. 37-01-14 N, Long. 082-34-42 W; The town was named for former governor of Virginia, Henry A. Wise.

WOODSTOCK, Town; Shenandoah County Seat; Pop. 2,627 / 3,900; Zip Code 22664; Lat. 38-52-49 N, Long. 078-30-39 W; Named by founder Jacob Miller in 1761.

WYTHEVILLE, Town; Wythe County Seat; Pop. 7,135 / 8,148; Zip Code 24382; Elev. 2,284; Lat. 36-56-47 N, Long. 081-05-04 W; Named for George Wythe, the first professor of law in America, teacher of Thomas Jefferson, John Marshall and James Monroe, and first Virginia signer of Declaration of Independence.

WASHINGTON
The Evergreen State

Mount Saint Helens

The Space Needle - Seattle

GOVERNOR
Gary Locke

North Head Lighthouse

Downtown Seattle

Mount Rainier

National Historic Site - Fort Vancouver

INTRODUCTION

EVERGREEN STATE

Washington offers a multitude of outstanding natural endowments for inhabitants and visitors alike. Washington's forests are vocal with the sounds of many birds. Woodland trails, mountain summits, deep gorges, turbulent streams with cascading waterfalls, and clear alpine lakes exemplify the beauty of nature. Outdoor lovers and sports enthusiasts are enticed by rugged mountains and blue-white glaciers; secluded lakes, streams, and saltwater channels; deep canyons and surf-pounded beaches; and the channels of Puget Sound and many enchanted islands.

A number of historical sites in the State of Washington tell a story of conquering the wilderness. War canoes, tomahawks, arrowheads, feathered headdresses, and other mementos of the Indian culture (whose descendants now live primarily on reservations) give an account of the State's first inhabitants. Early mission houses, forts, blockhouses, and other pioneer buildings; crumbling tombstones in lonely prairie cemeteries; and markers on old trails all paint a picture of the State's earliest white settlers. All of these historical markers give one a clearer understanding of the region's history and the great changes the Evergreen State has undergone from its earliest days.

In the course of the State's rapid development, the country has been greatly altered. Forests have been cut, leaving vast scarred and denuded areas. Grasslands have been broken and planted to wheat; often the arid range has become the feeding ground of cattle and sheep, enclosed with barbed-wire fencing. Desert lands have been converted by irrigation into productive gardens, orchards, and alfalfa tracts; automobiles travel through areas that once were native trails; ships ply waters previously crossed only by primitive dugouts, and airplanes dot the skies.

Factories and mills stand where Indians once set their wares; on the sites or early communal Indian villages lie large cities with towering buildings and well-lighted, tree-lined streets.

The history of Washingtonians is also greatly diverse. Attracted by timber, free lands, minerals, railroad construction, the fish industry, irrigation and power developments, and wartime industries, many waves of settlers came into the Evergreen State after the early 1800s. They included dissatisfied and restless emigrants from older states, Southerners ruined and uprooted by the Civil War, immigrants from Europe and the Orient, discouraged farmers from eroded lands of the Midwest, and multitudes of war workers seeking new homes and lives. Each group brought its distinctive and unique folkways. And each culture ultimately modified and enriched the cultural life of its adopted homeland.

STATE NAME

On March 2, 1853, Washington Territory was carved out of Oregon Territory. The territory of Washington was named for George Washington, the first President of the United States. In a petition to Congress framed by the delegates of the citizens of northern Oregon on October 25, 1852, it was suggested that the territory be named the *Territory of Columbia*. When the bill came up for consideration in the House of Representatives on February 8, 1853, Representative Stanton of Kentucky suggested that, as there was already a *District of Columbia*, the name of the new territory be changed to Washington, thus expressing his desire to see "a sovereign State bearing the name of the Father of his Country." A motion was quickly made to strike out the word *Columbia*, and to insert the word *Washington*, which was done.

An early form of the name *Washington* is *Wessingatun*, which seems to have been used about 946-955 A.D., according to *Publications of the English Place-Name Society*, Volume 6, Part I. This publication discourages the idea that the words *waesc*, *waesse*, *wase*, denoting marshy land, are a part of the name Washington; the English Washington, it points out, is situated on a "spur of the downs, well out of the valley below. The soil of the valley is largely sand, so that neither from the site of Washington itself nor from the neighborhood are we justified in looking for any word *waesc*, *waesse*, or *wase* denoting marshy land as part of the name."

Mawer and Stenton also explain that the occasional variant vowel in the early forms of the word leading to the replacing of *ss* by *sh* was confused with the common words *gewaesc* and *waescan*, Middle English *wasshe*, *wesshe*. The word Washington is composed of a personal name, *Wassa*, plus the syllable *ing*, plus the suffix *ton*. The termination *ing* in place names signifies "the settlement of a family or clan community, in certain cases possibly the descendants of some one man." The suffix *ton* or *tun* means "primarily a piece of ground surrounded by a hedge or [a] rough palisade, inside [of] which there might or might not be placed a dwelling." It also carries the idea of a farm; consequently the name *Washington* means "farm" or "settlement of the people of Wassa."

STATE NICKNAMES

The State of Washington was nicknamed the *Evergreen State*, by C.T. Conover, pioneer Seattle realtor and historian, because of its abundant evergreen forests.

Inhabitants of the State of Washington have been nicknamed *Clam Grabbers*, doubtless from the fact that they gather vast quantities of clams annually from the shallow waters of Puget Sound and Wallapa Harbor.

The *Chinook State* was given as a nickname to the State of Washington because it was formerly the home of the "principal tribe of the Lower Chinook division of North American Indians;" it also referred to the State's salmon industry. However, this nickname is no longer commonly used.

STATE SEAL

The seal of the State of Washington was prescribed in the 1889 State Constitution and added to the body of law in 1967. The constitution, which was adopted on November 11, 1889, states that "the seal of the state of Washington shall be a seal encircled with the words: 'The Seal of the State of Washington,' with the vignette of General George Washington as the central figure, and beneath the vignette the figures '1889.'"

STATE FLAG

The flag of the State of Washington was officially adopted on March 5, 1923, and was amended slightly in 1925. The law is as follows: "The official flag of the State of Washington shall be of dark green silk or bunting and shall bear in its center a reproduction of the Seal of the State of Washington embroidered, printed, painted or stamped thereon. The edges of the flag may, or may not, be fringed. If a fringe is used the same shall be of gold or yellow color of the same shade as the seal. The dimensions of the flag may vary."

STATE MOTTO

Washington's motto is *Alki*, which signifies "bye and bye," from an American Indian dialect. This word is taken from the Chinook jargon, and it appeared on the territorial seal designed by J.K. Duncan.

Alki Point in Seattle was at first called Point Roberts, and was first settled in 1841. On November 13, 1851, this point was favored by the landing of the Denny colony, out of which Seattle grew. The Denny colony designated the place *New York* "As the one little store and the few cabin homes grew so slowly, they added a hyphen and the Indian jargon word *Alki*, meaning 'bye and bye.'" It was hoped that New York-Alki would "become the metropolis of the Pacific Coast in the near future." It is probable that this first use of the word influenced its selection as the State motto.

STATE BIRD

The willow goldfinch, *Astragalinus tristis salicamans*, was designated the official bird of the State of Washington in 1951 by an act of the State Legislature.

The willow goldfinch is found along the Pacific coast regions from southern California to Oregon. Its total length is 4½ inches, and its tail length is 1½ to two inches. It is similar to the eastern goldfinch, but the wings and tail are shorter and the coloration is darker than the eastern variety. The adult male summer plumage of the back is tinged with pale olive green, and in winter, adults and young are decidedly darker or browner than the eastern goldfinch, and have broader markings on the wings.

Called the willow goldfinch because of its gravitation to damp areas conducive to the growth of willows, this bird is a cheery singer and a graceful flyer. The willow goldfinch begins to nest earlier than its eastern counterparts, usually in April or May. It is primarily a seed eater, munching mostly on seeds from harmful or neutral plants, including sunflower seeds, weed and thistle seeds, the buds of bushes, and sycamore and alder seeds. It occasionally supplements its diet with harmful insects.

STATE FLOWER

The Pink Rhododendron, *Rhododendron machrophyllum*, was designated the State flower of Washington by the State Legislature in 1949. *The World Almanac* states that this flower was se-lected by the people. It was selected "because it blooms in all its beauty here...It does not grow everywhere in the State, however," according to one Reference Librarian of the Washington State Library. Another said of it, "hiding within the shade of these (wild fruits and berries), playing hide and seek with nature lovers who enjoy threading the romantic trails for which this section of the world is noted, is many a modest flower which in some sections blooms nearly the whole year round, so soft is the climate; while the pink petal rhododendron, of bolder nature, Washington's state flower, is prominent in June tossing its beautiful head among the dry logs and lining the course of many a pretty driveway."

STATE TREE

The official tree of the State of Washington is the western hemlock, *Tsuga heterophylla*. Designated in 1947, it is native to the Pacific Coast and northern Rocky Mountain regions north to Canada and Alaska. The western hemlock is a large tree with reddish-brown bark, deeply furrowed into broad, flat ridges. Needles are short-stalked and flat, from one-quarter to three-quarter inch long; they are dark green above and lighter beneath. Cones are brownish and from three-quarter to one inch long.

STATE SONG

The State song, 'Washington, My Home," was written by Helen Davis. It became the official State Song in 1959. In 1987, the State Legislature also designated an official folk song: "Roll On Columbia, Roll On," composed by Woody Guthrie.

STATE LICENSE PLATE

On May 2, 1905, S.A. Perkins of Tacoma became the first Washington citizen to register his vehicle. The two-dollar fee registration fee for his Pope-Toledo touring car did not include a license plate; motorists were obligated to make their own plates or stencil the numbers on the back and front of their vehicle until 1916, when the State issued its first plate, which was white on blue. Blue and white were used in 1923-1925 and 1936-1937. Green and white were used in 1926-1927, 1929-1934, 1938, 1940-1946, and 1950-1986. In 1987, in celebration of its centennial as a state, Washington issued a multi-year plate with patriotic colors: a white background, blue numerals, and "Washington" in red letters at the top and "Centennial Celebration" at the bottom, also in red, all overlaying a light blue graphic of Mount Rainier. In 1999, the plates were issued with the same design and colors but without the centennial designation. The motto "Evergreen State" appears on the bottom of the plate in red letters.

STATE POSTAGE STAMP

In 1939, Washington was one of four states, including North and South Dakota and Montana, to commemorate its fifty-year anniversary of statehood. A purple three-cent stamp was issued with all of the four states depicted; issue dates in each State capital corresponded to the anniversary date for each State's entry to the Union. For Washington, the stamp was issued on November 11, 1939 in Olympia. The stamp features each of the four states highlighted on a map of the northwestern United States, and the name of each state's capital. A.R. Meissner designed the stamp, and M.D. Fenton and W.B. Wells were the engravers. A total of 66,835,000 stamps were printed.

OTHER STATE DESIGNATIONS

Through the years, the Washington Legislature has occasionally adopted other official designations to symbolize the State's unique importance: The official dance is the Square dance (1979); the official fish is the Steelhead trout (1969); the State fruit is the apple (1989); and the official gem is petrified wood (1975).

CAPITOL BUILDING

Olympia became the territorial capital of Washington in 1855. At that time, a wooden capitol was built. When Washington entered the Union in 1889, a more suitable capitol was suggested. In 1893, the design submitted by Ernest Flagg was chosen, and work began in 1894, only to be delayed while the foundation and basement were being constructed. In 1901, what is now known as the "Old Capitol" was purchased by the State and was utilized as the Statehouse until 1928.

By 1909, the government decided that the Old Capitol had become inadequate. Ernest Flagg visited Olympia in 1911 and proposed a group concept for the building. Architects Walter R. Wilder and Harry K. White of New York were chosen to carry out Flagg's idea. In 1919, work began on an enlarged foundation for Flagg's original building. Construction began in 1922, and continued until completion in 1929.

The legislative building represents the Classical type of Renaissance architecture. It is constructed of native sandstone known as Wilkeson stone. This structure is 413 feet long and 179.2 feet wide. Its total height is twenty-two stories. The dome, crowned by the "Lantern of Liberty," rises 287 feet high. Doric columns adorn the colonnade around the building. Corinthian columns decorate the main north entrance and south portico. Total cost of the building was 6,798,596 dollars. However, this cost applies only to the legislative building, as the Statehouse was built on the group plan, which included six buildings; namely, the old capitol building, the Governor's mansion, the temple of justice, the insurance building, the power house and heating plant, and the legislative building.

OTHER FACTS ABOUT WASHINGTON

Total area: 68,139 square miles
Land area: 66,511 square miles
Water area: 1,627 square miles
Average elevation: 1,700 feet
Highest point: Mount Rainier, 14,410 feet
Lowest point: Pacific Ocean, sea level
Highest temperature: 118 degrees Fahrenheit
Lowest temperature: -48 degrees Fahrenheit
Population in 1990: 4,866,992
Population density in 1990: 73.09 persons per square mile
Population 1980-1990: +17.8 percent change
African American population in 1990: 149,801
Hispanic population in 1990: 214,570

Native American population in 1990: 81,483
European American (non-Hispanic) population in 1990: 4,308,937
Per Capita Income: 16,473
Capital: Olympia
Admitted to Union: November 11, 1889
Order of Statehood: 42
Electoral votes: 10

CHRONOLOGY

1579 Francis Drake sails to Pacific Northwest coast, naming the region New Albion (New England).

1592 Apostolos Valerianos (Juan de Fuca) allegedly finds a strait.

1774 Juan Perez sails along coast; he sights mountain (*Olympus*), which he names Sierra de Santa Rosalia.

1775 Bruno Heceta and Juan de Bodega y Quadra land on Washington coast (near present Point Grenville) and take possession for Spain.

1778 Captain James Cook, on his last voyage, names Cape Flattery; he misses discovery of Strait nearby, and makes survey from forty-fourth to seventieth parallel.

1787 Captain Charles W. Barkley finds strait northeast of Cape Flattery and "renames" it Juan de Fuca, after its legendary discoverer.

1788 Captain John Meares explores Juan de Fuca Strait, renames Mount Olympus, and, missing the River of the West, names Cape Disappointment.

1789 Spaniard Estevan Martinez confiscates British ships at Nootka Sound.

1790 Manuel Quimper, Spanish seaman, explores as far as San Juan Islands, and takes formal possession at Neah Bay.

1791 Francisco de Eliza, from temporary base at Discovery Bay, sends small boats as far as Bellingham Bay.
– Salvador Fidalgo sets up provisional establishment at Neah Bay.

1792 Captain Robert Gray discovers and names Bulfinch (Grays) Harbor.
– Gray discovers and names Columbia River while anchored on north side, trading for furs.
– Captain George Vancouver arrives to negotiate settlement between England and Spain with Bodega y Quadra; he explores Admiralty Inlet and Puget Sound; at a point near Everett, he takes possession for George III of England, renaming New Albion as New Georgia.
– Lieutenant Broughton, under Vancouver's orders, ascends Columbia River to Point Vancouver.

1794 Spain makes restitution for property seized by Martinez at Nootka Sound.

1803 United States purchases Louisiana Territory, increasing interest in Oregon country.

1805-06 Lewis and Clark reach mouth of Columbia River and return to St. Louis; their exploration gives United States further claim to Oregon country.

1810 North West Fur Company establishes Spokane Mouse (nine miles northwest of present Spokane), first white settlement within limits of present State.

1811 Astoria, in present Oregon, is founded by John Jacob Astor's Pacific Fur Company.
– David Thompson reaches mouth of Columbia River, after exploring from Kettle Falls to mouth of Snake River, and claims all land north of Snake River for England.
– Fort Okanogan is established by agents of Pacific Fur Company.

1812 Fort Spokane is established by Pacific Fur Company, near Spokane Mouse, to compete with North West Company.

1813 North West Company, taking advantage of War of 1812, purchases all property of Pacific Fur Company in valley of Columbia.

1818 Fort Nez Perce (Fort Walla Walla) is built by North West Company.
– Joint occupancy of Oregon country by Americans and British is established by convention to cover ten years.

1819 Florida Treaty with Spain gives United States all rights claimed by Spain to Oregon country.

1821 North West Company and Hudson's Bay Company amalgamate under name of latter.

1825 Hudson's Bay Company establishes Fort Vancouver on north bank of Columbia.

1826 Fort Colvile is built by Hudson's Bay Company; Spokane House is abandoned.

1827 Renewal of convention with Great Britain continues joint occupancy indefinitely; one year's notice is required to modify pact.

1831 Captain Bonneville arrives overland at Fort Vancouver, but is unable to purchase goods to compete with Hudson's Bay Company.
– Nathaniel Wyeth arrives at Fort Vancouver, but his business enterprises are temporarily halted by Dr. John McLoughlin of Hudson's Bay Company.
– First school at Fort Vancouver is taught by John Ball.

1833 Fort Nesqually, first trading post on Puget Sound, is established by Archibald McDonald.

1835 Lieutenant William Slacum of United States Army arrives on Columbia to report on conditions of trade and population.

1836 Missionaries Marcus Whitman and H.H. Spalding arrive with their wives; they are first American women in Oregon country.
– Whitman establishes mission at Waiilatpu near Fort Walla Walla.

1838 Walker-Eells Protestant mission to Spokane is begun.
– Fathers Blanchet and Demers arrive at Fort Vancouver by way of Columbia from Canada.

1839 Roman Catholic mission is established at Cowlitz Landing.
– Methodist mission is established at Fort Nesqually.

1840 Catholic mission is established on Whidbey Island.

1841 Wilkes Expedition arrives at Fort Nesqually; main field of exploration is Puget Sound, but small parties go to Fort Okanogan, Fort Colvile, Fort Walla Walla, Fort Vancouver, Grays Harbor, and Shoalwater Bay (Willapa Harbor).

1843 Influx of immigrants assumes large proportions.
– Oregon Provisional Government forms at Champoeg.

1844 Boundary slogan, "Fifty-four-forty or fight," is prominent in Presidential campaign.

1845 Lieutenants Warre and Vavasour of British Army arrive incognito on Columbia and survey territory, in view of possible war with United States.
– Michael T. Simmons and his party, first American settlers in Puget Sound region, reach Tumwater.

1846 United States-Canadian boundary is fixed at 49 degrees N.
– Hudson's Bay Company plans to move headquarters to site of Victoria on Vancouver Island.
– Settlement begins at site of Olympia.

1847 Band of Cayuse Indians at Waiilatpu kill Dr. and Mrs. Whitman and eleven others at mission.
– First American sawmill is erected at Tumwater by Michael Simmons.

1848 Oregon Territory, including all of present Washington, is created.

1849 Fort Steilacoom is established by United States Army, because Snoqualmie Indians have attacked Squally Indians at Fort Nesqually.

1850 Donation Land Claim Law is passed by Congress.

1851 Schooner *Exact* brings members of Denny pioneer party to Alki Point (now in Seattle).
– Cowlitz Convention memorializes Congress to create region north of Columbia as separate Territory to be named Columbia.

1852 Cowlitz Convention meets and again petitions Congress for Territory of Columbia.
– First settlers come to Bellingham Bay; Nicholas DeLin settles on Commencement Bay, at site of Tacoma.

– Claims are staked on Seattle metropolitan site by Denny, Boren, and Bell.
– First Washington newspaper, the *Columbian*, is printed in Olympia; it strongly advocates new Territory.

1853 Washington Territory is created.
– White population numbers 3,965.
– First northern-route transcontinental-railroad survey is begun, under Isaac I. Stevens.
– Isaac I. Stevens is appointed Territorial Governor and Supervisor of Indian Affairs.
– Olympia is named temporary capital.

1854 First Federal Court session in Washington Territory convenes.
– First Legislature meets and provides for University; Congress makes grant of two townships.
– December 26. Medicine Creek Treaty is concluded; it is first with Indians of Puget Sound Basin.
– Treaties are negotiated with Puget Sound and Juan de Fuca Strait tribes.

1855 Indian war is waged both east and west of Cascades.
– Klickitat Indians fail in attack upon Seattle and later are severely defeated at Connell's Prairie.
– Eastern Washington is closed to settlers and miners.

1857 Governor Stevens is elected to represent Territory in Congress.
– Territorial charter is granted to Northern Pacific Railroad.

1858 Lieutenant Colonel Steptoe is defeated near Rosalia.
– Colonel Wright defeats Indians at Spokane Plains and Four Lakes.
– Eastern Washington is opened to settlement.

1859 Fraser River gold rush begins.
– San Juan Islands boundary controversy between England and United States becomes acute.
– Gold rush to eastern Washington Territory (especially the part now Idaho) begins.
– Indian treaties negotiated by Governor Stevens are ratified by Congress.

1860 Population is 11,594.
– Walla Walla becomes outfitting point for gold rush.

1861 Territorial University is opened at Seattle, with Asa S. Mercer as teacher and president, and one student, Clarence Bagley, in college department.

1863 Territory of Idaho is created from Washington Territory, establishing present eastern boundary of State.

1864 "Mercer girls," women who are Civil War orphans and widows, are brought to Seattle by Asa Mercer; they find husbands waiting.
– First transcontinental telegraph lines are completed.

1866 Some 95 more "Mercer girls" arrive.

1867 Legislature memorializes Congress to admit Washington to statehood.
– Alaska, "the Great Country," is purchased from Russia.

1869 United States settles Hudson's Bay Company's claim for property in Territory.

1870 First bank in Territory is established at Walla Walla by Dorsey S. Baker.
– Work is begun on Northern Pacific Railroad, from Kalama on Columbia northward to Puget Sound.
– Population is 23,355.

1871 San Juan Islands boundary dispute with Great Britain is submitted to arbitration.

1871 Settlement of Spokane Falls is begun.
– San Juan dispute is settled; award, by Emperor William I of Germany, is in accord with United States contention.
– Dr. Dorsey S. Baker begins to build his railroad from Walla Walla to Wallula, on the Columbia.

1873 Northern Pacific Railroad from Kalama reaches Tacoma, which has won coveted terminal.

1875 Railroad from Walla Walla to Wallula is completed.

1876 Territory votes to hold constitutional convention and again apply for admission as State.
– Proposed State Constitution is adopted, but Congress fails to respond.

1880 Population is 75,116.

1881 Transcontinental line of Northern Pacific is completed to Spokane Falls.

1883 Railroad connections between Puget Sound and East are established via Columbia River route.

1885 Anti-Chinese riots occur in Issaquah, Coal Creek, Black Diamond, and Tacoma.

1886 Anti-Chinese riots occur in Seattle.

1887 Northern Pacific reaches Tacoma via switchbacks at summit of Cascades.

1888 Stampede Tunnel is opened, thus eliminating switchbacks.

1889 Enabling Act is passed in Congress and signed February 22.
– Constitutional Convention assembles at Olympia on July 4.
– Constitution is adopted October 1.
November 1. Washington is proclaimed State by President Harrison.

1890 Population is 337,232.

1891 Puget Sound Navy Yard is voted by Congress and located at Bremerton.

1892 State College of Washington is opened at Pullman.

1893 Great Northern Railroad reaches Seattle, having passed up new city of Everett as its terminus.

1895 University of Washington is moved to its present location.
– Barefoot Schoolboy Law is enacted, laying basis for Washington's common-school system.

1896 Trans-Pacific steamship service is inaugurated by Nipon Yusen Kaisya.

1897 Gold rush to Klondike begins.

1898 Washington contributes 1,332 men for Spanish-American War.

1899 March 2. Mount Rainier National Park is created.

1900 Population is 518,103.

1901 State Bureau of Labor is created.

1902 Federal Reclamation Act is passed by Congress; projects are begun in Okanogan and Yakima counties.

1905 State Railroad Commission and State Tax Commission are created.

1907 Direct primary law is passed.

1908 North Bank Railroad is built.

1909 Alaska-Yukon-Pacific Exposition opens in Seattle.
– Chicago, Milwaukee and St. Paul Railroad reaches western terminus at Tacoma.

1910 Population is 1,141,990.
– Women's suffrage is voted for State.

1911 Workman's Compensation Act is passed.

1912 Initiative, referendum, and recall measures are enacted.

1914 Statewide prohibition law is approved by referendum vote, with one year to elapse before it becomes effective.

1916 First transcontinental telephone service is extended to Seattle.
– Opening of Panama Canal helps trade with East Coast.

1917 Washington sets records in shipbuilding.
– Pierce County donates land for Camp (Fort) Lewis.
– Lake Washington Ship Canal is opened.

1918 Armistice; Washington has 67,694 men and 632 women in war service.

1919 Columbia Basin Survey Commission is appointed.
– First State American Legion Post is established.

November 11. Armed clash, fatal to several, occurs at Centralia between marchers in Armistice Day parade and I.W.W. members.

1920 Population is 1,356,621.
– Sand Point Naval Air Base is dedicated.
– Foreign airmail service begins between Seattle and Victoria.

1921 First airplane passenger service operates between Seattle and Vancouver, British Columbia.
– Anti-Alien Land Ownership Law is passed.

1922 Columbia Basin Irrigation League is organized at Pasco.

1924 United States Army's "round-the-world" flight begins at Sand Point Naval Air Base; journey of six months ends at Sand Point in September.

1928 Capitol building at Olympia is completed.

1930 Population is 1,563,396.
August. Olympic Loop highway is opened.

1933 Work starts at Bonneville Dam.
– Contracts are let on Grand Coulee Dam.

1934 State Liquor Law is passed, and control board is established.
– General maritime strike centers in Seattle.

1935 Seattle *Post-Intelligencer* suspends publication because of Newspaper Guild strike.
– November 30. Guild strike ends; *Post-Intelligencer* resumes publication.

1937 State Department of Social Security is established.

1938 January. President Roosevelt signs bill to create Olympic National Park.
May 31. Boeing Pan-American Airways launches 74-Passenger clipper.

1939 State celebrates Golden Jubilee, commemorating fifty years of statehood.

1940 Population is 1,736,191.
– S.F. Chadwick seeks Republican nomination for U.S. Senator.

1941 Legislature plans to investigate vote by which A.B. Langlie defeated C.C. Dill for Governor; Langlie's inauguration is set.
– Weyerhaeuser Corporation opens first U.S. tree farm near Aberdeen.
– Grand Coulee Dam, on Columbia, is completed.

1942 University and state colleges unite in war effort program.
– All Japanese persons of birth or ancestry, numbering 14,559 in all, are moved from Washington to World War II relocation camps.
– Washington receives billions in World War II contracts; Puget Sound yards produce warships, and Boeing's output includes B-17 and B-29 bombers.

1943 Bonneville Dam is ordered to supply power to Ft. George Wright and army hospital in Spokane.
– Hanford Engineering Works, operating in secrecy, produces plutonium for first nuclear weapons.

1944 M.C. Wallgren is elected Governor.

1945 Dr. L.P. Siege announces his retirement as president of University of Washington.
– World War II ends.

1946 Research Foundation at Washington State College in Pullman patents photoelectric device to determine auto traffic.

1947 Legislature votes to make strikes by government employees a misdemeanor.

1948 A.B. Langlie is elected Governor.
– University of Washington begins conducting cancer research.

1949 Former State administration and professors at University of Washington are under siege for alleged communist activities; committee on un-American activities conducts investigations.
– Washington ranks second among states in nation in pears, apricots, cherries, and green peas; it ranks third in peaches, prunes, strawberries, and asparagus.
– Population is 2,379,000.

1950 Social Security Department seeks to overhaul general assistance and health programs.
– Washington leads nation in production of aluminum.

1951 President Allen resigns from University of Washington, Seattle; H.P. Everest is named acting president.

1952 Governor Langlie is reelected.
– Dr. H. Schmitz becomes new president of University of Washington.

1953 State celebrates centennial of creation of Washington Territory; commemorative stamp is issued.

1954 Washington Water Power joins five companies participating in Pacific Northwest atomic energy project.

1955 Puget Sound Power seeks permit to build 85,000 KW hydroelectric plant on Upper Baker River.

1956 Rosellini is elected Governor.

1957 Funds are approved for work on capitol building.
– Chief Joseph Dam on upper Columbia River is completed.

1958 U.S. Senate approves bill consenting to compact with Oregon over permanent boundary.

1959 AMF Atomics is selected to design and build reactor for University of Washington.

1960 Population is 2,853,000.
– Rosellini is reelected Governor.

– Bonds are issued to finance second floating bridge across Lake Washington.

1961 University of Washington celebrates 100th anniversary.

1962 University of Washington researchers produce artificial kidney.
– Seattle hosts Century 21 Exposition.

1963 After long controversy, Federal panel affirms right of university to require loyalty oaths from employees and faculty.
– Floating bridge over Lake Washington is completed, two years after similar one spanning the Rood Canal.

1964 U.S. Supreme Court voids loyalty oaths for public employees.

1965 D.S. Evans is sworn in as Governor.

1966 NASA awards $3.2 million for space research to University of Washington and University of Wisconsin.

1967 Boeing Airplane Manufacturing is largest single industry in State.
– State fair-housing law adopted.

1968 Governor Evans is reelected.
– North Cascades National Park is established.

1969 Bomb blast damages administration building at University of Washington, Seattle; student unrest continues on campus.

1970 Population is 3,413,000.
– Students protest university's racist policies; Navy and Air Force ROTC hall on campus is bombed.
– President Richard Nixon orders FBI probe into bombing.

1971 Ex-Attorney General O'Connel, ex-Deputy Attorney General Faler, and Pierce County ex-Prosecutor McCutcheon, along with San Francisco Mayor Alioto, are indicted on Federal racketeering charges.
– Unemployment hits Boeing plants in Washington; from 95,000 in 1968, employment has dropped to 37,000 due to sharp drop in aircraft and aerospace orders.
– Governor Evans says State will seek Federal economic aid to replace supersonic airplane project funding canceled by Congress.

1972 D.J. Evans is elected to third term as Governor.
– State Equal Rights Amendment is adopted.
– Republican J.M. Pritchard is sole Republican winner of Congressional seat in State.

1973 Washington voters order legislators to take 5.5 percent increase in annual salary rather than 193 percent raise they seek.
– T. Bundy former employee of Washington Governor D.J. Evan's reelection committee admits that he posed as college student during 1972 election campaign in order to travel with Evan's Democratic opponent, A.D. Rosellini, and secretly report on his campaign activities.

1974 Seattle Pilots, American League baseball team, moves to Milwaukee.
– Supreme Court upholds strict disclosure law for public officials and lobbyists; it cites public's right to know how money and persuasion influence government, and rules that all state officials must file extensive yearly reports of personal finances and business dealings.
– Spokane's Expo '74 draws 5.2 million visitors.

1975 Vietnamese refugees settle in Washington.
– Dr. Dixy Lee Ray, resigning as State Department's top science official, announces she may consider running as Democratic candidate for governor in Washington in '76.

1976 Dixy Lee Ray becomes first woman Governor of Washington.
– Seattle's $60 million domed stadium, the King-dome, is dedicated.
– Senator Henry M. Jackson is reelected over relatively weak opposition.

1977 State workers strike, for first time in State's history.
January 12. Governor Dixy Lee Ray is sworn in.
– Ray's first 100 days in office are assessed; considered a political novice, she is controversial and her unorthodox style in administration upsets some voters.

1978 Joel Pritchard, Al Swift, Don Bonker, Mike McCormack, Thomas Foley, Norman Dicks, and Mike Lowry are elected to House of Representatives.
– Governor Ray says she will abolish State Women's Council.

1979 Washington gains an additional seat in House of Representatives, due to population shifts since 1970.
– U.S. Supreme Court upholds treaty rights of Washington Indians to catch half of all salmon returning to traditional off-reservation waters; provision incenses State's sports fishermen.

1980 Population is 4,132,000.
– John Spellman is elected Governor.
– Eruption of Mt. St. Helens in southwestern Washington leaves more than 60 dead; volcanic ash is spread over large areas.

1981 State inheritance tax is abolished.
– Governor John Spellman, warning conservatives that essential programs must be maintained, wants to raise taxes despite 1980 campaign promise not to do so.

1982 State unemployment rate rises to 13 percent; declines in timber and aerospace are seen as part of cause.
– Spokane elects first African American Mayor, Jim Chase.
– Democratic Senator Henry M. Jackson is reelected.

1983 110,000 acres surrounding Mt. St. Helens volcano is dedicated as national monument.
– Thirty-eight Japanese-Americans who lost State jobs in World War II are to receive up to $5,000 each under bill signed by Governor Speilman.
– Senator Henry M. Jackson, 44-year veteran of Congress and national politics, dies at age 71 of heart attack.

– Washington is third among states in wheat production, with record crop of 172.6 million bushels; it ranks second in potatoes.
– Washington Public Supply System defaults on over $2 billion worth of bonds intended to finance two nuclear power plants.

1984 Federal District Judge Jack Tanner orders State to compensate women employees found to have been paid less than men in jobs of comparable worth.

1985 Booth Gardner is inaugurated Governor.
– State law banning voter polling within 300 feet of polls is ruled unconstitutional.
– U.S. Navy makes Everett home headquarters for 15-ship battle group.

1986 Washington State employees receive first benefits from settlement regarding sexual bias in pay scales; Governor Gardner says program will erase wage discrimination in positions filled primarily by women.

1987 Senator Daniel J. Evans says he will not seek reelection in 1988.
– Robertson offends Seattle GOP conference.

1988 Bush and Quayle win 54 percent to 46 percent victory in population vote over Dukakis and Bentsen; Washington is one of scattering of states carried by Dukakis.
– Washington is one of eight states listed as hardest hit by fire season damage; six million acres are reported destroyed.
– Washington apple growers lose more than $145 million after reports that Alat, growth-inducing chemical sprayed on fruit, may cause cancer.

1989 Environmentalists admit that shutdown of Hanford Plutonium Uranium Extraction Plant (PUREX) in December 1988 had gone unnoticed.
– Norm Rice is elected first African American mayor of Seattle.

1990 Population is 4,866,000,
– It is disclosed that large amounts of radiation were secretly released from Hanford Nuclear Reservation in three-year period ending December 1947; Energy Department's report, part of five-year study, says that 13,700 residents in Washington and Oregon absorbed 33 rads of radiation, and a few could have been exposed to as much as 3,000 rads.
– *Seattle Times* wins Pulitzer Prize for reports on Exxon Valdez oil spill.

1991 In *Masey vs. Washington*, Supreme Court lets stand life sentence imposed for crime committed by 13-year old boy; he and accomplice killed Marine in 1987.
– Energy Secretary James D. Walkins informs Washington Governor Booth Gardner that cleanup work on Hanford Nuclear plant will be delayed at least one to two years.
– Olympic National Park beaches become covered with oil from spill after collision of Chinese freighter and Japanese fishing vessel.

1992 U.S. Geological Survey scientists suggest that Puget Sound is site of major fault line that could pose danger for Seattle area.

– University of Washington researchers find evidence of powerful earthquake 1000 years ago that reshaped Puget Sound coastline and created tidal wave that obliterated forests.

– Computer fraud network is discovered in San Diego, California; it is determined that electronic files at Atlanta-based credit rating company were changed, allowing millions of dollars to be used for credit card purchases; network computers and related equipment are seized in New York City, Philadelphia, and Seattle.

– Mike Lowry wins Washington gubernatorial race against State Attorney General Ken Eikenberry; he will succeed two-term Governor Booth Gardner.

1993 Westley Alan Dodd, previously convicted of 1989 murders of three boys, is executed by hanging in Walla Walla; it is nation's first execution by hanging since 1965; (Dodd's crimes and pledges to kill again if not executed helped prompt 1990 Washington law under which habitual sex offenders can be jailed indefinitely if a jury still finds them a threat after they have served their term.) Execution sparks debate over civil liberties of offenders for crimes not yet committed.

– Joseph Meling is found guilty of two counts of murder after lacing capsules in five packages of Sudafed (non-prescription decongestant) at local drug store in attempt to kill his wife for $700,000 in life insurance; Meling is found guilty of 11 charges in all, including insurance fraud and perjury; his wife survives poisoning.

1994 Seattle Federal District Court Judge William L. Dwyer rules that Washington State law imposing term limits for State Representatives in U.S. Congress violates U.S. Constitution; ruling is first by Federal court in case involving term-limit laws. Dwyer says term limits violates 14th Amendment against discrimination in politics by barring specific group (incumbents) candidacy for Federal office. He states that voters' freedom to choose Federal legislators must not be abridged by laws that make qualified persons ineligible to serve.

– Compassion in Dying, Seattle-based group that helps individuals with terminal illnesses to die joins three ill patients and five doctors in challenging State law prohibiting assisted suicide.

– U.S. District Judge Barbara Rothstein strikes down State law prohibiting assisted suicide, stating that law violating 14th Amendment guarantee that individual rights will not be infringed upon by State; Rothstein argues that individual has same right to end own life as to abort unwanted pregnancy or remove self from life-support system.

– Mark Kowalski, white supremist who bombed NAACP office in 1993, is sentenced to eleven years, eight months in prison; no injuries were reported in bombing.

1995 U.S. 9th Circuit Court of Appeals panel upholds Washington State law barring doctors from helping patients commit suicide; court bases ruling on law that protects vulnerable patients, keeps doctors from "killing" patients; decision overturns lower-court ruling in 1994.

– Toxic gas released outside Boeing Co. plant in Seattle, results in hospitalization of some 120 workers; gas cloud of nitrous oxide believed to have been caused by chemical reaction when supervisors transferred 300 gallons of nitric hydrofluoric acid into outdoor storage tank.

– Bill Gates, Microsoft Corporation founder donates $10 million to University of Washington; money is earmarked to establish fund for outstanding undergraduates, called Mary Gates Endowment for Students.

1996 Hanford nuclear facility is one of many sites across United States scheduled to disclose inventory of plutonium in report entitled *Phitotnum: the First 50 Years*; report marks first public disclosure of atomic data by any nation possessing nuclear weapons.

– Rivers overflow after heavy rains; Washington is hit with worst flooding in 30 years; at least eight deaths are reported in Washington, Oregon, and Idaho; President Clinton tours area and promises $38.4 million in federal disaster aid to State.

1997 Supreme Court rules unanimously in case regarding states' rights to ban doctor-assisted suicide; ruling overturns lower court ruling striking down statutes banning physician-assisted suicide as unconstitutional; decision also affects case in New York.

– Voters defeat gun-control measure that would require handguns sold in State to be equipped with trigger guard; measure was considered test case for expanding gun control at state level.

– State voters reject proposal to bar discrimination on basis of sexual orientation; proposal to legalize medicinal use of marijuana, LSD, and heroin; and plan allowing workers to keep their doctors if changing health care coverage.

– In case that becomes national issue, teacher Mary Kay Letourneau is charged with statutory rape for sexual affair with 13-year-old boy; she later gives birth to daughter fathered by boy.

1998 Mary Kay Letourneau is sentenced to seven and a half years in prison after violating court order that she refrain from contact with 14-year boy with whom she was previously sexually involved.

1999 April 12. The Snake River in southeastern Washington state is named the nation's most endangered river because of four dams that have brought salmon runs to the brink of extinction.

– November 29. In Seattle as many as 50,000 protesters gather to oppose "the march of corporate globalization."

– November 30. In Seattle riot police struggle with thousands of protesters who force the World Trade Organization to cancel the opening session of three day summit meeting. Mayor Paul Schell declares a state of emergency and a night curfew and Gov. Gary Locke calls in some 200 unarmed National Guard.

– December 14. In Seattle Ahmed Ressam was arrested after crossing the border at Port Angeles from Canada with a car trunk with over 150 pounds of bomb-making materials that include two hundred pounds of urea, timing devices and a bottle of RDX, cyclotrimethylene trinitramine. Canadian authorities later issue an arrest warrant for Abdelmajed Dahoumane for possessing or making explosives.

DIRECTORY OF STATE SERVICES

OFFICE OF THE GOVERNOR
Legislative Building
Olympia, WA 98504
Fax: 360-753-4110
Governor's Office: 360-753-6780

OFFICE OF THE LIEUTENANT GOVERNOR
304 Legislative Building
Olympia, WA 98504
Fax: 360-786-7520
Lieutenant Governor's Office: 360-786-7700

OFFICE OF THE ATTORNEY GENERAL
P.O. Box 40100
Olympia, WA 98504
Fax: 360-644-0228
Attorney General's Office: 360-753-6200

OFFICE OF THE SECRETARY OF STATE
P.O. Box 40220
Olympia, WA 98504
Fax: 360-586-5629
Secretary of State Office: 360-753-7121

OFFICE OF THE TREASURER
P.O. Box 40200
Olympia, WA 98504
Fax: 360-586-6147
Treasurer's Office: 360-753-7130

AGRICULTURE DEPARTMENT
P.O. Box 42560
Olympia, WA 98504
Fax: 360-902-2092
Director: 360-902-1801

AUDITOR
P.O. Box 40021
Olympia, WA 98504
Fax: 360-753-0646
State Auditor: 360-753-5280

CODE REVISER
P.O. Box 40551
Olympia, WA 98504
Fax: 360-586-6480
Code Reviser: 360-753-1440

COMMUNITY, TRADE AND ECONOMIC DEVELOPMENT DEPARTMENT
P.O. Box 48300
Olympia, WA 98504
Fax: 360-586-3582
Director: 360-753-7426

Building Code Council
P.O. Box 48300
Olympia, WA 98504
Chairman: 360-586-0486

Business Assistance Center
919 Lakeridge Way SW
Olympia, WA 98502
Director: 360-586-4848

CORRECTIONS DEPARTMENT
P.O. Box 41100
Olympia, WA 98504
Fax: 360-586-3676
Secretary: 360-753-2500

ECOLOGY DEPARTMENT
P.O. Box 47600
Olympia, WA 98504
Fax: 360-407-6989
Director: 360-407-7001

Waste Management Division
P.O. Box 47600
Olympia, WA 98504
Fax: 360-407-6989
Assistant Director: 360-407-7011

Water and Shorelands Division
P.O. Box 47600
Olympia, WA 98504
Fax: 360-407-6989
Assistant Director: 360-407-7013

EMPLOYMENT SECURITY DEPARTMENT
P.O. Box 9046
Olympia, WA 98507
Fax: 360-753-4851
Commissioner: 360-753-5114

GENERAL ADMINISTRATION DEPARTMENT
P.O. Box 41000
Olympia, WA 98504
Fax: 360-586-5898
Director: 360-753-5434

HEALTH DEPARTMENT
P.O. Box 47890
Olympia, WA 98504
Fax: 360-586-7424
Secretary: 360-753-5871

LABOR AND INDUSTRIES DEPARTMENT
P.O. Box 44001
Olympia, WA 98504
Fax: 360-956-4202
Director: 360-956-4203

LICENSING DEPARTMENT
P.O. Box 48001
Olympia, WA 98504
Fax: 360-753-7500
Director: 360-902-4050

MILITARY DEPARTMENT
Camp Murray
Tacoma, WA 98430
Fax: 206-512-8497
Adjutant General: 206-512-8201

NATURAL RESOURCES DEPARTMENT
P.O. Box 47001
Olympia, WA 98504
Fax: 360-902-1775
Commissioner of Public Lands: 360-902-1004

PERSONNEL DEPARTMENT
P.O. Box 47500
Olympia, WA 98504
Fax: 360-586-4694
Director: 360-753-5358

PRINTING DEPARTMENT
P.O. Box 798
Olympia, WA 98504
Fax: 360-586-8444

Director: 360-753-6820

PUBLIC INSTRUCTION DEPARTMENT
P.O. Box 47200
Olympia, WA 98504
Fax: 360-753-6712
Superintendent: 360-586-6904

Administrative and School Business Services
P.O. Box 47200
Olympia, WA 98504
Fax: 360-586-3946
Deputy Superintendent: 360-753-6742

Administrative Services
360-644-0759

School Business Services
360-753-1717

Board of Education Administration
P.O. Box 47206
Olympia, WA 98504
Fax: 360-586-2357
Executive Director: 360-753-6715

Instructional Programs
P.O. Box 47200
Olympia, WA 98504
Fax: 360-586-0247
Deputy Superintendent: 360-753-1545

FINANCIAL INSTITUTIONS DEPARTMENT
P.O. Box 41203
Olympia, WA 98504
Director: 360-902-8744

FISH AND WILDLIFE DEPARTMENT
600 N Capitol Way
Olympia, WA 98501
Fax: 360-902-2947
Director: 360-902-2226

RETIREMENT SYSTEMS DEPARTMENT
P.O. Box 48380
Olympia, WA 98504
Fax: 360-753-3166
Director: 360-753-5281

REVENUE DEPARTMENT
P.O. Box 47454
Olympia, WA 98504
Fax: 360-586-5543
Director: 360-753-5574

SOCIAL AND HEALTH SERVICES DEPARTMENT
P.O. Box 45010
Olympia, WA 98504
Fax: 360-586-5874
Secretary: 360-753-3395

Aging and Adult Services
P.O. Box 45040
Olympia, WA 98504

Fax: 360-586-5874
Assistant Secretary: 360-586-3768

Children, Youth and Family Services
P.O. Box 45060
Olympia, WA 98504
Fax: 360-586-5874
Assistant Secretary: 360-536-4031

Community Relations
P.O. Box 45100
Olympia, WA 98504
Fax: 360-664-0788
Assistant Secretary: 360-753-5230

Juvenile Rehabilitation Services
P.O. Box 45045
Olympia, WA 98504
Fax: 360-586-5874
Assistant Secretary: 360-753-7402

Economic Services
P.O. Box 45070
Olympia, WA 98504
Fax: 360-586-5874
Assistant Secretary: 360-586-3770

Health and Rehabilitative Services
P.O. Box 45060
Olympia, WA 98504
Fax: 360-586-5874
Assistant Secretary: 360-753-3327

Management Services
P.O. Box 45030
Olympia, WA 98504-5030
Fax: 360-586-5874
Assistant Secretary: 360-753-3424

Medical Assistance Services
P.O. Box 45500
Olympia, WA 98504
Fax: 360-586-5874
Assistant Secretary: 360-753-1777

TRANSPORTATION DEPARTMENT
P.O. Box 47316
Olympia, WA 98504
Fax: 360-705-6808
Secretary: 360-705-7054

Finance and Administration
P.O. Box 7400
Olympia, WA 98504
Fax: 360-705-6803
Assistant Secretary: 360-705-7400

Field Operations Support Service
P.O. Box 47300
Olympia, WA 98504
Fax: 360-705-6823
Assistant Secretary: 360-705-7801

VETERANS AFFAIRS DEPARTMENT
P.O. Box 41150
Olympia, WA 98504
Fax: 360-586-5540
Director: 360-753-5586

ACCOUNTANCY BOARD
P.O. Box 9131
Olympia, WA 98504
Fax: 360-664-9190
Chairman: 360-753-2585

ARTS COMMISSION
P.O. Box 42675
Olympia, WA 98504
Fax: 360-586-5351
Executive Director: 360-753-3860

CONSERVATION COMMISSION
P.O. Box 47721
Olympia, WA 98504
Fax: 360-407-6215
Executive Director: 360-407-6200

ENERGY OFFICE
P.O. Box 43165
Olympia, WA 98504
Fax: 360-956-2217
Director: 360-956-2000

FINANCIAL MANAGEMENT OFFICE
P.O. Box 43113
Olympia, WA 98504
Fax: 360-586-4837
Director: 360-753-5450

FOREST PRACTICES APPEALS BOARD
P.O. Box 40903
Olympia, WA 98504
Fax: 360-438-7699
Administrative Appeals Judge: 360-459-6327

GAMBLING COMMISSION
P.O. Box 42400
Olympia, WA 98504
Fax: 360-438-8652
Director: 360-438-7654

HEALTH CARE FACILITIES AUTHORITY
1212 Jefferson St., Ste. 201
Olympia, WA 98504
Fax: 360-586-9168
Executive Director: 360-753-6185

HIGHER EDUCATION COORDINATING BOARD
917 Lakeridge Way
Olympia, WA 98504
Fax: 360-753-1784
Executive Director: 360-753-7810

HISTORICAL SOCIETY
315 N Stadium Way
Tacoma, WA 98403
Fax: 206-597-4186

Director: 206-593-2830

HORSE RACING COMMISSION
7512 Martin Way, Ste. D
Olympia, WA 98506
Fax: 360-459-6461
Chairman: 360-459-6462

HUMAN RIGHTS COMMISSION
711 S. Capitol Way, Ste. 402
Olympia, WA 98504
Fax: 360-586-2282
Executive Director: 360-753-6770

HUMANITIES DIVISION
615 2nd Ave., Ste. 300
Seattle, WA 98104
Fax: 360-682-4158
Executive Director: 360-682-1770

INDETERMINATE SENTENCE REVIEW BOARD
P.O. Box 40907
Olympia, WA 98504
Fax: 360-493-9287
Chairman: 360-493-9266

INDUSTRIAL INSURANCE APPEALS BOARD
P.O. Box 2401
Olympia WA 98504
Fax: 360-586-5611
Chairperson: 360-753-6823

INSURANCE COMMISSION
P.O. Box 40255
Olympia, WA 98504
Fax: 360-586-3535
Insurance Commissioner: 360-753-7301

LIQUOR CONTROL BOARD
P.O. Box 43075
Olympia, WA 98504
Fax: 360-664-9689
Chairman: 360-753-6262

PHARMACY BOARD
P.O. Box 47863
Olympia, WA 98504
Fax: 360-586-4359
Executive Director: 360-753-6834

PUBLIC DISCLOSURE COMMISSION
P.O. Box 40908
Olympia, WA 98504
Fax: 360-753-1112
Executive Director: 360-753-1980

PUBLIC EMPLOYMENT RELATIONS COMMISSION
P.O. Box 40919
Olympia, WA 98504
Fax: 360-586-7091
Executive Director: 360-753-3444

PUBLIC POWER SUPPLY SYSTEMS
3000 George Washington Way
Richland, WA 99352
Fax: 509-372-5205
Managing Director: 509-372-5000

STATE INVESTMENT BOARD
P.O. Box 40916
Olympia, WA 98504
Fax: 360-664-8912
Executive Director: 360-664-8907

MEMBERS OF CONGRESS

SENATE

SEN. SLADE GORTON (R) (b. 1928); 3rd Term;
Phone: 202-224-3441; Fax: 202-224-9393; E-mail: (None).

www.senate.gov/~gorton

SEN. PATTY MURRAY (D) (b. 1950); 2nd Term;
Phone: 202-224-2621; Fax: 202-224-0238;
E-mail: senator_murray@murray.senate.gov.

www.senate.gov/~murray

HOUSE

JAY INSLEE (D-1st) (b. 1951); 1st Term;
Phone: 202-225-4501; Fax: 202-225-4656;
E-mail: ga06@mail.house.gov.

www.house.gov/isakson/

JACK METCALF (R-2nd) (b. 1927); 3rd Term;
Phone: 202-225-2605; Fax: 202-225-4420;
E-mail: w02@legislators.com.

www.house.gov/metcalf/

BRIAN BAIRD (D-3rd) (b. 1956); 1st Term;
Phone: 202-225-3536; Fax: 202-225-3478;
E-mail: brian.baird@mail.house.gov.

www.house.gov/baird

DOC HASTINGS (R-4th) (b. 1941); 3rd Term;
Phone: 202-225-1313; Fax: 202-225-1171;
E-mail: alcee.pubhastings@mail.house.gov.

www.house.gov/alceehastings/

GEORGE R. NETHERCUTT, Jr. (R-5th) (b. 1944); 3rd Term;
Phone: 202-225-2006; Fax: 202-225-3392;
E-mail: wa05@legislators.com.

www.house.gov/nethercutt/

NORMAN D. DICKS (D-6th) (b. 1940); 12th Term;
Phone: 202-225-5916; Fax: 202-226-1176;
E-mail: wa06@legislators.com.

www.house.gov/dicks

JIM McDERMOTT (D-7th) (b. 1936); 6th Term;
Phone: 202-225-3106; Fax: 202-225-6197;
E-mail: wa07@legislators.com.

www.house.gov/mcdermott/

JENNIFER DUNN (R-8th) (b. 1941); 4th Term;
Phone: 202-225-7761; Fax: 202-225-8673;
E-mail: dunnwa08@mail.house.gov.

www.house.gov/dunn/

ADAM SMITH (D-9th) (b. 1965); 2nd Term;
Phone: 202-225-8901; Fax: 202-225-5893;
E-mail: wa09@legislators.com.

www.house.gov/adamsmith/

TWENTIETH CENTURY GOVERNORS

ROGERS, JOHN RANKIN (1838-1901), third governor of Washington (1897-1903), was born in Brunswick, Maine on September 4, 1838. His great-grandfather, Captain John Rogers, commanded a privateer during the American Revolution, and held letters of marque and reprisal granted by the Continental Congress. Rogers acquired his early education in the area's common schools and afterward spent four years learning the drug business in Boston, Massachusetts.

In 1856, Rogers moved to Jackson, Mississippi; although he was only eighteen years old, he took charge of a drug store. He later moved to Illinois, where he taught school and subsequently bought a farm, which he cultivated for ten years. He then resided in Kansas for fourteen years and engaged in farming as well as in promoting the Farmers' Alliance; he also held several minor offices there.

In 1890, Rogers moved to the State of Washington. In 1892, he published *The Irrepressible Conflict*, which made a sensation and brought him prominently before the people of his adopted state. He was elected to the State Legislature in 1894 and took an avid interest in legislation pertaining to education, coal mining, and taxation. With great passion, he championed the cause of coal miners, who desired passage of a proper mine ventilation bill.

Rogers authored the measure known as the "barefoot schoolboy law," which required a tax to produce a sum amounting to six dollars for each child of school age; it was due to his energetic efforts that the bill became law after a memorable contest.

In 1896, Rogers was elected Governor by a large majority after a closely contested campaign, he was reelected in 1900. When he took office, a measure put before the Legislature sought financial support for an expensive foundation for a new capitol building; although the Legislature had previously passed a bill carrying a large appropriation to complete the building, there were no available funds, and he vetoed it.

In his second inaugural address, Rogers recommended to the Legislature that they buy the Thurston County Courthouse and appropriate 350,000 dollars to build an addition, which would give ample room to accommodate all the State officials. This recommendation was accepted, and the new building was completed in 1903.

Rogers was the author of a number of books and pamphlets on sociological topics, as well as one novel, entitled *Looking Forward; or the Story of an American Farm* (1898).

Rogers was married in 1861 to Sarah L. Greene of Illinois, and the couple had five children.

Rogers died on December 26, 1901 in Olympia, Washington, while serving his second gubernatorial term.

MCBRIDE, HENRY (1856-1937), fourth governor of Washington (1901-1905), was born in Utah on February 7, 1856. He was educated at the public schools of Utah and at Trinity College in Hartford, Connecticut. After studying law and being admitted to the bar, he established a law practice in Mount Vernon, Washington in 1884, and four years later, was elected prosecuting attorney of Skagit County, Washington.

In 1891, McBride was appointed by Governor Elisha P. Ferry to the office of Justice of the Supreme Court for Skagit and Island counties; in November of the following year, he was elected to the same office for a four-year term. After leaving that post, he resumed his law practice.

In November 1900, McBride was elected lieutenant governor of the State of Washington. Upon the death of Governor John R. Rogers in December 1901, he succeeded to the governor's chair. He remained in gubernatorial office until the expiration of Rogers' term in January 1905, and afterward returned to his professional duties in Seattle as a partner of McBride, Stratton & Dalton.

McBride was married to Alice Garrett. He died in 1937.

MEAD, ALBERT EDWARD (1861-1913), fifth governor of Washington (1905-1909), was born at Manhattan, Kansas on December 14, 1861. After receiving his education at local schools in Kansas, Iowa, and Illinois, he entered the Southern Illinois Normal University at Carbondale, and graduated in 1882. He then took a two-year course at the Union College of Law in Chicago, and was admitted to the bar of the Illinois Supreme Court in 1885.

For four years, Mead practiced law in Leoti, Kansas. He then moved to Washington and located in Blaine, where he soon established an extensive practice. He served as mayor of Blame in 1892, was a representative of the third legislature during 1893-95, and was prosecuting attorney from 1899 to 1903.

Mead was an active Republican. In 1904, after the most sensational fight in the political history of the State, he was nominated for governor, receiving 75,278 votes to 59,119 for Turner, the Democratic candidate. Among important measures adopted during his administration were provisions for a State Railway Commission and a State Tax Commission, a State Public Highway Department, direct primary elections, the establishment of a reformatory, indeterminate sentences for criminals, and creation of the office of State bank examiner.

Mead was married to Lizzie Brown; the couple had four children. After the death of his first wife, he married Mina J. Piper, a widow, with whom he had one son.

Mead died on March 19, 1913.

COSGROVE, SAMUEL GOODLOVE (1847-1909), sixth governor of Washington (1909), was born in Tuscarawas County, Ohio on April 10, 1841. He spent his childhood on a farm in Defiance County, Ohio.

When he was sixteen years old, Cosgrove enlisted in Company E, 14th Ohio Volunteer Infantry during the Civil War and was honorably discharged in July 1865. He taught school for a time in both Woodsfield and Brooklyn, Ohio to pay for his education, and graduated from Wesleyan University in 1873, receiving the degrees of M.A. and LL.B. He read law under Hollister & Okey at Woodsfield, Ohio, and was admitted to the bar in 1875.

Leaving Ohio in 1880, Cosgrove spent one year mining in Nevada, moved to California for a year, and finally in 1882, settled in Pomeroy, Washington, where he practiced law until his election to the governorship.

Cosgrove was mayor of Pomeroy for five terms. When he first accepted the position, the city was deeply in debt and was supporting only fourteen mills annually. The following year, they were reduced to nine mills, and finally to six mills, the entire debt being liquidated and the city put on a cash basis.

In politics, Cosgrove was a staunch Republican, and campaigned in every election after his move to Washington. He was a member of the Constitutional Convention and was an elector for McKinley and Roosevelt, and Roosevelt and Fairbanks; each time, he received the highest number of votes cast for any member of his party, and was chairman of two State conventions.

Cosgrove wrote and introduced every plank in the Republican State platforms relative to reducing and establishing maximum freight rates. In the Spokane convention of 1906, failing to get the plank in the platform in committee, he took it on the floor of the convention, and forced its adoption over the report of the committee. In the 1902 and 1904 conventions, he headed the delegation from his county, and supported the Railroad Commission forces.

Before it was positively known that Governor McBride could not be nominated in 1904, Cosgrove was offered the nomination himself if he would desert McBride and throw his influence in opposition to him; Cosgrove declined the honor. In 1904, he was offered a seat on the Supreme Court bench, but refused. Although he was receptive to candidacy as chief executive for many years, he never permitted his ambitions to bias his acts or hamper his freedom with unfair compacts.

Cosgrove was president of the school board of Pomeroy for eight years, during which a large debt was liquidated. He was also a member of the first city council. As a member of the Grand Army of the Republic, he served the jurisdiction of Washington and Alaska as department commander; in Louisville, Kentucky, he was elected junior vice-commander in chief, the third highest office in the army. While he was still practicing law, he also farmed over 1,400 acres of land in Washington and Idaho.

Cosgrove was elected Governor of Washington in November 1908. During his brief administration, a local option law was enacted by the State Legislature. Laws were also passed which placed telegraph and telephone companies under the jurisdiction of the Railroad Commission, and gave cities and towns of the State the power to oppose, purchase, and operate street railways. A law was also passed that made it a crime to sell, give away, or possess a cigarette.

Cosgrove died while serving the first year of his gubernatorial term. He was married to Zephorena Edgerton, and the couple had three children. He died at Paso Robles, California on March 28, 1909.

HAY, MARION F. (1865-1933), seventh governor of Washington (1909-1913), was born in Adams County, Wisconsin on December 9, 1865. He attended country schools and the Bayless Commercial Business College in Dubuque, Iowa.

Hay began his business career in 1888 as a partner with Charles Grutt, under the firm name of Hay & Grutt in Davenport, Washington. A year later, he moved to Wilbur, Washington and the firm became M.E. Hay. In 1901, the business was incorporated as M.E. & F.T. Hay.

In 1908, Hay was elected Lieutenant Governor of Washington. Upon the death of Governor Cosgrove in 1909, he succeeded to the chief executive's chair. He served until 1913.

Hay was married to Lizzie Muir, and the couple had five children. He died on November 21, 1933.

LISTER, ERNEST (1870-1919), eighth governor of Washington (1913-1919), was born in Halifax, England on June 15, 1870, the son of Ellen Hey and Jeremiah Lister. His family immigrated to the United States in 1884 and settled in Tacoma, Washington.

After finishing his early education, Lister began a woodworking shop and small iron foundry called the Lister Manufacturing Company. In 1894, he ran for Tacoma City Council on the Populist ticket and was elected. An admirer of the Populist leader, John R. Rogers, Lister became his campaign manager in 1896 and helped him win election as Governor of Washington. Soon after, Lister was appointed chairman of the State Board of Control.

Both Rogers and Lister abandoned the Populist Party in 1900 and returned to the Democratic Party. In 1912, Lister ran for governor on a platform that supported women's suffrage, anti-saloon laws, and direct legislation. He lost in the primary. However, just three weeks before the general election, Black, the Democratic Party's candidate, was declared ineligible for office; the State Democratic Central Committee selected Lister to take his place. He campaigned heavily in the remaining weeks, and managed to win the election against the Republican contender Hay. He was reelected in 1916.

During his administration, Lister supported State industrial accident insurance and agricultural legislation, which provided aid to irrigation and reclamation projects. He was against an anti-picketing measure, and he vetoed legislation that he believed would have denied civil rights to members of the Industrial Workers of the World. He took part in the Washington State Council of Defense during World War I. In labor matters, he was instrumental in establishing the eight-hour workday in Washington.

In the summer of 1918, Lister collapsed during a special session of the Legislature, and was diagnosed as having Bright's disease. He was able to continue in his duties until January 1919, when he became ill once again, and resigned his office to the lieutenant governor.

Lister died on June 14, 1919, just one day before his forty-ninth birthday. He was married to Alma Thornton in 1893. The couple had two children.

HART, LOUIS FOLWELL (1862-1929), ninth (acting) and tenth governor of Washington (1919 and 1919-1925), was born on January 4, 1862 in High Point, Missouri, the son of Harriet Van Artsdalin and Thomas Hart. After receiving his early education, he studied law. In 1884, he was admitted to the Missouri Bar.

Hart moved to the State of Washington in 1889 and engaged in a law practice with J.A. Coleman. He lived in Snohomish and Republic before settling in Tacoma in the early 1890s. Between 1901 and 1914, he was a member of the Elks, Masons, Shriners, Lions International, and the Independent Order of Odd Fellows, for which he served as Grand Secretary for a time.

Hart was elected Lieutenant Governor of Washington on the Republican ticket in 1912, and served as president of the State Senate and chairman of the Selective Service Appeals Board for Southwest Washington. Following Governor Lister's death in 1919, Hart became Acting Governor. He was elected in his own right the same year.

During his administration, Hart sought to improve the State Highway Department and the State Highway Patrol. He also supported reorganization of the State's administrative structure. He was against increasing taxes to support higher education, and also opposed federal child labor laws. His term saw the beginning of construction on the State capitol complex, the introduction of dairy herds at correctional institutions, and the reduction of administrative agencies from seventy-five to ten.

Hart chose not to run for reelection in 1924, due to ill health. He returned to his private law practice in Tacoma, where he died on December 5, 1929.

Hart was married to Lou Ella James in 1881. The couple had four children.

HARTLEY, ROLAND H. (1864-1952), tenth governor of Washington (1925-1933), was born on June 26, 1864 in Skogomoc, New Brunswick, the son of Rebecca Whitehead and Edward Hartley. While he was still a child, his family moved to Minnesota; he was educated in the public schools there and at Minneapolis Academy.

Hartley resided for a time in Brainerd, Minnesota, and worked as a logger, cook, hotel clerk, and bookkeeper. In 1885, he took employment with Clough Lumber and later became its manager. He served as private secretary to Governor David M. Clough of Minnesota in 1897 and was on the general staff of the Minnesota National Guard.

Hartley moved to Washington State in 1903, at the invitation of J.J. Hill of the Great Northern Railroad. In Everett, Washington, he helped establish the Clough-Hartley Lumber Company. He was elected Mayor of Everett in 1910, and served until 1911. From 1915-16, he was a member of the State House of Representatives.

Hartley won election as Governor of Washington in 1924 as a Republican, on a platform that supported child labor laws, funding for higher education, and unionization of the lumber industry. During his administration, he worked diligently to bring about the changes promised in his campaign.

Hartley also became embroiled in a controversy with University of Washington's president, Henry M. Suzzalo, which led to Suzzalo's removal from office in 1926 by a Board of Regents, which had been appointed by Hartley. After reelection to a second term in 1928, he ran again in 1936, after four years out of office, but was not successful in regaining the governorship. He then returned to his business in Everett.

Hartley was married to Nina M. Cough in 1888. The couple had three children.

Hartley died on September 21, 1952.

MARTIN, CLARENCE DANIEL (1887-1955), twelfth governor of Washington (1933-1941), was born on June 29, 1887 in Cheney, Washington, the son of F.M. and Pilena Martin. He attended the University of Washington, and graduated in 1906 with a BA.

In 1907, Martin went to work for the family-owned F.M. Martin Milling Company in Cheney. When his father died, he became president and general manager of the company. He entered politics while still in Cheney, serving as mayor of that city for three terms.

In 1932, Martin was elected Governor of Washington on the Democratic ticket. He was reelected again in 1936. While in office, Martin worked for tax reform, highway construction, and increase in public education and welfare. He was instrumental in helping to create the Washington Emergency Relief Administration and the State Planning Commission. Bonneville, Grand Coulee, Diablo, and Ross dams were built during his administration, as well as the Tacoma Narrows Bridge and the Lake Washington Floating Bridge.

After leaving office, Martin returned to his business interests in Cheney. He also served on the Board of Directors of the Seattle First National Bank.

In 1906, Martin was married to Margaret Mulligan, with whom he had three children. He was married a second time in 1951, to Lue Ekhardt.

Martin died in Cheney on August l, 1955.

LANGLIE, ARTHUR B. (1900-1966), thirteenth and fifteenth governor of Washington (1940-1945 and 1949-1957), was born in Lanesboro, Minnesota on July 25, 1900, the son of Carrie Dahl and Bjarne Langlie. His family moved to Bremerton, Washington in 1909.

Langlie attended the University of Washington and received his LL.B. degree in 1926. That same year he was admitted to the Washington Bar. He practiced law with the firm of Shank, Belt and Fairbrook from 1926 to 1936, and was elected to the Seattle City Council in 1935. From 1939-45, he served as a lieutenant, junior grade, in the U.S. Naval Reserve. He continued to seek political office, and in 1938 was elected mayor of Seattle. He served until 1941.

In 1940, Langlie was elected Governor of Washington. He ran for a second term in 1944, but was defeated. However, he returned in 1948, and was again elected to office. He was also reelected in 1952, becoming the first man to serve three terms as governor of Washington.

Part of Langlie's term in office spanned the World War II years. During that period, Washington received four million dollars in war contracts. In 1949, he helped create the Washington State Toll Bridge Authority. He served as a keynote speaker at the Republican National Convention in 1952; vice president of the National Municipal League; chairman of the Governor's Conference (1955-56); and delegate to the International Labor Organization Conference in Geneva, Switzerland.

Langlie declined to run for a fourth term in 1956. After leaving office, he became chief executive and president of McCalls Publishing Company from 1957-61, and served as chairman of the board of McCalls from 1961-65.

Langlie died on July 24, 1966, one day before his sixty-sixth birthday. He was married to Evelyn Pansy in 1928, and the couple had two children.

WALLGREN, MONRAD CHARLES (1891-1961), fourteenth governor of Washington (1945-3949), was born on April 17, 1891 in Des Moines, Iowa, the son of Carrie Helgeson and Swan Wallgren. His family moved to Washington in 1901, and he attended the Business College in Everett, and the Washington State School of Optometry in Spokane. He was graduated in 1914.

Wallgren served as a second lieutenant in the U.S. Coast Artillery during World War I, and was an adjutant in the Washington National Guard from 1923-22. Residing in Everett, he operated a retail jewelry and optometry business until 1933, when he was elected to the U.S. Congress. He served as a Representative from Washington's second district until 1941, and as a U.S. Senator from 1941-45.

In 1944, Wallgren ran for governor of Washington and won against the incumbent, Arthur Langlie. During his administration, he supported increasing State tourism and recreation, public ownership of electrical power production, and research in higher educational institutions. He advocated construction of a tunnel through the Cascade Mountains. In 1945, he successfully instituted unemployment compensation in Washington.

Wallgren ran for a second term in 1948, but was defeated by former Governor Langlie. From 1949-51, he served as chairman of the Federal Power Commission. He subsequently became involved with real estate investments in California.

Wallgren married Mabel C. Liberty in 1914. He died on September 18, 1961 in Olympia.

ROSELLINI, ALBERT DEAN (1910-), sixteenth governor of Washington (1957-1965), was born on January 21, 1910 in Tacoma, the son of Annuziata Pagni and John Rosellini. He attended the University of Washington, and received a LL.B. degree in 1933. Upon graduation, he entered a private law practice in Seattle. From 1933-41, Rosellini was the Assistant Deputy Prosecuting Attorney for King County. He was ejected to the State Senate, and served from 1938-56, where he was the Democratic floor leader. From 1941-43, he also served as Assistant State Attorney General.

In 1956, Rosellini was elected Governor of Washington. He was reelected in 1960. During his administration, he reorganized the Department of Institutions, and created the new Department of Commerce and Economic Development. He also worked to implement a new accounting system for State government. He supported improvements to prisons and mental hospitals, and helped to promote a salmon enhancement program through the State Fisheries Department. In public works projects, he saw construction of the second Lake Washington Bridge and the Hood's Canal bridges. Rosellini ran for a third term in 1964, but was defeated. He returned to his law practice in Seattle. He later became chairman of the State Transportation Commission.

Rosellini was married to Ethel K. McNeil in 1937. The couple has five children.

EVANS, DANIEL JACKSON (1925-), seventeenth governor of Washington (1965-1977), was born on October 16, 1925 in Seattle, the son of Irma Ide and Daniel Evans. He attended the University of Washington, and graduated with a M.S. in 1949. During World War II, he served in the U.S. Naval Reserve; after completing his education, he served again from 1951-53.

From 1953-59, Evans was assistant manager for the Mountain Pacific Chapter of Associated General Contractors, and was a partner in Gray & Evans Structural and Civil Engineers firm from 1959-65. He also served in the Washington House of Representatives from 1956-65, and was Republican floor leader for four years.

Evans was elected Governor of Washington in 1964, 1968, and 1972. He was the first candidate to serve three consecutive terms as governor of the State. During his administration, he gave strong support to the State's educational needs, and helped promote a number of programs including a school building project; programs for the disabled; establishment of a new four-year college; and creation of a community college system for the State. He also worked to curb air and water pollution with new legislation.

Evans served as chairman of the Campaign Committee of the National Republican Governors (1965-66), and was a member of the Executive Board of National Republican Governors (1966-67 and 1973-75). He was keynote speaker at the Republican National Convention (1968), chairman of the Western Governors' Conference (1968-69), and chairman of the National Governors' Conference (1973-74).

After his third term ended in 1977, Evans retired from office. In 1977, he became the second president of Evergreen State College in Olympia.

Evans was married to Nancy Ann Bell in 1959. The couple has three children.

RAY, DIXY LEE (1914-1994), eighteenth governor of Washington (1977-1981), was born on September 3, 1914 in Tacoma, the daughter of Frances Adams and Alvis Ray. She attended Mills College, where she received a B.A. in 1937 and a M.A. in 1938. In 1945, she earned her Ph.D. at Stanford University.

A marine biologist, Ray was a professor of zoology at the University of Washington from 1945-76. In 1952, she received a Guggenheim Fellowship; she also earned honorary degrees from over twenty colleges and universities.

From 1960-62, Ray was a special consultant on biological oceanography to the National Science Foundation. In 1963, she served as special assistant to the director of that organization. She was a member of the Presidential Task Force on Oceanography in 1969. From 1963-72, she was director of the Pacific Science Center in Seattle. In the latter year, President Nixon appointed her the first woman to serve on the Atomic Energy Commission; she chaired the commission from 1973-75. In addition, she was Assistant Secretary of State for the Bureau of Oceans, International Environmental and Scientific Affairs in 1975.

In 1976, Ray returned to Washington State and decided to run for governor. With a scorn for bureaucracy acquired during her service on governmental commissions, she ran a low budget, people's campaign, labeling herself a non-politician. Her platform called for governmental reorganization and austerity, and economic development in the State through the use of nuclear power. She surprised many pollsters by narrowly defeating Wes Uhlman in the Democratic primary then went on to win in the general election by attracting support of conservatives and business people from both parties. In doing so, she became the first woman governor in Washington's history.

Once in office, Ray attracted national attention with her outspoken and sometimes eccentric way of conducting both her private life and government affairs. She lived with her pet dogs in a mobile home on Puget Sound, and was reputed to have given herself a chainsaw for Christmas one year. As governor, she intimidated and fired members of her staff at will, antagonized the press, and polarized public opinion.

As Ray pushed for the growth of nuclear power, conservationists, farmers, and even businesspeople criticized Ray for pushing growth too quickly without regard to the environment. She caused a furor by insisting on maintaining the nuclear dump at Hanford to handle atomic waste from Washington and other states. She allowed supertankers to ship oil from Alaska through Puget Sound, despite strong opposition. She was criticized when her choice for Director of Transportation turned out to be a convicted drunk driver.

Despite the controversy surrounding her administration, Ray was instrumental in improving Washington's economy during her term. She was also credited with providing aid and effective crises management during the Mt. St. Helen's eruption of 1980. However, in 1981, she was named in a civil suit tiled on behalf of eight people who died in the eruption.

Ray ran for a second term in 1981 and was, for a time, a strong contender in the Democratic primary. She was defeated, however, by Senator Jim McDermott. After leaving office, Ray retired to Fox Island to live with her sister, and to write a book about her term as governor. She was also a consultant to TRW Engineering, and appeared on the radio show "Speaking Out."

Ray died in January 1994.

SPELLMAN, JOHN DENNIS (1926-), nineteenth governor of Washington (1981-1985), was born on December 29, 1926 in Seattle, the son of Lela Cushman and Sterling Spellman. He attended Seattle University, and served in the U.S. Navy during World War II. Following his discharge from the Navy, he entered Georgetown University, where he earned a law degree in 1953.

Spellman practiced law in Seattle for thirteen years. He entered politics in 1965 when he ran for mayor, but was defeated in the election. From 1967-69, he served as King County Commis-

sioner. He was elected King County Executive in 1969, 1973, and 1977, and was instrumental in completing the Kingdome, Seattle's domed stadium, while keeping costs within the proposed budget. During that time, he also served as first vice president of the National Association of Counties, chairman of the King-Snohomish Manpower Consortium, and chairman of the Citizens Committee for Revenue Sharing.

Spellman ran for governor in 1976 on the Republican ticket, but was defeated by Dixy Lee Ray. He ran again in 1980, this time capturing the vote of conservative Democrats as well as those of his own party, and won with fifty-seven percent of the vote.

After Dixy Lee Ray's unconventional tenure in office, Spellman's reputation as a capable though rather spiritless administrator brought traditional governing approaches back to the capitol. He served as chairman of the National Governors' Association Task Force on Export Finance; vice chairman of the National Governors' Association Committee on International Trade and Foreign Relations; founding cochairman of the Coalition for Employment Through Exports; and chairman of the U.S. Savings Bonds Campaign. He ran for a second term as governor in 1984, but was defeated by Democrat Booth Gardner, despite the national Republican landslide that year.

Spellman is married to Lois Elizabeth Murphy. The couple has six children.

GARDNER, BOOTH (1936-), twentieth governor of Washington (1985-1992), was born in Tacoma on August 21, 1936. He studied business at the University of Washington then attended Harvard University, where he received an M.B.A. degree in 1963.

While still a student in Washington, Gardner co-founded the Central Area Youth Association in Seattle to provide educational, sports, and social activities for disadvantaged and minority youths. After graduate school, he became director of the School of Business and Economics at the University of Puget Sound in Tacoma.

Gardner was elected to the Washington Senate and served from 1970 to 1973. During his term, he chaired the Education Committee, continuing his special interest in educational programs for the disadvantaged. In 1972, he became president of the building and supply firm of Laird Norton Company. He remained at that post until 1980. In 1981, he was elected Pierce County Executive, a position he held until 1984, when he ran for governor.

A Democrat, Gardner won the governorship with fifty-three percent of the vote against John Spellman's forty-seven percent. One of his top priorities was the State's economic development, and he worked to bring new industry to the State. He also continued his strong support of education. With a style he characterized as "management by walking around," he spent one day each month visiting public schools, and often dropped in unannounced at various State agency offices.

Gardner was reelected to a second term in 1988. Shortly after stepping down as chief executive in 1992, he received an appointment by President Bill Clinton as Ambassador to Japan. Currently his appointment has been held up due to trade conflicts.

Gardner and his wife Jean were married in 1960 and have two children.

LOWRY, MIKE (1939-), twenty-first governor of Washington (1992-1996) was born on March 8, 1939 in St. John, Washington. After graduating from Endicott High School in 1957, he attended Washington State University and graduated in 1962.

Lowry's public life began with an election to the King County Council in 1975; he became chairman of the council in 1977. In 1978, he was elected a member of the U.S. House of Representatives; he was reelected four times and served a total of ten years. Upon leaving Congress, he began to teach government at the Seattle University Institute for Public Service.

Lowry was elected Governor of Washington in 1992. During his campaign, he set a precedent by refusing to accept contributions over 1,500 dollars, believing that this would allow him to govern the State without undue pressure from lobbyists and special interest groups. He strongly emphasized a need to improve the State's economy by maintaining a strong educational system, investing in the infrastructure, and improving government efficiency.

Immediately after his inauguration, Lowry began a program to reduce spending and streamline operations in State agencies. His administration was able to cut more than 700 million dollars from 1993-1995 budgets. In addition, he took a 31,000 dollars pay cut himself and reduced the budget for the governor's office staff by 1.3 million dollars. Salaries of State workers with yearly incomes of 45,000 dollars or over were frozen, and additional steps were taken to restrict travel, cut equipment costs, and lower the number of mid-level managers.

Other innovations Lowry sought to accomplish during his tenure included health care reform, changes in the State's outdated civil service system, merging of agencies, and improved access to higher education. His administration was dedicated to improving government ethics, changing the State's regulatory climate, and making Washington the best State in the nation in which to do business.

Lowry is married to Mary Lowry; the couple has one daughter.

LOCKE, GARY (1950-), twenty-second governor of Washington (1997-), was born in Seattle, Washington on January 21, 1950. During his early years, he worked at his father's restaurant and small grocery store. He attended Franklin High School, graduating with honors in 1968. He then attended Yale University, working part-time jobs and earning scholarships and financial aid to pay for his tuition. In 1972, he graduated from Yale with a political science degree and went on to earn a law degree from Boston University in 1973

Locke was a prosecuting attorney in King County for several years, and worked as a community relation's manager for U.S. West. He was elected to the State House of Representatives in 1982, and kept his seat for eleven years. During his tenure, he served on the House Judiciary and Appropriations committees and was chairman of the latter committee for his last five years with the House. Some of the issues he addressed were improvements in health care for children, stronger environmental protections, and efforts to increase college and university enrollment.

In 1993, Locke was elected chief executive of King County, Washington's largest county and the thirteenth largest in the nation. Some efforts during his term included establishing a savings incentive program to reward county departments that saved money, developing a nationally acclaimed growth management plan for the county, streamlining the process for obtaining government permits, expanding bus service, and cutting the county's budget.

Locke was elected Washington's governor in 1996, winning a fifty-eight percent majority. His campaign and continuing efforts as chief executive have focused on education. During his first legislative session, he worked with the Republican controlled legislature to increase funding for job training, health care, and education. He signed into law a landmark welfare reform bill that put work first. His budget has provided more than 300 dollars in tax relief for homeowners and businesses.

In 1994, Locke was married to Mona Lee Locke, a former news reporter for KING television in Seattle. Their first daughter, Emily Nicole, was born in March 1997.

DICTIONARY OF PLACES

Population figures and demographic information are official U.S. Census Bureau finals for 1990. When two figures are shown, separated by a slash, the first figure is the 1990 and the second is the U.S. Census Bureau 1999 estimate—the most recent available. Year 2000 census supplements will be available in the Fall of 2001.

ABERDEEN, City; Grays Harbor County; Pop. 18,739 / 16,087; Zip Code 98520; Lat. 46-58-21 N, Long. 123-45-05 W; The city is named after the famous town in Scotland.

AIRWAY HEIGHTS, City; Spokane County; Pop. 1,730 / 4,370; Zip Code 99001; A descriptive name for the community.

ALBION, Town; Whitman County; Pop. 631 / 619; Zip Code 99102; Lat. 47-21-07 N, Long. 117-42-44 W; The town's name honors early English exploration of the region.

ALMIRA, Town; Lincoln County; Pop. 330 / 318; Zip Code 99103; Elev. 1915; Lat. 47-53-27 N, 117-21-07 W; The town's name honors Almira Davis, wife of the town's first merchant.

ANACORTES, City; Skagit County; Pop. 9,013 / 15,368; Zip Code 98221; Lat. 48-30-08 N, Long. 122-37-17 W; Civil engineer Amos Bowman platted the town site and named it for his wife's maiden name; Anna Curtis; the spelling was later changed to give it a Spanish sound.

ARLINGTON, City; Snohomish County; Pop. 3,282 / 7,012; Zip Code 98223; Lat. 48-11-34 N, Long. 122-07-16 W; Two railroad contractors purchased the townsite in 1890 and named it for Lord Henry Arlington, a member of the cabinet of Charles II.

ASOTIN, City; Asotin County Seat; Pop. 943 / 1,041; Zip Code 99402; Elev. 770; Lat. 46-20-13 N, Long. 117-02-10 W; A Nez Perce Indian word meaning "Eel Creek" and descriptively referring to the eels caught there.

AUBURN, City; King County; Pop. 26,417 / 38,460; Zip Code 980+; Originally called Slaughter, the name was later changed to the more euphonious Auburn.

BATTLE GROUND, City; Clark County; Pop. 2,774 / 6,103; Zip Code 98604; Lat. 45-46-54 N, Long. 122-31-57 W; The town's name commemorates a battle between the U.S. Army and local Indians during pioneer days.

BEAUX ARTS VILLAGE, Town; King County; Pop. 328 / 302; A euphonious name given by the town's settlers.

BELLEVUE, City; King County; Pop. 73,903 / 105,521; Zip Code 98004; Lat. 47-35-00 N, Long. 122-10-29 W; An old English name given by the town's founders.

BELLINGHAM, City; Whatcom County Seat; Pop. 45,794 / 63,019; Zip Code 98225; Lat. 48-44-54 N, Long. 122-28-52 W; George Vancouver's expedition honored Sir William Bellingham by naming the bay for him. The city gets its name from the bay.

BENTON CITY, City; Benton County; Pop. 1,980 / 2,208; Zip Code 99320; Lat. 46-15-55 N, Long. 119-29-16 W; The city was named in 1909 by two employees of the North Coast Railroad Co. possibly for a fellow employee.

BINGEN, City; Klickitat County; Pop. 644 / 659; Zip Code 98605; Elev. 1131; Lat. 45-43-00 N, Long. 121-27-58 W; Founded in 1892 and named for a city on the Rhine River in Germany.

BLACK DIAMOND, City; King County; Pop. 1,170 / 3,542; Zip Code 98010; Lat. 47-18-41 N, Long. 122-00-08 W; The city is named after the Black River, which runs through the county.

BLAINE, City; Whatcom County; Pop. 2,363 / 3,722; Zip Code 98230; Lat. 48-59-21 N, Long. 122-45-00 W; Blaine takes its name from 1884 Republican presidential nominee James G. Blaine.

BOTHELL, City; King County; Pop. 7,943 / 30,335; Zip Code 980+; Lat. 47-43-21 N, Long. 122-13-04 W; Named in honor of the Bothell family, who were local businessmen and politicians.

BREMERTON, City; Kitsap County; Pop. 36,208 / 40,612; Zip Code 983+; Lat. 47-34-46 N, Long. 122-39-59 W; The city's name comes from William Bremer, an early pioneer who founded the town.

BURLINGTON, City; Skagit County; Pop. 3,894 / 6,398; Zip Code 98233; Lat. 48-28-12 N, Long. 122-19-17 W; Founded in 1891 and named by early settlers for a former home.

CAMAS, City; Clark County; Pop. 5,681 / 11,621; Zip Code 98607; Lat. 45-35-13 N, Long. 122-24-23 W; The city is named the food plant, Camassia Esculenta, a favorite food of the original Indians.

CARBONADO, Town; Pierce County; Pop. 456 / 563; Zip Code 98323; Lat. 47-04-36 N, Long. 122-03-05 W; The town gets its name from the adjacent Carbon River, so called for the coal deposits on its banks.

CARNATION, City; King County; Pop. 913 / 1,583; Zip Code 98014; Lat. 47-38-56 N, Long. 121-54-54 W; The city was named for the flower by action of the state legislature in 1917.

CASHMERE, City; Chelan County; Pop. 2,240 / 2,777; Zip Code 98815; Elev. 795; Lat. 47-31-12 N, Long. 120-28-08 W; The city is named for the Valley of Cashmere in India.

CASTLE ROCK, City; Cowlitz County; Pop. 2,162 / 2,055; Zip Code 98611; Lat. 46-16-25 N, Long. 122-54-18 W; A descriptive name for a huge 150-foot high rock that resembles a castle.

CATHLAMET, Town; Wahkiakum County Seat; Pop. 635 / 489; Zip Code 98612; Elev. 53; Lat. 46-12-37 N, Long. 123-22-48 W; An Indian word meaning "Stone" and referring to the bed of the adjacent Columbia River.

CENTRALIA, City; Lewis County; Pop. 10,809 / 13,317; Zip Code 98531; Elev. 189; Lat. 46-43-42 N, Long. 122-58-43 W; Originally called Centerville, the name was later changed to Centralia after the city in Illinois.

CHEHALIS, City; Lewis County Seat; Pop. 6,100 / 6,680; Zip Code 98532; Elev. 226; Lat. 46-39-52 N, Long. 122-57-42 W; An Indian word meaning "sand," which early settlers incorrectly applied to the local Indians.

CHELAN, City; Chelan County; Pop. 2,802 / 3,597; Zip Code 98816; Lat. 47-50-16 N, Long. 120-00-42 W; An Indian word meaning either "deep water" or "bubbling water."

CHENEY, City; Spokane County; Pop. 7,630 / 8,198; Zip Code 99004; Lat. 47-29-27 N, Long. 117-34-44 W; The city is named in honor of Benjamin P. Cheney, a founder of the Northern Pacific Railroad.

CHEWELAH, City; Stevens County; Pop. 1,888 / 2,499; Zip Code 99109; Elev. 1671; Lat. 48-16-45 N, Long. 117-43-01 W; An Indian word meaning "snake" and possibly applied as a description to meandering streams.

CLARKSTON, City; Asotin County; Pop. 6,903 / 7,181; The town is named for Captain William Clark of Lewis and Clark expedition fame.

CLE ELUM, City; Kittitas County; Pop. 1,773 / 1,779; Zip Code 98922; Elev. 1905; Lat. 47-11-34 N, Long. 120-55-39 W; An Indian word meaning "swift waters."

COLFAX, City; Whitman County Seat; Pop. 1,780 / 2,588; Zip Code 99111; Elev. 1962; Lat. 46-52-55 N, Long. 117-21-57 W; Founded in 1872 and named in honor of U.S. Vice-President Colfax.

COLLEGE PLACE, City; Walla Walla County; Pop. 5,771 / 7,156; Zip Code 99324; Lat. 46-01-48 N, Long. 118-26-52 W; The town took its name from a local Seventh Day Adventist college.

COLTON, Town; Whitman County; Pop. 307 / 336; Zip Code 99113; Elev. 2562; Lat. 46-34-00 N, Long. 117-07-43 W; The town is named for an early settler.

COLVILLE, City; Stevens County Seat; Pop. 4,510 / 5,154; Zip Code 99114; Lat. 48-32-42 N, Long. 117-53-57 W; Colville takes its name from Andrew Colville who was governor of the Hudson Boy Company in the early 1800s.

CONCONULLY, Town; Okanogan County; Pop. 157 / 185; Zip Code 98819; Lat. 48-33-22 N, Long. 119-44-58 W; The town's name is a corrupt rendering of an Indian word meaning "cloudy."

CONCRETE, Town; Skagit County; Pop. 592 / 791; Zip Code 98237; Lat. 48-32-19 N, Long. 121-45-32 W; Settled in 1888 and later named for the cement industry that grew up in the area.

CONNELL, City; Franklin County; Pop. 1,981 / 2,971; Zip Code 99326; Elev. 840; Lat. 46-39-40 N, Long. 118-51-32 W; Named after an early settler.

COSMOPOLIS, City; Grays Harbor County; Pop. 1,575 / 1,482; Zip Code 98537; Elev. 12; Lat. 46-57-12 N, Long. 123-46-22 W; Following a practice common in the 19th century the town was given a classical name.

COULEE CITY, Town; Grant County; Pop. 510 / 652; Zip Code 99115; Lat. 47-36-45 N, Long. 119-17-10 W; The town is situated in the Grand Coulee. A Coulee is a steep-walled trench like valley created by a lava flow.

COULEE DAM, Town; Douglas, Grant & Okanogan Counties; Pop. 1,412 / 1,129; Zip Code 991+; Lat. 47-57-48 N, Long. 118-58-53 W; The town takes its name from the nearby world famous dam.

COUPEVILLE, Town; Island County Seat; Pop. 1,006 / 1,626; Zip Code 98239; Lat. 48-12-44 N, Long. 122-40-03 W; Founded in 1853 by Captain Thomas Coupe and named in his honor.

CRESTON, Town; Lincoln County; Pop. 309 / 243; Zip Code 99117; Elev. 2436; Lat. 47-45-24 N, Long. 118-31-12 W; Named by Northern Pacific Railway engineers after a local butte, the highest point in the county.

CUSICK, Town; Pend Oreille County; Pop. 246 / 208; Zip Code 99119; Lat. 48-20-10 N, Long. 117-17-47 W.

DARRINGTON, Town; Snohomish County; Pop. 1,064 / 1,257; Zip Code 98241; Elev. 549; Lat. 48-15-06 N, Long. 121-36-12 W; The town was named in honor of a man named Barrington, but the first letter got changed in the application.

DAVENPORT, City; Lincoln County Seat; Pop. 1,559 / 1,603; Zip Code 99122; Elev. 2369; Lat. 47-39-10 N, Long. 118-08-59 W; Named after an early settler.

DAYTON, City; Columbia County Seat; Pop. 2,565 / 2,477; Zip Code 99328; Elev. 1613; Lat. 46-52-16 N, Long. 122-15-47 W; Early settlers, Jesse and Elizabeth Day, founded the town in the 1870s. It is named in their honor.

DEER PARK, City; Spokane County; Pop. 2,140 / 2,889; Zip Code 99006; Lat. 47-57-14 N, Long. 117-28-11 W; A descriptive name for the good hunting of pioneer days.

DES MOINES, City; King County; Pop. 7,378 / 26,588; The city is named after the city in Iowa.

DUPONT, City; Pierce County; Pop. 559 / 1,137; Zip Code 98327; The town took its name from the DuPont powder company factory nearby.

DUVALL, City; King County; Pop. 729 / 4,329; Zip Code 98019; Lat. 47-44-31 N, Long. 121-58-56 W; Pioneer James Duval was the first landowner and the town was named in his honor.

EATONVILLE, Town; Pierce County; Pop. 998 / 1,825; Zip Code 98328; The town takes its name from an early pioneer named Eaton.

EDMONDS, City; Snohomish County; Pop. 27,526 / 40,751; Zip Code 98020; Lat. 47-47-09 N, Long. 122-20-07 W; With a slight name change the town was named in honor of famous Vermont Senator George Edmunds.

ELECTRIC CITY, Town; Grant County; Pop. 927 / 1,073; Zip Code 99123; Elev. 1655; Lat. 47-55-48 N, Long. 119-02-13 W; So called because of its relation to hydroelectric power.

ELLENSBURG, City; Kittitas County Seat; Pop. 11,752 / 14,512; Zip Code 989+; Lat. 46-59-51 N, Long. 120-32-24 W; Pioneer John Shoudy named the town in honor of his wife, Mary Ellen.

ELMA, City; Grays Harbor County; Pop. 2,720 / 3,133; Zip Code 98541; Lat. 47-00-11 N, Long. 123-24-25 W; The city's name honors early Puget Sound pioneer Miss Elma Austin.

ELMER CITY, Town; Okanogan County; Pop. 312 / 314; Zip Code 99124; Lat. 47-59-48 N, Long. 118-57-05 W; Named for an early settler.

ENDICOTT, Town; Whitman County; Pop. 290 / 290; Zip Code 99125; Elev. 1706; Lat. 46-55-45 N, Long. 117-41-10 W; The town is named for an early pioneer.

ENTIAT, Town; Chelan County; Pop. 445 / 604; Zip Code 98822; Lat. 47-40-45 N, Long. 120-12-28 W; An Indian word meaning "rapid water" and referring to the Entiat River.

ENUMCLAW, City; King County; Pop. 5,427 / 9,365; Zip Code 98022; Lat. 47-12-21 N, Long. 121-59-29 W; An Indian word meaning "home of the evil spirit."

EPHRATA, City; Grant County Seat; Pop. 5,359 / 6,791; Zip Code 98823; Lat. 47-19-06 N, Long. 119-32-46 W; Great Northern Railway Surveyors gave the town the ancient Biblical name for Bethlehem.

EVERETT, City; Snohomish County Seat; Pop. 54,413 / 87,352; Zip Code 982+; Lat. 47-58-03 N, Long. 122-12-19 W; The city is named in honor of Everett Colby, one of the city fathers.

EVERSON, City; Whatcom County; Pop. 898 / 1,786; Zip Code 98247; Elev. 90; Lat. 48-54-47 N, Long. 122-20-43 W; Named in honor of Ever Everson, the first white settler north of the Nooksack River.

FAIRFIELD, Town; Spokane County; Pop. 582 / 523; Zip Code 99012; Elev. 2559; Lat. 47-22-59 N, Long. 117-10-28 W; Named in 1888 by E.H. Morrison to describe the extensive grain fields surrounding the town.

FARMINGTON, Town; Whitman County; Pop. 176 / 109; Zip Code 99104; Elev. 2626; Lat. 47-05-35 N, Long. 117-09-43 W; Settler G.W. Truax named the town for the city in Minnesota.

FERNDALE, City; Whatcom County; Pop. 3,855 / 7,868; Zip Code 98248; Lat. 48-51-08 N, Long. 122-35-42 W; The town's first teacher named the future town for the first school location; a fern patch.

FIFE, City; Pierce County; Pop. 1,823 / 4,481; Named after the musical instrument.

FORKS, Town; Clallam County; Pop. 3,060 / 3,338; Zip Code 98331; Lat. 47-57-02 N, Long. 124-22-56 W; A descriptive geographical name.

FRIDAY HARBOR, Town; San Juan County Seat; Pop. 1,200 / 1,851; Zip Code 98222; Elev. 91; Lat. 48-30-08 N, Long. 122-37-17 W; A Hudson Bay Company engineer named "Friday" gave the town his name.

GARFIELD, Town; Whitman County; Pop. 599 / 537; Zip Code 99130; Lat. 47-00-35 N, Long. 117-08-27 W; The town's name honors President James Garfield.

GEORGE, City; Grant County; Pop. 261 / 346; Named for an early trapper and fur trader, Indian George.

GIG HARBOR, City; Pierce County; Pop. 2,429 / 5,593; Zip Code 98335; Lat. 47-19-32 N, Long. 122-35-01 W; Named by the 1841 Wilkes expedition who noted it "has sufficient depth for small vessels."

GOLD BAR, Town; Snohomish County; Pop. 794 / 1,777; Zip Code 98251; Lat. 47-51-26 N, Long. 121-41-43 W; Descriptively named by gold prospectors here in 1896.

GOLDENDALE, City; Klickitat County Seat; Pop. 3,414 / 3,626; Zip Code 98620; Elev. 1633; Lat. 45-49-22 N, Long. 120-49-09 W; The city is named after homesteader John J. Golden, who settled here in 1863.

GRAND COULEE, City; Grant County; Pop. 1,180 / 1,197; Zip Code 91333; Lat. 47-56-32 N, Long. 119-00-04 W; Descriptively named for its location near the gigantic coulee that was the ancient bed of the Columbia River.

GRANDVIEW, City; Yakima County; Pop. 5,615 / 8,170; Zip Code 98930; Lat. 46-15-09 N, Long. 119-54-30 W; The town was founded in 1906 and named for its view of Mt. Adams and Mt. Rainier.

GRANGER, Town; Yakima County; Pop. 1,182 / 1,800; Zip Code 98932; Elev. 731; Lat. 46-20-25 N, Long. 120-11-19 W; Founded in 1902 and named in honor of irrigation canal company president, Walter N. Granger.

GRANITE FALLS, Town; Snohomish County; Pop. 911 / 2,042; Zip Code 08252; Elev. 391; Lat. 48-04-56 N, Long. 121-57-58 W; The town is named for the falls in the granite rock canyon of the Stillaguamish River.

HARRAH, Town; Yakima County; Pop. 343 / 404; Zip Code 98933; Lat. 46-24-14 N, Long. 120-33-06 W; Originally called Saluskin after an Yakima Indian Chief, the town's name was changed in 1915 to honor prominent rancher J.T. Harrah.

HARRINGTON, City; Lincoln County; Pop. 507 / 440; Zip Code 99134; Elev. 2140; Lat. 47-28-43 N, Long. 118-15-19 W; In 1882, W.P. Harrington, a California banker, invested in the town and subsequently had it named in his honor.

HARTLINE, Town; Grant County; Pop. 165 / 206; Zip Code 99135; Lat. 47-41-11 N, Long. 119-06-09 W; Early settler John Hartline gave the town his name.

HATTON, Town; Adams County; Pop. 81 / 84; A combined name-for postmaster J.D. Hackett and a local settler named Sutton.

HOQUIAM, City; Grays Harbor County; Pop. 9,719 / 8,818; Zip Code 98550; Lat. 46-58-47 N, Long. 123-52-42 W; An Indian word meaning "hungry for wood" and referring to the large amount of driftwood at the river's mouth.

ILWACO, Town; Pacific County; Pop. 604 / 923; Zip Code 98624; Elev. 11; Lat. 46-18-27 N, Long. 124-02-14 W; Named for a petty Indian Chief, El-wah-ko.

INDEX, Town; Snohomish County; Pop. 147 / 134; Zip Code 98256; Elev. 532; Lat. 47-49-05 N, Long. 121-33-26 W; A descriptive name referring to Index Mountain that resembles an index finger pointing to the sky.

ISSOQUAH, City; King County; Pop. 5,536 / 10,945; Zip Code 98027; Lat. 47-33-29 N, Long. 122-04-15 W; A proper Indian name whose meaning is uncertain.

KAHLOTUS, Town; Franklin County; Pop. 203 / 211; Zip Code 99335; Elev. 901; Lat. 46-38-41 N, Long. 118-33-03 W; An Indian name meaning "hole-in-the-ground."

KALAMA, City; Cowlitz County; Pop. 1,216 / 1,794; Zip Code 98625; Lat. 46-00-42 N, Long. 122-50-46 W; An Indian word meaning "pretty maiden."

KELSO, City; Cowlitz County Seat; Pop. 11,129 / 12,348; Zip Code 98626; Lat. 46-08-38 N, Long. 122-54-08 W; Surveyor Peter Crawford named the town for his former home in Scotland.

KENNEWICK, City; Benton County; Pop. 34,397 / 50,727; Zip Code 993+; Lat. 46-12-17 N, Long. 119-08-02 W; An Indian word meaning "grassy place."

KENT, City; King County; Pop. 23,397 / 66,233; Zip Code 980+; Lat. 47-24-09 N, Long. 122-15-09 W; The city takes its name from the famous county.

KETTLE FALLS, City; Stevens County; Pop. 1,087 / 1,634; Zip Code 991+; Elev. 1625; A translation of the Salish Indian word for "kettle" or tightly woven basket.

KIRKLAND, City; King County; Pop. 18,779 / 45,635; Zip Code 980+; Lat. 47-40-34 N, Long. 122-11-36 W; The city takes its name from millionaire iron maker Peter Kirk who lived and died nearby.

KITTITAS, City; Kittitas County; Pop. 782 / 1,227; Zip Code 98934; Elev. 1647; Lat. 46-59-04 N, Long. 120-25-09 W; An Indian word meaning either "land of bread" or "clay gravel valley."

LA CENTER, City; Clark County; Pop. 439 / 899; Zip Code 98629; Lat. 45-51-36 N, Long. 122-40-13 W; A descriptive name referring to the town's geographical position.

LA CONNER, Town; Skagit County; Pop. 633 / 729; Zip Code 98257; Lat. 48-23-23 N, Long. 122-29-29 W; Early merchant J.J. Conner named the town in honor of wife Louisa Ann.

LA CROSSE, Town; Whitman County; Pop. 373 / 315; Zip Code 99136; Elev. 1481; Lat. 46-40-32 N, Long. 117-55-18 W; The town takes its name from the well-known sport.

LAKE STEVENS, City; Stevens County; Pop. 1,660 / 5,898; Zip Code 98258; Lat. 48-00-58 N, Long. 122-03-36 W; Named for an early settler.

LAMONT, Town; Whitman County; Pop. 101 / 90; Named for Daniel Lamont, Vice President of the Northern Pacific Railway Company.

LANGLEY, City; Island County; Pop. 650 / 1,077; Zip Code 98260; Lat. 48-02-20 N, Long. 122-24-14 W; The town is named in honor of Judge J.W. Langley of Seattle, one of the original land-owners.

LATAH, Town; Spokane County; Pop. 155 / 216; Zip Code 99018; Lat. 47-16-45 N, Long. 117-09-14 W; A corruption of an Indian word meaning "place where fish are caught."

LEAVENWORTH, City; Chelan County; Pop. 1,522 / 2,217; Zip Code 98826; Lat. 47-35-52 N, Long. 120-39-35 W; Named by early settlers for the famous Army post in Kansas.

LIND, Town; Adams County; Pop. 567 / 458; Zip Code 99341; Lat. 46-58-09 N, Long. 118-36-53 W; Named by the Northern Pacific Railway Company around the turn of century.

LONG BEACH, City; Pacific County; Pop. 1,199 / 1,439; Zip Code 98631; Lat. 46-21-18 N, Long. 124-03-07 W; A descriptive name for the twenty mile long beach in the area.

LONGVIEW, City; Cowlitz County; Pop. 31,052 / 34,256; Zip Code 98632; Elev. 21; Lat. 46-09-28 N, Long. 122-56-08 W; A descriptive name referring to the long view of the Columbia River.

LYMAN, Town; Skagit County; Pop. 285 / 329; Zip Code 98263; Lat. 48-31-30 N, Long. 122-03-42 W; The town is named for the first postmaster B.L. Lyman.

LYNDEN, City; Whatcom County; Pop. 4,022 / 8,917; Zip Code 98264; Elev. 103; Lat. 48-56-35 N, Long. 122-27-26 W; Named in 1870 by Mrs. Phoebe Judson who changed the name from Linden to Lynden.

LYNNWOOD, City; Snohomish County; Pop. 21,939 / 34,034; Zip Code 98036; Lat. 47-50-21 N, Long. 122-17-13 W; Named by early settlers for one of their former homes.

MABTON, City; Yakima County; Pop. 1,248 / 1,349; Zip Code 98935; Lat. 46-12-41 N, Long. 119-59-48 W; Named in honor of Mrs. Mabel Anderson, daughter of pioneer railroad builder Dorset Baker.

MALDEN, Town; Whitman County; Pop. 200 / 183; Zip Code 99149; Lat. 47-13-48 N, Long. 117-28-31 W; The town was by a railroad company official for a town in Massachusetts.

MANSFIELD, Town; Douglas County; Pop. 315 / 426; Zip Code 98830; Elev. 2262; Lat. 47-48-39 N, Long. 119-37-56 W; Settler R.E. Darling named the town in honor of his home town in Ohio.

MARCUS, Town; Stevens County; Pop. 174 / 156; Zip Code 99151; Lat. 48-39-54 N, Long. 118-03-49 W; The town's name honors Marcus Oppenheimer one of the two original settlers.

MARYSVILLE, City; Snohomish County; Pop. 5,080 / 21,632; Zip Code 98270; Lat. 48-03-56 N, Long. 122-09-51 W; Founded in the 1870s and named by early settlers for Marysville, California.

MCCLEARY, Town; Grays Harbor County; Pop. 1,419 / 1,485; Zip Code 98557; Lat. 47-03-22 N, Long. 123-15-57 W; Named in honor of timber company President Henry McCleary.

MEDICAL LAKE, City; Spokane County; Pop. 3,600 / 3,711; Zip Code 99022; Lat. 47-34-08 N, Long. 117-41-04 W; So named by early settlers because the Indians thought bathing in the nearby lake a cure for rheumatism.

MEDINA, City; King County; Pop. 3,220 / 2,880; Zip Code 98039; Lat. 47-37-29 N, Long. 122-13-24 W; The city is named after Medina, Turkey.

MERCER ISLAND, City; King County; Pop. 21,522 / 20,891; Zip Code 98040; Lat. 47-3-43 N, Long. 122-11-42 W; The city's name honors Asa Mercer, an early settler of the region.

MESA, City; Franklin County; Pop. 278 / 309; Zip Code 99343; Lat. 46-34-33 N, Long. 199-00-13 W; Descriptively named, the town's name means "table-land" in Spanish.

METALINE, Town; Pend Oreille County; Pop. 190 / 217; Zip Code 99152; Lat. 48-50-56 N, Long. 117-23-13 W; The town was named by early miners who thought the entire district a storehouse of minerals.

METALINE FALLS, Town; Pend Oreille County; Pop. 296 / 325; Zip Code 99153; Lat. 48-52-05 N, Long. 117-21-35 W; The town is on the Pend Oreille River at the site of a falls. Named by miners during gold rush days.

MILLWOOD, Town; Spokane County; Pop. 1,717 / 1,646; Descriptively named as the site of a sawmill.

MILTON, City; King & Pierce Counties; Pop. 3,162 / 6,022; Zip Code 983+; Lat. 47-14-21 N, Long. 122-18-42 W; The town is named after an early settler.

MONROE, City; Snohomish County; Pop. 2,869 / 9,545; Zip Code 98272; Lat. 47-51-17 N, Long. 121-58-53 W; The city is believed to be named after resident James Monroe.

MONTESANO, City; Grays Harbor County Seat; Pop. 3,247 / 3,434; Zip Code 98563; Elev. 66; Lat. 46-58-56 N, Long. 123-35-55 W; Named in 1860 by early pioneers and meaning "the promised place."

MORTON, City; Lewis County; Pop. 1,264 / 1,174; Zip Code 98356; Lat. 46-33-27 N, Long. 122-22-26 W; The town is named in honor of farmer Vice-president Levi Morton.

MOSES LAKE, City; Grant County; Pop. 10,629 / 16,304; Zip Code 98337; Lat. 47-08-32 N, Long. 119-17-59 W; It was named from the fact that the tribe of Chief Moses lived near the shares of the lake.

MOSSYROCK, City; Lewis County; Pop. 463 / 514; Zip Code 98564; Elev. 698; Lat. 46-31-48 N, Long. 122-31-34 W; Named in 1852 after a point of moss-covered rock about 200 feet high near the town.

MOUNT VERNON, City; Skagit County Seat; Pop. 13,009 / 23,894; Zip Code 98273; Lat. 48-25-19 N, Long. 122-19-28 W; Named in 1877 in honor of the Virginia Estate of George Washington.

MOUNTLAKE TERRACE, City; Snohomish County; Pop. 16,534 / 20,977; Zip Code 98043; Lat. 47-47-59 N, Long. 122-18-07 W; The city is descriptively named.

MUKILTEO, City; Snohomish County; Pop. 1,426 / 14,715; Zip Code 98275; Lat. 47-56-37 N, Long. 122-16-48 W; An Indian word meaning "good camping ground."

NACHES, Town; Yakima County; Pop. 644 / 686; Zip Code 98929; Lat. 46-52-47 N, Long. 121-16-51 W; An Indian place name whose meaning has been lost.

NAPAVINE, City; Lewis County; Pop. 611 / 1,131; Zip Code 98565; Elev. 444; Lat. 46-34-46 N, Long. 122-54-35 W; The name is derived from an Indian word "Nopavoon" meaning "small prairie."

NESPELEM, Town; Okanogan County; Pop. 284 / 200; Zip Code 99155; Lat. 48-09-54 N, Long. 118-58-19 W; The origin of the town's name is uncertain.

NEWPORT, City; Pend Oreille County Seat; Pop. 1,665 / 2,144; Zip Code 99156; Lat. 48-10-43 N, Long. 117-01-22 W; In 1890 when the first steamboat placed on the Pend Oreille River, a new landing place was selected and named Newport.

NOOKSACK, City; Whatcom County; Pop. 429 / 897; Zip Code 98276; Elev. 84; Lat. 48-55-39 N, Long. 122-19-23 W; An Indian word meaning "people who live on the root of the fern."

NORTH BEND, City; King County; Pop. 1,701 / 3,863; Zip Code 98045; Elev. 442; Lat. 47-29-44 N, Long. 121-46-40 W; Its name comes from its location where the South Fork of the Snoqualmie River bends to the north.

NORTH BONNEVILLE, City; Skamania County; Pop. 394 / 513; Zip Code 98639; Lat. 45-38-48 N, Long. 121-55-57 W; Descriptively named—Bonneville means "beautiful city."

NORTHPORT, Town; Stevens County; Pop. 368 / 334; Zip Code 99157; Lat. 48-54-55 N, Long. 117-47-06 W; So named for its northern position on the Columbia River.

OAKESDALE, Town; Whitman County; Pop. 444 / 326; Zip Code 99158; Elev. 2461; Lat. 47-07-52 N, Long. 117-14-45 W; Descriptive and euphoniously named after oak graves.

OAK HARBOR, City; Island County; Pop. 12,271 / 20,919; Zip Code 98278; Lat. 48-19-07 N, Long. 122-38-46 W; So named because of the large number of oak trees growing in the area.

OAKVILLE, City; Grays Harbor County; Pop. 537 / 628; Zip Code 98568; Elev. 90; Lat. 46-50-20 N, Long. 123-13-59 W; The city's name reflects the many oak trees in the area at the time of its founding.

OCEAN SHORES, City; Grays Harbor County; Pop. 1,692 / 3,309; Zip Code 98569; Lat. 47-04-19 N, Long. 124-09-51 W; The town is descriptively named for its position on the Pacific Ocean.

ODESSA, Town; Lincoln County; Pop. 1,009 / 956; Zip Code 99159; Elev. 1544; Lat. 47-19-48 N, Long. 118-41-02 W; Named in 1892 by Great Northern Railway officials on account of the Russian settlers living in the area.

OKANOGAN, City; Okanogan County Seat; Pop. 2,302 / 2,467; Zip Code 98840; Elev. 860; Lat. 48-21-53 N, Long. 119-34-45 W; An Indian word meaning "rendezvous."

OLYMPIA, City; Thurston County Seat and Capitol of Washington; Pop. 27,447 / 39,904; Zip Code 985+; The name Olympia comes from the Olympia Mountains and was suggested by Colonel Isaac N. Ebey.

OMAK, City; Okanogan County; Pop. 4,007 / 4,731; Zip Code 98841; Elev. 837; Lat. 48-24-37 N, Long. 119-31-22 W; An Indian word meaning "great medicine" and referring to a nearby lake with supposed curative powers.

OROVILLE, City; Okanogan County; Pop. 1,483 / 1,716; Zip Code 98844; Lat. 48-56-16 N, Long. 119-26-07 W; The town was founded by placer miners, Oro in Spanish means gold.

ORTING, Town; Pierce County; Pop. 1,763 / 1,763; Zip Code 98360; Lat. 47-05-43 N, Long. 122-12-09 W; The town is named after an early power.

OTHELLO, City; Adams County; Pop. 4,454 / 3,468; Zip Code 99332; Elev. 1038; Lat. 46-46-35 N, Long. 118-49-29 W; The town is named after the great Shakespearean tragic hero Othello.

PALOUSE, City; Whitman County; Pop. 1,005 / 885; Zip Code 99161; Elev. 2426; Lat. 46-54-46 N, Long. 117-04-21 W; Early French-Canadian fur trappers named the grass covered hills north of the Snake River "pelouse" or grasslands.

PASCO, City; Franklin County Seat; Pop. 17,944 / 27,779; Zip Code 99301; Lat. 46-14-23 N, Long. 119-07-22 W; Surveyor Virgil Bogue named the town after a city in Mexico.

PATEROS, Town; Okanogan County; Pop. 555 / 659; Zip Code 98846; Elev. 776; Lat. 48-03-26 N, Long. 119-53-30 W; The town is named after an early settler.

POMEROY, City; Garfield County Seat; Pop. 1,716 / 1,458; Zip Code 99347; Lat. 46-28-19 N, Long. 117-35-43 W; Original landowner Joseph Pomeroy founded the town in 1878.

PORT ANGELES, City; Clallam County Seat; Pop. 17,311 / 19,046; Zip Code 98362; Elev. 32; Lat. 48-06-29 N, Long. 123-24-25 W; Spanish explorers named it Port of our Lady of the Angels, but the British shortened that to Port Angeles.

PORT ORCHARD, City; Kitsap County Seat; Pop. 4,787 / 6,702; Zip Code 98366; Lat. 47-31-45 N, Long. 122-38-25 W; Named of Captain Vancouver in 1792 in honor H.M. Orchard, clerk of the ship "Discovery."

PORT TOWNSEND, City; Jefferson County Seat; Pop. 6,067 / 8,395; Zip Code 98368; Lat. 48-07-09 N, Long. 122-46-43 W; British explorer George Vancouver named the bay in honor of Marquis Townsend.

POULSBO, City; Kitsap County; Pop. 3,453 / 6,518; Zip Code 98370; Elev. 15; Lat. 47-44-09 N, Long. 122-38-19 W; Norwegian settler named the town in honor of their former home in Norway.

PRESCOTT, Town; Walla Walla County; Pop. 341 / 336; Zip Code 99348; Elev. 1055; Lat. 46-17-57 N, Long. 118-18-48 W; Named in 1881 in honor of C.H. Prescott, General Superintendent of the Oregon Railway and Navigation Company.

PULLMAN, City; Whitman County; Pop. 23,579 / 24,096; Zip Code 9916+; Lat. 46-43-53 N, Long. 117-10-32 W; Founded in 1882 and named in honor of railroad sleeping-car manufacturer George Pullman.

PUYALLUP, City; Pierce County; Pop. 18,251 / 31,538; Zip Code 9837+; Lat. 47-11-36 N, Long. 122-20-05 W; The town is named after the Puyallup River Valley. The Puyallup Indians, whose name means "generous people." gave their name to the valley.

QUINCY, City; Grant County; Pop. 3,535 / 4,875; Zip Code 98848; Lat. 47-14-04 N, Long. 119-51-02 W; The town is named after an early settler.

RAINIER, Town; Thurston County; Pop. 891 / 1,469; Zip Code 98576; Elev. 428; Lat. 46-53-11 N, Long. 122-41-07 W; Captain George Vancouver discovered and named the mountain for Rear Admiral Peter Rainier of the British Navy.

RAYMOND, City; Pacific County; Pop. 2,991 / 3,075; Zip Code 98577; Elev. 14; Lat. 46-40-59 N, Long. 123-43-52 W; The town is named for L.U. Raymond, the original landowner.

REARDON, Town; Lincoln County; Pop. 498 / 541; Zip Code 99029; Elev. 2496; Lat. 47-40-14 N, Long. 117-52-28 W; The town is named for a civil engineer who worked for the Washington Central Railroad Co.

REDMOND, City; King County; Pop. 23,318 / 44,708; Zip Code 98052; Lat. 47-38-30 N, Long. 122-09-07 W; Luke McRedmond arrived in Washington in 1852 and later founded the town and become its first postmaster.

RENTON, City; King County; Pop. 30,612 / 47,540; Zip Code 98055; Lat. 47-28-55 N, Long. 122-12-05 W; The town's name honors Captain William Renton of the Port Blakely Mill Company.

REPUBLIC, City; Ferry County; Pop. 1,018 / 988; Zip Code 99166; Lat. 48-38-46 N, Long. 118-44-00 W; The town is named for the famous Republic Mine discovered in 1896.

RICHLAND, City; Benton County; Pop. 33,578 / 37,553; Zip Code 99352; Lat. 46-17-32 N, Long. 119-18-44 W; A prominent landowner, Nelson Rich, named the town in 1904.

RIDGEFIELD, City; Clark County; Pop. 1,062 / 1,831; Zip Code 98642; Lat. 45-48-51 N, Long. 122-44-41 W; A descriptive name as the town site on a beautiful ridge.

RITZVILLE, City; Adams County Seat; Pop. 1,800 / 1,682; Zip Code 99169; Lat. 47-07-40 N, Long. 118-22-27 W; Ritzville honors early pioneer Phillip Ritz who settled in the area in 1878.

RIVERSIDE, Town; Okanogan County; Pop. 243 / 236; Zip Code 98849; Lat. 48-30-31 N, Long. 119-30-29 W; On the Okanogan River the town is named for its location.

ROCKFORD, Town; Spokane County; Pop. 442 / 506; Zip Code 99030; Elev. 2361; Lat. 47-27-00 N, Long. 117-07-49 W; Pioneer D.C. Farnsworth named the town for the many fords crossing Rock Creek, which ran through the townsite.

ROCK ISLAND, City; Douglas County; Pop. 491 / 615; Zip Code 98850; Lat. 47-22-15 N, Long. 120-08-11 W; A descriptive name given by the U.S. Coast Survey in 1854.

ROSALIA, Town; Whitman County; Pop. 572 / 524; Zip Code 99028; Elev. 2232; Lat. 47-19-19 N, Long. 117-23-06 W; A common Spanish name the town is the site of the Indian battle with Colonel Steptoe.

ROSLYN, City; Kittitas County; Pop. 938 / 852; Zip Code 98941; Lat. 47-13-20 N, Long. 120-59-33 W; A manager of the Northern Pacific Railroad Company named the town in 1886 as a compliment to his sweetheart, who lived in Roslyn, New York.

ROY, City; Pierce County; Pop. 417 / 281; Zip Code 98580; Lat. 47-00-07 N, Long. 122-32-34 W; Named in honor of an early settler.

ROYAL CITY, City; Grant County; Pop. 676 / 1,463; Zip Code 99357; Lat. 46-54-10 N, Long. 119-37-33 W; A euphonious name given by the town's incorporators.

RUSTON, Town; Pierce County; Pop. 612 / 718; Ruston is named in honor of W.R. Rust, one time president of the Tacoma Smelting Company.

ST. JOHN, Town; Whitman County; Pop. 529 / 487; Zip Code 99171; Lat. 47-05-29 N, Long. 117-35-02 W; Named after E.T. St. John, an early settler in the area.

SEATTLE, City; King County Seat; Pop. 493,846 / 537,150; Zip Code 980+; Lat. 47-45-37 N, Long. 122-14-27 W; The city takes its name from Chief Seattle of the Suquamish Indians.

SEDRO-WOOLLEY, City; Skagit County; Pop. 6,110 / 8,158; Zip Code 98284; Lat. 48-30-14 N, Long. 122-13-46 W; The town of Sedro and nearby Woolley merged at the turn of the century to become Sedro-Woolley.

SELAH, City; Yakima County; Pop. 4,372 / 6,745; Zip Code 98942; Lat. 46-39-15 N, Long. 120-31-55 W; An Indian word meaning "still water" and referring to a quiet section of the Yakima River.

SEQUIM, City; Clallam County; Pop. 3,013 / 4,834; Zip Code 98334; Elev. 183; Lat. 48-03-15 N, Long. 122-55-20 W; A Clallum Indian word meaning "quiet water."

SHELTON, City; Mason County Seat; Pop. 7,629 / 8,172; Zip Code 98584; Lat. 47-12-45 N, Long. 123-06-23 W; The city is named after David Shelton—pioneer and later mayor of his namesake city.

SKYKOMISH, Town; King County; Pop. 289 / 251; Zip Code 98288; Elev. 931; Lat. 47-42-47 N, Long. 121-21-40 W; An Indian word meaning "inland people."

SNOHOMISH, City; Snohomish County; Pop. 5,294 / 9,031; Zip Code 98290; Lat. 47-55-19 N, Long. 122-05-16 W; The name of the dominant Indian tribe in the area.

SNOQUALMIE, City; King County; Pop. 1,370 / 1,939; Zip Code 98065; Lat. 47-31-38 N, Long. 121-49-22 W; The name of a tribe of Indians. The name refers to a legend the tribe came from the moon.

SOAP LAKE, City; Grant County; Pop. 1,196 / 1,292; Zip Code 98851; Lat. 47-23-15 N, Long. 119-29-16 W; A descriptive name as the lake's water was soapy.

SOUTH BEND, City; Pacific County Seat; Pop. 1,686 / 1,743; Zip Code 98586; Lat. 46-39-53 N, Long. 123-47-32 W; So named because the Willapa River takes a bend to the south in what is now the city.

SOUTH PRAIRIE, Town; Pierce County; Pop. 202 / 344; Zip Code 98385; Lat. 47-08-22 N, Long. 122-05-34 W; Descriptively named in 1889 for its geographic location on South Prairie Creek.

SPANGLE, City; Spokane County; Pop. 276 / 215; Zip Code 99031; Lat. 47-25-51 N, Long. 117-22-43 W; The city's name honors William Spangle, the homesteader who platted the town in 1886.

SPOKANE, City; Spokane County; Pop. 171,300 / 184,323; Zip Code 990+; Lat. 47-33-23 N, Long. 117-12-46 W; The name stems from a Chief of the Spokane Indians called Illim-Spokane, or "chief of the sun people."

SPRAGUE, City; Lincoln County; Pop. 473 / 432; Zip Code 99017; Elev. 1899; Lat. 47-12-04 N, Long. 117-54-14 W; Sprague is named in honor of General John W. Sprague, a director of the Northern Pacific Railroad.

SPRINGDALE, Town; Stevens County; Pop. 281 / 297; Zip Code 99173; Elev. 2070; Lat. 48-03-27 N, Long. 117-44-21 W; Originally called Squire the Town's name was changed to Springdale after nearby Spring Creek.

STANWOOD, City; Snohomish County; Pop. 2,744 / 3,700; Zip Code 98292; Lat. 48-14-22 N, Long. 122-21-06 W; Settled in 1866 and named by Postmaster D.O. Pearson in honor of his wife's maiden name.

STARBUCK, Town; Columbia County; Pop. 198 / 185; Zip Code 99359; Elev. 645; Lat. 46-30-57 N, Long. 118-07-30 W; New York businessman, General Starbuck, gave the town church its first bell. The town is named in his honor.

STEILACOOM, Town; Pierce County; Pop. 4,089 / 6,174; Founded in 1851 and given the Indian name "Tchil-ac-cum" or "pink flower."

STEVENSON, City; Skamania County Seat; Pop. 1,172 / 1,165; Zip Code 98648; Lat. 45-41-29 N, Long. 121-52-55 W; Founded in 1894 by George Stevenson and named in his honor.

SULTAN, City; Snohomish County; Pop. 1,578 / 3,178; Zip Code 98294; Elev. 114; Lat. 47-51-54 N, Long. 121-48-27 W; The town is named after the Sultan River. The river received its name from Chief Tseultud.

SUMAS, City; Whatcom County; Pop. 712 / 873; Zip Code 98295; Lat. 48-59-41 N, Long. 122-15-49 W; Sumas is an Indian word meaning "big level opening."

SUMNER, City; Yakima County; Pop. 9,225 / 8,536; Zip Code 98390; Lat. 47-13-04 N, Long. 122-15-09 W; Founded by John Kincaid and named in honor of U.S. Senator and anti-slavery proponent Charles S. Sumner.

SUNNYSIDE, City; Yakima County; Pop. 9,225 / 13,284; Zip Code 98944; Lat. 46-19-23 N, Long. 120-00-36 W; Walter Granger, president of the Sunnyside Canal Co. founded the town in 1893. It is named in his honor.

TACOMA, City; Pierce County Seat; Pop. 158,501 / 180,020; Zip Code 98303; Lat. 47-11-05 N, Long. 122-42-11 W; The Indian name for Mt. Rainier is Tacoma—hence the city's name.

TEKOA, City; Whitman County; Pop. 854 / 711; Zip Code 99033; Elev. 2494; Lat. 47-13-36 N, Long. 117-04-20 W; Early settlers borrowed the Biblical Hebrew term *tekoa* or "settlement of tents" for the town's name.

TENINO, City; Thurston County; Pop. 1,280 / 1,347; Zip Code 98589; Lat. 46-51-29 N, Long. 122-50-43 W; A Chinook Indian term meaning "fork" or "junction."

TIETON, Town; Yakima County; Pop. 528 / 819; Zip Code 98947; Lat. 46-41-56 N, Long. 120-45-10 W; Named after the Tieton River. The word Tieton is an Indian word meaning "roaring water."

TOLEDO, City; Lewis County; Pop. 637 / 663; Zip Code 98591; Lat. 46-26-15 N, Long. 122-51-22 W; The town took its name from the riverboat Toledo, which worked in the area in 1879.

TONASKET, City; Okanogan County; Pop. 985 / 1,043; Zip Code 98855; Lat. 48-42-22 N, Long. 119-26-15 W; The town is named in honor of Chief Tonasket of the Colville Indians.

TOPPENISH, City; Yakima County; Pop. 6,517 / 8,039; Zip Code 98948; Lat. 46-22-38 N, Long. 120-18-18 W; A Yakima Indian word meaning "people from the foot of the hills."

TUKWILA, City; King County; Pop. 3,578 / 14,278; The town was renamed in 1905 after the Indian word "Tuckwilla" meaning "land of the hazelnuts."

TUMWATER, City; Thurston County; Pop. 6,785 / 11,712; On the falls of the Deschutes River and so named in Chinook jargon "Tun-water."

TWISP, Town; Okanogan County; Pop. 911 / 1,073; Zip Code 98856; Elev. 1614; Lat. 48-21-51 N, Long. 120-07-25 W; Twisp takes its name from the nearby Twisp River. The word twisp derives from the Indian word *twip*.

UNION GAP, City; Yakima County; Pop. 3,184 / 5,783; A descriptive name for the town's location near a gap in the Ahtanum Ridge that connects ports of the Yakima Valley.

UNIONTOWN, Town; Whitman County; Pop. 286 / 269; Zip Code 99179; Elev. 2572; Lat. 46-32-18 N, Long. 117-05-11 W; Settled 1879 and descriptively named by the junction of Union Creek and Union Flat.

VADER, City; Lewis; Pop. 406 / 455; Zip Code 98593; Lat. 46-24-15 N, Long. 122-57-10 W; Named by the state legislature in 1913 for an early settler named Vader.

VANCOUVER, City; Clark County Seat; Pop. 42,834 / 118,743; Zip Code 98660; Lat. 45-38-36 N, Long. 122-39-51 W; The city is named in honor of George Vancouver, the famous British explorer.

WAITSBURG, City; Walla Walla County Seat; Pop. 25,618 / 1,078; Zip Code 99361; Lat. 46-16-02 N, Long. 118-09-17 W; The town is named in honor of Sylvester M. Wait, who built a flour mill in the area in 1864.

WALLA WALLA, City; Walla Walla County Seat; Pop. 25,618 / 28,862; Zip Code 99362; Lat. 46-03-45 N, Long. 118-19-51 W; The city's name comes from the Nez Perce Indian word *Walatsa* meaning "running water."

WAPATO, City; Yakima County; Pop. 3,007 / 4,085; Zip Code 98951; Lat. 46-26-44 N, Long. 120-25-16 W; Named in 1902 with a variation of the Chinook word wappatoo or "potato."

WARDEN, City; Grant County; Pop. 1,479 / 2,108; Zip Code 98857; Lat. 46-58-02 N, Long. 119-02-38 W; The town was named by railroad official H.R. Williams after an eastern investor named Warden.

WASHOUGAL, City; Clark County; Pop. 3,824 / 6,209; Zip Code 98671; Lat. 45-34-47 N, Long. 122-20-50 W; Both the river and town take their name from an Indian word meaning "rushing water."

WASHTUCNA, Town; Adorns County; Pop. 266 / 242; Zip Code 99371; Elev. 1024; Lat. 46-45-13 N, Long. 118-18-41 W; The name of a Palouse Indian Chief was given to the town by its founders.

WATERVILLE, Town; Douglas County Seat; Pop. 908 / 1,113; Zip Code 98858; Elev. 2622; Lat. 47-38-40 N, Long. 120-04-12 W; Originally called Jumpers Flat the name was changed to Waterville when a 30-foot well produced water.

WAVERLY, Town; Spokane County; Pop. 99 / 103; Zip Code 99039; Lat. 47-20-19 N, Long. 117-13-45 W; Named by early settlers for their former home in Iowa.

WENATCHEE, City; Chelan County Seat; Pop. 17,257 / 24,733; Zip Code 98801; Lat. 47-25-39 N, Long. 120-18-47 W; Wenatchee is an adaptation of a Yakima Indian word meaning "river flowing from canyon."

WEST RICHLAND, City; Benton County; Pop. 2,938 / 7,384.

WESTPORT, City; Grays Harbor County; Pop. 1,954 / 2,002; Zip Code 98595; Elev. 12; Lat. 46-53-11 N, Long. 124-06-34 W; Formerly called Peterson's Point, the city is descriptively named as it is on the west side of Chehalis Point Spit.

WHITE SALMON, City; Klickitat County; Pop. 1,853 / 1,913; Zip Code 98672; Lat. 45-43-53 N, Long. 121-29-10 W; The town takes its name from the river. The river's name describes the color that spawning salmon have during their fall runs.

WILBUR, Town; Lincoln County; Pop. 1,122 / 953; Zip Code 99185; Elev. 2163; Lat. 47-45-19 N, Long. 118-42-22 W; Wilbur's name honors its founder, Samuel Wilbur Condit, who founded the town in 1887.

WILKESON, Town; Pierce County; Pop. 321 / 377; Zip Code 98396; Lat. 47-06-36 N, Long. 122-03-01 W; The town's name Samuel Wilkeson who was an official of the Northern Pacific Railroad. The railroad began a coal mine there in 1879.

WILSON CREEK, Town; Grant County; Pop. 222 / 216; Zip Code 98860; Lat. 47-25-21 N, Long. 119-07-17 W; The town takes its name from an early settler.

WINLOCK, City; Lewis County; Pop. 1,052 / 1,189; Zip Code 98596; Elev. 309; Lat. 46-29-32 N, Long. 122-56-10 W; The city is named in honor of original landowner, General Winlock E. Miller.

WINSLOW, City; Lewis County; Pop. 1,052; Winslow is named in honor of Winslow Hall, a founder of the Hall Brothers Shipbuilding Company.

WINTHROP, Town; Okanogan County; Pop. 413 / 391; Zip Code 98833; Elev. 1760; Lat. 48-35-37 N, Long. 120-24-15 W; New England author Theodore Winthrop wrote a well known book on the Washington region, *The Canoe and the Saddle*. The town is named in his honor.

WOODLAND, City; Clark & Cowlitz Counties; Pop. 2,341 / 3,494; Zip Code 986+; Lat. 45-54-16 N, Long. 122-44-56 W; A descriptive name given by the first postmaster, Christopher Bozgath, for the site's wooded surrounding.

YACOLT, Town; Clark County; Pop. 544 / 986; Zip Code 98675; Lat. 45-51-56 N, Long. 122-24-24 W; An Indian word meaning "haunted place."

YAKIMA, City; Yakima County Seat; Pop. 49,826 / 72,483; Zip Code 989+; Elev. 1066; Lat. 46-36-09 N, Long. 120-31-39 W; The city is named for the Indian tribe who originally live in the area.

WEST VIRGINIA
The Mountain State

Victoria Vaudeville Theater - Wheeling

The Majestic Blackwater Falls

GOVERNOR
Cecil Underwood

Stonewall Jackson's
Historical Home

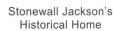

Civil War Reenactment - Bulltown

Charles Town Races

Penitentiary
Old West Virginia

INTRODUCTION

The southern State of West Virginia is one of the South Atlantic states. It is bordered on the north by Pennsylvania, Maryland, and the Potomac River; on the south by Virginia; on the east by Maryland; and on the west by Kentucky and Ohio. A thin peak of the State juts north with Pennsylvania on its eastern side and Ohio on its west. Its boundary is considered the most irregular of any state.

West Virginia ranks forty-first in area among all the states. Of its total area of 24,231 square miles, 24,087 square miles is land area, and 145 square miles is inland water area.

The State has the highest mean elevation (1,500 feet) of any state east of the Mississippi, dominated by the narrow peaks and valleys of the Appalachian Mountains. Two major mountainous regions create the State's rugged character, the Allegheny Plateau in the western two-thirds of the State, and the Appalachian Valley in the eastern third. Panhandles jut out from the east along the southern border of Maryland; to the north, panhandles partly divide Pennsylvania from Ohio. In climate, West Virginia is primarily humid continental.

Livestock (including dairy products, cattle, hogs, and poultry) is one of the State's leading economic mainstays. Important agricultural products include corn, barley, potatoes, and oats. The timber industry consists of hardwoods such as cherry and oak, and softwoods such as white pine and red spruce. Mined products, with bituminous coal the leader, also aid the State's economy. Leading manufactures include chemicals, rubber, primary and fabricated metals, processed foods, ceramics, fine glass and electrical machinery.

STATE NAME

West Virginia was a part of Virginia until 1861, when it became a separate territory. As part of Virginia, it was named after Queen Elizabeth of England, who was popularly called the "Virgin Queen." The name Virginia is the feminine form of the Latin word *virginius*.

After the break between Virginia and West Virginia, the people belonging to the newly separated group framed a new constitution in 1862. The newly formed state first proposed to call itself Kanawha, but finally the name West Virginia was decided upon. West Virginia was admitted into the Union as a separate state on June 20, 1863.

STATE NICKNAMES

Sobriquets for West Virginia include the Mountain State, the Panhandle State, and the Switzerland of America.

West Virginia merits the distinction of being designated as the Mountain State because more than one-third of the area of the State is a high plateau of the Allegheny Mountains. It is known as the Panhandle State on account of the resemblance of the shape of the State to a pan with a handle on it; the region representing the handle is called the Panhandle section. The Switzerland of America is applied to West Virginia because of its picturesque mountain scenery.

The use of the sobriquet Pan-handle-ites, applied to West Virginians, has the same origin and significance as that of the nickname the Panhandle State.

GREAT SEAL

The State constitution of West Virginia designated the seal chosen by a legislative committee and designed by Joseph H. Diss Debar in 1863 as the official great seal of the State. It was written as follows:

"The present seal of the State, with its motto, 'Montani Semper Liberi,' shall be the great seal of the State of West Virginia, and shall be kept by the secretary of state, to be used by him officially, as directed by law."

The report of the Joint Committee on Seals was adopted by an act of the State legislature on September 26, 1863. It described the seal of the State as follows:

"The disc of the great seal is to be two and one-half inches in diameter; the obverse to bear the legend, 'State of West Virginia,' the constitutional designation of our Republic, which with the motto 'Montani Semper Liberi—Mountaineers always free,'—is to be inserted in the circumference. In the center a rock with ivy, emblematic of stability and continuance, and on the face of the rock the inscription 'June 20, 1863,' the date of our foundation, as if graven with a pen of iron in the rock forever. On the right of the rock a farmer clothed in the traditional hunting garb, peculiar to this region, his right arm resting on the plow handles, and his left supporting a woodman's axe, indicating that while our territory is partially cultivated, it is still in the process of being cleared of the original forest. At his right hand a sheaf of wheat and a cornstalk on the left hand of the rock, a miner, indicated by a pick-axe on his shoulder, with barrels and lumps of mineral at his feet. On his left anvil, partly seen, on which rests a sledgehammer, typical of the mechanic arts, the whole indicating the principal pursuits and resources of the State. In front of the rock and the hunter, as if just laid down by the latter and ready to be resumed at a moment's notice, two hunter's rifles, crossed and surmounted at the place of contact by the Phrygian cap, or cap of liberty, indicating that our freedom and liberty were won and will be defended and maintained by the force of arms.

"The reverse of the great seal is to be encircled by a wreath composed of laurel and oak leaves, emblematical of valor and strength, with fruits and cereals, productions of the State. In the distance on the left of the disc a wooded mountain; and on the right a cultivated slope with the log farmhouse peculiar to this region. On the side of the mountain, a representation of the viaduct on the line of the Baltimore and Ohio Railroad in Preston County, one of the great engineering triumphs of the age, with a train of cars about to pass over it. Near the center a factory, in front of which a river with boats, on the bank and to the right of it nearer the foreground, a derrick and a shed, appertains to the production of salt and petroleum. In the foreground a meadow with cattle and sheep feeding and reposing, the whole indicating the leading characteristics, productions and pursuits of the State at this time. Above the mountain, etc., the sun merging from the clouds, indicating that former obstacles to our prosperity are now disappearing. In the rays of the sun the motto 'Libertas et Fidelitate,'

Freedom and Loyalty—indicating that our liberty and independence are the result of faithfulness to the Declaration and the National Constitution."

The committee further recommended that the above device and motto, for the obverse of the Great Seal be also adopted as the Coat-of-Arms of the State.

STATE FLAG

The State flag of West Virginia was adopted on March 7, 1929, after a number of other flags had come into use and then become unfeasible. The resolution says:

"Whereas, The legislature of West Virginia, by joint resolution passed on the twenty-fourth day of February, one thousand nine hundred and five, adopted a state flag, prescribing the design thereof; and

"Whereas, The design so adopted is impractical of manufacture, making the cost of purchase thereof prohibitive to the schools of the state and others desiring to purchase said flag; and

"Whereas, There has been worked out a design embodying all of the features of the first West Virginia state flag so adopted, but so designed as to be practical of manufacture at the reasonable cost to those desiring to purchase the same; and

"Whereas, It seems desirable to change the design of the West Virginia state flag; therefore, be it

"Resolved by the Legislature of West Virginia:

"That the legislature of West Virginia hereby adopts a state flag of the following design and proportions to-wit:

"The proportions of the flag of the state of West Virginia shall be the same as those of the United States ensign; the field shall be pure white, upon the center of which shall be emblazoned in proper colors, the coat-of-arms of the state of West Virginia, upon which appears the date of the admission of the state into the Union, also with the motto *'Montani Semper Liberi'* (Mountaineers Are Always Free) above the coat-of-arms of the state of West Virginia there shall be a ribbon lettered, state of West Virginia, and arranged appropriately around the lower part of the coat-of-arms of the state of West Virginia a wreath of rhododendron maximum in proper colors. A strip of blue on four sides shall border the field of pure white. The flag of the state of West Virginia when used for parade purposes shall be trimmed with gold colored fringe on three sides and when used on ceremonial occasions with the United States ensign, shall be trimmed and mounted in similar fashion to the United States flag as regards fringe cord, tassels and mounting."

STATE MOTTO

The motto of West Virginia is *Montant Semper Liberi*, meaning "Mountaineers Are Always Free." The motto was adopted along with the State seal in 1863.

Joseph H. Diss Debar of Doddridge County created the design of the seal. An Alsatian from Switzerland, Debar came to America in 1842 and became interested in the sale of lands to Swiss and French immigrants in Western Virginia. The motto seems to have been a favorite saying of the Swiss people. On the reverse of the State seal of West Virginia appear the words: *Libertas Et Fidelitate*. This phrase means "Freedom and loyalty" and indicates that the liberty and independence of West Virginia "are the result of faithfulness to the Declaration (of Independence) and the National Constitution."

STATE BIRD

The cardinal, (*Richmondena cardinalis*), was designated the official bird of the State of West Virginia in 1949. The cardinal ranges in the eastern United States, west to the Great Plains, southern Arizona, and northwestern Mexico, and south through Georgia to the Gulf States.

Total length of the cardinal is 7½ to eight inches; its tail length is four inches. A member of the finch species, it is crested and thick-billed. Its tail is longer than its short and rounded wings. Adult males are bright red, except for a black patchy band from the eye to the throat on both sides of the bill. The female is brownish above and dull tawny or pale buffy below, with a dull grayish patch on the face and throat. The crest, wings, and tail are dull reddish in color, and the underwing feathers are pinkish red.

Cardinals build their nests in shrubs and bushes, sometimes in areas in close proximity to humans. Eggs are whitish with brown spots; the incubation period lasts between twelve to thirteen days. Both parents attend to the young with frequent feedings of insects. As the young birds mature, they become primarily fruit and grain eaters, although insects still make up a third of their diet. The cardinal is a colorful bird. Its songs are loud, flute like whistles, the trills lasting about three seconds.

STATE FLOWER

On January 23, 1903, the West Virginia Legislature designated the *Rhododendron maximum*, or big laurel, as the official State flower, following a vote by school children of West Virginia on November 26, 1902.

The big laurel grows from Nova Scotia to Alabama, along streams and in low-lying wooded areas. It often forms dense thickets. Also called deer-laurel, rose bay, spoon-hutch, and cow-plant, the tall-branching shrub has rose colored or white flowers, lightly spotted with yellow or orange.

STATE TREE

The sugar maple, *Acer saccharum Marsh*, was designated the State tree of West Virginia in 1949. The State's civic clubs and school children voted to recommend the sugar maple because it is enjoyed for its maple syrup and it is used extensively in furniture building.

The sugar maple is also known as the hard maple, rock maple, and black maple. It is native to the eastern half of the United States and adjacent Canada.

The large tree has gray bark, furrowed into irregular ridges or scales. Leaves are paired, heart shaped, with three or five lobes, long pointed and sparingly, coarsely toothed; they are three to 5½ inches in diameter, dark green above and light green and usually smooth beneath, turning yellow, orange, or scarlet in the fall. Fruits are one to 1¼ inches long, and mature in the fail.

STATE SONG

Three songs have been adopted by the State of West Virginia. The first, "This Is My West Virginia," was written and composed by Mrs. Iris Bell of Charleston. The second song was "West Virginia, My Home Sweet Home," with words and music by Colonel Julian O. Hearne, Jr.; it was designated the official state song in 1947. The Reverend David King as a poem wrote the third song "The West Virginia Hills," in 1879 for his wife, Ellen King. Mrs. King's name may be found on the music, as this was the request of the poet. In 1885, H.E. Engle put the poem to music. The song was designated an official State song in 1961.

STATE LICENSE PLATE

West Virginia began issuing license plates in 1906. The first plate was white-on-blue. A variety of color combinations, usually including white, were used until the 1931 issue, when yellow and black became the color combination of all plates until 1956. Due to wartime shortages, in 1943 and 1944, new plates were not issued; instead, a black and white metal tab was used to validate 1942 for 1943, and a windshield sticker was used for 1944. Between 1956 and 1962, various color combinations were used; green and white were used in 1956, 1958, and 1959. A series of blue and yellow combinations were started.

West Virginia's current plate retains the colors of blue and yellow on a field of white. Blue numerals are superimposed over this across the center of the plate.

On the center at the bottom is the slogan "Wild, Wonderful" in blue letters.

STATE POSTAGE STAMP

A series of fifty stamps, all in thirteen-cent denominations, went on sale simultaneously in Washington, D.C. and the state capital on February 23, 1976. The stamps depicted the flag of each state. They were designed by Walt Reed and Peter Cocci and engraved by A. Saavedra. A total of 436,005,000 of the stamps were printed.

OTHER STATE DESIGNATIONS

West Virginia has designated several other symbols throughout the years to recognize the State. Included are the State animal (1973) as the black bear; the State fish (1973) as the brook trout; and the State fruit (1972) as the apple.

CAPITOL BUILDING

Wheeling was West Virginia's capital city until 1870. That year, the capital was moved to Charleston. In 1875, the capital was again located in Wheeling. In 1877, by a vote of citizens, the capital was again moved to Charleston. A capitol building was constructed in 1885 in downtown Charleston, but it was destroyed by fire in 1921. A temporary capitol was also destroyed by fire six years later.

The capitol now in use was built in three stages: the west wing was constructed in 1924-1925; the east wing was finished in 1927; and the center was built in 1932.

The West Virginia capitol was designed by Cass Gilbert of New York City, who also designed the U.S. Supreme Court. This building represents the Classical type of Renaissance architecture, and provides over fourteen acres of floor space. Limestone pillars that weigh eighty-six tons support porticoes at the north and south entrances. The west wing is three hundred feet long, sixty feet wide, and sixty-seven feet high. It has an ell seventy-three feet long. This wing is built of steel and of Indiana limestone. The east wing duplicates the west wing in size and in structure. The exterior is of buff Indiana limestone; an assortment

of marble was used to finish the interior. The dome reaches 293 feet, and is five feet higher than the dome of the U.S. Capitol. Total cost of construction of the capitol was ten million dollars.

OTHER FACTS ABOUT WEST VIRGINIA

Total area: 24,232 square miles
Land area: 24,119 square miles
Water area: 112 square miles
Average elevation: 1,500 feet
Highest point: Spruce Knob, 4,861 feet
Lowest point: Potomac River, 240 feet
Highest temperature: 112 degrees Fahrenheit
Lowest temperature: -37 degrees Fahrenheit
Population in 1990: 1,793,477
Population density in 1990: 74.46 persons per square mile
Population 1980-1990: -8.0 percent change
Population projected for year 2000: 1,722,000
African American population in 1990: 56,295
Hispanic American population in 1990: 8,489
Native American population in 1990: 2,458
White population in 1990: 1,725,523
Capital: Charleston
Admitted to Union: June 20, 1863
Order of Statehood: 35
Electoral votes: 5

CHRONOLOGY

1607 First permanent English colony in America is established at Jamestown, Virginia by 105 English colonists.

1641 New River is discovered by Walter Chiles, Rice Roe, Walter Austin, and Joseph Johnson.

1669-70 Crest of Blue Ridge near Harpers Ferry is reached on two occasions by John Lederer, German physician.

1671 Batts-Fallam expedition, sent out by Colonel Abraham Wood "for the finding out the ebbing and flowing of ye South Sea," reaches Falls of Great Kanawha.

1716 Lieutenant Governor Alexander Spotswood and Knights of the Golden Horse Shoe penetrate western Virginia to peaks of Alleghenies.

1725 John Van Meter of New York Dutch settlers visits valley of South Branch of Potomac.

1726-27 Morgan makes first permanent settlement of record in western Virginia at Bunker Hill on Mill Creek (Berkeley County).

1726-30 Germans from Pennsylvania settle at Mecklenburg, later Shepherdstown.

1730 Isaac and John Van Meter, sons of John Van Meter, receive patent for 40,000 acres, much of it in what are now Jefferson and Berkeley counties, West Virginia.

1742 John Peter Saucy and others discover coal on Coal River.

1744 All territory between Allegheny Mountains and Ohio River ceded to English by Six Nations for 400 pounds.

1746 Fairfax stone placed four miles north of Thomas, Tucker County to mark western limit of Fairfax Estate.

1747-48 Washington surveys land in western Virginia for Lord Fairfax and visits "ye famed Warm Springs at Bath" (Berkeley Springs).
– Draper and Ingles families found settlement of Draper's Meadows in New River Valley, near what is later Blacksburg, Montgomery County, Virginia.

1749 Captain Peter Joseph Celeron, Chevalier de Bienville, makes expedition down Ohio River and buries plates, taking possession for King of France.
– Jacob Marlin and Stephen Sewell build cabins at mouth of Knapp's Creek in Pocahontas County.

1750 Christopher Gist travels along Clinch, Bluestone, and New rivers while traveling to Ohio country.
– Dr. Thomas Walker, while traveling down Greenbrier River, writes in journal, "There are some inhabitants on the branches of Green Bryer but we missed their plantations."
– Fort Ohio, first frontier fort, is built at Ridgeley, in later Mineral County.

1751 Greenbrier Company is authorized by English government to locate 100,000 acres on Greenbrier River.

1753 First mention of school in what is now West Virginia names schoolmaster Schrock in Hampshire County.

1754 Baptist Church is organized at Opequon in later Berkeley County.

1755 July 8. Draper's Meadows settlement in New River station attacked by Shawnee Indians; nearly all settlers killed or captured.
– Mrs. Mary Ingles and other white captives of Indians credited with making first salt in State at Campbells Creek, east of Charleston, while being taken to Ohio following Ingles-Draper massacre.

1756 Lord Fairfax grants acreage and springs at Bath (Berkeley Springs) to Virginia, that "these, heating waters might be forever free to the publick, for the welfare of suffering humanity."

1762 Romney and Mecklenburg (Shepherdstown) established as towns by Virginia assembly in act signed December 23 by Governor Francis Fauquier.

– Virginia General Assembly authorizes Agricultural and Mechanical Fair at Mecklenburg (Shepherdstown).

1763 French and Indian War terminated by Treaty of Paris.

1764 John and Samuel Pringle live in hollow sycamore tree near Turkey Run on Buckhannon River near present site of Buckhannon.

1765 Matthew Arbuckle of Greenbrier settlement explores Great Kanawha Valley.

1766 Survey of Mason-Dixon Line reaches western boundary of Maryland.

1768 Nearly all of western Virginia north of Little Kanawba River ceded to King of England by Six Nations in Treaty of Fort Stanwix.
– First flood of Ohio River is recorded.

1769 Colonel Ebenezer Zane and brothers, Jonathan and Silas, begin settlement at mouth of Wheeling Creek.

1772 George Washington patents 10,990 acres of land on south side of Great Kanawha, two miles above confluence of Ohio and Great Kanawha rivers.
– George Rogers Clark explores Ohio and Great Kanawha rivers.

1773 First family settlement in Great Kanawba Valley made at Cedar Grove at mouth of Kellys Creek by Walter Kelly from North Carolina.

1774 April 30. Lord Dunmore's War precipitated by murder of Chief Logan's family by party of European men at mouth of Yellow Creek.
– Battle of Point Pleasant is fought; it is considered by some as first battle of Revolution.
– Fort Fincastle, later renamed Fort Henry, erected at Wheeling by Captain Angus McDonald.
– General Andrew Lewis, with 1,300 men, leaves Fort Savannah (Lewisburg) en route to Point Pleasant to oppose Indians.
– Lord Dunmore arrives at Fort Fincastle (Wheeling) with 1,200 men.

1775 First regular troops raised in Virginia for Continental service mobilized at Morgan's Springs and Winchester.

1776 Virginia adopts its first constitution.

1777 Cornstalk, his son Elinipsico, and Red Hawk murdered by whites at Fort Randolph.
– Indians led by Simon Girty, renegade European man, unsuccessfully besiege Fort Henry.

1782 Mason-Dixon Line continued to southwestern corner of Pennsylvania.
– Second siege of Fort Henry at Wheeling; it has sometimes been called the last battle of American Revolution.

1784 James Rumsey demonstrates model of mechanically propelled boat near Berkeley Springs on Potomac in presence of George Washington.
– Permanent survey of Mason-Dixon Line completed.

1785 Potomac Company is incorporated to build canal connecting Potomac River with Cheat River.
– James River Company is incorporated to construct canal to connect James River with Great Kanawba.
– George Washington is made president of Potomac and James River companies.

1788 Six new western counties send representatives to Virginia convention, which ratifies Constitution of the United States.

1789 Daniel Boone is commissioned lieutenant colonel of Kanawha Militia.

1790 Population of western Virginia reported at 55,873; it demands for equality in representation in assembly.
– *Potomack Guardian and Berkeley Advertiser*, first newspaper in western Virginia, is printed by Nathaniel Willis at Shepherdstown; it is removed to Martinsburg in 1797.

1792 Kanawha County is represented in Virginia assembly at Richmond by Daniel Boone and George Clendenin.

1794 December 19. Charlestown (Charleston) is established as town.
– Iron furnace is erected by Peter Tarr at Kings Creek.
Post office is established at Wheeling.

1795 Treaty of Greenville makes Virginia frontier safe from Indian attacks.
– Daniel Boone and family leave Kanawha Valley permanently.

1796 Old Stone Presbyterian Church erected at Lewisburg.

1800 Population of western Virginia increases to 78,592.
– Discontent because of unequal representation is reiterated in petition to Virginia assembly, citing that Warwick (with 614 white population) and Berkeley (with 17,832) have same number of representatives in assembly.

1806 First salt well is bored in Great Kanawha Valley at Great Buffalo Lick near Maiden by Joseph and Daniel Ruffner.
– National or Cumberland Road is authorized by Congress.
– Blennerhassett Island and Mansion confiscated by Virginia Militia as result of alleged Burr-Blennerhassett plot.

1810 Western Virginia, with 312,626 European inhabitants and four senators, protests unequal representation (eastern Virginia has 338,826 population and 20 senators).
– Parkersburg becomes established as a town.
– Blennerhassett Mansion is destroyed by fire.
– Oil is discovered in gravel beds along Hughes River in Wood County.

1814 Monongalia Academy at Morgantown, forerunner of West Virginia University, is incorporated.

1815 James Wilson, boring for salt near Charleston, brings in first natural gas well in America.

1816 Newspapers propose division of State into North Virginia and South Virginia at line of Rappahsanock River, then to confluence of Greenbrier with New, and down Kanawha to Ohio.

1817 First trust in United States, the salt trust, formed by salt manufacturers of Kanawita Valley.

1818 National Road opens to Wheeling.

1819 First steamboat on Great Kanawha River ascends stream to Red House.

1824 James River and Kanawha Turnpike completed from Lewisburg to Falls of Great Kanawba. Staunton and Parkersburg Turnpike authorized.

1827 Northwestern Turnpike authorized.
– Baltimore and Ohio Railroad chartered by Virginia Assembly.

1830 Discussion of abolition of slavery assumes alarming sectional aspect.
– Second Virginia constitution is ratified, but dissatisfied western Virginians hold mass meeting at Wheeling to consider annexation of Maryland.

1841 First industrial use of natural gas in United States takes place at Burning Springs (Kanawha County).

1842 Public meetings are held in western counties to deliberate "our restoration to equal political rights of which we are deprived."

1847 Jefferson County adopts free school system, first in western Virginia.
– Western Virginia studies ways to rid that part of State of slavery; Dr. Henry Rufiner publishes pamphlet.

1851 Third Virginia constitution is ratified; it extends suffrage to all European male adults.
– For first time, western Virginia has majority in House of Delegates.

1853 January 1. First through train from Atlantic Ocean to Ohio River reaches Wheeling over Baltimore & Ohio Railroad.

1859 John Brown's raid takes place at Harpers Ferry; Brown is convicted of treason and hanged at Charles Town.

1860 First commercial oil well in state drilled at Burning Springs, Wirt County.

1861 April 4. Fall of Fort Sumter begins Civil War.
April 17. Twenty-nine of 46 western Virginia counties vote against secession.
April 21. Harpers Ferry garrison burns arsenal, flees to Maryland.
May 13. First Wheeling convention, with 26 counties represented, opposes secession.

June 3. Confederate outposts are defeated at Philippi.

June 11. Second Wheeling convention opens; delegates from 40 counties take oath of loyalty to Union.

June 13. Convention adopts Declaration of Rights.

June 19. Convention adopts ordinance to recognize State government.

June 20. Convention votes unanimously to set up Restored Government of Virginia on loyal basis, With Francis H. Pierpont as governor; ordinance is submitted to people.

July 1. First Virginia Legislature in western Virginia meets at Wheeling.

July 9. John S. Carlile and Waitman T. Willey are elected United States senators.

July 11. Confederates driven from Rich Mountain.

July 13. Engagement takes place at Corrick's Ford.

July 7. Skirmish takes place at Scary Creek.

August. Wheeling convention resumes its work.

September 10. Engagement takes place at Carnifex Ferry.

September 12-13. Battle of Cheat Mountain fought; Lee is defeated.

September 25. Engagement takes place at Kanawha Gap.

October 3. Engagement takes place at Greenbrier.

October 24. New State ordinance ratified by the people.

November 26. Constitutional convention opens at Wheeling.

November 27. Convention chooses name of "West Virginia."

December 13. Engagement takes place at Buffalo Mountain.

1862 April 3. Constitution of West Virginia ratified by voters.

May 6. Legislature of Restored Government of Virginia approves formation of new State.

September 10. Engagement takes place at Fayetteville.

September 15. Jackson captures Harpers Ferry.

1863 June 20. West Virginia admitted as 35th state of the Union.

June 20. First legislature of West Virginia convenes at Wheeling.

August 5. Berkeley County transferred from Virginia to West Virginia.

August 26-27. Engagement takes place at Rocky Gap. Gap.

September 26. State seal is adopted.

October 18. Engagement takes place at Charleston.

November 2. Jefferson County transferred from Virginia to West Virginia.

November 6. Engagement takes place at Droop Mountain.

December 10. Present free school system created by legislative act.

1864 January 29–February 1. Cavalry skirmishes at Medley.

July 4–7. Confederates under General Early have engagements around Harpers Ferry.

– West Virginia Hospital, State's first public institution, opens at Weston; it was established by Virginia assembly in 1859.

1865 April 9. Civil War ends when Lee surrenders.

– First public free school in State is opened at Charleston.

– First railroad bridge over Ohio River is completed at Fast Steubenville.

1866 May 24. Voters ratify constitutional amendment barring citizenship from all who gave aid to Confederacy.

– Virginia demands payment of $15,000,000 from West Virginia as its part of debt at time of separation.

1867 January 16. Legislature ratifies Fourteenth Amendment.

– West Virginia University is chartered under name of Agricultural College of West Virginia; it absorbs Monongalia Academy (incorporated January 4, 1858) and Woodburn Female Seminary (incorporated January 4, 1858).

1868 December 4. Legislative act changes name of West Virginia Agricultural College at Morgantown to West Virginia University.

1869 February 20. Charleston designated as seat of government by legislature "on and after April 1, 1870."

March 3. Fifteenth Amendment ratified by legislature.

1870 U.S. Census lists population of 442,014.

– State School for Deaf and Blind established at Romney.

– State capital moves to Charleston.

1871 April 27. Flick Amendment, enfranchising all persons disfranchised in 1866, becomes effective.

1872 January 16–April 9. Constitutional Convention drafts new constitution.

August. Constitution is ratified by voters.

1875 February 20. Legislature passes act designating Wheeling as seat of government.

May 21. Wheeling becomes capital.

1880 Population is 618,457.

– First telephone exchange in State is erected in Wheeling.

– Nathan Goff is appointed Secretary of the Navy.

1881 Second capitol building at Charleston is erected.

– Seat of State government is removed from Wheeling to Charleston.

1885 Wesleyan Seminary, later West Virginia Wesleyan College, is established at Buckhannon.

1890 Population is 762,794.

1891 Stephen B. Elkins is appointed Secretary of War.

1895 William L. Wilson is appointed Postmaster General.

1898 West Virginia furnishes two regiments of volunteer infantry in Spanish-American War neither regiment sees active service, although many West Virginians see active service in other organizations.

1900 Population is 958,800.

– West Virginia's oil production for year is 16,195,675 barrels.

1901 Office of Commissioner of Banking is created.

– Republican Albert B. White becomes Governor.

1902 "Mother" Mary Jones begins campaign to unionize 7,000 miners in Kanawha Valley.

1903 January 23. Rhododendron is adopted by legislature as State flower.
– West Virginia State Federation of Labor organizes 60 craft unions.

1904 State Department of Archives is created.

1905 Republican William M.O. Dawson is Governor.

1907 Five mine explosions cause 537 deaths.

1909 Republican William E. Glascock is Governor.

1910 Population is 1,221,119.

1911 State Department of Agriculture is created.

1912 Paint Creek Miners strike to gain recognition of United Mine Workers of America (UMWA); Martial Law is imposed until January 1913.

1913 Republican Henry D. Hatfield is Governor.

1914 State prohibition law becomes effective.

1915 West Virginia-Virginia debt case is decided by United States Supreme Court, holding West Virginia's share of debt to be $12,393,929.

1917 Democrat John J. Cornwell is inaugurated as Governor.

1917-18 U.S. enters World War I; West Virginia Selective Service registrants number 323,383; 45,648 enter active service; 624 die in action; 375 die of wounds or other causes overseas; 722 die of disease or other causes in U.S.

1918 Government explosives plant, costing about $75,000,000 erected at Nitro.
– State Department of Public Safety created.

1919 West Virginia University placed under control of State Board of Education.
– Legislature authorizes payment of Virginia debt by issuance of 20-year bonds and cash payment of $1,062,867.

1920 Population is 1,463,701.
– Constitutional amendment passes; amendment issues $50,000,000 in road bonds to "lift West Virginia out of the mud."
– Following "Matewan Massacre," UMWA membership rises significantly in Mingo County.

1921 January 3. State Capitol at Charleston is destroyed by fire.
– Logan County coalfields are invaded by 4,000 armed miners who fight battle of Blair Mountain with 500 deputy sheriffs and State police; conflict is dispersed by Federal troops.
– Republican Ephriam F. Morgan serves as Governor.

1923 Hard-surfaced road constructed between Charleston and Huntington.
– Tax on gasoline becomes effective.

1924 Howard M. Gore of Harrison County appointed Secretary of Agriculture.
– Three-year strike begins against coal operators in north.

1925 Republican Howard M. Gore is Governor.

1927 Federal prison for women is erected at Aldenon.

1929 March 7. New State flag design is adopted by legislature.
– West Virginia ranks first in production of bituminous coal.
– Republican William G. Conley becomes Governor.

1930 Population is 1,729,205.
– Glass production from 17 counties valued at more than $50,000,000.

1930-1934 Hawks Nest Tunnel workers experience high death rate due to silicosis; State officials suppress details of tragedy in WPA State guide.

1932 June 30. Dedication ceremonies are held for new State Capitol at Charleston; building and grounds cost $9,493,180.
– Levy limitation and property classification amendment adopted by referendum.
– First radio station in State, WSAZ, begins broadcasting from Huntington.

1933 Legislature declares 5 percent beer "non-intoxicating."
– County unit plan of school administration is adopted.
– Democrat H. Guy Kump becomes Governor.

1934 State Prohibition Law is repealed.

1937 Democrat Homer A. Holt begins gubernatorial term.

1938 Mingo Oak, largest and oldest white oak tree of record in the United States, declared dead and felled with ceremony.
– State Treasurer announces funds on hand for last payment of Virginia Bond Debt (due July 1, 1939).

1939 Miners certificate law, requiring six months' apprenticeship in West Virginia mines to establish eligibility for work, is enacted by legislature.
– State Road Commission reports 13,068 miles of surfaced highways out of total of 34,350 miles of State roads, largely constructed during past 10 years.

1940 Explosion of mine at Battley, McDowell County, claims lives of 92 miners.

1941 Democrat M. Mansfield Neely is Governor.

1941-1945 First and largest synthetic rubber plant in country opens near Charleston.
– Industries in State furnish many chemical products during World War II.

1945 Democrat Clarence W Meadows begins term as Governor.

1949 First television station in West Virginia, WSAZTV, begins broadcasting in Huntington.

– Democrat Okey L. Patterson is Governor.

1953 William C. Marland (D) becomes chief executive of State.

1954 Legislature passes law allowing African Americans to attend state universities and colleges.

1956 New aluminum plant in Ravenswood begins operations.

1957 Republican Cecil H. Underwood is Governor.

1959 National Radio Astronomy Observatory at Green Bank begins operations.

1961 Democrat William W. Barron is Governor.

1962 State Legislature approves funds for supplying birth control information and aid to welfare recipients.

1965 Capital punishment is abolished.
– Democrat Hulett C. Smith is Governor.

1968 Farmington mine explosion kills 78 persons.

1969 Former Governor W.W. "Wally" Barron convicted to five-year prison term for tampering with a jury.
– Republican Arch A. Moore is inaugurated as Governor.

1972 Buffalo Creek coal waste dam collapses, causing flood that kills 118 people.

1973 Retired West Virginia coal miner, Arnold Miller, campaigns against incumbent "Toney" Doyle for president of UMWA on reformist Miners for Democracy ticket.

1977 Democrat John D. Rockefeller IV is Governor.

1978 State records second successive record-breaking winter; heavy rain, snow, and flash floods are problems.

1981 Economy of State has unstable pattern, with major gains in oil and gas industries, and depression in steel and coal mining industries.

1982 Unemployment rises to 13.6 percent; level is nearly the nation's highest.

1983 As State recession continues, Governor John D. Rockefeller IV imposes major cutbacks in government spending.

1985 West Virginia has highest unemployment rate in nation.
– Arch A. Moore (R) begins second term as Governor.

1987 Unemployment rate drops to single digit level for first time in several years; State government battles ongoing fiscal crisis.

1988 West Virginia University college football team has first undefeated season in its history of 98 years.

1989 Democrat Gaston Caperton is Governor.

1990 Population is 1,793,477
– West Virginia has lost more population between 1980 and 1990 than any other state (-8 percent).

1991 Discovery of wild marijuana growing in Moorefield brings significant increase of tourism to town; weed is destroyed by officials.
– Per capita income is $14,174, a 3.1 percent increase over 1990.

1992 State has three Democrats in U.S. House of Representatives.

1995 Lewisburg circuit court judge sentences former beauty queen Tracy M. Lippard for attempting to kill romantic rival and parents; former Miss Williamsburg, Virginia contest winner drove from home to Lewisburg with arms to murder the trio.

1996 Former Governor Cecil H. Underwood defeats former State Senator Charlotte Pritt for gubernatorial office; Underwood was previously elected in 1956, served as governor from 1957 to 1961.

1997 Thousands of West Virginia residents are hit by severe flooding of Ohio River Valley.
– State Supreme Court dismisses most claims by State Attorney General Darrell V. McGraw in suit against tobacco industry; McGraw filed suit to obtain compensation from tobacco companies for public funds that were spent on treatment of smoking-related illnesses.

1998 West Virginia is one of three states to ban controversial late-term abortions since April; at least 28 states have now banned the procedure.

1999 August 2. The Clinton administration declares West Virginia and parts of five other eastern states agricultural disaster areas due to heat and drought.

DIRECTORY OF STATE SERVICES

OFFICE OF THE GOVERNOR
1900 Kanawha Blvd. E, Capitol Bldg.
Charleston, WV 25305-0370
Fax: 304-342-7025
Governor: 304-558-2000

OFFICE OF ATTORNEY GENERAL
1900 Kanawha Blvd. E, Bldg. 1, Rm. E-26
Charleston, WV 25305-0220
Fax: 304-558-0140
Attorney General: 304-558-2021

OFFICE OF SECRETARY OF STATE
1900 Kanawha Blvd. E, Bldg. 1, Ste. 157-K
Charleston, WV 25305-0770
Fax: 304-558-0900
Secretary of State: 304-558-6000

DEPARTMENT OF TREASURY
145 East Wing, State Capitol Bldg.
Charleston, WV 25305
Fax: 304-346-6602
State Treasurer: 304-343-4000

ADJUTANT GENERAL
1703 Coonskin Drive
Charleston, WV 25311-1086
Fax: 304-341-6466
Adjutant General: 304-341-6316

ADMINISTRATION DEPARTMENT
1900 Kanawha Blvd. E, Bldg. 1, Ste. E-119
Charleston, WV 25305-0120
Fax: 304-558-2999
Secretary: 304-558-2300

Consolidated Public Retirement Board
Capitol Complex E, Bldg. 5, Rm. 1000
Charleston, WV 25305-0720
Fax: 304-558-6337
Executive Secretary: 304-558-3570

Education State Employees Grievance Board
808 Greenbriar St.
Charleston, WV 25311
Fax: 304-558-1106
Director: 304-558-3361

AGRICULTURE DEPARTMENT
Room 28 Main Unit, Capitol Bldg.
Charleston, WV 25305-0170
Fax: 304-558-0451
Commissioner: 304-558-3550

Charleston Farmer's Market
599 Eagan St.
Charleston, WV 25301
Manager: 304-558-0185

Gen. John McCausland Memorial Farm
Capitol Bldg.
Charleston, WV 25305-0170
Commissioner: 304-675-0875

State Soil Conservation Agency
1900 Kanawha Blvd. E, Bldg. 5
Charleston, WV 25305-0107
Fax: 304-558-1635
Chairperson: 304-558-2204

US West Virginia Agriculture Statistics
1900 Kanawha Blvd. B
Charleston, WV 25305-0170
Fax: 304-558-0297
State Statistician: 304-558-2217

AUDITOR'S OFFICE
1st Flr., 100 State Capitol
Charleston, WV 25305-0230
Fax: 304-558-5200
Auditor: 304-558-2251

COMMERCE BUREAU
State Capitol Bldg., Rm. M146
Charleston, WV 25305-0310
Fax: 304-558-4983
Bureau Head: 304-558-2200

Development Office
1900 Kanawha Blvd. E
Charleston, WV 25305
Director: 304-558-2234

District Export Council
P.O. Box 26
Charleston, WV 25321
Fax: 304-347-5408

Economic Development Authority
1018 Kanawha Blvd. E, Ste. 501
Charleston, WV 25301
Executive Director: 304-558-3650

Energy Efficiency Program Office
Capitol Complex, Bldg. 6, Rm. 553
Charleston, WV 25311-0311
Manager: 304-558-4010

Minority and Small Business Development Agency
1115 Virginia St. E
Charleston, WV 25301-0311
Director: 304-558-2960
Chairperson: 304-347-5123

Forestry Division
1900 Kanawha Blvd. E
Charleston, WV 25305
Fax: 304-558-0143
Director: 304-558-2788

Mine Health Safety and Training Division
1615 Washington St. E
Charleston, WV 25311-2126
Fax: 304-558-1282
Director: 304-558-1425

Natural Resources Division
Capitol Complex, Bldg. 3
Charleston, WV 25305-0661
Fax: 304-558-2768
Director: 304-558-2754

Tourism and Parks Division
2101 Washington St. E
Charleston, WV 25305
Fax: 304-558-2956
Commissioner: 304-558-2200

Water Development Authority
1201 Dunbar Ave.
Dunbar, WV 25064
Fax: 304-558-0299
Director: 304-558-3612

EDUCATION DEPARTMENT
1900 Kanawha Blvd. E, Bldg. 6, Capitol Complex
Charleston, WV 25305-0330
Fax: 304-558-0048
State Superintendent: 304-558-2681

EDUCATION AND THE ARTS
1900 Kanawha Blvd. E
State Capitol Bldg. 1, Rm. 151
Charleston, WV 25305-2827
Fax: 304-558-1311
Secretary: 304-558-2440

Culture and History Division
1900 Kanawha Blvd. E
Cultural Center, Capitol Complex
Charleston, WV 25305-0300
Commissioner: 304-558-0220

Educational Broadcasting Authority
600 Capitol St.
Charleston, WV 25301-1292
Fax: 304-558-4034
Executive Director: 304-558-3239

Library Commission
1900 Kanawha Blvd. E
Charleston, WV 25305-0620
Fax: 304-558-2044
Executive Secretary: 304-558-2041

State College and University Systems
1018 Kanawha Blvd. E, Ste. 700
Charleston, WV 25301
Fax: 304-558-0259
Administrator: 304-558-4016

West Virginia Education Loan Services
20 Kenton Drive
Charleston, WV 25311
President: 304-345-7211

EMPLOYMENT PROGRAMS BUREAU
112 California Ave.
Charleston, WV 25305-0112
Fax: 304-558-2992
Commissioner: 304-558-2630

Workmen's Compensation Division
601 Morris St.
P.O. Box 3151
Charleston, WV 25332
Executive Secretary: 304-558-0475

ENVIRONMENTAL PROTECTION BUREAU
10 McJunkin Road
Nitro, WV 25143-2506
Fax: 304-759-0526
Bureau Read: 304-759-0515

Air Quality Office
1558 Washington St. E
Charleston, WV 25311-2599
Chief: 304-558-4022

Rural Development Council
2 Players Club Drive
Charleston, WV 25311
Fax: 304-558-0596
Chairperson: 304-558-1240

Solid Waste Management Division
1615 Washington St. E
Charleston, WV 25311
Fax: 304-558-0899
Director: 304-558-0844

Waste Management Division
1356 Hansford St.
Charleston, WV 25301
Fax: 304-558-0256
Chief: 304-558-5929

GEOLOGICAL AND ECONOMIC SURVEY
P.O. Box 879
Morgantown, WV 26507
Fax: 304-594-2575
Director & State Geologist: 304-594-2331

HEALTH AND HUMAN RESOURCES DEPARTMENT
State Capitol Complex, Bldg. 3, Rm. 206
Charleston, WV 25305
Fax: 304-558-1130
Secretary: 304-558-0684

Aging Commission
1900 Kanawha Blvd. E, State Capitol Complex
Charleston, WV 25305
Fax: 304-558-0004
Executive Director: 304-558-3317

Developmental Disabilities Planning Council
1601 Kanawha Blvd. W, Ste. 200
Charleston, WV 25312-2500
Fax: 304-558-0941
Executive Director: 304-558-0416

Finance Bureau
Bldg. 3, 201 State Capitol
Charleston, WV 25305-0501
Fax: 304-558-0045
Deputy Secretary: 304-558-5208

Health Care Cost Review Authority
100 Dee Drive, Ste. 201
Charleston, WV 25305-1692
Fax: 304-558-7001
Chairperson: 304-558-7000

Hospital Finance Authority
910 Quarrier St., Ste. 402
Charleston, WV 25305
Executive Director: 304-558-0549

Human Resources Bureau
State Capitol Complex, Bldg. 6, Rm. 617
Charleston, WV 25305
Fax: 304-558-1008
Community Support Deputy Commissioner: 304-558-2400
Public Assistance Deputy Commissioner: 304-558-2400

Women's Commission
1900 Kanawha Blvd. E, Bldg. 6, Rm. 637
Charleston, WV 25305
Executive Director: 304-558-0070

Human Rights Commission
1321 Plaza E, Rm. 104-106
Charleston, WV 25301-1400
Fax: 304-558-2248
Executive Director: 304-558-2616

Medical Services Bureau
State Capitol Complex, Bldg. 6
Charleston, WV 25305
Fax: 304-926-1776
Commissioner: 304-926-1700

Operations Bureau
State Capitol Complex, Bldg. 3, Rm. 265
Charleston, WV 25305-0501
Fax: 304-558-1130
Deputy Secretary: 304-558-3217

Public Health Bureau
State Capitol Complex, Bldg. 3, Rm. 518
Charleston, WV 25305-0501
Fax: 304-558-1035
Commissioner: 304-558-2971

Chief Medical Examiner
701 Jefferson Road S
Charleston, WV 25309
Chief Medical Examiner: 304-558-3920

Environmental Health Office
815 Quarrier St., Ste. 418
Charleston, WV 25301-2616
Director: 304-558-2981

LABOR DIVISION
Capitol Complex, Bldg. 3, Rm. 319
Charleston, WV 25305
Fax: 304-558-3797
Commissioner: 304-558-7890

**MILITARY AFFAIRS AND PUBLIC SAFETY
DEPARTMENT**
1900 Kanawha Blvd. E
Mail to: P.O. Box 50155
Charleston, WV 25305-0155
Fax: 304-341-6466
Secretary: 304-558-2930

Armory Board
1703 Coonskin Drive
Charleston, WV 25311-1085
Fax: 304-341-6466
Executive Assistant: 304-341-6368

Parole Board
112 California Ave., Bldg. 4
Charleston, WV 25305
Chairperson: 304-558-6366

Corrections Division
112 California Ave., Bldg. 4
State Capitol Complex
Charleston, WV 25305
Fax: 304-558-5934

Commissioner: 304-558-2037

Emergency Services
State Capitol Bldg. EB 80
Charleston, WV 25305
Fax: 304-344-4538
Director: 304-558-5380

Public Safety Division/WV State Police
725 Jefferson Rd.
Charleston, WV 25309
Fax: 304-746-2246
WV State Police: 304-746-2111

Regional Jail and Prison Authority
P.O. Box 50285
Charleston, WV 25305-0285
Fax: 304-558-2115
Executive Director: 304-558-2110

State Fire Marshal
2100 Washington St. E
Charleston, WV 25305
Fax: 304-558-2537
State Fire Marshal: 304-558-2191

Veterans Affairs Division
1321 Plaza E
Charleston, WV 25301-1400
Fax: 304-558-3662
Director: 304-558-3661

TAX AND REVENUE DEPARTMENT
State Capitol Complex
Charleston, WV 25305
Fax: 304-558-3269
Secretary: 304-558-2500

Alcohol Beverage Control Commission
70th St. SE
Charleston, WV 25304
Fax: 304-558-0081
Commissioner: 304-558-2481

Banking Division
State Capitol, Bldg. 3, Rm. 311
Charleston, WV 25305-0240
Fax: 304-558-0442
Commissioner: 304-558-2294

Insurance Commission
2019 Washington St. E
Charleston, WV 25305
Fax: 304-558-0412
Commissioner: 304-558-3354

Licensing and Continued Education
2019 Washington St. E
Charleston, WV 25305
Fax: 304-558-0412
Agent: 304-558-0610

Lottery Commission
312 McCorkle Ave. SE

P.O. Box 2067
Charleston, WV 26327
Fax: 304-558-3321
Director: 304-558-0500

Municipal Bond Commission
812 Quarrier St., Ste. 300
Charleston, WV 25301
Fax: 304-558-1280
Executive Director: 304-558-3971

Racing Commission
Capitol Complex, Rm. 317
Mail to: P.O. Box 3327
Charleston, WV 25333-3327
Fax: 304-558-6319
Executive Secretary: 304-558-2150

TRANSPORTATION DEPARTMENT
1900 Kanawha Blvd. E, Bldg. 5
Charleston, WV 25305-0440
Fax: 304-558-1004
Secretary: 304-558-0444

Aeronautics Commission
1900 Kanawha Blvd. E, Bldg. 5
Charleston, WV 25305-0440
Fax: 304-558-1004
Executive Assistant: 304-558-0330

Highways Division
1900 Kanawha Blvd. E, Bldg. 5
Charleston, WV 25305-0440
Fax: 304-558-1004
Commissioner: 304-558-3505

Motor Vehicles Division
Capitol Complex, Bldg. 3
Charleston, WV 25317
Fax: 304-558-1987
Commissioner: 304-558-2723

Parkways Economic Development and Tourism Authority
P.O. Box 1469
Charleston, WV 25325
Fax: 304-926-1909
General Manager: 304-926-1900

Port Authority
1900 Kanawha Blvd. B, Bldg. 5, Rm. 931
Charleston, WV 25305
Fax: 304-558-4076
Chairperson: 304-558-0330

Railroad Maintenance Authority
P.O. Box 470
Moorefield, WV 26836
Fax: 304-538-7474
Executive Director: 304-538-2305

BOARD OF INVESTMENTS
E122 State Capitol Bldg.
Charleston, WV 25305
Fax: 304-344-9284

Executive Director: 304-558-5000

CONSUMER ADVOCATE DIVISION
723 Kanawha Blvd. E, 7th Fl.
Charleston, WV 25301
Fax: 304-558-3610
Director: 304-558-0526

ETHICS COMMISSION
1207 Quarrier St., 4th Fl.
Charleston, WV 25305
Fax: 304-558-2169
Executive Director: 304-558-0664

Finance Division
208 7th Ave. SW
S Charleston, WV
Fax: 304-558-2334
Director: 304-558-1369

Personnel Division
State Capitol, Bldg. 6
Charleston, WV 25305-0139
Fax: 304-558-1587
Director: 304-558-2300

Public Defenders Services
State Capitol, Bldg. 3, Rm. 330
Charleston, WV 25305-0730
Fax: 304-558-1098
Executive Director: 304-558-3905

Public Employees Insurance Agency
State Capitol, Bldg. 5, Rm. 1001, 10th Fl.
Charleston, WV 25305-0710
Fax: 304-558-2516
Director: 304-558-7850

Purchasing Division
1900 Kanawha Blvd. E, Bldg. 1, Rm. 107E
Charleston, WV 25305-0130
Fax: 304-558-3970
Director: 304-558-2309

Risk Insurance Management
307 Jefferson St., P.O. Box 50124
Charleston, WV 25305-0124
Fax: 304-558-0154
Director: 304-558-2291

HOUSING DEVELOPMENT FUND
814 Virginia St. E
Charleston, WV 25301
Fax: 304-345-4828
Executive Director: 304-345-6475

REAL ESTATE COMMISSION
1033 Quarrier St., Ste. 400
Charleston, WV 25301-2315
Fax: 304-558-6442
Executive Director: 304-558-3555

PUBLIC SERVICE COMMISSION
P.O. Box 812

Charleston, WV 25323
Fax: 304-340-0325
Chairperson: 304-340-0300

STATE COUNCIL ON VOCATIONAL EDUCATION
1206 Kanawha Blvd. E, Ste. 211
Charleston, WV 25301-2984
Fax: 304-558-0136
Executive Director: 304-558-3784

MEMBERS OF CONGRESS

SENATE

SEN. ROBERT C. BYRD (D) (b. 1917); 7th Term;
Phone: 202-224-3954; Fax: 202-228-0002;
E-mail: senator_byrd@byrd.senate.gov

www.senate.gov/~byrd/

SEN. JOHN D. ROCKEFELLER (D) (b. 1937); 3rd Term;
Phone: 202-224-6472; Fax: 202-224-7665;
E-mail: senator@rockefeller.senate.gov

www.senate.gov/~rockefeller

HOUSE

ALAN B. MOLLOHAN (D-1st) (b. 1943); 9th Term;
Phone: 202-225-4172; Fax: 202-225-7564; E-mail: (None)

ROBERT E. WISE, Jr. (D-2nd) (b. 1948); 9th Term;
Phone: 202-225-2711; Fax: 202-225-7856;
E-mail: bobwise@mail.house.gov

www.house.gov/wise/

NICK J. RAHALL II (D-3rd) (b. 1949); 12th Term;
Phone: 202-225-3452; Fax: 202-225-9061;
E-mail: nrahall@mail.house.gov

www.house.gov/rahall

TWENTIETH CENTURY GOVERNORS

ATKINSON, GEORGE WESLEY (1845-1925), ninth governor of West Virginia (1897-1901), author, lecturer, jurist, was born on June 29, 1845 in Kanawha County, Virginia, now West Virginia, the son of James and Miriam (Rader) Atkinson. A product of the "old field" schools of his state, he received his higher education at Ohio Wesleyan University, from which he graduated, with an A.B. degree in 1870, and an M.A. degree in 1873. The following year he graduated in law from Howard Atkinson University, Washington, D.C., and was admitted to the bar of his native state in 1875. He took a graduate course in literature in Mount Union College, Alliance, Ohio, from which he received the doctorate, *pro merito*, in 1885.

Literary interests occupied an important place in Atkinson's life, as is attested by an impressive list of works he'd written, including: *History of Kanawha County* (1876); *West Virginia Pulpit* (1878); *After the Moonshiners* (1881); *Hand Book for Revenue Officers* (1881); *A.B.C. of the Tariff* (1884); *Dont's or Negative Chips from*

Blocks of Living Truths (1887); *Prominent Men of West Virginia*, jointly with A.F. Gibbens (1895); *Psychology Simplified* (1897); *Public Addresses* (1901); and *Bench and Bar of West Virginia* (1919). Atkinson also contributed to the press as editor of the *Evening Standard* (Wheeling) 1877-78, and subsequently for a period of nine years, joint editor of the *West Virginia Journal*.

Throughout West Virginia, Atkinson was in demand as a public lecturer on Sunday school, prohibition, and literary themes. He was, however, best known politically. Before he graduated from college he was a member of the board of education of Charleston, West Virginia, where he served as postmaster from 1876 to 1881. As United States Marshal for the District of West Virginia, 1881-85, he won temporary publicity because of his war on moonshiners. He was Federal Collector of Internal Revenue from 1878-81. Meanwhile, Atkinson moved to Wheeling and in 1888 was elected to Congress as a Republican. He declined renomination and practiced law until 1896, when he was elected the first Republican governor of West Virginia in a quarter century.

As governor Atkinson was vigorous and constructive, standing, among other things, for better public schools, permanent roads, reforms in state election laws, the right of labor to organize, and encouragement of immigration. Almost immediately after the expiration of his term as governor, he became United States District Attorney for southern West Virginia, a post he held until April 15, 1905, when President Roosevelt appointed him judge of the United States Court of Claims.

On April 17, 1916, Atkinson retired to private life. He was twice married: first, on December 2, 1868, to Ellen Eagan of his native county, by whom he had five children, and who died in 1893; and second, on June 24, 1897, to Mrs. Myra (Hornor) Camden, widow of Judge G.D. Camden of Clarksburg, West Virginia.

Atkinson died on April 14, 1925.

WHITE, ALBERT BLAKESLEE (1856-1941), tenth governor of West Virginia (1901-1905), was born in Cleveland, Ohio on September 22, 1856.

White attended Marietta College, graduating in 1878. He went on to earn an L.L.D. degree from West Virginia University in 1910, then later received a second LL.D. from Marietta College in 1935. In 1878 he began working as a reporter for the *Lafayette Daily Journal* and was later made managing editor of that publication. He left that post in 1881 to purchase the Parkersburg *State Journal*, and after partnering with S.B. Baker, he turned the paper into a daily, serving as its editor until 1899. In 1884 White served as president of the West Virginia Press Association, and between 1887 and 1888 he was president of the National Editorial Association. He was named Collector of Internal Revenue for the District of West Virginia in 1889, serving until 1893, then held the post again between 1897 and 1901.

White ran for the West Virginia governorship on the Republican ticket in 1900, defeating his Democratic opponent, John H. Holt, and taking office on March 4, 1901. During his tenure a State Tax Commission was created and imbued with a certain amount of authority, in order to streamline citizen taxation within the State. In addition, the West Virginia State Federation of Labor organized several craft unions, and the State Department of Archives was established.

After stepping down from office on March 4, 1905, White served as the West Virginia Tax Commissioner during 1907-08. During 1918-19, he was involved in charity work in other countries, and between 1921 and 1925, once again served as Collector of Internal Revenue for the District of West Virginia. Between 1927 and 1931 he served in the West Virginia Senate, and was later involved in a manufacturing venture.

White was married to Agnes Ward, and the couple had five children. He died on July 3, 1941.

DAWSON, WILLIAM MERCER OWENS (1853-1916), eleventh governor of West Virginia (1905-1909), was born in Bloomington, Maryland on May 21, 1853.

After working at various jobs, including schoolteacher, Dawson was named editor of the *Preston County Journal* in 1873. Two years later he purchased that paper, and served as its publisher for nearly twenty years. Between 1881 and 1889 Dawson was a member of the West Virginia Senate. In 1895 he was Mayor of Kingwood, West Virginia, and in 1897 was appointed Secretary of State, a post he held for two more terms, until 1904.

Dawson ran for the West Virginia governorship on the Republican ticket in 1904, defeating the Democratic candidate, John J. Cornwell and taking office on March 4, 1905. During his tenure, both the State Board of Control and the Board of Regents were created, and an insurance law and a corrupt practice law were passed. After stepping down from office on March 4, 1909, he returned to his private law practice.

Dawson was married twice: to Luda Neff and to Maude Brown. He had one child from each union. Dawson died on March 12, 1916.

GLASSCOCK, WILLIAM ELLSWORTH (1862-1925), twelfth governor of West Virginia (1909-1913), was born near Arnettsville, Virginia (later West Virginia) on December 13, 1862.

Between 1880 and 1884 Glasscock was a schoolteacher, first in Iowa, then in Nebraska. After returning to Arnettsville, he served as Superintendent of Public Schools in Monongalia County, West Virginia, and held that post from 1887 to 1890. Between 1890 and 1902, Glasscock served as County Clerk of Monongalia County. In 1902 he began studying at West Virginia University Law School, passing the West Virginia Bar in 1903, and going into law practice in Morgantown, West Virginia. Between 1905 and 1908 he was named Collector of Internal Revenue for the District of West Virginia.

Glasscock ran for the West Virginia governorship on the Republican ticket, defeating Democrat Louis Bennett and taking office on March 4, 1909. During his tenure, the Public Service Commission was established, as were the Department of Public Roads and the State Tuberculosis Sanitarium. In addition, all public school children were required to get medical examinations, and the Workmen's Compensation Law was adopted.

After stepping down from office on March 4, 1913, Glasscock returned to his private law practice. He was married to Mary Alice Miller and the couple had one child. Glasscock died on April 12, 1925.

HATFIELD, HENRY DRURY (1875-1962), thirteenth governor of West Virginia (1913-1917), was born in Logan County, West Virginia on September 15, 1875.

Hatfield attended Franklin College in New Athens, Ohio, earning an A.B. degree in 1890. Initially pursuing a career in medicine, Hatfield took classes at New York Polyclinic Medical School and Hospital, Cornell University Medical College, and New York Post Graduate Medical School and Hospital. In 1895 he received an M.D. degree from the University of Louisville, as well as one in 1904 from New York University, Bellevue Hospital Medical College. Hatfield served as Commissioner of Health of Mingo County, West Virginia between 1895 and 1900. In the latter year he was one of the founders of the Miners' Hospital in Welch, West Virginia, and was that facility's chief surgeon until 1912.

Delving into politics, Hatfield served as Commissioner of District Roads in McDowell County, West Virginia between 1900 and 1905. From 1908 to 1912 he served in the West Virginia Senate. Still also involved in his medical work, Hatfield was the surgeon for the Norfolk and Western Railway Company from 1909 to 1913.

Hatfield ran for the West Virginia governorship on the Republican ticket in 1912, defeating Democrat William R. Thompson, and the Socialist nominee, W. Hilton, and taking office on March 4, 1913. At the start of his administration mining was a big issue, with Hatfield arbitrating a long coal miners' strike due to their insistence on joining the United Mine Workers Union, and coming up with an equitable settlement between the miners and the mine owners. Hatfield also backed reforms in the State's Workmen's Compensation Law after a mining explosion killed one hundred and eighty miners in Eccles, West Virginia. Also during his tenure two laws were passed, including the Klein Act, which gave voting rights to the women of West Virginia, and the Corrupt Practices Act, created to target election corruption. In addition, when Virginia divided to create West Virginia, the latter state held a huge debt, prompting the creation of the Virginia Debt Commission, to try and settle the case between the two states. Ultimately, the United States Supreme Court ruled that the amount West Virginia was responsible for was 12,393,929 dollars.

Hatfield stepped down from office on March 4, 1917. Later that year he served in the Medical Corps of the United States Army. He founded two medical facilities, the Hatfield-Lawson Hospital in Logan, West Virginia, in 1923, and in 1927, the Williamson Memorial Hospital. In 1928 he was elected to the United States Senate and served until 1935, failing to win a second term.

Hatfield was married to South Carolina Bronson, and the couple had one child. Hatfield died on October 23, 1962.

CORNWELL, JOHN JACOB (1867-1935), fourteenth governor of West Virginia (1917-1921), was born near Bennsboro, West Virginia on July 11, 1867.

Cornwell became a schoolteacher at the young age of sixteen, and taught for the next several years; during 1889-90, he served as principal of the Romney, West Virginia grade schools. In 1888 he studied at Shepherd College in Shepherdstown, West Virginia', then the following year, attended West Virginia University in Morgantown, receiving an LL.D. degree in 1890. Later that year, in partnership with his brother, Cornwell purchased the *Hampshire Review*, and was editor of that paper until 1917. Cornwell passed the West Virginia Bar in 1894.

Cornwell entered politics in 1898 when he was elected to the West Virginia Senate, winning a second term as well, in 1902. Cornwell made an unsuccessful attempt at the West Virginia governorship in 1904, on the Democratic ticket. In 1916 he ran again, this time winning the election over his Republican opponent, Ira E. Robinson, and taking office on March 4, 1917.

Two months after taking office, a special session of the State Legislature was called by Cornwell, during which a constitutional amendment was put to a popular vote regarding a budget system that would monitor treasury expenditures. World War I was taking place during his tenure, and he made sure that the State of West Virginia did its part for the war effort. In addition, both the State Road Commission and the Department of Public Safety were created. Also, the State Department of Agriculture's programs and duties were expanded, a mother's pension law was passed, and stricter enforcement of the State Prohibition Law was put into effect.

Cornwell stepped down from office on March 4, 1921 and was subsequently appointed director of the Baltimore and Ohio Railway Company. He was the author of two books, *Knock-about Notes* (1915), and *A Mountain Trail* (1939).

Cornwell was married to Edna Brady, and the couple had two children. He died on September 8, 1935.

MORGAN, EPHRIAM FRANKLIN (1869-1950), fifteenth governor of West Virginia (1921-1925), was born in Forksburg, West Virginia on January 16, 1869.

Morgan attended West Virginia University, earning an LL.B. degree in 1897. During the Spanish-American War, Morgan served in the United States Army. During 1902-03 he served as City Solicitor of Fairmont, and from 1906 to 1912, he was Judge of the Intermediate Court of Marion County. Between 1915 and 1919, he was a member of the West Virginia Service Commission.

Morgan ran for the West Virginia governorship on the Republican ticket in 1920, winning over the Democratic nominee, Arthur B. Koontz, and Independent candidate, S. Montgomery and taking office on March 4, 1921. During his tenure, several pieces of legislation were passed to facilitate statewide improvements, including the building of several State roads and a new State Capitol Building, the expansion and revamping of the Department of Health, the revitalization of the National Guard, and benefits for disabled World War I veterans. In addition, a Gross Sales Tax Law was created, as was a State Sinking Fund Commission and a Public School Commission.

Morgan stepped down from office on March 4, 1925, and returned to his law practice. Between 1927 and 1933 he was appointed Solicitor for the United States Department of Commerce. He was married to Alma Bennett and the couple had two children, one of whom died in infancy. Morgan died on January 15, 1950.

GORE, HOWARD MASON (1877-1947), sixteenth governor of West Virginia (1925-1929), was born in Clarksburg, West Virginia on October 12, 1877.

Gore and his three brothers grew up learning about farming and livestock breeding, and after graduating from West Virginia University in 1900, he returned to the family business. He and his siblings operated several ventures, including Portner, Highland Brothers and Gore, Gore Brothers, W.F Gore and Brothers, and H.M. Gore Brothers. Between 1912 and 1916 he was president of the West Virginia Livestock Association.

During those years Gore also served as Assistant Food Administrator for West Virginia and during World War I was assistant to the United States Food Administrator. In 1921, under the aegis of the Department of Agriculture, he was appointed overseer of trade practices in the Division of Packers and Stockyard Administration. In 1923 he was appointed Assistant Secretary of Agriculture, and after the death of Henry C. Wallace, was named Secretary of Agriculture in President Calvin Coolidge's administration, a post he served in from November 1924 to March 1925.

In 1924 Gore ran for the governorship of West Virginia on the Republican ticket, defeating Democratic opponent Jake Fisher, and taking office on March 4, 1925. While in office Gore stressed the need to raise both automobile license and gasoline taxes and use the funds to improve State highways. He requested that State institutions that dealt with education and medical care improve their services where needed, and also made an effort to solidify the Virginia-West Virginia debt settlement. In addition, he also requested legislation for clarification on how the Prohibition Law should be enforced.

In 1928 Gore made an unsuccessful attempt at the United States Senate, and after the election of William G. Conley to the West Virginia governorship, he stepped down from office on March 4, 1929. From 1931 to 1933 he served as West Virginia Commissioner of Agriculture, and for several years he was also a member of a number of farming and livestock cooperatives.

Gore was married to Roxalene Corder Bailey. He died on June 20, 1947.

CONLEY, WILLIAM GUSTAVUS (1866-1940), seventeenth governor of West Virginia (1929-1933), was born near Kingwood in Preston County, West Virginia on January 8, 1866.

Conley attended West Virginia University, earning an LL.B. degree in 1893, and was admitted to the State Bar that same year. He later returned to school and received an LL.D. degree in 1929. Between 1886 and 1891 he was a public school teacher, and after passing the bar, he started a private law practice in Parsons, West Virginia.

From 1896 to 1904 Conley was Prosecuting Attorney of Tucker County, West Virginia, between 1901 and 1903, he served as Mayor of Parsons, and in addition, from 1896 to 1903 he was also co-owner and editor of the *Parsons Advocate*. From 1903 to 1905 he served, as a member of the Kingwood, West Virginia City Council, and between 1906 and 1908, was mayor of that town. After the death of State Attorney General Clark W. May, Conley was appointed to that post, and in the subsequent election, was elected, serving from May 1908 to March 1913.

In 1929 Conley ran for the governorship of West Virginia on the Republican ticket, and defeated his Democratic opponent, Jake Fisher, taking office the following year. During his administration, the Game, Fishing and Forestry Commission, and the State Road Commission were reorganized, and a Department of Public Welfare was created, which absorbed such organizations as the Board of Children's Guardians, the Crippled Children's Council, and the Veterans' Service Office. In addition, a Water Power Bill was passed, and Charleston was the site of dedication ceremonies for the new State Capitol.

After the election of Herrnan G. Kump, Conley stepped down from the governorship on March 4, 1933. He was married to Bertie Isom Marton, and the couple had five children. Conley died on October 21, 1940.

KUMP, HERMAN GUY (1877-1962), eighteenth governor of West Virginia (1933-1937), was born in Capon Springs, West Virginia on October 31, 1877.

Kump attended Shenandoah Normal College, then studied law at the University of Virginia, earning an LL.B. degree in 1905. Kump was admitted to the West Virginia Bar that same year. After having his own law practice in Elkins, West Virginia, he was elected Prosecuting Attorney of Randolph County, Virginia in 1908, then again in 1916. After serving in the United States Army in World War I, be served as Mayor of Elkins, West Virginia, from 1921 to 1923.

In 1928 Kump was elected Judge of the Twentieth Judicial Circuit of West Virginia, and served until he resigned in 1932 in order to run for the governorship of West Virginia on the Democratic ticket. Kump won the election over his Republican opponent, T.C. Townsend, and took office on March 4, 1933.

During Kump's tenure, both the Public Land Corporation of West Virginia and a Civil Service Commission were created. Also the Small Bill Loan was passed, as was an amendment that limited taxation. In addition, State public officials had their salaries reduced, and unemployment compensation was put into effect.

The West Virginia Constitution of 1872 prohibited Kump from succeeding himself as Governor, and he stepped down on January 18, 1937, afterwards returning to his private law practice of Kump and Kump.

Kump was married to Edna Scott, and the couple had six children. He died on February 14, 1962.

HOLT, HOMER ADAMS (1898-1975), nineteenth governor of West Virginia (1937-1941), was born in Lewisburg, West Virginia on March 1, 1898,

Holt attended Washington and Lee University, earning an A.B. degree in 1918 and an LL.B. degree in 1923. Between 1920 and 1923 he was a mathematics instructor at his alma mater. During 1923-24 he was assistant professor of law at that facility, and during 1924-25, served as associate professor of law. From 1925 until 1927 he had his own private law practice, Hubard, Bacon and Holt, and again between 1927 and 1932, with Dillon, Mahan and Holt.

In 1932 Holt was elected Attorney General of West Virginia, a post he held until 1937. In 1936 Holt ran for the governorship of West Virginia on the Democratic ticket, defeating his Republican opponent, Summers H. Sharp, and taking office on January 18, 1937.

One of the first things Holt did while in office was offer protection to miners who did not want to join in on a strike. Also during his tenure, the State's probation and parole system was modernized, as was the distribution system of State aid to schools. In addition, the building and renovation of State institutions was made a top priority.

The State's Constitution of 1872 prevented Holt from succeeding himself in office and he stepped down on January 20, 1941. Upon leaving office Holt returned to his law practice, joining the firm of Brown, Jackson and Knight in Charleston, West Virginia, where he worked from 1941 to 1946. During 1944-45 Holt served as Director of Union Carbide and Carbon Corporation of New York; between 1947 and 1953, he was that firm's general counsel, and served as their vice-president from 1949 to 1953.

In 1953 Holt was a partner in the firm of Jackson, Kelly, Molt and O'Farrell, and later served as director of the Kanawha Valley Bank of Charleston, as well as the Slab Fork Coal Company. From 1957 to 1963 he served as chairman of the West Virginia Commission for Constitutional Revision.

Holt was married to Isabel Hedges Wood, and the couple had three children. He died on January 16, 1975.

NEELY, MATTHEW MANSFIELD (1874-1958), twentieth governor of West Virginia (1941-1945), was born in Grove, West Virginia on November 9, 1874.

After attending Salem College, Neely studied at West Virginia University where he earned an A.B. degree in 1901, and received an LL.B. degree in 1902, passing the West Virginia Bar in the latter year. During the Spanish-American War, Neely served in the First West Virginia Volunteer Infantry, and later held several ranks in the West Virginia National Guard.

In 1903 Neely went into private law practice with a partner, Henry A. Lively in Fairmont, West Virginia. Between 1908 and 1910 he was Mayor of Fairmont, then from 1911 to 1913 he was clerk of the West Virginia House of Delegates. After the resignation of U.S. Representative John W. Davis, Neely was elected to his seat on the Democratic ticket, and was reelected to three more terms (1913-1921). Failing to win a fourth term, Neely later ran for, and won, a seat in the U.S. Senate, serving from 1923 to 1929, then again from 1931 until 1941.

Neely ran for the West Virginia governorship on the Democratic ticket, and defeated his Republican opponent, Daniel Boone Dawson. He took office on January 20, 1941. During his tenure, the Child Welfare Law was improved so that there was better interaction and cooperation between the child welfare organizations, the Department of Public Assistance, and the State Department of Health. In addition, both State Council of Defense and a State Planning Board were established. Child adoption laws were also amended so that both the children and the adoptive parents benefitted.

Unable by law to succeed himself as governor, and Neely stepped down on January 15, 1945. After leaving office, Neely served once again as a member of the U.S. House of Representatives, from 1945 to 1947. He made an unsuccessful attempt at another term, but instead, served two more terms in the U.S. Senate from 1949, until his death in 1958.

Neely was married to Alberta Claire Ramage, and the couple had three children. He died on January 18, 1958.

MEADOWS, CLARENCE WATSON (1904-1961), twenty-first governor of West Virginia (1945-1949), was born in Beckley, West Virginia on February 11, 1904.

Meadows attended Washington and Lee University between 1921 and 1925, and in 1927, earned an LL.B. degree from the University of Alabama. He was admitted to the Alabama Bar that same year, and in 1929, was admitted to the West Virginia Bar. In later years he was admitted to all state and federal court bars, including the United States Supreme Court in 1934, and the Fourth Circuit, Circuit Court of Appeals in 1940.

In 1927 Meadows went into private law practice in Birmingham, Alabama, and two years later returned home to Beckley, West Virginia to set up another law practice there. In 1931 he was elected to the West Virginia House of Delegates, and then served as Prosecuting Attorney of Raleigh County, West Virginia from 1933 to 1936. The following year he was elected Attorney General of West Virginia, then was reelected again in 1941, but resigned in 1942 after being appointed Judge of the Tenth Judicial Circuit of West Virginia. Meadows were subsequently elected to another term in that post, serving until December 1944.

Meadows ran for the West Virginia governorship on the Democratic ticket, defeating his Republican opponent, Daniel Boone Dawson, and taking office on January 15, 1945. During his tenure, workmen's compensation premiums were changed from monthly to quarterly, with an advance deposit of three months being required instead of two. In addition, both the Department of Motor Vehicles and the West Virginia Turnpike Commission were established, as was the office of Insurance Commissioner of West Virginia. A law was also passed making it mandatory that all deaf and blind children over the age of six were to receive an education.

Unable by law to succeed himself as Governor, Meadows stepped down on January 17, 1949, and returned to his law practice, as well as other various business interests. Several years later, Meadows moved to Fort Lauderdale, Florida, where he continued to practice law and involve himself in Democratic politics.

Meadows was married to Nancy Ryals Massie, and the couple had four children. He died on September 12, 1961.

PATTESON, OKEY LEONIDAS (1898-1989), twenty-second governor of West Virginia (1949-1952), was born in Dingess, West Virginia on September 14, 1898.

Patteson attended Wesleyan College where he earned a B.A. degree, then continued his post-graduate studies at the Carnegie Institute of Technology.

Patteson pursued various business interests such as real estate and automobiles. His first public office was as President of the Fayette County Court between 1935 and 1941, then from the latter year until 1944, he was Sheriff of Fayette County. After working within the Democratic Party, he was appointed Executive Assistant to Governor Clarence Meadows in January 1945, a post he remained in until the next gubernatorial election, when he decided to run for the office himself. Patteson won the governorship, defeating his Republican opponent, Herbert S. Boreman, and took office on January 17, 1949.

During Patteson's tenure, West Virginia University established a four-year school encompassing medicine, nursing and dentistry. In addition the State Department of Health was reorganized and a State Board of Health was established. Also, the Workmen's Compensation Law was amended.

Unable by law to succeed himself as Governor, Patteson stepped down on January 19, 1953, and later that year, was named general manager of the West Virginia Turnpike Commission.,

Patteson was married to Viole Lee Hawse and the couple had two children. He died on July 3, 1989.

MARLAND, WILLIAM CASEY (1918-1965),

twenty-third governor of West Virginia (1953-1957), was born in Johnston City, Illinois on March 26, 1918.

Marland attended the University of Alabama, earning a B.A. degree in 1940. Continuing his studies at West Virginia University, he received an LL.B. degree in 1947, and was admitted to the West Virginia Bar that same year. While at the latter school, he served as president of the student board of editors of the *West Virginia Law Quarterly*. At the start of World War II Marland joined the U.S. Navy, serving overseas.

After the war, Marland went into private law practice in Charleston, West Virginia, and in 1948 became Assistant Attorney General of the State. He became Attorney General of West Virginia the following year, serving in that post until 1952. Marland resigned from office in order to pursue the West Virginia governorship. Running on the Democratic ticket, he won the election over his Republican opponent, Rush D. Holt, and took office on January 19, 1953.

During his time in office, Marland concentrated on developing West Virginia's industry, which included his efforts at preventing the Follansbee Steel Corporation from moving out of state. He also took part in the Governors Fuel Conference, which was held to persuade the U.S. Congress to establish a limit on the amount of foreign oil that could come into the United States. In addition, he was a supporter of the school integration ruling handed down by the U.S. Supreme Court, and asked for total compliance in the breaking up of the State's segregated schools and recreational facilities.

Unable by law by succeed himself as Governor, Marland stepped down on January 21, 1957. After making an unsuccessful attempt for a U.S. Senate seat in 1959, he was named Sales Director of the Western Kentucky Coal Company, a post he held until 1961. From 1962 to 1965 he was Associate Director at Edwards Enterprises.

Marland was married to Valerie Allen, and the couple had three children. He died on November 26, 1965.

UNDERWOOD, CECIL HARLAND (1922-),

twenty-fourth governor of West Virginia (1957-1961), was born in Joseph Mills, West Virginia on November 5, 1922.

Underwood attended Salem College where he earned an A.B. degree in 1943, and continued his studies at West Virginia University, receiving an M.A. degree in 1952. Between 1943 and 1946 Underwood was a high school biology teacher, and from 1946 until 1950, was assistant to the president of Marietta College. Between 1950 and 1956 he was vice president in charge of public relations at his alma mater, Salem College.

Entering the political arena, Underwood was elected to the West Virginia House of Delegates, a post he served in from 1944 to 1956. Underwood ran for the governorship of West Virginia on the Republican ticket in 1956, defeating his Democratic opponent, R. Mollohan, and taking office on January 21, 1957.

During Underwood's tenure, property taxation was no longer allowed on money kept in banks, and county school districts were given the authority to make improvements needed in public schools. In addition, a vocational training program was set up for unemployed people who wanted a second chance. Also, a Department of Mental Health was established.

Unable by law to succeed himself as Governor, Underwood stepped down on January 16, 1961. After leaving office he served as Vice President the Island Creek Coal Company, between 1961 and 1964. The following year he became Director of Civic Affairs for the Monsanto Company, serving in that post until 1967, when he became vice president of that firm. Between 1968 and 1975 he was President of the Franswood Corporation, and from 1976 to 1978 he was a field underwriter for New York Life Insurance Company. Along with his other corporate interests, Underwood also served as president of his own company, Cecil H. Underwood Associates from 1965 to 1980.

Various other business interests included: President, Morgantown (W.V.) Industrial Park, Inc., 1983; President, Software Valley, 1989-92; and President, Mon View Heights of West Virginia, 1993.

Underwood made two more attempts at the governorship, but was defeated by Democrat Huiett C. Smith in 1964, and by Democrat John D. Rockefeller in 1976.

Underwood is married to Hovah Hall, and the couple has three children.

BARRON, WILIAM WALLACE (1911-),

twenty-fifth governor of West Virginia (1961-1965), was born in Elkins, West Virginia on December 8, 1911.

Barron attended Washington and Lee University, earning an A.B. degree in 1934, then continued his studies at West Virginia University, receiving an LL.B. degree in 1941. After passing the West Virginia Bar in the latter year, he went into private law practice. During World War II, Barron served in the U.S. Army, and after the war, was elected Mayor of Elkins, West Virginia, serving from 1949 to 1951. In 1950 and 1952, he was also a member of the West Virginia House of Delegates. In subsequent years he held such posts as Deputy Land Commissioner, Commissioner of Accounts, and Commissioner of the Chancery of Randolph County.

During 1957 to 1961 Barron served as Attorney General of West Virginia. In 1960 he ran for the governorship of West Virginia on the Democratic ticket, defeating his Republican opponent, Harold F. Neely, and taking office on January 16, 1961. During his tenure, tighter controls were placed on strip-mining, the State income tax laws were updated to coincide with federal income tax law revisions, and the coroner system was replaced by a more comprehensive medical examiner system.

Unable by law to succeed himself as Governor, Barron stepped down on January 18, 1965. He returned to his own law practice at the firm of Barron and Davis in Charleston, West Virginia.

Barron is married to Opal Wilcox, and the couple has three children.

SMITH, HULETT CARLSON (1918-),

twenty-sixth governor of West Virginia (1965-1969), was born in Beckley, West Virginia on October 21, 1918.

After attending Beckley College, Smith studied at the Wharton School of Finance and Commerce at the University of Pennsylvania, graduating with honors. In subsequent years he was Vice President of the First Beckley Corporation, President of Investment Securities, Inc., and President of the Home Insurance Agency, in Beckley. Between 1947 and 1959 he was a member of the West Virginia State Aeronautics Commission, and from 1956 to 1961, served as Democratic State Chairman.

Smith ran for the governorship on the Democratic ticket, defeating his Republican opponent, former Governor Cecil H. Underwood, and taking office on January 18, 1965. During his time in office, the death penalty was revoked, family planning clinics were opened, and the State sales tax went up. In addition, controls were tightened considerably for strip-mining, and workmen's compensation was increased.

Unable by law to succeed himself as Governor, Smith stepped down on January 13, 1969. Between 1968 and 1972 Smith was a member of the Democratic National Committee for West Virginia.

MOORE, ARCH ALFRED, JR. (1923-), twenty-seventh and twenty-ninth governor of West Virginia (1969-1977, 1985-1989), was born in Moundsville, West Virginia on April 16, 1923.

Moore attended Lafayette College in Easton, Pennsylvania during 1943, then continued his studies at West Virginia University, earning an A.B. degree in 1948, and an LL.B. degree in 1951, passing the West Virginia Bar in the latter year. Between 1943 and 1946 he served in the U.S. Army, and was awarded the Purple Heart.

Moore began his own private law practice in Moundsville, in 1951. Between 1953 and 1955 he served in the West Virginia House of Delegates. In 1956 he was elected to the U.S. House of Representatives, and was elected for five more terms, ending his tenure in 1969.

Moore ran for the West Virginia governorship on the Republican ticket, defeating his Democratic opponent, James M. Sprouse, and taking office on January 13, 1969. During his tenure, workmen's compensation laws were amended to cover black lung disease (pneumoconiosis), a malady often suffered by coal miners. In addition, laws pertaining to water pollution were tightened when and wherever gas or oil drilling was to take place. Also, regulations concerning elections, divorce or banking were revised. State voting rights were given to eighteen year-olds, a board of regents was organized for higher education facilities, and a state-wide kindergarten system was implemented.

A 1970 amendment to the West Virginia Constitution of 1872 allowed Moore run for a second consecutive term, which he did, defeating his Democratic opponent, John D. Rockefeller, IV, and taking office on January 15, 1973. During this term, public school teachers received across-the-board raises, a consumer credit and protection hill was passed, and low-income groups and the elderly received property tax relief.

Moore faced scandal when he was accused of trying to extort 25,000 dollars from a State banker during his 1972 run for the governorship; however, a federal jury acquitted him of the charge. Unable by law to seek a third term, he stepped down on January 17, 1977.

Moore is married to S. Shelley Riley, and the couple has three children.

ROCKEFELLER, JOHN DAVISON, IV (1937-), twenty-eighth governor of West Virginia (1977-1985), was born in New York City, New York on June 16, 1937. He is related to the famous, wealthy Rockefeller family, including John D. Rockefeller, his great-grandfather, who founded the Standard Oil Company.

After studying the Japanese language at International Christian University in Tokyo from 1957 to 1960, Rockefeller attended Harvard, earning an A.B. degree in 1961. He then did his post-graduate work at the Yale University Institute of Far Eastern Languages. In 1961 he was appointed a member of the National Advisory Council of the Peace Corps, serving as special assistant to the director of that organization in 1962. During 1964 Rockefeller worked has a field hand in the Action for Appalachian Youth Program, and was also a consultant on the President's Commission on Juvenile Delinquency and Youth Crime.

From 1966 to 1968 Rockefeller, a Democrat, was a member of the West Virginia House of Delegates, then from 1968 to 1972, he was Secretary of State of West Virginia. Between 1973 and 1975 he served as President of West Virginia Wesleyan College.

Rockefeller made his first attempt at the West Virginia governorship in 1972, but lost to Republican Arch A. Moore. However, in his second try four years later, he was successful, defeating Republican candidate, former State Governor Cecil H. Underwood, and taking office on January 17, 1977.

During Rockefeller's tenure the nation was experiencing an energy crisis, and West Virginia was investigated as a source of "fossil fuels," with oil and natural gas being sought out by wild-catters looking to cash in. In addition, West Virginia wanted to build the first commercial plant that would create synthetic fuel from coal. Also, the State purchased a large piece of the Chessie System, a non-commuter railroad line.

Rockefeller, in his attempt at a second term, defeated John Rogers in the Democratic primary. A bitter contest then ensued between the incumbent and his Republican opponent, former Governor Arch Moore. Moore blasted Rockefeller for his extravagant campaign spending, estimated at over 11.7 million dollars, and Rockefeller reminded voters of Moore's trial on extortion charges during his term in office. Rockefeller won a second term, and served without taking a salary, although State employees received a raise in 1982. Unable by law to succeed himself for a third term, Rockefeller ran for, and won, a seat in the U.S. Senate in 1984.

Rockefeller is married to Sharon Percy, and the couple has four children.

CAPERTON, GASTON (1940-), thirtieth governor of West Virginia (1989-1997), was born in 1940 in the state he later governed. He attended the University of North Carolina, where he earned a B.S. degree in 1963.

Before his political career, Caperton was a highly successful businessman as principal owner and chief operating officer of McDonough-Caperton Insurance Group. Soon after being elected to the governorship, Caperton came up with a plan that was dubbed Revolution '89. In an attempt to stem a near bankruptcy of the State, he made massive changes that included the slashing of government spending and the streamlining of several government agencies. Through his efforts, the State budget not only got out of the red, but also built up a healthy surplus to work with, a situation Time magazine described as "a near miracle." He also created the INSPIRE program, a quality management system implemented throughout West Virginia in which State employees were able to have input into how their jobs and departments could be improved.

One of Caperton's most passionate causes was the revitalization of the State's educational system. Under a comprehensive ten-year, seventy million dollars program launched by him, thousands of computers were placed in classrooms, starting from kindergarten up through the fifth grade. Also, using 800 million dollars earmarked for the State's public school system, over sixty new schools were built and hundreds more were renovated. In addition, the Center for Professional Development helped train over 15,000 instructors and educators, statewide.

Caperton's first term also included many other important improvements for West Virginia, including the 1991 Rural Health

Initiative Act, stringent environmental legislation, highway renovations, and over 75,000 new jobs. Caperton's impressive job performance garnered him a second term by a landslide in 1992.

Caperton is married to Maestra Rachael Worby. He has two sons.

UNDERWOOD, CECIL HARLAND (1922-), twenty-fourth and thirty-first governor of West Virginia (1957-1961, 1996-), was born in Joseph Mills, West Virginia on November 5, 1922.

Underwood attended Salem College where he earned an A.B. degree in 1943, and continued his studies at West Virginia University, receiving an M.A. degree in 1952. Between 1943 and 1946 Underwood was a high school biology teacher, and from 1946 until 1950, was assistant to the president of Marietta College. Between 1950 and 1956 he was vice president in charge of public relations at his alma mater, Salem College.

Entering the political arena, Underwood was elected to the West Virginia House of Delegates, a post he served in from 1944 to 1956. Underwood ran for the governorship of West Virginia on the Republican ticket in 1956, defeating his Democratic opponent, R. Mollohan, and taking office on January 21, 1957.

During Underwood's tenure, property taxation was no longer allowed on money kept in banks, and county school districts were given the authority to make improvements needed in public schools. In addition, a vocational training program was set up for unemployed people who wanted a second chance. Also, a Department of Mental Health was established.

Unable to succeed himself by law as Governor, Underwood stepped down on January 16, 1961. After leaving office he served as Vice President the Island Creek Coal Company, between 1961 and 1964. The following year he became Director of Civic Affairs for the Monsanto Company, serving in that post until 1967, when he became vice president of that firm. Between 1968 and 1975 he was President of the Franswood Corporation, and from 1976 to 1978 he was a field underwriter for New York Life Insurance Company. Along with his other corporate interests, Underwood also served as president of his own company, Cecil H. Underwood Associates from 1963 to 1980.

Various other business interests included: President, Morgantown (W.V.) Industrial Park, Inc., 1983; President, Software Valley, 1989-92; and President, Mon View Heights of West Virginia, 1993.

Underwood made two more attempts at the governorship, but was defeated by Democrat Hulett C. Smith, in 1964, and by Democrat John D. Rockefeller, in 1976. However, in 1996, he was re-elected to another term as governor of West Virginia, defeating his Democratic opponent, Charlotte Pritt.

Underwood is married to Hovah Hall, and the couple has three children.

DICTIONARY OF PLACES

Population figures and demographic information are official U.S. Census Bureau finals for 1990. When two figures are shown, separated by a slash, the first figure is the 1990 and the second is the U.S. Census Bureau 1999 estimate—the most recent available. Year 2000 census supplements will be available in the Fall of 2001.

ALDERSON, Town; Greenbrier & Monroe Counties; Pop. 1,375 / 1,160; Zip Code 24910; Elev. 1552; Lat. 37-43-36 N, Long. 080-38-38 W; The town is named in honor of pioneer Baptist preacher, Rev. John Alderson.

ANAWALT, Town; McDowell County; Pop. 652 / 259; Zip Code 24808; Elev. 1687; Lat. 37-20-06 N, Long. 081-26-22 W; The town was incorporated in 1949 and named after local business manager C. Anawalt.

ANMOORE, Town; Harrison County; Pop. 865; Zip Code 26323; Elev. 1010; Lat. 39-15-27 N, Long. 080-17-27 W; Originally called Steelton, the name was later changed to recall a local woman, Ann Moore.

ANSTED, Town; Fayette County; Pop. 1,952 / 1,609; Zip Code 25812; Elev. 1312; Lat. 38-08-12 N, Long. 081-06-02 W; Incorporated in 1891 and named after London geologist Professor D.T. Anstead.

ATHENS, Town; Mercer County; Pop. 1,147 / 1,068; The site of a teachers college, the town is named after the ancient center of learning. Athens.

AUBURN, Town; Ritchie County; Pop. 116 / 89; Zip Code 26325; Lat. 39-05-45 N, Long. 080-51-14 W; Named for an early settler.

BANCROFT, Town; Putnam County; Pop. 528 / 462; Zip Code 25011; Elev. 587; Lat. 38-30-37 N, Long. 081-50-28 W; The town is named after local coal mine operator, George Bancroft.

BARBOURSVILLE, Village; Cabell County; Pop. 2,871 / 3,344; Zip Code 25504; Lat. 38-24-31 N, Long. 082-17-29 W; Founded in 1813 and named in honor of Phillip Barbour.

BARRACKVILLE, Town; Marion County; Pop. 1,815 / 1,360; Zip Code 26559; Lat. 39-30-18 N, Long. 080-10-01 W; The town's name honors George Barrack, the first settler.

BATH (BERKELEY SPRINGS), Town; Morgan; Pop. 789 / 844; Zip Code 25411; Elev. 612; Lat. 39-37-42 N, Long. 078-13-31 W; Descriptively named for the warm mineral springs in the town.

BAYARD, Town; Grant County; Pop. 540 / 413; Zip Code 26707; Lat. 39-16-13 N, Long. 079-22-02 W; Named in 1882 for President Grover Cleveland's cabinet member, Thomas Bayard.

BECKLEY, City; Raleigh County Seat; Pop. 20,492 / 19,228; Zip Code 258+; Lat. 37-46-57 N, Long. 081-11-17 W; The town's name honors U.S. soldier and government official John Beckley.

BEECH BOTTOM, Village; Brooke County; Pop. 507 / 295; Zip Code 26030; Elev. 689; Lat. 40-13-35 N, Long. 080-39-05 W; First settled in 1773 and descriptively named for its location along a beech covered river shallow, or bottom.

BELINGTON, Town; Barbour County; Pop. 2,038 / 1,969; Zip Code 26250; Elev. 1704; Lat. 39-01-20 N, Long. 079-56-13 W; The town's name remembers pro-Civil War merchant John Begun.

BELLE, Town; Kanawha County; Pop. 1,621 / 1,242; Zip Code 250+; Lat. 38-15-11 N, Long. 081-33-05 W; Named after the first postmaster, Belle Gardner Reynolds.

BELMONT, City; Pleasants County; Pop. 887 / 1,086; Zip Code 26134; Lat. 39-22-45 N, Long. 081-15-46 W; Founded in 1853 and named for one of two prominent men whose first name was Benjamin.

BENWOOD, City; Marshall County; Pop. 1,994 / 1,563; Zip Code 26031; Lat. 40-01-34 N, Long. 080-45-09 W; Founded in 1853 and honoring one of two prominent men whose first name was Benjamin.

BETHANY, Town; Brooke County; Pop. 1,336 / 1,041; Zip Code 26032; Lat. 40-12-21 N, Long. 080-33-34 W; Settled in 1847 and given a Biblical town name.

BETHLEHEM, Village; Ohio County; Pop. 2,677 / 2,648; Named for the biblical village where Jesus was born.

BEVERLY, Town; Randolph County; Pop. 475 / 818; Zip Code 26253; Lat. 38-50-34 N, Long. 079-52-23 W; Founded in 1790 and named in honor of Beverly Randolph, mother of a governor of Virginia during this time.

BLACKSVILLE, Town; Monongalia County; Pop. 248 / 157; Zip Code 26521; Lat. 39-43-06 N, Long. 080-12-42 W; The town was laid out in 1829 by David Black. It is named in his honor.

BLUEFIELD, City; Mercer County; Pop. 16,060 / 12,361; Zip Code 24701; First settled in 1887 and named for the blue flowers growing locally.

BOLIVAR, Town; Jefferson County; Pop. 672 / 1,009; The town's name honors General Simon Bolivar, Democrat-Liberator of South America.

BRAMWELL, Town; Mercer County; Pop. 989 / 542; Zip Code 24715; Elev. 2253; The town's name remembers an English engineer who lived in the area.

BRIDGEPORT, City; Harrison County; Pop. 6,604 / 7,790; Zip Code 26330; Elev. 987; Lat. 39-17-28 N, Long. 080-15-07 W; Descriptively named when the first bridge in the county was built here in 1803.

BRUCETON MILLS, Town; Preston County; Pop. 296 / 129; Zip Code 26525; Lat. 39-39-32 N, Long. 079-38-28 W; Settled in 1853 and named by pioneer John Huffman for his stepfather.

BUCKHANNON, City; Upshur County Seat; Pop. 6,820 / 6,628; Zip Code 26201; Elev. 1443; Lat. 38-59-14 N, Long. 080-13-03 W; The town takes its name from the Buckhannon River.

BUFFALO, Town; Putnam County; Pop. 1,034 / 1,041; Zip Code 25033; Elev. 580; Lat. 38-37-10 N, Long. 081-58-43 W; Established in the 1840s and named for an old bison trail in the area.

BURNSVILLE, Town; Broxton County; Pop. 531 / 483; Zip Code 26335; Lat. 38-51-28 N, Long. 080-39-31 W; The town's name remembers lumber businessman John Miller Burns.

CAIRO, Town; Ritchie County; Pop. 428 / 295; Zip Code 26337; Elev. 678; Lat. 39-12-30 N, Long. 081-09-23 W; The first settlers named the area after Cairo, Egypt because of its fertile river land.

CAMDEN-ON-GAULEY, Town; Webster County; Pop. 236 / 157; Zip Code 26208; Elev. 2029; Lat. 38-21-55 N, Long. 080-35-41 W; Named for Senator John Camden combined with its location on the Gauley River.

CAMERON, City; Marshall County; Pop. 1,474 / 1,150; Zip Code 26033; Elev. 1060; Lat. 39-49-44 N, Long. 080-34-06 W; Founded in 1861 and named for railroad agent Samuel Cameron.

CAPON BRIDGE, Town; Hampshire County; Pop. 191 / 234; Zip Code 26823; Lat. 39-07-30 N, Long. 078-29-15 W; Descriptively named as a bridge site across the Cacapon River.

CASS, Town; Pocahontas County; Pop. 148; Zip Code 24927; Lat. 38-23-50 N, Long. 079-54-55 W; The town is named after 1890s era lumber businessman Joseph Cass.

CEDAR GROVE, Town; Kanawha County; Pop. 1,479 / 1,108; Zip Code 25039; Elev. 618; Lat. 38-13-13 N, Long. 081-25-42 W; First settled in 1774 and descriptively named for a large cedar grove in the area.

CEREDO, City; Wayne County; Pop. 2,255 / 1,859; Zip Code 25507; Elev. 552; Lat. 38-23-54 N, Long. 082-34-07 W; Settled in 1857 and named for the roman goddess of agriculture, Ceres.

CHAPMANVILLE, Town; Logan County; Pop. 1,164 / 1,201; Zip Code 25508; Elev. 650; Lat. 37-58-26 N, Long. 082-01-10 W; Established in 1800 and named after early postmaster Ned Chapman.

CHARLES TOWN, City; Jefferson County Seat; Pop. 2,857 / 3,019; Zip Code 25414; Lat. 39-17-14 N, Long. 077-51-32 W; The town's name honors George Washington's brother, Charles.

CHARLESTON, City; Kanawha County Seat and Capital of West Virginia; Pop. 63,968 / 54,598; Zip Code 253+; Lat. 38-20-53 N, Long. 081-37-53 W; Settled in 1794 and named in honor of Charles Clendenin.

CHESAPEAKE, Town; Kanawha County; Pop. 2,364 / 1,835; Named after the local Chesapeake and Ohio Railroad.

CHESTER, City; Hancock County; Pop. 3,297 / 2,648; Zip Code 26034; Elev. 703; Lat. 40-36-51 N, Long. 080-33-58 W; Founded in 1896 and named after the English city.

CLARKSBURG, City; Harrison County Seat; Pop. 22,371 / 17,297; Zip Code 26301; Elev. 1011; Lat. 39-16-29 N, Long. 080-19-11 W; Clarksburg's name honors Revolutionary War patriot George Rogers Clark.

CLAY, Town; Clay County Seat; Pop. 940 / 606; Zip Code 25043; Elev. 708; Lat. 38-28-30 N, Long. 081-05-00 W; Named in honor of statesman Henry Clay.

CLENDENIN, Town; Kanawha County; Pop. 1,373 / 1,058; Zip Code 25045; Elev. 629; Lat. 38-29-22 N, Long. 081-20-53 W; First settled in 1877 and named for pioneer Charles Clendenin.

COWEN, Town; Webster County; Pop. 723 / 512; Zip Code 26206; Lat. 38-24-35 N, Long. 080-33-24 W; Founded in 1899 and named in honor of railroad director John Cowen.

DANVILLE, Town; Boone County; Pop. 727 / 571; Zip Code 25053; Elev. 692; Lat. 38-04-42 N, Long. 081-49-57 W; Danville's name remembers Dan Rock, the first postmaster.

DAVIS, Town; Tucker County; Pop. 979 / 734; Zip Code 26260; Elev. 3099; Lat. 39-07-52 N, Long. 079-27-50 W; Named in honor of U.S. Senator from West Virginia, Henry G. Davis.

DAVY, Town; McDowell County; Pop. 882 / 320; Zip Code 24828; Elev. 1189; Lat. 37-28-43 N, Long. 081-39-04 W; Named after Davy Creek, which runs through the town.

DELBARTON, Town; Mingo County; Pop. 981 / 574; Zip Code 25670; Lat. 37-42-26 N, Long. 082-11-12 W; The town is named after an official of a local land company.

DUNBAR, City; Kanawha County; Pop. 9,285 / 8,271; Zip Code 25064; Elev. 603; Lat. 38-22-31 N, Long. 081-44-35 W; Incorporated in the 1920s and named in honor of Charleston banker Dunbar Baines.

DURBIN, Town; Pocahontas County; Pop. 379 / 284; Zip Code 26264; Elev. 2732; Lat. 38-32-51 N, Long. 079-49-38 W; Founded in the late nineteenth century and named after bank clerk Charles Durbin.

EAST BANK, Town; Kanawha County; Pop. 1,155 / 796; Zip Code 25067; Lat. 38-11-11 N, Long. 081-27-51 W; Descriptively named for its location on the east bank of the Kanawha River.

ELEANOR, Town; Putnam County; Pop. 1,282 / 1,377; Zip Code 25070; Elev. 574; Lat. 38-32-26 N, Long. 081-56-10 W; Named in honor of Eleanor Roosevelt.

ELIZABETH, Town; Wirt County Seat; Pop. 856 / 991; Zip Code 26143; Elev. 646, Lat. 39-03-40 N, Long. 081-23-54 W; The town's name remembers the daughter-in-law of founded William Beauchamp.

ELK GARDEN, Town; Mineral County; Pop. 291 / 261; Zip Code 26717; Elev. 2288; Lat. 39-23-08 N, Long. 079-09-26 W; Descriptively named by the early settlers for the abundant elk.

ELKINS, City; Randolph County Seat; Pop. 8,536 / 8,349; Zip Code 26241; Elev. 1930; Lat. 38-55-31 N, Long. 079-51-04 W; Settled in 1889 and named in honor of Senator Stephen Elkins.

ELLENBORO, Town; Ritchie County; Pop. 357 / 453; Zip Code 26346; Elev. 807; Lat. 39-15-52 N, Long. 081-03-24 W; Named after the daughter of the family, the Williamson's, who donated the right-of-way to the railroad.

FAIRMONT, City; Marion County Seat; Pop. 23,863 / 20,029; Zip Code 265+; Elev. 991; Lat. 39-28-12 N, Long. 080-09-37 W; Descriptively named in 1843 for the town's location on a hill.

FAIRVIEW, Town; Marion County; Pop. 759 / 418; Zip Code 26570; Elev. 1000; Lat. 39-35-36 N, Long. 080-14-45 W; Incorporated in 1891 and named for the clear view of the countryside from the townsite.

FALLING SPRING, Town; Greenbrier County; Pop. 240 / 177; Named for the spring that ran through the town.

FARMINGTON, Town; Marion County; Pop. 583 / 378; Zip Code 26571; Lat. 39-30-47 N, Long. 080-14-54 W; Originally Underwood, the railroad renamed the town after the many farmers in the area.

FAYETTEVILLE, Town; Fayette County Seat; Pop. 2,366 / 2,101; Zip Code 25840; Elev. 1821; Lat. 38-03-20 N, Long. 081-06-07 W; The town's name honors Revolutionary War hero Marquis Lafayette.

FLATWOODS, Town; Braxton County; Pop. 405 / 335; Zip Code 26621; Elev. 1071; Lat. 38-43-25 N, Long. 080-39-10 W; The town is descriptively named for the wooded level land in the area.

FLEMINGTON, Town; Taylor County; Pop. 452 / 338; Zip Code 26347; Lat. 39-16-03 N, Long. 080-07-47 W; Founded in 1860 and named for an early settler.

FOLLANSBEE, City; Brooke County; Pop. 3,994 / 3,229; Zip Code 26037; Lat. 40-06-15 N, Long. 080-05-38 W; The city takes its name from the Follansbee Brothers Steel Mill Company.

FORT GAY, Town; Wayne County; Pop. 886 / 840; Zip Code 25514; Lat. 38-07-17 N, Long. 082-35-42 W; The site of a Civil War fort combined with a local settlers surname titled the town.

FRANKLIN, Town; Pendleton County Seat; Pop. 780 / 860; Zip Code 26807; Elev. 1739; Lat. 38-38-51 N, Long. 079-19-48 W; Named for the surveyor who mapped the area in 1769.

FRIENDLY, Town; Tyler County; Pop. 242 / 133; Zip Code 26146; Lat. 39-30-53 N, Long. 081-03-41 W; The town is named after Friend Williamson, a descendent of the first settler.

GARY, City; McDowell County; Pop. 2,233 / 1,047; Zip Code 24836; Lat. 37-21-47 N, Long. 081-32-56 W; Named in honor of Elbert Gary, an official of U.S. Steel Corporation.

GASSAWAY, Town; Braxton County; Pop. 1,225 / 977; Zip Code 26624; Elev. 841; Lat. 38-40-23 N, Long. 080-46-22 W; Senator Henry Gassaway Davis is remembered in the town's name.

GAULEY BRIDGE, Town; Fayette County; Pop. 1,177 / 669; Zip Code 25085; Lat. 38-09-56 N, Long. 081-11-02 W; Named after the Gauley River, which flows through the town.

GILBERT, Town; Mingo County; Pop. 757 / 425; Zip Code 25621; Elev. 829; Lat. 37-37-01 N, Long. 081-52-02 W; An early traveler named Gilbert was killed near here. Both the creek and town are named after him.

GLASGOW, Town; Kanawha County; Pop. 1,031 / 859; Zip Code 25086; Lat. 38-12-47 N, Long. 081-25-29 W; Founded in 1914 and named after Glasgow, Scotland.

GLEN DALE, City; Marshall County; Pop. 1,875 / 1,596; Zip Code 26038; Lat. 40-01-48 N, Long. 080-43-07 W; The city is named after Glendale, a local farm.

GLENVILLE, Town; Gilmer County Seat; Pop. 2,155 / 1,835; Descriptively named for a sheltered place, or glen, here at the bend of the little Kanawha River.

GRAFTON, City; Taylor County; Pop. 6,845 / 5,685; Zip Code 26354; Lat. 39-20-03 N, Long. 080-01-06 W; Named in honor of civil engineer John Grafton, who brought the Baltimore and Ohio Railroad here in 1856.

GRANT TOWN, Town; Marion County; Pop. 987 / 544; Zip Code 26574; Lat. 39-33-25 N, Long. 080-10-44 W; Robert Grant, a Boston investor, held mining claims in the area. The town is named after him.

GRANTSVILLE, Town; Calhoun County Seat; Pop. 788; Zip Code 26147; Elev. 713; Lat. 38-55-19 N, Long. 081-05-39 W; Established shortly after the Civil War and named in honor of General U.S. Grant.

GRANVILLE, Town; Monongalia County; Pop. 992 / 808; Zip Code 26534; Elev. 833; Lat. 39-38-44 N, Long. 079-59-25 W; Captain Felix Scott named the town after an island in the nearby river.

HAMBLETON, Town; Tucker County; Pop. 403 / 250; Zip Code 26269; Elev. 1685; Lat. 39-04-48 N, Long. 079-38-37 W; Founded in 1889 and named in honor of Baltimore banker John Hambleton.

HAMLIN, Town; Lincoln County Seat; Pop. 1,219; Zip Code 25523; Elev. 673; Lat. 38-16-45 N, Long. 082-06-17 W; Named after the Methodist Hamlin Chapel founded here.

HANDLEY, Town; Kanawha County; Pop. 633 / 294; Zip Code 25102; Lat. 38-11-19 N, Long. 081-22-12 W; Named for an official of the Wyoming Manufacturing Company.

HARMAN, Town; Randolph County; Pop. 181 / 123; Zip Code 26270; Elev. 2360; Lat. 38-55-16 N, Long. 079-31-30 W; The Rev. Asa Harman donated the land for the town. It is named in his honor.

HARPERS FERRY, Town; Jefferson County; Pop. 361 / 317; Zip Code 25410; Elev. 484; Lat. 39-21-43 N, Long. 077-45-53 W; Robert Harper built a ferry across the rivers that merge here. The town was named for him.

HARRISVILLE, Town; Ritchie County Seat; Pop. 1,673 / 1,942; Zip Code 26362; Elev. 873; Lat. 39-12-34 N, Long. 081-03-15 W; Named in honor of the Harris family, who settled here in 1808.

HENDRICKS, Town; Tucker County; Pop. 390 / 287; Zip Code 26271; Lat. 39-04-32 N, Long. 079-37-55 W; Founded in 1894 and named in honor of Vice-President, Thomas Hendricks.

HILLSBORO, Village; Pocahontas County; Pop. 276 / 200; Zip Code 24946; Elev. 2303; Lat. 38-08-09 N, Long. 080-12-46 W; John Hill founded the town. It is named in his honor.

HINTON, City; Summers County Seat; Pop. 4,622 / 3,351; Zip Code 25951; Elev. 1449; Lat. 37-40-10 N, Long. 080-53-03 W; The town's name honors lawyer John Hinton, on early pioneer in the county.

HUNDRED, Town; Wetzel County; Pop. 485 / 330; Zip Code 26575; Elev. 1021; Lat. 39-41-04 N, Long. 080-27-21 W; Pioneer Henry Church died here in 1860 at age 109. The town's name recalls that memorable feat.

HUNTINGTON, City; Cabell & Wayne Counties; Cabell County Seat; Pop. 63,684 / 52,273; Zip Code 257+; Elev. 569; Lat. 38-24-34 N, Long. 082-26-59 W; Founded in 1871 and named in honor of Collis Huntington. president of the Chesapeake and Ohio Railroad.

HURRICANE, City; Putnam County; Pop. 3,751 / 5,900; Zip Code 25526; Lat. 38-26-08 N, Long. 082-01-21 W; The city is named after nearby Hurricane Creek.

HUTTONSVILLE, Town; Randolph County; Pop. 242 / 232; Zip Code 26273; Elev. 2053; Lat. 38-42-54 N, Long. 079-58-34 W; Pioneer Jonathan Hutton settled here in 1795. The town is named after him.

IAEGER, Town; McDowell County; Pop. 833 / 452; Zip Code 24844; Elev. 981; Lat. 37-27-49 N, Long. 081-49-03 W; Colonel William Iaeger owned 45,000 acres here in the 1880s. The town is named after him.

JANE LEW, Town; Lewis County; Pop. 406 / 440; Zip Code 26378; Elev. 1007; Lat. 39-06-40 N, Long. 080-24-35 W; Settled in 1835 and named in honor of the mother of town founder, Lewis Maxwell.

JUNIOR, Town; Barbour County; Pop. 591 / 526; Zip Code 26275; Lat. 38-58-51 N, Long. 079-57-05 W; Senator Henry Davis named the town for his son, or junior, John Davis.

KENOVA, City; Wayne County; Pop. 4,454 / 3,647; Zip Code 25530; Elev. 561; Lat. 38-24-01 N, Long. 082-34-51 W; Established in 1889 and named as the meeting place of three states, Kentucky, Ohio, and West Virginia.

KERMIT, Town; Mingo County; Pop. 705 / 308; Zip Code 25674; Elev. 625; Lat. 37-50-28 N, Long. 082-24-11 W; Founded in 1906 and named in honor of President Theodore Roosevelt's son Kermit.

KEYSER, City; Mineral County Seat; Pop. 6,569 / 5,532; Zip Code 21726; Elev. 810; Lat. 39-26-26 N, Long. 078-59-00 W; Named for railroad official William Keyser in 1874.

KEYSTONE, City; McDowell County; Pop. 902 / 493; Zip Code 24852; Lat. 37-25-00 N, Long. 081-26-52 W; Originally named Cassville, the name was later changed after the Keystone Cool and Coke Company.

KIMBALL, Town; McDowell County; Pop. 871 / 428; Zip Code 24853; Elev. 1492; Lat. 37-25-38 N, Long. 081-30-29 W; Founded in 1911 and named in honor of Frederick Kimball, president of the Norfolk and Western Railroad.

KINGWOOD, City; Preston County Seat; Pop. 2,877 / 3,416; Zip Code 26537; Elev. 1863; Lat. 39-28-15 N, Long. 079-41-01 W; Named by the Pocahontas Coal Company when they opened a mine here at the beginning of the century.

LEON, Town; Mason County; Pop. 228 / 134; Zip Code 25123; Elev. 569; Lat. 38-44-56 N, Long. 081-57-24 W; Originally Cologne, the name was changed in 1880 to Leon.

LESTER, Town; Raleigh County; Pop. 626 / 417; Zip Code 25865; Lat. 37-44-17 N, Long. 081-18-02 W; The town is named after early settler Champ Lester.

LEWISBURG, City; Greenbrier County Seat; Pop. 3,065 / 3,823; Zip Code 24901; Elev. 2099; Lat. 37-47-59 N, Long. 080-26-42 W; Named in honor of Revolutionary War hero General Andrew Lewis.

LITTLETON, Town; Wetzel County; Pop. 335 / 174; Zip Code 26581; Elev. 946; Lat. 39-41-49 N, Long. 080-30-42 W; Probably named for an early settler.

LOGAN, City; Logan County Seat; Pop. 3,029 / 3,823; Zip Code 25601; Elev. 680; Lat. 37-52-28 N, Long. 081-59-08 W; Originally called Lawnsville and later renamed after Chief Logan of the Cayugas.

LOST CREEK, Town; Harrison County; Pop. 604 / 396; Zip Code 26385; Lat. 39-09-40 N, Long. 080-21-04 W; The town is named after Lost Creek, which runs nearby.

LUMBERPORT, Town; Harrison County; Pop. 939 / 964; Zip Code 26386; Elev. 994; Lat. 39-22-36 N, Long. 080-20-44 W; Founded in 1838 and named for a lumber trade on the nearby Tenmile Creek.

MABSCOTT, Town; Raleigh County; Pop. 1,668 / 1,453; Zip Code 25871; Lat. 37,46-18 N, Long. 081-12-30 W; Incorporated in 1906 and named for the wife of a local coal mine owner.

MADISON, City; Boone County Seat; Pop. 3,228 / 3,267; Zip Code 25130; Elev. 716; Lat. 38-03-37 N, Long. 081-49-28 W; The city is named in honor of President James Madison.

MAN, Town; Logan County; Pop. 1,333 / 853; Zip Code 25635; Elev. 733; Lat. 37-44-38 N, Long. 081-52-34 W; The town is named after the last syllable of representative Ulysses Hinchman who served the state in the 1860s.

MANNINGTON, City; Marion County; Pop. 3,036 / 2,240; Zip Code 26582; Elev. 975; Lat. 39-31-39 N, Long. 080-20-27 W; Founded in 1856 and named for a railroad official.

MARLINTON, Town; Pocahontas County Seat; Pop. 1,352 / 1,514; Zip Code 24954; Elev. 2130; Lat. 38-13-17 N, Long. 080-04-56 W; The town's name honors Jacob Marlin, who was the first settler in the region in 1749.

MARMET, City; Kanawha County; Pop. 2,196 / 1,835; The town took the name of the Marmet Coal Company.

MARTINSBURG, City; Berkeley County Seat; Pop. 13,063 / 15,754; Zip Code 25401; Elev. 457; Lat. 39-27-54 N, Long. 077-58-09 W; Named in honor of Colonel Thomas Martin, a large landowner in the 18th century.

MASON, Town; Mason County; Pop. 1,432 / 1,115; Zip Code 25260; Elev. 581; Lat. 39-01-09 N, Long. 082-01-55 W; Mason is named after George W. Mason, a Virginia statesman.

MASONTOWN, Town; Preston County; Pop. 1,052 / 765; Zip Code 26542; Lat. 39-33-03 N, Long. 079-47-57 W; Storekeeper William Mason left his name on the town when it was founded in 1856.

MATEWAN, Town; Mingo County; Pop. 822 / 567; Zip Code 25678; Elev. 700; Lat. 37-37-18 N, Long. 082-09-36 W; The town is named after Matteawan. New York.

MATOAKA, Town; Mercer County; Pop. 613 / 317; Zip Code 24736; Elev. 2362; A nickname for the famous Indian princess, Pocahontas, given to the town in 1903.

MCMECHEN, City; Marshall County; Pop. 2,402 / 1,453; Zip Code 26040; Elev. 669; Lat. 40-00-23 N, Long. 080-44-29 W; Named in honor of the McMechen family who first settled here in the 1780s.

MEADOW BRIDGE, Town; Fayette County; Pop. 530 / 317; Zip Code 25976; Elev. 2427; Lat. 37-51-42 N, Long. 080-51-17 W; The area is known for its meadows and is named for a bridge over the nearby Meadow Creek.

MIDDLEBOURNE, Town; Tyler County Seat; Pop. 941 / 931; Zip Code 26149; Elev. 745; Lat. 39-29-38 N, Long. 080-54-29 W; Middlebourne means "middle point." The town is named for its location as a middle point to some geographic feature.

MILL CREEK, Town; Randolph County; Pop. 801 / 691; Zip Code 26280; Elev. 2067; Lat. 38-43-53 N, Long. 079-58-16 W; Descriptively named for a large grist mill built on the adjacent creek.

MILTON, Town; Cabell County; Pop. 2,178 / 2,306; Zip Code 25541; Elev. 584; Lat. 38-26-12 N, Long. 082-07-56 W; Milton Reece owned the land when the town was laid out in 1872. It is named for him.

MONONGAH, Town; Marion County; Pop. 1,132 / 996; Founded in 1891 and named after the Monongahela River with the last three letters left off.

MONTGOMERY, City; Fayette & Kanawha Counties; Pop. 3,104 / 1,936; Zip Code 25136; Lat. 38-10-49 N, Long. 081-21-12 W; Named for James Montgomery, on early settler.

MONTROSE, Village; Randolph County; Pop. 129 / 141; Zip Code 26283; Lat. 39-04-02 N, Long. 079-48-38 W; Wild roses grow profusely in the local mountains and gave the town its name.

MOOREFIELD, Town; Hardy County Seat; Pop. 2,257 / 2,487; Zip Code 26836; Elev. 829; Lat. 39-03-24 N, Long. 078-58-09 W; Settled in the 1700s and named after the original landowner, Conrad Moore.

MORGANTOWN, City; Monongalia County Seat; Pop. 27,605 / 29,017; Zip Code 265+; Lat. 39-38-39 N, Long. 079-58-15 W; First settled in 1768 by Zackquill Morgan and named for his family.

MOUNDSVILLE, City; Marshall County Seat; Pop. 12,419 / 9,847; Zip Code 26041; Elev. 692; Lat. 34-55-57 N, Long. 070-38-37 W; Founded in 1831 and descriptively named for a nearby Indian mound.

MOUNT HOPE, City; Fayette County; Pop. 1,849 / 1,580; Zip Code 25880; Elev. 1661; Lat. 37-53-58 N, Long. 081-10-17 W; The city is named for nearby Mount Hope School.

MULLENS, City; Wyoming County; Pop. 2,919 / 1,774; Zip Code 25882; Elev. 1426; Lat. 37-34-47 N, Long. 081-22-47 W; A.J. Mullins donated the land to the Virginia Railroad in exchange far naming the new town for him.

NEW CUMBERLAND, City; Hancock County Seat; Pop. 1,752 / 1,236; Zip Code 26047, Lat. 40-30-05 N, Long. 080-36-38 W; Founded in 1839 as Vernon and later named after the Cumberland Trail.

NEW HAVEN, Town; Mason County; Pop. 1,723 / 1,736; Zip Code 25265; Lat. 38-59-09 N, Long. 081-58-20 W; Settled in the 1850s and named after New Haven, Connecticut.

NEW MARTINSVILLE, City; Wetzel County Seat; Pop. 7,109 / 6,503; Zip Code 26155; Elev. 628; Lat. 39-39-14 N, Long. 080-51-26 W; The city is named after an early settler, Presley Martin.

NEWBURG, Town; Preston County; Pop. 418 / 369; Zip Code 26410; Lat. 39-23-15 N, Long. 079-51-03 W; Settled in the 1850s and named for its being a new town, or burg, on the railroad line.

NITRO, City; Kanawha & Putnam Counties; Pop. 8,074 / 6,727; Zip Code 25143; Lat. 38-25-14 N, Long. 081-50-02 W; The U.S. Government founded on explosives factory here during World War I. The town's name reflects this project.

NORTHFORK, Town; McDowell County; Pop. 660 / 498; Zip Code 24868; Elev. 1708; Lat. 37-24-51 N, Long. 081-26-04 W; Named for its location on the Northfork of the Elkhorn River.

OAK HILL, City; Fayette County; Pop. 7,120 / 6,986; Zip Code 25901; Elev. 1961; Lat. 37-58-43 N, Long. 081-08-59 W; Descriptively named as the town's post office was located on a hill near a large oak tree.

OCEANA, Town; Wyoming County; Pop. 2,143 / 1,697; Zip Code 24870; Elev. 1269; Lat. 37-41-28 N, Long. 081-38-00 W; Founded in 1853 and given a popular female name, Ode.

OSAGE, Town; Monongalia County; Pop. 285; Zip Code 26543; Elev. 907; Lat. 39-39-28 N, Long. 080-00-23 W; The town's name remembers the Osage Indians who lived in the area in the early 1800s.

PADEN CITY, City; Tyler & Wetzel Counties; Pop. 3,671 / 2,857; Zip Code 26159; Lat. 39-36-07 N, Long. 080-56-08 W; Obediah Paden settled here in 1790. The town is named after him.

PARKERSBURG, City; Wood County Seat; Pop. 39,967 / 32,212; Zip Code 261+; Elev. 649; Lat. 39-16-57 N, Long. 081-32-27 W; Alexander Parker was a prominent landowner here by 1810. The town is named after him.

PARSONS, City; Tucker County Seat; Pop. 1,937 / 1,571; Zip Code 26287; Lat. 39-05-41 N, Long. 079-40-42 W; Ward Parsons owned the land upon which the town arose. It is named in his honor.

PAW PAW, Town; Morgan County; Pop. 644 / 546; Zip Code 25434; Elev. 572; Lat. 39-31-57 N, Long. 078-27-34 W; Descriptively named for the many paw paw trees in the area.

PAX, Town; Fayette County; Pop. 274 / 148; Zip Code 25904; Lat. 37-54-36 N, Long. 081-15-51 W; A corrupt spelling of the name of Samuel Pack who settled here in the 1840s.

PENNSBORO, City; Ritchie County; Pop. 1,652 / 1,225; Zip Code 26415; Elev. 867; Lat. 39-17-06 N, Long. 080-58-04 W; A surveyor named Penn laid out the town in the early 1800s. It is named for him.

PETERSBURG, City; Grant County Seat; Pop. 2,084 / 3,075; Zip Code 26847; Lat. 38-59-38 N, Long. 079-07-13 W; Jacob Peterson built the first store here in pioneer days. It is named for him.

PETERSTOWN, Town; Monroe County; Pop. 648 / 594; Zip Code 24963; Elev. 1624; Lat. 37-24-00 N, Long. 080-47-49 W; The town's name remembers Christian Peters who settled here in the 1780s.

PHILIPPI, City; Barbour County Seat; Pop. 3,194 / 3,137; Zip Code 26416; Elev. 1307; Lat. 39-09-19 N, Long. 080-02-35 W; Founded in 1844 and named in honor of Phillip P. Barbour.

PIEDMONT, Town; Mineral County; Pop. 1,491 / 930; Zip Code 26750; Lat. 39-28-43 N, Long. 079-02-43 W; A French word meaning "foot of the mountain," and referring to a ridge that divides the Potomac River watershed from the Ohio River watershed.

PINE GROVE, Town; Wetzel County; Pop. 767 / 634; Zip Code 26419; Elev. 1155; Lat. 39-33-49 N, Long. 080-40-48 W; Descriptively named for a large grove of nearby pines.

PINEVILLE, Town; Wyoming County Seat; Pop. 1,140 / 782; Zip Code 248+; Elev. 1321; Lat. 37-36-16 N, Long. 081-36-50 W; Named for the many pine trees in the region.

POCA, Town; Putnam County; Pop. 1,142 / 1,382; Zip Code 25159; Lat. 38-28-26 N, Long. 081-48-53 W; Named after the Pocatalico River. This is an Indian word meaning "fat dog."

POINT PLEASANT, City; Mason County Seat; Pop. 5,682 / 5,350; Zip Code 25550; Lat. 38-51-44 N, Long. 082-07-430 W; The junction of the Kanawha and Ohio Rivers, the place is descriptively name for its location.

PRATT, Town; Kanawha County; Pop. 821 / 608; Zip Code 25162; Lat. 38-12-32 N, Long. 081-25-27 W; The Charles Pratt Company owned land in the area and gave its name to the town.

PULLMAN, Town; Ritchie County; Pop. 196 / 107; Zip Code 26421; Lat. 39-11-17 N, Long. 080-56-51 W; Pullman was named by the Past Office, probably for George M. Pullman, the owner of the Pullman Palace Car Company.

QUINWOOD, Town; Greenbrier County; Pop. 460 / 511; Zip Code 25981; Lat. 38-03-29 N, Long. 080-42-24 W; The city was founded in 1919 by Quin Morton and W.S. Wood, settlers from Charleston.

RAINELLE, Town; Greenbrier County; Pop. 1,983 / 1,722; Zip Code 25962; Lat. 37-58-09 N, Long. 080-46-02 W; The town is named after lumber businessmen John and W.T. Raine.

RANSON, Town, Jefferson County; Pop. 2,471; Zip Code 25438; Lat. 39-18-01 N, Long. 077-51-37 W; The Ransom family owned the land where the town was built. The town was incorporated in 1910 and named for them.

RAVENSWOOD, City; Jackson County; Pop. 4,126 / 4,603; Zip Code 26164; Lat. 38-57-23 N, Long. 081-45-41 W. The town was laid out in 1852. It was originally known as Ravensworth, but the name was misspelled consistently on early maps as Ravenswood. It was probably named for an English family.

REEDSVILLE, Town, Preston County; Pop. 564 / 497; Zip Code 26547; Lat. 39-30-39 N, Long. 079-47-55 W; James Reed, owner of the town site, settled here in 1827. The town was named for him.

REEDY, Town; Roane County; Pop. 338 / 262; Zip Code 25270; Lat. 38-53-59 N, Long. 081-25-29 W; The town takes its name from Reedy Creek, which flows through the town.

RHODELL, Town; Raleigh County; Pop. 472 / 226; Zip Code 25915; Elev. 1618; Lat. 37-36-24 N, Long. 081-18-11 W; Founded in 1907 by I.J. Rhodes, among others, it is named in his honor.

RICHWOOD, City; Nicholas County; Pop. 3,568 / 2,760; Zip Code 26261; Lat. 38-13-30 N, Long. 080-31-55 W; Named in 1881 to reflect the rich timber stock in the area.

RIDGELEY, Town; Mineral County; Pop. 994 / 716; Zip Code 26753; Lat. 39-38-28 N, Long. 078-46-21 W; Named after the original landowner of the site.

RIPLEY, City; Jackson County Seat; Pop. 3,464 / 3,564; Zip Code 25271; Lat. 38-48-58 N, Long. 081-42-17 W; The town's name remembers preacher Harry Ripley who died here in 1831.

RIVESVILLE, Town; Marion County; Pop. 1,327 / 3,564; Zip Code 265+; Lat. 39-32-35 N, Long. 080-08-41 W; Named in honor of William C. Rives, a U.S. Senator from Virginia in the early 1800s.

ROMNEY, City; Hampshire County Seat; Pop. 2,094 / 2,520; Zip Code 26757; Lat. 39-20-39 N, Long. 078-45-23 W; Lord Fairfax named the area after an English seaport in 1762.

RONCEVERTE, City; Greenbrier County; Pop. 2,312 / 1,687; Zip Code 24970; Elev. 1668; Lat. 37-44-57 N, Long. 080-28-06 W; On the Greenbrier River, the name is French for Greenbrier.

ROWLESBURG, Town; Preston County; Pop. 966 / 641; Zip Code 26425; Elev. 1406; Lat. 39-20-48 N, Long. 079-40-34 W; Given its name in 1852 for a railroad official named Rowles.

RUPERT, Town; Greenbrier County; Pop. 1,276 / 1,048; Zip Code 25984; Elev. 2432; Lat. 37-57-47 N, Long. 080-41-23 W; Dr. Cyrus Rupert practiced here for several decades. The town is named after him.

ST. ALBANS, City; Kanawha County; Pop. 12,402 / 11,861; Zip Code 25177; Lat. 38-22-45 N, Long. 081-48-51 W; Founded in 1816 and later named by a railroad engineer after the English city.

ST. MARYS, City; Pleasants County Seat; Pop. 2,219 / 2,068; Zip Code 26170; Elev. 628; Lat. 39-24-21 N, Long. 081-11-30 W; Established by Alexander Creel who had a religious vision here in 1849.

SALEM, City; Harrison County; Pop. 2,706 / 2,832; Zip Code 26426; Elev. 2144; Settlers from New Salem, New Jersey arrived here in 1788 and named the place for their former home.

SHEPHERDSTOWN, Town; Jefferson County; Pop. 1,791 / 1,903; Zip Code 25443; Elev. 406; Lat. 39-25-57 N, Long. 077-48-23 W; Named in honor of Thomas Shepard who laid out the town in 1764.

SHINNSTON, City; Harrison County; Pop. 3,059 / 2,684; Zip Code 26431; Lat. 39-23-40 N, Long. 080-17-40 W; Quaker Levi Shinn settled here in 1773. The town is named for him.

SISTERSVILLE, City; Tyler County; Pop. 2,367 / 1,764; Zip Code 26175; Elev. 647; Lat. 39-33-47 N, Long. 080-59-47 W; Two sisters, Delilah and Sarah Wells, owned the site in 1839 when the town incorporated and so suggested the name.

SMITHERS, City; Fayette & Kanawha Counties; Pop. 1,482 / 1,148; Zip Code 25186; Elev. 643; Lat. 38-10-53 N, Long. 081-20-24 W; The city is named after an early pioneer family.

SMITHFIELD, Town; Wetzel County; Pop. 278 / 183; Zip Code 26437; Lat. 39-30-04 N, Long. 080-33-52 W; Henry Smith, a local merchant, had the town named after him in the 1880s.

SOPHIA, Town; Raleigh County; Pop. 1,216 / 1,313; Zip Code 25921; Lat. 37-42-40 N, Long. 081-14-55 W; Named for Sophia McGinnis, a relative of a prominent official, when the town incorporated in 1912.

SOUTH CHARLESTON, City; Kanawha County; Pop. 15,968 / 14,203; Descriptively named for its location near Charleston.

SPENCER, City; Roane County Seat; Pop. 2,799 / 2,343; Zip Code 25276; Elev. 749; Lat. 38-48-11 N, Long. 081-21-11 W; Originally Tanners Crossroads, the name was later changed to honor Judge Spencer Roan.

STAR CITY, Town; Monongalia County; Pop. 1,464 / 1,347; The site of a glass-making industry, the town was incorporated in 1907 and named for the Star Glass Company.

STONEWOOD, City; Harrison County; Pop. 2,058 / 2,393; Incorporated in 1947 and given the made-up name of Stonewood, which was chosen as a result of a naming contest for the new community.

SUMMERSVILLE, Town; Nicholas County; Pop. 2,972 / 3,698; Zip Code 26651; Elev. 1894; Lat. 38-16-52 N, Long. 080-51-06 W; Founded in 1824 and named in honor of Judge Lewis Summers.

SUTTON, Town; Braxton County; Pop. 1,192 / 894; Zip Code 266+; Lat. 38-39-53 N, Long. 080-42-39 W; John D. Sutton arrived here in 1808. The town is named in his honor.

SYLVESTER, Town; Boone County; Pop. 256 / 189; Zip Code 25193; Lat. 38-00-37 N, Long. 081-33-30 W; Named for a local family when incorporated in 1952.

TERRA ALTA, Town; Preston County; Pop. 1,946 / 1,948; Zip Code 26764; Elev. 2559; Lat. 39-26-38 N, Long. 079-32-34 W; Originally Green Glades, the name was later changed to Terra Alta, Latin for "high land." The name reflects the Communities 2559-ft. altitude.

THOMAS, City; Tucker County; Pop. 747 / 550; Zip Code 26292; Lat. 39-08-55 N, Long. 079-29-44 W; Named in 1892 for prominent landowner Colonel Thomas Davis.

TRIADELPHIA, Town; Ohio County; Pop. 1,461 / 678; Zip Code 26059; Lat. 40-06-11 N, Long. 080-36-18 W; Three brothers donated the land for the townsite in 1829. The name is a Greek word meaning "three brothers."

TUNNELTON, Town; Preston County; Pop. 510 / 328; Zip Code 26444; Elev. 1816; Lat. 39-23-34 N, Long. 079-44-50 W; Descriptively named for its location near a Baltimore and Ohio Railroad tunnel.

UNION, Town; Monroe County Seat; Pop. 743 / 608; Zip Code 24983; Elev. 2071; Lat. 37-35-26 N, Long. 080-32-35 W; Founded in 1800 and named for its function as a meeting place for soldiers in the various Indian wars.

VALLEY GROVE, Village; Ohio County; Pop. 597 / 529; Zip Code 26060; Lat. 40-05-26 N, Long. 080-33-48 W; Named around 1900 for a favored picnic spot, Valley Grove.

VIENNA, City; Wood County; Pop. 11,618 / 11,273; Dr. Joseph Spencer laid out the town in 1795 and named it after Vienna, Virginia.

WAR, City; McDowell County; Pop. 2,158 / 849; Zip Code 24892; Lat. 37-18-13 N, Long. 081-41-12 W; Named after War Creek, a name that remembers the various Indian wars that occurred in the region.

WARDENSVILLE, Town; Hardy County; Pop. 241 / 366; Zip Code 26851; Elev. 1011; Lat. 39-04-33 N, Long. 078-35-33 W; William Warden built a fort here in 1750. The town's name honors its early founder.

WAYNE, Town; Wayne County Seat; Pop. 1,495 / 1,171; Zip Code 25570; Elev. 708; Lat. 38-13-23 N, Long. 082-26-32 W; Established in 1842 and named in honor of Revolutionary War General Anthony Wayne.

WEIRTON, City; Brook. B Hancock Counties; Pop. 24,736 / 21,080; Zip Code 26062; Lat. 40-19-22 N, Long. 080-25-04 W; The Weir brothers started a tin plate factory here in 1909 and gave their name to the town.

WELCH, City; McDowell County Seat; Pop. 3,885 / 2,640; Zip Code 24801; Lat. 37-26-12 N, Long. 081-35-05 W; Former confederate officer, Captain Welch, founded the town in 1893. It is named after him.

WELLSBURG, City; Brook. County Seat; Pop. 3,963 / 2,618; Zip Code 26070; Lat. 40-16-46 N, Long. 080-26-34 W; Founded in 1791 as Charles Town, but later changed after a Mr. Alexander Wells.

WEST HAMLIN, Town; Lincoln County; Pop. 643 / 450; Zip Code 25571; Elev. 590; Lat. 38-17-18 N, Long. 082-11-43 W; Descriptively named for its location west of Hamlin.

WEST LIBERTY, Town; Ohio County; Pop. 744 / 435; Zip Code 26074; Lat. 40-10-12 N, Long. 080-35-41 W; Settled in the 1770s and named for its function as a meeting place for Revolutionary War patriots.

WEST LOGAN, Town; Logan County; Pop. 630 / 533; Descriptively named for its location west of Logan.

WEST MILFORD, Town; Harrison County; Pop. 510 / 564; Zip Code 26451; Lat. 39-12-06 N, Long. 080-24-03 W; Two settlers built a mill here in 1821 on the West Fork River, and thus named the town.

WEST UNION, Town; Doddridge County Seat; Pop. 1,090 / 860; Zip Code 26456; Elev. 828; Lat. 39-17-46 N, Long. 080-46-38 W; Originally Lewisport, the town grew on both sides of the Middle Island Creek and later had the name changed to West Union.

WESTON, City; Lewis County Seat; Pop. 6,250 / 5,020; Zip Code 26452; Elev. 1017; Lat. 39-02-36 N, Long. 080-28-06 W; Founded in 1818 on the West River and thus named.

WESTOVER, City; Monongalia County; Pop. 4,884 / 4,113; The town is across the Monongalia River to the west of Morgantown and hence received it's name.

WHEELING, City; Marshall & Ohio Counties; Ohio County Seat; Pop. 43,070 / 32,526; Zip Code 26003; Elev. 678; Lat. 40-02-21 N. Long. 080-38-14 W. The town was established in 1769 by Ebenezer Zone of Virginia as the site of Fort Henry. It was the scene of the last bottle of the Revolutionary War in 1782. It was known as Zonesburg until 1795, when the name was changed to Wheeling. According to local legend, the name refers to on incident in which the Indians killed some white settlers and put the head on a stake as a warning to other would-be settlers. The name Wheeling is derived from an English version of an Indian word "weeling." meaning "place of the head."

WHITE SULPHUR SPRINGS, City; Greenbrier County; Pop. 3,371 / 2,710; Zip Code 24986; Lat. 37-47-50 N, Long. 080-17-52 W; Descriptively named for the nearby mineral springs. The heavily-sulphured water leaves deposits of white sulphur on everything over which it flows.

WILLIAMSON, City; Mingo County Seat; Pop. 5,219 / 3,875; Zip Code 25661; Lat. 37-40-31 N, Long. 082-16-03 W; Named for prominent businessman Wallace J. Williamson, who once owned the town's site.

WILLIAMSTOWN, City; Wood County; Pop. 3,095 / 2,676; Zip Code 26187; Lat. 39-24-01 N, Long. 081-27-07 W; Settled by frontiersman Isaac Williams in 1786 and named after him.

WISCONSIN
The Badger State

Waterfowl on Horicon Marsh

Milwaukee waterfront

GOVERNOR
Tommy G.Thompson

Little Manitou Falls
Pattison State Park

Madison Skyline

Round Barn - Wood County

Birthplace of the Republican Party - Ripon

INTRODUCTION

Wisconsin covers 56,523 square miles of total geographical area, with 54,426 square miles of land area and 1,727 square miles of water area. The State ranks twenty-third in size of all the states in the nation. All of its major cities are located on some body of water, including lakes, streams, and major rivers—such as the headwaters of the Mississippi. Even the State's name comes from the Wisconsin River, the principal river that courses through the center of it.

Water provided the impetus for the great logging industry that thrived in the nineteenth century, and for the later paper milling, fishing, and beer brewing industries that became so important to the economic development of the State. Today, Wisconsin's lakes and rivers attract not only industrial developers, but also people who seek recreational activities. With more than 8,000 interior lakes and some 20,000 miles of rivers, ample opportunity is provided for a wide variety of sports and hobbies.

STATE NAME

In the early history of Wisconsin, its lands were part of the Northwest Territory; it later became part of the Indiana, Illinois and Michigan territories. Then on May 29, 1848, Wisconsin was admitted as a state into the Union by an act of Congress; thus it became a territory in its own right.

Historians generally agree that the aboriginal word from which the State's present name is derived is not definitively known. In the 1890s, Reuben Gold Thwaites stated that although "the meaning of the aboriginal word...is now unknown, popular writers declare that it signifies *gathering of the waters*, or *meeting of the waters*, having reference, possibly, to the occasional mingling of the divergent streams over the low-lying watershed at Fox-Wisconsin portage; but there is no warrant for this."

The *Wisconsin Magazine of History* said "Wisconsin is named for its principal river, but the origin of that name has never been satisfactorily determined; it had over twenty spellings on the early maps ranging from *Miscous* to the ordinary French form, *Ouisconsin*, anglicized as Wisconsin."

Several writers have stated that the name Wisconsin is of Chippewa origin, and means "grassy place." However, Alfred Brunson, an early place name historian, explained "the state derives its name from the principal river which runs centrally through it." He further stated that, upon the authority of an Indian trader, "the Chippewas upon its head waters call this river *Wees-kon-san*, which signifies 'the gathering of the waters.'"

According to Brunson, the original idea of the name referred to the fact that several streams gather to make up the Wisconsin River at its head and this river flows for a long way with few tributaries. The French changed the form of the word to *Ouistonsin*, which brings the first syllable nearer to the Indian sound of the original word than does the present day word "his." He further states that the last syllable, *sin*, "is evidently a derivation from" the original term in both the French and the English forms.

One finds in the records of the early French explorers several forms of the name, some of which are: *Ouisconsin*, or *Misconssin*, *Misconsing*, and *Mesconsin*. Louise Phelps Kellogg, a former research associate of the State Historical Society of Wisconsin, said in 1925 that the names *Meskousing* and *Miskous*, by which the guides of Marquette designated the Wisconsin River, were changed by Pierre Margry to *Misconsing* "in a report appearing under Joliet's name, the n' being a typographical error for 'u.' One finds in the records of Hennepin that the following forms of the name appear: *Misconsing*, *Mesconsin*, *Misconsin* and *Ouisconsin*. Thus it is seen that the initial 'ou' of the word began to appear very early in the French documents."

Brunson said "an attempt was made, a few years since, to restore the second syllable of this name to its original Indian sound by substituting 'k' for 'c', but that the Legislature decided that the name should be spelled 'Wisconsin.'"

The name Wisconsin was given in the act establishing the territorial government of Wisconsin dated April 20, 1836.

Various other spellings of this name were: *Ouisconsin*, *Misconsing*, *Ouisconching*, *Ouiskensing*, *Wiskonsan*, and *Wiskonsin*.

STATE NICKNAMES

Wisconsin is generally known as "The Badger State," or "America's Dairy Land," although in the past it has also been nicknamed "The Copper State."

Historians of the nineteenth century spoke of Wisconsin as "the land of the badgers," and this sobriquet had its origin in the early mining days of Wisconsin. It was begun for the lead miners who, upon first arriving at a new location, dug into the side of a hill and lived underground as protection from the cold, much as a badger digs in his burrow. In the southwest part of the State, several lead mines were prosperous when the Madison State Journal declared in 1879 that "the term Badger was first applied to the occupants of these temporary subterranean residences in derision—as the term Sucker was applied to the migratory inhabitants of Southern Illinois, who, like the fish of the carp family, came to the mines in the spring and returned on the approach of winter—and afterward to all the inhabitants of the lead mine region, and by not unnatural adaptation has been applied to the people of the state and to the state itself."

Wisconsin has been called "America's Dairy Land" because dairy production is the single most important agricultural pursuit in the State. Cheese and other dairy products are distributed to all parts of the U.S. from Wisconsin's small farms. Enough cheese produced here each year to make it the leading dairy state in the nation.

The nickname "The Copper State" refers to the copper mines once lucrative in the northern part of the State.

STATE SEAL

In 1848, when Wisconsin became a State of the Union, a new seal was designed to replace the revised territorial seal of 1839. In 1851, the State seal was again revised and was prescribed by an act of the Legislature in 1881. The law reads as follows:

"The great seal of the state consists of a metallic disc, 2-3/8 in diameter, containing, within an ornamental border, the following devices and legend: The coat of arms of the state above the arms, in a line parallel with the border, the words, "Great Seal of the State of Wisconsin"; in the exergue, in a curved line, thirteen stars."

The coat of arms is described as follows:

"The coat of arms of the state of Wisconsin is declared to be as follows:

"*Arms*. Or, quartered, the quarters bearing respectively a plow, a crossed shovel and pick, an arm and held hammer, and an anchor, all proper; the base of shield resting upon a horn of plenty and pyramid of pig lead, all proper; overall, on fesse point, the arms and motto of the United States, namely: Arms, palewise of thirteen pieces argent and gules; a chief azure; motto (on garter surrounding in escutcheon), 'E pluribus unum'.

"*Crest*. A badger, passant, proper.

"*Supporters*. Dexter, a sailor holding a coil of rope, proper; sinister, a yeoman resting on a pick, proper.

"*Motto*. Over crest, 'Forward.'"

STATE FLAG

Wisconsin adopted its State flag in 1913. In 1979, the Legislature revised the flag. The law became effective in 1981 and set out the following requirements:

"(1)   The Wisconsin State flag consists of the following features:

"(a)   Relative dimensions of two to three, hoist to fly.

"(b)   A background of royal blue cloth.

"(c)   The state coat of arms, as described under s. 1.07 in material of appropriate colors, applied on each side in the center of the field, of such size that, if placed in a circle whose diameter is equal to fifty percent of the hoist, those portions farthest from the center of the field would meet, hut not cross, the boundary of the circle.

"(d)   The word 'WISCONSIN' in white, capital, condensed Gothic letters, one-eighth of the hoist in height, centered above the coat of arms, midway between the lowermost part of the coat of arms and the top edge of the flag.

"(e)   The year '1848' in white, condensed Gothic numbers, one-eighth of the hoist in height, centered below the coat of arms and the bottom edge of the flag.

"(f)   Optional trim on the edges consisting of yellow-knotted fringe.

"(2)   The department of administration shall ensure that all official state flags that are manufactured on or after May 1, 1981 conform to the requirements of this section. State flags manufactured before May 1, 1981 may continue to be used as state flags."

STATE MOTTO

The motto of the State of Wisconsin is "Forward." It was adopted when the seal and coat of arms were revised in 1851. The seal was designed by Edward Ryan and John H. Lathrop. The motto was a compromise between the two men when Ryan objected to Lathrop's Latin motto.

Wisconsin's motto signifies the progressive sentiment of the State's residents throughout its history. Governor Nelson Dewey had the motto engraved on the state seal in 1851. He is said to have been inspired by New York State's motto, "Excelsior," and wanted the idea of "Onward and Upward," to symbolize the new State.

STATE BIRD

In 1926, a vote of the school children of Wisconsin selected the robin (*Turdus migratorius*) as the state bird. Mrs. Walter Bowman, Conservation Chairman of the State Federated Women's Clubs, conducted the campaign.

The robin ranges in eastern and northern North America; westward to the Rocky Mountains; north westward to Alaska; it winters southward to Florida and along the Gulf coast to Texas.

The robin has a total length of 8½ to nine inches; its tail length is four inches. The bird is the largest thrush in North America. The male is colored most deep mouse gray or brownish slate gray on the back. The head is black with white spots from the eye to the bill and on both the upper and lower eyelids; the chin is white; the feathers of the neck are black in the center, margined with brownish slate gray or mouse gray; the tail is a dull slate black or sooty black with a large and conspicuous white spot. The chest flanks, breasts, and upper abdomen are white. The female is much duller in color, with gray of upper parts lighter and chest browner than the male.

In behavior, the robin is easily jittery and upset. However, he may sail through the air without faltering, with his chest out and back straight. The robin fits the saying of "the early bird gets the worm," as he arises early and sings his songs in a loud and energetic voice.

Eggs of the robin are pale blue, and usually laid in sets of three or four. The male cares for the young almost exclusively, while the female prepares for a new brood. Three separate sets of eggs may be laid on one year.

Robins subsist primarily on beetles and caterpillars, supplemented by spiders, earthworms, and snails. Since the robin also likes fruits, both cultivated and wild, he may pose a potential threat to orchards. However, when there is a plentiful supply of insects or wild fruit, he will leave fruit crops alone.

STATE FLOWER

In 1949, the Legislature of Wisconsin officially adopted the wood violet (*Viola papilionacea*) as the State flower. The violet received this designation in an election by which it won over three other choices: wild rose, trailing arbutus, and white water lily. The wood violet was previously chosen on Arbor Day in 1909 by a vote of school children, but the choice was unofficial until the 1949 vote.

STATE TREE

The Wisconsin Legislature adopted the sugar maple (*Acer saccharum*) as the official State tree in 1949. It was chosen after an election of school children in 1948; after the election, some sought to overrule the vote by lobbying for the white pine. However, the Legislature accepted the recommendation of the Youth Centennial Committee, and the sugar maple became the official choice.

The sugar maple is also known as the hard maple, rock maple, and black maple. It is native to the eastern half of the United States and adjacent Canada. The tree is large, with gray bark, furrowed into irregular ridges or scales. Leaves are paired, heart shaped, with three or five lobes. They are long pointed and sparingly, coarsely toothed, from three to 5½ inches in diameter. They are dark green above and light green and usually smooth underneath. Leaves turn yellow, orange, or scarlet in the fall. Fruits are one to 1¼ inches long and mature in the fall.

The sugar maple is important to Wisconsin's economy. It is a timber and shade tree whose hard wood is used for a variety of manufactured products including furniture, flooring, and musical instruments.

STATE SONG

In 1959, "On Wisconsin" was designated the official State song. It was composed in 1909 by William T. Purdy as a fight song for football. The song was unofficially recognized as the State song for fifty years before its official adoption. However, several different lyrics were used during that time. When the song became officially designated in 1959, the law also prescribed the words to be used.

STATE LICENSE PLATE

In 1904, the cities of Madison and Milwaukee began to register automobiles. However, the State did not furnish official license plates until July 1, 1905. The first plate was undated, and had aluminum numbers riveted on a black zinc base. These plates were used until 1912, except for new registrations, which were aluminum-on-green plates issued between July 1 and the end of 1911.

In 1912, new annual plates were aluminum-on-red. In 1913, plates were aluminum-on-blue. Beginning in 1914, black-on-white plates were issued, and aluminum was never again used as a color for Wisconsin plates. A variety of plate colors were used throughout the years. In 1917, olive drab was used; in 1961, it was jonquil yellow; and in 1965, Polaris maroon colored Wisconsin plates.

The slogan of "America's Dairy Land" was first used on the 1940 red-on-white plate; the slogan remains today. The first graphic plates were issued in 1986. The current plate for Wisconsin is graphically depicted. "Wisconsin" appears in blue letters at the upper left top of the plate. Green and blue lines cross the plate below the state name and define the graphic in the upper right of the plate. The blue line represents water on which a sailboat is sailing against the orange sun. Also depicted are geese flying toward the sun from a farm scene in the extreme upper right of the plate. Numerals and letters are colored red.

STATE POSTAGE STAMP

The Wisconsin Statehood Commemorative stamp was issued on May 29, 1948, one hundred years after Wisconsin entry into the Union. The purple three-cent stamp was designed by V.S. McCloskey, Jr., and was engraved by R. M. Bower and C.A. Smith. It has two main features. To the left is an unrolled scroll with the state of Wisconsin in dark outline and the centennial dates of 1848-1948 to the left and right of the state. To the right is the State capitol, and above it the word "Forward," the State motto. A total of 115,250,000 of the stamps were printed.

OTHER STATE DESIGNATIONS

Through the years, the Wisconsin Legislature has designated a number of other symbols to represent the State. Included are: the State animal (1957) as the badger (*Taxidea taxus*); the State beverage (1986) as milk; the State domestic animal (1971) as dairy cow; the State fish (1955) as muskellunge (*Esox masquinongy masquinongy mitchell*); the State fossil (1988) as trilobitc (*Calynieme celehra*); the State grain (1991) as corn; the State insect (1977) as honeybee; the State mineral (1971) as ga-lena; the State rock (1971) as red granite; the wildlife animal (1957) as the white-tailed deer; and the State symbol of peace (1971) as the mourning dove.

CAPITOL BUILDING

The State capitol in Madison is the fifth capitol building in Wisconsin, and the third to be built in Madison. The first Madison capitol was used from 1838 to 1863. The second building was destroyed by fire in 1904. The current building was designed by George B. Post and Sons of New York. Construction was begun in 1906, and was completed in 1917.

The capitol, which is located between Monona and Mendota lakes, has been built on a 13.4-acre park. Designed in Roman Renaissance style, it is constructed of marble and granite, and occupies 2.42 acres.

Built in the form of a Greek cross, the structure is 438 8/10 feet long from east to west. It rises to a height of 285.9 feet from the ground to the top, which has Daniel Chester French's gilded bronze statue entitled "Wisconsin." The capitol has the only granite-domed capitol in the nation. The capitol is situated atop a grassy hill. The interior is finished in forty-three varieties of stone, glass mosaics, and murals. The structure cost 7½ million dollars to build, and has been restored.

OTHER FACTS ABOUT WISCONSIN

Total area: 56,153 square miles
Land area: 54,426 square miles
Water area: 1,727 square miles
Average elevation: 1,050 feet
Highest point: Timms Hill, 1,951 feet
Lowest point: Lake Michigan, 581 feet
Highest temperature: 114 degrees Fahrenheit
Lowest temperature: -54 degrees Fahrenheit
Population in 1990: 4,891,769
Population density in 1990: 90.07 persons per square mile
Population 1980-1990: +4.0 percent change
Population projected for year 2000: 4,784,000
Black population in 1990: 244,539
Hispanic population in 1990: 93,194
Native American population in 1990: 39,387
White population in 1990: 4,512,523
Capital: Madison
Admitted to Union: May 29, 1848
Order of Statehood: 30
Electoral votes: 11

CHRONOLOGY

WISCONSIN UNDER FRENCH DOMINION

1634 Jean Nicolet, emissary of New France, lands on shores of Green Bay.

1654-56 Medard Chouart, Sieur de Groseilliers, fur trader, accompanied by companion of uncertain identity, winters among Potawatomi around Green Bay; the following spring, he ascends Fox River and crosses Wisconsin River at Portage.

1656-57 Groseilliers, with his brother-in-law, Pierre Esprit Radisson, visits Green Bay; they proceed south on uncertain route.

1658-60 Same two explorers skirt south shore of Lake Superior; somewhere between Ashland and Washburn, they build rude waterside hut; it is probably first white habitation in Wisconsin.
– Explorers visit Ottawa on Lac Court Oreilles, and accompany Sioux to site of city of Superior and into eastern Minnesota; upon their return, they build post at Chequamegon Bay and return to Montreal.

1660-61 Father Rene Menard follows Hurons into Wisconsin, winters at Keweenaw Bay and visits Hurons of Chippewa and Black Rivers; becoming lost in dense forest along tributary of Chippewa River, he is never heard from again.

1665-67 Father Claude Jean Allouez, Jesuit missionary, reopens Huron mission on shore of Chequamegon Bay.

1668-67 Nicholas Perrot, fur trader, visits Winnebago, Potawatomi, Fox, Sauk, and Mascouten villages near Green Bay; he gains Potawatomi trade for New France.

1669 Father Jacques Marquette relieves Father Allouez, who goes to Green Bay.

1670 May 20. Father Allouez returns to Sault, Ste. Marie after visiting Fox village on Wolf River and Mascouten village on upper Fox (near present Berlin); in autumn, he and Father Claude Dablon begin three missions: St. Francois for Menominee and Potawatomi, St. Marc for Fox, and St. Jacques for Mascouten.

1671 In Sault, Ste. Marie, Simon Francois Daumont, Sieur de St. Lusson, takes official possession of Northwest in name of French King.

1673 May. Louis Joliet and Father Jacques Marquette leave Mackinac, enter Green Bay and Fox River; they reach Mascouten village on June 7, and portage into Wisconsin River.
June 17. Joliet and Marquette discover Mississippi River.

1673-78 Father Allouez, aided by Fathers Andre and Silvy, continues missionary work around Green Bay.

1675 May 19. Father Marquette dies on eastern shore of Lake Michigan.

1678-80 Daniel Greysolon, Sieur du Luth (du Lhut), discovers Bois Brule-St. Croix route to Mississippi. (Historians differ, some believing he went by way of St. Louis River into interior.)

1679 September. Robert Cavalier, Sieur de la Salle, arrives off Green Bay in *Grifton*, first sailing vessel on Great Lakes; he explores west coast of Lake Michigan.

1680 Father Louis Hennepin explores upper Mississippi.

1683 Dr. Luth defends De Pere mission against Iroquois; he punishes Indian murderers of French at Sault Ste Marie and makes Lake Superior safe for French traders.

1684 First French post at Green Bay is built by La Durantaye.

1685 Perrot is appointed "Commandant of the West"; he crosses Fox-Wisconsin route with 20 soldiers and winters on east bank of Mississippi above Trempealeau.

1686 Perrot establishes trading posts on Mississippi, among them Fort St. Nicolas near Prairie du Chien, and Fort St. Antoine on Lake Pepin; he presents silver ostensorium to De Pere mission; it is oldest relic of Wisconsin, which is still preserved at Green Bay.

1689 Perrot takes possession of Fort St. Antoine, St. Croix, St. Peter, and upper Mississippi valley for French king.

1690-92 Perrot discovers and starts operating lead mines in Iowa and Wisconsin region; he adjusts peace among Sioux, Fox, and their allies.

1693 Indian War makes Fox-Wisconsin waterway unsafe; Pierre Le Sueur is sent to command Chequamegon and keep open route from Lake Superior to Mississippi; he builds stockade village at La Pointe.

1696 Fur trade licenses are revoked; posts are evacuated.

1698 October 4. Father Jean Francois Buisson de St. Cosine camps at Potawatomi village on supposed site of Sheboygan, visits sites of Milwaukee and Racine.

1700 Le Sueur and 30 French miners ascend Mississippi and build fort on Blue Earth River (Minnesota).

1701 Peace builds between Iroquois and northwestern Indians; Cadillac invites Wisconsin Indians to Detroit.

1702 Juchereau de St. Denis pays Fox Indians 1,000 crowns to pass his fleet of trading canoes to Mississippi by Fox-Wisconsin route.

1710 Many Fox Indians move to Detroit.

1712-16 Hostile Fox Indians from Green Bay imperil trade routes between Great Lakes and Mississippi.

1716 Louis de la Porte, Sieur de Louvigny, leads 800 men into Little Lake Buttes des Morts region; peace is negotiated with Fox.

1717 Fort is built at Green Bay; Philippe d'Amours, Sieur de la Morandiere, is commander.

1718 Paul le Gardeur, Sieur de St. Pierre, founds Chequamegon post.

1721 Father Pierre Francois Xavier de Charlevoix, Jesuit historian, visits Wisconsin with Jacques Testard, Sieur de Montiguy, who supersedes La Morandiere as commandant at La Baye.

1724-26 Marchand de Lignery, commandant at Mackinac, and Francois d'Amariton, commandant at Green Bay, aided by Jesuit missionaries, attempt to make peace among warring tribes; by 1726, truce permits building of post among Sioux.

1727 Fort Beauharnois is established on west bank of Lake Pepin (near Frontenac, Minnesota), to separate Sioux from Fox allies; Rene Boucher, Sieur de la Rerriere, takes command.

1728 August. Lignery, with expedition of French and Indians, advances up Fox River, destroys villages and crops of Fox; upon return, they destroy French fort at La Bayer and warn Fort Beauharnois garrison; fort is evacuated October 3; roving Mascoutens and Kickapoos capture and retain garrison as hostage.

1729 French captives detach Mascouten and Kickapoo from Fox alliance; peace is made between them and Illinois.
– Commandant at Chequamegon reports copper mines on Lake Superior.

1730 Pierre Paul Martin, commanding Menominee, aids Winnebago against Fox on Little Lake Butte des Morts.
– In eastern Illinois, French defeat Fox seeking asylum with Iroquois.

1731 Kiala, principal Fox Chief, surrenders as hostage to commandant at Green Bay.

1732 Fort La Baye at Green Bay is rebuilt on later site of Fort Howard, under command of Nicolas Antoine Coulon de Villiers.
– Rene Godefroy, Sieur de Linctot, rebuilds Lake Pepin post.

1733 Sauk and Fox amalgamate after severe battle at Sauk village near Green Bay; they retreat to lead regions.

1737 St. Pierre abandons Lake Pepin fort.

1738 Louis Denis, Sieur de la Ronde, obtains permit to work Lake Superior copper mines.

1739-43 Mann pacifies all Wisconsin Indians, thus ending Fox wars.
– Lead mining is begun in southwestern Wisconsin.

1750 Mann reestablishes post among Sioux; he and his partner, Governor Marquis de La Jonquiere, obtain annual net profit of 150,000 livres from Wisconsin fur trade.

1752 Joseph Mann relieves his father at Sioux post.

1753 La Baye post is granted to Francois Rigaud, brother of Governor Vaudreuil.
– Mann and St. Pierre make peace between Sioux, Cree, and Chippewa.

1755 Charles de Langlade and Indians take part in Braddock's defeat.

1756 Joseph Mann abandons Sioux post.

1757 Hubert Couterot is last French commandant at La Bayer; Pierre Joseph Hertel, Sieur de Beaubassin, is last at Chequamegon.

1759 Wisconsin Indians take part in siege of Fort William Henry on Lake George, and in defense of Quebec.

1760 Louis Lienard de Beanjeau-Villemonde, last French commandant, evacuates Fort Mackinac; he retires to Mississippi, taking with him La Baye garrison.

WISCONSIN UNDER BRITISH DOMINION

1760 Upon surrender of New France to Britain on September 8, Wisconsin becomes British territory governed by Mackinac and Quebec.

1761 October 12. Capt. Henry Balfour, British Infantry, arrives at Green Bay to assume command of abandoned French stockade renamed Port Edward Augustus; he leaves garrison under command of Ensign James Gorrell.

1762 Gorrell makes treaties with Menominee, Winnebago, Ottawa, Sauk, Fox, and Iowa, and also promotes treaty between Chippewa and Menominee.

1763 Wisconsin, with other parts of New France, is formally ceded to Britain.
– Gorrell makes treaty with Sioux.
– Pontiac's conspiracy begins; Indians attack British posts on upper Great Lakes.
June 21. Gorrell abandons Green Bay post, which is never again garrisoned by British.

1764 Augustin de Langlade, with his wife and son Charles, leave Mackinac and settle at La Baye.

1765 Alexander Henry and Jean Baptiste Cadotte reopen trading post on Chequamegon Bay.

1766 Jonathan Carver, colonial officer in French and Indian War, visits Wisconsin; he leaves valuable records descriptive of region.

1773-75 Peter Pond, Connecticut fur trader, visits Wisconsin and writes about inhabitants.
– Pond finds French ex-soldier, Pinnashon, at Fox-Wisconsin portage (now Portage) transporting boats and cargoes.

1774 By Quebec Act, Wisconsin becomes part of British Province of Quebec.

1776-78 Langlade leads Indians to Canada to defend Montreal and Quebec against Americans.

1778 George Rogers Clark allies Wisconsin Indians with Americans.

1780 British build small fort at Prairie du Chien, send expedition against St. Louis.
– Spanish attack; fort is burned by Langlade.

1781 Traditional date of settlement of Prairie du Chien by Basil Girard, Augustin Ange, and Pierre Antaya (although French traders have long dwelled there).

1783 Treaty of Paris is concluded; British territory east of Mississippi is ceded to United States.

WISCONSIN UNDER AMERICAN DOMINION
(Under British influence until 1815)

1784 Northwest and Mackinac Fur companies are organized.

1785 Julien Dubuque visits Prairie du Chien, explores lead mines.

1787 July. Congress passes ordinance for government of Northwest Territory, including Wisconsin.

1788 At general council meeting at Prairie du Chien, Fox Indians agree to allow Dubuque to work lead mines.

1791 Jacques Porlier comes to Green Bay.

1792 John Johnston builds trading post on Chequamegon Bay.

1792-93 Charles Reauine winters on St. Croix River; Porlier is on upper Mississippi.

1792 Laurent Barth builds cabin at Fox-Wisconsin portage, transports boats and cargoes.

1795 Pierre Grignon, Sr., son-in-law of Charles de Langlade, dies at Green Bay.
– Jacques Vieau establishes posts at Kewaunee, Sheboygan, Manitovoc, and Milwaukee.

1796 British evacuate western posts.
– Mackinac is occupied by American garrison.

1797 Incited by Spanish, Sauk and Fox pillage British traders at Prairie du Chien.
– Sioux-Chippewa war is fought in northern Wisconsin.

1799 XY Company is organized to compete with Northwest & Mackinac companies.
– John Lawe, clerk for Jacob Franks, reaches Green Bay.

1800 May 7. Congress creates Territory of Indiana with jurisdiction over vast Northwest Territory, including Wisconsin.

1801 Charles de Langlade dies at Green Bay.

1802 John Campbell, British trader, is appointed Indian agent at Prairie du Chien.
– Governor Harrison of Indiana grants commissions as justices of peace to John Campbell and Robert Dickson of Prairie du Chien; he also organizes militia.

1803 Charles Reaume is commissioned American magistrate for Green Bay; Henry Monroe Fisher takes same commission for Prairie du Chien.

1804 At St. Louis, Governor Harrison makes treaty with Sauk and Fox, who relinquish title to their lands, including lead mines, in southern Wisconsin.
– Northwest and XY companies amalgamate.

1805-06 Zebulon M. Pike is sent from St. Louis to inform Indians and traders along upper Mississippi about Louisiana Purchase; he spends several days at Prairie du Chien.

1806 Nicolas Boilvin is appointed assistant Indian agent for Sauk and Fox.

1809 February 3. Act of Congress creates Territory of Illinois, whose bounds include Wisconsin.

1810 John Jacob Astor purchases Mackinac Company, organizes Southwest Fur Company.

1812-13 Robert Dickson leads Wisconsin Indians to aid of British in Ohio and Michigan.

1814 Fort Shelby, first United States post in Wisconsin, is built at Prairie du Chien.

1814 July 17. Fort Shelby surrenders to British and Indian forces led by Major William McKay and Robert Dickson.
August 4. Wisconsin traders, Indians, and British defend Mackinac against United States attack.

1815 British abandon Fort McKay after Treaty of Ghent; U.S. jurisdiction resumes under Nicolas Boilvin, Indian agent and justice of peace.

1816 Gen. Thomas A. Smith erects Fort Crawford at Prairie du Chien on site of Fort McKay, formerly Fort Shelby.
– Col. John Miller erects Fort Howard at Green Hay on site of former French and British posts.
– Act of Congress restricts fur trading to U.S. citizens.
– Astor's American Fur Company continues operating in Wisconsin.
– Government fur trade factories are established at Green Bay and Prairie du Chien.
– First flourmill, using horsepower, is built at Fort Crawford; flour is made for soldiers.

1817 February. First school in Wisconsin opens at Green Bay.
– First priest visits Prairie du Chien.

1818 School is opened at Prairie du Chien by Willard Keyes.

– Brown, Crawford, and Michilimackinac counties organize; they embrace whole of present Wisconsin, part of Minnesota, and upper Michigan peninsula.

– Solomon Juneau arrives at Milwaukee.

December 3. Wisconsin region is attached to Michigan Territory upon elevation of Illinois Territory to statehood.

1818-21 French inhabitants of Green Bay plan to remove to Red River.

1820-21 Land claims of French settlers at Prairie du Chien and Green Bay are adjusted.

1821 First steamer to navigate Lake Michigan brings New York Indians to arrange transfer to Wisconsin.

– Code of Michigan Territory is made basis of law; no courts are organized except those of justice of peace.

1822 Government fur trade factory system is abolished.

– New York Indians begin removal to Wisconsin.

– Speculators and prospectors rush to southwestern Wisconsin following opening of lead mines at Galena, Illinois.

1823 May 12. First session of Crawford County Court is held at Prairie du Chien.

October 17. First session of U.S. Circuit Court is held at Prairie du Chien; James D. Doty is judge.

– *Virginia* is first steamboat to ascend upper Mississippi.

1824 July 12. First session of Brown County Court opens at Green Bay; Jacques Porlier is Chief Justice.

October 4. Judge Doty holds first U.S. Circuit Court at Green Bay.

1825 William Clark and Lewis Cass, government commissioners, conclude treaty at Prairie du Chien with Indians of Illinois, Minnesota, and Wisconsin; they establish boundaries and make peace among tribes.

1826 Fort Crawford's garrison is removed.

1827 Winnebago outbreak causes renaming of Fort Crawford.

– Winnebago mining lands are ceded to U.S. as condition of pardon for leaders of insurrection.

1828 September. Fort Winnebago is begun at Portage.

1829-32 Col. Zachary Taylor rebuilds Fort Crawford on new site at Prairie du Chien.

1829 July. Chippewa, Ottawa, and Potawatomi at Green Bay cede lands between Rock and Wisconsin rivers.

– Thousands of miners settle in lead regions.

1831 Daniel Whitney's company begins erecting shot tower at Old Helena on Wisconsin River.

1832 Black Hawk War; Indians are defeated; they cede lands east and south of Fox and Wisconsin rivers.

1833 Chippewa, Ottawa, and Potawatomi cede lands south and west of Milwaukee River.

December 11. *Green Bay Intelligence*, first Wisconsin newspaper, is established.

1834 Land offices open at Mineral Point and Green Bay.

– First public land sale takes place at Mineral Point.

– First public road is laid out.

– Settlers begin to arrive at Milwaukee.

1835 June 17. First steamboat arrives at Milwaukee.

– First bank opens at Astor, part of Green Bay.

– Influx of settlers begins in southern and eastern Wisconsin.

1836 April 20. Territory of Wisconsin is organized by Act of Congress.

– Henry Dodge becomes first Governor; John S. Homer is secretary; George W. Jones is first delegate to Congress.

July 4. Officers are sworn in at Mineral Point.

– Supreme Court is constituted: Charles Dunn, David Irvin, and William Frazer become justices.

October 25. First Territorial assembly meets at Old Belmont (now Leslie).

November 24. Madison is chosen as capital.

– Because of depression, all four banks in Territory fail.

– *Milwaukee Advertiser* begins publishing.

– Land office opens in Milwaukee; there are no sales until 1839.

– Menominee cede to United States about 4,000,000 acres in Michigan and Wisconsin.

1837 Winnebago Chief's sign treaty at Washington ceding Wisconsin lands, agree to remove from Territory.

– Town site of Madison is surveyed and platted; first capitol is begun.

1838 Congress appropriates land to endow University of Territory of Wisconsin.

– Eighty post offices and thirty-five mail routes are established.

– Second Territorial assembly meets at Madison; lack of accommodations forces it to adjourn.

– Milwaukee and Rock River Canal Company is chartered.

1839 Adjourned session of second Territorial assembly meets at Madison.

– First school taxes are levied.

– Wisconsin Marine & Fire Insurance Company (Mitchell's Bank) is chartered.

1840 Population is 30,945 according to U.S. census.

1841 James Duane Doty is appointed governor (1841-44).

1843 Cooperative industrial community, chiefly English, settles at North Prairie, Waukesha County, under Thomas Hunt.

1844 Wisconsin Phalanx, Utopian socialist community promoted by Warren Chase, settles at Ceresco (now Ripon).

– Nathaniel P. Talmadge is appointed governor (1844-45).

1845 Tallmadge is removed; Dodge is reappointed (1845-48).

– Swiss colony settles at New Glarus.

– Mormon colony organizes near Burlington, Racine County.

1846 State government is voted upon.
– Congress passes enabling act.
October 15. First constitutional convention opens at Madison.

1847 First constitution is rejected by popular vote.
November 21. Propeller *Phoenix* burned off Sheboygan; 148 persons are lost, including 127 immigrants from Holland.
December 15. Second constitutional convention opens at Madison.
– Population is 219,456 (Special census).

WISCONSIN AS U.S. STATE

1848 March 13. Second State constitution is adopted.
May 29. Wisconsin is admitted as State.
– First State officers are Nelson Dewey, governor (1848-52); Henry Dodge and Isaac P. Walker, U.S. Senators; Mason C. Darling and William P. Lynde, U.S. representatives; Andrew G. Miller, U.S. District Court judge.
June 5. First State Legislature convenes.
– Free school system is established.
– Land grant for university is made by Congress; university is chartered.
– Menominee, by treaty, cede lands east of Wisconsin and north of Fox River to U.S.
– Large numbers of Germans settle at Milwaukee and in eastern counties.

1849 Construction of railroad from Milwaukee westward begins.
– State Historical Society organizes.
– University of Wisconsin opens at Madison.
– First telegram is received in Milwaukee.
– Cholera epidemic hits Statewide.
– Gold rush to California begins.

1850 Population is 305,391.

1851 First railroad train in State runs from Milwaukee to Waukesha.

1852 Several railroad enterprises begin in southern Wisconsin.
– Leonard J. Farwell is governor (1852-54).

1853 July. Act abolishing capital punishment passes in Wisconsin.
– Milwaukee and Mississippi Railroad is completed to Madison.

1854 February 28. State Republican Party is founded at Ripon (reorganized at Madison, July 13).
– University of Wisconsin holds first class graduation.
– State Historical Society is reorganized; Lyman C. Draper becomes secretary.
– Wisconsin Supreme Court declares fugitive Slave Act void.

1856 Reelection of Gov. William A. Barstow, Democrat, is declared fraudulent.
– Coles Bashford, Republican, is declared elected governor (1856-58).

1857 Milwaukee & Mississippi Railroad is completed to Prairie du Chien.

– Legislature passes law against kidnaping to neutralize effect of Fugitive Slave Law.
– Severe monetary panic begins.

1858 Excursion train celebrating opening of Chicago and Fond du Lac Railway (later C & NW) crashes at Johnson's Creek; fourteen are killed.
– Legislative investigation exposes bribery of officials by railways, and improper use of United States railway land grants.
– Alexander W. Randall is governor (1858-1862).

1859 Byron Payne is elected to State Supreme Court on anti-slavery platform.
September 30. Abraham Lincoln delivers address at State Fair in Milwaukee.

1860 September 9. Milwaukee excursion steamer, *Lady Elgin*, sinks; 225 persons are drowned.
– State votes for Lincoln.
– Grand League of Farm Mortgagors is organized.
– Population is 775,881.

1861 April 15. Gov. Alexander W. Randall calls for volunteers in Civil War; sixteen regiments muster during year.
July 2. George C. Drake, Co. A, 1st Infantry, dies at Falling Waters, Virginia; he is first Wisconsin soldier killed in Civil War.

1862 April 19. Gov. Louis P. Harvey, while visiting Wisconsin soldiers wounded at Shiloh, drowns in Tennessee River; Edward Saloman becomes governor (1862-64).
April. 700 captured Confederate soldiers are received at Camp Randall, Madison.
– Wisconsin sends about 15,000 volunteers into war service during year.

1863 September 17. War Democrats hold convention in Janesville; they repudiate Ryan address of September 3, 1862, criticizing Federal administration.
– Military hospitals open in Milwaukee and Prairie du Chien through efforts of Mrs. Harvey.

1864 James T. Lewis is inaugurated fourth wartime governor (1864-66).
February 23. Father Mazzuchelli, missionary to Green Bay and southwestern Wisconsin since 1833, dies; he was founder and builder of churches, schools, and other public buildings, and was chaplain of first Territorial legislature.
– Chester Hazen establishes first Wisconsin cheese factory at Ladoga, Fond du Lac County.

1865 April 9. Civil War ends.
– Wisconsin ceases recruiting; State has furnished 91,379 men to North during war; deaths total 10,752.

1866 February. State university reorganizes.
– College of agriculture is created under Morrill Grant.
– James R. Doolittle, U.S. senator, is asked to resign by Legislature because of support to President Johnson's reconstruction policy; Lucius Fairchild is governor (1866-72).

1867 First practical typewriter is invented by Christopher Latham Sholes of Milwaukee.

1868 March 9. Fifteenth Amendment to United States Constitution is ratified by Wisconsin.
– Legislature defeats bill to regulate railway.

1870 May 24. Bishop Jackson Kemper dies at Delafield; he was missionary of West, builder and founder of schools, churches, colleges, and convents.
– Contest over railway legislation continues; cities, towns, and villages are authorized to issue bonds in aid of new railways.
– Population is 1,054,670.

1871 October 8-10. Great fires occur in Door, Oconto Shawano, Kewaunee, Brown, and Manitowoc counties; 1,000 perish and 3,000 are homeless.

1872 Wisconsin Dairymen's Association organizes at Watertown.
– C.C. Washburn is governor (1872-74).

1873 Financial panic begins.
– Democrats, on issue of railway legislation, elect State ticket for first time since Civil War.
– Winnebago are forcibly removed to Nebraska.

1874 Potter Law, limiting railroad rates, is enacted; law is upheld in State Supreme Court.
– William R. Taylor is governor (1874-76).

1875 Republicans, opposing Potter Law and "Grangerism," elect State ticket.
– Women are made eligible to vote for school offices.
April 28. Oshkosh is almost entirely destroyed by fire.
September 14. Increase A. Lapham, famous scientist, dies.

1876 Potter Law is repealed.
– Harrison Ludington is governor (1876-78).

1877 John F. Appleby perfects twine binder on principle of "knotter" he invented in 1858.
– State law is enacted enabling women to practice law in Wisconsin.

1878 William E. Smith is governor (1878-82).

1880 John Stevens of Neenah patents roller flour mill.
October 19. Chief Justice Edward G. Ryan dies.
– Population is 1,315,497.

1881 September. First serious labor disturbance begins: Eau Claire sawmill operatives demand reduction of hours; National Guard is called out.

1882 Constitution is amended to provide for biennial legislative sessions.
– Jeremiah M. Rusk is governor (1882-89).

1883 Agricultural Experiment Station is established at Madison.

1885 March 6. William F. Vilas is appointed postmaster general in cabinet of President Cleveland.
– High-grade iron ore is discovered on Gogebic Range.

1886 Agricultural Short Course opens at college of agriculture.
– Milwaukee workmen strike for 8-hour workday; National Guard is called out; several strikers are killed.

1887 June 27. Marshfield is almost destroyed by fire; property loss is between $2,000,000 and $3,000,000.

1888 January 16. William F. Vilas is appointed U.S. Secretary of Interior.

1889 Legislature passes "Bennett Law" making English compulsory in schools.
March 4. Gen. Jeremiah M. Rusk is appointed first U.S. Secretary of Agriculture.
– William D. Hoard is governor (1889-91).
– Strike of railway builders begins at West Superior.

1890 Democrats elect entire State ticket on Anti-Bennett law platform.
– Wisconsin Supreme Court declares Bible reading in public schools unconstitutional.
– Dr. S.M. Babcock discovers method of determining butterfat content of milk.
– University dairy school is established.
– Population is 1,686,880.

1891 "Bennett Law" is repealed.
– Reapportioned congressional and legislative districts under 1890 census are unsatisfactory to Republicans.
– George W. Peck is governor (1891-95).

1892 Special legislative session adopts new apportionment; it is uncontested.
October. Third Ward Fire, Milwaukee, causes $5,000,000 damage; six lives are lost.

1893 Medford is virtually destroyed by fire.
November 21. Three-time governor, General Jeremiah Rusk, dies.
– Panic causes failure of several Milwaukee banks.

1895 William H. Upham is governor (1895-97).

1896 May 23. Three-time governor, Gen. Lucius Fairchild, dies; he was Minister to Spain, National Commander of G.A.R.
– Wisconsin Free Library Commission organizes.
– Traveling library system is initiated in Dunn.
– Immigration into northern Wisconsin is substantial.

1897 Corrupt Practices Act, requiring statements of campaign expenses, passes Legislature.
– Edward Schofield is governor (1897-1901).

1898 Wisconsin raises 5,496 men for Spanish American War, equips four regiments of infantry and one battery.
– Strike of woodworkers in Oshkosh results in violence.
– Forest fires in Barron and Polk counties cause $500,000 loss.

1899 Third Regiment is mustered out in January, and Fourth Regiment in February at Anniston, Alabama.
– Anti-Railway-Pass Law is enacted.
– State tax commission is created.

June 12. Tornado destroys New Richmond, resulting in losses of $1,000,000.

1900 May 1-8. Forest fires on Chequamegon Bay and Menominee River cause more than $1,000,000 damage.
June 12. Belle Boyd, famous woman spy during Civil War, dies at Kilbourn.
October 19. New State Historical Library building, Madison, is dedicated.
– Lead and zinc mining arc revived in southern Wisconsin.
– Population is 2,069,042, gain of 22.6 percent in 10 years.

1901 January 7. Robert M. La Follette, first native-born governor, is inaugurated; he is twice reelected (1901-06).

1903 Primary election law passes.
– Ad valorem railroad tax, mortgage tax, and inheritance tax are chief features of year's legislation.

1904 February 27. Fire destroys south wing and much of interior of State Capitol.
June 5-9. State university celebrates golden jubilee; Charles R. Van Hise is inaugurated president, first alumnus to hold the office.
November 8. Voters endorse primary election law.

1905 January 25. Robert M. La Follette is elected to U.S. senate.
– Civil Service for State employees is adopted.
– State Board of Forestry is organized.
– Railroad Regulation Law is passed.
– Railroad Commission is established.

1906 Gov. Robert M. La Follette resigns to take seat in U.S. Senate (he serves as senator until his death on June 18, 1925).
– James O. Davidson is governor (1906-11).

1907 Construction of new State Capitol begins.

1908 Will of former Senator William F. Vilas creates trust fund from which $30,000,000 eventually will accrue to State University.

1909 Cities are permitted to adopt commission form of government.

1910 U.S. Forest Products Laboratory is established at university.
– Milwaukee elects Socialist municipal ticket; it is first large city to be governed by this party.
February 17. Eau Clair adopts commission form of government.
November 8. Socialists carry Milwaukee County and elect Victor Berger first Socialist Congressman.
– Population is 2,333,860.

1911 Two new commissions—public affairs and industrial—are created.
– State laws pass regarding income tax, labor regulations, workmen's compensation, state life insurance, corrupt practices, teachers' pensions, control of water power, second choice primary, board of vocational education.
– Francis F. McGovern is governor (1911-15).

1913 Legislation passes, including mothers' pensions; minimum wage law for women; compulsory workmen's compensation; waterpower control; eugenic marriage law.
October 22. Dr. Reuben Gold Thwaites, Superintendent of State Historical Society, dies.

1914 Wisconsin Cheese Federation is organized.
– John Muir, writer and naturalist, dies.

1915 State departments are consolidated.
– Conservation Commission, State Board of Agriculture, State Department of engineering, State Board of Education is created.
– Mothers' Pension Act is made compulsory.
– Emanuel L. Philipp is governor (1915-21).

1916 Wisconsin National Guard is sent to Mexican border.

1917-18 World War I begins.

1917 Wisconsin National Guard is mobilized, equipped by State at expense of $780,000; three companies are transferred to 42nd Division at Camp Mills; remaining troops are sent to Camp MacArthur.
– State organizes for wartime activities through State and County councils of defense.
– Law is enacted providing State aid and hospital treatment for crippled and deformed children.
– State Capitol is completed at total cost of $7,258,763.
October 21. U.S. Senator Paul O. Husting dies in accident.

1918 Wisconsin has approximately 120,000 men in military service; deaths total approximately 4,000.
– Civil Service preference to veterans is passed by Legislature.
November 19. Charles R. Van Hise, president of university, dies.
November 22. William D. Hoard, former governor, dies.

1919 Divisions of rural planning, markets, and land settlement board are made part of State Board of Agriculture.

1920 Population is 2,632,067.

1921 John J. Blaine is governor (1921-27).
– New legislation includes teachers' retirement fund law; increase in inheritance tax rates; several dairy standards laws.
March 4. Charles McCarthy, promoter of "Wisconsin Idea," dies.

1922 Law requires publication of income tax returns.

1923 Farmers and laborers obtain representation on Board of University Regents.
– Military training at University of Wisconsin is made optional.

1924 Wisconsin State General Hospital opens.
– Senator Robert M. La Follette, Wisconsin's first candidate for U.S. presidency, runs on Progressive platform; he carries only Wisconsin.

1925 January 5. Wisconsin wins when United States Supreme Court upholds injunction against Chicago's lowering level of Lake Michigan.

– Glenn Frank, editor of *Century Magazine*, is elected president of State University.
June 18. Senator Robert M. La Follette dies in Washington.
– Legislature unanimously chooses La Follette for remaining place allotted to Wisconsin in National Hall of Fame.
– Robert M. La Follette, Jr., is elected U.S. Senator.
– New legislation includes prohibition of sale of oleomargarine; constitutional amendment for recall of elective officials; liberalized absentee voters law; ratification of child labor amendment; new minimum wage law for women; old age pension law optional with counties.

1926 U.S. Supreme Court upholds Wisconsin's Workmen's Compensation and insurance laws.

1927 February 8. Wisconsin's Progressive Republican congressmen refuse to enter Republican caucus at Washington.
October 19. Congressman Victor L. Berger from Milwaukee is chosen national chairman of Socialist Party.
– Fred R. Zimmerman is governor (1927-29).

1928 President Coolidge makes Cedar Island Lodge on Brule River his summer White House.

1929 Prof Harry Steenbock, University of Wisconsin, announces commercialization of his vitamin U patent; profits to go to university.
August 7. Victor L. Berger, Socialist, dies.

1930 Gov. Walter J. Kohler is exonerated of charges of violating Corrupt Practices Act in 1928 campaign.
– Population is 2,939,006.

1931 Dr. Stephen Moulton Babcock, famous scientist, dies.
– Chris L. Christensen is appointed dean of College of Agriculture.
– New legislation includes making Wisconsin first state to enact labor code to protect workers' rights in disputes with employers; workmen's compensation act is made compulsory for employers of three or more persons; enactment of compulsory old-age pension law will become effective in 1933.
– Philip F. La Follette is governor (1931-33).

1931-32 November 24–February 4. Special session of Legislature results in first American unemployment compensation law being enacted.
– Emergency chain store tax law is enacted.

1932 Gov. Philip La Follette loses primary election; it is first time in 42 years that member of La Follette family is defeated by popular vote.
– State goes Democratic nationally for first time since 1912 by largest majority in its history.
– Albert G. Schmedeman is elected governor; he is first Democrat since 1895.
– F. Ryan Duffy is elected senator.
– Federal government advances $3,000,000 for highway construction jobs.
– New U.S. Forest Products Laboratory, world's largest wood research laboratory, is erected at Madison at cost of $737,000.

1933 Three farm strikes, led by Wisconsin Cooperative Milk Pool and Farmers Holiday Association, involve more than 17,000 farmers; rioting, milk dumping, and pitched battles ensue between farmers and deputies.
– Gen. Immell calls out National Guard; one farmer is fatally shot.

1934 Tercentenary of French discovery of Wisconsin is celebrated for eight weeks at Green Bay.
– Public Service Commission authorizes municipal competition with privately owned utility, and denies private utility damages in addition to purchase price in ease of municipal acquisition of local plant.
– One hundred and twenty strikes take place, 65 of major importance.
– Strike at Kohler results in rioting, two men killed, 40 wounded; one man is killed during Milwaukee Electric Railway and Light Company strike.
– Philip La Follette is elected governor; Robert M. La Follette, Jr., is reelected U.S. Senator.

1935 University launches Science Inquiry—new step in scientific appraisal and education.

1936 March 2. Rasmus B. Anderson, diplomat, scholar, "father of Norse literature in America," dies.
– Centennial of organization of Territory is celebrated at Madison and other cities.
– Franklin Roosevelt and Philip F. La Follette sweep Wisconsin by large majorities.
– Wisconsin, with 2.37 percent of nation's population, pays over $51,000,000 internal revenue tax.

1937 Supreme Court Judge Martin is reelected.

1938 State Supreme Court reverses earlier ruling and holds Development Authority constitutional, but curtails use of State funds.

1939 Commerce Department is abolished; new Securities Department is created.
– Muskellunge is named official State fish.

1940 La Follette is reelected to U.S. Senate.

1941 Bill is signed barring Communist Party from ballot.
– L.H. Smith is elected to succeed Representative S. Bolles in Congress.

1942 O.S. Loomis is elected governor, but dies before he can take office; Supreme Court appoints Lt. Gov. Goodland to fill vacancy.

1944 Date of primary election is changed to August 15 to allow armed forces to vote.
– Goodland is elected governor.

1946 Progressives liquidate party and join Republicans.
– La Follette, running for Senate on Republican ticket, is defeated by McCarthy.

– University of Wisconsin Pharmacy School prepares packages labeled "aspirin" which kill two public school children stricken with flu.

1947 Goodland, at age 84, is inaugurated for third term as governor.
March. Goodland dies; Rennebohm becomes acting governor.

1948 State celebrates centennial.
– Rennebohm is elected governor.

1949 Interstate Commerce Commission approves protective committee for preferred stock in reorganization of Wisconsin Central Railway Company.

1950 Senator Wiley is reelected; N.J. Kohler is elected governor.
– Senator Joseph McCarthy of Appleton begins career, claims State Department of harboring Communists.

1951 Wisconsin Central Railway reorganization is still in question; Interstate Commerce Commission reopens case to hear new company plan.

1952 McCarthy is reelected in controversial Senate race; Kohler retains governorship.
– Wisconsin Central Railway reorganization plan is approved.

1953 Constitutional amendment to base State Senate districts on area and population is passed.

1954 Senator McCarthy probes "un-American activities," in witch-hunt against Communists.
– Anti-McCarthy sentiment grows.
– Kraft Foods Co. wins exclusive right to make rindless Swiss cheese in 4-year old patent case; court holds Wisconsin (which tried to make process available to all state producers) not liable for patent infringement.

1955 Mrs. G. Wise becomes first woman appointed as Wisconsin State Secretary.
– Governor Kohler is inaugurated.
– Support for Senator McCarthy ebbs.

1956 Mrs. Wise briefly serves as acting governor; she is first woman ever to hold the post in Wisconsin.
– Wiley is reelected to Senate.

1957 Senator McCarthy dies; Proxmire wins his seat in special election, becomes first Democrat elected since 1932.
– Mrs. O. Smith is named State Treasurer.

1958 Menominee Indian Tribe votes to organize their reservation as county.
– Democrats score major victories in November election when Proxmire is reelected and Gaylord Nelson is voted in as governor.

1959 Professor Tatum of University of Wisconsin wins Man of the Year award.

1960 University of Wisconsin's Dr. Senn is named to direct biotron, world's first controlled environment lab.

1961 U.S. Supreme Court upholds State law requiring attorneys to belong to single bar association.
– Menominee Indian Reservation becomes Wisconsin's 72nd County, known as Menominee County.

1962 Gaylord Nelson defeats Wiley for senator.

1963 Tax Commissioner Gronouski is appointed U.S. Postmaster General.
– NAACP launches black voter registration drive.

1964 Congress of Racial Equality (CORE) demonstrators disrupt legislative session, force Assembly to adjourn.
– Proxmire wins Senate race; Republican W.P. Knowles is elected governor.

1965 H.C. La Follette is sworn in as State Attorney General.
– Capitol building is dedicated.

1966 NAACP Youth Council demands State law barring members of segregated organizations from holding public office.
– Wisconsin wins "Keep America Beautiful" award.
– Knowles is reelected governor; Republicans regain control of assembly.

1967 State Supreme Court orders new trial for Assemblyman Alfonsi, charged with bribery to promote bill; Alfonsi was reelected in 1966, but was deprived of his seat; he is afterwards sworn in for 9th term.
– Students demonstrate against job recruiting at university by Dow Chemical Company, manufacturers of napalm for Vietnam War.
– Disorderly student protests over CIA and armed forces recruitment on campus shut down Madison bus system.
– Green Bay Packers football team brings $8.5 million to State in season.

1968 Knowles is reelected governor; Nelson holds on to senate seat.
– Students rampage administration building at State University, demand action on black student union, and more Afro-American courses; ninety-one students, mostly black, are suspended.
– Firebombs at University of Wisconsin damage 15,000 undergrad records.
– 300 students occupy administration building in sit-in over alleged university investments in South Africa.

1969 Anti-draft protestors disrupt Knowles Inauguration ceremony.
– State government is under complete Republican control for first time since 1959.
– National Guard troops are ordered to University of Wisconsin campus to put down student demonstrations; use of troops to control student protectors is believe to be first in nation.

1970 Legislature grants Knowles' request for expanded emergency police powers to put down anti-war protests.
– Capitol is evacuated after bomb threat.

– Proxmire is reelected to senate; Patrick Lucey wins race for governor.
– Students continue to demonstrate on university campus.
– University President Harrington resigns in wake of continued protests.
– University of Wisconsin's Army Math Research Center is destroyed by bomb explosion; one student is killed, four injured in blast.
– Population is 4,417,821.

1971 Patrick Lucey is inaugurated; he becomes first Governor elected to four-year term.
– Rev. J.E. Groppi is jailed for contempt of State Legislature for leading sit-in at State Capitol.

1972 Royal Canadian Mounted Police arrest K.L. Armstrong for bombing of Army Math Research Center at University of Wisconsin, Madison.

1973 State Supreme Court rules Wisconsin police in disguise must make a reasonable effort to identify them when making arrests.

1974 Lucey and Nelson win reelection.
– Universities face rising costs, declining enrollment.

1975 Karleton Armstrong is imprisoned for arson and second degree murder in 1970 anti-war bombing of University of Wisconsin building in Madison he is denied parole.
– Menominee County fails politically and economically, is returned to reservation status.

1976 David Sylvan Fine is arrested; one of four men connected to 1970 bombing of Math Center, he is sentenced to seven years' imprisonment.

1977 Lucey resigns governorship to become Ambassador to Mexico. Lt. Col. Martin Sehreiber becomes acting governor.
– Thousands of State workers go on strike; National Guard is called in to assist in hospitals, mental institutions, and prisons.
– Dwight Alan Armstrong arrested in connection with 1970 Math Center bombing; he pleads no contest, receives seven-year sentence.
– No-fault State law substitutes "irretrievable breakdown of marriage" for all existing grounds for civil divorce.
– Livestock and dairy products make up more than 80 percent of State's agricultural receipts.

1978 Republican Lee Dreyfus is elected governor in close race with acting governor Schreiber.

1979 Anti-war activist David Fine is released after serving three years for 1970 bombing of Army Math Research Center.

1980 Rev. Robert Cornell, candidate for Congress, drops out of race as result of decree from Pope John Paul II forbidding priests to run for political office.
– Karleton Armstrong is released on parole after eight years in prison.

1981 Col. Dreyfus asks former Beatle Paul McCartney to waive royalties due him on State song, "On Wisconsin"; McCartney ob-

tained rights several years previously when he purchased Edward H. Marsh Company, music publisher; McCartney turns down request.
– In Milwaukee, Joseph Schlitz Brewing Company, "the beer that made Milwaukee famous," closes brewery after 133 years of operation.

1982 Proxmire is reelected to Senate; Anthony S. Earl is voted in as governor.
– 600 people storm bridge at Menominee after University of Wisconsin homecoming celebration; 175 are arrested.
– New $70 million downtown Milwaukee shopping center opens.

1983 Sales tax increases from 4–5 percent.

1984 Gerald Klezcka is elected to Congressional Seat left vacant by death of longtime Representative, Clement Zablocki.

1985 Kenneth Shaw is named president of University of Wisconsin system.

1986 Menominee Indians protest inclusion of their reservation among dozen proposed sites for nuclear waste.

1987 Republican Governor Tommy C. Thompson takes office.
– Dr. Donna E. Shalala is named Chancellor of University of Wisconsin, Madison.
– State voters approve constitutional amendments to legalize pail-mutual betting and Wisconsin lottery.

1988 Democrat Herbert H. Kohl defeats State Senator Susan Engeleiter in race to fill long-held seat of William Proxmire, who declines to run.
– Only months after acquiring American Motors, Chrysler Corporation announces closing of Kenosha plant; some 5,500 employees will lose jobs.
– After 28 years in office, Milwaukee Mayor Henry Maier steps down; his mayoral election was longest for big city mayors in history of U.S.

1989 University of Wisconsin faculty votes to petition Board of Regents to shut down ROTC program because it denies entry to homosexuals.

1990 Oshkosh man, Mark A. Peterson, is convicted of raping woman whom psychiatrists describe as having 46 personalities. Peterson argues that one of woman's personalities agreed to have sex with him; woman alleges that Peterson manipulated by waiting for her to turn into "Jennifer," one of personalities, so he could seduce her; some jurors say (afterwards) they were not convinced woman suffered from multiple personality disorder, but it appeared she suffered from some type of mental illness, and Peterson should have been aware of it.

1991 U.S. district judge in Milwaukee revokes citizenship of Anton Baumann, believed to have worked as guard at Nazi concentration camp; Baumann is ordered to relinquish naturalization certificate for lying on visa application in 1950; Judge Thomas I. Curran says it has not been proven that Baumann was at Stutthof camp near Gdansk, Poland during World War II, but enough evidence shows that Baumann was member of SS, Nazi elite security force.

1992 Serial killer Jeffrey L. Dahmer, after pleading guilty in January on charges of murdering 15 young men and boys and mutilated their bodies, is found sane by jury in Milwaukee Feb. 15; he is sentenced to serve 15 consecutive life terms in prison. (Wisconsin does not have death penalty.)

1998 Green Bay Packers lose Superbowl XXXII to Denver Broncos, 31 to 24; game is considered one of most competitive and exciting in history of championship football.
– Agriculture Secretary Dan Glickman reveals plans to simplify nation's complex milk-pricing system and make milk prices more responsive to market forces; current pricing makes milk prices dependent on producers' distance from Eau Claire; another proposed change would diminish government's regional price differentials, which keeps prices artificially low in Midwest compared to rest of U.S.

1999 **January 27.** In two votes the Senate votes along party lines, 56-44, to reject a Democratic proposal to dismiss the impeachment case against President Clinton and to subpoena three witnesses including Monica Lewinsky. Wisconsin Democrat Feingold makes the only crossover vote.

DIRECTORY OF STATE SERVICES

OFFICE OF THE GOVERNOR
P.O. Box 7863
Madison, WI 53707-7863
Fax: 608-267-8983
Governor: 608-266-1212

Washington, DC Office
444 N. Capitol St., Ste. 613
Washington, DC 20001

OFFICE OF THE LIEUTENANT GOVERNOR
22 E. State Capitol
Madison, WI 53702
Fax: 608-267-3571
Lieutenant Governor: 608-266-3516

ATTORNEY GENERAL (JUSTICE DEPARTMENT)
P.O. Box 7857
Madison, WI 53707-7857
Fax: 608-267-2223
Attorney General: 608-266-1221

SECRETARY OF STATE
P.O. Box 7848
Madison, WI 53707-7848
Fax: 608-267-6813
Secretary of State: 608-266-8888

TREASURER
P.O. Box 7871
Madison, WI 53707
Fax: 608-266-2647
Treasurer: 608-266-1714

ADMINISTRATION DEPARTMENT
P.O. Box 7864
Madison, WI 53707-7864
Fax: 608-267-3842

Secretary: 608-266-1714

Claims Board
101 S. Wilson St.
Madison, WI 53702
Fax: 608-267-3842
Secretary: 608-266-2765

Reviser of Statutes Bureau
131 W. Wilson St., Ste. 800
Madison, WI 53703-3233
Fax: 608-267-0410
Reviser of Statutes: 608-267-3536

Sentencing Commission
P.O. Box 8457
Madison, WI 53708-8457
Fax: 608-261-8141
Executive Director: 608-267-2437

Tax Appeals Commission
101 E. Wilson St.
Madison, WI 53702
Chairman: 608-266-1391

AGRICULTURE, TRADE AND CONSUMER PROTECTION DEPARTMENT
P.O. Box 8911
Madison, WI 53708
Fax: 608-224-5045
Secretary: 608-224-5012

Central Animal Health Laboratory
6101 Mineral Point Rd.
Madison, WI 53705
Fax: 608-267-0636
Director: 608-266-2465

CORRECTIONS DEPARTMENT
P.O. Box 7925
Madison, WI 53707-7925
Fax: 608-267-3661
Secretary: 608-266-4548

DEVELOPMENT DEPARTMENT
P.O. Box 7970
Madison, WI 53707
Fax: 608-267-0436
Secretary: 608-266-7088

EMPLOYMENT RELATIONS DEPARTMENT
P.O. Box 7855
Madison, WI 53707-7855
Fax: 608-267-1020
Secretary: 608-266-9820

EMPLOYEE TRUST FUNDS DEPARTMENT
201 E. Washington, Rm. 171
Madison, WI 53702
Fax: 608-267-0633
Secretary: 608-266-1071

HEALTH AND SOCIAL SERVICES DEPARTMENT
P.O. Box 7850
Madison, WI 53707-7850
Fax: 608-266-7882
Secretary: 608-266-9622

Care and Treatment Facilities Division
P.O. Box 7850
Madison, WI 53707-7850
Fax: 608-266-2579

Community Services Division
P.O. Box 7850
Madison, WI 53707-7850
Fax: 608-266-2579
Administrator: 608-266-0554

Economic Support Division
P.O. Box 7850
Madison, WI 53707-7850
Fax: 608-261-6376
Administrator: 608-266-3035

Directory of State Services
Health Division
P.O. Box 7850
Madison, WI 53707-7850
Fax: 608-267-2832
Administrator: 608-266-1511

Management Services Division
P.O. Box 7850
Madison, WI 53707-7850
Fax: 608-267-2147
Administrator: 608-266-6954

Vocational Rehabilitation Division
P.O. Box 7850
Madison, WI 53707-7850
Fax: 608-267-3657
Administrator: 608-266-5466

INDUSTRY, LABOR AND HUMAN RELATIONS DEPARTMENT
P.O. Box 7946
Madison, WI 53707
Fax: 608-266-1784
Secretary: 608-266-7552

MILITARY AFFAIRS DEPARTMENT
P.O. Box 8111
Madison, WI 53708-8111
Fax: 608-242-3111
Adjutant General: 608-242-3001

NATURAL RESOURCES DEPARTMENT
P.O. Box 7921
Madison, WI 53707
Fax: 608-266-6983
Secretary: 608-266-2121

PUBLIC INSTRUCTION DEPARTMENT
P.O. Box 7841
Madison, WI 53707-7841

Fax: 608-267-1052
State Superintendent: 608-266-1771

Learning Support Instructional
Services Division
P.O. Box 7841
Madison, WI 53707-7841
Fax: 608-267-1052
Assistant Superintendent: 608-266-3361

Management and Budget Division
P.O. Box 7841
Madison, WI 53707-7841
Fax: 608-267-1052
Assistant Superintendent: 608-266-3903

School Financial Resources and Management Services Division
P.O. Box 7841
Madison, WI 53707-7841
Fax: 608-267-1052
Assistant Superintendent: 608-266-3851

School for the Deaf and Hearing Impaired
309 W. Walworth Ave.
Delavan, WI 53115
Fax: 414-728-7160
Superintendent: 414-728-7120

School for the Visually Handicapped
1700 W. State St.
Janesville, WI 53545
Fax: 608-758-6161
Superintendent: 608-755-2950

REGULATION AND LICENSING DEPARTMENT
P.O. Box 8935
Madison, WI 53708-8935
Fax: 608-267-0644
Secretary: 608-266-8609

REVENUE DEPARTMENT
P.O. Box 8933
Madison, WI 53708
Fax: 608-266-5718
Secretary: 608-266-1611

TRANSPORTATION DEPARTMENT
P.O. Box 7910
Madison, WI 53707-7910
Fax: 608-266-9912
Secretary: 608-266-1113

VETERANS AFFAIRS DEPARTMENT
P.O. Box 7843
Madison, WI 53707
Fax: 608-267-0403
Secretary: 608-266-1315

AGING AND LONG TERM CARE BOARD
214 N. Hamilton St.
Madison, WI 53707
Fax: 608-261-6570
Executive Director: 608-266-8944

ARTS BOARD
101 E. Wilson St., 1ˢᵗ Fl.
Madison, WI 53702
Fax: 608-267-0380
Executive Director: 608-266-0190

BANKING COMMISSION
P.O. Box 7876
Madison, WI 53707-7876
Fax: 608-267-6889
Commissioner: 608-266-1621

BUILDING COMMISSION
P.O. Box 7866
Madison, WI 53707
Fax: 608-267-2710
Chairman: 266-1031

CREDIT UNIONS COMMISSIONER
101 E. Wilson St., 4ᵗʰ Fl.
Madison, WI 53702
Fax: 608-267-0479
Commissioner: 608-266-0438

EDUCATIONAL COMMUNICATIONS BOARD
3319 Beltine Hwy.
Madison, WI 53713-4296
Fax: 608-264-9622
Executive Director: 608-264-9697

ELECTIONS BOARD
132 E. Wilson St., 3ʳᵈ Fl.
Madison, WI 53702
Fax: 608-267-0500
Chairman: 608-266-8087

EMPLOYMENT RELATIONS COMMISSION
P.O. Box 7870
Madison, WI 53707-7870
Fax: 608-266-6930
Chairman: 608-266-1381

ETHICS BOARD
44 E. Mifflin St., Ste. 601
Madison, WI 53703-2800
Fax: 608-264-9309
Executive Director: 608-266-8123

GAMING COMMISSION
P.O. Box 8979
Madison, WI 53708-8979
Fax: 608-267-4879
Chairman: 608-264-6607

HEALTH EDUCATIONAL FACILITIES AUTHORITY
18000 W. Sarah Ln., Ste. 140
Brookfield, WI 53045-5843
Fax: 414-792-0649
Executive Director: 414-792-0466

HIGHER EDUCATIONAL AIDS BOARD
P.O. Box 7885
Madison, WI 53707
Fax: 608-267-2808

Executive Secretary: 608-267-2208

HISTORICAL SOCIETY
816 State St.
Madison, WI 53706
Fax: 608-264-6404
Director: 608-264-6400

HOUSING AND ECONOMIC DEVELOPMENT AUTHORITY
P.O. Box 1728
Madison, WI 53701-1728
Fax: 608-267-1099
Executive Director: 608-266-7884

INSURANCE COMMISSION
P.O. Box 7873
Madison, WI 53707-7873
Fax: 608-266-9935
Commissioner: 608-266-3585

JUDICIAL COMMISSION
110 E. Main St., Ste. 606
Madison, WI 53703
Fax: 608-266-8647
Executive Director: 608-266-7637

JUDICIAL COUNCIL
25 W. Main St., Rm. 777
Madison, WI 53703
Fax: 608-267-4507
Executive Secretary: 608-266-1319

LABOR AND INDUSTRY REVIEW COMMISSION
P.O. Box 8126
Madison, WI 53708
Fax: 608-267-4409
Chairman: 608-266-9850

LEGISLATIVE AUDIT BUREAU
131 W. Wilson St., Ste. 402
Madison, WI 53703
Fax: 608-267-0410
State Auditor: 608-266-2818

PERSONNEL COMMISSION
131 W. Wilson St., Rm. 1004
Madison, WI 53702
Chairperson: 608-266-1995

PUBLIC DEFENDER
P.O. Box 7923
Madison, WI 53707
Fax: 608-267-0584
State Public Defender: 608-266-0087

PUBLIC SERVICE COMMISSION
P.O. Box 7854
Madison, WI 53707-7854
Fax: 608-266-1401
Chairman: 608-267-7897

SAVINGS & LOAN COMMISSION
4785 Hayes Rd., Ste. 202
Madison, WI 53704-7365
Fax: 608-242-2187
Commissioner: 608-242-2180

SECURITIES COMMISSION
P.O. Box 1768
Madison, WI 53701
Fax: 608-256-1259
Commissioner: 608-266-3431

STATE FAIR
P.O. Box 14990
West Allis, WI 53214-0990
Fax: 414-266-7007
Director: 414-266-7000

TECHNICAL COLLEGE SYSTEM
P.O. Box 7874
Madison, WI 53707-7874
Fax: 608-266-1285
Director: 608-266-1207

MEMBERS OF CONGRESS

SENATE

SEN. HERBERT H. KOHL (D) (b. 1935); 2nd Term;
Phone: 202-224-5653; Fax: 202-224-9787;
E-mail: senator_kohl@kohl.senate.gov

www.kohl.senate.gov

SEN. RUSS FEINGOLD (D) (b. 1953); 2nd Term;
Phone: 202-224-5323; Fax: 202-224-2725;
E-mail: russell_feingold@feingold.senate.gov

www.senate.gov/~feingold

HOUSE

PAUL D. RYAN (R-1st) (b. 1970); 1st Term;
Phone: 202-225-3031; Fax: 202-225-3393;
E-mail: wi01@legislators.com

www.gov/ryan

TAMMY BALDWIN (D-2nd) (b. 1962); 1st Term;
Phone: 202-225-2906; Fax: 202-225-6942;
E-mail: tammy.baldwin@mail.house.gov

www.house.gov/baldwin/

RON J. KIND (D-3rd) (b. 1963); 2nd Term;
Phone: 202-225-5506; Fax: 202-225-5739;
E-mail: ron.kind@mail.house.gov

www.house.gov/kind

JERRY KLECZKA (D-14th) (b. 1943); 9th Term;
Phone: 202-225-4572; Fax: 202-225-8135;
E-mail: wi04@legislators.com

www.house.gov/kleczka

THOMAS BARRETT (D-5th) (b. 1953); 4th Term;
Phone: 202-225-3571; Fax: 202-225-2185;
E-mail: telltom@mail.house.gov

www.house.gov/barrett/

THOMAS E. PETRI (R-6th) (b. 1940); 11th Term;
Phone: 202-225-2476; Fax: 202-225-2356;
E-mail: wi06@legislators.com

www.house.gov/petri/

DAVID R. OBEY (D-7th) (b. 1938); 16th Term;
Phone: 202-225-3365; Fax: 202-225-3240; E-mail: (None)

MARK GREEN (R-8th) (b. 1960); 1st Term;
Phone: 202-225-5665; Fax: 202-225-5729;
E-mail: mark.green@mail.house.gov

www.house.gov/markgreen

F. JAMES SENSENBRENNER, Jr. (9th) (b. 1943); 11th Term;
Phone: 202-225-5101; Fax: 202-225-3190;
E-mail: sensen09@mail.house.gov

www.house.gov/sensenbrenner/

TWENTIETH CENTURY GOVERNORS

SCOFIELD, EDWARD (1842-1925), eighteenth governor of Wisconsin (1897-1901), was born in Clearfield, Pennsylvania on March 28, 1842, the son of Isaac and Mary (Collins) Scofield. He attended the district school until the age of thirteen, when he became a printer's apprentice, and at the start of the Civil War enlisted in the 11th Pennsylvania Infantry. Meritorious service led to his promotion, first as a lieutenant, then to the rank of captain, the latter for gallantry on the field at Gettysburg, and finally major. At the battle of the Wilderness on May 5, 1864, Scofield was captured by the Confederates and held in southern prisons for ten months.

After the war, Scofield was engaged in railway surveying from 1865-68, then became foreman of a lumber business on his own account in 1876. In 1890, he formed a partnership with George R. Arnold under the name of Edward Scofield & Company, the business being incorporated four years later as the Scofield & Arnold Lumber Company.

In 1887 Scofield was elected as the Republican candidate to the Wisconsin State Senate, and was reelected for a second term two years later, serving until 1891. Twice elected Governor of Wisconsin, Scofield served from January 1897 to January 1901. His administration was distinguished for the reform effected in the state institutions; he established, through the State board of control, an efficient system of civil service, and upon his recommendation, a tax commission was appointed for the purpose of working out a system of tax reform.

After retiring from the executive office, Scofield returned to the management of his business. He died February 3, 1925.

LA FOLLETTE, ROBERT MARION (1855-1925), nineteenth governor of Wisconsin (1901-1906), was born in Primrose, Wisconsin on June 14, 1855, the son of Josiah and Mary (Ferguson)

La Follette. His parents were pioneer settlers of the Wisconsin wilderness, and he was born in the log cabin house on his father's farm. His early education was obtained in the district school, and at a private academy in Madison, where the family settled in 1873.

By earnest study in between farm work, La Follette completed his preparation for college, and entered the Wisconsin State University in 1875. As an undergraduate, he gained distinction, particularly in literature and oratory, winning the university contest in oratory in his senior year, and also the state oratorical contest and the interstate contest at Iowa City, Iowa. After his graduation in 1879, La Follette began the study of law and was admitted to the bar in the following February. He began a practice in Madison, and from the very first achieved such success and reputation that in the fall of 1880 he was elected District Attorney of Dane County on the Republican ticket; in 1882 he was reelected in spite of strong opposition.

In 1884, at the age of twenty-nine, La Follette was elected to represent the third district of his state in the 49th Congress, and although the youngest man in that body, La Follette at once gained a national reputation for his brilliant speeches, particularly those on the iron and harbor bill, Mills bill, the Lodge force bill, and his reply to Speaker Carlisle in the tariff debate of 1888. La Follette was reelected in 1886 and 1888, and was defeated in 1890, only through the compulsory education clause in the Republican platform. In December 1889, he was appointed to the Committee of Ways and Means, and took a conspicuous part in preparing the McKinley tariff bill.

After La Follette retired from Congress, he was offered the comptrollership of the currency by President McKinley in 1896, but declined on account of his professional duties. He was, however, a delegate to the National Convention in 1896 and member of the Committee on Platform. Among his most famous addresses were "The Menace of the Machine" before the Chicago University in 1897, and "The Nomination of Candidates by Australian Ballot" before the University of Michigan in 1898.

In 1900, La Follette was elected by the Republican Party as governor of Wisconsin, and was reelected in 1902, his term expiring in January 1905. Through his efforts a primary election law was enacted in Wisconsin, by which all nominations were made by Australian ballot. During his administration, the Capitol in Madison was destroyed by fire (February 27, 1904). Governor La Follette was married December 31, 1881, to Belle Case, of Baraboo, Wisconsin. She was his classmate at the University of Wisconsin, and later took the law course there. In later years, she was prominent in the cause of physical culture among women, delivering lectures on the subject.

La Follette died June 18, 1925.

DAVIDSON, JAMES O. (1854-1922), Wisconsin's twentieth governor (1906-1911), was born in Upper Aardal, Sogn, Norway on February 10, 1854, the son of Ole and Ingeborg Davidson. His family came to the United States when he was eighteen, and eventually settled near Boscobel, Wisconsin. As a young man, Davidson worked as a farmhand, a tailor, and a clerk in a general store then moved to Soldiers Grove where he established his own general store arid null. In 1883, he married Helen M. Bliss, a schoolteacher who helped him complete his education. They had two daughters.

In 1888, Davidson was elected Village President for Soldiers Grove. He served as village treasurer in 1892, 1893, 1897 and 1898, and in 1892 was elected to the State Assembly. He won reelection to the Assembly in 1894 and 1896, and in 1898 became Wisconsin State Treasurer. In 1902, on the ticket with Governor La Follette, Davidson ran for lieutenant governor and was elected.

He won a second term in 1904, and when Governor La Follette resigned in 1906 to join the Senate, Davidson became the new State governor.

During his administration, Davidson worked to continue La Follette's reform programs. He extended State regulation of public utilities; telegraph companies, streetcars, telephones, water, and electricity companies. He also began an investigation into insurance company practices in the state.

Davidson left office in 1911, after two terms. In 1915 he was appointed President of the State Board of Control.

He died in Madison on December 16, 1922.

McGOVERN, FRANCIS E. (1866-1946), twenty-first governor of Wisconsin (1911-1915), was born in Sheboygan County, Wisconsin on January 21, 1866, the son of Lawrence and Ellen (Wren) McGovern. He attended the University of Wisconsin, graduated in 1890, then worked as a high school principal in Brodhead and Appleton, Wisconsin. He studied law in his spare time and in 1897 was admitted to the Wisconsin Bar. Seven years later, he was elected District Attorney for Milwaukee. When the Republican Party failed to endorse him for a second term in 1906, he ran as an Independent and won the election. He ran for the U.S. Senate in 1908, but was defeated.

In 1910 McGovern decided to run for governor, and formed an alliance with the progressive La Follette, who was seeking reelection to the Senate. Both won their respective elections. As governor, McGovern pushed through numerous reforms. He established the first workers' compensation pro-grain in the U.S., mandated a minimum wage for women, signed legislation regulating working hours for women and children, adopted the first successful state income tax, and reorganized state government to include a Highway Commission and Forest Commission. McGovern was also attentive to the needs of farmers and supported laws that encouraged the formation of farm cooperatives, increased agricultural education, and provided loans for farmers.

In 1912, McGovern was elected to a second term. By now he had parted ways with La Follette, and this caused friction with the Progressives in the Legislature. They effectively blocked McGovern's proposals, thereby incapacitating his administration.

At the end of his second term in 1914, McGovern ran for a Senate seat, but lost the election, partly due to a lack of support from Progressives. He made an unsuccessful bid for the governorship in 1916, losing to Emanuel Philipp. From 1917 to 1920, he served in the Army Judge Advocate Department. He became ex-officio chairman of the Claims Board of the United States Emergency Fleet Corporation in 1920, and the following year, returned to his law practice. McGovern ran for Senate once again in 1925 and 1934, losing both times. He won the Democratic nomination for governor in 1940, but lost in the general election.

McGovern died on May 16, 1946. He was not married.

PHILIPP, EMANUEL L. (1861-1925), Wisconsin's twenty-second governor (1915-1921), was born near Honey Creek, Wisconsin on March 25, 1861, the son of Luzi and Sabina (Ludwig) Philipp. After completing high school, he became a telegrapher and agent for the Chicago and Northwestern Railroad. In the years that followed he worked as a train dispatcher and a contracting freight agent. He married Bertha Schweke in 1887. They had three children.

Between 1889 and 1897, Philipp worked as a general agent for the Gould lines, including the American Refrigerator Transit Company; as a traffic manager of the Schlitz Brewery; and as manager of a lumber company. He became president of the American Refrigerator Transit Company of St. Louis in 1897, and six years later he bought the organization and moved it to Wisconsin.

Philipp became active in Republican politics about 1900 when he served as chairman of the Milwaukee County Convention. At one time a supporter of La Follette, Philipp broke with him in 1904 and published The Truth About Wisconsin Freight Rates, a paper refuting La Follette's stance on the issue.

Philipp served as police commissioner of Milwaukee from 1909 to 1914. In 1914, he ran for governor and won. He was elected to two subsequent terms in 1916 and 1918.

Philipp's administration was marked by state contributions to the war effort in World War I and aid to returning veterans. The State Legislature passed the Prohibition Enforcement Act in 1919 to conform to federal law.

Philipp returned to his businesses after three terms as governor. He was a regent of Marquette University and also supported efforts of the Wisconsin Humane Society.

He died on June 15, 1925.

BLAINE, JOHN J. (1875-1934), twenty-third governor of Wisconsin (192 1-1927), was born in Wingville, Wisconsin on May 4, 1875, the son of James and Elizabeth (Brunstadt Johnson) Blaine. He attended Valparaiso University in Indiana, where he studied law and graduated in 1896. He was admitted to the Wisconsin Bar and began to practice in Montfort. After a year, he moved to Boscobel. He was elected Mayor of that city for four successive terms, and also served as county supervisor for four years. In 1904, he married Anna McSpaden. They had one adopted daughter, Helen.

In the Republican State Conventions of 1902 and 1904, Blaine supported La Follette for governor. Blaine was elected to the State Senate in 1908. He ran for governor in 1914, but lost the election. In 1918, he was elected Attorney General and served for two years. He became Governor of Wisconsin in 1920, an office he held for three terms. During his administration, Blame was a strong proponent of tax reform. He presented himself as the "Economy Governor" and strove to reduce state expenditures. In 1926, he was elected to the U.S. Senate. He served a single term, and then was appointed director of the Reconstruction Finance Corporation by President Roosevelt.

Blaine died suddenly of pneumonia on April 16, 1934.

ZIMMERMAN, FRED R. (1880-1954), twenty-fourth governor of Wisconsin (1927-1929), was born on November 20, 1880 in Milwaukee, the son of Charles and Augusta (Fiesenhauser) Zimmernimn. His father died when he was five, and Zimmerman worked to help support the family. He finished grammar school, and for a short time attended night school. In 1902, he became a milkman for the Bee Hive Dairy in Milwaukee. He married Amanda Freedy in 1904. They had two sons.

Zimmerman held a series of jobs over the next several years, including salesman, bookkeeper, and head of his own business, Berthlet & Company, which sold building materials. He entered politics in 1908 when he ran for the Wisconsin Assembly and won by six votes. Between 1912 and 1915, he was a board member for the town of Lake. He became director of industrial relations for Nash Motor Company in 1920. Two years later his political career continued when he was elected Secretary of State. He served two terms, and in 1926 ran for governor on the Republican ticket, winning over Independent Charles B. Perry and Democrat Virgil H. Cady.

Zimmerman's administration was marked by passage of the first drivers' license law in Wisconsin, establishment of a system for permanent voter registration in cities of over 5,000, creation of a six-man conservation commission, and modifications to income tax.

Zimmerman ran for governor again in 1928, but finished third in the primary. In 1929, President Hoover named him envoy to the Spanish-American Exposition in Seville, Spain. He returned to Wisconsin and ran for governor in 1934, losing again in the primary. From 1935 to 1936, he was a certifying officer for the Works Progress Administration. He ran an unsuccessful race for Congress in 1936. Two years later, he helped establish the firm Better Properties, Inc. of Milwaukee, and became its president. That same year he was elected Secretary of State, a post he held for nine consecutive terms. He tried unsuccessfully for a seat on the Supreme Court in 1945.

Fred Zimmerman died on December 14, 1954.

KOHLER, WALTER J. (1875-1940), twenty-fifth governor of Wisconsin (1929-1931), was born on March 3, 1875 in Sheboygan, Wisconsin, the son of John and Lilly (Vollrath) Kohler. His father was the founder of Kohler Company, which manufactured farm tools, and at the age of fifteen, Walter left school to work in his father's business. He married Charlotte H. Schroeder in 1900, and they had four sons. Two days after his wedding, his father died, and Walter became superintendent of the Kohler Company plant. In the years that followed, he served as president and chairman of the board for the company.

In 1916, Kohler was chosen as a presidential elector. This led him to become more involved in politics. In 1918, Governor Philipp appointed him to the Board of Regents of the University of Wisconsin, a position he held until 1924. In 1928, he ran for governor on the Republican ticket and won. During his term in office, Kohler attempted to reorganize state administrative offices. He brought his own businesslike methods to this task, which resulted in creation of the Department of the Budget and Accounts, the Bureau of Purchasing, the Bureau of Personnel, the Bureau of Engineering, and the Highway Commission. Kohler also expanded the Department of Agriculture and Markets, and added 800 positions to civil service.

Walter Kohler ran for a second term as governor in 1930, but lost in the primary to Philip La Follette. He ran again in 1932, beating La Follette in the primary, but losing to Democrat Albert Schmedeman in the general election. Kohler retired to business, which included concerns with Kohler Company, Vollrath Company, a Salt Lake City supply company, and several railroads.

Kohler died in River Bend, Wisconsin on April 21, 1940.

LA FOLLETTE, PHILLIP F. (1897-1965), Wisconsin's twenty-sixth and twenty-eighth governor (1931-1933 and 1935-1939), was born in Madison on May 8, 1897, the son of the famous Progressive leader and governor, Robert La Follette, and Belle (Case) La Follette. He attended the University of Wisconsin, graduating in 1919. During World War I, he served as a second lieutenant in the U.S. Army. He subsequently studied law in Washington, D.C. and at the University of Wisconsin Law School. He was admitted to the Bar, and entered his father's old law firm of La Follette, Rogers and Roberts. He married Isabel Bacon in 1923. They had three children.

In 1924, La Follette was elected District Attorney for Dane County. He served one term, and between 1926 and 1931 was a lecturer for the University of Wisconsin Law School. He ran for governor in 1930, winning against incumbent Walter Kohler in the primary, and Democrat Charles E. Hammersley in the general election. As governor, La Follette asked for greater government control over banks and the electric power industry. He also increased public works projects, especially highway building, and attempted to push through various anti-Depression measures. Although a conservative Senate blocked many of his proposals, he did see an Unemployment Compensation Act and a new State Labor Code passed. La Follette's Depression era administration was also marked by the failure of 116 banks, a fall in farm income of thirty-three percent in two years, and the closure of 1,500 businesses.

La Follette ran for a second term in 1932, but was defeated in the primary by his old adversary Walter Kohler. He responded to this defeat by throwing his support to Franklin D. Roosevelt and other Democrats. But rather than actually join the Democratic Party, he formed a third, Progressive Party, and returned in 1934 to win the gubernatorial election by a narrow margin.

During his second administration, La Follette promoted programs for public power, public works and general relief, with little success from the conservative-controlled Senate. He won a third term in office in 1936, and with a new, more progressive group in the Legislature, forced passage of the Wisconsin Labor Relations Act. He founded the National Progressives of America in 1938, the same year he ran for a fourth term as governor. Fighting claims that some of the policies of the new progressives resembled that of European fascists, La Follette lost the election. Disheartened by his defeat, he returned to his law practice, and refused further association with Wisconsin politics.

He died in Madison on August 10, 1965.

SCHMEDEMAN, ALBERT G. (1864-1946), twenty-seventh governor of Wisconsin (1933-1935), was born on November 25, 1864 in Madison, Wisconsin, the son of Henry and Wilhelmina (Camien) Schmedeman. He attended Northwestern Business College, and upon graduation began work for the clothing firm of Olson, Winder and Veerhusen as a bundle boy. He eventually became a member of the firm, and it was reorganized as Winder, Grinde and Schmedeman in 1892, he married Katherine Regan, and they had two children.

In 1904, Schmedeman was elected Alderman for the city of Madison. He served two terms, then became City Fire and Police Commissioner and a member of the Board of Education. He ran for Congress in 1910, but lost the election. He also tried for mayor of Madison in 1912, but was defeated. In 1913, he served as treasurer of the Democratic State Committee and supported Woodrow Wilson. Wilson reciprocated by appointing him Minister to Norway, a position he held for the next eight years. Schmedeman returned to Wisconsin and was employed at the National Guardian Life Insurance Company.

In 1925, Schmedeman was elected Mayor of Madison, and served until 1932, when he won the governorship. (He had run a previous unsuccessful campaign for the governor's office in 1928.) His administration was faced with the problems of the Great Depression. Schmedeman ordered the banks closed, and attempted to secure a moratorium on farm and home loans, he also sent state troops to maintain order during dairy strikes. During his term, the Prohibition Enforcement Act was repealed.

Schmedeman ran for a second term in 1934. That summer, while dedicating Rib Mountain State Park at Wausau, he fell and hurt his foot. Neglecting to care for it properly in the midst of his political campaign, he developed gangrene, and eventually lost the leg. He was defeated in the election by Progressive Philip La Follette; however, the legislature voted him compensation for his injury. In 1935, President Roosevelt named him Federal Housing Administrator for Wisconsin. He retired from this post in 1942, in poor health.

Albert Schmedeman died in Madison on November 26, 1946.

HEIL, JULIUS PETER (1876-1949), twenty-ninth governor of Wisconsin (1939-1943), was born on July 24, 1876 in Duesmond an der Mosel, Germany, the son of Franz and Barbara (Krebs) Heil. His family came to Wisconsin in 1881 and he attended Mill Valley rural school until the age of twelve. In 1888, he began work as an assistant in a general store. Later he went to Milwaukee, where he worked a series of jobs including drill press operator, newspaper vendor on trains, streetcar conductor, boiler fireman, and assistant blacksmith. He also worked as a rail joints salesman, a job that took him to many parts of the world. In 1900, he married Elizabeth Conrad. They had one son.

Heil settled in Milwaukee again in 1901 and established the Heil Rail Joint Company, which later became known as Heil Company. He ran for Milwaukee city treasurer in 1908, but lost the election and devoted himself to his business until 1938, when he made a reentry into politics with his candidacy for governor. A Republican, he won against Progressive Philip La Follette, who was running for an unprecedented fourth term. Once in office, Heil began to reorganize State government, using business methods. He created a Motor Vehicle Department, and the controversial Division of Departmental Research, and consolidated the Department of Welfare. Reelected in 1940, he created the State Guard to replace the National Guard during World War II. He also signed into law the Industrial Peace Act. He ran for a third term in 1942, but lost to Orland Loomis.

Heil returned to Heil Company, where he was made resident, a position he held until 1946, when he turned it over to his son, Joseph. He subsequently served as chairman of the board for the company until his death on November 30, 1949.

LOOMIS, ORLAND S. (1893-1942), governor-elect (1942), was born on November 2, 1893 in Mauston, Wisconsin, the son of Morgan and Clara (Steen) Loomis. He attended Ripon College and the University of Wisconsin, where he received a law degree in 1917. He married Florence Ely in 1918. They had three children. That same year, he enlisted in the U.S. Army and was sent to France with a medical supply unit. Returning in 1919, he practiced law in Mauston.

In 1922, Loomis was elected Mauston City Attorney, and served until 1931. He also served three terms as district attorney of Juneau County. In 1928, he was elected to the State Assembly, where he emerged as a leader of the Progressives. He won election to the Senate in 1930 on the Republican ticket, but in 1934 changed allegiance and joined the newly created Progressive Party. He ran as their candidate for attorney general in 1934, but lost.

In 1935, Loomis was appointed director of the state Rural Electrification Authority. He was elected Attorney General in 1935 and served a single term, losing a second election to John C. Martin. Loomis ran as the Progressive candidate for governor in 1940, but was narrowly defeated. He returned two years later to win the governorship. Tragically, in December of 1942, before he could enter the office, he suffered a series of heart attacks and died. He was forty-nine at the time of his death.

GOODLAND, WALTER S. (1862-1947), Wisconsin's thirtieth governor (1943-1947), was born in Sharon, Wisconsin on December 22, 1862, the son of John and Carolina (Clark) Goodland. He attended Lawrence College for one year, and then found work as a schoolteacher in the rural area near Appleton, Wisconsin. In 1883, he married Christena Lewis. They had four children.

After teaching school for five years, Goodland studied law in his father's law office. He was admitted to the Wisconsin Bar in 1886, and soon moved to Wakefield, Michigan where he started a law practice. He also established a newspaper, The Wakefield Bulletin, which failed when the town was destroyed by fire a year later. His wife Christena died in 1896, and two years later, he married her sister, Annie Lewis. He had one daughter by his second marriage. Also in 1888, Goodland founded the newspaper, *Ironwood Times*, which remained in print until 1895.

Goodland served as postmaster of Ironwood until 1899 when he moved to Beloit, Wisconsin and became part owner and publisher of the Daily News. In 1900, he became editor and publisher of the Racine Times, and in 1915 was president of Call Publishing Company, which owned the Racine paper.

While in Racine, Goodland served as president of the Water Commission for twelve years, and mayor of the city for one term. He was elected to the State Senate in 1926, and won reelection in 1930. His wife Annie died in December of that year, and three years later, he married Madge (Roach) Risney. In 1938, under Governor Heil, Goodland was elected Lieutenant Governor. He was reelected to the office in 1940 and 1942. Shortly before inauguration in 1942, Governor-elect Loomis died of a heart attack, and the Supreme Court named Goodland Acting Governor. He was elected to the office in 1944, and again in 1946.

During his administration, Goodland took advantage of World War II prosperity to build up the state treasury. Many of these funds were devoted to rehabilitation and veterans' benefits. Goodland was a strong supporter of the Thomson Anti-Gambling Act of 1945. He also helped develop a fifteen-point program to improve conditions for state employees. Walter Goodland died on March 12, 1947, just after the start of his third term as governor.

RENNEBOHM, OSCAR (1889-1968), thirty-first governor of Wisconsin (1947-1951), was born in Leeds, Wisconsin on May 25, 1889, the son of William and Julia (Brandt) Rennebohm. His family moved to Milwaukee, and he attended high school there, graduating in 1908. He worked in a drug store for a year then entered the University of Wisconsin in Madison, where he studied pharmacy. Upon graduation in 1911, he worked for a druggist, and then bought a pharmacy. During World War I, he attended officer's candidate school and was commissioned Ensign. In 1920, he married Mary Fowler. They had one daughter.

Rennebohm entered politics in 1944 when he was elected Lieutenant Governor under Governor Goodland. Both he and Goodland were reelected in 1946, and when the governor died the following year, Rennebohm became Acting Governor. In 1948, he was officially elected to the office of governor. During his administration, Rennebohm supported changes to public education, began a veterans' housing program, and charged the State Building Commission with a new program for construction in the state.

At the end of Rennebohm's term in 1950, he returned to his pharmaceutical activities. He was president of the Wisconsin Pharmaceutical Association, vice-president of the American Pharmaceutical Association, and treasurer of the National Association of Retail Druggists. He also served on the Board of Regents for the University of Wisconsin. Rennebohm died in Maple Bluff, Wisconsin on October 15, 1968.

KOHLER, WALTER J., JR. (1904-1976), thirty-second governor of Wisconsin (1951-1957), was born in Sheboygan, Wisconsin on April 4, 1904, the son of Walter and Charlotte (Schroeder) Kohler. His father was governor of Wisconsin from 1929 to 1931. Walter Jr. attended Phillips Academy in Andover, Massachusetts and Yale University, where he earned a Ph.D. degree in 1925. In 1932, he married Celeste McVoy Holden. They had two children.

After graduation from the university, Kohler began a job with the family business, working first in engineering and ceramic research, and later in marketing and sales. He was named director of the Kohler Company in 1936, and in 1937 became its secretary. During World War II, Kohler was commissioned a lieutenant in the Naval Reserve; he was called to active duty, and served in the Western Pacific. After the war, he returned to Kohler Company, where he was president from 1945-47. He then became president of the Vollrath Company, another family business.

In 1946, Kohler and his wife, Celeste, were divorced. He married Charlotte McAleer in 1948. That same year, he entered politics as a delegate-at-large at the Republican National Convention. He ran for governor in 1950 and won. He won reelection in 1952 and 1954, defeating Democrat William Proxmire both times, but by a slim margin in the second race. During his three terms as governor, Kohler sought to reduce state income tax, raise salaries for state employees, and continue Wisconsin's state building program. The Rosenberry Act, which reapportioned state voting districts on a population basis, was passed during his administration. In addition, a program to eradicate dairy cattle disease was begun in the state.

Kohler declined reelection in 1956, and the following year, ran for the senate seat vacated by the death of Senator Joseph R. McCarthy. He met his Democratic adversary, William Proxmire, once again in the election, and this time Proxmire won. Kohler returned to his position as president of Vollrath Company.

Kohler died in Sheboygan on March 21, 1976.

THOMSON, VERNON W. (1905-), Wisconsin's thirty-third governor (1957-1959), was born on November 5, 1905 in Richland Center, Wisconsin, the son of Alva and Ella (Wallace) Thomson. He attended Carroll College and the University of Wisconsin, where he graduated in 1927. Thomson taught at Viroqua High School, and later at Madison Vocational School while studying law at the University of Wisconsin Law School. He was admitted to the Wisconsin Bar in 1932. From 1933-35, he worked as an enrolling officer for the Civilian Conservation Corps. He also was Assistant District Attorney of Richland County during that time. He served as Richland Center City Attorney from 1933 to 1937, and again from 1942 to 1944. In 1936, he married Helen Davis. They had three children.

Thomson was elected to the Wisconsin Assembly in 1935, and served for eight terms, until 1949. In 1950 he ran for State Attorney General and was elected to three consecutive terms. Following this service, in 1956, he tried for the governorship and won against Democrat William Proxmire. As governor, Thomson worked to enact one of the strictest lobbying laws in the United States. He also signed legislation, which provided group life insurance for state employees and overhauled the public retirement system. Thomson sought reelection in 1958, but was defeated by Gaylord Nelson.

Thomson returned to Madison to practice law for two years then ran for the U.S. House of Representatives in 1960. He was reelected twelve times, serving until 1974 when he declined to run again. He was appointed to the Federal Election Commission in 1975.

NELSON, GAYLORD ANTON (1916-), thirty-fourth governor of Wisconsin (1959-1963), was born on June 4, 1916 in Clear Lake, Wisconsin, the son of Anton and Mary (Bradt Hogan) Nelson. After receiving his education at San Jose State College in California and the University of Wisconsin Law School, he was admitted to the Wisconsin Bar in 1942. During World War II, he served in the U.S. Army in the Pacific Theater. In 1946, he returned and began a law practice in Madison. He ran as a Republican for the Wisconsin State Assembly that same year, but lost the election, in 1947, he married Carrie Lee Dotson. They had three children.

Nelson changed his affiliation to the Democratic Party in 1948, and ran for the State Senate. He served for three consecutive terms, until 1958. In 1954, he ran for the U.S. House of Representatives, but lost to Glenn R. Davis. Nelson ran for the governorship of Wisconsin in 1958, and was elected, becoming the first Democratic governor since 1932. He served for two terms.

During his administration, Nelson reorganized the state government, creating a Department of Economic Development, Department of Administration, and a State Commission on Aging. He supported conservation efforts with the passage of the Outdoor Recreation Act of 1961.

Nelson decided not to run for a third term as governor. In 1964, he ran for a seat in the U.S. Senate and won.

Nelson served on numerous committees including the Finance Committee, the Select Committee on Small Business, the Subcommittee on Private Pension Plans, the Subcommittee on Monopoly, and the Subcommittee on Employment, Poverty, and Migratory Labor.

REYNOLDS, JOHN W. (1921-), thirty-fifth governor of Wisconsin (1963-1965), was born in Green Bay, Wisconsin on April 4, 1921, the son of John and Madge (Flatley) Reynolds. He attended the University of Wisconsin and graduated in 1942. During World War II, he served in the army infantry, where he rose to the rank of master sergeant. He was commissioned in 1944 and sent to the Counter Intelligence Corps, where he served until 1946. He was discharged with the rank of first lieutenant. In 1947, he married Patricia Ann Brody. They had three children.

After his discharge from the army, Reynolds studied law at the University of Wisconsin Law School. He graduated in 1949 and began a law practice in Green Bay. In 1950, he ran for the House of Representatives, but was defeated. From 1951-52, he served as district director of the Office of Price Stabilization. He was chairman of the Brown County Democratic Party from 1952 to 1956, and from 1955 to 1958 was the U.S. Commissioner for the Eastern Judicial District of Wisconsin. He also served on the State Administration Commission.

Reynolds was elected State Attorney General in 1958. Four years later, he became Governor of Wisconsin. As governor, Reynolds championed civil rights and supported social services. He sought to expand Wisconsin's health, education, and welfare programs. He also worked to extend research facilities of the University of Wisconsin and to attract more businesses to the state.

Reynolds acted as a stand-in for Lyndon Johnson in the 1964 Wisconsin Democratic presidential primary. He emphasized the civil rights issue in his campaign, and won easily over Alabama Governor George Wallace. The same year, Reynolds also sought reelection as governor, but lost to Warren P. Knowles. Reynolds became the U.S. District Judge for Wisconsin's Eastern District in 1965. He remained in that post for many years.

In 1967, his wife, Patricia, died. Reynolds later married Jane Conway, and with her has two children.

KNOWLES, WARREN P. (1908-1993), Wisconsin's thirty-sixth governor (1965-1971), was born on August 19, 1908 in River Falls, Wisconsin, the son of William P. Knowles II and Anna (Deneen) Knowles. He attended Carleton College in Minnesota, and the University of Wisconsin, where he graduated with a law degree in 1933. He was admitted to the Wisconsin Bar and became a partner in a law firm in New Richmond, Wisconsin.

Knowles was elected to the New Richmond County Board in 1935, and served five years. In 1940 he became a state senator, but World War II interrupted his time in the State Senate. He en-

tered the U.S. Navy and took part in the invasions of Attu, Normandy and southern France. In 1946 he was discharged with the rank of lieutenant, and returned to the State Senate where he remained until 1953, serving as Majority Floor Leader for a time. Meanwhile, in 1943, he married Dorothy C. Guidry, a union that ended in divorce in 1968.

Knowles continued his political career in 1954, when he was elected Lieutenant Governor of Wisconsin. Twice reelected, he served until 1964, when he won the governorship in a race against incumbent John W. Reynolds. During his administration, Knowles attempted to curb what he called excessive spending. He promoted the development of industry and other economic expansion in the state. He was reelected in 1966 and 1968. His later terms were concerned with the expansion of the state college system, vocational education, improvements to highways, water pollution control, and the provision of new outdoor recreation areas. He appointed the Kellett Commission to make recommendations on how to reorganize state government and control the state debt. He also created the Tarr Task Force to advise on fiscal management.

Knowles declined reelection in 1970. He became the chairman of the board for Inland Financial Corporation in 1971. After leaving the governorship, he also remained active in philanthropic and civic activities.

LUCEY, PATRICK J. (1918-), thirty-seventh governor of Wisconsin (1971-1977) was born on March 21, 1918 in La Crosse, Wisconsin, the son of Gregory and Ella (McNamara) Lucey. He attended St. Thomas College from 1936 to 1939 then managed his father's grocery store for three years. In 1941 he joined the army and was sent to the Caribbean. He was discharged in 1945 with the rank of captain. For the following six years, he managed fourteen farms in southwestern Wisconsin. He also returned to school and finished his B.A. at the University of Wisconsin in 1946. In 1951, he married Jean Vlasis. They had three children.

Lucey entered politics in 1948 when he was elected to the State Assembly. Two years later he ran for U.S. Representative, but was defeated. Between 1951 and 1953, he was executive director of the Wisconsin Democratic Party. He later served as chairman of that body. Lucey also worked as a campaign manager. In 1952, he managed Thomas Fairchild's bid for Senate; in 1954, he was in charge of James E. Doyle's race for governor; and in 1957, he took control of William Proxmire's run for the U.S. Senate. He was a campaign aide for John F. Kennedy in the 1960 presidential election, and for Robert Kennedy in 1968.

Lucey ran his own successful campaign for lieutenant governor of Wisconsin in 1964. He tried for the governorship two years later, but was defeated by incumbent Warren P. Knowles. He ran again in 1970 and won, becoming the first Wisconsin governor ever elected to a four-year term.

During his administration, Lucey supported changes to the tax system and the campaign financing law. The legislature passed an ethics code for state officials, and reformed the state revenue sharing system with municipalities. Lucey was reelected to a second term in 1974. He served until July 7, 1977, when he resigned to take an appointment as U.S. Ambassador to Mexico.

SCHREIBER, MARTIN J. (1939-), thirty-eighth governor of Wisconsin (1977-1979), was born in Milwaukee on April 8, 1939, the son of Martin and Emeline (Kurz) Schreiber. He received his education at Valparaiso University, the University of Wisconsin, and Marquette University, where he earned an LL.B. degree in 1964. In 1961, he married Elaine Thaney. They had four children.

In 1962, while still at the university, Schreiber was elected to the Wisconsin Senate. He was reelected in 1964 and 1968. Schreiber ran for lieutenant governor in 1966, but lost the election. He served as Democratic Caucus Chair in 1967 and 1969; then, in 1970, he ran once again for lieutenant governor on the Democratic ticket with Patrick Lucey. Schreiber won, becoming the first lieutenant governor in Wisconsin elected to a four-year term.

In 1974, Schreiber was reelected and, in 1977, when Lucey resigned to become Ambassador to Mexico, Schreiber became Acting Governor. In the remainder of the four-year governor's term, he sought to continue efforts started by Lucey. He signed into law an income tax relief bill for low-income and elderly persons, a new code of ethics for public employees, tighter lobbying regulations, and a tough drunk-driver law. Although he originally disapproved it, he also signed a bill to prohibit the use of state funds for non-therapeutic abortions.

Schreiber ran for governor in 1978, but was defeated by Lee Sherman Dreyfus. He subsequently moved to Stevens Point, where he became vice-president of Sentry Insurance. He tried for the governorship once again in the 1982 election, but was defeated in the primary by Anthony Earl. Schreiber then resumed work with Sentry Insurance.

DREYFUS, LEE SHERMAN (1926-), Wisconsin's thirty-ninth governor (1979-1983), was born in Milwaukee on June 20, 1926, the son of Woods Orlow and Clare (Bluett) Dreyfus. He attended the University of Wisconsin, and graduated in 1957 with a Ph.D.) in communications. During World War II, he served in the U.S. Navy as an electronic technician. In 1947, Dreyfus married Joyce Mae Unke. They had two children.

While still at the university, Dreyfus began work as a radio actor for station WISN in Milwaukee. He was an instructor at the University of Wisconsin for three years. Over the next ten years, he had various positions including general manager of radio station WDFT in Detroit; and assistant professor, associate professor of Speech, and associate director of Mass Communications at Wayne State University. From 1962-65, he was general manager for WHA television in Madison. He was professor of Speech, and Chairman of the Radio-TV and Films Division at the University of Wisconsin-Madison from 1962 to 1967. He also served as Director of Instructional Resources. From 1967 to 1969, he was president (later called chancellor) of Wisconsin State University at Stevens Point.

Dreyfus entered politics in 1978 as the Republican candidate for governor. His prominence in education and media around the state had allowed him to cultivate many friends, and although he ran a grass roots campaign, he won against Martin Schreiber by a vote of 816,056 to 673,813. His effectiveness in communicating via the media gained him popularity.

As governor, Dreyfus was faced with an opposition legislature, which attempted to block many of his programs. He was successful in reducing income taxes and deregulating the trucking industry. He created the Department of Development, supported tough sentencing for criminals, and signed into law a bill to prohibit discrimination because of sexual preference.

Later in Dreyfus's term he attempted to diminish the soaring state deficit through reducing state spending, imposing a five-cent per gallon gasoline tax, and increasing the state sales tax. He declined to seek reelection in 1982. Following his term in office, Dreyfus went to work as president of Sentry Insurance.

EARL, ANTHONY S. (1936-), Wisconsin's fortieth governor (1983-1987), was born in Michigan on April 12, 1936. He attended Michigan State University at East Lansing, where he re-

ceived a bachelor's degree in political science in 1958. In 1961, he graduated from the University of Chicago Law School and passed the bar in both Wisconsin and Minnesota. From 1962 to 1965, Earl served in the U.S. Navy. He married Sheila Coyle of Chicago in 1962. They had four daughters.

In 1965, Earl was appointed Assistant District Attorney of Marathon County, Wisconsin. He served for a year then became the first full-time City Attorney of Wausau. In 1969, he ran for State Assembly and won, serving the remainder of a term left open by the departure of David Obey. He was reelected to a full term in 1970, and was named to the Joint Committee on Finance. In 1971, his colleagues selected him to serve as majority leader. He held that position until he left the legislature in January 1975.

Earl ran for state attorney general in 1974, but was defeated. Later that year, Governor Lucey appointed him Secretary of the Department of Administration, a cabinet position. The following year, he became Secretary of the Department of Natural Resources. Earl served as Wisconsin's chief environmental officer from December 1975 until 1980, when he returned to private law practice as a partner in the firm of Foley and Lardner.

Earl ran for governor in 1982, and defeated Republican Terry Kohler by a margin of fifty-seven to forty-two percent. He was inaugurated on January 3, 1983. In addition to his work as governor, Earl held various national posts, including that of chairman of the National Governors Association's Standing Committee on Energy and the Environment. He was also a member of the Democratic National Committee's Fairness Commission and Policy Commission. He was chair of the Council of Great Lakes Governors from 1983-85. Earl completed his term as governor in January 1987.

THOMPSON, TOMMY G. (1941-), forty-first Governor of Wisconsin (1987-2001), was born on November 19, 1941 in Elroy, Wisconsin. During his youth, he worked in his father's grocery store. After graduating from Elroy High School, he earned a bachelor's degree in political science (1963) and a law degree (1966) from the University of Wisconsin - Madison.

Thompson's career in public service began in 1966, when he was elected to the State Assembly; he became assistant minority leader in 1973, and minority leader in 1981.

Thompson ran for gubernatorial office in 1986, and won the chief executive's chair on a platform of reducing State spending, creating a positive business climate, bringing new jobs to the State, reforming the welfare system, and solving problems in the State prison system. Many attributed his success at the point to a philosophy of management that sought to make Wisconsin more competitive in an increasingly interdependent national and world economy.

During his years of tenure, Thompson has helped Wisconsin to create more than 450,000 new jobs, and to become first in the nation in creating manufacturing jobs. The State unemployment rate remained below the national average for six years, and the city of Madison had the lowest rate in the nation. Wisconsin was the only state to reduce personal income tax rates, balance its budget every year, and not raise any major taxes. Thompson cut State taxes by 3.8 billion dollars, and vetoed over 603 million dollars in tax increases.

In his efforts to address welfare reform, Thompson's administration has initiated several programs that have gained national recognition, including Workfare, Learnfare, the Parental and Family Responsibility initiative, the Children First program, and two-tiered welfare; the programs have become models for the nation. These programs, plus a healthy economy, have resulted in a decrease in Wisconsin's welfare rolls by twenty-five percent, in a time when the national average increased thirty-five percent.

Thompson's concern in the area of education has resulted in a program called Parental School Choice. The program allows low-income Milwaukee families to send their children to the private or public school of their choice. In addition, Thompson's budget proposal expands public school choice statewide, and extends the Milwaukee program to include religious schools. He is leading a statewide effort designed to prepare high school students for the workforce through his School-to-Work initiative, which provides both education and training to junior and senior students.

A number of environmental programs have been established by the Thompson administration, all based on the philosophy that economic development and environmental protection can go hand-in-hand. Thompson is also a strong advocate of international trade, and his overseas missions to many other countries have created new markets for Wisconsin products. Exports have increased from 3.9 billion dollars to 8.7 billion dollars during his years in office.

Thompson was elected to a second term in the Governor's office in 1990. In 1994, he became the first chief executive of the State to be elected to a third, four-year term.

Thompson is a member of the State Bar Association and the Juneau County Bar Association; he assumed the chairmanship of the National Governor's Association in August 1995. Thompson and his wife, Sue Ann, have three children.

DICTIONARY OF PLACES

Population figures and demographic information are official U.S. Census Bureau finals for 1990. When two figures are shown, separated by a slash, the first figure is the 1990 and the second is the U.S. Census Bureau 1999 estimate—the most recent available. Year 2000 census supplements will be available in the Fall of 2001.

ABBOTSFORD, City; Clark County; Pop. 1,901 / 2,135 Zip Code 54405; Lat. 44-57-14 N, Long. 090-18-34 W; Named for Edwin H. Abbot, an official for the Wisconsin Central Railway.

ADAMS, City; Adams County; Pop. 1,744 / 1,943; Zip Code 53910; Elev. 960; Lat. 43-57-28 N, Long. 089-48-55 W; Named in honor of President John Quincy Adams, the town was first called South Friendship.

ALBANY, Village; Green County; Pop. 1,051 / 1,188; Zip Code 53502; Lat. 42-42-45 N, Long. 089-26-09 W; Settled by former residents of Albany, New York and named for their hometown.

ALGOMA, City; Kewaunee County; Pop. 3,656 / 3,340; Zip Code 54201; Elev. 600; Lat. 44-36-24 N, Long. 087-26-29 W; The name is either from the Indian words *Algonquin* and *goma* meaning "Algonquin waters," or from *Algoma* meaning "park of flowers" or "snow shoe."

ALLOUEZ, Village; Brawn County; Pop. 14,882 / 14,574; Named for Father Claude Allouez, a French missionary who preached to the Indians around 1650.

ALTOONA, City; Eau Claire County; Pop. 4,393 / 6,607; Zip Code 54720; Lat. 44-48-14 N, Long. 091-26-49 W; Platted in 1881 as East Eau Claire; Upon incorporation in 1887, it was renamed for Mr. Beols hometown of Altoona, Pennsylvania.

AMERY, City; Polk County; Pop. 2,404 / 3,047; Zip Code 54001; Lat. 45-18-29 N, Long. 092-21-27 W; Named in 1887 for William Amery, an Englishman who settled in St. Croix, Wisconsin.

ANTIGO, City; Langlade County Seat; Pop. 8,653 / 8,587; Zip Code 54409; Lat. 45-08-37 N, Long. 089-08-25 W; Antigo comes from a Chippewa Indian name meaning "balsam evergreen river" or "place where evergreens can be found."

APPLETON, City; Outagamie County Seat; Pop. 59,032 / 67,178; Zip Code 54911; Lat. 41-11-34 N, Long. 082-15-05 W; Named for Samuel Appleton, one of the founders of Lawrence University.

ARCADIA, City; Trempealeau County; Pop. 2,109 / 2,305; Zip Code 54612; Elev. 728; Lat. 44-16-22 N, Long. 091-29-57 W; Named for the state of Arcadia in ancient Greece.

ASHLAND, City; Ashland County Seat; Pop. 9,115 / 8,723; Zip Code 54806; Elev. 671; Lat. 46-34-47 N, Long. 090-52-50 W; Named in 1885 for Henry Clay's home in Kentucky; Earlier names include Zhom-o-wa-mik, Ojibwa for "the long stretched beaver" and Wittlesey for Adolph Wittlesey, the town's first postmaster.

ASHWAUBENON, Village; Brown County; Pop. 14,486 / 17,488; The village was named for the great Menominee Chief Ashwaubamie, who left this land to his descendants, the Franks and La Rose families.

ATHENS, Village; Marathon County; Pop. 988 / 1,001; Zip Code 54411; Lat. 45-01-17 N, Long. 090-03-49 W; Probably named for the capital city of Greece.

AUGUSTA, City; Eau Claire County; Pop. 1,560 / 1,455; Zip Code 54722; Lat. 44-40-36 N, Long. 091-07-14 W; First known as Ridge Creek, later changed to Augusta, either in honor of Charles Buckmon's hometown in Maine, or for August Rickard, who was voted the prettiest girl in town.

BALDWIN, Village; St. Croix County; Pop. 1,620 / 2,502; Zip Code 54002; Lat. 44-58-01 N, Long. 092-22-54 W; Named either for D.A. Baldwin, an early settler, or for D.H. Baldwin of the West Wisconsin Railway Company. The town was earlier known as Clarksville.

BANGOR, Village; La Crosse County; Pop. 1,012 / 1,077; Zip Code 54614; Lat. 43-53-22 N, Long. 090-59-22 W; Named by Welsh settlers for the town of Bangor, Wales.

BARABOO, City; Sauk County Seat; Pop. 8,081 / 10,082; Zip Code 53913; Elev. 894; Lat. 43-28-06 N, Long. 089-44-58 W; Named for any of three Frenchmen called Baribeau; two brothers who had a mill at the mouth of the Baraboo River, or another Baribeau, who later had a trading post there.

BARRON, City; Barron County Seat; Pop. 2,595 / 3,262; Zip Code 54812; Elev. 1115; Lat. 45-23-51 N, Long. 091-51-01 W; Named in honor of Henry D. Barron, a judge and state senator; Previously known as Quaderer's Camp for John Quaderer, foreman of the lumber camp here.

BAYSIDE, Village; Milwaukee County; Pop. 4,724 / 4,629; Incorporated in 1953, a suburb of Milwaukee, and named for its geographical location on Lake Michigan.

BEAVER DAM, City; Dodge County; Pop. 14,149 / 14,844; Zip Code 53916; Elev. 879; Lat. 43-27-21 N, Long. 088-50-35 W; Named by James P. Brower for the many beaver that built dams in nearby streams.

BELGIUM, Village; Ozaukee County; Pop. 892 / 1,459; Zip Code 53004; Elev. 736; Established in 1864; Townspeople wanted the name Luxembourg, offer their country in Europe, but when application papers came back from Washington the name Belgium had been assigned by mistake.

BELLEVILLE, Village; Dane County; Pop. 1,302 / 1,881; Zip Code 53508; Elev. 870; Lat. 42-51-44 N, Long. 089-32-47 W; Founded by John Frederick who came to the area in 1845; Named for his former home of Belleville in Canada.

BELOIT, City; Rock County; Pop. 5,457 / 35,728; Zip Code 53511; Lat. 42-31-28 N, Long. 089-02-32 W; Earlier known as Turtle Creek and New Albany; Around 1837 settler Major Johnston suggested calling the city Beloit because he liked a name similar to Detroit.

BERLIN, City; Green Lake County; Pop. 5,478 / 5,509; Zip Code 54923; Elev. 764; Lat. 43-58-52 N, Long. 088-56-25 W; Named in 1851 for Berlin, Germany; The city was previously called Strong's Landing and later Strongville.

BIG BEND, Village; Waukesha County; Pop. 1,345 / 1,532; Zip Code 53103; Lat. 42-52-57 N, Long. 088-12-15 W; The Indians named this place for the bend in the Fax River, which flows on the west side of the village.

BLACK CREEK, Village; Outagamie County; Pop. 1,097 / 1,179; Zip Code 54106; Elev. 790; Lat. 44-28-12 N, Long. 088-26-45 W; Originally called Middleburg by a settler; It later became known as Black Creek, for a dark creek on the edge of town.

BLACK EARTH, Village; Dane County; Pop. 1,145 / 1,357; Zip Code 53515; Elev. 818; Lat. 43-08-38 N, Long. 089-44-53 W; Incorporated as Berry in 1848; The village was called Black Earth in 1851, after a creek that ran through town; The name changed again to Ray and then back to Black Earth in 1858.

BLACK RIVER FALLS, City; Jackson County Seat; Pop. 3,434 / 3,798; Zip Code 54615; Elev. 796; Lat. 44-17-21 N, Long. 090-50-43 W; Called The Falls by Europeans who set up camp at the falls here in 1819; Later, the full name, Black River Falls, came into use.

BLAIR, City; Trempealeau County; Pop. 1,142 / 1,135; Zip Code 54616; Elev. 859; Lat. 44-19-12 N, Long. 091-14-04 W; Platted as Porterville, after the Porter family; Renamed Blair, in 1873, for John Insley Blair, a stockholder in the railroad company.

BLOOMER, City; Chippewa County; Pop. 3,342 / 3,380; Zip Code 54724; Elev. 1011; Lat. 45-05-57 N, Long. 091-29-12 W; Known as Bloomer Prairie for Mr. Bloomer, an Illinois merchant who came to build a sawmill an the Chippewa River, and had to scout for hay from the nearby prairie; The name was later shortened to Bloomer.

BONDUEL, Village; Shawano County; Pop. 1,160 / 1,423; Zip Code 54107; Lat. 44-44-41 N, Long. 088-26-18 W; Named for Father Floribrant Bonduel, a Jesuit priest who started a chapel here for the Menominee Indians.

BOSCOBEL, City; Grant County; Pop. 2,662 / 2,755; Zip Code 53805; Elev. 672; Lat. 43-08-10 N, Long. 090-42-16 W; Possibly named either for the Boscobel Wood in England, or from the Spanish words *basque bello* meaning "beautiful wood."

BOYCEVILLE, Village; Dunn County; Pop. 862 / 1,181; Zip Code 54725; Elev. 948; Lat. 45-02-51 N, Long. 092-02-13 W; Named for the Boyce family which owned a mill at the west end of town.

BRILLION, City; Calumet County; Pop. 2,907 / 3,051; Zip Code 54110; Lat. 44-10-23 N, Long. 088-03-59 W; Originally called Brandon, the name was changed in 1854 to Brillian, because there was already another Brandon in the next county.

BROADHEAD, City; Green County; Pop. 3,153 / 3,255; Zip Code 53520; Elev. 798; Lat. 42-37-35 N, Long. 089-22-19 W; Named for Edward H. Broadhead of the Chicago, Milwaukee and St. Paul Railway.

BROOKFIELD, City; Waukesha County; Pop. 34,035 / 38,290; Zip Code 53005; Elev. 828; Incorporated in 1984 and named after the numerous brooks and fields in the area.

BROWN DEER, Village; Milwaukee County; Pop. 12,921 / 11,886; First called White Deer after an albino deer was seen in the area; The named was changed because brown deer were more common to the vicinity.

BURLINGTON, City; Racine County; Pop. 8,385 / 10,099; Zip Code 53105; Lat. 42-39-50 N, Long. 088-15-51 W; E.D. Putnam proposed the name Burlington, after his favorite city in Vermont.

CADOTT, Village; Chippewa County; Pop. 1,247 / 1,415; Zip Code 54727; Elev. 979; Lat. 44-57-10 N, Long. 091-09-06 W; Named for Jean Baptiste Cadotte, who ran a trading post near here; Known for many years as Cadotte Falls.

CAMBRIDGE, Village; Dane County; Pop. 844 / 1,187; Zip Code 53523; Lat. 42-59-21 N, Long. 089-02-09 W; In 1847, landowner Alvin B. Carpenter named this village for Cambridge, New York, the hometown of his sweetheart.

CAMERON, Village; Barron County; Pop. 1,115 / 1,458; Zip Code 54822; Elev. 1097; Lat. 45-24-33 N, Long. 091-44-34 W; Settled in 1879 and named for Wisconsin State Senator Cameron of La Cross.

CAMPBELLSPORT, Village; Fond du Lac County; Pop. 1,740 / 1,893; Zip Code 53010; Named Crouchville in 1843, for settler Ludlow Crouch; Later called New Cassel, after Hesse-Cassel, Germany, and finally named Campbellsport for landowner Stuart Campbell.

CASHTON, Village; Monroe County; Pop. 827 / 1,091; Zip Code 54619; Lat. 43-46-11 N, Long. 090-46-38 W; First called Mt. Pisgah, later Hazen's Corner; In 1879, the village was named for Henry Harrison Cash, who built the railroad through town.

CASSVILLE, Village; Grant County; Pop. 1,270 / 1,091; Zip Code 53806; Elev. 621; Lat. 42-42-56 N, Long. 090-59-36 W; Founded in 1827 and named for Lewis Cass, Governor of the Michigan Territory, which at that time encompassed Wisconsin.

CEDAR GROVE, Village; Sheboygan County; Pop. 1,420 / 1,824; Zip Code 53013; Elev. 711; Lat. 43-33-49 N, Long. 087-49-08 W; Named for a forty acre tract of cedar trees at the south end of town.

CEDARBURG, City; Ozaukee County; Pop. 9,005 / 10,651; Zip Code 53012; Lat. 43-17-18 N, Long. 087-58-21 W; Possibly named for the house of Dr. Fred Luening, which stood on a hill surrounded by cedars.

CHETEK, City; Barron County; Pop. 1,931 / 2,099; Zip Code 54728; Lat. 45-19-04 N, Long. 091-39-07 W; The Chippewa Indian word for Chetek is *Jede-Sagaigan* meaning "swan" or "pelican" and "inland lake."

CHILTON, City; Calumet County Seat; Pop. 2,965 / 3,621; Zip Code 53014; Elev. 902; Lat. 44-01-41 N, Long. 088-09-34 W; Originally named Chillington, after John Marygold's home in England; The name became Chilton due to an error in recording it.

CHIPPEWA FALLS, City; Chippewa County Seat; Pop. 12,270 / 13,136; Zip Code 54729; Lat. 44-54-5-4 N, Long. 091-22-41 W; Named by Jean Brunet in 1836 for the falls here an the Chippewa River; The word *Chippewa* is an adaptation of *Ojibwa*, a tribal name meaning "to roast until puckered up."

CLEAR LAKE, Village; Polk County; Pop. 899 / 1,010; Zip Code 54005; Elev. 1201; Lat. 45-14-47 N, Long. 092-15-54 W; The proposed name was Clark's Lake, for one of the town's oldest families, but it had to be changed to Clear Lake since there was already a Clark's Lake in the state.

CLEVELAND, Village; Manitowoc County; Pop. 1,270 / 1,506; Zip Code 53015; Elev. 640; Lat. 43-55-04 N, Long. 087-45-10 W; Founded in 1850 and named Birch for the birch trees in the area; In 1885 it was renamed for President Grover Cleveland.

CLINTON, Village; Rock County; Pop. 1,751 / 2,168; Zip Code 53525; Elev. 949; Lat. 42-33-17 N, Long. 088-51-43 W; Probably named for DeWitt Clinton, Governor of New York.

CLINTONVILLE, City; Waupaca County; Pop. 4,567 / 4,890; Zip Code 54929; Elev. 825; Lat. 44-37-42 N, Long. 088-46-04 W; First called Pigeon Lake, later changed to Clintonville for the Norman Clinton family, the first permanent settlers.

COLBY, City; Clark County; Pop. 1,496 / 1,696; Zip Code 54421; Elev. 1350; Lat. 44-55-20 N, Long. 090-18-25 W; Named for Charles L. Colby, President of the Wisconsin Central Railroad.

COLFAX, Village; Dane County; Pop. 1,149 / 1,210; Zip Code 54730; Lat. 44-59-51 N, Long. 091-44-21 W; Originally called Begga Town for the rutabagas raised here; Renamed around 1868 for Senator Schuyler Colfax.

COLUMBUS, City; Columbia County; Pop. 4,049 4,468; Zip Code 53912; Elev. 871; Lat. 43-19-52 N, Long. 088-56-20 W; Named by Molar Dickason, one of the first white men in the area.

COMBINED LOCKS, Village; Outagamie County; Pop. 2,573 / 2,368; Zip Code 54113; Lat. 43-26-18 N, Long. 086-40-37 W; The canal locks on the Fox River gave this village its name.

CORNELL, City; Chippewa County; Pop. 1,583 / 1,554; Zip Code 54732; Lat. 45-09-45 N, Long. 091-09-13 W; First called Brunet's Falls for Jean Brunet who ran a trading post here; Later named for Ezra Cornell, president of Cornell University, which had large land holdings in Wisconsin.

COTTAGE GROVE, Village; Dane County; Pop. 888 / 3,494; Zip Code 53527; Elev. 888; Lat. 43-04-30 N, Long. 089-12-00 W; Settler William C. Wells named the town for a grove of burr oaks that surrounded his house.

CRANDON, City; Forest County Seat; Pop. 1,969 / 2,218; Zip Code 54520; Lat. 45-34-01 N, Long. 088-54-13 W; Originally named Ayr, from the city in Scotland; In 1885 the town was named for Molar Frank P. Crandon of the Chicago and North Western Railway.

CRIVITZ, Village; Marinette County; Pop. 1,041 / 1,189; Zip Code 54114; Elev. 681; Lat. 45-14-14 N, Long. 088-01-05 W; Called Ellis Junction after the Ellis family; The name was later changed to Crivitz, for Judge Bartels' home in Germany.

CROSS PLAINS, Village; Dane County; Pop. 2,156 / 3,247; Zip Code 53528; Elev. 859; Lat. 43-06-43 N, Long. 089-39-31 W; In 1838, Postmaster Berry Honey named this village after his hometown in Tennessee.

CUBA CITY, City; Grant County; Pop. 2,129 / 2,055; Zip Code 53807; Elev. 1012; Lat. 42-36-22 N, Long. 090-25-35 W; First called Western; It was platted as Yuba around 1871, but the Y was changed to C because there was another Yuba in the state.

CUDAHAY, City; Milwaukee County; Pop. 19,547 / 8,143; Zip Code 53110; Lat. 42-58-01 N, Long. 087-53-12 W; Named for Patrick Cudahay, who grew up in the area and, with his brother John, started the firm of Cudahay Brothers.

CUMBERLAND, City; Barron County; Pop. 1,983 / 2,181; Zip Code 54829; Elev. 1251; Lot 45-32-04 N, Long. 092-01-44 W; Established as Lakeland in 1876; In 1879 John A. Humbird renamed the city after his hometown of Cumberland, Maryland.

DARIEN, Village; Walworth County; Pop. 1,152 / 1,514; Zip Code 53114; Elev. 948; Lat. 42-36-14 N, Long. 088-42-31 W; First known as Bruceville, after landowner John Bruce; Renamed around 1838 by settlers from Darien, New York.

DARLINGTON, City; Lafayette County Seat; Pop. 2,300 / 2,213; Zip Code 53530; Elev. 817; Lat. 42-40-39 N, Long. 090-06-43 W; Purchased in 1850 and named for land agent Joshua Darling of New York.

DE FOREST, Village; Dane County; Pop. 3,367 / 7,231; Zip Code 53532; Elev. 949; Lat. 43-15-00 N, Long. 089-20-38 W; Named for Isaac DeForest, who purchased land here in 1854.

DE PERE, City; Brown County; Pop. 14,892 / 19,978; Zip Code 54115; Lat. 44-27-34 N, Long. 088-01-33 W; Possibly named for a French settler or missionary; In French *pere* means "father."

DEERFIELD, Village; Dane County; Pop. 1,466 / 1,873; Zip Code 53531; Lat. 43-03-29 N, Long. 089-03-36 W; Settled mainly by Norwegians and named for the many deer that lived in the area.

DELAFIELD, City; Waukesha County; Pop. 4,083 / 6,221; Zip Code 53018; Lat. 43-04-38 N, Long. 088-23-26 W; First known by the Indian name *Nehamabin* or *Nemahbin*; Settlers called it Hayopolis; The city was later named after Charles Delafield, who started a mulberry grove here in 1843.

DELAVAN, City; Walworth County; Pop. 5,684 / 7,648; Zip Code 53115; Lat. 42-37-23 N, Long. 088-37-08 W; Named for Edward Cornelius Delavan, a prominent temperance leader from New York.

DENMARK, Village; Brown County; Pop. 1,475 / 1,747; Zip Code 54208; Lat. 44-20-56 N, Long. 087-49-38 W; Settled by immigrants from Denmark and named for their homeland.

DICKEYVILLE, Village; Grant County; Pop. 1,156 / 985; Zip Code 53808; Elev. 957; Lat. 42-37-41 N, Long. 090-35-33 W; Settled around 1849 and named for Mr. Dickey, an early resident.

DODGEVILLE, City; Iowa County Seat; Pop. 3,458 / 4,408; Zip Code 53533; Lat. 42-57-42 N, Long. 090-07-54 W; First called Minersville; The name was changed to honor Henry Dodge, a settler here, who in 1836 became the first governor of the Wisconsin Territory.

DOUSMAN, Village; Waukesha County; Pop. 1,153 / 1,765; Zip Code 53118; Lat. 43-00-46 N, Long. 088-28-17 W; First called Bull Frog Station, for the marshy land at the railroad Station here; Renamed either for Talbot C. Dousman or for Colonel John Dousman.

DURAND, City; Pepin County Seat; Pop. 2,047 / 2,057; Zip Code 54736; Elev. 721; Lat. 44-37-35 N, Long. 091-57-39 W; Named in honor of Miles Durand Prindle, who with Charles Billings, platted the town in 1856.

EAGLE, Village; Waukesha County; Pop. 1,008 / 1,446; Zip Code 53119; Elev. 949; Lat. 42-52-46 N, Long. 088-28-21 W; Variously called Eagle Prairie, Eagleville, and Eagle Center; The place got its name when a group of prospectors saw a bald eagle on the prairie here in 1836.

EAGLE RIVER, City; Vilas County Seat; Pop. 1,326 / 1,667; Zip Code 54521; Elev. 1647; Lat. 45-55-16 N, Long. 089-15-01 W; From the Indian name *Mi-gis-iwis-ibi* meaning "eagle;" The place was named for the many eagles that nested in the area.

EAST TROY, Village; Walworth County; Pop. 2,385 / 3,620; Zip Code 53120; Lat. 42-47-36 N, Long. 088-24-28 W; Named by settlers for their hometown of Troy, New York; At first there was a single township called Troy; When it split, this port became East Troy.

EAU CLAIRE, City; Eau Claire County Seat; Pop. 51,509 / 60,223; Zip Code 547+; Lat. 44-48-27 N, Long. 091-28-54 W; Platted and named in 1855 for the nearby Eau Claire River; In French *eau claire* means "clear water."

EDGAR, Village; Marathon County; Pop. 1,194 / 1,448; Zip Code 54426; Lat. 44-56-46 N, Long. 089-57-19 W; Platted in 1891 and named for railroad employee, William Edgar.

EDGERTON, City; Rack County; Pop. 4,335 / 4,507; Zip Code 53534; Lat. 42-50-18 N, Long. 089-04-00 W; Named for Benjamin Edgerton, chief surveyor for the railroad.

ELKHART LAKE, Village; Sheboygon County; Pop. 1,054 / 1,335; Zip Code 53020; Elev. 938; Lat. 43-48-16 N, Long. 088-00-52 W; Named after the lake, which is said to be shaped like the heart of an elk; German settlers to this village first called it Rhine.

ELKHORN, City; Walworth County; Pop. 4,605 / 7,060; Zip Code 53121; Elev. 1033; Lat. 43-28-19 N, Long. 087-57-09 W; Named by Colonel Samuel F. Phoenix, who while traveling through in 1836, saw the horns of an elk that someone had hung in a tree.

ELLSWORTH, Village; Pierce County Seat; Pop. 2,143 / 2,969; Zip Code 540+; Elev. 1226; Lat. 44-43-39 N, Long. 092-29-05 W; First called Perry; Later renamed in honor of Colonel E.E. Ellsworth.

ELM GROVE, Village; Waukesha County; Pop. 6,735 / 6,035; Zip Code 53122; Elev. 746; Lat. 42-55-23 N, Long. 087-49-26 W; Named for the beautiful elm trees in the area.

ELROY, City; Juneau County; Pop. 1,504 / 1,568; Zip Code 53929; Elev. 959; Lat. 43-43-59 N, Long. 090-15-53 W; James Madison Brintnall called the city LeRoy, after his hometown of LeRoy, New York; The first two letters of the name were reversed because there was already another LeRoy in Wisconsin.

EVANSVILLE, City; Rock County; Pop. 2,835 / 3,747; Zip Code 53536; Elev. 897; Lat. 42-47-07 N, Long. 089-18-03 W; Originally called The Grove; Later changed to Evansville in honor of physician, Dr. Calvin (or J.M.) Evans.

FALL CREEK, Village; Eau Claire County; Pop. 1,148 / 1,159; Zip Code 54742; Lat. 44-45-35 N, Long. 091-16-40 W; Originally called Cousins, for Mr. Henry Cousins; Renamed Foil Creek after the stream that ran by the village.

FALL RIVER, Village; Columbia County; Pop. 850 / 1,000; Zip Code 53932; Elev. 858; Lat. 43-23-12 N, Long. 089-03-04 W; Alfred Brayton, a settler here, named the village for the hometown of his father's family in Fall River, Massachusetts.

FENNIMORE, City; Grant County; Pop. 2,212 / 2,441 Zip Code 53809; Lat. 42-58-56 N, Long. 090-39-04 W; Called Fennimore Center, after John Fennimore, who farmed in the area, and disappeared during the Black Hawk War; In 1881, "Center" was dropped from the name.

FOND DU LAC, City; Fond du Lac County Seat; Pop. 35,863 / 40,987; Zip Code 54935; Elev. 760; Lat. 44-17-11 N, Long. 088-20-44 W; Menominee Indians called this place *Wanikamiu* meaning "end of lake;" The French translated this to Fond du Lac.

FONTANA-ON-GENEVA LAKE, Village; Walworth County; Pop. 1,764 / 1,764; Pioneers named this village by the lake, Fontana, a word they thought was French for "a place of many springs."

FORT ATKINSON, City; Jefferson County; Pop. 9,785 / 11,163; Zip Code 53538; Elev. 790; Lat. 42-55-02 N, Long. 088-50-30 W; First established as Fort Koshkonong, a stockade commanded by Brigadier General Henry Atkinson during the Indian uprising of 1832; In 1836, settlers changed the name in honor of Atkinson.

FOUNTAIN CITY, City; Buffalo County; Pop. 963 / 1,202; Zip Code S4629; Elev. 663; Lat. 44-07-11 N, Long. 091-41-09 W; Originally called *Wha-ma-dee* by Sioux Indians, later Holmes' Landing for pioneer, Thomas A. Holmes; In 1855 it was renamed Fountain City for the many springs along the bluff's near here.

FOX LAKE, City; Dodge County; Pop. 1,373 / 1,430; Zip Code 53933; Elev. 920; Lat. 43-33-44 N, Long. 088-54-25 W; From *Hos-a-rac-atah*, the Indian name for the lake meaning "fox;" The village was later platted under the English translation, Fox Lake.

FOX POINT, Village; Milwaukee County; Pop. 7,649 / 6,737; Called Dutch Settlement by immigrants from Holland; The village eventually became Fox Point, a surveyor's name for the point of land at Doctor's Park.

FREDERIC, Village; Polk County; Pop. 1,039 / 1,205; Zip Code 54825; Lat. 45-41-20 N, Long. 092-17-37 W; Landowner William J. Starr named this village for his son, Frederic.

FREDONIA, Village; Ozaukee County; Pop. 1,437 / 1,939; Zip Code 53021; Originally called Stanley Creek; Renamed for the town of Fredonia, New York.

GALESVILLE, City; Trempealeau County; Pop. 1,239 / 1,399; Zip Code 54630; Elev. 712; Lat. 44-05-40 N, Long. 091-21-20 W; Named for Judge George Gale, who purchased land here and founded Gale College.

GENOA CITY, Village; Walworth County; Pop. 1,202 / 1,654; Zip Code 53128; Lat. 42-30-02 N, Long. 088-19-25 W; Named after the town of Genoa, New York.

GERMANTOWN, Village; Washington County; Pop. 10,729 / 17,859; Zip Code 53022; Elev. 863; Lat. 43-13-22 N, Long. 088-07-11 W; Named for German settlers who made up the entire village.

GILLETT, City; Oconto County; Pop. 1,356 / 1,246; Zip Code 54124; Elev. 812; Lat. 44-53-19 N, Long. 088-17-24 W; Named for Rodney and Mary Roblee Gillett, who settled here in 1858; Originally called Gillett Center.

GLENDALE, City; Milwaukee County; Pop. 13,882 / 13,637; Also called Lake; Townspeople later voted for the name Glendale, descriptive of the surroundings.

GLENWOOD CITY, City; St. Croix County; Pop. 950 / 1,151; Zip Code 54013; Lat. 45-03-49 N, Long. 092-11-01 W; Named for the Glenwood Manufacturing Company which came to the area in 1885.

GRAFTON, Village; Ozaukee County; Pop. 8,381 / 10,679; Zip Code 53024; Lat. 42-14-02 N, Long. 085-45-45 W; First known as Homburg; Renamed Grafton, possibly from Grafton Street in Dublin, or the Grafton in New Hampshire, Massachusetts or West Virginia; The name changed to Manchester in 1857 and back to Grafton in 1862.

GRANTSBURG, Village; Burnett County Seat; Pop. 1,153 / 1,368; Zip Code 54840; Lat. 45-46-36 N, Long. 092-41-16 W; The Indians called this place *Kitchi-Maski-gimi-tika-ning* meaning "at the great cranberry place;" Renamed by white settlers in honor of Ulysses S. Grant.

GREEN BAY, City; Brown County Seat; Pop. 87,899 / 98,362; Zip Code 54300; Elev. 594; Lat. 44-30-48 N, Long. 088-01-10 W; Menominee Indians called it *Putci-wikit* or *puji-kit* meaning "a boy in spite of itself;" The French named it *La Bale Verte* or Green Bay, for the greenish color of the water.

GREEN LAKE, City; Green Lake County Seat; Pop. 1,208 / 1,203; Zip Code 54941; Lat. 43-50-32 N, Long. 088-57-12 W; Established as Dartford, for a Mr. Dart who built a dam and a ford across the river here; Renamed Green Lake after the greenish lake at the center of the county.

GREENDALE, Village; Milwaukee County; Pop. 16,928 / 14,931; Zip Code 53129; Lat. 42-54-49 N, Long. 087-58-58 W; One of the Greenbelt Towns built around 1936 by the Resettlement Administration; This one became Greendale.

GREENFIELD, City; Milwaukee County; Pop. 31,467 / 35,246; Nathan Dennison named this city for his hometown of Greenfield, Massachusetts.

GREENWOOD, City; Clark County; Pop. 1,124 / 1,089; Zip Code 54437; Elev. 1168; Lat. 44-45-34 N, Long. 090-35-41 W; Named for the numerous pine and hardwood trees in the area.

HALES CORNERS, Village; Milwaukee County; Pop. 7,110 / 7,409; Zip Code 53130; Lat. 42-55-43 N, Long. 088-02-04 W; The town got its named from William Hale, who built the first log cabin here in 1837.

HAMMOND, Village; St. Croix County; Pop. 991 / 1,191; Zip Code 54015; Lat. 44-58-34 N, Long. 092-26-30 W; Named for R.B. Hammond who built the first sawmill here.

HARTFORD, City; Washington County; Pop. 7,046 / 10,122; Zip Code 53027; Lat. 43-18-53 N, Long. 088-22-54 W; First called Wright after a Mr. Wright; The name Hartford may have come from the ford at heart-shaped Pike Lake nearby, an Indian name for the area meaning "heart" or from the city of Hartford, Connecticut.

HARTLAND, Village; Waukesha County; Pop. 5,559 / 8,813; Zip Code 53029; Lat. 43-06-54 N, Long. 088-23-15 W; Early names include; Warren, for settler Steve Warren; Hersheyvill and Hershey's Mills, for Mr. Christ Hershey and the Indian *Sha-ba-qua-nole* meaning "a growing group;" The current name probably descriptive of the area, the heartland.

HAYWARD, City; Sawyer County Seat; Pop. 1,698 / 2,161; Zip Code 54843; Elev. 1198; Lat. 46-00-34 N, Long. 091-28-57 W; Chippewa Indians called this place *Ba-ke-abash-kang* meaning "swamp which is a branch of a bigger swamp;" Later named for Judson Hayward, who built a sawmill here.

HAZEL GREEN, Village; Grant County; Pop. 1,282 / 1,282; Zip Code 53811; Lat. 42-32-05 N, Long. 090-25-56 W; First called Hardy's Scrape, later Hard Scrabble; Renamed either for Captain Charles McCoy's hometown of Hazel Green, Kentucky, or for the hazel bushes in the area.

HILBERT, Village; Calumet County; Pop. 1,176 / 1,276; Zip Code 54129; Lat. 44-08-11 N, Long. 088-09-48 W; The source of the name is unknown; The village was first called Hilbert Junction, later shortened to Hilbert.

HILLSBORO, City; Vernon County; Pop. 1,263 / 1,515; Zip Code 54634; Elev. 1001; Lat. 43-39-13 N, Long. 090-20-33 W; Named for Vilentia Hill who laid the first claim here in 1850; The original spelling was Hillsborough.

HOLMEN, Village; La Crosse County; Pop. 2,411 / 5,005; Zip Code 54636; Elev. 718; Lat. 43-57-49 N, Long. 091-15-10 W; Early names were Frederickstown and Cricken; Later called Holmen, probably for Senator Holmen of Indiana, who once surveyed this territory.

HORICON, City; Dodge County; Pop. 3,584 / 3,718; Zip Code 53032; Elev. 884; Lat. 43-26-35 N, Long. 088-38-10 W; Originally a Winnebago village called *Maunk-shak-kah* or "White Breast;" Later known as Elk Village, Indian Ford, Hubbard's Ford and finally Horicon, from the home of settlers at Lake Horicon (now Lake George) New York.

HORTONVILLE, Village; Outagamie County; Pop. 2,016 / 2,249; Zip Code 54944; Elev. 794; Lat. 44-20-00 N, Long. 088-37-23 W; Named for Alonzo Erastus Horton who founded the village in 1849.

HOWARD, Village; Brown County; Pop. 8,240 / 13,900; Named in honor of Brigadier General Benjamin Howard, who fought in the War of 1812.

HOWARDS GROVE, Village; Sheboygan County; Pop. 1,838 / 2,828; Originally called Pitchville; Later named for H.B. Howard who established a trading post here in 1850.

HUDSON, City; St. Croix County Seat; Pop. 5,434 / 8,453; Zip Code 54016; Lat. 44-59-08 N, Long. 092-45-15 W; First called Willow River; The name was changed to Hudson when travelers remarked on a resemblance between the St. Croix River and the Hudson River in New York.

HURLEY, City; Iron County Seat; Pop. 2,015 / 1,755; Zip Code 54534; Lat. 46-26-36 N, Long. 090-11-39 W; Platted in 1885 and named for Judge M.A. Hurley, a lawyer and iron ore mine operator.

HUSTISFORD, Village; Dodge County; Pop. 874 / 1,064; Zip Code 53034; Lat. 43-20-16 N, Long. 088-36-08 W; First called Rock River Rapids for the half mile of rapids here; Renamed Hustis Rapids, and later, Hustisford after John Hustis, the first settler.

INDEPENDENCE, City; Trempealeau County; Pop. 1,180 / 1,083; Zip Code 54747; Elev. 782; Lat. 44-23-19 N, Long. 091-25-33 W; So named because the city was platted during the year of the Centennial celebration of American Independence.

IOLA, Village; Waupaca County; Pop. 957 / 1,309; Zip Code 54945; Elev. 955; Lat. 44-30-24 N, Long. 089-07-24 W; Named for a Potawatomi Indian girl, Iola, who was said to be the daughter of Old Red Bird, brother of Chief Waupaca.

IRON RIDGE, Village; Dodge County; Pop. 766 / 1,034; Zip Code 53035; Lat. 43-23-48 N, Long. 088-32-08 W; Named for iron ore mines in the vicinity.

JACKSON, Village; Washington County; Pop. 1,817 / 4,591; Zip Code 53037; Elev. 896; Lat. 43-19-26 N, Long. 088-10-21 W; Named in honor of Stonewall Jackson.

JANESVILLE, City; Rock County Seat; Pop. 51,071 / 60,255; Zip Code 53542; Elev. 858; Lat. 42-38-21 N, Long. 089-09-45 W; Winnebago Indians had a village here called *E-nee-poro-poro* or "round rock"; Later names include Monteray Point, Block Hawk and finally Janesville, for Henry F. Jones, who ran a ferry service here.

JEFFERSON, City; Jefferson County Seat; Pop. 5,647 / 6,962; Zip Code 53549; Lat. 43-00-17 N, Long. 088-48-18 W; Named in honor of Thomas Jefferson.

JOHNSON CREEK, Village; Jefferson County; Pop. 1,136 / 1,633; Zip Code 53038; Elev. 812; Lat. 43-05-21 N, Long. 088-46-28 W; First called Belleville; Renamed Johnson Creek after Timothy Johnson, who had an early land claim here.

JUNEAU, City; Dodge County Seat; Pop. 2,045 / 2,326; Zip Code 53039; Lat. 43-24-06 N, Long. 088-42-27 W; First called Victory, later Dodge Center; It was renamed Juneau in honor of Solomon Juneau, founder of Milwaukee.

KAUKAUNA, City; Outagamie County; Pop. 11,310 / 12,807; Zip Code 54130; Lat. 44-17-13 N, Long. 088-16-41 W; Derived from the Menominee Indian name *okakaning* or *kokaning* for rapids in the Fox River; In translation the word means "place where they fish for pike," "long portage" or "crow nesting place."

KENOSHA, City; Kenosha County; Pop. 77,685 / 89,447; Zip Code 53140; Lat. 41-50-32 N, Long. 086-19-11 W; Potawatomi Indians called their villages *kenosha* meaning "pike" or "pickerol;" White settlers adopted the name Pike, which was changed to Southport, and finally Kenosha, the Indian name.

KEWASKUM, Village; Washington County; Pop. 2,381 / 3,256; Zip Code 53040; Lat. 43-30-48 N, Long. 088-13-54 W; Named for a Potawatomi Indian Chief who died here around 1847; The name means "a man able to turn fate whichever way he wants" or "his tracks ore toward home."

KEWAUNEE, City; Kewaunee County Seat; Pop. 2,801 / 2,717; Zip Code 54216; Lat. 44-27-18 N, Long. 087-30-24 W; An Indian name meaning either "the way around or across a paint of land" or "prairie chicken."

KIEL, City; Manitowoc County; Pop. 3,083 / 3,336; Zip Code 53042; Elev. 933; Lat. 43-54-39 N, Long. 088-02-16 W; First called Abel, for settler D. Abel and later Schleswig; The town was renamed for Colonel Belitz's home in Kiel, Germany.

KIMBERLY, Village; Outagamie County; Pop. 5,881 / 5,917; Zip Code 54136; Elev. 734; Lat. 44-03-27 N, Long. 087-55-12 W; Known as The Cedars because the Treaty of Cedars was signed here; Renamed for Kimberly Clark and Company, which built a pulp and paper mill here in 1889.

KOHLER, Village; Sheboygan County; Pop. 1,651 / 1,956; Zip Code 53044; Elev. 676; Lat. 43-42-58 N, Long. 087-47-04 W; First named Riverside; Renamed for the Kohler Manufacturing Company, which moved its plant her, in 1912.

LA CROSSE, City; La Crosse County Seat; Pop. 48,347 / 49,409; Zip Code 54601; Elev. 669; Lat. 43-48-34 N, Long. 091-13-54 W; So named because when French explorers first arrived, they saw Indians playing a ball game that resembled the French game "la crosse."

LADYSMITH, City; Rusk County Seat; Pop. 3,826 / 3,820; Zip Code 54848; Elev. 1144; Lat. 45-27-46 N, Long. 091-05-47 W; Earlier called Corbett, Flambeau Falls and Warner; Renamed in 1900 for Lady Smith, the wife of a factory manager, as an enticement for him to move his woodenware company to the town.

LAKE GENEVA, City; Walworth County; Pop. 5,607 / 7,216; Zip Code 53147; Lat. 42-36-11 N, Long. 088-27-34 W; Originally called *Muck-Suck* or Big Foot, for a Potawatomi Chief; The French called it Gras Pied, but settler John Brink renamed it for the village of Geneva on Seneca Lake in New York.

LAKE MILLS, City; Jefferson County; Pop. 3,670 / 4,655; Zip Code 53551; Lat. 43-05-23 N, Long. 088-54-33 W; Called Keyes Mills, for Captain Joseph Keyes, who owned mills here; He later changed the name to Lake Mills; In 1870, however, for one year the town was called Tyranena, before changing back to Lake Mills.

LANCASTER, City; Grant County Seat; Pop. 4,076 / 4,134; Zip Code 53813; Lat. 42-50-55 N, Long. 090-42-36 W; Platted in 1837 and named for Lancaster, Pennsylvania, the hometown of one of the settlers.

LINDEN, Village; Iowa County; Pop. 395 / 442; Zip Code 53553; Elev. 1101; Lat. 42-55-08 N, Long. 090-16-34 W; Originally called Peddler's Creek, after a nearby stream; Renamed Linden in 1855 for a big linden tree that grew outside the general store.

LITTLE CHUTE, Village; Outagamie County; Pop. 7,907 / 10,698; Zip Code 54140; Elev. 728; Lat. 44-06-56 N, Long. 087-58-29 W; French explorers called the falls in the Fox River *La Petite Chute*; The name is believed to have been translated by Father Vanden Broek, who built the first church here in 1836.

LODI, City; Columbia County; Pop. 1,959 / 2,849; Zip Code 53555; Elev. 833; Lat. 43-18-53 N, Long. 089-31-52 W; Possibly named after Lodi, Italy or Lodi, New York.

LOMIRA, Village; Dodge County; Pop. 1,446 / 2,330; Zip Code 53048; Elev. 1039; Lat. 43-35-30 N, Long. 088-27-01 W; First called Springfield; Renamed in 1849, probably for Lamira Schoonover; The name may also refer to the loamy soil here.

LOYAL, City; Clark County; Pop. 1,252 / 1,323; Zip Code 54446; Lat. 44-43-48 N, Long. 090-29-25 W; The name was a tribute to the townsmen who fought in the Civil War; It is claimed that every eligible man in the township enlisted.

LUCK, Village; Polk County; Pop. 997 / 1,173; Zip Code 54853; Lat. 45-33-57 N, Long. 092-28-21 W; Possibly named by settlers who used this place as a stopover on their trips to Minnesota for supplies; If they arrived at the site by nightfall they were said to be "lucky." Thus the place came to be called Luck.

LUXEMBURG, Village; Kewaunee County; Pop. 1,040 / 1,839; Zip Code 54217; Lat. 44-32-18 N, Long. 087-42-19 W; Named by settlers from Luxemburg, Belgium.

MADISON, City; Dane County Seat and Capital of Wisconsin; Pop. 170,616 / 210,674; Zip Code 53562; Elev. 863; Lat. 39-39-06 N, Long. 082-16-20 W; Winnebago Indians had a village here called *De-jop* or "four lakes;" Incorporated in 1846 as the capital of the Wisconsin Territory and named for President James Madison.

MANAWA, City; Waupaca County; Pop. 1,205 / 1,376; Zip Code 54949; Lat. 44-27-35 N, Long. 088-55-16 W; First called Brickley, then Elberton, after postmaster Elbert Scott; Renamed Manawa after the hero of an Indian legend.

MANITOWOC, City; Manitowoc County Seat; Pop. 32,547 / 33,491; Zip Code 54220; Elev. 606; Lat. 44-05-32 N, Long. 087-40-43 W; Derived from Indian words meaning "river of bad spirits" or "devil's den."

MAPLE BLUFF, Village; Dane County; Pop. 1,351 / 1,315; Incorporated in 1930 as Lakewood Bluff; Later renamed for the maple trees growing on a bluff near the lake.

MARINETTE, City; Marinette County; Pop. 11,965 / 12,010; Zip Code 54143; Elev. 598; Lat. 45-05-44 N, Long. 087-37-29 W; Named for Marguerite Chevallier, nicknamed Marinette, who started a fur trading business on the banks of the Menominee River.

MARION, City; Waupaca County; Pop. 1,348 / 1,431; Zip Code 54950; Lat. 44-40-33 N, Long. 088-53-20 W; First called Perry's Mills for J.W. Perry, who had a sawmill here; Renamed Marion, wither after Marion, Ohio; General Francis Marion of the Revolutionary War; or after Marion Ransdell, a settler.

MARKESAN, City; Green Lake County; Pop. 1,446 / 1,776; Zip Code 53946; Elev. 847; Lat. 43-42-22 N, Long. 088-58-50 W; Earlier known as Granville; The present name, Markesan, is said to have come from the Marquises Islands.

MARSHALL, Village; Dane County; Pop. 2,363 / 3,249; Zip Code 53559; Lat. 43-10-48 N, Long. 089-03-36 W; First called Bird's Ruins, after the settlement started by A.A. Bird and Zenas Bird, burned in a prairie fire; Later named Hanchettville, for postmaster Hanchett, then Howard City, for a railroad contractor, and finally Marshall, after property buyers Porter and Marshall.

MARSHFIELD, City; Wood County; Pop. 18,290 / 19,706; Zip Code 544+; Lat. 44-33-11 N, Long. 089-57-39 W; Either named for J.J. Marsh, or for his uncle, Samuel Marsh, one of the early owners of the land.

MAUSTON, City; Juneau County Seat; Pop. 3,284 / 3,795; Zip Code 53948; Elev. 883; Lat. 43-47-26 N, Long. 090-04-32 W; There was an Indian village here called *To-ko-nee*; White settlers named the place Maughs Mills, for M.M. Maughes who managed a mill here; He platted the city in 1854 as Maughstown, which was shortened to Mauston.

MAYVILLE, City; Juneau County; Pop. 2,284 / 4,790; Zip Code 53050; Elev. 776; Lat. 43-30-41 N, Long. 088-33-37 W; Named for Eli P. May, who established a trading post here in 1845.

MAZOMONIE, Village; Dane County; Pop. 1,248 / 1,535; Zip Code 53560; Lat. 43-11-06 N, Long. 089-48-14 W; Derived from one of several Indian words; *May-Zhee-Mou-nee* or Walking Mat, a Winnebago Chief; *Mo-zo-mee-nan* meaning "mooseberries" or *mo-so-min-um* meaning "moon berries."

MCFARLAND, Village; Dane County; Pop. 3,783 / 6,398; Zip Code 53558; Lat. 40-59,19 N, Long. 085-02-07 W; Named for William H. McFarland, who bought land here and laid out the village; For a short time the name was spelled MacFarland.

MEDFORD, City; Taylor County Seat; Pop. 4,035 / 4,364; Zip Code 54451; Lat. 45-08-20 N, Long. 090-20-37 W; Possibly named for Medford, Massachusetts, the hometown of a young man who passed through here in 1873.

MELLEN, City; Ashland County; Pop. 1,046 / 957; Zip Code 54546; Lat. 46-19-37 N, Long. 090-39-31 W; Platted as Iron City; When the railroad depot was built, the town was called Mellen, after Charles Sanger Mellen, a railroad official.

MENASHA, City; Winnebago County; Pop. 14,728 / 15,689; Zip Code 54952; Lat. 44-00-41 N, Long. 088-00-19 W; The name comes from a Menominee Indian word meaning "thorn" or "island."

MENOMONEE FALLS, Village; Waukesha County; Pop. 27,845 / 31,925; Zip Code 53051; Lat. 43-09-39 N, Long. 088-06-44 W; Named after the Indian tribe that lived here; The word *menomonee* means "wild rice;" An early name for the village was Nehsville, for Frederich Nehs, a settler.

MENOMONIE, City; Dunn County Seat; Pop. 12,769 / 15,304; Zip Code 54751; Elev. 877; Lat. 44-52-44 N, Long. 091-55-30 W; A variation of the Indian tribal name, which translates as "wild rice."

MEQUON, City; Ozaukee County; Pop. 16,193 / 22,321; Derived from the Wau-Mequon or White Feather, the name of Chief Waubaka's daughter.

MERRILL, City; Lincoln County Seat; Pop. 9,579 / 10,433; Zip Code 54452; Lat. 45-11-09 N, Long. 089-41-34 W; First known as Jenny Bull Falls, shortened to Jenny Falls and then Jenny, for the daughter of a Potawatomi Chief; In 1881 the city was named for S.S. Merrill, General Manager of the Wisconsin Central Railroad.

MERTON, Village; Waukesha County; Pop. 1,045 / 1,894; Zip Code 53056; Lat. 43-08-34 N, Long. 088-19-06 W; Called Warren, for Sylvanus Warren and his family; In 1849 the village was named after the English town of Moreton; The spelling later changed to Morton.

MILWAUKEE, City; Milwaukee County Seat; Pop. 636,212 / 572,424; Zip Code 53200; Elev. 634; Lat. 43-07-21 N, Long. 088-00-31 W; Derived from on Indian word; possibly from any one of the following; *Millecki* or *Melchi* meaning "good land;" *Millicki* meaning "there is a good point," *Milwarkik* meaning "great council place" or *Milwauky* meaning "good earth."

MINERAL POINT, City; Iowa County; Pop. 2,259 / 2,616; Zip Code 53565; Elev. 1135; Lat. 42-51-41 N, Long. 090-10-56 W; Named for the lead and zinc found at a high rocky point between two streams.

MINONG, Village; Washburn County; Pop. 557 / 654; Zip Code 54859; Elev. 1064; Lat. 46-06-01 N, Long. 091-49-43 W; The name comes from an Indian word meaning either a good high place," "a place where blueberries grow" or "a pleasant valley."

MISHICOT, Village; Manitowoc County; Pop. 1,503 / 1,445; Zip Code 54228; Lat. 44-14-13 N, Long. 097-38-44 W; Probably named for Chief Mishicot of the Ottawa; His name means "hairy legs;" In 1853, settlers called the town Saxonburgh, but it was later changed back to Mishicot.

MONDOVI, City; Buffalo County; Pop. 2,545 / 2,665; Zip Code 54755; Lat. 44-34-01 N, Long. 091-40-32 W; First called Pan Cake Valley, later Farringtons, for Harvey Farrington, the first settler; Renamed for Mondovi, for Mondovi, Italy, where Napoleon won against the Sardinians.

MONONA, City; Dane County; Pop. 8,809 / 8,773; The name is probably of Indian origin, a word meaning "beautiful."

MONROE, City; Green County Seat; Pop. 10,027 / 10,985; Zip Code 53566, Elev. 1099, Lat. 42-35-52 N, Long. 089-38-14 W; Probably named in honor of President James Monroe.

MONTELLO, City; Marquette County Seat; Pop. 1,273 / 1,858; Zip Code 53949; Elev. 782; Lat. 43-47-45 N, Long. 089-19-17 W; First called Serairo, later Hill River; The name Mantella may have come from the French words *Mont l'eau* or "hill by the water."

MONTICELLO, Village; Green County; Pop. 1,273 / 1,238; Zip Code 53570; Elev. 84; Lat. 42-44-54 N, Long. 089-35-16 W; Named Monticello or "little mountain" in 1845 because of the mounds or bluffs along the valley.

MOSINEE, City; Marathon County; Pop. 3,015 / 3,975; Zip Code 54455; Elev. 1153; Lat. 44-51-44 N, Long. 089-42-24 W; First called Little Bull Falls, because the rapids on the river here sounded like a roaring bull; Later renamed in honor of Old Chief Mosinee.

MUKWONAGO, Village; Waukesha County; Pop. 4,014 / 6,578; Zip Code 53149; Elev. 837; Lat. 42-52-02 N, Long. 088-20-01 W; The name is derived from an Indian word that probably means "place of the bear;" An earlier spelling of the name was Mequanigo.

MUSCODA, Village; Grant County; Pop. 1,331 / 1,293; Zip Code 53573; Lat. 43-11-32 N, Long. 090-26-24 W; Called English Prairie or English Meadow because an English trader and his son were murdered here; The present name, Muscoda, is derived from *Mash-ko-deng*, an Indian word for "meadow" or "prairie."

MUSKEGO, City; Waukesha County; Pop. 15,277 / 22,055; Zip Code 53150; Lat. 42-54-35 N, Long. 088-07-09 W; Derived from the name for the original Potawatomi Indian settlement here; It meant either "fishing place," "sunfish," "swamp," or "cranberry bog."

NASHOTAH, Village; Waukesha County; Pop. 513 / 1,135; Zip Code 53058; Lat. 43-06-13 N, Long. 088-24-32 W; Named for the Upper and Lower Nashotah Lakes; The name is of Indian origin and means "twins."

NEENAH, City; Winnebago County; Pop. 22,432 / 23,913; Zip Code 54956; Lat. 41-54-52 N, Long. 083-55-32 W; First called Winnebago Rapids; Later renamed from the Winnebago Indian word for "running water."

NEILLSVILLE, City; Clark County Seat; Pop. 2,780 / 3,013; Zip Code 54456; Lat. 44-33-12 N, Long. 090-35-20 W; First known as O'Neill's Mills, and later Neillsville for James O'Neill, who ran a sawmill here.

NEKOOSA, City; Wood County; Pop. 2,519 / 2,450; Zip Code 54457; Lat. 44-19-09 N, Long. 089-54-13 W; Named Whitney's Rapids, and then Point Boss, Point Basso, or just Boss; In 1893, the town was named Nekoosa from an Indian word meaning "running water."

NEW BERLIN, City; Waukesha County; Pop. 30,529 / 38,360; Named Mentor in 1838; In 1840 it was changed to New Berlin, after the hometown in New York of settler, Sidney Evans.

NEW GLARUS, Village; Green County; Pop. 1,763 / 2,141; Zip Code 53574; Lat. 42-49-07 N, Long. 089-38-07 W; Named by Swiss settlers, for Canton Glarus, in which authorities in Switzerland decided to send families to the United States to escape the famine and unemployment in their homeland.

NEW HOLSTEIN, City; Calumet County; Pop. 3,412 / 3,509; Zip Code 53061; Elev. 935; Lat. 43-56-42 N, Long. 088-05-32 W; Named for the home of settler Ferdinand Ostenfeld in Schleswig-Holstein, Germany.

NEW LISBON, City; Juneau County; Pop. 1,390 / 1,599; Zip Code 53950; Elev. 891; Lat. 43-52-20 N, Long. 090-09-52 W; Indians called this site of their winter camps *Wa-du-shuda* meaning "we leave canoe here;" White settlers named the place Mill Haven, and later New Lisbon, probably after Lisbon, Ohio.

NEW LONDON, City; Waupaca County; Pop. 6,210 / 7,372; Zip Code 54961; Elev. 789; Lat. 44-23-22 N, Long. 088-43-54 W; Established in 1852 and named for New London, Connecticut, the birthplace of the father of Reeder Smith, one of the city developers.

NEW RICHMOND, City; St. Croix County; Pop. 4,306 / 6,484; Zip Code 54017; Elev. 982; Lat. 45-07-10 N, Long. 092-32-25 W; First called Foster's Crossing; Later named for Richmond Day, the town surveyor.

NIAGARA, Village; Marinette County; Pop. 2,079 / 2,393; Zip Code 54151; Lat. 45-46-26 N, Long. 087-59-52 W; Probably derived from the Iroquois Indian word *Oh-nia-ga* meaning "bisected bottom land."

NORTH PRAIRIE, Village; Waukesha County; Pop. 938 / 1,651; Zip Code 53153; Lat. 42-56-19 N, Long. 088-24-08 W; Settled in 1836 and named for the beautiful prairie land here; Because there was another prairie two miles to the south, this one was termed "north."

OAKFIELD, Village; Fond du Lac County; Pop. 990 / 1,108; Zip Code 53065; Elev. 894; Lat. 43-41-07 N, Long. 088-32-40 W; Earlier names for this area were Avoca, and Lime, for the limestone quarries; Renamed Oakfield for the oak trees that grew on the edges of fields.

OCONOMOWOC, City; Waukesha County; Pop. 9,909 / 11,675; Zip Code 53066; Elev. 873; Lat. 43-06-22 N, Long. 088-28-39 W; An Indian name, from the word *Coo-no-mo-wauk*

meaning "waterfall," "beautiful waters," or "river of lakes," referring to the string of lakes joined by the Oconomowoc River.

OCONTO, City; Oconto County Seat; Pop. 4,505 / 5,017; Zip Code 54153; Elev. 591; Lat. 44-53-57 N, Long. 087-51-32 W; Named for the river, whose name was probably derived from *okato*, *o-kon-to* or *oak-a-toe*, Menominee Indian word meaning "pike place," "boat paddle," "river of plentiful fishes," or "block bass;" or from the Chippewa word *okando* meaning "he watches" or "lies in ambush."

OCONTO FALLS, City; Oconto County; Pop. 2,500 / 2,949; Zip Code 54154; Elev. 735; Lat. 44-52-31 N, Long. 088-07-57 W; Named for falls on the Oconto River.

OMRO, City; Winnebago County; Pop. 2,763 / 3,195; Zip Code 54963; Lat. 44-02-19 N, Long. 088-44-21 W; First called Smalley's Landing, later Beckwith Town, for settler, Nelson Beckwith; Platted in 1849 as Omro, in honor of Charles Omro, an Indian trader.

ONALASKA, City; La Crosse County; Pop. 9,249 / 14,826; Zip Code 54650; Elev. 716; Lat. 43-53-01 N, Long. 091-13-36 W; The name may either come from an Indian word meaning "bright water," or from Campbell's poem "Pleasure of Hope," which has the line "The wolf's long howl from Oonalaskas shore."

OOSTBURG, Village; Sheboygan County; Pop. 1,647 / 2,507; Zip Code 53070; Lat. 43-36-34 N, Long. 087-47-59 W; Settled by the Dutch and named for a village in Holland.

OREGON, Village; Dane County; Pop. 3,876 / 7,322; Zip Code 53575; Elev. 949; Lat. 37-37-43 N, Long. 078-13-41 W; First called Rome Corners; In 1847 it was renamed Oregon, after the state.

ORFORDVILLE, Village; Rock County; Pop. 1,143 / 1,249; Zip Code 53576; Lat. 42-37-49 N, Long. 089-15-33 W; Named after the town of Orford, New Hampshire; The "ville" was added later because of confusion with Oxford.

OSHKOSH, City; Winnebago County Seat; Pop. 49,678 / 60,333; Zip Code 549+; Lat. 43-01-43 N, Long. 086-33-22 W; Named for Indian Chief Oshkosh; Over a period of time the first "H" was added and the emphasis placed on the lost syllable.

PALMYRA, Village; Jefferson County; Pop. 1,515 / 1,686; Zip Code 53156; Elev. 848; Lat. 42-51-36 N, Long. 088-35-22 W; Named after Palmyra, Syria, the oasis city mentioned in the Bible; The name means "sandy soil" and is appropriate since this village has sandy earth.

PARDEEVILLE, Village; Columbia County; Pop. 1,594 / 1,981; Zip Code 53954; Elev. 815; Lat. 43-32-19 N, Long. 089-17-49 W; Named for John S. Pardee, a Milwaukee merchant and the U.S. consul to San Juan del Sur, Nicaragua.

PARK FALLS, City; Price County; Pop. 3,192 / 3,240; Zip Code 54552; Elev. 1490; Lat. 45-56-09 N, Long. 090-26-51 W; First called Muskallonge Falls; In 1885 the name was changed to Park Falls, both for the falls an the river and for the park like landscape in the area.

PESHTIGO, City; Marinette County; Pop. 2,807 / 3,346; Zip Code 54157; Lat. 45-03-39 N, Long. 087-45-05 W; The name is Indian, for either "snapping turtle" or "wild goose."

PEWAUKEE, Village; Waukesha County; Pop. 4,637 / 7,501; Zip Code 53072; Elev. 591; Lat. 35-54-06 N, Long. 073-28-23 W; The village took its name from the lake, which Potawatomi Indians called *Pewaukeewinick* or "snail lake."

PHILLIPS, City; Price County Seat; Pop. 1,522 / 1,635; Zip Code 54555; Lat. 45-37-06 N, Long. 090-20-43 W; Platted in 1876 and named for Elijah B. Phillips, general manager of the Wisconsin Central Railroad Company.

PLATTEVILLE, City; Grant County; Pop. 9,580 / 9,857; Zip Code 53818; Elev. 994; Lat. 42-44-19 N, Long. 090-28-42 W; Named Platte River Diggings in 1827; Later called Lebanon, and then Platteville, after the Platte River.

PLOVER, Village; Portage County; Pop. 5,310 / 10,574; Zip Code 54467; Elev. 1075; Lat. 44-27-20 N, Long. 089-32-34 W; Chippewa Indians called this place a name meaning "prairie;" Later renamed for the Plover River.

PLYMOUTH, City; Sheboygan County; Pop. 6,027 / 7,843; Zip Code 53073; Lat. 43-43-35 N, Long. 087-58-38 W; Settled in 1845 by Henry Davidson and his son Thomas; The city was named for Plymouth, Massachusetts, the home of Thomas's girlfriend.

PORT EDWARDS, Village; Wood County; Pop. 2,077 / 1,858; Zip Code 54469; Elev. 975; Lat. 44-21-23 N, Long. 089-51-46 W; First called Frenchtown, for the large French population; Later named for John Edwards, Sr., who built a sawmill here in 1840.

PORT WASHINGTON, City; Ozaukee County; Pop. 8,612 / 10,716; Zip Code 53074; Elev. 612; Lat. 43-23-18 N, Long. 087-52-49 W; Originally named Green Bay, then Wisconsin Bay, and later Washington, after George Washington, "Port" was added to the name after a pier was built and the city become a center for commerce.

PORTAGE, City; Columbia County Seat; Pop. 7,896 / 7,896; Zip Code 53901; Lat. 43-32-39 N, Long. 089-27-37 W; The French named this place *le portage*, and throughout Wisconsin history, this portage on the Fox-Wisconsin River has been on important landmark.

POYNETTE, Village; Columbia County; Pop. 1,447 / 2,269; Zip Code 53955; Elev. 847; Lat. 43-23-20 N, Long. 089-24-12 W; Named Pauquette, after Pierre Pauquette, on Indian interpreter and trader; The name was corrupted to Poynette.

PRAIRIE DU CHIEN, City; Crawford County Seat; Pop. 5,829 / 5,980; Zip Code 53821; Elev. 632; Lat. 43-02-41 N, Long. 091-08-41 W; The name came from a Fox Indian Chief know as Dog; Prairie du Chien or Dog's Prairie was the name the French gave to this place.

PRAIRIE DU SAC, Village; Sauk County; Pop. 2,145 / 3,104; Zip Code 53578; Lat. 43-15-41 N, Long. 089-43-14 W; French for Sauk Prairie, for a Sauk Indian village once located here on the prairie.

PRESCOTT, City; Pierce County; Pop. 2,654 / 3,906; Zip Code 54021; Lat. 44-44-53 N, Long. 092-47-08 W; First called Mouth of the St. Croix and Lake Mouth; Later named Elizabeth, for Elizabeth Schasser, and then Prescott, after Philander Prescott, on Indian interpreter.

PRINCETON, City; Green Lake County; Pop. 1,479 / 1,513; Zip Code 54968; Lat. 43-51-14 N, Long. 089-07-20 W; Originally called Treat's Landing, for settler Royal C. Treat; He and his brother later obtained title to 132 acres and laid out a town they called Princeton; The source of the name is not known.

PULASKI, Village; Brown County; Pop. 1,875 / 2,508; Zip Code 54162; Lat. 44-40-14 N, Long. 088-14-54 W; Named in honor of Count Cosimir Pulaski of Revolutionary War fame.

RACINE, City; Racine County Seat; Pop. 85,725 / 80,902; Zip Code 534+; Lat. 42-43-36 N, Long. 087-48-21 W; Known as Belle City of the Great Lakes; The name Racing comes from the French translation of the Potawatomi title for the river here, "Roots."

RANDOLPH, Village; Dodge County; Pop. 1,691 / 1,832; Zip Code 539+; Elev. 964; Lat. 43-32-15 N, Long. 089-00-13 W; Originally called LeRoy, then Conversville, for settler Jon Converse, and later Westford. In 1870, the village was incorporated as Randolph, after Randolph in Vermont.

RANDOM LAKE, Village; Sheboygan County; Pop. 1,287 / 1,636; Zip Code 53075; Elev. 901; Lat. 43-32-50 N, Long. 087-57-40 W; Known as Greenleaf, for E.D. Greenleaf, a financial agent for the railroad company; Later named for nearby Random Lake.

RED GRANITE, Village; Waushara County; Pop. 976 / 1,150; Zip Code 54970; Elev. 789; Lat. 44-02-36 N, Long. 089-06-50 W; Built up around a red granite quarry, and named for the stone.

REEDSBURG, City; Sauk County; Pop. 5,038 / 7,432; Zip Code 53959; Elev. 926; Lat. 43-32-21 N, Long. 090-00-08 W; Named for David C. Reed, who founded the city in 1850.

REEDVILLE, Village; Manitowoc County; Pop. 1,134 / 1,273; Zip Code 54230; Lat. 44-09-15 N, Long. 087-57-16 W; First called Mud Creek; Later named in honor of Judge George Reed of Manitowoc.

RHINELANDER, City; Oneida County Seat; Pop. 7,873 / 8,363; Zip Code 54501; Elev. 1554; Lat. 45-38-22 N, Long. 089-24-39 W; Originally named Pelican Rapids; Later changed to Rhinlander, after F.W. Rhineland, president of the railroad company.

RICE LAKE, City; Barron County; Pop. 7,691 / 8,696; Zip Code 54868; Lat. 45-30-07 N, Long. 091-44-21 W; The area was once a swamp where Indians gathered wild rice; Around 1868, the Knapp Stout Lumber Company built a dam here that turned the swamp into Rice Lake.

RICHLAND CENTER, City; Richland County; Pop. 4,997 / 5,101; Zip Code 53581; Elev. 731; Lat. 43-19-57 N, Long. 090-27-10 W; So named for its location at the center of Richland County.

RIVER FALLS, City; Pierce County; Pop. 9,036 / 12,438; Zip Code 54022; Lat. 44-51-21 N, Long. 092-37-17 W; First called Kinnickinnic, the Indian name for the river; Later named Greenwood, but changed to River Falls, for the falls here, after it was discovered there was already a Greenwood in the state.

RIVER HILLS, Village; Milwaukee County; Pop. 1,642 / 1,599; Edwin B. Bartlett suggested the name River Hills, because he considered river and hills to be pleasant country.

ROBERTS, Village; St. Croix County; Pop. 833 / 1,107; Zip Code 54023; Lat. 44-58-57 N, Long. 092-33-19 W; Originally located in Warren Township; Later moved south and named Roberts, after a railroad man.

ROCHESTER, Village; Racine County; Pop. 746 / 1,026; Zip Code 53167; Elev. 777; Lat. 42-44-24 N, Long. 088-13-24 W; Settlers named this village after their former home in Rochester, New York.

ROTHSCHILD, Village; Marathon County; Pop. 3,338 / 4,155; Zip Code 54474; Lat. 44-55-33 N, Long. 089-36-58 W; Named for a local man who was nicknamed Baron de Rothschild.

ST. CROIX FALLS, City; Polk County; Pop. 1,497 / 1,920; Zip Code 54024; Lat. 45-24-15 N, Long. 092-37-53 W; St. Croix is a French name for Holy Cross; When the city was founded there was a waterfall here on the St. Croix River, now altered by a power company dam.

ST. FRANCIS, City; Milwaukee County; Pop. 10,066 / 9,204; Indians called this place *No-gosh-ing* meaning "snake" or "enemies;" The source of the present name is not known.

ST. NAZIANZ, Village; Manitowoc County; Pop. 738 / 723; Zip Code 54232; Lat. 44-00-27 N, Long. 087-55-35 W; Founded by German immigrants who came to escape religious persecution; They named the village for St. Gregory Nazianz.

SAUK CITY, Village; Sauk County; Pop. 2,703 / 3,154; Zip Code 53583; Elev. 757; Lat. 43-14-39 N, Long. 089-43-36 W; The village was first called Harszthy, after Count Augustine Harszthy; Later changed to Westfield, then to the traditional name for the area, Sauk Prairie, which eventually became Sauk City.

SAUKVILLE, Village; Ozaukee County; Pop. 3,494 / 4,401; Zip Code 53080; Lat. 43-23-03 N, Long. 087-56-24 W; The present town encompasses the early settlements of Voelker's Mills, Schmit's Mill, Mechanicsville and St. Finbars; Named for a Sauk Indian village once located here.

SCHOFIELD, City; Marathon County; Pop. 2,226 / 2,391; Zip Code 54476; Elev. 1,198; Lat. 44-56-29 N, Long. 089-35-59 W; Originally called Scholfield Mill, for Dr. William Scholfield, who built a sawmill here; The "l" was later dropped from the name.

SEYMOUR, City; Outagamie County; Pop. 2,530 / 3,332; Zip Code 54165; Lat. 44-30-31 N, Long. 088-19-50 W; Named in honor of Horatio Seymour, Governor of New York.

SHARON, Village; Walworth County; Pop. 1,280 / 1,285; Zip Code 53585; Elev. 1027; Lat. 42-30-06 N, Long. 088-43-55 W; Probably named for the former home of settlers, in Sharon, New York.

SHAWANO, City; Shawano County Seat; Pop. 7,013 / 8,199; Zip Code 54166; Elev. 821; Lat. 44-46-48 N, Long. 088-35-59 W; Named after Shawano Lake, which was called *Sha-wah-no-hah-pay-sa*, the Menominee words for "lake to the south."

SHEBOYGAN, City; Sheboygan County Seat; Pop. 48,085 / 49,558; Zip Code 530+; Lat. 43-43-54 N, Long. 087-45-34 W; Named from any of several Indian words; The meanings vary from "pipe stem" or "hollow bone" to "underground river" or "underground noise."

SHEBOYGAN FALLS, City; Sheboygan County; Pop. 5,253 / 6,596; Zip Code 53085; Elev. 659; Lat. 43-42-23 N, Long. 087-48-55 W; First called Rochester after the city in New York; Later named for falls on the Sheboygan River.

SHELL LAKE, City; Washburn County Seat; Pop. 1,135 / 1,348; Zip Code 54871; Lat. 45-44-15 N, Long. 091-55-08 W; Chippewa Indians called the lake *Makokesese Sohkiagin* or "frog's novel." In 1855, it was named Frog Lake, and in 1881 a town was laid out and called Summit; Both town and lake were renamed Shell Lake in 1883, because the lake was said to resemble the shape of a shell.

SHERWOOD, Village; Caumet County; Pop. 372 / 1,389; Zip Code 54169; Elev. 1065; Lat. 44-10-23 N, Long. 088-15-30 W; Established as Limo in 1858; Later called Nicolai's Corners for settler, Steven Nicolai, and then Sherwood for a Civil War veteran of that name.

SHOREWOOD, Village; Milwaukee County; Pop. 14,327 / 12,589; Platted in 1836 as Mechanicsville; In 1900, the village was incorporated under the name East Milwaukee, later changed to Shorewood, for its location on the shore of Lake Michigan.

SHULLSBURG, City; Lafayette County; Pop. 1,484 / 1,242; Zip Code 53586; Elev. 1021; Lat. 42-34-08 N, Long. 090-13-48 W; Founded around 1827 and named for Jesse W. Shull, who came to the area in 1818 and established a settlement called Old Shullsburg.

SILVER LAKE, Village; Kenosha County; Pop. 1,598 / 2,201; Zip Code 53170; Lat. 42-32-53 N, Long. 088-10-07 W; Named for the silvery sheen on the water here.

SIREN, Village; Burnett County; Pop. 896 / 1,044; Zip Code 54872; Elev. 996; Lat. 45-46-45 N, Long. 092-22-34 W; Charles F. Segerstrom, first postmaster, suggested Syren, the Swedish name for lilacs, because his house was surrounded by the flowers; The spelling was later corrupted to Siren.

SLINGER, Village; Washington County; Pop. 1,612 / 3,790; Zip Code 53086; Elev. 1069; Lat. 43-19-50 N, Long. 088-17-34 W; Called Schleisingerville after B. Schleisinger Weil, who purchased land here; The name was shortened to Slinger in 1921.

SOMERSET, Village; St. Croix County; Pop. 860 / 2,028; Zip Code 54025; Lat. 45-07-29 N, Long. 092-40-38 W; Founded by General Samuel Harriman, who named the village after his father's home of Somerset County, England.

SOUTH MILWAUKEE, City; Milwaukee County; Pop. 21,069 / 20,289; Zip Code 53172; Lat. 42-55-22 N, Long. 087-53-41 W; Named for its location, just south of the city of Milwaukee.

SPARTA, City; Monroe County Seat; Pop. 6,934 / 8,602; Zip Code 54656; Elev. 793; Lat. 43-56-28 N, Long. 090-48-37 W; Named after Sparta of ancient Greece.

SPENCER, Village; Marathon County; Pop. 1,754 / 1,859; Zip Code 54479; Lat. 44-49-56 N, Long. 090-16-40 W; Known by the names Waltham, and then Irene, after the wife of James L. Robinson, who built a sawmill here; Later named for Spencer, Massachusetts.

SPOONER, City; Washburn County; Pop. 2,365 / 2,682; Zip Code 54801; Elev. 1065; Lat. 45-49-37 N, Long. 091-53-27 W; Named for John C. Spooner, a lawyer for the Chicago, St. Paul, Minneapolis and Omaha Railroad Corporation, who later become a U.S. senator.

SPRING GREEN, Village; Sauk County; Pop. 1,265 / 1,479; Zip Code 53588; Elev. 729; Lat. 43-07-56 N, Long. 090-04-01 W; Mrs. Turner Williams suggested the name, after hollows nearby which become green earlier in spring than the rest of the surrounding country.

SPRING VALLEY, Village; Pierce County; Pop. 987 / 1,086; Zip Code 54767; Lat. 44-50-37 N, Long. 092-14-25; Probably named for two principal streams in this valley; Eagle Springs and Berghardt Springs.

STANLEY, City; Chippewa County; Pop. 2,095 / 2,025; Zip Code 54768; Lat. 44-57-50 N, Long. 090-56-14 W; Platted in 1881 and named for L.C. Stanley of the Northwest Lumber Company.

STEVENS POINT, City; Portage County Seat; Pop. 22,970 / 23,266; Zip Code 54481; Elev. 1093; Lat. 44-30-44 N, Long. 089-33-33 W; The Indians called this a name that meant Hemlock Island; Later it was called First Island, and then Stevens Point, after George Stevens, who started the settlement here.

STOUGHTON, City; Dane County; Pop. 7,589 / 11,701; Zip Code 53589; Lat. 42-55-05 N, Long. 089-14-32 W; Named for Luke Stoughton, who bought the land in 1847 and platted the village.

STRATFORD, Village; Marathon County; Pop. 1,385 / 1,624; Zip Code 54484; Lat. 44-52-02 N, Long. 090-03-44 W; The Connors family, who bought land and built a mill here, named this for their original home in Stratford, Ontario.

STRUM, Village; Trempealeau County; Pop. 944 / 1,057; Zip Code 54770; Lat. 44-35-22 N, Long. 091-23-50 W; First known as Tilden, for statesman Samuel J. Tilden; Renamed in 1890 for Louis (or Peter) Strum, who was later a state senator from this district.

STURGEON BAY, City; Door County Seat; Pop. 8,847 / 9,478; Zip Code 54235; Elev. 588; Lat. 44-49-54 N, Long. 080-22-14 W; Called Graham in 1855, then Ottumba, and then Graham again; In 1860, it was named Sturgeon Boy because the bay here had a lot of sturgeon fish.

STURTEVANT, Village; Racine County; Pop. 4,130 / 5,100; Zip Code 53177; Elev. 727; Lat. 42-44-04 N, Long. 087-51-47 W; First named Johnson, for postmaster William M. Johnson; Later called Western Union junction, then Corliss, and finally, Sturtevant, after the B.F. Sturtevant Company.

SUN PRAIRIE, City; Dane County; Pop. 12,931 / 20,391; Zip Code 53590; Lat. 43-11-35 N, Long. 089-13-05 W; So named because, for a group of workmen traveling out of Milwaukee in 1837 and breaking the wilderness, this was the first place they saw sun on their ten day trip.

SUPERIOR, City; Douglas County Seat; Pop. 29,571 / 27,339; Zip Code 54836; Elev. 642; Lat. 46-29-39 N, Long. 092-16-41 W; Incorporated and named for Lake Superior; Champlain, the explorer, called the lake Grand Lac, and later Father Marquette named it Lac Superieur de Tracy.

SUSSEX, Village; Waukesha County; Pop. 3,482 / 8,891; Zip Code 53089; Lat. 43-08-04 N, Long. 088-13-23 W; The village was laid out by the Weaver brothers to resemble their former home of Sussex, England.

THERESA, Village; Dodge County; Pop. 766 / 1,004; Zip Code 53091; Lat. 43-31-05 N, Long. 088-27-45 W; Founded by Solomon Juneau, who named the village after his mother, Theresa.

THIENSVILLE, Village; Ozaukee County; Pop. 3,341 / 3,273; Zip Code 53092; Lat. 42-47-16 N, Long. 087-09-53 W; First known as Mequon River; Later named for Joachim Heinrich Them, a German settler who built the first mill and laid out the village.

TOMAH, City; Monroe County; Pop. 7,204 / 8,271; Zip Code 54660; Lat. 43-58-39 N, Long. 090-30-08 W; Named for Chief Thomas Carron of the Menominee; The French pronounced his name Tomah.

TOMAHAWK, City; Lincoln County; Pop. 3,527 / 3,630; Zip Code 54487; Lat. 45-28-25 N, Long. 089-43-40 W; Named after the Tomahawk River, which got its name when warring Sioux and Chippewa Indians buried a tomahawk, or Indian hatchet, here as a symbol of peace between the two tribes.

TREMPEALEAU, Village; Trempealeau County; Pop. 956 / 1,267; Zip Code 54661; Elev. 691; Lat. 44-00-29 N, Long. 091-26-21 W; First known as Reeds Landing or Reeds Town, then Montoville or Mountainville; Later changed to Trempealeau after the nearby island mountain which Indians called "mountain soaked in water" and the French named *La Montogne qui trempe a l'eau*.

TWIN LAKES, Village; Kenosha County; Pop. 3,474 / 4,863; Zip Code 53181; Lat. 42-31-26 N, Long. 088-15-24 W; The village took its name from two lakes, known as twin lakes.

TWO RIVERS, City; Manitowoc County; Pop. 13,354 / 13,171; Zip Code 54241; Lat. 44-09-13 N, Long. 087-35-08 W; Named for its location between the North and South Twin Rivers.

UNION GROVE, Village; Racine County; Pop. 3,517 / 4,102; Zip Code 53182; Lat. 42-41-05 N, Long. 088-03-05 W; Governor Dodge is said to have named this village, for the Union School established here in 1846, and for a grove of burr oak trees nearby.

VERONA, City; Dane County; Pop. 3,336 / 6,992; First called The Corners because two main roads crossed here; Later named Verona Corners, and then Verona, by settlers from Verona, New York.

VESPER, Village; Wood County; Pop. 554 / 6,225; Zip Code 54489; Elev. 1110; Lat. 44-29-11 N, Long. 089-57-40 W; An early suggestion for the name was Hardscrabble; Around 1882, the post office was asked to select a better name, and came up with Vesper.

VIROQUA, City; Vernon County Seat; Pop. 3,716 / 4,338; Zip Code 54665; Lat. 43-33-20 N, Long. 090-53-17 W; Platted in 1850 and named Farwell, after Governor Farwell; In 1854 the name was changed to Viroqua, said to be the name of an Indian girl.

WALES, Village; Waukesha County; Pop. 1,992 / 2,748; Zip Code 53183; Elev. 1002; Lat. 43-00-23 N, Long. 088-22-45 W; Settled by Welsh immigrants and named for their home country.

WALWORTH, Village; Walworth County; Pop. 1,607 / 1,975; Zip Code 53184; Elev. 998; Lat. 42-31-59 N, Long. 088-35-39 W; Named Douglass Corners, for settler, Christopher Douglass; Later changed to Walworth, after the county, which was named in honor of Reuben Hyde Walworth.

WATERFORD, Village; Racine County; Pop. 2,051 / 3,639; Zip Code 53185; Lat. 42-45-47 N, Long. 088-12-48 W; The name is said to be from on old Indian ford across the Fox River at this site.

WATERLOO, City; Jefferson County; Pop. 2,393 / 3,047; Zip Code 53594; Elev. 819; Lat. 43-12-29 N, Long. 088-59-21 W; Indians called this place *Maunesa*; Settler, Bradford Hill renamed the spot after the bottle of Waterloo.

WATERTOWN, City; Jefferson County; Pop. 18,113 / 21,006; Zip Code 53094; Elev. 823; Lat. 43-12-17 N, Long. 088-43-14 W; The Indian name was *Ka-Ka-ree* or "ox bow," referring to the bend here in the Rack River; White settlers called the place Johnson's Rapids, and later Watertown, after Watertown, New York.

WAUKESHA, City; Waukesha County Seat; Pop. 63,261; Zip Code 531+; Elev. 821; Lat. 41-25-29 N, Long. 084-55-28 W; First called Prairieville; When Waukesha County was farmed, the town was made county seat, and named Waukesha, the Potawatomi word for "fox."

WAUNAKEE, Village; Dane County; Pop. 3,866 / 9,252; Zip Code 53597; Elev. 925; Lat. 41-13-19 N, Long. 085-23-20 W; The village was wither named for a friendly Indian who camped near here, or from an Indian word said to mean "you win," "sharpshooter," "he lies," or "he lives in peace."

WAUPACA, City; Waupaca County Seat; Pop. 4,472 / 5,958; Zip Code 54981; Lat. 44-20-59 N, Long. 089-04-41 W; Derived from an Indian word that could mean; "where one waits for deer." "looking on," "white sand bottom," "pale water," or "tomorrow."

WAUPUN, City; Dodge County; Pop. 8,132 / 10,060; Zip Code 53963; Elev. 904; Lat. 43-37-50 N, Long. 088-44-08 W; First named Madrid, after Madrid, Vermont; Later renamed from the Indian word *Waubun* meaning "dawn" or "early light of day."

WAUSAU, City; Marathon County Seat; Pop. 32,426 / 36,726; Zip Code 54401; Lat. 44-58-05 N, Long. 089-38-15 W; The name is a Chippewa Indian word meaning "far away."

WAUTOMA, City; Waushara County Seat; Pop. 1,629 / 2,082; Zip Code 54982; Elev. 867; Lat. 44-04-21 N, Long. 089-17-24 W; The name is a combination of the Indian words *wau* meaning "good," "life," or "earth," and *tomah* for "land of Tomah," the name of an Indian Chief.

WAUWATOSA, City; Milwaukee County; Pop. 51,308 / 45,405; Settlers called this place Hart's Mills, after mill owner Charles Hart; Later named for Wauwautosa an Indian chief, whose name is said to mean "great walker."

WEST ALLIS, City; Milwaukee County; Pop. 63,982 / 59,332; Parts of this city formerly were called North Greenfield and Honey Creek; The present name came from Allis-Chalmers, a manufacturing plant established here.

WEST BEND, City; Washington County; Pop. 21,484 / 29,095; Zip Code 530+; Elev. 893; Lat. 43-25-05 N, Long. 088-11-25 W; The city combines the early settlements of Salisbury's Mills (later called Barton), and West Bend; West Bend got its name from a curve in the Milwaukee River.

WEST SALEM, Village; La Crosse County; Pop. 3,276 / 4,357; Zip Code 54669; Elev. 742; Lat. 43-53-44 N, Long. 091-04-49 W; First called Salem because it means "peace" and was considered a good amen for the town, "West" was added later to distinguish the village from Salem in Kenosha County.

WESTBY, City; Vernon County; Pop. 1,797 / 2,014; Zip Code 54667; Elev. 1298; Lat. 43-39-20 N, Long. 090-51-29 W; Named for Ole T. Westby, who built a store here in 1867.

WESTFIELD, Village; Marquette County; Pop. 1,033 / 1,393; Zip Code 53964; Elev. 865; Lat. 43-53-09 N, Long. 089-29-20 W; Founded by Robert Cochrane and named for his former home in Westfield, New York.

WEYAUWEGA, City; Waupaca County; Pop. 1,549 / 1,900; Zip Code 54983; Lat. 44-19-00 N, Long. 088-55-54 W; Originally an Indian village by this name was located here; The name means "here we rest."

WHITEHALL, City; Trempealeau County Seat; Pop. 1,530 / 1,579; Zip Code 54773; Elev. 820; Lat. 44-23-42 N, Long. 091-19-19 W; Named after Whitehall, Illinois.

WHITEFISH BAY, Village; Milwaukee County; Pop. 14,930 / 12,841; Incorporated in 1892 and named for the many whitefish found in the bay.

WHITEWATER, City; Walworth County; Pop. 11,520 / 13,569; Zip Code 53190; Lat. 42-49-51 N, Long. 088-44-42 W; Translated from the Indian name for the river, *Wau-be-gon-naw-po-cat* which means "white water."

WILLIAMS BAY, Village; Walworth County; Pop. 1,763 / 2,219; Zip Code 53191; Lat. 42-34-28 N, Long. 088-32-34 W; Named for Israel Williams, a settler.

WINNECONNE, Village; Winnebago County; Pop. 1,935 / 2,275; Zip Code 54986; Elev. 753; Lat. 44-06-41 N, Long. 088-42-37 W; The name is an Indian word meaning "place of skulls," which came from a battle here in which Sauk and Fox tribes fought against the French, Menominee and Chippewa.

WISCONSIN DELLS, City; Columbia County; Pop. 2,337 / 2,475; Zip Code 53965; Elev. 912; Lat. 43-38-03 N, Long. 089-46-34 W; Originally called Kilbourn, after Byron Kilbourne; In 1931 it was changed to Wisconsin Dells, a name descriptive of the location.

WISCONSIN RAPIDS, City; Wood County; Pop. 17,995 / 18,718; Zip Code 54494; Lat. 44-24-45 N, Long. 089-48-00 W; Indians called this "rabbit's place;" It was later named for rapids on the Wisconsin River.

WITTENBERG, Village; Shawano County; Pop. 997 / 1,252; Zip Code 54432; Lat. 44-42-49 N, Long. 089-15-44 W; First called Carbenero, for charcoal kilns; The name Wittenberg was suggest by Pastor E.J. Homme, who came here with the intention of establishing a home for orphans and the aged.

WOODVILLE, Village; St. Croix County; Pop. 725 / 1,144; Zip Code 54028; Lat. 44-57-17 N, Long. 092-17-53 W; First known as Kelly's Switch; Later named Woodville, either for an early settler, or for the Woodlands that stood here before the logging companies came.

WRIGHTSTOWN, Village; Brown County; Pop. 1,169 / 1,844; Zip Code 54180; Lat. 44-19-39 N, Long. 088-10-07 W; Named for Hoel S. Wright, who settled here around 1833; At one time the village was called Wright's Ferry.

WYOMING
The Equality State

Buffalo in Yellowstone Park

Oregon-Mormon trail rut near Guernsey

GOVERNOR
Jim Geringer

Old Faithful
Yellowstone

A trail of covered wagons follows the original trail carved out by early settlers

Mount Moran
Grand Teton National Park

Aspen Valley
in the Sierra Madres

INTRODUCTION

Wyoming is the ninth largest state in the nation; its area of 97,809 square miles shares boundaries with six other Great Plains and Mountain states. Montana lies to the north and northwest; Colorado is to the south; South Dakota and Nebraska are on the east; Idaho is to the west; and Utah lies to the southwest.

During the nineteenth century, tens of thousands of pioneers crossed Wyoming along the Oregon, Overland, Mormon, Bozeman, and Bridger trails. In 1861, the route of the short-lived Pony Express crossed the State along the Oregon Trail. In the latter part of the decade, the tracks of the Union Pacific also cut across the State when they first connected the east and west coasts.

Most State residents live in small mining settlements, ranching towns, and communities that offer numerous opportunities for recreation. Yellowstone and Grand Teton national parks are very popular tourist areas, and these and other attractions bring in millions of visitors each year.

STATE NAME

The name of Wyoming is derived from the Delaware Indian, *mecheweamiing*, which means "at the big flats" or "land of vast plains." Legh Richmond Freeman, who published *The Frontier Index* in Kearney, Nebraska, is said to have been the first to suggest the name of Wyoming for the Dakota Territory's southwestern half.

STATE NICKNAME

Wyoming has several nicknames, including the Equality State, the Big Wyoming, and the Cowboy State. The first sobriquet is given to recognize Wyoming as the first state to extend to women the right to vote; it is also used because the State motto is "Equality." The Big Wyoming and the Cowboy State are both used because of Wyoming's reputation as a state with vast open lands and cowboys.

STATE SEAL

The legislature of Wyoming adopted an official seal in 1893, three years after the State joined the Union. The seal was revised in 1921. The current seal is described as follows: "There shall be a great seal of the state of Wyoming, which shall be of the following design, viz: A circle one and one-half (1½) inches in diameter, on the outer edge or rim of which shall be engraved the words 'Great Seal of the State of Wyoming.' The design shall conform substantially to the following description: A pedestal, showing on the front thereof an eagle resting upon a shield, the shield to have engraved thereon a star and the figures, '44,' being the number of Wyoming in the order of admission to statehood. Standing upon the pedestal shall be a draped figure of a woman, modeled after the statue of the 'Victory of the Louvre,' from whose wrists shall hang links of a broken chain, and holding in her right hand a staff from the top of which shall float a banner with the words, 'Equal Rights' thereon, all suggesting the political position of woman in this state. On either side of the pedestal and standing at the base thereof, shall be male figures typifying the livestock and mining industries of Wyoming. Behind the pedestal, and in the background, shall be two (2) pillars, each supporting a lighted lamp, signifying the light of knowledge. Around each pillar shall be a scroll with the following words thereon: On the right of the central

figure the words 'Livestock' and 'Grain,' and on the left the words 'Mines' and 'Oil.' At the base of the pedestal, and in front, shall appear the figures '1869-1890,' the former date signifying the organization of the territory of Wyoming and the latter date of its admission to statehood."

STATE FLAG

A State flag for Wyoming was officially adopted in 1917. Designed by Mrs. A.C. Keyes of Casper, the flag was created with colors having important symbolism: the red border to signify the Indian and the blood of the pioneers; the white to symbolize purity; and the blue to signify fidelity and justice. A description of the flag is as follows: "A state flag is adopted to be used on all occasions when the state is officially and publicly represented. All citizens have the privilege of use of the flag upon any occasion they deem appropriate. The width of the flag shall be in red, the width of which shall be one-twentieth (1/20) of the length of the flag; next to the border shall be a stripe of white on the four (4) sides of the field, which shall be in width one-fortieth (1/40) of the length of the flag. The remainder of the flag shall be a blue field, in the center of which shall be a white silhouetted buffalo, the length of which shall be one-half (1/2) of the length of the blue field; the other measurements of the buffalo shall be in proportion to its length. On the ribs of the buffalo shall be the great seal of the state of Wyoming in blue. The seal shall be in diameter one-fifth (1/5) the length of the flag. Attached to the flag shall be a cord of gold with gold tassels. The same colors shall be used in the flag, red, white, and blue, as are used in the flag of the United States of America."

STATE MOTTO

The motto for Wyoming is "Equal Rights." The motto was used earlier on the seal, and was officially adopted in 1955. It was chosen to recognize the fact that Wyoming women had attained political rights in 1869, many years before they were given voting rights in national elections.

STATE BIRD

The legislature of Wyoming officially designated the meadowlark, genus *Sturnella*, as the State bird in 1927.

The meadowlark is found in the Western United States, southwestern Canada, northwestern Mexico, east to the prairie areas of the Mississippi Valley, in Minnesota, Iowa, Missouri, and Texas.

In size, the meadowlark has a total length of eight to nine inches, and a tail length of 2½ to three inches. The head and back of the neck are a pale dull buff or white, with broad lateral crown stripes of pale grayish brown. The lower sides of the head are largely yellow, topped by a dull grayish white area streaked with gray; mostly buff of grayish brown above streaked with black; the outermost tail feathers are mostly white; the throat, breast, and abdomen are a deep yellow, sometimes with an orange hue. The yellow area is relieved by a black horseshoe-shaped patch on the chest.

The meadowlark feeds mostly on insects, with perhaps one third of its diet consisting of grain. Its loud, distinctive song is considered one of its most appealing qualities; it sometimes hammers out as many as 200 notes per minute. The young leave the nest early, unable to fly but still under the protection of the parents until able to care for themselves. Fledglings may become easy prey for weasels, skunks, snakes, owls, and hawks.

STATE FLOWER

In 1917, the legislature of Wyoming designated the Indian paintbrush, *Castilleja linariaefolia*, as the official State flower. It is also called the prairie fire, bloody warrior, and nosebleed. A scarlet member of the figwort family, it is parasitic on plant roots, and can be found in meadows and damp thickets from Maine to Wyoming and Texas.

STATE TREE

The cottonwood tree, *Populus sargentii*, was adopted by the 1947 and 1961 Wyoming legislatures as the official State tree. It is also commonly called the plains cottonwood, and plains poplar.

The plains cottonwood is a large tree with gray, deeply furrowed bark. Leaves are light green and smooth, shiny, and broadly oval in shape; they are often wider than they are long, from three to four inches in length, wide and long pointed, with coarse, curved teeth. Leafstalks are flat.

STATE SONG

In 1955, the marching song, "Wyoming" with words by Charles E. Winter and music by George E. Knapp, became the official State song.

STATE LICENSE PLATE

The first Wyoming license plate was issued in 1913. The plate had a white background and red letters; it was undated. Plates remained undated until 1918, when the State issued a white on brown plate. A variety of color combinations was used in annual plates issued each year until 1975, when multiyear plates were first used. A brown on white plate was used in 1978; in 1983, a brown on gold plate was used; and in 1988, Wyoming's plate had a red, white, and blue bicentennial design.

The current plate for Wyoming features graphics that depict a green and sand-colored prairie at the bottom, which runs into blue foothills and mountains to the center of the plate. "Wyoming" is lettered at the top right in dark blue. Numerals are centered, also in dark blue, and are separated by a cowboy on a bucking horse. The bucking horse was first used on the 1936 issue plate.

STATE POSTAGE STAMP

The Wyoming Statehood Commemorative stamp was issued in Cheyenne on July 10, 1940, to celebrate fifty years of statehood. The

stamp, designed by A.R. Meissner, depicts the State seal in purple. C.A. Brooks designed the vignette, and E.H. Helmuth did the lettering. A total of 50,034,400 of the stamp was printed.

OTHER STATE DESIGNATIONS

Over the years, the Wyoming legislature has adopted a number of additional symbols to officially represent the State. Included are the State fish as the cutthroat trout (1987); the State fossil as fossilized fish *Knightia* (1987); the State gem as jade (1967); and the State mammal as the American bison (1985).

STATE CAPITOL

When Wyoming became a State of the Union in 1890, Cheyenne was already the territorial capital. In 1886, the first of three separate contracts for a capitol was let. The firm of David W. Gibbs and Company was the architect. In 1887, the cornerstone for the statehouse was laid. The pseudo-Corinthian building was reminiscent of the U.S. Capitol. By 1888, the structure was ready for use. The first wings were completed in 1890, and new east and west wings were approved in 1915 and were completed in 1917. Cost for the original building and additions were 389,569 dollars.

Between 1974 and 1980, renovations were done to the sandstone structure at a cost of almost seven million dollars. The dome, covered in twenty-four karat gold leaf, is 145 feet high. The dome has been leafed several times.

OTHER FACTS ABOUT WYOMING

Total area: 97,809 square miles
Land area: 96,989 square miles
Water area: 820 square miles
Average elevation: 6,700 feet
Highest point: Gannett Peak, 13,804 feet
Lowest point: Belle Fourche River, 3,009 feet
Highest temperature: 114 degrees Fahrenheit
Lowest temperature: -63 degrees Fahrenheit
Population in 1990: 453,588
Population density in 1990: 4.67 persons per square mile
Population 1980-1990: -3.4 percent change
Population projected for year 2000: 489,000
Asian/Pacific Islander population in 1990: 2,806
Black population in 1990: 3,606
Hispanic population in 1990: 25,751
Native American population in 1990: 9,479
White population in 1990: 412,061
Capital: Cheyenne
Admitted to Union: July 10, 1890
Order of Statehood: 44
Electoral votes: 3

CHRONOLOGY

1743 Verendryes and companions are first white men to sight Big Horn Mountains in Wyoming.

1803 Louisiana Purchase (including present Wyoming) is completed.

1805 General James Wilkinson is appointed governor of region embracing Wyoming.
– Lewis and Clark employ Sacajawea as guide.

1806 John Colter comes to region; he is credited with being first native-born American to enter what is now Wyoming.

1807 Ezekiel Williams heads trapping party that enters Wyoming.
– John Colter is first white man to enter Tog-Wo-Tee.

1807-08 Edward Rose takes up permanent residence in Big Horn Basin; he is first American to do so.

1809 Many white trappers operate in what now is eastern Wyoming.

1811 Wilson Price Hunt's party, employed by John Jacob Astor, crosses Wyoming.

1812 Robert Stuart and companions returning from Astoria (it is believed) discover South Pass; they build first cabin erected by whites in Wyoming.

1822 General William Ashley establishes trading post on Yellowstone.
– Jim Bridger arrives with Ashley.

1824 Ashley party names Sweetwater River.
– South Pass is crossed by Ashley trappers, headed by Thomas Fitzpatrick and Jedediah Smith.

1825 Ashley and his men descend Green River; they are first white men to navigate that stream.

1826 General Ashley sells his trapping interests in Wyoming.

1827 First wheeled vehicle, a four-pound cannon, crosses South Pass.

1828 First of Wyoming posts, known as "Portuguese Houses," is established on Middle Fork of Powder River, 11 miles east of Kaycee.

1829 Smith, Jackson, and Sublette bring supplies to rendezvous near mouth of Popo Agie in wagons drawn by mules; wagons are first ever brought to Wyoming.

1830 Kit Carson, noted scout, arrives.

1832 Captain B.L.E. Bonneville, with 110 men, 20 wagon loads of provisions, goods and ammunition, heads for Pierre's Hole; he takes first wagons through South Pass and establishes temporary fortification on tributary of Green River.
– Bonneville records presence of oil in Popo Agie region of Wyoming.

1834 Fort William (later called Fort John, and then Fort Laramie), is established; it is first permanent trading post in Wyoming.

1835 Samuel Parker and Marcus Whitman are first missionaries to traverse Wyoming.

1836 Mrs. H.H. Spalding and Mrs. Marcus Whitman accompany their missionary husbands across Wyoming.

1838 Jim Baker joins American Fur Company; he becomes noted scout and guide.

1840 Father P.J. De Smet celebrates first mass in Wyoming on Green River.

1842 Fort Bridger is established.
– John C. Fremont leads expedition to select sites for line of military posts with view to territorial acquisitions in Far West.
– Elijah White leads large party of missionaries and settlers across Wyoming to Oregon. Gold is discovered near South Pass.

1843 Fort Bridger is opened to trade.
– Fremont's second expedition crosses Laramie Plains.

1845 Federal troops under Colonel Stephen W. Kearny march from Fort Leavenworth to Fort Laramie.

1846 President Polk approves act to establish military posts along Oregon Trail.

1847 Brigham Young leads first group of Mormons across Wyoming.
– Mormons build ferry across Platte River near Fort Caspar site.

1849 Fort Laramie is purchased by United States for $4,000.

1851 Captain Howard Stansbury completes reconnaissance for railway route.
– Steamboat *El Paso* sails up Platte River to Guernsey; it is first steamship on Platte River in Wyoming.

1853 Party of Mormons form settlement at old Fort Bridger.

1854 Grattan Massacre occurs near Fort Laramie.

1855 General W.S. Harney leads military expedition against Sioux.

1856 Mormon "hand-cart" exodus enters Wyoming, en route to Utah.

1857 Colonel A.S. Johnston's expedition marches across Wyoming against Mormons.
– Mormons burn buildings at Fort Bridger and Fort Supply.
– Camp Scott is established as winter quarters for Johnston's army.

– Jim Bridger leases Fort Bridger to government.
– Lieutenant G.K. Warren explores Wyoming from Fort Laramie to western slope of Black Hills.
– Colonel E.V. Sumner leads troops against Cheyenne.

1858-59 Russell, Majors, and Waddell transport more than 16,000,000 pounds of freight to Utah, passing through Wyoming on Oregon Trail.

1859 Central, Overland, California and Pike's Peak Express Company is established by Russel, Majors, and Waddell.
– Fort Bridger becomes government military reservation.

1860 Pony Express riders cross Wyoming.

1861 Creighton completes transcontinental telegraph line across Wyoming.

1862 March. Ben Holladay takes over equipment of Russell, Majors, and Waddell.
– Indians raid stage line and steal equipment.
July. Government mail route is changed from central Wyoming to southern part of State because of Indian depredations.

1863 Bozeman Trail through Wyoming is established.
– Cargo of soda is freighted to Salt Lake by Mormon; it is first known export of mineral from territory.
– Troops under General P.E. Connor are sent to Wyoming to suppress Indians.
– De Lacy prospecting expedition discovers Shoshone Lake.

1864 Indians wage war along Platte in Wyoming as result of Sand Creek Massacre in Colorado.

1865 January 5. First proposal for temporary government for Territory of Wyoming is made by James M. Ashley, later governor of Montana Territory.
July. Platte Bridge Fight occurs.

1866 Forts Reno and Phil Kearny are built along Bozeman Trail.
– Fetterman Massacre occurs.
– Fort Sanders is built on Laramie Plains.

1867 January 9. Laramie County is created by Dakota Legislature.
December 27. Carter County is created.
– Union Pacific builds into Wyoming.
– Fort Fetterman is established.
– Town of Cheyenne is founded.
– Wagon Box Fight takes place in Big Horns.
– Fort D.A. Russell (now Fort F.E. Warren) is established.
– Carissa lode is discovered at South Pass.

1868 Peace Commission signs treaties with Sioux, Crow, and Arapaho at Fort Laramie, and with Bannock and Eastern Shoshone at Fort Bridger.
– Shoshone Reservation is established.
July 25. Territory of Wyoming is created by Congress.
– Camp Augur is established (it is later called Camp Brown and is renamed Fort Washakie in 1878.
– Fort Fred Steele is established.
– Albany and Carter counties are organized.

– Episcopal Church builds first church building in Wyoming at Cheyenne.

1869 April 15. J.A. Campbell is inaugurated first governor of Wyoming.
– Cheyenne is designated as territorial capital.
October 12. First territorial legislature convenes.
December 10. Act granting suffrage to women is approved; it is first in United States.
– Union Pacific Railway is completed across territory.
– Act is passed prohibiting intermarriage of whites and blacks.
– Carter County is changed to Sweetwater County.
– Uinta County is organized.

1870 U.S. Census population totals 9,118.
– First homestead entry is made in territory.
– Women serve on grand and petit juries at Laramie.
– Esther M. Morris of South Pass is appointed first female justice of the peace.
– Washburn and Doane Expedition explores Yellowstone National Park region.

1871 Legislature passes Militia Act; three militia districts are created.

1872 "Yellowstone Wonderland" is established as first national park.
– State Penitentiary is built at Laramie; it is destroyed by fire soon after, and is partially rebuilt in 1873.

1873 Wyoming Stock Growers Association organizes.

1876 Cheyenne and Black Hills stage line is launched.
– Custer leads expedition in northern Wyoming.
– Custer Massacre occurs in Montana.

1877 Arapaho are moved to Shoshone Reservation for 'temporary' quarters (they have remained there ever since).

1879 Lotteries and games of chance are outlawed by legislation.

1880 Population is 20,789.

1883 Cheyenne completes incandescent lighting system.

1884 Fremont County is organized.

1885 Anti-Chinese "Riot" occurs in Rock Springs.

1886 Governor Warren approves act providing for capitol building.
– Commission is appointed to build capitol and State university.
– Legislature provides for construction of Institution for Deaf, Dumb and Blind at Cheyenne.
– Severe winter kills thousands of cattle.
– Fremont and Elkhorn Valley Railroad builds branch to Douglas called Wyoming and Central.

1887 Corner stone of capitol building is laid at Cheyenne.
September 6. University of Wyoming opens at Laramie.
– Crook and Pease (Johnson) counties are organized.

1888 Four hundred Mormon families move into Big Horn Basin.
– Wyoming National Guard is established.
– Legislature appropriates funds for penitentiary at Rawlins.
– Converse, Natrona, and Sheridan counties are created.

1889 November. Wyoming adopts State constitution.

1890 Population is 62,553.
July 10. Wyoming is admitted into Union as forty-fourth State.
October 14. Francis E. Warren (last territorial governor) is inaugurated governor of State.
– First Wyoming congressmen are elected; Joseph M. Carey (last delegate) and Francis E. Warren are U.S. senators; Clarence D. Clark is representative-at-large.
– Big Horn and Weston counties are created.
– First oil well is brought in by Pennsylvania Oil and Gas Company in Shannon field of Salt Creek district.

1891 President Harrison establishes Yellowstone Timber Land Reserve, first in United States.

1892 Johnson County Cattle War is fought.

1895 Oil refinery is built at Casper.
– Dupont Powder Company begins development of soda deposits in Wyoming.

1896 Hot Springs is purchased from Shoshone Indians.

1897 First Cheyenne Frontier Day is celebrated.

1898 New penitentiary is completed at Rawlins.
– Legislature enacts law taxing migratory stock from adjoining States.

1899 Union Pacific mail train is robbed of $60,000 in unsigned bank notes at Wilcox.

1900 Population is 92,531.

1901 Stinking Water River is renamed Shoshone by legislature.

1903 Tom Horn is hanged in Cheyenne.

1905 Governor's mansion is ready for occupancy.
– State Fair is established at Douglas.

1906 Riverton townsite is thrown open to settlers.
– First auto accident in Wyoming occurs.
– Devil's Tower National Monument is established.

1909 Pathfinder Dam is completed.
– Park County is organized.

1910 Population is 145,965.
– Willis Van Devanter of Wyoming is appointed associate justice of U.S. Supreme Court.
– Colonel Theodore Roosevelt visits Cheyenne Frontier Days Celebration.

1911 Campbell, Goshen, Hot Springs, Lincoln, Niobrara, Platte, and Washakie counties are organized.

1913 First automobile license in Wyoming is issued to J.M. Schwoob.
– Wolf is trained to carry mail over deep snows.

1915 Workmen's Compensation Law is enacted.

1916 Non-partisan Judiciary Law is passed.
– "Bill" Carlisle robs Union Pacific train.
– Sunrise is made model town by Colorado Fuel & Iron Company.
– Homestead tax exemption is increased to $2,500.

1917 Buffalo Bill dies in Denver.
– State Flower and State Flag are adopted by legislature.
– State highway department is created.
– Jim Baker's cabin is moved to Cheyenne.
– Wyoming male citizens register for World War I draft.

1918 Wyoming purchases $10,000,000 worth of Liberty bonds.
– State votes for prohibition by three-to-one margin.

1919 All Wyoming breweries suspend operations during national emergency.
– President Wilson makes several stops in Wyoming.
– "Bill" Carlisle, train bandit, escapes from penitentiary.

1920 Population is 194,531.
– Transcontinental airmail planes are launched.
– Night airmail flying is inaugurated across Wyoming.

1921 Great oil well roars in at Teapot Dome.
– Prize fighting is legalized in Wyoming.
– Teton and Sublette counties are organized.
– Number of homesteaders reaches peak of 15,044, covering 5,145,427 acres; much of land is later abandoned or sold.

1922 Union Pacific stores six months' supply of coal along tracks as precautionary measure in strike situation.
– Teapot Dome oil reserve's 9,481 acres is leased without competitive bidding; major scandal results.

1923 Governor William B. Ross dies in office.
– Frances Warren Pershing Memorial Hospital is dedicated in Cheyenne.
– Ninety-nine coal miners die in explosion at Kemmerer mine.
– State's oil production hits peak of 44 million barrels.

1924 Senator Francis E. Warren obtains $3,000,000 appropriation for aid in night flying service.
– State receives $1,700,000 from oil royalties for schools.
– Nellie Tayloe Ross is made governor; she is first woman to hold gubernatorial office in United States.
– Low post World War I farm prices result in 35 of Wyoming's 120 banks closing.

1925 Teapot Dome oil case is tried before Judge Kennedy at Cheyenne; decision upholds Sinclair lease.
– 3,500,000 pounds of honey are produced in Wyoming.
– New Douglas airplane makes first flight across State.

– Gros Ventre River is dammed by huge slide.
– State legislature votes for ratification of Colorado River Compact.

1926 John E. Higgins wills entire estate of $500,000 to Wyoming.
– Queen Marie of Roumania visits Wyoming.

1927 Wyoming aeronautics law is passed.
– Gros Ventre dam breaks; flooding wipes out town of Kelley.

1929 Senator Francis E. Warren dies; he served as U.S. senator from 1890-93; 1895-1929.
– Grand Teton National Park is created.
– Honorable Patrick J. Sullivan is appointed to fill unexpired term as U.S. Senator on December 5.

1930 Population is 225,565.
– Fort D.A. Russell is officially renamed Fort Francis E. Warren.
– 6,000 people stage outdoor celebration at Independence Rock.
– Legislature adopts taxes on business profits; it also sets up graduated rates on personal and corporate income, uniform rates for all tangible property.

1931 Governor Frank Emerson dies in office.
– Wyoming Air Service officials fly to Sheridan from Casper with passengers and mail.

1933 Allocation of $22,700,000 is made for Casper-Alcova Reclamation Project.
– New federal building is completed in Cheyenne.
– Senator John B. Kendrick dies in office.
– Hon. Joseph C. O'Mahoney, assistant U.S. postmaster general, is designated U.S. senator on December 18 for remainder of Kendrick's term.
– Great Depression results in one out of five Wyoming residents receiving some form of public relief; unemployed number 20,000.

1934 Wyoming Air Service begins airmail route between Cheyenne, Wyoming, and Billings, Montana.
– Democrats win every State elective office and majority of seats in State legislature.

1935 Lethal gas is made official method of capital punishment.
– Two percent sales tax is put into effect.
– Wyoming Democratic regime takes over entire State government for first time.
– State liquor commission is created; State becomes wholesaler of intoxicating liquors, not including beer.
– Sixty-day divorce law is enacted.
December 10. Designated as Wyoming Day, commemorating Governor John A. Campbell's signing of act granting women in Wyoming Territory right of suffrage.

1936 Aeronautical Commission is created.
– Terms of county elective officers are lengthened to 4 years.
– Columbus Day, October 12, is made public holiday by legislature.
– Wyoming home for dependent children is completed in Casper.
– General John Pershing visits Cheyenne.
– Old Cheyenne Club, landmark, is demolished.
– President Franklin D. Roosevelt visits Wyoming three times during summer.

– Dr. Grace Raymond Hebard, historian, dies.
– Harry H. Schwartz is elected U.S. senator for term ending 1943.

1937 New Supreme Court and Library Building are dedicated.
– Justice Willis Van Devanter resigns from United States Supreme Court.
– Ex-Senator Robert D. Carey dies.
– Social Security and Unemployment Insurance laws are enacted.
– Old Fort Laramie is purchased by Wyoming Landmark Commission.
– University of Wyoming holds Semi-Centennial Celebration.
– United Airlines passenger plane crashes in Wasatch Mountains with 19 aboard.

1938 Fort Laramie is taken over by federal government and made 74th National Monument.
– Alcova Dam is completed.
– Republicans gain political control of State government by electing three out of five State officials and majority of legislators.
– Final judgment of $6,364,677, less costs of suit and all of government's non-treaty expenditures for Shoshone since 1868, is granted to Shoshone Tribe in satisfaction of claims brought against federal government for value of land in Shoshone Reservation occupied by Arapaho for 60 years; decision clears title to 2,343,540 acres of Wyoming land, gives legal status to homes of more than 1,000 Arapaho, and brings to Shoshone about $4,000,000.

1939 Earl Durand, 26, kills four peace officers in northern Wyoming; he attracts nationwide attention as "Tarzan of the Tetons." World War II begins.

1941 Wyoming Senator Joseph C. O'Mahoney (D) urges Congress to call national conference to draft "national economic constitution" to "abolish the economic uncertainties" that threaten U.S. political system.

1942 Relocation center for persons of Japanese birth or ancestry is established in Heart Mountain area of northwestern Wyoming; it will house almost 11,000 through end of war.

1945 Total cash receipts from farming, ranching are double 1939 figures.

1949 UMW leader halts payments from depleted union welfare fund; eight thousand Utah and Wyoming miners hold strike.
– Four-day blizzard hits Wyoming, two other states; Chicago-California rail traffic is disrupted.

1950 President Truman signs bill creating Grand Teton National Park.

1952 Mining, refining of trona for soda ash begins in Sweetwater County; industry supplies most of nation's output.

1960 Wyoming produces 1,357,225 tons of uranium ore; State is second in nation in production.

1962 U.S. Steel iron-ore mine and mill complex in South Pass begins production.

1963 Right to work law abolishes closed shop.

1965 Minutemen intercontinental ballistic missiles installation at Warren Air Force Base near Cheyenne is completed.

1968 State voters approve constitutional amendment to establish initiative and referendum.

1969 One percent mineral severance tax is adopted.

1970 Wyoming's peak oil production of 160 barrels puts State in fifth place in nation.

1973 Interior secretary approves commercial leasing plan for experimental development of oil shale deposits on six federal land tracts in Utah, Wyoming, Colorado.
– Equal Rights Amendment (ERA) is ratified.
– In effort to save fuel, President Nixon signs bill to put most of U.S. on year-round daylight savings time for two years; only Alaska and Hawaii are exempted.
– Supreme Court rules that states cannot discriminate against illegitimate children in enforcement of state child support laws; decision affects cases in Wyoming, two other states.

1974 Gasoline shortage situation worsens; federal allocations are reduced in Wyoming, nine other states.
– Under experimental federal program, sixth potential shale oil tract, located in Wyoming, fails to attract bids.

1975 Interior Department designates grizzly bear as "threatened species," after declining numbers in Wyoming, two other states.

1976 Supreme Court approves coal strip mining in Wyoming, three other states; approval rejects Sierra Club request for delay until regional environmental impact study is completed.

1978 Ed Herschler (D) is elected governor.

1979 Forest fires in Wyoming, four others states burn some 171,000 acres.

1980 U.S. Census Bureau reports population total of 470,816 in 1980; State will have one representative in 98th Congress in 1982; population has grown 41 percent since 1970 census.

1981 Wyoming's unemployment rate is 3.7 percent, second lowest in nation.
– In address to legislature, Governor Ed Herschler reports that key issues in coming year will include protection of State environment and lifestyle, and mounting pressure for development of mineral resources.

1982 Republicans are left with majorities in State house and senate.

1983 Wyoming is one of only four states that have not adopted austerity measures to combat budget problems.
– Amtrak discontinues passenger trains in State; Wyoming has no passenger rail service.

1984 Wyoming is one of five states showing smallest gains in per capita income.
– Cody voters reject measure outlawing sale of pornographic material within city limits.

1985 Grasshopper infestation in Wyoming, several other Western nations prompts 25 million federal effort to spray about 9.7 million acres with pesticide.

1986 Democrat Mike Sullivan is governor.
– Wyoming has six of 10 largest coal mines in nation (all strip mines); total of 136.8 million tons ranks State second in coal production.
– Nation's first operational MX intercontinental ballistic missiles are installed at Warren Air Force Base.

1987 Study says state tax systems are riddled with inequities that allow "super-rich" to pay smaller share of income in state, local taxes than poor; list is headed by Wyoming, where wealthiest pay at rate of 0.9 percent, while poor pay 4.4 percent.

1988 Senator Alan K. Simpson is reelected Minority Whip by Republican senators.
– Widespread forest fires burn large area of Yellowstone National Park.

1989 State tax collections rose 7 percent in fiscal year 1987-88; Wyoming ranks near bottom in State tax revenue.

1990 Governor Mike Sullivan wins reelection.

1991 State House committee kills bill to outlaw abortion except in cases of rape or incest reported to police in five days, or in cases where pregnancy poses threat to woman's health; bill would have given doctors possible prison term of 14 years for performing illegal abortions.
– Population is 453,588; figure is 3.4 percent lower than 1980.
– State is one of ten in which poor pay highest rate of taxes as compared with rich.

1992 State voters approve measure to limit terms of State and federal legislators, 77 percent to 23 percent.

1993 Executions in State since 1976 reinstitution of capital punishment (1976-1993) total four.

1994 Republican Jim Geringer wins election to governor's office.

1995 Federal government begins program to reintroduce endangered North American gray wolf to Yellowstone National Park and Idaho wilderness area amid protests from western ranching interests; opponents fear wolves will prey on sheep and livestock; while supporters assert that wolves prefer wild game species that thrive in areas designated for release of wolves.

1996 In referendum, State voters back congressional term limits, 54 percent to 46 percent.

1997 National Transportation Safety Board (NTSB) study concludes that instructor of seven year old Jessica Dubroff (child who attempted to become youngest person to pilot airplane across U.S.), was responsible for fatal 1996 crash in Cheyenne; NTSB says instructor Joe Reid, killed in crash along with Jessica and father, Lloyd Dubroff, should not have allowed child to take off during snowstorm, but was concerned about keeping schedule for media interviews planned for stops during flight.

1998 Chastity Pasley pleads guilty to accessory charges in first-degree murder of Matthew Shepard, Wyoming college student beaten to death because he was gay; Pasley was girlfriend of one of Shepard's attackers.

1999 Russell Henderson pleads guilty to 1998 kidnapping, beating death of Matthew Shepard; Henderson avoids death penalty, but is sentenced to two consecutive life terms in prison; second man, Aaron McKinney, is scheduled for trial later in 1999 for his part in murder.

DIRECTORY OF STATE SERVICES

OFFICE OF THE GOVERNOR
State Capitol
Cheyenne, WY 82002-0010
Governor: 307-777-7434
Fax: 307-632-3909

ATTORNEY GENERAL
State Capitol
Cheyenne, WY 82002-0010
Governor: 307-777-7841
Fax: 307-777-6889

Law Enforcement Academy
1556 Riverbend Dr.
Douglas, WY 82633
Director: 307-358-3617
Fax: 307-358-9603

Peace Officers Standards and Training Commission
1710 Pacific Ave.
Cheyenne, WY 82002
Executive Director: 307-777-7718

SECRETARY OF STATE
State Capitol
Cheyenne, WY 82002-0020
Secretary of State: 307-777-7378
Fax: 307-777-6217

TREASURER
State Capitol
Cheyenne, WY 82002
Treasurer: 307-777-7408
Fax: 307-777-5411

ADJUTANT GENERAL
P.O. Box 1709
Cheyenne, WY 82003-1709
Adjutant General: 307-777-5234
Fax: 307-772-5910

Emergency Management Division
P.O. Box 1709

Cheyenne, WY 82003-1709
Director: 307-777-4900
Fax: 307-635-6017

ADMINISTRATION AND INFORMATION DEPARTMENT
2001 Capitol Ave., Rm. 104
Cheyenne, WY 82002
Director: 307-777-7201
Fax: 307-777-6725

Library Division
Supreme Court Building
Cheyenne, WY 82002-0650
State Librarian: 307-777-7281
Fax: 307-777-6289

AGRICULTURAL DEPARTMENT
2219 Carey Ave.
Cheyenne, WY 82002-0100
Director: 307-777-6569
Fax: 307-777-6593

State Fair
Drawer 10
Douglas, WY 82633
Director: 307-358-2398
Fax: 307-358-6030

AUDIT DEPARTMENT
Herschler Building, 3rd Fl. E
Cheyenne, WY 82002
Director: 307-777-6605
Fax: 307-777-5341

AUDITOR
Capitol Building, Rm. 114
Cheyenne, WY 82002
State Auditor: 307-777-7831
Fax: 307-777-6983

CORRECTIONS DEPARTMENT
1 East Herschler Building
Cheyenne, WY 82002
Director: 307-777-7405
Fax: 307-777-7479

COMMERCE DEPARTMENT
Barrett Building, 2301 Central Ave.
Cheyenne, WY 82002
Director: 307-777-6303
Fax: 307-777-5840

Tourism Division
125 & College Dr.
Cheyenne, WY 82002
Director: 307-777-7777
Fax: 307-777-6940

EDUCATION DEPARTMENT
Hathaway Building 2nd Fl., 2300 Capitol Ave.
Cheyenne, WY 82002-0050
Superintendent: 307-777-7675
Fax: 307-777-6234

EMPLOYMENT DEPARTMENT
Herschler Building 2nd Fl. E
Cheyenne, WY 82002
Director: 307-777-7672
Fax: 307-777-5805

Mine Inspector's Office
P.O. Box 1094
Rock Springs, WY 82902
State Inspector: 307-362-5222

Vocational Rehabilitation
117 Hathaway Building
Cheyenne, WY 82002-0710
Director: 307-777-7191

Workers Safety and Compensation Division
122 W 25th St.
Cheyenne, WY 82002-0700
Director: 307-777-7441

ENVIRONMENTAL QUALITY DEPARTMENT
Herschler Building, 4th Fl. W
Cheyenne, WY 82002
Director: 307-777-7938
Fax: 307-777-7682

FAMILY SERVICES DEPARTMENT
Hathaway Building, 3rd Fl., 23000 Capitol Ave.
Cheyenne, WY 82002-0490
Director: 307-777-7564
Fax: 307-777-7747

FIRE PREVENTION AND ELECTRICAL SAFETY DEPARTMENT
Herscler Building, 122 W 25th St.
Cheyenne, WY 82002
Director & State Fire Marshall: 307-777-7288
Fax: 307-777-7119

GAME AND FISH DEPARTMENT
5400 Bishop Blvd.
Cheyenne, WY 82006
Director: 307-777-4601
Fax: 307-777-4610

HEALTH DEPARTMENT
117 Hathaway Building
Cheyenne, WY 82002-0710
Director: 307-777-7821
Fax: 307-777-7439

Aging Division
139 Hathaway Building
Cheyenne, WY 82002-0710
Administrator: 307-777-7986
Fax: 307-777-5340

Behavioral Health Division
446 Hathaway Building
Cheyenne, WY 82002-0710
Administrator: 307-777-7094
Fax: 307-777-5580

Preventive Medicine Division
117 Hathaway Building
Cheyenne, WY 82002-0710
Administrator: 307-777-6004
Fax: 307-777-5402

Public Health Division
Hathaway Building, 4th Fl.
Cheyenne, WY 82002-0710
Administrator: 307-777-6186
Fax: 307-777-5402

INSURANCE DEPARTMENT
122 W 25th St.
Cheyenne, WY 82002-0440
Commissioner: 307-777-7401
Fax: 307-777-5895

REVENUE DEPARTMENT
122 W 25th St., Herschlet Building
Cheyenne, WY 82002
Director: 307-777-7961
Fax: 307-777-7722

TRANSPORTATION DEPARTMENT
P.O. Box 1708
Cheyenne, WY 82003-1708
Director: 307-777-4484
Fax: 307-777-4163

Aeronautics Division
P.O. Box 1708
Cheyenne, WY 82003-1708
Chairman: 307-777-4880
Fax: 307-637-7352

ARCHITECTS BOARD
2310 Central Ave. 3rd Fl.
Cheyenne, WY 82002
President: 307-777-7788
Fax: 307-777-6005

CAPITOL BUILDING COMMISSION
801 W 20th St.
Cheyenne, WY 82002
Chairman: 307-777-7767
Fax: 307-635-7049

COMMUNITY COLLEGE COMMISSION
2020 Carey Ave., 8th Fl.
Cheyenne, WY 82002
Executive Director: 307-777-7763
Fax: 307-777-6567

DEVELOPMENTAL DISABILITIES PLANNING COUNCIL
122 W 25th St., Herschler Building, 4th Fl.
Cheyenne, WY 82002
Executive Director: 307-777-7230
Fax: 307-777-5690

GEOLOGICAL SURVEY
Box 3008 University Station
Laramie, WY 82071
State Geologist: 307-766-2286

Fax: 307-766-2605

LIQUOR COMMISSION
1520 E 5th St.
Cheyenne, WY 82005
Director: 307-777-7231
Fax: 307-777-6255

LIVESTOCK BOARD
2020 Carey Ave., 4th Fl.
Cheyenne, WY 82002
Executive Officer & State Veterinarian: 307-777-7515
Fax: 307-777-6561

MEDICAL EXAMINERS BOARD
Barrett Building, 2nd Fl.
Cheyenne, WY 82002
Executive Secretary: 307-777-6463
Fax: 307-777-6478

MUNICIPAL POWER AGENCY
P.O. Box 900
Lusk, WY 82225
Executive Director: 307-334-2170
Fax: 307-334-2407

PUBLIC EMPLOYEES ASSOCIATION
P.O. Box 2100
Cheyenne, WY 82003
President: 307-635-7901
Fax: 307-637-3932

STATE LANDS AND FARM LOAN OFFICE
Herschler Building 122 W 25th St.
Cheyenne, WY 82002-0600
Director: 307-777-6629
Fax: 307-777-5400

PUBLIC SERVICE COMMISSION
700 W 21st St.
Cheyenne, WY 82002
Chairman: 307-777-7427
Fax: 307-777-5700

RETIREMENT SYSTEM BOARD
Herschler Building, 1st Fl., E
Cheyenne, WY 82002
Director: 307-777-7691
Fax: 307-777-5995

STATE ENGINEER
Herschler Building, 4th Fl. E
Cheyenne, WY 82002
State Engineer: 307-777-7354
Fax: 307-777-5451

WATER DEVELOPMENT COMMISSION
Herschler Building, 4th Fl. West, 122 W 25th St.
Cheyenne, WY 82002
Director: 307-777-7626
Fax: 307-777-6819

MEMBERS OF CONGRESS

SENATE

SEN. CRAIG THOMAS (R) (b. 1933); 1st Term;
Phone: 202-224-6441; Fax: 202-224-1724;
E-mail: craig@thomas.senate.gov

www.senate.gov/~thomas/

SEN. MICHAEL B. ENZI (R) (b. 1944); 1st Term;
Phone: 202-224-3424; Fax: 202-228-0359;
E-mail: senator@enzi.senate.gov

www.senate.gov/~enzi/

HOUSE

BARBARA CUBIN (R-At Large) (b. 1946); 3rd Term;
Phone: 202-225-2311; Fax: 202-225-3057;
E-mail: barbara.cubin@mail.house.gov

www.house.gov/cubin

TWENTIETH CENTURY GOVERNORS

RICHARDS, DEFOREST (1846-1903), fourth governor of Wyoming (1899-1905), was born in Charlestown, New Hampshire on August 6, 1846. After his schooling, he moved to Alabama and made his living as a farmer. In 1867 he entered politics with a seat in the Alabama State Legislature, then between 1868 and 1871 he served as Sheriff and Treasurer of Wilcox County, Alabama. In 1888 Richards relocated to Douglas, Wyoming Territory, where he founded a bank and engaged in the mercantile business. Returning to politics, from 1891 to 1894 he served as Mayor of Douglas, and during 1893, held one term in the Wyoming State Senate. Also between 1891 and 1894, Richards served in the Wyoming National Guard.

In 1898 Richards successfully ran for the Wyoming governorship on the Republican ticket, and won a second term in 1902. Richards likened his new job to the businesses he ran and approached it as such, making it his first order of business to pay off the State debts, and reduce expenditures. He also requested that a large amount of federally-owned acreage be turned over to the State of Wyoming. In addition, the State Board of Health was established, funding was set aside for local health boards, plus the Pure Food Act was adopted. Institutions organized during that time included a hospital, prisons, a school for the deaf, dumb and blind, as well as a veterans facility. The establishment of railroads was also a priority.

He was married to Elise Jane Ingersol, and the couple had two children. Richards died on April 28, 1903.

CHATTERTON, FENIMORE (1860-1958), acting governor of Wyoming (1905-1906), was born in Oswego, New York on July 21, 1860. In 1878 he relocated to Wyoming Territory, founding his own mercantile store. He subsequently attended the University of Michigan, earning a law degree in 1892, and went into private law practice.

Chatterton entered politics in 1888, with his election as Probate Judge and Treasurer of Carbon County. Between 1890 and 1893 he served in the Wyoming Senate, made an unsuccessful bid for the United States Senate in 1894, then between 1895 and 1897, was Wyoming's Prosecuting Attorney. In 1898 Chatterton, a Republican, was named Secretary of State. As such, upon the death of the incumbent, Governor Deforest Richard, on April 28, 1903, Chatterton assumed the governorship. During that time he served both as Acting Governor and Secretary of State.

During his tenure, Chatterton rejected expansion of the State's forest preserves, including Yellowstone Park. His biggest priority was industrial growth, saying: "Let us organize Wyoming into an Industrious Industrial Industry." He urged the construction of railroads and the development of irrigation, and while in office, served as attorney and general manager for the Wyoming Central Irrigation Company. He also requested from the federal government that a part of the Wind River Indian Reservation be divided to allow settlement and irrigation.

In the 1904 election, the Republican Party did not nominate him for the governorship, and Chatterton left office and returned full time to his Secretary of State post, stepping down in January of 1907.

Continuing with his various business enterprises, Chatterton helped plat and set up irrigation for the town of Riverton. In 1927 Chatterton served on the State Board of Equalization and the Public Service Commission.

Chatterton was married to Stella Wyland, and the couple had two children. Chatterton died on May 9, 1958.

BROOKS, BRYANT BUTLER (1861-1944), fifth governor of Wyoming (1906-1911), was born on February 5, 1861 in Bernardston, Massachusetts. At the age of eighteen he moved to Nebraska, where he did farm work, then migrated to Wyoming in 1880, where he engaged in ranching. The following year he started his own business.

Entering politics, Brooks, a Republican, served as County Commissioner during 1891-92, and in 1893, he was a member of the Wyoming State Legislature. Brooks was elected to the Wyoming governorship in November, 1904, to fill the seat vacated after the death of Governor DeForest Richards, taking office on January 2, 1905.

During his administration, irrigation throughout the State was an important issue, and Brooks also sought to preserve Wyoming's animal wildlife. In addition, the production of oil in Wyoming increased dramatically, creating enough revenue to construct badly needed institutions, and upgrade existing ones.

Brooks stepped down from office on January 2, 1911, and returned to his business ventures. In subsequent years he was president of the Consolidated Royalty Oil Company, and the Wyoming National Bank of Casper.

Brooks was married to Mary Naomi Willard, and the couple had five children. He died on December 7, 1944.

CAREY, JOSEPH MAULL (1844-1924), sixth governor of Wyoming (1911-1915), was born in Milton, Delaware on January 19, 1844. He moved to New York to attend Union College, then studied at the University of Pennsylvania Law School, graduating in 1864.

Between 1869 and 1871, Carey served as United States Attorney to the region that had just become Wyoming Territory, and in the latter year, he was appointed Associate Justice of the Territorial Supreme Court, a post he held until 1876. Between 1881 and 1885 Carey was Mayor of Cheyenne, and from 1885 to 1890, was a Territorial Delegate to the United States Congress. Carey was responsible for introducing the Wyoming statehood bill and guiding its eventual passage, then subsequently served as the first United States Senator from the new State between 1890 and 1895.

After losing his reelection bid, Carey stepped down from that post and involved himself in his law work and various business enterprises, which included ranching, livestock, irrigation, and real estate.

Carey revived his political career in 1910 in a unique way. After failing to receive the Republican nomination for the Wyoming governorship, Carey immediately switched parties and accepted the Democrats' offer of nomination, although running on what he termed the Independent ticket, and he went on to secure the office of governor.

During his tenure, Carey, a progressive on many issues, was able to secure such reforms as the secret ballot, direct primaries, and the adoption of a corrupt practices act, and plans were laid for a workmen's compensation law. Also during that time, the State Legislature adopted the Seventeenth Amendment to the United States Constitution, granting direct election of Senators.

Carey decided to step down after one term. He remained active in politics as a member of the Progressive Party, serving as delegate in 1916, to the Progressive National Convention. He left politics for two years, returning to his law work and other various business ventures. In 1918 he came back to support his son, who successfully ran for the Wyoming governorship on the Republican ticket.

Carey was married to Louisa David, and the couple had two children. He died on February 5, 1924.

KENDRICK, JOHN BENJAMIN (1857-1933), seventh governor of Wyoming (1915-1917), was born in Cherokee County, Texas on September 6, 1857. His formal schooling ended at the seventh grade. In 1879 he became a cattle herder who brought the animals from Texas to Wyoming, and eventually owned and expanded his own herd for a number of years. In the early 1900s he settled in Sheridan, Wyoming, and became a successful ranch owner. In 1909 he held the post of President of the Wyoming Stock Growers.

Kendrick, a Democrat, entered politics with his election to the Wyoming Legislature in 1910, and two years later, made an unsuccessful bid for the United States Senate. However, in 1914 he was successful in his run for the Wyoming governorship. During his tenure, State surveys were implemented to research possible reclamation and irrigation locations, plus the Public Service Commission was organized. Also, in 1915, the State Legislature joined Kendrick in a protest to the United States Congress regarding the withdrawal by President Woodrow Wilson of public acreage attached to mineral rights, as well as power sites that controlled water sources.

In 1916 Kendrick ran successfully for the United States Senate, and resigned from the governorship to assume his new post. He subsequently served seventeen years as a Senator, during which time he was an influential presence in Washington, D.C. He was behind the passage of legislation regarding meat-packing, was one of the first to investigate the Teapot Dome scandal, and also sponsored the Casper-Alcova reclamation bill.

Kendrick was married to Eula Wulgjen, and the couple had two children. He died on November 3, 1933.

HOUX, FRANK L. (1860-1941), acting governor of Wyoming (1917-1919), was born in Lexington, Missouri on December 12, 1860. He graduated from Shaw's Business College in Kansas City, Missouri, in 1884. In 1885 he migrated to Montana, where for a decade he was a cattleman, then relocated to Cody, Wyoming, where he went into real estate and also worked in the fire insurance business.

Houx, a Democrat, entered politics in 1901 when he became the first Mayor of Cody, also serving at that time as Police Judge. He subsequently won a second mayoral term in 1905. In 1910 and 1914, he successfully won the post of Secretary of State. As such, when the incumbent, Governor John Kendrick was elected to the United States Senate, Houx assumed the governorship on February 26, 1917. While in office, World War I was already in progress, and he was in charge of the mobilization of not only the economic necessities, but also of the Wyoming National Guard's participation in the war effort. In addition, he organized the Wyoming Council for National Defense, and helped choose the officials ultimately responsible to oversee the Selective Service draft.

Houx lost his reelection bid in 1918 and stepped down from office on January 6, 1919. Later that year Houx relocated to Texas where he started up an oil refining enterprise, and stayed until 1935, when he returned home to Wyoming.

Houx was married twice: to Augusta Camp, and after her death, to Ida Mason Christy. He had three children from his first union, and four from his second. Houx died on April 3, 1941.

CAREY, ROBERT DAVIS (1878-1937), eighth governor of Wyoming (1919-1925), was born in Cheyenne, Wyoming on August 12, 1878, the son of former Wyoming Governor, Joseph M. Carey. He received his education in Pennsylvania, then attended Yale University, from which he was graduated in 1900. From 1911 to 1915, Carey served on his father's staff while the elder was Governor. Initially a Republican, Carey was a member of the Progressive Party for a time, then returned to his former party, with whom he won the Wyoming governorship in 1918.

During Carey's tenure, a State highway system was implemented, with a new State Highway Department being organized to oversee it. Wanting to attract more settlers to Wyoming, he restored the State Board of Immigration, and within a decade, nearly ten million acres of land were established under the Homestead Laws. Carey also sought to support State farmers, advocating the Farm Loan Act, which offered long-term, low interest funding to farmers. In addition, workmen's compensation was increased, and "blue sky" legislation was passed. Carey did the best he could to cut State expenditures during a time of agricultural depression that was taking place during the early twenties, but when he ran for reelection, he was defeated, and stepped down from office in 1923.

Carey resumed his various business ventures, but returned to the political arena with his successful 1930 run for the United States Senate. Defeated in his reelection bid, he left that post in 1937.

Carey was married to Julia Blanchard Freeman, and the couple had two children. He died on January 17, 1937.

ROSS, WILLIAM BRADFORD (1873-1924), ninth governor of Wyoming (1923-1924), was born on December 4, 1873 in Dover, Tennessee. Receiving a common school education, he attended Nashville's Peabody Normal School. In 1901 Ross relocated to Cheyenne, Wyoming and during 1906-07, served as Prosecuting Attorney of Laramie County. Between 1910 and 1922, he served on the Board of Law Examiners. In the latter year, Ross successfully ran for the Wyoming governorship on the Democratic ticket, taking office on January 1, 1923. During his short tenure, he sought to run a frugal administration by merging a number of governmental departments. In addition, he recommended that all products taken out of state be given a severance license tax.

Ross was only twenty-one months into his term when he died, and was eventually succeeded in the governorship by his widow, Nellie Tayloe Ross. The couple had four children.

LUCAS, FRANK E. (1876-1948), acting governor of Wyoming (1924-1925), was born in Grant City, Missouri. He received his early schooling in Bedford, Iowa, then dropped out of school in the eighth grade in order to apprentice in the printing field. After working on two Iowa newspapers, Lucas relocated to Wyoming in 1899, where he had a long newspaper career as owner and operator of the *Buffalo Bulletin* for thirty-six years.

Since the *Bulletin* was a Republican paper, Lucas was eventually drawn to a political career. In 1915 and 1917, he was elected to the Wyoming House of Representatives, and also served in the Wyoming Senate for two terms. Lucas was elected Wyoming's Secretary of State in 1922 on the Republican ticket. On October 2, 1924, the incumbent Governor, William B. Ross, died. As such, Lucas ascended to the governorship for a short period. On January 5, 1925, the widow of Ross, Nellie Tayloe Ross, was inaugurated into office. During his short tenure, Lucas served in both posts, but would only accept the governor's salary. While Mrs. Ross held the governorship, he continued as Secretary of State until 1927. He made two bids for the governorship, in 1926 and 1934, but was unsuccessful. Lucas continued to publish and edit the *Buffalo Bulletin*, finally selling it in 1946.

Lucas married Ina Belle Craven, with whom he had three children, one of whom died in infancy. Lucas died on November 26, 1948.

ROSS, NELLIE TAYLOE (1876-1977), tenth governor of Wyoming (1925-1927), was born in St. Joseph, Missouri on November 29, 1876. Receiving both a public and private education, Ross subsequently took a two-year course at a kindergarten training school in Omaha, Nebraska. Sources differ on whether she had a teaching career, with one saying her health was too frail for her to teach, and another claiming she taught kindergarten for two years.

While visiting relatives in Tennessee, the young woman met the man she would eventually marry, William B. Ross. A year after William settled in Wyoming, Nellie joined him, and the two were wed. William Ross was eventually elected to the Wyoming governorship. During his tenure, although she spent most of her time as a wife, and mother to their four children, Mrs. Ross, a charming, intelligent woman, became prominent both in political circles, and to her husband's constituency. As such, upon the death of her husband on October 2, 1924, it seemed a natural progression that Mrs. Ross would be the logical choice to serve out her husband's unexpired term. Until a special election could be held, Secretary of State, Frank E. Lucas, assumed the office as Acting Governor.

In a State that had a majority of Republican voters, Nellie Ross was elected to the Wyoming governorship on the Democratic ticket, receiving 43,323 votes, the largest number of votes any public official had ever received in the State up to that time. Ross, who took office on January 5, 1925, was the first woman in the United States to be inaugurated as Chief Executive of a state. During her tenure, she became a national figure with her advocacy of women's suffrage. In addition, Ross sought to implement stringent safety standards for coal miners, and urged the ratification of the Child Labor Amendment to the United States Constitution. The only program she couldn't convince the State Legislature to adopt was a strong statute against the selling of alcohol.

Ross lost her reelection bid of 1926 by a very small margin of 1,365 votes, and stepped down from office on January 3, 1927. She remained active within the Democratic Party, guiding the women's' vote during the presidential campaign of Franklin D. Roosevelt. In 1933, President Roosevelt appointed Ross Director of the United States Bureau of the Mint. She was the first woman to hold that post as well, and also the first to have her image inscribed on a mint medal. During her long tenure of twenty years, Ross oversaw the construction of the mints at San Francisco, West Point, and Fort Knox.

In earlier days, it was assumed that women who participated in politics would lose their femininity, but according to a 1927 writer, Mrs. Ross was "visual evidence to the contrary," a "charming, soft-voiced gentlewoman," who proved the exception to the rule. The periodical, *Collier's Weekly*, noting in an editorial the success of her time in office, said, "By common consent, Mrs. Ross' administration ranks high in the history of her state."

Ross died on December 19, 1977, at the age of one hundred and one.

EMERSON, FRANK C. (1882-1931), eleventh governor of Wyoming (1927-1931), was born in Saginaw, Michigan, on May 26, 1882. He attended the University of Michigan, earning a B.S. degree. Emerson subsequently relocated to Cora, Wyoming, where he was named chief engineer for the Wyoming Land and Irrigation Company. He also served as superintendent of the Big Horn Canal Association and the Lower Hanover Canal Association, plus he was engineer for the Wyoming Sugar Company and the Worland Drainage District. During this later period, between 1919 and 1927, Emerson was State Engineer. While in this post, Emerson was one of the main architects of the Colorado River Compact, in which seven western states attempted to share the river water equitably.

In 1923, while serving as State Engineer, Governor William Ross removed him from that office. Emerson fought back, however, taking his cause to the Wyoming Supreme Court. After a ten-month struggle, Emerson was reinstated. As a longtime foe of the Ross's, he later waged a successful gubernatorial campaign on the Republican ticket against Ross' widow, Nellie Tayloe Ross, who had already served one term. Emerson won the election by a slim margin, and went on to secure a second term in 1930.

During his tenure, Emerson sought to develop Wyoming's natural resources, as well as the State's highways. Also, due to his past expertise, Emerson was asked by the United States Secretary of the Interior to act as special advisor on all issues concerning the Colorado River.

Six weeks into his second term, Emerson took ill, and died on February 18, 1931. He was married to Zennia Jean Reynders, and the couple had three children.

CLARK, ALONZO M. (1868-1952), acting governor of Wyoming (1931-1933), was born in Flint, Indiana, on August 13, 1868. He attended Nebraska State Teachers College, earning a teaching certificate in 1898. Clark subsequently taught school in Nebraska, and later served as Superintendent of Schools for Dawes County. In 1901 he migrated to Wyoming, where he oversaw a homestead, and also continued his teaching career.

Clark, a Republican, entered politics in 1926 with his election to the office of Secretary of State, also winning a second term. While in that post he ascended to the Wyoming governorship upon the death of the incumbent, Governor Frank C. Emerson, on February 18, 1931. During his tenure, Wyoming, liked the rest of the country, was still reeling from the Great Depression. Clark was an advocate of the position taken by the Hoover administration, by which State self-reliance was the key to getting through the rough period. He sought to have cooperative marketing of agricultural products, plus during that time, prohibition was repealed. He also urged an end to the selling of crude oil drawn from the State's federally-owned lands, but Joseph M. Dixon, Acting Secretary of the Interior, rejected the suggestion.

In 1932 Clark failed in his reelection bid, and stepped down from office on January 2, 1933. He continued as Secretary of State, leaving that post in January of 1935. He made another attempt at the governorship in 1934, but lost in the general election. Clark returned to his teaching career soon after. He made two more bids for political office: for the United States Congress in 1938, and the U.S. Senate in 1942, but failed both times.

Clark was married twice: to Lucy M. Smith, and after her death, to Florence Russell. He had one child from his first union. Clark died on October 12, 1952.

MILLER, LESLIE A. (1886-1970), twelfth governor of Wyoming (1933-1939), was born in Junction City, Kansas on January 29, 1886. His formal schooling ended at the eighth grade, but he continued to learn on his own by doing a lot of reading. As a young man he made his way to Wyoming, where he worked for the Union Pacific Railroad in Laramie. Miller subsequently found success as an oil executive, starting his own firm, the Aero Oil Company.

Deciding to pursue politics, Miller was elected to two terms in the State House of Representatives, serving from 1911 to 1913, and again from 1923 to 1925. In 1929 he was elected to the Wyoming State Senate. However, he resigned from the latter post the following year to run for the governorship, which he failed to win. He ran again a second time in a special election, after the death of the incumbent, Frank Emerson, and won to serve the unexpired short term, taking office on January 2, 1933. In 1934, Miller was reelected to a full term.

Miller, like his predecessors, had to try and keep the State running in the midst of the Great Depression, and while he was in office, a sales tax was implemented. Although it could have been beneficial to the State, legalized gambling was vetoed as a form of income for Wyoming. Also during that time, Miller was the lone voice in support of the expansion of the Grand Teton National Park, and in addition, helped mediate the plans for the division of the North Platte River between Colorado, Nebraska and Wyoming.

Miller lost his bid for reelection in the 1938 race, and stepped down from office. From 1940 to 1970 he was a board member of Jackson Hole Preserve, Incorporated, and between 1942 and 1944, he served as Regional Director of the War Production Board.

Miller was married to Margaret Morgan, and the couple had two children. He died on September 29, 1970.

SMITH, NELS H. (1884-1976), thirteenth governor of Wyoming (1939-1943), was born on August 27, 1884 in Gayville, South Dakota. He attended the University of South Dakota, earning a B.A. degree in 1904. The following year he engaged in the cattle business, and in 1907 he migrated to Crook County, Wyoming, where he partnered with his brother in a ranching and livestock breeding venture, until 1911.

Politically active, Smith served for a time on the Wyoming Highway Commission. A Republican, he was elected to the Wyoming House of Representatives in 1918. In 1938 he ran for and won the Wyoming governorship on the Republican ticket. While in office, State property taxes were eventually abolished, a vocational training program was implemented at the State Industrial Institute, and the Game and Fish Commission was reorganized. In addition, Smith sought to construct 300 miles of roads linking farmlands to markets throughout the State.

After losing his reelection bid in 1942, Smith returned to his ranching and livestock breeding businesses. Married to Marie Christensen, the couple had two children. Smith died on July 5, 1976.

HUNT, LESTER CALLOWAY (1892-1954), fourteenth governor of Wyoming (1943-1949), was born in Isabel, Illinois, on July 8, 1892. He attended Illinois Wesleyan University for a time, but was forced to drop out due to financial difficulties. Later, deciding to pursue dentistry, Hunt attended the St. Louis University College of Dentistry, graduating in 1917. He established a dental practice in Lander, Wyoming, then during World War I, Hunt served in the Army Dental Corps between 1917 and 1919, and was discharged at the rank of major. He subsequently returned to school to complete his graduate work at Northwestern University during 1919-20.

Politically active in Democratic politics, Hunt secured a seat in the Wyoming Legislature in 1932, and in 1934, he became Secretary of State, being reelected to that post in 1938. In 1942 Hunt, running on the Democratic ticket, was successful in his bid for the Wyoming governorship, and also won a second term in 1946. During his tenure, Hunt was a staunch supporter of states' rights, even opposing the establishment of a national park in Jackson Hole. In addition, while seeking to maintain a balanced budget, he also advocated the construction of a number of State buildings, plus financial support for the State university. Hunt served two years of his second term, then stepped down to successfully run for the United States Senate. Initially deciding to run for a second term, Hunt changed his mind and withdrew from the race.

On June 19, 1954, Hunt took his own life. He was survived by his wife Emily Nathelle Higby, and their two children.

CRANE, ARTHUR GRISWOLD (1877-1955), acting governor of Wyoming (1949-1951), was born in Davenport Center, New York, on September 1, 1877. He moved to Northfield, Minnesota to attended Carleton College, earning a B.S. degree in 1902. Crane subsequently settled in Minot, North Dakota where, from 1902 to 1905, he served as Superintendent of Schools. Between 1905 and 1907 Crane was principal of Fergus County Free High School in Lewiston, Montana, then returned to Minot where he was president of the State Normal School from 1912 to 1920. Deciding to continue his education, he attended Columbia University, taking his M.A. degree in 1918, and a Ph.D. in 1920. Also, during that time, with World War I in progress, Crane served at the rank of major in the Army Sanitary Corps, and authored the thirteenth volume of *The Official Medical History of the War*. From 1922 to 1941, Crane served as president of the University of Wyoming, and during that time, was also president of the National Association of State Universities.

Deciding to enter politics, Crane, a Republican, was elected Wyoming's Secretary of State. As such, upon the resignation in 1948 of the incumbent, Governor Lester Hunt, Crane assumed the governorship. During his time in office, Crane backed the construction of several State institutions, including the Wyoming Home and Hospital for the Aged, located in Thermopolis. Also during that time the State endured natural disasters, including a grasshopper plague, and the 1949 blizzard. The latter had Crane requesting financial help from the federal government in order to aid livestock businesses.

After his term as Acting Governor ended, Crane stepped down from office and retired from politics. He was married to Lura May DeArment, and the couple had two children. He died on August 12, 1955.

BARRETT, FRANK A. (1892-1962), fifteenth governor of Wyoming (1951-1953), was born on November 19, 1892. He studied at Creighton University, earning a B.A. degree in 1913 and an LL.D. degree in 1916. Barrett moved to Lusk, Wyoming, where he engaged in law work and also owned a ranch.

Politically active, Barrett became a member of the United States House of Representatives in 1942, serving in that body until 1950. In the latter year he successfully ran for the Wyoming governorship on the Republican ticket. Known as a very frugal administrator, Barrett supported several types of industry, including mining, oil, and livestock, and rejected proposed tax hikes on these industries.

Barrett stepped down from office after two years and successfully ran for the United States Senate, serving in that post from 1953 to 1959. He was married to Alice C. Donoghue, with whom he had three children. Barrett died on May 30, 1962.

ROGERS, CLIFFORD JOY (1897-1962), acting governor of Wyoming (1953-1955), was born near Clarinda, Iowa on December 20, 1897. By the age of seven, he had lost both parents, and was therefore raised by an uncle. Rogers studied at the University of Iowa for a time, then after the start of World War I, joined the United States Army, serving in Europe and Mexico. After his discharge, he moved to Gillette, Wyoming in 1920, where he ran a homestead and was the football coach at Gillette High School. In 1924 he resettled in Sheridan, Wyoming, and found employment at the Veterans Hospital. In 1928 he moved once again, this time to Cheyenne, where he made his living as a motor vehicle inspector.

Entering the political arena, between 1931 to 1933, Rogers was secretary to Governor Alonzo M. Clark, then from 1933 to 1935, was Deputy Secretary of State. Deciding he wanted to own his own business, Rogers constructed the Top Rail Motel, which he operated from 1935 to 1958. Continuing in politics, between 1947 and 1951 he was State Treasurer, and from the latter year until 1953, Rogers, a Republican, was Wyoming's Secretary of State. As such, upon the resignation of the incumbent, Governor Frank Barrett, Rogers ascended to the governorship on January 2, 1953.

During Rogers's tenure, State records were preserved within the newly-created Central Microfilm Department, plus the new State motto, "Equal Rights," was adopted in 1955. In addition, veterans saw their property tax exemption benefits reduced, plus the property tax homestead exemption was nullified. Also, the first junior college, Casper College, was established in Wyoming in 1955. Rogers lost his reelection bid in 1954, and stepped down from office on January 3, 1955. In 1959 he was elected State Treasurer of Wyoming, serving until 1962.

Rogers and his wife Mabel had one child. He died on May 18, 1962.

SIMPSON, MILWARD L. (1897-1993), sixteenth governor of Wyoming (1955-1959), was born on November 12, 1897. As a young man, he held a number of jobs, including day laborer, cattle herder, coal miner, and semi-professional baseball player. During World War I, Simpson served in the Infantry as a 2nd Lieutenant. After his discharge he attended the University of Wyoming where he earned a B.S. degree in 1921. He continued his studies at Harvard Law School, and in 1926, passed the Wyoming bar.

Simpson entered politics by way of a seat in the Wyoming House of Representatives from 1927 to 1929. In 1940 he made an unsuccessful bid for the United States Senate. He subsequently pursued a business career, serving on the board of the Husky Oil Company, and was also president of the University of Wyoming Board of Trustees between 1943 and 1955.

In 1954 Simpson ran for and won the Wyoming governorship on the Republican ticket. During his tenure, Simpson sought to run a fiscally-sound State government, and reorganize it as well. He submitted thirty-three legislative proposals, with only three failing to pass. Laws adopted included the organization of a commission to research the possibility of establishing concessions within Yellowstone National Park, plus the reduction of tax exemptions for veterans. Simpson opposed the federal land policies in place at the time, and lobbied to have federal acreage placed under the State's autonomy. Simpson pushed for an expanded highway patrol, as well as a comprehensive study of all State programs and institutions, and also during that time, closed down gambling and liquor establishments, and cut State employee perks.

Simpson lost his reelection bid in 1958, and stepped down from office. In 1962 he was elected to fill a United States Senate seat vacated by the death of Edwin Keith Thompson. He did not seek a second term, due to frail health.

Simpson married Lorna Kooi, and the couple had two children. He died on June 10, 1993 of Parkinson's disease.

HICKEY, JOHN JOSEPH (1911-1970), seventeenth governor of Wyoming (1959-1961), was born in Rawlins, Wyoming on August 22, 1911. He attended the University of Wyoming, earning an LL.B. degree in 1934. Later, in 1959, he returned to that school and received his LL.D. degree.

In 1934 Hickey established a law practice in Rawlins, and the following year, entered politics with his becoming City Treasurer, a post he held until 1940. Between 1939 and 1942, and again from 1946 to 1949, Hickey, a Democrat, served as Carbon County Attorney. In the interim, he served in the United States Army during World War II, spending over two years fighting in the European Theater of Operations, and was discharged in 1946.

In 1949 Hickey was named by President Harry Truman to the post of United States District Attorney for Wyoming, where he served until 1952. During 1954 he served as Wyoming State Chairman of the Democratic Party. In the 1958 governor's race, Hickey won, taking office on January 5, 1959. On January 2, 1961, Hickey resigned his post to fill the unexpired United States Senate seat left by the death of Edwin Keith Thomas. Hickey ran for a full term in 1962, but lost and stepped down. He returned to his law practice for a time, then was appointed to the United States Tenth Circuit Court of Appeals in 1966 by President Lyndon Johnson.

Hickey was married to Winfred Espy, and the couple had two children. He died on September 22, 1970.

GAGE, JACK ROBERT (1899-1970), acting governor of Wyoming (1961-1963), was born on January 13, 1899, in McCook, Nebraska. After high school Gage enlisted in the United State Army Coast Artillery Corps, where he served almost a year. Gage attended the University of Wyoming, taking a degree in agriculture in 1924. He worked for a time as a schoolteacher and also operated a bookstore. In 1934 he was elected to the post of State Superintendent of Public Instruction, serving a four-year term.

From 1942 until 1958, Gage served as Postmaster of Sheridan, Wyoming. In the latter year, he was elected Secretary of State. As such, when incumbent Governor Joseph Hickey resigned to take the vacant United States Senate seat left by the death of Edwin Keith Thompson, Gage assumed the governorship on January 3, 1961. While in office he sought to maintain Wyoming's financial stability, but opposed a higher sales tax. He also asked the federal government for additional funds, as well as more acreage. In 1962 he was unsuccessful in his attempt to secure another term in office, and after stepping down, subsequently went into a private business venture. In addition, he wrote a number of books concerning Wyoming, and the West. He made one more attempt in 1966 for the governorship, but was unsuccessful.

In his final years, Gage became prominent with his colorful and humorous lectures regarding the State of Wyoming. He was married to Leona Switzer, and the couple had two children. Gage died on March 14, 1970.

HANSEN, CLIFFORD P. (1912-), eighteenth governor of Wyoming (1963-1967), was born in Jackson Hole, Wyoming on October 16, 1912. He attended the University of Wyoming, earning a B.A. degree in 1934. He subsequently engaged in his family's ranching enterprise in Jackson Hole.

Entering politics in 1943, Hansen served two terms as Teton County Commissioner, stepping down in 1951. Between 1946 and 1966, Hansen was a member of the University of Wyoming Board of Trustees.

In 1962 Hansen won the race for governor on the Republican ticket, taking office on January 7, 1963. During his tenure several social reforms were put into place regarding such issues as funding for public schools, welfare programs, the upgrading of State institutions, and employment practices. It was his opinion that the social needs of the individual were of the utmost importance, and he sought to curb the control of the federal government by creating a solid State government. Hansen completed his term, stepping down from office in 1967, and immediately made a successful bid for the United States Senate, winning a second term as well.

Hansen is married to Martha Close, and the couple has two children.

HATHAWAY, STANLEY KNAPP (1924-), nineteenth governor of Wyoming (1967-1975), was born in Osceola, Nebraska on July 19, 1924. Upon the death of his mother in 1926, Hathaway was adopted. He studied at the University of Wyoming until 1943, when he left to enlist in the Army Air Force during World War II. Afterward, he continued his schooling at the University of Nebraska, earning an A.B. degree in 1948, and an LL.B. degree in 1950. He passed the Wyoming bar soon after, and began his own law practice in Torrington, Wyoming.

Politically active in the Republican Party, Hathaway served on the Young Republican National Committee from 1958 to 1960, was State Committeeman for the Republican Party during 1960-61, and County Chairman during 1962-63.

In 1966 Hathaway was a successful candidate for the Wyoming governorship, taking office on January 2, 1967. He also won a second term in 1970. During his administration, Hathaway sought to reorganize the State government. In addition, he was instrumental in the development of the Wyoming Quality Growth Plan, which encompassed rules for environmental protection and proposals for upgrading the State's economy. During his time in office, he chaired the Federation of Rocky Mountain States and the Western Governors' Conference, and he served on the Executive Committee of the National Governors' Conference.

Hathaway decided to step down from office after his second term, and subsequently returned to his law work. In June of 1975, Hathaway took the oath for the post of Secretary of the Interior, but was forced to resign a little over a month later due to frail health.

Hathaway is married to Roberta Harley, and the couple has two children.

HERSCHLER, EDGAR J. (1918-1990), was twentieth governor of Wyoming (1975-1987), born near Kemmerer, Wyoming, on October 27, 1918. He attended the University of Colorado, graduating in 1941, then studied at the University of Wyoming Law School, where he took his LL.B. degree in 1949. In the interim, Herschler served in the South Pacific during World War II as a member of the United States Marine Corps, and after being wounded, received both the Purple Heart and the Silver Star.

Politically active in the Democratic Party, Herschler was Kemmerer Town Attorney between 1949 and 1974. Also during those years, he served as the Lincoln County Prosecuting Attorney (1951-1959) as a member of the Wyoming House of Representatives (1959-1969) and on the State Parole Board (1972-1974).

In 1970 Herschler made an unsuccessful bid for the United States House of Representatives. In 1974 he ran for and won the Wyoming governorship, making him the first Democrat to win that post in a regular election since 1958. During his tenure, Herschler zeroed in on a number of issues that he wanted to address while in office, including aid to ranchers and farmers, drought, water development, the energy shortage, and environmental protection. He was an avid supporter of states' rights, especially in regard to mining laws, public lands, and water.

In 1978 Herschler ran for reelection, and although he won, he had to endure a growing scandal that was coming out of the mineral boom town of Rock Springs, where gambling and prostitution were supposedly being run by organized crime. The fallout involved the indictment of Attorney General Frank Mendecino, and corruption charges were even being thrown at Governor Herschler. Although he won his second term by a very small margin, most of Wyoming's voters did not believe Herschler was involved himself. After he won the nomination, he responded to the allegations by firing Mendecino, and asking for the resignation of State Democratic Chairman Don Anselmi, who was also named in the scandal.

Herschler, upon his reelection, became the first Democrat to serve more than one term since 1949. During his second term, Herschler was outspoken in his opposition to Wyoming being looked at by the federal government as the "energy breadbasket of the nation." His anger came from a proposed amendment that would have loosened controls on coal strip mining within the State. In addition, much of Wyoming's acreage was federally-controlled land, and Herschler publicly denounced the overabundance of bureaucratic red tape that the State had to endure, claiming it was detrimental to the needs of Wyoming and its citizens.

In 1982 Herschler won a third term by a solid margin. While in office, Governor Herschler served as Chairman of the Interstate Oil Compact Commission, was Co-Chairman of the National Governors' Association Subcommittee on Range Resources Management, and Chairman of the Subcommittee on Coal.

Herschler decided to step down from office at the end of his third term. He was married to Kathleen Colter, and the couple had two children. He died on February 5, 1990.

SULLIVAN, MICHAEL "MIKE" JOHN (1939-), twenty-first governor of Wyoming (1987-1995), was born in Omaha, Nebraska, on September 22, 1939. He attended the University of Wyoming, earning a B.S. degree in 1961, then continued his studies at the University of Wyoming Law School, taking his law degree with honors in 1964. Sullivan subsequently joined the law firm of Brown, Drew, Apostolos, Massey and Sullivan.

Although having no political experience, Sullivan ran for and won the Wyoming governorship on the Democratic ticket in 1986, serving two terms. He stepped down from office in 1995.

Sullivan is married to Jane, and the couple has three children.

GERINGER, JAMES, (1944-), twenty-second governor of Wyoming (1995-current), was born in Wheatland, Wyoming on April 24, 1944. He attended Kansas State University, earning a B.S. degree in 1967. Between 1967 and 1977, Geringer served in the United States Air Force, during which time he was stationed in California and assigned to various space development programs. Some of his projects included the creation of different types of booster rockets for not only the Air Force, but NASA as well. They included an upper stage booster on the space shuttle, NASA's Viking Mars lander, the Global Positioning Satellite System, plus reconnaissance satellites.

In 1977 Geringer left active duty, and was assigned to the Air Force Reserves. Later that year he relocated with his family to Wyoming, where he became employed as a contract administrator at the Missouri Basin Power Project's Laramie River Station, working in that post until 1979. He then engaged in farming and cattle-ranching full time. By 1987 the Geringers owned their own farm.

Geringer entered politics in 1982, securing a seat in the House of Representatives for six years, then serving another six in the State Senate. In 1994 Geringer was elected to the Wyoming governorship on the Republican ticket. During his administration, Geringer has zeroed in on the State's educational system, urging higher standards, and the implementation of technology in the classrooms. In addition, he has stressed the importance of economic growth, helping organize the Wyoming Business Council, and setting about bringing new business into the State. During his tenure, he has chaired the Interstate Oil and Gas Compact Commission, as well as the Western Governors' Association.

In 1998 Geringer was reelected to office. His term expires in January of 2003. He and his wife Sherri have five children.

DICTIONARY OF PLACES

Population figures and demographic information are official U.S. Census Bureau finals for 1990. When two figures are shown, separated by a slash, the first figure is the 1990 and the second is the U.S. Census Bureau 1999 estimate - the most recent available. Year 2000 Census supplements will be available in the fall of 2001.

AFTON, Town; Lincoln County; Pop. 1,461 / 1,690; Zip Code 831+; Lat. 42-43-36 N, Long. 110-55-44 W; Founded in 1879 and named by a Scotch settler for the line from poet Robert Burns; "Flow gently, sweet Afton."

ALBIN, Town; Laramie County; Pop. 128 / 127; Zip Code 82050; Elev. 5340; Lat. 41-24-52 N, Long. 104-05-55 W; Founded in 1905 by John Albin Anderson, the first postmaster, and named for him.

BAGGS, Town; Carbon County; Pop. 433 / 230; Zip Code 62321; Elev. 6247; Lat. 41-02-07 N, Long. 107-39-26; Established in 1876 as Dixon and later renamed Baggs for a nearby prominent ranch family.

BASIN, Town; Big Horn County Seat; Pop. 1,349 / 1,343; Zip Code 82410; Elev. 3873; Lat. 44-22-41 N, Long. 108-02-14; Settled in 1897 and named after the Bighorn Basin.

BIG PINEY, Town; Sublette County; Pop. 530 / 483; Zip Code 83113; Lat. 42-32-51 N, Long. 110-06-35 W; The town is named after nearby Big Piney Creek.

BUFFALO, City; Johnson County Seat; Pop. 3,799 / 3,907; Zip Code 828+; Lat. 44-21-02 N, Long. 106-41-55 W; First settled in 1879 and descriptively named, as the main street was an old buffalo trail. Mail sent to the residents of what is now Buffalo was sent in care of Fort Kearney for nearly one hundred years because the town had no name. In 1880, the residents decided the town needed a name. A meeting was held in which each man chose a name and put it in a hat. The winning draw was Buffalo, after Buffalo, New York. The town was incorporated in 1884.

BURNS, Town; Laramie County; Pop. 268 / 265; Zip Code 82053; Lat. 41-11-39 N, Long. 104-21-34 W; The town was founded in 1907 and named for a railroad engineer.

BYRON, Town; Big Horn County; Pop. 633 / 455; Zip Code 82412; Lat. 44-47-47 N, Long. 108-30-13 W; Byron Sessions, an early Mormon settler, influenced the region's development and had the town named for him.

CASPER, City; Natrona County Seat; Pop. 51,016 / 48,233; Zip Code 82601; Lat. 42-50-29 N, Long. 106-22-59 W; The city is named after Fort Casper. Originally called Camp Platte, and once known as the "Crossroads of the West." Fort Casper honors Lt. Caspar Collins who was killed by the Indians near here.

CHEYENNE, City; Laramie County Seat and Capital of Wyoming; Pop. 47,283 / 53,925; Zip Code 82001; Lat. 41-07-34 N, Long. 104-48-59; The city is named after the Cheyenne Pass to the west of the city.

CHUGWATER, Town; Platte County; Pop. 282 / 209; Zip Code 82210; Lat. 41-45-29 N, Long. 104-49-12; The town was named after Chugwater Creek.

CLEARMONT, Town; Sheridan County; Pop. 191 / 131; Zip Code 82835; Lat. 44-38-33 N, Long. 106-22-57; Named after Clear Creek, the town is a livestock shipping center.

CODY, City; Park County Seat; Pop. 6,790 / 9,083; Zip Code 824+; Lat. 44-31-24 N, Long. 109-03-31; Incorporated in 1901 and named in honor of "Buffalo Bill" Cody.

COKEVILLE, Town; Lincoln County; Pop. 515 / 495; Zip Code 83114; Lat. 42-05-02 N, Long. 110-57-21; Settled in 1874 and named for the good coking coal in the area.

COWLEY, Town; Big Horn County; Pop. 455 / 549; Zip Code 82420; Lat. 44-53-02 N, Long. 108-28-14; The town was settled in 1901 and named for Mormon apostle Mathias F. Cowley.

DAYTON, Town; Sheridan County; Pop. 701 / 621; Zip Code 82836; Lat. 44-52-25 N, Long. 107-15-52; Dayton was founded in 1882 and named for banker Joseph Dayton Thorn.

DEAVER, Town; Big Horn County; Pop. 178 / 239; Zip Code 82421; Lat. 44-53-21 N, Long. 108-35-46 W; The town's name honors D.C. Deaver, a railroad agent for the Burlington Railroad.

DIAMONDVILLE, Town; Lincoln County; Pop. 1,000 / 899; Zip Code 83116; Lat. 41-46-41 N, Long. 110-32-11; Settled in the 1890s and named for the diamond-like quality of the coal found here.

DIXON, Town; Carbon County; Pop. 82 / 56; Zip Code 82323; Elev. 6359; Lat. 41-02-01 N, Long. 107-31-59 W; The town's name honors Robert Dixon, an old trapper who lived in the area before the coming of the railroad.

DOUGLAS, Town; Converse County Seat; Pop. 6,030 / 5,677; Zip Code 82633; Lat. 42-45-15 N, Long. 105-22-48 W; Named in honor of U.S. Senator Stephen A. Douglas.

DUBOIS, Town; Fremont County; Pop. 1,067 / 1,055; Zip Code 82513; Lat. 43-32-07 N, Long. 109-37-49; Founded in the 1880s and named after U.S. Senator from Idaho, a Mr. Dubois.

EAST THERMOPOLIS, Town; Hot Springs County; Pop. 359 / 204; Lat. 43-38-47 N, Long. 108-11-51; Named for the natural hot springs in the area.

EDGERTON, Town; Natrona County; Pop. 510 / 255; Zip Code 82635; Lat. 43-24-52 N, Long. 106-14-41; Located on the edge of the Salt Creek oil field and so descriptively named.

ELK MOUNTAIN, Town; Carbon County; Pop. 338 / 167; Zip Code 82324; Lat. 41-41-13 N, Long. 106-24-37; The town is named after nearby Elk Mountain.

ENCAMPMENT, Town; Carbon County; Pop. 611; Zip Code 82325; Lat. 41-12-46 N, Long. 106-47-09 W; Founded as a copper town and named after the Encampment River.

EVANSTON, City; Uinta County Seat; Pop. 6,421 / 11,436; Zip Code 82930; Elev. 6749; Lat. 41-16-06 N, Long. 110-57-52; Union Pacific Railroad officials founded the town in 1869. They named it for surveyor James A. Evans. The discovery of natural gas in the area in the 1980s cause the town's most recent population boom that lasted less than a decade.

EVANSVILLE, Town; Natrona County; Pop. 2,652 / 1,538; Zip Code 82636; Lat. 42-51-07 N, Long. 106-14-55 W; Blacksmith W.T. Evans homesteaded here in the 1800s. The town is named after him.

FORT LARAMIE, Town; Goshen County; Pop. 356 / 250; Zip Code 82212; Lat. 42-12-43 N, Long. 104-31-03 W; The town is named for the Laramie River. Laramie is derived from Jacques La Ramie, a French-Canadian trapper killed by Indians in 1818.

FRANNIE, Town; Big Horn County; Pop. 121 / 169; Zip Code 82423; Lat. 44-58-10 N, Long. 108-37-18; Railroad officials named the town for Frannie Morris, an early pioneer.

FRANNIE, Town; Park County; Pop. 17; Named for Frannie Morris, an early pioneer woman.

GILLETTE, City; Campbell County Seat; Pop. 12,134 / 19,860; Zip Code 82716; Elev. 4550; Lat. 44-17-34 N, Long. 105-29-55; Edward Gillette, a surveyor and civil engineer, directed the railroad's construction through the area. It is named in his honor. The town was homesteaded by Frank Murrey, Robert and George Durley, and Charles T. Weir. When the railroad passed through their land, the Lincoln Land and Livestock company purchased the land and planned the town of Gillette. Gillette is known as the "Energy Capital of the Nation," because of the hundreds of oils wells found here and the gas produced here.

GLENDO, Town; Platte County; Pop. 367 / 198; Zip Code 82213; Elev. 4714; Lat. 42-30-12 N, Long. 105-01-28 W; The site of an attractive glen, it was christened when railroad officials arrived in 1887.

GLENROCK, Town; Converse County; Pop. 2,736 / 2,307; Zip Code 82637; Lat. 42-51-27 N, Long. 105-52-18 W; Originally Mercedes, it was later changed to describe a large rock in a glen nearby.

GRANGER, Town; Sweetwater County; Pop. 177 / 108; Zip Code 82934; Elev. 6268; Lat. 41-35-45 N, Long. 109-57-47 W; Originally a stagecoach stop, the town is named after General Goroon Granger.

GREEN RIVER, City; Sweetwater County Seat; Pop. 12,807 / 12,887; Zip Code 82935; Elev. 6109; Lat. 41-31-17 N, Long. 109-27-59 W; The town is named after the Green River. So called for its deep green color.

GREYBULL, Town; Big Horn County; Pop. 2,277 / 1,870; Zip Code 82426; Elev. 3787; Lat. 44-29-32 N, Long. 108-03-05; Named for the river, itself named after an albino buffalo bull that roamed here in Indian days.

GUERNSEY, Town; Platte County; Pop. 1,512 / 1,261; Zip Code 82214; Lat. 42-16-03 N, Long. 104-44-21; The town's name honors rancher and author Charles A. Guernsey, who said "A dreamer lives forever; a toiler but a day."

HANNA, Town; Carbon County; Pop. 2,288 / 984; Zip Code 82327; Lat. 41-52-19 N, Long. 106-32-59 W; A coal mining town named for financier Mark Hanna in 1886.

HARTVILLE, Town; Platte County; Pop. 149 / 78; Zip Code 82215; Lat. 42-19-43 N, Long. 104-43-27 W; The town is named after Major V.K. Hart, who owned a copper mine in the vicinity.

HUDSON, Town; Fremont County; Pop. 514 / 405; Zip Code 82515; Lat. 42-54-13 N, Long. 108-34-49 W; Rancher John G. Hudson was the original landowner. It is named in his honor.

HULETT, Town; Crook County; Pop. 291 / 531; Zip Code 82720; Lat. 44-41-05 N, Long. 104-36-08; Hulett is named after its first postmaster, Lewis M. Hulett.

JACKSON (Jackson Hole), Town; Teton County Seat; Pop. 4,511 / 6,326; Zip Code 830+; Lat. 43-28-43 N, Long. 110-45-37 W; The first residents of what is now Jackson Hole were Blackfoot, Crow, Gros Ventre, and Shoshone Indians, all of whom occupied the land during the summer months. European fur trappers and traders began to occupy the area in the early to mid-180s. Early trappers referred to a high valley as a "hole." The territory in which Jackson Hole lies belonged to trapper Davey Jackson, and so the town was named Jackson Hole. Jackson Hole elected the first all-female town council in the United States in 1920.

KAYCEE, Town; Johnson County; Pop. 271 / 292; Zip Code 82639; Lat. 43-42-36 N, Long. 106-38-13 W; The town is named after the K.C. Ranch, which flourished here in the 1880s. Kaycee was the site of the Johnson County War.

KEMMERER, Town; Lincoln County Seat; Pop. 3,273 / 2,979; Zip Code 83101; Lat. 41-47-42 N, Long. 110-32-24 W; Founded in 1897 and named after the Kemmerer Coal Company.

LA BARGE, Town; Lincoln County; Pop. 302 / 533; Zip Code 83123; Lat. 42-15-41 N, Long. 110-11-38; The town is named for La Barge Creek. The creek's name remembers Capt. Joseph La Barge, a Missouri River pilot.

LA GRANGE, Town; Goshen County; Pop. 232 / 223; Zip Code 82221; Lat. 41-38-23 N, Long. 104-09-51 W; Incorporated in 1889 and named for rancher Kale La Grange. Primary economic activities in the area are agriculture and ranching.

LANDER, City; Fremont County Seat; Pop. 9,126 / 7,034; Zip Code 82520; Lat. 42-50-09 N, Long. 108-45-04 W; Once called Push Root, the town was renamed after surveyor General F.W. Lander in 1857.

LARAMIE, City; Albany County Seat; Pop. 24,410 / 24,905; Zip Code 82057; Elev. 7163; Lat. 41-04-43 N, Long. 106-09-13 W; The city is named after the Laramie River.

LINGLE, Town; Goshen County; Pop. 475 / 483; Zip Code 82223; Elev. 4171; Lat. 42-08-04 N, Long. 104-20-33 W; Hiram Lingle was a major promoter of the valley's agriculture. The town is named in his honor.

LOVELL, Town; Big Horn County; Pop. 2,447 / 2,268; Zip Code 82431; Elev. 3837; Lat. 44-50-01 N, Long. 108-23-17; Founded in 1900 and named for area rancher Henry T. Lovell.

LUSK, Town; Niobrara County Seat; Pop. 1,650 / 1,649; Zip Code 82225; Lat. 42-45-25 N, Long. 104-27-03; Begun as a mining town and named for rancher Frank Luck.

LYMAN, Town; Uinta County; Pop. 2,284 / 2,119; Zip Code 82937; Lat. 41-19-47 N, Long. 110-17-46 W; Francis Lyman, a Mormon apostle, started the town in 1898.

MANDERSON, Town; Big Horn County; Pop. 174 / 85; Zip Code 82432; Lat. 44-16-13 N, Long. 107-57-28; Originally called the Alamo, it was renamed in 1889 after a lawyer for the Burlington Railroad.

MANVILLE, Town; Niobrara County; Pop. 94 / 114; Zip Code 82227; Lat. 42-46-32 N, Long. 104-36-39 W; The town is named after H.S. Manville, who organized the Converse Cattle Co. in 1880.

MARBLETON, Town; Sublette County; Pop. 537 / 712; Lat. 42-33-13 N, Long. 110-06-31; Founded in 1912 and named for A.H. Marble.

MEDICINE BOW, Town; Carbon County; Pop. 953 / 370; Zip Code 82329; Elev. 6563; Lat. 41-53-49 N, Long. 106-11-36 W; The town is named after the Medicine Bow Mountains. The mountains were of source of ash wood for bows and medicinal compounds.

MIDWEST, Town; Natrona County; Pop. 638 / 473; Zip Code 82643; Lat. 43-24-39 N, Long. 106-16-24; Originally Shannon Camp, it was later renamed after the Midwest Oil Company.

MILLS, Town; Natrona County; Pop. 2,139 / 2,375; Zip Code 82644; Lat. 42-51-00 N, Long. 106-23-07 W; Named for the Mills brothers, who helped found the town in 1919.

MOORCROFT, Town; Crook County; Pop. 1,014 / 796; Zip Code 82713; Lat. 44-29-21 N, Long. 104-48-00; Named for the first white settler in the area, Alexander Moorcroft.

MOUNTAIN VIEW, Town; Uinta County; Pop. 628 / 1,335; Zip Code 82939; Lat. 41-16-18 N, Long. 110-20-27; Founded in 1891 and named after a local ranch.

NEWCASTLE, City; Weston County Seat; Pop. 3,596 / 3,263; Zip Code 82701; Elev. 4317; Lat. 43-51-08 N, Long. 104-12-19 W; Settled in 1889 and named for the English city of Newcastle upon-Tyne.

PAVILLION, Town; Fremont County; Pop. 287 / 141; Zip Code 82523; Lat. 43-14-37 N, Long. 108-41-26 W; The town is named for a nearby pavillion shaped butte.

PINE BLUFFS, Town; Laramie County; Pop. 1,077 / 1,091; Zip Code 82082; Elev. 5040; Lat. 41-11-07 N, Long. 104-03-51; Descriptively named for the pines on nearby bluffs.

PINEDALE, Town; Sublette County Seat; Pop. 1,066 / 1,322; Zip Code 82941; Lat. 42-52-00 N, Long. 109-51-31; Postmaster Charles Peterson named the town for its location on Pine Creek.

POWELL, City; Park County; Pop. 5,310 / 5,395; Zip Code 82435; Lat. 44-45-15 N, Long. 108-45-21; The town's name honors Major John Wesley Powell, engineer and explorer.

RANCHESTER, Town; Sheridan County; Pop. 655 / 743; Zip Code 82839; Lat. 44-54-32 N, Long. 107-09-47; Founded in 1894 by Englishman S.H. Hardin, who combined the word ranch with Chester, the name of an English City.

RAWLINS, City; Carbon County Seat; Pop. 11,547 / 8,839; Zip Code 823+; Elev. 6769; Lat. 41-47-14 N, Long. 107-14-13 W; The town's name honors General John A. Rawlins, who helped build the Transcontinental Railroad in 1868.

RIVERSIDE, Town; Carbon County; Pop. 55 / 70; Elev. 7136; Lat. 41-13-03 N, Long. 106-46-42; Descriptively named for its location on the Encampment River.

RIVERTON, City; Fremont County; Pop. 9,588 / 10,782; Zip Code 82501; Lat. 43-01-42 N, Long. 108-23-04 W; Pioneer residents named the town for the nearby convergence of four rivers.

ROCK RIVER, Town; Albany County; Pop. 415 / 202; Zip Code 82083; Elev. 6891; Lat. 41-44-13 N, Long. 105-58-39 W; Descriptively named for a nearby rocky river.

ROCK SPRINGS, City; Sweetwater County; Pop. 19,458 / 19,230; Zip Code 829+; Lat. 41-35-12 N, Long. 109-12-48 W; A pony express rider discovered springs here in 1861. The good water led to the founding of the town. The Union Pacific Railroad passed through the area of Rock Springs in 1868, at which time the town became the Central Terminal for stock herds. Coal mining has been one of the most important economic activities of Rock Springs for over one hundred years.

SARATOGA, Town; Carbon County; Pop. 2,410 / 1,806; Zip Code 82331; Lat. 41-27-01 N, Long. 106-48-27 W; Founded in 1878, it was originally called Warm Springs. It was renamed in 1884 by Fenimore C. Chatterton, after Saratoga, New York. *Saratoga* comes from an Indian word *Sarachtogue*, meaning "place of miraculous water in the rock."

SHERIDAN, City; Sheridan County Seat; Pop. 15,146 / 14,657; Zip Code 82801; Lat. 44-47-50 N, Long. 106-57-29; Settled in 1878 and named in honor of Civil War General, Phillip Sheridan. Fort Phil Kearney is found nearby, which was active during the war between the United States and the Sioux Indians, which took place in the 1860s.

SHOSHONI, Town; Fremont County; Pop. 879 / 542; Zip Code 82649; Lat. 43-14-21 N, Long. 108-06-21; Shoshoni is the name of an Indian tribe (also spelled Shoshone). The name means "grass lodge people."

SINCLAIR, Town; Carbon County; Pop. 586 / 393; Zip Code 82334; Elev. 6593; Lat. 41-46-31 N, Long. 107-06-57; First named Parco, the town was renamed Sinclair in 1943, after the Sinclair Oil Company that owns the refinery in town.

SOUTH SUPERIOR, Town; Sweetwater County; Pop. 586; The town is named after the Superior Coal Company.

SUNDANCE, Town; Crook County Seat; Pop. 1,087 / 1,218; Zip Code 82710; Elev. 4765; Lat. 44-38-25 N, Long. 104-10-54; Founded in 1879 and named after the Sundance Mountains.

TEN SLEEP, Town; Crook County Seat; Pop. 1,087 / 318; Zip Code 82442; Lat. 44-02-06 N, Long. 107-26-50; Named for Indian method of telling time. Town was also ten days "sleeps" from Yellowstone Park and Fort Laramie. The town was officially incorporated in 1933.

THAYNE, Town; Lincoln County; Pop. 256 / 300; Zip Code 83127; Lat. 42-55-11 N, Long. 11-00-04; Named for Henry Thayne, first postmaster.

THERMOPULIS, Town; Hot Springs County Seat; Pop. 3,852 / 3,071; Zip Code 82443; Lat. 43-38-41 N, Long. 108-12-13 W; Name chosen by Dr. Julius A. Schuelkle: a combination of the latin *therme* (hot baths) and the Greek word *polis* (city). The town was established in 1897 on land that the Arapaho Indians sold to the United States, allegedly so that the healing powers of the hot springs would be available to all. Settlement began in the 1870s.

TORRINGTON, Town; Goshen County; Pop. 5,441 / 6,190; Zip Code 82240; Lat. 42-04-00 N, Long. 104-10-52; Name selected by William Curtis after the city in Connecticut in 1889.

UPTON, Town; Western County; Pop. 1,193 / 937; Lat. 44-05-52 N, Long. 104-37-30; First known as Irontown, later named for George S. Upton, an early surveyor in the region.

WAMSUTTER, Town; Sweetwater County; Pop. 681 / 244; Zip Code 82336; Lat. 41-40-03 N, Long. 107-58-23; First known as Washakie, later changed to present name after a bridge-builder on the Union Pacific Railroad.

WHEATLAND, Town; Platte County Seat; Pop. 5,816 / 3,501; Zip Code 82201; Lat. 42-03-13 N, Long. 104-57-18; First named Gilchrist; later changed to present name descriptive of the local wheat fields.

WORLAND, City; Washkie County Seat; Pop. 6,391 / 5,973; Elev. 4748; Lat. 43-48-17 N, Long. 108-10-49 W; Named for C.R. "Dad" Worland, who had built an early camp in the area. The population of the area was less than one hundred when surveying began for the railroad in 1903. The railroad came through in 1906, but on the opposite side of the Big Horn River. For economic prosperity, the decision was made to move the community across the river, and there the present town of Worland was incorporated in 1906.

YODER, Town; Goshen County; Pop. 110 / 139; Zip Code 82244; Lat. 41-54-57 N, Long. 104-17-46; Named for Jess and Frank Yoder, pioneer residents in the area.

BIBLIOGRAPHY

BOOKS ABOUT ALABAMA

Abernathy, T.P. *The Formative Period in Alabama.* Montgomery, AL: Brown Printing Company, 1922.

Berney, Saffold. *Handbook on Alabama.* Birmingham, AL: Roberts and Son, 1892.

Beverly, J.W. *History of Alabama.* Montgomery, AL. Private publication, 1904.

Boyd, Minnie Claire. *Alabama in the Fifties.* New York, Columbia University Press, 1931.

Brewer, Willis. *Alabama History.* Montgomery, AL: Barrett and Brown, 1872.

Carmer, Carl Lamson. *Stars Fell on Alabama.* Farrar and Rinehart, New York, NY: 1934.

Clark, Willis G. *History of Education in Alabama, 1702-1889.* Washington, D.C.: Government Printing Office, 1889.

Damer, Dyre. *When the Ku Klux Rode.* New York, NY: The Neale Publishing Co., 1912.

Denman, Clarence P. *The Secession Movement in Alabama.* Montgomery, AL: Alabama State Department of Archives and History, 1933.

Dubose, J.C. *Alabama History.* Richmond, VA: Johnson Publishing Co., 1908.

Encyclopedia of Alabama. Somerset Publishers. Michigan, 1999.

Gosse, Philip Henry. *Letters From Alabama.* London, Morgan and Chase, 1859.

Graves, John Turner, II. *The Book of Alabama and the South.* Birmingham, AL: Commercial Printing Company, 1933.

Hill, Isaac William. *How We are Governed in Alabama.* Richmond, VA: The Bell Company, 1914.

History of Alabama and Her People. New York, NY: American Historical Society, Inc., 1927.

Little, J.B. *History of Butler Co., Alabama from 1815 to 1885.* Cincinnati, OH: Elm St. Printing Co., 1885.

Little Journeys to Interesting Points in Alabama. Montgomery, AL: Paragon Press, 1931.

Makers and Romance of Alabama History. Private publication, Birmingham, AL, 1914.

Mathews, Mrs. P. L. *History Stories of Alabama.* Dallas, TX: Southern Publishing Company, 1929.

McCorvey, T. C. *Government of the People of the State of Alabama.* Philadelphia, PA: Eldridge, 1902.

Montgomery, W. D. Brown. Alabama Polytechnic Institute. Department of Agriculture. *A General Description of the State of Alabama.* 1884.

Owen, Marie Bankhead. *Our State Alabama.* Birmingham, AL: Birmingham Printing Co., 1927.

Owen, Thomas M. *History of Alabama and Dictionary of Alabama Biography.* Chicago, IL: S. J. Clarke Publishing Co., 1921.

Riley, B. F. *Alabama As It Is.* Atlanta, GA: Constitution Publishing Co., 1888.

Saunders, James Edmonds. *Early Settlers of Alabama.* With Notes and Genealogies by his Granddaughter, Elizabeth Saunders Blair Stubbs. New Orleans, LA: L. Graham & Son, 1899.

BOOKS ABOUT ALASKA

Alaska Almanac. Alaska Northwest. (Annual).

Clinton, Susan. *The Story of Seward's Folly.* Childrens Press, 1987.

Dunnahoo, Terry. *Alaska.* Watts, 1987.

Fradin, Dennis B. *Alaska.* Childrens Press, 1993.

Hedin, Robert and Holthaus, G. H., eds. *Alaska: Reflections on Land and Spirit.* 1989. Rep. University of Arizona Press, 1994.

Heinrichs, Ann. *Alaska.* 1990. Rep. Childrens Press, 1992.

Hinckley, Ted C. *The Americanization of Alaska, 1867-1897.* Pacific Books, 1972. Rep. 1994.

Hunt, William R. *Alaska: A Bicentennial History.* Norton, 1976.

Johnston, Joyce. *Alaska.* Lerner, 1994.

Milepost editors. *Alaska A to Z.* Vernon Publications, 1993.

Murphy, Claire R. *A Child's Alaska.* Alaska Northwest, 1994.

Naske, Claus-Michael and Slotnick, H. E. *Alaska: A History of the 49th State.* 2nd ed., 1987. Rep. University of Oklahoma Press, 1994.

Oberle, Joseph. *Anchorage.* Dillon Press, 1990.

Sgroi, Peter P. *The Purchase of Alaska, March 30, 1867: A Bargain at 2 Cents an Acre.* Watts, 1975.

Sherwood, Morgan B. *Exploration of Alaska, 1865-1900.* Yale, 1965.

Shumaker, Virginia O. *The Alaska Pipeline.* Messner, 1979.

Stefansson, Evelyn and Yahn, L.C. *Here is Alaska.* 4th ed. Scribner, 1983.

BOOKS ABOUT ARIZONA

Bancroft, Hubert Howe. *The History of Arizona and New Mexico, 1530-1888.* San Francisco, CA, 1889.

Barnes, Will C. *Arizona's Place Names.* University of Arizona Press, 1988.

Carpenter, Allan. *Arizona.* Rev. ed. Childrens Press, 1979.

Cremony, John C. *Life Among the Apaches.* San Francisco, CA, 1868.

Encyclopedia of Arizona. Somerset Publishers. Michigan, 1999.

Filbin, Dan. *Arizona.* Lerner, 1991.

Fireman, Bert M. *Arizona: Historic Land.* Knopf, 1982.

Goddard, Pliny Earle. *Indians of the Southwest.* New York, NY, 1931.

Hansen, Gerald E. and Douglas A. Brown, eds. *Arizona: its Constitution and Government,* 2nd ed. University Press of Am., 1987.

Hewett, Edgar Lee. *Ancient Life in the American Southwest.* Indianapolis, IN, 1930.

Leshy, John D. *The Arizona State Constitution.* Greenwood, 1993.

Luckingham, Bradford. *Phoenix.* University of Arizona Press.

Miller, Tom, ed. *Arizona.* University of Arizona Press, 1986.

Miller, Tom. *Arizona: The Land and the People.* University of Arizona Press, 1986.

Officer, James E. *Hispanic Arizona:* 1536-1856. University of Arizona Press, 1987.

Powell, Lawrence Clark. *Arizona: A Bicentennial History.* Norton, 1976.

Sheridan, Thomas E. *Arizona.* University of Arizona Press, 1995.

The Early Navajo and Apache. Washington DC, 1895.

Trimble, Marshall. *Arizona: A Panoramic History of a Frontier State.* Doubleday, 1977.

Wagoner, Jay J. *Arizona Territory, 1863-1912: A Political History.* University of Arizona Press, 1970.

Weaver, Thomas, ed. *Indians of Arizona.* University of Arizona Press, 1974.

Weir, Bill and Blake, Robert. *Arizona Traveler's Handbook.* 6th ed. Moon Travel, 1996.

Woznicki, Robert. *History of Arizona.* 4th ed. R. Woznicki, 1987.

BOOKS ABOUT ARKANSAS

Ashmore, Harry S. *Arkansas: A Bicentennial History.* New York, NY: Norton, 1978.

Bradley, Matt. *Arkansas.* Little Rock, AR: Bradley Publishing, 1996.

Clayton, Powell. *The Aftermath of the Civil War in Arkansas.* New York, NY: Neale Publishing Co., 1915.

Clinton, Bill. *Preface to the Presidency.* University of Arkansas Press, 1997.

Delano, Patti. *Arkansas: Off the Beaten Path.* Old Saybrook, CT: Globe Pequot Press, 1997.

Du Vall, Leland. *Arkansas: Colony and State.* Little Rock, AR: Rose, 1973.

Encyclopedia of Arkansas. Somerset Publishers. Michigan, 1999.

Ferguson, Jim C. *Minerals in Arkansas.* Little Rock, AR: Bureau of Mines, Manufactures and Agriculture, 1922.

Fletcher, John Gould. *Arkansas.* Chapel Hill, NC: University of North Carolina Press, 1947.

Hallum, John. *Biographical and Pictorial History of Arkansas.* Albany, NY: Weed, Parsons and Co., 1887.

Henry, James P. *Resources of the State of Arkansas.* Little Rock, AR: Price and McClure, 1872.

Highlights of Arkansas History. Little Rock, Arkansas History Commission, 1922.

Hubbell, George Allen. *A History of Arkansas.* Little Rock, AR: Democrat Printing and Lithographing Co., 1932.

Little Rock: One From the Heart. Towery Pub., 1996.

Makers of Arkansas History. Chicago, Silver, Burdette and Co., 1911.

McNutt, Walter Scott. *Government of Arkansas and the Nation.* Little Rock, AR: Democrat Printing and Lithographing Co., 1933.

Moneyhon, Carl H. *Arkansas and the New South, 1874-1929.* 1997.

Pope, William F. *Early Days in Arkansas.* Little Rock, AR: Fred W. Allsopp, 1895.

Shetrone, Henry Clyde. *The Mound Builders.* New York, NY: D. Appleton and Co., 1930.

Shinn, Josiah Hazen. *Pioneers and Makers of Arkansas.* Little Rock, AR: Democrat Printing and Lithographing Co., 1908.

Staples, Thomas S. *Reconstruction in Arkansas,* New York, NY: Columbia University, 1923.

Sutherland, Diann. *The Arkansas Handbook.* Fly-by-Night Press, 1996.

The Arkansas Handbook: 1937-1938. Little Rock, Arkansas History Commission, 1938.

Thomas, David Y., ed. *Arkansas and Its People.* New York, NY: American Historical Society, 1930.

Williams, C. Fred. *A Documentary History of Arkansas.*

BOOKS ABOUT CALIFORNIA

A History of California: the American Period. New York, NY, 1922.

Altman, Linda Jacobs. *California (Celebrate the States).* 1997.

Altschul, Jeffrey M. and Grenda, Donn R, eds. *Islanders and Mainlanders: Prehistoric Context for the Southern California Coast and Channel Islands.* 2000.

Bancroft, Hubert Howe. *History of California.* (7 vols.) San Francisco, CA, 1884-90.

Bell, C.G. and Price, C.M. *California Government Today.* 3rd ed. 1987.

Blashfield, Jean F. *The California Gold Rush.* 2000.

Bolton, Herbert Eugene. *Anza's California Expeditions.* (5 vols.) Berkeley, CA, 1931.

Bradley, Glenn. *The Story of the Pony Express.* Chicago, IL, 1914.

Caushey, John W. *California: A Remarkable State's Life History.* 4th ed., 1982.

Chapman, Charles E. *A History of California: the Spanish Period.* New York, NY, 1921; rev. ed. 1928.

Curry, Jane Louise. *Down from the Lonely Mountain: California Indian Tales.* 2000.

Durrenberger, Robert W. *California: The Last Frontier.* New York, NY, 1969.

Eldredge, Zoeth Skinner, ed. *History of California.* (5 vols.) New York, NY, 1915.

Encyclopedia of California. Somerset Publishers. Michigan, 2000.

Englehardt, Fr. Zephyrin. *The Missions and Missionaries of California.* (4 vols.), San Francisco, CA, 1908-16 (2nd ed. in 2 vols., 1929-30).

Farmer, Arla Gridley. *Dairyville Days: Life in Rural California.* 2000.

Forbes, Alexander. *A History of Upper and Lower California.* London, 1839 (later ed. San Francisco, 1937).

Forbes, Mrs. Harrie R. Piper. *California Missions and Landmarks.* Los Angeles, CA, 1903. (8th ed., 1925).

Gregory, James N. *American Exodus: The Dust Bowl Migration and Okie Culture in California.* 1991.

Heizer, Robert Fleming and Whipple, M.A., eds. *The California Indians: A Source Book.* 1983.

Hyink, Bernard L. and Provost, David H. *Politics and Government in California.* 2000.

Kroeber, Alfred L. *Handbook of the Indians of California.* Washington, DC: Bureau of American Ethnology. Bulletin No. 78., 1925.

Lantis, Davis W., Steiner, Rodney and Karinen, Arthur. *California, Land of Contrasts.* Belmont, CA, 1963.

Lavender, D.S. *California-A Place, a People, a Dream.* 1986.

Mayo, Morrow. *Los Angeles.* New York, NY, 1933.

Ritchie, Robert Welles. *The Hell-Roarin' Forty-niners.* New York, NY, 1928.

The Rumble of California Politics, 1848-1970. New York, NY, 1970.

Wallers, Dan. *The New California.* 1986.

BOOKS ABOUT COLORADO

Abbott, Carl. *Colorado, a History of the Centennial State.* 1982.

Baker, James H. and Hafen, LeRoy R. *History of Colorado.* State Historical Society of Colorado. 1927.

Bluemel, Elinor. *One Hundred Years of Colorado Women.* 1973.

Brown, Robert L. *Ghost Towns of the Colorado Rockies.* 1968.

The Great Pikes Peak Gold Rush. 1985.

Busch, Paul. *Colorado Sketchbook: A Graphic History of the Early Years.* 1976.

Chamblin, Thomas S. *The Historical Encyclopedia of Colorado.* 1975.

Colorado Legislative Council. *A Directory of Colorado State Government.* 1984.

Davis, Carlyle Channing. *Olden Times in Colorado.* 1916.

De Smet, Pierre Jean. *Life, Letters, and Travels of Father Pierre Jean de Smet, S.J., 1801-1873; Missionary Labors and Adventures among the Wild Tribes of the North American Indians.* New York, NY: F.P. Harper, 1905.

Denver Public Library. *Nothing Is Long Ago: A Documentary History of Colorado, 1776-1976.* 1975.

Dorset, Phyllis F. *The New Eldorado: The Story of Colorado's Gold and Silver Rushes.* 1970.

Eichler, George R. *Colorado Place Names, Communities, Peaks, Passes; with Historical Love and Facts, Plus a Pronunciation Guide.* 1977.

Encyclopedia of Colorado. Somerset Publishers. Michigan, 1999.

Federal Writer's Project. *Colorado: A Guide to the Highest State.* 1940.

Hafen, LeRoy R. *Colorado and Its People: A Narrative and Topical History of the Centennial State.* 1948.

Hill, Alice Polk. *Tales of the Colorado Pioneers.* 1884.

Hughes, J. Donald. *American Indians in Colorado.* 1960.

Jessen, Kenneth. *Colorado Gunsmoke: True Stories of Outlaws and Lawmen on the Colorado Frontier.* 1960.

Knight, Harold V. *Working in Colorado: A Brief History of the Colorado Labor Movement.* 1971.

May, Stephen. *Pilgrimage: A Journey Through Colorado's History and Culture.* 1987.

Shikes, Robert H. *Rocky Mountain Medicine: Doctors, Drugs and Disease in Early Colorado.* 1986.

Ubbelohde, Carl. *A Colorado History.* (3d. ed. 1972).

Wood, Myron. *Colorado: Big Mountain Country.* (Rev. ed. 1972).

Wright, James Edward. *The Politics of Populism: Dissent in Colorado.* 1974.

BOOKS ABOUT CONNECTICUT

Anderson, Ruth O.M. *From Yankee to American: Connecticut, 1865-1914.* Chester, CT: Pequot Press, 1975.

Beardsley, Thomas R. and Shuldiner, David P. (ed.) *Connecticut Speaks for Itself: Firsthand Accounts of Life in the Nutmeg State from Colonial Times to the Present Day.* 1997.

Bingham, Harold J. *History of Connecticut.* New York, NY: Lewis, 1962.

Bixby, William. *Connecticut: A New Guide.* New York, NY: Scribner & Sons, 1974.

Bushman, Richard L. *From Puritan to Yankee: Character and the Social Order in Connecticut, 1690-1765.*

Carpenter, W.H. and Arthur, T.S. *The History of Connecticut, from Its Earliest Settlement to the Present Time.* Philadelphia, PA: Lippincott, Grambo and Co., 1854.

Clark, George L. *History of Connecticut, Its People and Institutions.* New York, NY: G.P. Putnam's Sons, 1914.

Collier, Christopher. *Connecticut in the Continental Congress.* 1973.

Connecticut's Place in Colonial History. New Haven, CT: Yale University Press, 1924.

DeForest, John Williams. *History of the Indians of Connecticut from the Earlier and Known Period to 1850.* Hartford, CT, 1853.

Encyclopedia of Connecticut. Somerset Publishers. Michigan, 1999.

Fennelly, Catherine. *Connecticut Women in the Revolutionary Era.* 1975.

Hollister, Gideon H. *This History of Connecticut, from the First Settlement of the Colony to the Adoption of the Present Constitution.* New Haven, CT: Durrie and Peck, 1855.

Horton, Wesley W. *The Connecticut State Constitution.* 1933.

Janick, Herbert F.A. *A Diverse People: Connecticut, 1914 to the Present.* Chester, CT: Pequot Press, 1975.

Main, Jackson Turner. *Connecticut Society in the Era of the American Revolution.* 1977.

Perry, C.E. *Founders and Leaders of Connecticut, 1633-1783.* Boston, MA, 1934.

Peters, Rev. Samuel Andrew. *General History of Connecticut.* New York, NY: D. Appleton and Company, 1857.

Roth, David M. *Connecticut: A Bicentennial History.* New York, NY: Norton, 1979.

State of Connecticut. *First Laws of the State of Connecticut.* 1981.

Thompson, Kathleen. *Connecticut (Portrait of America).* 1996.

Todd, Charles Burr. *In Olde Connecticut: Being a Record of Quaint, Curious and Romantic Happenings There in Colonial Times and Later.* New York, NY: 1906.

Weld, Ralph Foster. *Slavery in Connecticut.* New Haven, CT: Yale University Press, 1935.

Welsbacher, Anne. *Connecticut.* 1998.

Whipple, Chandler. *The Indian in Connecticut.* Stockbridge, MA: Berkshire Traveller Press, 1972.

BOOKS ABOUT DELAWARE

Brown, Dottie. *Delaware.* Lerner, 1994.

Carpenter, Allan. *Delaware.* Rev. ed. Childrens Press, 1978.

Christensen, Gardell D. and Burney, Eugenia. *Colonial Delaware.* Nelson, 1975.

Delaware: A Guide to the First State. Rev. ed. Scholarly, 1976.

Dolan, Paul and Soles, J.R. *The Government of Delaware.* University of Delaware, 1976.

Encyclopedia of Delaware. Somerset Publishers. Michigan, 1999.

Hagley Museum. *Delaware in Two Centuries: Practical Approaches to Economic History.* 1984.

Hancock, Harold B. *Delaware During the Civil War: A Political History.* University of Delaware Press, 1961.

Hancock, Harold B. *Delaware Two Hundred Years Ago: 1780-1800.* Middle Atlanta Press, 1987.

Hoffecker, Carol E. *Delaware: A Bicentennial History.* Norton, 1977.

McDonough, Margo, et al., *Delaware First Place: A Contemporary Portrait.* Windsor Publications, 1990.

Munroe, John A. *Colonial Delaware: A History.* KTO Press, 1978.

Munroe, John A. *History of Delaware,* 2nd Edition. University of Delaware Press, 1984.

Swindler, William F. and Frech, Mary, eds. *Chronology and Documentary Handbook to the State of Delaware.* Oceana Publications, 1973.

Thompson, Kathleen. *Delaware.* 2nd Edition. Raintree Steck Vaughn, 1996.

Thompson, Kathleen. *Delaware.* Raintree, 1987.

Weslager, Clinton A., *The Delaware Indians: A History.* Rutgers, 1972. Rep. 1990.

BOOKS ABOUT FLORIDA

Abbey, Kathryn T. *Florida, Land of Change,* 2nd ed., 1948.

Anderson, Edward. *Florida Territory in 1844: A Diary.* Alabama. 1977.

Ballinger, Kenneth. *Miami Millions: The Dance of the Dollars in the Great Florida Land Boom of 1925.* Miami, FL, 1936.

Barrietos, Bartolome (trans. Kerrigan, Anthony). *Pedro Menendez de Aviles, Founder of Florida.* Florida Facsimile and Reprint Series. 1965.

Blackman, Lucy W. *The Women of Florida.* (2 vols.) 1940.

Bouvier, L., and Weller, B. *Florida in the 21ˢᵗ Century: The Challenge of Population Growth.* 1922.

Brinton, Daniel G. *Notes on the Floridian Peninsula, Its Literary History, Indians Tribes, and Antiquities.* 1859.

Burnett, Gene M. *Florida's Past: People and Events That Shaped the State.* 1986.

Carson, Ruby Leach, and Tebeau, Charlton W. *Florida: From Indian Trails to Space Age.* (3 vols.) 1966.

Chandler, David L. *Henry Flagler: The Astonishing Life and Times of the Visionary Robber Baron Who Founded Florida.* 1986.

Davis, William. *The Civil War and Reconstruction in Florida.* 1913. Rep. Gainesville, 1964.

Doster, James. *The Creek Indians and Their Florida.* 1974.

Dovell, Junius E. *Florida: Historic, Dramatic, Contemporary.* (4 vols.) 1952.

Encyclopedia of Florida. Somerset Publishers. Michigan, 1999.

Florida: A Bicentennial History. 1976.

Frazure, Hoyt. *Memories of Old Miami.* 1969.

History of Florida From Its Discovery by Ponce de Leon in 1512, to the Close of the Florida War in 1842. 1871.

Hopkins, James. *Fifty Years of Citrus: The Florida Citrus Exchange, 1909-1959.* 1960.

Jackson, W.R. *Early Florida Through Spanish Eyes.* 1954.

Johns, John E. *Florida During the Civil War.* 1963.

Lanier, Sidney. *Florida: Its Scenery, Climate, and History.* Gainesville. 1973.

Oceana Publications. *Chronology and Documentary Handbook of the State of Florida.* 1973.

Read, William A. *Florida Place-Names of Indian Origin.* Baton Rouge, LA. 1934.

Smith, Julia F. *Slavery and Plantation Growth in Ante-Bellum Florida, 1821-1860.*

Williams, Joy. *Florida Keys: A History and Guide.* 1986.

BOOKS ABOUT GEORGIA

A History of Georgia, Containing Brief Sketches of the Most Remarkable Events... Savannah, GA: Seymour and Williams, 1811-1816.

A History of Georgia. Athens, GA: University of Georgia Press, 1977.

Alexander, Adele Logan. *Ambiguous Lives: Free Women of Color in Rural Georgia, 1789-1879.* 1991.

Bartley, Numan V. *From Thurmond to Wallace: Political Tendencies in Georgia, 1948-68.* Baltimore, MD: John Hopkins Press, 1970.

Bridges, Edwin C. *Georgia's Signers and the Declaration of Independence.* 1981.

Coleman, Kenneth. *American Revolution in Georgia, 1763-1789.* 1958.

Cook, James F. *The Governors of Georgia.* 1977.

Drago, Edmund L. *Black Politicians and Reconstruction in Georgia.* 1992.

Dubois, W.E. Burghardt. *Black Reconstruction: An Essay Toward a History of the Part Which Black Folk Played in the Attempt to Reconstruct Democracy in America, 1860-1880.* New York, NY: Harcourt, Brace & Co., 1935.

Encyclopedia of Georgia. Somerset Publishers. Michigan, 1999.

Garrison, Webb B. *Oglethorpe's Folly: The Birth of Georgia.* 1982.

Georgia History and Government. Austin, Steck Vaughn, 1973.

Hepburn, Lawrence R. *The Georgia History Book.* Athens, GA: University of Georgia Institute of Government. 1982.

History of Georgia. Boston, MA and New York, NY: Mentzer & Co., 1913.

Jackson, Harvey H., and Spalding, Phinizy. *Forty Years of Diversity: Essays on Colonial Georgia.* 1984.

Johnson, Michael P. *Toward a Patriarchal Republic: The Secession of Georgia.* 1977.

Martin, Harold H. *Georgia: A Bicentennial History.* New York, NY: Norton, 1977.

Northern, William J. *Men of Mark in Georgia.* Atlanta, GA: A.B. Caldwell, 1907-12.

Phillips, Ulrich Bonnell. *Annual Report for 1901: "Georgia and State Rights, a Study of the Political History of Georgia from the Revolution to the Civil War..."* Washington, DC: American Historical Association, 1902.

Scott, Thomas Allan. *Cornerstones of Georgia History: Documents That Formed the State.* 1995.

Stevens, Rev. William Bacon. *A History of Georgia, from Its First Discovery by Europeans to the Adoption of the Present Constitution, in MDCCXCVIII.* Savannah, GA: W.T. Williams. 1847. Reprinted Savannah, GA: Beehive Press, 1972.

The Revolutionary Records of the State of Georgia. Atlanta, GA: Franklin-Turner Co., 1908.

The Story of Georgia and the Georgia People, 1732 to 1860. Macon, GA: G. G. Smith, 1900.

Thompson, C. Mildred. *Reconstruction in Georgia, Economic, Social, Political, 1865-1872.* New York, NY: Columbia University, 1915. Reprinted Savannah, GA: Beehive Press, 1974.

Wood, Betty. *Slavery in Colonial Georgia, 1730-1775.* 1984.

BOOKS ABOUT HAWAII

Craig, Robert D. *Historical Dictionary of Honolulu and Hawaii.* Scarecrow, 1998.

Culliney, John L. *Islands in a Far Sea: Nature and Man in Hawaii.* Sierra Club, 1988.

Daws, Gavan. *Shoal of Time: A History of the Hawaiian Islands.* 1968. Rep. University of Hawaii Press, 1974.

Feeney, Stephanie and Fielding, Ann. *Sand to Sea: Marine Life of Hawaii.* University of Hawaii Press, 1989.

Fradin, Dennis B. *Hawaii.* Childrens Press, 1994.

Johnston, Joyce. *Hawaii.* Lerner, 1995.

Kuykendall, Ralph S. *The Hawaiian Kingdom.* 3 vols. University of Hawaii Press, 1938-1967.

Lind, Andrew W. *Hawaii's People.* 4ᵗʰ ed. University of Hawaii Press, 1980.

McNair, Sylvia. *Hawaii.* Childrens Press, 1989.

Michi Kodama-Nishimoto, et al., eds. *Hanahana: An Oral History Anthology of Hawaii's Working People.* University of Hawaii Press, 1984.

Nordyke, Eleanor C. *The Peopling of Hawaii.* 2ⁿᵈ ed. University of Hawaii Press, 1989.

Rayson, Ann. *Modern Hawaiian History.* Bess Press, 1984.

Siy, Alexandra. *Hawaiian Islands.* Dillon Press, 1991.

Tregaskis, Moana, et al. *Hawaii.* 4ᵗʰ ed. Compass American Guides, 1988.

BOOKS ABOUT IDAHO

Arrington, Leonard J. *History of Idaho.* 2 vols. University of Idaho Press, 1994.

Attebery, Louis W., ed., *Idaho Folklife: Homesteads to Headstones.* University of Utah Press, 1985.

Beal, Merrill D. and Wells, M.W. *History of Idaho.* 3 vols. Lewis Historical Publishing Company, 1959.
Blank, Robert H. *Regional Diversity of Political Values: Idaho Political Culture.* University Press of Am., 1978.
Carpenter, Allan. *Idaho.* Rev. ed. Childrens Press, 1979.
Colson, Dennis C. *Idaho's Constitution: The Tie that Binds.* University of Idaho Press, 1990.
Encyclopedia of Idaho. Somerset Publishers. Michigan, 1999.
Hanson, Sam, et al., Hard *Times in Idaho Between the Great Wars, 1920-1941.* Idaho State University Press, 1984.
Jensen, Dwight W. *Discovering Idaho: A History.* Caxton Printers, 1977.
Pelta, Kathy. *Idaho.* Lerner, 1995.
Peterson, Frank Ross *Idaho: A Bicentennial History.* Norton, 1976.
Schwantes, Carlos A. *In Mountain Shadows: A History of Idaho.* University of Nebraska Press, 1991.
Schwantes, Carlos A. *So Incredibly Idaho! Seven Landscapes that Define the Gem State.* University of Idaho Press, 1996.
Stapilus, Randy. *Paradox Politics: People and Power in Idaho.* Ridenbaugh Press, 1988.
Strahorn, Robert E., *The Resources and Attractions of Idaho Territory.* University of Idaho Press, 1990.
Thompson, Kathleen. *Idaho.* 2nd ed. Raintree Steck Vaughn, 1996.
Walker, Deward E., Jr. *Indians of Idaho.* University of Idaho Press, 1978.
Wells, Merle and Hart, Arthur. *Idaho: Gem of the Mountains.* Windsor Publishers, 1985.
Young, Virgil M. *The Story of Idaho.* University of Idaho Press, 1977.

BOOKS ABOUT ILLINOIS

Andreas, A.T. *History of Chicago.* (3 vols.) 1884-86.
Alvord, Clarence W. and Carter, C.E. *The Illinois Country, 1673-1818, 1917-1920.* 1965.
Bateman, Newton and Selby, Paul. *Historical Encyclopedia of Illinois, With Commemorative Biographies.* 1915.
Carpenter, John Allan. *Illinois, From its Glorious Past to Present.* 1963.
Chicago Sun Times. *20th Century Chicago: 100 Years, 100 Voices.* 2000.
Clayton, John. *The Illinois Fact Book and Historical Almanac, 1673-1968.* 1970.
Cohen, Adam and Taylor, Elizabeth. *American Pharaoh: Mayor Richard J. Daley: His Battle for Chicago and the Nation.* 2000.
Encyclopedia of Illinois. Somerset Publishers. Michigan, 2000.
Dedmon, Emmett. *Fabulous Chicago.* 1953.
Faragher, John Mack. *Sugar Creek: Life on the Illinois Prairie.* 1987.
Farber, David. *Chicago '68.* 1995.
Farr, Finis. *Chicago; a Personal History of America's Most American City.* 1973.
Federal Writers' Project. *Illinois; A Descriptive & Historical Guide.* 1939. Rep. 1971.
Ford, Thomas. *A History of Illinois.* 1854.
Illinois: A History. 1978.
Jensen, Richard J. *Illinois Government.* Rev., ed. 1974.
Kay, Betty Carlson. *Illinois from A to Z.* 2000.
Marsh, Carole. *Discover Illinois (The Illinois Experience).* 2000.
Reynolds, John. *The Pioneer History of Illinois.* 1887.
Shetrone, Henry Clyde. *The Mound Builders.* New York, NY: D. Appleton and Co., 1930.
Simeone, James. *Democracy and Slavery in Frontier Illinois: The Bottomland Republic.* 2000.
Spinney, Robert G. *City of Big Shoulders: A History of Chicago.* 2000.
Thompson, Kathleen. *Illinois (Portrait of America).* 1996.
Trestrall, Joanne. *Illinois: The Spirit of America (Art of the State).* 2000.
Wheeler, Adade, with Wortman, Marlene S. *The Roads They Made; Women in Illinois History.* 1977.

BOOKS ABOUT INDIANA

Barnhart, John D. and Carmony, Donald F. *Indiana: From Frontier to Industrial Commonwealth.* (4 vols.) 1954.
Burnet, Mary Q. *Arts and Artists of Indiana.* 1921.
Burns, Lee. *Architects and Builders of Indiana.* 1935.
Cavinder, Fred D. *The Indiana Book of Records, Firsts, and Fascinating Facts.* 1985.
Cayton, Andrew R.L. *Frontier Indiana.* 1998.
Cockrum, William M. *Pioneer History of Indiana; Including Stories, Incidents, and Customs of the Early Settlers.* 1980.
Cottman, George S. *Centennial History and Handbook of Indiana.* 1915.
Encyclopedia of Indiana. Somerset Publishers. Michigan, 1999.
Ewbank, Louis B. *Morgan's Raid in Indiana.* 1923.
Federal Writers' Project. *Indiana: A Guide to the Hoosier State.* 1941.
Funk, Arville L. *A Sketchbook of Indiana History.* 1969.
Gray, Ralph D. *Gentlemen from Indiana: National Party Candidates, 1836-1940.* 1977.
Hawkins, Hubert H. *Indiana's Road to Statehood: A Documentary Record.* 1964.
Jonsson, Ingrid E. *Reference Guide to Indiana.* 1977.
Kellar, James H. *An Introduction to the Prehistory of Indiana.* 1983.
Levering, Julia H. *Historic Indiana.* 1909.
Madison, James H. *Indiana Through Tradition and Change: A History of the Hoosier State and its People, 1920-1945.* (The History of Indiana, Vol. V). 1982.
Moore, Leonard J. *Citizen Klansmen: The Ku Klux Klan in Indiana, 1921-1928.* 1997.
Noland, Jeannette C. *Hoosier City, the Story of Indianapolis.* 1943.
Phillips, Clifton J. *Indiana in Transition: The Emergence of an Industrial Commonwealth 1880-1920.* (The History of Indiana, Vol. IV) 1968.
Starr, George W. *Industrial Development of Indiana.* 1937.
The Indiana Way: A State History. 1986.
Thornbrough, Emma Lou. *Indiana in the Civil War Era, 1850-1880.* (The History of Indiana, Vol. III). 1965.
VanderMeer, Phillip R. *The Hoosier Politician: Officeholding and Political Culture in Indiana 1896-1920.* 1985.
Wilson, William E. *Indiana, a History.* 1966.

BOOKS ABOUT IOWA

Barrows, Willard. *Notes on Iowa Territory.*
Black Hawk. *Life of Black Hawk, Ma-ka-tai-me-she-kia-kiak.* Iowa City, IA: State Historical Society of Iowa, 1932.
Brigham, Johnson. *Iowa, Its History and Its Foremost Citizens.* Chicago, IL: S.J. Clarke Publishing Co., 1915.

Clarke, S.J. *Prominent Iowans.* Chicago, IL: S. J. Clarke Publishing Co., 1915.

Cody, Mrs. Louisa. *Memories of Buffalo Bill.* New York, NY, 1919.

Cole, Cyrenus. *The History of the People of Iowa.* Cedar Rapids, IA: The Torch Press. 1921.

De Smet, Pierre Jean. *Life, Letters, and Travels of Father Pierre Jean de Smet, S.J., 1801-1873; Missionary Labors and Adventures among the Wild Tribes of the North American Indians.* New York, NY: F.P. Harper, 1905.

Dwelle, Jessie M. *Iowa, Beautiful Land.* 1954.

Encyclopedia of Iowa. Somerset Publishers. Michigan, 1999.

Federal Writers' Project. *Iowa: A Guide to the Hawkeye State.* New York, NY: Somerset, 1938.

Gallaher, Ruth A. *Legal and Political Status of Women in Iowa.* Iowa City, IA: State Historical Society of Iowa, 1918.

Glazer, Rabbi Simon. *The Jews in Iowa.* Des Moines, IA: Koch Brothers Printing Co., 1904.

Gue, Benjamin F. *History of Iowa.* New York, NY: Century History Co., 1903.

Harlan, Edgar R. *A Narrative History of the People of Iowa.* Chicago, IL: American Historical Society. 1931.

Iowa Stories. Iowa City, IA: Clarence R. Aurner, 1917-21.

Keyes, Charles Reuben. *Prehistoric Man in Iowa.* (vol. 8) Palimpsest. June 1927.

Mott, Frank L. *The Lewis and Clark Expedition in its Relation to Iowa History and Geography.* IA: Annals of Iowa (Third Series). 1921-22.

Peterson, William J. *Iowa History Reference Guide.* Iowa City, IA: State Historical Society of Iowa, 1952.

Progressive Men of Iowa. Des Moines, IA: Conaway & Shaw Publishing Co., 1899.

Ross, Earl. *History of Agriculture in Iowa.* 1950.

Ross, Russell. *Government and Administration of Iowa.* 1957.

Sage, Leland. *A History of Iowa.* Ames, IA: Iowa State University Press, 1974.

Shetrone, Henry Clyde. *The Mound Builders.* New York, NY: D. Appleton and Co., 1930.

Swisher, Jacob A., and Erbe, Carl H. *Iowa History as Told in Biography.* Cedar Falls, IA: Holst Printing Co., 1932.

Wall, Joseph Frazier. *Iowa: A Bicentennial History.* New York, NY: Norton, 1978.

BOOKS ABOUT KANSAS

Carpenter, Allan. *Kansas.* Rev. ed. Children's Press, 1979.

Davis, K.S. *Kansas: A Bicentennial History.* Norton, 1976.

Drury, James W. *Government of Kansas.* 3rd rev. ed. Regents Press of Kansas, 1980.

Encyclopedia of Kansas. Somerset Publishers. Michigan, 1999.

Haywood, C. Robert. *Victorian West: Class and Culture in Kansas Cattle Towns.* University Press of Kansas, 1991.

Rita Napier, ed. *History of the Peoples of Kansas: An Anthology.* Division of Continuing Education, University of Kansas, 1985.

Isern, Thomas D. and Wilson, Raymond. *Kansas Land.* 2nd ed. Gibbs Smith Pub, 1992.

Painter, Nell Irvin. *Exodusters: Black Migration to Kansas after Reconstruction.* Knopf, 1977.

Richmond, Robert W. *Kansas, A Land of Contrasts.* 3rd ed. Forum Press, 1989.

Socolofsky, Homer E. *Kansas Governors.* University Press of Kansas, 1990.

Thompson, Kathleen. *Kansas.* Raintree, 1988.

BOOKS ABOUT KENTUCKY

Archambeault, James. *Kentucky.* Portland, OR: Graphic Arts Center Pub. Co., 1982.

Bowman, Mary Jean and Haynes, W. Warren. *Resources and People in East Kentucky.* New York, NY: AMS Press, 1983.

Brown, J.M. *The Political Beginnings of Kentucky.* Louisville, KY: J.P. Morton & Company, 1889.

Bruce, H. Addington. *Daniel Boone and the Wilderness Road.* New York, NY: Macmillan, 1910.

Clark, T.D. *A History of Kentucky.* New York, NY: Prentice-Hall, 1937.

Collins, L. and R.H. *History of Kentucky.* Covington, KY: Collins & Company, and later by other publishers. 1874 and subsequent reprints.

Connelley, W.E. and Coulter, E.M. *History of Kentucky.* Chicago, IL and New York, NY: American Historical Society, 1922.

Coulter, E.M. *The Civil War and Readjustment in Kentucky.* Chapel Hill, University of North Carolina Press, 1926.

Encyclopedia of Kentucky. Somerset Publishers. Michigan, 1999.

Filson, John. *The Discovery of Kentucky and the Adventures of Daniel Boone.* New York, NY: Garland Publishing, 1979.

Funkhouse, W.D. *Wild Life in Kentucky.* Frankfort, KY: Kentucky Geological Survey. 1925.

Harrison, Lowell H., ed. *Kentucky's Governors, 1792-1985.* Lexington, KY: University Press of Kentucky, 1985.

Hood, Fred J., compiler. *Kentucky, Its History and Heritage.* St. Louis, MO: Forum Press, 1978.

Johnson, L.F. *Famous Kentucky Tragedies and Trials.* Louisville, KY: Baldwin Law Book Company, 1916.

Kentucky Historical Society. *Kentucky Profiles.* Frankfort, KY, 1982.

Marshall, Humphrey. *History of Kentucky.* 2d ed. Frankfort, KY: G. S. Robinson, 1824.

McElroy, R. McNutt. *Kentucky in the Nation's History.* New York, NY: Moffat, Yard & Company, 1909.

Mutzenberg, C.G. *Kentucky's Famous Feuds and Tragedies.* New York, NY: R.F. Fenno & Company, 1917.

Newcomb, Rexford. *The Architecture of Old Kentucky.* Kentucky State Historical Society Register, Frankfort, KY: July, 1933.

Southard, M.Y. and E.C. Miller. *Who's Who in Kentucky.* Louisville, KY: Standard Printing Company, 1936.

Thomas, W.R. *Life Among the Hills and Mountains of Kentucky.* Louisville, KY: Standard Printing Company, 1926.

Trabue, Daniel. *Westward into Kentucky.* Lexington, KY: University Press of Kentucky, 1981.

Twenhofel, W.H. *The Building of Kentucky.* Frankfort, KY: 1931.

Vexler, Robert I., ed. *Chronology and Documentary Handbook of the State of Kentucky.* Dobbs Ferry, NY: Oceana Publications, 1978.

Webb, Ross Allan. *Kentucky in the Reconstruction Era.* Lexington, KY: University Press of Kentucky, 1979.

BOOKS ABOUT LOUISIANA

Asbury, Herbert. *The French Quarter.*

Cajun, Andre. *Louisiana Voodoo. Stories of New Orleans.*

Dubois, W.E. Burghardt. *Black Reconstruction: An Essay Toward a History of the Part Which Black Folk Played in the Attempt to Reconstruct Democracy in America, 1860-1880.* New York, NY: Harcourt, Brace & Co., 1935.

Dufour, Charles L. and Huber, Leonard V. *The Battle of New Orleans.* 1965.

Encyclopedia of Louisiana. Somerset Publishers. Michigan, 1999.

Evans, Melvin. *Study in the State Government of Louisiana.* 1931.

Federal Writers' Program. *New Orleans City Guide.* 1938.

Ficklen, John Rose. *History of Reconstruction in Louisiana.* 1914.

Harvard, William C. *The Government of Louisiana.* 1958.

Howard, Perry H. *Political Tendencies in Louisiana, 1812-1852.* 1971.

Kendall, John S. *Golden Age of New Orleans.*

Kriegel, Leonard. *Life on the Mississippi, by Mark Twain.* 1961.

Lynn, Stuart M. *New Orleans.*

Martin, Thomas. *Dynasty, the Longs of Louisiana.* 1960.

McIntire, William J. *Prehistoric Indian Settlements of the Changing Mississippi River Delta.* 1958.

Parkinson, Keyes. *All This is Louisiana.* 1950.

Rand, Clayton. *Stars in Their Eyes; Dreamers and Builders in Louisiana.*

Ricciut, Italo W. and Hamlin, Talbot F. *New Orleans and its Environs, the Domestic Architecture, 1727-1870.*

Rousseve, Charles B. *The Negro in Louisiana.* 1937.

Saxon, Lyle. *Fabulous New Orleans.* 1928.

Saxon, Lyle. *Father Mississippi.* 1928.

Smith, Fraser J. *White Pillars, the Architecture of the South.*

Taylor, Joe Gray. *Negro Slavery in Louisiana.* 1963.

Williams, Harry T. *Huey Long, a Biography.* 1969.

BOOKS ABOUT MAINE

Attwood, Stanley B. *The Legend and Breadth of Maine.* 1973

Banks, Ronald F. *Maine Becomes a State; the Movement to Separate Maine from Massachusetts.* 1970.

Barrington, Richard E. *A Maine Manifest.* 1972.

Bradford, Peter A. *Fragile Structures: A Story of Oil Refineries, National Security, and the Coast of Maine.* 1975.

Burrage, Henry S. *Beginnings of Colonial Maine.* Portland, OR, 1914.

Caldwell, Bill. *Islands of Maine: Where America Really Began.* 1981.

Caldwell, Bill. *Rivers of Fortune: Where Maine Tides and Money Flowed.* 1983.

Chase, Edward E. *Maine Railroads: A History of the Development of the Railroad System.* Portland, OR, 1926.

Coe, Harrie B. *Maine: Resources, Attractions, and Its People.* New York, NY, 1928-31.

Conkling, Philip W. *Islands in Time: A Natural and Human History of the Islands of Maine.* 1981.

Dunnack, Henry E. *Manual of Maine Government.* Augusta, ME, 1921.

Dunnack, Henry E. *The Maine Book.* Augusta, ME, 1920.

Encyclopedia of Maine. Somerset Publishers. Michigan, 1999.

Hale, Robert. *Early Days of Church and State in Maine.* Brunswick, ME, 1910.

Holmes, Herbert E. *The Makers of Maine: Essays and Tales of Early Maine History.* Lewiston, ME, 1912.

Maine Historical Society. *Documentary History of the State of Maine.* Portland, OR, 1869-1916.

Moulton, Augustus F. *Memorials of Maine: A Life Record of Men and Women of the Past.* New York, NY, 1916.

Rowe, William H. *The Maritime History of Maine, Three Centuries of Shipbuilding and Seafaring.* 1966.

Smith, W.B. *Indian Remains of the Penobscot Valley and their Significance.* Orono, 1926.

Spencer, Wilbur D. *Maine Immortals.* Augusta, ME, 1932.

Starkey, Glenn W. *Maine: Its History, Resources, and Government.* Boston, MA, 1930.

Sterling, Robert T. *Lighthouses of the Maine Coast, and the Men Who Keep Them.* Brattleboro, VT, 1935.

Thoreau, Henry D. *The Maine Woods.* Boston, MA, 1864.

Verrill, A. Hyatt. *Romantic and Historic Maine.* New York, NY, 1933.

Willougby, Charles C. *Prehistoric Burial Places in Maine.* Cambridge, MA, 1898.

BOOKS ABOUT MARYLAND

Andrews, Matthew P. *The Founding of Maryland.* 1933.

Bard, Harry. *Maryland, State and Government: In New Dynamic.* 1974.

Barker, Charles. *The Background of the Revolution in Maryland.* 1940.

Bodine, Aubrey. *The Face of Maryland.* 3d. ed. 1970.

Brugger, Robert J. *Maryland: A Middle Temperament, 1634-1980.* 1988.

Carr, Lois G. and Jordan, David W. *Maryland's Revolution of Government, 1689-1962.* 1973.

Crowl, Philip A. *Maryland During and After the Revolution: A Political and Economic Study.* 1943.

Dozer, Donald M. *Portrait of a Free State: A History of Maryland.* 1976.

Encyclopedia of Maryland. Somerset Publishers. Michigan, 1999.

Federal Writers Project. *Maryland, a Guide to the Old Line State.* 1940.

Goldsborough, William W. *The Maryland Line in the Confederate Army, 1861-1865.* 1972.

Guide to the Research Collections of the Maryland Historical Society: Historical and Genealogical Manuscripts and Oral History. 1981.

Hall, Clayton C. *Narratives of Early Maryland, 1633-1684.* 1910.

History of Maryland from Earliest Times to the Present Day. 1879.

Hoffman, Ronald. *A Spirit of Dissention: Economics, Politics, and the Revolution in Maryland.* 1973.

Lemay, J.A. *Men of Letters in Colonial Maryland.* 1972.

McConnell, Roland C. *Three Hundred and Fifty Years: Chronology of the Afro-American in Maryland, 1634-1984.*

McSherry, James. Bartlett *B. James: History of Maryland.* 1904.

Meyer, Eugene L. *Maryland Lost and Found: People and Places from Chesapeake to Appalachia.* 1986.

Pedley, Avril J.M. *The Manuscript Collections of the Maryland Historical Society.* 1968.

Quinn, David B. *Early Maryland in a Wider World.* 1982.

Rollo, Vera F. *The Black Experience in Maryland.* 1980.

Walsh, Richard, and Fox, William Lloyd. *Maryland: A History 1632-1974.*

White, Frank Jr. *The Governors of Maryland.* 1970.

Wright, James. *The Free Negro in Maryland, 1634-1860.* 1921.

BOOKS ABOUT MASSACHUSETTS

Adams, Charles F. *Three Episodes of Massachusetts History,* (2 vols.). Boston, MA, 1892 and New York, NY, 1965.

Allen, Gardner W. *Massachusetts Privateers of the Revolution,* Boston, 1927.

Battis, Emery. *Saints and Secretaries: Anne Hutchinson and the Antinomian Controversy in the Massachusetts Bay Colony.*

Baum, Dale. *The Civil War Party System: The Case of Massachusetts, 1848-1876.* 1984.

Biographical History of Massachusetts. (3 vols.) Boston, MA, 1911.

Blodgett, Geoffrey. *The Gentle Reformers: Massachusetts Democrats.* 1966.

Bolton, Charles K. *The Real Founders of New England.* Boston, 1929.

Boyer, Paul. *Salem Possessed: The Social Origins of Witchcraft.* Cambridge, MA, 1974.

Brown, Richard. *Massachusetts: A Bicentennial History.* New York, NY, 1978.

Reynolds, Michael M. *Maryland: A Guide to Information and Reference Sources.* 1976.

Colonial Society of Massachusetts. *Seafaring in Colonial Massachusetts.* 1980.

Cronon, William. *Changes in the Land: Indians, Colonists, and the Ecology of New England.* 1983.

Demos, John. *A Little Commonwealth: Family Life in the Plymouth Colony.* 1970.

Dentler, Robert A. and Scott, Marvin B. *Schools on Trial: An Inside Account of the Boston Desegregation Case.* 1981.

Duniway, Clyde A. *The Development of Freedom of the Press in Massachusetts.* New York, 1906.

Ellis, George. *Puritan Age and Rule in the Colony of the Massachusetts Bay, 1629-1685.* Boston, 1888.

Emilio, Luis, et al. *A Brave Black Regiment: The History of the Fifty-Fourth Regiment of Massachusetts Volunteer Infantry, 1863-1865.* 1995.

Encyclopedia of Massachusetts. Somerset Publishers. Michigan, 1999.

Everyday Life in the Massachusetts Bay Colony. rev. ed. 1988

Formisano, Ronald P. *The Transformation of Political Culture: Massachusetts Parties, 1790s-1840s.* 1893.

Fryatt, Norma. *Boston and the Tea Riots.* 1972.

Gill, Crispin. *Mayflower Remembered: A History of Plymouth Colony.* 1970.

Hall, Van Beck. *Politics without Parties: Massachusetts, 1780-1791.* 1972.

Hart, Albert, ed. *Commonwealth History of Massachusetts.* (5 vols.) New York, NY, 1930.

Labaree, Benjamin. *Colonial Massachusetts: A History.* 1979.

Litt, Edgar. *The Political Cultures of Massachusetts.* 1965.

BOOKS ABOUT MICHIGAN

Angelo, Frank. *Yesterday's Michigan.* Miami, FL 1975.

Barfknecht, Gary W. *Mich-again's Day: A Panorama of Major and Trivial, Human-Interest and Historical, and Informative and Entertainers Events that Have Taken Place on each of Michigan's Past Days.* Davison, MI, 1984.

Brazer, Harvey E. *Michigan's Fiscal and Economic Structure.* Ann Arbor, MI, 1982.

Brown, Alan Scouler. *Michigan Perspectives: People, Events, and Issues.* Dubuque, IA, 1974.

Campbell, J.V. *Outlines of the Political History of Michigan.* Detroit, MI, 1876.

Carr, Robert. *The Government of Michigan.* rev. ed. 1967; rep. 1980.

Catton, Bruce. *Michigan: A Bicentennial History.* New York, NY, 1976.

Cleland, Charles E. *A Brief History of Michigan Indians.* 1975.

Clive, Alan. *State of War—Michigan in World War II.* Ann Arbor, MI, 1979.

Cooley, Thoams M. *Michigan: A History of Governments.* Boston, MA, 1892.

Cox, William J. *A Primer of Michigan History.* Lansing, MI.

Davies, Nancy Millichap. *Michigan.* 1992.

Epstein, Ralph. *The Automobile Industry.* Chicago, IL, 1928.

Encyclopedia of Michigan. Somerset Publishers. Michigan, 1999.

Federal Writers' Project. *Michigan, A Guide to the Wolverine State.* St. Clair Shores, MI: Somerset Publishers.

Grimm, Joe. *Michigan Voices: Our State's History in the Words of People Who Lived It.* 1987.

Kuhn, Madison. *Michigan State: The First Hundred Years.* East Lansing, MI, 1955.

Lanman, C. *The Red Book of Michigan: A Civil, Military and Biographical History of Michigan.* Washington, DC, 1871.

Michigan, A Centennial History of the State and Its People. Chicago, IL, 1939.

Michigan Through the Centuries. New York, NY, 1955.

Rural Michigan. 1922.

Severance, Henry O. *Michigan Trailmakers.* Ann Arbor, MI, 1930.

Sheldon, Mrs. E.M. *Early History of Michigan, from the First Settlement to 1815.* New York, NY, 1874.

Stieber, Carolyn. *The Politics of Change in Michigan.* East Lansing, MI: Michigan State University, 1970.

The First People of Michigan. Ann Arbor, MI, 1930.

BOOKS ABOUT MINNESOTA

Brook, Michael. *Reference Guide to Minnesota History: A Subject Bibliography of Books, Pamphlets, and Articles in English.* St. Paul, MN: Minnesota Historical Society, 1971.

Burnquist, Joseph A. Arner. *Minnesota and Its People.* Chicago, IL: S. J. Clarke Publishing Co., 1924.

Carpenter, John Allan. *Minnesota.* Chicago, IL: Children's Press, 1978.

Daughters of the American Revolution. *Old Rail Fence Corners: Frontier Tales Told by Minnesota Pioneers.* St. Paul, MN: Minnesota Historical Society Press, 1976.

Encyclopedia of Minnesota. Somerset Publishers. Michigan, 1999.

Fearing, Jerry. *The Story of Minnesota.* St. Paul, MN: Minnesota Historical Society, 1977.

Federal Writers' Project. *Minnesota: A State Guide.* New York, NY: Somerset, 1938, reprinted 1954.

Gilman, Rhoda R. *Minnesota Politics and Government: A History Resource Unit—Minnesota: Political Maverick.* St. Paul, MN: Minnesota Historical Society, 1975.

Hage, George S. *Newspapers on the Minnesota Frontier, 1849-1860.* 1967.

Heilbron, Bertha L. *The Thirty-Second State: A Pictorial History of Minnesota.* 1958.

Holmquist, June Drenning. *They Chose Minnesota.* St. Paul, MN: Minnesota Historical Society Press, 1981.

Hubbard, Lucius F., Baker, James H., Murray, William P., and Upham, Warren. *Minnesota in Three Centuries, Semi-Centennial Edition, 1655 to 1908.* MN and NY: The Publishing Society of Minnesota and New York, 1908.

Hunt, Ron. *A Living Past: 15 Historical Places in Minnesota.* St. Paul, MN: Minnesota Historical Society, 1978.

Jenks, Albert E. *Minnesota History—"Recent Discoveries in Minnesota Prehistory."* March 1935, v. 16.

Lass, William E. *Minnesota: A Bicentennial History.* New York, NY: Norton, 1977.

Minnesota: A History of the State. Minneapolis, MN: University of Minnesota Press, 1963, rep. 1975.

Minnesota Historical Collections —"Civilization and Christianization of the Ojibways in Minnesota." (vol. 9), St. Paul, MN.

Minnesota Historical Society. *Minnesota History.* 1938.

Minnesota in Three Centuries, 1655-1908. Mankato, MN: Free Press Printing Co., 1908.

Minnesota, Its History and Its People: A Study Outline with Topics and References. Minneapolis, MN: University of Minnesota Press, 1937.

Minnesota, the Land of Sky-tinted Waters: A History of the State and Its People. Chicago, IL, and New York, NY: The American Historical Society, 1935.

Neill, Edward Duffield. *The History of Minnesota, from the Earliest French Explorations of the Present Time* (c. 1858). New York, NY: Arno Press, 1975.

Upham, Warren, and Dunlap, Rose B. *Minnesota Biographies, 1655-1912.* St. Paul, MN: Minnesota Historical Society, 1912.

Vexler, Robert I. *Chronology and Documentary Handbook of the State of Minnesota.* Dobbs Ferry, NY: Oceana Publications, 1978.

Winchell, Newton, H. *The Aborigines of Minnesota.* St. Paul, MN: Minnesota Historical Society, 1911.

BOOKS ABOUT MISSISSIPPI

Butts, Alfred B. *The Court System of Mississippi.* 1930.

Carpenter, Barbara. *Ethnic Heritage in Mississippi.* 1992.

Cobb, Joseph B. *Mississippi Scenes.* Philadelphia, PA, 1851.

Davis, Reuben. *Recollections of Mississippi and Mississippians.* Boston, MA, 1891.

Dennis, Frank A. *Index to the Journal of Mississippi History, 1939-1958.* 1984.

Dorsey, Florence. *Master of the Mississippi: Henry Shreve and the Conquest of Mississippi.* 1941.

Encyclopedia of Mississippi. Somerset Publishers. Michigan, 1999.

Fant, Mabel, and John C. *History of Mississippi.* Jackson, MS, 1928.

Garner, James W. *Reconstruction in Mississippi.* New York, NY, 1901.

Hall, James. *A Brief History of the Mississippi Territory.* Oxford, MS, 1906.

Korn, Jerry. *War on the Mississippi; Grant's Vicksburg Campaign.* 1985.

Lana, Meredith. *Defender of the Faith: The High Court of Mississippi.* 1977.

Lincecum, Gideon. *The Choctaw Traditions: About Their Settlements in Mississippi and the Origin of Their Mounds.* Oxford, 1904.

McLemore, Richard A. *A History of Mississippi.* 1973.

Mississippi: An Encyclopedic History. Atlanta, GA, 1917.

Mississippi Department of Archives and History. *Guide to Official Records in the Mississippi Department of Archives and History.* 1975.

Mississippi: Storm Center of Secession, 1856-1861.

Rainwater, Percy Lee. *An Economic Interpretation of Secession. Opinions in Mississippi in 1850s.* Baton Rouge, LA, 1935.

Riley, Franklin L. *A Contribution to the History of the Colonization Movement in Mississippi.* Oxford, 1906.

Rowland and Sanders. *Mississippi Provincial Archives.* Jackson, MS, 1927.

Rowland, Dunbar. *Biographical Guide to the Mississippi Hall of Fame.* Jackson, MS, 1935.

Rowland, Dunbar. *Mississippi: the Heart of the South.* Chicago, IL, 1925.

Shetrone, Henry Clyde. *The Mound Builders.* New York, NY: D. Appleton and Co., 1930.

Snydor, Charles S. *Slavery in Mississippi.* New York, NY, 1933.

Wall, E.G. *Handbook of the State of Mississippi.* Jackson, MS, 1882.

BOOKS ABOUT MISSOURI

Bradley, Glenn. *The Story of the Pony Express.* Chicago, IL, 1914.

Breckenridge, A.C. and Colman, W.G. "Missouri as a Pioneer in Criminal Court Reform." *Missouri Historical History.* St. Louis, MO. 1939.

Coffin, Tristram. *Missouri Compromise.* 1947.

Darby, Ada. *"Show Me" Missouri.* Kansas City, MO: 1938.

Encyclopedia of Missouri. Somerset Publishers. Michigan, 1999.

Farnham, Laurie. *A Handbook on Women and the Law in Missouri.* 1974.

Federal Writer's Project. Works Project Administration. *Missouri, A Guide to the "Show Me" State.* New York, 1941. (Rep. St. Clair Shores) 1978.

Foley, William E. *The Genesis of Missouri: The Wilderness Outpost to Statehood.* 1989.

Hardy, Richard J. and Dohm, Richard R. *Missouri Government and Politics.* 1985.

Houck, Louis. *A History of Missouria from the Earliest Explorations and Settlements Until the Admission of the State Into the Union.* Chicago, IL: 1908. (rep. NY, 1971).

Kirkendall, Richard S. *A History of Missouri, 1919-1953.* (vol. V. 1986).

Kremer, Gary R., and Holland, Antonio F. *Missouri's Black Heritage.* 1993.

LeSueur, Stephen C. *The 1838 Mormon War in Missouri.* 1987.

Lewis, Meriwether, and Clark, William. *Original Journal of the Lewis and Clark Expedition, 1804-1806.* New York, NY: Dodd, Mead & Co., 1904-05.

Mallinckrodt, Anita M. *Missouri.* 1994.

March, David. *The History of Missouri.* (4 vols.) New York. 1967.

Missouri's Struggle for Statehood. Jefferson City, MO, 1969.

Nagel, Paul C. *Missouri, a Bicentennial History.* New York. 1977.

Parrish, William. *Missouri, the Heart of the Nation.* 1992.

Reynolds, Edwin. *Missouri, A History of the Crossroads State.* 1962.

Rogers, Ann. *Lewis and Clark in Missouri.* 1981.

Shoemaker, Floyd. *Missouri and the Missourians: Land of Contrasts and People of Achievement.* Chicago. 1943.

Stevens, Walter. *Slavery in Missouri, 1804-1865.* Baltimore, MD. 1914.

Waal, Carla, and Kormer, Oliver Barbara (eds.) *Hardship and Hope: Missouri Women Writing About Their Lives, 1820-1920.* 1997.

Wlesbacher, Anne. *Missouri.* 1998.

BOOKS ABOUT MONTANA

Abbot, N.C. *Montana Government* Billings, MT: Gazette Print. Co., 1937.

Bancroft, Hubert Howe. "History of Montana." (In his *History of the Pacific States of North America: Washington, Idaho, and Montana, 1845-1889.*) San Francisco, CA, The History Co., 1890.

Dimsdale, Thomas J. *The Vigilantes of Montana; or, Popular Justice in the Rocky Mountains. Narrative of the chase, capture, trial, and execution of Henry Plummer's road agent band...interspersed with sketches of life in the mining camps.* Butte, MT: W.F. Bartlett, 1915.

Encyclopedia of Montana. Somerset Publishers. Michigan, 1999.

Fisher, Arthur. *Montana, Land of the Copper Collar.* New York, NY: Boni & Liveright, 1924.

Grimsby, Oscar Melvin P. *The Contribution of Scandinavian and Germanic People to the Development of Montana.* Missoula, MT: University of Montana, 1926.

Hennen, Jennings. *The History and Development of Gold Dredging in Montana.* Washington, DC: Govt. Print. Off., 1916.

Housman, Robert. L. *The Beginnings of Journalism in Frontier Montana.* Missoula, MT, 1935.

Palladino, Lawrence B.S.J. *Indian and White in the Northwest; A History of Catholicity in Montana, 1831-1891.* Lancaster, PA: Wickersham Pub. Co., 1922.

Phillips, Paul C. "The Archives of the State of Montana." (*In American Historical Association. Annual Report, 1912.* Washington, DC, 1914.)

Richardson, Jessie E. *The Quality of Living in Montana Farm Homes.* Bozeman, 1932.

Shields, George O. *The Battle of the Big Hole. A History of General Gibbon's Engagement with Nez Perce Indians in the Big Hole Valley, Montana, August 9, 1977.* Chicago, IL and New York, NY: Rand McNally & Co., 1889.

"The Montana National Bison Range." *Journal of Mammalogy*, Feb. 1926.

Thompson, Mrs. Margaret. *High Trails of Glacier National Park.* Caldwell, ID: Caxton Printers, 1936.

BOOKS ABOUT NEBRASKA

Andreas, A.T. *History of Nebraska.* 1882.

Bennett, Mildred R. *The World of Willa Cather.* 1988.

Bremer, Richard G. *Agricultural Change in an Urban Age. The Country of Nebraska, 1910-1970.* 1976.

Bucklin, Clarissa. *Nebraska Art and Artists.* 1932.

Cherny, Robert B. *Populism, Progressivism and the Transformation of Nebraska Politics, 1885-1915.* 1981.

Condra, George E. *The Nebraska Story.* 1951.

Creigh, Dorthy W. *Nebraska.* A Bicentennial History of States and the Nations Series, 1977.

Encyclopedia of Nebraska. Somerset Publishers. Michigan, 1999.

Faulkner, Virginia. *Roundup.* A Nebraska Reader, 1957.

Federal Writers Project. *Origin of Nebraska Place Names.* 1938.

Fink, Deborah. *Agrarian Women, Wives and Mothers in Rural Nebraska.* 1992.

Hanna, Robert. *Sketches of Nebraska.* 1984.

Holmes, Louis A. *Fort M. Pherson.* Nebraska, Fort Cottonwood, Guardian of the Trucks and Trails. 1963.

Johnson, John R. *Representative Nebraskans.* 1954.

Larson, Lawrence H. and Cottrell, Barbara J. *History of Omaha.* 1982.

Lee, Wayne C. *Wild Towns of Nebraska.* 1988.

Manley, Robert N. *Nebraska: Our Pioneer Heritage.* 1981.

Miewald, Robert D. *Nebraska Government and Politics.* 1984.

Morton, J. Sterling, and Watkins, Albert. *Illustrated History of Nebraska, 1905-1913.*

Olson, James C. *History of Nebraska.* 1966.

Sheldon, Addison E. *Nebraska, The Land and the People.* 1931.

Sittig, Robert. *Nebraska Government Sources and Literature.* 1983.

Stilgebouer, Forster G. *Nebraska Pioneers. The Story of Sixty-Five Years of Pioneering in Southwest Nebraska, 1875-1940.* 1944.

Webb, Walter P. *The Great Plains.* 1931.

Welsch, Roger L. *A Treasury of Nebraska Pioneer Folklore.* 1966.

BOOKS ABOUT NEVADA

American Guide Series. *Nevada: A Guide to the Silver State.* 1940. Rep. 1972.

Bushnell, Eleanore and Driggs, D.W. *The Nevada Constitution.* 6th ed. University of Nevada Press, 1984.

Bushnell, Eleanore and Driggs, Don. *The Nevada Constitution: Origin and Growth.* 6th ed. University of Nevada Press, 1984.

Carpenter, Allan. *Nevada.* Rev. ed. Childrens Press, 1979.

Castleman, Deke. *Nevada Handbook.* 3rd ed. Moon Publications, 1993.

Elliott, Russel R. *Nevada's Twentieth Century Mining Boom: Tonopah, Goldfield, Ely.* University of Nevada Press, 1966.

Elliott, Russel R. and Rowley, W.D. *History of Nevada* 2nd ed. University of Nebraska Press, 1987.

Encyclopedia of Nevada. Somerset Publishers. Michigan, 1999.

Hulse, James W. *The Nevada Adventure.* 6th ed. University of Nevada Press, 1990.

Hulse, James W. *The Nevada Adventure: A History.* 5th ed. University of Nevada Press, 1981.

Hulse, James W. *The Silver State: Nevada's Heritage Reinterpreted.* University of Nevada Press, 1991.

Laxalt, Robert. *Nevada.* Coward, 1971.

Laxalt, Robert. *Nevada: A Bicentennial History.* Norton, 1977.

Lillegard, Dee and Stoker, Wayne. *Nevada.* Children's Press, 1990.

Sirvaitis, Karen. *Nevada.* Lerner, 1992.

Toll, David W. *The Compleat Nevada Traveler: A Guide to the State.* Rev. ed. Gold Hill, 1985.

Trimble, Stephen. *The Sagebrush Ocean, A Natural History of the Great Basin.* University of Nevada Press, 1989.

Wuerthner, George. *Nevada Mountain Ranges.* American and World Geographic Publications, 1992.

BOOKS ABOUT NEW HAMPSHIRE

Belknap, Jeremy. *History of New Hampshire.* Boston, MA, 1792.

Campbell, Catherine H. *New Hampshire Scenery: A Dictionary of Nineteenth-Century Artists of New Hampshire Mountain Landscapes.* 1985.

Carpenter, Allan. *New Hampshire.* Rev. ed. Childrens Press, 1979.

Churgin, Jonah R. *From Truman to Johnson: New Hampshire's Impact on American Politics.* 1972.

Daniel, Jere R. *Colonial New Hampshire – A History.* 1981.

Encyclopedia of New Hampshire. Somerset Publishers. Michigan, 1999.

Farmer, John, and Moore, Jacob B. *Gazetteer of New Hampshire.* Concord, NH, 1823.

Fradin, Dennis B. *The New Hampshire Colony.* Macmillan, 1988.

Fry, W.H. *New Hampshire as a Royal Province.* New York, NY, 1908.

Hammond, Otis G. *Check List of New Hampshire Local History.* 1971.

Haskell, John D. and T.D. Seymour Bassett. *New Hampshire: A Bibliography of Its History.* 1979.

Heffernan, Nancy C. and Stecker, A.P. *New Hampshire: Cross-currents in Its Development.* Tompson & Rutter, 1986.

Hill, Ralph. *Yankee Kingdom: Vermont and New Hampshire.* 1960.

Jager, Ronald and Grace. *New Hampshire: An Illustrated History of the Granite State.* 1983.

Kingsbury, John M. *Oil and Water, the New Hampshire Story.* 1975.

Leavitt, Richard F. *Yesterday's New Hampshire.* 1974.

McNair, Sylvia. *New Hampshire.* Childrens Press, 1992.

Morison, Elizabeth F. and Elting E. *New Hampshire: A Bicentennial History.* 1976.

New Hampshire – 1937. Concord, NH, 1937.

Nutting, Wallace. *New Hampshire Beautiful.* New York, NY, 1937.

Sanborn, Franklin B. *New Hampshire (American Commonwealth Series)* Boston, MA, 1904.

Scheller, William G. *New Hampshire: Portrait of the Land and Its People.* American Geographic Pub., 1988.

Stackpole, E.S. *History of New Hampshire.* New York, NY, 1917.

Turner, Lynn W. *The Ninth State: New Hampshire's Formative Years.* University of North Carolina Press, 1983.

Water Bodies in the State of New Hampshire. Concord, NH, 1934.

BOOKS ABOUT NEW JERSEY

Barber, John Warner, and Howe, Henry. *Historical Collections of New Jersey.* Rev. ed. New Haven, CT: J.W. Barber, 1868.

Burr, Nelson R. *A Narrative and Descriptive Biography of New Jersey.* Princeton, NJ: Van Nostrand, 1964.

Carpenter, John Allan. *New Jersey From its Glorious Past to the Present.* Chicago, IL: Children's Press.

Cooley, Henry Scofield. *A Study of Slavery in New Jersey.* Baltimore, MD: Johns Hopkins Press, 1896.

Cunningham, John T. *This is New Jersey.* Rev. ed. New Brunswick, NJ: Rutgers University Press, 1968, 1983.

Encyclopedia of New Jersey. Somerset Publishers. Michigan, 1999.

Erdman, Charles R., Jr. *The New Jersey Constitution: A Barrier to Governmental Efficiency and Economy.* Princeton, NJ: University Press, 1934.

Federal Writer's Project. *New Jersey: A Guide to the Present and Past.* Reprint. New York, NY: Somerset (orig. 1939).

Gordon, Thomas F. *Gazetteer of the State of New Jersey and History of New Jersey.* Trenton, NJ: D. Fenton, 1834.

Hannau, Hasn W. *New Jersey.* Garden City, NJ: Doubleday, 1968.

Knapp, C.M. *New Jersey Politics During the Period of the Civil War and Reconstruction.* New York, NY: W.F. Humphrey, 1924.

Kull, Irving S., ed. *New Jersey: A History.* New York, NY: American Historical Society, 1930.

League of Women Voters of New Jersey. *New Jersey: Spotlight on Government.* New Brunswick, NJ: Rutgers University Press, 1983.

Lee, Francis Bazley. *New Jersey as a Colony and as a State.* New York, NY: Publishing Society of New Jersey, 1902.

Mappen, Marc. *Jerseyana: The Underside of New Jersey History.* 1992.

McCormick, Richard Patrick. *New Jersey from Colony to State, 1609-1789.* 1981.

Miers, Earl Schenck. *Down in Jersey: An Affectionate Narrative.* New Brunswick, NJ: Rutgers University Press, 1973.

Mustead, Harley P. *New Jersey Geography and History.* Philadelphia, PA: Winston, 1960.

New Jersey: A Bicentennial History. New York, NY: Norton, 1977.

New Jersey: A History. 1985.

Parsons, Floyd William, ed. *New Jersey: Life, Industries and Resources of a Great State.* Newark State Chamber of Commerce, 1928.

Pomfret, John E. *Colonial New Jersey—A History.* New York, NY: Scribners, 1973.

Resnick, Abraham, and Rosenfelt, W.E., (ed. Consultant). *New Jersey: Its People and Culture.* Minneapolis, MN: T.S. Denison, 1974.

Stockton, F.R. *Stories of New Jersey.* New York, NY: American Book Co., 1896.

Tanner, Edwin P. *The Province of New Jersey, 1664-1738.* New York, NY: Columbia University Press, 1908.

BOOKS ABOUT NEW MEXICO

Bailey, Vernon. *Life Zones and Crop Zones of New Mexico.* Washington, DC, 1931.

Bancroft, Hubert Howe. *The History of Arizona and New Mexico, 1530-1888.* San Francisco, CA, 1889.

Bloom, Lansing B. and Donnelly C. *New Mexico History and Civics.* Albuquerque, NM, 1933.

Carpenter, Allan. *New Mexico.* Rev. ed. Childrens Press, 1978.

Cremony, John C. *Life Among the Apaches.* San Francisco, CA, 1868.

Dozier, Edward P. *The Pueblo Indians of North America.* Waveland Press, 1983.

Duffus, Robert L. *The Santa Fe Trail.* New York, NY, 1930.

Encyclopedia of New Mexico. Somerset Publishers. Michigan, 1999.

Expeditions Into New Mexico by Antonio de Espejo, 1582-1583. Los Angeles, CA, 1929.

Goddard, Pliny Earle. *Indians of the Southwest.* New York, NY, 1931.

Hammond, George P. *Don Juan de Onate and the Founding of New Mexico.* Santa Fe, NM, 1927.

Haury, Emil W. *The Mongolian Culture of Southwestern New Mexico.* Globe, 1936.

Hewett, Edgar Lee. *Ancient Life in the American Southwest.* Indianapolis, IN, 1930.

Leading Facts of New Mexico History. Cedar Rapids, IA, 1911-1912.

Mammals of New Mexico. Washington DC, 1931.

Mera, Harry P. *Ceramic Clues to the Prehistory of North Central New Mexico.* Santa Fe, NM, 1935.

Native Tales of New Mexico. Philadelphia, PA, 1932.

Prince, L. Bradford. *Spanish Mission Churches of New Mexico.* Cedar Rapids, IA, 1915.

Reeve, Frank D. and Cleaveland, A.A. *New Mexico: Land of Many Cultures.* Rev. ed. Pruett, 1980.

Segale, Sister Blandina. *At the End of the Santa Fe Trail.* Columbus, OH, 1932.

Stein, Conrad R. *New Mexico.* Childrens Press, 1988.

Sunseri, Alvin R. *Seeds of Discord: New Mexico in the Aftermath of the American Conquest, 1846-1861.* Nelson-Hall, 1979.

The Early Navajo and Apache. Washington DC, 1895.

Twitchell, Ralph Emerson. *Old Santa Fe.* Santa Fe, NM, 1925.
Villagra, Gaspar Perez de. *History of New Mexico.* Los Angeles, CA, 1933.

BOOKS ABOUT NEW YORK

Alexander, D.S. *A Political History of the State of New York.* (3 vols.) New York, NY, 1906-09.
American Guide Series. *New York: A Guide to the Empire State.* New York, NY, 1940.
Becker, Carl L. *The History of Political Parties in the Province of New York, 1760-76.* Madison, WI, 1909.
Beveridge, Charles E., et al. *Creating Central Park 1857-1861: The Papers of Frederick Law Olmsted.* (Vol. 3.) 1983.
Burgess, Anthony. *New York.* New York, NY, 1977.
Colby, P.W., and J.K. White, eds. *New York State Today.* 1989.
Condon, Thomas J. *New York Beginnings.* New York, NY, 1968.
Davis, Elmer. *History of the New York Times, 1851-1921.* New York, NY, 1921.
Encyclopedia of New York. Somerset Publishers. Michigan, 2000.
Federal Writer's Project. *New York. A Guide to the Empire State.* 1940. Rep., 1972.
Halsey, Francis W. *The Old New York Frontier, 1614-1800.* New York, NY, 1902.
Howes, Kelly King. *Harlem Renaissance.* 2000.
Irving, Washington. *Knickerbocker's History of New York.* Edited by Anne C. Moore. 1959.
Lach, William, ed. *New York, New York: The City in Art and Literature.* 2000.
McKay, Ernest A. *The Civil War and New York City.* 1991.
McNamara, Brooks and MacDonald, Robert R. *Day of Jubilee: The Great Age of Public Celebrations in New York, 1788-1909.* 1997.
Morris, Lloyd. *Incredible New York.* New York, NY, 1951.
New York, State and City. Ithaca, NY, 1979.
Nutting, Wallace. *New York Beautiful.* New York, NY, 1927.
Odell, G.C.D. *Annals of the New York Stage.* New York, NY, 1927-39.
Oppenheim, Samuel. *The Early History of the Jews in New York.* New York, NY, 1909.
Patterson, Jerry. *First 400: New York and the Gilded Age.* 2000.
Peiss, Kathy. *Cheap Amusements: Working Women and Leisure in Turn-of-the-Century New York.* 1987.
Sleeper, Jim. *Closest of Strangers: Liberalism and the Politics of Race in New York.* 1991.
The American Revolution in New York, Its Political, Social and Economic Significance. Albany, NY, 1926.

BOOKS ABOUT NORTH CAROLINA

Alexander, Roberta Sue. *North Carolina Faces the Freedmen.* Durham, NC: Duke University Press, 1985.
Barnett, John Gilchrist. *The Civil War in North Carolina.* 1995.
Bassett, J. S. *Constitutional Beginnings of North Carolina, 1663-1729.* 1854.
Butler, Lindley S. and Alan D. Watson. *The North Carolina Experience: An Interpretive Documentary History.* Chapel Hills, NC: University of North Carolina Press, 1984.
Church and State in North Carolina. 1893.
Claiborne, Jack, and Price, William (eds.) *Discovering North Carolina: A Tar Heel Reader.* 1993.

Clements, John. *Flying the Colors: North Carolina Facts. A Comprehensive Look At North Carolina Today, County by County.* Dallas, TX: Clements Research II, 1988.
Cooper, Richard. *Biographical Dictionary of Famous Tar Heels.* Raleigh, NC: Raleigh, 1988.
Crow, Vernon H. *North Carolina Government, 1585-1979.* 1981.
Encyclopedia of North Carolina. Somerset Publishers. Michigan, 1999.
Fenn, Elizabeth A., and Wood, Peter H. *Natives and Newcomers: The Way We Lived in North Carolina Before 1770.* Chapel Hill, NC: University of North Carolina Press, 1983.
Franklin, J.H. *The Free Negro in North Carolina, 1790-1860.* 1943. Rep. 1995.
Gilmore, Glenda Elizabeth. *Gender and Jim Crow: Women and the Politics of White Supremacy in North Carolina, 1896-1920.*
Gilpatrick, D.H. *Jeffersonian Democracy in North Carolina, 1789-1816.* 1931.
Hill Wheeler, John. *Historical Sketches of North Carolina from 1584-1581; Compiled from Original Records...* Philadelphia, PA: Lippincott, Grambo and Company, 1851.
History of North Carolina. (6 vols.) Chicago, IL and New York, NY: The Lewis Publishing Company, 1919.
Jones, H. G. *For History's Sake, The Preservation and Publication of North Carolina History, 1663-1903.* Chapel Hill, NC: University of North Carolina Press, 1965.
North Carolina During Reconstruction. Raleigh, NC: State Department of Archives and History, 1969.
North Carolina Through Four Centuries. Chapel Hill, NC: University of North Carolina Press, 1989.
O'Donnell, James H. *The Cherokees of North Carolina in the American Revolution.* 1976.
Reconstruction in North Carolina. 1914.
Russell, Phillips. *North Carolina in the Revolutionary War.* 1965.
Simmons-Henry. *The Heritage of Blacks in North Carolina: Volume I.* Raleigh, NC: North Carolina African-American Heritage Foundation, 1990.
Sitterson, J.C. *The Secession Movement in North Carolina.* 1939.
Slavery and Servitude in the Colony of North Carolina. 1896.

BOOKS ABOUT NORTH DAKOTA

Berg, Francis M. *Ethnic Heritage in North Dakota.* 1983.
Brand, Wayne L. *North Dakota Decision Makers.* 1972.
Buttree, J. Edmond. *The Despoilers; Stories of the North Dakota Grain Fields.* 1920.
Bye, John E. *North Dakota Institute for Regional Studies: Guide to Manuscripts and Archives.* 1985.
Crawford, Lewis. *History of North Dakota.* New York, NY and Chicago, IL, 1931.
Encyclopedia of North Dakota. Somerset Publishers. Michigan, 1999.
Fossum, Paul Robert. *The Agrarian Movement in North Dakota.* Baltimore, MD, 1925.
Hager, Dorothy. *First Ladies of North Dakota.* 1967.
Hennessey, William B. *History of North Dakota.* Bismarck, ND, 1910.
Howard, Thomas W. *The North Dakota Political Traditions.* 1981.
Kingsbury, G.W. *History of Dakota Territory.* Chicago, IL: Clarke Publishing Co., 1915.

Lindgren, H. Elaine. *Land in Her Own Name: Women as Home-steaders in North Dakota.* 1991.

North Dakota Biography. Chicago, IL, 1900.

Norton, Sister Mary Aquinas. *Catholic Missions and Missionaries Among the Indians of Dakota.* 1931.

Oihus, Colleen A. *Compendium of History and Biography of North Dakota Containing a History of North Dakota.* 1980.

Omdahl, Lloyd. *Organization and Administration of the State Government of North Dakota.* 1942.

Raaen, Aagot. *Grass of the Earth; Immigrant Life in North Dakota.* 1950.

Reese, John B. *Some Pioneers and Pilgrims on the Prairies of Dakota, or From the Ox Team to the Areoplane.* Mitchell, Author, 1920.

Robinson, Elwyn B. *Heroes of North Dakota.* 1947-1948.

Rylance, Daniel F. *North Dakota Government and Politics: A Selected Annotated Bibliography.* 1975.

Schneider, Mary J. *North Dakota Indians: An Introduction.* 1986.

State Historical Society of North Dakota Collection. Bismarck, ND, 1906-24.

Tweton, Jerome D. and Rylance, Daniel F. *North Dakota: The Heritage of a People.* 1976.

Tweton, Jerome D. and Rylance, Daniel F. *The Years of Despair: North Dakota in the Depression.* 1973.

Waldo, Edna LaMoore. *Dakota: An Informal Study of Territorial Days.* Caldwell, ID, 1936.

BOOKS ABOUT OHIO

A History of Ohio. 2nd ed. 1967.

Atwater, Caleb. *A History of the State of Ohio.* Cincinnati, OH, 1838.

Boryczka, Raymond and Cary, Lorin L. *No Strength Without Union: An Illustrated History of Ohio Workers, 1803-1980.* 1982.

Burke, J.L. and Davison, K.E. *Ohio's Heritage.* 1984.

Cutler, Julia P. *The Founders of Ohio.* Cincinnati, OH, 1888.

Downes, Randolph. *Frontier Ohio: 1788-1803.* Columbus, OH, 1935.

Encyclopedia of Ohio. Somerset Publishers. Michigan, 2000.

Eszterhas, Joe. *Thirteen Seconds: Confrontation at Kent State.* New York, NY: Dodd, Mead & Co., 1970.

Hopkins, Charles E. *Ohio the Beautiful and Historic.* Boston, MA, 1931.

Howe, Henry. *Historical Collections of Ohio...An Encyclopedia of the State.* Columbus, OH, 1890-91.

Howells, William Cooper. *Recollections of Life in Ohio, 1813-1840.* Cincinnati, OH, 1895.

Kent, Deborah. *America the Beautiful: Ohio.* 1989.

Knopf, Richard. *Indians of the Ohio Country.* 1959.

Martzolff, Clement Luther. *Fifty Stories from Ohio History.* Columbus, OH, 1917.

Ohio: A Bicentennial History. New York, NY: W. W. Norton & Co., 1976.

Potter, Martha A. *Ohio's Prehistoric People.* 1968.

Randall, E.O. and Ryan D.J. *History of Ohio.* (5 vols.) New York, NY, 1912.

Shetrone, Henry Clyde. *The Mound Builders.* New York, NY: D. Appleton and Co., 1930.

Slocum, Charles E. *The Ohio Country Between the Years 1785 and 1815.* 1991.

"The Foundations of Ohio." (*Sesquicentennial History of the State of Ohio, Vol. 1*). 1941.

The Indians of Ohio. 1918.

The Mysteries of Ohio's Underground Railroad. 1951.

Weisenburger, Francis. P. "The Passing of the Frontier, 1825-1850." *(Sesquicentennial History of Ohio, Vol. 3).* 1941.

Wheeler, Kenneth W. *For the Union; Ohio Leaders in the Civil War.* 1967.

Wittke, Carl Frederick, ed. *History of the State of Ohio, 1941-44.* Columbus, Ohio State Arch. and Hist. Society.

BOOKS ABOUT OKLAHOMA

Baird, W. David and Goble, Danney. *The Story of Oklahoma.* University of Oklahoma Press, 1994.

Chapman, Berlin B. *Federal Management and Disposition of the Lands of Oklahoma Territory, 1866-1907.* Ed. by Stuart Bruchey. Ayer, 1979.

Encyclopedia of Oklahoma. Somerset Publishers. Michigan, 1999.

Federal Writers' Project Staff. *Oklahoma: A Guide to the Sooner State.* Rprt. Serv. 1989.

Fradlin, Dennis B. *Oklahoma.* Children's Press, 1995.

Franks, Kenny A. *The Oklahoma Petroleum Industry.* University of Oklahoma Press, 1980.

Gibson, Arrell M. *Oklahoma: A History of Five Centuries, Guide to the Sooner State.* 2nd ed. University of Oklahoma Press, 1988.

Goble, Danney. *Progressive Oklahoma: The Making of a New Kind of State.* University of Oklahoma Press, 1980.

Heinrichs, Ann. *Oklahoma.* Childrens Press, 1989.

LaDoux, Rita C. *Oklahoma.* Lerner, 1992.

Morgan, David R., et al. *Oklahoma Politics and Policies: Governing the Sooner State.* University of Nebraska Press, 1991.

Morgan, H. Wayne and Morgan, Anne H. *Oklahoma: A History.* Norton, 1984.

Oklahoma: New Views of the Forty-sixth State. Ed. by Anne H. Morgan and H.W. Morgan. University of Oklahoma Press, 1982.

Seals, James R. and Goble, Danny. *Oklahoma Politics: A History.* University of Oklahoma Press, 1982.

Stein, Howard F. and Hill, Robert E. *The Culture of Oklahoma.* University of Oklahoma Press, 1993.

Strickland, Rennard. *The Indians in Oklahoma.* University of Oklahoma Press, 1980.

Thompson, Kathleen. *Oklahoma.* Rev. ed. Raintree Steck Vaughn, 1996.

BOOKS ABOUT OREGON

Bancroft, Hubert Howe. *History of Oregon.* (2 vol.) San Francisco, 1986.

Brown, J. Henry. *Political History of Oregon.* Portland, OR. 1892.

Carey, Charles H. *A General History of Oregon.* (2 vol.) Portland, OR. 1935.

Clarke, S.A. *Pioneer Days of Oregon History.* Portland OR. 1905.

Coues, Dr. Elliot. *New Light on the Early History of the Great Northwest.* New York, NY, 1897.

Dawson, Charles. *Pioneer Tales of the Oregon Trail.* Topeka, KS. 1912.

De Smet, Pierre Jean. *Life, Letters, and Travels of Father Pierre Jean de Smet, S.J., 1801-1873; Missionary Labors and Adventures among the Wild Tribes of the North American Indians.* New York, NY: F.P. Harper, 1905.

Duniway, Abigail Scott. *Path Breaking: An Autobiographical History of the Equal Suffrage Movement in Oregon.* Portland, OR. 1914.

Dunn, John. *History of the Oregon Territory.* London, 1844.

Encyclopedia of Oregon. Somerset Publishers. Michigan, 1999.

Evans, Elwood. *History of the Pacific Northwest: Oregon and Washington.* Portland, OR: North Pacific History Co., 1899.

Federal Writers' Project. *The Oregon Trail.* New York, NY. 1938.

Gaston, Joseph. *Centennial History of Oregon.* Chicago, IL. 1912.

Gray, W.H. *History of Oregon, 1742-1849.* Portland, OR. 1870.

Howard, Oliver Otis. *Nez Perce Joseph; An Account of His Ancestors, His Lands, His Confederates, His Enemies, His Murders, His War, His Pursuit and Capture.* Boston, MA: Lee & Shepard, 1881.

Josephy, Alvin M., Jr. *The Nez Perce Indians and the Opening of the Northwest.* New Haven: Yale University Press, 1965.

Lewis, Meriwether, and Clark, William. *Original Journal of the Lewis and Clark Expedition, 1804-1806.* New York, NY: Dodd, Mead & Co., 1904-05.

Lyman, Horace S. *History of Oregon.* (4 vols.) New York, NY. 1903.

Parkman, Francis. *The Oregon Trail.* New York, NY. 1933.

Schafer, Joseph. *Oregon Pioneers and American Diplomacy.* New York, NY. 1910.

Steel, W.G. *The Mountains of Oregon.* Portland, OR. 1890.

Taylor, Arthur Samuel. *Guide to the Reading and Study of the History of the Pacific Northwest.* Portland, OR: Metropolitan Press, 1935.

Turnbull, George S. *History of Oregon Newspapers.* Portland, OR. 1939.

Victor, Frances Fuller. *The Early Indian Wars of Oregon.* Salem, MA. 1894.

Woodward, W.C. *Rise and Early History of Political Parties in Oregon, 1843-1868.* Portland, OR. 1913.

BOOKS ABOUT PENNSYLVANIA

Beers, Paul. *Pennsylvania Politics, Today and Yesterday.* 1980.

Benhart, John. *The Encyclopedia of Pennsylvania.* 1984.

Blair, William Alan and Pencak, William, eds. *Making and Remaking Pennsylvania's Civil War.* 2000.

Blockson, Charles. *Pennsylvania's Black History.* 1975.

Bolles, Albert S. *Pennsylvania Province and State, 1690-1790.* Philadelphia, PA, 1899.

Brunn, Stanley. *Final Report on the Social Survey of Three Mile Island.* 1979.

Carpenter, Allan. *Pennsylvania.* Children's. 1978.

Coleman, John E. *The Disruption of Pennsylvania Democracy, 1848-1860.* 2000.

Davidson, Robert. *War Comes to Quaker Pennsylvania, 1682-1756.* 1957.

Dobree, Bonamy. *William Penn, Quaker and Pioneer.* 1948.

Doutrich, Paul E. *To Form a More Perfect Union: The Federal Constitution and Pennsylvania.* 2000.

Encyclopedia of Pennsylvania. Somerset Publishers. Michigan, 2000.

Federal Writers' Project. *Philadelphia: A Guide to the Nation's Birthplace.* Philadelphia, PA, 1937.

Frost, J. William. *A Perfect Freedom: Religious Liberty in Pennsylvania.* 1993.

Hanna, William. *Benjamin Franklin and Pennsylvania Politics.* 1964.

Heckwelder, J.G.E. *History, Manners and Customs of the Indian Nations who Inhabited Pennsylvania.* Philadelphia, PA, 1876.

Illick, Joseph. *Colonial Pennsylvania, A History.* 1976.

Indian Chiefs of Pennsylvania. Rep. 1971, 2000.

Indian Wars of Pennsylvania. 1929, 1971, 2000.

Kroll, Steven. *William Penn: Founder of Pennsylvania.* 2000.

Myers, Albert Cook. *Narratives of Early Pennsylvania, 1630-1707.* Rep. 1967.

Pennsylvania's Natural Beauty (Pennsylvania's Cultural and Natural Heritage). 2000.

Raber, Paul A. *The Archaic Period in Pennsylvania: Hunter-Gatherers of the Early and Middle Holocene Period.* 2000.

Romance of Old Philadelphia. Philadelphia, PA, 1918.

To Secure the Blessings of Liberty: Pennsylvania and the Changing U.S. Constitution. 2000.

BOOKS ABOUT RHODE ISLAND

Bates, Frank Greene. *Rhode Island and the Formation of the Union.* New York, NY, 1898.

Beals, Carleton. *Colonial Rhode Island.* Thomas Nelson, 1970.

Bridenbaugh, Carl. Fatt Mutton and Liberty of Conscience: Society in Rhode Island, 1636-1690.

Carpenter, Allan. *Rhode Island.* Rev. ed. Childrens Press, 1979.

Carroll, Charles. *Rhode Island, Three Centuries of Democracy.* New York, NY, 1932.

Chapin, Howard Millar. *Rhode Island Privateers in King George's War, 1739-48.* Providence, RI, 1926.

Coleman, Peter J. *The Transformation of Rhode Island, 1790-1860.* Brown University Press, 1963.

Conley, Patrick T. *An Album of Rhode Island History: 1636-1986.* Donning, 1986.

Daniels, Bruce C. *Dissent and Conformity on Narragansett Bay: The Colonial Rhode Island Town.* Wesleyan, 1983.

Dearden, Paul F. *The Rhode Island Campaign of 1778: Inauspicious Dawn of Alliance.* Rhode Island Bicentennial Foundation, 1980.

Encyclopedia of Rhode Island. Somerset Publishers. Michigan, 1999.

Gleeson, Alice Collins. *Colonial Rhode Island.* Pawtucket, RI, 1926.

Isham, Norman Morrison and Brown, Albert Fred. *Early Rhode Island Houses.* Providence, RI, 1895.

James, Sydney V. *Colonial Rhode Island: A History.* Scribner, 1975.

McLoughlin, William G. *Rhode Island: A Bicentennial History.* Norton, 1978.

Milner, Lillian Burleigh. *Our State, Rhode Island.* Providence, RI, 1925.

National Society of Colonial Dames in the State of Rhode Island. *Old Houses in the South County of Rhode Island.* Boston, MA, 1932.

Office of the Secretary of State. *Know Rhode Island.* Providence, RI, 1936.

Rhode Island Historical Society, Collections. Providence, RI, 1827-92; 1901-16; 1893-1901.

Richman, Irvine Berdine. *Rhode Island, Its Making and Its Meaning.* New York, NY, 1902.

State Bureau of Information. *The Book of Rhode Island.* Providence, RI, 1930.

Webb, Robert N. *The Colony of Rhode Island.* Watts, 1972.

Weeden, William Babcock. *Early Rhode Island*. New York, NY, 1910.

Withey, Lynne. *Urban Growth in Colonial Rhode Island: Newport and Providence in the Eighteenth Century*. State University of New York Press, 1984.

BOOKS ABOUT SOUTH CAROLINA

Ball, William Watts. *The State That Forgot: South Carolina's Surrender to Democracy*. Indianapolis, IN: The Bobbs-Merrill Co., 1932.

Barnwell, John. *Love of Order: South Carolina's First Secession Crisis*. Chapel Hill, NC: University of North Carolina Press, 1982.

Bassett, John Spencer. *The Life of Andrew Jackson*. Garden City, NY: 1911.

Boucher, C.S. *Nullification Controversy in South Carolina*. 1916.

Carroll, B.R. *Historical Collections of South Carolina; Embracing Rare Pamphlets, and Other Documents, Relating to the History of That State...to 1776*. New York, NY: Harper and Brothers, 1836.

Cauthen, Charles E. *South Carolina Goes to War, 1860-65*. Chapel Hill, NC: University of North Carolina Press, 1950.

Encyclopedia of South Carolina. Somerset Publishers. Michigan, 1999.

Gould, Christopher, and Morgan, Richard Parker. *South Carolina Imprints, 1731-1800: A Descriptive Bibliography*. Santa Barbara, CA: ABC-Clio Information Services, 1984.

Gragg, Rod. *Pirates, Planters, and Patriots: Stories From the South Carolina Grand Strand*. Winston-Salem, NC: Peace Hill Publishers, 1985.

Green, Edwin Luther. *Indians of South Carolina*. Columbia, SC: University Press, 1920.

Hamer, P.M. *Secession Movement in South Carolina, 1847-1852*.

Herd, E. Don. *The South Carolina UpCountry: Historical and Biographical Sketches*. Greenwood, SC: Attic Press, 1981.

Joyner, Charles W. *Down by the Riverside: A South Carolina Slave Community*. Urbana, IL: University of Illinois Press, 1984.

Kohn, August. *The Cotton Mills of South Carolina*. Charleston, SC: Press of Daggett Printing Co., 1907.

Lander, Ernest M. *A History of South Carolina, 1856-1960*. Columbia, SC: University of South Carolina Press, 1970.

McCrady, Edward. *History of South Carolina under the Proprietary Government, 1670-1783*. New York, NY: Macmillan, 1902.

Moss, Bobby Gilmer. *Roster of South Carolina Patriots in the American Revolution*. Baltimore, MD: Genealogical Publications Co., 1983.

Pancake, John S. *This Destructive War: The British Campaign in the Carolinas, 1780-1782*. AL: University of Alabama Press, 1985.

Simms, William Gilmore. *A History of South Carolina*. Columbia, SC: The State Company, 1927.

Sirmans, M. Eugene. *Colonial South Carolina: A Political History, 1663-1763*. Chapel Hill, NC: University of North Carolina Press, 1966.

South Carolina. *Know Your State: South Carolina Government*. Columbia, SC: League of Women Voters of South Carolina, 1984.

Taylor, Rosser H. *Ante-Bellum South Carolina: A Social and Cultural History*. New York, NY: Da Capo Press, 1970.

Weir, Robert M. *Colonial South Carolina: A History*. Millwood, NY: KTO Press, 1983.

Wolfe, J.H. *Jeffersonian Democracy in South Carolina*. 1940.

Wright, Louis B. *South Carolina: A Bicentennial History*. New York, NY: Norton, 1976.

BOOKS ABOUT SOUTH DAKOTA

Aken, David. *Pioneers of the Black Hills, or Gordon's Stockade Party of 1874*.

Atherton, Loren G. *The Government of South Dakota, State and Local* Pierre, SD, Olander, 1927.

Black Hills, South Dakota. Casper, WY, Prairie Publishing Co. 1937.

Briggs, Harold E. *Early Freight and Stage Lines in Dakota*. 1929.

Briggs, Harold E. *Pioneer River Transportation in Dakota*. 1929.

Burdick, Usher L. *Last Battle of the Sioux Nation*. WI, 1929.

Coursey, O.W. (compiler and editor) *The First Woman in the Black Hills. As Told by Herself, Mrs. Annie D. Talent*. Mitchell, Educator Supply Co., 1923.

Custer, Mr. Elizabeth Bacon. *"Boots and Saddles;" or, Life in Dakota with General Custer*. New York, NY: Harper, 1885.

DeLand, Charles Edmund. *The Aborigines of South Dakota*. South Dakota Historical Collections, Vol. III, Vol. IV.

DeLand, Charles Edmund. *The Sioux Wars*. South Dakota Historical Collection, Vol. XV, Vol. XVI.

Encyclopedia of South Dakota. Somerset Publishers. Michigan, 1999.

Fox, Lawrence K. *Fox's Who's Who Among South Dakotans*. Pierre, SD: Statewide Service Co., 1924-28.

Hans, Red M. *The Great Sioux Nation*. Chicago, IL: Donohue, 1907.

Hebert, Frank. *Forty Years Prospecting in the Black Hills of South Dakota*. Rapid City, SD: *Rapid City Daily Journal*, 1921.

Hunkins, Ralph V. and Lindsey, John. *South Dakota; Its Past, Present, and Future*. New York, NY: Macmillan, 1932.

Kane, Lucile M. *Military Life in Dakota: The Journal of Philippe Regis de Troobriand*. 1951.

Kingsbury, G.W. *History of Dakota Territory*. Chicago, IL: Clarke Publishing Co., 1915.

Lamar, Howard R. *Dakota Territory, 1861-1889: A Study of Frontier Politics*. 1956.

Lowe, Barrett. *Heroes and Hero Tales of South Dakota*. Minneapolis, MN: Hale, 1931.

Norton, Sister Mary Aquinas. *Catholic Missions and Missionaries Among the Indians of Dakota*. 1931.

Reese, John B. *Some Pioneers and Pilgrims on the Prairies of Dakota, or From the Ox Team to the Areoplane*. Mitchell, Author, 1920.

Peterson, Purl D. *Through the Black Hills and Bad Lands of South Dakota*. Pierre, SD: Olander, 1929.

Robinson, Doane. *Doane Robinson's Encyclopedia of South Dakota*. Pierre, SD: Robinson, 1925.

Smith, G.M. and Young, C.M. *History and Government of South Dakota*. New York, NY: American Book Co., 1913.

Waldo, Edna LaMoore. *Dakota: An Informal Study of Territorial Days*. Caldwell, ID, 1936.

BOOKS ABOUT TENNESSEE

Alderson, W.T. and Thomas, Hulan Glyn. *Historic Sites in Tennessee*. 1965.

Alderson, W.T. and White, Robert H. *A Guide to the Study and Reading of Tennessee History*. Nashville, TN: Tennessee Historical Commission. 1959.

Alexander, Thomas B. *Political Reconstruction in Tennessee.* 1950.

Allison, John. *Dropped Stitches in Tennessee History.* Nashville, TN: Marshall & Bruce Co., 1897.

Atkins, Jonathan M. *Parties, Politics, and the Sectional Conflict in Tennessee, 1832-1861.* 1997.

Beard, William Ewing. *Nashville, The Home of History Makers.* Nashville, TN: Civitan Club, 1929.

Bergeron, Paul H. *Antebellum Politics in Tennessee.* Lexington, KY: University Press of Kentucky, 1982.

Caldwell, Joshua W. *Studies in the Constitutional History of Tennessee.* Cincinnati, OH: Robert Clarke Co., 1907.

Cimprich, John. *Slavery's End in Tennessee, 1861-1865.* AL: University of Alabama Press, 1985.

Connelly, T.L. *Civil War Tennessee: Battles and Leaders.* Knoxville, TN: University of Tennessee Press, 1979.

Coppock, Paul. *Memphis Memoirs.* Memphis, TN: Memphis State University Press, 1980.

Corlew, Robert Ewing. *Statehood for Tennessee.* Nashville, TN: Bicentennial Commission, 1976.

Dykeman, Wilma. *Tennessee: A Bicentennial History.* New York, NY. Norton, 1975.

Elder, Randy and Charles. *A History of Tennessee from the Earliest Times.* Nashville, TN: Goodspeed Publishing Co., 1886-87, 1970.

Encyclopedia of Tennessee. Somerset Publishers. Michigan, 1999.

Ewing, James. *A Treasury of Tennessee Tales.* Nashville, TN: Rutledge Hill Press, 1985.

Federal Writers' Project. *Tennessee: A Guide to the State.* New York, NY: Somerset, 1939.

Folmsbee, Stanley J., Corlew, Robert E., and Mitchell, Enoch L. *History of Tennessee.* New York, NY: 1960.

Frontier Tales of Tennessee. 1989.

Garrett, William Robertson, and Goodpasture, Albert Virgil. *History of Tennessee, Its People and Its Institutions.* Nashville, TN: The Brandon Printing Co., 1900.

Goodspeed, Weston A., et al. *History of Tennessee from the Earliest Times.* Nashville, TN: Goodspeed Publishing Company, 1886.

Hale, Will T., and Merritt, Dixon L. *A History of Tennessee and Tennesseans; the Leaders and Representative Men in Commerce, Industry, and Modern Activities.* Chicago, IL and New York, NY: Lewis Pub. Co., 1913.

Hamer, Philip May. *Tennessee: A History; 1673-1832.* New York, NY: American Historical Society, 1933.

Phillips, Margaret I. *The Governors of Tennessee.* 1978.

Tennessee: A Short History. Knoxville, TN: University of Tennessee Press, 1981.

BOOKS ABOUT TEXAS

Adair, Anthony Garland. (ed.). *Heroes of the Alamo.* 1957.

Allen, Charles Fletcher. *David Crockett, Scout, Small Boy, Pilgrim, Mountaineer Solder, Bear Hunter, and Congressman; Defender of the Alamo.* Philadelphia and London: Lippincott. 1911.

Barr, Alwyn. *Black Texans: A History of Negroes in Texas, 1528-1971.* Austin, TX, 1973.

Benedict, H.Y. and Lomax, John. *The Book of Texas.* Garden City, NJ, 1916.

Bishop, Curtis. *The First Texas Ranger, Jack Hays.* 1959.

Calvert, Robert A. *Black Leaders: Texans for Their Times.* 1981.

Carleton, Don E. *Red Scare: Right Wing Hysteria, Fifties Fanaticism, and Their Legacy in Texas.* 1985.

Clark, L.D. *Civil War Recollections of James Lemuel Clark: Including Previously Unpublished Material of the Great Hanging at Gainesville, Texas in October 1862.* 2000.

Clarke, Mary. *Chief Bowles and the Texas Cherokees.* 1971.

Crawford, Ann F. and Ragsdale, Crystal S. *Women in Texas.* 1982.

Day, James M., et. al. *Indian Tribes of Texas.* 1971.

Dumont, Ella E.B. *Ella Elgar Bird Dumont: An Autobiography of a West Texas Pioneer.* 1988.

Encyclopedia of Texas. Somerset Publishers. Michigan, 2000.

Fehrenbach, T.R. *Lone Star: A History of Texas and the Texans.* New York, NY, 1985.

Foote, Henry. *Texas and the Texans, or Advance of the Anglo-Americans to the Southwest.* (2 vols.) Philadelphia, PA, 1841.

Frantz, Joe B. *Texas: A Bicentennial History.* 1976.

Gallaway, B.P. *The Dark Corner of Confederacy; Accounts of Civil War Texas.* Dubuque, IA, 1968.

Jenkins, John Holland. *Recollections of Early Texas.* 1987.

Kingston, Mike. *A Concise History of Texas.* 1991.

Malone, Ann P. *Women on the Texas Frontier.* 1983.

Merk, Frederick. *Slavery and the Annexation of Texas.* 1972.

Ruff, Ann. *Unsung Heroes of Texas: Stories of Courage and Honor from Texas History and Legend.* 1985.

Texas Monthly. *Texas, Our Texas; 150 Moments That Made Us the Way We Are.* 1986.

The Legends of Texas. Austin, TX, 1916. Rep., 1975.

The Life of Stephen A. Austin, Founder of Texas. Nashville, TN, 1925.

BOOKS ABOUT UTAH

Bancroft, Hubert Howe. *History of Utah.* San Francisco, CA, 1890.

Baskin, R.N., *Reminiscences of Early Utah.* Salt Lake City, UT, 1914.

Beardsley, Harry M. *Joseph Smith and His Mormon Empire.* Boston, MA, 1931.

Carpenter, Allan. *Utah.* Rev. ed. Childrens Press, 1979.

Creer, Leland Hargrave. *Utah and the Nation.* Seattle, WA, 1929.

Encyclopedia of Utah. Somerset Publishers. Michigan, 1999.

Evans, John Henry, *Joseph Smith, an American Prophet.* New York, NY, 1933.

Evans, John Henry, *The Story of Utah: The Beehive State.* New York, NY, 1933.

Ferris, Benjamin, G., *Utah and the Mormons.* New York, NY, 1854.

Harris, Chauncy Dennison. *Salt Lake City: A Regional Capital.* Chicago, IL, 1940.

Histories of Utah. Salt Lake City, 1889.

History of Salt Lake City, and its Founders. Salt Lake City, 1886.

Kenner, Scipio Africanus. *Utah As It Is.* Salt Lake City, UT, 1904.

Linn, W.A. *The Story of the Mormons From the Date of Their Origin to the Year 1901.* New York, NY, 1902.

Luce, Willard and Celia. *Utah.* Rev. ed. G. M. Smith, 1980.

Neff, Andrew Love. *History of Utah, 1847-1869.* Salt Lake City, UT, 1940.

Peterson, Charles S. *Utah: A Bicentennial History.* Norton, 1977.

Roberts, Brigham H. *A Comprehensive History of the Church of Jesus Christ of Latter-Day Saints.* Salt Lake City, UT, 1930.

Stansbury, Howard. *Explorations and Survey of the Valley of the Great Salt Lake of Utah.* Philadelphia, PA, 1852.

Thomas, George. *Civil Government of Utah.* Chicago, IL, 1912.

Utah: A Guide to the State. Rev. ed. Western Epics, 1982. From the American Guide Series.

Utah's History. Ed. by Richard D. Poll and others. Brigham Young University Press, 1978.

Warrum, Noble. *History of Utah Since Statehood.* Chicago, IL and Salt Lake City, UT, 1919.

Werner, M.R. *Brigham Young.* New York, NY, 1924.

Young, Levi Edgar. *The Founding of Utah.* Boston, MA and New York, NY, 1923.

BOOKS ABOUT VERMONT

Allen, Ira. *The Natural and Political History of the State of Vermont.* London, 1798.

Bryan, Frank M. *Yankee Politics in Rural Vermont.* 1974.

Carpenter, Allan. *Vermont.* Rev. ed. Childrens Press, 1979.

Carroll, Daniel B. *The Unicameral Legislature in Vermont.* Montpelier, VT, 1932.

Chappell, George S. *Colonial Architecture in Vermont.* 1918.

Cheney, Cora. *Vermont: The State with the Storybook Past.* Rev. ed. New England Press, 1986.

Crockett, Walter H. *History of Vermont.* New York, NY, 1921.

Encyclopedia of Vermont. Somerset Publishers. Michigan, 1999.

Hard, Walter and Margaret. *This Is Vermont.* Brattleboro, VT, 1936.

Haviland, William A. and Power, Marjory W. *The Original Vermonters: Native Inhabitants, Past and Present.* 1981.

Hemenway, Abby M. *Abby Hemenway's Vermont: Unique Portrait of a State.* 1972.

Hill, Ralph N. *Contrary Country: A Chronicle of Vermont.* Shelburne, VT, 1982.

Kent, Dorman B.E. *Vermonters.* Montpelier, VT, 1937.

Lee, John Parker. *Uncommon Vermont.* Rutland, 1926.

Morrissey, Charles T. *Vermont: A Bicentennial History (States and the Nation Series).* 1981.

Parks, Roger. *Vermont: A Bibliography of its History.* 1989.

Robbins, Daniel. *The Vermont Statehouse: A History and Guide.* 1980.

Rural Vermont: A Program for the Future. Burlington, VT, 1931.

Slade, William, Jr. *Vermont State Papers: Records and Documents Relative to the Early History of the State.* Middlebury, VT, 1823.

Stevens, Ethel M. *Footprints Down the Centuries; a Vermont Heritage.* 1961.

Swift, Esther M. *Vermont Place-Names: Footprints of History.* 1977.

Thompson, Zadock. *History of Vermont, Natural, Civil, and Statistical.* Burlington, VT, 1842.

Van de Water, Frederic F. *The Reluctant Republic: Vermont, 1724-1791.* Countryman, 1974.

Wardner, Henry Steele. *The Birthplace of Vermont.* New York, NY, 1927.

BOOKS ABOUT VIRGINIA

Ballagh, James Curtis. *A History of Slavery in Virginia.* Baltimore, MD: John Hopkins Press, 1902.

Bayne, Howard R. *A Rebellion in the Colony of Virginia.* New York, NY: Society of Colonial Wars in the State of New York, 1904.

Beverely, Robert. (ed. Louis B. Wright). *The History and Present State of Virginia.* 1705.

Buckley, Thomas E. *Church and State in Revolutionary Virginia, 1776-1787.* 1977.

Caperton, Helena Lefroy. *Legends of Virginia.* Richmond, VA: Garrett and Massie, 1931.

Carroll, Nan. *Gentlemen of Virginia: Biographical Sketches of Twenty Virginians Who Were Instrumental to the American Revolution.* 1975.

Cooke, John Esten. *Virginia: A History of the People.* New York, NY: Houghton, Mifflin and Co., 1891.

Eckenrode, Hamilton James. *Political History of Virginia During the Reconstruction.* Baltimore, MD: John Hopkins Press, 1904.

Edmunds, Pocahontas W. *Virginians Out Front.* 1972.

Encyclopedia of Virginia. Somerset Publishers. Michigan, 1999.

Federal Writers' Project. *Virginia: A Guide to the Old Dominion.* New York, NY: Somerset, 1980. (orig. 1940)

Four Hundred Years of Virginia, 1584-1984. Lanham, MD: University Press of America, 1985.

Freehling, Alison Goodyear. *Drift Toward Dissolution: The Virginia Slavery Debate of 1831-1832.* Louisiana State University Printing, 1982.

History of Virginia. Chicago, IL and New York, NY: American Historical Society, 1924.

Jordan, Daniel P. *Political Leadership in Jefferson's Virginia.* 1983.

Kilpatrick, James Jackson. *The Sovereign States: Notes of a Citizen of Virginia.* Chicago, IL: Henry Regnery, 1957.

Lebsock, Suzanne. *Virginia Women: A Share of Honour.* 1987.

Lewis, Jan. *The Pursuit of Happiness: Family and Values in Jefferson's Virginia.* 1985.

Rubin, Louis D., Jr. *Virginia: A Bicentennial History.* New York, NY: Norton, 1977.

Morton, Richard L. *Colonial Virginia.* Chapel Hill, NC: University of North Carolina Press, 1960.

Separation of Church and State in Virginia. Richmond, VA: D. Bottom, Supt. Public Printing, 1910.

Shanks, Henry T. *The Secession Movement in Virginia, 1847-1861.*

Social Life of Virginia in the Seventeenth Century. Lynchburg, VA: J. P. Bell, Inc., 1927.

Tyler, Lyon Gardiner. *Narratives of Early Virginia.* New York, NY: Charles Scribner's Sons, 1907.

Younger, Edward. *The Governors of Virginia, 1860-1978.* Charlottesville, VA: University Press of Virginia, 1982.

BOOKS ABOUT WASHINGTON

Allen, Paul. *History of the Expedition of Lewis and Clark.* New York, NY: Bradford and Inskeep, 1814.

Avery, Mary W. *Washington: A History of the Evergreen State.* University of Washington Press, 1965.

Coues, Dr. Elliot. *New Light on the Early History of the Great Northwest.* New York, NY, 1897.

Encyclopedia of Washington. Somerset Publishers. Michigan, 1999.

Hanford, C.M. *Seattle and Environs.* Seattle, WA: Pioneer History Publishing Col., 1924.

Hines, Rev. Harvey K. *An Illustrated History of the State of Washington, Containing...Biographical Mention of Its Pioneers and Prominent Citizens ...* Chicago, IL: The Lewis Publishing Co., 1893.

History of the State of Washington. New York, NY: Macmillan, 1924.

Howard, Oliver Otis. *Nez Perce Joseph; An Account of His Ancestors, His Lands, His Confederates, His Enemies, His Murders, His War, His Pursuit and Capture.* Boston, MA: Lee & Shepard, 1881.

Hunt, Herbert and Kaylor, Floyd C. *Washington, West of the Cascades: Historical and Descriptive: The Explorations, the Indians, the Pioneers, the Modern.* Chicago, IL: and Seattle, WA: S. J. Clarke Publishing Co., 1917.

Josephy, Alvin M., Jr. *The Nez Perce Indians and the Opening of the Northwest.* New Haven: Yale University Press, 1965.

Leedy, E.C. *Washington.* St. Paul: Great Northern Railway Co., 1934.

Lewis, Meriwether, and Clark, William. *Original Journal of the Lewis and Clark Expedition, 1804-1806.* New York, NY: Dodd, Mead & Co., 1904-05.

Lewis, Paul M. *The Beauty of Washington.* Beaverton, OR: Beautiful America Publishing Co., 1981.

Majors, Harry M. *Exploring Washington.* Van Winkle Publications, 1975.

Meeker, Ezra. *Seventy Years of Progress in Washington.* Tacoma, WA: Allstrom Printing Co., 1921.

Mullen, W. Frank. *The Government and Politics of Washington State.* Pullman, WA: Washington State University Press, 1978.

Oliphant, Orin J. *A Brief Outline of the History of Washington.* Olympia, WA: O.N. Olson, 1933.

Pollard, Lancaster, and Spencer, Lloyd. *A History of the State of Washington.* New York, NY: American Historical Society, 1937.

Roberts, Philip. *A Date with Washington History.* Skyline West Press, 1986.

Snowden, Clifton A. *History of Washington: The Rise and Progress of an American State.* New York, NY: The Century History Co., 1909.

Ruffner, William H. *Report on Washington Territory.* New York, NY: Lakeshore and Eastern Railway, 1889.

Sperlin, O. B. and Miles, Charles. *Building a State: Washington, 1889-1939.*

Taylor, Arthur Samuel. *Guide to the Reading and Study of the History of the Pacific Northwest.* Portland, OR: Metropolitan Press, 1935.

Veiler, Robert I. *Chronology and Documentary Handbook of the State of Washington.* Dobbs Ferry, NY: Oceana Publications, 1979.

Washington State: National Parks, Historic Sites, Recreation Areas, and Natural Landmarks. WA: University of Washington Press, 1974.

BOOKS ABOUT WEST VIRGINIA

Ash, Jerry W. and Douthat, S.L. *West Virginia USA.* Seawell Multimedia Corp., 1976.

Bastress, Robert M. *The West Virginia State Constitution.* Greenwood, 1995.

Bice, David A. and Jones, Helen. *West Virginia and the Appalachians.* Jalamap Publishing, 1983.

Carpenter, Allan. *West Virginia.* Rev. ed. Childrens Press, 1979.

Coffey, William E., et al. *West Virginia Government.* Education Foundation, 1984.

Cohen, Stan B. and Pauley, Michael J. *Historic Sites of West Virginia,* 2nd ed. Pictorial Hists., 1985.

Di Piazza, Domenica. *West Virginia.* Lerner, 1995.

Encyclopedia of West Virginia. Somerset Publishers. Michigan, 1999.

Federal Writers' Project Staff. *West Virginia: A Guide to the Mountain State.* 1939. Rep., 1989.

Hammock, Allan S. and Peterson, Sophia, eds. *West Virginia Policy Issues.* West Virginia University Press, 1979.

Morgan, John G. *West Virginia Governors, 1863-1980.* 2nd ed. Charleston Newspapers, 1980.

Rice, Otis K. ***West Virginia: A History.*** **2nd ed. University Press of Kentucky, 1993.**

Rice, Otis K. *The Allegheny Frontier: West Virginia Beginnings, 1730-1830.* University Press of Kentucky, 1970.

Rice, Otis K. *West Virginia: The State and Its People.* McClain, 1979.

Soltis, Stephen and Stacy. *West Virginia: Off the Beaten Path.* Globe Pequot, 1995.

Stutler, Boyd B. *West Virginia in the Civil War.* 2nd ed. Education Foundation, 1966.

Tams, W. P. *The Smokeless Coal Fields of West Virginia: A Brief History.* West Virginia University Press, 1983.

Thompson, Kathleen. *West Virginia.* 2nd ed. Raintree Steck Vaughn.

West Virginia: A Guide to the Mountain State. Somerset, 1974.

Williams, John A. *West Virginia and the Captains of Industry.* West Virginia University Press, 1976. Rep. 1997.

Williams, John A. *West Virginia.* Norton, 1984.

BOOKS ABOUT WISCONSIN

Algire, Tom. *Wisconsin.* Portland, OR: Graphic Arts Center Publishing Co., 1981.

Bruce, William George. *A Short History of Milwaukee.* Milwaukee, Bruce Publishing Co., 1936.

Campbell, Henry Colin. *Wisconsin in Three Centuries, 1634-1905.* New York, NY: The Century History Co., 1906.

Current, Richard Nelson. *Wisconsin: A Bicentennial History.* New York, NY: Norton, 1977.

Davidson, John N. *In Unnamed Wisconsin.* Milwaukee, WI: S. Chapman, 1895.

Encyclopedia of Wisconsin. Somerset Publishers. Michigan, 1999.

Fitzpatrick, Edward A. *Wisconsin.* New York, NY: The Bruce Publishing Co., 1931.

Gale, Zona. "Wisconsin, a Voice from the Middle Border." *These United States.* 1st series. New York, NY: Boni & Liveright, 1923.

Howe, Frederic Clemson. *Wisconsin: An Experiment in Democracy.* New York, NY: Scribner, 1912.

Kellogg, Louise Phelps. *The British Regime in Wisconsin and the Northwest.* Madison, WI: Wisconsin State Historical Society, 1935.

McCarthy, Charles. *The Wisconsin Idea.* New York, NY: Macmillan, 1912.

McDonald, Grace. *History of the Irish in Wisconsin in the Nineteenth Century.* (c. 1954) New York, NY: Arno Press, 1976.

McMurtrie, Douglas Crawford. *Early Printing in Wisconsin.* Seattle, WA: McCaffrey, 1931.

Merk, Frederick. *Economic History of Wisconsin During the Civil War Decade.* Madison, WI: Wisconsin State Historical Society, 1916.

Paul, Justus F. and Barbara D. *The Badger State.* Grand Rapids, MI: Eerdmans, 1978.

Pederson, Jane Marie. *Between Memory and Reality: Family and Community in Rural Wisconsin, 1870-1970 (History of American Thought and Culture)*. 1992.

Smith, William Rudolph. *Observations on the Wisconsin Territory. (c. 1838)* New York, NY: Arno Press, 1975,

Strong, Moses McCure. *History of the Territory of Wisconsin, from 1836 to 1848*. Madison, WI: 1885.

Thomson, Alexander McDonald. *A Political History of Wisconsin*. Milwaukee, WI: E. C. Williams Co., 1900.

Thwaites, Reuben Gold. *The Story of Wisconsin*. Boston, MA: Lothrop, 1980 (rev. ed. 1988).

Trask, Kerry A. *Fire Within: A Civil War Narrative from Wisconsin*. 1998.

Turner, Jennie McMullin. *Wisconsin Pioneers*. Appleton C. C. Nelson Publishing Co., 1929.

Vexler, Robert I., (ed.) *Chronology and Documentary Handbook of the State of Wisconsin*. Dobbs Ferry, NY: Oceana Publications, 1978.

Woodward, David, et al. *Cultural Map of Wisconsin: Wisconsin's History, Culture, Land & People*. 1996.

Zeitlin, Richard H. and Hale, Frederick. *Germans in Wisconsin*. 1977.

BOOKS ABOUT WYOMING

Bancroft, Hubert Howe. *History of Wyoming*. San Francisco, CA, 1890.

Bartlett, Ichabod S. *History of Wyoming*. Chicago, IL, 1918.

Beach, Mrs. Cora May. *Women of Wyoming*. Casper, WY, 1927-28.

Beard, Frances. *Wyoming from Territorial Days to the Present*. Chicago, IL and New York, NY, 1933.

Bragg, William F. *Wyoming: Rugged but Right*. Pruett, 1979.

Bragg, William F. *Wyoming: Wild and Wooly*. 1983.

Brooks, Bryant B. *Memoirs of Bryant B. Brooks. Cowboy, Trapper, Lumberman, Stockman, Oilman, Banker, and Governor of Wyoming*. Glendale, CA, 1939.

Carpenter, Allan. *Wyoming*. Rev. ed. Childrens Press, 1979.

Chapman, W.E. *Some of the Early Newspapers in Wyoming*. Laramie, WY, 1919.

Cody, Mrs. Louisa. *Memories of Buffalo Bill*. New York, NY, 1919.

Coutant, C.G. *The History of Wyoming from the Earliest Known Discoveries*. Laramie, WY, 1899.

Department of Commerce and Industry. *Dude Ranches of Wyoming*. 1938.

Department of Commerce and Industry. *Wyoming Worth Knowing*. Casper, WY, 1928.

Encyclopedia of Wyoming. Somerset Publishers. Michigan, 1999.

Fuller, Robert P. *Wonderful Wyoming, the Undeveloped Empire*. Cheyenne, WY, 1911.

Guernsey, Charles. *Wyoming Cowboy Days*. New York, NY, 1936.

Hebard, Grace Raymond. *The History and Government of Wyoming*. San Francisco, CA, 1919.

Larson, Taft A. *Wyoming: A Bicentennial History*. Norton, 1977.

Murray, Robert A. *The Bozeman Trail: Highway of History*. Pruett, 1988.

Righter, Robert W. *Crucible for Conservation: The Creation of Grand Teton National Park*. Colorado Associated, 1982.

Ross, Nellie. *Governor Lady; Autobiography*. 1927.

Thompson, Kathleen. *Wyoming*. Raintree, 1988.

U.S. National Park Service. *Yellowstone National Park, Wyoming*. Washington, DC, 1938.

Walker, Tacetta. *Stories of Early Days in Wyoming*. Casper, WY, 1936.

Wyoming Historical Society. *Collections of the Wyoming Historical Society*. Cheyenne, WY, 1897.